CREDIT DERIVATIVES AND CREDIT LINKED NOTES

Second Edition

CREDIT DERIVATIVES AND CREDIT LINKED NOTES
Second Edition

Satyajit Das

John Wiley & Sons (Asia) Pte Ltd

Singapore   New York   Chichester   Brisbane   Toronto   Weinheim

Published in 2000 by John Wiley & Sons (Asia) Pte Ltd
2 Clementi Loop, #02-01, Singapore 129809

Other Wiley Editorial Offices

John Wiley & Sons, Inc., 605 Third Avenue, New York, NY 10158-0012, USA
John Wiley & Sons Ltd, Baffins Lane, Chichester, West Sussex PO19 1UD, England
John Wiley & Sons (Canada) Ltd, 22 Worcester Road, Rexdale, Ontario M9W 1L1, Canada
John Wiley & Sons Australia Ltd, 33 Park Road (PO Box 1226), Milton, Queensland 4064, Australia
Wiley-VCH, Pappelallee 3, 69469 Weinheim, Germany

Library of Congress Cataloging-in-Publication Data
ISBN 0-471-84031-9

Typeset in 10/13 points, Times by Linographic Services Pte Ltd
Printed in Singapore by Saik Wah Press Pte Ltd
10 9 8 7 6 5 4 3 2 1

WILEY FRONTIERS IN FINANCE
SERIES EDITOR: EDWARD I. ALTMAN, NEW YORK UNIVERSITY

To

My friend and partner Jade Novakovic
And my parents Sukumar and Aparna Das
For their support and encouragement

Contents

List of Contributors

1. **Editor and Principal Contributor**
   SATYAJIT DAS

2. **Other Contributors**

NELS ANDERSON
Moody's Investors Service, London, UK

PETER CROSBIE
KMV Corporation, San Francisco, USA

LEA CARTY
Moody's Investors Service, New York, USA

JEROME S. FONS
Moody's Investors Service, New York, USA

GREG GUPTON
J.P. Morgan, New York, USA

DAVID HAMILTON
Moody's Investors Service, New York, USA

ANDREW J. HICKMAN
eRisks.com, New York, USA

SEAN KEENAN
Moody's Investors Service, New York, USA

ROBERT REOCH
Bank of America, San Francisco, USA

HAYDN STEDMAN
Citibank, Sydney, Australia

TOM WILDE
Credit Suisse First Boston, London, UK

CHRISTOPHER WHITELEY
Allen & Overy, Paris, France

PRICEWATERHOUSECOOPERS
Regina Fikkers, Ian Hammond, Bill Testa – Australia
Steffen Gnutzmann, Georg Klusak, Manfred Kühnle – Germany
Marc Bertschy, Urs Landolf, Andreas Risi – Switzerland
Jonathan Davies, Matthew Davidson, Emma Lubbock – UK
John T Lawton, Nabi Niang, Viva Hammer – US

About the Contributors

1. Editor and Principal Contributor

Satyajit Das

Satyajit Das is an international specialist in the area of financial derivatives and risk management. He presents seminars on financial derivatives/risk management and capital markets in Europe, North America, Asia, and Australia. He acts as a consultant to financial institutions and corporations on derivatives and financial products, risk management, and capital markets issues.

Between 1988 and 1994, Mr Das was the Treasurer of the TNT Group, an Australian-based international transport and logistics company. Between 1977 and 1987, he worked in the banking industry, with the Commonwealth Bank of Australia, Citicorp Investment Bank, and Merrill Lynch Capital Markets.

Mr Das is the author of *Swaps and Financial Derivatives: The Global Reference to Products, Pricing, Applications and Markets* (1994, LBC Information Services; McGraw-Hill), *Exotic Options* (1996, LBC Information Services), and *Structured Notes and Derivative Embedded Securities* (1996, Euromoney Publications). He is also the major contributor and editor of *The Global Swaps Market* (1991, IFR Publishing Ltd), *Financial Derivatives & Risk Management: A Guide to the Mathematics* (1997, LBC Information Services; McGraw-Hill; MacMillan Publishing), and *Credit Derivatives* (1998, John Wiley & Sons).

2. Other Contributors

Nels Anderson

Nels Anderson is a senior vice president at Moody's Investors Service in London. Working in the structured finance group, he leads the CDO team, which specializes in credit derivatives, collateralized bond and loan obligations, and other structured products. He joined Moody's from the fixed-income derivatives desk of Goldman Sachs. Prior to entering finance, he earned a bachelor's degree in physics from the Massachusetts Institute of Technology and a PhD in astrophysics from Princeton University, and conducted astrophysical research at institutions in the US, France, and Germany.

Lea V Carty

Lea V Carty is a managing director at Moody's Investors Service's Risk Management Services Group. He has published research articles on various aspects of corporate credit risk and trends in corporate credit quality in academic journals, professional journals, and books. Prior to joining Moody's in 1992, Mr Carty worked at Bear, Stearns, and Company, Inc., New York and Thomson-CGR, Paris. He holds a BA in Mathematics and French from Washington University in St. Louis, an MA in Mathematics from the University of Colorado, and a PhD. in Economics from Columbia University. Dr Carty's thesis — written in the academic disciplines of corporate finance and economic history — was awarded a distinction.

Peter Crosbie

Peter Crosbie is a managing director of KMV Corporation and is responsible for its Portfolio Management products. He joined KMV in 1995 and has worked in both product development and with clients to implement KMV's technology. Prior to joining KMV, he was director of Portfolio Management for Barclays Bank in New York.

Dr Crosbie began his career as a consultant to Barclays Bank in 1986, teaching executive development courses in corporate finance and derivatives, and was on the business faculty of Santa Clara University from 1990 to 1992. Dr Crosbie is a native of New Zealand and holds a BSc. Honours degree in Management Science from Canterbury University and a PhD in Marketing Science and Economics from Purdue University.

Jerome S Fons

Jerome S Fons is a managing director in the Financial Institutions and Sovereign Risk Group at Moody's Investors Service in New York. He is responsible for Moody's ratings on East Asian banks, including Japanese banks. From 1990 through 1994, Mr Fons was the principal author of Moody's corporate bond and commercial paper default studies and has published widely in the field of credit risk. Prior to joining Moody's, Mr Fons was an economic advisor at Chemical Bank, New York and an economist with the Federal Reserve Banks of New York and Cleveland.Mr Fons holds a BA in Economics from San Diego State University and a PhD in Economics from the University of California at San Diego.

Greg M Gupton

Greg M Gupton is a vice president at JP Morgan, where he has worked for 14 years. He was the lead author and principal researcher in the development of CreditMetrics™. He has been central in developing credit risk and pricing methodology across JP Morgan's internal applications for the past eight years. Mr Gupton's prior assignments include economic risk-based equity allocation, and primary bond and preferred stock issuance to fund JP Morgan's Tier-II capital position.

Mr Gupton received a BA in Accounting from the University of Washington and an MS in Industrial Administration from Carnegie-Mellon University in 1985 when he joined J.P. Morgan. In addition to CreditMetrics™, Mr Gupton was published in *The Journal of Lending and Credit Risk Management*, August 1997 and *Heuristic Programming in Artificial Intelligence* (1st edition).

David T Hamilton

David T Hamilton specializes in the areas of defaults, bankruptcies, and distressed debt performance for the Risk Management Services Group at Moody's Investors Service. He devised and produces Moody's Bankrupt Bond Index, and his analyses appear regularly in Moody's *Speculative Grade Comment* and *Credit Perspectives*. Prior to joining Moody's as an associate analyst in 1997, Mr Hamilton worked in the Regional Economics group at the Federal Reserve Bank of Philadelphia. Mr Hamilton holds a BA in Economics and Classical Studies from Texas A&M University, an MA in Economics from The Pennsylvania State University, and is a CFA candidate. Mr Hamilton is also an instructor at the New York Institute of Finance.

Andrew Hickman

Andrew Hickman is director of Research & Development for eRisks.com, responsible for designing methods and models, and providing technical content for the website. His contribution was written while he was a vice president in Risk Management & Measurement at Credit Suisse First Boston, where he was primarily responsible for modeling counterparty credit exposure on structured derivatives. Prior to joining Credit Suisse Financial Products, which subsequently merged into CSFB, Mr Hickman was a management consultant with Oliver, Wyman & Company, where he specialized in risk management. He graduated *magna cum laude* from the Wharton School of Business, University of Pennsylvania, with a BSc in Economics, concentrating in Finance and Political Science.

Sean C Keenan

Sean C Keenan is a vice president/senior analyst in the Risk Management Services Group at Moody's Investors Service in New York. His research includes the authorship of Moody's annual corporate bond default study and statistical modeling related to credit risk and credit risk dynamics. Prior to joining Moody's, Mr Keenan was senior econometrician at Loan Pricing

Corporation, Inc.Mr Keenan holds a BA in History/Economics from New York University and a PhD in Economics, also from New York University.

Robert Reoch

Robert Reoch is managing director, head of Asia Credit Fixed Income at Bank of America in Hong Kong. Prior to this appointment, Mr Reoch was based in London as global co-head of Structured Credit Products, a group responsible for credit derivatives and synthetic securitizations. Prior to joining the bank in 1997, Mr Reoch was director at Nomura International, where he was responsible for credit derivatives. Before joining Nomura in 1996, he spent 10 years at JP Morgan. In 1998, he transferred to Hong Kong and worked in the JP Morgan's M & A Group, focusing on the Philippines, Indonesia, and Hong Kong. Mr Reoch returned to London in early 1993 to join the Investor Derivatives Marketing Group. His responsibilities included the development of JP Morgan's credit derivatives business that started with the formation of a European credit derivatives group in 1994. He holds a degree in Law and Oriental Studies from the University of Cambridge.

Haydn Stedman

Haydn Stedman completed his BSc in 1980 with first class honours, winning the university medal in Pure Mathematics. Over the past 16 years, he has worked in a quantitative capacity in the financial markets, both in the design and development of software and as a market practitioner. He has also undertaken a post-graduate study in both Pure Mathematics (stochastic calculus) and Computer Science. He is currently with Citibank where he runs the cross-markets and exotic options desk in Sydney, Australia.

Christopher Whiteley

Christopher Whiteley is an associate with Allen & Overy, based in their Paris office, having qualified as a Solicitor in England and Wales in 1994 and Hong Kong in 1997. He specializes in advising on the privately-negotiated (OTC) derivative transactions (relating to interest rates, currencies, equities, and credit risk), repurchase and stock lending transactions, including regulatory and capital adequacy requirements in relation to such transactions. He also advises on collateral, including the taking of security over, or a transfer of title to, assets. He has experience in dealing with, and acting for, a wide range of counterparties, including banks, AAA -rated SPV's, fund managers, project finance and securitization SPV's, corporate end-users, mutuals, and individuals in both Europe and Asia. He acted for a large number of creditors of the Peregrine group in relation to their transactions.

Tom Wilde
Tom Wilde is a director at Credit Suisse First Boston in London, with responsibility for credit risk measurement methodologies. Mr Wilde is the technical architect of CREDITRISK+™, Credit Suisse First Boston's portfolio model which was made public in October 1997. Mr Wilde has a PhD in Pure Mathematics from Warwick University and a BA in Mathematics from Cambridge University, UK, and is a UK chartered accountant.

PricewaterhouseCoopers
Matthew Davidson — is a senior tax manager, currently on secondment to PricewaterhouseCoopers' Financial Management and Treasury group in London. He specializes in international tax structuring and products with emphasis on finance and treasury matters. He joined Price Waterhouse in 1991 and was seconded to the London office in 1997 from Perth, Australia. He holds a Bachelor of Business degree from Edith Cowan University and is also a Chartered Accountant.

Jonathan Davies — is based in London and set up PwC Credit Derivatives Practice in 1998. This is a group with global capability that supports clients in all aspects of using credit derivatives. The group has performed a number of assignments from infrastructure projects to gap analysis. Mr Davies has a number of credit derivative clients whom he advises on accounting, regulatory, risk management, and infrastructure issues. His role includes knowledge transfer, liaison, and global support for credit derivative assignments. Prior to joining PwC in 1995, He has spent four years in the industry working in the credit trading areas of investment banks.

Regina Fikkers — is a financial reporting director of PricewaterhouseCoopers based in Sydney, Australia. She specializes in advising on the practical applications of Australian and international accounting standards, in particular financial instrument standards, and in training on the implementation of new standards. She was principal author of the firm's IAS Illustrative Bank Financial Statements and has contributed to numerous other publications on financial reporting.

Steffen Gnutzmann — is a corporate and tax lawyer. He specializes in derivatives and international finance and is a member of the German Capital Markets Group of PricewaterhouseCoopers in Frankfurt.

Viva Hammer — is a principal consultant in the Financial Services Industry group at PricewaterhouseCoopers in New York. Prior to joining the financial services practice, Ms Hammer specialized in US and international tax, and was involved with designing and implementing global tax planning for multinational corporate clients. She has a Bachelor of Economics, and a first class honours degree in Law, both from the University of Sydney, Australia.

Ian Hammond — is the Assurance & Business Advisory Services practice leader of PricewaterhouseCoopers Australia Financial Services Industry Group. Based in Sydney, he is currently an Australian representative on the International Accounting Standards Board and was a member of the Australian Accounting Standard Board during 1992–1999. He has specialist experience in financial reporting aspects of treasury and capital markets.

Georg Klusak — is a lawyer based in Frankfurt. After having worked for Deutsche Bank, he joined Coopers & Lybrand. He is now heading the Capital Markets and the Investment Management Groups of PricewaterhouseCoopers in Germany.

Manfred Kühnle —is an audit senior manager in the financial services division of PricewaterhouseCoopers. After serving an apprenticeship in banking, Mr Kuhnle graduated with majors in Economics and Business Administration and joined PricewaterhouseCoopers in 1992. He is qualified as a German tax consultant (Steuerberater) and as a German chartered accountant (Wirtschaftsprüfer). He has specialized in the field of trading activities, especially forex transactions, equities, securities and derivatives, including credit derivatives, and in the field of risk management and risk control.

Urs Landolf — is a European partner in PricewaterhouseCoopers Tax & Legal Services, Zurich, Switzerland and partner in charge of the PricewaterhouseCoopers Financial Services Industry Tax Practice in Switzerland. He is a specialist in international tax, consulting for banking and financial services institutions including investment management operations, and in transfer pricing. He graduated with majors in Business Administration and Economics, and holds a PhD in Law from the University of St Gallen, Switzerland.

John T Lawton — is a partner in the Assurance and Business Advisory Services, Capital Markets Industry Practice of PricewaterhouseCoopers LLP. He specializes in providing auditing, accounting, and business advisory services to financial institutions, particularly money center and international banks, and broker/dealers. Mr Lawton is a former Practice Fellow of the Financial Accounting Standard Board. During his two-year fellowship, he participated in establishing new accounting standards for financial instruments. Mr Lawton has an MBA from Columbia and a bachelors degree in Accounting from the

University of Notre Dame. He is licensed as a CPA in the states of New York and Connecticut.

Emma Lubbock — is a tax partner in PricewaterhouseCoopers Finance Treasury Group in London. She is responsible for the firm's European Finance and Treasury Network. She has lectured on a wide range of banking, capital markets, and treasury subjects, and has contributed to a number of books and publications. She joined PricewaterhouseCoopers London in 1974 after graduating from Oxford University and became a partner in 1986. She is a chartered accountant and a member of both the Chartered Institute of Taxation and the Association of Corporate Treasurers.

Nabi Niang — is a member in the Assurance and Business Advisory Services group, Banking Practice of PricewaterhouseCoopers LLP. Before assuming his current position in 1996 in New York, he worked for three years in France on the audit of large banking institutions. He has provided assistance to several firms' banking clients on accounting issues related to various financial instruments. Mr Niang holds a Masters degree in audit and finance from the University of Paris IX, and a Graduate diploma in finance from the London School of Economics. He is licensed as a CPA in the state of Delaware.

Andreas Risi — is a senior manager in PricewaterhouseCoopers Tax and Legal Services, Zurich, Switzerland. He worked with Revisuisse Price Waterhouse/ PricewaterhouseCoopers from 1992 to 1998, and rejoined PricewaterhouseCoopers in December 1999 again. Mr Risi is a specialist in banking and financial services, in international tax planning for multinational corporations including mergers and acquisitions and ESOP's. He has led a number of international FS projects, proving his extensive technical knowledge. He holds degrees in Business Administration and Economics, Law and Political Sciences from the University of St Gallen, Switzerland. He is a certified Swiss tax onsultant and holds a doctorate in Economics at the University of Zurich.

Bill Testa — is a tax partner in the Specialist Financial Services Tax Group in PricewaterhouseCoopers, Sydney. He has 15 years experience in providing taxation services to the banking financial services industry, with particular experience advising on the income tax issues for derivatives and other complex financial transactions, as well as structured finance, leasing, funds management, offshore banking and cross border financing transactions. He is an Eonomics/ Law graduate from Sydney University and a qualified chartered accountant.

Introduction

Background to the second edition of *Credit Derivatives and Credit Linked Notes*

Credit derivatives have emerged as an area of significant interest in global derivatives and risk management practice. These instruments promise to revolutionize the management of credit risk in banking and capital markets, enhancing the liquidity of and facilitating the trading in counterparty credit risk. The first edition of **Credit Derivatives** was aimed at meeting the high interest in the study of these instruments and helped in the gaining of familiarity with these instruments.

This second edition is written in response to both the success of the first edition and the rapid changes in the market for credit derivatives. Since publication of the first edition, the credit derivative market has developed rapidly in various respects:

- The instruments have become more standardized.
- The market for credit-linked notes has grown rapidly with important developments in the techniques for securitizing the credit risk of bank credit portfolios.
- The range of applications has expanded with the rapid development of applications of credit derivatives in managing the credit risk of portfolios within financial institutions.
- The pricing of default risk is now more clearly defined, with a number of competing approaches emerging — the focus is increasingly on data problems, implementation issues, and model validation.
- The documentary framework for credit derivatives has evolved rapidly with the development of the ISDA-standard confirmation and definitions.
- The accounting and taxation aspects of credit derivatives have also developed as various proposals for derivatives have emerged.

Objectives of Credit Derivatives and Credit Linked Notes

The main objective of **Credit Derivatives and Credit Linked Notes** is to function as a complete reference work on credit derivatives.

It consists of a collection of papers from leading market practitioners providing comprehensive information on:
- all major credit-derivative structures, including credit derivatives and credit linked notes
- credit derivative applications
- pricing and valuation approaches and models
- documentation, accounting, and taxation aspects of credit derivative structures
- general implications of credit derivatives for banking and credit management

Key areas of this new and enhanced coverage include:
- credit linked notes, including repackaging structures and portfolio securitization
- pricing models and valuation approaches
- updated default statistics
- credit portfolio management
- regulatory framework for credit derivatives
- market developments and prospects

The book adopts a practical approach, with emphasis on examples to convey concepts associated with the instruments.

It is targeted at:
- staff at financial institutions, particularly commercial and investment banks, as well dealers who are active in credit derivative products
- liability and investment managers who utilize or are planning to utilize credit derivatives
- service industries, consultants, information technology (IT) firms, and accountants, who are active in advising traders or are users of these instruments
- supervision and policy staff at regulatory agencies

This book can also be used as the basis for practical in-house training programs, as·well as in postgraduate programs, such as MBA or Applied Finance courses in credit risk management, either as the primary text or supplementary reading.

Content and Structure

Credit Derivatives and Credit Linked Notes is structured around several themes:

- **Part 1 — Products and Structures**

  Chapter 1 outlines the basic building blocks of credit derivatives: total return loan swaps, credit spread products, and credit default products. Chapters 2, 3, and 4 examine credit linked structured notes, synthetic credit linked notes that were created using special-purpose repackaging vehicles, and credit risk portfolio securitization structures. These chapters have been extensively rewritten since the first edition, in response to market developments since then. In particular, the coverage on repackaged notes, repackaging vehicles, and portfolio securitization structures is new, reflecting the emergence of these products.

- **Part 2 — Applications**

  Comprising a single chapter, i.e. Chapter 5, which covers the applications of credit derivatives by banks and financial institutions, investors, and corporations, this section has been remodeled to reflect emerging applications of credit derivatives, including convertible arbitrage and corporate credit risk hedging.

- **Part 3 — Pricing and Valuation Issues**

  This section covers the pricing of credit or default risk. Chapter 6 provides an overview of the generic approaches to measuring and pricing default risk. It has been completely rewritten to cover recent developments in valuation methodologies. Chapter 7 outlines the use of estimated default rates to create models of term structures of credit risk. Chapter 8 describes mathematical approaches to pricing credit default derivative products. Chapter 9 outlines KMV's Expected Default Frequency approach, which is based on the Merton Model, to estimate the likelihood of default. This chapter has also been revised to reflect changes in the KMV Corp's modeling. Chapter 10 examines rating-agency models to estimate the risk of default, based on current rating levels. Chapter 11 focuses on the risk of rating revisions and its potential impact on default probabilities. Chapters 10 and 11 have both been updated with recent default statistics generated by Moody's Investors Service from its default database.

- **Part 4 — Credit Portfolio Management**

  This is a completely new section and it covers the emerging approaches to credit portfolio management. Chapter 12 gives an overview of and compares the credit portfolio models that are currently in use. Chapter 13 covers J.P. Morgan's CreditMetrics^{TM} approach to the management of credit risk.

Chapter 14 sets out Credit Suisse (CSFB)'s CREDITRISK$^+$ approach to the management of credit risk.

- **Part 5 — Markets**

  This section, consisting of only Chapter 15, focuses on the current market for credit derivatives, with a special focus on applications and participants. This chapter has been extensively revised to focus on current developments and the structure of the credit derivative markets.

- **Part 6 — Rating, Documentation, Accounting, Taxation, and Regulatory Issues**

  This section covers many of the critical support issues that need to be addressed when entering into any credit derivative transactions. Chapter 16 focuses on the rating of structured notes with embedded credit derivative elements and the impact of credit derivatives on ratings in general. This chapter has been extensively updated to reflect current approaches used to rate credit linked structures. Chapter 17 focuses on documentation and legal issues raised by credit derivatives. It is a new chapter, supplying information on the revised ISDA standard form confirmation and new ISDA credit derivative definitions. Chapters 18 and 19 examine the issues in the accounting for and taxation of credit derivatives. Both chapters have been extensively updated to reflect developments in various jurisdictions. Chapter 19, a new chapter, examines the regulatory treatment of credit derivatives. It covers the existing framework, as well as the June 1999 BIS reform proposal.

- **Part 7 — Conclusion**

  Chapter 20 bring the book to a conclusion with an examination of the evolution of the market and its impact on financial markets and risk management. In particular, it examines current market problems, including the key issue of the optimal structure and organization of the credit derivative function within a financial institution.

This book is designed either to be read from start to finish or to function as a reference source, where individual sections can be read separately.

Acknowledgements

I would like to thank all the contributors to the book. They are all busy practitioners whose expertise adds a valuable dimension to the work. I would also like to thank Claude Brown, who contributed to the first edition but was unavailable to continue his participation in this edition.

Thanks also go to the following organizations, which kindly consented to the use of material that greatly enhanced this work: *Financial Analyst's Journal* (which has given its permission for the inclusion of the article on "Using Default Rates To Model Term Structures Of Credit Risk" and Tullet & Tokyo (Vinayek Singh and Derek Simpkins).

My appreciation also goes to the Publishers, John Wiley & Sons (Asia) — Nick Wallwork and Gael Lee — for agreeing to publish the book, to Elizabeth Daniel who edited this book, and to Katherine Krummet who proofread it.

But above all, I would like to thank my parents, Sukumar and Aparna Das, for their encouragement and continued support of my work. In particular, I would like to thank my friend and partner, Jade Novakovic. Without her support, help, patience, and encouragement, this book, like so many others before, would never have been completed. This book is dedicated to these three people.

Satyajit Das
May 2000

PART ONE
PRODUCTS & STRUCTURES

1
Credit Derivatives — Products[1]

Satyajit Das

1.1 Overview

The emergence of credit derivatives must be understood against a background of a progressive redefinition of risk and financial derivatives. This change may ultimately prove to be as important as the advent of derivatives themselves and their use in capital markets.

The concept of financial derivatives is increasingly becoming one of trading attributes of assets. The move to combine the trading, sales, distribution, and risk management of physical assets and that of the derivatives on these physical assets, and the broader trends in the measurement, quantification, and management of market risk all reflect this important shift in focus.

A simple asset, such as a physical bond, is a complex bundle of attributes, which include:

- **Liquidity:** Represented by the investment of funds and the ultimate return of the investment, where the amount and timing of the cash flow (i.e. principal and interest) determine the return on or value of the investment.
- **Interest rates or debt prices:** Where the return is represented by fluctuations in the asset price that represents the present value of cash flow driven by interest rate movements or changes in the discount rate. The applicable

---

[1]   Earlier versions of the material in this chapter have appeared in:
Das, Satyajit 1996, "Credit Derivatives — Products & Applications," *IFR Financial Products*, Issue 49, pp 16–19
Das, Satyajit 1996, *Structured Notes And Derivative Embedded Securities*, Euromoney Publications, London, Chapter 13

discount rate, which combines a risk-free rate and a risk margin (to compensate for credit risk), is utilized to value the cash flow. The risk in this case also includes exposure to a series of discount rates (i.e. the zero curve) — in effect the risk of changes in yield-curve shape — that will interact with the movement of time (i.e. maturity and term-structure risk).

- **Currency:** Reflecting changes in the value of the currency in which the cash flow is paid.
- **Contingent elements:** Relating to embedded option features, such as prepayment or other rights.
- **Default risk:** Relating to the exposure to the potential failure of the issuer to perform its obligations under the contract.

The process of decomposition is illustrated in Figure 1.1.

Figure 1.1   Risk Decomposition

Assume the following bond:

Issuer	Company A
Amount	DM 100 million
Maturity	10 years
Coupon	6.25% pa, payable annually on the basis of a 30/360 day year
Issue Price	100
Yield to Maturity	6.25% pa, equivalent to 45 bp over the equivalent German risk-free rate
Call Option	The bond is redeemable at par after five years
Rating	A

The bond can be decomposed into and reconstructed from a number of distinct transactions. The decomposition set out below is from the perspective of a US$ investor. The steps are as follows:

1. Invest US$ equivalent of DM100 million (i.e. US$62.5 million, assuming a spot exchange rate of US$1/DM 1.60) in a risk-free, 10-year asset yielding floating-rate US$ money market rates.
2. Enter a 10-year cross currency floating-to-floating (basis) swap, where the investor receives DM floating rates and pays US$ floating rates (as funded by his/her US$ investment).
3. Enter a DM interest rate swap, where the investor receives fixed-rate DM for 10 years against payment of DM floating rates (as funded by the cross currency basis swap outlined in Step 2).

All these steps create a DM 10-year bond. To add the aspect of default risk to the transaction, the following additional transaction is required:

4. The investor enters into a default risk swap, where it assumes the default risk of Company A in return for receipt of an annual fee.

The effect of Step 4 is to create a corporate bond from which the investor suffers a loss of coupon and/or principal (subject to be recovered in bankruptcy) upon the default of the issuer. The spread over the equivalent risk-free rate that is derived from the fee received in exchange for entry into the default swap is designed to compensate for the credit risk assumed.

The investor can also add the call option when entering into a final transaction:

5. Enter a sale of a DM European exercise receiver swaption, through which the counterparty has the option to receive 6.25% pa against payment of DM floating rate for a period of five years, exercisable in five years' time.

These five steps are set out in the chart on the following page.

The pricing of the bond should equal the sum of its individual components. This ignores both the transaction costs and additional credit risks assumed within each of the different elements.
This decomposition illustrates the distinct risks that exist in each transaction, and the capacity to unbundle these risks and trade them separately.[2] This is set out in the following table.

Risk	Source
Liquidity	Step 1: Floating-rate investment
Currency risk	Step 2: Cross-currency basis swap
Interest-rate risk	Step 3: DM interest rate swap
Call or prepayment risk	Step 5: DM swaption
Default risk	Step 4: Default swap

This analysis is designed to highlight that derivative instruments, in conjunction with a cash investment, can be used to replicate physical assets. Moreover, reversing the process allows the deconstruction of physical assets into the constituent elements, thus facilitating separate trading in individual risk aspects, including credit risk.

Derivatives, above all else, facilitate the separate trading of *individual* attributes of the asset in *isolation* from the asset itself. In the above case, traditional derivatives, which involve interest rates and currencies, can be utilized to manage the risk of many of the attributes embedded in it. However, these traditional derivatives do not, except indirectly, allow the separate trading

---

[2] The decomposition is a simplification. For example, the swaps and swaptions need to be capable of termination in the event of a default by the underlying credit in order to reflect more accurately the actual underlying transaction

STEP 1:   US$ MILLION FLOATING-RATE CASH INVESTMENT

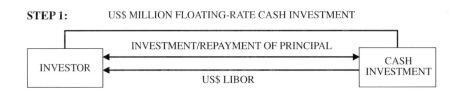

STEP 2:   DM/US$ CROSS CURRENCY FLOATING-TO-FLOATING
(BASIS) SWAP

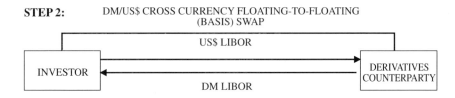

STEP 3:   DM INTEREST RATE SWAP

STEP 4:   CREDIT DEFAULT SWAP ON COMPANY A

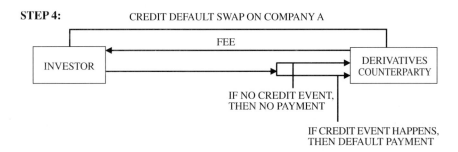

STEP 5:

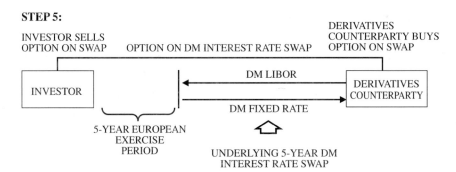

of two risks, namely, the risk of change in the risk margin and the risk of default. These attributes constitute both aspects of the credit risk of the security or the issuer. Traditionally, these risks have been viewed as impacting the price of the *overall* security. Consequently, exposure to these risks is managed through trading in the *asset* or *security* itself. Credit derivatives are specifically designed to allow the separate trading in and management of these risks.

1.2 Definition of Credit Derivatives

Credit derivatives may be defined as a specific class of financial instruments, the value of which is derived from an underlying market value that is driven by the credit risk of private or government entities, other than the counterparties to the credit derivative transaction itself. The last component of the definition is critical. In essence, it captures the role of credit derivatives in trading the credit risk of a particular entity (credit spread or price fluctuations arising from changes in credit quality, including default) by two parties who may, in some cases, have no commercial or financial relationship with the entity whose credit risk is being traded. Credit derivatives are, in essence, traditional derivatives (forwards and options, both on a standalone basis or embedded in the form of structured notes) re-engineered to have a credit orientation.

The principal feature of this instrument is that it separates and isolates credit risk, thus facilitating the trading of credit risk for the purpose of:
- Replicating credit risk
- Transferring credit risk
- Hedging credit risk

Credit derivatives also create new mechanisms for taking on credit risk in non-traditional formats within defined risk/reward parameters.

The principal demand for credit derivative products has, to date, been from the banks, financial institutions, and other institutional investors.

The use of credit derivatives by banks has been motivated by the desire to hedge or assume credit risk, improve (synthetically) portfolio diversification, and to improve the management of credit portfolios.

Investor demand is motivated by a mixture of factors:
- The ability to add value to portfolios through trading in credit as a separate dimension. This particularly entails the assumption of specific types of credit risk *without the acquisition of the credit asset itself.*

- The opportunity to manage the credit risk of investments.
- The inability of traditional institutional investors and asset managers to participate in loan markets, partly as a result of the absence of the necessary origination and loan administration infrastructure.
- The ability to arbitrage the pricing of credit risk in and between separate market sectors.

In the longer term, it is probable that credit derivatives will dictate a profound change in the activity of both these groups:

- Institutional investors will add credit risk as a *distinct* asset class, which will be managed within the general asset-allocation framework.
- Banks will alter their role into that of the *originator* of credit assets, which are then distributed to investors.

Corporate use of credit derivatives is also likely to develop as a mechanism for the management of financing risk or project risk (particularly in emerging markets), increase range of business counterparties, as well as insulate against default of major suppliers or purchasers.

Figure 1.2 sets out the product groupings of credit derivative instruments.

The principal products usually referred to as credit derivatives encompass three instruments:

- Total rate of return or total return swaps (also known as loan swaps)
- Credit spread products
- Credit default products

Figure 1.2   Credit Derivatives Product Hierarchy

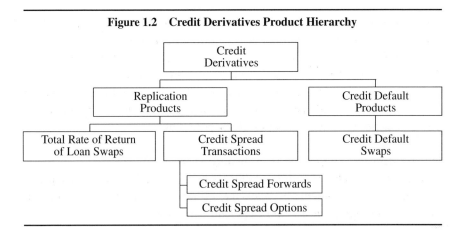

Total return swaps are adaptations of the traditional swap format to synthetically create loan or credit asset-like investments for investors, or hedge or short credit risk. The defining characteristic of these structures is their appearance off-balance sheet and their not necessitating entry into loan or bond purchase arrangements (in the traditional sense), and the concomitant obligation to fund.

Credit spread products are generally forwards or options on the credit risk margins on credit sensitive assets (primarily bonds, loans, or other credit assets). These instruments allow the separate trading of this attribute of assets for the purpose of risk reduction, speculation, or return enhancement.

Total return swaps and credit spread products can be regarded as replication products as they allow the synthetic creation of certain positions. These positions can be created in the physical market, but the derivative format offers significant advantages in terms of efficiency and transaction cost savings.

Credit default products, which are not dissimilar in structure to put options on credit sensitive assets, are usually structured as instruments that give an agreed payoff (either fixed or calculated based on a specific mechanism) upon the occurrence of a specific event — generally, the payment default of the subject credit. Credit default products thus allow the transfer and assumption of pure credit risk in relation to the event of default of a nominated issuer (however defined).

The market for credit derivatives is segmented along the following lines:
• Investment-grade credits
• Non-investment-grade/high-yield credits
• Distressed credit assets
• Emerging market credits

Predictably, given the relatively low default risk of investment grade issuers, the principal products relevant to this group are the replication products, in particular, the credit spread products). However, credit concentration problems, for example, in derivatives trading by dealers with high-quality investment grade credits may necessitate the use of credit default products for these counterparties. The other three sectors encompass both the replication and credit default products.

The availability of credit derivative products adds an interesting dimension to these market segments for the following reasons:
• The value in these markets is influenced significantly by credit factors.
• Value shifts, such as the spread decrease or increase experienced in emerging

market credits, or bond or loan price fluctuations that are driven by changing expectations of the risk of default or recovery rates in the event of default, are principally credit driven.

- The underlying credits may be of a credit standing that would not be acceptable to the investor, whereas a higher-rated counterparty providing the opportunity to create exposure to the underlying credit, indirectly may be an acceptable format.
- Regulatory and legal constraints may make it difficult to take the credit exposure directly, necessitating the use of synthetic means for creating the position sought.

1.3 Total Return Swaps

1.3.1 Structure[3]

The central concept of this credit derivative structure is the replication of the total performance of a loan asset. The basic structure of a total return swap is set out in Figure 1.3.

Figure 1.3   Total Return Swap — Basic Structure

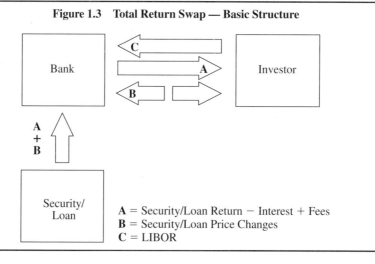

A = Security/Loan Return − Interest + Fees
B = Security/Loan Price Changes
C = LIBOR

---

[3] For a discussion on total return swaps, see James, Jessica and Thomas, Phyllis 1998, in *Credit Derivatives: Applications for Risk Management, Investment, and Portfolio Optimisation*, Risk Books, London, Chapter 7 "Total return swaps"

The key elements of the total return swap structure are:
* The investor assumes all risk and cash flow of the underlying asset. The term investor is used to merely differentiate the parties; in reality, both parties may well be banks. The term loan is used generically to cover all credit assets, including bonds and loans; most transactions use traded bonds and loans as the underlying asset.
* The bank passes through all payments of the underlying asset.
* The investor, in return, effectively makes a payment akin to a funding cost.
* The investor bears the full risk of capital price fluctuations of the underlying asset. This risk is structured as:
  — payments by the investor to the bank where the price of the underlying asset decreases
  — payments by the bank to the investor where the price of the underlying asset increases
This adjustment is made at specified times throughout the term of the transaction in accordance with an agreed mechanism that is based on the actual market price of the underlying security.

The investor may fund fully the total return swap (in effect, eliminating all leverage) by investing cash equivalent to the notional principal of the transaction in an asset yielding a return related to money market interest rates, which match the investor's payments to the bank. Figure 1.4 charts this structure.

Figure 1.4   Total Return Swap — Funded Structure

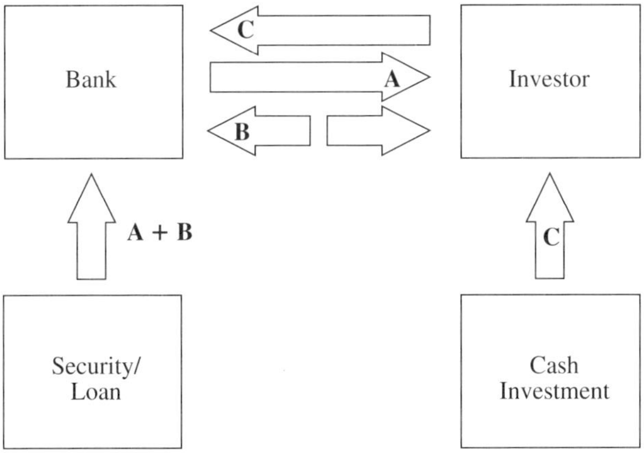

A = Security/Loan Return − Interest + Fees
B = Security/Loan Price Changes
C = LIBOR

The quotation convention for total rate of return swaps is for the return to be paid or received against the payment or receipt of the money-market return plus or minus a margin. The margin is used to adjust the return to the purchaser of the underlying bond or loan asset. Appendix A at the end of this chapter sets out an extract from a screen service showing the form of commonly used quotation.

1.3.2   Key Terms

Figure 1.5 sets out an abbreviated list of terms and confirmation of a total return swap.[4]

**Figure 1.5   Total Rate of Return Loan or Credit Swap —
Confirmation and Terms**

Underlying Credit Asset	A participation in a loan to [Corporation ABC] dated [March 15, 2001] or the [6.50%] coupon [November 15, 2012] final maturity bond issued by [Corporation ABC]
Total Return Payer	[Bank]
Total Return Receiver	[Investor]
Initial Notional Principal	US$[20] million × the Initial Price
Current Notional Principal	Initial Notional Principal adjusted for any principal reductions in the Underlying Credit Asset since the Commencement Date
Commencement Date	5 business days after entry into transaction
Maturity Date	The earlier of:
	1. One year from Commencement Date.
	2. The next succeeding payment date following repayment of the full principal and interest due on the Underlying Credit Asset.
	3. The occurrence of a Credit Event on the Underlying Credit Asset.
	4. Default or termination event caused by Total Return Payer or Total Return Receiver
Initial Price	[100.00]
Current Price	The [bid or offer] price of the Underlying Credit Asset as calculated by the Calculation Agent in accordance with the Calculation Method at 11.00am (New York time), [5] business days prior to the Final Settlement
Total Return Payment	All coupons and fees on the Underlying Credit Asset received by the Total Return Payer
Total Return Payment Date	2 business days after Total Return payments are received

---

[4]   For a detailed analysis of terms and documentation issues of total return swaps, see Chapter 17

Floating-rate Payment	3-month LIBOR plus Floating-rate Margin calculated on the Current Notional principal. (LIBOR is as quoted on Telerate page 3750, two business days prior to each the commencement of each floating-rate interest period.)
Floating-rate Margin	[0.50]% pa
Floating-rate Payment Date	Quarterly in arrears, commencing three months after the Commencement Date
Total Return Payment	The Total Return Payer pays to the Total Return Receiver the Total Return Payment on the Total Return Payment Date
Floating-rate Payment	The Total Return Receiver pays the Floating-rate Payment to the Total Return Payer on the Floating-rate Payment Date
Final Settlement	On Maturity Date, the Total Return Receiver will, at its option, receive from the Total Return Payer, either:

1. Cash settlement calculated as:

$$\frac{\text{Current Price} - \text{Initial Price}}{\text{Initial Price}} \times \frac{\text{Current Notional}}{\text{Principal Amount}}$$

and, the final Total Return Payment. In the event the cash settlement amount is negative, the Total Return Receiver will make the payment to the Total Return Payer.

2. Physical delivery of the Underlying Credit Asset including any existing cash or successor debt in exchange for payment to the Total Return Payer of the Current Notional Principal × the Initial Price + the final Total Return Payment

Credit Event	[Bankruptcy or insolvency event], [failure to pay or payment default above a nominated minimum amount which stays uncured for a nominated period], [restructuring event as defined], affecting the underlying credit asset or [Corporation ABC]
Collateral (optional)	10% of the Initial Notional Principal, i.e. US$[2.0] million in cash or US government securities. The transaction is to be marked-to-market and the collateral requirement may be adjusted on a [daily, weekly, monthly] basis.
Calculation Agent	[Bank]
Calculation Method	Choose one of these three methods:

1. In the sole opinion of the Calculation Agent
2. By dealer poll under which the Calculation Agent will poll 4–6 dealers in the loan on agreed dates and utilize the quoted prices to determine an average price for the underlying credit asset
3. By reference to a screen or quote service

The key terms of the total return swap structure include:

- **Reference bond/loan or underlying credit asset:** The typical total return swap is referenced to any widely quoted and traded bond or loan. This is essential to allow the price of the asset to be determined from an objective source. This requirement has meant that most swaps are based on traded obligations. In cases where an illiquid and non-traded loan assets is utilized, the terms loan asset and the total return swap must coincide with the final price of the loan becoming the actual final principal repayment made by the borrower.

- **Notional amount:** The transaction is based of a notional principal amount. No initial exchange is undertaken. The notional principal decreases with any amortization of the underlying bond or loan.

- **Term:** Typically, total return swaps have relatively short terms, of about six months to one year, although longer terms are not unknown. In practise, the typical documented term may be three years, with the option on each annual anniversary of the transaction by either party to terminate the swap. This structure provides the flexibility of a 1-year renewable annually, which has the added benefit of reducing the documentation costs in such a swap. The term of the total return swap need not coincide with the maturity of the underlying credit asset. The swap is also terminated in case of a credit event on the underlying bond or loan, as well as the default by either party to the total return swap itself. Where there is a credit event on the underlying bond or loan, there may be an additional requirement for materiality conditions to be met (see discussion on credit default swaps).

- **Asset price:** The initial price is agreed between the parties based on the current trading price of the asset. In the case of a new bond or loan, the initial price will be set at or close to 100% or par value. In the case of an existing bond or loan, it will be the prevailing market price (which may be greater or lower than the face or par value). The current price is necessary to calculate the final settlement under the transaction. This will be at maturity in the absence of default on the underlying bond or loan or default by either party to the total return swap. The current price may also be needed to calculate the mark-to-market value of the swap for the purpose of valuation or collateral calculations. The current loan price is determined by one of a number of ways, including:
  1. Independent quotes obtained from dealers in the asset over an agreed period, which are then averaged.
  2. Publicly available price information (screen or quote services) on the asset.

3. The dealer's own quote.

The problem of determination of the loan or security price is common to both total return swaps and credit default swaps. This is discussed later in the context of credit default structures.

- **Payments:** Under the total return swap structure, the investor receives:
  — Interest payments
  — Any loan fees, including commitment fees

The investor pays:
  — LIBOR (or the equivalent money market interest rate in the relevant currency) ± an agreed margin

All payments are calculated on the notional principal, which is adjusted for any amortization or repayments on the underlying bond or loan. Payments are usually made quarterly on the floating-rate money market side, while loan payments are passed through as close as possible to actual receipt. The payments may be netted when they are made on the same date.

- **Final settlement:** At maturity, upon default on the underlying loan or bond or default by one of the counterparties to the total return swap, a price settlement based on the change in the value of the bond or loan is made. The price used is that determined in accordance with the agreed relevant price calculation mechanism. Should the loan price appreciate, the investor receives a payment equal to the change in value of the loan. Should the loan price depreciate, the investor makes a payment equal to the change in the value of the loan. While it is usual to make the loan value settlement at maturity or default, as already noted, more frequent adjustments effectively marking the loan to market, including as at each payment date, can be made. These more frequent adjustments may be made for the purposes of collateral calculations or notionally in order to mark the position to market for valuation purposes.

The above structure assumes a total return swap indexed to a single loan. Total return swaps indexed to a basket or a specified loan index are also feasible. A total return swap indexed to a specific loan index would be structurally similar to a bond index swap.[5] Total return swaps are increasingly linked to a loan index despite problems including:

---

[5] See Das, Satyajit 1996, *Structured Notes & Derivative Embedded Securities*, Euromoney Books, London, Chapter 4

- The illiquidity of the index
- Occasional divergences between loan trading and index values, making these structures difficult to hedge

However, the index structures have the advantage of creating diversified exposure that may be sought by investors seeking either to hedge or assume exposure to the credit risk of the assets.

Indexes used include the Lehman Brothers Corporate Loan Index as well as various indexes published by other investment banks/dealers including Salomon Brothers, Goldman Sachs, and JP Morgan. An interesting index in this regard is the Citicorp/IFR European Impaired Loan Index,[6] which tracks a basket of distressed of impaired loan assets.

1.3.3   Transaction Rationale

The explicit rationale of the total return swap is to facilitate the purchase of or investment in (or sale or divestment of) credit assets (bond or loan) in a synthetic format. The receiver of the total return under the total return swap structure has full exposure to the underlying credit asset. The payer of the total return, on the other hand, effectively short sells or hedges its exposure to the underlying asset. It is important to note that the total return swap transfers the full risk of the underlying asset covering:

- **Credit spread risk:** Effectively a credit improvement of deterioration short of default, this is achieved by the final payment mechanism, where there is a payment between the counterparties of the transaction, reflecting the price change in the underlying bond or loan. As this price change reflects market changes in credit spread, the risk would effectively have been assumed and transferred under the structure.
- **Default risk:** This is also achieved through the final payment mechanism. In the event of default, the total return swap final payment will reflect the impact of default through the fall in price of the underlying bond or loan (effectively, the expected recovery level on the asset). The final payment mechanism will, therefore, effectively indemnify the payer under the total return swap against any loss as a result of default, through the receipt of the difference between the price at the commencement of the transaction and the price following default. The receiver in the total return swap correspondingly will bear the loss upon default via the payment to be made.

---

[6] See January 20, 1996, *International Financing Review*, Issue 1116 pp. 76

The total return swap structure is similar to and achieves the same economic outcome as a number of transactions involving the physical asset including:
- Sale of the asset
- A subparticipation transaction
- A repurchase (repo) arrangement

Advantages of the total return swap include:
- The off-balance sheet nature of the structure
- The capacity to short sell the loan market to hedge or position credit assets
- Potential cost of funding advantages
- The ability, because of the off-balance sheet nature of the structure, to leverage the exposure by utilizing a fraction of asset value as collateral to leverage the credit view
- The separation of the transaction from the underlying security or loan transaction, which effectively allows the *de facto* transfer of the credit risk to be affected without the consent of the issuer or borrower. This also allows the transfer of the economic rights relating to the obligation to be undertaken in complete confidentiality.
- The ability to separate the maturity of the exposure from that of the underlying credit asset

Advantages such as the off-balance sheet nature of the transaction and potential funding cost advantages provide significant benefits for banks and investors with lower credit ratings and higher funding costs in certain markets. The known advantages of the structure are especially attractive to certain institutional investors seeking to participate in loan markets. These investors may lack the essential infrastructure to undertake such transactions or suffer from significant barriers to trading credit default risk as part of broad macro-economic views or suffer high funding costs in holding such assets. Hedge funds have been a significant component of this last group.

The structure of total return swaps also creates certain issues. There is no direct relationship or contractual nexus between the borrower and the investor, assuming the economic risk exposure to the bond or loan. This means that there may be problems of confidentiality or representation in the case of default, distress short of default requiring restructuring of liabilities or dispute resolution.

Confidentiality issues may arise in respect of confidential financial information and other information that is not in the public domain but provided by the borrower to the lender on record (as opposed to the economic risk holder of the bond or loan). This is because the investor in the bond or loan through the total return swap may not be able to access this information without breach of the confidentiality provisions. In the event of default or other matters requiring creditors' agreement to a restructuring of the obligation or amendment to the terms of the original bond or borrowing, the investor via the total return swap may not be entitled to be directly represented at any such meeting, or be able to participate in such process to protect its economic interests. The investor may thus be forced to rely on the lender on record to act on its behalf, presumably based on its advised intentions and views in relation to the matter.[7]

1.4 Credit Spread Products

1.4.1 Structure

Credit spreads represent the margin relative to the risk-free rate designed to compensate the investor for the risk of default on the underlying security. Credit spread is calculated as:

$$\text{Credit spread} = \frac{\text{Yield of}}{\text{security/loan}} \times \frac{\text{Yield of corresponding}}{\text{risk} - \text{free security}}$$

Two general formats of credit spread derivatives exist:
- Credit spread relative to the risk-free benchmark (the absolute spread)
- Credit spreads between two credit sensitive assets (the relative spread)

Both linear (forward) and non-linear (option) format of investments are available.

Figure 1.6 illustrates the structure of a credit spread swap.

In the transaction depicted in Figure 1.6, under the absolute spread, the counterparty gains if the spread between the nominated security and either a risk-free security or another risky security decreases. If the spread increases, the counterparty suffers a loss of value. In the relative spread, the counterparty gains (loses) where the spread on the second security decreases (increases) relative to that on the first security. The relative spread transaction, in reality, is merely the absolute spread case where the counterparty enters into two credit spread swaps, where the risk-free component is offset and eliminated.

---

[7] Refer to the discussion in Chapter 17

Figure 1.6   Credit Spread Swap — Structure

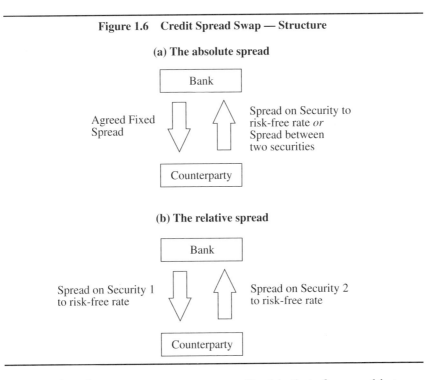

(a) The absolute spread

Bank

Agreed Fixed
Spread

Spread on Security to
risk-free rate *or*
Spread between
two securities

Counterparty

(b) The relative spread

Bank

Spread on Security 1
to risk-free rate

Spread on Security 2
to risk-free rate

Counterparty

In practice, the most common structure utilized is that of a spread between a security (bond or loan) and the risk-free rate. In practise, the asset swap[8] spread to US\$ LIBOR (or less frequently the LIBOR or equivalent in the relevant currency) is often utilized. This is despite the fact that LIBOR is not strictly a risk-free rate.

The credit spread swap structurally is a forward on the credit spread. In reality, it does not need to be structured as a swap or exchange of cash flow. It is capable of being structured as a simple forward similar to a Forward Rate Agreement (FRA), where upon maturity of the contract, there is a net cash settlement based on the difference between the agreed spread and the actual spread.

Options on credit spreads or credit spread swaps allow the creation of non-linear payoffs on the underlying credit spread movement. The types of options are:

---

[8]   For a detailed discussion of asset swaps, see Das, Satyajit 1994, *Swaps & Financial Derivatives*, LBC Information Services, Sydney, McGraw-Hill, Chicago, Chapter 18

- **Call options on credit spreads:** Where the buyer has the right to purchase the spread and benefits from a decreasing spread
- **Put options on credit spreads:** Where the buyer has the right to sell the spread and benefits from an increase in the spread

Figure 1.7 lists the traditional format for premiums for options on the bond credit spreads for a hypothetical range of securities.

Figure 1.7   Indicative Pricing of Bond Credit Spread Options

Type of Option	European call options on the spreads at the strike spread		
Issuer	Corporation A	Corporation B	Corporation C
Rating	Baa3/BBB-	A2/A	Baa2/BBB
Underlying Bond Issue	8.000% July 15, 2031	6.875% January 15, 2006	8.625% April 15, 2012
Reference Treasury	6.25% August 2031	6.25% February 2006	6.25% August 2012
Spot Spread (bp)	180	80	160
Strike Spread (bp)	150	70	140
Premium (bp)	28	6	10
Type of Option	**European put options on the spreads at the strike spread**		
Issuer	Corporation A	Corporation B	Corporation C
Rating	Baa3/BBB-	A2/A	Baa2/BBB
Underlying Bond Issue	8.000% July 15, 2031	6.875% January 15, 2006	8.625% April 15, 2012
Reference Treasury	6.25% August 2031	6.25% February 2006	6.25% August 2012
Spot Spread (bp)	180	80	160
Strike Spread (bp)	220	95	160

1.4.2   Spread Duration

Credit spread products entail the use of the concept of spread duration. Spread duration can be defined as the sensitivity of the capital value of a security to a movement in the credit spread. It represents the effective change in the capital price of the bond, reflecting the impact of a change in the spread on the discount rate used to calculate the present value of the security. It, therefore, captures the impact of the spread changes *over the full life of the security* in the present value price of the cash flows.

It is typically calculated by measuring the change in the value of the underlying bond price for a change in credit spread of, say, 1 bp at current yield levels. Figure 1.8 shows an example of the calculation of spread duration.

Figure 1.8   Calculation of Spread Duration

Assume the following security:

Issuer	Company A
Term	10 years
Coupon	7.25% pa, payable semi-annually
Yield	7.55% pa, semi-annual
Spread (to Treasury)	64 bp over Reference Treasury bond, which yields 6.91% pa

The spread duration of the security is 6.8. This signifies that for every 0.01% pa (1 bp pa) change in yield at current yield levels, the value of the underlying bond will change by 0.068% (6.8 bp).

The sensitivity of the spread duration (expressed as basis-point change in price) to changes in yield and spread levels is summarized in the table below:

Yield level (% pa Treasury yield)	5.91	6.91	7.91
Spread to Treasury (bp pa)			
34	7.7	7.0	6.4
64	7.5	6.8	6.3
94	7.3	6.7	6.1

Spread duration is also maturity sensitive as set out in the table below:

Maturity (years)	1	3	5	7	10	20	30
Coupon (% pa semi-annual)	8.00	8.00	8.00	8.00	8.00	8.00	8.00
Yield level (% pa Treasury yield)	8.00	8.00	8.00	8.00	8.00	8.00	8.00
Spread to Treasury (bp pa)	50	50	50	50	50	50	50
Spread duration (bp in price)	0.9	2.6	4.0	5.1	6.5	9.2	10.3

Note that the spread duration is characterized by convexity, that is the spread duration alters at different yield levels and with changes in the level of credit spread. It is feasible to adjust for the convexity of the credit spread.[9]

1.4.3   Transaction Rationale

The central concept of credit spread oriented credit derivatives is the isolation and capture of value from:
• Relative credit value changes independent of changes in interest rates
• Trading forward credit spread expectations
• Trading the term structure of credit spreads

The central concept underlying credit spread products is the ability to use credit spread derivatives to trade, hedge, or monetize expectations on future credit spreads.

The key dimension related to trading and hedging credit spreads is the term structure and volatility of credit spreads.[10]

The forward credit spread is calculated as follows:
1.   Identify the spot price of the security and the risk-free benchmark security
2.   The forward price of both securities are calculated and converted to the corresponding forward yield
3.   The forward credit spread is taken as the forward security yield minus the forward risk-free rate

From a theoretical perspective, the credit spread should increase in line with increasing default risk and maturity. In practise, the mathematics of the calculation indicates that with a positive sloped yield curve, the forward credit spreads increase. This merely reflects the inherent mathematics of the calculation of forward prices and yields, where the slope of the forward rate on the security increases at a faster rate than the forward on the risk-free rate, thus reflecting the increasing credit spread.

---

[9] For a discussion of adjustments for convexity in pricing derivatives, see Hull, John 1997, *Options, Futures and Other Derivative Securities*, Prentice Hall, New Jersey, US, pp 395, 405, 406–411, 414–415, 450–452; Brotherton-Ratcliffe, R and Iben, B 1993 "Yield Curve Applications of Swap Products," in *Advanced Strategies In Financial Risk Management*, eds Schwartz Robert, and Smith, Jr. Clifford, New York Institute of Finance, New York, US

[10] For a more detailed discussion and the mathematics of credit spreads, see Chapter 6

The implied forward credit spreads, in practise, seem to exhibit the following characteristics:
- They do not appear to accurately reflect investor expectations
- The forward credit spreads appear to be poor indicators of futures spot spreads

The forward credit spreads also appear to be relatively more volatile than the underlying securities. This higher spread volatility reflects the following:
- Lower absolute level of spread
- Imperfect correlation between the security and risk-free rate[11]

These factors allow the use of credit spread forwards or options for the following purposes:
- Trading credit spread as an isolated variable
- Trading the credit spread without assuming the interest rate risk
- Structuring specific risk reward profiles on credit spreads

In contrast to total return swaps, which transfer both the spread risk and the default risk, credit spread forwards and options only transfer the risk of changes in the credit spread. In reality, the transfer of spread risk may provide default protection as the spread could be expected to increase following default. The credit spread forward also provides symmetric payoffs, with participants benefitting from improvements in the credit and suffering a loss from adverse changes in the spread.

The use of credit spread products rather than physical transactions to replicate the positions is favored by the fact that the transactions are off-balance sheet and generally have lower transactional costs.

Figures 1.9 and 1.10 show examples of credit spread derivatives while Figure 1.11 shows an example of a credit spread derivative transaction involving emerging market securities.

---

[11] The volatility of credit spreads and their behavior are discussed in detail in the context of valuation of credit spread transactions in Chapter 6

Figure 1.9   Credit Spread Forward — Example 1

Assume that the widening of credit spreads on bonds issued by Company ABC allows the structuring of the following transaction:

Notional Amount	(up to) US$10 million
Maturity	1 year
Payoff of Spread Rate at Maturity	4.9 × (Strike Spread minus Final Spread) × Notional Principal
Strike Spread	150 bp
Final Spread	Reference Yield minus Reference Treasury Yield
Issuer	Corporation ABC
Reference Yield	Issuer's 7.75% of February 15, 2006
Reference Treasury Yield	US Treasury 6.00% of May 15, 2006

The investor entering into the transaction effectively receives the fixed strike spread and pays the floating credit spread on the credit spread swap. The result of the transactions is that the investor receives a fixed percentage of the notional amount for every basis point (the spread duration) that the spread on the Issuer's bonds decreases, relative to the strike spread of 150 bp. If the spread increases, the investor pays a fixed amount per basis point of the widening spread.

The transaction effectively segregates the spread duration of the underlying 8-year corporate bond from its interest rate risk. This type of transaction would be undertaken in an environment where spreads for these bonds have increased and are expected to decline over the 1-year horizon of the transaction.

The breakeven analysis for the investor in this type of transaction is set out below:

Final Spread (bp)	75	100	125	150	175	200	−225
Payoff on Spread Agreement (% of Notional Amount)	3.675	2.45	1.225	0	−1.225	−2.45	−3.675

The investor benefits within this structure as long as the spread on the spreads tightens from the spot level of say 150 bp (the forward is set at the spot spread level).

The spread forward may be combined with an investment in a 1-year security. The yield on the combination of a 1-year investment and the spread forward may provide a return in excess of the return on the security. Given the symmetric nature of the instrument, the investor would suffer losses where the spread continues to widen.

In an interesting variation, a number of these structures are combined with an option that effectively guarantees the investor a minimum spread on the investment (say, at 4.00% pa). This is achieved through embedding an option in the spread in the structure that limits the downside from a continued increase in the credit spread.

Figure 1.10 Credit Spread Option — Example 1

Assume an investor perceives that the credit spread on bonds issued by Company ABC is likely to narrow over a 1-year period. The investor can monetize its expectations by selling the following put option on the credit spread:

Notional Amount	(up to) US$25 million
Expiry Date	1 year
Option Premium	0.75% flat
Current Offer Spread (bp)	85
Strike Spread (bp)	100
Reference Bond	Company ABC's 7.75% 10-year bonds
Reference Treasury	Current US Treasury benchmark 10 year (as agreed by the parties)
Reference Spread	Yield of Reference Bonds minus Yield of Reference Treasury
Option Payoff	The purchaser of the option has the right to put the Reference Bonds to the seller of the option at the Strike Spread over the yield on the Reference Treasury at the Expiry Date.

Under the terms of the transaction, the investor is selling an out-of-the-money forward spread option where the purchaser can sell the reference securities of the issuer to the investor at a spread of 100 bp over the relevant Treasury benchmark. The investor receives 75 bp in premium for the sale of this option.

Based on spread duration of the Company ABC bonds at maturity of the option (i.e. the price of the bond changes 6.81% for each 100-bp change in the spread), the investor's breakeven level is around 11 bp. This is calculated as the premium divided by the spread duration. This breakeven point is some 26 bp above the spot spread.[12] This means that the spread on the bonds would have to increase to a spread in excess of 27 bp above current levels (around 32% increase in the spread), before the investor suffered a loss.

The investors would, through this trade, be seeking to monetize their neutral to positive view on the credit spread outlook. The sale of put option may be superior to an outright position in the bonds for the following reasons:
- The absence of direct interest rate risk
- The capture of return from the high volatility of the spread relative to the volatility on the underlying bonds
- The ability, through the strike level, to adjust the spread level at which the bonds are acquired if the put option is exercised

The purchaser in this case obtains protection against an increase in the spread on these bonds above the strike level.

---

[12] It is not strictly correct to view this option as being out-of-the-money. The in- or out-of-the-money nature of the option is determined by looking at the implied *forward* credit spread (*not* the current spot spread)

Figure 1.11   Credit Spread Forward — Example 2

In the aftermath of the emerging market sell-off in early 1995, the mispricing in relative value terms of various emerging market securities created interesting trading opportunities. For example, the following transaction, involving a credit spread forward, is designed to take advantage of the relative pricing of two types of Brady Bonds of an emerging market issuer. As of early 1995, the following bonds were trading as follows:

Security	Stripped Yield (% pa)	Stripped Spread (bps pa)	Stripped Duration (years)
Bond 1 (around 26 years final maturity)	15.84	943	3.5
Bond 2 (around 9 years final maturity)	14.42	870	4.1

The current spread of 142 bp between the two securities is at the upper end of the range over the immediate past 12–24 months. Given the similar stripped duration between the two securities, an investor, who believes that the two bonds should trade closer to each other, could monetize this expectation with the following transaction:

Notional Amount	US$10 million
Maturity	6 months
Payment	Notional Amount × (Current Spread minus Final Spread) × Average of Stripped Spread Duration of the two bonds
Payment Flows	If the payment is positive, then the dealer pays the investor. If the payment is negative, then the investor pays the dealer.
Final Spread	Bond 1 Stripped Yield at Maturity minus Bond 2 Stripped Yield at Maturity.
Bond 1	[Issuer; type of bond; coupon; final maturity]
Bond 2	[Issuer; type of bond; coupon; final maturity]
Bond 1 Stripped Yield	This is the semi-annual yield to maturity of cash flows resulting from a long position in the Bond and a short position in the US Treasury zero corresponding to its final maturity.
Bond 2 Stripped Yield	This is calculated by using a coupon bond amortizing similar to the bond and a price, which is the sum of the offer price on the Bonds, and the unwind value of an interest rate swap to pay LIBOR plus an agreed margin and receive the coupon.

The spread indexed swap outlined allows the investor to profit (lose) from a narrowing (widening) of the spread between the two securities.

1.5 Credit Default Products

1.5.1 Structure

Credit default products are designed to isolate the risk of default on credit obligations. These instruments can be structured as:
- Credit default swaps
- Credit default options
- Indemnity agreements

The exact structure is often regulation-driven or jurisdiction-driven. However, the essential elements are common to all forms of the transaction. The underlying default risk sought to be traded is capable of a high level of definition, including:
- Static exposures (such as bonds or loans) or dynamic exposures (such as those occurring in market value-driven instruments, primarily, derivatives) can be isolated and transferred.
- All obligations or a nominated subset of credit assets of the issuer can be identified. This categorization may be by seniority of debt or by market of issue (bank versus bond/public markets).
- The instrument can be linked to an individual credit or a basket of credits to create a specific or diversified exposure to default risk.

Figure 1.12 shows the diagrammatic structure of a credit default swap, while Figure 1.13 shows an example of a credit default swap. The transaction would operate as follows: if there is a credit event by the reference credit, then in this

Figure 1.12   Credit Default Swap — Structure

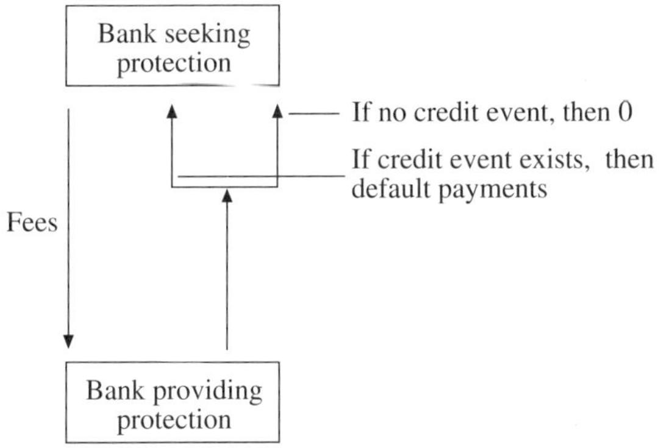

example, the bank would pay the counterparty the agreed default payment. In effect, the counterparty has acquired protection from the risk of default of the reference credit and, in return, pays a periodic fee to the bank.

Figure 1.13   Credit Default Swap

Assume investors own long maturity bonds issued by a company (Company ABC). The issuer's bonds have seen a widening of credit spreads with 3-year spreads currently quoted at 115 bp and 12-year spreads at 203 bp. The investor could, if concerned with shorter-term default risk, hedge with the following credit default swap:

Maturity	3 years
Reference Credit	Company ABC
Reference Bond	Company ABC's 8.50% 3-year bond
Credit Event	On the first business day following a default on its senior debt or a bankruptcy filing by reference credit
Default Payment	Notional amount × [100% minus Fair Market value of Reference Bond after default]
Default Swap Premium	3.20% (flat) payable by the entity purchasing protection.
Payment of Default Payment	The Default Payment is payable by the entity providing protection upon the occurrence of a Credit Event.

The transaction would have allowed the investor to hedge its exposure to a default by reference credit. An investor purchasing the underlying 12-year bond could have hedged its default risk for the first three years and still have enjoyed a positive spread on reference credit 12-year bonds of around 80 bp over Treasuries.

1.5.2   Key Terms

Appendix A sets out an extract from a screen service showing the form of quotation commonly utilized. Figure 1.14 lists an abbreviated form of term sheet/confirmation utilized in connection with these types of transactions.[13]

---

[13] For a detailed analysis of terms sheets and documentation issues of credit default swap, see Chapter 17

Figure 1.14   Credit Default Swap — Confirmation/Term Sheet

Buyer of Protection	Bank A, London branch
Seller of Protection	Bank X
Reference Entity	[Corporation ABC] and any successors
Calculation Amount	US$[10,000,000]
Trade Date	[date of entry into transaction]
Effective Date	[3–5] business days after Trade Date
Scheduled Termination Date	1 year from Effective Date
Termination Date	The Scheduled Termination Date; or [5–10] Business Days following the occurrence of a Credit Event [and the Materiality Requirement exists] as evidenced by the delivery by either the Seller of Protection or the Buyer of Protection of a Credit Event Notice, provided that this is on or before the Scheduled Termination Date.
Fixed-rate Payer	Buyer of Protection
Fixed Rate	[1.00]% pa (calculated on a 365/360 day count basis)
Fixed-rate Payment Dates	Quarterly in arrears with the Fixed-rate Payer paying the Fixed Rate up to the Termination Date
Floating-rate Payer	Seller of Protection
Floating-rate Payment	If there is no Credit Event prior to the Scheduled Termination Date, then there is no payment.
	If there is a Credit Event prior to the Scheduled Termination Date, then the Floating-rate Payer will either
	a) make a Cash Settlement; or
	b) undertake a Physical Settlement.
Floating-rate Payment Dates	Following Termination Date as specified in Cash Settlement or Physical Settlement
Cash Settlement	Floating-rate Payer pays:
	a) Variable Amount = Calculation Amount × Percentage Change in Price where:

$$\text{percentage change in price} = \frac{\text{initial price} - \text{final price}}{\text{initial price}}$$

	b) Fixed Amount = [50]% of the Calculation Amount
	The Floating-rate Payment is due and payable [5] business days after the Final Price Calculation Date.
Physical Settlement	Floating-rate Payer pays:
	Calculation Amount × Initial Price

	Fixed-rate Payer delivers: Face value equivalent to the Calculation Amount of the Deliverable Obligations where: Deliverable Obligations means the Reference Asset or where delivery of the Reference Asset is illegal or prohibited by regulation any obligation of the Reference Entity where the traded bond or loan obligation is: a) of equivalent priority in payment with the Reference Asset b) denominated in US\$ c) repayable in an amount equal to the principal amount and is not repayable in an amount determined by any formula or index d) of a maturity not exceeding [10] years. Physical Settlement must be affected [10–20] business days after the Termination Date in the event of the occurrence of a Credit Event.

Reference Asset	Means the following obligation:
	    Issuer/Borrower: [Corporation ABC]
	    Maturity: [November 15, 2012]
	    Coupon: [6.50]% pa
	    CUSIP/ISIN: [ ]
	    Original Issue Amount: US\$[500] million
	If the amount of the Reference Asset (or a Substitute Asset) is, in the reasonable opinion of the Calculation Agent, materially reduced, the Calculation Agent may substitute an alternative Reference Asset (the Substitute Asset) issued or guaranteed by the Reference Entity of the same credit quality as the Reference Asset.

Initial Price	[94]% of Face or Par Value, excluding accrued interest
Final Price	Means the price determined by the Calculation Agent determined by the Calculation Agent in accordance with the Calculation Method
Initial Spread (to US\$ LIBOR on an asset swap basis	0.85% pa
Final Spread (to US\$ LIBOR on an asset swap basis)	The spread of the Reference Asset to US\$ LIBOR on an asset swap basis calculated by the Calculation Agent on the Calculation Date(s) after the Termination Date in the event of the occurrence of a Credit Event
Credit Event	Credit Event means the existence of at least one of the following events:

a) Failure to Pay: The failure by the Reference Entity to make a due and payable amount exceeding US$[10] million on any Obligation after giving effect to an applicable grace period not exceeding [5] business days

b) Cross Default: The occurrence of a default event or similar event in respect of the Reference Entity under any Obligation in any amount exceeding US$[10] million which has resulted in such Obligations becoming capable of being declared due and payable before their original due date

c) Bankruptcy: The occurrence of any event set forth in Section 5(a) (vii) of the ISDA Multi-currency Cross Border Master Agreement, 1992 edition with respect to the Reference Entity

d) Restructuring: Waiver, deferment, restructuring, rescheduling, standstill agreement, debt or payment moratorium, Obligation exchange or other adjustment occurs with respect to any obligation of the Reference Entity and the effect of such is that the terms of such Obligations are overall materially less favored from an economic, credit or risk perspective to any holder of such obligation

e) Rating Downgrade [optional]: The Reference is downgraded by either Moody's Investors service or Standard & Poor's rating service to a long-term senior debt rating below BBB-/Baa3

where:

Obligation means any external obligation whether present or future contingent or otherwise as principal, surety or otherwise for payment or repayment of money incurred by the Reference Entity

Credit Event Notice — Means an irrevocable notice that sets out the occurrence of a credit event based on Publicly Available Information

Publicly Available Information — Means information that has been published or electronically displayed by at least two internationally recognized financial news sources. However, if either the Buyer of Protection or the Seller of Protection is cited as the source for the information, then such

	information shall be deemed not to be Publicly Available Information.
Materiality Requirement [optional]	The materiality requirement is taken to exist if after the Termination Date in the event of the occurrence of a Credit Event the Final Spread exceeds the Initial Spread by [1.50]% pa on [any one/majority/all] the Calculation Dates
Business Days	London and New York as adjusted by the Modified Following business day convention
Calculation Agent	[Bank X]
Calculation Method	The Final Price will be determined as the arithmetic average of the [bid] prices provided to the Calculation Agent by [4–6] Dealers on the Calculation Date(s)
Calculation Fates	[10–20] business days after the Termination Date in the event of the occurrence of a Credit Event; or [4–6] successive samples provided over a [4–6]-week period after the Termination Date in the event of the occurrence of a Credit Event
Dealers	[list agreed dealer panel members]
Documentation	Standard ISDA documentation
Governing Law	[London or New York]

The key terms and condition of the Credit Default Swap include:

- **Reference entity:** This is in effect the reference obligor the occurrence of a credit event in respect of which triggers the payout under the swap. The concept of Reference Entity is unique to credit default swaps. In the case of both total return swaps and credit spread transactions, a reference asset is needed. In contrast, in the case of a credit default swap, a reference entity concept is required. A reference asset is only required where there is cash settlement (based on the post-default price of the bond or loan) or physical settlement. It may also be needed to determine materiality.
- **Reference asset:** The relevant traded bond or loan asset issued or guaranteed by the reference credit must be nominated. The initial price of the asset must be agreed between the parties as at the commencement of the transaction. This is particularly important where the default payment is based on the post-default price of the security. The initial spread to US$ LIBOR on an asset swap basis is also agreed to enable determination of materiality where this is a condition of the transaction.
- **Transaction dates:** The key transaction dates include:
  — the trade date on which the effective terms of the transaction are agreed between the buyer and seller of protection

— the effective date (usually 3–5 business days after the trade date) when the transaction becomes effective

— termination date when the transaction ends

The effective date is important in that credit protection is only valid commencing from that date and any credit event that occurs prior to that date is not covered. Termination is usually after the agreed period of credit protection or where there is a credit event prior to the scheduled maturity the date of the credit event.

- **Credit event:** The occurrence of the credit event triggers the obligation of the seller of default protection to make the default payment to the purchaser of default protection. There are a number of possibilities:

  1. Payment default on obligations above a nominated threshold (say, in excess of US$10 million) after expiration of a specific grace period (say, 2–5 business days)
  2. Cross default or cross acceleration on other obligations
  3. Bankruptcy or insolvency event
  4. Restructuring, administration or Chapter 11 or the equivalent bankruptcy protection filing by the issuer
  5. Ratings downgrade below agreed threshold

  [The ratings downgrade provision is infrequently used and is not included in the revised ISDA credit default swap confirmation.]

  Given the heterogeneous nature of credit obligations (sometimes even for the same borrower), there are significant difficulties in defining the credit events. Reflecting the early stage of market evolution, there is also a lack of standard practises. However, in general, possibilities 1, 2, 3, and 4 are commonly used as the nominated credit or default event based on their importance, transparency, and lack of ambiguity.

- **Materiality:** The default event is usually linked to some concept of materiality to avoid an inadvertent or unintended triggering of a credit event. The concept of materiality is based on a minimum change in either the price of the bond or loan, or in the spread of the bond or loan relative to a benchmark rate such as US$ LIBOR or US Treasury bonds. The market practise has evolved around the concept of an increase in the asset-swap spread (over US$ LIBOR) by a pre-specified amount (say, 150 bp). This is calculated by specifying the spread at the time of entry into the credit default swap, and then comparing the initial spread to the prevailing market spread following a credit event. This provision is designed to ensure that there has been a true credit event triggering the requirement to make the default payment and to avoid the possibility of triggering a credit event when there has not, in reality, been an event of default. Materiality is usually determined simultaneously with the post-default price sampling used to determine the settlement payment. It is important to note that where materiality is a requirement it is not an independent trigger but must co-exist with the credit event to trigger the default payment. The materiality provision is controversial with considerable debate about its desirability and efficacy between major market practitioners.

- **Publicly available information:** The existence of a credit event is usually determined on the basis of publicly available information. This is required because it is assumed that either seller or buyer of protection has a contractual relationship with the reference entity and, therefore, will only become aware of the occurrence of a credit event from public sources of information. This approach is standard to all credit default swaps and total return swaps. The standard requirement is for a minimum of two reputable information sources. Information from interested parties is excluded to ensure that there is no conflict of interest. In order to avoid problems, a dispute resolution process is usually incorporated. Figure 1.15 illustrates this process in diagrammatic form.

- **Default payment:** Following a credit event, the buyer of protection is compensated by the receipt of a payment from the seller of protection designed to match the erosion of value in the underlying bond or loan arising from the credit event. There are at least three possible types of default payment:

Figure 1.15   Credit Default Swap — Determination of Credit Event

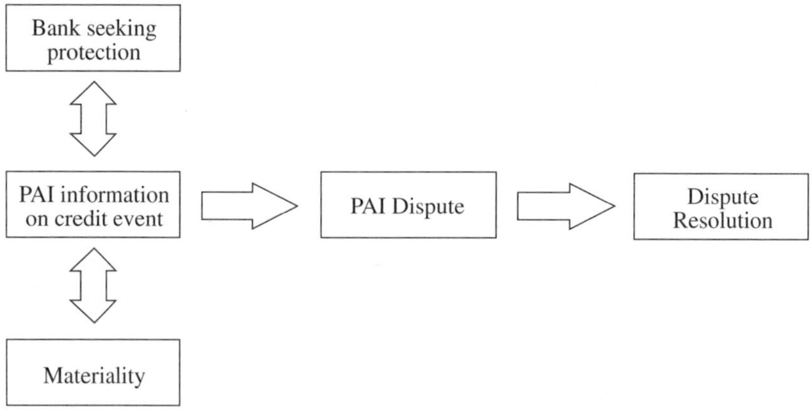

1. Post-default price: The transaction principal × the percentage change in the reference asset, as determined by dealer poll or from price quote services. Typically, (up to) six dealers are polled either on a single date or on a pre-agreed frequency over a (maximum) 3-month period following the credit event. The post-default price reflects the market price or the average of the prices obtained.
2. Fixed payout: Pre-agreed fixed percentage of notional principal.
3. Physical settlement: Payment of par or initial price by default protection provider in exchange for delivery of defaulted credit asset.

In practice, types 1 and 3 pre-dominate. They may be used in conjunction with the choice of default payment mechanism resting with the buyer of protection. The choice usually must be made at a pre-specified time around the time the post-default price is established. However, limitations on the universe of available liquid and publicly traded securities, as well as concerns about the effectiveness and transparency of dealer polls or market prices, have led to the use of type 2. Fixed payouts are typically based on historical loss experience in cases of default. These statistics may be internal to the organization or derived from rating agency statistics. The evidence of loss experience, somewhat predictably, points to average losses upon default being related to the seniority of the obligation and the secured or unsecured nature of the exposure.[14] Possible loss ratios include:

| Secured Obligations | 20–30% |
| Unsecured Senior Obligations | 40–60% |

The use of physical settlement assumes the availability of adequate face value of the reference asset. In the event that there are insufficient securities available or there are legal or regulatory impediments to physical settlement, a process of substitution is provided with cash settlement option as a final option. The market standard for substitutability allows for any US$-denominated standard obligation (bond or loan) of equivalent seniority with a maximum maturity of 10 years.

• **Payment timing:** The settlement timing varies between the different default payment structures. The fixed payout option has the simplest timing. This takes place an agreed number of business days after the termination of the agreement as a result of the occurrence of a credit event. The post-default

---

[14] See discussion of recovery statistics in Chapters 6 and 10

price and the physical settlement option are more complex. Where the post-default price mechanism is used, payment is made an agreed number of days after the post-default price has been made. Where physical settlement is used, the timing is around 10–20 business days from the termination arising from the occurrence of the credit event.

- **Payment for credit/default protection:** The buyer of default protection pays a premium. This premium is usually structured as an annual fee paid quarterly or semi-annually. It is expressed as the fixed rate in the default swap and is accrued up to the termination date. In certain transactions, this fee is paid as an upfront lump sum. This amount is calculated as the fixed annual fee discounted back to the effective date at an agreed interest rate. The upfront lump sum structure is primarily utilized to avoid credit exposure for the protection seller to the protection buyer. Where this structure is utilized, there is an adjustment or "claw back" provision requiring the protection seller to repay the unamortized amount of the fee in the event of an early termination of the swap.

Several of the key terms and conditions of credit default derivatives require comment. The two other terms that, in practise, create the greatest difficulties are the definition of the credit event, determination of the occurrence of a credit event and the calculation of the default payment.[15] The definition of these terms impact not only credit default swaps but, as already noted, also total return loan swaps (where the fluctuations in loan value are transferred between the counterparties and, therefore, the loan value must be calculated periodically).

The definition of default, as already noted, is confined to payment, as well as certain reasonably clear events of financial distress. In practise, the definition of default usually combines a trigger credit event, the existence of *public information* regarding the credit event, and, increasingly, the concept of materiality.

In examining the definition of default event, a distinction between private sector and sovereign obligors is essential. The discussion on credit events to date has focused on private sector obligors. Where the obligor is sovereign while many of the same types of default events are relevant, additional factors must be considered. For example, the concept of a bankruptcy-driven credit event is less applicable. Typical credit event for sovereign obligors include:

---

[15] For detailed discussion of the definition of these terms, see Chapter 17. See also Brown, Claude March 5, 1997, "Credit Derivative Payout Mechanisms," *IFR Financial Products*, Issue 61, pp 18–22

- Payment default
- Cross default or cross acceleration on other obligations.
- Ratings downgrade below agreed threshold.

Additional credit events would generally include:
- Debt moratorium or suspension of payment obligations or similar action
- Restructuring of the obligation, where the new terms are materially less favorable to the lenders

The possibility of differential treatment of different types of obligations (public versus bank, domestic versus international, local versus foreign currency) also has the potential to create significant problems.

The calculation of default payment presents greater problems. The fixed payout structure is the only default mechanism that is relatively free from doubt. The need to work out a post-default value to effect a cash settlement or physical settlement presents a series of problems.

The calculation of a post-default value assumes:
- A tradable and reasonably liquid loan or bond
- A transparent and objective polling process

In reality, the first condition is generally satisfied through the avoidance of variable payout structures where the underlying bond or loan is not sufficiently traded or liquid. The second condition is met in practise through a series of provisions:
- A sufficient number of dealers are included in the dealer poll
- The prices must be of a size comparable to the relevant transaction
- There is usually some provision for excluding quotes that are too high or too low, or where the bid-offer spread is unrealistically high
- The inclusion of a series of polls rather than the reliance on a single poll (often referred to as anniversary polling). Under these structures, an agreed sequence of polls is conducted at intervals of one week or two weeks between polls for a fixed period. This raises the difficulty of extending the time before actual settlement is effected.

Also needed is the inclusion of a provision to defer valuation where a satisfactory poll is not conducted. Figure 1.16 shows a typical timeline of events that establish a default payment.

Physical delivery avoids some of difficulties. However, it creates different problems including:

Figure 1.16   Credit Default Swap — Determination of Payout

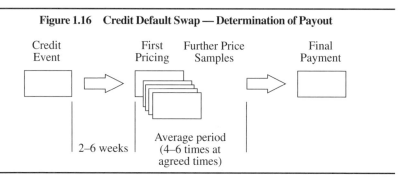

- The availability of the underlying securities to be delivered
- The ability to legally effect a secure and effective transfer of the defaulted securities

The lack of certainty of both of these means there is usually provision to deliver substitute securities (usually pre-agreed) or to revert to a dealer poll mechanism.

These choices and the problems they create in structuring these types of transactions are very real. For example, the fixed payout structure, which has considerable advantage of avoiding some of the identified mechanical difficulties, creates economic risks for the counterparties, as the agreed payout may not provide a true hedge for the party seeking to hedge the underlying risk.

The final problem regarding default payment relates to the necessity of selecting one of these mechanisms. This can be agreed at the start of the transaction or at the time that the credit event has occurred. The potential for disagreement on the mechanism for setting the default payment is substantial.

1.5.3   Transaction Rationale

The principal application of credit default structures is the transfer of credit risk. It is used primarily by financial institutions to manage credit risk arising from intermediation activities. Investment applications include the ability to transfer or, more commonly, assume credit risk synthetically to enhance portfolio return. Other applications include:

- Management of concentration risk within credit portfolios, particularly in improvements in the diversification of portfolios
- Adjustment of term requirements of credit by aligning supply of credit assets with internal constraints on the maximum term of investment funds
- Synthesis of credit risks with highly structured return profiles or the creation of credit risk-affected investments that are not directly available

- Creation of and investment in non-funded and off-balance sheet credit exposures
- Pre-determination of and trading in recovery rates, which are not generally available in capital markets
- Management of return on credit risk including optimizing returns unaffected by funding constraints or balance sheet restrictions

In considering the role of credit default swaps, it important to note the difference between these transactions and total return swaps or credit spread transactions. Credit default swaps transfer price risk on the underlying bond or loan in the event of a credit event. However, they do not transfer any price risk arising from changes in credit quality falling short of default. This is because there is no settlement between the parties unless there is a credit event. In contrast, both total return swaps and credit spread forwards transfer the risk of price changes as a result of changes in credit quality falling short of default, as embodied in changes in credit spread and, hence, in the price of the bond or loan.

1.6 Product Variations

The product structures within credit derivatives have evolved rapidly. Several structures that have emerged as important instruments include:
- First-to-default baskets (including a related structure—credit exchange agreements)
- Swap guarantees (or market risk contingent credit default swaps)
- Synthetic lending facilities, also referred to as asset swaptions[16]
- Variations on these structures including Volume/Size Remarketing Options and Currency Convertibility Agreements

1.6.1 First-to-Default Baskets and Variations

First-to-Default Basket[17]

The first-to-default basket concept is based on a credit default that is in turn based on a basket of underlying assets with different issuers. Figure 1.17 sets out an example of a basket-linked credit default swap.

---

[16] There is no consistent terminology in relation to these structures. The term synthetic lending facility is most often associated with Merrill Lynch

[17] For a more detailed discussion on the structure and value dynamics of first-to-default baskets, see Chapter 5

Figure 1.17   Basket-Linked Credit Default Swap

Counterparties	[Dealer] and [Investor]
Notional Principal	US$50 million
Adjustment of Notional Principal	In the event that any of the Issuers make an early repayment in respect of a Underlying Credit Asset, the Notional Principal will be reset on the next payment date to reflect the outstanding value of the remaining bonds.
Maturity	5 years from Commencement Date
Commencement Date	5 business days
Payments	Dealer pays Enhanced Payments. Investor pays Interest Payments.
Enhanced Payments	3-month LIBOR plus 0.35%, paid quarterly on an actual/360 basis
Interest Payments	3-month LIBOR, paid quarterly on an actual/360 basis
Underlying Credit Assets	**Issuer Maturity** Entity A December 2000 Entity B June 1999 Entity C April 2000 Entity D December 2000 [Average Coupon: LIBOR plus [20] bp pa]
Event of Default	If any one of the Issuers files for bankruptcy protection or incurs a payment default on any debt that remains uncured for 5 business days, the swap will be terminated and the Investor will pay the Termination Payment to the Dealer, who will pay to the Investor the Termination Asset.
Termination Payment	Equal to the Notional Principal
Termination Asset	The defaulted Underlying Credit Assets to the amount of face value equal to the Notional Principal
Calculation Agent	[Dealer]

The critical aspect of these transactions is the concept of first-to-default. This effectively entails that the relevant credit event that triggers the default payment or physical settlement under the transaction in respect of the underlying credit assets, is the first default of any of the credit assets included in the basket of credits.

The rationale for a first-to-default basket is that the combination of credit risks in the structure creates a lower credit quality than the individual credit

standing of the credit assets. This reflects the combination of two factors:
- The low default correlations between the credit assets included in the basket.
- The fact that there is an element of inherent leverage in the structure. Effectively, in a US$50 million transaction on four underlying credit assets, the provider of default protection on a first-to-default basis provides protection on any of the four assets up to a face value of US$50 million. The seller of default protection is providing protection on US$200 million of credit assets at least until one of the entities defaults.

In practice, the earliest first-to-default structures entailed high-quality underlying credit assets such as Scandinavian sovereign issuers and other large European borrowers. The motivation for these transactions was the need for commercial and investment banks to hedge large credit exposures to these entities. These credit exposures related to capital market activity, such as interest rate and currency swaps, standby credit facilities to support funding of these borrowers, and limits to facilitate trading in securities issued by these entities.

The providers of protection under these structures were primarily institutional investors seeking higher yields on high-quality securities. The higher yield obtained on these first-to-default baskets was attractive to investors, who did not properly quantify the additional marginal risk of the structure, or because they were indifferent to the risks as the underlying credit assets were eligible investments for these investors on a standalone purchase basis. Far Eastern investors, including Japanese institutions, European and Middle Eastern investors were the major providers of these types of credit default protection. The attraction of these structures from the perspective of the parties purchasing protection, was that these structures enabled them to reduce large credit concentrations within their portfolios at an attractive cost.

Recently, the structure has been used primarily by Japanese banks and emerging markets credits. The emergence of significant credit problems within the Japanese banking system in the mid-1990s prompted a significant volume of transactions, which primarily entailed the sale of default risk on the weaker Japanese financial institutions through these first-to-default credit structures. The driving force was the necessity to reduce the large credit concentration within bank portfolios to this group of obligors. The protection was provided by Far Eastern investors, including *better capitalized* Japanese financial institutions, primarily institutional investors, as well as investors in other markets *with low levels of exposure to Japanese bank risk*.

The emerging market transactions involved trading baskets of Latin, Southeast Asian and, more recently, East European risk. The underlying rationale of these transactions was for large international money-center commercial and investment banks active in these markets to diversify or trade out of large risk concentration to particular counterparties to allow them to continue to transact business with these counterparties. The providers of default protection was again institutional investors and hedge funds willing to take the default risk to these issuers/counterparties.

In all of these transactions, a major driving force was the attractiveness to the investors assuming the default risk of the format for the transfer of credit risk created in the first-to-default basket. The structures embedded in notes/securities provided an elegant mechanism for creating the desired exposure while allowing the investors to generate incremental yield, which provide outperformance relative to the underlying benchmarks against which the performances of these investors were measured.

In reality, the first-to-default basket structures are essentially predicated on allowing providers of protection to trade default correlation. As default correlation has not historically been easy to trade, the ability to trade it and the use of this factor to generate incremental income were the major drivers of the structure. The capacity to create hidden leverage was also attractive.

Credit Exchange Agreements

Credit exchange agreements are based on the same essential premise as first-to-default baskets. These structures provide the purchaser with the capacity to substitute one credit for another within an asset swap framework. In return for offering essentially default protection, the writer of the credit exchange option receives a return on the asset swap, which is usually higher than the spread on either underlying credit on an asset swap basis. The available return is generally closer to the combined spread of the two underlying asset swaps. Figure 1.18 lists the terms of a typical credit exchange transaction. This transaction is also known as switch asset swap or asset swap switch option.

Figure 1.18   Credit or Asset Swap Exchange Agreement

Credit or asset swap exchange agreements allow investor who are seeking to enhance returns on asset swaps, to engineer incremental yield through entry into credit exchange swaps. This structure allows the investor to combine the spreads of two issuers and earn an incremental return that is greater than the spread over the LIBOR available for the lower quality issuer.

A typical credit or asset swap exchange agreement is structured as follows:

	Asset
Issuer	A rated issuer
Principal Amount	US$20 million
Maturity	5 years
Coupon	7.25% pa on a bond basis
	Payments
Investor Pays To Counterparty	Par for bonds, swaps and coupons on Asset, Credit Exchange Event (if appropriate)
Investor Receives From Counterparty	3-month LIBOR plus 75 bp reset payable quarterly on an actual/360-day basis
	Credit Event Exchange
Exchange Option	The Counterparty in the event of the occurrence of a Credit Event may cancel the asset swap. Upon such cancellation, the Counterparty will deliver US$25 million of senior debt claims on a nominated BBB- Company in return for the cancellation of the swap and the delivery of the Asset from the Investor.
Credit Event	Any of the following with respect to BBB-rated Company:
	1. Payment default on interest or principal on any senior debt or other monetary obligation above US$[10] million and after a 3-day grace period
	2. Cross default or cross acceleration event
	3. Event of bankruptcy
	4. Restructuring

Under the terms of the transaction, the investor combines the credit of a single A credit with that of a BBB-rated company. The A-rated credit would swap into LIBOR plus 20 bp. A similar maturity bond issued by the BBB-rated issuer would swap into LIBOR plus 65 bp. The credit exchange swap allows the investor to receive closer to the combined credit spread.

Upon occurrence of a default event with respect to the BBB-rated company, the counterparty has the right to cancel the swap and deliver the notional amount of (defaulted) senior debt claims on the BBB-company in exchange for delivery of the A-rated security.

In structural terms, credit exchange transactions are similar to the first-to-default basket credit structures identified above. The enhancement to the underlying credit is achieved through taking advantage of the underlying default risk correlations. The incremental spread generated is dependent upon the individual spreads and on the correlation between the probability of default of the two issuers.

1.6.2 Swap Guarantees/Market Risk Contingent Credit Default Swaps[18]

The credit default structures considered to date assume that the underlying credit exposure being hedged or assumed is fixed and known. This is the case with credit exposure on bond and loan structures. However, where the underlying transaction is a derivative transaction (such as an interest rate swap, cross currency swap, etc), the credit exposure is a function of movements in markets variables (interest rates, foreign exchange rates, implied volatility) and the remaining time to maturity (affected by the passage of time). For example, in any swap, forward, or option position, the credit exposure as between the counterparties is a function of two factors: the current mark-to-market value of the transaction (effectively its replacement value at current market rates) and an estimate of the expected future replacement costs (derived using expected volatility of the variables affecting the contract value).

The static structure of the traditional credit default swap is not designed to effectively hedge or transfer this type of dynamic credit risk. Swap guarantees or market risk contingent credit default swap evolved during 1995–1996 to enable this type of credit risk.[19]

The swap guarantee is a credit default swap, where the notional principal is linked directly to the credit exposure on a swap transaction (that is, the mark-to-market valuation of the reference transaction). In the event of credit event or default on the swap, the bank providing protection will pay the bank purchasing protection an amount related directly to the mark-to-market value of the swap as at the time of default. The default event may be defined generally or with reference to default on the swap itself. Figure 1.19 shows the structure of this contract.

The credit default swap linked to the swap value is different from a normal credit swap in that amount of the default payment is dynamic and linked to the value of the swap which is a function of *market variables*. Bank buying

---

[18] For a further discussion of the structure and value dynamics of swap guarantee structures, see Chapter 5

[19] The major portion of these types of transactions relate to swaps (particularly, currency swaps). Consequently, the term swap guarantee is utilized to designate these types of structure

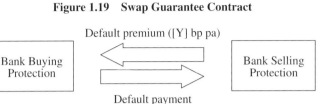

Figure 1.19   Swap Guarantee Contract

protection will only suffer a loss if the swap counterparty defaults, there is an amount owing under the swap, and the bank providing protection under the swap also defaults. This multiple contingency structure significantly enhances the credit quality of the exposure that will generally be superior to that of both the swap counterparty and the swap guarantee counterparty.

The credit default swap linked to the value of the swap is capable of being structured in a number of ways:

1.   The default swap may cover any exposure under the swap.
2.   The default swap may cover exposure to a pre-agreed amount.
3.   The default swap may cover exposure above a minimum amount.

The term of the protection can also be varied, with protection being obtained for periods up to the remaining term of the swap.

1.6.3   Asset Swaptions/Synthetic Lending Facilities

Structure

The central concept underlying these structures is an instrument that provides institutional investors the capacity to derive fee income in return for the provision of a forward commitment to purchase a security. The decomposition of these structures reveals embedded credit spread optionality that is sold to generate premium income.

Structurally, the synthetic lending facilities are undertaken as effectively as a put option on a revolving bank credit facility or, more typically, an asset swap transaction in relation to an identified reference security. In effect, the transaction entails a participation in an unfunded revolving loan, which at agreed dates either terminates or converts, at the option of the purchaser, into term credit commitment with a predetermined credit spread. Figure 1.20 shows the terms of a typical synthetic lending facility.

Figure 1.20   Asset Swaption/Synthetic Lending Facility

	Issuer
Issuer	Company ABC
Credit Rating	Ba1/BBB-
Reference Bond	7.50% January 2012
Ranking	Senior Unsecured Debt
	Structure
Structure	Synthetic Revolving Credit Facility
Notional Principal	US$50 million
Maturity	3 years
Form of Commitment	Commitment to enter into an Asset Swap
Settlement Type	Physical or cash
Settlement Date	First business day of each month
Notification Date	5 business days prior to Settlement Date
	Pricing
Upfront Fee	30 bp (flat), payable as at Commencement Date
Annual Commitment Fee	25 bp pa, payable quarterly
Interest Rate on Asset Swap	3-month LIBOR plus 60 bp, payable quarterly in arrears
All-In Spread	Drawn—71 bp
	Undrawn—36 bp

The terms of the transaction, in particular the structure of the revolving credit, are agreed as between the parties. A key element is the specification of the reference bond (or less commonly traded loan) that can be delivered in asset swap form under the synthetic lending facility.

The synthetic lending facility operates as follows:

- The investor receives the upfront fee at the commencement of the transaction.
- The investor also receives the commitment fee until the synthetic funding facility is called upon.
- If the facility is exercised, the reference bond will be sold in an asset swap format to the investor yielding the agreed margin over the floating interest rate benchmark. The arrangement can be either cash settled or concluded by physical delivery.

The key terms of the instrument are as follows:

- **Upfront fee:** Payable at commencement on the Notional Amount of the transaction.
- **Commitment fee:** Paid, usually, quarterly, at the agreed rate until the synthetic lending facility is drawn or expires unexercised.

- **Spread:** Refers to the margin over the nominated floating-rate index which is payable on the credit facility or asset swap if the synthetic lending facility is drawn upon.
- **Settlement mechanics:** The transaction is usually settled in one of two ways:
  1. If settlement is by delivery, the reference bonds are delivered to the investors in return for payment of par or a pre-agreed value. The investor enters into an interest swap with the counterparty where it pays the bond coupon and receives the agreed floating-rate index plus the agreed spread.
  2. If settlement is by cash, then the asset swap is valued by polling a number (typically, 3 or 4) of dealers, with the quotes being averaged out. The difference in value from par or a pre-agreed value, if negative, (positive) is paid by (to) the investor.

The synthetic lending facility structure can include covenant protection, which offers the investor additional protection. The format has occasionally incorporated increases in the fees or spread in line with any credit rating downgrade.

The structure is essentially a structured sale of a Bermudan put option on the credit spread on the underlying asset. The option is sold by the investor in the facility.

The primary advantage of the synthetic lending swap is its customized and more liquid form of a traditional bank revolving credit facility. In particular, it offers investors, as opposed to financial institutions, the ability to gain exposure to the loan markets.

Major benefits include:

- The capacity to participate in, essentially, bank markets without the need to establish the necessary infrastructure of a bank
- The ability to customize the terms to a very high degree
- The choice of cash versus physical settlement
- The enhanced liquidity offered by the capacity to trade the position in the asset swap market (which assumes the liquidity of the underlying bond or swap market)

The major participation in synthetic lending facilities has to date emerged from investors seeking the fee earnings from these transactions without the necessity to invest cash in the underlying security. In addition, the fact that the implied spread is usually greater than the spread available on existing revolving credits offers investors some protection against any potential increase in the credit spread. The buyers of protection in these structures have included banks with significant asset swap inventory seeking protection against a widening in the credit spread. Other parties include investors in high yield assets who combine the purchase of a bond with the simultaneous entry into a synthetic lending transaction/ asset swaption. This combination means that the investor receives the higher return on the high-yield asset, but can limit its loss in the event of a deterioration of credit quality by exercising its rights under the facility and putting the bond on asset swap basis with the seller of protection. This limits its losses to a pre-nominated amount.

Figure 1.21 shows the typical format of quotation of the structure and pricing of available synthetic lending facilities for a number of hypothetical credits.

Figure 1.21   Asset Swaption/Synthetic Lending Facilities Quotations

Issuer	Security	Ratings	Maturity (years) (flat)	Upfront Fee (bppa)	Commitment Fee	Spread to LIBOR
Corporation A	8.25% April 1, 2000	A−/Baa1	2	30	25	75
Corporation A	7.90% July 1, 2012	BBB+/Baa1	3	31.5	5	90
Corporation B	0% July 15, 2017	BBB−/Ba1	3	50	40	150
Corporation C	9.25% September 15, 2010	BBB−/Ba1	3	35	30	125
Corporation D	MTN < December 1, 2006	A/Baa1	1	10	30	55

The synthetic lending facility, also referred to as a remarketing option, was originally devised by securities traders who sought to protect inventory positions, either in physical securities or asset swaps, as yield fell to historically low levels during the 1990s. These transactions provided protection against losses on inventory in a sudden reversal in the decline of credit spreads or an erosion of the (often) very substantial capital gains that had accrued on some of these positions as a result of the fall in credit spreads.

The providers of these facilities included traders and investors, who sought exposure to credit spreads, in anticipation of decreasing credit spreads, but on an off-balance sheet basis in order to decrease capital committed to these transactions. A significant issue for traders and investors was that as spreads declined to lower levels, the fact that the potential declines became progressively smaller meant that increased degrees of leverage were required to amplify the profit impact of moves in changes in credit spread.

Structural Variations

A number of structural variations on the basic asset swaption/synthetic lending facility have evolved. These include callable/puttable asset swaps and volume/size options.

Callable/Puttable Asset Swaps

The concept of a callable asset swap represents a variation of the standard asset swaption, where the dealer placing the asset swap with an investor or a bank retains a call option on the asset. The call option entitles the dealer to repurchase the asset swap at a nominated spread over LIBOR at specific dates.

The asset swap is typically callable at the spread at which the asset swap is placed with the investor, i.e. at par. Call options are either European or Bermudan in exercise structures being exercisable either at the end of 6–12 months or at each interest payment date, say quarterly, in a year. If the credit spread on the underlying credit asset decreased, then the call would be exercised enabling the dealer to capture the value from the fall in the spread. The value capture is achieved by the dealer reselling the asset swap package to other banks or investors at the lower credit spread. The transaction basically entails the investor in the asset swap simultaneously selling a call option on the spread to the counterparty.

The bank or investor purchasing the callable asset swap is compensated by receiving a higher spread than that available in the market at that time. In return for this additional spread, the bank writes the call option on the credit spread on the underlying asset. The major attraction for the bank or investor writing the call option was the capacity to receive higher yields than currently available to meet target rates of return or enhance yield. From the dealer's point of view, the callable asset swap is an attractive mechanism for maintaining exposure to further tightening in the credit spread but on an off-balance sheet basis and without exposure to an increase in the spread.

The transactions were generally designed to be settled through a physical settlement entailing sale of the asset and an assignment or cancellation of the swap. A variation on this form of settlement was the recouponing or spread reset option. Under this structure, the asset remained with the bank or investor, but the spread was merely reset at the new market level with the usual swap cash flows being adjusted. This might also incorporate an option for the bank or investors to resell the call, but at a lower strike spread level to enhance returns through the capture of the call premium.

A variation on this structure evolved around 1997 and 1998 during a period of unprecedented volatility in merging markets. As emerging markets in Asia, Latin America and Eastern Europe collapsed, dealers in emerging markets were increasingly left with large inventories of emerging market debt with large mark-to-market losses.[20] As markets eventually stabilized, at least, in relative terms, dealers seeking to divest themselves of this "toxic" paper had to develop special structures to entice investor interest. One such structure was the puttable asset swap.

The structure entailed the dealer selling a tranche of emerging market paper to an investor on an asset swap basis. In order to protect the investor against any loss in value, the asset swap would incorporate a provision whereby the investor would have the right to put the asset swap back to the dealer at a designate spread (typically, the same spread as the asset swap itself or a slightly higher spread) at pre-agreed dates during the life of the asset swap. In effect, the investor was buying and the dealer was selling a put option on the credit spread. The put option premium was usually funded by a reduction in the asset swap spread.

The major attraction of these structures was the ability for dealers to reduce inventory and gain liquidity. The capacity to achieve disposition at prices that were above those that could be achieved by direct sale was also important. The attraction for investors was the ability to gain exposure to emerging markets at relatively attractive prices (even after the reduction in spread to fund the purchase of the put option) in anticipation of an improvement in values.

Volume/Size Options

These transactions evolved from the standard asset swaptions/synthetic lending facilities and callable asset swaps. The major driving factors were the decline in credit spreads to historically low levels. Dealers who had either earned

---

[20] It was during this time that the term "submerging markets" was coined

significant returns (often unrealized) from the ongoing contraction in credit spreads, or had or were acquiring inventory at these lower spread levels, became concerned about an increase in credit spreads. The volume/size options, also known variously as double up options or variable size asset swaps, were designed in effect to hedge this exposure to the risk of credit spreads increasing.

The transactions were structured as assets swaps that were placed with the investors or banks at a credit spread above that which was available in the market at the time. The dealer had the right under the structure to place or put an additional volume in face value of the asset swap at the agreed spread to the bank or investor within 6–12 months. The exercise structure was similar to that described in connection with callable asset swaps.

The transaction effectively combines the placement of an asset swap with the sale by the bank or investor of an asset swaption or synthetic lending facility for a face value equivalent to the additional amount the dealer can put with the buyer of the original asset swap. The premium received for the sale of the asset swaption is utilized to increase the return on the original asset swap. If the spreads widen, than the additional volume of asset swaps is placed with the investors. If spreads do not increase above the nominated levels, than the asset swap volume remains unaltered.

The bank or investor was originally attracted to this structure as a mechanism for enhancing the return on assets in a period of narrow credit spreads. They were prepared to accept the credit spread risk on the basis of the premium captured and the fact that they would have been prepared to purchase the assets at values higher than the current market spreads had they been available. During the market crisis that prevailed in 1997 and 1998, this structure was used by dealers to reduce inventory of emerging market paper with large mark-to-market losses. The major investors were aggressive investors who held the view that markets had "overshot" and would ultimately correct to normal levels.

Both the callable/puttable asset swaps and volume/size options are typically documented as asset swap structures. Both structures are also frequently embedded and sold in the form of structured note products

1.6.4   Currency Inconvertibility Agreements

A number of structures that deal with specific aspects of sovereign risk in financial transactions have emerged. These structures are mainly utilized in relation to emerging markets transactions. This reflects both the higher level of sovereign risk evident in such transactions and the central role played by sovereign risk in emerging markets trading.[21]

There are various levels of credit risk in transactions involving emerging markets. They range from regulatory risk, market risk (currency, interest rate, and equity price risk), counterparty default risk, and sovereign risk.

The sovereign risk element involves a series of risks including the inconvertibility of the currency or non-transferability of the currency. For example, a borrower with foreign currency debt or other payment obligations may not be able to exchange local currency to meet these obligations even if it has the cash resources to make the relevant transfer. This risk is a central concern of foreign investors in emerging markets (both direct and portfolio equity investors, and purchasers of debt securities). It is also a concern for traders in emerging market debt and financial products including emerging market securities and derivative contracts. Currency inconvertibility agreements have emerged as a mechanism for dealing with these types of risks.

The aspect of sovereign risk most commonly dealt with in the credit derivatives market is the risk of currency inconvertibility or restrictions placed on the free flow of funds. This reflects the fact that this is a central concern of foreign investors and the fact that structures linked to default have certain problems in the context of emerging market transactions and sovereign risk generally. In particular, there are a number of events short of actual default that have a material impact on transactions involving emerging market debt. In addition, the actual event of default on sovereign debt is likely to be somewhat remote.

Hence, several types of currency inconvertibility agreements have emerged, generally in the context of credit derivatives. Figure 1.22 shows an example of a possible transaction structure. Structures where this element is embedded in a security are also utilized. Figure 1.23 shows the structure of an inconvertibility agreement in diagrammatic form.

---

[21] For a perspective on the use of credit derivatives in emerging markets, see Gheerbant, Mark 1998, "Managing Country Risk Using Credit Derivatives", *Credit Derivatives: Applications for Risk Management, Investment, and Portfolio Optimisation*, Risk Books, London, Chapter 3; Van Der Maas, Paul and Naqui, Nabeel 1999, "Credit Derivatives Within An Emerging Market Framework", *Credit Derivatives: Key Issues*, 2nd ed, edited by Storrow, Jamie, British Bankers Association, London, Chapter 6

Figure 1.22   Currency Inconvertibility Agreement — Example

Assume an investor has investments in an emerging market (in the form of debt issued by non-sovereign issuers located in the relevant jurisdiction). The investor is concerned about the risk of inconvertibility and transfer of funds and decides to hedge the currency conversion risk on its investments. The specific exposure under consideration is that the issuer may be prevented by government regulations from converting local currency into the foreign currency (say, US$ or other hard currencies in which the debt obligation is denominated) in order to make payments to the investor.

The currency inconvertibility transaction is structured as follows:
* The agreement is structured to provide protection for a fixed period, say 1 year, against currency inconvertibility in the relevant jurisdiction on a specified face value, which is related to the amount of the investor's exposure by way of its investment (say, US$25 million). The exact value under security or investment does not need to be defined, as the protection is not necessarily related to the underlying investment.
* The investor pays a premium to the provider of protection of say 1.00% pa based on the face value (US$25 million), equivalent to US$250,000.
* The payoffs under the currency inconvertibility agreement are as follows:
    1. If during the 1-year tenure of the agreement, there is no currency inconvertibility event, then the investor receives no benefit and the agreement expires normally.
    2. If during the 1-year tenure of the agreement, there is a currency inconvertibility event, which continues at the maturity of the agreement or alternative upon the occurrence of the inconvertibility event (usually two business days after exercise), the investor receives the benefit of currency inconvertibility protection as follows:
        — The investor receives the face value of the contract (US$25 million) from the party providing protection (usually in New York).
        — In return, the investor pays the equivalent amount of local currency of the emerging market country in the emerging market location at the then current prevailing exchange rate (the rate determination mechanism is prescribed).

The inconvertibility event will generally be defined to include the imposition of regulations (described in broad terms) that have the effect of:
* Preventing or making illegal the conversion of the local currency into foreign currency
* Preventing or making illegal the payment of the local currency to accounts outside the jurisdiction and/or transferring any funds outside the jurisdiction
* Prohibiting the receipt or repatriation outside the jurisdiction of any capital, principal of any security, interest, dividend, capital gain, or proceeds of the sale on any assets owned by foreign persons or entities
* Making the US$ unavailable in any legal exchange market in the jurisdiction in accordance with normal commercial practise

Other events that would trigger the inconvertibility event include:
* A general banking moratorium on suspension of payments by banks or government entities in the jurisdictions

- A general expropriation, confiscation, nationalization, or other compulsory acquisition or similar action by the government of the jurisdiction that derives OECD banks of all or substantially all of their assets in the jurisdiction
- Any war, revolution, insurrection, or hostile act that has the effect of preventing convertibility of the local currency or transfer of funds to overseas accounts

The rate at which the conversion is undertaken is usually the exchange rate as at the date of settlement. The rate used is usually either the central bank published rates or, in the absence of such a rate or where such a rate is manifestly incorrect, a rate determined by a poll of dealers or in some other commercially realistic method under the circumstances.

The effect of the transaction is to enable the investor seeking protection against restriction on currency conversion that might impact unfavorably on its ability to receive payment in hard currency, to transfer funds out of the emerging market country despite the imposition of currency controls.

Figure 1.23   Currency Inconvertibility Agreement — Structure

(a)   Convertibility agreement structure

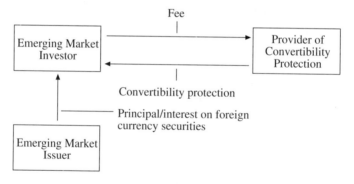

(b)   If inconvertibility event occurs

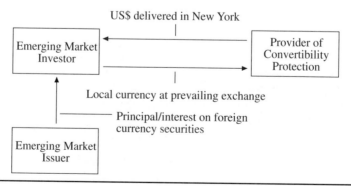

The parties providing currency inconvertibility protection in effect assume the risk of the local currency obligation, at least in relation to currency convertibility. The risk assumed is not significantly different from that when purchasing a foreign currency denominated security issued by an issuer in an emerging market country. The transaction effectively separates the credit risk from the currency conversion risk. This separation is important, for example, for issuers such as subsidiaries of large creditworthy multinationals whose credit risk is low (perhaps through parent company credit support) but currency conversion risk is high.

This relationship allows the pricing of the currency inconvertibility agreement to be derived from the pricing of comparable maturity bonds of the emerging market country but issued by either sovereign or non-sovereign issuers and denominated in hard currencies. This security will exhibit risk premiums similar to that evident in these transactions. The risk premiums derived are generally adjusted for the possible illiquidity of the currency inconvertibility agreement relative to the investment in the bond itself. Another source of risk premiums includes trade finance transactions.

The party providing the protection against currency inconvertibility will generally be motivated by the following objectives:

- The risk of inconvertibility is seen as slight and/or the premium received is seen as a fair value compensation for the risk assumed, in terms of expected loss
- An underlying requirement to purchase local currency to finance planned investments

The first objective may motivate a financial institution or an emerging market investor seeking to earn premium income. The second objective is relevant to industrial corporations that have entered into commercial transactions to undertake relevant investments and cannot withdraw from this obligation. The currency inconvertibility agreement provides this group the ability to effectively monetize this obligation through the capture of the premium.

These types of structures, in practise, are characterized by the following:

- They tend to be more expensive than similar export credit or officially provided sovereign risk, reflecting either the non-commercial nature of the insurance provided and the impact of inter-governmental influence.
- Protection may be available for transactions that traditionally would not qualify for protection under other insurance arrangements.
- The terms for which protection is available are relative short. The market still

exhibits limited liquidity. However, the ability to hedge these transactions using emerging market bonds despite considerable basis risk, is increasingly allowing the structuring of quite sophisticated instruments for hedging aspects of sovereign risk.

1.7 Summary

Credit derivatives represent a diverse and heterogeneous group of transactions that are concerned with principally the isolation of credit risk as a separately traded market variable. The different products essentially are focused on structuring instruments to allow trading in this risk attribute in varied formats to allow hedging or risk assumption by market participants.

Selected References

BZW June 1997, "An Investor's Guide to Credit Derivatives". *Derivatives Strategy Credit Derivatives Supplement*, pp 1–8

Chase Manhattan Bank April 1997, "Credit Derivatives: A Primer". *Asiamoney Derivatives Guide*, pp 2–5

(1998) *Credit Derivatives: Applications For Risk Management*, Euromoney Books, London

(1998) *Credit Derivatives: Applications for Risk Management, Investment and Portfolio Optimisation*, Risk Books, London

Fallon, William "Credit Where Credit's Due" (March 1994) *Risk*, vol 7, no 3, pp 9–11

Francis, Jack Clark, Forst, Joyce A., and Whittaker, J. Gregg (Editors) (1999) *The Handbook of Credit Derivatives*, McGraw-Hill, New York

Ghose, Ronit (Editor) *Credit Derivatives: Key Issues* (1997, British Bankers Association, London)

Howard, Kerrin (Winter 1995), "An Introduction To Credit Derivatives", *Derivatives Quarterly*, pp 28–37

Iacono, Frank "Credit Derivatives" in Schwartz, Robert J. and Smith Jr., Clifford W.(Editors) (1997) *Derivatives Handbook: Risk Management and Control*, John Wiley & Sons, Inc., New York at Chapter 2

(1999) *The J.P. Morgan Guide To Credit Derivatives*, Risk Publications, London

Masters, Blythe "A Credit Derivatives Primer" (May 1996), *Derivatives Strategy*, pp 42–44

Masters, Blythe and Reoch, Rob (March 1996), *Credit Derivatives: Structures And Applications*, J.P. Morgan, New York and London

Masters, Blythe and Reoch, Rob (March 1996), *Credit Derivatives: An Innovation in Negotiable Exposure*, J.P. Morgan, New York and London

Nelken, Dr, Israel (1999), *Implementing Credit Derivatives*, McGraw-Hill, New York

Reoch, Rob and Masters, Blythe "Credit Swaps: An Innovation In Negotiable Exposure" (1995), *Capital Market Strategies*, 7 pp 3–8

Scott-Quinn, Brian and Walmsley, Julian K. (1998) *The Impact Of Credit Derivatives On Securities Markets*, International Securities Market Association, Zurich

Smith, Bradley E. "Total Return Swaps" (1994), *Capital Market Strategies*, 3, pp 37–39

Smithson, Charles with Holappa. Hal "Credit Derivatives" (December 1995) *Risk*, vol 8, no 12, pp 38–39

Storrow, Jamie (1999), *Credit Derivatives: Key Issues — 2nd Edition*, British Bankers Association, London

Tavakoli, Janet M. (1998), *Credit Derivatives: A Guide To Instruments And Applications*, John Wiley & Sons, Inc., New York

Whittaker, Greg J. and Kumar, Sumita "Credit Derivatives: A Primer" in Atsuo Konishi and Ravi Dattatreya (Ed), *The Handbook of Derivative Instruments*, (Irwin Publishing, 1996) pp595–614

Appendix A

Market Quotations[22]

```
TUCD                                        DG40n Corp   T U C D

        ┌──────────────────────┐           Americas :  212-208-4075
        │     TULLETT          │           Europe   :  171 827 2225
        └──────────────────────┘


                    CREDIT  DERIVATIVES

                ┌─────────────────────────────┐
                │  1) Emerging Markets         │
                │  2) North America            │
                │  3) Europe                   │
                │  4) Australia/Asia           │
                │  5) Disclaimer               │
                │  6) Contacts                 │
                │  7) To Request Information   │
                └─────────────────────────────┘
```

1   DG8 0a Corp   T U C D

Tullett & Tokyo - Emerging Markets Credit Derivatives

Last	Rating	Credit	Term	Bid	Offer	Type	Ref 22-Dec-99 14:14 GMT
		Sovereign					
12-10-99	BB3	Argentina	6 mos.	225	415	DF	FRB
	BB3	Argentina	9 mos			DF	FRB
12-02-99	BB3	Argentina	1yr	425	525	DF	FRB
	BB3	Argentina	3yr			DF	FRB
	BB3	Argentina	4yr			DF	FRB
	BB3	Argentina	5yr			DF	FRB
	BB3	Argentina	1yr			CV	
	B1	Brazil	1yr			DF	EI
12-07-99	B1	Brazil	2yr	430		DF	EI
12-08-99	B1	Brazil	3yr	530		DF	EI
12-08-99	B1	Brazil	3.5yr	530	615	DF	EI
12-08-99	B1	Brazil	5yr		680	DF	EI
	B1	Brazil	90 days			CV	
	B1	Brazil	6 mos			CV	
	B1	Brazil	1yr			CV	
	B1	Brazil	2yr			CV	

Page 1 of 3

[22] Copyright: Tullet & Tokyo and Bloomberg; reproduced with the permission of Tullet & Tokyo

```
Page                                          DG8   a Corp   T U C D
Tullett & Tokyo - Emerging Markets Credit Derivatives
  Last   Rating  Credit     Term    Bid    Offer    Type Refere22-Dec-99 14:14 GMT
          B2    Bulgaria   6 mos                    DF
          B2    Bulgaria   1yr                      DF

          NR    Chile      1yr                      DF
          NR    Chile      3yr                      DF
          NR    Chile      5yr                      DF

          BBB3  Colombia   1yr                      DF
          BBB3  Colombia   2yr                      DF
          BBB3  Colombia   4yr                      DF

          B1    Ecuador    1yr                      DF
          B1    Ecuador    3yr                      DF
          B1    Ecuador    5yr                      DF
12-02-99  BB2   Mexico     6mos    45      90       DF
          BB2   Mexico     1yr                      DF
          BB2   Mexico     2yr                      DF
12-07-99  BB2   Mexico     3yr     180             DF
12-21-99  BB2   Mexico     9yr     240     285      DF


                                          Page 2 of 3
Copyright 1999 BLOOMBERG L.P.    Frankfurt:69-920410  Hong Kong:2-977-6000  London:171-330-7500   New York:212-318-2000
Princeton:609-279-3000     Singapore:226-3000     Sydney:2-9777-8686     Tokyo:3-3201-8900     Sao Paulo:11-3048-4500
                                                                          I967-381-1 22-Dec-99  9:33:20
```

Bloomberg PROFESSIONAL

```
Page                                          DG8   a Corp   T U C D
Tullett & Tokyo - Emerging Markets Credit Derivatives
Last Rating      Credit      Term    Bid    Offer    Type Refer22-Dec-99 14:34 GMT
          BB2    Peru        1yr                      DF
          BB2    Peru        3yr                      DF
          BB2    Peru        5yr                      DF

          BB1    South  Africa  5yr                   DF

          BB3    Venezuela   1yr                      DF
          BB3    Venezuela   3yr                      DF
          BB3    Venezuela   5yr                      DF
Corporates

  Brazil
          B1     Petrobras   1yr                      DF




                                          Page 3 of 3
Copyright 1999 BLOOMBERG L.P.    Frankfurt:69-920410  Hong Kong:2-977-6000  London:171-330-7500   New York:212-318-2000
Princeton:609-279-3000     Singapore:226-3000     Sydney:2-9777-8686     Tokyo:3-3201-8900     Sao Paulo:11-3048-4500
                                                                          I967-381-1 22-Dec-99  9:34:10
```

Bloomberg PROFESSIONAL

2   DG8 0a Corp   **T U C D**

Tullett & Tokyo - North American Credit Derivatives

Last	Rating	Credit	Term	Bid	Offer	Typ22-Dec-99c13:49 GMT

United States Industrials

Last	Rating	Credit	Term	Bid	Offer	Typ
12-02-99	AA2	Wal-Mart	6mo		10	DF
12-22-99	AA3	Associates Corp	3yr	23		DF
11-19-99	AA3	Associates Corp	5yr	25		DF
11-19-99	A1	Motorola	5yr	18	26	DF
12-14-99	A1	AT&T Corp	1yr	10	14	DF
12-03-99	A1	AT&T Corp	5yr		33	DF
12-14-99	A1	Lucent Tech	3yr	15	22	DF
12-14-99	A1	CIT Group	5yr	27	45	DF
12-17-99	A1	Disney	5yr	14	22	DF
12-20-99	A2	Xerox	5yr	35	54	DF
12-10-99	A2	Goodyear	3.5		34	DF
12-22-99	A2	Ford Motor Co	3yr	21	24	DF
12-21-99	A2	Ford Motor Credit	5yr	24	30	DF
12-21-99	A2	Kodak	3yr	16	21	DF
12-21-99	A2	Household	5yr	31	42	DF
12-13-99	A2	Caterpillar Inc	5yr		30	DF
12-21-99	A3	Sears	5yr	55	65	DF
12-21-99	A3	GMAC	5yr	25	30	DF

Page 1 of 3

Page   DG8 a Corp   **T U C D**

Tullett & Tokyo - North American Credit Derivatives

Last	Rating	Credit	Term	Bid	Offer	Typ22-Dec-99c13:50 GMT	
12-14-99	BBB3	Time Warner	3.25yr	40	56	DF	
12-02-99	BBB1	Quaker Oats	4yr		32	DF	
12-03-99	BBB3	Raytheon	5yr		85	DF	
12-07-99	BBB2	WorldCom	3yr	20	27	DF	
12-21-99	BBB1	JC Penney	5yr	155	180	DF	
12-07-99	BBB3	Seagrams	5yr	45	95	DF	
12-07-99	BBB3	Viacom Inc	5yr		67	DF	
12-09-99	BBB3	Delta	5yr	65	95	DF	
12-03-99	BBB3	Philip Mo	4yr		100	DF	
United States Non-Investment Grade							
12-07-99	BB1	Kmart	5yr		300	DF	
	BB1	Columbia/HCA	2yr			DF	Revolver
	BB2	ComCast Cell	3yr			DF	
	BB2	Circus Circus	3yr			DF	
	BB1	Medpartners Inc	3yr			DF	
			5yr			DF	
North American Financial Institutuions							
12-12-99	AAA	FSA	5yr	26	28	DF	Senior
12-12-99	AAA	MBIA Ins	5yr	25	39	DF	Sub Debt
12-13-99	AA3	MBIA Inc	5yr	28	42	DF	Senior

Page 2 of 3

Page   DG8   a Corp   **T U C D**
Tullett & Tokyo - North American Credit Derivatives

Last	Rating	Credit	Term	Bid	Offer	Type	22-Dec-99e13:48 GMT
	AA3	TD	5yr			DF	
	AA3	CIBC	5yr			DF	
12-21-99	AA3	Bank One Bank	5yr	19		DF	Senior
12-20-99	A2	Bear Stearns	5yr	35	45	DF	Senior
12-01-99	A3	Charles Schuab	5yr		50	DF	Senior
12-21-99	A1	Keybank	5yr	17	24	DF	Senior
12-07-99	A2	Chase Bank	4+yr	11	19	DF	Senior
12-06-99	A1	CitiGroup	5yr	18	26	DF	Senior
12-14-99	A1	Chase Holding Co	3+yr	16	20	DF	Senior
12-06-99	A1	Chase Holding Co	5yr	18	26	DF	Senior
12-21-99	A1	Morgan Stanley	5yr	21	28	DF	Senior
12-21-99	A1	Goldman	5yr	26	31	DF	Senior
12-21-99	AA3	Merrill Lynch	5yr	23	30	DF	Senior
12-06-99	A1	BOA Holding Co	5yr	19	26	DF	Senior
12-14-99	A3	Lehman	4yr		68	DF	Senior
12-07-99	BBB1	Paine Webber	5yr		68	DF	Senior

Page 3 of 3

---

3   DG8 0a Corp   **T U C D**
Tullett & Tokyo - European Credit Derivatives

Last	Rating	Credit	Term	Bid	Offer	Type	T21-Dec-99e14:35 GMT
European Financial Institutions							
27-09-99	AA2	ABN	5yr	9	15	DF	Senior
17-11-99		Argentaria	5yr	13	17	DF	Senior
26-09-99		BGB	5yr	10	17	DF	Senior
	A1	BBV	4yr			DF	Senior
14-12-99		Banco Pop di Brescia	3yr	24	29	DF	Senior
14-12-99		Banco di Napoli	5yr		32	DF	Senior
13-12-99	A2	Banca di Roma	5yr	18	24	DF	Senior
		BCI	5yr			DF	
16-09-99	AA2	Bk Austria	5yr	10	17	DF	Senior
13-09-99	A1	BNP	5yr	9	16	DF	Senior
	AA2	BVB	5yr			DF	Senior
16-09-99	AA3	Commerzbank	5yr	10	17	DF	Senior
18-08-99		Credit Lyonnais	5yr	21	28	DF	Senior
13-12-99		Deutschebank	5yr		43	DF	Sub
20-08-99	AA2	Dresdner	5yr	13	17	DF	Senior
03-09-99	AA3	Ing	4yr	10		DF	Senior
	AA2	Kredietbank	5yr			DF	
29-11-99	A3	Lavoro	5yr	23		DF	Senior
15-09-99	AAA	Rabobank	5yr	5		DF	Senior
10-12-99	A	Santander sub	4yr		40	DF	sub

Page 1 of 7

Page DG8 a Corp TUCD

Tullett & Tokyo - European Credit Derivatives

Last	Rating	Credit	Term	Bid	Offer	Type 21-Dec-99 14:35 GMT	
29-11-99		San Paulo-IMI	5yr	17	25	DF	Senior
01-09-99	A1	Soc Gen	5yr	12	16	DF	Senior
10-12-99	A3	Skandi Enskilda	4yr		19	DF	Senior
01-09-99	AA1	West LB	5yr	11	17	DF	Senior
European Corporates							
France							
06-12-99	AA3	Carrefour	5yr	14	20	DF	
06-12-99	AA1	France Telecom	5yr	26	31	DF	
01-12-99	NR	Michelin	4.5yr		42	DF	
	NR	Pechiney	4yr			DF	
09-11-99		Peugeot	5yr	22	30	DF	
09-11-99	NR	Renault	5yr	30	45	DF	
19-11-99	BBB3	Rhone-Poulenc	2yr	24	33	DF	
13-12-99		Saint Gobain	5yr		28	DF	
29-10-99	BBB2	Usinor Sacilor	5yr	50	70	DF	
17-11-99	BBB	Vivendi	5yr	55		DF	
Italy							
29-11-99	A3	Fiat	5yr	22	30		
		Olivetti	3yr				
19-11-99		Tecnost	5yr	65	85		

Page 2 of 7

Copyright 1999 BLOOMBERG L.P. Frankfurt:69-920410 Hong Kong:2-977-6000 London:171-330-7500 New York:212-318-2000
Princeton:609-279-3000 Singapore:226-3000 Sydney:2-9777-8686 Tokyo:3-3201-8900 Sao Paulo:11-3048-4500
I967-381-1 22-Dec-99 9:35:17

Bloomberg PROFESSIONAL

Page DG8 a Corp TUCD

Tullett & Tokyo - European Credit Derivatives

Last	Rating	Credit	Term	Bid	1	Type21-Dec-99e14:35 GMT
Germany						
	AA2	Bayer AG	5yr	15	25	DF
18-08-99	A1	BMW	5yr	22	26	DF
06-12-99	AA3	Deutsche Telecom	5yr	27	31	DF
07-12-99	A2	Lufthansa	5yr	20	25	DF
03-12-99	A2	Mannesman	5yr	50	58	DF
05-10-99	NR	Metro AG	5yr		38	DF
01-10-99	NR	Thyssen	5yr		40	
Netherlands						
13-12-99		Akzo Nobel	5yr		30	DF
29-11-99	A3	Wolters Kluwer	7yr		50	DF
Scandis						
02-12-99	A1	Ericsson	3yr		24	DF
03-12-99		Nokia	5yr		27	DF
01-12-99	NR	Scania	5yr	25		DF
13-12-99	A3	Volvo	5yr	22	30	DF
2Spain						
01-12-99	AA3	Repsol	5yr	28	38	DF
21-10-99	AA3	Endesa	5yr		33	DF
13-12-99	A1	Iberdrola	5yr	19	25	DF

Page 3 of 7

Copyright 1999 BLOOMBERG L.P. Frankfurt:69-920410 Hong Kong:2-977-6000 London:171-330-7500 New York:212-318-2000
Princeton:609-279-3000 Singapore:226-3000 Sydney:2-9777-8686 Tokyo:3-3201-8900 Sao Paulo:11-3048-4500
I967-381-1 22-Dec-99 9:35:20

Bloomberg PROFESSIONAL

Page   DG8   a Corp   **T U C D**
Tullett & Tokyo - European Credit Derivatives

Last	Rating	Credit	Term	Bid	Offer	Typ21-Dec-99c14:35 GMT
Switzerland						
	NR	Swiss Air	5yr			DF
UK						
09-11-99	A2	Allied Domecq	5yr		30	DF
		Anglian Water PLC	5yr			DF
04-11-99	A3	BAT	5yr	55	75	DF
07-12-99		Bass	5yr		27	DF
		B-Sky-B	5yr			DF
13-12-99		British Aerospace	5yr	25	32	DF
10-12-99	A2	British Air	5yr	25	32	DF
16-12-99	A2	Brti Gas Transco	5yr	28	38	DF
22-11-99		British Steel	5yr	37	47	DF
03-12-99		British Telecom	5yr	22	26	
03-12-99		Cable & Wireless	5yr	28	36	DF
13-12-99	A2	Diageo PLC	3.5yr		22	DF
03-12-99	A3	Dixons	4yr	20	28	DF
07-12-99		Eastern Group	10yr	60		DF
16-11-99	BBB1	Hyder	4yr	52		DF
08-12-99		ICI	5yr	40	50	DF

Page 4 of 7

Page   DG8   a Corp   **T U C D**
Tullett & Tokyo - European Credit Derivatives

Last	Rating	Credit	Term	Bid	Offer	Type 21-Dec-99 14:35 GMT
07-12-99		Kingfisher	5yr	19	25	DF
	AA2	Marks&Spencer	5yr			DF
09-11-99	AA2	National Grid	5yr	18	25	DF
09-11-99	BBB1	P & O	5yr	25	35	DF
07-12-99	BBB1	Pearson PLC	5yr	32	42	DF
01-10-99	A1	Railtrack	5yr	20	30	DF
16-11-99	Baa1	Rank Plc	5yr		115	DF
07-12-99	A3	Rolls Royce	5yr	25	30	DF
	A3	Safeway Plc	5yr			DF
10-12-99	A1	Sainsbury	5yr	20	28	DF
21-09-99	A1	Scottish Power	5yr		30	DF
	AA3	Southern Elec	5yr			DF
16-11-99	AA3	Tesco	5yr	22	27	DF
14-09-99	A2	United Utilities	5yr		40	DF
10-12-99	A2	Vodafone	5yr	45	50	DF
SOVEREIGN						
	AAA	Austria	5yr			DF
06-09-99	AA1	Belgium	5yr		11	DF

Page 5 of 7

Page   DG8   a Corp   T U C D

Tullett & Tokyo - European Credit Derivatives

Last	Rating	Credit	Term	Bid	Offer	Type	21-Dec-99 14:35 GMT
	BBB3	Croatia	6yr			DF	
08-11-99	BBB3	Croatia	5yr	450	500	DF	
16-11-99	NR	Czech Republic	3yr		45	DF	
05-11-99	NR	Czech Republic	5yr		63	DF	
	A2	Greece	2yr			DF	
03-12-99	A2	Greece	5yr	17	22	DF	In Euro
26-11-99	A2	Greece	10yr	32	40	DF	
06-12-99	BBB3	Hungary	3yr	33	40	DF	
06-12-99	BBB3	Hungary	5yr	41	47	DF	
26-11-99	BBB3	Hungary	10yr	65	75	DF	
	AA1	Ireland	5yr			DF	
	AA3	Italy	1yr			DF	
27-09-99	AA3	Italy	5yr	5	10	DF	
	AA3	Italy	10yr			DF	
	BBB3	Poland	2yr				
	BBB3	Poland	5yr			DF	
	BBB3	Poland	10yr			DF	
		Russia	1yr			DF	
		Russia	5yr			DF	
	NR	Slovokia	1yr			DF	
	NR	Slovokia	3yr	3yr		DF	

Page 6 of 7

Page   DG8   a Corp   T U C D

Tullett & Tokyo - European Credit Derivatives

Last	Rating	Credit	Term	Bid	Offer	Type	Ref 21-Dec-99 14:35 GMT
01-10-99	A3	Slovenia	3yr	27	40	DF	
10-11-99	BB1	South Africa	1yr	90	140	DF	
10-11-99	BB1	South Africa	2yr	115	150	DF	
01-10-99	BB1	South Africa	3yr	150	210	DF	
	BB1	South Africa	5yr			DF	
	AA2	Spain	1yr			DF	
22-09-99	AA2	Spain	5yr	3	8	DF	
	AA2	Spain	10yr			DF	
01-10-99	B2	Turkey	6mo			DF	
03-11-99	B2	Turkey	2yr	550		DF	
15-12-99	B2	Turkey	3yr	600	675	DF	

Page 7 of 7

4

DG8 0a Corp **T U C D**

Tullett & Tokyo - Australian/Asian Credit Derivatives

Last	Rating	Credit	Term	Bid	Offer	Type	Refer21-Dec-99 14:34 GMT
Japan							
Sovereign							
12-01-99	AA	Japan	5yr	9	12	DF	
12-06-99	AA	Japan	10yr	12	14	DF	
Financial	Institutions						
11-26-99	A2	BOTM	10yr	26	37	DF	Senior
11-30-99	BBB1	Sumi	4.5yr	18.5	23	DF	Senior
11-24-99	BBB1	Sumi	10yr	27	38	DF	Senior
11-12-99	BBB1	Sanwa	5yr	19	23	DF	Senior
11-29-99	BBB1	Sanwa	10yr	25	35	DF	Senior
11-17-99	BBB2	DKB	10yr	29		DF	Senior
11-16-99	BBB2	IBJ	10yr	29		DF	Senior
11-17-99	BBB2	Fuji	10yr	29		DF	Senior
12-01-99	A3	DKB	10yr	80		DF	Subordinated
12-01-99	A3	BOTM	10yr	65	85	DF	Subordinated
12-17-99	BBB2	Sumi	10yr	75	85	DF	Subordinated
12-17-99	BBB1	Sakura	10yr	85		DF	Subordinated
12-02-99	BBB1	Sanwa	10yr	80	84	DF	Subordinated
12-08-99	BBB2	IBJ	5yr	50	65	DF	Yen Subordinated
12-01-99	BBB2	IBJ	10yr	80		DF	Subordinated
12-01-99	BBB3	Fuji	10yr	80		DF	Subordinated

Page 1 of 7

Page

DG8 a Corp **T U C D**

Tullett & Tokyo - Australian/Asian Credit Derivatives

Last	Rating	Credit	Term	Bid	Offer	Type	Ref21-Dec-99 14:34 GMT
Corporates							
10-20-99	AA3	Ito-Yokado	5yr		30	DF	Senior
10-08-99	AA1	Toyota	5yr	12	17	DF	Senior
	AA1	TEPCO	1yr			DF	Senior
10-20-99	A2	Hitachi (Yen)	5yr		35	DF	Senior
	A3	Mitsui & Co.	1yr			DF	Senior
11-09-99	A2	Sharp Corp	5yr	15	25	DF	Senior
10-20-99	A3	NEC (Yen)	0 5yr		40	DF	Senior
	A3	Nippon Oil	5yr			DF	Senior
10-01-99	BBB1	Nissan	5yr	130	190	DF	Senior
10-20-99	NR	Acom (Yen)	3yr	65	100	DF	Senior

Page 2 of 7

Page   DG8   a Corp   T U C D
Tullett & Tokyo - Australian/Asian Credit Derivatives

Last	Rating	Credit	Term	Bid	Offer	Type	Refe21-Dec-99 14:34 GMT
Australia/Asia excluding Japan							
Sovereign							
	AA2	Australia	10yr			DF	
11-16-99	BBB1	China	08-02	45		DF	
12-07-99	BBB1	China	4yr	70	82	DF	
12-08-99	BBB1	China	5yr	75	85	DF	
12-08-99	BBB1	China	10yr	87	125	DF	
	NR	Hong Kong	5yr			DF	
	CCC1	Indonesia	1yr			DF	
11-17-99	BBB3	Korea	1yr		95	DF	
11-15-99	BBB3	Korea	2yr		105	DF	
12-06-99	BBB3	Korea	2.5yr	75		DF	
11-16-99	BBB3	Korea	3yr		110	DF	
11-18-99	BBB3	Korea	5yr		120	DF	
11-17-99	BBB3	Korea	04-08	100		DF	
11-16-99	BBB3	Malaysia	3yr	90		DF	
12-07-99	BB1	Philippines	6mo	55		DF	
11-16-99	BB1	Philippines	3yr	170	195	DF	
12-06-99	BB1	Philippines	5yr		240	DF	
11-17-99	BB1	Philippines	04-08	240		DF	

Page 3 of 7

Bloomberg PROFESSIONAL

Page   DG8   a Corp   T U C D
Tullett & Tokyo - Australian/Asian Credit Derivatives

Last	Rating	Credit	Term	Bid	Offer	21-Dec-99r14:34 GMT
	AAA	Singapore	5yr			
	BB1	Thailand	1yr			
11-24-99	BB1	Thailand	5yr	120	135	DF
	BB1	Thailand	04-07			DF
Corporates/Financial Institutions						
Australia/NZ						
	AA3	ANZ	5yr			DF
	A3	BHP	3yr			DF
11-09-99	A3	BHP	5yr	55		DF
	A3	BHP	7yr			DF
11-05-99	A3	Mayne Nickless	5yr	105	115	DF
	BBB2	Fletcher Challenge	1yr			DF
		Pacific Dunlop	3yr			DF
	BBB1	QANTAS	4yr			DF
China						
	BBB2	Bank of China	1yr			
12-08-99	BBB2	China Development Bk	1yr	35		
12-08-99	BBB2	China Commercial Bk	1yr	40		

Page 4 of 7

Bloomberg PROFESSIONAL

Page   DG8   a Corp   **T U C D**
Tullett & Tokyo - Australian/Asian Credit Derivatives

Last	Rating	Credit	Term	Bid	Offer	T21-Dec-99r14:34 GMT
Hong Kong						
	A2	HSBC Sub	6yr		DF	
	A2	StandChart	5yr		DF	
	A3	Swire	5yr		DF	
	A3	MTRC	5yr		DF	
	NR	Hong Kong Land	02-01		DF	Convertible
	NR	Hong Kong Land	3yr		DF	Senior
India						
	BB2	Reliance Industries	2yr		DF	
	BB2	TATA Elect	5yr		DF	
	NR	ICICI	5yr		DF	
	NR	IDBI	5yr		DF	
	NR	ONGC	2yr		DF	
Thailand						
11-26-99	B2	Bangkok Bank	22mo	170		DF
11-23-99	B2	Bangkok Bank	2yr	240	325	DF
	NR	IFCT	5yr		DF	

Page 5 of 7

Page   DG8   a Corp   **T U C D**
Tullett & Tokyo - Australian/Asian Credit Derivatives

Last	Rating	Credit	Term	Bid	Offer	Type21-Dec-99e14:34 GMT
Korea						
11-29-99	BBB3	KDB	1yr		100	DF
12-06-99	BBB3	KDB	19mo		100	DF
11-27-99	BBB3	KDB	2yr		110	DF
11-27-99	BBB3	KDB	3yr		115	DF
11-27-99	BBB3	KDB	5yr		125	DF
	BBB3	KDB	05-06		DF	
	BBB3	Kexim	1yr		DF	
	BBB3	Kexim	2yr		DF	
	BBB3	Kexim	3yr		DF	
	BBB3	Kexim	5yr		DF	
	BBB3	Kepco	5yr		DF	
	B1	Hanvit	1yr		DF	
	NR	LG Electronics	1yr		DF	
	NR	Samsung	1yr		DF	
	BBB3	Pohang	1yr		DF	
Malaysia						
	BBB3	Petronas	3yr		DF	
	BBB3	Petronas	5yr		DF	
	BBB3	Telekom Malaysia	5yr		DF	

Page 6 of 7

Tullett & Tokyo – Australian/Asian Credit Derivatives

Last Rating	Credit	Term	Bid	Offer	Type	Refer	21-Dec-99 14:34 GMT
Philippines							
BB2	PLDT	2yr			DF		
NR	RFM Capital Ltd	4yr			DF		

Page 7 of 7

Bloomberg PROFESSIONAL

TULLETT GLOBAL CREDIT DERIVATIVES

GLOBAL DIRECTOR   Vinayek Singh   212-208-3794

NEW YORK   212-208-4075
80 Pine Street, 26th Floor
New York, NY 10005

Tad Lundborg
Nelson Negron
Derek B. Simpkins
George Spencer

LONDON   171-827-2225
Cable House
54-62 New Broad Street, 4th Floor
London EC2M 1JJ

Carolyn Garzon
Conor McEvoy
Brian O'Callaghan
Tim Pasco
Peter Tamaro

Bloomberg PROFESSIONAL

2
Credit Linked Notes — Structured Notes[1]

Satyajit Das

2.1 Overview

Credit linked notes are part of the class of transactions of credit derivatives involving the isolation and separate trading in the aspect of credit risk. Credit linked notes entail the combination of a fixed income security with an embedded credit derivative. The credit linked note enables the investor to replicate exposure to the credit risk inherent in a bond or a loan without the necessity of undertaking a direct investment in the security itself. The credit linked note is designed to allow the investor to capture value from movements in the value of an underlying loan asset or bond, credit spreads, or default risk itself. In this and the next two chapters, the background, structure, and applications of credit linked notes are examined. In this chapter, credit linked notes are examined. Repackaged credit linked notes, synthetic bonds, and credit portfolio securitization are examined in Chapters 3 and 4.

2.2 Types of Credit Linked Notes

There is a large variety of credit linked notes transactions as seen in Figure 2.1. The various types of credit linked notes include:

- **Credit linked structured notes:** These are traditional types of structured notes where a fixed income security is combined with a credit derivative (a

---

[1] This chapter draws on material from Das, Satyajit 1996, *Structured Notes And Derivative Embedded Securities*; Euromoney Publications, London, Chapter 13. Earlier versions of this chapter were published as Das, Satyajit, "Credit linked Notes — Structured Notes: Parts 1 and 2" March 23, 1999, *Financial Products*, Issue 110, pp 20–24 & April 9, 1999 *Financial Products*, Issue 111, pp 16–23

total return swap, credit default swap, or credit spread forward or option). They feature a linkage of either the coupon or the principal to the underlying credit risk component as specified by the investor. A high-quality issuer (rated AAA or AA) issues the notes. The issuer in turn hedges its exposure fully with a back-to-back credit derivative transaction with a dealer.

- **Repackaged credit notes:** These involve a special-purpose issuance vehicle or asset repackaging structure to create credit linked structured notes. The repackaging vehicle purchases securities in the secondary market, and then reprofiles the cash flow and the credit risk of the underlying securities by entering into derivative transactions with a dealer. The repackaged cash flow is then bundled up as a security and placed with investors. The repackaged credit notes are similar to and complement credit linked structured notes and asset swap transactions.

- **Synthetic bonds:** These entail the issue of corporate or sovereign debt by a special purpose issuance or asset repackaging vehicle. The underlying credit risk exposure is created through a combination of cash securities and a credit derivative transaction. The synthetic bond is designed to replicate the characteristics of a fixed-interest security issued by the underlying issuer. These transactions are typically similar to repackaging transactions that utilize the credit derivatives mentioned above.

- **Credit portfolio securitization:** This entails repackaging *portfolios* of credit risk (both from loans/securities and counterparty risk on derivatives/ off-balance sheet transactions), utilizing securitization concepts into multiple tranches of securities that are then sold to investors. The issuer of the securities reduces or eliminates the credit risk to existing obligors through the issues.

Figure 2.1   Types of Credit Linked Notes

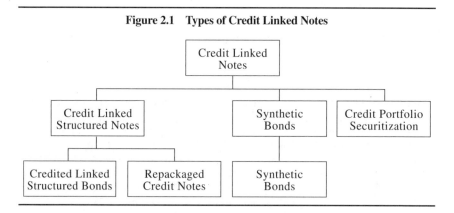

There is naturally some overlap among the structures. The principles used to construct and hedge the different types of notes also are similar.

2.3 Utilization of Credit Linked Notes

Credit linked notes have primarily been used by investors. The major attraction of this type of credit derivative is its capacity to create synthetic exposure to the underlying cash market asset without the need to undertake an actual physical investment in the associated security. The fact that this can be done using an acceptable and traditional securities format makes it especially favorable.

The advantage of being able to avoid direct investment is derived from a number of sources. In developed capital markets, the advantages are derived primarily from the capacity to avoid withholding taxes, the elimination of the requirement for custody, and the minimization of foreign exchange transactions. However, in high-yield/non-investment grade securities and emerging markets, the advantages are derived from a wider range of factors:

- The regulatory framework that may prevent investors directly purchasing the underlying security
- The presence of often complex and cumbersome procedures to obtain approval in order to make a direct investment
- The lack of underlying securities of the type sought by the investors
- The difficulties of trading in the underlying market, including lack of liquidity and high transaction costs
- Lack of development of the infrastructure of investment (particularly, for foreign investors) including the absence of well-developed settlement, custody, and foreign exchange markets

The difficulties of direct investment co-exist with increased demand for investment in the high-yield and emerging markets. This demand is driven by:

- The search for higher investment returns in an environment of low nominal returns and low spreads
- The volatility of asset prices and credit spreads in these markets, which provides significant trading opportunities
- The attractive longer-term prospects of these market segments, which may be less efficient and less fully arbitraged than more developed markets, therefore, offering relative value opportunities
- The need for diversification of credit risk
- The increased search for currency diversification within investment portfolios

The combination of increased demand for foreign investment and the presence of these significant barriers to direct investment has encouraged the development of the market for credit linked notes that allow economic investment in the underlying asset without the necessity to make direct investments in these markets. The use of credit default notes to overcome the absence of suitable cash investments can also be devised. The capacity to create customized and highly structured risk-reward profiles within these structures is also attractive.

The identified advantages are particularly important to credit linked notes and repackaged credit assets. However, synthetic bonds and credit portfolio securitization are driven by different considerations. These include:

- Banks and financial institutions with portfolios of credit risks seeking to hedge and restructure their risk profiles. These transactions enable the issuers to hedge the credit risk of individual counterparties or an entire credit portfolio
- Investors seeking credit risk may find these structures to be more attractive on relative value basis or offering higher liquidity than comparable securities issued by individual issuers.

2.4 Credit Linked Structured Notes

The re-engineering of credit derivatives into a structured note format is motivated by the traditional factors that dictate the use of these structures generally.[2] However, there are a number of additional factors that are also relevant, including:

- The capacity to participate in markets that traditionally have excluded participation from investors, such as the bank loan market
- The ability to create exposures to particular markets, where direct exposure is either prohibited or difficult or expensive as a result of either regulations or high transaction costs
- The ability to assume exposure to credit risk where *the performance obligation* (i.e. the issuer) is separate in a credit sense from *the underlying credit risk*, allowing investment in assets or asset classes, which traditionally have not been available
- The capacity to create rated formats for investment in traditionally unrated assets

---

[2] See Das, Satyajit 1996, *Structured Notes & Derivative Embedded Securities*, Euromoney Books, London

- The ability to add credit risk as a unique and specific asset class or risk factor to investment portfolios

These are in addition to more conventional advantages of these structures, such as customization of exposure and structured forms of tradable risk.

The major types of credit linked structured notes include:
- Total return swap embedded notes
- Credit spread linked notes
- Credit default linked notes

A central feature of credit linked notes is the capacity to create exposure to unrated credits through the introduction of a rated issuer and engineering the exposure to the unrated underlying loan asset synthetically. The key issue in this regard is the basis of the rating.

There are two possible approaches:
- A separation of the performance obligation (the risk on the issuer) and the market risk element (effectively, the exposure to the reference credit asset)
- A rating based on the credit risk of both the issuer and the reference credit using the so-called expected loss approach

The first approach is consistent with the approach used in connection with structured notes with other embedded risk factors (such as interest rate, currency, and commodity). The position of rating agencies is evolving in this regard. Major rating agencies generally favor the second approach, arguing that it more accurately portrays the investment credit risk profile.[3]

2.5   Total Return Credit Linked Notes

2.5.1   Structure

The principal object of total return credit linked notes is the simulation of an investment in the underlying loan asset (bank loan or bond) or an index based

---

[3]   For a detailed analysis of the rating of credit linked notes, see Chapter 16. See also Pimbley, Joseph March 1996, "Credit Derivatives And Credit Ratings," *Financial Derivatives and Risk Management* 5, pp 34–38; Cifuentes, Arturo; Efrat, Isaac, Gluck, Jeremy, and Murphy, Eileen, "Buying And Selling Credit Risk: A Perspective On Credit Linked Obligations" 1998, in *Credit Derivatives: Applications for Risk Management, Investment and Portfolio Optimization*, Risk Books, London, Chapter 8

on a basket of the underlying loan assets. This structure also allows a separation of the risk profile with direct credit risk on the issuer and the underlying market risk exposure to the high yield issuers underlying the index.

Figure 2.2 shows an example of a total return credit linked note.

Figure 2.2   Total Return Credit Linked Note

Issuer	AA/AAA rated institution
Principal Amount	US$50 million
Maturity (years)	The earlier of:
	1. 1year from Commencement Date.
	2. The next succeeding payment date following occurrence of a Credit Event on the Underlying Credit Asset.
Underlying Credit Asset	Loan to Corporation ABC dated March 15, 2001 or 8% pa March 15, 2012 Bonds issued by Corporation ABC
Coupon	3-month LIBOR plus Margin, payable quarterly on an actual/360-day basis
Margin	[250] bp pa
Principal Redemption	At par plus Capital Price Adjustment, subject to the Minimum Redemption Level
Minimum Redemption Level	0%
Capital Price Adjustment	Principal Amount × Change (either positive or negative) in the Price of the Underlying Credit Asset. The Price of the Underlying Credit Asset Change is calculated as:

$$\frac{\text{Currency price} - \text{Initial price}}{\text{Initial price}}$$

Initial Price	100.00
Current Price	The [bid or offer] price of the Underlying Credit Asset as calculated by the Calculation Agent in accordance with the Calculation Method at 11.00am (New York time) 2 business days prior to each Payment Date
Calculation Method	Choose one of these:
	1. In the sole opinion of the Calculation Agent
	2. By dealer poll under which the Calculation Agent will poll at least 4 and no more than 6 dealers in the loan and utilize the quoted prices to determine an average price for the loan
	3. By reference to a screen or quote service
Calculation Agent	[Dealer]

The structure can be decomposed into two separate transactions:

1.   An investment by the investor in a floating-rate asset (such a LIBOR-based floating-rate note (FRN)
2.   The simultaneous entry by the investor into a total return swap where the investor pays the floating interest rate index (LIBOR) and receives the total return on the underlying loan asset

The issuer will, in this case, enter into the total return swap to eliminate any exposure to fluctuations in the index and allow generation of a known cost of funds (consistent with its funding cost objectives).

Figure 2.3 illustrates the decomposition of this type of structure. The first part shows the construction on the transaction from the viewpoint of the issuer. The second part shows the transaction components from the perspective of the investor.

Two aspects of this type of note merit comment: the ability to introduce leverage and the capacity to effectively short sell the relevant loan or bond market to capture value from a decline in the price of loans from either a deterioration in the credit or increase in credit spreads.

In the above case, the transaction could readily be structured to incorporate leverage. This would be achieved by embedding a higher face value of total return swaps relative to the face value of the underlying floating rate cash investment in the note structure.

Figure 2.3   Total Return Credit Linked Note — Decomposition

(a)   Issuer's perspective

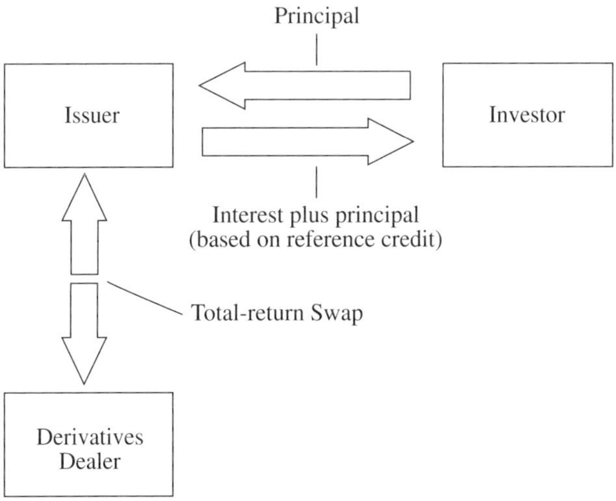

(b) Investor's perspective

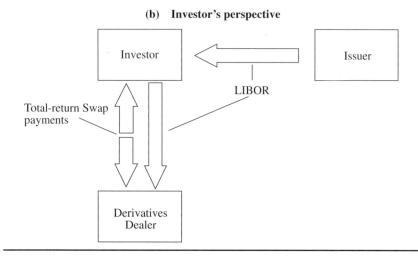

Figure 2.4 sets out an example of a structure that features eight times the leverage. Note that the coupon is calculated as:

$$\left(\begin{array}{c}\text{Leverage} \\ \text{factor}\end{array} \times \begin{array}{c}\text{Net margin on} \\ \text{total return swap}\end{array}\right) + \text{LIBOR}$$

Figure 2.4   Leveraged Total Return Credit Linked Indexed Note

Issuer	AA/AAA-rated institution
Principal Amount	US$50 million
Maturity (years)	The earlier of:
	1. 1 year from Commencement Date
	2. The next succeeding payment date following occurrence of a Credit Event on the Underlying Credit Asset
Underlying Credit Asset	Loan to Corporation ABC dated March 15, 2001 or 8% pa March 15, 2012 Bonds issued by Corporation ABC
Coupon	(Leverage Factor × Margin) plus 3-Month LIBOR, payable quarterly on an actual/360-day basis
Margin	[250] bp pa
Principal Redemption	At par plus Capital Price Adjustment, subject to the Minimum Redemption Level
Minimum Redemption Level	0%
Capital Price Adjustment	[Leverage Factor] × Principal Amount × Change (either positive or negative) in the Price of the Underlying Credit Asset. The Price of the Underlying Credit Asset Change is calculated as:

$$\frac{\text{Current price} - \text{Initial price}}{\text{Initial price}}$$

Leverage Factor	8
Initial Price	100.00
Current Price	The [bid or offer] price of the Underlying Credit Asset as calculated by the Calculation Agent in accordance with the Calculation Method at 11.00am (New York time) 2 business days prior to each Payment Date
Calculation Method	Choose one of the following:
	1. In the sole opinion of the Calculation Agent
	2. By dealer poll under which the Calculation Agent will poll at least 4 and no more than 6 dealers in the loan and utilize the quoted prices to determine an average price for the loan
	3. By reference to a screen or quote service
Calculation Agent	[Dealer]

Figure 2.5 sets in diagram form the construction and hedging of the leveraged note.

Use of leverage requires caution as fluctuations in the value may have the effect of eroding the capital value of the underlying FRN in full. Consequently, in order to hedge the leveraged note it is necessary to combine the total return loan swap on the larger total principal with an option to effectively cap the losses at a level which equates to total loss of principal. This is designed to avoid negative redemption values under the note. This aspect of construction of

Figure 2.5   Leveraged Total Return Credit Linked Note

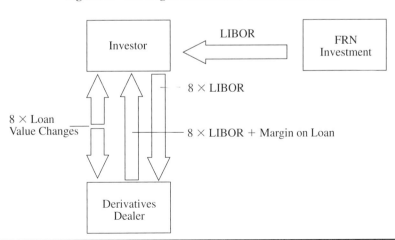

leveraged structures is also relevant to leveraged versions of other types of credit linked notes including credit linked notes as well credit default linked notes.

Shorting the loan market is traditionally difficult to achieve in the physical market because of the difficulty of borrowing non-government bonds for the purposes of creating the short sale. The ability to utilize the embedded total rate of return loan swap to create the short position is advantageous in this respect.

2.5.2   Product Variations

Figure 2.6 sets out an example of credit linked note where the investor has specific exposure to a high yield index. Figure 2.7 sets out an example of a transaction where the investor has specific exposure to an emerging market index.

Figure 2.6   High-Yield Credit Linked Note

Issuer	AAA/AA rated institution
Principal Amount	US$50 million
Maturity	3 years
Coupon	3-Month LIBOR + 200 bp
Principal Redemption	Principal Amount + Leverage Factor × Change In Underlying Credit Asset
Minimum Redemption Level	0%
Leverage Factor	3
Underlying Credit Asset	Nominated High-Yield Bond Index
Initial Price	Price of Underlying Credit Asset as at the date of issue
Current Price	The [bid or offer] price of the Underlying Credit Asset as at the maturity
Change In the Underlying Credit Asset	Percentage Change in the Underlying Credit Asset as calculated from the Initial Price and the Final Price

---

Figure 2.7   Emerging Market Credit Linked Note

Issuer	AA rated issuer
Amount	US$10 million
Maturity	3 years
Issue Price	100.00
Coupon	0.00% pa
Redemption Value	Redemption amount is based on the following formula:

$$\text{Amount} \times \frac{\text{Index}}{131.8}$$

	where:
	Index is the JP Morgan Emerging Local Markets Index (in US$) on the Value Date
Minimum Redemption	0.00
Value Date	5 business days before maturity

In these cases, the note structure allows the investor the following advantages:

- Assumption of a diversified exposure to the high-yield sector, which allows reduction of the specific risk of individual counterparties
- The benefits of a liquid and tradable instrument on the index
- Avoidance of the difficulties that would be associated with directly replicating the index
- The leverage inherent in this transaction, which entails embedding additional total return index swaps or entering into a total return swap with a larger notional principal amount. This is optional depending on the requirement of the investor
- The ability to short sell the index

The capacity to effectively short sell loan assets can be illustrated with the following example. Assume an investor holds an illiquid emerging market or high-yield bond and is concerned about the price exposure arising primarily from potential deterioration in the credit outlook for the issuer. The traditional physical solution to deal with this problem would be to either:

- Sell the securities that would give rise to immediate realization of a capital gain or loss (which may have tax and other implications)
- Short sell the securities which may be difficult to engineer as a results of the unavailability of securities to borrow as well as the risks and ongoing management of the short position

A potential synthetic solution would be to purchase a total rate of return credit linked note either on the security or an index — the corresponding emerging market or high yield index — which is correlated in its price behavior to the securities held. The note has embedded within the structure a total return swap where the investor, effectively, receives the floating rate of interest (LIBOR) and pays the total rate of return on the security or index.

This, effectively, provides a hedge for the investor while potentially overcoming the problems of the transaction costs in the physical market and the practical difficulties of shorting the securities.

2.6 Credit Spread Linked Notes

2.6.1 Structure

The use of credit spread linked notes allows the creation of highly specific and structured exposure to the credit spread without the need to either have direct credit exposure to the counterparty whose credit spread underlies the transaction and any absolute exposure to interest rate risk. The ability to mismatch or vary the duration of the underlying investment and the credit spread to which exposure is sought is also a potential source of additional value.

Figure 2.8 sets out an example of a credit spread linked note. The structure seeks to monetize the investor's expectations in respect of the implied forward credit spread. The investor gains if the spread decreases and loses if the spread increases.

Figure 2.8   Credit Spread Linked Notes — Example 1

Issuer	AAA/AA rated institution
Principal Amount	US$50 million
Term	3 years
Issue Price	100
Coupon	3-Month LIBOR + 125 bp
Reference Security	[Identified] bonds issued by [Sovereign State]
Reference Treasury Benchmark	[Identified US Treasury Bond]
Principal Redemption	Face Value + [(Spread Duration Factor = 5) × (120 bp — Credit Spread)]
Credit Spread	Defined as the Yield at Maturity of the Reference Security minus Yield at Maturity of the Reference Treasury Benchmark

---

Analytically, a fixed income bond is combined with a credit spread forward (where the investor purchases the spread) in this structure. Figure 2.9 sets out the detailed construction and hedging of the structure.

The face value amount of the credit spread forward can be higher than the face value of the note to create leverage, if required. Additional yield on the note can be engineered by structuring the spread forward at an off-market rate. For example, the transaction can be structured such that the investor can buy the spread forward at a price relative to the forward price (above the theoretical forward price), which creates an intrinsic value that is then present valued and used to enhance the yield on the security.

Figure 2.9   Credit Spread Linked Notes — Decomposition

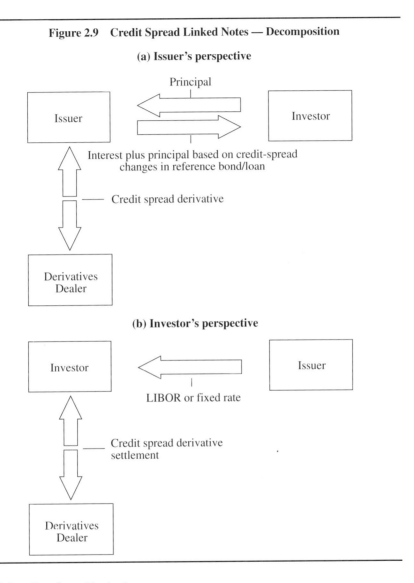

(a) Issuer's perspective

Principal

Issuer   Investor

Interest plus principal based on credit-spread
changes in reference bond/loan

Credit spread derivative

Derivatives
Dealer

(b) Investor's perspective

Investor   Issuer

LIBOR or fixed rate

Credit spread derivative
settlement

Derivatives
Dealer

2.6.2   Product Variations

Figure 2.10 sets out an example of a credit spread linked note where the return profile is linked to the performance of the credit spread, relative to US Treasuries, of a sovereign issue. The rationale of the transaction is that the investor assumes an exposure to the credit spread and seeks to monetize the expectation that the spread will stay within the identified range. The investor benefits if the spread stays within the range. If the credit spread increases or decreases outside the range, then the investor receives a minimum coupon but clearly suffers a reduction in return[4].

Figure 2.10   Credit Spread Linked Notes — Example 2

Issuer	AAA/AA rated institution
Principal Amount	US$50 million
Term	3 years
Issue Price	100
Coupon	Zero
Reference Security	[7.25% September 2031] bonds issued by [Sovereign State]
Reference Treasury Benchmark	[Identified US Treasury Bond 6.25% February 2031]
Principal Redemption	If Credit Spread at maturity is between 95 bp and 140 bp, then at 126% of Face Value (implied yield to maturity of 8.01% pa).
	If Credit Spread at maturity is below 95 bp or above 140 bp, then at 109% of Face Value (implied Yield at Maturity of 2.91% pa)
Credit Spread	Defined as the Yield at Maturity of the Reference Security minus Yield at Maturity of the Reference Treasury Benchmark

---

The structure effectively can be decomposed into a series of digital put and call option on the credit spread with the premium received for the sale of these options being used to enhance the return on the note. The digital payout on the embedded options has the effect of lowering the return to the note investor in case the spread is outside the nominated range triggering either the call or put option on the spread. The issuer in turn on sells the embedded option to hedge its own exposure and reduce its cost of funds to its target level.[5]

Figure 2.11 gives an example of a credit spread linked note where the underlying securities are emerging market issues. In this structure, the investor

---

[4] This structure is focused on the credit spread at maturity. An alternative that is also common entails the coupon being determined daily depending on whether the spread is within or outside the nominated range

[5] The structure is modeled on the range or accrual note structure that evolved in the early 1990s. See Das, Satyajit 1996, *Structured Notes & Derivative Embedded Securities*, Euromoney Books, London, Chapter 12; Das, Satyajit 1996, *Exotic Options*, LBC Information Services, Chapter 13

uses the foregone coupon to purchase a call option on a basket of four countries, which is then embedded in the note. The structure links redemption to changes in four Brady bonds. The return profile provide for unlimited potential gains but with an assured return of principal.

Figure 2.11   Credit Spread Linked Note — Example 3

In early 1995, following a major sell-off in emerging markets, a number of structured notes linked to emerging market securities, usually Brady Bonds, were issued. The following note was typical of the securities issued:

Issuer	AAA or AA rated
Maturity	1 year
Coupon	0%
Principal Redemption	The higher of:
	100 + (Final Basket Price − 48%)
	Minimum Redemption
Minimum Redemption	100%
Basket	40% Par Bond of Latin American Country A
	30% Par Bond of Latin American Country B
	30% Par Bond of Latin American Country C
Current Basket Price	48%

The note combines a zero coupon note with a call option on a basket of three Brady bonds. The call option is engineered through the linking of the redemption value to the price of the Brady bonds. The call option is financed through the forgone interest on the note.

The issue was designed to allow investors to increase exposure on a risk averse basis to emerging market debt following the Mexican crisis where emerging market Brady bond spreads widened between 100 bp and 400 bp bringing the spreads to their highest levels for many years.

The economics of the transaction was as follows:
- The 1-year yield on AAA or AA rated notes at the time of issue was around 7.00% to 7.25% pa. The breakeven price on the note to equate the return to that on a conventional note was around 93.25/93.50.
- The breakeven price increase on the basket such that the noteholder would earn the yield on 1-year securities was around 14.60%/15.10%, implying a final basket price of 55%–55.25%.

These notes have been frequently structured and used in the context of emerging market bonds where the credit spreads can be extremely volatile. The major investors have included institutional investors seeking exposure to the emerging market sector without the need to assume direct credit exposure to emerging market issuers. An added advantage is the ability to avoid the risks of trading in emerging markets debt.

2.7 Credit Default Linked Notes

2.7.1 Structure

Credit default linked notes are primarily used to assume or reduce counterparty default exposure. Investors have traditionally used credit default structures to assume credit default exposure to generate premium income to enhance yield. However, structures that entail shifting of credit exposure, while less common, are also feasible.

Figure 2.12 sets out an example of a credit default linked note. The note structure depicted sets out a note linked to a single issuer credit. The credit default note is constructed by combining a cash investment with a default swap.

Figure 2.12   Credit Default Linked Note — Example 1

Issuer	AAA/AA rated institution
Principal Amount	US$50 million
Term	5 years
Issue Price	100 or Face Value
Coupon	LIBOR + 150 bp
Reference Security	[Identified Bond or Loan of Nominated Borrower]
Principal Redemption	If no credit event has occurred before or as at Maturity, then at Face Value.
	If a credit event has occurred before or as at maturity, then Par minus Default Payment.
Credit Event	Any of the following with respect to Nominated Borrower:
	1. Failure to pay interest or principal on any senior debt security
	2. Event of bankruptcy
	3. Cross default or cross acceleration on any senior unsecured obligation
	4. Restructuring event
Default Payment	Any one of the following:
	1. An agreed US$ amount equal to [60]% of Principal Amount
	2. Change in price of the Reference Security as between the issue date and date an agreed period after default as determined by a poll of selected dealers in the Reference Security

3. Payment of par or the price of the security as at issue date in exchange for delivery of the defaulted Reference Security

The notes are structurally created from the combination of a fixed interest security (fixed or floating coupon) and the entry by the investor into a credit default swap where the investor is the provider of default protection. The default payment or recovery rate is engineered into the principal redemption structure. The issuer enters into an offsetting default swap with a counterparty to eliminate its default risk position and generate a known cost of funds for the issuer.

The payment for the default swap is used to generate the return above the underlying interest rate on the credit default linked note. In the event of default, the principal repayment to the investor is reduced by the amount of the default payment (effectively the loss suffered as a result of the occurrence of the credit event). The default payment can be calculated either as a fixed amount or an amount reflecting the actual recovery amount (calculated using changes in the value of the underlying bond following default using a dealer polling mechanism). The calculation mechanics are identical to those applicable to credit default swaps.

Figure 2.13 sets out the construction and hedging of a typical credit default linked note.

The major advantages of the structure include:
- Providing yield enhancement in return for assuming the risk of default
- Allows utilization of credit risk assumption capacity that might not otherwise be capable of being utilized through the absence of available investments
- Separation of default risk and principal credit risk which are attributable to different underlying issuers
- Ability to create capped and known loss profile in the event of default

The structure has some significant credit enhancement aspects. The fact that the credit default swap is embedded in the note that is purchased by the investor dictates that the performance obligation to make the default payment in the case of default under the reference asset is fully cash collateralized. This results from the fact that in the event of default the issuer merely adjusts the payment to the investor reducing the principal repayment by the default payment obligation.

This allows substitution of the *credit of the issuer for the credit of the investor* in the provision of default protection. This significantly broadens the range of institutions able to provide credit default protection through the unbundling of the assumption of default risk from the actual counterparty credit risk of the

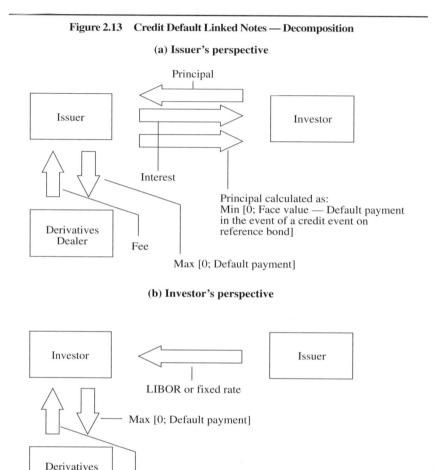

Figure 2.13   Credit Default Linked Notes — Decomposition

(a) Issuer's perspective

(b) Investor's perspective

party providing default protection.[6] By extending this concept to the synthetic bond framework (discussed in detail below), high-quality collateral (government or high credit rated-Aa/AA or better-bonds) can be utilized to significantly increase the range of providers of default protection *irrespective of the credit quality of the entity or person providing the protection.*

Figure 2.14 sets out an additional example of credit default linked notes.

---

[6]   This is a structural phenomenon that is common with all types of structured notes. See Das Satyajit, 1996, *Structured Notes & Derivative Embedded Securities*, Euromoney Books, Chapter 1

Figure 2.14   Credit Default Linked Note — Example 2

Issuer	AAA/AA rated institution
Principal Amount	US$ 20 million
Maturity	3 months
Issue Price	96.65% of Principal Amount
Coupon	0.00% pa
Reference Security	Republic of Korea 8.75% April 15, 2003
Principal Redemption	If no credit event has occurred before or as at Maturity, then at Face Value.
	If a credit event has occurred before or as at Maturity, then Default Payment.
Credit Event	Any of the following with respect to Reference Security
	1. Failure to pay interest or principal on any senior debt security
	2. Cross default or cross acceleration on any senior unsecured obligation
	3. Debt moratorium, suspension of interest or principal repayments on debt or any material restructuring event
Default Payment	The Issuer will deliver Reference Securities to the value of the Principal Amount to the noteholder

---

2.7.2   Product Variations

One variation on the credit default note structure to emerge is the callable credit default note. Figure 2.15 sets out the detailed structure of this type of credit default linked note.

Figure 2.16 sets out an example of a credit default note where the investors is guaranteed return of principal but risks the coupon through linkage to a default event. Figure 2.17 sets out an additional example of this structure. It also introduces the addition of a leverage factor that modulates the exposure in line with the investor's desired risk profile.

Figure 2.15   Callable Credit Default Linked Note

This structure entails a security where the final maturity of the note is, say, 5 years. The redemption of the note is linked to a reference asset and in the event of default the principal repaid is adjusted by the amount of the agreed default payment. The major differences in the callable versus the non callable structure are the following additional features:

• The note can be called annually or sometimes semi-annually or quarterly (upon provision of appropriate notice) at the option of the issuer

- In the event, the note is not called, then the coupon on the security increases by a preset amount
- The call and the increase in coupon mechanism is repeated as at specified date during the life of the note until final maturity unless the note is called at any of the call dates

In effect the issuer (in practise, the ultimate buyer of default protection through the credit default swap used by the issuer to hedge its own exposure) can continue as of each call date to maintain protection against the cost of default of the underlying credit but at an increasing cost. This increasing cost of protection is embedded in the higher coupons.

Economically, this type of structure can be used to secure protection against default over the near term with the option to extend but at higher cost. The investor is, in turn, the receiver of increased remuneration for assumption of the default risk. In effect, if the note is not called, than it is probable that the credit risk of the underlying credit asset has increased but the investor receives additional income, by way of higher yield, to compensate for the increased default risk.

In practise, this structure was used extensively by banks, in particular Japanese banks, to purchase protection against credit risk on certain obligations. However, most of these transactions were not designed to achieve real transfer of risk. They were intended as period end risk management strategies with the issuers exercising the call at the earliest opportunity.[7]

Figure 2.16   Principal Guaranteed Credit Default Linked Note — Example 1

Issuer	AAA/AA rated institution
Principal Amount	US$20 million
Term	5 years
Issue Price	100 or Face Value
Coupon	• If there is no Credit Event, then US$ LIBOR + 125 bp
	• If there is a Credit Event, then coupon terminates
Reference Security	[Identified Bond or Loan of Nominated Emerging Market Borrower]
Principal Redemption	Principal Amount. If there is a Credit Event, then the Principal Amount is repayable immediately.
Credit Event	Any of the following with respect to Reference Security:
	1. Failure to pay interest or principal on any senior debt security
	2. Cross default or cross acceleration on any senior unsecured obligation
	3. Debt moratorium, suspension of interest or principal repayments on debt or any material restructuring event

---

[7] For examples, see Mahtani Arun, November 21, 1998, "Credit Derivatives Bolster Balance Sheets" *International Financing Review*, Issue 1260 pp 91

Figure 2.17   Principal Guaranteed Credit Default Linked Note — Example 2

Issuer	AAA/AA rated institution
Principal Amount	US$50 million
Term	3 years
Issue Price	100
Coupon	4.50% pa; coupon terminates upon occurrence of Credit Event
Reference Security	[Identified Bond or Loan of Nominated Emerging Market Borrower]
Principal Redemption	Greater of Face Value or Face Value + [Market Value of Reference Security × Factor]
Credit Event	Any of the following with respect to Reference Security:
	1. Failure to pay interest or principal on any senior debt security
	2. Cross default or cross acceleration on any senior unsecured obligation
	3. Debt moratorium, suspension of interest or principal repayments on debt or any material restructuring event

A similar structure which has developed to allow risk averse investors to assume credit risk with guaranteed principal returns entails a note where:
• The capital value of the note is returned at maturity
• The investor participates in any upside performance of the underlying credit asset (loan or security) as captured by the increase in price of the asset above a pre-agreed level

The note has the return profile of a call option on the underlying credit asset. The note is constructed as either a risk free bond combined with a call on the underlying asset or the purchase of the loan that is hedged by the purchase of a default put on the asset. In each case the option is paid for by the forgone or reduced income from the underlying assets. This type of investment has been attractive for investors seeking to invest in higher risk loan transactions within a low risk format. Figure 2.18 sets out an example of this type of structure.

Figure 2.18   Principal Guaranteed Credit Default Linked Note — Example 3

Issuer	AAA/AA rated institution
Principal Amount	US$20 million
Maturity	5 Years
Issue Price	100
Coupon	• If there is no Credit Event, then 0.00% pa.
	• If there is a Credit Event, then 5.75% pa (accruing from issue date to the date of the Credit Event)

Redemption Value	• If there is no Credit Event, then 150% of Principal Amount
	• If there is a Credit Event, then 100% of Principal Amount (payable at Maturity)
Reference Security	[Identified Bond or Loan of Nominated Emerging Market Borrower]
Credit Event	Any of the following with respect to Reference Security:
	1. Failure to pay interest or principal on any senior debt security
	2. Cross default or cross acceleration on any senior unsecured obligation
	3. Debt moratorium, suspension of interest or principal repayments on debt or any material restructuring event

Other variants on the basic credit default note structures include the use of basket credit default notes linked to the first to default within the basket to enhance yield. For example, an investor seeking to enhance yield within a AA rating constraint would generally seek relative value within the universe of available asset within this credit category. An alternative would be to invest in a basket credit default note where the default event is indexed to multiple (say, 3 to 4) AA rated sovereign issuers. The investor receives an enhanced return (say, around 10 bp to 15 bp) relative to the return on any individual asset. This higher return compensates the investor for the higher risk as the default payment can be triggered by default on the first of the three names to default.[8]

Another example of a basket credit note may entail an investor seeking to increase exposure to a particular sovereign issuer within the constraint that it will withdraw from the sector upon reduction in the credit rating or from an increase in bond spreads. The traditional physical solution would be to purchase the relevant securities and sell the portfolio upon the occurrence of the relevant credit event.

Two possible derivative solutions, entailing basket credit default notes are also potentially available:

• Purchase a basket credit default note linked to the reference sovereign assets with the investor's risk linked to the first to incur the credit event.
• Purchase the physical securities and simultaneously purchase a basket credit default note on a first to default basis where the exposure under the note is capable of being extinguished by delivery of the underlying physical securities at an agreed price.

---

[8]   See detailed discussion in Chapter 1

Figure 2.19 shows an example of a credit default note where the reference credit is an emerging market nation with the return of principal being contingent on performance on external credit obligations and on continuation of currency convertibility. Another interesting feature of this issue is the shortness of tenor of the issue. Figure 2.20 and Figure 2.21 sets out additional examples of this type of structure.

Similar structures have emerged in recent years to facilitate synthetic investor exposure to Eastern European domestic. Significant regulatory and administrative burdens in making investments in and holding domestic securities in these markets has encouraged the use of these types of structures to gain effective economic exposure to the domestic.[9] Figure 2.22 sets out details of one example of these types of synthetic emerging market structured notes as applied to Eastern Europe. Figure 2.23 sets out details of an additional example as applied in Asia.

Figure 2.19   Credit Default Linked Note — Default/Inconvertibility Structure, Example 1

In 1995, following the financial crisis in Mexico, a special type short-term security was issued. The credit derivative embedded structure issued by a number of issuers was designed to allow investors to monetize their expectation that Mexico would continue to meet its credit obligations and that the convertibility of the Mexican peso would continue. The typical structure of these transactions was as follows:

Issuer	A1+/P1 rated issuer
Principal Amount	(up to) US$20 million
Maturity	Between 30 days and 90 days
Coupon	Zero
Issue Price	Issued at discount to give investor required yield to maturity
Credit Event	Any default on any Reference Security or inconvertibility of the Mexican peso into US$.
Reference Credit	Government of Mexico
Reference Security	Cetes, Tesobonos, Bondes, Ajustabones or other securities issued or guaranteed by the Reference Credit.
Principal Redemption	If there is no Credit Event, at par (100%). If there is a Credit Event, the Issuer can satisfy its obligations under the note by delivery of any of the Reference Securities or its cash equivalent.

---

[9]   See Kim Theodore, April 1997 "Open All Hours" *Euromoney* pp 109–111; Kim, Theodore, August 1997 "No KO for GKOs," *Futures & Options World*, pp 15–17

These short dated securities were priced to yield the equivalent of LIBOR + 350 bp to 450 bp depending on market conditions. The investors received significant yield enhancement in return for their willingness to risk the principal investment to the risk of credit default by the Mexican government or the restriction of currency convertibility (between the Mexican Peso and the US$) by the Mexican authorities.

Figure 2.20   Credit Default Linked Note — Default/Inconvertibility Structure — Example 2

Issuer	AA rated issuer
Principal Amount	(up to) US$75 million
Maturity	2 years
Coupon	8.00% pa payable semi-annually
Issue Price	100.00
Credit Event	• The Government of Brazil restricts the convertibility of the Brazilian Real into US$
	• Default, rescheduling, moratorium or suspension of payments on Government of Brazil debt
	• War, civil strife or similar event occurs involving Brazil
Interest Payments & Principal Redemption	• If there is no Credit Event, the payment of interest as scheduled and redemption of principal at par (100%)
	• If there is a Credit Event, then the Issuer can defer its payment obligation under the note until 10 days after cessation of such credit event or satisfy its obligations under the note by delivery of any Real-denominated securities issued by the Government of Brazil.

The investors received significant yield enhancement in return for their willingness to risk deferral of payments on the investment in the event of default by the Brazilian government or the restriction of currency convertibility (between the Real and the US$).

Figure 2.21   Credit Default Linked Note — Default/Inconvertibility Structure — Example 3

Issuer	A rated issuer
Principal Amount	(up to) US$50 million
Maturity	1 year
Coupon	0.00% pa
Issue Price	88.00%
Final Redemption	• If there is no Credit Event, then: Principal Amount × (1530/FX) where: FX is the US$/Lebanese pound Exchange Rate
	• If there is a Credit Event, then final redemption will be in Lebanese pounds in an amount equal to: Principal Amount × US$: Lebanese Pounds 1532

Credit Event	The Government of Lebanon restricts the convertibility of the Lebanese pound into US$

The investors received significant yield enhancement (a return of 13.64% pa) and the ability to gain from any appreciation in the Lebanese Pound against the US$. The risk of the investment is that the investor may receive non convertible Lebanese Pounds as payment where restrictions on currency convertibility (between the Lebanese Pound and the US$) is imposed.

Figure 2.22   Synthetic Emerging Market Structured Notes — Example 1

An example of this type of structure includes investments in short dated notes linked to Russian GKOs effectively Treasury Bills. In 1996, the Russian capital markets were de-regulated to allow foreign investment in fixed interest securities. This was facilitated by the introduction of the S account for foreign fixed income investment. Previous to this initiative, foreign investors were unable to repatriate the proceeds from the GKO (effectively Treasury bills) and OFZ sovereign debt markets. However, the establishment of the S account was administratively complex. This encouraged foreign investment indirectly through the use of structured notes where the price performance of the note was linked to the underlying GKO securities.

The transactions were typically structured as follows:

- The investor invested US$ and received an interest rate and principal redemption based on the underlying GKO settled *in US$*. The return received by the investor reflected the interest rate on the GKO as well as the final principal repayment (in the absence of default) converted from roubles into US$ *at the currency rate at maturity*.
- The structure of the transaction transferred the credit risk, interest rate risk, and currency risk to the investor. The structure effectively replicated an investment in the GKO itself.
- The seller of the structured note (typically an investment bank with an S account) hedged its risk by purchasing the GKO itself and transferring the economic risk and returns through the issue of the notes.

The impact of these types of transactions can be seen in the following statistics

- The GKO market has increased to approximately US$60 billion by end 1997 with foreign investment representing around 50% of total outstandings.
- GKO interest rates have fallen from around 40% pa to a pre crisis low of 16.75% pa, in part due to the impact of foreign participation.[10]

The structure has also been used in other markets. For example, set out below is a representative structured note that passed through Polish government Treasury bill risk to the investor. The structure is designed, as above, to allow investors who might not otherwise be able to invest to participate in the market.

Issuer	Investment bank
Maturity	3 months
Amount	(multiples of) US$5 million equivalent

Redemption	Amount $\times$ (1 + Interest Rate) $\times$ Currency Adjustment
Interest Rate	Polish zloty 3-month Treasury Bill yield (on an actual/ 360 day basis) plus/minus a margin
Currency Adjustment	(.45 $\times$ US$1/US$2) + (.35 $\times$ DEM 1/DEM 2) + (.10 $\times$ GBP 1/GBP 2) + (0.05 $\times$ FFR 1/FFR 2) + (.05 $\times$ SFR 2/ SFR 2)

The note effectively is a US$ settled investment which replicates an investment in Polish zloty Treasury bills. The currency adjustment is designed to embed a basket weighted forward currency position in the Note matching the Polish zloty basket peg in order to reduce the currency risk of the investment.

Figure 2.23   Synthetic Emerging Market Structured Notes — Example 2

The structure set out below is a representative structured note that passed through Philippines government Treasury bill risk to the investor. The structure is designed, as above, to allow investors who might not otherwise be able to invest to participate in the market.

Issuer	Investment bank
Maturity	2 years
Amount	(multiples of) US$5 ·million equivalent
Issue Price	100
Interest Rate	• If there is no credit event, then US$ 6 Month LIBOR plus 150 bp
	• If there is a credit event, then Default Payment will apply
Principal Redemption	• If there is no credit event, then Amount in US$
	• If there is a credit event, then Default Payment will apply
Reference Credit	Bangko Sentral ng Pilipinas (BSP) (the Central Bank of the Republic of Philippines)
Reference Securities	Treasury Bills issued by BSP equal to the Amount
Credit Event	• Default, rescheduling, moratorium, suspension of payments or material restructuring of BSP or Republic of Philippines debt
	• BSP restricts the convertibility of the Philippine Peso into US$
Default Payment	The Issuer will not be required to pay any unpaid Interest rate coupons or Principal Amount. The Issuer will have the option to:
	1. Deliver the Reference Securities to the investor; or
	2. Pay the net proceeds that would result from the sale of the Reference Securities.

---

[10] The default by Russia on its debt in 1998 created significant problems with the large volume of GKO linked structured notes on issue.

The note effectively is a US$ settled investment which replicates an investment in Treasury Bills issued by BSP.

2.8 Summary

Structured notes are established instruments in capital markets. They are typically used by investors to acquire exposures to financial market movements in a highly customized fixed income security framework. The major advantages of the structure include the ability to avoid entering into derivative transactions as well the ability of these structures to provide credit enhancement and therefore access to a number of participants to these instruments.

The structured note concept has been readily adapted to credit linked structures. A wide variety of credit linked structured notes have been issued. In addition to the traditional benefits of structured notes, credit linked structured notes through its embedded cash collateral feature greatly broadens the range of counterparties able to sell or provide credit protection in financial markets.

Selected References

BZW June 1997, "An Investor's Guide to Credit Derivatives," *Derivatives Strategy Credit Derivatives Supplement* 1–8

Chase Manhattan Bank April 1997, "Credit Derivatives: A Primer," *Asiamoney Derivatives Guide* 2–5

Flesaker, Bjorn, Hughston, Lane, Schreiber, Laurance, and Sprung, Lloyd, September 1994, "Taking All The Credit," *Risk* vol 7, no 9, 104–108

Francis, Jack Clark, Forst, Joyce A., and Whittaker, J. Gregg (Editors) 1999, *The Handbook of Credit Derivatives*, McGraw-Hill, New York

Howard, Kerrin Winter 1995, "An Introduction To Credit Derivatives," *Derivatives Quarterly*, 28–37

Iacono, Frank "Credit Derivatives" in Schwartz, Robert J. and Smith Jr., Clifford W.(Editors) 1997, *Derivatives Handbook: Risk Management and Control*, John Wiley & Sons, Inc., New York, Chapter 2

Nelken, Dr, Israel (1999) *Implementing Credit Derivatives*, McGraw-Hill, New York

(1999) *The J.P. Morgan Guide To Credit Derivatives*, Risk Publications, London

Smithson, Charles with Holappa, Hal "Credit Derivatives" (December 1995) *Risk*, vol 8, no 12, 38–39

Whittaker, Greg J. and Kumar, Sumita "Credit Derivatives A Primer" in Atsuo Konishi and Ravi Dattatreya (Ed) 1996, *The Handbook of Derivative Instruments*, Irwin Publishing, 595-614

3
Credit linked Notes — Repackaged Notes and Repackaging Vehicles

Satyajit Das

3.1 Overview[1]

Repackaged credit linked notes are a special class of credit linked structured notes. They involve using a special purpose issuance vehicle or asset-repackaging structure to repackage the credit risk of securities to create credit linked structured notes. The repackaging vehicle purchases securities in the secondary market and then re-profiles the cash flows and the credit risk of the underlying securities by entering into derivative transactions with a dealer. The repackaged cash flows are then bundled up as a security and placed with investors. Structurally, repackaged notes are based on asset-swap technology.

The motivation underlying repackaged notes and repackaging vehicles is similar to that underlying the market for credit linked notes generally. These include:

- Investor demand for credit risk that is not directly available in the market
- Relative value considerations under which the credit exposure can be created at a more attractive value through structured notes
- Regulatory and market considerations that favor indirect assumption of the credit exposure relative to direct investment in the security

---

[1] Earlier versions of this chapter were published as Das, Satyajit, May 6, 1999, "Credit Linked Notes: Repackaged Notes And Repackaging Vehicles: Part 1," *Financial Products*, Issue 113, pp 16–21; June 4, 1999, "Credit Linked Notes: Repackaged Notes And Repackaging Vehicles: Part 2," *Financial Products*, Issue 115, pp 16–22

However, the demand for repackaged credit assets over traditional structured notes is predicated upon the following additional factors:

- The lack of requirement to compensate the issuer for issuing the structured note (effectively, the sub-LIBOR margin requirement).
- Relative value considerations whereby the repackaging structure has the inherent opportunity to allow purchase of undervalued securities in the secondary market to collateralize the structure reducing the cost.
- Greater flexibility to structure investments, consistent with investor requirements, without the restriction of needing to satisfy the requirements of the note issuer.[2]
- Enhanced freedom to select the credit and issuer profile of the underlying securities, which allows both customization of issuer risk and diversifies the universe of issuers of structured notes.

These factors (in particular, the first two) have greatly contributed to the development of repackaged notes in general. Repackaged credit notes complement and compete with credit linked structured notes. The market also operates parallel to the asset-swap market.

In this chapter, the structure, design, and trading of repackaged credit notes are examined. The origin and evolution of repackaging vehicles out of asset-swap securitization are first examined. This is followed by a discussion of the structure and design of repackaging vehicles. The adaptation of the repackaging concept to create credit linked notes is then analyzed and, finally, the extension of asset repackaging into synthetic bonds is discussed.

3.2 Evolution of Repackaging Vehicles

3.2.1 History

The concept of repackaging vehicles evolved out of the asset-swap market.[3] The term "asset swap" is a generic term covering repackaging of the cash flows of any security into a required cash-flow configuration for an investor. Traditional asset swaps focused on repackaging the interest-rate and/or currency-risk profile of a security for placement with an investor.

---

[2]   This is relevant despite the fact that the issuer is perfectly insulated against the impact of the embedded derivative and is fully hedged back into LIBOR-based funding at an attractive cost

[3]   For a detailed discussion of asset swaps, see Das, Satyajit 1994, *Swaps & Financial Derivatives*, LBC Information Services, Sydney, McGraw-Hill, Chicago, Chapter 18

Asset swaps were predicated on the reverse of the liability arbitrage and focused on creating synthetic assets for investors. The dominant drivers of this market were: the opportunity to create securities that are not directly available in the market; the opportunity to generate returns in excess of those available from conventional securities of similar characteristics; and repackaging illiquid assets.

Traditional asset swaps were a combination of the purchase of a security and entry by the investor into a derivative transaction to transform the security's interest-rate or currency characteristics. This was problematic for a number of reasons including:

- The inability of a number of investors to transact derivatives
- The credit risk inherent in the derivative transaction
- The lack of liquidity of the package and the difficulty in trading the synthetic asset except by unbundling it into its components, which could be expensive
- The administrative complexity of marking to market both the security and the derivative, and the complexity of accounting for and establishing the taxation treatment of the transaction

These problems led investment banks to evolve the concept of securitized asset swaps. Securitized asset swaps were the effective precursors of the repackaging vehicle.

3.2.2 Securitized Asset Swaps

Until September 1985, asset swaps had traditionally been undertaken as private transactions, being structured primarily as investor-manufactured swaps. In September 1985, the concept of the public or securitized asset swap was introduced with two transactions, one led by Hill Samuel and the other by Merrill Lynch Capital Markets (Merrill Lynch). An analysis of the Merrill Lynch transaction provides an insight into the mechanics of the securitized asset swap. This structure is set out in Figure 3.1.

Figure 3.1   MECS Securitized Asset Swap Structure

Towards the end of September 1985, the UK raised US$2.5 billion through the issuance of seven-year floating-rate notes (FRNs), due October 1992. The notes were originally priced at 99.7% of face value, net of fees, with a coupon of three-month US$ LIBID and were non-callable for three years from the time of issuance. Following the launch of this issue, the sales force of Merrill Lynch noted that there was considerable interest from its investors in fixed-rate UK government US$-denominated debt. In particular, the sales force had reported a coupon of approximately 9.375% pa with a three-year maturity as acceptable to these investors. However, no fixed-rate UK government debt denominated in US$ was available. Consequently, the Merrill Lynch swap and Eurobond syndicate desk set about designing, at that time, the largest securitized asset swap.

The structure of the transaction was as follows:

1. Merrill Lynch bought US$100m of UK 1992 FRNs.
2. The US$100m of UK FRNs were then sold into a special-purpose vehicle (SPV) known as Marketable Eurodollar Collateralized Securities Ltd (MECS).
3. Simultaneously, Merrill Lynch arranged a swap with Prudential Global Funding Corp (rated AAA) between MECS and the swap counterparty under which MECS made payments of US$ LIBID every three months in return for Prudential making payments equivalent to 9.375% pa to MECS. This effectively converted the floating-rate US$ cash flow that MECS trust earned from the UK FRNs into a fixed-rate US$ flow.

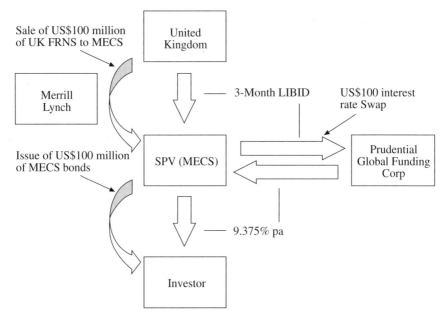

Merrill Lynch then arranged a Eurodollar bond issue in the name of MECS with a coupon of 9.375% pa and a maturity of October 1988. The bonds issued by MECS were collateralized with the assets of the trust, which was a holding of US$100m of UK FRNs and also the contingent liability reflecting the interest rate swap with Prudential. Essentially, the package constituted a high quality (AAA) credit risk.

The end result of the repackaging was the creation of a conventional fixed interest security for the investor. The investor, through the mechanism of the securitized asset-swap structure, avoided any need to either purchase the underlying securities or enter into a derivative transaction. The structure met investor requirements in terms of:

- Credit quality
- Interest rate and currency requirements
- Capacity to have the security listed, rated and cleared, and settled through existing clearing systems
- Liquidity and ability to be traded

The basic structure described continues to be the basis of the design of all repackaging vehicles.

3.2.3 Structured Note Repackaging Vehicles

The use of the structure described gradually gained in popularity as a means for repackaging secondary markets assets.[4] An important step in the evolution of the repackaging markets was the development of a secondary market in structured notes.[5]

The impetus to secondary-market trading in structured notes derived from the market distress period of 1994–5. Prior to that, secondary-market interest had been spasmodic. The activity that had occurred had been related to investors exiting structured investments, with the dealer purchasing the note, engineering the reversal of the derivative component(s), and distributing the security as a higher-yielding fixed- or floating-note security to conventional investors in asset-swap products. The latter continues to be the basic mechanism for providing any required secondary-market liquidity and establishing benchmark secondary-market bid prices for these notes.

However, in the market conditions that prevailed in late 1994 and early 1995, the volume of structured notes that began to appear for sale increased dramatically as investors exited their investments.[6] These market conditions resulted in dealers rapidly re-positioning their secondary market trading in these instruments to allow them to be repackaged. As noted above, the major buyers of the structured notes were asset-swap buyers prepared to purchase structured notes which had been asset swapped to reverse engineer the market-risk

---

[4] For a detailed discussion of the evolution of the market, see Das, Satyajit 1994, *Swaps & Financial Derivatives*, LBC Information Services, Sydney; McGraw-Hill, Chicago, pp 594–598. See also Das, Satyajit 1989, *Swap Financing*, LBC Information Services, Sydney; IFR Publishing, London, pp 336–345

[5] See Das, Satyajit 1996, *Structured Notes and Derivative Embedded Notes*, Euromoney Publications, Chapter 15

[6] The most notable transaction during this period was the sale of the very large portfolio of structured notes held by Orange County.

component. The asset swap was used to create, typically, an FRN priced off LIBOR targeted to banks and, to a lesser extent, a fixed-rate bond priced off US treasuries targeted to the fixed-income investor.

The development of the secondary market in structured notes saw the introduction of a number of structured note repackaging vehicles. These vehicles were modeled on the securitized asset-swap vehicles identified above. Such vehicles include Merrill Lynch's Structured Enhanced Return Trusts (STEERS), Salomon Brothers' Trust Investment Enhanced Return Securities (TIERS) as well as similar vehicles operated by other investment banks.

The central concept of these trust-based structures is their ability to create trust receipts that represent either repackaged structured notes or structured notes specifically created through repackaging that are sold to investors. The trust receipts are rated by one or more of the major rating agencies and the trust receipt is tradable to facilitate liquidity. In essence, it is the conversion of asset swaps into public and tradable securities.

The process of utilizing a trust vehicle is set out in Figure 3.2. The diagram illustrates the creation of a trust receipt on a structured note. The transaction entails the following steps:
- Purchase of a security in, generally, secondary markets
- The lodgment of this security in the trust vehicle
- The entry by the trust into a series of derivative transactions with a counterparty to engineer the required cash-flow/risk profile. This can entail either reverse engineering a structured note to remove the derivative element to allow the security to be placed as a fixed-income bond. Alternatively, a

Figure 3.2   Repackaging Vehicle

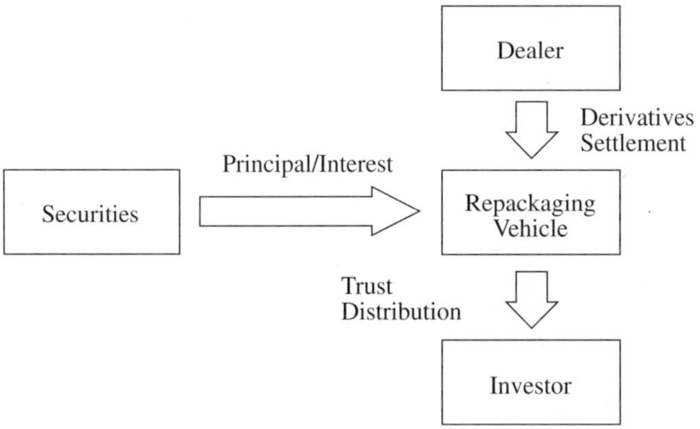

conventional fixed- or floating-rate security can be combined with the relevant derivative components to create a structured note
• The trust then issues trust certificates or notes representing the restructured cash flows of the security (combining the security and the derivative transactions) to the investor in return for payment of the face value
• The trust collects all cash flows (principal, interest, and derivative settlements from the relevant counterparties), and passes them through to the investor over the life of the transaction

The credit rating of this trust arrangement is the rating of the bond plus the derivative transactions. The typical counterparty to the derivative transaction is an AAA or AA entity. The credit quality of the underlying security is selected by the issuer. The resulting transaction can be, at the option of the investor, be issued as a rated or unrated security.

The original purpose of these repackaging vehicles was to re-engineer large volumes of structured notes that investors wanted to sell into conventional fixed income (primarily, floating- or fixed-rate straight bonds) for replacement with investors. However, the capacity of these structures to create structured notes, as distinct from reverse engineering them into conventional securities, came to be recognized. This led to the emergence of the modern structure of repackaging vehicles, which currently operates in both the primary and secondary markets.

3.2.4 Primary Market Repackaging Vehicles

The use of these special purpose repackaging vehicles in both the creation of new structured notes (the primary market) and in repackaging existing structured notes (the secondary market) was predicated on the advantages of the structure. The major advantages of the repackaging vehicle structures include:
• Relative value considerations
• Restructuring risk exposure
• Credit selection
• Liquidity
• Flexibility

These structures can provide significantly higher returns to the investors. The sources of this enhanced return is derived from a number of sources:
• The ability to purchase undervalued securities in the secondary market
• The avoidance of paying the issuer the required funding margin on a customized structured note issue

The higher costs of the repackaging vehicle structure do not significantly affect the return as the majority of costs are fixed, and on a per-transaction basis, may be substantially less than the enhanced return that can be generated from the identified sources (see further discussion below).

A major advantage relates to the reprofiling of the investor's exposure under the structured note. The restructuring of risk under a traditional structured note requires the entry into an offsetting series of derivatives transactions to adjust the cash flow and risks. The required transactions may be difficult for regulatory or credit reasons for the investor to undertake. The alternative is to sell the structured note and, if appropriate purchase a new structured note with the new risk profile. The second alternative is expensive in practise.

Under the repackaging vehicle structure, the restructuring is achieved by selling back the trust certificate to the vehicle. The vehicle executes a series of derivative trades designed to, firstly, eliminate the original exposure, and, secondly, create the desired profile. The trust re-issues a certificate with adjusted cash flows. The cost or benefit of the reprofiling is captured by either payment at the time of the restructuring or over the life of the transaction. The flexibility and the cost economies of this flexibility are considerable.

As the repackaging vehicle enables the use of any available security, it allows significant expansion in credit selection processes that are no longer constrained by the issuer universe prepared to undertake the issue of the required structured note.

Secondary market liquidity should be comparable or enhanced by the repackaging vehicle structure as the receipts or notes are tradable and the underlying process of gaining liquidity is, at worst, unaltered and, at best, improved.

Overall, the structure significantly enhances the potential of both repackaging of structured notes by effectively allowing securitized and tradable asset swaps and the creation of new structured notes as an alternative to new issues of such products. In fact, the repackaging vehicles currently operate in competition to the primary issuer market in these types of transactions.

3.3 Structure and Design

3.3.1 Generic Structure

The basic design of the repackaging vehicles is largely standardized. It follows the structure set out in Figure 3.2.

The basic repackaging vehicle used is either a trust structure (favored in the

US) or a single-purpose special company. The vehicles are associated with, but not owned by, the dealer or investment banks. The critical issue in this regard is to ensure that the vehicle is bankruptcy-remote to the sponsoring entity (that is, the default or bankruptcy of the sponsor does not result in the default or bankruptcy of the special vehicle).

The steps in creating a structured note utilizing a repackaging vehicle take the following (fairly standardized) steps:

- The investor requirements are determined in terms of credit risk and risk profile and exposure required
- The investment bank purchases the required collateral in the secondary market
- The investment bank sells the collateral for value into the repackaging vehicle. The repackaging vehicle generates the liquidity needed to purchase the collateral from the issue of the structured note to the investor
- The repackaging vehicle enters into derivative transactions with the investment bank to:
  1. Convert a structured security into a conventional fixed- or floating-rate bond by hedging out the derivative elements through the derivative transaction
  2. Convert a conventional security into a structured note with a defined risk profile by embedding the required exposure into the transaction through the derivative transaction. The derivative transaction is secured over the assets of the repackaging vehicle, the collateral securities.
- The repackaging vehicle issues either notes (in the case of a company) or trust receipts (in the case of a trust) to the investor in return for value (this cash is used to purchase the collateral securities and, if necessary, to finance any payment required under the derivative contract).
- The repackaging vehicle collects the cash flows from the underlying collateral as well as the settlements under the derivative contracts. The net cash flow is paid to the investor over the term of the transaction and at maturity. The structured note is cleared and settled through normal accepted mechanics.
- In the event of default under either the collateral securities or the derivative contract, the investor in the notes is fully exposed to the risk of loss and receives any payment received by the repackaging vehicle.
- The structured notes issued by the vehicle can be, if required, rated by a rating agency. The rating is dependent on both the collateral and the credit risk of the derivative counterparty.

In effect, the repackaging vehicle acts as a conduit to allow the investor to access the underlying security and overlay the specific risk exposure required through the derivative contract. The repackaging vehicle funds itself through the issue of the structured notes. The risk and return profile of the structured note is attributable to the underlying collateral and the derivative contract.

Repackaging vehicles active in the market include the vehicles mentioned above as well as J.P. Morgan's Custom Repackaged Asset Vehicle Trust (CRAVE) and Barclays's Asset Linked Trust Securities (ALTS).

3.3.2 Types of Vehicle

The types of vehicles used are:
- **Single-purpose standalone issuers:** Where a separate entity is established for each issue of structured notes.
- **Multiple issuance structures:** Where a broad flexible structure is in place that allows the same entity to undertake different issues of structured notes.

The selection between these types of vehicles is dictated by the desire to maximize administrative flexibility and speed of execution, and to minimize the costs of establishing the repackaging vehicles.

Multiple issuance structures have grown in popularity, which is derived from:
- The lower cost of such structures reflecting the capacity to amortize the set up and ongoing costs over a larger volume of issues
- The speed of execution as the structure is permanently in place enabling transactions to be completed in a relatively short time scale
- The benefits of administration of fewer vehicles
- The opportunity for individual investment banks to brand their repackaged products. The brand awareness has significant benefits in terms of achieving the status of an established issuer facilitating ready acceptance by investors

Two types of multiple issuance vehicles are commonly used:
- Program issuers
- Multiple issuer or "Umbrella" programs.

Program issuers are designed as single legal entities that issue multiple series of structured notes. Each note is specifically secured over the specific assets and derivatives used to create the note. This is achieved by limiting the recourse of the investor (as creditor) to specified identified assets and derivative transactions through a non-recourse agreement. Each series of notes is isolated from other assets and contracts held by or entered into by the issuer through this non-recourse mechanism — often referred to as a "firewall."

Figure 3.3 sets out the program issuer structure.

Figure 3.3   Program Issuer Structure

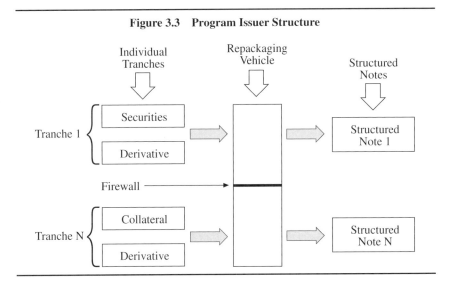

The program issuer format is especially attractive because of its low cost, lower administrative requirements, and speed and flexibility in use. However, the critical issue is in relation to the effective segregation of assets. This is important both from a legal and ratings perspective as well as from the investors' point of view.

In the event that the assets underlying one issue were in default and the required separation had not been achieved, the investors could potentially seek recourse to *all assets and contracts of the vehicle*. This result (referred to as "tainting") would have far-reaching effects. The issuer itself could be in default, compromising *all issues* and not just the one in default. This may lead to litigation *against the issuer* and could prevent the operation of the vehicle.

This means that the program issuance format is not used in all jurisdictions. It is only utilized in jurisdictions where an appropriate level of legal comfort on the firewalls can be established. In practise, two other provisions are also generally utilized to manage this risk:

- Program issuance structures are not utilized where the underlying assets being securitized vary significantly in terms of credit quality from one issue of structured notes to another.

- The structure incorporates substitution rights enabling assets to be removed from the structure in order to protect the rating of the vehicle.[7]

The alternative is the multiple issuers or umbrella structure, where a separate vehicle is used for each issue but a master documentary framework governing the individual issuers is established. Figure 3.4 sets out the structure

Figure 3.4   Umbrella Multiple Issuance Program

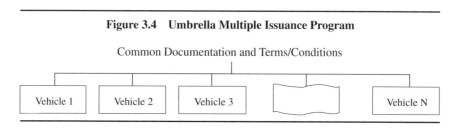

Common Documentation and Terms/Conditions

This type of structure has the following characteristics:
- The problems of tainting are avoided
- Individual companies must still be established and administered over the transaction term
- The process is facilitated by the common master documentation with speed being increased by advance creation of a number of issuance vehicles
- The cost is higher and the threshold size of the transaction and/or its profitability must be larger to support the higher cost

The multiple issuer structure is generally favored where the underlying assets are of higher risk or the underlying assets are of significantly different credit risk.

The vehicles are generally based in favorable tax and regulatory environments such as Holland, the Netherlands Antilles, Jersey, or Cayman Islands. The major factors driving selection as between the jurisdictions include:
- Tax regimes, including tax treaties in place with key investor jurisdictions
- Legal framework, particularly in terms of contract law, segregation, and bankruptcy remoteness
- A benign regulatory framework
- Political stability

---

[7] Following the collapse of emerging markets in 1997–98, this provision was used to, for example, remove South Korean assets from some vehicles. This reflected the sharp deterioration in the South Korean credit rating during this period.

- Cost factors
- Availability of services such as legal firms, accounting firms, and management companies
- Physical location, in terms of distance from major financial centers
- Time zones that allow trading overlap with normal trading hours in key trading jurisdictions

The vehicles are generally rated by the major rating agencies.[8] The rating is based on the individual issue and key factors driving ratings include:
- The credit quality of the collateral
- The credit quality of the derivatives counterparty
- The market risks, such as currency, interest rate risk and term to maturity
- The structure of the transaction including legal risks and taxation risks

3.4 Repackaged Credit Linked Notes

3.4.1 Concept

The concept of repackaged credit linked notes is based firmly on the asset-swap/asset repackaging principles already outlined. The rationale is to deliberately create credit exposure to selected counterparties using a credit derivative contract. The process is identical to that already described. Assets are bought in the secondary market lodged in a repackaging vehicle. The repackaging vehicle enters into credit derivative transactions to reprofile the credit risk on the asset. The repackaging vehicle then issues a security to the investor consistent with the investor's requirements. The distinguishing feature of repackaged credit linked notes is the focus on reprofiling the credit risk of the underlying securities. This reprofiling is typically achieved with either total return swaps or credit default swaps.

3.4.2 Types

In general, there are two types of repackaged credit linked note transactions:
- **Creation of exposure to high-quality credits** (referred to here as asset credit swaps): This is done by buying an asset in the secondary market and entering into a credit derivatives transaction to reduce the risk to the obligor/issuer of the underlying security. The repackaged security enables the investor to acquire exposure to the derivatives counterparty (via the credit derivative).

---

[8] See Chapter 16.

The repackaged security generates a return that is lower than that on the underlying security but higher than the normal return that would be available on an equivalent security for the higher-rated credit (the derivatives counterparty). This type of transaction may be motivated by relative value considerations whereby the asset swap is used to arbitrage the valuation of different credits in the capital market.

- **Creation of exposure to a selected credit(s)** (referred to as synthetic credit assets): This is done by purchasing high-quality collateral assets that are then converted through a credit derivative to provide exposure to a selected credit nominated by the investor. The repackaged security in this case provides the investor with indirect exposure to the selected underlying credit. This type of transaction is motivated by the ability of the investor to access the underlying asset (which may not be available in the cash market), the ability to circumvent regulatory and legal constraints on the investment, the capacity to structure the exposure in a manner desired by the investor, or relative value considerations.

Figure 3.5 sets out an example of the structures of an asset credit swap.

Figure 3.5   Repackaged Credit Linked Notes — Example 1: Credit Asset Swap

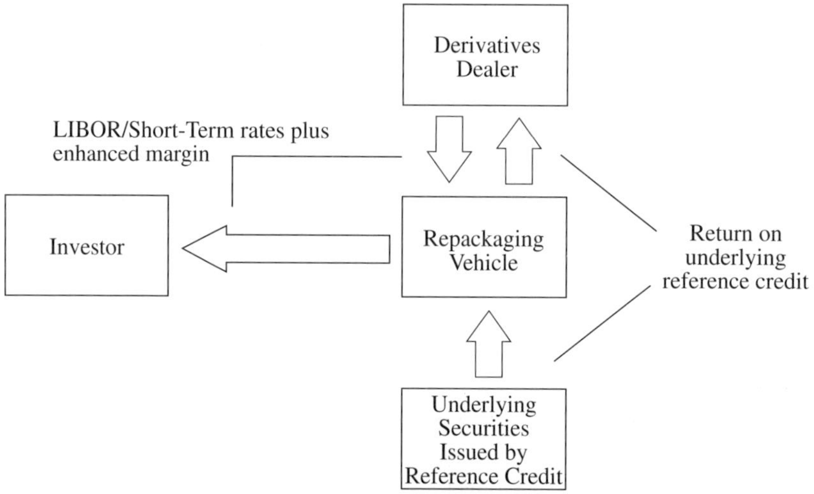

The mechanics of the transaction are as follows:

- The underlying securities issued by the reference credit are purchased by the repackaging vehicle.

- The vehicle enters into a total return swap with the derivative dealer. Under the swap, the dealer receives the return on the underlying securities and pays LIBOR plus a margin the repackaging vehicle.
- At maturity, the derivatives dealer pays par to the vehicle (unless it is in default) and receives the maturing proceeds of the underlying securities, unless the obligor on the underlying securities is in default, in which case it receives the liquidation proceeds.

It is important that credit risk transfer of the repackaging structure be recognized. The objective is to immunize the investor from any credit exposure to the underlying asset. However, the repackaging structure inevitably creates an exposure to the underlying securities and the derivatives counterparty. In this structure, to avoid any exposure to the underlying securities, the obligation of the derivative counterparty to pay is absolute irrespective of the performance of the obligor. In effect, the derivative counterparty's obligation to pay the LIBOR plus margin stream is unconditional. The derivatives counterparty has an entitlement to receive the return on the underlying securities (both interest and principal). In this way, the only exposure assumed by the investor is to the higher-rated derivatives counterparty.

Figure 3.6 sets out the construction of a synthetic credit asset.

Figure 3.6   Repackaged Credit Linked Notes – Example 2: Synthetic Credit Asset

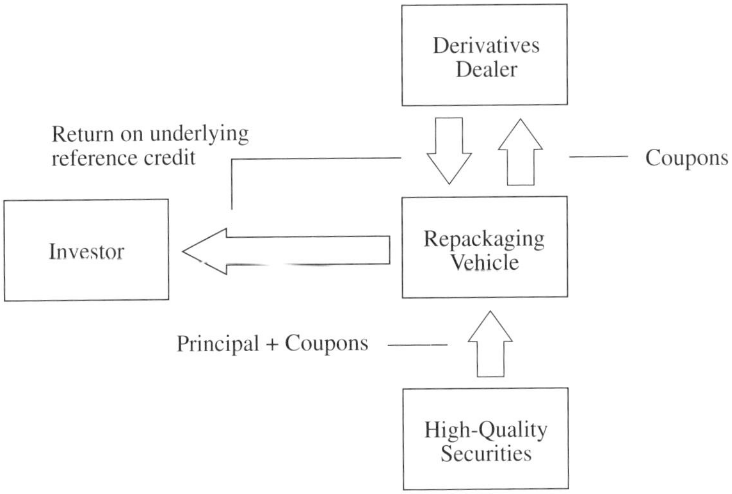

The mechanics of the structure are as follows:
- The repackaging vehicle purchases high-quality securities in the market

- The repackaging vehicle enters into a credit derivative transaction with a derivative counterparty. This can be a total return swap or a credit default swap linked to reference credit or reference security
- The repackaging vehicle issues securities that pay a return to the investor that equates to the return on the reference security. The security issued by the repackaging vehicle at maturity pays out the principal value of the transaction, but in the event of default, pays out the post-default value of the reference securities calculated through either a screen price, dealer poll, or as calculated by deducting a pre-agreed quantification of the expected loss on default

The cash flow structure of the synthetic credit asset structure is dependent on the type of credit derivative embedded:

- In the case where a total return swap is used, the return on the underlying high-quality securities is paid thorough to the derivatives counterparty. In return, the counterparty pays the return on the reference security. This return corresponds to the return received by the investor on the note. At maturity, the counterparty effects a cash settlement with the repackaging vehicle based on the change in value of the reference security. Where the reference security increases in value, the counterparty pays the net settlement amount to the repackaging vehicle to increase the value paid out to the investor. Where the reference security falls in value, the counterparty receives the net settlement amount from the repackaging vehicle. The repackaging vehicle funds this payment from the high-quality securities held by the vehicle. This reduces the payment to the investor
- In the case of a credit default swap, the derivatives counterparty pays a periodic fee in return for the repackaging vehicle agreeing to make a default payment in the event of a default by the reference credit. This fee, combined with the return on the high-quality underlying securities, makes up the return to the investor. At maturity, if there has been no default on the reference credit, the investor receives the principal of its investment financed by the maturing high-quality securities. If there is a default on the reference credit, there is a cash settlement between the repackaging vehicle and the derivative counterparty based on the decline in value in a reference security. This settlement is paid to the derivatives counterparty. The repackaging vehicle funds this payment from the high-quality securities held by the vehicle. This reduces the payment to the investor.

The mechanics of the synthetic credit asset structures ensures that the investor has a direct exposure to the reference credit.

3.4.3   Examples

In this section, some examples of repackaged credit assets are set out. The principal focus is on synthetic credit assets. The asset credit swaps are more straightforward transactions, which are designed to pay a floating rate return on a high quality underlying credit targeted to, in general, money market investors looking for a yield pick-up. However, one example of a repackaging of longer-term securities for investors seeking short-term exposure is set out. The synthetic credit asset structures discussed focus on synthesizing exposures to reference credits in a non-traditional manner. The examples described here are in addition to the more traditional structures of credit linked structured notes which were described in Chapter 2. These types of credit linked notes can and are structured using repackaging vehicles, in addition to the more traditional direct issuance structures.[9]

Figure 3.7 shows an example of a transaction to create short-term exposure to underlying assets that have longer maturities.

Figure 3.7   Repackaged Credit Assets — Example 1

A popular form of repackaging has been the restructuring of the cash flows of assets with a longer maturity into a structured note where the investor has exposure to the asset for a shorter term. Generally, these transaction have been structured as follows:
- The repackaging vehicle purchases the longer-dated security.
- The repackaging vehicle enters into a credit spread swap with a derivatives counterparty for a period of say, one year, corresponding to the maturity of the structured note issued by the repackaging vehicle. Under the terms of the swap, which is equivalent to a forward on the spread on the security, at maturity of the swap:
  1. The derivatives counterparty pays a settlement amount equal to the amount of any depreciation in the value of the security in the event that the value of the security falls.
  2. The derivatives counterparty receives a settlement amount equal to the amount any appreciation in the value of the security in the event of the value of the security increasing.
- The repackaging vehicle may also enter into additional derivatives transactions (usually an interest or currency swap) with the derivatives counterparty to re-profile the cash flow of the underlying security into the desired framework (generally, US$ floating-rate LIBOR).

---

[9] For an indication of the size of the market in these types of notes, see Arun Mahtani "Synthetic Structures Facilitate Leverages Loan Boom," November 28, 1998, *International Financing Review*, Issue 1261, pp 85

- The repackaging vehicle issues a structured note for a maturity that is identical to that of the credit spread swap. The structured note is collateralized by the underlying longer-dated security and the credit spread swap.
- The structured note pays a return to the investor equivalent to US$ LIBOR plus a spread generated off the coupon on the security and interest rate/currency swap.
- At maturity, the structured note pays out at par. This is achieved as follows:
  1. The underlying securities are liquidated in the market.
  2. The credit spread swap is settled with the derivative counterparty with the repackaging vehicle paying (receiving) cash in the event of an increase (decline) in the value of the underlying security. Where the repackaging vehicle has to make the payment, the payment is financed by the excess of liquidation value over the amount required to redeem the structured note at par.
  3. The combination of the liquidation amount and the credit spread swap settlement equates to the total cash available for payment to the investor.

The investor's risk in this type of transaction is on the underlying asset and the derivatives counterparty. The transaction enables the investor to complete the maturity

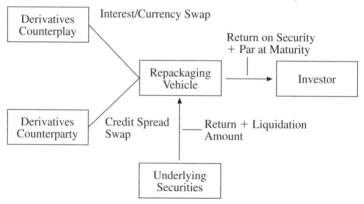

spectrum of investments using the credit spread swap to hedge the market risk on sale as on the underlying longer dated asset as at maturity of the shorter structured note.

Figure 3.8 sets out an example of using a repackaging vehicle to create diversified exposure to a portfolio of bonds/credits.

Figure 3.8   Repackaged Credit Assets — Example 2

The objective in this case is to create an investment where the investor has exposure to a diversified portfolio of securities. The transaction is structured as follows:
- The repackaging vehicle issues a structured note to the investor.
- The cash proceeds of the note are used to make an investment in high-quality bonds.
- The repackaging vehicle enters into a series of total return swaps with a derivative counterparty to gain exposure to a variety of bonds/credits. The total return swaps

have total notional principal equivalent to the value of the investments in the high-quality bonds that are used to fully collateralize the swaps.

- The structured note returns to the investor (usually) a floating-rate return calculated as LIBOR plus a margin. The return is equivalent to the payments received under the total return swaps. The return from the underlying high-quality bond investments is used to fund the floating rate payments under the total return swaps.
- At maturity, the structured note pays out the value of the securities underlying the total return swaps. An appreciation in value adds to the pool of funds generated from the liquidation of the high quality collateral pool and is available for distribution to the investor. Any depreciation in the value of the securities underlying the total return swaps is funded by the collateral pool and reduces the payment to the investor in the structured note.

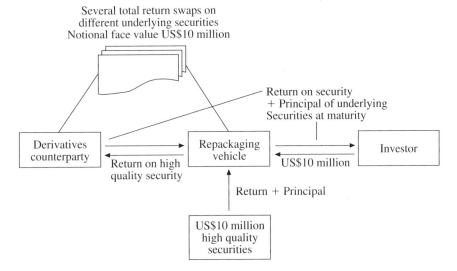

The structure is designed to allow an investor through the investment in the structured note issued by the repackaging vehicle to obtain economic exposure to the diversified portfolio of securities. The major benefits include the higher level of diversification that is obtained as a result of the lower threshold size of total return swaps (versus investment in the bonds) and the elimination of administration costs of managing a portfolio of securities.

Figure 3.9 sets out an example of a transaction where the repackaging vehicle creates exposure to one or more credits on a leveraged basis.

Figure 3.9   Repackaged Credit Assets — Example 3

The objective of this type of structure is to create leveraged exposure to a portfolio of securities or loans. The essential transaction dynamics are exactly the same as those identified in Figure 3.8. The only additional element is that the total return swap entered into is for a notional principal greater than the face value of the collateral.

The structure will operate as follows:

- As in the previous case, the repackaging vehicle uses the proceeds of the issue of structured notes to purchase high-quality securities, which are then used to collateralize the total return swaps.
- The collateral will represent approximately 10–20% of the notional principal of the total return swaps entered.
- The structured note redeems at maturity as in the previous example. However, the investor can only lose the principal face value of the structured note, not the notional value of the total return swaps entered into (that is, there is an effective put on the value of the underlying securities written by the counterparty to the total return swap in favor of the repackaging vehicle).

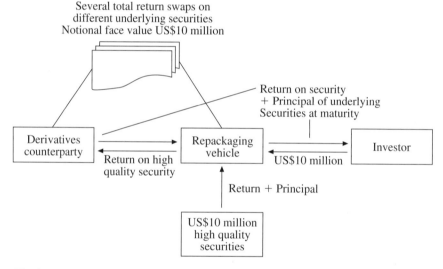

The investor has exposure to both the collateral and the securities underlying the total return swaps.

The rationale for the structure is the very high returns an investor can generate from the leverage embedded in the transactions. However, unlike traditional forms of leverage (such as purchasing the underlying securities on margin), the loss that can be suffered by the investor is constrained to the face value of the structured notes (effectively, the collateral amount).

Figure 3.10 sets out an example of using a repackaging vehicle to create a first to default security.

Figure 3.10   Repackaged Assets — Example 4

The underlying concept in this case is to create a higher-yielding structured note through leveraged exposure to multiple credit risks through a first-to-default basket.

The structure will operate as follows:
- The repackaging vehicle issues a structured note for, say, face value of US$10 million.
- The proceeds of the note are invested in high-quality securities.
- The repackaging vehicle enters into a credit default swap on a first-to-default basis with a counterparty. The first-to-default swap operates as follows:
  1. The repackaging vehicle receives a fee in return for assuming the credit risk on a portfolio of securities (say, US$40 million made up of four securities of US$10 million).
  2. In the event of default on any of the securities, the first default swap is triggered, and the defaulted security is put to the repackaging vehicle.
  3. The repackaging vehicle uses the proceeds from the sale of the high-quality securities to purchase the defaulted securities.
- The investor in the structured note receives the return on the portfolio of high-quality collateral together with the fee under the credit default swap.
- At maturity, where there has been no default, the settlement under the structured note is at par from the proceeds of the maturing high-quality collateral. In the event of default, the investor can physically settle (by receiving delivery of the defaulted bonds) or cash settle (the repackaging vehicle selling the defaulted bonds at the post default price in the market).

A number of variations are feasible. For example, the credit default swap may be structured on the basis of a pre-agreed default loss amount (an assumed recovery rate). This would mean that instead of physical delivery of the defaulted security the repackaging vehicle would make a pre-agreed payment (the loss or par minus the recovery rate assumed) to the derivatives counterparty. This structure has the advantage of a known loss in the event of default for the investor.

The rationale for the structure is that the investor provides first loss protection on a first-to-default basis on a portfolio of securities, allowing the magnetization of expectations on default risk. The structure enables the value to be released to the investor by way of enhanced return on the note.

An additional driver for these transactions has been the ability to use these structures to create securities that may not be available in the market. For example, assume the investor is seeking a B-rated investment that is unavailable. However, the investor can synthesize the B credit rating exposure by purchasing a first to default note of the type described, where the first-to-default portfolio consists of say four BB-rated securities. The combined risk of the portfolio on a first-to-default basis is higher than the risk of default on any individual security. This higher risk equates to a single B-type exposure.[10] This allows the creation of specific types of credit exposures unavailable directly in the market.

---

[10] Assume a BB-rated issuer has a 2% likelihood of defaulting over a one-year holding period. Assuming zero default correlations, the probability of any one of the four issuers defaulting can be approximated as $1 - (1-.02)^4$ which equates to 0.08% or 8.00%. This is equivalent to the approximate likelihood of default on a B-rated issuer over a one-year time horizon. This horizon reflects the maturity of the structured note and the term of first-to-default credit swap.

Figure 3.11 sets out an example of transactions involving recovery-rate expectations using a repackaging vehicle to structure it as a note.

Figure 3.11   Repackaged Credit Assets — Example 5

This type of structure is designed to create a higher-yielding investment by monetizing expectations on recovery rates. The structure operates as follows:

- The repackaging vehicle issues a structured note to the investor. The return on the note is linked to the price performance on a specified reference security.
- The repackaging vehicle pays an enhanced return to the investor while there is no event of default on the underlying securities.
- In the event of default, the investor suffers a loss equal to the full face value of the note. The investor has no right to take physical delivery of the underlying reference security. The investor does not have any recourse against the issuer of the structured note or the repackaging vehicle in terms of any recovery value on the defaulted securities.

In effect, the structure provides the investor in the note an enhanced return predicated on the investor giving up *any recovery value on the underlying security.*

The repackaging vehicle generates the enhanced return by using the structured note proceeds to purchase the reference security. Simultaneously, the repackaging vehicle enters into a credit derivative transaction with a counterparty that agrees to purchase the asset in the event of default at nominal value (say, US$0.01 per US$1 million face value of bonds) in the event of default. The counterparty pays a periodic fee for that right which is passed on to the investor in the structured note.

The process of repackaging has been applied increasingly to the leveraged loan market.[11] These transactions combine the techniques of repackaging and portfolio securitization.[12] An example of this type of transaction is Synthetic Equity Loan Securitization (SEQUILS) and Morgan Intermediated Collateralized Loan Obligations (CLO) Securities (MINCS) transactions introduced in 1999 by J.P. Morgan. Figure 3.12 sets out a description of the structure.

Figure 3.12   Repackaged Credit Assets — SEQUILS/MINCS Structure

In April 1999, J.P. Morgan launched the SEQUILS/MINCS transactions.[13] The objective of the transaction was to allow investors to invest in leveraged loans.

---

[11] See discussion in Chapter 20
[12] See discussion in Chapter 4
[13] See Mahtani, Arun April 17, 1999 "JPM Launches Next Generation Credit Vehicle," *International Financing Review*, Issue 1279, pp 99

The structure operates as follows:
- SEQUILS and MINCS are special-purpose vehicles.
- SEQUILS issues US$712.5 million in AA-rated senior notes. The proceeds are used to purchase leveraged loans from the primary market, the secondary market and from J.P. Morgan's own portfolio.
- SEQUILs enters into a credit default swap on US$114 million (16% of the total portfolio) with J.P. Morgan. SEQUILS pays a fee out of the interest income received from the underlying portfolio of leveraged loans. The credit enhancement provided through the credit default swap enables the portfolio to achieve the high investment-grade ratings on the notes issued out of the SEQUILS vehicle.
- J.P. Morgan in turn enters into a transaction with MINCS to reduce the credit risk assumed under its credit default swap with SEQUILS. This is done through the issue of credit linked notes by J.P. Morgan to MINCS. The payments on the credit linked notes are linked to the credit performance of the underlying leveraged loan portfolio in SEQUILS. MINCS finances the purchase of these credit linked notes through the issue of US$114 million of BBB rated notes to investors.
- The transaction operates as follows:
  1. In the event there is no default on the underlying loans, SEQUILS receives the interest on the loans, which is used to make payments to investors in the notes and J.P. Morgan under the credit default swap. J.P. Morgan uses the fee received to make payment to MINCS that in turn uses the receipts to finance payments to noteholders. At maturity, the cash flow from maturing loans is used to make principal repayments to SEQUILS noteholders. At maturity, J.P. Morgan repays the principal of the credit linked notes to MINC that in turns repays the noteholders in MINCS.
  2. In the event of default on the underlying loans, SEQUILS claims under the credit default swap with J.P. Morgan (to a maximum of US$114 million). J.P. Morgan covers any default payment to SEQUILS by reducing the principal repaid to MINCS under the credit linked notes. MINCS in turn reduces the principal paid on the notes issued to investors by MINCS.

The structure of the notes issued is as follows:
- All notes issued by SEQUILS and MINCS are floating-rate notes with a legal final maturity of 12 years.
- Notes issued by SEQUILS were offered as a standard structured AA-rated issue to investors at a small yield premium to comparable issues.
- Notes issued by MINCS were offered to investors at an expected return of LIBOR plus 400 bp. The expected coupon was LIBOR plus 150 bp and a potential return of LIBOR plus 550/600 bp.

The SEQUILS/MINCS vehicle structures were cash-flow based. This contrasts with market-value based structures. The cash flow based structures rely on expected cash flows generated from the underlying asset pool. In contrast, market value structures rely on changes in market values of the underlying assets.[14] Cash-flow based structures are

---

[14] See discussion in Chapter 4

more stable in high stress scenarios where market values may move in a very volatile manner.

The objective of the structure was to provide investor access to a diversified portfolio of leveraged loans. The structure also effectively bifurcates the returns — SEQUILS investors obtain exposure to the lower risk component while MINCS investors obtain exposure to the higher risk elements through assuming the first loss position.[15]

3.5 Synthetic Bonds

3.5.1 Structure

Synthetic bonds entail the issue of "corporate" or "sovereign" debt out of a special-purpose issuance or asset repackaging vehicle where the underlying credit risk exposure is created through a combination of cash securities and credit derivative transaction. The synthetic bond is designed to replicate the characteristics of a fixed interest security issued by the underlying issuer.

These transactions are typically similar to asset repackaging transactions involving the use of a special-purpose repackaging vehicle. The central concept of these structures is their ability to create securities (trust receipts or bonds/ notes) that represent either repackaged cash flows that approximate a conventional bond created through repackaging which are sold to investors. The securities are rated by one or more of the major rating agencies and the trust receipt is tradable to facilitate liquidity.

The distinguishing characteristics of these transactions, which differentiate the synthetic bond transactions from typical repackaged credit linked note transactions are:

- The transactions are driven by the desire by the counterparty (usually a bank/ financial institution) to shed risk to the relevant credit. This contrasts with the typical asset repackaging transactions which tend to be driven by investors seeking exposure to a particular underlying obligation or wishing to create the exposure in a structured manner.
- The size of the transactions. Typical synthetic bond transactions have been significant (above US$400 million). This contrasts with typical asset repackaging that are in the range US$10–50 million (on average).
- The synthetic bond is designed as public or quasi-public issue that is expected to trade in the secondary market. Asset repackaging is generally

---

[15] MINCS investors are approximately six times leveraged to the performance of the portfolio. This is not dissimilar to the logic of the BISTRO structure discussed in Chapter 4

structured as private placements that are to be held to maturity. In the event that the investor needs secondary market liquidity, in the case of a typical asset repackaging, this is achieved by restructuring the security into a format (a US$ LIBOR-based FRN) by reverse engineering the derivative components.

3.5.2 Examples of Synthetic Bonds

There have been a number of examples of synthetic bonds. The most notable examples of these transactions involves J.P. Morgan which issued two synthetic bonds[16] to open this market: a US$594 million transaction where the underlying credit exposure is to Wal-Mart, the US retailing corporation; and, a US$460 million transaction where the underlying exposure is to Walt Disney, the US entertainment company.[17] Other transactions are thought to have been completed including one for BAT. Figure 3.13 sets out the structure including the construction and hedging of the Wal-Mart synthetic bond.

Figure 3.13   Example of Synthetic Bond Transaction

Transaction

In late 1996, JP Morgan arranged an issue of a synthetic bond where the underlying credit was Wal-Mart. The unique feature of the transaction was that the transaction was completely independent of the participation of Wal-Mart itself insofar as Wal-Mart did not issue the bonds nor guarantee the payment of interest and/or principal.

The transaction details are as follows:

Issuer	A special-purpose trust
Underlying Credit Risk	Wal-Mart
Amount	US$594 million (issued as US$576 million in notes and US$18 million in subordinated certificates
Maturity	10-year final with amortization giving an average life of 5.8 years.
Yield	Treasury plus 65 bp
Market	Rule 144 A issue

---

[16] See Irving, Richard "Credit Notes In Record Deals" January 1997, *Risk*, Vol 10, No 1, pp 9

[17] The second transaction for Walt Disney was originally not confirmed although it is mentioned in the press, see "More Credit To J.P. Morgan" February 5, 1997, *IFR Financial Products*, pp 16—17

The transaction operates as follows:
- The investor purchases the note for value.
- The investor receives repayment of interest and principal, provided Wal-Mart was not in default.
- In the event of default, the investor receives repayment of principal equivalent to the recovery value of Wal-Mart debt.

The relevant default event under the terms of this transaction is the default of Wal-Mart under a referenced credit obligation. The specific terms of default of Wal-Mart were as follows:

1. Payment default or event of bankruptcy or insolvency (as established by publicly available information); *and*
2. The satisfaction of a materiality test whereby the definition of default required any event of default was not deemed to have occurred unless the spread on Wal-Mart's public debt increased by a prespecified amount (believed to be 150 bp pa). This was designed to ensure that there was no spurious triggering of the default.

A specified process establishes the recovery value of Wal-Mart debt. It was linked to the traded market value of existing Wal-Mart bonds. The process required a dealer poll of five market makers in the reference obligations. The poll is to be conducted every two weeks for three months following default. The investor has the option of requiring either early redemption based on a dealer poll conducted as soon as possible after default or redemption based on actual recovery values within an 18-month period. In the event that the 18-month period proves to be insufficient to derive actual recovery values, the recovery value is calculated using a dealer poll mechanism at the end of 18 months. This process was designed to replicate the actual payoffs where the investor held physical bonds issued by Wal-Mart as closely as possible.

Construction

The construction of the synthetic bond is feasible in one of two ways:
- **Structure 1:** This would entail collateralizing the issuing vehicle with floating-rate securities purchased from the proceeds of the synthetic bond issue itself. The securities which generate floating rate returns (LIBOR plus or minus a margin) could be either floating rate securities or fixed rate bonds which are swapped using an interest rate swap. The issuing vehicle would simultaneously enter into a total rate of return swap where it pays a floating rate (LIBOR plus/minus a margin) and receives the return on the Wal-Mart bonds or debt. The combined cash flows effectively create the cash flow and credit risk profile described above.
- **Structure 2:** This structure is identical to the first with the exception that the credit risk profile is created by the entry by the trust into a credit default swap whereby it receives a fee (payable per annum) in return for agreeing to make a payment based on the recovery rate following default of Wal-Mart debt. The compensation received for assuming the default risk effectively enhances the return to the investor over and above the return on the collateral held in the trust.

Credit Derivative (Total Return Swap/Default Swap on Wal-Mart)

The quality of the collateral in this case need only be of a credit quality sufficient to ensure that the rating of the structure equates to that of the underlying credit on a combined basis.

It is understood that the Wal-Mart transaction was constructed using a combination of the above techniques.

3.5.3 Risks of Synthetic Bonds

The structure of synthetic bonds (consistent with repackaged credit linked notes involving asset repackaging vehicles) entails three levels of risk:
- Risk to the reference credit
- Risk to the underlying collateral
- Risk to the credit derivative counterparty

The primary objective of structuring is to create exposure only to the reference credit. The risk to the other two risk elements is sought to be minimized. This is sought to be achieved in a number of ways:
- Utilizing high-quality collateral such as US Treasury securities or AAA rated securities
- The risk to the derivative counterparty is similarly managed by transacting with AAA or AA rated counterparties
- Credit enhancement may also be used in the form of cash/high-quality

collateral being used to manage the credit risk on the derivative. One approach that has been used is the concept of a contingency derivative counterparty that steps into the position of the derivatives counterparty in the event of default to perform the originally contracted obligations under the swap.

3.5.4 Implications of Synthetic Bonds

The issue of these synthetic bonds raises both a series of difficulties for the underlying credits and opportunities for intermediaries. The problems relate to the fact that the underlying credit effectively suffers a diminution in its control of the market in its own debt securities. For example, the Wal-Mart transaction was priced at a yield spread to Treasuries of 65 bp (at issue) which compares favorably to publicly traded Wal-Mart debt that trades at approximately 40–45 bp spread to Treasuries. This discrepancy, which is partially attributable to inherent additional risks of the synthetic bond structure, may create pricing pressures as well as constrain the issuers access to the underlying credit market.

The opportunities for intermediaries relate to the prospect of synthetically repackaging credit exposure in the form of bank debt or other types of financial transactions into a format that is capable of distribution in public markets to investors. The major advantage in this context is the opportunity to separate the issuer's desire to undertake the transactions from the creation of publicly tradable obligation allowing the investors to create the required exposure through the embedded credit derivative.

3.6 Summary

Repackaged credit linked notes are a special class of credit linked structured notes. They involve using a special-purpose issuance vehicle or asset repackaging structure to repackage the credit risk of securities to create credit linked structured notes. The repackaging vehicle purchases securities in the secondary market and then reprofiles the cash flows and the credit risk of the underlying securities by entering into a derivative transaction with a dealer. The repackaged cash flows are then bundled up as a security and placed with investors. Structurally, repackaged notes are based on asset-swap technology. Synthetic bonds are an extension of the basic repackaging concept being designed to allow bank and financial institutions to repackage credit risk for the purpose of selling it down in capital markets.

The market for repackaged credit linked notes is extremely large. It functions as a mechanism for enabling investors to access credit risk in a manner consistent with investment requirements and risk-reward profiles. The asset repackaging market, in performing this function, allows the reprofiling of credit risk and facilitates the transfer of credit risk between market segments. It also brings increased transparency and consistency to credit risk pricing in capital markets.

4
Credit Linked Notes — Credit Portfolio Securitization Structures[1]

Satyajit Das

4.1 Concept

Credit linked notes entail the combination of a fixed-income security with an embedded credit derivative. The credit linked note enables the investor to replicate exposure to a bond or a loan without the necessity of undertaking a direct investment in the security itself. The credit linked note is designed to allow the investor to capture value from movements in the value of an underlying loan asset or bond, credit spreads, or default risk itself. Both credit linked structured notes and repackaged credit linked notes represent this type of technology.

Credit portfolio securitization entails repackaging portfolios of credit risk (both from loans/securities and counterparty risk on derivatives/off-balance-sheet transactions). It utilizes securitization concepts to repackage credit risk into multiple tranches of securities that are then distributed to investors. The issue of the securities is designed to reduce or eliminate the credit risk to existing obligors. While building on existing credit linked note technology, credit portfolio securitization structures are characterized by a number of distinctive features:

---

[1] Earlier versions of this chapter were published as Das, Satyajit "Credit linked Notes: Credit Portfolio Securitization Structures: Part 1," *Future & OTC World*, pp 57–64; November 1999, Das, Satyajit December 1999, "Credit Linked Notes: Credit Portfolio Securitization Structures: Part 2," *Futures & OTC World*, pp35–43

- The transaction encompasses a portfolio of credit risks rather than an individual counterparty credit risk.
- The transaction is issuer-driven being primarily motivated to transfer credit risk and also, in some cases, access funding.
- The credit portfolio securitization structures are predicated upon credit derivatives techniques (in particular, credit linked note technology) and asset repackaging structures as well as securitization technology (particularly the techniques commonly used in Collateralized Bond Obligations (CBOs) and Collateralized Loan Obligations (CLOs) transactions).

In this chapter, the concept, rationale, and structuring of credit portfolio securitization transactions are examined. The rationale of these transactions is first examined. Then, the structure of CLOs generally is addressed and a series of portfolio securitization transactions are analyzed.[2]

4.2 Rationale

The key driving forces underlying the development of these structures include:
- **Capital management:** The reduction of the regulatory capital committed to support loan portfolios, particularly, the low-yielding loans to highly rated corporations
- **Balance sheet management:** The ability to shift assets off-balance sheet and enhance return on equity through these structures
- **Funding:** For lower-rated banks (such as Japanese banks suffering from the effect of Japanese funding premium), these structures have been an effective mechanism for raising funding[3]
- **Credit risk management:** These structures can be effective in transferring the credit or counterparty risk of assets with certain credit quality or particular credit characteristics from the financial institution's balance sheet, enabling more effective risk management
- **Management of client relationships:** These structures allow banks and financial institutions to continue to maintain relationships with clients, even where that relationship would normally create concentration of credit risk,

---

[2] For a good overview, see Tierney, John and Punjabi, Sanjeev "Synthetic CLOs and Their Role In Bank Balance Sheet Management" in Storrow, Jamie 1999, *Credit Derivatives: Key Issues*, 2nd ed, British Bankers Association, London

[3] See Paul-Choudhury, Sumit, "Fables of Reconstructions" March 1998, *Credit Risk Supplement to Risk*, pp 20–24; Rutter, James May 1998, "Selling The Securitization Story," *Euromoney*, pp 8–10.

because it allows the bank to shed or manage its exposure through these techniques

From the investors' point of view, some of the appeal of these securitized structures is:

- **Access to asset/risk:** These structures allow investors to access diversified portfolios of corporate risk in a highly effective format. They have also allowed diversification of the range of highly rated assets (AAA/AA) available for investment.
- **Performance history:** The performance history in respect of portfolio defaults and erosion of returns (in CBOs/CLOs) has been favorable, encouraging institutional investor participation in the market.[4]
- **Returns:** The credit spreads available on these types of transactions have been attractive compared with those of equivalent risk providing relative value investors with a significant yield enhancement opportunity.
- **Liquidity:** The market has developed in terms of secondary market trading and liquidity, and offers an investment alternative to the less liquid corporate bond market.

  In essence, the credit portfolio securitization structure represents an evolution of the more common credit derivative applications of credit risk management. It represents a shift in focus to portfolio level and strategic applications. These include:

  1. Management of systemic or portfolio credit risk, including creating strategic short positions to reduce systemic credit risk
  2. Transferring credit risk without undertaking loan sales, assignments, or participation by using synthetic sales and securitization techniques
  3. Banks seeking to manage the institution's credit ratings and portfolio credit quality
  4. Management of regulatory capital and managing concentration risk

4.3 CBO/CLO Techniques

4.3.1 Market History

CBO structures were originally developed around 1987. However, the market did not show significant volume until the mid-1990s, when the segment emerged

---

[4] The collapse of emerging markets has resulted in increased scrutiny of the risks of these structures. See Spinner, Karen November 1998 "CDOs Under Fire," *Derivatives Strategy*, pp 18–25

as one of the fastest growing arz2eas of the bond market and asset-backed securities.

The original driver for the market was the repackaging of high-yield bonds for placement with investors. A major factor underlying the development of the market was insurance companies who found that their holdings of high-yield bonds were problematic for two reasons: the lack of liquidity of some of these securities and the application of the National Association of Insurance Commissioners' (NAIC) risk-weighted reserve requirements made these securities very expensive to hold. In response to these pressures, insurance companies repackaged these high-yield assets into CBOs, enabling the riskier tranches to be transferred to their holding companies (which were not subject to the reserve requirements). The insurance companies continued to hold the repackaged higher-credit-quality securitized debt that was subject to lower capital requirements.[5]

In a precursor to the more recent activity in the market, CLO structures also emerged in connection with banks that had problem loans and sought to securitize these loans using asset-backed structures.

However, there was only limited interest in these structures. In the 1990s, the factors identified above became more important, encouraging rapid development of the market.

4.3.2   Concept[6]

In concept, CBOs and CLOs represent an application of traditional concepts of securitization and asset backed securities (ABS) to bonds and commercial loans.

CBO/CLO structures are similar to ABS structures:

- A standalone special-purpose issuing vehicle (SPV) is established. The vehicle is bankruptcy-remote to the loan originator.
- The SPV purchases a portfolio of assets (bonds or loans) from the originator(s).

---

[5]   The reserve requirements are as follows: NAIC 1–1 %, NAIC 2–2%, NAIC 3–5%, NAIC 4–10%

[6]   For an overview, see Linda Feinne, Albert Papa, Bradford Craighead, and Brian Arsenault September 19, 1997, *CBOs/CLOs: An Expanding Securitization Product*, J.P. Morgan Securities, Inc; Lawrence Richter Quinn December 22, 1997, "Slicing Up Bank Loans", *Investment Dealers' Digest*; "Bank Collateralized Loan Obligations: An Overview", December 18, 1997, Fitch Research Structured Finance Asset-Backed Special Report; "CLOs Meet Investor appetite For Loans", November 4, 1996, *Fitch Research Structured Finance Special Report*

- The SPV funds the purchase through an issue of several tranches of securities and a residual equity portion.
- The securities issued are rated on the basis of the credit quality of the asset pool, and the credit is enhanced through the use of several types of credit enhancement.
- The investors rely on the cash flow from the underlying asset pool to receive interest and principal payments.

The structures of a CBO and a CLO are set out in Figures 4.1 and 4.2.

The differences between these two structures are:

- CBOs: The SPV issues a mix of investment grade and non-investment-grade debt against a purchased collateral pool consisting of typically US$ high-yield securities and, more recently, emerging-market debt.
- CLOs: While structurally similar to the CBO, the underlying collateral consists of bank loans, typically investment-grade, but some high-yielding non-investment-grade loans may be included.

The nature of the underlying collateral pool also dictates the nature of the structure to some degree. For instance, the ability to transfer bonds into the SPV is relatively straightforward. However, the transfer of loan assets, essentially bilateral loan obligation, is more problematic. It would require assignments of or participation in the loans to be entered into by the SPV. These may require the consent of the obligor.

4.3.3 Structural Dynamics

There are several structural issues in these types of structures:

- **Single versus master trust structure:** Traditional CBO/CLO structures utilize a single purpose vehicle. However, recent CLO transactions have been structured using a master trust structure that permits the issue of multiple series out of a single vehicle
- **Revolving structure:** Some CBO/CLO transactions include:
  1. A ramp-up period: This refers to a period during which the initial collateral is purchased by the SPV
  2. A revolving period: During this period, the collections on the underlying asset pool are reinvested in new assets followed by a period in which the bond principal is repaid.
- **Management of asset pool:** Typical CBO/CLO transactions nominate a manager (usually for CBOs, this is an asset manager with expertise in the

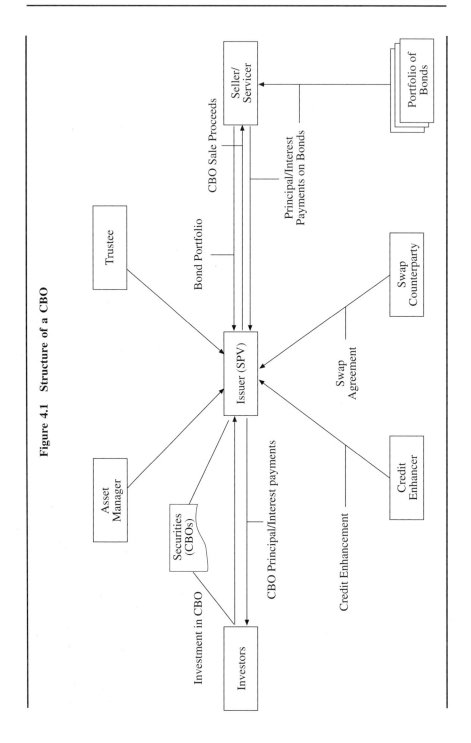

Figure 4.1   Structure of a CBO

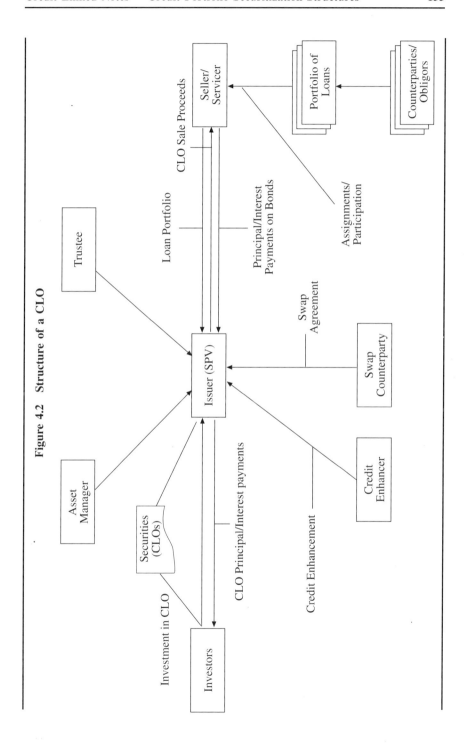

Figure 4.2   Structure of a CLO

underlying assets and for CLOs, it is the originator of the assets or a related entity) to actively manage the asset pool.

- **Cash flow versus market value structures:** There are basically two types of CBO/CLO structures:
    1. Cash flow structures: Where all payments to the investors in the securities are met from and secured over the cash flows from the underlying collateral asset pool.
    2. Market value structures: Where reliance is placed on periodic (daily or weekly) mark-to-market values of the collateral portfolio. If the market value of collateral assets declines below threshold levels, a portion of the collateral is sold and some notes are retired to allow the over-collateralization level to be preserved.

Cash-flow structures are used for both CBOs and CLOs. In contrast, market-value structures are used generally only with CBOs. Market-value structures are generally designed to allow the inclusion of certain assets that are currently non-income-producing, such as distressed bonds, but which are attractive from a return perspective. The structures also require different levels of trading. Cash-flow structures require only limited trading by the manager of the asset pool within prescribed investment guidelines. The market-value structure requires more active trading.

4.3.4   Rating Issues[7]

The rating of CBO/CLOs is based on the techniques used to evaluate other structured transactions, such as ABS transactions, generally. The generic approach by rating agencies is based on the following criteria:

- **Asset quality:** This examines the credit quality of the collateral assets in terms of repayment ability, diversification of the portfolio (default quality), and asset maturity.
- **Cash flow analysis:** This focuses on timing of cash flows, any mismatch between cash inflows and outflows, and the impact of reduced cash flows from default on any portfolio asset.

---

[7]   See Falcone, Yvonne Fu and Gluck, Jeremy April 3, 1998, *Moody's Approach To Rating Market Value CDO*, Moody's Investor Service Global Credit Research; March 17, 1997, "CBO/CLO Rating Criteria", Fitch Research Structured Finance Asset-Backed Special Report; February 1998, *CBO/CLO Criteria Update: Market Innovations*: Standard & Poor's Structured Finance Ratings Asset Backed Securities

- **Market risk:** This examines any interest-rate or currency mismatch as between the cash flow from the asset pool, the required payments on the securities to be issued, and the derivative transactions in place to manage these risks. This analysis will include evaluation of the credit quality of the counterparty to any derivative transaction.
- **Legal risks:** This includes review of the legal structure to ensure insulation from bankruptcy of the SPV, the effectiveness of the transfer of title to the collateral, legal enforceability of the contracts, and other legal issues associated with the structure.
- **Asset manager:** This analyses the ability of the asset manager to perform the ongoing management of the asset portfolio and the credit quality of the asset manager.[8]

The ratings will depend on the evaluation of the following:

- **Expected credit losses:** A major component of the risk of the CBO/CLO securities is the level of expected credit losses for the assets in the portfolio. This is a function of:
  1. The expected default rate: Each obligor is assigned a rating to establish a default probability that is based on historical default rates and maturity.
  2. Timing of defaults: The timing of defaults and the impact of differences in default timing are considered
  3. Recovery rates or default severity: This focuses on the level of recovery following default and the timing of any such recovery. This is estimated based on historical data of defaults and recoveries.
- **Stress testing:** The rating process emphasizes stressing the asset portfolio in terms of default rates, default timing, recovery rates and recovery timing with a view to analyzing the ability of the asset portfolio to meet the obligations issued by the SPV.
- **Credit enhancement:** The structure will incorporate one or more types of credit enhancement. The level and type of credit enhancement will be determined by the rating desired on the securities issued by the SPV. Typical types of credit enhancement include:
  1. Subordination/over-collateralization: Over-collateralization entails creating an excess of assets (collateral) over liabilities (the highly rated debt tranches). This is achieved through tranching the debt, that is, issuing different series of debt with different payment priorities, in particular, the

---

[8] See analysis in December 8, 1997, "Management of CBOs/CLOs," Fitch Research Structured Finance Special Report

issuance of subordinated debt and equity tranches. The tranching ensures that there is over-collateralization of the more highly rated tranches. The lower-rated subordinated debt bears a higher risk of loss that is compensated for by the higher return received.

2. Payment structure: The allocation of cash flow from the asset pool to repayment of the issued securities is also used to engineer the credit risk. Common techniques include:
   - Sequential pay: This requires repayment of senior debt in full before payment of more junior tranches of debt.
   - Fast pay/slow pay: This requires a more rapid paydown of senior debt than that on more junior debt.

3. Excess spread: There is usually a surplus of cash flow from assets over the level that is required to service the securities on issue. This excess spread can be maintained within the SPV to build up reserves against future credit losses and liquidity risks to provide additional protection for bondholders.

4. Cash reserves: A cash reserve account (held in the form of highly rated securities) can be created by over-funding the structure to enhance the credit quality of the structure.

5. Financial guarantees: This involves a third-party financial guarantee or insurance policy typically provided by a monoline insurer (known as the insurance wrap). This transfers the risk of the assets to a guarantor, typically the highly rated (AAA) insurance company, who guarantees timely payment of principal and interest.

6. Other: This would include variations on the above as well as guarantees of collateral or noteholder payments, liquidity puts on bond payment dates, or credit default swaps.

Within the rating framework, the rating agency will typically require certain specified tests to be met:
- **Collateral quality tests:** This entails ensuring that the asset portfolio complies with certain criteria:
  1. Diversity test: A minimum level of diversity (issuer, industry, and country) must be maintained.
  2. Maximum maturity profile: A minimum amount of principal must be available for amortization of the bonds on each payment date.
  3. Weighted average rating factor: A minimum average weighted credit rating for the asset portfolio is specified
     These tests must be satisfied initially and over the life of the structure in the case of a revolving structure, where the asset manager has the ability

to sell and purchase assets from the pool in purchasing new assets for the pool.

- **Coverage tests:** These tests are designed to ensure that specified levels of over-collateralization are maintained for CBO/CLO notes. These tests include:

    1. Par value tests: The principal outstanding on the asset portfolio must exceed or equal the level of outstanding bonds.
    2. Interest coverage ratio: The interest due to the bondholders will be payable from the interest to be received from the asset portfolio during the collection period.

    In the event of breach, early amortization of the notes may be necessitated.

The above describes the overall approach adopted in establishing the rating of CBO/CLO securities. There are obviously differences of emphasis between different rating agencies in relation to their analysis. There are a number of additional issues with regard to the rating of CLOs. These relate to:

- The documentation of the loan is less standardized than for bonds and can be more complex.
- Loan terms can vary in terms of principal repayments, interest payment dates, interest rates payable, etc. In addition, loan terms can be renegotiated or restructured by mutual agreement between the lender and borrower.
- The secondary market for loans is less liquid than the bond market.
- The mechanism for transfer of the lender's rights in the loan to the SPV is more problematic.

In practise, it is the last issue that creates the greatest problems in a CLO transaction. Unlike CBOs, where the transfer of the interest in the bonds can be effected relatively simply (by delivery in the case of a bearer bond or registration of a transfer of the interest in the case of a registered bond), there are a number of means for transferring the seller's interest in a loan. These include:

- **Participation:** This represents a right to receive the cash flows of the referenced loan. However, if the sale is undertaken without the knowledge and agreement of the borrower, the participation creates a contractual relationship only between the seller (the original lender) and the SPV (as buyer). This means that if the seller becomes insolvent, the SPV may be an unsecured creditor in bankruptcy of the selling lender without direct recourse to the borrower. This will generally have a rating impact on the structure and will create a rating linkage between the rating of the seller and the rating of the notes.[9] For US banks, an additional complication is the right of set-off. Under the law, the Federal Deposit Insurance Corporation may, in the event of insolvency of a bank, reduce the amount of any outstanding loan by the by the amount of the deposit held by the institution. This would have the effect of diminishing the cash flows due to the SPV. This risk can be managed by contractual waivers of rights to set-off or by tracking set-off exposure.

- **Assignment:** These represent the full legal assignment of the rights of the seller in the loan. This requires notification and (in some cases) approval of the borrower. This allows a direct contractual nexus to be established as between the SPV (as buyer) and the borrower.

The advantage of non-disclosure dictates that sponsors prefer participations. However, the legal problems with participation favor assignments. Some hybrid structures have also developed:

- **Contingent assignments:** Where the selling bank would only be obligated to assign in the event of decline in its credit rating below an agreed threshold.
- **Credit derivatives/credit linked notes:** Where the risk on the loan is transferred synthetically using credit derivatives technology. This approach is detailed below.

4.3.5 Types of CBO/CLOs

The CBO/CLO market can be classified into two distinct market segments that are differentiated by the motivation/objectives of the sponsor.

- **Arbitrage structures:** These are generally secondary market transactions initiated by an investment bank or trading entity designed to take advantage of relative value opportunities in the market. Undervalued assets are purchased and repackaged to lock in a value differential which is realized by the sponsor as the spread between the cash flow from the asset portfolio and

---

[9] There is a notable exception to this general rule. The NationsBank Commercial Loan Master Trust has a rating of the highest-rated tranche of AAA, higher than that of NationsBank, the sponsor bank, which is rated AA-. Fitch IBCA based this rating on a review of the security interest in each eligible loan, the legal documentation, and the enforceability of the security interest in the event of the insolvency of the sponsor banks. It concluded that the default risk of the relevant securities was substantially independent of the seller's insolvency. The current position for US federally regulated banks appears to be that where the asset transfer is structured as a participation with a back-up first perfected security interest, the rights of the purchaser under the participation will be protected in the event of an insolvency of the selling bank under the FIRREA regulations.

the servicing requirements on the bond issued to finance the purchase. Assets will typically include high-yield bonds and emerging-market bonds. Some more recent structures may include high-yield bank loans. The senior higher-rated tranches are sold to normal asset investors while the subordinated junior tranches are targeted at investors seeking a leveraged exposure to a pool of assets.

- **Balance-sheet structures:** These are transactions that have been driven by the desire to obtain regulatory capital relief, access funding, and reduce balance sheet size. The underlying assets have been bank loans, primarily of investment grade. In these transactions, the sponsor bank has generally held the first loss or equity component of the structure. This has forced the sponsor bank to focus on investment-grade loans in order to reduce the size of the equity component required to be contributed and to ensure favorable regulatory capital treatment. These structures have also attracted insurance companies. These companies, as noted above, have used CBO/CLO techniques to re-tranche existing assets to obtain capital relief in terms of reserves to be held against assets.

In the remainder of this chapter, the focus is on balance-sheet structures. This is done through the analysis of a series of transactions. First, a classical CLO transaction is analyzed. Second, a credit linked note-based CLO transaction is examined. Finally, a synthetic credit portfolio securitization structure is considered. The objective is to explore the structural dynamics in terms of the capacity of each of the structures to meet the objectives of the sponsor bank.

4.4 Transaction Examples

4.4.1 Classical CLO Transaction

The first completed major collateralized loan transaction was by National Westminster Bank Plc (NatWest) of UK. The transaction: Repeat Offering Securitization Entity (ROSE) Funding: represented the securitization of a US$5 billion portfolio of corporate loans from NatWest's balance sheet.[10] The structure of the transaction is set out in Figure 4.3.

---

[10] See Caplen, Brian October 1996, "Will NatWest's Deal Backfire?" *Euromoney* pp 38–40; Hagger, Euan and Ball, Matthew "How Sweet is NatWest's ROSE?" November 1998, *Corporate Finance*, pp 22–26

Figure 4.3   CLO Structure: ROSE Transaction

Overview

ROSE Funding is a securitization collateralized by a portfolio of US$5 billion of NatWest's corporate loans. The transaction was completed in November 1996 and was for a period of five years. The transaction appears to have been designed to free capital by selling down a portion of the bank's low-yielding corporate loan portfolio.

Structure

The overall structure is set out in the diagram below:

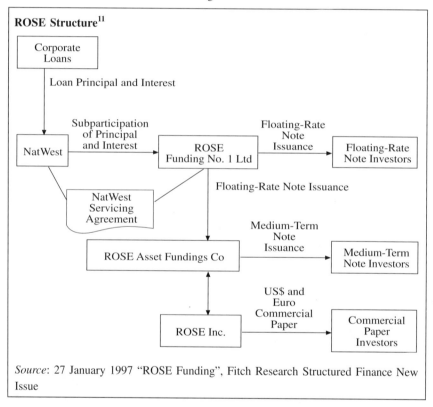

ROSE Structure[11]

Source: 27 January 1997 "ROSE Funding", Fitch Research Structured Finance New Issue

The basic structure was as follows:

1. ROSE purchased a portfolio of US$ and £ loans from NatWest (see details of asset portfolio below).

---

[11] The description of the structures is based on January 27, 1997, "ROSE Funding", Fitch Research Structured Finance New Issue

2. ROSE financed this purchase through the issue of multiple tranches of securities:

Tranche	Rating	US$m	£m	Pricing (Margin over US$ or £ LIBOR)
Senior Class A1	AA	750	600	8 bp
Senior Class A2	AA	750	600	18 bp
Senior Class A3	AA	500	600	22 bp
Mezzanine A4	A	25	16	40 bp
Mezzanine A5	BBB	27	18	65 bp
Class	Unrated	100		

Several structural aspects of the transaction should be noted:
- ROSE purchased subparticipations in drawn and undrawn loan commitments entered into by NatWest. Under the subparticipations, ROSE paid to NatWest the total US$ and £ amounts of the loans subparticipated and received from NatWest all amounts received by NatWest under the loans. The subparticipations do not represent a purchase of the loans themselves and the legal title to the loans remains with NatWest. ROSE does not have recourse to NatWest for payment defaults under the loans. It is also understood that the identities of the underlying loan obligors were not disclosed.
- The loan portfolio includes revolving credit facilities. ROSE is structured so that repayments under revolving facilities are maintained in a cash pool from which further advances under revolving facilities.
- During an initial period of 18 months (the substitution period), ROSE may use funds from redemptions to purchase substitute subparticipations if the relevant loan meets all eligible criteria.
- After the completion of the substitution period, the notes will be subject to mandatory redemption in accordance with the following priorities:

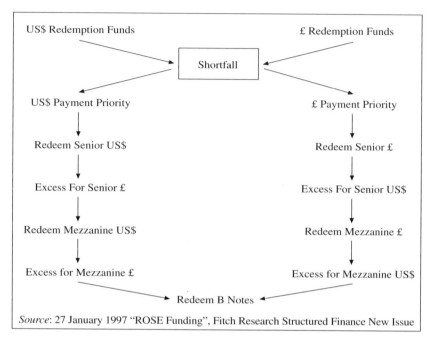

Source: 27 January 1997 "ROSE Funding", Fitch Research Structured Finance New Issue

Asset Portfolio

The asset portfolio consisted of some 201 loans with a value of US$4.97 billion entered into by NatWest. The characteristics of the loans were as follows:

- Types: Numerous structures including revolving facilities, term loans, etc.
- Maturity: All loans had a maturity of five years or less.

The rating of the asset portfolio was predicated on the following:

- Obligor credit quality: This was based on an analysis of the NatWest internal credit scoring system by comparing internal ratings with rating agency categories and comparing actual default experience with external studies.
- Diversification: The portfolio was geographically diversified (13 countries including UK–60%, US–27% and other investment-grade countries–13%). The industry exposure was also well diversified, with the largest exposure to any one industry totaling 7.79% (food industry). The portfolio was also well diversified in terms of individual obligors, with the largest single obligor being £75 million.
- Market risk profile: This consists of basis risk (mismatches between the interest rates received and the interest rate obligations on the CLOs in terms of interest rate benchmarks) and currency risk (multicurrency options). The basis risk is managed through a swap with NatWest that fully hedged any mismatch. The currency risk is managed by NatWest and through conversion of any drawing other than in US$ or £ into the one of those two currencies.

NatWest operates as a loan administrator. The rating agencies conducted due diligence on NatWest's capabilities in administering the transaction. This was an important element in rating the transaction.

Credit Enhancement

The major form of credit enhancement was the use of subordinated tranches of securities. The credit enhancement levels (effectively, the sizes of the lower-rated tranches of securities) were based on stress tests conducted by the rating agencies. The stress test focused on default probabilities, recovery rates, timing and obligor concentration levels within the portfolio.

As already noted, a number of similar transactions have also been completed subsequently. These are thought to include transactions for US banks (NationsBank, Citibank), European banks (ABN-Amro), and Japanese banks (IBJ, Tokyo-Mitsubishi, DKB, and Sumitomo Bank). These transactions are all predicated on a similar approach although individual transactions are characterized by (often significant) structural differences.

The classical CLO-type transactions assist the sponsor banks in achieving the following objectives:

- Credit risk reduction at both an economic level (reducing exposures to selected clients, often freeing up lines to large clients) and at a regulatory capital level (reducing the level of regulatory capital by lowering risk assets). The overall exposure is typically reduced to the level of the equity component of the transaction retained by the sponsor bank.
- Improved balance-sheet management by removing assets off-balance sheet (other than the equity component) and assisting in improving certain accounting/performance ratios.
- Increasing the diversification of funding sources by allowing capital market access in the form of funding through the ABS market, effectively separating the credit quality of the sponsor bank from the funding, which relies on the quality of the collateral assets.

However, the CLO structure as described, may suffer from some significant disadvantages from the viewpoint of certain banks:

- The bank's asset portfolio may be unsuitable for securitization where there is a predominance of non-funded types of exposures: revolving credits, unfunded commitments, and counterparty exposure on market value instruments such as derivatives.
- The transfer of the loan obligations without advising the borrower or the co-operation of the borrower may be difficult in some jurisdictions. The potential for damage to the client relationship may limit the utility of the structure.
- Economic and regulatory capital requirement may be unchanged as the sponsor bank retains, in a typical transaction the major component of the

credit risk in the form of the equity tranche. Under regulatory guidelines, there is an advantage in minimizing the equity or first-loss component of the transaction in order to allow the bank to benefit from the low-level recourse rules (see discussion below). This means that in practise, there is a tendency to focus on investment-grade loan commitments in these transactions lowering their value to banks.

- The actual cost of funding achieved through these transactions may be unattractive for banks with low cost of funds. The comparative cost of funds is evident from the table below:

Type	Rating	Spread (bp to 3-Month LIBOR)	Rating	Spread (bp to 3-Month LIBOR)
Collateralized Mortgage-Backed Securities	AA	25–30	BBB	80–90
Corporations	AA	0–5	BBB	50–70
Credit Card Asset-Backed Securities	AA	10–15	BBB	100–120
Collateralized Loan Obligations	AA	18–23	BBB	110–160
Collateralized Bond Obligations	AA	35–45	BBB	130–180

Source: Linda Feinne, Albert Papa, Bradford Craighead, and Brian Arsenault 19 September 1997, *CBOs/CLOs: An Expanding Securitization Product*, J.P. Morgan Securities Inc, pp 5

Other issues may include:
- The cost and long-time needed (around 4–6 months) needed to complete a CLO.
- The need to change bank loan administration operations to accommodate the CLO operation.

4.4.2   Credit Linked Note CLO Transaction

In 1997, a variation on the traditional CLO was introduced with the credit linked note CLO transaction. Swiss Bank Corporation (SBC) launched the first transaction: SBC Glacier Ltd. It was followed by a transaction for Credit Suisse, launched by CSFB: Triangle.

The concept underlying these transactions is the use of credit linked notes to transfer the credit exposure from the sponsor bank to the SPV and to use the credit linked note itself as the collateral for the issue of securities.

The credit linked note is structured normally. It is issued by the CLO sponsor and references the payment obligations of an individual obligor under a loan or other transaction. The defining element is the use of the credit linked note to transfer the credit risk and hedge the sponsor bank's credit exposure without the transfer of the actual loan or contract.[12]

Figure 4.4 describes the structure of the SBC Glacier transaction.[13]

Figure 4.4   Credit Linked Note CLO Transaction: SBC Glacier Transaction[14]

Overview

SBC completed the Glacier transaction in September 1997. The transaction for approximately US$1.7 billion in total was successful, with the issue of bonds being oversubscribed. The transaction was predicated on transferring the risk on a portfolio of corporate loans to enable the bank to reduce the capital held against the loan in order to improve the bank's return on risk capital. The interesting aspect of the transaction is its combination of CLO and credit derivative technology.

Following the success of the initial transaction, Credit Suisse completed a similar larger transaction: Triangle. This transaction was motivated by a similar factor as with the SBC Glacier transaction. A number of transactions have subsequently been completed based on the template developed.

Structure

SBC Glacier Finance Ltd (Glacier) is a Cayman Islands-incorporated limited liability company that acts as the issuer of the CLO securities. It is an SPV that is bankruptcy-remote to SBC. The issuer is structured a Master Trust Facility enabling Glacier to undertake further CLO issues for SBC.

---

[12] See Chapter 2

[13] See Peter Lee October 1997, "SBC Taps Its Credit Pool For Cash", *Euromoney*, pp 16; Robert Chow January 1998, "A New Leaf for the ROSE", *Institutional Investor* pp 74–75

[14] The description of the structure is based on SBC Glacier Finance Ltd (November 1997) Standard & Poor's Structured Finance

The overall structure of the transaction is set out in the diagram below:

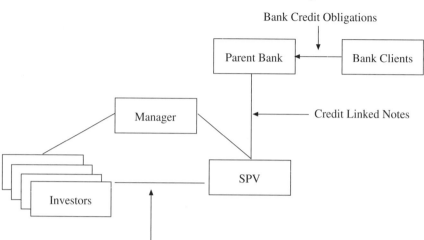

The transaction operates as follows:

- Glacier issues two series of notes each totaling US$870 million floating rate and zero coupon notes. The notes are expected to mature in five and seven years. The notes were issued in the following tranches:

Type	Series 1997 – 1	Series 1997 – 2
Class A	US$798.225 million floating rate notes	US$798.225 million floating rate notes
Class B	US$36.105 million floating rate notes	US$29.58 million floating rate notes
Class C	US$20.88 million floating rate notes	US$10.44 million floating rate notes
Class D	US$10.875 million floating rate notes	US$26.1 million floating rate notes
Class E	US$3.915 million zero coupon rates	US$5.655 million zero coupon rates

- The proceeds of the notes are used to purchase credit linked notes issued by SBC under its MTN program. As described in more detail below, the credit linked notes are linked to the credit risk of SBC's corporate customers. These credit linked notes constitute the collateral for the notes issued by Glacier.
- The notes issued by Glacier are direct and limited recourse obligations guaranteed by SBC (acting through its New York Branch) payable solely from the collateral consisting of the credit linked notes.
- The investors in the Glacier notes receive repayments of interest and principal derived from the corporate loans underlying the credit linked notes. SBC acts as administrator of the loan facilities to collect and pass through payments.
- In the event of losses on the underlying loan obligations, investors in the Glacier notes bear the losses. These losses are calculated as the face value of the credit linked notes

less the post credit event redemption amounts paid upon the defaulted obligations. This is calculated as the post-default market value of the reference security nominated under the credit linked notes or a fixed percentage (51%). The allocated principal and interest are paid on each payment date sequentially within a series in accordance with a specified priority structure to protect the highest-ranking Class A notes.

The structure also incorporates a number of special features:

- Asset transfer: The loans and commitments undertaken by SBC which underlie the credit linked notes are not transferred to Glacier but continue to remain on SBC's balance sheet. SBC receives cash from the sale of credit linked notes, which can effectively be utilized to finance the loans (retiring existing borrowings).
- Revolving structure: The collateral asset portfolio is dynamic in structure. The proceeds of the issue are used to purchase the initial portfolio of credit linked notes. However, the credit linked notes are optionally redeemable at par on every quarterly interest payment date. Where credit linked notes are redeemed or mature, or where there are additional issues of notes, Glacier can purchase additional credit linked notes within the specified collateral guidelines (see below). This dynamic feature is available during the revolving period that continues until the earlier of an amortization event or expected maturity. This feature is designed to allow SBC to adjust its credit hedge. Where the loan has been repaid or the exposure on derivatives contract has changed due to market price movements, the existing credit linked note may not match SBC's underlying credit exposure. SBC then repays the relevant credit linked note and issues a new credit linked note that matches the current exposure profile.

Asset Portfolio

The underlying asset portfolio consists of, as already noted, credit linked notes issued by SBC referencing underlying corporate loans that have been entered into by SBC. The characteristics of the credit linked notes included:

- They are US$ denominated senior unsecured debt obligation of SBC acting through its New York Branch issued under its medium-term note program.
- Each credit linked notes references a specified individual borrower or counterparty. SBC establishes the face value of the credit linked note based on its estimate of credit exposure to the underlying obligor under either a loan or a derivative transaction.
- Each credit linked note pays a floating rate of interest based on three month LIBOR plus a designated spread. The credit linked notes all have a bullet maturity.
- Each credit linked note has both an optional redemption (at par on any quarterly interest payment date) and a mandatory redemption date which is triggered by a default or credit event occurring on the underlying reference obligation.
- Credit event in respect of the notes and a reference obligor is defined as payment default, bankruptcy, insolvency, debt restructuring, or similar event.
- In the event of default, the recovery amount is calculated in one of two ways:
  1. Reference security note: this is calculated as the average bid price on the basis of quotations from five dealers on the specified senior unsecured security of the reference obligor payable on a redemption date 25 business days after the credit event.
  2. Fixed percentage notes: This is specified as 51% of the face value of the notes (effectively, a pre-estimate of the recovery rate) payable on a redemption date five business days after the credit event.

The rating agencies placed stringent guidelines on the composition of the credit quality of the underlying asset portfolio of credit linked notes. These criteria must be satisfied both initially when the initial collateral is purchased and also in the event of further purchases of credit linked notes.

The guidelines are as follows:

- Minimum SBC internal rating of C9 (around a B) on reference obligor at the time of credit linked note purchase.
- Maximum concentration limits:
  1. 8% for any single industry.
  2. 5% aggregate exposure to countries with a sovereign rating of less than AA−.
  3. 2% to any single obligor.
  4. 50% for aggregate exposures to obligors with SBC internal rating of C5–C9 (effectively below BBB−, that is, non-investment grade).
- Maturity limit of:
  1. Weighted average credit linked maturity of no more than 4.25 years.
  2. Maturity date of each credit linked note at the time of acquisition must not exceed the expected maturity date of the last maturing series.
- Minimum 25% in fixed percentage notes.
- Credit linked portfolio must total 106% of all but the principal outstanding of the last maturing series.

The rating of the asset portfolio of credit linked notes was predicated on the following:

- The credit rating of SBC (AA+).
- Obligor credit quality: This was based on an analysis of the SBC's internal credit scoring system by comparing internal ratings with rating agency categories and compared actual default experience with external studies. The guidelines also restrict the types of underlying obligor risks that can be purchased through the credit linked notes.
- Diversification and maturity profile: The portfolio was structured to maintain a high degree of diversification and limit maturity through the portfolio collateral guidelines.
- Interest rate risk profile: Glacier at closing entered into an interest rate swap with SBC designed to cover the risk of narrowing spreads between performing credit linked note assets and note liabilities. This was structured as basis swap whereby:
  1. SBC paid Glacier quarterly an amount equal to the positive difference between the weighted average rate on Glacier's notes and the weighted average rate on the performing (non-defaulted) credit linked notes based on the notional amount equal to the weighted average principal amount of performing credit linked note collateral.
  2. Glacier paid SBC where the weighted average performing credit linked note rate exceeds the weighted average note rate, an amount equal to any excess spread over 0.25% on the notional amount.

SBC operates as administrator of credit linked note collateral portfolio and of ensuring the portfolio is managed in accordance with the collateral guidelines. The rating agency (Standard & Poor's) maintains continuous surveillance based on a monitoring process.

Credit Enhancement

The credit enhancement embedded in the CLO structure included:

- Subordination: About 8.25% of each series of notes was subordinated to provide credit enhancement to the more highly rated tranches.
- Early amortization provisions: Both series had early amortization triggers based on adverse changes in portfolio credit quality (as evidenced by charge-offs exceeding 2% of the initial principal balance) and accompanying negative carry from post-default cash recoveries. These are designed to protect investors.

The use of credit linked notes in a CLO transactions represents an interesting combination of securitization and credit derivatives technology.

The major benefits of the structure include:

- The ability to avoid the issues in respect of perfecting the asset transfer without the necessity of an assignment. This has numerous aspects including avoiding any impediment to the client relationship, the maintenance of confidentiality in respect of the client, and simplification of the legal issues in terms of perfection of the security (which is now focused on the credit linked note).
- The ability of the sponsor bank to hedge and manage credit risk through the credit linked note. This should achieve reductions for the bank in terms of both economic capital and regulatory capital. The regulatory capital relief will be achieved if the criteria in respect of normal default swaps is satisfied.

However, some of the disadvantages in respect of the CLO structure identified above persist. The actual cost of funding achieved through these transactions may be unattractive for banks with low cost of funds. This will depend on the implicit rate on the credit linked note after stripping out the embedded credit default swap transaction and the rate demanded by investors in the securities issued collateralized by the credit linked notes. In particular, the potential funding disadvantage will be governed by the extent to which these notes are treated as different from ABS transactions.

In addition, the balance sheet benefits of the classical CLO structure are not achieved as the underlying transaction continue to remain on the balance sheet of the sponsor bank despite the fact that the credit linked note effectively transfers the credit risk to the SPV and thence to the investors.

The credit linked note CLO structure also introduces new issues:

- The transaction is fundamentally dependent on the credit standing of the issuer of the credit linked notes: the sponsor bank. This is because there is no effective separation of the underlying credit obligation in the portfolio of the selling bank. In effect, there is full performance risk on the seller. This dictates that this structure is restricted inevitably to sponsor banks with a strong issuer credit rating. This is necessary because the rating agencies will treat the credit linked notes as a primary debt obligation of the sponsor bank, which is contractually obligated to pass through the credit linked note's underlying reference obligations payments to the CLO SPV. This effectively limits the rating of the highest rating tranche of CLO securities to that of the sponsor bank.

• The ability to create the required credit linked notes themselves may be subject to practical limitations. The necessity to link loss estimates to reference securities means that the universe of obligors to which this technique can be applied is restricted primarily to those with some liquid outstanding traded securities, although the use of fixed recovery amount notes can overcome this problem to some degree.

4.4.3   Synthetic Credit Portfolio Securitization

In December 1997, J.P. Morgan completed an innovative synthetic transaction that highlighted the potential for synthetic portfolio securitization using credit default swaps (also known as synthetic CLOs). The transaction: Broad Index Secured Trust Offering (BISTRO): was effectively a massive capital market securitization of a US$9.722 billion credit default swap executed by J.P. Morgan against its underlying corporate credit exposures. The transaction was designed to hedge the bank's credit risk to these obligors.[15]

Figure 4.5 sets out the structure and details of the BISTRO transaction.[16]

Figure 4.5   Synthetic Credit Portfolio Securitization: BISTRO Transaction

Overview

In December 1997, J.P. Morgan, through BISTRO, an SPV, launched a US$700 million issue of credit linked notes. In effect, BISTRO issued bonds to finance a collateral pool of US$ Treasury securities that were used to collateralize a credit default swap entered into by BISTRO with J.P. Morgan. Under the terms of the swap, J.P. Morgan hedged the credit exposure on US$9.722 billion of credit exposure to its corporate customers. The innovative structure differs from the classical CLO or credit linked note CLO in that it transfers the pure credit risk of the underlying credit exposures without providing any financing for J.P. Morgan and has no balance sheet impact.

---

[15] See Paul-Choudhury, Sumit January 1998, "BISTRO Opens For Business," *Risk* pp 8–9

[16] See Efrat, Isaac 21 August 1998, *BISTRO Trust 1997-1000*, Moody's Investors Service Structured Finance New Issue Report

Structure

The overall structure of the BISTRO transaction is set out in the diagram below:

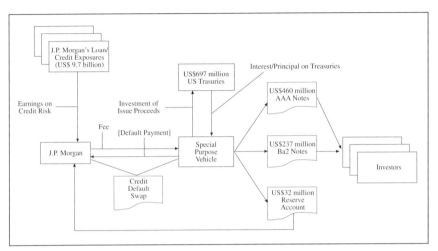

The specific steps entailed in the transaction are as follows:

• BISTRO issues US$697 million of five-year notes in two tranches:

Type	Senior Notes	Subordinated Notes
Amount (US$m)	460	237
Rating	AAA	Ba2
Yield (Spread bp over US$ Treasuries)	60	375

• The issue proceeds were used by BISTRO to purchase US Treasury notes.
• BISTRO enters into a five-year credit default swap on a portfolio of credit exposure with a total notional face value of US$ 9.722 billion with J.P. Morgan. The swap is structured so that in return for a fee BISTRO assumes the default risk on this portfolio that is static and consists of identified reference entities. BISTRO's obligations under the credit default swap are collateralized by a pledge of the US Treasury Notes.
• BISTRO also holds a US$32 million reserve account funded for five years. This represents the equivalent of the equity component of the transaction. It is refundable to J.P. Morgan in the event it is not required.
• During the term of the transaction, BISTRO pays out the coupons on the issued debt out of the coupon received from the US Treasuries and the fee on the credit default swap received from J.P. Morgan.
• In the event of a credit event on any of the underlying reference credits, any loss suffered (net of any recovery) will be met in the following order:
  1. Reserve account.
  2. The treasury collateral pool.

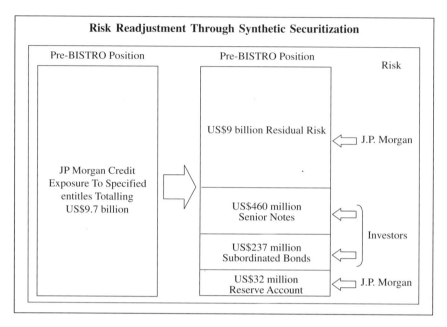

Where losses exceed the reserve account, the drawings on the treasury collateral pool reduce the amount available to meet repayment of the notes issued. The holders of the subordinated debt meet any loss first. The senior debt holders incur losses only after losses exceed the subordinated debt amount.

- The loss amount on the underlying reference credits is calculated as either:
    1. The average work-hour recovery value.
    2. Physical delivery of senior unsecured claims against individual reference credits.
- Any default payment is made at maturity, that is after five years.

Risk Profile

The risk profile of the credit portfolio after the BISTRO transaction is set out above:

As is evident, under the structure, J.P. Morgan retains the following risk on its underlying credit portfolio:

- First loss piece of US$32 million (0.33%).
- Final loss piece of US$8,993 million (92.5%).

The first loss component is equivalent to the expected loss on the credit portfolio. The next US$697 million (7.17%) is borne by the BISTRO subordinated and senior noteholders in that order. The final loss piece represent losses exceeding US$729 million. This is borne by J.P. Morgan . However, based on the fact that the senior notes are rated AAA, the risk of this loss is obviously remote.

Asset Portfolio

The credit portfolio in respect of which J.P. Morgan purchased protection has the following characteristics:

- Obligor credit quality: The portfolio was of relatively high-credit-quality obligors. The weighted average credit quality was A2/A. The lowest credit quality was A3/BBB+. As a proportion of the overall portfolio, A3 obligors represent 22.7% of the portfolio and BBB+ obligors represent 4.4% of the portfolio.
- Portfolio diversification: The portfolio was well diversified in terms of geography (US–80.4%; Canada–2.3%; EuropE–17.3%); industry (29 industries); and individual obligors (307).

The asset portfolio was characterized by some interesting features:

- All obligors were identified in the prospectus, both by name and amount of exposure (not exceeding a maximum of US$37 million).
- The asset portfolio included obligors to whom J.P. Morgan had no exposure. This effectively creates a short credit position for J.P. Morgan which either enables the bank to undertake transactions with that obligor in the future on fully credit hedged basis or to profit from changes in the pricing of the obligor's credit risk.
- The asset portfolio is completely static and cannot be altered during the life of the transaction.
- The credit exposure could be derived from any type of transaction ranging from drawn loans, unfunded standby loan commitments, and counterparty exposures on derivatives.

Credit Enhancement

The credit enhancement within the structure is primarily based on the following:
- The first loss retention by J.P. Morgan.
- The senior subordinated tranche structure of the issue.

Investor Perspective

The BISTRO securities were placed successfully in a difficult market in December 1997. The major attraction for investors in the transaction included:
- The ability to earn attractive returns on a relative value basis on the notes compared to equivalent rated securities.
- The absence of prepayment risk and no extension risk unlike comparable ABS transactions.

The most significant appeal of the BISTRO notes was that the inherent risk on the underlying portfolio was to a high-grade universe of obligors. This was particularly attractive in the subordinated tranche as in effect the investor was taking a leveraged exposure to this high-grade obligor universe to generate extra yield from the consequent lower rating. This compared favorably in terms of risk to taking direct exposure to lower rated corporate credits. This is particularly so as at the end of the credit cycle where the BISTRO subordinated notes may well offer more attractive returns and lower risk than comparable conventional corporate bonds of equivalent rating.

An interesting aspect of the investor analysis of the BISTRO securities was the disclosure of the underlying obligors and the static nature of the portfolio. This contrasts with the aggregate disclosure in terms of broad portfolio characteristics and the revolving and dynamic nature of more conventional CLO structures. This allows the investor to base the investment decision on both the ratings analysis and its own analysis of the underlying asset portfolio.

The synthetic securitization structure represented by the BISTRO transaction is significantly different from the more traditional CLO structures and the variants on CLO structures. These include:

- **Credit risk reduction:** Traditional CLOs achieve both economic and regulatory capital release by reducing risk. The regulatory capital reduction is contingent on certain condition being met (see discussion below). The synthetic securitization structures achieve economic risk reduction. However, they may not achieve regulatory capital reduction.

- **Balance sheet management:** Unlike traditional CLOs, the synthetic securitization structure do not have any balance-sheet management implications. This is because they shift the credit risk of the underlying transaction through the credit default swap but the assets remain on the sponsor bank's balance sheet.

- **Funding:** The synthetic securitization unlike traditional CLOs also does not generate funding. As the underlying asset/transaction is not transferred or credit linked notes referenced to it are not issued no financing is created. This means the synthetic securitizations do not allow access to new sources of funding. However, for highly rated banks, it means that the CLO disadvantage of a higher funding cost relative to the sponsor bank's own cost of funds is avoided.

A significant benefit of the synthetic securitization structure is that it significantly reduces the amount of securities required to be placed with capital market investors. This is because the transaction does not necessitate the total collateral portfolio being purchased or financed. The quantum of securities sold is dependent on the level of capital needed to be raised to collateralize the underlying credit default swap. In the BISTRO transaction, this was only US$697 million (US$729 million inclusive of the reserve account) on a portfolio of US$9.722 billion.

The structure has proved attractive and popular.[17] J.P. Morgan is estimated to have issued approximately US$2 billion in synthetic CLO BISTRO offerings covering the credit risk of portfolios totaling in excess of US$20 billion during 1998.[18] Other dealers and investment banks have launched similar structures.

---

[17] See Mahtani October 3 1998, "Synthetic CLOs Move To The Fore," *International Financing Review* Issue 1253 pp 77

[18] See Booth, Tamzin January 1999, "The Good, The Bad And The Ugly," *Institutional Investor* pp 65-66

One of these competing structures was launched by Warburg Dillon Read in October 1998. The structure: Eisberg Finance: is similar structurally to BISTRO format of synthetic CLO.[19] The initial issue was for five years and for an amount of US$211.25 million (three tranches: US$82.5 million AAA/Aaa; US$65 million A/A2; US$63.75 million BB/Ba2). All tranches were floating-rate being priced off LIBOR. The issue was used to securitize a US$2.5 billion credit default swap hedging a part of the corporate loan portfolio for United Bank of Switzerland AG, the parent of Warburg Dillon Read.[20] A similar structure was used by Credit Suisse First Boston in the Triangle II transaction. Synthetic securitizations have been used in the Asia-Pacific – primarily Australia.[21]

In an interesting variation on the concept, in late 1998 J.P. Morgan and Commerzbank completed synthetic securitization transactions of mortgage portfolios. The transactions utilized credit default swaps to transfer the default risk on mortgages to institutional investors. The J.P. Morgan transaction (reported to be around US$1.5 billion) was undertaken on behalf of a German bank. The Commerzbank transaction (reported to be around US$1.0 billion) was in respect of its own portfolio. The transactions were very similar in structure to the basic synthetic securitization format described and were driven by the desire to achieve regulatory capital relief.[22]

A number of other synthetic securitization structures have also been completed. Citibank engineered a transaction on behalf of a European bank.[23] The banks sought to transfer the risk on approximately DM 6 billion of corporate risk in the form of term loans, undrawn commitments, letters of credit, and guarantees. The European bank did not want funding. The major motivation of the transaction was the transfer of the credit risk. The transaction was complicated by the fact that a portion of risk assets was from small to medium-sized unrated obligors. In addition, the bank was subject to stringent bank secrecy laws and transfer of assets would have required the cooperation of

---

[19] One noteworthy difference was the withholding of the identity of the obligors whose loans were covered by the credit default swap. In addition, the Eisberg structure, unlike BISTRO, retains the capacity to dynamically manage the credit pool.

[20] See October 10 1988, "Warburg Launches Tip of Eisberg," *International Financing Review*, Issue 1254 pp 39

[21] See Wood, August 1999, Duncan "CBA Secures First For Credit Risk Exposure," *AsiaRisk* 8; see discussion of Asian potential for synthetic securitization in "Asian Banks Get Taste For Synthetic CLOs) (October 9 1999) *International Financing Review*, Issue 1304, 1997. Satyajit Das February 7, 2000.

[22] See January 25 1999, "First Synthetic Securitizations Surface" *Derivatives Week* vol VIII no 4 1,14

[23] See March 1999, "European Credit Risk Hedge", *Global Finance*, pp 27

obligors. To avoid these difficulties, the European bank segregated the portfolio into several rated tranches. The bank then entered into two series of transactions:

• Entry into a credit default swap with Citibank in respect of the AAA-rated tranche (93% of the portfolio).

• Hedged the credit risk through the sale of credit linked notes to Citibank and third-party investors in respect of the AA and BBB rated tranches.

The European bank continued to hold the risk on the unrated assets.

The result of the transaction was to transfer a substantial portion of the economic credit risk, obtain regulatory capital relief, and avoid payment of high funding costs of CLOs.

In a separate transaction, Gerling Credit Insurance (an affiliate of Gerling Konzern AG, an insurance company) hedged the credit risk on small to medium-sized company exposures through an issue arranged by Goldman Sachs.[24] The Euro-denominated transaction entailed the issue of a series of three year credit linked FRNs. There were three classes of notes rated Aa2, A2, and Baa2. The payoffs on the FRNs are linked to a reference portfolio of over 90,000 obligors in Europe. The investor's returns were contingent on annual insolvency rates remaining below nominated levels. If annual solvency rates exceed 2.1%. 2.6%, or 3.3%, then the principal and coupons in each of the three classes of notes decline according to the extent of any excess in accordance to a formula. In addition, if the cumulative losses exceed 5.4%, 5.9% or 6.6%, then the principal and coupons in each of the three classes of notes also decline according to the extent of any excess in accordance to a formula. The solvency index is compiled by Dun & Bradstreet. The major driver for the transaction is the ability to hedge the credit exposure on a large diverse unrated universe of obligors on a cost effective basis.

The European synthetic securitisations are similar to the BISTRO transaction described above. However, there are significant differences. These differences are driven by a number of factors. The major driver is the regulatory capital treatment. An example of these structures is set out in Figure 4.6.

---

[24] See Rhode, William, May 1999, "Credit, The Final Frontier," *Risk* 7

Figure 4.6   Synthetic Credit Portfolio Securitization – C*Star Transaction[25]

Overview

In June 1999, Citibank/Salomon Smith Barney launched a synthetic securitization - C*Strategic Asset Redeployment Program 1999-1 Limited (C*Star). The transaction represented the first public synthetic securitization of a European credit portfolio. The transaction was repeated in November 1999 with C*Star 1999-2 Corp and also in a transaction for a credit portfolio involving Banca Commercial Italiana (SCALA 1 Limited). Similar transactions have been used by a number of other European banks including Deutsche Bank.

Structure

The basic structure of C*Star is similar to the BISTRO transaction described in **Figure 4.5**. However, there are a number of interesting differences driven primarily by regulatory considerations.

The basic structure is as follows:
- Citibank assembled a portfolio of €4 billion of corporate credit risk.
- Citibank hedges its risk on this portfolio through a series of separate transactions:
  1. Citibank retains the first loss portion of €40 million (1% of the portfolio).
  2. Citibank enters into a credit default swap with C*Star, a SPV domiciled in Jersey, covering €280 million of credit risk (7% of the portfolio). This swap is collateralized with German government bonds (see below).
  3. Citibank enters into a credit default with OECD banks covering €3,680 million (92% of the portfolio).
- C*Star issues the following tranches of 10-year notes:
  1. €100 million Class A notes (rated AAA/ Aaa) bearing interest at Euribor + 21 bps (2.5% of the portfolio).
  2. €128 million Class B notes (rated A/A2) bearing interest at Euribor + 48 bps (3.2% of the portfolio).
  3. €52 million Class C notes (rated BB/ Ba2) bearing interest at Euribor + 48 bps (1.3% of the portfolio).
     The €280 million proceeds of the Note issue are invested in German government bonds to collateralise the credit default swap with Citibank.

---

[25] See Murra, Francesca September 1999, "C*Star Points The Way Forward", *International Securitisation Review*, Issue 40; I am grateful to Herman Watzinger of Citibank/Salomon Smith Barney for providing information on the above transaction

The risk transfer within this structure is set out below:

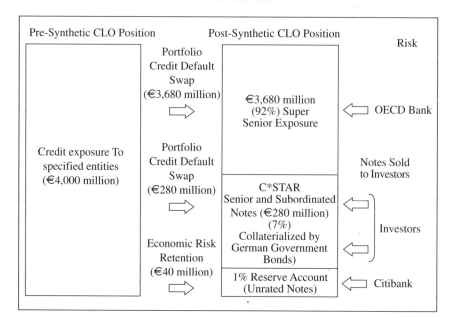

The transaction structure dictates that Citibank bears the first 1% of losses. The investors in the C*STAR notes bear the next 7% of credit losses. The remaining 92% of loss (usually referred to as the super AAA tranche – reflecting the fact that the risk is very low in a ratings sense) is borne by the OECD bank counterparties to the credit default swap.

The C*STAR structure is very similar to the BISTRO structure and has similar advantages including:

- Credit risk transfer: Citibank sheds credit exposure to the underlying counterparties.
- Cost effective risk transfer: The fact that Citibank retains the underlying transactions and only the risk is hedged means that the higher funding spread on the transaction is only paid on about 7% of the total portfolio. Given that the coupon on the AAA/ Aaa tranche is around 21 bp and assuming a funding cost for a highly rated bank of around LIBOR minus 15 bp, this translates into a cost saving of around 36 bps pa.
- Separation of underlying transaction from credit hedge: This enables a wide variety of transactions to be hedged.

The differences between BISTRO and C*STAR relate primarily to the super AAA tranche. In BISTRO, this is retained by the sponsor bank (although it may then be separately hedged). In C*STAR, this risk is hedged through a credit default swap with OECD banks. The primary motivation of this structure is BIS credit capital relief. The C*STAR structure enables a reduction in risk capital to 20% from 100% for the underlying portfolio. The credit default swap on the super AAA tranche is usually attractively priced reflecting the very low risk on this tranche.

Asset Portfolio

The underlying portfolio of €4 billion consisted of 164 transactions to 152 obligors. The transactions are primarily loans of which 67% are currently undrawn. The obligors were primarily from Europe (excluding Greece), Norway and Switzerland.

Individual obligors were not specifically identified. The structure is rated with the rating being based on a mixture of external ratings and Citibank's internal credit ratings (mapped to rating agency external ratings). Approximately 40% of the portfolio has to have ratings at all time and the other 60% has mapped ratings. The portfolio is subject limits on industry and individual obligor concentration limits.

Credit Enhancement

The structure uses the sponsor retained first loss provision and the tranched notes to enhance the credit structure of the portfolio.

4.5 Regulatory Capital Considerations[26]

As is evident, a significant driving factor behind these transactions is the regulatory capital treatment of credit risk. In this section, the current position of the different structures is considered.

The basic regulatory capital position in respect of credit risk in terms of the BIS credit capital accord as expressed in the risk weighting calculations is as follows:
- Term loans and the funded component of revolving credit facilities to a corporate counterparty are 100% risk weighted.
- Unfunded commitments have risk weighting of 50%.
  Where the credit risk is sought to be eliminated/hedged, the bank can enter into three classes of transactions:
- Participation and assignments.
- Securitizations, such as CLOs.
- Credit derivatives, such as credit default swaps.

The impact of these types of risk reduction transactions varies in terms of its regulatory treatment. Participation and assignments reduce the risk weighting of both funded loans and unfunded commitments to 0%.

The treatment of securitization transactions is more complex. For example, US regulators (the Federal Reserve Board, FDIC, and OCC) apply the so-called low level recourse rules. Under this approach, in bank securitization

---

[26] For a consideration of the regulatory treatment of credit derivatives, see Chapter 19.

transactions, capital must be held against the retained first loss position. Retention of a first loss position of more than 8% results in treatment of the transaction as a financing rather than a sale. This results in the requirement to hold capital equal to 8% of the underlying pool. Retention of a first loss position of less than 8% allows capital to be reduce proportionally to the face value of the retained position.

Recent inter-agency proposals, which would be applicable to both a bank's own securitization and third-party securitization transactions would alter the treatment as follows:

- AAA rated second loss positions would be 20% risk weighted.
- Other investment-grade positions would be risk weighted at either 100% of par amount or 50% of the underlying pool from which the risk of loss derives.
- Below investment-grade recourse provisions would be 100% risk weighted based on the entire pool from which the risk of loss derives.

   Securitizations, such as the CLO structures described, have been effective means for reducing risk. However, in order to achieve favorable regulatory capital treatment, the first loss retained loss position must be less than 8%. This can typically only be achieved where the underlying portfolio is investment grade.[27]

This means that CLO transactions are difficult to justify economically because of the high funding cost for banks with access to low cost funding except as a mechanism for creating regulatory relief. It has the perverse aspect of allowing banks to shed lower risk assets and create higher levels of credit risk on their retained assets. In effect, this is a form of credit capital arbitrage which forces the existing credit capital guidelines to reflect lower risk weighting for investment grade risk.

Under proposed changes to the BIS Capital Accord[28], the treatment of securitization transactions for credit capital will change. The proposed approach is reliant on rating and is designed to avoid the problems of capital arbitrage. The primary proposal is that securitization tranches should be weighted in accordance with the risk weighting categorization set out in Figure 4.7. The

---

[27] In a typical CLO transaction, the size of the unrated first loss piece for an investment grade portfolio would be in the region of 3 % where the mezzanine tranche of debt to be issued against the asset pool is sought to be rated investment grade (BBB).

[28] See Chapter 19.

most important change is that holdings of securitization tranches rated B+ or below and all unrated tranches will be deducted in full from capital.

Figure 4.7   BIS Risk Weighting – Proposed

Credit Rating	AA– or above	A+ to A–	BBB+ to BBB–	BB+ to B–	B– and below	Unrated
Sovereign	0%	20%	50%	100%	150%	100%
Bank (Option 1)	20%	50%	100%	100%	150%	100%
Bank (Option 2)	20%	50%	50%	100%	150%	50%
Corporate	20%	100%	100%	100%	150%	100%
Securitization SPV	20%	50%	100%	150%	Full deduction	Full deduction

Bank regulators generally allow regulatory capital relief where credit derivatives are utilized to hedge credit exposure. Under the current position[29], the treatment of credit defaults swaps is as follows:

- **Banking Book:** Where the transaction is in the banking book, where protection is sold, the credit exposure assumed is treated as analogous to that on a letter of credit or guarantee, and risk weighted according to the reference credit rather than the counterparty. Where protection is purchased and the transaction provides virtually complete protection (that is the notional principal, seniority of debt, maturity, and obligations are matched) and certainty of the recovery amount, the protection afforded is recognized through the reduction of the counterparty risk weighting to that of the seller of protection. This means that where the seller of protection is an OECD bank, the risk weight declines for a corporate 100% risk weighted asset from 100% to 20% (for a funded obligation) or 50% to 10% (for commitments).
- **Trading Book:** Where the credit default swap is in the trading book, the transaction is treated as follows under the market risk capital guidelines (not the credit capital rules):
  1. The transaction must be marked-to-market.
  2. Capital must be held against the general market risk (effectively the VaR of the transaction), specific risks, and counterparty credit risk.
  3. Market risk can be calculated either by reference to internal models or using the BIS standard model.

---

[29] This is problematic insofar as there is no definitive regulations on the treatment of credit derivatives. The statements reflect discussion /guidance papers published by regulators.

4. Specific risk charges (which in practise are the most problematic) are designed to cover the change in the value of reference asset that is unique to the issuer and in effect represents unsystematic or diversifiable risk. It can also be calculated using either internal models or standard models.
5. Counterparty credit risk is only applicable to the buyer of protection under a credit default swap. It is calculated as the mark-to-market amount (if positive) and an add-on factor for potential future exposure.

If specific risk is not modeled, the standardized specific risk charges are as follows:

Category	Remaining Term to Maturity	Weighting Factor	Conventional Risk Weighting Equivalence
Government	Not applicable	0	0
Qualifying (debt of OECD banks;	< 6 months	0.25	3.125
Government agencies; investment grade	6–24 months	1.00	12.5
Corporations)	> 24 months	1.60	20
Other	Not applicable	8.00	100

The standardized rules allow offsets only where the structure, maturity, and reference asset is identical.

The counterparty risk add-ons are as follows:
• Equity conversion factors for investment-grade reference assets.
• Commodity conversion for non investment-grade reference assets.

These factors (as % of notional principal) are:

Maturity	Equity	Commodity
< 1 year	6	10
1–5 years	8	12
> 5 years	10	15

The treatment of credit derivatives is relevant to both the credit linked note CLO structure and the synthetic securitization structures.

In the case of the credit linked note structure, provided the virtually complete protection test is satisfied, regulatory capital relief on the assets on which the risk is transferred should be achieved. The low-level recourse test may also have to be satisfied.

However, the synthetic securitization structures, such as BISTRO, do not necessarily *prima facie* achieve regulatory capital relief. This is despite the fact that it may act as an economic hedge of the credit risk on the underlying transaction. This is because based on the current risk based capital rules, the mismatch in collateral underlying the credit default swap dictates that the reduction in risk weighting to 0% is only available on the notional amount of the Treasury collateral.

In practise, additional capital relief may be possible by structuring the transaction as an internal credit default swap between the banking book and the trading book within the sponsor bank. Under this structure, the banking book achieves at least a reduction in the risk weighting. In the trading book, the credit default swap is subject to mark-to-market and the risk capital rules. If the transaction has been economically efficiently structured, this would enable the regulatory capital relief to be achieved. This is because the retained risk in a transaction like BISTRO would be minimal in terms of economic risk models. However, it is far from clear whether this strategy is one that would be accepted by regulators who have yet to indicate their position on such transactions.

The current regulatory position for synthetic securitization transactions (referred to as Synthetic CLOs in the regulatory guidelines) is not settled. The US Federal Reserve and OCC issued guidelines in November 1999.[30] The approach taken covered the treatment of sponsor bank and investors in notes issued under these structures. The guidelines appear to apply to the banking book.

The treatment of the investor in notes issued under synthetic securitization transactions is relatively straightforward. Investors in notes must assign risk weights appropriate to risk-weighted assets underlying the notes.

The regulatory position for synthetic securitization is based on classification into three separate types of transactions:

• **Transaction 1:** This entails a banking organization hedging the whole notional amount of the reference asset portfolio through a synthetic CLO. The proposed regulatory treatment requires the cash proceeds to be treated as collateral and the capital required is reduced to collateral risk weighting.

---

[30] See Pelham, Mark November 23–29 1999, "US Regulators Address Synthetic CLOs," *Financial Products* 1, 11; Cass, Dwight December 1999, "Fed Issues CLO Guidelines," *Risk* 11, Satyajit Das February 7, 2000

- **Transaction 2**: This covers a banking organization hedging part of notional amount of a reference asset portfolio through a synthetic CLO. The bank retains a high quality risk position (that is, it absorbs loss in excess of a junior loss position). The proposed treatment is that there will be a reduction in capital on the part hedged with synthetic CLO (to collateral risk weight). There is a requirement that capital is to be held against the high quality (super senior) position.
- **Transaction 3:** This covers a banking organization hedging part of the notional amount of a reference asset portfolio through a synthetic CLO. The bank retains a first loss risk position. The proposed treatment is for capital to be the higher of:
  1. Approach 1: Hold $ for $ capital against loss retained but no capital against additional risk
  2. Approach 2: Hold 8% against loss retained with second loss position is viewed as completely collateralized (at collateral risk weight).

Under the proposed approach, the US regulators provide the possibility of the sponsoring bank obtaining regulatory capital relief on the so-called super senior or super AAA tranche (effectively the risk retained by the sponsor bank after the first loss and external cash collateralised component has been exhausted. The capital relief would be available *without the need to enter into a credit default swap* with an OECD bank.

This capital relief is contingent on the sponsor bank being able to satisfy three requirements:

- The sponsor bank must demonstrate that it has transferred virtually all the risk on the underlying credit risk portfolio through the synthetic securitization. Indicia of virtual total protection will include:
  1. The issuance of notes rated by a major rating agency.
  2. The most senior tranche based must be rated AAA/Aaa.
  3. The structure must include a first loss provision that is retained by the sponsor bank. This first loss position must be equal to (certainly no greater than) a reasonable estimate of the expected loss on the reference portfolio. This first loss provision must be deducted from the capital of the sponsor bank.
- The sponsor bank must be able to demonstrate that it can evaluate the remaining banking book risk exposures and also demonstrate adequate capital resources to support these exposures. This may take the form of an internal rating system and credit modeling process. Any such system must be based on credible and verifiable capital assessment methodology including stress testing.

- The sponsor bank must also ensure adequate public disclosure of the risk profile and capital adequacy consequences of synthetic securitization transactions. This would include economic, regulatory and accounting consequences of the transaction.

If the bank fails to meet the requirement, the regulators may assign the unhedged senior position to the 20% risk weighting category.

The US regulators will assess individual transaction structures separately on a case-by-case approach. It is not possible that based on the structure of individual transactions, the capital treatment may be varied or adjusted from transaction to transaction.

4.6 Summary

The pressure to manage capital (both economic and regulatory) while preserving relationships with clients has led banks to examine a variety of financial structures to shed credit exposure. Traditionally this has taken the form of securitization transactions, including CLO structures. However, increasingly alternatives to securitization usually involving credit derivative structures have emerged. These have included the credit linked note CLO structures (SBC Glacier and Triangle) and synthetic securitizations using credit default swaps (BISTRO).

The evolution of the structures has created competitive alternatives for banks seeking to manage the capital committed to credit exposure assumed in servicing their corporate relationships. Figure 4.8 sets out the comparative features of the competing structures.

Figure 4.8   Comparison of CLO, Credit Linked Note CLO and Synthetic Securitization

Feature	CLO	Credit Linked Note CLO	Synthetic Securitization
Asset Transfer Mechanism	Assignment or participation	Credit linked note	Credit default swap
Economic Capital	Risk is reduced by the amount of assets transferred less the first loss position retained	Risk is reduced to the extent that the credit linked note hedges the underlying credit exposure less any equity piece in the CLO retained	Risk is reduced to the extent that the credit exposure is transferred less the first loss position assumed (which is less than that needed for CLO) and to the extent that losses exceed the protection purchased triggering the final loss position retained by the sponsor bank
Regulatory Capital	Relief available dependent on quantum of first-loss position	Relief available dependent on the extent the credit linked notes provides virtually complete protection	Limited relief available *prima facie* but may be able to be achieved by structuring
Balance Sheet Impact	Assets are transferred off balance sheet	Assets remain on balance sheet	Assets remain on balance sheet
Funding	Funding generated as a result of the sale	Funding generated as a result of sale of credit linked notes	No funding generated
Client Relationship	Clients may need to be advised where an assignment is required. Client particulars are not usually disclosed in the offering document	Clients do not need to be advised. Client particulars are not usually disclosed in the offering document	Clients do not need to be advised. Client particulars disclosure optional in the offering document

Figure 4.8   (Cont'd)

Feature	CLO	Credit Linked Note CLO	Synthetic Securitization
Credit Rating of Selling Bank	Important in rating where participation structure is used; not important where assignment structure is used	Important in rating	Not relevant
Amount of Securities	Equal to approximately face value of loans sold	Equal to approximately face value of loans sold	Equal to the level required to shed economic risk but will generally be significantly lower than face value of asset hedged

The emerging structures also highlight the deficiencies of the existing BIS credit risk capital regulations. The discrepancies between economic capital and regulatory capital have been exposed by the use of the structure identified. The current position means that often transactions that reduce economic credit risk may not achieve regulatory capital relief. The divergence is clearly inefficient. The solution will require a revision of credit capital standards and will in all probability see the introduction of model based approaches to credit risk analogous to those in use in relation to market risk.

PART TWO
APPLICATIONS

5
Credit Derivatives — Applications

Satyajit Das

5.1 Market for credit risk

The volume of credit risk within capital markets is very large. The total volume of *new* issuance of bonds and loan transactions undertaken in international markets now runs in the order of several trillion dollars each. In addition, substantially larger volumes of derivative transactions and other off-balance sheet-instruments are transacted creating significant counterparty credit risk. There is also a substantial parallel market in credit risk outside the market for credit risk among financial institutions. This market relates to the credit risk incurred by non-financial institutions in their normal trading operations. This pertains to the credit risks relating to supplier credits and other trade receivables, supply and purchase contracts, insurance arrangements, employee-share acquisition schemes on a deferred payment basis, and contract prepayments.

Credit risk has historically been regarded as illiquid. The applications of credit derivatives are focused on isolating or unbundling the credit risk (effectively the risk of value changes driven by changes in credit quality) from other risks and structuring it in a format that allows these risks to be traded within capital markets. This is to facilitate both the reduction of these risks through hedging and the assumption of these risks where appropriate.

The application of credit derivatives is predicated on a shift in the *approach* to the management of credit risk. Traditionally, credit risk has been regarded as static in nature. The process of credit risk management has focused on assessing credit risk and matching it with capital or provisions to cover expected losses from default. The principal management techniques have been diversification of the credit risk and the use of credit enhancement (for example, collateral) to manage the credit risk incurred.

In contrast, credit derivatives allow credit risk to be viewed as a disaggregated commodity, separate from other risks such as interest rate or currency risk. This risk is more than capable of being managed dynamically through hedging techniques previously associated with market risk.

The primary advantages of this new approach to the management of credit risk emphasizes the following:

- The increased liquidity of credit risk.
- The reduction in transaction costs and market frictions in hedging and trading in credit risk.
- The increase in opportunities to both diversify credit risk and to assume credit risk in a format that either allows the creation of risk profiles not directly available or allowing access to credit risk that is traditional inaccessible for some investors.

This chapter examines the principal applications of credit derivatives. The major application opportunities are first considered. The use of credit derivatives in the management of credit risk is then examined. A number of application examples are also considered.

5.2 Application Opportunities[1]

5.2.1 *Underlying Key Factors*

The principal impetus for applications of credit derivative products derives from the following factors:

- The capacity to isolate and disaggregate credit risk
- The ability to trade credit risk in a relatively liquid format with *relatively* low transaction costs

---

[1] For a general discussion on the application of credit derivatives, see Gontarek, Walter 1998, "Hedging With Credit Derivatives: Practical Applications and Considerations," *Credit Derivatives: Applications for Risk Management, Investment and Portfolio Optimisation*; Risk Books, London, Chapter 2; Gontarek, Walter "Today's Credit Derivatives Market" in Storrow, Jamie 1999, *Credit Derivatives: Key Issues* (2nd ed), British Bankers Association, London, Chapter 2; Reoch, Robert "An Introduction To Credit Derivatives" in Storrow, Jamie 1999 *Credit Derivatives: Key Issues* (2nd ed), British Bankers Association, London, Chapter 3

These factors allow trading in credit risk to achieve the following objectives:

- **Enhance diversification**: The enhanced liquidity of credit risk should facilitate the diversification of existing credit portfolios. This increases efficiency (in terms of optimizing the risk-return trade-off) by allowing reduction in risk exposures to certain issuers to whom the lender is over-exposed while simultaneously increasing exposure to issuers to whom the lender has suboptimal exposures. The fact that credit derivatives may allow investors to access credit risks that traditionally have been difficult to access is an element in this process.
- **Trade forward expectations or anomalies of credit risk pricing**: Forward credit spreads and default risk probabilities are implied by the market price of traded instruments. These forward credit risk parameters imply trading opportunities. There may be inconsistencies in the pricing of credit risk for the same issuer (that is, different instruments issued by the same issuer may imply different credit risks) or for similar issuers of comparable credit risk allowing arbitrage. The implied forward credit spreads or default probabilities may not accord with an investor's expectations, allowing monetization of the view that actual credit risk will vary from the implied forward credit risk.[2]
- **Attract new investment to credit risk**: Access to credit risk through credit derivatives allows non-traditional investors to assume credit risk or facilitates traditional investors assuming credit risk to which they previously had no, limited, or expensive access. This process, which should allow greater diversification of credit risk, will assist in broadening the range of institutions which can commit capital to support credit risk in capital markets.[3]

Within this framework, the key applications of credit derivatives entail using the building-block credit derivative structures to create mechanisms to either transfer credit risk or customized risk-reward profiles. The key factors in this regard are:

---

[2] This is conceptually no different to monetisation of expectations that actual spot currency or interest rates will differ from implied forward currency and interest rates.

[3] An example of a market that traditionally has been difficult to access and invest in by institutional investors has been the loan market. For a discussion of the role of credit derivatives in facilitating access to this market, see Culp, Christopher L. and Neves, Andrea M.P. "Financial Innovations In Leveraged Commercial Loan Markets" (Summer 1998) *Journal of Applied Corporate Finance*, Vol 11, No 279-93; Barnish, Keith, Miller, Steve, and Rushmore, Michael "The New Leveraged Loan Syndication Market" (Spring 1997) *Journal of Applied Corporate Finance*, Vol 10, No 1 79–88; Mahtani, Arun "Synthetic Structures Facilitate Leveraged Loan Boom" (28 November 1998) *International Financing Review*, Issue 1261, pp 85

- Enhancing the available term structure of credit risk
- Modifying the type of credit risk that is assumed
- Allowing the assumption of highly structured exposure profiles on:
  — Recovery rates upon default
  — Differentiation of relative default risk on different classes of obligations.
- Allowing assumption of credit exposure within a framework of structural flexibility.

5.2.2   Term Structures

Credit derivatives fundamentally allow the separation of the term for which credit risk is assumed from the term of the underlying credit obligation.

Traditional instruments entailing credit risk, such as bonds or loans, link the term of the transaction and the term of the credit risk. The disaggregation of risk underlying credit derivatives allows this separation. This has the impact of removing the inherent constraint on an investor that its management of the credit risk of a portfolio is linked to the term of the available instruments. This allows:

- Expression of views on credit sensitive assets for maturities which are different from the maturity of the referenced security.
- Construction of a complete credit risk term structure.

The application of this concept can be illustrated with the following examples:

- **Specific Credit Duration:** Assume a bank or investor is seeking to acquire credit exposure to a particular issuer for a term of two years. This maturity is dictated by available credit lines. However, the issuer in question has no two-year securities/credit assets outstanding although it has longer term (say, five years or more in remaining maturity) securities outstanding. The bank or investor could acquire the credit exposure it requires by investing in a structured note where the default risk of the two year security is linked to the default risk on the available longer term securities of the target issuer. This structure allows the bank or investor to overcome the lack of availability of the desired assets.
- **Forward Start Credit Derivatives:** Assume a bank or investor has no available term credit lines to a particular issuer. This reflects that its term credit lines (up to five years) are currently being used by existing loans that mature after 18 months. This use of the credit lines represents a suboptimal use of credit capital. This is because the returns being obtained against the capital committed reflects the shorter maturity of the credit asset. The available credit capacity is not fully utilized; that is, there is a forward gap

in utilization of this line from 18 months to five years. In order to optimize the use of its credit capital, the bank or investor can enter into a transaction entailing the sale of a credit default put or the sale of credit protection for a period of three and a half years commencing in 18 months time (effectively, a forward credit default swap). The return earned on that credit risk would have two separate effects: first, it would fully utilize the credit capital available; and, second, depending on the pricing of the forward default swap, it would boost the returns on capital over the full term of the credit lines.

- **Structured Term Exposure:** An investor willing to assume credit exposure to a particular issuer may only be willing to do so at an increasing cost as the maturity of the risk increases. This can be designed as a structured note where the principal redemption is linked to the default of the reference issuer. The note pays a coupon that increases after an initial period if the note is not called at the end of the period. This note would operate in the following manner. If the credit risk of the issuer improves or if the issuer of the notes requirement for default risk protection decreases, than the issuer will call the note. However, if as at the call date, the issuer on the note still requires default protection, it does not call the note but pays the higher coupon rate. The investor in the note will continue to bear the risk of default in the event of the call not being exercised but will be compensated at a higher rate that presumably, in its judgement, adequately covers an risk of loss from default.

5.2.3 Credit Risk

Credit derivative structures will also generally allow flexibility in the creation of different types of credit exposure or particular trading opportunities in credit. These opportunities may not be readily available in the physical market that restricts the type of risk that can be assumed to the universe of available securities. The choice of risk in these physical securities and loans is usually delineated by two factors:
- Choice of credit rating or credit quality
- Seniority or type of obligation

The application of this approach to flexible assumption of very structured credit risks can be illustrated with the following examples:
- **First-to-Default-Baskets:** A bank or investor can create simultaneous exposure to multiple credits by assuming the credit exposure to a basket of reference issuers under a first-to-default structure, where it will be required to make a default payment where any of the underlying credits defaults. This

structure entails an increase in the credit risk to the bank or investor assuming the risk of default as the credit risk of the first-to-default structure is higher than the individual credits which is compensated for in a higher return to the bank or investor. In effect, the structure allows trading in default correlations. This specific form of exposure is unavailable in the physical market and can only be created through credit derivatives.

- **Ratings Protection:** An investor subject to a minimum credit rating investment constraint can utilize credit derivatives to achieve its investment objectives. Assume the investor has a minimum rating constraint of investment grade (BBB–/Baa–). Assume it seeks to purchase the following securities: Issuer A who is BBB– rated (therefore eligible but a downgrade would require liquidation); and Issuer B who is BB rated (therefore, ineligible). The investor seeks to invest in both securities for normal investment reasons: diversification of industry and issuer risk, and perceived attractive returns relative to risk. There are two possible means to structure these investments:

  1. The investor purchases Issuer A's securities while simultaneously purchasing a credit default swap that is triggered on a downgrade allowing the investor to sell the security at a pre-agreed price. This allows the investor in return for the cost of purchasing the downgrade protection to lower its risk of selling the security following the fall in credit rating. The availability of the downgrade protection may allow the investor to purchase these types of securities (that is, those close to its credit constraints) rather than avoid such investments to minimize the price risk on sale after downgrade. The latter problem entails many investors pursuing a policy of only purchasing securities at a rating level well above its minimum criteria (referred to as a credit gap or ratings cushion) which result in suboptimization of portfolio performance.

  2. The investor purchases Issuer B's securities while simultaneously purchasing a credit default swap on Issuer B from a counterparty within its acceptable credit criteria. This structure allows the investor to acquire assets that would otherwise be unavailable to it. This may be important in allowing investors to participate in certain industry sectors (for example, the airlines sector) where the industry rating average would preclude investment.

The capacity to customize credit risk allows access to investments that would otherwise be extremely difficult for banks and investors.

- **Seniority Choices:** Assume a bank or investor has purchased a loan asset that is a senior obligation of the issuer. In order to increase its return from the investment, it can sell default protection on subordinated or junior obligations of the same issuer to alter its risk profile without the necessity to trade in the underlying asset. Alternatively, holders of a subordinated obligation can, through the simultaneous purchase of protection on subordinated obligations and the sale of protection on senior obligations of the issuer, alter its risk within the capital structure. For example, a number of transactions involving convertible preferred shares have been completed where the subordinated nature of the obligations precluded purchase of these securities by certain banks and investors. The investments combined with the default puts produced returns, which even after adjustment for the cost of the conversion in seniority status provided attractive returns relative to other available fixed interest senior obligations.

- **Static versus Non-Static Exposures:** Assume a bank is seeking protection on credit exposures under existing derivative transactions with a client. Movements in interest and currency rates have meant that the credit exposure on these transactions has increased to levels in excess of prudential levels. Another bank may offer to sell a credit default swap on the market credit exposure on these derivatives. The rationale of the bank selling the exposure is the projected exposure on the portfolio based on its projected exposure of currency and interest rates is lower than current exposure levels. Given that the bank seeking protection is prepared to pay fees based on higher levels of assumed credit exposure than that anticipated by the second bank, the latter is prepared to assume the exposure as it believes that it can effectively generate economic profits based on its expectations.

Each of the examples discussed above highlights the capacity to construct customized exposure to credit risks that moreover will generally not be directly available in the credit market.

5.2.4 Recovery Rate Structures

Credit default swaps facilitate banks or investors trading their expectations of recovery rates upon default. The bank or investor providing protection has considerable structural flexibility in nominating the payout due in the event of default, including:

- Cash settlement based on a dealer poll of the post default value of the security
- Cash settlement based on a pre-agreed payout amount (say, 40–60%) of the nominal face value of the transaction

- Physical delivery of the defaulted securities in exchange for receipt of a pre-agreed amount (usually, the value of the security at the time of entry into the transaction)

The availability of these options allows the default payout to be structured to allow the bank or investor to vary the risk-reward profile. This facilitates the following types of trading opportunity:
- Selling default protection at recovery levels that are lower than expected recovery rates to allow creation of value through assumption of risks that are considered unlikely.
- Trade credit risk to maximize return on credit risk allocated to credit risk by using default swaps to adjust expected loss rates on portfolios of credit assets

The application of this approach to flexible assumption of and trading in recovery rate risks can be illustrated with the following example.

Assume Bank A is willing to take senior unsecured credit exposure on Company X at credit spread of 80 bp pa. It expects that in the event of default the expected loss rate will be 50% of notional value (i.e. recovery rate of 50%). Assume another bank, Bank B, prices the equivalent exposure to Company X at the same spread level. Bank B estimates that in the event of default its loss rate will be 40% (i.e. recovery rate of 60%). The two banks' pricing of the credit risk is identical although its recovery rate expectations are different.

This difference in recovery rate expectations allows the construction of a credit default swap predicated on the differential recovery rates. Under the proposed transaction, Bank A should rationally be willing to sell a default swap to Bank B on the following terms:
- Bank A will pay a fixed amount in the event of the default of Company X
- The fixed amount payable will be 50% (that is, the fixed payout option is selected rather than a variable payout option dependent upon the price performance of the defaulted security)

The price paid by Bank B for the purchase of this protection should be 100 bp pa. This is calculated as follows:
Credit Spread × Loss Rate Assumed By Bank A/Loss Rate Assumed By Bank B
= 80 bp pa × 50%/40% = 100 bp

Bank A is prepared to sell this protection at a return equal to or greater than 80 bp pa. This is because it produces an equivalent or higher return from holding the asset or providing protection under a credit default swap with a variable payout dependent on the price performance of the defaulted security, based on it recovery rate expectations. Bank B should be prepared to pay this amount for the default protection as the default swap offers protection at a higher level than that the bank would receive based on its recovery rate expectations. This would be the case whether bank held the credit risk directly or by providing protection under a credit default swap with a variable payout dependent on the price performance of the defaulted security. A transaction between the banks at anywhere between 80 bp pa and 100 bp pa would effectively benefit both counterparties based on their individual recovery rate expectations.[4]

This type of trading recovery rate expectations is only feasible through credit derivatives. This reflects the capacity to isolate the separate aspects of credit risk that is not readily available in direct transactions entailing the assumption of credit risk through traditional forms of credit.

5.2.5 Default Risk Structures

Credit default products also provide flexibility in terms of the definition of credit event that triggers the default payout. The credit event can be selected from the following range of definitions:[5]

- Payment default (non-trivial or exceeding a de minimus rule) which remains unremedied after an agreed grace period, including cross-default and cross-acceleration on other monetary obligations
- Bankruptcy, restructuring, or administration
- Credit rating downgrade below trigger level
- A material change in the credit spread or price of a security[6]

The capacity to select the credit event allows a bank or investor to structure the credit event which triggers default to reflect its expectations on likely treatment of different classes of securities issued by the same issuer. For example, a distressed issuer may default on its domestic but not its international obligations

---

[4] This transaction is hypothetical and designed to illustrate the opportunity to monetise views on recovery rates. In reality, given the current stage of development of the market and the level of trading liquidity, such structures are difficult to establish

[5] The definition of credit event is not comprehensive and many other structures are also feasible

[6] As noted in Chapter 1, this type of provision (referred to as the materiality requirement) is used in conjunction with other credit events to determine the trigger in a credit event. However, there is no reason why a material change in spread or price can of itself constitute a credit event

or vice versa.[7] Alternatively, the public securities of an issuer may be treated quite differently from its bank debt. These discrepancies of treatment have been experienced in emerging market sovereign debt as well as the obligations of a number of distressed corporations. The use of credit default products can allow trading in the value of credit obligations through the selection of the definition of credit event and nomination of the universe of reference obligations. This, in combination with the capacity to structure the recovery rate, can provide interesting trading opportunities for market participants.

5.2.6 Structural Flexibility

All credit derivative derivatives provide considerable structural flexibility. These include:

- **Ease of administration:** Allowing investors, other than banks, to participate in loan transactions through the use of total rate of return loan swaps. Similarly, credit spread structures allow monetization of credit spread expectations without the need to trade in the underlying assets while credit default products facilitate the assumption of pure default risk without the need to acquire the securities of the reference credit.
- **Ease of creation of position:** Allowing the creation of synthetic credit assets (total rate of return loan swaps) or credit risk attributes (credit spread or default risk products) on an off-balance sheet basis without the necessity of trading in the underlying credit markets. This includes the creation of positions not directly available in the credit markets.
- **Capacity to short credit risk:** Allowing banks and investors to effectively short sell the credit market which is practically difficult to achieve through direct trading in credit assets. This is of course fundamental to being able to hedge existing portfolios of loan and other credit assets.
- **Liquidity benefits:** Facilitating the trading in these risks with lower transaction costs and market friction because of the off-balance sheet form of these instruments.

5.3. Management of Concentration Risk in Credit Portfolios

5.3.1 Concept

The application of credit derivatives, in particular, credit default products, to manage the concentration risk within credit portfolio of financial institutions

---

[7]   The default by Russia on its debt is a case in point. Russia initially defaulted on some but not all of its obligations

represents a special application of these instruments. It is also among the most important applications of credit default products.

The concept of concentration risk focuses on the additional risk of credit losses in portfolios of credit assets where the portfolios of credit risk are not well diversified. This is predicated on the assumption that consistent with the dictates of portfolio theory where the correlation as between the risk of default of individual obligors is imperfect a portfolio of assets will demonstrate reductions in risk with increases in diversification. Accordingly, an inadequately diversified credit portfolio will generally be characterized by concentration risk that quantitatively can be measured as the excess of expected and unexpected credit loss for the poorly diversified relative to a well diversified portfolio of similar size and characteristics.

5.3.2 Concentration Risk — Key Factors

The presence of concentration risk in credit portfolios of financial institutions is the result of a number of factors:

- **Specialization of banks/financial institutions:** Limited resources and competitive forces, such as the knowledge and competencies of the institution, relative competitive position and return requirements, have inevitably forced banks into specialization. This specialization may take the form of industry specialization, geographic specialization (by country or region) or specialization of type of client as classified by credit rating. This has the consequence of leading to higher degrees of concentration in the credit composition of portfolios.

- **Mismatch between origination capacity and diversification objectives:** There is a parallel limitation in the scope of a financial institution being able to directly originate credit assets outside its natural markets. This reflects the focus of its client relationships, the presence and knowledge requirements of penetrating new markets, as well as the competitive behavior of institutions with established market positions in the relevant market segments. This is exacerbated by the increased trend to specialization that creates higher levels of concentration risk.

- **Incompleteness of credit markets:** Credit markets are generally incomplete in that they lack of available credit assets with the required term, structure, and industry characteristics in the institution's markets may itself increase concentration. A bank located in and focusing on a particular geography is naturally captive to the industrial bias of the region as well as the borrowing characteristics of the entities active in that region. This creates a natural bias in portfolio structure of credit risk that increases concentration risk.

- **Changing structure of credit markets:** Several trends in the pattern of capital market activity also creates concentration risks:

  1. The trend to direct issuance of securities to investors by higher quality issuers as an alternative to bank financing has resulted in a change in the composition of the credit risk structure of bank loan portfolios. These portfolios now have higher proportionate levels of exposure to lower-rated borrowers who do not enjoy the same access to capital markets.

  2. The trend to corporations reducing the size of their core banking groups has increased the relative size and scale of bank exposure to individual clients. For example, in recent years, a number of borrowers have raised bank loans of several billions of dollars (say, US$5 billion) from a small group of banks (say, 10 banks). While these loans are often of short duration, for example, associated with acquisitions/mergers, and are frequently refinanced in other markets quite quickly, the substantial size of these exposures can substantially skew the credit portfolio.

  These factors have combined to significantly increase the level of concentration risk in portfolios.

- **Client relationship pressures:** Banks have increased individual loan exposures to clients as a primary resource in establishing and maintaining major relationships. This has been done in the expectation that the dominant position as a major lender will allow the bank to gain access to other non-credit business from the clients. The inability to reduce these direct credit exposures often creates substantial concentration risks within credit portfolios.

These factors are collectively referred to as the credit paradox. The factors identified have the capacity to significantly increase concentration risk in the credit portfolios of financial institutions to unacceptable levels.

5.3.3 Concentration Risk in Credit Portfolios[8]

The impact of concentration risk within credit risk portfolios is best understood from the viewpoint of portfolio theory. Traditional mean-variance portfolio theory is not directly applicable to credit portfolio. This reflects the characteristics of credit portfolios that include:

---

[8] For a discussion of concentration risk in credit portfolios see Chapter 6, 12–14.

- The returns in credit portfolios appear to be skewed in well-diversified portfolios
- Credit risk appears to be non-linear in nature
- Credit risk appears to be exacerbated by the traditional illiquidity of credit risk
- Increasing the size of the portfolio and increasing diversification can reduce credit risk. However, the size of portfolio required to reach full diversification is large

This quantitative approach to credit portfolio management would indicate that the return on credit assets should be related to the return/pricing, the size of the exposure, and the default correlation between credit assets. This is consistent with the fact that concentration risk arises from an increase in the expected loss of the portfolio due to large exposures to a particular issuer, industry, region, or other grouping of credit assets that have a high default correlation. This analysis indicates that it is desirable in a risk-return trade-off sense to reduce exposure to issuer to whom the institution is over exposed or increase exposure to issuers to whom the institutions is underexposed.

The price that an institution should be prepared to economically pay to achieve this optimization of portfolio credit risk shows surprising characteristics. The portfolio manager to adequately cover the increased risk of concentration requires returns, which increases in a non-linear fashion (at an increasing rate) reflecting the fact that the portfolio risk is a function of the individual exposures squared. Figure 5.1 sets out this relationship diagrammatically.

Figure 5.1   Managing Concentration Risk in Credit Portfolios

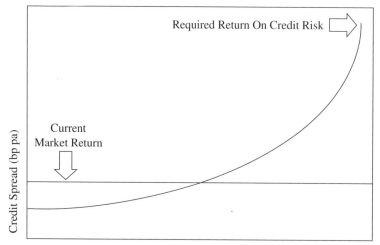

Required Target Return on Credit Risk
Exposure in Portfolio Context

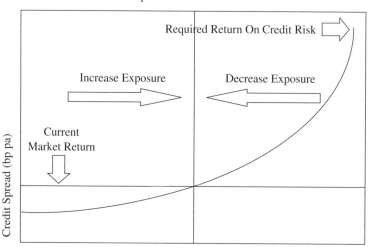

Required Portfolio Actions

This dictates that the institution that has high levels of exposure to a particular credit should be prepared to pay a premium to market returns to reduce the risk of concentration. Similarly, the institution may require a lower than market return in increasing its exposure to credits to which it is underexposed.

This is predicated on the fact that while the returns on individual credits are determined by market prices, the return required to compensate for risk for a particular investor is related to the portfolio structure. In effect, the marginal return required is related to the marginal risk contribution to the portfolio risk. This relationship requires increasing returns, which are above market returns, where there is already substantial exposure to a particular credit. Interestingly, traditional methods of managing credit risk which are based on fixed limits do not necessarily incorporate this return on marginal risk component.

This type of portfolio-based approach to management of credit assets is gradually being accepted. The implementation of such approaches forces institution to address the management of concentration risk within credit portfolios to increase the efficiency of returns on capital within a risk-return framework.

5.3.4 Approaches to Management of Concentration Risk

The recognition of the impact of concentration risk does not dictate in itself the use of credit derivatives. It does, however, emphasize the importance of diversification of credit risk and the reduction of exposure to issuer to whom the institution is overexposed compensated by the increase in exposure to credits to which the institution is under exposed.

Traditional methods of adjusting exposure levels would have entailed participation in the secondary loan market as well as boosting credit asset origination efforts in the relevant markets. These approaches have certain inherent problems:

- The secondary loan market is not liquid (albeit secondary loan trading has been increasing) and suffers from high transaction costs.
- The sale of loans where the borrower must consent or where the borrower becomes aware of the sale, may damage the relationship between the bank and its client.
- The capacity to originate assets in non-traditional markets may be difficult and may expose the bank to new risks.
- Even where the asset can be originated, the lack of availability of funding in a particular currency, or the cost of that currency may prevent the investment or reduce returns to the bank to unacceptable levels.

These factors underlie the traditional illiquidity of credit markets.

Credit derivatives provide a viable alternative to these mechanisms for adjusting credit risk profiles. Total rate of return loan swaps can be employed to transfer the credit exposure to other banks or investors without the necessity of selling the credit asset. Exposure to other issuers to whom the bank is less exposed can similarly be generated through entry into total return loan swaps in which the bank assumes the credit exposure.

Alternatively, a bank overexposed to a particular issuer can purchase default protection against that issuer from an acceptable counterparty to reduce its exposure to optimal levels. As noted above, it can pay above market prices to achieve this reduction in risk as on a portfolio risk-return basis the improvement in portfolio risk allows achievement of target risk relative to risk after factoring in the cost of purchasing the default protection.

Similarly, the portfolio diversification may be enhanced by selling default swaps on the relevant credits to which it is underexposed. This can be done simultaneously to or in conjunction with the default swap whereby protection is purchased. The total effect of this set of transactions should be to enhance the overall risk-return characteristics of the overall credit portfolio with minimal cost (assuming the two premiums are similar in size).

5.4 Application Examples — Overview

The major types of applications involving credit derivatives, within the above framework, focus on:

- **Yield enhancement:** This entails the ability to trade expectations about credit risk attributes (credit spreads or default risk) and monetization of these expectations. This can be done in derivative format off-balance sheet or in the form of structured notes as investments. The use of structured notes can allow the gains from the monetization of these credit risk expectations to be incorporated in the yield or return of the fixed income securities thereby assisting in enhancing portfolio returns. In this context, the investor is allowed access to credit risk in isolation from other risks for the purpose of trading/positioning.
- **Credit risk management within financial institutions:** This entails either the transfer of credit risk through total rate of return credit swaps or purchase of credit default swaps to reduce the entity's exposure to a particular counterparty. It also entails the use of these types of instruments to enhance the management of credit portfolios through portfolio diversification in order to enhance the risk-return characteristics of the portfolio.

- **Credit risk management within non-financial institutions:** This entails similar objectives to that within financial institutions. It entails the ability to isolate and reduce undesired credit exposures incidental to the primary operating activities of the entity such as that arising from trade receivables, and supplier financing. This exposure may be to individual entities or to a geographic region or industry sector. The exposure may arise from the normal course of trading or from a specific project. It will also entail the management of the cost of funding of the entity through the use of credit derivatives or investment in default swaps as a higher-yielding source of return on surplus funds.

Figure 5.2 sets out the type of application analyzed by user group.

Figure 5.2   Applications of Credit Derivatives

Type of User	Type of Application
Banks/Financial Institutions	• Credit exposure reduction • Portfolio management/diversification
Fixed Income Investors	• Yield enhancement • Credit exposure reduction
Corporations	• Credit exposure reduction • Management of financing costs • Yield enhancement

5.5   Bank/Financial Institution Applications

5.5.1   Credit Portfolio Management[9]

In this section, examples of applications of credit derivatives by banks/financial institutions in the reduction of credit exposure or management of portfolios of credit assets are considered.

---

[9]   For an overview, see Allen, Robert 1998, "Approaches to Bank Credit Diversification: Credit Derivatives and their Alternatives" *Credit Derivatives: Applications for Risk Management, Investment and Portfolio Optimisation*, Risk Books, London, Chapter 1; Gontarek, Walter 1998, "Hedging With Credit Derivatives: Practical Applications and Considerations," *Credit Derivatives: Applications for Risk Management, Investment and Portfolio Optimisation*, Risk Books, London, Chapter 2; Gontarek, Walter "Today's Credit Derivatives Market," in Storrow, Jamie 1999, *Credit Derivatives: Key Issues (2nd Ed.)*; British Bankers Association, London, Chapter 2; Watzinger, Herman "Credit Derivatives In Bank Loan Portfolio Management – A Practitioner's Approach," in Storrow, Jamie 1999, *Credit Derivatives: Key Issues (2nd Edition)*, British Bankers Association, London, Chapter 4

Example 1 — Reducing Loan Exposure

Assume Bank A has a high level of credit exposure to Company X and the automobile industry generally. Within its portfolio, Bank A considers it would benefit from a reduction in its exposure to both this specific borrower and the sector. The exposure is primarily in the form of medium-term loans.

The physical solution for Bank A would traditionally be to seek to sell off some of the exposure to Company X in the secondary loan market. The major difficulties may include:

- The lack of liquidity in the secondary loan market.
- The documentary problems in any secondary market asset sale.
- The potential damage to the bank's relationship with its client (caused by either advising or seeking consent to the sale).

Several alternative solutions to this problem, utilizing credit derivatives, are feasible:

- **Total return swap:** This would entail Bank A entering into a total return swap with a counterparty where it pays the total return on a loan or loans extended to Company X in exchange for receiving US$ LIBOR. The effect of the transaction is to shift the full credit exposure of its loans to Company X to the counterparty, substituting the credit of the counterparty (on the loan swap) for the full credit risk on the loans.
- **Credit default swap:** This would entail Bank A entering into a credit default swap whereby it would purchase protection from the counterparty against the default of Company X on the reference obligations. The transaction effectively substitutes the counterparty credit of the counterparty providing protection for its exposure to Company X.

In each case, the derivative transaction avoids the difficulty of the physical transaction in the secondary loan market. This is possible because of the fact that the credit derivative-based solutions do not require the sale of the loan assets. The loan assets continue to remain on the balance sheet of the Bank.

The following aspects of the derivative solutions should be noted:

- Bank A can, as noted previously, pay theoretically a higher rate of return on the risk of Company X than current market rates. This is because of the improvement in its portfolio risk. This is a result of the benefits of the reduction in concentration risk through reduction in the exposure to individual obligors to which the bank is overexposed. This should make it feasible to transfer this exposure to counterparties who will be receiving higher than market returns as an incentive to assume the risk.[10]

---

[10] While intellectually tractable, this is in practise difficult primarily for organizational and income/earnings attribution reasons; see discussion in Chapter 20

- Bank A can offset any cost of the derivatives (the net cash flow loss from the credit spread lost in the case of the total return loan swap or the default swap premium paid away to purchase protection) by taking on credit risk. This can be done by selling protection on credit risk to which it is underexposed. This can be in the form of either a total return swap where it assumes the credit risk or a credit default swap where it is the seller of protection. As also noted above, Bank A can facilitate its purchase of the credit risk by requiring lower than market returns on underexposed counterparties, reflecting the fact that increasing credit exposure to these counterparties results in a proportionately higher increase in portfolio return relative to an increase in portfolio risk.
- The credit derivatives entail the bank assuming the credit risk of the counterparty on the derivative transaction to reduce its risk to Company X. Therefore, it utilizes credit lines and deploys credit capital against the entity selling its protection on Company X.

Example 2 — Unfunded Credit Risk

Assume Bank A has term credit lines available to Company X. The market price for Company X credit is now LIBOR plus 40 bp. Bank A's target return on risk for Company X is 45 bp pa on fully funded assets and 35 bp pa on unfunded obligations. Bank A can exceed its target return in US$ because it enjoys funding at LIBOR minus 10 bp reflecting its strong credit rating (AA) and its superior access to US$ funding. The only asset currently available is a £ asset reflecting Company X's current borrowing requirements. Bank A's £ cost of fund is £ LIBOR plus 5 bp, reflecting its relatively less advantageous access to £ funding. This funding cost disadvantage means that Bank A is unable to fund this £ loan at a level that ensures a return commensurate either with its target returns or the return on US$ assets for the same credit.

The physical solution to this problem would entail trading in the secondary loan market to seek to acquire a US$ loan asset that satisfies Bank A's targets. This approach to the problem is subject to the same difficulties noted above in Example 1.

Several alternative solutions to this problem utilizing credit derivatives are feasible:

- **Total return swap:** This would entail Bank A entering into a total return swap with a counterparty, where it receives the total return on the £ loan extended to Company X (that is, £ LIBOR plus 40 bp) in exchange for paying £ LIBOR plus a margin. As long as the margin payable is less than 5 bp, Bank A is able to achieve its target return. This reflects the fact that the swap effectively provides it with £ funding. The unfunded and off-balance sheet nature of the transaction also lowers the threshold return target. The effect of the transaction is to allow Bank A to assume the full credit exposure of the £ loans to Company X without the necessity of funding the £ asset directly.

- **Credit default swap:** This would entail Bank A entering into a credit default swap where it would sell protection to the counterparty against the default of Company X on the reference obligations. As long as this default swap nets Bank A a net fee of 35 bp pa, it meets the bank's target return levels on unfunded obligations (the default swap is off-balance-sheet).

The total return swap and the credit default swap transaction in this example is attractive to the counterparty transferring the credit exposure of Company X to Bank A. This reflects the fact that under each transaction, it creates a synthetic AA rated asset (based on the rating of Bank A). This is done through the extension of the £ loan to Company X while simultaneously transferring the credit exposure of Company X to Bank A. The return on this asset is approximately LIBOR plus 5 bp which may compare favorably to direct returns on AA rated assets.

Example 3 — Credit Line Utilization/Forward Start Credit Derivatives

Assume Bank A (AA+) has medium-term (five-year) credit lines for Company X (BBB+). The comparative term structure of credit spreads for Company B is as follows:

Maturity (years)	Bank A (AA+)	Company X (BBB+)
1–2	LIBOR – 15 bp pa	LIBOR + 30 bp pa
3–4	LIBOR – 10 bp pa	LIBOR + 40 bp pa
5	LIBOR – 10 bp pa	LIBOR + 50 bp pa

Assume Bank A's target return on its exposure to Company X is around 40 bp pa for funded exposures and 30 bps for unfunded exposures for maturity up to five years.

On a portfolio basis, Bank A's lines to Company X are currently utilized by a two-year loan that is yielding LIBOR plus 35 bp (this is the remaining term to maturity of an existing loan). The asset does not meet Bank A's return criteria.

The physical solution to this problem would entail the sale of the existing loan in the secondary market and the entry into or purchase of a longer term loan that meets the return criteria. However, the secondary market transactions are subject to the difficulties identified while the alternative assets might not be readily available.

The credit derivative solution would entail one of the following transactions:

- **Total return swap:** Bank A enters into a total return swap transferring the return on the two-year loan to Company X to a counterparty while simultaneously entering into a swap whereby it receives the return on a five-year loan asset of Company X. If both transactions are done at current market levels, then Bank A will generate a credit asset at an effective return of around 52 .2 bp pa over LIBOR (the slight premium reflecting the additional 5 bp pa in return excess in the first two years amortized at 6.0% pa). This would allow Bank A to meet its target returns and enhance its utilization of risk capital committed to the available credit lines.

- **Credit default swap:** Bank A may enter into a forward start credit default swap protecting the counterparty against default by Company X. The swap will cover a period of three years commencing in two years from the present. Over the first two years, Bank A continues to hold its loan exposure to Company X. The default swap does not operate allowing the bank to allocate part of the premium received to enhance its returns on the loan asset. At the end of Year 2 where the loan has expired, Bank A has effectively an unfunded exposure to Company X that is earning a rate of return which is above the target rate of return. Bank A may continue to maintain this unfunded exposure or buy back the default swap and acquire new exposure to Company X either in the loan market or synthetically. The total return (combining the existing two-year loan and the three-year credit default swap commencing two years forward) is around 52.2 bp pa over LIBOR over the full five-year period. This is in excess of its return target.

The above transaction is based on the fact that the counterparty to each of the credit derivative is able to create a synthetic AA+ equivalent asset. This is done through purchasing a credit exposure to Company X and purchasing protection against that exposure from Bank A for the last three years of the transaction. This may generate a return on a funded asset in excess of that available directly on a AA+ asset.

The increasing structure of credit spreads creates a natural trading opportunity for Bank A. At the end of Year 2, the value of the default put, which has a remaining term of three years out of spot, is calculated off the credit margins for Years 1 to 3. As these are lower than the margin for five-year risk, assuming no change in the credit spread structure, Bank A should be able to reverse its position in the credit default swap for a gain.

Example 4 — Credit Spread Risk Management

Assume Bank A has a substantial portfolio of loans to a particular industry. It is concerned that credit spreads to the industry may increase. It is seeking to reduce its exposure to this expected increase in spreads.

The only traditional mechanism for reducing this exposure to credit spreads would be to sell off its loan exposures in the secondary market, which is unlikely to be able to be effected on a cost efficient basis.

An alternative mechanism would be for Bank A to enter into a one-year synthetic lending or standby credit facility. It pays a fee. In return, Bank A has the right at the end of one year, at its option, to require the counterparty to:
- Provide a three-year revolving credit to a number of leading companies in the relevant industry sector (at pre-agreed spreads over LIBOR); or
- Enter into an asset swap (on underlying bonds issued by these companies) at a pre-agreed yield over LIBOR.

The transaction is structured on a cash settlement basis. The payment to be received by Bank A is calculated upon exercise of its rights under the agreement as the difference between the agreed spreads and secondary market spreads (loans and/or asset swaps) on the reference companies.

The transaction operates as follows:
- Bank A pays the fee.
- At the end of one year, if credit spreads on the industry as represented by the reference credits have not increased above an agreed level, the facility expires unutilized.
- At the end of one year, if credit spreads on this industry sector have increased above the agreed level over LIBOR, the facility is exercised. Bank A receives a cash payment that is designed to offset the loss in value in its portfolio as a result of the increase in credit spreads.

The advantage to Bank A of this structure includes:
- The known cost of the increase in credit spreads as represented by the fee paid.
- The ability to protect its portfolio from erosion in value from increases in credit spreads. This is particularly the case where spreads have declined and continuing to extend credit or acquire assets at these historically low levels exposes the lenders to high risk from spread changes.

The effectiveness of the hedge is contingent upon the extent of correlation as between the reference credits and the underlying portfolio sought to be hedged.

The risk that can be hedged using this structure includes individual issuers and specific geographic or country exposures as well as industry sectors.

5.5.2   Managing Syndication Risk

In this section, examples of applications of credit derivatives by banks/financial institutions in the syndication process of credit assets are considered.

Example 1 — Hedging Syndication Risk

Assume Bank A is approached by a major client (Company X) to assist it in raising US$2,000 million to facilitate an acquisition. The loan is to be provided by four banks, each committing US$500 million. Each bank will be asked to underwrite US$500 million of which it plans to syndicate US$250 million, leaving it with a final exposure of US$250 million. The loan will have a term of three years, although it is anticipated that the loan will be either repaid prior to maturity from the proceeds of asset sales planned following the acquisition or refinanced in the capital markets.

Bank A wishes to meet this client requirement for the following reasons:
- It wishes to support a major client and protect its existing relationship.
- It believes that the transaction will generate significant collateral business (foreign exchange, hedging, and capital markets transaction associated with the refinancing) for which it wishes to position itself.

It is conscious that entry into this transaction will have the following difficulties:
- The large quantum of the exposure will mean that Bank A will be close to its internal and external prudential limits for exposure to Company X.
- The exposure may in fact prevent Bank A from undertaking the ancillary business that it views as the rationale for entering into this transaction.
- Bank A is aware that Company X will seek to restrict it ability to sell down it exposure on the loan through sub-participation or assignment transactions (by requiring Company X's consent to any such transaction). Company X's reasoning is that it seeks to limit its banking relationship to enable more effective control of its lending groups.

Bank A agrees to provide the loan. It now has two levels of risk (exposure to credit spread changes in the loan market and default risk on the borrower) which it seeks to manage using credit derivatives. The following strategies are available:
- **Credit spread risk:** Bank A can seek to hedge the exposure to credit spread risk on its underwriting position. This is through entry into a credit spread

forward or through the purchase of a credit spread put enabling it to effectively short the spread (as it is effectively long the credit spread through the underwriting). The credit spread may be on the specific borrower (which, in practise, for a transaction of this size would be difficult) or on a basket of similar credit quality issuers. The latter does not provide direct protection on changes in the credit spread of Company X. However, it provides general protection on unexpected changes in the credit spread as a result of changes in credit conditions in the syndication market.

- **Credit default risk:** Bank A can purchase a credit default swap to protect against a default of Company X. This swap will effectively reduce the exposure to the issuer to a level sought by Bank A while allowing it to undertake the transaction for its clients. The protection can be purchased initially to protect it until syndication is complete as well as following syndication to maintain the exposure within it desired levels.
- **Synthetic syndications:** Bank A can enter into total return swaps to effectively reduce its exposure on its final participation in this financing by paying the return on the loan in return for receiving LIBOR. This will simultaneously allow it to free up its credit capacity for the other transactions that it wishes to undertake for the client without the need to sell off the loan assets. As it remains the lender of record for the transaction, Company X will not have to deal with the lenders or investors who have effectively acquired the credit exposure thereby at least partially meeting its objectives.

Several aspects of the credit derivative based hedging strategies are noteworthy:
- The term of the protection against default is capable of being customized. For example, Bank A may choose to sell down its exposure for a period shorter than the scheduled term of the loan (three years). This allows it to manage the risk dynamically while also potentially arbitraging the default valuation curve as the risk of default and the credit spread should increase over time.
- The structure of the transactions allows Bank A pricing flexibility. For example, it may be prepared to pay a premium over the market price of Company X's risk to reduce its risk. This reflects the fact that it may be overexposed in a portfolio sense to this issuer or the earning potential from the ancillary business which it is targeting (for which it needs to free up credit lines).
- The credit derivatives transactions are also attractive to market participants as a means of acquiring credit exposure to Company X. The size of the transaction and the minimum participation amounts in syndications has increased rapidly to the point where the credit derivatives market as depicted

may be an attractive mechanism for banks to take smaller participations in these transactions consistent with their risk appetites. This process creates an opportunity for Bank A (as the wholesaler) to capture value by way of adjustments in pricing from the banks seeking to participate but only at levels below the minimum levels in the primary markets (the retail buyers).

Example 2 — Synthetic Syndication[11]

In 1997, CIBC/CIBC Woody Gundy, the Canadian banking group, in conjunction with co-arranger Ceskoslovenka Obchodni Banka (CSOB) agreed to arrange a US$500 million loan to Aero Vodochody (AV), a Czech aerospace manufacturer. The loan package included import financing, a letter of credit facility, and a revolving loan.

However, a bridge loan of US$100 million became necessary. This was because of a lengthy government process for the approval of the loan. During the approval process, AV had commitments to make payments on contracts associated with the project to vendors/contractors. These payments were intended to be financed by the facilities negotiated. CIBC agreed to make a US$100 million bridge loan to meet this interim financing requirement.

However, CIBC needed to reduce its exposure on the bridge loan as soon as possible due to credit concentration issues. In order to hedge its credit risk on the bridge loan, CIBC entered into two credit default swaps for a total of US$50 million. Under these swaps, CIBC pays the two counterparties an agreed fee in return for the counterparties assuming the risk of default. The swaps were for a period of around one year. In effect, the credit default swaps reduced CIBC exposure on the bridge loan by 50%.

The reference credit for the default swap was a US$250 million five-year bond issued by Czech Export Bank and guaranteed by the Czech Republic. The rationale for use of the bond as the reference credit and asset was the fact that AV was also state owned and from a legal and commercial perspective, there was sufficient similarity between the obligor on the loan and the reference credit to provide reasonable protection.

Example 3 — Maturity Restriction for Loan Participants

Assume Bank A is syndicating a project loan for Company X (the project's principal sponsor) for US$350 million for a term of 12 years (average life of eight years). The complexity of the project makes the syndication difficult. A

---

[11] The example set out was reported in Fortune, Mark October 18, 1997, "Default Swaps Enable Czech Loan," *International Financing Review*, Issue 1205, pp 109

major problem encountered is that some of the banks invited have internal restrictions that prevent them from extending credit beyond a final maturity of 10 years. The participation of these banks is important from not only the point of view of securing the finance, but in providing reassurance to other banks in the syndicate.

Bank A has two choices. The first entails restructuring the loan debt repayment schedule. This may be difficult for operational reasons and may alter the economics and risk profile of the project. The second is to use credit derivatives to seek to redefine the risk exposure of the relevant banks.

Two possible credit derivatives strategies are feasible:

- **Total return swap:** The final two years exposure of the relevant banks could be hedged. Protection could be provided by another bank (within the syndicate or outside the syndicate) or the project sponsor through entry into a forward loan swap (for two years commencing in 10 years' time). This effectively transfers the credit exposure for the project from the banks in the syndicate subject to the constraint of final maturity.
- **Credit default swap:** The final two years of exposure could be also hedged by the relevant banks purchasing default protection for the final two years from other banks or the sponsor.

In both cases, the project loan would be undertaken normally with the relevant banks entering into separate hedges for their exposure with the indemnifying banks or the sponsor. This has the effect of allowing the syndicate and loan structure to be preserved with the minority lenders constraints being satisfied separately and without disruption to the project financing.

The hedges can be put in place permanently or for a period of two years only. The later would be designed to ensure that the 10-year constraint was honored with the exposure reverting upon the project's remaining term falling within the restriction.

5.5.3 Hedging Dynamic Exposure on Derivatives

Credit derivatives structures are also feasible in the management of variable credit exposure instruments such as derivative transactions.

Example 1 — Managing Cross-Currency Swap Exposure

Assume Bank A enters into a 12-year cross-currency swap with Bank B. The swap is for a notional principal of US$100 million and entails Bank A receiving at a fixed rate of 6.00% pa and paying US$ LIBOR. The exchange rate at commencement is US$1: ¥160.00. At the time of entry, the expected credit exposure is expected to peak at US$30 million (30% of US$ principal) with an average exposure of around US$20 million (20% of US$ principal). The credit limits and returns on risk capital on this transaction are based on these anticipated credit exposures. The transaction is set out in Figure 5.3.

Figure 5.3   US$/¥ Cross-Currency Swaps

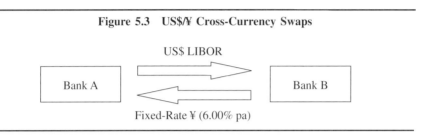

US$ LIBOR

Bank A   Bank B

Fixed-Rate ¥ (6.00% pa)

Assume that four years have elapsed and the US$/¥ exchange rate is at 90 and the ¥ interest rate for the remaining term of the swap has fallen to 2.80% pa. The replacement value for the swap is now about US$218 million, representing an effective mark-to-market credit exposure of US$118 million (118% of US$ principal). This exposure is significantly above that which was anticipated reflecting the unexpected volatility and directional change in the exchange and interest rates.

During this period, Bank B that was AA+ rated at the commencement of the transaction has been downgraded to a A– with a negative credit outlook. This has further exacerbated the credit exposure.

The increase in exposure has the following implications for Bank A:

• The higher than expected credit exposure has worsened the transaction exposure such that the bank is incurring a loss on the transaction in return on capital terms.

• The increase in exposure may have caused the bank to sharply increase its utilization of or breach its counterparty limits to Bank B. It may also breach its prudential exposures to a single counterparty.

• The increased exposure may have created higher than acceptable concentration risk levels within Bank A's portfolio and also significantly reduced its trading liquidity by tying up it interbank counterparty credit lines.

Correcting this exposure problem is difficult for Bank A. This reflects the difficulty and cost of unwinding the swap in the market, which might not be possible because of the counterparty's lower credit rating, the cash impact on the counterparty in unwinding the trade, and the impact that this request might have on the relationship between the banks. The counterparty might also not be prepared to implement credit enhancement measures (not provided for in the terms of the original documentation covering the swap) such as re-couponing, mark-to-market or cash collateralization.

An alternative to the termination of the swap or provision of additional credit enhancement is the purchase by Bank A of a credit default swap where the counterparty (Bank C) will make a payment to Bank A in the event of a default by Bank B of an amount equal to the mark-to-market value of the swap as at the time of default. The default event may be defined generally or with reference to default on the swap itself. This transaction is set out in Figure 5.4.

Figure 5.4   Swap Guarantee Structure

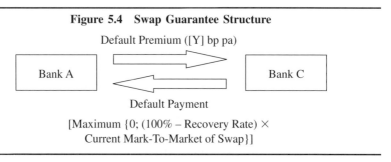

Default Premium ([Y] bp pa)

Bank A   Bank C

Default Payment
[Maximum {0; (100% – Recovery Rate) ×
Current Mark-To-Market of Swap}]

The transaction operates in a manner analogous to a normal default swap:
• The bank seeking protection pays a premium (on an upfront or periodic basis).
• The bank providing protection agrees to make a payment if the Swap/ Derivatives Counterparty defaults.

The principal distinguishing feature is that the default payment is linked to the mark-to-market value of the swap/derivatives transaction at the time of default. The default payout will be specified as:

Default payment = (100% minus Agreed Recovery Rate) × Current Mark-to-Market Value of the Transaction

In practice, for reasons of certainty and convenience, the recovery rate is frequently fixed as an agreed percentage at the commencement of the transaction.

The credit default swap linked to the swap value is different from a normal credit swap in that amount of the default payment is dynamic and linked to the value of the swap which is a function of market variables. Bank A will only suffer a loss if Bank B defaults, there is an amount owing to Bank A under the swap, and the counterparty providing protection under the swap also defaults. This multiple contingency structure significantly enhances the credit quality of the exposure that will generally be superior to that of both Bank B and the credit swap counterparty.

The credit swap linked to the value of the swap is capable of being structured in a number of alternative ways:

- The default swap may cover any exposure under the swap.
- The default swap may cover exposure by to a pre agreed amount.
- The default swap may cover exposure above a minimum amount.

The term of the protection can also be varied with protection being able to be obtained for periods up to the full remaining term of the swap.

Example 2 — Managing Contingent Interest Rate Exposure

Assume Company A, an asset finance/leasing company, leases equipment at fixed rentals. The company raises floating-rate funding, which is hedged into fixed rate to provide an asset liability match between its funding and the leasing assets. In the event of default, the company takes possession of the asset and re-leases the equipment. The re-leasing risk is combined with interest rate risk. This interest rate risk derives from the fact that if interest rates fall from the level prevailing when the original lease is undertaken, Company A will be exposed to the risk of loss from the termination of the interest rate swap.

In order to manage its exposure to this contingency, Company A could enter into a credit default swap where the payoff is linked to the mark-to-market exposure on the interest rate swap. The reference credit for the default swap would be the lessee of the equipment. The structure of the transaction would be as follows:

- Company A pays a commitment fee on the overall notional amount. This fee would be a fraction of the normal fee payable on a default swap.
- Company A would be liable to pay an additional amount (the full premium on a default swap) if the mark-to-market exposure in any period becomes negative (that is, in the event of a default the termination of the swap would result in a loss to Company A). This calculation would typically be done quarterly or monthly. In the event that the mark-to-market exposure under the swap becomes positive, the additional fee is not payable.
- In the event of the lessee defaults, Company A would receive a payment equal to the mark-to-market value of the swap (provided it is negative).

This type of structure has the advantage of being more cost effective as the party seeking protection only is liable to pay the full fee where it requires protection with its only ongoing cost being the commitment fee. The effect of this structure is to provide default protection only where underlying market movements would result in a termination loss on the swap in the event of default of the lessee.

5.5.4 Optimizing Balance Sheet Capital Utilization and Return on Risk Capital

Credit derivatives represent an effective mechanism for assuming credit risk within return on risk capital constraints.

Example 1 - Balance Sheet/Funding Arbitrage

Assume Bank A is a lower-rated bank. Its higher cost of funding makes it difficult to generate a positive spread on loans to highly rated issuers, at least a spread which provides it with its required rate of return on capital. This pressure has forced the bank to make loans to more risky lower-rated borrowers at a much higher level of its asset portfolio, to the point where it is now overexposed to these categories of credits.

Bank A may be able to address these difficulties by assuming credit exposures to higher-rated credits by entering into credit default swaps where it provides protection against default. This strategy has the following effects:

- The default swap does not need to be funded, thereby minimizing the impact of Bank A's unfavorable funding costs.
- Any problems regarding the counterparty risk of Bank A as a counterparty to the default swap can be addressed by some form of credit enhancement (collateralization and periodic mark-to-market provisions).
- The ability to diversify away the concentration to lower credit quality borrowers should allow the overall risk-return on the credit portfolio to be significantly enhanced.

  There are significant advantages to the counterparty to the default swap obtaining protection against default on the better credit quality assets. These include:

- Maximization of the advantage of its lower funding cost. This reflects the fact that the premium paid for obtaining the protection against default may be less than the effective spread (asset return less the lower cost bank's funding cost) allowing it to increase its overall returns.
- The strategy allows an effective increase in the diversification of its own credit portfolio but conceivably on economically more attractive terms.

Example 2 — Credit Capital Arbitrage

Assume Bank A is about to extend credit to a borrower. The loan is to a

corporation rated investment grade (BBB/Baa) for five years and attracts a
spread of 45 bp over LIBOR. The bank has the choice of booking the loan in
one of the following ways:

- Extend a traditional loan that is held on the bank balance sheet and fully
  funded.
- Arrange for the loan to be made by another entity (Bank B) with Bank A
  assuming the risk of the underlying loan through either a total return swap on
  the loan or selling credit protection to the loan provider through a credit
  default swap.

The two sets of transactions are depicted in Figure 5.5.

Figure 5.5   Traditional Loan versus Credit Derivatives Structures

Traditional Loan Structure

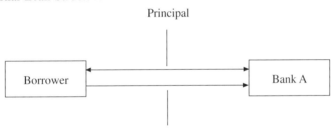

**Non-Funded Loan – Risk Assumed Through Total Return Swap or
Credit Default Swap**

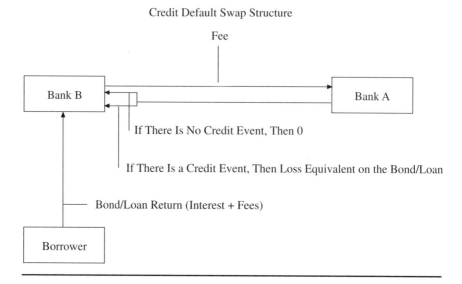

Credit Default Swap Structure

Under each structure, Bank A assumes the credit risk of the bond purchased or loan made to the ultimate borrower. However, the capital required to be held against the underlying risk position may be different.[12]

The bank loan is booked in the banking book and 8% capital must be held against the underlying risk (equivalent to face value multiplied by the counterparty risk weighting which for a corporate is 100%). The total return swap or the credit default swap can be booked in the trading book. In order to qualify for trading book treatment, the bank must be able to mark-to-market the underlying reference asset. If held in the trading book, the capital charge is lower than the banking book for qualifying assets. The capital charge on qualifying assets is set as follows:

- 0.25% (residual maturity six months or less)
- 1.00% (residual maturity between 6 and 24 months)
- 1.60% (residual maturity exceeding 24 months)

The "qualifying" category would apply to securities issued by public sector entities and multilateral development banks, plus other securities that are:
- Rated investment grade (rates Baa or higher by Moody's and BBB or higher by Standard & Poor's) by at least two credit agencies specified by the relevant supervisor

---

[12] For a detailed discussion of regulatory treatment of credit derivatives, see Chapter 19

- Rated investment grade by one rating agency and not less than investment grade by any other rating agency specified by the supervisor (subject to supervisory oversight)
- Unrated, but deemed to be of comparable investment quality by the bank or securities firm, and the issuer has securities listed on a recognized stock exchange (subject to supervisory approval)

In the situation described, the capital to be held in the trading may be as low as 1.60%, some 80% lower than that required under the banking book treatment. The return on risk capital is set out in the table below:

Calculation of Risk Adjusted Return

Nominal Value	$1,000,000
Loan Spread	0.45%
Total Return Swap Margin/Credit Default Swap Fee	0.45%
Counterparty Risk Weighting	100.0%
Capital Requirement	
Banking Book	8.00%
Trading Book	1.60%

Return Calculations

	Banking Book	Trading Book
Net Income	$4,500	$4,500
Capital Required	$80,000	$16,000
Return on Capital	5.625%	28.125%
% increase in Return		500.0

The calculation of return assumes that Bank A receives the full net spread on the loan. However, even where the net spread received is lower than that on the loan, the return to the bank on a return on risk capital basis is greater than for the direct loan. For example, if the net spread received on the total return swap or feed for the credit default swap is say 30 bp, the return on capital to Bank A is 18.75% (an increase of over three times).

The decision to seek to take advantage of the trading book treatment requires the bank to mark to market the asset with an gain or loss being taken to profit and loss creating potential volatility in the earnings. Inclusion of the transaction in the trading book may also require market risk capital to be held against the position where the position incurs general market risk (for example if the asset is not match funded).

Example 3 — Credit Capital/Funding Arbitrage

Assume a loan to Company X for $10 million for five years priced at LIBOR plus 40 bp. The following are the banks that are prepared to participate in the transaction:

- Bank A rated AA that is able to fund the loan at LIBOR minus 20 bp.
- Bank B rated BBB that is able to fund the loan at LIBOR plus 10 bp.

Assume that both banks are subject to regulatory capital requirements where each bank is required to hold capital of 8% against risk weighted assets. The risk weighting for assets is 100% for corporations (the loan to Company X) and 20% for OECD Banks (both Bank A and Bank BBB).

Where both counterparties provided the loan on balance sheet, the resulting return to the banks is summarized in the table below:

Loan Returns

Bank	A	B
Interest Income	$640,000	$640,000
Interest Expense	-$533,600	-$561,200
Net Interest Margin	$106,400	$78,800
Capital Held	$800,000	$800,000
Return On Capital	13.30%	9.85%

Notes:
1. The interest calculations assume a LIBOR rate of 6.00% pa.
2. Both banks are assumed to hold capital of 8% exactly against the loan.
3. The funding for the loan is: $9,200,000 in loans at an interest expense charged at LIBOR plus/minus the bank's funding spread; and $800,000 in capital is not specifically charged for. The calculation, therefore, is $ 9,200,000 × 5.80% (6.00% minus 0.20%) and $ 9,200,000 × 6.10% (6.00% + 0.10%).
4. Return on capital is calculated as the Net Interest Margin divided by the Capital held ($800,000).

Assume the transaction is restructured as follows:
- The higher-rated bank (Bank A) extends the loan.
- Bank A then enters into a default swap whereby it pays a fee to Bank B in return for Bank B assuming the default risk of Company X.

Economically, the transaction has the effect of allowing Bank B to create exposure to the credit/default risk of Company X while limiting the funding cost disadvantage suffered by Bank B.

Assuming that the fee paid by Bank A to Bank B for entering into the default swap is equal to the credit spread of 40 bp. The transaction economics are set out in the tables below:

Return for Bank A

Interest Income	$640,000
Interest Expense	-$570,720
Net Interest Margin	$69,280
Credit Default Swap Fee	-$40,000
Net Income	$29,280
Capital Held	$160,000
Return On Capital	18.300%
Change In Return (%)	38%
Equivalent Loan Margin	0.80%
Incremental Loan Margin	0.40000%

Notes:
1. Assumes that the counterparty risk weighting is reduced from 100% to 20% implying a reduction in capital from $800,000 (8% of $10 million × 100%) to $160,000 (8% of $10 million × 20%).
2. The funding for the loan is calculated as $9,840,000 × 5.80% (6.00% − 0.20%).
3. Change in Return (%) refers to the percentage change in the return on credit derivatives based transaction compared to the conventional loan described previously.
4. The concept of equivalent loan margin is based on deriving the margin required to generate the return on capital achieved under a traditional loan structure.

Return for Bank B

Credit Default Swap Fee	$40,000
Interest On Capital	$46,400
Net Income	$86,400
Capital Held	$800,000
Return On Capital	10.80%
Change In Return (%)	10%
Equivalent Loan Margin	0.476%
Incremental Loan Margin	0.0760%

Notes:
1. Assumes that the capital required to be held is invested to yield LIBOR-20 bp, that is $800,000 \times 5.80\%$ (6.00% − 0.20%).
2. Change in Return (%) refers to the percentage change in the return on credit derivatives based transaction compared to the conventional loan described previously.
3. The concept of equivalent loan margin is based on deriving the margin required to generate the return on capital achieved under a traditional loan structure.

As is evident, the transaction enables both banks to significantly enhance returns on capital as a result of the transaction.

Example 4 — Synthetic Loan/Credit Capital Arbitrage

Assume Bank A has available credit lines for Company X. The credit lines are for a maturity of (up to) five years. Under current market conditions, the pricing for three-year assets for Company X is around LIBOR plus 30 bp pa. Bank A requires a return of around LIBOR plus 40 bp pa for Company X risk. This return is not available directly in the market.

Bank A may be able to acquire Company X risk through entry into a one-year (usually 364 days) synthetic lending or standby credit facility. It receives a fee of 17.5 bp flat in return for agreeing to provide at the end of one year, at the option of the counterparty, a three-year revolving credit to Company X (spread of LIBOR plus 40 bp pa; undrawn fee of 20 bp pa), or enter into an asset swap (on an underlying security issued by Company X) at a yield of LIBOR plus 40 bp pa.

The transaction operates as follows:
- Bank A receives the fee
- At the end of one year, if credit spreads on Company X have not increased, the facility expires unutilized
- At the end of one year, if credit spreads on Company X have increased above LIBOR plus 40 bp, the facility is exercised by the entry into the revolving credit facility or, more realistically, the counterparty placing an asset swap with Bank A at LIBOR plus 40 bp pa

The advantage to Bank A of this structure includes:
- The transaction meets the target return levels that cannot be met in the direct loan market.
- The transaction may receive favorable regulatory treatment for capital adequacy where the transaction is for maturity less than one year

5.6 Investor Applications

5.6.1 Synthetic/Non-accessible Asset

In this section, examples of applications of credit derivatives by institutional investors and asset managers to create synthetic assets are considered.

The examples discussed do not entail generally the use of leverage to increase the exposure of the investor to changes in the value of the underlying credits. In each case, the transaction could be leveraged, usually by increasing the notional principal of the credit derivative transaction, to increase the sensitivity of the investment return for the investor. The examples also focus generally on the use of credit derivatives in off balance sheet format. In practise, the credit derivative may be combined with a fixed-income instrument as a structured note where the investor does not wish to transact the credit derivative directly or seeks a fully funded cash investment.

Example 1 — Synthetic Bank Loan Investment
Assume Investor M seeks to invest in commercial bank loans for its money market funds. The rationale is to acquire these assets to generate risk adjusted returns which are above those available from other comparable floating rate investments.

The direct physical solution would be to directly participate in loans in the primary syndications market or acquire loan participations in the secondary markets. These approaches suffer from a number of inherent difficulties including:
- The absence of a loan syndication infrastructure making participation in the primary loan market difficult
- The identified difficulties inherent in the secondary loan market will constrain acquiring loan assets through this avenue

A credit derivatives-based solution would be to acquire this exposure synthetically by entering into the following transactions:
- **Total return swap:** This would entail Investor M entering into a total return loan swap with a counterparty whereby it receives the total return on the relevant loan(s) in exchange for paying LIBOR plus a margin.
- **Credit default swap:** This would entail Investor M entering into a credit default swap whereby it would sell protection to the counterparty against the default of the relevant borrowers on the reference obligations.

In each case, the credit derivative is combined with a cash investment equivalent to the face value of the swaps to effect fully fund the transaction (in effect, eliminating any leverage) to create a synthetic loan asset investment for the investor which avoids the issues identified with direct investment in the loans.

Example 2 — Synthetic Portfolio Investment

Assume Investor M wishes to invest in a diversified portfolio of high-yield bonds. The primary objective being to create a diversified investment in this asset class which is comparable to the high-yield index to which the performance of this portfolio is benchmarked.

The direct physical solution to this investment would be to replicate the high-yield index through direct investment in the underlying assets constituting the index. This approach has a number of issues associated with it including:

- The necessity to trade in a significant number of securities some of which may not be very liquid.
- The requirement for often odd-lot parcel sizes that might impact on the acquisition price.
- The potential lack of liquidity of the portfolio.
- The need for rebalancing if the index composition is altered or where the index weighting is changed.
- The issue of tracking error where the tracking portfolio of bonds fails to exactly replicate the index may lead to under performance.

A credit derivative-based solution would be to acquire this exposure synthetically by entering into a total rate of return loan swap based on the relevant high-yield index. This would entail Investor M entering into a total return loan swap with a counterparty whereby it receives the total return on the relevant index in exchange for paying LIBOR plus a margin.

This transaction together with a cash investment to effectively fund the LIBOR payments would effectively replicate the desired exposure to the high-yield index more efficiently than the physical investments. In particular, the problems identified above may be substantially avoided allowing the investor to achieve a diversified exposure to the high yield sector in a tradable format.

If required the investment in cash and the swap could be combined into a structured note issued by an acceptable issuer of suitable credit standing to provide the required exposure.

Example 3 — Synthetic Structured Investment

Assume Investor M is seeking to increase its exposure to Italian lira assets within its fixed income investment portfolio. However, it is subject to the following constraints:

1. It is at the upper limit of its exposure to the Republic of Italy and is not able to increase its exposure to Italian risk.
2. It has available credit capacity on Canadian risk particularly to those of the Canadian provinces to whom it is significantly underexposed on a portfolio risk basis.
3. It has a target maturity of three years.

The direct investment solution available would entail the Investor purchasing C\$ securities issued by the Canadian provinces and entering into a currency swap to convert the C\$ investment into lira. This direct solution has a number of difficulties:

• The available C\$ issues are of maturities significantly longer than three years.
• The entry into the C\$/lira cross-currency swap would require commitment of large counterparty credit limits.

One credit derivative-based solution would be to create the following synthetic asset in the form of a credit default structured note. The final maturity of the note is three years (consistent with the investor's target maturity), denominated in lira (as desired) with the redemption linked to the default of the reference securities issued by the Canadian provinces (to which the investor wishes to increase exposure).

In this particular case, the transaction is consistent with the investor achieving its investment objectives with the credit default structured note allowing it to effectively diversify its credit exposures within its investment currency and maturity constraints.

Example 4 — Synthetic Emerging Market Investment[13]

Assume Investor M wishes to increase its exposure within its fixed-income portfolio to the sovereign debt of an emerging market issuer – Country C. The investor is subject to a number of investment constraints:

1. The issuer must be the sovereign itself.
2. The investment must be principal protected.

---

[13] This particular type of synthetic asset is suggested in Wheat, Allen May 1995, "Developments in the OTC Derivatives Markets," *Financial Derivatives and Risk Management*, Vol 1, pp 37-44

3. The term of the investment must be not exceeding three years.
4. The investment must have liquidity.

The investor is focusing on Country C's outstanding Brady Bonds that satisfy criteria 1, 2, and 4. However, as the Brady bonds have a maturity of 30 years, they would violate criteria 3 making them ineligible investments.

A credit derivative-based synthetic asset may allow the investor to overcome the maturity constraint. This would entail the creation of a structured note issued by an issuer of acceptable credit quality which has a final maturity of three years where the redemption is linked to the Brady Bonds of Country C. This note will perform in a manner consistent with the performance of the underlying reference securities of the emerging markets issuer but the disaggregation of the maturity of the investment and the reference securities allows the synthetic note to meet the relevant investment criteria.

Example 5 — Convertible Arbitrage

In recent times, there has been increased interest in trading convertible bonds as a fixed-income security.[14] This has been the case in particular in relation to convertibles where the embedded equity option has little value as a result of a decline in the price of the underlying stock to levels well below the strike price of the option. Under these conditions, convertible and fixed-income arbitrage traders have looked to unbundle the security and repackage it through an asset swap.[15]

This form of trading has taken two forms:

- **Convertible arbitrage**: This structure entails a trader purchasing a convertible and separating the transaction into a conventional fixed-income bond and the embedded equity option. The equity option is sold to an equity derivative counterparty and the bond cash flows re-profiled into a floating-rate bond. The yield achievable is higher than would be available from a direct investment in a comparable bond issued by the underlying issuer.
- **Convertible and credit arbitrage:** This structure is the same as the above form of convertible arbitrage with an added feature. The additional feature is that the trader will typically purchase protection against the risk of default by the issuer in the form of a credit default swap. This has the effect of creating

---

[14] See Mahtani Arun, March 13, 1999, "Asset Swappers, Bond Investors Target Convertibles," *International Financing Review* Issue 1274, pp 75

[15] For a discussion of an asset swap, see Das, Satyajit 1994, *Swaps And Financial Derivatives*; LBC Information Services, Sydney; McGraw-Hill, Chicago, Chapter 18

a fixed-income security where the underlying credit risk is transformed from that of the issuer to that of the counterparty providing credit protection. The motivation is again the return achievable from this transaction relative to that on a comparable transaction where the underlying credit is the provider of credit protection.

The major drivers underlying these forms of transactions include:

- **Returns:** The yields available from these transactions have been very attractive on a relative value basis. This higher return, in the case of standard convertible arbitrage, is relative to returns available on comparable securities issued by the issuer or equivalent credit or, credit arbitrage, in the case of convertible and relative to returns available on the credit risk of the seller of credit protection or equivalent risk. As relative value groups in financial institutions and hedge funds systematically traded away pricing discrepancies in the conventional fixed income markets, the pricing anomalies in pricing equity linked securities were the center of trading focus. These pricing anomalies related to both the pricing of the bond itself (including any embedded optionality) and also the equity component.
- **Availability of investments:** The lack of the availability of fixed-income securities issued by the relevant issuer also contributed to the development of this type of transactions. Investors seeking fixed-income exposure to a particularly issuer may have been constrained by the lack of availability of securities issued by that particular issuer. Where the issuer has outstanding convertibles, the capacity to asset swap these securities to create a fixed income investor has proved attractive. For example, the lack of European corporate bond issuance in the period 1998–2000 contrasts with the significant volume of convertible and exchangeable bond issuance by European issuers. This created the opportunity to synthesize the credit risk of these issuers through convertible asset swaps. The risk is sold in two possible formats. The first form is as a conventional asset swap where the investor creates a floating rate investment returning a margin relative to LIBOR (in the currency of the investor's choice) by combining the purchase of the convertible, sale of the equity option back to the trader, and entry into an interest rate or currency swap. The second form entails assuming the credit risk indirectly through the sale of credit protection under a credit default swap. Under the second format, the trader purchases the convertible, sells the equity option to another trader, and purchases credit protection from the investor wanting to create credit exposure to the issuer. The trader is left with a substantially hedged position and an arbitrage profit. The investor can

assume the credit risk is a funded (credit linked note) or unfunded form (credit default swap).

The transactions are not free of risk. The presence of the equity option and the call features of the convertible (where the drivers are both the equity price and interest rates) make this type of transaction more complex than conventional asset swaps. These risks require the swap structure to be customized to the underlying asset to avoid any residual risk of the transaction. For the investor in the asset swap, the major residual issue is the uncertainty regarding the duration of the investment.[16]

Assume the investor purchases the following convertible bond:

Issuer	**Company A**
Maturity	November 15, 2010
Face Value Amount	US$10 million
Coupon	3.00% pa, payable annually (30/360 bond basis)
Current Price	73.75 plus accrued interest 2.35
Trade Date	August 22, 2001
Settlement Date	August 27, 2001
Purchase Price	US$7,609,412

The investor purchases the bond, sells the equity option to the trader, and enters into an interest rate swap to convert the cash flows into a synthetic floating-rate note paying a margin over LIBOR. The cash flows of the swap are as follows:

- **Initial cash flows:** There is no initial cash flow unless the investor want to adjust the amount invested to a round amount.[17]
- **Periodic payments:** The following exchanges take place over the life of the bond:
    1. On each annual coupon date of the convertible, the investor passes through to the swap counterparty the coupons on the convertible (US$ 30,000 calculated as 3.00% on US$30,000. Typically, the investor passes through

---

[16] See Das, Satyajit 1998, "Pricing & Risk Management of Equity Derivatives Transactions: Part 1," *Financial Products*, Issue 87, pp 18–23; "Pricing & Risk Management of Equity Derivatives Transactions: Part 2" (1998) *Financial Products*, Issue 89 pp 18–26

[17] For a discussion of the detailed structure of asset swaps, see Das, Satyajit (1994), *Swaps and Financial Derivatives*; LBC Information Services, Sydney; McGraw-Hill, Chicago, Chapter 18

the complete coupon including the initial full coupon despite the fact that the swap commences only a short time prior to the first coupon payment. The swap counterparty adjusts for this extra receipt in the margin paid on the floating rate side of the swap.

2. Every quarter (February 15, May 15, August 15, and November 15, commencing November 15, 2001 and ending November 15, 2010 unless terminated early), the investor receives a payment equivalent to 3-month US$ LIBOR plus a margin (say, 95 bps).[18]

- **Final termination:** Unless terminated early, the investor receives from the counterparty the purchase price paid for the convertible bond at the commencement of the asset swap and pays to the counterparty the US$10 million face value of the maturing convertible bond.
- **Early termination:** If the bond is converted or called prior to final maturity, the investor receives from the counterparty the purchase price paid for the convertible bond at the commencement of the asset swap and pays to the counterparty the amount received from the call of the convertible bond or transfers ownership of the convertible or the stock received as a result of conversion.

The diagram on the next page sets out the transaction cash flows:

The result of the transaction is that the investor has synthesized a floating-rate investment at a return of US$ LIBOR plus 95 bp. This compares to a return on a conventional bond issued by the issuer of comparable maturity which would swap into US$ LIBOR plus 71 bp. This represents an additional return of 24 bp pa that is in return for the sale of the embedded equity option and assuming the call risk on the underlying convertible bond. In case of conversion or call, the swap counterparty has the right to effectively terminate the asset swap.

In the case of a convertible and credit arbitrage transaction, the mechanics would be similar. The major differences would be as follows:

- The trader would hold the convertible bond, sell the equity option and enter into the swap.
- The trader would enter into a transaction with the investor whereby the investor paid the spread (95 bp pa) to the investor in return for the investor agreeing to assume any loss on the convertible bond in the event that the issuer defaulted on its obligations. The term of the credit default swap would be till maturity or termination by conversion or call. The return could also be

---

[18] Interest payments can be priced of US$ 3-month LIBOR, swapped into fixed-rate or swapped into a currency of the investor's choice

INITIAL CASH FLOWS

PERIODIC CASH FLOWS

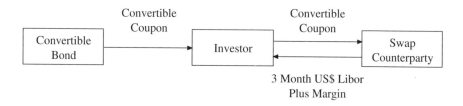

TERMINATION CASH FLOWS

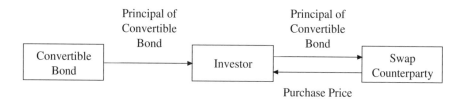

EARLY TERMINATION CASH FLOWS

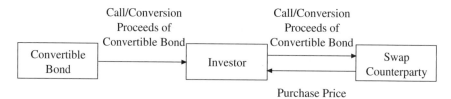

structured as the coupon on a credit linked note issued by the trader to the investor.

5.6.2   Yield Enhancement

In this section, examples of applications of credit derivatives by institutional investors and asset managers to enhance the return on asset portfolios are considered. While the examples below are not leveraged, the addition of leverage could increase the yield enhancement potential of these structures. The incorporation of leverage would also however increase the risk of the investment.

Example 1 — First To Default Basket[19]

Assume Investor M manages a portfolio of bonds subject to a minimum credit rating level of AA/Aa. The investor is seeking opportunities to increase the yield on the portfolio.

Traditional direct approaches to yield enhancement would emphasize seeking to identify relative value by purchasing undervalued AA/Aa rated assets in the primary or secondary markets to enhance portfolio performance. The capacity to enhance yield in this manner is limited by strong competition to identify these relative value opportunities and the generally efficient structure of the markets.

A credit derivative-based solution would focus on investing in a credit default structured note where the default on the note is linked to a basket of, say, four AA/Aa credits on a first-to-default basis. In the event that any one of the reference credits defaults, the redemption value of the structured note is reduced by either a pre-agreed fixed amount or the fall in the value of the first defaulted security. For a 5-year maturity, such an investment provides an additional return of around 20 bp pa relative to the current yield levels on any of the reference securities on an individual basis.

The increased return compensates for the fact that a first-to-default basket is inherently more risky than the individual issuers. In effect, a first-to-default basket of AA/Aa issuers may have a default risk equivalent to lower credit levels although it satisfies the actual minimum threshold credit rating level imposed upon the investor.

Example 2 — Monetizing Credit Spread Expectations with Spread Forwards Or Collars

In this example and the following two examples, monetization of the value of forward credit spreads are used to highlight the opportunities to create yield on fixed interest portfolio utilizing credit spread products.

---

[19] For an example outlining the use of first-to-default baskets to create synthetic leverage as well as pricing issues, see discussion below.

Assume Investor M manages a money market portfolio. Authorized portfolio investments are floating interest rate assets that must have a final maturity not exceeding three years. The minimum credit rating is A1/P1 or AA/Aa. Investor M is seeking opportunities to enhance the returns on the portfolio in a period of very tight credit spreads.

The investor expects that credit spreads will increase for certain borrowers (one such borrower is Company X). However, it expects that the spread shift will be most marked in longer maturities. For example, assume that Company X's credit spreads for three years are around 20 bp pa and for 10 years, it is 45 bp pa. Investor M expects that the spreads on the shorter securities will increase to 30 bp pa (increase of 10 bps) while spreads on the longer maturities will increase to 75 bp pa (increase of 30 bp). The greater spread duration at the longer maturities combined with the larger increase provides greater opportunities to extract value from the 10-year spreads.

Investor M can seek to capture value from this expectation by disaggregating its expectations on changes in credit spreads from other aspects of the underlying securities, such as the term or interest rate exposure.

Examples of the types of transactions that are feasible are set out below. Each example entails a structured note issued by a AA/Aa rated issuer where the redemption is linked to the credit spread on the 10-year securities issued by Company X. The note has a maturity of two years. The return on the note is above that available for a conventional security for an equivalent credit quality issuer. This added return is generated from one of the following sources:

- **Sale of the forward spread:** Under this structure, the investor sells the credit spread of Company X two years forward (effectively, a 2-year forward on 8-year credit spreads reflecting the shortening in the remaining term to maturity). The forward spread is around 49 bp pa. In order to extract value from the transaction, the forward embedded in the note is structured at a forward rate of, say, 54 bp pa. This means that the forward is effectively in the money and the embedded value can be discounted back to the start of the transaction and allocated over the life of the note to increase the yield on the shorter dated transaction. The investor benefits if the credit spreads for Company X widens above 54 bp pa (this is reflected in the adjusted redemption value of the note) or suffers a loss (reflected as a loss of principal) if the spread falls below 54 bp pa.

- **Credit spread collar:** Under this structure, the investor purchases a put on the forward credit spread while financing the put through the sale of a call on the spread. The collar created has the effect of allowing the Investor to benefit from an increase in the spread but suffer a loss from a contraction.

The strikes are arranged so that the value received from the sale of the call is higher than that required to purchase the put. For example, in this case, the call could be sold with a strike of 55 bp. The option is in the money based on a forward spread of 49 bp. The put could be purchased at a strike of 60 bp pa that is out of the money. This means that Investor M benefits if the spread widens above 60 bp pa while losing if the spread fall below 55 bp pa. The structure of the strikes is designed to ensure that the collar will provide net premium income that will then be used to enhance the coupon return on the note itself.

This structure allows Investor M to seek to improve its returns on its money market investments through monetization of its expectations on credit spreads. The investment is consistent with its investment parameters. The structure allows the investor to obtain exposure to the spread duration without altering its overall interest rate risk profile. The structure would typically be utilized to enable the investor to outperform its return benchmark (e.g. LIBOR average).

Example 3 — Monetizing Credit Spread Expectations with Targeted Put Selling

Assume Investor M is managing a portfolio of emerging market bonds. Assume that following a crisis in one of the Latin American emerging markets, there has been a significant sell-off in emerging market debt and the spread (for 10 year maturities) on an Asian BBB/Baa rated sovereign issuer has widened from 125 bp pa to 155 bp pa over US$ Treasury yields. The rise in credit spreads has been accompanied by a significant increase in the volatility of these investments.

Investor M expects that this rise in credit spreads is likely to be short-lived as the fundamentals assert themselves and the pattern of trading in the Asian emerging market issuer decouples from that of the Latin issuers. It seeks to monetize this expectation through the sale of a put option on the credit spread (relative to a nominated benchmark treasury). The option is for 1 year with a strike yield of 175 bp (some 20 bp above the current spot spread). The investor receives a premium of, say, 1.30% flat of the principal of the transaction.

The investor's payoff profile is as follows:

- If the investor's expectations are realized and the issuer's credit spreads remain at current levels or fall, then the put will not be exercised and the premium received will enhance portfolio returns.
- If the issuer's credit spreads increase to a level above the strike spread of 175 bp, then the put will be exercised. The exercise of the put will in effect equate to the purchase of the issuer's 10-year securities (which will have 9 years to

reach maturity) at the strike spread. The transaction may in fact be structured to allow the purchaser of the option to sell that security to the investor at the current Treasury yield at option maturity plus the strike spread facilitating this acquisition. The investor may well be prepared to accept that risk on the basis that it considers these securities to represent value at these levels. From a purely economic perspective, the premium received equates to providing protection against an increase in the spread of around 22 bp pa. In effect, where the spread increases above around 197 bp pa over the US treasury yield, the investor suffers an economic loss.

Two aspects of the sale of this covered credit spread put should be noted:
• The transaction may be motivated by the higher volatility for credit spreads relative to the volatility of the underlying yield on these securities. This allows extraction of additional value from the sale of the put on the credit spread.
• The option position may benefit from the shortening in the maturity of the underlying securities (from 10 to 9 years) over the life of the put option transaction. Assuming a positively shaped credit spread curve, the shortening of the maturity of the underlying securities should assist Investor M as it will benefit from the expected fall in the credit spread arising from the fall in maturity.

Example 4 — Monetizing Credit Spread Expectations with Digital Options
Assume that Investor M manages a fixed-interest portfolio of high-credit quality (minimum rating AA/Aa). The contraction in credit spreads means that portfolio returns are not adequate. This example describes a common means available for utilization by Investor M to capture additional returns from this portfolio.

Assume that Investor M has available capacity to purchase 10-year securities issued by Company X (the reference security has a coupon of 6.75% pa and a maturity of approximately 10 years). Investor M observes that the credit spread on these securities (currently, 40 bp pa) has traded in a range of 35–50 bp pa relative to US Treasury yields for the previous 12 months. Investor M also expects that the bond will continue to trade within this credit spread range.

To capitalize on its views, Investor M purchases the underlying 10-year bonds issued by Company X. Simultaneously, it enters into a derivative transaction with a dealer whereby it will receive a payment over the next one-year (the term of the transaction) of, say, 35 bp in exchange for making payment(s) equivalent to 2.00% pa to the dealer if the credit spread on this reference security is outside the range of 30–55 bp pa.

The effect of this transaction is the following:
- If the credit spread stays within the nominated range, then the Investor enjoys an enhanced yield (the additional yield being equivalent to the payment received from the counterparty) relative to the return that it would have received on its investment in the bonds.
- If the credit spread moves outside the range, then the investors return is reduced by around 165 bp pa (the net loss being the amount received of 35 bp pa and the payment due to the counterparty of 200 bp pa). This loss is effectively funded by the allocation of part of the coupon on the reference securities effectively reducing the portfolio returns.

The transaction structure entails the Investor selling digital options (both calls and puts) on the credit spread with the payout being fixed to the amount (200 bp pa) willing to be forgone by the investor. The structure is identical to Range or Accrual Note structures introduced in the early 1990s.[20] The premium received allows the investor to enhance the return on the portfolio in return for taking on the exposure to potential movements of the spread outside the historical range (the strikes are set slightly outside the historical trading range).

The actual payoffs on the digital options sold will typically be calculated on the basis of daily accruals of the payment amount based on the number of days on which over the full one-year period that the spread is outside the range. The structure itself is capable of adjustment. For example, by varying the amount of the coupon on the underlying bond that Investor M is willing to risk or the strike levels, the level of credit enhancement achieved can be increased or decreased. The structure can also be embedded in a structured note if required by the investor.

The structure, in effect, captures value from the volatility of credit spreads and their historical performance. The Investor achieves enhanced returns if the credit spreads behave consistent with its expectations. However, the investor does not risk principal and is guaranteed a minimum return as the digital option specifically limits its level of loss.

---

[20] See Das, Satyajit, August 3, 1994, "Range Finders," *IFR Swaps Weekly*, Issue 80, pp 4-5; 10 August, 1994, *IFR Swaps Weekly*, Issue 81, 1996, *Exotic Options*; IFR Publishing, London/LBC Information services, Sydney, Chapter 13; 1996, *Structured Notes & Derivative Embedded Securities*, Euromoney Books, London, Chapter 12

5.6.3   Exposure Reduction

In this section, examples of applications of credit derivatives by institutional investors and asset managers to reduce the credit risk on asset portfolios are considered.

Example 1 — Ratings Downgrade Protection

Assume Investor M is planning to increase its exposure to a specific industry group (say, automobiles). This exposure will be created by purchasing a basket of bonds issued by companies within the industry. The increase in exposure is predicated on macroeconomic and business-cycle factors.

The investor is risk-averse and is considering a contingent exit strategy. This strategy would entail selling the bonds upon the default by or a downgrade of the outstanding debt of any one of the issuers. It is based on the logic that the default or downgrade (below a threshold level) of any of the issuers within the basket will adversely affect the value of the other bonds (that is, there is a positive correlation as between default/credit risks in this industry basket).

The traditional physical solution is to establish the position by investing in the bonds and then exiting the sector by liquidation of the holdings upon default or downgrade. This suffers from a number of difficulties:

- The assumption about market liquidity, in practise, may not be reasonable.
- The occurrence of the contingent event is likely to trigger a fall in prices for all the issuers in the basket and may lead to both price pressures, and reduction in liquidity in the non-defaulted or non-downgraded securities.
- In the absence of liquidity, it may be difficult, under the circumstances considered, to hedge or reduce the credit risk of the portfolio.

Two possible credit derivative solutions are feasible:

- **First-to-default note:** As an alternative to purchasing the bonds, the investor invests in a structured note where the payoff is linked to the default or downgrade of a basket of the underlying issuers. Under this structure, the investor assumes the risk to the issuers included in the basket on a first-to-default basis. In the event of default, the investor suffers a loss based on the loss on the defaulted or downgraded securities but is effectively repaid the rest of its investment (replicating its exit strategy objectives). In return for this arrangement, the investor pays a premium (in effect, a reduction of the return on the underlying securities) in return for this set of rights. The major benefit of this arrangement is that the investor achieves an immediate reduction of its exposure to default risk to the industry upon the default of any one of the issuers.

- **First-to-default swap:** The investor purchases the bonds. Simultaneously, the investor enters into a default swap (on a first-to-default basis) where the investor can settle the swap by delivery of the securities included in the basket at pre agreed prices.

Both strategies have the desired effect of achieving a rapid reduction in the exposure to the industry in case of any deterioration in credit quality in the industry.

Example 2 — Emerging Market Portfolio Hedge

Assume Investor M is an emerging-market investor with a substantial investment portfolio of Brady Bonds. The investor is now seeking to reduce its exposure to this sector. This decision reflects the fall in spreads prompting Investor M to lock in its capital gains.

However, Investor M does not wish to sell its holdings, at least not immediately, for a number of reasons:

- The portfolio is very large and would create price pressures if rapid liquidation was attempted.
- The physical sale of the securities would also result in the realization of gains resulting in acceleration of tax liabilities, which is to be avoided if practicable.

Another factor may be its expectations that US Treasury interest rates are likely to decline in the near future.

Against this background, Investor M decides to hedge its Brady Bond portfolio for the next one year. This is designed to hedge the price risk and allow a systematic sale of the portfolio if desired over a longer time period.

The physical hedge, entailing shorting the Brady Bonds themselves, is difficult because of the problems of shorting emerging market debt, including availability of securities for borrowing, the cost of borrowing securities, the term of any such borrowing, and the interest rate uncertainties introduced.

A credit derivative-based solution would be to enter into a total return loan swap where Investor M pays the total rate of return on a reference emerging market index (e.g. the IFC Index or a private index published by a financial institution) in exchange for receiving LIBOR.

The transaction would have the following impact:

- Transferring the price risk on the portfolio to the counterparty creating a hedge against the value of the bonds. This assumes that the underlying portfolio is similar in composition to the index used to hedge — that is, there is limited basis risk.

- The index may well be a more liquid vehicle to effect the hedge allowing avoidance of liquidity and other problems alluded to above.
- The bonds can continue to be held as the price risk has been substantially reduced allowing the issue of realization to be deferred.

5.6.4 Leverage

In this section, examples of applications of credit derivatives by institutional investors and asset managers to specifically create leverage are considered. A key attraction of credit derivatives (both total return swaps and credit default swaps) is the capacity to use these instruments to take leveraged positions on credit risk. This advantage derives from the off-balance-sheet nature of the transactions and also the ability to use default correlations to create complex multiple risk positions on credit.

Example 1 — Simple Leveraged Structure

A total return swap is a purely off-balance sheet transaction. However, where the party seeking to receive the return on the bond or loan (effectively, to acquire synthetic exposure to the asset) invests in a cash asset it can create a synthetic on balance sheet asset. This transaction structure is set out in Figure 5.6.

However, the bank or investor (Bank B, in the above example) seeking exposure to the underlying bond or loan asset need not fund the swap fully as in the above case. It may choose to undertake the transaction on an unfunded basis. This structure is set out in Figure 5.7.

Figure 5.6   Funded Total Return Swap

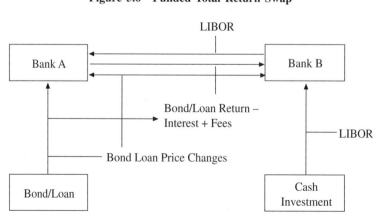

Figure 5.7   Unfunded/Leveraged Total Return Swap

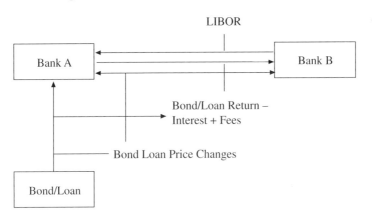

The economics of this leveraged investment can be illustrated with a numerical example. Assume that Bank B assumes exposure to a high-yield asset that is currently yielding LIBOR plus 2.75% pa. It is a new loan that is priced at 100% of face value or par. Assume that in return for receiving the return on the loan Bank B will have to pay LIBOR plus 0.80% pa. This reflects a net spread of 1.95% accruing to Bank B. The transaction requires Bank B to post collateral of 10% of the nominal face value of the total return swap (assumed to be US$10 million). The collateral earns interest at 5.50% pa. The swap has a term of one year.

The return to Bank B is set out in the table on the next page.

The highly leveraged structure of returns (on the capital invested that is equal to the collateral posted) is evident from the table. These are typically attractive to aggressive leveraged investors in credit assets including hedge funds and emerging market banks.

From the viewpoint of Bank A that facilitates the entry by Bank B into the leveraged swap, it obtains a return of 80 bp for a 10% cash collateralized exposure. The swap will typically have ongoing mark-to-market provisions such that Bank B is required to post additional collateral if the swap is out-of-the-money at specific intervals or if at any time if the swap mark-to-market exposure exceeds a given trigger amount. This decreases the credit exposure under the transaction for Bank A.

Bond/Loan Price at Maturity (%)	Net Spread on Total Return Swap ($)	Gain (Loss) on Total Return Swap ($)	Collateral Interest ($)	Rate of Return (% pa)
105.00	195,000	500,000	55,000	75.00
104.50	195,000	450,000	55,000	70.00
104.00	195,000	400,000	55,000	65.00
103.50	195,000	350,000	55,000	60.00
103.00	195,000	300,000	55,000	55.00
102.50	195,000	250,000	55,000	50.00
102.00	195,000	200,000	55,000	45.00
101.50	195,000	150,000	55,000	40.00
101.00	195,000	100,000	55,000	35.00
100.50	195,000	50,000	55,000	30.00
100.00	195,000	–	55,000	25.00
99.50	195,000	–50,000	55,000	20.00
99.00	195,000	–100,000	55,000	15.00
98.50	195,000	–150,000	55,000	10.00
98.00	195,000	–200,000	55,000	5.00
97.50	195,000	–250,000	55,000	0.00
97.00	195,000	–300,000	55,000	–5.00
96.50	195,000	–350,000	55,000	–10.00
96.00	195,000	–400,000	55,000	–15.00
95.50	195,000	–450,000	55,000	–20.00
95.00	195,000	–500,000	55,000	–25.00

Example 2 — Leveraged Note Structure

Assume an investor wishes to create a leveraged exposure to a diversified portfolio of securities (either bonds or traded loans). A repackaging vehicle mayused to create diversified exposure to a portfolio of bonds/credits. The transaction is structured as follows:

- The repackaging vehicle issues a structured note to the investor.
- The cash proceeds of the note are used to make an investment in a high quality bond(s).
- The repackaging vehicle enters into a series of total return swaps with a derivative counterparty to gain exposure to a variety of bonds/credits. The total return swaps have total notional principal equivalent to the value of the investments in the high quality bonds that are used to fully collateralize the swaps.
- The structured note returns to the investor (usually) a floating-rate return

calculated as LIBOR plus a margin. The return is equivalent to the payments received under the total return swaps. The return from the underlying high-quality bond investment is used to fund the floating rate payments under the total return swaps.

- At maturity, the structured note pays out the value of the securities underlying the total return swaps. An appreciation in value adds to the pool of funds generated from the liquidation of the high quality collateral pool and is available for distribution to the investor. Any depreciation in the value of the securities underlying the total return swaps is funded by the collateral pool and reduces the payment to the investor in the structured note.

The structure is designed to allow an investor, through the investment in the structured note issued by the repackaging vehicle to obtain economic exposure to the diversified portfolio of securities. The major benefits include the higher level of diversification that is obtained as a result of the lower threshold size of total return swaps (versus investment in the bonds) and the elimination of administration costs of managing a portfolio of securities.

The only additional element required to engineer leverage is that the total return swap entered into is for a notional principal greater than the face value of the collateral. The leveraged structure will operate as follows:

- As in the previous case, the repackaging vehicle uses the proceeds of the issue of structured notes to purchase high quality securities, which are then used to collateralize the total return swaps.
- The collateral will represent approximately 10–20% of the notional principal of the total return swaps entered.
- The structured note redeems at maturity as in the previous example. However, the investor can only lose the principal face value of the structured note not the notional value of the total return swaps entered into (that is, there is an effective put on the value of the underlying securities written by the counterparty to the total return swap in favor of the repackaging vehicle).

The investor has exposure to both the collateral and the securities underlying the total return swaps.

The rationale for the structure is the very high returns an investor can generate from the leverage embedded in the transactions. However, unlike traditional forms of leverage (such as purchasing the underlying securities on margin), the loss that can be suffered by the investor is limited to the face value of the structured notes (effectively, the collateral amount).

The structure is set out in Figure 5.8.

Figure 5.8   Leveraged Credit Note Structure

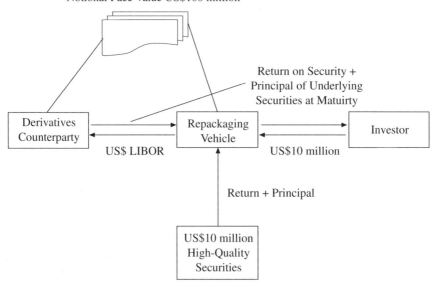

Several Total Return Swap on Different Underlying Securities
Notional Face Value US$100 million

Return on Security +
Principal of Underlying
Securities at Matuirty

Derivatives Counterparty

Repackaging Vehicle

Investor

US$ LIBOR

US$10 million

Return + Principal

US$10 million
High-Quality
Securities

Example 3 — Utilizing First-to-Default Baskets to Create Leveraged Exposure

A less obvious manner in which to create leverage is the concept of the first-to-default basket. Assume Investor A manages a portfolio of bonds subject to a minimum credit rating level of AA/Aa. The investor is seeking opportunities to increase the yield on the portfolio.

A credit derivative-based solution would focus on investing in a credit default structured note or swap where the default on the note or swap is linked to a basket of, say, four AA/Aa credits on a first-to-default basis. In the event that any one of the reference credits defaults, then the seller of first-to-default protection is required to purchase the defaulted securities. For a 2-year maturity, such an investment provides an additional return (say, around 20 bp pa) relative the current yield levels on any of the reference securities on an individual basis.

The rationale for a first-to-default basket is that the combination of credit risks in the structure creates a lower credit quality than the individual credit standing of the credit assets. In effect, a first-to-default basket of AA/Aa issuers may have a default risk equivalent to lower credit levels although it satisfies the actual minimum threshold credit rating level imposed upon the investor. The higher risk reflects low default correlations between the credit assets included in the basket. It also reflects the fact that there is an element of inherent leverage in the structure (effectively, in a US$50 million transaction on four underlying credit assets, the provider of default protection because it provides protection on any of the four assets up to a face value of US$50 million on a first-to-default basis it is providing protection on US$200 million of credit assets). The increased return compensates for the fact that a first-to-default basket is inherently more risky than the individual issuers.

A major driving force of these transactions is the fact that the format for the transfer of credit risk created in these first-to-default basket is attractive for the investors assuming the default risk. The structures whether in swap form or embedded in notes/securities provided an elegant mechanism for creating the desired exposure while allowing the investors to generate incremental yield. This provides outperformance relative to the underlying benchmarks against which the performance of these investors is measured. Where the investor have the capacity to enter into purchases of securities of any of the issuers included in the basket, the structure of the first-to-default basket allows investors to create leverage through the position on default correlations.[21]

5.7 Corporate Applications[22]

5.7.1 Managing Credit Exposure to Major Customer

Example 1 — Credit Exposure Management
Most enterprises incur significant credit exposures in the process of conducting their day-to-day operations. These may include:
• Direct credit risk on:
  1. Trade receivables
  2. Vendor or supplier financing associated with the supply of, say, capital equipment
• Contract prepayments in advance of performance.

---

[21] For a discussion of pricing of first-to-default baskets, see Chapter 6.

[22] For an overview, see Buy, Richard, Kaminski, Pinnamaneni, Krishnarao, and Shambhogue, Vasant, 1998, "Actively Managing Corporate Credit Risk: New Methodologies and Instruments For Non-Financial Firms," *Credit Derivatives: Applications for Risk Management, Investment and Portfolio Optimisation*; Risk Books, London, Chapter 5

- Business losses (including additional set-up or switching costs) where as the default of a major supplier or customer the operations of the enterprises are disrupted.

The following example illustrates the risks and the opportunities to hedge this risk through credit derivatives.

Assume Company X sells it products to a few large customers. The product is sold on trade credit terms where the terms of payments are usually 90 days. The customers are in an industry that has poor credit characteristics (the industry is largely non-investment grade). The risk of its receivables impacts upon the credit quality of Company X because of the high concentration of its sales to this industry group.

Traditionally, Company X has managed its exposure to the credit risk on its receivables through provisions against non-payment and limits on individual customers. However, as its sales has grown, the competitive nature of the market has forced Company X to increase its limits to the individual customers and diminishing profit margins is placing pressure on the provisioning practises.

Company X can utilize the credit derivatives market to manage its exposure to its major customers by entry into credit default swaps, where it pays a fixed premium in return for receipt of a payment in the event of default by the customer. The structure of the hedge can be designed to fit the requirements of Company X:

- The payment receipt upon default is usually a fixed amount reflecting the non-tradable nature of the debt obligations.
- The company can purchase protection on all or a portion of the customers in accordance with its risk management objectives.

  The use of credit derivatives to hedge this exposure will generally provide cost-effective protection for Company X as a result of the following factors:
- Company X's credit exposure shows a high level of industry and specific counterparty concentration reflecting its business. It also has limited opportunities to diversify its credit risks. This means that its exposure to the risk of credit losses is significantly above that it would expect in a more completely diversified portfolio.
- The concentration of risk means that, on a portfolio basis, it should be prepared to pay a premium to reduce its credit risk. Conversely, banks and financial institutions may be prepared to accept the credit risk for a lower cost than the current cost to Company X (as represented by commitment of capital in the form of provisions) because of its opportunities to more fully diversify its portfolio. This reflects the fact that the banks/financial institutions are not

constrained in diversifying their exposures in the same way that Company X is as they are not subject to the business constraints. This will usually mean that the purchase of credit risk protection will be positive for Company X in that it will allow it to free up capital which can be used in its core business. This will be reflected in the lower cost of protection on default purchased externally relative to the economic cost of maintaining the exposure with provisioning.

- The protection can be purchased on a short-term basis with the default protection being renewed at maturity. This allows the level of exposure to be adjusted continually while also benefiting from riding the default risk curve. The latter will assist Company X insofar that it will only be required to pay for short term protection.

- Company X also gains certainty in terms of its loss levels and cash flow. This may have business benefits in allowing expansion of trading relationships with a counterparty where credit considerations may have reduced the capacity to trade. It also adds a greater degree of pricing precision in Company X's business dealings in that its profit margin on sales must cover the known cost of the default swap (representing the market cost of the credit risk of the transaction). This should allow more accurate quantification of its business profitability.

- There may be additional benefits in the form of cost savings as the expense of making credit assessments on a business counterparty is made redundant through entry into the default swap. In effect, Company X gains a benefit from the credit infrastructure of the financial institution providing it with protection.

Example 2 — Managing Exposure to Credit Impaired Buyer[23]

Assume Company X sells a significant amount of its product to a retailer. The sales are on 45-day credit terms. The retailer experiences financial difficulties and goes into Chapter 11 bankruptcy (or its equivalent in the relevant jurisdiction). The effect of this is to significantly increase the credit risk to Company X on its receivables. However, the inability to extend credit terms will have the effect of resulting in a substantial loss of sales to the retailer.

Company X has two courses of action available to it:

---

[23] For a practical example, see "Credit Risk Hedge For Corporation" (March 1999) *Global Finance*, pp 27

- Continue to transact with the retailer — this would mean that Company X
  will incur the additional credit risk that may ultimately result in bad debt
  losses which will impact upon Company X's financial position.
- Continue to transact but hedge credit risk — this would mean that Company
  X will incur the additional risk but will simultaneously hedge its credit risk
  through the credit derivative market.

The credit derivative could be structured as the purchase by Company X of a
credit default swap. The reference credit is the retailer and the face value amount
of the transaction is amount of trade receivables. Company X pays a fee and in
return the seller of protection agrees to pay Company X 100 of the face value
of receivables in the case where a credit event occurs. Credit event is defined
in these circumstances to include:

- Failure to pay receivables which are due after a grace period of say 30 days.
- Plan to cease operations or liquidate assets under Chapter 11 is approved.
- The Chapter 11 bankruptcy is converted into full bankruptcy under Chapter
  7 bankruptcy (or its equivalent in the relevant jurisdiction).

The effect of this transaction is to enable Company X to estimate the cost of any
losses and continue to trade with the Retailer.

5.7.2   Credit Spread Risk on New Borrowing

Assume corporate credit spreads have declined significantly. The current rate
structure is as set out in the table below:

Maturity (years)	Treasury Rate (% pa)	Company X's Rate (% pa)	Credit Spread (bp pa)
1	6.00	6.25	25
5	6.45	6.95	50
6	6.50	7.00	50

Company X expects to issue new 5-year debt in one year's time. It is concerned
that credit spreads might rise above implied forward spreads (the implied
forward spread is 55 bp pa). Company X, therefore, seeks to lock in its credit
spread on its expected borrowing. It seeks to isolate its exposures on its credit
spreads as it is of the view that the underlying benchmark yields (the US
Treasury rates) are unlikely to be above the current implied forward rate (6.60%
pa).

The physical solution would require Company X to issue debt immediately and invest the proceeds in cash or other liquid securities until the funds are required in one year's time. This approach has a number of problems:

- The transaction may significantly increase the size of the balance sheet as both the borrowing and the cash investment would utilize the balance sheet. It would also increase the gearing of the company where gross debt is utilized.
- There would be an earnings impact (in this case, 1.00% pa or US$1 million pa on a borrowing of US$100 million), which would potentially reduce current earnings from the following sources:
  1. The credit spread between borrowing and investment for Company X (in this case, 50 bp pa).
  2. The shape of the yield curve whereby a positive (negative) yield curve would result in a cost (benefit) to Company X from the difference as between the 1 year and 6 year rates. In the current case, this equates to an additional cost of 50 bp pa
- The necessity to borrow for longer maturities than actually the financing required. In the above case, the borrowing would be for six years rather than for the required five years. This has the impact of forcing up the cost (potentially, both the interest rate and the spread) and also may create access issues particularly for lower rated entities where longer maturities may be less readily available or only at higher rates.

An alternative to the physical transactions would be for Company X to enter into a credit spread forward with a counterparty to lock in the current forward credit spread. The credit spread would be at the current implied forward spread level of 55 bp pa to a forward date of one year. The hedge would operate as follows:

- If spreads increased, then the credit spread forward would increase in value resulting in a positive cash flow settlement. For example, assuming a spread duration of 4.08, an increase in the 5-year credit spread to 70 bp pa would result in a payment received of 61.2 bp on the forward. This would offset the lower receipts on the issue of debt or higher cost as a result of the widening of the spread.
- If spreads decreased, then Company X would incur a loss on the spread which would be offset by higher receipts or lower cost on the issue of the debt.
  Some aspects of the hedge should be noted:
- The efficiency on the hedge will be affected by changes in the absolute level of the spread and underlying rates. For example, if the 5-year Treasury rate is 6.45% pa and the corresponding 5-year issue rate for Company X is 7.15%

pa equating to a credit spread of 70 bp pa, the loss on the borrowing from the wider spread is around 61.50 bp compared to a gain on the credit spread forward of 61.2 bp. The small slippage reflects the changing spread duration. Changes in the underlying interest rates may exacerbate this problem. Assume that the 5-year Treasury rate falls to 6.25% pa implying an issue cost of 6.95% pa. The higher spread equates to a loss of 61.8 bp that is not exactly offset by the gain on the credit forward. This convexity effect of rates and spreads will typically create hedging errors that will lower but not eliminate the risk exposure.

• In practise, it may be necessary, where Company X does not have large universe of outstanding traded securities of sufficient liquidity available, to undertake the transaction on a very liquid equivalent security issued by another issuer or on a basket of such issuers. This will reduce the efficiency of the hedge because of the inherent basis risk.

An alternative to the above strategy would entail the purchase of a put option on the spread to hedge any increase in the credit spread.

5.7.3 Project Finance Country Risk

It is feasible to utilize credit derivatives to seek to isolate and hedge the sovereign credit risk incurred in cross border investments, particularly, in emerging markets.

Assume Company X is committed to undertake a major investment in an emerging Eastern European country. The company believes the political environment is uncertain and it is possible that the country risk may deteriorate in the near term. However, they are confident that the project will provide above average returns over the longer term. However, the short-term potential for deterioration may have a deleterious impact on Company X in terms of credit ratings and market perception.

The planned investment is significant and the company wishes to isolate the political risk and hedge it to the maximum extent possible. While it is not feasible to hedge the risk of the project itself, the company believes that the risk of the project is reasonably correlated with the performance of the Eastern European country itself. It is willing to accept the correlation risk between the risk of sovereign debt and the project risk (the basis risk).

The physical solution would entail shorting or purchasing a put option on the sovereign debt of the relevant country. This assumes that the emerging market nation has outstanding internationally traded securities that can form the basis of the transaction. The physical solution has a number of difficulties associated with it including:

- The cost of creating the hedge may be high reflecting difficulties in borrowing the securities for the purpose of shorting and the difficulty in managing the short position.
- The risk of losses on price fluctuations in the security resulting in losses on the hedge where these are caused by factors which is unrelated to changes in the political risk.

The credit derivatives-based alternative would entail Company X entering into a credit default swap where it pays a premium in return for which it receives protection against any event of default on the sovereign's outstanding debt. This is achieved by linking the default payment to a reference security (securities) of the sovereign issuer. In the event of default, the issuer receives a payment based on the price performance of the sovereign bonds or a fixed sum. The structure provides protection to the Company from a potential loss resulting from political risk. The following aspects of the transaction should be noted:

- The hedge will only be effective where there is a default under the sovereign debt. If the increase in political risk affects the project (for example, by way of expropriation) without default on the reference obligations, then the hedge will not be effective.
- The actual loss suffered by the Company X as a result of its political risk must be similar to the change in the value of the bonds or the fixed pre-estimate of loss for the hedge to be effective. In practise, a fixed pre-estimate is preferred, for example, an amount equating to the equity investment in the project or some portion thereof is utilized. This and the issue noted above are symptomatic of the basis risk of the hedge.
- The credit default swap does not have the problems noted above in relation to the physical solution.

The credit default swap based hedge allows Company X to isolate and manage its political risk using market based instruments and prices. This type of approach provides an alternative or supplement to traditional insurance based approaches to political risk management.

5.7.4 Hedging Currency Convertibility Risk

It is also feasible to use credit derivatives to seek to hedge currency convertibility risk (a different facet of sovereign credit risk).

Assume Company X has a subsidiary located in an Asian country. The subsidiary operates purely within the country and all cash flows are in local currency. Profits of the subsidiary are paid out to Company X, the parent company, each year. Assume an emerging market crisis occurs and extreme market volatility is experienced. The local currency falls sharply in value as international investors withdraw capital. The country experiences balance of payments difficulties. There is increasing risk that the country may impose foreign exchange controls restricting the convertibility of its currencies and/or places restriction on foreign currency remittances to overseas entities.

A possible means for Company X to hedge its exposure to the imposition of foreign exchange controls is to entry into a currency inconvertibility hedge with a bank. Company X pays a fee to the counterparty based on the expected dividend remittance sought to be hedged. In return, the counterparty agrees to the following payments:

- If foreign exchange controls are not imposed, then there is no payment.
- If foreign exchange controls are imposed and the remittance of dividends to the parent are prevented, the counterparty will pay the US$ equivalent of the dividend amount to Company X in New York. In return, Company X will deliver the equivalent in local currency (calculated at the then prevailing spot exchange rate) in the Asian country where the subsidiary is domiciled.

The transaction has the effect of hedging Company X's currency conversion risk. However, it does not hedge its currency risk on the dividend that must be managed separately.

5.7.5   Investment in Credit Default Swaps As A Use of Corporate Surplus Funds

An alternative utilization of credit derivatives would entail corporations providing credit protection through credit default swaps whereby the company agreed to make an agreed payment on default in return for receipt of a premium. This type of activity would be based on the following approaches:

- Acting as a financial investor seeking additional return on its cash surpluses through assumption of credit risks on a diversified portfolio of credit exposures.
- Selling default protection on entities where the default risk assumed is poorly correlated on an industry or individual basis to credit exposures in its existing business operations. This would allow the generation of income that would offset the potential credit losses on its existing credit exposures.

- Selling default protection on competitors within the industry in the sense that this would provide a competitive hedge. For example, a default by a competitor would have a favorable earnings impact on the company. This gain would offset any loss on the default swap where the company has assumed default risk.

Companies with available capital resources additional to their business requirements may, in time, be attracted to deploying it to assume certain credit risks which either diversify their existing, usually concentrated credit exposures or are related to their industry positions.

5.8 Summary

Credit derivative structures offer interesting mechanisms for the isolation or disaggregation of credit exposures. This allows the effective trading of this type of risk between counterparties facilitating the hedging and assumption of risk.

The application of credit derivatives is in its relatively early stages of development. The principal applications to date have focused on: first, financial institutions seeking to hedge credit risk, improve portfolio diversification, and improve returns on available credit capital; and, second, fixed-income investors prepared to assume credit risk as a mechanism for return enhancement or exposure management. The application of credit derivatives by corporations to manage the credit risks incurred in the course of normal trading is also feasible and is developing.

The development of additional applications is likely as understanding of credit derivative structures increases, markets in these instruments gain in liquidity and pricing becomes increasingly transparent. The enhancement of credit pricing and increased understanding of credit portfolios and the risk of credit concentration is also likely to be a major factor in the evolution of applications.

Selected References

Francis, Jack Clark, Forst, Joyce A., and Whittaker, J. Gregg (Editors) 1999, *The Handbook of Credit Deriatives*, McGraw-Hill, New York
(1999) *The J.P. Morgan Guide to Credit Derivatives*, Risk Publications, London.
Nelken, Dr, Israel, 1999, *Implementing Credit Derivatives*, McGraw-Hill, New York
Rai, Shaun, Hatstadt, Philippe, Gill, Ala, and Minton, Lyle July 1997 "Using Credit Swaps To Enhance Credit Portfolio Management," *Risk Credit Risk Supplement - Sponsorship Statement*
Reoch, Rob, March 1996, "Credit Derivatives And Applications," *Financial Derivatives and Risk Management*, 5, pp 4–10

Reoch, Rob and Masters, Blythe, 1995 "Credit Swaps: An Innovation In Negotiable Exposure," *Capital Market Strategies*, Chapter 7, pp 3–8

Smithson, Charles with Holappa Hal, December 1995, "Credit Derivatives," *Risk*, Vol 8 No 12, pp 38–39

Tavakoli, Janet M, 1998, *Credit Derivatives: A Guide To Instruments And Applications*, John Wiley & Sons, Inc., New York

Theodore, Samuel S and Madelain, Michael, March 1997, "Modern Credit Risk Management and The Use of Credit Derivatives: European Banks' Brave New World (And Its Limits)," Moody's Investors Service – Global Credit Research

Whittaker, Greg J and Kumar, Sumita, 1996, "Credit Derivatives: A Primer" in Atsuo Konishi and Ravi Dattatreya (Ed) *The Handbook of Derivative Instruments*, Irwin Publishing, pp 595-614

Wong, Ming and Song, Shang, June 1997 "A Loan In Isolation," *AsiaRisk*, pp 21–23

PART THREE
PRICING & VALUATION ISSUES

6
Modeling Credit Risk/ Pricing Credit — Derivative Instruments[1]

Satyajit Das

6.1 Introduction

The rapid development of the market for credit derivatives has prompted increasing focus upon the modeling of credit risk. This is in part predicated upon the necessity of pricing credit derivatives transactions but also because at a more fundamental level an understanding of the value dynamics of credit risk is inevitably a precursor to effectively applying credit derivatives to the management of credit risk and credit portfolios.

This interest has lead to increasing interest in credit and default risk modeling. This interest has manifested itself in a number of ways including a significant increases in the volume of academic literature and the release of products such as CreditMetrics^{TM} and CREDITRISK^{+}. However, the fact remains that implementation of the academic models/approaches has been limited. In practise, the pricing of credit risk and by implication, credit derivatives remain driven by the pricing of debt securities in capital markets. As will be discussed in greater detail later this reflects the necessity of hedging, valuation, and price discovery in the spot market.

---

[1] Earlier versions on this chapter were published as Das, Satyajit "Modelling Credit Risk—Part 1" January 2000, *Futures & OTC World*, 31–38; Das, Satyajit "Modelling Credit Risk—Part 2" February 2000, *Futures & OTC World*, 31–38; Das, Satyajit "Modelling Credit Risk—Part 3" March 2000, *Futures & OTC World*, 59–66

In this chapter, the approaches to pricing and modeling credit/default risk and the pricing and hedging of default risk are examined. The structure of the chapter is as follows: the pricing relationships are first considered; the methodology of pricing in practise is analyzed; the nature of default risk is then examined; the modeling of credit risk is then presented; and the pricing of individual structures (total return swaps, credit spread products, and first-to-default baskets) is finally considered.

6.2 Pricing Relationships

In substance, the pricing of credit derivative instruments is not generally significantly different from the pricing of default risk. The inherent credit risk of a conventional loan or credit transaction must be compensated for by way of return (calculated as the credit spread received) commensurate with the risk assumed. This risk is measured as the risk of default—both on expected (average) and unexpected (extreme) losses—the credit exposure, and the recovery rate in the event of default.

The pricing of credit, in general terms, is evident from the traded prices of securities in financial markets generally. However, the available prices must be put into a tractable framework for the pricing, valuation, and hedging of credit derivatives.

The basic approach to pricing follows the underlying product structures as follows:

- **Replication products:** Such as total return swaps and credit spread derivatives are priced off the capacity to replicate the credit derivative with transactions in the cash market.
- **Credit default products:** Are priced as a function of the exposure under the loan or asset, the default probability of the reference credit, and the expected recovery rate.

There is a tendency to approach the pricing on individual credit derivatives products separately. In reality, the pricing of each of these instruments is integrated. This reflects the fundamental fact that the underlying source of risk and the corresponding return is driven by the risk of the issuer's default. Figure 6.1 sets out this interrelationship in a diagrammatic format.

Figure 6.1 Pricing Relationships

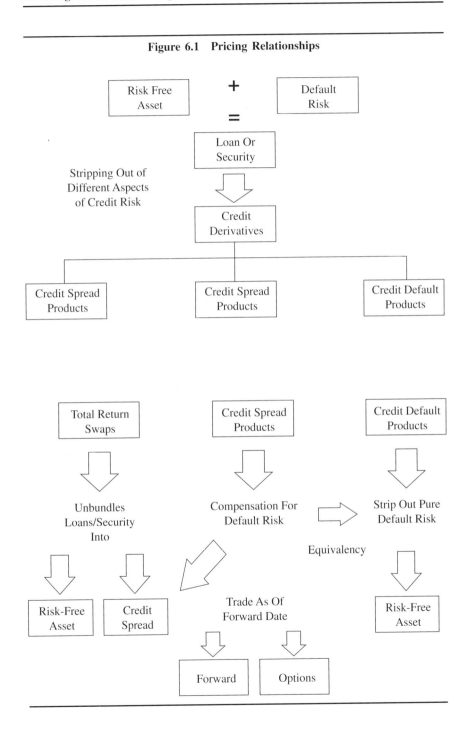

The fundamental relationships may be summarized as follows:
- The pricing of any risky security must reflect the return on a risk free asset plus a risk margin. The risk margin must compensate the investor for the risk assumed which in this instance is the risk of default.[2]
- Credit derivative transactions merely strip out and isolate the default risk in order to facilitate the separate trading of aspects of default risk.

The inherent relationships, in turn, imply pricing and valuation interdependence between the different types of credit derivative transactions:
- Credit default swaps allow separate trading of the default risk. Therefore, the pricing of the default swap should reflect the stripped-out value of the credit spread (which is the effectively the compensation for assuming credit risk).
- Total return swaps are a mechanism for synthetically creating a loan or security. The end economic outcome of a total return swap is to create the equivalent of the underlying loan or security (assuming the total return swap is combined with a cash investment). It is equivalent to an investment in a risk-free cash asset combined with the sale of protection under a credit default swap where the investor assumes the risk of default. The incremental return (above the risk-free rate) should reflect the value of the credit default swap or its equivalent stripped out credit spread as noted above.
- Credit spreads are inherent in both credit default and total return swap products as the essential return compensation for credit risk. Credit spread products allow the trading of these spreads as at forward dates in either forward or option formats. The pricing of the spot or current credit spread should reflect the default risk. This is because if the credit spread is stripped out the remaining security return should be equivalent to the risk-free return.

In understanding the pricing relationships, it is also important to focus on the fact that the different products transfer different components of the underlying credit risk:
- A credit default swap transfers only the risk of a credit event (however defined, but usually covering default). It does not in itself transfer the risk of price changes arising from a deterioration in credit quality as manifested by way of changing credit spreads, where the deterioration in credit quality falls short of default. This is only a significant issue where the credit default swap has a maturity shorter than that of the underlying obligation being hedged.

---

[2]   In this context, credit pricing represents an extension of the Capital Asset Pricing Model for the pricing of all risky assets in that the holder of a risky bond must receive a return in a risk-neutral world whereby the excess return (the spread) compensates the holder for the additional risk (default of losses from changes in credit quality)

- A total return swap transfers both default risk and spread risk. This reflects the fact that the swap transfers the returns on the underlying reference asset and re-transfers the asset to the original holder at the current price at maturity where the swap maturity is less than that of the underlying obligation.
- A credit spread swap or option transfers the pure spread risk and the default risk at least to the extent that the default risk manifests itself as a change in spread.

The analysis set out above highlights the fact that the key to pricing credit default products is the pricing of default risk and the derivation of credit spreads.

6.3 Pricing in Practice

In practice, the pricing of credit default derivatives is based on fundamental arbitrage relationships based on actual traded market instruments. This process is illustrated using an example in Figure 6.2.

Figure 6.2   Pricing Credit Derivatives Utilizing Asset Swap Prices

Assume a 5-year asset swap for Corp ABC (rated BBB) is trading at US$ LIBOR plus 58 bp. The underlying asset is a bond with an interest rate swap with an AAA rated counterparty. Assume risk free US$ floating rate assets (taken in this instance to be AAA rated US$ FRNs) are trading at LIBOR minus 10 bp).

This market scenario implies a credit spread for Corp ABC of 68 bp pa calculated as follows:

Risk-free return (AAA rated FRN Return)	LIBOR – 10 bp pa
Risky return (Corp ABC Asset Swap)	LIBOR + 58 bp pa
Credit Spread	68.0 bp pa

The implied credit default cost can be calculated as follows:

Company	ABC
Rating	BBB
Maturity (Years)	5
Swap Rate	6.50%
Asset Swap Pricing	
Benchmark	LIBOR
Margin	0.580%
Default Swap Pricing	
Risk Free (Aaa) Margin	–0.100%
Required Additional Margin	0.000%
Credit Default Swap Pricing (pa)	0.680%
Credit Default Swap Pricing (Upfront)	2.826%

The credit spread is the compensation received by the investor for the default risk assumed on Corp ABC.[3] Using a discount rate for 5 years of 6.50% pa, the net present value of this credit spread is 283 bp. This present value amount can be equated to the price of a credit default swap.

The process of replication can demonstrate the relationship. The investor can purchase the AAA rated risk free FRN and enter into a credit default swap where it provides protection against the risk of default. The investor would require 283 bp up front or 68 bp pa to equate its position to that under the asset swap. The equivalence is necessitated by the fact that the asset swap and the FRN plus the default swap embody identical risk and therefore should attract identical returns. Failure of this condition would enable arbitrage to take place.

The key role occupied by the market for asset swaps in credit pricing merits special comment.[4] Increasingly, all credit assets are traded on a spread to LIBOR basis. This reflects the increased availability and liquidity of global swap and derivative markets which allow the ready transformation of assets irrespective of currency and interest rate basis into a floating rate asset in US$ in the first place and through a cross-currency basis swap into other currencies. The availability of asset swaps and the depth and size of the market means that it provides a ready and reasonably price transparent means for establishing the relative value of credit assets. This characteristic dictates that the asset swap market serves as the principal market information source for credit pricing.

In practise, the asset swap market provides the benchmark returns that are used to derive the default swap values. In effect, it places a floor under these values as it allows:

- A traded benchmark
- The ability to value and mark-to-market existing positions
- A mechanism for the traders to hedge transactions

The capacity to use the asset swap market to hedge is illustrated in Figure 6.3.

---

[3]   It is being assumed that the counterparty risk on the interest rate swap is negligible (reflecting its very high credit standing). If required this could be incorporated

[4]   For a detailed discussion of asset swaps, see Das, Satyajit 1994, *Swaps and Financial Derivatives: The Global Reference to Products, Pricing, Applications and Markets*, LBC Information Services, Sydney, McGraw-Hill, Chicago, Chapter 18

Figure 6.3   Using Asset Swaps to Hedge a Credit Default Swap

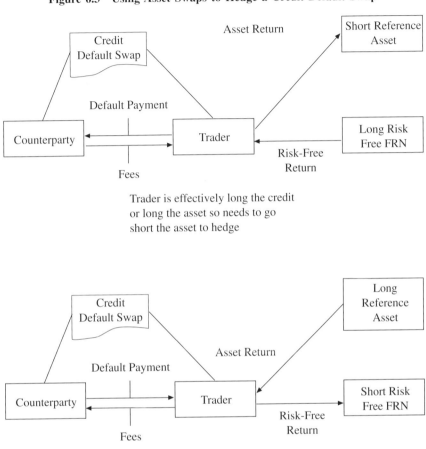

It is important to note that the hedge is far from perfect. For example, the hedge does not protect against deterioration of the credit (increase in credit spreads resulting in a fall in asset value) where the credit default swap is for a maturity shorter than the underlying reference asset. This is because the change in value of the hedge is not offset by a corresponding cash payout on the credit default swap itself.

The practical approach (entailing stripping out the market price of credit risk from existing securities) and the more complex approach of derivation of the price of default from the default risk, recovery rate, and loss expectations are consistent. In an efficient market, where, by definition, market prices for securities accurately and fully reflect the default risk pricing, the two approaches would yield identical results. In practise, credit markets are not fully efficient. This reflects the lack of transparency of credit markets. Potential differences between the two approaches dictate that both approaches are frequently used simultaneously to seek to derive the price of the default swap. A significant element of that process is to arbitrage possible pricing anomalies in the pricing of credit risk in markets.

6.4 Credit Risk Modeling Approaches

The major impetus to the credit risk modeling approaches has been the increase in volumes of credit derivatives traded. Traders entering into matching transactions drove the early development of the market. However, as the market has developed, participants have demanded non-standard structures, instantaneous execution, and liquidity. This has forced traders increasingly to enter into trades with a counterparty that is then hedged, not with an offsetting transaction, but a hedge entailing trading in the underlying bonds issued by the relevant issuer. This hedging approach required the credit derivative to be decomposed into component elements to allow the hedges to be established and managed. This requires models for credit risk to be available to engineer the necessary hedges. The models for pricing credit derivatives in turn require the modeling of credit risk generally.[5]

This interest in credit risk modeling is multidimensional. It is driven by two primary factors:
- The interest in pricing and trading credit derivatives on an individual credit, indirectly focusing attention on the pricing of credit assets generally.
- The interest in managing credit portfolios.

Credit risk modeling encompasses a variety of issues:
- The analysis of default risk and loss experience.

---

[5] For an interesting overview of credit risk assessment approaches see Keating, Con, March 1999, "Opening Credit", *Futures & OTC World*, 40-46; Keating, Con, April 1999 "If And When", *Futures & OTC World*, 40–44; Keating, Con, May 1999, "Bond Experiences", *Futures & OTC World*, 26–34; Keating, Con, June 1999, "Construction Time Again", *Futures & OTC World*, 37-44; Keating, Con, July 1999,"Fuzzy Bearings", *Futures & OTC World*, 66–71

- The approach to quantification of credit risk on an individual and aggregate basis.
- The development of pricing models for both valuations of individual credits and portfolios.

6.5 Default Risk

As is evident from the above discussion, the central element in pricing credit derivatives is the measurement of default risk. In theoretical terms, the risk of default can be best characterized as the sale by the lender or investor in the risky bond of deep out-of-the-money puts on the net asset value of the firm (see detailed discussion below).[6] However, the problems of quantifying market risk are similar to the processes of managing market risk (such as in options) but there are additional complexities. The empirical research[7] on the nature of default risk highlights a number of key difficulties that both distinguish it from credit risk and also increase the problems associated with measuring this risk accurately. The key issues include:

- The difficulty in estimating the variability of credit risk (the problem of expected versus unexpected losses).
- The nature of the distribution of credit losses (the problem of the loss distribution).
- The low correlation between default risks (the problem of portfolio diversification).

The risk of loss arising from the default by an obligor can be separated into two specific components: the expected loss and the unexpected loss or uncertainty/volatility of loss (this is discussed in greater detail below). Expected losses are derived from the size of exposure and the probability of default (however calculated). The risk of credit loss derives from the volatility of the expected loss. This is particularly important for a number of reasons:

- The variability of default risk within a portfolio is substantial (that is, the largest default probability may be significantly larger (say, 100 times) than the smallest default probability).
- The default risk itself is dynamic and subject to large fluctuations.

---

[6] This framework was first suggested by Merton, R. 1974, "On The Option Pricing Of Corporate Debt: The Risk Structure Of Interest Rates" , *Journal of Finance*, Vol 29, 449–470

[7] See (1995) *Derivative Credit Risk: Advances in Measurement and Management*, Risk Publications: London at Chapter 3, 4, 5, and 6

- Within a well diversified portfolio, the loss behavior is characterized by lower than expected default credit losses for much of the time but with a high probability of a very large losses that are incurred infrequently and the portfolio loss distribution exhibits a skewed pattern (reflecting the impact of correlations).

It is clear that estimation of the uncertainties of loss in credit portfolios present significant difficulties. This reflects the highly skewed distribution of credit losses and the fact that meaningful probabilities of loss in a credit portfolio occur many standard deviations away from the mean.

The nature of credit risk is manifested in the shape of the credit loss distribution. A typical credit loss distribution compared to a market risk loss distribution is set out in Figure 6.4.

Figure 6.4   Credit Loss Distribution

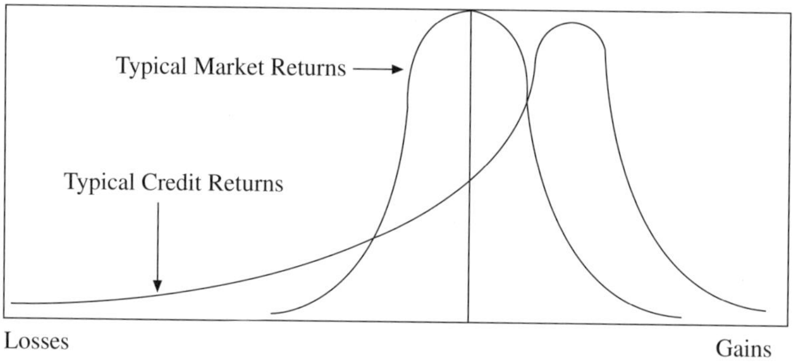

The diagram illustrates the fundamental differences in loss distributions between traditional financial assets (debt, equity, currency and commodity) and credit. Market returns (price changes) are relatively symmetrical and can be well approximated by normal or log normal distributions, although the distribution may be fat-tailed. In contrast, credit returns are asymmetric, highly skewed and are not well-approximated by normal or log normal distributions. The problems of credit pricing derive from this basic structure of credit or risky debt returns, which trades off a small excess return (the credit spread received) against the risk of losses (zero or small if there is no default versus very large in case of default).

This means that the full distribution of losses is significantly more difficult to generate than a corresponding market risk distribution and requires more information beyond simple summary statistics such as a mean and standard deviation. Typically, the generation of the full distribution of a credit risk portfolio will require every possible combination of credit states and value changes contingent upon the credit states being generated usually through simulation methodology.

The nature of the correlation between default events also significantly affects the nature of credit risk. In practice, default correlations are low. For example, an equity portfolio will typically feature correlations between returns on the individual components of the portfolio of 0.3–0.6. In contrast, a portfolio of credit risk will typically feature correlations between defaults of around 0.01 or lower. This low level of default correlations means that the systematic risk of a portfolio is small relative to the unsystematic risk of the portfolio (that is, the individual contribution of risks to the portfolio is greater).

This higher level of non-systematic risk dictates that the benefits of diversification are greater. In effect, a high degree of diversification is essential as an inadequately diversified portfolio may result in a significantly lower return on risk than would have been the case had the level of non systematic risk been lower. This points to a significant problem in credit-risk management in that a large portfolio of obligors will typically be less diversified than say an equivalent portfolio of equities. In effect, it requires a significantly higher number of names to fully diversify a credit portfolio than an equivalent portfolio of equities. One researcher has argued that it requires 350 names to achieve an equivalent level of diversification in a debt portfolio as 30 names in an equity portfolio.[8]

Default risks can be effectively managed through diversification but may require active management reflecting the dynamic nature of risk. This reflects a different phenomenon. As noted above, credit risk approximates the risk of the sale of deep out-of-the-money options on the value of the obligor firm's net assets. This approach dictates that as the quality of an individual credit or portfolio declines, the portfolio become more leveraged.[9] This increase in risk is exacerbated by the fact of serial dependence in changes in credit quality changes (the historical tendency of a downgrade in credit rating to be followed by subsequent downgrades) as against the independence of daily changes/returns in other financial market assets (in effect, the efficient market hypothesis of random returns). This serial dependence can increase the volatility of a credit

---

[8] See Ron Levin 1997, *Challenges of Managing Credit Portfolios*, J.P. Morgan Securities Inc

[9] In effect, the delta of the options is increasing

portfolio and accelerate portfolio risk. This necessitates that portfolio rebalancing is necessary as a means of materially reducing this effect. However, in practise, the illiquidity of credit markets may impede this adjustment process. This means that the consequences of lack of liquidity may be significantly greater for a credit portfolio as compared to a market risk portfolio.

The significant differences between credit risk and market risk imply:

- Market risk exhibits higher correlation as between risk (both within asset classes and across asset classes) which allows hedging as well as positioning/ trading whereby outright price risk is traded for basis risk.
- Credit risk exhibits lower correlations creating difficulties in hedging and trading forcing reliance on portfolio diversification mechanisms.

These factors which tend to differentiate credit risk from types of risk such as market risk (see discussion below) dominate both the quantification and pricing of credit risk in general and credit derivatives specifically.

6.6 Credit Spreads

6.6.1 Concept

Credit spreads are central to the market for default risk. Credit spreads represent the margin relative to the risk free rate designed to compensate the investor for the risk of default on the underlying security. In essence, it is the market price of default risk. The fact that it is the major traded measure of default risk means that it is central to all credit-risk modeling. It is particularly important in that it is the single most important indicia of issuer specific credit risk that is market driven.

The credit spread itself is calculated as:

Credit Spread = Yield of Risky Security or Loan minus Yield of
corresponding Risk-Free Security

The derivation of credit spreads focus on the concept of the risk neutral credit spread and the term structure of credit spreads.

6.6.2 Risk Neutral Credit Spreads

A threshold issue relates to the definition of the yield curve for credit risk affected instruments. This problem is analogous to the issues in modeling the yield curve generally. However, the definition of a credit risk adjusted yield curve is affected by a number of additional complicating factors:

- The absence in many markets of well-defined credit spread structures.
- The absence of a complete term structure of credit spreads with rather infrequent data points.
  These problems may be the result of:
- Inefficiency or illiquidity of the underlying debt markets.
- Absence of or friction in trading in secondary markets.
- Lack of a clearly defined rating-based credit-quality tiering structure.
- Lack of issuance across the whole maturity spectrum by particular issuer groups due to issuer or investor preferences.

Consequently, where the term structure of credit spreads is not observable or the data is for any reason not tractable, the credit spreads must be estimated. An approach utilized to overcome these definitional problems is the concept of the risk neutral credit spread.[10]

The concept of a risk neutral yield credit spread relative to a comparable risk free benchmark is predicated on estimating a credit spread that compensates the investor for the default risk assumed. The underlying logic is that the risk neutral credit spread would in an efficient capital market make an investor indifferent between a risky bond and a risk free security.

The risk neutral spread calculation typically assumes par bonds, a holding period equal to maturity or default (whichever occurs first), risk neutrality and arbitrage free capital markets. Within this framework, the risk neutral spread can be defined as:

$$C = Y - Rf$$

Where

C = Risk neutral credit spread

Y = Yield of risky bond

Rf = Yield on risk free bond

C is a function of the default risk of the risky bond. It is feasible to utilize marginal default risk and recovery rates estimates to approximate C. Given Rf and C, it is feasible to solve for Y which using weighted average cash flows equates to Rf. This requires weighting each cash flow of the risky bond by the probability of default and the recovery rate to calculate the default risk adjusted risky bond cash flows (effectively, certainty equivalent cash flows).

---

[10] See Chapter 7; Fons Jerome S. September–October 1994, "Using Default Rates To Model The Term Structure Of Credit Risk," *Financial Analysts Journal*, 25–32; this paper is reproduced in Satyajit Das 1998, *Credit Derivatives*, John Wiley & Sons, Chapter 5

Figure 6.5 sets out an example of derivation of a risk neutral credit spread.

Figure 6.5   Derivation of a Risk Neutral Credit Spread

In the example below, the risk neutral credit spread for a bond is derived as follows:
- The cash flows of the bond are identified and placed in the appropriate time period.
- The default probabilities for the issuer and the recovery rate for the type of obligation are identified.
- The survival probability (1 minus the default probability) is calculated.
- The recovery adjusted default payment is calculated from the default probability and the recovery rate assumed.
- The original bond cash flows are then adjusted for the risk of default by calculating the expected cash flows assuming the risk of default.
- The adjusted bond cash flows are then discounted using the risk free rate to solve for the credit spread that equates the internal rate of return on the adjusted cash flows of the bond to the risk free rate.

Inputs

Maturity	5
Interest Rates	
Risk Free	6.0000%
Credit Spread	0.1852%
Issuer Rates	6.1852%

Years	0	1	2	3	4	5
Cash Flows	$(100.0000)	$6.1852	$6.1852	$6.1852	$6.1852	$106.1852
Default Probability		0.12%	0.39%	0.76%	1.27%	1.71%
Recovery Rate		47.54%	47.54%	47.54%	47.54%	47.54%
Survival Probability		99.88%	99.61%	99.24%	98.73%	98.29%
Recovery Adjusted Default Payment		0.0570%	0.1854%	0.3613%	0.6038%	0.8129%
Adjusted Cash Flows	$(100.0000)	$ 6.1813	$ 6.1725	$ 6.1605	$ 6.1440	$ 105.2326
Adjusted Cash Flows (IRR or YTM)	6.00%					
Discount Factor (Risk-Free Rate)		0.9434	0.8900	0.8396	0.7921	0.7473
Discounted Cash Flows	$ 100.0000	$ 5.8314	$ 5.4935	$ 5.1725	$ 4.8666	$ 78.6359
Cash Flow Difference	$ 0.0000					

The approach outlined allows the derivation of a credit spread given a term structure of risk free rates, default probabilities and recovery rates. Alternatively, given credit spreads it can be used to recover one of the other three variables provided two of these are known. Importantly, the approach does not incorporate the variability in (or distribution of) default probabilities or recovery rates.[11]

The generation of risk neutral credit spreads allows the modeling of a complete term structure of risk from limited observations. It also allows the calibration of default rates from market data.

6.6.3   Term Structure of Credit Spreads

The theory of term structure of interest rates is relatively well developed. However, the term structure of credit risk is relatively less well understood although it has begun to attract increased attention.[12]

From a theoretical perspective, the credit spread should increase in line with increasing default risk and maturity. The observed behavior of credit spreads is set out in Figure 6.6. In practise, the credit spread seems to increase with maturity only for higher credit quality bonds. The credit spread decreases for lower credit quality bonds.

Figure 6.6   Term Structure of Credit Spreads

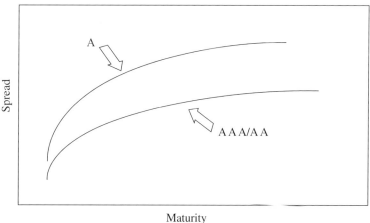

---

[11] The approach outlined is a simplification designed to illustrate the approach to derivation of risk neutral spreads. One particular simplification is the assumption that the principal remains payable at the original contracted maturity in the event of default. It is possible to develop more complex simulations (using conditional probabilities) where the principal is accelerated in the event of default

[12] See Fons, Jerome S. September–October 1994 "Using Default Rates To Model The Term Structure Of Credit Risk," *Financial Analysts Journal*, pp 25-32; Litterman, R. and Iben, T. 1988, *Corporate Bond Valuation And The Term Structure Of Credit Spreads*, Goldman Sachs Financial Strategies Group, New York

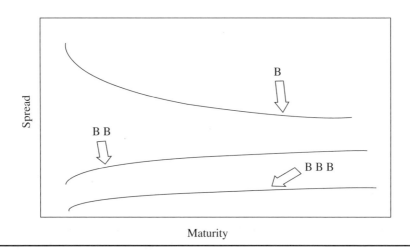

Maturity

The behavior of credit spreads reflects the impact of the following factors:[13]
- The concept of "crisis at maturity" — predicated on the risk generated by the liquidity pressures created by the need to refinance near-term maturing debt, which is often confronted by lower credit quality and highly leveraged firms.
- The pattern of default risk for lower credit quality firms whereby default risk is higher in absolute terms but the marginal default risk for lower rated firms decreases with maturity. In contrast, the marginal default risk of higher rated firms increase with maturity (see discussion below).

The pattern of marginal default risk for lower credit quality firms is consistent with the following:
- Life cycle of ratings outlook whereby lower-rated firms face higher short-term risk which is resolved by survival or default.
- Mean reversion processes in ratings outlook whereby lower-rated issuer improve, middle-rated issuer stay the same, and higher-rated firms tend to decline on average.

The derived risk neutral credit spreads, incorporating the rating sensitive term structure model, is utilized in practise to derive a complete set of credit spreads to allow the valuation and pricing of credit derivatives.[14]

---

[13] See Jerome S., September–October 1994, "Using Default Rates To Model The Term Structure Of Credit Risk", *Financial Analysts Journal*, 25–32
[14] For an overview of how credit curves are constructed in practice, see Li, David "Constructing A Credit Curve", November 1998, *Risk — Credit Risk Special Report*, 40–44

6.7 Pricing Default Risk

6.7.1   Pricing Approaches

All credit products to a lesser or greater degree revolve around the measurement of default risk and the required return to compensate for that risk. As noted above, credit default products are priced as a function of the exposure under the loan or asset, the default probability of the reference credit and the expected recovery rate. In this section, the modeling process for each of these variables is considered together with the combination of these into an integrated formal model for pricing credit derivatives.

There are two pricing approaches required:
• Individual transactions
• Portfolios

Individual transaction approaches cover the pricing of single transactions on a standalone basis. The pricing components include: the loss exposure, the default probability, the recovery rate, and the correlation between these components. Figure 6.7 sets out the pricing approach for individual credit derivatives.

Portfolio approaches require capture of the pricing interactions between the risk on individual transactions. The pricing components for a portfolio include the exposure on individual transactions and the correlation between exposures. This includes not only capture of the correlations between defaults within the portfolio (that is, the joint default probability) but also the correlation between loss exposure and also recovery rate. In practise, the latter correlations are difficult to model. Figure 6.8 sets out the pricing approach for a portfolio of credit derivatives.

Figure 6.7   Pricing Approach — Individual Transactions

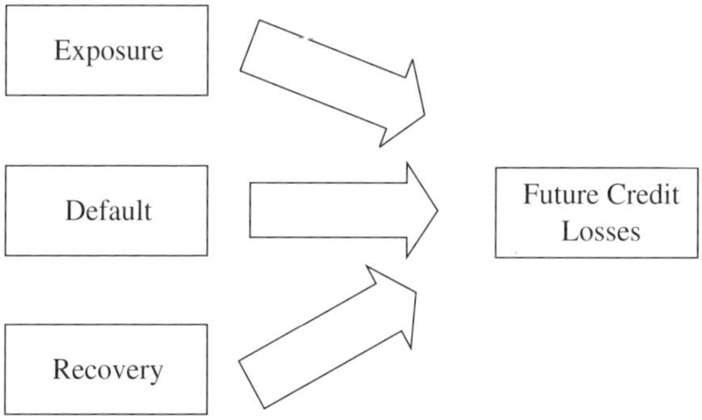

6.7.2   Modeling Credit (Loss) Exposure

Credit or loss exposure refers to the amounts exposed to risk of loss upon default occurring. In effect, this is the amount at risk in the event of default prior to adjustment for recovery.

Loss exposure can be classified into two categories:

- **Static:** Which encompasses loan type exposures, which by their inherent nature are relatively stable and independent of changes in market variables. The typical methodology for measurement of loss exposure is based on the face value of the loan (adjusted for accrued interest).
- **Non-static:** Which encompasses loss exposure, which are dynamic in nature, being usually a function of a stochastic market variable, generally a market price for an asset. Typically examples include derivative products. The loss exposure is measured utilizing the replacement cost based on the mark-to-market value of the transaction. For these instruments, the credit or loss exposure, at least, at any point of time, can be equated to the market risk of the transaction.[15]

Figure 6.9 sets out diagrammatically the nature of credit exposure in financial instruments.

---

[15] For a good overview of credit risk in derivative transactions, see Banks, Eric 1993, *The Credit Risk Of Financial Instruments*, MacMillan Publishers, England; Banks, Eric 1994, *Complex Derivatives: Understanding and Managing the Risks of Exotic Options, Complex Swaps, Warrants and Other Synthetic Derivatives*, MacMillan Publishers Ltd, England; Sorensen, Eric H. and Bollier, Thierry F. October 1993, *Pricing Of Interest Rate Swap Default Risk*, Salomon Brothers Inc., New York; 1995, *Derivative Credit Risk: Advances in Measurement and Management, Risk Publications: London; Smithson, Charles* October 1996 "Exposure Measures" *Risk*, Vol 9, No 10, pp 70–73; Zangari, Peter First Quarter 1997 "On Measuring Credit Exposure," *RiskMetrics^{TM} Monitor*, pp 3–22; Jarrow, Robert and Turnbull, Stuart "When Swaps Are Dropped," (May 1997) *Risk*, Vol 10, No 5, pp 70–75

Figure 6.8   Pricing Approach — Portfolios

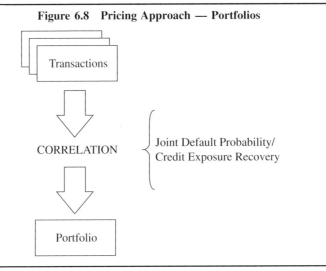

Figure 6.9   Credit Exposure in Financial Instruments

1. Static exposures

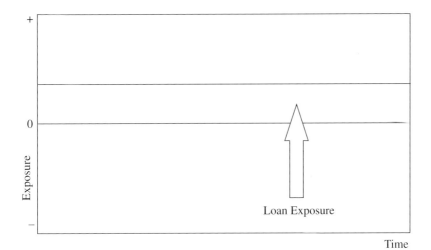

2. Dynamic exposures

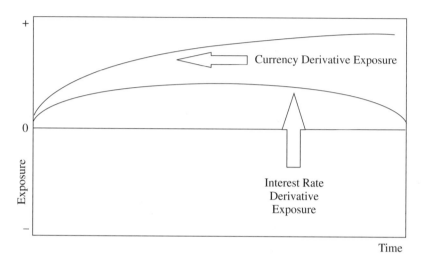

Loan types exposures are driven by the face value of the transaction. However, this approach masks the fact that changes in market rates (both absolute and credit spreads) have the ability to affect the value of the transaction and the credit risk to the investor. In this regard, the true exposure is not the face value but the present value of the remaining cash flows over the nominated risk horizon. This would be calculated using zero coupon rates derived from the current yield curve (incorporating the credit risk of the obligation) to discount the remaining cash flows. The zero rates used will need to be the forward zero curve as at the nominated risk horizon.

Undrawn commitments present different problems. The exposure is a function of the amount currently drawn under the facility, expected changes in the level of drawings, and the spreads and fees needed to revalue the drawn and undrawn portions of the facility. The amount drawn under the commitment is related to credit quality. As obligor credit quality deteriorates, the drawings under the facility will typically increase. Similarly, as obligor credit quality improves, drawings tend to be repaid. The evolution of exposure is complicated by the fact that drawings are influenced by covenants required to be satisfied prior to drawings and pricing structures. These tend to reduce volatility being designed to allow the lenders to be released from their obligation to fund where the obligor credit quality declines beyond certain pre-nominated levels.

Various models can be used to capture this pattern on exposure. CreditMetrics[TM] for example, seeks to capture commitment behavior by assuming that drawings increase upon downgrade and decrease with an upgrade in credit quality. Other models often assume simply that the lender's exposure is to the full face value of the facility.

Financial guarantees (including letters of credit) are simpler in that they will be called in the case of default. Consequently, they are equated to loans.

The exposure under dynamic market risk instruments is taken as the replacement value of the transaction plus an additional factor for future exposure. The replacement value is driven by the market factors used to price the instrument being based on the expected average exposure assuming certain levels of volatility. The future exposure is designed to cover changes (often rapid) in the level of exposure and is calculated with reference to the volatility of the relevant market factors.

The exposure under non-static transactions features two characteristics: the stochastic nature of the exposure and the possibility of zero or negative exposures. The key point to note is that exposure on a non-static transaction will alter with changes in the underlying market risk factor that dictates exposure and the time to maturity. In the case of interest rate derivatives, the exposure increases and then decreases over time as the remaining term to maturity becomes shorter. In the case of currency derivatives, the exposure increases but does not decrease reflecting the exposure on the principal amount of the transaction.

Depending on the changes in the market risk variable, it is possible that the transaction will result in zero or negative exposure, that is in the event of default, the non-defaulting party will not have any amount owing as the result of the default but will in fact owe the counterparty a termination sum. In this case, there is obviously no credit risk on the counterparty although it is not possible to predict this in advance.

The exposure under both interest rate and currency derivatives is therefore not predictable with certainty in advance but, usually, will be less than the face value of the transaction.[16]

In measuring the loss exposure it is useful to differentiate between the expected and unexpected credit loss. The expected credit loss is usually calculated as the loss exposure as at the relevant points in time and the average

---

[16] For a discussion of approaches to dealing with market driven exposures, see Rowe, David M. and Reoch, Robert D. "Aggregating Market Driven Credit Exposures: A Parameterised Monte Carlo Approach and Implications for the Use of Credit Derivatives," in 1998, *Credit Derivatives: Applications for Risk Management, Investment and Portfolio Optimisation*; Risk Books, London, Chapter 4

expected credit exposure is calculated as the average of the expected credit exposures over a given period of time (generally, the life of the transaction). The unexpected credit loss is the worst-case loss exposure calculated as the maximum exposure at a point in time. The average unexpected loss is the average worst case exposure calculated as the average of the worst case exposures over a given period of time.

6.7.3   Modeling Recovery Rates

The concept of recovery rate focuses on the amount of any loss exposure likely to be recovered from a counterparty following default. In most defaults, often after a significant period, investors in the securities recover some portion of their investment. This recovery may take a number of forms including cash, securities (debt or equity), and occasionally, assets of the business. The recovery rate may be defined as the percentage of par value of the security recovered by the investor.

There are two separate elements to the recovery rate: first, the recovery rate itself, and second, the adjustment for time value reflecting the discounting of the recovery rate from the eventual date of recovery to the date of default. The potential for delay arises from the time taken to complete the legal process required to facilitate the recovery of amounts owed as well as the time taken to realize the value of the counterparty's assets, if relevant.

There are two general approaches to modeling recovery rates:

- Utilizing recovery experience on public and/or rated securities collated by the major rating agencies.
- Information internal to the organization based on its experience in the case of default.

Figure 6.10 sets out the recovery rates published by Moody's Investor Services.[17]

---

[17] For a detailed discussion of recovery rates see Chapter 10; Carty Lea V, and Lieberman Dana , "Historical Default Rates of Corporate Bond Issuers" in Satyajit Das 1998, *Credit Derivatives*, John Wiley & Sons, Chapter 9; Altman, Edward I., and Kishore, Vellore M. "Almost Everything You Wanted To Know About Recoveries On Defaulted Bonds" November/ December 1996, *Financial Analysts Journal*, pp 57–64

Figure 6.10   Recovery Rates

Moody's Recovery Rates 1977–1998

Class of Debt	Recovery Rate (%)	Standard Deviation (%)
Senior Secured Bank Debt	70.26	21.33
Equipment Trust	65.93	28.55
Senior Secured Public Debt	55.15	24.31
Senior Unsecured Public Debt	51.31	26.3
Senior Subordinated Public Debt	39.05	24.39
Subordinated Public Debt	31.66	20.58
Junior Subordinated Public Debt	20.39	15.36
All Subordinated Public Debt	34.12	22.35
All Public Debt	45.02	26.77

Moody's Defaulted Bond Price Distribution 1974–1995

Class Of Debt	Average	Median	Std Deviation	Percentile 10th	90th
Senior Secured	53.11	56.00	24.27	18.50	85.32
Unsecured	49.86	46.56	26.32	11.46	87.88
Subordinated	32.83	30.17	19.67	9.18	60.40

Source: Carty, Lea; Lieberman, Dana; and Fons, Jerome S, January 1995, *Corporate Bond Defaults And Default Rates 1970-1994*, Moody's Investors Service Global Credit Research, New York; Carty, Lea, and Lieberman, Dana January 1997, *Historical Default Rates of Corporate Bond Defaults 1920-1996*: Moody's Investors Service Global Credit Research, New York; Keenan, Sean C., Shtogrin, Igor, and Sobehart, Jorge January 1999, *Historical Default Rate Of Corporate Bond Issuers, 1920–1998*, Moody's Investors Service Global Credit Research, New York

The recovery rates are, generally, based on the trading price of the defaulted instrument. This price is used as a proxy of the present value of the expected ultimate recovery. This approach is based on the fact that it provides an immediate measure of recovery and it corresponds to a traded market estimate of the anticipated recovery rate.

It is valid insofar as an investor can effectively liquidate any position in the securities and cap its losses or achieve recovery at the recovery level equivalent to the spot traded price of the defaulted bonds. This has the advantage of avoiding the necessity of tracking payments on defaulted bonds for a potentially long period and then discounting back these payments to generate a recovery rate. It also avoids potential valuation difficulties with securities issued in exchange for the original obligation that may prove problematic to value, given that they are issued by a defaulted or restructured issuer.

The recovery rates identified merit the following comments:
- The recovery rate, predictably, is related to the seniority of the obligation and its place in the counterparty's capital structure.
- The distribution of recovery rates does not appear to be normal.
- The recovery rates feature significant variability.
- The volatility statistics indicate that subordinated debt has a lower volatility than other classes of debt indicating that the value of these obligations in the event of default is likely to result in recovery rates close to its indicated mean.

The recovery rates also appear to be characterized by linkages to overall economic conditions. Declining GDP appears to coincide with a fall in the average recovery rates. There also appears to be some differences in the recovery rates as between securities markets and bank loans.[18]

6.7.4 Modeling Default Risk — Overview

The modeling of default risk is clearly central to pricing credit derivatives. Models for valuing default risk are not unique to credit derivatives. Default risk affects all financial transactions involving loss exposures in the event of the counterparty failing through insolvency to perform its obligations.

The difficulty in measuring and managing default risk can be illustrated by comparing default risk with market risk. Market risk characteristics include:
- Correlation between market risks particularly within but even extending across asset classes.
- The presence of these correlation relationships facilitates hedging as well as trading as taking an opposite position in one asset, price movements in which are correlated with those in the asset exposure to which is sought to be hedged, can reduce risk.

---

[18] See Carty, Lea V. and Lieberman, Dana, November 1996, *Defaulted Bank Recoveries*, Moody's Investor Service Global Credit Research; Grossman, Robert J, Brennan, William T. and Vento, Jennifer October 22, 1997, Syndicated Bank Loan Recovery Study; Fitch Research – *Structured Finance, Credit Facilities, Special Report*

In contrast, default risk appears characterized by:
- Lower correlations between default events (that is low joint default frequency).
- This lack of correlation increases the difficulty of hedging default risk with tradable instruments.
- The absence of strong correlation allows the use of diversification as a basis for reduction of default risk.

There are several different approaches to modeling default. The principal approaches include:
- **Default models:** These use of rating-based models of default and ratings migration to capture value changes in a security arising from changes in credit risk or credit spread based approaches.
- **Replication models:** These use the pricing in comparable markets such as credit insurance or guarantee product markets or how the transaction could be replicated by trading in a bond or asset swap.

In practice, default models or replication using hedges constructed from traded instruments are the dominant approaches to default modeling.

Ratings models utilizes historical data to estimate the probability of a change in value of the security resulting from a change in credit spread as a result of changes in rating (ratings migration) or default. This approach raises a number of issues:
- The default probabilities are sample specific and there may be significant differences between markets.
- Pricing is based on aggregate statistics and issuer level information is lost.

Credit spread models are based on the default probability being derived from the term structure of credit spreads of a particular issuer observable in the market. This is done using the risk neutral credit methodology outlined above. While having the obvious advantage of being issuer specific, the credit spread approach also raises a number of difficult issues:
- There are a number of mutually dependent unknowns (credit spread, default probability, and recovery rate). Consequently, assumptions must be made about either the default probability or the recovery rate in order to solve for the unknown variable given a credit spread.
- A complete term structure of credit spreads may not be available for an issuer requiring estimates.
- The impact of non-default or credit factors such as liquidity, tax and regulations, may affect the credit spread.

In the following section, two general classes of default risk models are examined:
- Rating agency based models that predict the marginal and cumulative risk of default based on rating categories.
- Proprietary models developed for the purposes of default prediction (which are generally issuer specific).

6.7.5   Rating Agency-Based Models[19]

Rating agency default models can be used to identify the risk of default for a counterparty with a known current rating. These models, which are based on historical default experience and incorporate macro-economic cycles, specify default risk as a function of two primary factors: current rating and time to maturity of the obligation.

There are two distinguishable types of default risk:
- **Cumulative risk of default:** Measures the total default probability of a counterparty over the term of the obligation.
- **Marginal risk of default:** Measures the change in default probability of a counterparty over a sequence of time periods.

Figure 6.11 sets out the cumulative and marginal default probabilities published by Moody's.[20] The marginal default probabilities in these tables are taken as the simple arithmetic differences between the cumulative default probability as at each year. Figure 6.12 sets out this information in graphical form.

The analysis shows that cumulative default probabilities increase with a decline in ratings levels but that marginal default risks decrease in the lower rating categories. The pattern of marginal default probabilities is consistent with the behavior of credit spreads discussed previously.

---

[19] For a detailed discussion of default rates, see Chapter 10 and 11

[20] See Keenan, Sean C, Shtogrin, Igor, and Sobehart, Jorge January 1999, "Historical Default Rate Of Corporate Bond Issuers, 1920-1998," Moody's Investors Service Global Credit Research, New York; Carty, Lea, March 1996, "Corporate Bond Defaults And Default Rates, 1938–1995", *Financial Derivatives and Risk Management*, 5, pp 39-50; Carty, Lea, and Lieberman, Dana January 1997, "Historical Default Rates of Corporate Bond Defaults, 1920–1996", Moody's Investors Service Global Credit Research, New York; Carty Lea V and Lieberman Dana, "Historical Default Rates of Corporate Bond Issuers" in Das Satyajit 1998, *Credit Derivatives*, John Wiley & Sons, Chapter 9

Figure 6.11   Default Probabilities

Moody's Cumulative Default Rates (%) 1970–1998

Years	1	2	3	4	5	6	7	8	9	10
Aaa	-	-	-	0.04	0.14	0.24	0.35	0.47	0.61	0.77
Aa	0.03	0.04	0.09	0.23	0.36	0.50	0.64	0.80	0.91	0.99
A	0.01	0.06	0.20	0.35	0.50	0.68	0.85	1.05	1.29	1.55
Baa	0.12	0.38	0.74	1.24	1.67	2.14	2.67	3.20	3.80	4.39
Ba	1.29	3.60	6.03	8.51	11.10	13.37	15.20	17.14	18.91	20.63
B	6.47	12.77	18.54	23.32	27.74	31.59	35.04	37.97	40.70	43.91
Investment Grade	0.05	0.15	0.33	0.58	0.81	1.06	1.34	1.63	1.94	2.27
Speculative Grade	3.82	7.69	11.27	14.44	17.49	20.14	22.33	24.46	26.38	28.32
All Corporate	1.15	2.30	3.37	4.33	5.21	5.99	6.66	7.31	7.93	8.55

Moody's Cumulative Default Rates (%), 1970–1998

Years	11	12	13	14	15	16	17	18	19	20
Aaa	0.94	1.13	1.35	1.47	1.59	1.73	1.88	2.05	2.05	2.05
Aa	1.08	1.18	1.30	1.56	1.63	1.72	1.92	2.04	2.17	2.32
A	1.81	2.09	2.35	2.56	2.86	3.19	3.52	3.86	4.24	4.45
Baa	5.04	5.71	6.35	7.02	7.72	8.46	9.19	9.88	10.44	10.89
Ba	22.50	24.54	26.55	28.21	29.86	31.70	33.28	34.66	35.88	36.99
B	45.98	47.25	48.53	49.69	51.07	52.20	52.90	52.90	52.90	52.90
Investment Grade	2.62	2.99	3.35	3.72	4.10	4.52	4.95	5.36	5.73	5.99
Speculative Grade	30.16	31.96	33.74	35.23	36.74	38.36	39.73	40.87	41.87	42.80
All Corporate	9.17	9.77	10.37	10.91	11.47	12.07	12.65	13.16	13.62	13.98

Moody's Marginal Default Rates (%), 1970–1998

Years	1	2	3	4	5	6	7	8	9	10
Aaa	-	-	-	0.04	0.10	0.10	0.11	0.12	0.14	0.16
Aa	0.03	0.01	0.05	0.14	0.13	0.14	0.14	0.16	0.11	0.08
A	0.01	0.05	0.14	0.15	0.15	0.18	0.17	0.20	0.24	0.26
Baa	0.12	0.26	0.36	0.50	0.43	0.47	0.53	0.53	0.60	0.59
Ba	1.29	2.31	2.43	2.48	2.59	2.27	1.83	1.94	1.77	1.72
B	6.47	6.30	5.77	4.78	4.42	3.85	3.45	2.93	2.73	3.21
Investment Grade	0.05	0.10	0.18	0.25	0.23	0.25	0.28	0.29	0.31	0.33
Speculative Grade	3.82	3.87	3.58	3.17	3.05	2.65	2.19	2.13	1.92	1.94
All Corporate	1.15	1.15	1.07	0.96	0.88	0.78	0.67	0.65	0.62	0.62

Moody's Marginal Default Rates (%), 1970–1998

Years	11	12	13	14	15	16	17	18	19	20
Aaa	0.17	0.19	0.22	0.12	0.12	0.14	0.15	0.17	-	-
Aa	0.09	0.10	0.12	0.26	0.07	0.09	0.20	0.12	0.13	0.15
A	0.26	0.28	0.26	0.21	0.30	0.33	0.33	0.34	0.38	0.21
Baa	0.65	0.67	0.64	0.67	0.70	0.74	0.73	0.69	0.56	0.45
Ba	1.87	2.04	2.01	1.66	1.65	1.84	1.58	1.38	1.22	1.11
B	2.07	1.27	1.28	1.16	1.38	1.13	0.70	-	-	-
Investment Grade	0.35	0.37	0.36	0.37	0.38	0.42	0.43	0.41	0.37	0.26
Speculative Grade	1.84	1.80	1.78	1.49	1.51	1.62	1.37	1.14	1.00	0.93
All Corporate	0.62	0.60	0.60	0.54	0.56	0.60	0.58	0.51	0.46	0.36

Source: Moody's Investors Service

Figure 6.12   Default Probabilities — Graphical Format

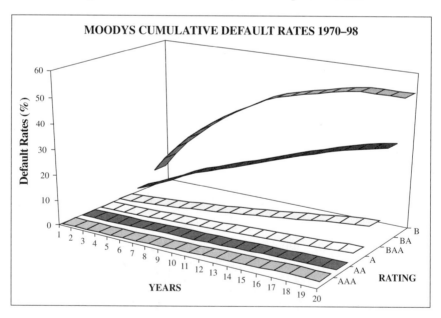

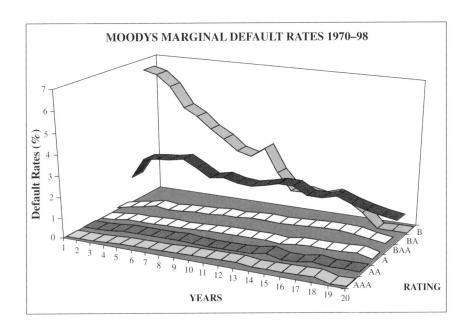

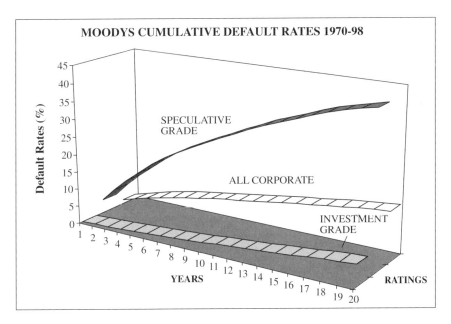

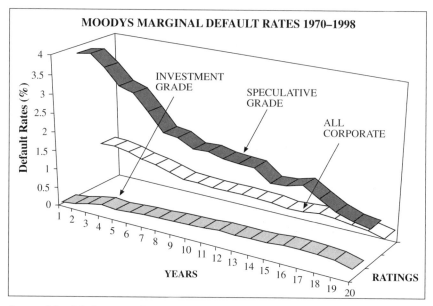

Source: Moody's Investors Service

Where a firm or entity is not rated, it is still possible to utilize rating agency default models and statistics. This will usually entail a three step process:

- Use the firm's financial data to calculate key accounting ratios. The accounting ratios usually used are those utilized by the rating agencies themselves.
- The accounting performance as captured by the ratios is compared to the comparable median for rated firms in both the industry and the universe of rated entities. The comparison is designed to allow a rating equivalent to be determined.
- Based on the theoretical rating, the default probabilities appropriate for that particular rating categories is then utilized.

6.7.6   Proprietary Models

Proprietary default prediction models are based on the original thesis by Fischer Black, Myron Scholes, and Robert Merton. This approach assumes that the equity in a risky firm is equivalent to a call option on the net asset value of the firm.[21] The net asset value is calculated as market value of the firm's assets minus the claims on the assets which include traditional financial claims such as debt and other claims including erosion of asset values that may result upon default. The position of the bond holder is a combination of the long position in the underlying bond plus the sale of a put option on the company's assets where the option has a strike price equal to the value of the debt of the entity.

The dynamics of asset behavior are as follows:

- Asset values evolve over time as a function of volatility of the asset values.
- If asset values are less than the claims on the asset value then the firm defaults which is to say the call option held by the shareholders is abandoned or the shareholders exercise the put option written by the debt providers.
- The extent to which the asset values of the entity are below that of the value of the debt equates to the loss suffered on the bond as a result of default.
- The premium paid by the shareholders for the option that is equivalent to the share price paid by the shareholder is lost in the event of default.

This model allows derivation, calculated from the distribution of asset values, of the default probability as the probability that asset values will be lower than the value of the claims on the asset. Figure 6.13 sets out the approach underlying the option based model diagrammatically.

---

[21]   See Black, Fischer and Scholes, Myron May,-June 1973, "The Pricing Of Options And Corporate Liabilities", *Journal of Political Economy*, 81, pp 637–659; Merton, R., 1974, "On The Option Pricing Of Corporate Debt: The Risk Structure Of Interest Rates", *Journal of Finance*, Vol 29, pp 449–470. For a more recent approach using the traditional option pricing framework, see Crouhy, Michael, Galai, Dan, and Mark, Robert, March 1998, "Credit Risk Revisited", *Risk – Credit Risk Supplement*, pp 40–44

Figure 6.13   Black-Scholes Merton-Based Default Model

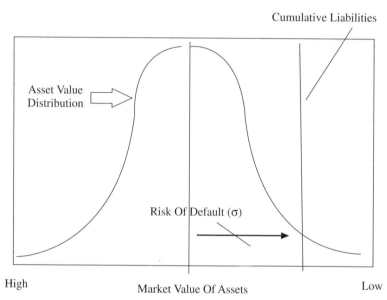

The best known of the proprietary default risk models is the Expected Default Frequency Model (EDF) developed by KMV Corp.[22] The work of Stephen Kealhofer, John McQuown and Oldrich Vasichek, the EDF model is used by a number of commercial banks and other entities to measure default risk.[23]

The implementation of this type of model requires the computation of the following parameter estimates:

- Asset values
- Asset value volatility
- Claims on asset values

The estimation of the required parameters is subject to some difficulties:

- The market value of real assets is difficult to determine because of the absence of liquid secondary markets, the difficulty in valuing intangible

---

[22] Other default risk or distress prediction models include Edward Altman's Z-score; see Altman, Edward I. 1983, *Corporate Financial Distress: A Complete Guide to Predicting, Avoiding, and Dealing With Bankruptcy*, John Wiley & Sons, New York

[23] For a detailed discussion, see Chapter 9; see also Brady, Simon, November 1998, "The Cutting Edge of Credit", *Euromoney*, pp 76–79

assets and the conventions and assumption underlying the measurement and presentation of accounting based financial information. This difficulty is compounded by the fact that the asset value must be established to incorporate any potential diminution in the value of the asset in the event of default.

- The volatility of these asset values is similarly difficult to measure. This reflects the absence of traded markets and the requisite levels of price transparency in the real underlying assets.
- The measurement of liabilities is complicated by the fact that the claims may have different maturities and are governed by different credit conditions.

There are a number of estimation approaches that seek to overcome these difficulties including that which underlies this methodology. The asset volatility can be estimated using the option pricing approach developed by Black, Scholes, and Merton that captures the relationship between asset value and asset volatility and equity value and equity volatility. Using this approach, the available equity value and equity volatility can be used to solve for the market value of asset and asset volatility. This approach requires an initial simplification that the claims are represented by a single liability due at a single date.[24] If this simplification is not applicable, then the approach remains the same, but a more complex process is required.

The asset value, asset volatility, and the cumulative liabilities allow the default risk of the firm to be calculated. The measure is calculated by determining the distance in volatility measures (standard deviations) between the asset value and the point at which the asset value will fall below the liabilities. The default probability is then determined based on the distance to default.

Models, such as EDF, utilize large databases of companies in combination with proprietary technology (predicated on the above general approach) to determine historical default frequencies. The default probabilities captured through this measure are then used as an accurate indicator of future default rates (EDF in the KMV model).[25]

---

[24] If it is assumed that all the debt is linked through cross default and cross acceleration provisions in the underlying documentation, then this simplification has more merit.

[25] The approach described here seeks to explain in general terms the theoretical approaches underpinning proprietary prediction models of default risk such as EDF. Chapter 8 contains a more detailed description of the KMV EDF model and approach. It is not designed to be a complete or comprehensive description of these complex models. Persons wishing to learn more about the models are advised to contact the vendor of the models such as KMV directly.

The major advantages of this type of approach include:
- The capacity to derive default within a volatility framework.
- The ability to estimate expected as well as unexpected default losses within a probability framework at specified confidence levels.
- The determination of the cost of dynamically hedging credit risk and trading credit risk.

One difficulty with this type of approach is the requirement that the equity of the firm whose default risk is being modeled is publicly traded. This is necessary for the derivation of equity volatility which is central to the calculation of default probabilities in allowing the asset price distribution to be generated.

In practice, the absence of traded equity can be overcome. This is achieved through the utilization of various proprietary models.[26] The basic approach is predicated on the basis that the fundamental process of default and default drivers are the same as between private companies and companies whose equity securities are traded publicly. The key default drivers (market value of assets, volatility of asset values, level of external liabilities) must be determined in the absence of equity prices. Typical private company models (such as those used by firms such as KMV) estimate the firm's equity value and volatility of asset values from accounting data. This is then transformed into asset values and volatility and combined with data on liabilities (obtained directly) to generate default risk estimates.

6.8. Modeling Expected versus Unexpected Losses

Amalgamation of the identified factors — loss exposure, recovery rate, and default probability — to determine the valuation of credit default derivatives requires incorporation of the concept of expected and unexpected losses.

Expected losses can be defined as the average expected credit loss. It is analogous to a credit loss provision. In contrast, unexpected credit loss is the worst-case credit loss. It is equivalent to the economic risk capital required to be held against the risk of this unexpected loss.

Expected loss, in a simplified case, is calculated as follows:

Expected loss = Loss Exposure × Default Probability × (1 minus Recovery Rate)

---

[26] See McQuown, J.A. "Market Versus Accounting Based Measures Of Default Risk" in Nelken, Israel (Ed) 1997, *Option Embedded Bonds: Price Analysis, Credit Risk And Investment Strategies*, Irwin Professional Publishing, Chicago, Chapter 5

This assumes statistical independence and no correlation between the factors. A more complex approach would entail incorporating the statistical dependence and correlation between the factors.

Expected loss, in this more complex case, is calculated as follows:

Expected loss = Loss Exposure × Default Probability × (1 minus Recovery Rate) × Multi-variate probability density function

Unexpected loss is calculated as the worst-case loss exposure based on the worst case probability of default. This is calculated as the expected loss plus the variance of the expected loss based on a nominated level of confidence (say, 95% or 99% confidence).

Figure 6.14 sets the pattern of expected and unexpected loss exposure. Figure 6.15 sets out in a diagrammatic form the relationship between the expected loss and the unexpected loss.

The major significance of these concepts is that the pricing of the credit default swap must reflect the following:
- The expected loss must be charged and recovered in full.
- The unexpected loss must be covered by capital committed against that exposure and the required return on the credit derivative transaction must recover the cost of risk capital committed.

Figure 6.14   Expected Versus Unexpected Loss

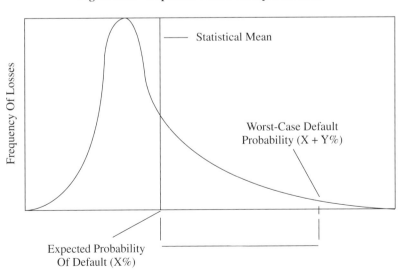

Figure 6.15   Expected Versus Unexpected Credit Losses And Implications

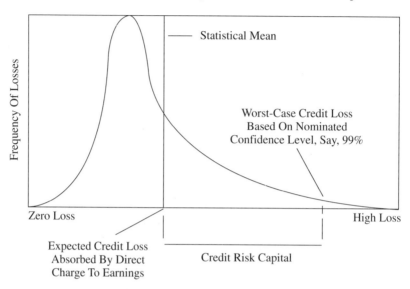

The calculation of the expected versus the unexpected credit loss entails certain problems. The expected loss is equivalent to the average default probability for the relevant maturity for the relevant entity adjusted for the recovery rate. The calculation of the unexpected losses is more difficult. Two approaches are possible:

- In the case of rating agency type default models, the unexpected loss can be modeled as the distribution of default probabilities. This can be calculated as the range of defaults for a particular credit rating category for a specific maturity. This data is available from the cohort group studies done by rating agencies. However, the often low small size of defaults, particularly at the higher rating levels, and the fact that the distribution of defaults is unlikely to be normal makes the use of this data as the basis for prediction of unexpected loss extremely risky. Figure 6.16 sets out Moody's estimates of one-year default rate volatility.[27]

---

[27] See also Carty, Lea V and Lieberman, Dana "Historical Default Rates of Corporate Bond Issuers" in Satyajit Das (Ed) 1998, *Credit Derivatives*, John Wiley & Sons, Chapter 9

Figure 6.16   One Year Default Rate Volatility

Rating	One-Year Default Rate Volatility (%) (1920–1998)	One-Year Default Rate Volatility (%) (1970–1998)
Aaa	0.00	0.00
Aa	0.18	0.11
A	0.23	0.05
Baa	0.48	0.28
Ba	1.72	1.37
B	4.57	4.99

Source: Keenan, Sean C., Shtogrin, Igor, and Sobehart, Jorge, January 1999 "Historical Default Rate Of Corporate Bond Issuers, 1920-1998," Moody's Investors Service Global Credit Research, New York, pp 18

- In case of option based default prediction models, the unexpected loss can be calculated off the distribution of asset values using a nominated confidence level. This approach also needs to make assumptions about the nature of the underlying distribution that may prove to difficult to predict in practise.

The difficulty with the determination of the unexpected loss is particularly problematic given the importance of this parameter in pricing credit default.

6.9   Pricing Models — Approach

The default pricing models seek to combine the loss exposure, recovery rate, and default probability into a quantification of the credit risk of a transaction and the fair value that compensates for that risk. Where portfolios are involved, the various correlations between the individual components, most significantly the default correlations, must be incorporated. Using this basic framework, it would be feasible to value a credit derivative, combining the loss exposure, recovery rate, and default probability.

Figure 6.17 sets out a simple calculation of the pricing of credit risk for both a static (loan exposure) and a non-static exposure (an interest rate and a currency transaction).

Figure 6.17   Pricing Default Risk

Approach

The pricing is done for different categories of credit — AA and BBB. The pricing is done for two maturities — 5 and 10 years. In each case, the following assumptions are made:

1. The credit exposure for loans is assumed to be the face value of the transaction while for derivatives it is assumed to be percentages of face value (a lower percentage for average expected exposure and a higher for expected worst case exposure).
2. In the case of derivatives, the probability for positive exposures to the bank is set at 50%. This implies that 50% of the time, there will be no exposure under the transaction as market price fluctuations will result in the bank owing a termination payment to the counterparty in the case of a default.
3. The expected loss is calculated based on the expected default probabilities for the relevant maturity for the particular credit rating.
4. The unexpected loss is subjectively set at a multiple of the expected loss.
5. The recovery rate assumed is that for unsecured obligations.
6. The cost of capital is assumed to be 15% pa pre-tax and the interest rate for amortization purposes is set at the swap rate for the relevant maturity.

The model is used to derive an arbitrage-free or risk-neutral price for the assumption of the credit risk. This is calculated as the sum of the expected loss charge and the cost of capital required to be held against the unexpected losses. The pricing is shown on both a flat fee and an amortized per annum charge basis.

Note that the approach here is very simplistic and is for illustrative purposes only. For example, for simplicity, the calculation takes the expected loss charge and adds the capital charge for the unexpected loss to it to drive the pricing. In reality, the expected loss is contained within the unexpected loss. Therefore, in practise, the capital charge would be lower reflecting that the capital held would be reduced by the expected loss providing that is already charged to capital by being expensed in the profit and loss account and reducing capital in this way.

Please note that the pricing examples set out below are merely intended as an example. The assumed unexpected losses, etc, are merely hypothetical and are, in no way, intended to provide an indication of suggested pricing levels for default risk.

Pricing Default Risk — AA/Aa Rated Credit – 5 years

Counterparty Rating	Aa	Aa	Aa
Transaction Final Maturity (Years)	5	5	5
Type Of Transaction	Static Loan Or Security Exposure	Non Static Interest Rate Derivative	Non Static Currency Derivative
Seniority Of Exposure	Senior Unsecured	Senior Unsecured	Senior Unsecured
Interest Rate	6.000%	6.000%	6.000%
Cost Of Capital	20.00%	20.00%	20.00%
Face Or Notional Value	$1,000,000	$1,000,000	$1,000,000
Average Credit Exposure	$1,000,000	$50,000	$200,000
Worst-Case Credit Exposure	$1,000,000	$100,000	$400,000

Probability Of Counterparty Default			
Cumulative Default Probability	0.40%	0.40%	0.40%
Worst-Case Default Probability	1.80%	1.80%	1.80%
Probability Of Positive Exposures	100.00%	50.00%	50.00%
Recovery Rate	47.54%	47.54%	47.54%

Default Pricing

Expected Loss			
Expected Loss Amount (Pre-Recovery)	$4,000	$100	$400
Expected Loss Amount (Post-Recovery)	$2,098.40	$52.46	$210
Expected Loss Amount (Post-Recovery)	0.2098%	0.0052%	0.0210%
Unexpected Loss			
Unexpected Loss	$18,000	$1,800	$7,200
Economic Capital Requirement	$18,000	$1,800	$7,200
Capital Cost Recovery (pa)	$3,600	$ 360	$1,440
Capital Cost Recovery (Present Value)	$15,165	$1,516	$6,066
Unexpected Loss Charge	1.5165%	0.1516%	0.6066%
Total Charge	1.7263%	0.1569%	0.6276%
Total Charge	$17,263	$1,569	$6,276
Total Charge (pa)	0.4098%	0.0372%	0.1490%

Pricing Default Risk — AA/Aa Rated Credit – 10 years

Counterparty Rating	Aa	Aa	Aa
Transaction Final Maturity (Years)	10	10	10
Type Of Transaction	Static Loan Or Security Exposure	Non Static Interest Rate Derivative	Non Static Currency Derivative
Seniority Of Exposure	Senior Unsecured	Senior Unsecured	Senior Unsecured
Interest Rate	6.000%	6.000%	6.000%
Cost Of Capital	20.00%	20.00%	20.00%
Face Or Notional Value	$1,000,000	$1,000,000	$1,000,000
Average Credit Exposure	$1,000,000	$100,000	$400,000
Worst-Case Credit Exposure	$1,000,000	$200,000	$800,000
Probability Of Counterparty Default			
Cumulative Default Probability	1.13%	1.13%	1.13%
Worst-Case Default Probability	2.40%	2.40%	2.40%
Probability Of Positive Exposures	100.00%	50.00%	50.00%
Recovery Rate	47.54%	47.54%	47.54%

Default Pricing

Expected Loss			
Expected Loss Amount (Pre-Recovery)	$11,300	$565	$2,260
Expected Loss Amount (Post-Recovery)	$5,928	$296	$1,186
Expected Loss Amount (Post-Recovery)	0.5928%	0.0296%	0.1186%
Unexpected Loss			
Unexpected Loss	$24,000	$4,800	$19,200
Economic Capital Requirement	$24,000	$4,800	$19,200
Capital Cost Recovery (pa)	$4,800	$ 960	$3,840
Capital Cost Recovery (Present Value)	$35,328	$7,066	$28,263
Unexpected Loss Charge	3.5328%	0.7066%	2.8263%
Total Charge	4.1256%	0.7362%	2.9448%
Total Charge	$ 41,256	$ 7,362	$ 29,448
Total Charge (pa)	0.5605%	0.1000%	0.4001%

Pricing Default Risk — BBB/Baa Rated Credit – 5 years

Counterparty Rating	Baa	Baa	Baa
Transaction Final Maturity (Years)	5	5	5
Type Of Transaction	Static Loan Or Security Exposure	Non Static Interest Rate Derivative	Non Static Currency Derivative
Seniority Of Exposure	Senior Unsecured	Senior Unsecured	Senior Unsecured
Interest Rate	6.000%	6.000%	6.000%
Cost Of Capital	20.00%	20.00%	20.00%
Face Or Notional Value	$1,000,000	$1,000,000	$1,000,000
Average Credit Exposure	$1,000,000	$50,000	$200,000
Worst-Case Credit Exposure	$1,000,000	$100,000	$400,000
Probability Of Counterparty Default			
Cumulative Default Probability	1.71%	1.71%	1.71%
Worst-Case Default Probability	4.80%	4.80%	4.80%
Probability Of Positive Exposures	100.00%	50.00%	50.00%
Recovery Rate	47.54%	47.54%	47.54%

Default Pricing

Expected Loss			
Expected Loss Amount (Pre-Recovery)	$17,100.00	$427.50	$1,710.00
Expected Loss Amount (Post-Recovery)	$8,970.66	$224.27	$897.07
Expected Loss Amount (Post-Recovery)	0.8971%	0.0224%	0.0897%
Unexpected Loss			
Unexpected Loss	$48,000	$4,800	$19,200
Economic Capital Requirement	$48,000	$4,800	$19,200
Capital Cost Recovery (pa)	$9,600	$ 960	$3,840
Capital Cost Recovery (Present Value)	$40,439	$4,044	$16,176
Unexpected Loss Charge	4.0439%	0.4044%	1.6175%
Total Charge	4.9409%	0.4268%	1.7073%
Total Charge	$49,409	$4,268	$17,073
Total Charge (pa)	1.1730%	0.1013%	0.4053%

Pricing Default Risk — BBB/Baa Rated Credit – 10 years

Counterparty Rating	Baa	Baa	Baa
Transaction Final Maturity (Years)	10	10	10
Type Of Transaction	Static Loan Or Security Exposure	Non Static Interest Rate Derivative	Non Static Currency Derivative
Seniority Of Exposure	Senior Unsecured	Senior Unsecured	Senior Unsecured
Interest Rate	6.000%	6.000%	6.000%
Cost Of Capital	20.00%	20.00%	20.00%
Face Or Notional Value	$1,000,000	$1,000,000	$1,000,000
Average Credit Exposure	$1,000,000	$100,000	$400,000
Worst-Case Credit Exposure	$1,000,000	$200,000	$800,000
Probability Of Counterparty Default			
Cumulative Default Probability	4.61%	4.61%	4.61%
Worst-Case Default Probability	9.40%	9.40%	9.40%
Probability Of Positive Exposures	100.00%	50.00%	50.00%
Recovery Rate	47.54%	47.54%	47.54%

Default Pricing

Expected Loss			
Expected Loss Amount (Pre-Recovery)	$46,100	$2,305	$9,220
Expected Loss Amount (Post-Recovery)	$24,184	$1,209	$4,837
Expected Loss Amount (Post-Recovery)	2.4184%	0.1209%	0.4837%
Unexpected Loss			
Unexpected Loss	$94,000	$18,800	$75,200
Economic Capital Requirement	$94,000	$18,800	$75,200
Capital Cost Recovery (pa)	$18,800	$3,760	$15,040
Capital Cost Recovery ($ Present Value)	$138,370	$27,674	$110,696
Unexpected Loss Charge	13.8370%	2.7674%	11.0696%
Total Charge	16.2554%	2.8883%	11.5533%
Total Charge	$162,554	$28,883	$115,533
Total Charge (pa)	2.2086%	0.3924%	1.5697%

The approach outlines provides a broad overview into the process of pricing credit risk. In particular, it highlights the crucial importance of the default rate volatility (the loss distribution) as captured through the unexpected loss component of the pricing structure. In practise, the valuation of credit exposure is more complex and a more rigorous approach is required.

6.10 Types of Pricing Models

6.10.1 Overview[28]

Mathematical default pricing approaches are designed to take the identified individual parameters and combine them into a generalized pricing model for

---

[28] For an overview, see Brooks, Robert and Yan, David Yong "Pricing Credit Default Swaps And The Implied Default Probability", *Derivatives Quarterly*, Winter 1998, 34-41; Skora, Richard "Rational Modelling of Credit Risk and Credit Derivatives" in (1998) *Credit Derivatives: Applications for Risk Management, Investment and Portfolio Optimisation*; Risk Books, London at Chapter 10; Arvantis, Angelo, Browne, Christopher, Gregory, Jon and Martin, Richard "A Credit Risk Toolbox" (December 1998) *Risk*, 50–55; James, Jessica "Pricing and Other Risks of Credit Dervatives" in Storrow, Jamie 1999, *Credit Derivatives: Key Issues — 2nd Edition*, British Bankers Association, London at Chapter 7; Duffies, Darrell, January/February 1999, "Credit Swap Valuation," *Financial Analyst's Journal*, 73–87; Blacher, Guillame, 28–29 November 1999, "Guidelines For Pricing And Risk Managing Credit Derivatives", *Financial Products*, 8–9; J.P. Morgan, December 1999, "The Price Of Credit", *Risk*, 68–71; Hayt, Greg, January 2000, "How To Price Credit Risk", *Risk*, 87–88

valuing the individual credit derivative transaction. Two classes of models exist: transactional models and portfolio models.

Transaction-based models require specification of the individual parameters:

- Loss exposure — specified as follows:
  - For static exposures, as the default payout structure for each component combined with a risk-free term structure to value the remaining cash flows as at future dates.
  - For non-static exposures, a market risk factor-based model is specified for determining the loss exposure at future dates as a function of the path of the market risk factor.
- The credit default process is specified in terms of the default risk process that captures the total loss distribution.
- Recovery rate is specified as a defaulted bond price or equivalent process incorporating the distribution of security market prices. This may include specification of the volatility and distribution of recovery rates.
- The correlations between the following are also specified:
  - Default risk and exposure process (it is often assumed to be independent)
  - Default probability and recovery rate (predicated on their joint dependency on the business cycle).

The portfolio model incorporates the individual transaction exposures and adjusts these to recognize correlation between default events.[29] This is measured in a number of ways including using equity correlations.[30] The intuitive rationale for incorporating these correlations is the commonality of industry factors, meaning changes will affect the default probability for firms in the industry. The individual firm impact will also reflect individual risk factors (like financial leverage) and industry economics, where the exit of one party may enhance the viability of existing competitors.

The parameters are then modeled as distributions of the value of the cash flows through price space over the period to maturity. The exposure is estimated at each node of the price space by calculating a distribution of loss exposures, the expected and unexpected losses, and the expected recovery rate. The expected payoffs are then calculated and discounted back to the present. The

---

[29] Referred to as joint default frequency (JDF) in KMV's EDF model

[30] It is understood that KMV utilizes an indirect technique to measure JDF from individual EDFs. This is based on the rationale that if the businesses of two firms are correlated, then the asset values and volatilities are correlated. The asset value JDFs are then used to calculate JDFs.

techniques used to model the distribution include Binomial trees or Monte Carlo simulations.

As already noted, the key element in modeling and pricing credit risk is the need to model default rate volatility and the loss distribution. The types of pricing models utilized in practise are dictated to a large degree by the approach to modeling this parameter.

Several types of approaches are available:

- **Modeling default rate volatility as a discrete variable:** Under this approach, the possible default rates are mapped by using historical data of ratings and rating transitions.[31] The underlying logic of this approach is that it captures the distribution of rating changes and by using forward rates and credit spreads at different levels, it can be used to capture changes in value of the underlying obligations. The credit risk of the portfolio requires correlation between defaults to be used. This is often referred to as the rating transition approach. JP Morgan's CreditMetrics[TM] approach is an example of this type of modeling technique.

- **Modeling default rate volatility as continuous variable:** Under this approach, the possible default rate is generated by a default rate and volatility of default rate. The underlying logic is to incorporate consideration of both the probability of loss (the default rate) and the severity of loss (the volatility). This approach is based on a non-life insurance approach. Portfolio risk can be captured in terms of spread correlations and can be built into the model. This approach is referred to as the credit spread approach. CSFP's CREDITRISK[+] is an example of this approach.

A third approach that has been used is the arbitrage-free approach.[32] This type of technique relies on calculating the implied default rate from spread data for individual issuers and spread data for generic rating groups. Implied spread volatility is generated from volatility of credit spreads in bond markets, spread options, and also standby credit facilities in the loan markets. The credit instruments are priced using market data as at a specified risk horizon using current and implied values for default and spreads.

---

[31] See Chapter 11, Carty, Lea V, "Moody's Rating Migration and Credit Quality Correlation, 1920–1996" in Das Satyajit, (Ed) 1998, *Credit Derivatives*, John Wiley & Sons, Chapter 10

[32] See Geoff Chaplin, "The Credit Balance," *Financial Products*, Issue 78, pp 12–13

The arbitrage approach is motivated by the fact that other approaches often generate values where the actual and calculated prices of credit instruments do not agree. This lack of insistence that the derived price replicates market prices can create significant difficulties in hedging credit derivatives in the cash markets. The major benefit of the arbitrage-free approach is that it avoids the possibility of arbitrage between the credit derivative and the replicating portfolio.[33]

Within this framework, a number of models have been proposed.[34] The models are predicated on the theoretical approaches to the valuation of risky debt using the evolution of firm value as its fundamental basis.[35] However, in general, the pricing models, which are increasingly favored, model the risky debt directly (the so-called reduced form models). These reduced form models fall into three categories:

---

[33] This occurs in other areas of derivative pricing such as interest-rate term structure models like equilibrium-type models. In order to overcome this, no arbitrage model may be utilized to ensure that the model recovers traded market prices through a calibration process.

[34] For a comparison of the different modeling approaches, see Koyluoglu, H. Ugur and Hickman, Andrew, October 1998, "Reconciliable Differences", *Risk*, pp 56–62; see also Locke, Jane, September 1998, "Credit Check", *Risk*, 40– 44; Locke, Jane, November 1998, "Off-the-peg, Off-the-mark?" *Risk – Credit Risk Special Report*, pp 22-27; Paul-Choudhury, Sumit, November 1998, "A Model Combination", *Risk – Credit Risk Special Report*, pp 18–20

[35] For literature on credit modeling, see Black, Fischer and Scholes, Myron, May–June 1973, "The Pricing Of Options And Corporate Liabilities", *Journal of Political Economy* 81, pp 637–659; Merton, R. 1974, "On The Option Pricing Of Corporate Debt: The Risk Structure Of Interest Rates", *Journal of Finance*, Vol 29, pp 449–470; Black, F. and Cox, J., 1976, "Valuing Corporate Securities: Some Effects of Bond Indenture Provisions", *Journal of Finance*, Vol 31, No 3, pp 361–367; Bhattacharya, S. and Mason, S., 1981, "Risky Debt, Jump Processes and Safety Covenants", *Journal of Financial Economics*, Vol 9, No 3, pp 281–307; Shimko, D, Tejima, N, and Van Deventer, D., 1993, "The Pricing of Risky Debt When Interest Rates Are Stochastic", *The Journal of Fixed Income*, Vol 3, pp 58–65; Leland, H., 1994, "Corporate Debt Value, Bond Covenants, and Optimal Capital Structure", *Journal of Finance*, Vol 49, pp 1213–1252

- **Credit rating models:** These models utilize credit ratings that are assumed to change over, driven by a Markov process to model default and to create a matrix of ratings transitions.[36]
- **Credit spread models:** These models use a specified process for the credit spread to generate the loss distribution.[37]
- **Default models:** These models specify a stochastic process for the default event itself and use this as the basis of modeling credit losses.[38]

An issue with reduced form models is the fact that they make no assumptions as to the cause of default.[39] Default is treated as almost a chance event. The default arrival rate must be estimated, in practise, from the observed price of the issuer's debt obligations. This assumes the efficiency of the underlying debt market. In practise, the hedge ratio derived from these models is necessarily subject to potentially significant error.[40]

---

[36] See Jarrow, R, Lando, D, and Turnbull, 1997, S "A Markov Model For The Term Structure of Credit Risk Spreads", *Review of Financial Studies*, Vol 10, pp 481–523; Das, Sanjiv Ranjan and Tufano, Peter, June 1996, "Pricing Credit-Sensitive Debt When Interest Rates, Credit Ratings and Credit Spreads Are Stochastic", *The Journal of Financial Engineering*, Vol 5, No 2, pp 161–198; Lando, David 1998, "On Rating Transition Analysis and Correlation" in *Credit Derivatives: Applications for Risk Management, Investment and Portfolio Optimisation*, Risk Books, London, Chapter 11

[37] See Ramaswamy, K. and Sunderesan, S. 1986, "The Valuation of Floating Rate Instruments: Theory And Evidence", *Journal Of Financial Economics*, pp 261–272; Das, Sanjiv Ranjan, Spring 1995, "Credit Risk Derivatives", *Journal of Derivatives*, pp 7–23;

[38] See Jarrow, R. and Turnbull, S., 1995, "Pricing Options On Financial Securities Subject To Default Risk", *Journal of Finance*, Vol 50, pp 53–86; Longstaff, F. and Schwartz, E., 1995, "A Simple Approach To Valuing Fixed and Floating Rate Debt", *Journal of Finance*, Vol 50, pp 789–819; Duffie, D. and Huang, M., 1996, "Swap Rates and Credit Quality", *Journal of Finance*, Vol 51; Duffie, D., Schroeder, M., and Skidas, C., 1996, "Recursive Valuation of Defaultable securities And The Timing Of Resolution of Uncertainty", *Annals of Applied Probability*, Vol 6, pp 1075–1090; Flesaker, Bjorn, Hughston, Lane, Schreiber, Laurance, and Sprung, Lloyd, September 1994, "Taking All The Credit", *Risk*, Vol 7, No 9, pp 104–108; Hughston, L.P., March 1996, "Pricing Of Credit Derivatives", *Financial Derivatives and Risk Management* 5, pp 11–16

[39] This should be contrasted with models based on equity prices (such as the Black-Scholes- Merton approach) where default is assumed to be the insufficiency of assets to meet liabilities rather than a chance event

[40] For an interesting exchange regarding the merits of different approaches to modeling, see Letter to the Editor (October 1998) *Risk* 19; Arvantis, Angelo and Laurent, Jean-Paul, October 1999, "On The Edge Of Completeness, *Risk*, pp 61–65

Variations on these structures have also emerged. One notable variation is a model developed by McKinsey & Co. This model focuses on the risk of a credit portfolio that explicitly link credit default and credit migration behavior to the macroeconomic factors that are major drivers of the credit quality of the portfolio. The McKinsey approach is also broader in its focus having been designed to be applied to all customer segments and product types. This would encompass liquid loans and bonds (which are the principal focus of the other approaches) but also less liquid classes of credit assets such as medium-sized/ small corporate loans and retail mortgage and credit card portfolios.[41]

6.10.2   Credit Rating Models

Credit rating models utilize credit ratings that are assumed to change over driven by a specified process to model default and to create a matrix of ratings transitions. In this section, the approach used by CreditMetrics[TM] is used to illustrate the technique.[42]

The basic technique uses historical rating migration information to build a distribution of credit outcomes at a nominated future date that coincides with the nominated risk horizon (CreditMetrics[TM] assumes a one-year risk horizon). The key steps are as follows:

1. A historical transition matrix is derived (usually from ratings data).
2. Current and implied forward zero rates (incorporating risk-free rates and credit spreads) for the relevant rating levels.
3. The bond is the valued as of the forward date utilizing:
   — Current market values
   — Expected values based on the probability of specific rating levels being attained and the bond price based on the implied forward rate and spread levels.
4. The price information is used to derive a distribution of values allowing the calculation of the economic risk capital required to be held consistent with a nominated confidence level (this is analogous to a credit based value at risk).
5. For a portfolio, estimates of correlations are then used to aggregate portfolio risks.

Figure 6.18 sets out an example of this approach.

---

[41]   See Wilson, Thomas "Portfolio Credit Risk (I)" (September 1997) *Risk*, Vol 10 No 9, pp 111–117; Wilson, Thomas "Portfolio Credit Risk (II)" (October1997) *Risk*, Vol 10 No 10, pp 56–61
[42]   For a detailed description of the CreditMetrics[TM] Approach see Chapter 13; (2 April 1997) CreditMetrics[TM] – Technical Document ; J.P. Morgan Securities Inc, New York

Figure 6.18   CreditMetrics™ Example

Assume an investor is holding a BBB rated bond. The bond has a coupon of 6.00% pa and a 5-year maturity.

In order to determine its credit exposure defined in terms of the volatility of a standalone instrument, the investor will need to:

1. Determine the possibility of the issuer's credit quality changing.
2. Establish the value of the instrument held as at the relevant risk horizon based on either the forward zero curve for each credit rating category and in case of default, based on the recovery rate that will be derived from the seniority of the exposure.
3. The volatility of value due to credit quality changes is then derived from combining the previous two steps.

Assume the credit quality migration is given by the following 1-year transition matrix:

Initial Rating At Year-end

(%)	AAA	AA	A	BBB	BB	B	CCC	Default
AAA	90.81	8.33	0.68	0.06	0.12	0.00	0.00	0.00
AA	0.70	90.65	7.79	0.64	0.06	0.14	0.02	0.00
A	0.09	2.27	91.05	5.52	0.74	0.26	0.01	0.06
BBB	0.02	0.33	5.95	86.93	5.30	1.17	0.12	0.18
BB	0.03	0.14	0.67	7.73	80.53	8.84	1.00	1.06
B	0.00	0.11	0.24	0.43	6.48	83.46	4.07	5.20
CCC	0.00	0.00	0.22	1.30	2.38	11.24	64.86	19.79

Source: Standard & Poor's *Creditweek*, April 15, 1996

Based on the probability of the credit quality of the instrument changing, each instrument must be revalued. The revaluation parameters are as follows:

- Revaluation in case of default based on recovery rates — see table below:

Seniority Class	Mean (%)	Standard Deviation (%)
Senior Secured	53.80	26.86
Senior Unsecured	51.13	25.45
Senior Subordinated	38.52	23.81
Subordinated	32.74	20.18
Junior Subordinated	17.09	10.90

Source: Moody's Investors Service

- Revaluation based on bond values using different rates and credit spreads based on rating levels as at the risk horizon. The following 1-year forward zero rates are used:

Rating Category	Year (%)			
	1	2	3	4
AAA	3.60	4.17	4.73	5.12
AA	3.65	4.22	4.78	5.17
A	3.72	4.32	4.93	5.32
BBB	4.10	4.67	5.25	5.63
BB	5.55	6.02	6.78	7.27
B	6.05	7.02	8.03	8.52
CCC	15.05	15.02	14.03	13.52

This information can now be used to determine the possible range of 1-year forward values for the BBB rated bonds plus the coupon as follows:

Rating Category	Price 1-Year Forward
AAA	109.35
AA	109.17
A	108.64
BBB	107.53
BB	102.01
B	98.09
CCC	83.63
Default	51.13

The estimate of the volatility of value can now be derived as follows:

Year-End Rating	AAA	AA	A	BBB	BB	B	CCC	Default
State Probability	0.02%	0.33%	5.95%	86.93%	5.30%	1.17%	0.12%	0.18%
Fwd Bond Value	109.35	109.17	108.64	107.53	102.01	98.09	83.63	51.13
Probability Weighted Value	0.02	0.36	6.46	93.48	5.41	1.15	0.10	0.09

The bond value distribution is as follows:

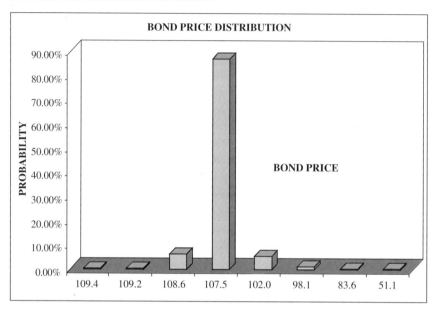

The credit risk can now be derived from the value (or loss distribution) set out below:

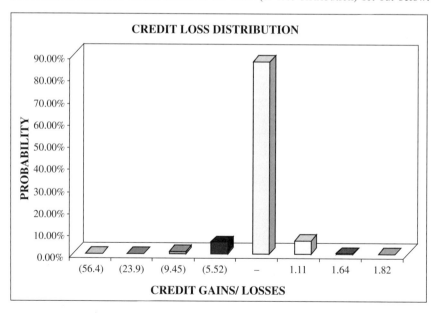

The bond/credit loss distribution can be utilized to derive the credit risk by calculating the standard deviation or using percentile measures to generate the risk statistics.

The standard deviation of the bond values is set out below:

Mean Value	$107.09
Standard Deviation	$2.99
Adjustment For Recovery Value Uncertainty	
Standard Deviation	$3.18

The mean value of the bond when compared to the estimated value of the bond (assuming no change in credit quality — that is, no credit risk) can be used to calculate the expected loss. The volatility of loss as calculated from the standard deviation using a nominated confidence level can be used to derive the unexpected loss. The adjustment for recovery value uncertainty relates to the fact that the recovery rate is not fixed and is quite volatile. This uncertainty adds to the credit risk of holding of the bond. The adjustment uses a mathematical procedure to derive an allowance for this additional risk.[43]

An alternative manner in which the risk may be derived uses the calculation of percentile level as a measure of risk. The percentile technique is useful given the asymmetric nature of the distribution. Based on a 99% confidence level, in this case the derived value is $98.10 (a loss of $8.99 relative to the mean projected bond value). This equates to the economic capital requirement against credit risk at a 99% confidence level.

Source: April 2, 1997, *Introduction to CreditMetrics*[TM]; J.P. Morgan Securities Inc, New York, pp 23–33

The application of this approach to a portfolio requires incorporation of credit default correlations. This reflects the joint likelihood of credit quality changes as ratings outcomes of different obligors are not independent of each other.

The choices available to estimate default correlations include:
- Actual rating and default correlations based on rating agency data
- Bond spread correlations
- Uniform constant correlations
- Equity price correlations.

CreditMetrics[TM] uses equity price correlations at industry and country level. The correlations are used are as follows:
- Individual obligors are mapped to industry and country on the basis of the classification that is most likely to determine its credit performance.

---

[43] For a description of this methodology see, April 2, 1997 *CreditMetrics*[TM] – *Technical Document*, J.P. Morgan Securities Inc, New York, Appendix D

- Firms are then related to one another via common sensitivity to industry and/ or country sectors.

Figure 6.19 outlines the process by which the credit exposures are consolidated under this approach.

Figure 6.19   Consolidating Exposures Under CreditMetrics

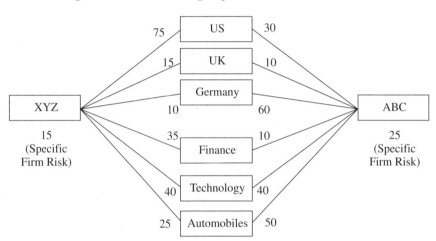

Source: April 2, 1997, *Introduction to CreditMetrics^{TM}*; J.P. Morgan Securities Inc, New York, pp 23–33

The advantage of this approach includes the fact that it allows the size of the axes of the correlation matrix to be reduced. It also allows correlations to be calculated for certain types of firms such as private firms or illiquid stocks. However, the approach does not capture specific risks associated with an individual obligor. In essence, the approach is focused on industry and country level risk factors, rather than firm specific risk factors. This means this approach is best suited to large well diversified risk portfolios.

The approach can be used to generate the following types of credit risk data:
- For an individual position, a risk estimate based on the loss distribution.
- For a portfolio it allows marginal risk statistics of the portfolio to be generated to derive both the average risk of the portfolio and the marginal risk contribution of individual transactions.

This allows the model to be used for a variety of applications including: credit portfolio management; risk-based exposure limits; risk-based pricing; and risk-based capital allocation.[44]

The model has significant numerical implementation issues. The number of values required is very large. This can be illustrated as follows:

- For individual exposures, a single position and 8 state outcomes (the credit migration possibilities) equates to 8 possible value states that can be observed at the risk horizon. For n bonds and 8 state outcomes, this corresponds to 8n possible value states that must be observed at the risk horizon.
- For a portfolio of n bonds and 8 state outcomes, calculation of portfolio risk requires estimation of correlations between credit quality migrations to 8n possible outcomes.

For a large portfolio with a large number of obligors, the number of possible outcomes becomes very large. This means that it is practically not feasible to use all possible portfolio states to obtain the value distribution. CreditMetrics overcomes this problem by relying on a reduced set of portfolio values. This reduced set is selected through random sampling to avoid selection bias. The process is designed so that the plot of the calculated distribution starts to approach the smooth underlying distribution. The process is numerically intensive and utilizes monte carlo simulation techniques.

6.10.3 Credit Spread Models

Credit spread models use a specified process for the credit spread to generate the loss distribution. As noted above, CSFP's CREDITRISK$^+$ model is an example of this approach.[45]

The basic approach is analogous to a non-life insurance framework where claims are assessed on a case-by-case basis and then losses are combined to form a severity distribution (the Pareto curve). The frequency loss distribution is modeled as a Poisson distribution or a negative binomial distribution. This allows aggregate loss distribution and associated percentiles/summary statistics to be generated for a portfolio.

---

[44] See Chapter 13, April 2, 1997, *CreditMetrics^{TM} — Technical Document*, J.P. Morgan Securities Inc, New York

[45] See Chapter 14, 1997 *CREDITRISK^1: A Credit Risk Management Framework*, Credit Suisse Financial Products

The distinguishing features of this approach include:

- Default rates are treated as continuous variable and a volatility of default rate is used to capture the uncertainty in the level of default rates. In contrast, the credit rating migration approach (such as CreditMetrics[TM]) treats default as a discrete variable which is modeled using the rating transition matrix.
- Default correlations are incorporated through the use of default rate volatility and sector volatility rather than as explicit default correlations. This has the merit of avoiding the problems of estimation of default correlations and the lack of stability of default correlations. It also has the advantage of making it easier to perform scenario analysis on the default rate volatility.

The model is based on the insurance approach whereby the portfolio consists of a large number of small risks where each risk has a low probability of occurring. The model generates the distribution of default events at a given time (the effective risk horizon). If the volatility of default rates are ignored, this distribution approximates a Poisson distribution. The model incorporates the uncertainty of default rates by specifying a default rate and a default rate volatility which is then used to generate a distribution of portfolio losses. Figure 6.20 sets out the typical distribution of default and losses generated using this approach.

Figure 6.20   Distribution of Defaults and Losses

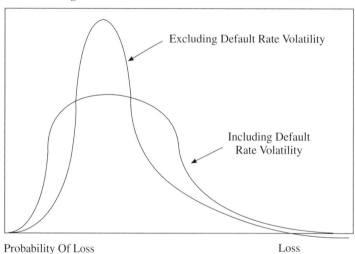

Probability Of Loss   Loss

Source: (1997) CREDITRISK[+]: *A Credit Risk Management Framework*, Credit Suisse Financial Products

The distribution of losses and defaults have the same level of expected losses but the distribution incorporating the volatility of default is skewed with a fatter tail. The distribution of losses differs significantly from the distribution of defaults in terms of the risk of experiencing large losses. This reflects the variation in size of exposure. This is based on the fact that the loss severity on a single default depends on the exposure to that obligor. The fatter tail of the distribution also dictates that the variance of the distribution ahs increased. The rise reflects the default correlations between borrowers.

Portfolio diversification in this approach is modeled by a factor sensitivity model whereby the default rate and volatility of default rate on an individual borrower will reflect specific factors which overall explain the volatility of default rates in the portfolio.

The model is similar to credit rating models in terms of applications. It can be used for provisioning for credit risk, risk credit limits and credit portfolio management.[46]

6.10.4   Credit Default Models

Default models specify a stochastic process for the default event itself and use this as the basis of modeling credit losses. The various default models are differentiated by the process by which the default probabilities are modeled. Figures 6.21 and 6.22 set out two possible approaches to this modeling process.

Figure 6.21   Credit Default — Model 1[47]

1. Framework

The model assumes that all debt securities can be decomposed into discount (or zero coupon) bonds. A risky bond (one capable of default) consists of a series of risk free zero coupon bonds plus a credit spread. The credit spread may be determined by calculating the risky zero rates and taking away the risk free zero rates to isolate the credit spread.

Using this structure of a term structure of discount securities, the assumption of a multifactor Brownian motion to generate market randomness and market completeness, it is possible to model the pricing of a risky bond within a Heath-Jarrow-Morton (HJM) framework[48].

---

[46] For a variation on the basic model that enables it to incorporate ratings changes, see Rolfes, Bernd and Broeker, Frank, November 1998, "Good Migrations", *Risk*, 72–73

[47] This figure sets out the model described in Hughston, L.P., March 1996, "Pricing Of Credit Derivatives", *Financial Derivatives and Risk Management*, pp 5, 11–16

[48] See Heath, D., Jarrow, R., and Morton, A., 1992, "Bond Pricing And The Term Structure of Interest Rates: A New Methodology For Contingent claims Pricing", *Econmetrica*, pp 77–105

The HJM framework states that the value of a derivative can be stated as:

$F_a/B_a \qquad = E_a [F_b/B_b]$

where:

F_a is the value of the derivative at time a

B_a is the value at time a for a unit initialized money market interest rate accumulating interest at the instantaneous rate

E_a is the conditional expectation given the information given information up to time a

F_b is the random payoff of an interest rate derivative at time b

B_b is the value at time b for a unit initialized money market interest rate accumulating interest at the instantaneous rate

This martingale relation allows the determination of a unique pricing measure at time a (which is earlier than b) of an interest rate derivative. The theory also provides suitable general formulae for the money market account process B_b and the bond price P_{ab}.

2. Incorporation of Default Risk

The valuation of risky bonds requires the HJM framework to incorporate the risk of default. This can be done by introducing a jump process, in practise a Poisson process is utilized, to incorporate the risk of default. The Poisson process models the random arrival of discrete events as on average a certain number of events per unit of time determined by the hazard rate, which itself can change randomly over time. The Poisson process models default on a risky bond as the payment of fixed unit of currency unless there has been default in which case the bond payment is reduced to zero. The default is modeled as the first arrival time of the Poisson process the intensity of which can be linked to interest rates in general even in a path dependent way if desired.

3. Valuing Risky Bonds

Within this framework, the value of a risky bond can be stated as:

$Q_{ab} \qquad = B_a E_a [Q_b/B_b]$

where:

$Q_b \qquad = 1 + (R_b - 1) n_b$

The terminology is as above except as follows;

Q_{ab} is the value of a risky bond with maturity of b at time a

Q_b is the default process as specified above

n_b is the default process indicator which is 1 if default has occurred and 0 if no default has occurred.

R_b is the recovery rate which specifies how much the bond would pay out in the event of default.

The above can be generalized for n_b as the first arrival indicator in a point process with random intensity λ_s where λ_s is adapted to the underlying Brownian motion driving the default free term structure. This allows specification of the conditional probability of default by time b as follows:

$$P [(n_a = 0) \text{ \& } (n_b = 1)] = 1 - \exp \int_a^b \lambda_s \, ds$$

Utilizing the fact that at continuous compounded interest earnings the value of the money market investment is the exponential of the integral of the risk free rate short term interest rate and assuming constant recovery rates of R, Hughston shows that the value of a risky bond is given by:

$$Q_{ab} = RP_{ab} + (1-R) E_a \left[\exp \left\{ -\int_a^b (r_s + \lambda_s) \, ds \right\} \right]$$

The above assumes that there is no default as at time a. An alternative formulation can be used allowing an immediate recovery on default based on a function of the value of the claim immediately before the default.

Source: The above is based on Hughston, L.P., March 1996, "Pricing Of Credit Derivatives" (March 1996) *Financial Derivatives and Risk Management*, pp 5, 11–16. The above represents an abbreviated version of the model and readers are referred to the original for the full exposition.

Figure 6.22   Credit Default — Model 2[49]

The Jarrow-Turnbull model uses a basic foreign exchange analogy to value credit pricing. The basic approach uses two currencies (US$ and a foreign currency stated in terms of expected US$). Both currencies have a term structure of interest rates and therefore, a defined present value and are free of default risk in its own currency. The exchange rate between US$ and the other currency is stochastic. The exchange rate is, say, 1 but can decrease. This risk of change creates uncertainty, namely exchange rate risk. In the case of credit derivatives, suing this analogy, the risk is driven by the risk of default rather than changes in currency values.

The approach is as follows:
- Assume a loan to an entity for an amount X.
- The price of the loan is:
$V_0 = E [P /(1+ R_0)]$
where:
V_0 = the present value of the cash flow
E = an expectations operator using risk adjusted probabilities
P = the actual payment in terms of the promised payment X
R_0 = the riskless interest rate over a time period [0,1]

- Using the above analogy, the actual payment can be restated as:
$P = e X$
where:
e = the exchange rate for agreed $ to actual $ where $e < 1$ in the event of default or
$e = 1$ where there is no default.

---

[49] This figure sets out the model developed by Robert Jarrow and Stuart Turnbull, see Jarrow, R., May/June 1998, "Current Advances In The Modeling Of Credit Risk", *Journal of Derivatives Taxation & Regulation*, pp 196–200

- The default rate can be elaborated as follows:
  $e = \delta < 1$ if default occurs with probability λ; or
  $e = 1$ if no default with probability $1 - \lambda$.
  where:
  λ = the cumulative risk adjusted probability of default by time 1
  δ = the recovery rate in the event of default

- This allows the value of the loan or bond to be written as:
  $V_0 = E\ [X\delta/(1+R_0) \mid \text{default}]\ \lambda + E\ [X\ /(1+R_0) \mid \text{no default}]\ (1 - \lambda)$

The approach states the value of risky loan or bond is equal to the discounted payoff in default times the probability of default plus the discounted payoff if no default occurs times the no default probability. The approach is capable of generalization covering multiple periods and multiple cash flows.

The key element of this approach is that the use of the foreign exchange analogy assists in the process of hedging and pricing. In essence, the key element of this process is modeling e that relies on modeling the default probability and the recovery rate.

Source: The above is based on Jarrow, R, May/June 1998, "Current Advances In The Modelling Of Credit Risk", *Journal of Derivatives Taxation & Regulation*, pp 196–200. The above represents an abbreviated version of the model and readers are referred to the original for the full exposition.

6.10.5 Assumptions Underlying Credit Modeling

The credit modeling described above is based on a number of assumptions which must be clearly understood. This is because the failure of many of these assumptions in real markets will inevitably weaken the ability to utilize these models.[50] The assumptions include:

- Market structures
- The data availability
- Numerical implementation

Consistent with other derivative pricing models, credit modeling generally assumes the conditions of perfect markets, namely:

---

[50] For a discussion of the problems of credit modeling see Jarrow, R., May/June 1998, "Current Advances In The Modelling Of Credit Risk", *Journal of Derivatives Taxation & Regulation* pp 196–200; "Round Table Discussion — Credit Risk" (November 1998) *Middle Office* III–XV; "The Crisis in Credit Modelling" (1998) *Derivatives Strategy*, pp 29–34; "Why We Missed The Asian Meltdown" (1998) *Derivatives Strategy*, pp 16–21; "Modelling Asia: A Roundtable" (1998) *Derivatives Strategy*, pp 21–23

- Competitive markets
- No transaction costs
- No taxes

For credit markets, these assumptions may be less applicable than for other asset markets. This reflects the relative lack of liquidity in trading in non government debt. It also reflects differences in tax treatment as between types of securities in a particular jurisdiction and as between jurisdictions. This may imply that factors such as liquidity risk will need to be specifically encompassed in credit modeling to reduce the risk of model specification errors. The nature of asset trading in credit markets may also be significantly different. For example, the market might be more discontinuous in nature. Trading might be essentially more prone to exhibiting greater gaps etc.[51]

The availability of data on credit (e.g., credit spread changes, defaults, and recovery rates) is crucial to the implementation of these modeling approaches. The relevant data is usually derived from historical information. This process is subject to not inconsiderable difficulty. The data weakness is evident at both a theoretical and practical level. At a theoretical level, these include:

- There is a paradox in seeking to estimate the likelihood of a particular obligor defaulting or suffering some sort of serious credit event. This is because that particular firm has not defaulted. This forces the use of analogous firms (classified by factors such as ratings levels) to infer the default probabilities and recovery rates of the relevant obligor.
- The difficulty of finding a representative firm is significant. This requirement is driven by the need to identify a representative or analogous firm that has suffered the credit event to allow derivation, through a process of analogy, of the data parameters needed. The difficulty is that such a representative firm may not be readily available and even if available may not be a very good approximation of the firm whose default risk is being considered. This merely restates that the systematic risk component of credit risk (the component driven by market wide factors) is lower than the unsystematic risk component (the component driven by obligor specific factors).

These theoretical difficulties make it difficult to apply traditional procedures used in the context of modeling the price behavior of financial prices (in interest rate, currency, equity and commodity prices) to combine historical and implicit

---

[51] For example, see Krakovsky, Andrey, March 1999, "Gap Risk In Credit Trading", *Risk* pp 65–67

estimation techniques and to calibrate results. Traditional approaches in these markets derive historical estimates based on past price observations that are then calibrated using market prices (implicit estimation or calibration being used to solve for the parameters that equate model price and market prices).

At a practical level, the difficulties include:

- Sample sizes are generally small for default data (particularly at higher credit quality levels).
- The data samples have inherent geographic biases. The rating data has historically been skewed in favor of the rated US market. Foreign issuers as a percentage of Moody's rated universe constituted only 15% as at January 1930, 18% as at January 1990, rising to 35% as at 1997.[52]
- The non stationary nature of many of the estimates (default rates, recovery rates, default correlations) are also problematic. Similarly, the skewed and asymmetric nature of the distribution of these variables as well as the large standards errors in many of these estimates create problems in credit modeling.

The problems identified are even more acute in the case of obligors whose debt is not publicly traded. These entities require the use of further inferential techniques to derives estimates which may introduce further errors in the modeling process. Given that the universe of traded obligations of non-government obligors with a large and liquid market in their obligations is small, these data problems are formidable.

To date there has been limited work in seeking to examine the performance of the credit models identified to establish the empirical validity of the models themselves.

The numerical implementation of the models themselves are considerable. This complexity derives from the large number of factors, multiple term structures and complex cross correlations (that is, they are typically high dimensional problems). In practise, tree structures (generally non-recombinant), implicit and explicit difference models involving the solution of partial differential equations, or Monte Carlo simulation techniques are used. The procedure adopted is used to generate a distribution for future cash flows from which the default expectation is inferred. The large scale computational requirements dictate that reduced forms of the models are the only forms that are

---

[52] Scott-Quinn Brian and Walmsley Julian K., 1998, *The Impact of Credit Derivatives On Securities Markets*, ISMA, Zurich, Switzerland, pp 54–55

practical. This creates a different level of model risk into the process of credit modeling.[53]

6.11 Hedging and Trading Default Risk

6.11.1 Dynamic Default Hedges

The pricing and valuation of credit default derivatives must be extended, in practise, to hedging and trading default risk.

Traditional concepts for managing default risk revolve around the concept of diversification of credit risk as the mechanism for reducing exposure utilizing the low correlations between defaults. More recent efforts seek to dynamically hedge the default risk through positions in underlying market risk instruments. The former approach is well suited to a portfolio manager. The later approach is necessary to enable traders creating credit default derivatives to synthesize the positions and trade these instruments.

The basic hedge of default risk as set out above entails trading in the underlying obligations (typically using asset swaps) to replicate the risk assumed or hedged in the credit derivative. An alternative approach entails a dynamic hedge. The dynamic hedge approach is predicated on the option based default risk framework (outlined above). As noted above, the bond investor is selling the shareholder a put on the company's assets (in effect the right to default). The position can be offset by creating the following hedge that must then be managed dynamically:

- Purchase the bond.
- Short the stock of the issuer.
  The behavior of the hedge will be as follows:
- If the asset value falls, then the stock price falls by more than the bond price reflecting the position in the capital structure of the securities and the corresponding recovery rates.
- The gains on the short stock position will offset the erosion of the bond value. Alternatives or variations to the above strategy include:
- The use of put options as an alternative to the short stock positions.
- The use of basis hedges using beta adjusted positions in the market equity index to enhance hedge liquidity.

---

[53] For examples of modeling currently in use by practitioners, see Browne, Christopher, Gregory, Jon, and Martin, Richard, December 1998, "A Credit Risk Toolbox", *Risk*, pp 50–55

The major problem with this dynamic hedge is the risk of decoupling of the performance of the two securities (basis risk). This can be illustrated with the example of a takeover announcement. Under these circumstances, the stock price rises creating losses on the short stock position that may not be offset by matching gains on the bond price. This reflects the fact that the credit position of the bond holders may not be affected to the same degree by the takeover as that of the equity holders. This risk favors the use of equity put options as the hedging vehicle.

Dynamic hedges are feasible on both a transactional and portfolio basis. The latter effectively incorporates the default correlations between the transactions.

The dynamic hedges, at least in theory, can be both direct or indirect. Direct hedges would entail using the specific underlying loan assets and options on the stock of the issuer. Indirect would entail using bond futures and equity indexes to structure the hedge based on the correlation relationships between the risky asset and the bond and the stock's correlation to the index. In practise, the instability of these relationships makes indirect hedging hazardous.

6.11.2 Potential Hedging Strategies

Future prospects for structuring dynamic hedges include the introduction of loan value or credit indexes and the supply of credit risk adjusted securities.

There are a number of loan value or credit indexes including the Citicorp Loan Index and bond indexes produced by a number of investment indexes. The possibility of introducing traded futures and options on these indexes exists if the indexes attain market acceptability. The advent of these markets would allow the structuring of hedges based on trading in the listed futures and options contract. The Chicago Mercantile Exchange (CME) has introduced traded futures and option contracts on the Quarterly Bankruptcy Index (QBI).[54] The contract is primarily designed to transfer default risk on various types of consumer credit risk. However, given the nature of default risk generally, in particular the absence of correlation would probably limit the use of these types of instruments to hedge individual transaction although they may be useful in portfolio hedging.

A number of securities where the behavior of the security is linked to credit factors have emerged. These include:

- Loans where the credit spread are a predetermined function of rating.

---

[54] See Arditti, Fred, and Curran, John, November 1998, "Futures Contract On The Cards", *Risk — Credit Risk Special Report* pp 30–32; for an analysis of trading performance, see Payne, Beatrix, January 1999, "Design Faults Stymie QBI", *Risk*, 12

- Bonds where the interest paid is a function of rating (issued by Chrysler and Unisys).
- Spread is a function of a periodic auction process which presumably reflects alterations in perceived default risk (issued by Merrill Lynch as Spread Adjusted Notes (SPANs)).
- Bond with a pre-determined put to the issuer in the event that the companies credit quality deteriorates. For example, the ill fated Korean Development Bank bond issue with an investor out at par in the event that the issuer was downgraded below A-.[55]

These securities may allow traders to hedge credit risk through trading in the credit sensitive notes to offset exposure to credit derivatives sold.

6.11.3   Issues in Modeling, Pricing, and Hedging Default Risk

There are a number of issues in the management of default risk and the pricing and valuation of credit risk. They include the impact of credit enhancement and the pricing and hedging difficulties in trading these instruments.

The discussion to date assumes that the loss exposure is clean, that is it is not subject to any enhancement. In reality, increasingly, credit exposures are enhanced through a variety of measures includes:

- Collateralization
- Netting of exposures
- Other techniques, including re-couponing, credit puts, right to break, or termination of downgrade provisions

In addition, default exposure may, in theory, be affected by the correlation between market risk factors (embedded in a single transaction), default risk and exposure,[56] and default correlations.

Credit enhancement would generally lower default losses and alter the exposure. Similarly, the correlations may increase or reduce exposures. In practise, the impact of credit enhancement and all the potential correlations is difficult.

---

[55] See Steven Irvine, July 1997, "Credit Where Credit's Due For KDB", *Euromoney*, 16
[56] Anecdotal evidence suggests that lower-rated credits make up a significant portion of the payers on fixed rate in interest rate swaps. These entities are more vulnerable to default in a high interest rate environment. However, higher rates equate to low or zero loss exposure under the contract. Therefore, the interaction of market and default risk should reduce the default cost.

The principal issue in modeling and ultimately pricing and hedging relates to the interaction of complex and interdependent variables. The practical econometrics in modeling and estimating these variables is considerable. Even where the estimates can be generated, the attendant assumption that must be made relating to the assumed stationarity of the estimates, particularly correlations, is difficult to defend, at least, over longer terms.

Other problems include:
- The absence of availability of a complete credit spectrum
- The degree of definition of credit-risk structure
- The degree of trading in credit assets and liquidity
- The rationale for loan trading

These factors vary significantly also as between different market segments of the market for credit derivatives, such as the investment grade market, the high-yield segment, distressed loan assets, and emerging market credits.

These factors dictate that the process of modeling, pricing, and valuing derivatives remains at an early stage with the market not yet at a true liquid trading stage. The emphasis continues to be on counterparty transactions and physically hedged transactions. In practise, the pricing of credit default products owes more to the current trading levels on asset swaps, supply and demand for individual credits and liquidity than the default models. However, increasing sophistication in pricing and hedging is becoming evident.

In the next sections, specific pricing methodologies for total return swaps, credit spread products and first-to-default baskets are outlined. While priced consistent with the techniques and approaches outlined above, it is evident that more traditional derivative pricing concepts can be used to derive the value of these structures.

6.12 Specific Pricing Methodologies — Total Return Swaps

6.12.1 Pricing Approach

Total return swaps can be priced off the risk-free return combined with the pricing of a credit default swap. In practise, this price is derived off the replication source utilized by the dealer to create the transaction cash flows.

The replication sources available include:
- Counterparty transactions
- Synthetic — entailing either a physical investment in the underlying loan assets or by proxy using an indirect correlation based hedge

Counterparty transactions are predicated upon banks and financial institutions with existing loan assets wishing to transfer the underlying credit risk of the asset. Dealers, seeking to replicate these transactions in the absence of an offsetting counterparty, would need to make an investment in the underlying loan (or, less likely, in a similar loan asset). Figure 6.23 sets out the structure of the hedge.

The valuation basis for counterparties is based on factors which generally affect the pricing of credit risk affected assets including current secondary market prices for the actual loans or securities (if available) or similar assets (if the assets themselves are not directly traded). Supply and demand for specific class of exposures, in terms of country, industry and borrower would be the principal driving force for the price of the underlying asset.

In addition, particularly where the transaction is synthesized from a specific investment undertaken to hedge the trade, the pricing of the transaction would reflect the cost of the synthetic hedge including:

- Balance sheet or capital utilization (both economic and regulatory)
- Counterparty risk exposure
- Transaction costs
- Adjustments for the position of the parties relative to access to the asset and funding cost

The theoretical pricing should also factor in a reduction of concentration, the diversification benefit, default risk expectation, the reduction in transaction cost and additional liquidity of the synthetic structure. The diversification benefit and default risk expectation can only be valued within the framework of a default

Figure 6.23   Hedging A Total Return Swap Transaction

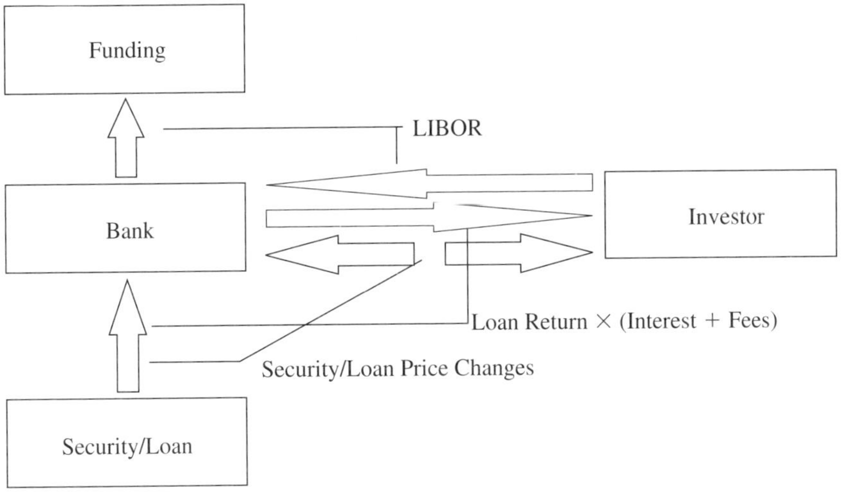

risk model (see discussion below). In practise, the pricing, at least currently, rarely reflects the full attribution of these benefits.

6.12.2 Developing Proxy Hedges

The method of replication, entailing purchase and funding of the underlying asset, is inefficient and expensive. An alternative methodology is to replicate the loan characteristics by surrogate instruments.

This entails, usually, a combination of credit or loan indexes, and/or financial market indicators (principally, interest rates, equity prices, and (to a lesser degree) commodity prices). The rationale underlying this approach is the correlation between the return on loans, the default risk and the other financial market variables. This approach is only applicable in defined circumstances. To date it has only been used in the US high-yield market.

The use of proxy hedges has developed in the US high-yield markets within a framework which views a corporate debt obligation as a combination of an investment in a risk free asset such as a government bond and an investment in the equity of the issuer. The empirical research[57] indicates that the correlation between the returns on corporate debt and US Treasury yields decreases as the credit quality, as measured by rating parameters, decreases. This decrease in correlation to risk free debt returns is paralleled by an increase in the correlation between the bonds and equity of a the issuer as the credit quality declines. The relationship can be seen from the comparison of the correlations (see Figure 6.24).[58]

---

[57] See Bookstaber, Richard and Jacob, David P., March/April 1986, "The Composite Hedge: Controlling The Credit Risk Of High Yield Bonds", *Financial Analysts Journal*, pp 25–36; Grieves, Robin, Summer 1986, "Hedging Corporate Bond Portfolios", *The Journal of Portfolio Management*, pp 23–25; Ramaswani, Murali, September–October 1991, "Hedging The Equity Risk Of High Yield Bonds", *Financial Analysts Journal* pp 41–50

[58] The underlying logic of this relationship is based on the theoretical model that specifies that all corporate securities are claims on the value of the firm. Equity being characterised as a residual claim akin to a call option on the net asset value of the firm (i.e. assets net of liabilities). Using put call parity, this means that corporate debt equates to the security combined with the sale of a put option structure on the assets of the firm. This analysis is fundamental to the derivation of default risk discussed in detail below. For more detailed discussion of this approach, see Black, F., and Scholes, M., 1973, "The Pricing of Options and Corporate Liabilities", *Journal of Political Economy*, Vol 81, pp 637–754; Merton, R., 1974, "On The Option Pricing Of Corporate Debt: The Risk Structure Of Interest Rates", *Journal of Finance*, Vol 29, pp 449–470; Geske, R., 1977, "The Valuation Of Corporate Liabilities As Compound Options", *Journal of Financial and Quantitative Analysis*, pp 541–552

Figure 6.24   Correlation Between Corporate Bonds, Treasury Bonds And Equity

Rating Level	Correlation With Treasury Bonds	Correlation With Equity
Aaa — A	0.86	0.09
Baa — Ba	0.77	0.25
B — Caa	0.51	0.28

Source: Bookstaber, Richard and Jacob, David P., March & April 1986, "The Composite Hedge: Controlling The Credit Risk Of High Yield Bonds", *Financial Analysts Journal*, pp 25–36

Based on this evidence, the possibility of utilizing a composite hedge, combining positions in government bonds (or government bond futures) and position in the individual stock (or the equity index) has been explored. There is evidence that a dynamically managed composite hedge significantly outperforms a conventional interest rate hedge.

This logic can be extended to use a mixture of government securities or futures on government securities and positions in equity stocks or in the equity index to replicate high-yield bond indexes. The direct application of this technology to valuing total return swaps derives from the fact that the underlying instruments can be used to hedge and therefore price and value index based total return swaps. This avoids the inefficiencies and high transaction costs of replication or hedging using physical assets.

The pricing of total return swaps, insofar as they entail the assumption or transfer of credit risk, can also be equated to the pricing of credit default swap. This reflects the fact that the total return swap can be equated to an investment in a risk free asset and the entry into a credit default swap to replicate the economic exposure to the underlying credit asset.

6.13   Specific Pricing Methodologies — Credit Spread Forwards and Options

6.13.1   Pricing Approach

As noted above, credit spread represent the compensation for credit risk assumed. This dictates that the credit spread plays a significant role in the pricing of all credit derivatives.

There are a number of specific components to the pricing of credit spread products. The most significant of which is the determination of the credit spread.

This, in turn, can be separated into two specific issues:
- The nature, behavior and logic of credit spreads
- Pricing forwards and options on credit spreads

The second component of pricing is the pricing of the products themselves which are merely forwards and options on the credit spread. The pricing, valuation, and trading of credit spread products themselves entails the adaptation of traditional derivative pricing techniques for deriving forward and option pricing on a different underlying asset — the credit spread.[59]

The derivation of value for the credit spread forwards and options is based on both theoretical valuation tools and the capacity to replicate the specific exposure sought through, usually, trading or transactions in the underlying cash securities.

6.13.2   Pricing Forwards on Credit Spread

The calculation of the forward on the credit spread follows traditional pricing logic. The forward credit spread is calculated as follows:
1. Identify the spot price of the security and the risk-free benchmark security.
2. The forward prices of both securities are calculated and converted to the corresponding forward yield.
3. The forward credit spread is taken as the forward security yield minus the forward risk-free rate.

The forward credit spread can also be calculated using the yields of the underlying securities. The above steps are usually done with traditional forward pricing methodologies entailing the construction of appropriate zero coupon rates across the maturity term structure for both the risk free rates and the risky security.

The forward rates are usually calculated in accordance with the following formula:

$$(1 + R_{t1}) \, t1 \, \times \, (1 + R_{t1x2})^{t2-t1} = (1 + R_{t2})^{t2}$$
where

For an overview of the pricing of forward and option contracts, see Das, Satyajit (Editor) 1998, *Risk Management And Financial Derivatives: A Guide To The Mathematics*, LBC Information Services, Sydney, McGraw-Hill, Chicago; MacMillan Publishing, Basingstoke, Chapters 4, 5, 7, 8, 10, 11

R_{t1} = the interest rate to time $t1$
R_{t2} = the interest rate to time $t2$
R_{t1x2} = the forward interest rate between time $t1$ and $t2$
$t1,t2$ = the time to maturity in days from the present divided by 365

Rearranging to solve for the forward interest rate:
$$R_{t1x2} = [(1 + R_{t2})^{t2} /(1 + R_{t1})^{t1}]^{1/(t2-t1)} - 1$$

The above assumes that all rates are expressed in consistent time units, usually annual effective rates.

The forward credit spreads can be calculated in one of two ways. The implied forward rates for both the risk-free curve and the risky curve can be calculated and the forward yield spread determined by subtracting the risk free forward rate from the risky forward rate. Alternatively, a zero coupon spread can be determined by calculating the spot credit spread from the two zero coupon rates. The forward credit spreads can then be calculated from the zero coupon derived spot credit spread curve.

Figure 6.25 sets out an example of the calculation of forward spreads. The term structure of spot credit spread creates significant richness in the pattern of forward credit spreads. The mathematics of the calculation indicates that in the case of a positive (negatively) sloped yield curve that the forward credit spreads increase (decrease).

Figure 6.25   Forward Credit Spread Calculations

In each of the examples set out below, the forward credit spread is calculated as the difference between the forward yield for the underlying government bond rates and the yield applicable on the issuer security (issuer in this context is used to merely signify a non risk free issuer). The principal point to observe is the difference between the spot spread and the implied forward spread. The difference, in strict terms, should be carefully considered in that the spot spread is for the securities to the final maturity date. In contrast, the implied forward spread is for a slightly shorter maturity out of the forward date.

1. Example 1

Date	August 20, 1998	
Forward Date	February 20, 1999	
Final Maturity	November 15, 2002	
Security Type	Risk-Free Security	Issuer Security
Yields		
To Forward Date	5.3200%	5.6000%

To Final Maturity	6.1000%	6.6200%
Credit Spreads		
To Forward Date	0.28%	
To Final Maturity	0.52%	
Forward Credit Spread		
Forward Yields	6.1452%	6.6792%
Forward Credit Spread	0.5340%	
Difference Between Current And Implied Spreads (bp)	1.40	
Difference Between Current And Implied Spreads (%)	2.69%	

2. Example 2

Date	August 20, 1998	
Forward Date	February 20, 1999	
Final Maturity	November 15, 2002	
Security Type	Risk-Free Security	Issuer Security
Yields		
To Forward Date	5.3200%	6.5700%
To Final Maturity	6.1000%	7.9000%
Credit Spreads		
To Forward Date	1.25%	
To Final Maturity	1.80%	
Forward Credit Spread		
Forward Yields	6.1452%	7.9772%
Forward Credit Spread	1.8321%	
Difference Between Current And Implied Spreads (bp)	3.21	
Difference Between Current And Implied Spreads (%)	1.78%	

3. Example 3

Date	August 20, 1998	
Forward Date	February 20, 1999	
Final Maturity	November 15, 2002	
Security Type	Risk-Free Security	Issuer Security
Yields		
To Forward Date	7.1500%	8.1000%
To Final Maturity	6.2800%	7.5200%
Credit Spreads		

To Forward Date	0.95%	
To Final Maturity	1.24%	
Forward Credit Spread		
Forward Yields	6.2300%	7.4866%
Forward Credit Spread	1.2566%	
Difference Between Current And		
Implied Spreads (Bp)	1.66	
Difference Between Current And		
Implied Spreads (%)	1.34%	

Figure 6.26 sets out an analysis of forward credit spreads under a variety of yield curve shapes.

Figure 6.26   Forward Credit Spread — Patterns

In each of the following cases, the term structure of implied forward credit spreads is estimated. The term structure is calculated from an assumed government yield curve and an assumed corporate (non-government issuer) yield curve. The forward credit spreads are calculated for a number of separate forward dates — 1 year forward, 3 years forward, and 5 years forward — as well spot or current date. The credit spreads calculated as of these dates is for all maturities up to 5 years at six month intervals. The results are set out as a series graphs showing the spot credit spread and the implied forward credit spread across the yield curve as of each of the forward dates compared to the spot spread. The objective of the analysis is to principally highlight the pattern of implied forward credit spreads relative to the current spot spreads.

Example 1
Assume the following yield curve and credit spreads:

Maturity (Years)	Government Bond Rate (% pa)	Issuer Bond Rate (% pa)	Issuer Credit Spread (% pa)
0.5	6.0000	6.2500	0.250
1	6.2500	6.5500	0.300
3	6.4000	6.8500	0.450
5	6.5000	7.2500	0.750
7	6.7500	7.5500	0.800
10	7.0000	7.9000	0.900

The spot and forward spreads are as follows:

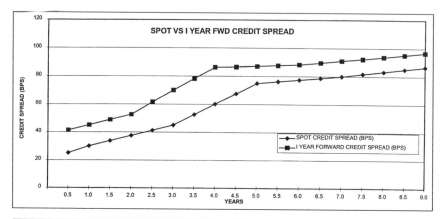

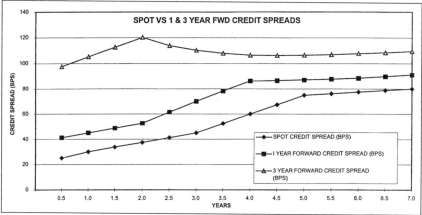

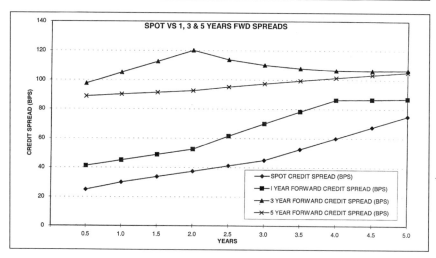

Example 2

Assume the following yield curve and credit spreads:

Maturity (Years)	Government Bond Rate (% pa)	Issuer Bond Rate (% pa)	Issuer Credit Spread (% pa)
0.5	5.5000	6.4000	0.900
1	5.7800	7.2800	1.500
3	5.8400	7.8400	2.000
5	6.2600	9.0100	2.750
7	6.3000	9.2000	2.900
10	6.3500	9.5000	3.150

The spot and forward spreads are as follows:

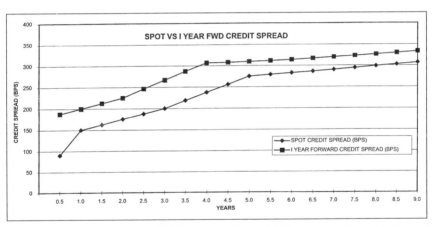

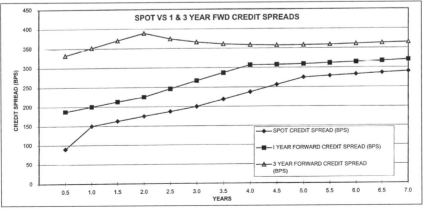

Example 3

Assume the following yield curve and credit spreads:

Maturity (Years)	Government Bond Rate (% pa)	Issuer Bond Rate (% pa)	Issuer Credit Spread (% pa)
0.5	5.5000	10.2500	4.750
1	5.8000	11.0500	5.250
3	6.0000	10.0000	4.000
5	6.1000	9.6000	3.500
7	6.2700	9.7700	3.500

The spot and forward spreads are as follows:

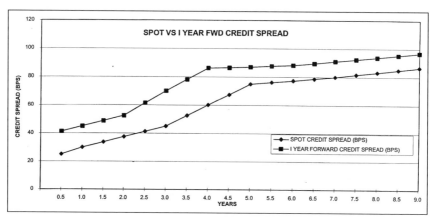

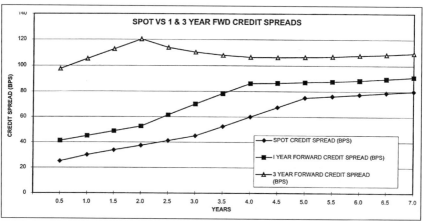

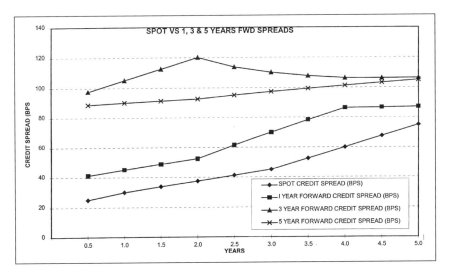

The forward credit spread behavior, in practise, seems to reflect the following pattern of behavior:

- They do not appear to accurately reflect investor expectations.
- The forward credit spreads appear to be poor indicators of futures spot spreads.

The forward credit spreads also appear to be relatively more volatile than the underlying securities (see discussion below in the context of spread volatility).

The calculation of forward credit spreads may under certain circumstances require adjustment for convexity.[60] This reflects the fact that a forward interest rate will not always correspond to the yield on the corresponding forward bond because the relationship between the bond price and bond yield is non linear. This may require a convexity adjustment to be incorporated.[61]

---

[60] The convexity adjustment is usually not required where there is no natural time lag (a phrase suggested by John Hull). This indicates that the convexity adjustment is not required where the payoff on a derivative depends on an n-period rate and the corresponding payoff takes place n periods after the rate being observed: see Hull, John, 1997, *Options, Futures, and Other Derivatives (3rd ed)*, Prentice Hall, New Jersey, pp 406–408

[61] For a methodology to make the convexity adjustment, see Hull, John, 1997, Chapter 16; Brotherton- Ratcliffe, R. and Iben, Ben "Yield Curve Applications Of Swap Products" in Schwartz, R. and Smith, C (Ed), 1993, *Advanced Strategies In Financial Risk Management*, New York Institute of Finance, New York, Chapter 15

6.13.3   Pricing Credit Spread Options

Key Parameters

The key determinants of value in credit spread options is the forward spread and
the volatility of this parameter. The dynamics of the forward credit spread have
already been discussed. Approaches to estimation of the volatility of the yield
spread are examined in the next section. Other parameter inputs include the
strike spread and the time to expiry (both givens) and the risk-free rate
effectively the discount factor (which is readily available).

As noted above, the credit spread option structure is effectively an option on
the forward credit spread between the nominated securities. The forward spread
is economically the differential between the forward rates of the two securities
as at the option expiration date. The forward rates are usually estimated using
the current spot yield for the security and the financing rate (repo, LIBOR rate)
to the option maturity. As noted above, technically, the forward rate estimated
using this technique is not exactly equal to the security's forward yield at the
theoretical forward price because the security has a non-zero convexity but
particularly for short dated options the difference is not material. Importantly,
the underlying pricing dynamic of credit spread options dictates that the price of
the option prior to expiration is sensitive to both the spot rates for the relevant
securities and the interest rate to expiration which in combination determines the
forward spread.

Volatility Estimation

The volatility of the forward spread is complex. It in effect is made up of the
volatility of the underlying securities and the correlation between yield
movements between the two securities.

This results in a number of ways to model the volatility of the forward
spread:
- The historical volatility of the spread between the actual two securities.
- The historical volatility of the spread between two securities having constant
  maturities equivalent to the actual underlying securities.
- The estimated yield spread volatility based on the average yield of each
  security, the historical yield volatility of each security, and the historical
  correlation between the two.
- The estimated expected future spread based the actual yields on the securities
  at transaction date, the implied volatility of options on each security, and an
  estimate of the future correlation coefficient.

In practice, the forward credit spreads appear to be relatively more volatile than the underlying securities. This higher spread volatility reflects the following:
- Lower absolute level of spread (a 1 bp change in credit spread results in larger percentage change than an equivalent change in the absolute yield level on the security).
- Imperfect correlation between the security and risk-free rate.

Figure 6.27 sets out an example of the calculation of the volatility of the credit spread as well as the yield volatility of the underlying security.

Figure 6.27   Spread Volatility

Assume the following rates and spreads:

Period	Risk Free Interest Rate (%)	Spread (%)
0	6.030	0.450
1	6.010	0.460
2	5.990	0.430
3	5.990	0.430
4	6.000	0.410
5	6.040	0.440
6	6.010	0.450
7	6.020	0.430
8	6.050	0.430
9	6.040	0.410
10	5.980	0.420
11	5.950	0.440
12	5.960	0.430
13	5.960	0.410
14	5.930	0.450
15	5.950	0.420
16	5.980	0.440
17	5.970	0.410
18	6.010	0.410
19	6.040	0.420
20	6.020	0.400

The rates and spreads are depicted in the graphs on the next page:

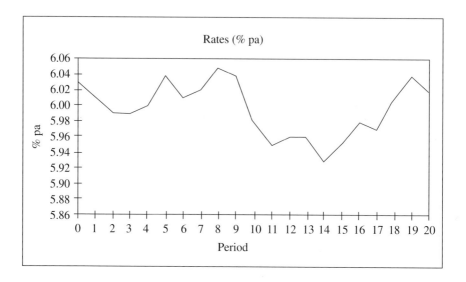

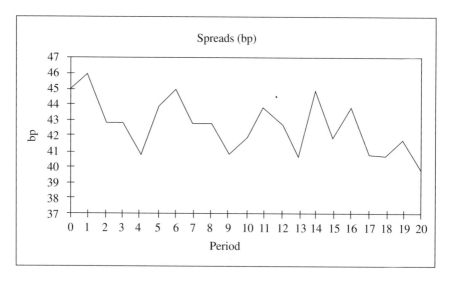

The rate and spread volatility are calculated in the table below:

Period	Risk Free-Interest Rate (%)	Spread (%)	Interest Rate (%)	Yield Volatility Spread Relative $(S_t/(S_{t-1}))$	Calculations Daily Return $U_i=\ln(S_t/(S_{t-1}))$	Spread Volatility Yield Relative $(S_t/(S_{t-1}))$	Calculations Daily Return $U_i=\ln(S_t/(S_{t-1}))$
0	6.030	0.450	6.480				
1	6.010	0.460	6.470	1.02222	0.02198	0.99846	(0.00154)
2	5.990	0.430	6.420	0.93478	(0.06744)	0.99227	(0.00776)
3	5.990	0.430	6.420	1.00000	0.00000	1.00000	0.00000
4	6.000	0.410	6.410	0.95349	(0.04763)	0.99844	(0.00156)
5	6.040	0.440	6.480	1.07317	0.07062	1.01092	0.01086
6	6.010	0.450	6.460	1.02273	0.02247	0.99691	(0.00309)
7	6.020	0.430	6.450	0.95556	(0.04546)	0.99845	(0.00155)
8	6.050	0.430	6.480	1.00000	0.00000	1.00465	0.00464
9	6.040	0.410	6.450	0.95349	(0.04763)	0.99537	(0.00464)
10	5.980	0.420	6.400	1.02439	0.02410	0.99225	(0.00778)
11	5.950	0.440	6.390	1.04762	0.04652	0.99844	(0.00156)
12	5.960	0.430	6.390	0.97727	(0.02299)	1.00000	0.00000
13	5.960	0.410	6.370	0.95349	(0.04763)	0.99687	(0.00313)
14	5.930	0.450	6.380	1.09756	0.09309	1.00157	0.00157
15	5.950	0.420	6.370	0.93333	(0.06899)	0.99843	(0.00157)
16	5.980	0.440	6.420	1.04762	0.04652	1.00785	0.00782
17	5.970	0.410	6.380	0.93182	(0.07062)	0.99377	(0.00625)
18	6.010	0.410	6.420	1.00000	0.00000	1.00627	0.00625
19	6.040	0.420	6.460	1.02439	0.02410	1.00623	0.00621
20	6.020	0.400	6.420	0.95238	(0.04879)	0.99381	(0.00621)
Standard Deviation (Per Period)					4.894%		0.527%
Annualized Volatility (Days)			250.0000		77.386%		8.334%

The relative volatilities are as follows:
Rate volatility: 8.334% pa
Spread volatility: 77.386% pa

Valuation Approach

The spread option is then priced using one of a variety of models. A number of separate approaches exist to the valuation of credit spread options themselves.[62] These include:

• Modeling the spread itself as an asset price.
• Modeling the option as an exchange option.
• Utilizing Multi-(Two) Factor Options models.

The advantage of the first approach is its relative simplicity. However, the approach creates significant problems. It assumes that the probability that the spread will ever become negative is nil. This may be a reasonably tractable assumption where the absolute credit spread (yield on a risky security is compared to the yield on a risk free security) is concerned. This is clearly inconsistent where relative credit spreads (between two risky securities) are concerned where negative spreads are feasible. This problem is introduced by the implicit assumption of the log normal distribution of the spread as an asset price.

In addition, the log normal assumption suggests that spread fluctuation size would increase for large spreads and decrease for small ones — the proportionality impact—which is not supported by evidence. One possible means of coping with the difficulties posed by the assumption of log normality (particularly in respect of the spread price being negative) is to assume a normal as opposed from log normal distribution where volatility is calculated on the absolute price change annualized standard deviation.

The other two approaches incorporate both the separate volatility of the underlying assets and the correlation between the two assets to derive the credit spread option value. This approach is preferable in that it does not suffer the same restrictions as the first approach.

---

[62] See Garman, Mark, December 1992, "Spread the Load", *Risk*, Vol. 5, No. 11, pp 68–84; McDermott, Scott "A Survey of Spread Options For Fixed Income Investors" in Klein, Robert A. and Lederman, Jess (Eds) 1993, *The Handbook of Derivatives & Synthetics*, Probus Publishing: Chicago, Illinios; Ravindran, K., October 1993, "Low Fat Spreads", *Risk*, Vol. 6, No. 10, pp 66–67; Ravindran, K., 1994, "Exotic Options" in Dattatreya, Ravi E. and Hotta, Kensuke, *Advanced Interest Rate and Currency Swaps: State-of-the Art Products, Strategies & Risk Management Applications*, Probus Publishing, Chicago, Illinios

Spread Option Pricing Models

An example of a closed form option pricing model for these instruments adapting the approach of Black's commodity option pricing model[63] is set out in Figure 6.28. An example of a calculation of the value of a spread option using this type of model is set in Figure 6.29.[64]

Figure 6.28   Spread Option Pricing Formula

The pricing of a call option is:

$$C_t = e^{-rt} [(S_t - K) N (h) + \sigma \sqrt{t} \, N'(h)]$$

where

$$h = (1/ \sigma \sqrt{t}) (S_t - K)$$

where

K	= strike yield spread
S_t	= forward yield spread at time t
σ	= volatility (standard deviation of yield spread)
r	= risk free rate
t	= time to option maturity
N(h)	= standard normal distribution

The equivalent pricing for a put option is:

$$P_t = e^{-rt} [(K - S_t)(1 - N (h)) + \sigma \sqrt{t} \, N'(h)]$$

where

$$h = (1/ \sigma \sqrt{t}) (S_t - K)$$

Source: McDermott, Scott "A Survey of Spread Options For Fixed Income Investors" in Klein, Robert A. and Lederman, Jess (editors) 1993, *The Handbook of Derivatives & Synthetics*, Probus Publishing: Chicago, Illinios, Chapter 4, at pp 109–110

Figure 6.29   Spread Option Pricing — Example

Assume the following parameters for a spread option: the trade date is 15 April 2002; option expires on October 15, 2002 (six months); the current forward spread is 85 bp; the option is struck at a spread of 90 bp; the spread volatility is 65% pa; and the risk free rate is 5.75% pa.

The option price is calculated below:

---

[63] See Black, Fischer, March 1976, "The Pricing of Commodity Contracts", *Journal of Financial Economics*, 3, pp 167–179

[64] For other single-factor approaches, see Bhansali, Vineer 1998, *Pricing and Managing Exotic and Hybrid Options*, McGraw-Hill, New York, pp 29–33

Pricing Inputs

Underlying Asset Price (bp)	85.00
Strike Price (bp)	90.00
Trade Date (bp)	April 15, 2002
Expiry Date	October 15, 2002
Volatility	65.00%
Risk Free Rate	5.75%
Number Of Steps (Binomial Model)	500

Option Premium	Black		Binomial	
Model Outputs	**Call**	**Put**	**Call**	**Put**
Option Premium (bp)	13.16	18.02	13.23	18.13
Option Premium (% of asset price)	15.48%	21.20%	15.56%	21.33%

European option prices are calculated using an adapted Black model while the American option prices are calculated using a binomial model.

Approaches incorporating the separate volatilities and correlations fall into a number of groups: exchange option structures; bivariate binomial schemes; or other numerical structures.

Credit spread options can be equated to Exchange Options in certain circumstances and valued utilising techniques similar to those applicable to minimum/maximum option structures. William Magrabe provides a valuation model for valuing an exchange option where both assets are denominated in the same currency[65] (see Figure 6.30).[66]

---

[65] See Margrabe, William, 1978, "The Value Of An Option To Exchange One Asset For Another", *Journal of Finance*, Vol 33, pp 177–186. For a version of this model, which shows where the second asset is denominated in a foreign currency, see Brotherton-Ratcliffe, R. and Iben, Ben, 1993, "Yield Curve Applications Of Swap Products," in Schwartz, R. and Smith, C (Ed) *Advanced Strategies In Financial Risk Management*, New York Institute Of Finance, New York, Chapter 15

[66] For an adoption of the Margrabe approach, see Bhansali, Vineer, 1998, *Pricing and Managing Exotic and Hybrid Options*, McGraw-Hill, New York, pp 69–79

Figure 6.30   Exchange Option Pricing Model[67]

$S_2 e^{-q2t} N(d1) - S_1^{-q1t} N (d2)$

Where

$d1 = [\ln (S_2/S_1) + (q1 - q2 + \sigma^2/2) t]/\sigma \sqrt{t}$

$d2 = d1 - \sigma \sqrt{t}$

$\sigma = \sqrt{(\sigma1^2 + \sigma2^2 - 2 \rho \sigma1\sigma2)}$

Where

$S_1 ; S_2$ = Spot price of assets 1 and 2

q1;q2 = Yields on assets 1 and 2

$\sigma1;\sigma2$ = Volatility of assets 1 and 2

ρ = Correlation between asset 1 and 2

t = time to expiry

Source: Margrabe, William, 1978, "The Value Of An Option To Exchange One Asset For Another", *Journal of Finance*, Vol 33, pp 177–186

Researchers have suggested binomial types model to price spread options.[68] Other numerical models include approaches which factor in the joint density of the terminal prices of the underlying assets into the product of univariate marginal and conditional densities to derive the available analytic expression for the integral of the option payoffs.[69] Monte Carlo approaches are also feasible.[70]

6.13.4   Trading and Hedging Credit Spread Products

Credit Forwards

Credit spread products are, in practise, replicated for trading and hedging purposes through trading in the underlying cash instruments or near surrogates.

---

[67] For an American version, see Rubinstein, Mark, July–August 1991, "One For Another", *Risk*, 30–32

[68] See Ravindran, K., "Exotic Options" in Dattatreya, Ravi E. and Hotta, Kensuke, 1994, *Advanced Interest Rate and Currency Swaps: State-of-the Art Products, Strategies & Risk Management Applications*, Probus Publishing, Chicago, Illinios; Ravindran, K., 1998, *Customised Derivatives: A Step-by-Step Guide to Using Exotic Options, Swaps and Other Customised Derivatives*, McGraw-Hill, New York, pp 274–278

[69] See Pearson. Neil D, Fall 1995, "An Efficient Approach For Pricing Spread Options", *The Journal Of Derivatives*, pp 76–91

[70] See Ravindran, K., 1998, *Customised Derivatives: A Step-by-Step Guide to Using Exotic Options, Swaps and Other Customised Derivatives*, McGraw-Hill, New York pp 331–332

Credit spread forwards are capable, in practise, of replication from a number of sources:

- Counterparty transactions
- On balance replication
- Off-balance sheet replication

Counterparty transaction rely on the presence of a number of natural counterparties for credit spread transactions given the underlying positions of these parties. These include loan and bond underwriters who are naturally long credit spreads from their underlying activities and who could as a result trade in the credit spread as a mechanism for managing the risk.

On balance sheet replication entails the establishment of physical long and short positions in the underlying credit assets and the management of these positions over the life of the transaction. Figure 6.31 sets out the structure for hedging both long and short forward positions in credit spreads.

The hedge is not exact:[71]

- **Convexity:** The hedge as structured does not incorporate any adjustment for convexity (the non linearity in the relationship between prices and yields). In practise, the hedge would need to be dynamically managed to adjust for the convexity changes as the yields on the underlying instruments changed. In the structure, the dealer will tend to be long or short convexity as the convexity and volatility of the underlying bond will generally be different from that of the risk free security. This risk is difficult in practise for the trader to hedge perfectly.
- **Market structure:** Difficulties in shorting the relevant bonds (that is the absence of an effective bond borrowing) mechanism may create significant difficulties in hedging.
- **Cost issues:** Some of the hedge costs (the repo rate, the bond borrowing cost) may be difficult to estimate at the time of establishing the hedge. For example, where the trader is long the risky bond, its receipt of the coupon is dependent upon the absence of default. In the event of default, the coupon flows are lost. This exposure is difficult in practise to hedge and must be covered by a pricing adjustment.

---

[71] For a discussion on some of the hedging issues, see Iacono, Frank "Credit Derivatives" in Schwartz, Robert J. and Smith, Jr., Clifford W. (Ed), 1997, *Derivatives Handbook: Risk Management and Control*, John Wiley & Sons, Inc., New York, Chapter 2

Figure 6.31   Replication of Credit Spread Forward Position

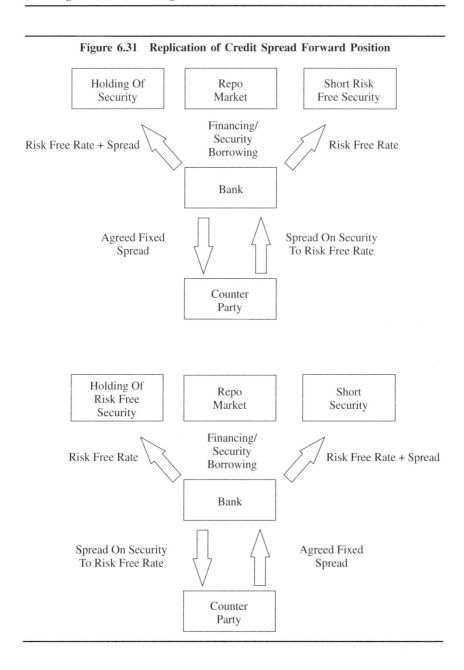

The key issues in this type of trading or hedging include:
- The utilisation of balance sheet and/or capital to support the positions.
- Liquidity of underlying asset.
- The availability of mechanisms for short selling securities.
- Transaction costs, including uncertainty regarding certain costs such as the cost of shorting securities.

Off-balance-sheet replication overcomes some of the problems of replicating credit spread forwards using physical securities. Using this form of replication requires the identification of the correlation of the credit spread to tradeable off balance sheet instruments. In practise, this usually entails using futures contracts on the relevant treasury or risk free rate and interest rate swaps. The latter being used as a surrogate for the risky security based on the observed relationship between swap spreads and corporate credit spreads in certain markets.[72] The alternative is to use a mixture of interest rate and equity index futures to replicate high yield bond spreads.

The issues in using these forms of replication is the tradeoff between the lower transaction costs and greater balance sheet/capital efficiency and the basis or correlation risk assumed.

Credit Spread Options

Credit spread options are usually created dynamically through trading in the underlying assets. Credit spread options cannot usually be efficiently replicated by trading in options on the underlying bonds. The portfolio of options is generally more expensive reflecting the separate payoff which allows each option to be separately exercised to maximise the value of individual options. This reflects the fact that the spread option is insensitive to absolute rate levels while the option portfolio is generally sensitive to the overall absolute level of rates.[73]

It should be noted that the one factor approach creates significant hedging difficulties. This reflects the fact that this type of model indicates a single delta governing synthetic replication or hedging of the spread option.

---

[72] For a discussion of swap spreads, see Das, Satyajit, 1994, *Swaps and Financial Derivatives*, LBC Information Services, Sydney, McGraw-Hill, Chicago; Evans, Ellen and Parente, Gloria M, 1987, "What Drives Interest Rate Swap Spreads," New York, Salomon Brothers Inc Bond Market Research.

[73] This is often expressed as the fact that the $ duration of the option portfolio is not zero, while the $ duration of the yield spread option is zero

The two-factor model will usually entail structures simulating the price fluctuations in the two relevant assets. The two-factor approach creates more complex valuation parameters including two deltas, multiple gammas, and at least two vegas. It requires, for computation purposes as already noted, the volatility of both assets involved in the spread and the correlation between them.

A particularly significant factor of credit spread options, when priced utilising multi factor options approaches, is the phenomenon of a negative vega. This reflects the fact that lower volatility levels, under certain circumstances, may result in higher option premiums. This reflects the fact that if the volatility of one asset diminishes (at least, with other variables held constant) the diminished volatility in one asset price performance can, in fact, increase the value of the spread option as it increases the possibility of the spread increasing or decreasing. Hence, the negative vega. This phenomenon is not unique to credit spread options and is, in fact, present in all multi-factor options structures.

6.14 Specific Pricing Methodologies — First-To-Default Baskets

The first-to-default basket structures entail using leverage (the credit protection is on an underlying amount greater than the notional principal of the transaction) and the default correlations (the risk of default on the basket is greater than on the component credits). Pricing the structures entail significant challenges.

From an intuitive perspective, the pricing of the structure should be bound by the sum of the default risk premiums on the issuers within the basket (the upper bound) and the risk premium on the weakest credit risk within the basket (the lower bound). The upper bound will clearly overestimate the risk as the purchaser of protection does not obtain protection on all the components within the basket as the protection is only on the first to default and protection on the non defaulting entities is lost when the first-to-default event occurs. The lower bound is insufficient, as the probability of default on the basket is greater than the probability of default by a single counterparty.

This process can be understood using a simple example. Assume a BB rated issuer has a 2% likelihood of defaulting over a one-year holding period. Assuming zero default correlations, the probability of any one of the four issuers defaulting can be approximated as the survival probability (1 minus the cumulative probability of default) of the components of the basket multiplied together. This in this example is calculated as $1-(1-.02)^4$ that equates to 0.08 or 8.00%.

Using this approach, assuming zero correlations, the first to default basket
probabilities for a series of first to default baskets is in Figure 6.32.

Figure 6.32   Risk of First-To-Default Baskets

AA Credit First-to-Default Basket

Cumulative Probability of First-to-Default Basket (Two Credits)

		Cumulative Probability of Default			
Issuer	Maturity (Years) Rating	1	3	5	10
A	AA	0.03%	0.10%	0.40%	1.13%
B	AA	0.03%	0.10%	0.40%	1.13%
	Survival Probability				
Issuer	Maturity (Years) Rating	100.00%	3	5	10
A	AA	99.97%	99.90%	99.60%	98.87%
B	AA	99.97%	99.90%	99.60%	98.87%

Basket					
	Maturity (Years)	1	3	5	10
Probability of Survival		99.94%	99.80%	99.20%	97.75%
Probability of Default		0.06%	0.20%	0.80%	2.25%
Times (×) Increase In Default Risk		2.00	2.00	2.00	1.99

Cumulative Probability of First-to-Default Basket (Four Credits)

		Cumulative Probability of Default			
Issuer	Maturity (Years) Rating	1.0	3	5	10
A	AA	0.03%	0.10%	0.40%	1.13%
B	AA	0.03%	0.10%	0.40%	1.13%
C	AA	0.03%	0.10%	0.40%	1.13%
D	AA	0.03%	0.10%	0.40%	1.13%

		Survival Probability			
	Maturity (Years)	1	3	5	10
Issuer	Rating				
A	AA	99.97%	99.90%	99.60%	98.87%
B	AA	99.97%	99.90%	99.60%	98.87%
C	AA	99.97%	99.90%	99.60%	98.87%
D	AA	99.97%	99.90%	99.60%	98.87%

Basket					
	Maturity (Years)	1	3	5	10
Probability of Survival		99.88%	99.60%	98.41%	95.56%
Probability of Default		0.12%	0.40%	1.59%	4.44%
Times (×) Increase In Default Risk		4.00	3.99	3.98	3.93

BB Credit First-to-Default Basket

Cumulative Probability of First-to-Default Basket (Two Credits)

		Cumulative Probability of Default			
	Maturity (Years)	1	3	5	10
Issuer	Rating				
A	BB	1.36%	6.29%	11.57%	20.94%
B	BB	1.36%	6.29%	11.57%	20.94%
		Survival Probability			
	Maturity (Years)	100.00%	3	5	10
Issuer	Rating				
A	BB	98.64%	93.71%	88.43%	79.06%
B	BB	98.64%	93.71%	88.43%	79.06%

Basket					
	Maturity (Years)	1	3	5	10
Probability of Survival		97.30%	87.82%	78.20%	62.50%
Probability of Default		2.70%	12.18%	21.80%	37.50%
Times (×) Increase In Default Risk		1.99	1.94	1.88	1.79

Cumulative Probability of First-to-Default Basket (Four Credits)

		Cumulative Probability of Default			
Issuer	Maturity (Years)	1.0	3	5	10
	Rating				
A	BB	1.36%	6.29%	11.57%	20.94%
B	BB	1.36%	6.29%	11.57%	20.94%
C	BB	1.36%	6.29%	11.57%	20.94%
D	BB	1.36%	6.29%	11.57%	20.94%
		Survival Probability			
	Maturity (Years)	1	3	5	10
Issuer	Rating				
A	BB	98.64%	93.71%	88.43%	79.06%
B	BB	98.64%	93.71%	88.43%	79.06%
C	BB	98.64%	93.71%	88.43%	79.06%
D	BB	98.64%	93.71%	88.43%	79.06%

Basket					
	Maturity (Years)	1	3	5	10
Probability of Survival		94.67%	77.12%	61.15%	39.07%
Probability of Default		5.33%	22.88%	38.85%	60.93%
Times (×) Increase In Default Risk		3.92	3.64	3.36	2.91

As is evident the risk of default on the first to default basket is significantly higher. Based on cumulative default probabilities:

- The two- and four-credit AA rated basket would be approximately A/BBB rated credit.
- The two- and four-credit BB rated basket would be approximately B/CCC rated credit.

The increase in risk is noticeably greater where underlying credit risks are non investment grade. The estimates above have been based on zero default correlations. The probability of default on the first to default basket increases with increasing default correlations within the basket. As discussed above, default correlations are in practise extremely difficult to calculate.

In practise, this means that pricing first to default structures is not scientific. Typically, the pricing drivers are the reasons for doing the transaction. Thus transactions are driven by the fact that the buyer of protection gets default protection at a lower overall cost than separately hedging each of the individual credits and the fact that they are useful in managing concentration risk within the portfolios. The pricing of the structures tend to reflect these prerogatives.

6.15 Summary

Credit derivative pricing is rapidly developing. Increasing research on default risk pricing by academic researchers is increasing the sophistication of credit risk modeling. However, the difficulties of parameter estimation, the instability of relationships as well as the problems of efficient numerical implementation are still formidable. One of the collateral benefits of this increases rigour in the pricing of default risk is that the modelling should ultimately improve the understanding of pricing and management of credit risk in financial services more broadly. Credit derivatives have significantly advanced the measurement and quantification of credit exposures and the return required to compensate for the risk assumed.

7

Using Default Rates to Model the Term Structure of Credit Risk[1]

Jerome S Fons,[2] Moody's Investors Service

Economists have paid a great deal of attention to the term "structure of interest rates." However, relatively little is known about the term "structure of credit risk," defined here as the behavior of credit spreads as maturity varies. Early studies of the term structure of credit risk noted an upward-sloping risk structure for highly rated bonds. That is, the difference or spread between the promised yield-to-maturity of a default-prone bond and the yield-to-maturity of a default-free bond of equivalent maturity widens as maturity increases. Conversely, when credit quality was low, researchers found a downward-sloping risk structure. A "crisis-at-maturity" model was used to explain this unusual pattern.[3] The "crisis-at-maturity" hypothesis assumes that highly leveraged firms with debt maturing over the near term may encounter refinancing problems. The higher default risk associated with debt maturing in the near term is reflected in higher spreads at shorter maturities.

---

[1] Reproduced by permission of the Association for Investment Management and Research (AIMR)

[2] The author thanks Douglas Lucas, Roger Stein and Pat Corcoran for their comments, and Lea Carty for his assistance and comments

[3] See Johnson, RE 1967, "The term structure of corporate bond yields as a function of risk of default," *Journal of Finance*, Issue 22; Silvers, JB 1973, "An alternative to the yield spread as a measure of risk," *Journal of Finance*, Issue 28; Van Horne, JC 1978, *Financial Market Rates and Flows*, Prentice Hall, Englewood Cliffs, US, pp 164–173

Recent theoretical models of credit risk, based on contingent claims models of debt pricing, take a much more sophisticated approach to this question.[4] In contrast, this chapter introduces a relatively straightforward, risk neutral bond-pricing model employing observed multi-period corporate bond default rates. Although more elaborate techniques could be used to reveal this fundamental relationship, the simple approach used here has the advantage of being highly intuitive and easy to implement. We find that for some levels of default risk, credit spreads indeed decrease with maturity. Furthermore, while our conclusions rely on the results of Moody's corporate bond default studies, the patterns exhibited in these studies can also be found in other studies of corporate bond defaults.[5]

7.1 Patterns in Default Rates

Moody's default studies summarize the default experience of all corporate issuers of long-term public debt holding Moody's ratings as of January 1, 1970. More than 473 issuers that ever held a Moody's corporate bond rating defaulted between that date and December 31, 1993. By comparing historical ratings of defaulting issuers with ratings for the thousands of public issuers that did not default, we construct default rates in order to estimate the default risk associated with each rating category. The most important concepts presented in these studies are marginal and cumulative default rates. We begin with a brief summary of these terms.

Let $m_t^Y(R)$ be the number of issuers rated R (where R = Aaa, Aa, ...), that were originally part of the cohort (or set) of all outstanding issuers with rating R at the start of year Y (where Y = 1970, 1971, ...), that defaulted in the tth year

---

[4] See Nielsen, LT, Saá-Requejo, J, and Santa-Clara, P 1993, "Default risk and interest rate risk: The term structure of default spreads," INSEAD Working Paper, May; Kim, IJ, Ramaswamy, K, and Sundaresan, S, 1993, "Does default risk in coupons affect the valuation of corporate bonds?: A contingent claims model," *Financial Management*, Autumn; Ginzburg, A, Maloney, K and Willner, R 1993, "Risk rating migration and the valuation of floating rate debt," Working Paper, December; Jones, EP, Mason, SP, and Rosenfeld E 1984, "Contingent claims analysis of corporate capital structures: An empirical investigations," *Journal of Finance* **39**; Litterman, R and Iben, T 1988, "Corporate bond valuation and the term structure of credit spreads," Goldman Sachs Financial Strategies Group

[5] As a matter of policy, Moody's Investors Service does not make, buy, or sell recommendations. We present the model in this chapter as just one of many possible ways to factor credit risk into the price of a bond

after cohort Y was formed. Let $n_t^Y(R)$ be the total number of issuers with rating R at the start of year Y that have not defaulted by year t. The marginal default rate $d_t(R)$ is the average issuer-weighted default rate for R-rated issuers in their t^{th} year. Formally:

$$d_t(R) = \frac{\sum_{Y=1970}^{T} m_t^Y(R)}{\sum_{Y=1970}^{T} n_t^Y(R)}, \text{ where } T = 1994 - t \qquad (1)$$

The variable T restricts the summations to only those cohorts for which t years of history are available, in this case, the years 1970–1993.

For example, $d_5(\text{Baa})$ would be the probability that a bond will default in the fifth year after holding the Baa rating. The likelihood that a bond rated R will not default in year t is the marginal survival rate $(1 - d_t(R))$. On the other hand, the probability that a bond rated R will not default by year t is the cumulative survival rate $S_t(R)$ defined as the product:

$$S_t(R) = \prod_{i=1}^{t} (1 - d_i(R)) \qquad (2)$$

That is, the cumulative survival rate is the product of intervening marginal survival rates. In turn, the cumulative default rate $D_t(R)$ is the probability that a bond rated R will default by year t. It is found as:

$$D_t(R) = 1 - S_t(R) \qquad (3)$$

In other words, the path of marginal default rates through period t completely describes the cumulative survival likelihood as well as the cumulative default likelihood.

Figures 7.1 and 7.2 present marginal and cumulative default rates from 1–20 years for Moody's broad letter rating categories. These estimates are derived from Moody's long-term default studies covering the years 1970–1993. The cumulative default rates, in particular, show that over any time horizon there is a clear pattern of increasing risk as rating quality declines.

In Figures 7.3 and 7.4 we plot marginal default rates for the investment-grade ratings and the speculative grades as the investment horizon grows from 1–20 years. These are the historical probabilities of an issuer defaulting t years after having a rating R. In general, the trend is for investment grade (Aaa, Aa, A, and Baa) marginal default rates to rise as the time horizon lengthens and for speculative grade (Ba and B) marginal default rates to decline. Stated differently, the year-on-year risk of default, though always non-decreasing in the cumulative

Figure 7.1   Weighted Average Marginal Default Rates, 1970–1993

	Year									
	1	2	3	4	5	6	7	8	9	10
Aaa	0%	0%	0%	0.04%	0.09%	0.10%	0.11%	0.12%	0.14%	0.15%
Aa	0.02%	0.01%	0.05%	0.12%	0.12%	0.11%	0.10%	0.11%	0.13%	0.15%
A	0.01%	0.08%	0.20%	0.18%	0.16%	0.21%	0.24%	0.25%	0.31%	0.35%
Baa	0.16%	0.35%	0.40%	0.56%	0.52%	0.50%	0.65%	0.68%	0.67%	0.59%
Ba	1.79%	2.64%	2.66%	2.67%	2.69%	2.19%	1.80%	1.67%	1.67%	1.64%
B	8.31%	7.13%	6.50%	5.52%	4.79%	4.89%	3.59%	3.64%	2.64%	2.57%

	Year									
	11	12	13	14	15	16	17	18	19	20
Aaa	0.17%	0.19%	0.22%	0.25%	0.29%	0.34%	0.21%	0.25%	0%	0%
Aa	0.17%	0.20%	0.23%	0.26%	0%	0%	0.13%	0.16%	0.20%	0.25%
A	0.35%	0.36%	0.35%	0.30%	0.34%	0.35%	0.32%	0.33%	0.40%	0.28%
Baa	0.64%	0.66%	0.62%	0.73%	0.77%	0.82%	0.85%	0.84%	0.69%	0.71%
Ba	1.69%	1.74%	1.70%	1.28%	1.24%	1.31%	1.16%	1.06%	1.14%	1.24%
B	1.86%	1.12%	1.22%	1.03%	1.15%	1.30%	1.50%	0.58%	0%	0%

Figure 7.2   Weighted Average Cumulative Default Rates, 1970–1993

	Year									
	1	2	3	4	5	6	7	8	9	10
Aaa	0%	0%	0%	0.04%	0.12%	0.22%	0.33%	0.45%	0.58%	0.73%
Aa	0.02%	0.04%	0.08%	0.20%	0.32%	0.43%	0.52%	0.6%	0.76%	0.91%
A	0.01%	0.09%	0.28%	0.46%	0.62%	0.83%	1.06%	1.31%	1.61%	1.96%
Baa	0.16%	0.51%	0.91%	1.46%	1.97%	2.46%	3.09%	3.75%	4.39%	4.96%
Ba	1.79%	4.38%	6.92%	9.41%	11.85%	13.78%	15.33%	16.75%	18.14%	19.48%
B	8.31%	14.85%	20.38%	24.78%	28.38%	31.88%	34.32%	36.71%	38.38%	39.96%

	Year									
	11	12	13	14	15	16	17	18	19	20
Aaa	0.90%	1.09%	1.30%	1.55%	1.84%	2.18%	2.38%	2.63%	2.63%	2.63%
Aa	1.09%	1.29%	1.51%	1.76%	1.76%	1.76%	1.89%	2.05%	2.24%	2.48%
A	2.30%	2.65%	2.99%	3.29%	3.62%	3.95%	4.26%	4.58%	4.96%	5.23%
Baa	5.56%	6.19%	6.77%	7.44%	8.16%	8.91%	9.69%	10.45%	11.07%	11.70%
Ba	20.84%	22.22%	23.54%	24.52%	25.46%	26.43%	27.29%	28.06%	28.88%	29.76%
B	41.08%	41.74%	42.45%	43.04%	43.70%	44.43%	45.27%	45.58%	45.58%	45.58%

sense, rises for investment-grade issuers and falls for speculative-grade issuers. This shifting pattern of marginal default rates by rating category is further supported by Moody's studies of changes in corporate credit quality and suggests an underlying "mean reversion" with respect to a company's credit outlook.

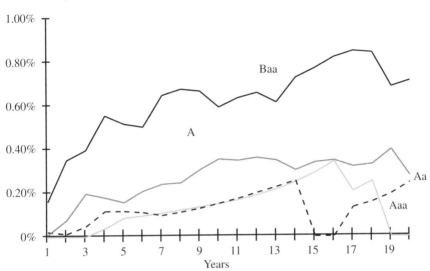

Figure 7.3   Marginal Default Rates — Investment-Grade Ratings

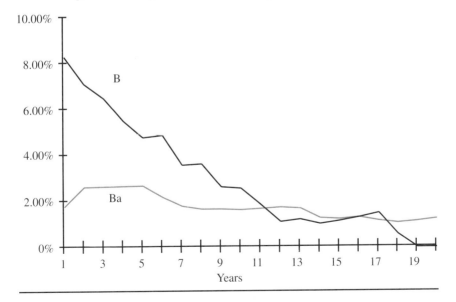

Figure 7.4   Marginal Default Rates — Speculative-Grade Ratings

To a certain extent, corporate bond issuers exhibit life-cycle patterns that, in the long run, cause their ratings to settle at average levels. Relatively small but growing firms, for example, tend to face a great deal of near-term uncertainty with respect to their ability to meet their obligations. The same is generally true of mature firms that significantly alter their capital structures by assuming more debt. Either type of firm can be rated as speculative grade and tends to face substantial near-term risks. Once past these obstacles and having survived without a default, these issuers may be upgraded or they may pay down their borrowings and withdraw from the public debt markets. In other words, the risk of default 10 or more years hence is relatively low, given that these companies survived the first few years without a default.

Investment-grade issuers, on the other hand, face very low default risk over the near term. They tend to be large, well-established leaders in their industry with a solid track record of meeting obligations. However, their credit outlook over the long-term is somewhat less certain. Any number of risks can surface over the course of 10 or more years. An industry can shrink altogether as new technologies emerge or the political climate changes. Furthermore, in terms of credit quality, top-rated firms have only two prospects—stable ratings or declining ratings.

The pattern that emerges is that, over the long term, surviving low-rated issuers tend to rise to the middle ratings. Middle-rated firms tend to stay middle-rated, and top-rated firms eventually slip to the middle ratings. As we show later, this has implications for the term structure of credit risk.

7.2 Risk Neutral Bond Pricing

In this section, we develop a yield spread model for new-issue bonds using the default concepts presented earlier in the context of a standard bond pricing formula. A coupon bond paying an annual coupon C, which matures N years from now, has a yield to maturity, Y, that solves the expression:

$$Price = \sum_{t=1}^{N} \frac{C}{(1 + Y)^t} + \frac{1}{(1 + Y)^N} \tag{4}$$

For simplicity, the price, coupon, and the principal terms are expressed as a fraction of unity. Equation (4) states that the price of a coupon bond (default prone or default free) is the present value of a stream of cash flows C and a terminal principal payment, 1, where the discount rate is Y.[6]

---

[6] We assume annual coupon payments to simplify the mathematics. The analysis extends easily to semiannual coupon payments as well

In order to use our default data to compute a yield spread over a comparable maturity default-free debt instrument, we will invoke four assumptions:

- Bonds are priced at par. Typically, a coupon bond is priced at par when first issued. When price equals 100% of par, the coupon rate C equals the promised yield to maturity Y.
- Investors hold bonds until maturity or default, whichever occurs first. In the event of default, the bond is sold immediately. This assumption removes the complexity introduced by possible changes in credit rating prior to maturity.
- Investors are risk neutral. That is, they are indifferent between taking a gamble with expected payout X and receiving X with certainty. A risk neutral individual would be indifferent about participating in a lottery with a ticket price of $1.00 and an expected pay-out of $1.00. Holding the ticket price at $1.00 and raising the expected payout to, say, $1.10, however, would lead the utility-maximizing, risk neutral individual to step up and take a chance.
- Capital markets are arbitrage free. In the present context, this means that risk-adjusted expected yields are equal for all securities.

We denote the yield of a default-prone bond by Y and the yield of a comparable-maturity default-risk free issue by i. If a bond has default risk, the yield must be high enough to compensate investors for this risk and the difference $(Y-i)$ is referred to as the credit spread. When the bond is priced at par, the credit spread will be $(C-i)$.

Using the notation introduced above, we weight a bond's risky coupon and principal payments by their probability of being paid when promised. Let S_t be the likelihood that an issuer with a given rating survives t years from the issuance date without a default. It is also the probability that a payment due t years after issuance will be received as promised. Otherwise, the issuer will default on the payment due in year t with probability $S_{t-1}d_t$, which is the probability that the issuer survives through year $(t-1)$ multiplied by the probability of a default during year t. In the event of a default, the bond holder sells the bond and expects to recover a fraction of the missed coupon plus principal.

This gives us a certainty-equivalent version of Equation (4):

$$Price = \sum_{t=1}^{N} \frac{S_t C + S_{t-1}d_t\mu(C+1)}{(1+i)^t} + \frac{S_N}{(1+i)^N} \tag{5}$$

where $S_0 = 1$.

The numerator of the summand is a default-risk adjusted payment stream based on expected default and survival rates. The probability of receiving a coupon payment t years from now is S_t. A default will occur in year t with probability d_t, given that the bond has survived to year t without a default — the probability of this being S_{t-1}. In the event of default, the investor receives a fraction μ of $(C+1)$, representing the coupon plus principal owed. The numerator of the last term on the right is the likelihood of receiving the final principal payment when due.

Equation (5) is identical to Equation (4) except that the latter payment stream is adjusted for default-risk. The risk neutral investor is indifferent between receiving this risk-adjusted payment stream and a certain stream with the same expected value. The appropriate discount rate for this stream is, therefore, the risk-free interest rate i.

Setting the bond price to par (100%) and given an array of marginal default rates (which, in turn, imply a set of survival rates), an estimate of the recovery rate and a default-free yield of appropriate maturity, Equation (5) implicitly determines the risky coupon rate. The difference $(C-i)$ is the credit spread required of the default-prone bond to perfectly compensate a buy-and-hold risk neutral investor for a set of marginal default rates d_t and an expected recovery rate μ. Such an investor will be indifferent between investing in this bond and investing in an equivalent-maturity, default-free bond yielding i. It is anticipated that most investors are risk-averse and would expect to be *more* than compensated for expected default risk because of the uncertainty surrounding point estimates of default likelihood.

Historical marginal default rates, by senior unsecured rating category, are presented in Figure 7.1. Recovery rates, on the other hand, depend on many factors, but chief among these is a bond's standing within the firm's capital structure. Moody's long-term default study presents estimates of recovery rates by bond seniority, based on defaulted bond prices measured one month after default. Figure 7.5 reveals that average recovery rates decline uniformly with seniority. For our sample of defaulted bonds, the average recovery rate at the senior unsecured level — associated with most debentures such as bonds and notes — was 48.38% of par. We use this figure in the simulations presented later.

Figure 7.5   Recovery Rates By Seniority

Seniority	Average recovery rate
Senior secured	64.59%
Senior unsecured	48.38%
Senior subordinated	39.79%
Subordinated	30.00%
Junior subordinated	16.33%

7.3 The Term Structure of Credit Risk

This section presents simulations based on the model introduced in the earlier section, using historical default rates and a recovery rate estimate. We compare modeled spreads to those recently observed in the corporate bond market.

Figures 7.6 and 7.7 are plots of risk neutral spreads from 1–20 years for each rating category, as determined by solving Equation (5). The results are also presented in Figure 7.8. The figures use the marginal default rates presented in Figure 7.1, and assume a fixed recovery rate of 48.38%. To arrive at the appropriate default-free yield for each maturity, we fit a (log linear) regression model to the US Treasury constant-maturity schedule (as of September 30, 1993) and use the modeled value.

Risk neutral spreads calculated for the investment-grade rating categories exhibit, with minor variations, a steady upward trend as bond maturity increases. To a very small extent, this is due to the upward slope of the Treasury yield curve as of September 30, 1993. At the Ba rating level, however, credit spreads rise through the fifth year but then slowly taper off. At the single-B rating, credit spreads fall from Year 1.

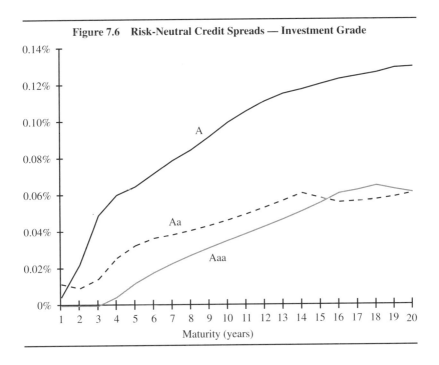

Figure 7.6   Risk-Neutral Credit Spreads — Investment Grade

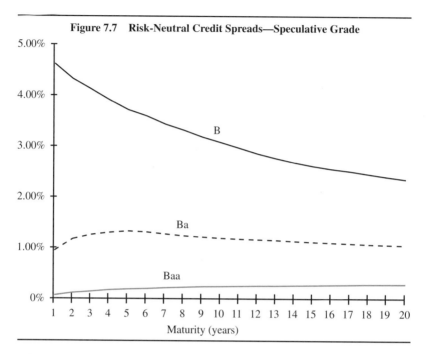

Figure 7.7   Risk-Neutral Credit Spreads—Speculative Grade

Although these patterns roughly match those of the corresponding marginal default rates, it is nonetheless surprising to find that spreads against comparable-maturity treasuries might actually decline as maturity is increased, especially at the lowest rating categories. As the threat of default recedes, even if initially high, risk neutral investors require a smaller yield spread to compensate them for expected default loss.

We should note that credit spreads generated using Equation (5) are highly sensitive to the recovery rate estimate. Lowering the estimated recovery rate leads to much wider spreads; higher recovery estimates give much smaller spreads. On the other hand, the model is much less sensitive to changes in the level of the risk-free yield.

Figure 7.8   **Risk Neutral Credit Spreads by Rating Category, as of September 30, 1993**

Years to maturity	Aaa	Aa	A	Baa	Ba	B
1	0%	0.01%	0%	0.09%	0.96%	4.64%
2	0%	0.01%	0.02%	0.14%	1.20%	4.34%
3	0%	0.01%	0.05%	0.16%	1.28%	4.14%
4	0%	0.03%	0.06%	0.19%	1.32%	3.93%
5	0.01%	0.03%	0.06%	0.21%	1.35%	3.74%

6	0.02%	0.04%	0.07%	0.22%	1.33%	3.61%
7	0.02%	0.04%	0.08%	0.24%	1.29%	3.45%
8	0.03%	0.04%	0.08%	0.25%	1.26%	3.34%
9	0.03%	0.04%	0.09%	0.26%	1.23%	3.20%
10	0.04%	0.05%	0.10%	0.26%	1.21%	3.10%
11	0.04%	0.05%	0.11%	0.27%	1.19%	2.99%
12	0.04%	0.05%	0.11%	0.28%	1.18%	2.88%
13	0.05%	0.06%	0.12%	0.28%	1.17%	2.78%
14	0.05%	0.06%	0.12%	0.28%	1.15%	2.70%
15	0.06%	0.06%	0.12%	0.29%	1.14%	2.63%
16	0.06%	0.06%	0.12%	0.30%	1.12%	2.58%
17	0.06%	0.06%	0.13%	0.30%	1.11%	2.54%
18	0.07%	0.06%	0.13%	0.31%	1.09%	2.48%
19	0.06%	0.06%	0.13%	0.31%	1.08%	2.42%
20	0.06%	0.06%	0.13%	0.31%	1.08%	2.37%

7.4 Market Behavior

Yield spreads, calculated using recent market data, indicate that our model helps explain observed pricing behavior. We collected yields as of September 30, 1993 for over 4,000 rated, straight, domestic US corporate bonds. To minimize the effects of call schedules on yields, we eliminated all bonds callable within one year. After deleting major outliers as well as those bonds with a maturity greater than 20 years, we were left with 2,848 bonds. They break down as follows: 108 bonds rated Aaa, 374 bonds rated Aa, 1235 bonds rated A, 725 bonds rated Baa, 183 bonds rated Ba, and 223 bonds rated single B. To compute spreads for each of these, we fit a spline regression to the US Treasury yield curve as of September 30, 1993, and calculate spreads against this function. The scatter plots in Figures 7.9–7.14 show the resulting market credit spreads for each rating category. Included in these diagrams is a line fitted using standard linear regression methods.

No clear trend emerges in the plot of the Aaa spreads against comparable maturity Treasury bonds as term varies. However, bonds rated Aa and A exhibit a significant, positive relationship between spread and maturity. Bonds rated Baa also show a positive relationship, although not as strong as that for bonds rated A. Consistent with the modeled behavior, credit spreads for bonds rated Ba decline only slightly as maturity increases. As anticipated, we found a significant negative spread versus maturity relationship for single-B-rated bonds. Furthermore, the lower bounds of the Aa and A spreads exhibit the convexity seen in their corresponding theoretical spread models.

Regression results, presented in Figure 7.15, also support these observations.

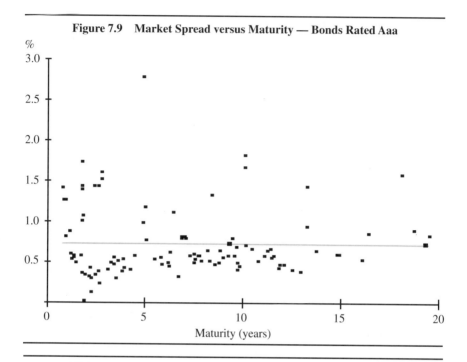

Figure 7.9   Market Spread versus Maturity — Bonds Rated Aaa

Figure 7.10   Market Spread versus Maturity — Bonds Rated Aa

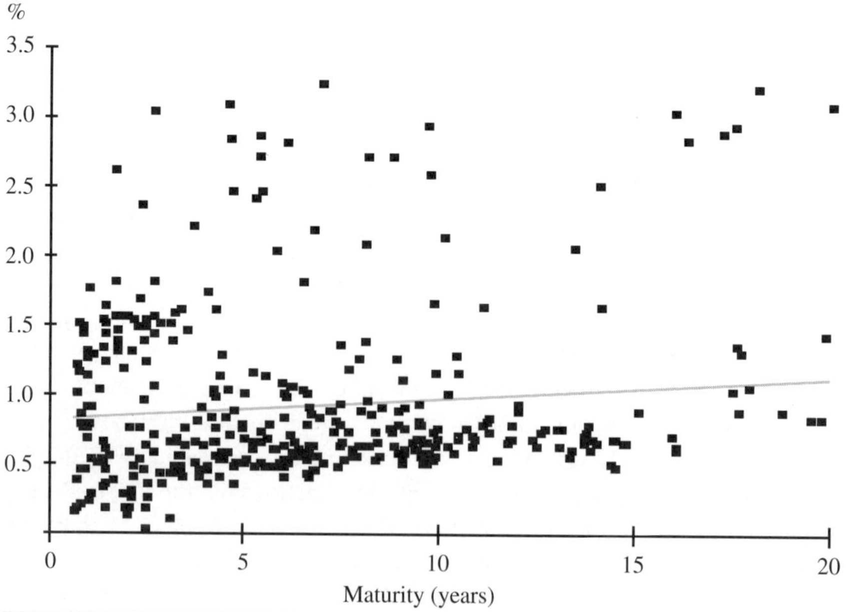

Figure 7.11   Market Spread versus Maturity — Bonds Rated A

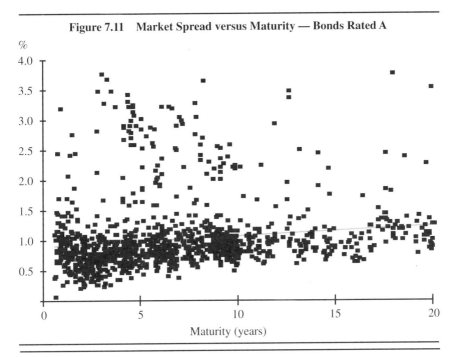

Figure 7.12   Market Spread versus Maturity — Bonds Rated Baa

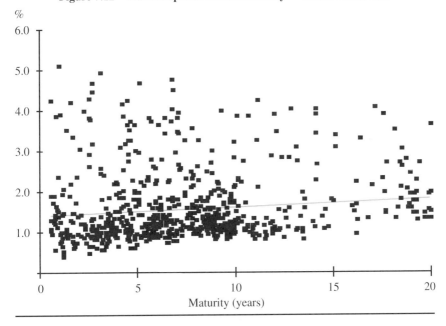

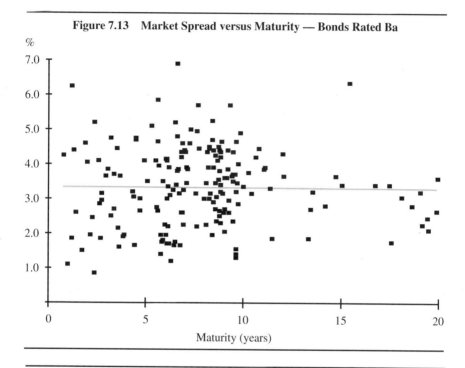

Figure 7.13   Market Spread versus Maturity — Bonds Rated Ba

Figure 7.14   Market Spread versus Maturity — Bonds Rated B

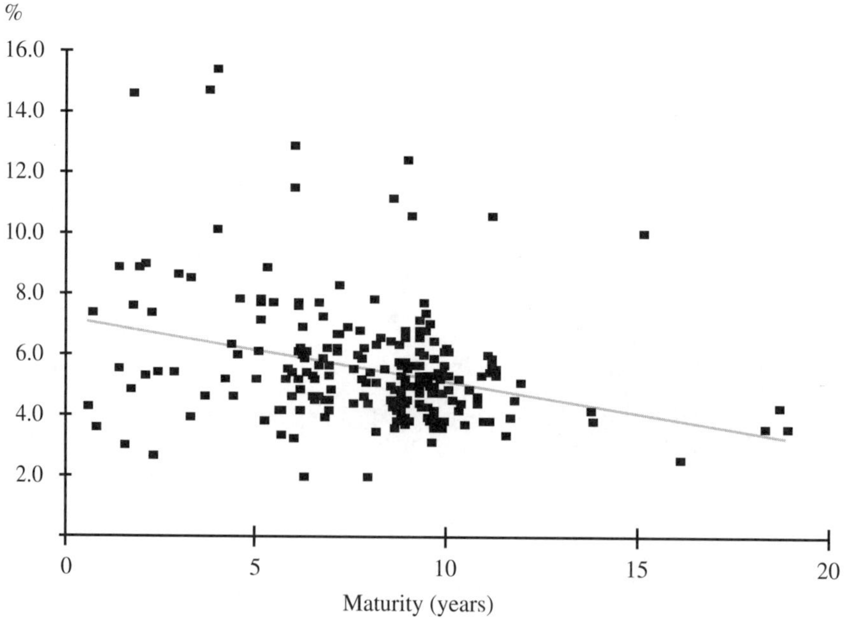

Due in part to the noise contained in the price data, the overall fit of the regressions is quite low. In two cases — bonds rated Aaa and bonds rated Ba — the slope coefficients of lines fitted through spreads as a function of maturity are not significantly different from zero. All other slope terms are significantly different from zero at the 5% level of confidence. The steepest positive slope corresponds to bonds rated single A, and spreads for bonds rated single B are negatively related to maturity. All intercept terms appear significant at the 5% level and rise as credit quality falls.

For each rating category, the fitted line lies above its theoretical counterpart. The difference is particularly apparent at the investment-grade categories (Aaa, Aa, A, and Baa). For these ratings, the 20-year theoretical credit spread ranges between 0.06% and 0.31%, while the 20-year maturity market spreads (as of September 30, 1993) averaged 0.74% for bonds rated Aaa, 1.14% for bonds rated Aa, 1.27% for bonds rated A, and 1.85% for bonds rated Baa. Theoretical risk neutral spreads for speculative-grade bonds more closely fit measured spreads. The modeled spreads for bonds rated Ba peak at 1.35% in Year 5, whereas market spreads for these bonds averaged 3.37%. Based on historical default rates, risk neutral spreads for bonds rated B should range between 4.64% (at 1-year maturity) and 2.37% (for 20-year maturity). Market spreads for bonds rated B averaged 7.05% at Year 1 and 3.09% at Year 20.

| | **Figure 7.15   Regression Results** | | |
Bond rating	Slope coefficient (*t*-statistic)	Intercept (*t*-statistic)	Adjusted R^2
Aaa	−0.0003 (−0.04)	0.742 (10.04)	−0.94% .
Aa	0.015 (2.13)	0.837 (14.70)	0.94%
A	0.0174 (4.89)	0.916 (31.63)	1.82%
Baa	0.0212 (2.96)	1.425 (23.02)	1.06%
Ba	−0.002 (20.09)	3.372 (18.36)	−0.55%
B	−0.208 (−4.71)	7.254 (19.45)	8.71

There are many reasons for the discrepancies between our modeled and market credit spreads. Among them are:

- By virtue of its size and activity level, the liquidity of the market for US Treasury securities far exceeds that of any other bond market. Investors in less liquid issues may require a premium as compensation for liquidity risk.
- We assumed that bond investors are risk-neutral. While individuals may exhibit risk neutral behavior with small portions of their wealth (such as lotteries), they are likely to be risk-averse when large sums are concerned. As will be shown later, default rate estimates (as well as recovery rate estimates) contain higher-order risk factors.
- We assumed that investors could not sell their bonds except in the case of default. Clearly, individuals are free to trade bonds, and may suffer paper losses if the credit worthiness of their bonds decline after the purchase date. Investors in highly rated bonds, in particular, may want compensation for this risk.
- Interest earned on US Treasury securities is exempt from state and local income taxes. As a result, individual investors, in particular, are often willing to accept a lower yield on these securities.
- Although we made an effort to minimize complications due to the call provisions found in many corporate bonds, residual effects remain. When a firm has the right to call its bonds, investors will demand compensation in the form of a higher promised yield.

As already mentioned, risk-neutral credit spreads are quite sensitive to the recovery rate estimate, and it is important to reiterate that our derived risk neutral spreads should establish a lower bound to actual market spreads. While introducing risk aversion will lead to wider theoretical spreads, other risks play a role in the pricing of corporate bonds as well. These risks could, under certain circumstances, dominate concerns about default risk.

7.5 Stability of Default Rate Estimates

The default rates used in the pricing model represent point estimates. However, history shows that default rates are not particularly stable, especially at low rating levels. By taking the number of issuers defaulting in a year — with a given rating at the start of that year — and dividing by the total number of issuers with that rating at the beginning of the year, we can form a time series of 1-year default rates by rating category. Presented in Figure 7.16, this chart illustrates the increased default rate volatility seen at the lower rating categories over the years 1970–1993. Moreover, it suggests at least a mild correlation between default rates and the overall business cycle.

The recessions of 1974, 1982, and 1990, as well as the slowdown of 1985, are each represented above by surges in speculative-grade default rates. (The large spike in 1970 is due to the default of Penn Central Railroad and its affiliates.) Broader trends in corporate leverage are a factor as well, particularly in the last half of the 1980s.

The increased volatility of default rates at lower-rating categories, as well as their cyclical nature, introduce a source of uncertainty to the pricing relationship. Risk-averse investors may require added compensation for this uncertainty. Likewise, though not presented here, there is considerable volatility across recovery rates, measured as the bond's trading price one month after

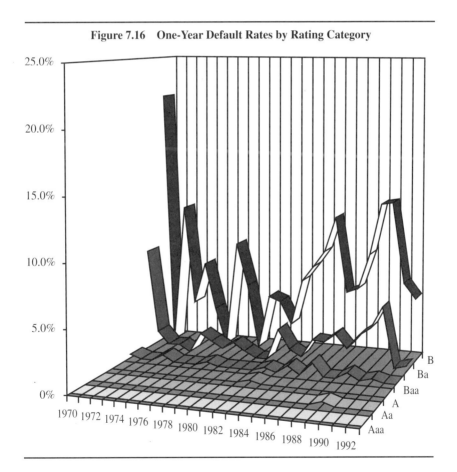

Figure 7.16   One-Year Default Rates by Rating Category

default. This too might induce risk-averse investors to seek compensation above actuarially neutral yields.

Left for future research is the question of how the spread versus maturity relationship might evolve through time, and its role as an indicator for the timing and phase of the credit cycle.

7.6 Summary

This chapter presents multi-year default rates from Moody's long-term default study and, using a risk neutral pricing model, relates these to the term structure of credit risk. We compare theoretical credit spreads by rating category and maturity to recent market data and find strong similarities. We attribute differences between predicted and observed patterns to other risk factors and differences between the US Treasury securities market and the corporate bond market.

8
Analytics and Algorithms for Credit Derivatives[1]

Haydn Stedman, Citibank

8.1 Introduction

The notion of a credit derivative (CD) used in this chapter is a contract under which the parties thereto undertake to exchange cash or other specified financial assets at set times or upon the occurrence of specified events in accord with a specified function of the value of a portfolio of notional short and long positions in a number of credit spread bonds (CSBs).

In this chapter we outline a mathematical framework for valuing and hedging credit derivatives. To obtain a notion of fair value we have to make some assumptions about liquidity; where fair value is defined as that value that cannot be arbitrated. In many cases these liquidity assumptions are patently false; however, one can always enter a (derivative) contract which obliges one party thereto to make and receive certain payments which mimic the effect of a specified position in an underlying credit spread bond portfolio. Notwithstanding, it is useful to have a notion of fair market value, the failure of the liquidity assumption can by modelled later as a wide bid/ask spread loosely based around fair value.

We commence in Section 8.2 with a simple compound interest/discreet probability model that is somewhat actuarial in nature. This is quite appropriate as many credit derivatives are as difficult to hedge as mortality rates. We calculate the underlying and credit spread term structures and default probabilities then value forward credit swaps and CSBs. This simple model, coupled with some simple arbitrage arguments, enables us to value default puts in addition to the margins on 'first-to-default' virtual portfolios and default puts

---

[1] Reproduced by permission of Haydn Stedman

on first-to-default virtual portfolios. A numerical example is developed to accompany the exposition.

Section 8.3 sees the introduction of martingales and the development of option formula. Notwithstanding the valuation of default puts in Part 1, there are many derivative structures on portfolios of credit spread bonds that cannot be valued from the model in Part 1. For example, a call on a CSB or a put on a CSB which is only valid as long as no default has taken place. For this wider class of derivatives the model should extend a 'conventional' swaption and bond option model and further converge in a reasonable fashion to the conventional model as the default probabilities approach zero. We briefly compare this model with the CreditMetrics^{TM} of J.P. Morgan as described by the articles available from their web site.

Section 8.4 develops an approach to Value-at-Risk (VaR) for positions in portfolios of CSBs and CDs. For the purposes of this article the usual methodology of taking 1.65 standard deviations of some underlying normal distribution is of limited applicability here. We take the principal the VaR is the amount the participant can make or lose in the event that outcomes are as good as they get with 5.0% probability or as bad as they get with 5.0% probability. For example if one has a 2.5% chance of losing $4 and a 10.0% chance of making $1.00 then the two-sided VaR numbers are −$2.00 and +$1.00.

Finally, the epilogue presents some comments and caveats on Sections 8.2–8.4.

8.2   Elementary Approach

Firstly, let us set some conventions and notation. We work with a 10-year horizon on monthly rests; quarterly or semi annual rates are then easily derived, i.e. effectively on a 30/360 day basis:

t_i for $i = 0$ to n ($= 20$) t_0 is now t_1 1 month from now, etc.

s_i is the i period underlying rate for $i = 1$ to n.
For example, the s_n would constitute a (30/360) treasury curve in USD, Gilt curve in GBP or JGB curve in JPY. s_n is specified on an effective per period basis so in this case if the annual monthly n period rate were 6.0% p.a. then s_n would be 0.005. This makes the maths tidier.

m_i is the i period CSB margin for $i = 1$ to n.
For example, if a 3-year CSB was trading 24 over T-bonds, m_{36} would be 0.0002.

y_i is the i period CSB yield, that is $y_i = m_i + s_i$.

f_i is the ith period forward underlying rate for $i = 1$ to n. Note that $f_0 = s_0$.

g_i is the ith period forward CSB margin for $i = 1$ to n. Note that $g_0 = m_0$.

z_i is the ith period forward CSB yield for $i = 1$ to n. That is, $z_i = g_i + f_i$.

V_i the ith period underlying discount factor for $i = 1$ to n. Note that

$$V_i = \prod_{j=1}^{i} \left(\frac{1}{(1 + f_j)} \right)$$

W_i is the ith period CSB discount factor for $i = 1$ to n. Note that

$$W_i = \prod_{j=1}^{i} \left(\frac{1}{(1 + f_j + g_j)} \right) = \prod_{j=1}^{i} \left(\frac{1}{(1 + z_j)} \right)$$

p_i is the probability of default in period i.

Q_i is the probability of no default prior to the end of period i. That is,

$$Q_i = \prod_{j=1}^{i} (1 - p_j)$$

r_i is the recovery fraction available in period i. We assume all $r_i = r$ constant.

In order to calculate all the terms above we start from the values that are available in the market usually the underlying curve and some of the margins. From there we interpolate to obtain all the values of s_n and m_n. From there we can use a bootstrap procedure to find the implied forward margin structure. Once all of the above terms are calculated we can then value the forward price of any CSB (of the same credit rating) or forward swap.

Typically the underlying rate and the margin are observable at various tenors and one can then interpolate the other values of s_n and m_n using a crafted spline or other viable technique. We develop a numerical example based on the following assumptions relating to underlying yield curve and credit spreads. Our assumed recovery rate is 60.00%.

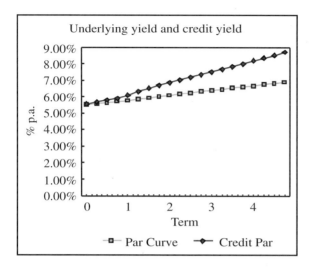

Term	Yield	CSB Yield
0.25	5.50%	5.55%
0.50	5.57%	5.67%
0.75	5.63%	5.78%
1.00	5.70%	5.90%
1.25	5.78%	6.10%
1.50	5.85%	6.30%
1.75	5.93%	6.50%
2.00	6.00%	6.70%
2.25	6.08%	6.86%
2.50	6.15%	7.03%
2.75	6.23%	7.19%
3.00	6.30%	7.35%
3.25	6.38%	7.51%
3.50	6.45%	7.68%
3.75	6.53%	7.84%
4.00	6.60%	8.00%
4.25	6.68%	8.18%
4.50	6.75%	8.35%
4.75	6.83%	8.53%
5.00	6.90%	8.70%

We would like to see our implied forward margin term structure and default probability term structure. To do this we must calculate them from our observable data. For each period we know that the expected present value of the margin paid must equal the size of the expected loss from default.

$$(1 - p_1) * g_i = p_i * ((1 + f_i) - r(1 + f_i + g_i))$$

or

$$(1 - p_i(1 - r))(1 + f_i + g_i) = (1 + f_i)$$

or, rearranging to isolate p

$$p_i = \frac{g_i}{(1 + f_i + g_i) * (1 - r)}$$

or, rearranging to isolate g

$$g_i = \frac{p_i(1 - r) * (1 + f_i)}{(1 - p_i)}.$$

On the assumption of sufficient liquidity to buy and sell CSBs of all maturities we can calculate values for forward using the following observation. By buying the n period floating CSB, going short the $n - 1$ period CSB and writing a FRA on f in period n, we can lock in either the receipt of g (for period n); or the payment of the default loss for period n or no cashflows at all if default occurs prior to the end of period $n - 1$. There are no net cash flows prior to period $n - 1$, the long and short positions cancel in both the default and no default cases, and by arbitrage the expected value of g in period n is equal to the expected default loss in that period. Hence the probabilities are as given above.

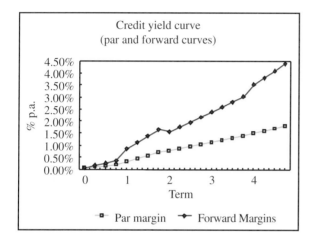

Term	g	p
0.25	0.05%	0.06%
0.50	0.15%	0.19%
0.75	0.25%	0.31%
1.00	0.35%	0.44%
1.25	0.85%	1.04%
1.50	1.11%	1.36%
1.75	1.38%	1.69%
2.00	1.65%	2.02%
2.25	1.56%	1.91%
2.50	1.75%	2.15%
2.75	1.96%	2.39%
3.00	2.16%	2.64%
3.25	2.37%	2.89%
3.50	2.59%	3.15%
3.75	2.81%	3.42%
4.00	3.04%	3.69%
4.25	3.53%	4.29%
4.50	3.81%	4.62%
4.75	4.10%	4.97%
5.00	4.40%	5.32%

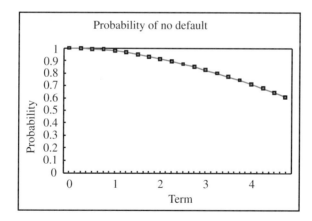

We calculate the forward margins g using $z = f + g$ and

$$y_n = \frac{\sum_{i=1}^{n} W_i z_i}{\sum_{i=1}^{n} W_i}$$

to obtain the expression

$$\frac{(y_n - z_n)}{(1 + z_n)} = \frac{\left(y_n \sum_{i=1}^{n-1} W_i - \sum_{i=1}^{n-1} W_i z_i \right)}{W_{n-1}}.$$

The result of this methodology is that we have calculated the full forward margin term structure, in addition to the term structure of default probabilities from the market data consisting of the underlying curve and the margins for different spot CSBs (of the same credit rating). This simple model allows us to value forward margin swaps and to find the forward price of CSBs of the same credit rating.

8.2.1 Forward Margin

The forward margin on a CSB starting at the start of period k and date maturity period n is just

$$m_{k,n} = \left(\frac{\sum_{i=k}^{n} W_i(g_i + f_i)}{\sum_{i=k}^{n} W_i} \right) - \left(\frac{\sum_{i=k}^{n} V_i f_i)}{\sum_{i=k}^{n} V_i} \right).$$

Note the forward par margin m is not just the weighted sum of the forward margins g. There is an additional term which captures the interest rate effect of the change in timing. We can give effect to this by entering the following transactions — Buy the n period floating rate CSB and sell the $(k - 1)$ period floating rate CSB and write a forward swap for the period k to n. These transactions mean that the holder has locked in the forward margins at their stated level. Theoretically if there are quotes different from these in the market, participants can lock in the difference, thereby forcing the validity of the above formula through arbitrage.

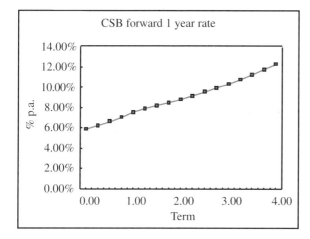

Forwards	
Term	1 year
0.00	5.90%
0.25	6.24%
0.50	6.63%
0.75	7.07%
1.00	7.56%
1.25	7.89%
1.50	8.22%
1.75	8.52%
2.00	8.81%
2.25	9.18%
2.50	9.55%
2.75	9.94%
3.00	10.33%
3.25	10.79%
3.50	11.27%
3.75	11.77%
4.00	12.29%

Example graph and table showing the 1-year CSB forward yield out to 4 years.

8.2.2 Mark-to-Market of Forward Swap

The mark-to-market value for a forward margin swap set at rate s for the same period is

$$Value = \sum_{i=k}^{n} W_i (s - g_i)$$

assuming that the receiver is released from their obligation to receive if there is a default prior to the start of period k.

8.2.3 Forward CSB Price

The value at the start of period k of a CSB with coupon c and maturity n is

$$Value - \sum_{i=k}^{n} W_i c + W_n \text{ where } W_i = \prod_{j=1}^{i} \left(\frac{1}{(1 + f_j + g_j)} \right)$$

assuming that the purchaser is released from their obligation to purchase if there is a default prior to the start of period i.

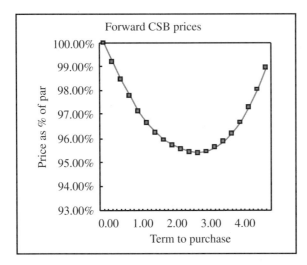

Delay	Price
0.00	100.00%
0.25	99.21%
0.50	98.47%
0.75	97.78%
1.00	97.14%
1.25	96.64%
1.50	96.25%
1.75	95.94%
2.00	95.73%
2.25	95.54%
2.50	95.43%
2.75	95.40%
3.00	95.46%
3.25	95.61%
3.50	95.86%
3.75	96.21%
4.00	96.67%
4.25	97.30%
4.50	98.05%
4.75	98.95%

8.2.4 Default Put Price

The premium payable today for a default put on a CSB can be calculated as follows. Consider the position of one who buys the CSB and borrows the full amount at the riskless rate (i.e. sells some treasuries). They receive the margin net and if default occurs pay the default loss. This must be equivalent to selling a default put, hence the default put premium must equal the present value of the margin up to default occurring or the option life, whichever is shorter.

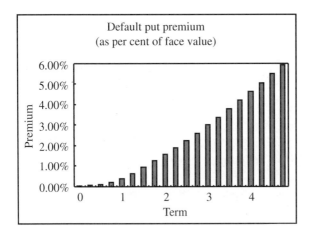

Term	Premium
0.25	0.01%
0.50	0.05%
0.75	0.11%
1.00	0.19%
1.25	0.38%
1.50	0.63%
1.75	0.92%
2.00	1.26%
2.25	1.56%
2.50	1.89%
2.75	2.24%
3.0	2.61%
3.25	2.99%
3.50	3.38%
4.00	4.19%
4.50	5.08%
5.00	5.94%

Default put premiums for our sample CSB are shown in the above table and graph.

8.2.5 Portfolio Techniques

To value forward margin swaps on CSB portfolios and first-to-default virtual CSB portfolios we proceed as follows. A portfolio of CSBs can first be approximated by setting the margin term structure to be equal to the weighted sum of the component margin term structures and the weighted sum of the recovery rates. From this we can then infer a margin term structure from the relations above. The portfolio margin term structure, apart from being used to value forward positions in the portfolio and swaps thereon, can provide an estimate of the effective credit rating of the portfolio at various tenors. As an example of an application we could answer the following questions. What level of leverage could be introduced into a CSB portfolio of AAA and AA bonds to produce a BB equivalent instrument, or what quantity and maturity profile of CC rated CSBs can I add to my AAA and AA portfolio to produce no worse than a BBB term structure? It may be the case that BBB bonds with the required characteristics are not readily available, but a mixed portfolio can be constructed from combinations of available bonds. Clearly this technique also lends itself to assisting with arbitrage identification and construction.

8.2.6 First-to-default Virtual Portfolio

The first-to-default virtual portfolio operates as follows. There are equal amounts A of b CSBs in the portfolio, the portfolio is purchased by A in equity and $(b - 1)A$ in non-recourse borrowings secured by the $(b - 1)$ bonds that are not the first to default (if kCSBs default at the same time the holder absorbs $1/k$th the loss on each). In the case where the default probabilities are independent the margin is simply the sum of the margins less the value of a put on the other $(b - 1)$ bonds in the event that one defaults.

This put option would normally require other techniques to value it. On the other hand we can find the probabilities by noting if there is no first to default then none have defaulted. Hence in the independent case

$$Q_n^{Portfolio} = \prod_{j=1}^{b} Q_n^j$$

given the Qs we can calculate easily and recall from above

$$g_n^{Portfolio} = \frac{p_1(1 - r) * (1 + f_1)}{(1 - p_1)}$$

so that we can then bootstrap the g and hence the m. That is, we use the implied probability of default of the portfolio which is derived from the implied probability of default of the underlying CSBs, which as we have seen above can be calculated from their margin term structure. Thus, for this style of portfolio we can value all the derivatives that we can in the single bond case, in particular forward credit spread swaps and first-to-default puts. (Our example consists of four independent bonds which have the same parameters as our example above.)

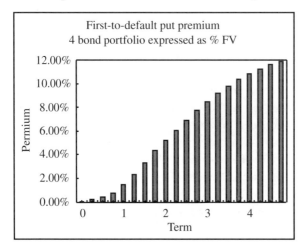

Term	Premium
0.25	0.05%
0.50	0.19%
0.75	0.43%
1.00	0.75%
1.25	1.46%
1.50	2.33%
1.75	3.29%
2.00	4.33%
2.25	5.20%
2.50	6.08%
2.75	6.93%
3.00	7.73%
3.25	8.49%
3.50	9.18%
3.75	9.80%
4.00	10.34%
4.25	10.84%
4.50	11.26%
4.75	11.60%
5.00	11.88%

The graph and table above shows the value of a first-to-default put, that is a put on a virtual portfolio that has an imbedded put on second to default, effectively knocked in when the first default occurs.

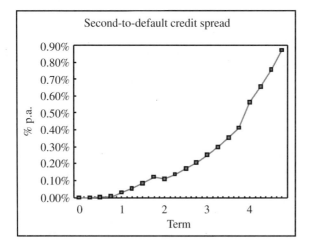

Term	Margin
0.25	0.00%
0.50	0.00%
0.75	0.00%
1.00	0.01%
1.25	0.03%
1.50	0.05%
1.75	0.08%
2.00	0.12%
2.25	0.11%
2.50	0.14%
2.75	0.17%
3.00	0.21%
3.25	0.25%
3.50	0.30%
3.75	0.35%
4.00	0.41%
4.25	0.56%
4.50	0.65%
4.75	0.76%
5.00	0.87%

The above graph and table show the proportion of the portfolio spread margin that should be alloccated to the second and subsequent defaults. Given that defaults are independent, the probability of two bonds defaulting in the same period is relatively small.

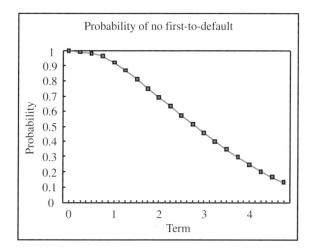

Term	Pr(No FtD)	Prob
0.25	0.9975	0.0025
0.50	0.9901	0.0074
0.75	0.9778	0.0124
1.00	0.9608	0.0174
1.25	0.9211	0.0413
1.50	0.8713	0.0540
1.75	0.8131	0.0668
2.00	0.7483	0.0798
2.25	0.6918	0.0755
2.50	0.6331	0.0848
2.75	0.5734	0.0943
3.00	0.5139	0.1039
3.25	0.4554	0.1137
3.50	0.3990	0.1238
3.75	0.3456	0.1340
4.00	0.2956	0.1445
4.25	0.2462	0.1672
4.50	0.2019	0.1799
4.75	0.1630	0.1929
5.00	0.1293	0.2063

The above table shows the derived probabilities for the first-to-default portfolios in addition to the cumulative probability that there has been no default up to the period in question.

8.3 Stochastics

We saw in Section 8.2 that a swap-style model can be used to value some derivatives and, furthermore, that the model implicitly implies some option values. In this section we develop a serviceable model for options on various credit derivatives. One immediate problem for software developers in coding options on CDs is that they are effectively mathematically intractable given the tremendous variety of instruments and no clear underlying process. You could just select to use a Black Scholes variant on certain options, but this will most certainly lead to some surprise revaluations down the track. This section assumes some familiarity with martingale techniques which we now briefly review.

8.3.1   Overview of Semi-martingales

We work over a collection of independent Brownian motions ω_i^i, $i = 1$ to N, that is all linear martingales are of the form

$$L_t = \int_0^t \sum_{i=1}^N h_i(s) \, d\omega_s^i \text{ for some } h_i \in L^2([0, T]).$$

Recall that linear martingales have the property at any fixed time they have normal distributions. In interest rate models the functions h determine the volatility term structure. Central to our model is the notion of a geometric martingale associated to a linear martingale, the martingale exponential. We use $\Xi()$ to denote the martingale exponential. X is the geometric martingale associated to L when

$$X_t = \Xi(L_t) = \exp\left(\frac{L_t - \langle L, L \rangle_t}{2}\right).$$

Now let f be a nice monotonic function and X a martingale and let

$$g(t) = -\log\left(\frac{E(f(X_t))}{f(x_0)}\right)$$

then

$$E(e^{g(t)} f(X_t)) = \frac{((X_0))}{(E(f(X_t))E(f(X_t)))} = f(X_0)$$

so $e^{g(t)} f(X_t)$ looks a lot like a martingale.

In practise we often use the following approximation, if then

where L is chosen to minimize the expectation of the quadratic variation of the difference.

It is assumed that all sources of randomness in the CSB market can be expressed as functions of these Brownian motions.

8.3.2   Setting the Distributions

Following from above we note that the margin term structure is implicitly tied to the probabilities of default and the recovery. It seems that a good place to start is to find a recovery distribution. It should have the following properties:

$$\Pr ob(r > (1 - \delta)) = Q$$

$$E(r|r < (1 - \delta)) = \text{recovery rate}$$

where δ is small enough. This means that the default probability distribution must be 0 outside [0,1] and have large mass at 0. Hence is it not a simple function of a Brownian motion. We consider allowing the forward margins g to be semi-martingales. In this case, using the above we see that the p would then inherit a semi-martingale structure with the required characteristics; that is the recovery rate is still fixed but the probability of default varies randomly over time in [0,1]. One can now propose a distribution for the recovery rate given that default has occurred; however, this adds nothing to the analysis, as prior to default only the expected recovery rate is relevant.

We require that in addition to producing 'reasonable' prices and hedge ratios the model must have the following properties:

- As the probability of default approaches 0, the option formula must approach a 'conventional' interest rate model.
- As the quadratic variation of the recovery semi-martingale and the volatility of interest rates approach zero, the prices must approach those calculated using the above elementary model.
- Option prices must agree with the option prices implied by the elementary model (see for example first-to-default CSB portfolios above).
- The model must have the generality to handle a wide variety of default probability term structures in addition a wide variety of instruments such as options on the CSBs directly, options on forward margin swaps (forward total return swaps) and options on portfolios consisting of CSBs and CDs.

The underlying interest rate model we use is a simplistic adaptation of the log-normal HJM model. That is we assume that

$$f_{i,t} = f_{i,0} \Xi \left(\int_0^i h_i(s) \, d\omega_s^i \right)$$

where we use $\Xi()$ to denote the martingale exponential

$$\Xi(L_t) = \exp\left(\frac{L_t - \langle L, L \rangle_t}{2} \right).$$

Note in this model caps and floors can be valued easily. Swaptions and bond options can be calculated for all practical purposes by assuming the relevant swap rate or bond yield is log-normal and then numerically integrating the valuation function over the relevant set. For options on long-dated swaps or bonds one needs to incorporate a drift term to correct for the convexity, a simple exp(xt) will suffice with x calculated to preserve at the money put-call parity. We assume initially that the g are also geometric martingales. That is,

$$g_{i,t} = g_{i,0} \Xi \left(\int_0^t k_i(s) \, d\varpi_s^i \right)$$

for some Brownian motion in our set. Note that and are probably correlated. Note that ϖ_s^i and ω_s^i the proposed g distribution is conditional upon there being no default at or before period i but closely related to the probability of default after period i. This overcomes one of the standard problems with CSBD models which tend to overvalue calls by including the implied probability of default as a yield volatility.

8.3.3   Pricing Options

Recall buying the forward rate for period i can be accomplished by buying the i period CSB and selling either the $i - 1$ period CSB or selling the underlying $i - 1$ period bond. In the first case the buyer has not effectively granted the default put in periods 1 to $i - 1$, and in the second case the buyer has effectively granted a default put for this period. The first case models the cap and floor options and the second case models swaptions and CSB puts and calls that have an implied default put over the term of the option. In the second case the premium can be factored into the forward term structure in which case the actual single period forward rate is the forward from the elementary model plus the future conditional value of the margin from now to the start of the forward, namely

$$g_i + \left(\frac{Q_{i-1}}{V_i} \right) \sum_{j=1}^{i-1} g_j W_j.$$

For the case of forward bond yields and swaps the future conditional margin value is subtracted from the price and the yield calculated for that new price is the forward yield.

   The simplest option to value on this model is one that it would be virtually impossible to hedge. A cap on CSB on period yield that the right to be paid so many dollars per point for each point that the period yield of the CSB is above the strike if there is no default to the end of period i plus, if the default occurs in that period, the payment of $(1 - r)$. The cap holder gets paid in the event that either there is a default in the period or if there is no default in the period or any prior period but the forward probability of default in the period increases. The caplet price can be given by

$$Cap = E(V_i Q_i (f_{i,t} + g_{i,t} - K)^+) + W_i Q_{i-1} p_i (1 - r).$$

The first term can be calculated as a simple bivariate integral, the second can be read from the elementary model as (assuming that interest rates are independent of default)

$$W_i Q_{i-1} p_i (1 - r) = \left(\sum_{i=1}^{n-1} Q_i W_i (m_n - m_{n-1}) + Q_{n-1} W_n m_n \right).$$

While a floor being exercised assumes no default and the floor holder gets paid if the forward probabilities of default fall, i.e. forward margins fall. The floor price is given by

$$Floor = E(W_i Q_i (K - f_{i,t} - g_{i,t})^+).$$

What about put-call parity? Namely, buy the call and sell the put should be zero cost at the forward. In this case, given f and g are martingales, the price of the bought cap sold floor is

$$W_i Q_i (f_{i,0} + g_{i,0} - K) + W_i Q_{i-1} p_i (1 - r).$$

That is, given there is no default prior to period i the value is $(f + g - K)$ and $(1 - r)$ if there is a default. The same as the forward, and hence we have one of the credit derivative put-call parity analogues. So one can value caps and floors on various credit ratings on the basis that a default effects only the period in which it occurs.

For swaptions and bond options we just substitute the semi-martingales $f_{i,t}$ and $g_{i,t}$ for f and g in the elementary pricing formula. We then make the approximation that the yield in question is log-normal (a general geometric semi-martingale when the full term structure of volatility is included) with an additional drift term to ensure that the tradeable forward instrument is a martingale. The difficult part, apart from the multi factor integration, is to ensure put-call parity. This is typically achieved by ensuring that the underlying forward instrument is a martingale. In our case we cannot make both CSBs and swaps martingales simultaneously as the same maturity bond can have a variety of coupons and hence slightly different convexities. In this case we set our martingale correction drift factors so that a CSB with coupon equal to the swap rate is a martingale. Consider a CSB with coupon c and maturity period n. A European put on the CSB with strike price K and expiring at t $(=i)$ can be exercised only if no default has occurred prior to expiration. If the price process is written as

$$P_t = P(s_{i,t}, m_{i,t}) = P(y_t)$$

where y the CSB yield is of the form $y_t = \exp(xt)\Xi(L_t)$ for L a linear martingale, this eliminates multi-factor integrations rather cheaply. Recall x is defined to make P look like a martingale.

The put option price can be written as

$$Put = Q_i E(W_i(K - P_t))^+$$

with the call formula the obvious analogue

$$Call = Q_i E(W_i(P_t - K))^+.$$

The put option that is American in default is also easy to value, being equal to the European plus the value of a default put over option life, namely

$$Q_i E(W_i(K - P_t)^+) + \sum_{j=1}^{i} Q_j W_j g_j.$$

The same correction term applies for the European swaption which is American in default. The value of the underlying swaption call is

$$Swaption\ Call = Q_i E(W_i((K - m_{i,n,t}) \sum_{j=i+1}^{n} Q_j W_j)^+)$$

and the put is defined analogously.

In regard to practical implementation we use the same approximation as in the underlying model. Namely forward swap rates and bond yields are the product of a drift term (martingale correction) and a geometric martingale of a linear Brownian motion. We approximate a weighted sum of geometric martingales by a geometric martingale which works well in practise. For example, on a single CSB we proceed as follows: since

$$P_t = \sum_{j=1}^{n} (1 + y_t)^{-j} c + (1 + y_t)^n$$

where

$$y_t = \exp(xt)\Xi(L_t) \text{ and } L_t = \int_0^t \sum_{i=1}^{N} h_i(s)\, d\omega_s^i$$

and x is set to make P look like a martingale: note when P is a sum of eigenvectors of the heat operator there is a continuous function f such that $\exp(f(t))$ is the correction, in practise a piecewise linear will suffice. Note the y has the form

$$y_t = \sum_{i=1}^{N} \alpha_i g_{i,t}$$

where the alphas sum to 1 and represent the present value weighting. Although the alphas do depend upon the g and the g are themselves assumed to be geometric martingales, the computational error introduced by setting y to a geometric semi-martingale (including drift) is small and has the advantage that the forward traded instruments are martingales and put-call parity follows immediately.

8.4 VaR

One can use the above models to calculate the VaR on a portfolio of CSBs and CDs. The VaR will not, of course, be symmetric. As in the case of a sold call position the most one can gain is the premium while any loss could be substantial. In the case of a CSB the maximum profit over standard returns is the PV of the margin, while the default loss could clearly be much larger.

However, recall that VaR is the technique of accessing the position in the event of a move in the underlying random factors of 5% probability at a given time t $(=i)$. If one can identify the price process as a function of the underlying normal distribution one can find the up and down VaR by simply substituting the values $+1.65$ and -1.65 for the normal variable in the valuation semi-martingale expression and adjust for events prior to the horizon. For other (non-normal) distributions (as in the option prices above) one calculates the 5.00 and 95.00% values and uses those values in the valuation function.

For example on a simple (underlying) bond we proceed as follows. In this case the valuation semi-martingale expression for the value of the bond at time t is given by

$$P_t = \left(\sum_{j=1}^{n} (1 + y_t)^{-j} c + (1 + y_t)^{-n} \right)$$

where $y_t = y_0 \exp(xt) \Xi(L_t)$, L linear and y_i is the forward bond yield at t.

We simply take the value of L at ± 1.65 standard deviations and substitute into the pricing formula. In this case then the up VaR to time t is given by

$$VaR_{t,\mathrm{up}} = \sum_{j=1}^{n} (1 + y_0 e^{xt} e^{\frac{\sigma \sqrt{t}1.65 - \sigma^2 t}{2}})^{-j} c + (1 + y_0 e^{xt} e^{\frac{\sigma \sqrt{t}1.65 - \sigma^2 t}{2}})^{-n} - P_t$$

where

$$\sigma_t = \sqrt{t^{-1} \int_0^t h^2(s) ds}$$

For the down VaR substitute -1.65 for 1.65 in the above expression.

For the case of a CSB the underlying random variables are:

I.   the Brownian motion driving the underlying bond yield ω_i;
II. the Brownian motion driving the credit margin v_i; and
III. the probability of default to the horizon date $1 - Q_n$.

To calculate the VaR at time t we need to derive the CSB price distribution at time t. We can proceed by using the fact that price is monotonic in both Brownian motions. From this it follows that given a CSB price the values of one Brownian motion are a function of the other, namely:

$$\omega_t = \left(\log\left(\frac{(c - m_k e^{\frac{\sigma_2 v_t - \sigma_2^2 t}{2}})}{s_k} \right) + \frac{\sigma_1^2 t}{2} \right)$$

where c is the yield for the set price. This fibres the $\omega_t - v_t$ plane into a line bundle — integrating the conditional distribution over the fibres leaves a probability distribution on the base space. The base space can then be parameterized by price, and the distribution is then the price distribution.

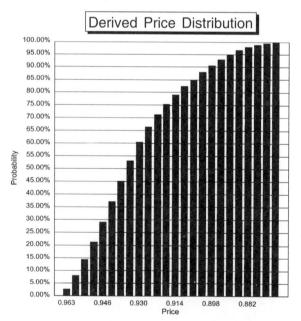

Price	Prob >
0.963	0.0272
0.958	0.0816
0.954	0.1440
0.950	0.2128
0.946	0.2912
0.942	0.3728
0.938	0.4512
0.934	0.5312
0.930	0.6048
0.926	0.6656
0.922	0.7136
0.918	0.7536
0.914	0.7904
0.910	0.8240
0.906	0.8512
0.902	0.8800
0.898	0.9072
0.894	0.9312
0.890	0.9520
0.886	0.9680
0.882	0.9808
0.877	0.9888
0.873	0.9952
0.869	1.0000

From the above table we can read off the 5.00 and 95.00% probability levels. Now the asymmetry of CSB risk demands that the up and down VaR have quite different forms. The up VaR can simply be read off from the table (assuming the risk of default is less than 95.00%).

The down VaR must include the excess probability of default before the horizon. However, this is just

$$(1 - Q) * \left(\frac{2}{0.5 - 1} \right)$$

Hence the VaR for a CSB are given by

$$VaR_{t,\text{up}} = P_{0.05} - P_t$$

$$VaR_{t,\text{down}} = P_t - P_{0.95} + 9 * (1 - Q_n) * (1 + s_n + m_n).$$

The same methodology can be applied to calculate VaR for any of the derivatives mentioned above. That is, express the future value of a financial instrument as a deterministic function of manageable random variables, typically normal distributions and discrete distributions, to derive the price distribution. Then one can simply read off the values and then adjust for events prior to the horizon. For a CSB portfolio or a virtual first-to-default portfolio the methods are similar. In either case find the yield components and their volatility from the data and proceed as above.

8.4.1 Comparison with CreditMetrics^{TM}

There are some very substantial differences in approach and outcome between the above model and the CreditMetrics^{TM} methodology. These differences centre around three aspects, described below.

8.4.2 The Role of Historical Data

The above model is based entirely upon the observation of market data and the spread term structure as traded on the day. The historical rate of default of rated securities is the basis of the risk assessment in CreditMetrics^{TM}. The particular approach taken depends very much on the nature of the exposure. If one is an active market participant whose notional turnover exceeds average holding one would most probably be best served with a market-based model. For example most swap and option traders value positions and exposures on the basis of market rates and volatilities not historical rate averages and historical volatilities. Historical data are, of course, important but the market can respond quickly to changing conditions and outlook, which would take a long time to surface with appropriate weight in historical data.

8.4.3   The Role of Credit Rating Bands

The above model makes no mention of credit rating. It is true that like-rated bonds tend to trade together in the absence of other factors. However, the above model allows spread to range continuously as opposed to forcing spreads into one of six or seven buckets determined by historical data. Individual businesses have different risk profiles with differing term structures. To restrict to a maximum of seven or eight with transition probabilities between the bands prescribed by historical data seems restrictive.

8.4.4   Completeness

CreditMetrics^{TM}, I would say, comprises the work of many academics and market participants over a considerable period and covers many aspects not addressed here. Multi-asset correlations, historical data estimation of volatility, the impact of levels of subordination, etc. CreditMetrics^{TM} is a valuable contribution to risk analysis and pricing. It is hoped that, as this level of sophistication spreads through the market, market-based models will automatically inherit the benefits. The above method of calculating VaR is by definition completely consistent with the market price of risk on a real-time basis.

8.5   Summary

We have seen the relationship between margin term structure and default probability in the elementary model and from there been able to value forward bonds and swaps, in addition to some options on some types of portfolio. The introduction of martingales in Section 8.3 enabled us to value various options and identify satisfactory approximations to the various price processes. In Section 8.4 the option model was used to calculate VaR as a special case.

One final comment on the nature of risk. The kind of risk taken when one makes a price on say a Eurodollar future option is essentially different from the default risk in a CSB or CD. The former can be hedged with futures, the latter cannot really be hedged. One may like to try some indices which have high correlations to default events. The risk one takes is more of an insurance style of risk which is borne, or 'kind of' hedged, through diversity. The model should treat these risks as essentially different in character. The default risk cannot be continuously hedged while the monatization of the perceived value of those risks, namely the margin term structure, can be hedged by positions in a large liquid CSB or CD market, if it exists.

9
Modeling Default Risk

Peter J Crosbie, KMV Corporation

9.1   Overview

Default risk is the uncertainty surrounding a firm's ability to service its debts and obligations. Prior to default, there is no way to discriminate unambiguously among firms that will default and those that will not. At best, we can only make probabilistic assessments of the likelihood of default. As a result, firms generally pay a spread over the default-free rate of interest that is proportional to their default probability to compensate lenders for this uncertainty.

Default is a deceptively rare event. The typical firm has a default probability of around 2% in any year. However, there is considerable variation in default probabilities across firms. For example, the odds of a firm with a AAA rating defaulting are only about 2 in 10,000 pa. A single A rated firm has odds of around 10 in 10,000 pa, five times higher than a AAA. At the bottom of the rating scale, a CCC rated firm's odds of defaulting are 4 in 100 (4%), 200 times the odds of a AAA rated firm.

The loss suffered by a lender or counterparty in the event of default is usually significant and is determined largely by the details of the particular contract or obligation. For example, typical loss rates in the event of default for senior secured bonds, subordinated bonds, and zero coupon bonds are 49%, 68%, and 81%, respectively.

Cross-default clauses in debt contracts usually ensure that the default probabilities for each of the classes of debt for a firm are the same. That is, the default probability of the firm determines the default probability for all of the firm's debt or counterparty obligations. However, the loss in the event of default for each of the classes of obligations can vary widely depending on their nature (security, collateral, and seniority).

Although in general a poor investment strategy, it is possible to be rewarded for taking on large concentrations of risk in equities because these concentrations at times produce large returns. However, overwhelming evidence of the ineffectiveness of this stock-picking strategy has been available since the early 1970s and, as a result, the majority of equity investments are managed in diversified portfolios. Unlike equities, debt has no upside potential and thus, the case for managing default risk in well-diversified portfolios is even more compelling. The limited upside potential of debt spreads means that there are no possible circumstances under which an investor or counterparty can be rewarded for taking on concentrations of default risk. Like other rare events with high costs, default risk can only be effectively managed in a portfolio.

In addition to knowing the default probability and loss given default, the portfolio management of default risk requires the measurement of default correlations. Correlations measure the degree to which the default risks of the various borrowers and counterparties in the portfolio are related. The elements of credit risk can therefore be grouped as follows:

- **Standalone Risk**
  1. Default probability, the probability that the counterparty or borrower will fail to service its obligations.
  2. Loss given default, the extent of the loss incurred in the event the borrower or counterparty defaults.
  3. Migration risk, the probability, and value impact of changes in default probability.

- **Portfolio Risk**
  1. Default correlations, the degree to which the default risks of the borrowers, and counterparties in the portfolio are related.
  2. Exposure, the size, or proportion, of the portfolio exposed to the default risk of each counterparty and borrower.

While each of these items is critical to the management of credit portfolios, none are more important or more difficult to determine, than the default probability. The remainder of this chapter will focus on the determination of default probability using information from a firm's financial statements and the market price of its equity.

9.2   Measuring Default Probability — The Problem

There are three main elements that determine the default probability of a firm:
- **Value of Assets:** The market value of the firm's assets. This is a measure of the present value of the future free cash flows produced by the firm's assets

discounted back at the appropriate discount rate. This measures the firm's prospects and incorporates relevant information about the firm's industry and the economy.

- **Asset Risk:** The uncertainty or risk of the asset value. This is a measure of the firm's business and industry risk. The value of the firm's assets is an estimate and is thus uncertain. As a result, the value of the firm's assets should always be understood in the context of the firm's business or asset risk.
- **Leverage:** The extent of the firm's contractual liabilities. Whereas the relevant measure of the firm's assets is always their market value, the book value of liabilities relative to the market value of assets is the pertinent measure of the firm's leverage, since that is the amount the firm must repay.

For example, Figure 9.1 illustrates the evolution of the asset value and book liabilities of Venture Stores, a Midwestern retailer which defaulted in January 1998.

Figure 9.1   Venture Stores Inc.

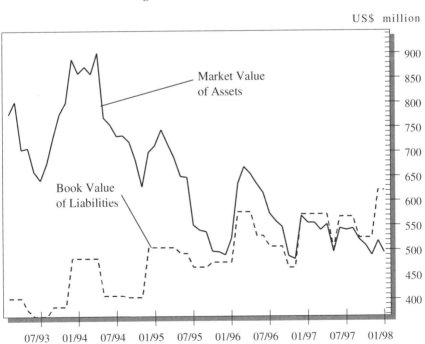

US$ million

The default risk of the firm increases as the value of the assets approaches the book value of the liabilities, until finally the firm defaults when the market value of the assets is insufficient to repay the liabilities.

In our study of defaults, we have found that, in general, firms do not default when their asset value reaches the book value of their total liabilities. While some firms certainly default at this point, many continue to trade and service their debts. The long-term nature of some of their liabilities provides these firms with some breathing space. We have found that the default point, the asset value at which the firm will default, generally lies somewhere between total liabilities and current, or short-term, liabilities.

The relevant net worth of the firm is therefore the market value of the firm's assets minus the firm's default point:

$$\text{Market Value of Assets} - \text{Default Point}$$

A firm will default when its market net worth reaches zero.

Like the firm's asset value, the market measure of net worth must be considered in the context of the firm's business risk. For example, firms in the food and beverage industries can afford higher levels of leverage (lower market net worth) than high-technology businesses because their businesses, and consequently their asset values, are more stable and less uncertain.

For example, Figure 9.2 shows the evolution of asset values and default points for Compaq Computer and Anheuser-Busch. Figure 9.3 shows the corresponding evolution of the annual default probabilities. The default probabilities shown in this figure are the one-year default rates, the probability that the firm will default in the ensuing year, and are displayed on a logarithmic scale.

The effect of the relative business risks of the two firms is clear from a comparison of the two figures. For instance, as of January 1998, the relative market values, default points, asset risks, and resulting default probabilities for Compaq Computer and Anheuser-Busch were:

	Anheuser-Busch	Compaq Computer
Market Value of Assets	28.7	52.1
Default Point	5.4	4.3
Market Net Worth (US$ billion)	23.3	47.8
Asset Volatility (%)	14	33
Default Probability (% pa)	0.02	0.16

Figure 9.2   Market Net Worth

US$ million

Compaq Computer: Market Value of Assets

Anheuser-Busch: Market Value of Assets

Compaq Computer:
Book Value
of Liabilities

55,000
50,000
45,000
40,000
35,000
30,000
25,000
20,000
15,000
10,000
5,000

07/93   01/94   07/94   01/95   07/95   01/96   07/96   01/97   07/97   01/98

Anheuser-Busch: Market Value of Assets ————
Compaq Computer: Market Value of Assets ▬▬▬
Anheuser-Busch: Book Value of Liabilities ·············
Compaq Computer: Book Value of Liabilities ▬ ▬ ▬

Figure 9.3   Default Probability

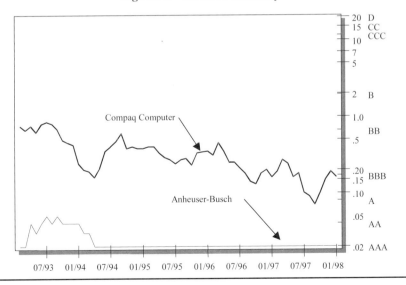

20 D
15 CC
10 CCC
7
5

2   B

1.0
     BB
.5

.20 BBB
.15
.10 A

.05 AA

.02 AAA

Compaq Computer

Anheuser-Busch

07/93   01/94   07/94   01/95   07/95   01/96   07/96   01/97   07/97   01/98

The asset risk is measured by the asset volatility, the standard deviation of the annual percentage change in the asset value. For example, Anheuser-Busch's business risk is 14%, which means that a one standard deviation move in their asset value will add (or remove) US$4 billion from its asset value of US$28.7 billion. In contrast, a one standard deviation move in the asset value of Compaq Computer will add or remove US$17.2 billion from its asset value of US$52.1 billion. The difference in their default probabilities is thus driven by the difference in the risks of their businesses, not their respective asset values or leverages.

As you would expect, asset volatility is related to the size and nature of the firm's business. For example, Figure 9.4 shows the asset volatility for several industries and asset sizes.

Asset volatility is related to, but different from, equity volatility. A firm's leverage has the effect of magnifying its underlying asset volatility. As a result, industries with low asset volatility (for example, banking) tend to take on larger amounts of leverage while industries with high asset volatility (for example, computer software) tend to take on less. As a consequence of these compensatory differences in leverage, equity volatility is far less differentiated by industry and asset size than is asset volatility.

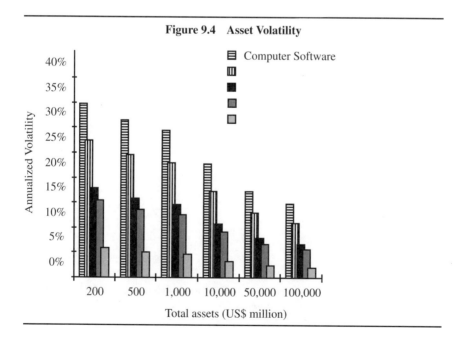

Figure 9.4   Asset Volatility

Asset value, business risk, and leverage can be combined into a single measure of default risk that compares the market net worth to the size of a one standard deviation move in the asset value. We refer to this ratio as the distance-to-default and it is calculated as:

$$[Distance-to-Default] = \frac{[Market\ Value\ of\ Assets] - [Default\ Point]}{[Market\ Value\ of\ Assets][Asset\ Volatility]}.$$

For example, in January 1998, Anheuser-Busch was approximately 5.8 standard deviations away from default while, in contrast, Compaq Computer was only 2.8 standard deviations away from default. That is, it would take a 5.8 standard deviation move in the asset value of Anheuser-Busch before it will default while only a 2.8 standard deviation move is required in Compaq's asset value to result in its default.

The distance-to-default measure combines three key credit issues: the value of the firm's assets, its business and industry risk, and its leverage. Moreover, the distance-to-default also incorporates, via the asset value and volatility, the effects of industry, geography, and firm size.

The default probability can be computed directly from the distance-to-default if the probability distribution of the assets is known, or, equivalently, if the default rate for a given level of distance-to-default is known.

9.3 Measuring Default Probability — A Practical Approach

There are three basic types of information available that are relevant to the default probability of a firm: financial statements, market prices of the firm's debt and equity, and subjective appraisals of the firm's prospects and risk. Financial statements, by their nature, are inherently backward looking. They are reports of the past. Prices, by their nature, are inherently forward looking. Investors form debt and equity prices as they anticipate the firm's future. In determining the market prices, investors use, among many other things, subjective appraisals of the firm's prospects and risk, financial statements, and other market prices. This information is combined using their own analysis and synthesis, and it results in their willingness to buy and sell the debt and equity securities of the firm. Market prices are the result of the combined willingness of many investors to buy and sell, and thus prices embody the synthesized views and forecasts of many investors.

The most effective default measurement, therefore, derives from models that utilize both market prices and financial statements. There is no assertion here that markets are perfectly efficient in this synthesis. We assert only that, in general, it is difficult to do a better job than they are doing. That is, in general, it is very difficult to consistently beat the market. Consequently, where available, we want to utilize market prices in the determination of default risk because prices add considerably to the predictive power of the estimates.

KMV Corporation has developed a model of default probability, Credit Monitor^{TM}, that uses equity prices and financial statements. Credit Monitor^{TM} (CM^{TM}) calculates the Expected Default Frequency^{TM} (EDF^{TM}), which is the probability of default during the forthcoming year, or years (CM^{TM} calculates EDFs^{TM} for Years 1 to 5). Default is defined as the non-payment of any scheduled payment, interest, or principal. The remainder of this section describes the procedure used by CM^{TM} to determine a public firm's probability of default.

There are essentially three steps in the determination of the default probability of a firm:

• Estimate asset value and volatility: In this step the asset value and asset volatility of the firm is estimated from the market value and volatility of equity and the book value of liabilities.

• Calculate the distance-to-default: The distance-to-default (DD) is calculated from the asset value and asset volatility (estimated in the first step) and the book value of liabilities.

• Calculate the default probability: The default probability is determined directly from the distance-to-default and the default rate for given levels of distance-to-default.

9.3.1   Estimating Asset Value and Volatility

If the market price of equity is available, the market value and volatility of assets can be determined directly using an options-pricing-based approach, which recognizes equity as a call option on the underlying assets of the firm. For example, consider a simplified case where there is only one class of debt and one class of equity. See Figure 9.5.

The limited liability feature of equity means that the equity holders have the right, but not the obligation, to pay off the debt holders and take over the remaining assets of the firm. That is, the holders of the other liabilities of the firm essentially own the firm until those liabilities are paid off in full by the equity holders. Thus, in the simplest case, equity is the same as a call option on the firm's assets with a strike price equal to the book value of the firm's liabilities.

Figure 9.5

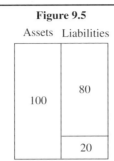

CM^{TM} uses this option nature of equity to derive the underlying asset value and asset volatility implied by the market value, volatility of equity, and the book value of liabilities. This process is similar in spirit to the procedure used by option traders in the determination of the implied volatility of an option from the observed option price.

For example, assume that the firm is actually a type of levered mutual fund or unit trust. The assets of the firm are equity securities and thus can be valued at any time by observing their market prices. Further, assume that our little firm is to be wound up after five years and that we can ignore the time value of money (discounting adds little to our understanding of the relationships and serves only to complicate the picture). That is, in five years' time, the assets will be sold and the proceeds divided between the debt and equity holders.

Initially, assume that we are interested in determining the market value of the equity from the market value of the assets. This is the reverse of the problem we face in practice, but provides a simpler perspective to initially understand the basic option relationships. See Figure 9.6.

To be specific, assume that we initially invest US$20 in the firm and borrow a further US$80 from a bank. The proceeds (US$100) are invested in equities. At the end of five years, what is the value of equity? For example, if the market value of the assets at the end of Year 5 is US$60, then the value of equity will be zero. If the value of the assets is US$110, then the value of the equity will be US$30, and so on. Thus, in Figure 9.6, the lines from US$0 to US$80 and from US$80 to point B represent the market value of the equity as a function of the asset value at the end of Year 5.

Now assume that we are interested in valuing our equity prior to the final winding up of the firm. For example, assume that three years have passed since the firm was started and that there are two years remaining before we wind the firm up. Further, we have marked the equities to market and their value is

Figure 9.6

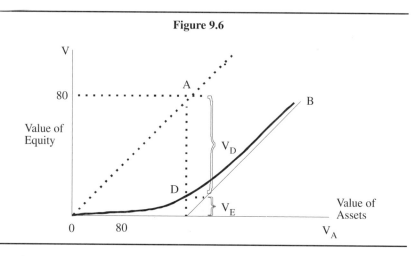

determined to be US$80. What is the value of the equity? Not zero. It is actually something greater than zero because it is the value of the assets two years hence that really matters and there is still a chance that the asset value will be greater than US$80 in two years' time. In Figure 9.6, the value of the equity with two years to go is represented by the curve joining 0 and point B.

The higher the volatility of the assets, the greater is the chance of high asset values after two years. For example, if we were dissatisfied with our fund's performance after three years because it has lost US$20 in value, dropping from US$100 to US$80, we may be tempted to invest in higher-potential, higher-risk, equities. If we do, what is the effect on the equity value? It increases. The more volatile assets have higher probabilities of high values, and consequently, higher payouts for the equity. Of course, there are accompanying higher probabilities of lower asset values, because volatility works both ways. But with limited liability, this does not affect the equity value. At the end of the five years, it makes no difference to the equity if the final asset value is US$79 or US$9; its payout is the same, 0.

Where did the increase in the equity's value come from? It did not come from an increase in the asset value. We simply sold our original portfolio for US$80 and purchased a new portfolio of higher-risk equities for US$80. There was no value created there. The value of course came from the bank holding our firm's debt. In Figure 9.6, the value of the firm can be divided between the debt and equity holders along the line joining the points US$80 and A, where the line 0 to A plots the asset value against itself. Thus, the only way the value of equity can increase while the asset value remains constant is to take the value from the market value of the debt. This should make sense. When we reinvested the firm's assets in higher-risk equities, we increased the default risk of the debt and consequently reduced its market value.

The value of debt and equity are thus intimately entwined. They are both really derivative securities on the underlying assets of the firm. We can exploit the option nature of equity to relate the market value of equity and the book value of debt to determine the implied market value of the underlying assets. That is, we solve the reverse of the problem described in our simple example. We observe the market value of the equity and solve backwards for the market value of assets, see Figure 9.7.

In practise, we need to take into account the more complex capital structures and situations that exist in real life. For example, we need to consider the various terms and nature of debt (for example, long- and short-term debt, and convertible instruments), the perpetuity nature of equity, the time value of money, and of course, we also have to solve for the volatility of the assets at the same time. Thus, in practice, we solve the following two relationships simultaneously:

$$\begin{bmatrix} \text{Equity} \\ \text{Value} \end{bmatrix} = OptionFunction\left(\begin{bmatrix} \textbf{Asset} \\ \textbf{Value} \end{bmatrix}, \begin{bmatrix} \textbf{Asset} \\ \textbf{Volatility} \end{bmatrix}, \begin{bmatrix} \text{Capital} \\ \text{Structure} \end{bmatrix}, \begin{bmatrix} \text{Interest} \\ \text{Rate} \end{bmatrix} \right)$$

$$\begin{bmatrix} \text{Equity} \\ \text{Volatility} \end{bmatrix} = OptionFunction\left(\begin{bmatrix} \textbf{Asset} \\ \textbf{Value} \end{bmatrix}, \begin{bmatrix} \textbf{Asset} \\ \textbf{Volatility} \end{bmatrix}, \begin{bmatrix} \text{Capital} \\ \text{Structure} \end{bmatrix}, \begin{bmatrix} \text{Interest} \\ \text{Rate} \end{bmatrix} \right)$$

Figure 9.7

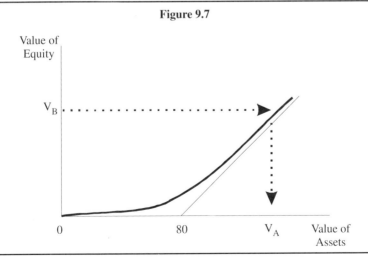

Asset value and volatility are the only unknown quantities in these relationships and thus, the two equations can be solved to determine the values implied by the current equity value, volatility, and capital structure.

9.3.2 Calculating the Distance-to-Default

There are six variables that determine the default probability of a firm over some horizon, from now until time H (see Figure 9.8):

1.   The current asset value.
2.   The distribution of the asset value at time H.
3.   The volatility of the future assets value at time H.
4.   The level of the default point, the book value of the liabilities.
5.   The expected rate of growth in the asset value over the horizon.
6.   The length of the horizon, H.

The first four variables, asset value, future asset distribution, asset volatility, and the level of the default point, are the critical variables. The expected growth in the asset value has little default discriminating power and the analyst defines the length of the horizon.

Figure 9.8

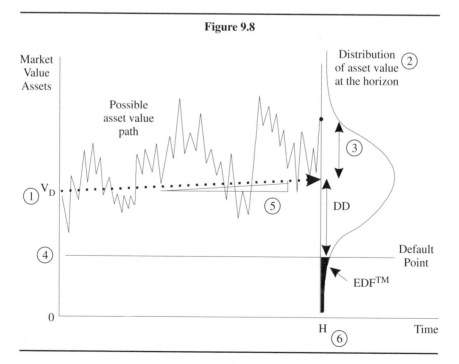

If the value of the assets falls below the default point, then the firm defaults. Therefore, the probability of default is the probability that the asset value will fall below the default point. This is the shaded area (EDF^{TM}) below the default point in Figure 9.8.

Figure 9.8 also illustrates the causative relationship and trade-off among the variables. This causative specification provides the analyst with a powerful and reliable framework in which they can ask what-if questions regarding the model's various inputs and examine the effects of any proposed capital restructuring. For example, the analyst can examine the effect of a large decrease in the stock price or the effects of an acquisition or merger.

If the future distribution of asset values was known, the default probability (EDF^{TM}) would simply be the likelihood that the final asset value was below the default point (the shaded area in Figure 9.8). However, in practice, the distribution of the asset values is difficult to measure. Moreover, the usual assumptions of normal or log normal distributions cannot be used. For default measurement, the likelihood of large adverse changes in value are critical to the accurate determination of the default probability. Consequently, CM^{TM} measures the distance-to-default as the number of standard deviations the asset value is away from default and uses empirical data to determine the corresponding default probability. As discussed in a previous section, the distance-to-default is calculated as:

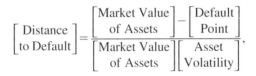

$$\left[\begin{array}{c} \text{Distance} \\ \text{to Default} \end{array}\right] = \frac{\left[\begin{array}{c} \text{Market Value} \\ \text{of Assets} \end{array}\right] - \left[\begin{array}{c} \text{Default} \\ \text{Point} \end{array}\right]}{\left[\begin{array}{c} \text{Market Value} \\ \text{of Assets} \end{array}\right]\left[\begin{array}{c} \text{Asset} \\ \text{Volatility} \end{array}\right]},$$

and is marked as DD in Figure 9.8.

9.3.3 Calculating the Default Probability

We obtain the relationship between distance-to-default and default probability from data on historical default and bankruptcy frequencies. Our database includes over 100,000 company-years of data and over 2,000 incidents of default or bankruptcy. From this data, we can generate a look-up or frequency table that relates the likelihood of default to various levels of distance-to-default.

For example, assume that we are interested in determining the default probability over the next year for a firm that is 7 standard deviations away from default. To determine this EDF^{TM}, we query the default history for the proportion of the firms, 7 standard deviations away from default that defaulted over the next year. The answer is about 5 bp, or 0.05%, or an equivalent rating of AA .

We have tested the relationship between distance-to-default and default frequency for industry, size, time, and other effects, and have found that the relationship is constant across all of these variables. This is not to say that there are no differences in default rates across industry, time, and size but only that it appears that these differences are captured by the distance-to-default measure. Our studies of international default rates are continuing but the preliminary results of studies by KMV Corporation and some of its clients indicate that the relationship is also invariant across countries and regions.

9.3.4   Putting It All Together

In summary, there are three steps required to calculate an EDF^{TM}:
(1)   estimate the current market value and volatility of the firm's assets
(2)   determine how far the firm is from default, its distance-to-default and
(3)   scale the distance-to-default to a probability. For example, consider Chrysler Motors, which at the end of January 1998 had a one-year EDF^{TM} of 21 bp, close to the median EDF^{TM} of firms with a BBB rating. Figure 9.9 illustrates the relevant values and calculations for the EDF^{TM}.

Figure 9.9   Relevant Values and Calculations for the EDF^{TM}

Variable	Value	Notes
Market value of equity	US$22,572 billion	(Share Price) × (Shares Outstanding)
Book Liabilities	US$49,056 billion	Balance sheet
Market value of assets	US$71,994 billion	Option-pricing model
Asset volatility	10%	Option-pricing model
Default point	US$36,993 billion	Liabilities payable within one year
Distance-to-default	4.8	Ratio: $\dfrac{72-37}{72 \times 10\%}$ (In this example we ignore the growth in the asset value between now and the end of the year)
EDF^{TM} (one year)	21 bp	Empirical mapping between distance-to-default and default frequency

9.4   A Closer Look at Calculating EDF^{TM}

Merton's general derivative pricing model was the genesis for understanding the link between the market value of the firm's assets and the market value of its equity. It is possible to use the Black-Scholes (BS) option-pricing model, as a special case of Merton's model, to illustrate some of the technical details of estimating EDF^{TM}. The BS model is too restrictive to use in practise but is widely understood and provides a useful framework to review the issues involved. This section works an example of the calculation of an EDF using the BS option-pricing model. The section also discusses some of the important issues that arise in practise and, where necessary, highlights the limitations of the BS model in this context.

Equity has the residual claim on the assets after all other obligations have been met. It also has limited liability. A call option on the underlying assets has the same properties. The holder of a call option on the assets has a claim on the assets after meeting the strike price of the option. In this case, the strike of the call option is equal to the book value of the firm's liabilities. If the value of the assets is insufficient to meet the liabilities of the firm, then the shareholders, holders of the call option, will not exercise their option and will leave the firm to its creditors.

We exploit the option nature of equity to derive the market value and volatility of the firm's underlying assets implied by the equity's market value. In particular, we solve backwards from the option price and option price volatility for the implied asset value and asset volatility.

To introduce the notation, recall that the BS model posits that the market value of the firm's underlying assets follows the following stochastic process:

$$dV_A = \mu VAdt + \sigma_A V_A\, dz \tag{1}$$

where

V_A, dV_A are the firm's asset value and change in asset value

μ, σ_A are the firm's asset value drift rate and volatility

dz is a Wiener process

The BS model allows only two types of liabilities, a single class of debt and a single class of equity. If this is the book value of the debt which is due at time then the market value of equity and the market value of assets are related by the following expression:

$$V_E = V_A N(d1) - e^{-rT} X N(d2) \tag{2}$$

where

V_E is the market value of the firm's equity

$$d1 = \frac{\ln\left(V_A/X\right) + \left(r + \frac{\sigma_A^2}{2}\right)T}{\sigma\sqrt{T}}$$

$d2 = d1 - \sigma_A\sqrt{T}$

r is the risk-free interest rate

It is straightforward to show that equity and asset volatility are related by the following expression:

$$\sigma_E = \frac{V_A}{V_E}\Delta\sigma_A \tag{3}$$

where

σ_E is the volatility of the firm's equity

Δ is the hedge ratio, $N(d1)$, from Equation (2).

Consider the example of a firm with a market capitalization of US$3 billion, an equity volatility of 40% pa, and total liabilities of US$10 billion. The asset value and volatility implied by the equity value, equity volatility, and liabilities are calculated by solving the call price and volatility equations, Equations (2) and (3), simultaneously. In this case,[1] the implied market value of the firm's assets is US$12.511 billion, and the implied asset volatility is 9.6%.

In practise, it is important to use a more general option-pricing relationship that allows for a more detailed specification of the liabilities and that models equity as perpetuity. CM currently incorporates five classes of liabilities, short-term, long-term, convertible, and preferred and common equity.

The model linking equity and asset volatility given by Equation (3) holds only instantaneously. In practise, the market leverage moves around far too much for Equation (3) to provide reasonable results. Worse yet, the model biases the probabilities in precisely the wrong direction. For example, if the market leverage is decreasing quickly, then Equation (3) tends to overestimate the asset volatility and thus the default probability will be overstated as the firm's credit risk improves. Conversely, if the market leverage is increasing rapidly, then

---

[1] All liabilities are assumed to be due in one year, $T = 1$, and the interest rate r is assumed to be 5%

Equation (3) will underestimate the asset volatility and thus the default probability will be understated as the firm's credit risk deteriorates. The net result is that default probabilities calculated in this manner provide little discriminatory power.

Instead of using the instantaneous relationship given by Equation (3), CM uses a more complex iterative procedure to solve for the asset volatility. The procedure uses an initial guess of the volatility to determine the asset value and to de-lever the equity returns. The volatility of the resulting asset returns is used as the input to the next iteration of the procedure that in turn determines a new set of asset values and hence a new series of asset returns. The procedure continues in this manner until it converges. This usually takes no more than a handful of iterations if a reasonable starting point is used. In addition, the asset volatility derived above is combined in a Bayesian manner with country, industry, and size averages to produce a more predictive estimate of the firm's asset volatility.

The probability of default is the probability that the market value of the firm's assets will be less than the book value of the firm's liabilities by the time the debt matures. That is:

$$p_t = \Pr\left[V_A^t \le X_t \mid V_A^0 = V_A\right] = \Pr\left[\ln V_A^t \le \ln X_t \mid V_A^0 = V_A\right] \tag{4}$$

where
p_t is the probability of default by time t

V_A^t is the market value of the firm's assets at time t

X_t is the book value of the firm's liabilities due at time t

The change in the value of the firm's assets is described by Equation (1) and thus the value at time t, V_A^t, given that the value at time 0 is V_A, is:

$$\ln V_A^t = \ln V_A + \left(\mu - \frac{\sigma_A^2}{2}\right)t + \sigma_A \sqrt{t}\,\varepsilon \tag{5}$$

where
    μ is the expected return on the firm's asset
    ε is the random component of the firm's return

The relationship given by Equation (5) describes the evolution in the asset value path that is shown in Figure 9.8. Combining Equations (4) and (5), we can write the probability of default as:

$$p_t = \Pr\left[\ln V_A + \left(\mu - \frac{\sigma_A^2}{2}\right)t + \sigma_A \sqrt{t}\, \varepsilon \le X_t\right] \tag{6}$$

and after rearranging:

$$p_t = \Pr\left[-\frac{\ln \dfrac{V_A}{X_t} + \left(\mu - \dfrac{\sigma_A^2}{2}\right)t}{\sigma_A \sqrt{t}} \le \varepsilon\right] \tag{7}$$

The BS model assumes that the random component of the firm's asset returns is Normally distributed, $\varepsilon \sim N(0, 1)$ and as a result we can define the default probability in terms of the cumulative Normal distribution:

$$p_t = N\left[-\frac{\ln \dfrac{V_A}{X_t} + \left(\mu - \dfrac{\sigma_A^2}{2}\right)t}{\sigma_A \sqrt{t}}\right] \tag{8}$$

Recall that the distance-to-default is simply the number of standard deviations that the firm is away from default and thus in the BS world is given by:

$$DD = \frac{\ln \dfrac{V_A}{X_t} + \left(\mu - \dfrac{\sigma_A^2}{2}\right)t}{\sigma_A \sqrt{t}} \tag{9}$$

Continuing with our example, assume that the expected return on the assets, μ, is equal to 7% and that we are interested in calculating the one-year default probability. The distance-to-default, DD, in this case,[2] is 2.8, and the corresponding default probability from Equation (8) is 25 bp.

In practise, we need to adjust the distance-to-default to include not only the increases in the asset value given by the rate $\left(\mu - \dfrac{\sigma_A^2}{2}\right)$ but also any cash

---

[2]   The distance-to-default is calculated by Equation (9):

$$DD = \frac{\ln \dfrac{12.5116}{10} + \left(0.05 - \dfrac{0.0092}{2}\right)}{0.0961}$$

outflows to service debt, dividends and so on. In addition, the Normal distribution is a very poor choice to define the probability of default. There are several reasons for this but the most important is the fact that the default point is in reality also a random variable. That is, we have assumed that the default point is described by the firm's liabilities and amortization schedule. Of course we know that this is not true. In particular, firms will often adjust their liabilities as they near default. It is common to observe the liabilities of commercial and industrial firms increase as they near default while the liabilities of financial institutions often decrease as they approach default. The difference is usually just a reflection of the liquidity in the firm's assets and thus their ability to adjust their leverage as they encounter difficulties.

Unfortunately ex ante we are unable to specify the behavior of the liabilities and thus the uncertainty in the adjustments in the liabilities must be captured elsewhere. We include this uncertainty in the mapping of distance-to-default to EDF^{TM}. The resulting empirical distribution of default rates has much wider tails than the Normal distribution. For example, a distance-to-default of 4, 4 standard deviations, maps to a default rate of around 45 bp. The equivalent probability from the Normal distribution is essentially zero.

9.5 Calculating Long-Term EDF^{TM}

The extension of the model to longer terms is straightforward. The default point, asset volatility, and expected asset value are calculated as before except they take into account the longer horizon (see Figure 9.10). For example, suppose we are interested in calculating the EDF^{TM} for a three-year horizon. Over the three years, we can expect that the default point will increase as a result of the amortization of long-term debt. This is a conservative assumption that all long-term debt is refinanced short-term. We could just as easily model the asset value decreasing as the debt is paid down but in practise, debt is usually refinanced. In any case, it really doesn't matter whether the assets go down by the amount of the amortization or the default point increases by the same amount. The net effect on the default point is the same.

In addition to the default point changing, as we extend the horizon, the future expected asset value is increasing as is our uncertainty regarding its actual future value. The expected asset value increases at the expected growth rate and the total asset volatility increases proportionally with the square root of time.[3]

---

[3] The asset variance is additive and therefore increases linearly with time. The asset volatility is the square root of the variance and therefore increases with the square root of time

Figure 9.10

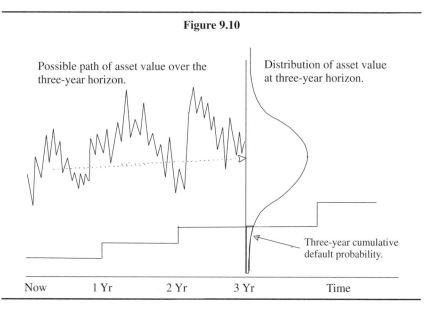

The distance-to-default is therefore calculated using the relevant three-year asset value, asset volatility, and default point. The scaling of the default probability again uses the empirical default distribution mapping three-year distance-to-defaults with the cumulative default probability to three years. That is, the mapping answers the question, what proportion of firms with this three-year distance-to-default actually default within three years. The answer to this question is the three-year cumulative default probability. EDF^{TM} is annual default probabilities and the three-year EDF^{TM} is calculated as the equivalent average annual default probability.[4] For example, suppose the three-year cumulative probability is 250 bp, then the three-year EDF is 84 bp.

9.6 Some Frequently Asked Questions About EDF^{TM}

How does the model deal with off-balance-sheet liabilities?

This is a critical question for many firms, particularly financial institutions where these liabilities can obviously be quite significant. Fortunately, the model

---

[4]   The EDF^{TM} is calculated from the cumulative default probability using survival rates. For example, the three-year cumulative probability of default and the three-year EDF^{TM} are related by the following expression: $1 2 CEDF_3 5 (1 2 EDF^{TM}_3)^3$. The probability of not defaulting within three years, $1 2 CEDF_3$, and the average annual probability of not defaulting, $1 2 EDF^{TM}_3$

is surprisingly robust to the precise level of the liabilities.

For example, consider the firm used previously in our BS example. Assume that in addition to the US$10 billion in liabilities, the firm has a further US$5 billion in off-balance-sheet commitments. That is, the true default point is actually $15 billion, not US$10 billion. The actual EDF^{TM} of the firm can therefore be calculated using the BS model as follows. The firm's market capitalization remains US$3 billion, and its equity volatility is still 40% pa. The implied asset value and volatility, with liabilities of US$15 billion, are calculated again by solving the call price and volatility equations, Equations (2) and (3), simultaneously. In this case,[5] the implied market value of the firm's assets is US$17.267 billion, and the implied asset volatility is 6.9%. The asset value is about US$5 billion higher and the asset volatility is lower reflecting the higher leverage of the firm. (Recall the equity volatility was kept the same but we increased the leverage, as a result the implied asset volatility must be lower.)

The corresponding distance-to-default is 2.7 and the implied EDF^{TM} is 34 bp. Compare this with the 2.8 distance-to-default and 25 bp EDF^{TM} calculated using only the on-balance-sheet liabilities of US$10 billion. This is a difference in about one minor rating grade, BBB− to BB+, for an increase in liabilities of 50%.

Obviously if you have more complete or up-to-date information on the firm's liability structure it should be used in the model. Credit Monitor^{TM} includes an add-on product called EDF Calculator^{TM} (EDFCalc^{TM}), which enables the user to enter a more complete, or more recent, statement of the firm's liabilities.

Does the model incorporate the possibility of large changes in the market value of the firm?

Yes. In addition to incorporating the uncertainty in the liability structure of the firm, the empirical distance-to-default to EDF^{TM} captures the possibility of large changes, up or down, in the firm's market value. The empirical distribution includes data from several serious market downturns including the crash of October 1987.

Can the model be used to simulate market downturns or crashes?

The EDF^{TM} already includes the effects of market downturns and crashes weighted by their appropriate probabilities. However, it is quite straightforward

---

[5] All liabilities are assumed to be due in one year, $T = 1$, and the interest rate r is assumed to be 5%

to ask questions such as, in the event of a 30% drop in the market, what will be the effect on a firm's, or a portfolio of firms', EDF^{TM}? The effect of a market downturn on the equity value of any particular firm can be estimated using the firm's equity beta.

$$\Delta V_E = \beta_E \Delta V_m \qquad (10)$$

Should EDF^{TM} be averaged or smoothed to remove its variation over time?

No. It is certainly true that the EDF^{TM} of a firm can vary over time, but these variations are reflecting changes in credit quality as perceived by the equity market. Therefore, any smoothing or averaging is simply masking the signals from the market.

The volatility in EDF^{TM} over time can pose problems for some bank's credit processes, where the EDF^{TM} directly determines the grade. However, this issue is usually simply overcome by determining actions by range of EDF^{TM}. That is, action triggers are attached to grades that are defined in terms of EDF^{TM} ranges. As a result, small, economically insignificant, movements within a grade do not trigger any action, and movements between grades trigger an appropriate review. A related question is whether or not there is any trend information in EDF^{TM}. There is not. EDF^{TM} is driven by market price and thus is directly analogous to price. If there isn't any trend information in the equity price, there isn't any in the EDF^{TM}.

What is the confidence interval around an EDF^{TM}?

Confidence intervals are commonly used in statistics to account for sampling error. That is, because a survey or other measure covers the entire population the statistic of interest, the average, for example, can only be known within certain limits and the limits are generally referred to as the confidence interval. There is not an analogous concept for an EDF^{TM}. With the exception of parts of the volatility estimation, EDF^{TM} is calculated from the option-pricing based causal model linking debt and equity. There really is no sampling measure.

In addition, the concept of a confidence interval around a probability really leads you to some quite philosophical issues.[6] Probabilities already encode a measure of uncertainty. Low EDF^{TM} means that we are quite confident that the firm will not default. Conversely, high EDF^{TM} implies that we are less confident that the firm will not default. For example, what is the expected default frequency when there is a 50% chance the default probability is 30 bp and a

50% chance the default probability is 20 bp? The answer is of course 25 bp, the average of the confidence interval.

In practise, it is better to understand the sensitivity of the EDF^{TM} to changes in the underlying variables, leverage, volatility, and asset value. The EDFCalc^{TM} is the most common tool used by analysts to conduct this type of analysis.

Why isn't information from the bond or credit derivatives market included?

There is a whole class of models, usually called reduced-form models, that relate credit spreads and default probabilities. Our experience implementing these approaches has not been successful to date. There is nothing wrong with the models per se, indeed in theory, they hold the promise of some advantages over the causal model described in this chapter. However, the data required to calibrate and implement reduced-form models is not yet widely available. In most cases, credit risk simply is not as actively and cleanly traded as equities at the moment. This situation will undoubtedly change as the credit derivative and other markets grow, but to date, we have not found credit spread information to be of sufficient quality to support the estimation of individual level default probabilities.

To date, the most successful use of credit spread data that we are aware of has been in the cross-sectional[7] estimation of credit spread curves. These curves describe the typical market spread for a given level of credit quality.

Are the default probabilities applicable across countries and industries?

The distance-to-default measure incorporates many of the idiosyncrasies of different countries and industries. For example, the business risk, as measured by the asset volatility, varies for a given industry across countries. Volatilities tend to be the lowest in Europe and the highest in the US, with Asian countries usually in-between. With exception of the difficulty posed by differing accounting standards, the default point can be measured appropriately for each firm regardless of its country of incorporation. The different economic prospects for countries are obviously captured by the individual equity and asset

---

[6]   There are some Bayesian decision models that can incorporate uncertainty in probabilities, but these models are complicated and are not in common use

[7]   Cross-sectional in this context means combining data from many different firms and issues. This is in contrast to the problem tackled in this chapter — the estimation of the default probability for each individual firm

valuations. As a result, we believe that the distance-to-default captures most of the relevant intercountry differences in default risk. However, the question remains whether differences in bankruptcy codes, culture and so on may result in different default rates for a given distance-to-default. That is, is the distance-to-default to EDF^{TM} mapping constant across countries?

The empirical default distribution that is used to map distance-to-default and EDF^{TM} is built from publicly listed defaults in the US. As a result, its translation to other countries should be questioned. However, we believe that the default probabilities resulting from this US-based mapping are good measures of economic default risk. That is, it is possible as a result of political or other intervention that a firm will be saved from default in say, Europe, when in the US it might have been left to fail. However, these interventions are not free and are costly to someone, often the taxpayer, or in the case of Asia, more commonly the shareholders of related firms. It seems unwise to us to measure default risk incorporating a reliance on the uneconomic behavior of another group. The uneconomic behavior may well continue, but it certainly seems unwise to institutionalize it in a measure of default risk. We do not believe it is possible to reliably model uneconomic behavior and thus we aim to provide a hard economic measure of default and allow the analyst to factor in their own measure of implied government or other support.

Philosophy aside, our experience with EDF^{TM} internationally has been very good. Over half the users of EDF^{TM} operate outside the US. During the recent credit problems in Asia, the model performed extremely well (see Figure 9.11) The model has also been tested anecdotally in most European countries. We continue to collect default data internationally and expect to be able to release a comprehensive study of Credit Monitor^{TM}'s performance as this data accumulates.

Does the EDF^{TM} contain any measure of country (translation) risk?

We believe there is some measure of country risk impounded in EDF^{TM} but exactly how much we don't know. The calculations for EDF^{TM} are done in the local currency and therefore the country risk measure comes from the discount in the local equity price as a result of international investors' concerns regarding the convertibility of the currency. Obviously, it is impossible to separate this influence from all the others, and as a result, we do not know how much country risk, if any, is present in the EDF^{TM}. The amount is likely to vary by country as a function of the accessibility of their equity market and on the interest of international investors.

Figure 9.11

Daito Kogyo, a Japanese construction company, defaulted in July 1997. Bangkok Metropolitan Bank (Thailand) was taken over in Jnuary 1998.

Daito Kogyo Co Ltd

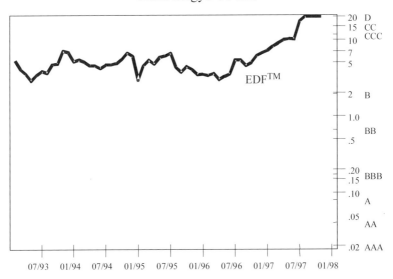

Bangkok Metropolitan Bank

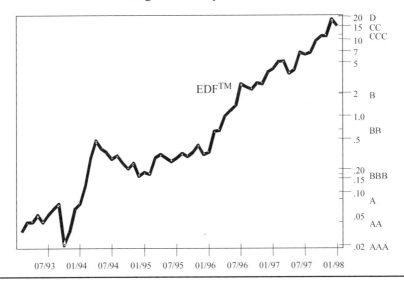

How well does the EDF^{TM} work on thinly traded or closely held firms?

Surprisingly well. This question often arises in connection with efficient markets and the culture of Anglo-Saxon markets. While the results of the international default studies will have to speak for themselves, we already know quite a lot about the performance of the model in thinly traded markets.

Our experience with these firms is drawn from the bottom end of the US equity market, where the companies are smaller and less actively traded than most of the firms on international exchanges. Our coverage of the US is almost total and the bottom 2,000 or so companies have market caps of less than US$20 million, (almost 1,000 companies have market capitalization of less than US$7 million). Most of these companies are not even listed on an exchange and are instead traded over-the-counter. Obviously, trading in these companies is going to be thin and many are likely to be very closely held.

This is also a group of firms that default a lot and thus we have a large body of evidence on the model's performance on these firms. It is very good. It appears that it doesn't seem to take many economically motivated investors to move the equity price to reflect the risk of the firm.

Does the model assume that the equity market is efficient?

No. The efficiency of a market usually refers to the degree to which the current price reflects all the relevant information about a firm's value. While we do not necessarily assume that the price reflects all the relevant information about a firm, we do know that it is difficult to consistently beat the market. For example, over 90% of managed funds were unable to outperform the market in 1998. That is, it is difficult to pick stocks consistently and difficult to know when the market is under- or overvaluing a firm. The market reflects a summary of many investors forecasts and it is unusual if any individual's or committee's forecast is better. Consequently, we believe that the best source of information regarding the value of a firm is the market.

The market though can be caught by surprise as in Figure 9.12. Burns, Philip and Co an Australian food company (spices and the like), caught the market and rating agencies by surprise although some credit analysts undoubtedly worried that it was overvalued.

Fraud is often the cause of extremely large and sudden changes in credit quality. For example, in Figure 9.13 it is not hard to spot when the announcement regarding the improprieties in the reporting of Mercury Finance's assets was made.

However, most of the time the market will be well aware of problems, or opportunities, and this information will be fairly reflected in the EDF™, (see Figure 9.14).

Figure 9.12

Burns, Philip and Co

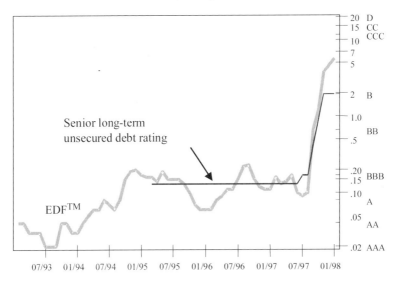

Burns, Philip and Co

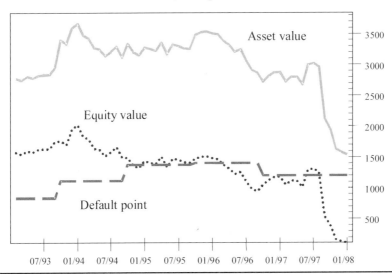

Figure 9.13

Mercury Finance Co

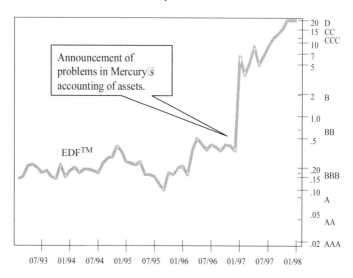

Mercury Finance Co

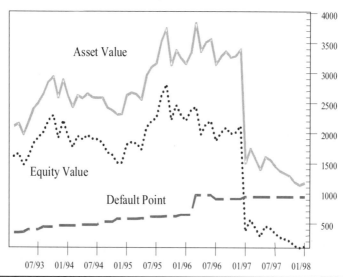

Figure 9.14

Toshoku, a Japanese food trading company, failed in December 1997. The equity value of Safeway, a US food retailer, has increased by US$12.5 billion over the past four years while its liabilities have increased by only US$1.5 billion.

Toshoku Ltd

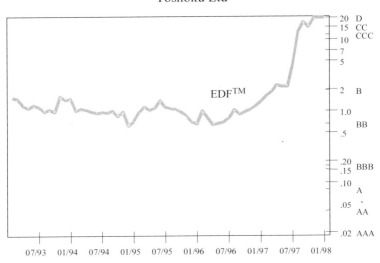

Safeway Inc

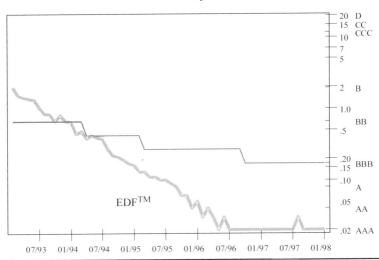

How well does the model work on financial institutions?

The credit risk of financial institutions is notoriously difficult to assess. Financial institutions are typically very opaque and thus judging the quality of their assets and determining the extent of their liabilities is almost always very difficult. In addition, the liquidity of their assets means that their true size is sometimes difficult to judge. The window dressing of balance sheets at reporting dates is common place.

The equity market is well aware of these issues and no doubt does better than most at sorting them out. In addition, we are fortunate that EDF^{TM} is relatively robust to the understatement of a firm's liabilities (see our earlier discussion on this issue). However, it is undoubtedly true that many financial institutions stretch this property of the model to its limits. In addition to these challenges, most financial institutions are tightly regulated and thus the appropriate definition of default may not be the point when their asset value falls below their liabilities. Unfortunately, there are very few financial institution defaults and thus testing and calibrating the model on just financial institutions is difficult. Overall, despite these challenges, we believe that the model performs very well on financial institutions, certainly better than any alternative approach that we know of. The lack of actual defaults means it is difficult for us to determine if the level of the EDF^{TM} is as precise as it is for commercial and industrial firms, but the anecdotal evidence is clear — the model provides timely and reliable early warning of financial difficulty (see Figures 9.15 and 9.16).

How does this apply to firms that do not have publicly traded equity?

One of the themes of this chapter has been that the equity value of the firm conveys a considerable amount of information regarding the firm's credit quality. When this information is not available, we are forced to fall back on peer comparisons to determine the asset value and asset volatility. We do this analysis in a companion product to Credit Monitor^{TM} called Private Firm Model^{TM} (PFM^{TM}).[8]

PFM^{TM} uses the same framework as CM^{TM} except that the asset value and asset volatility are estimated using financial statement data, and industry and country comparables. The estimation of the asset volatility is relatively straightforward. As we have seen, size, industry, and country can explain asset volatility quite well. Estimating the asset value is much more challenging. PFM^{TM}

---

[8] PFM^{TM} is discussed more fully in other publications, available from KMV Corporation

Figure 9.15

Yamaichi Securities defaulted in November 1997 and Siam City Bank (Thailand) was taken over by regulators in February 1998.

Yamaichi Securities

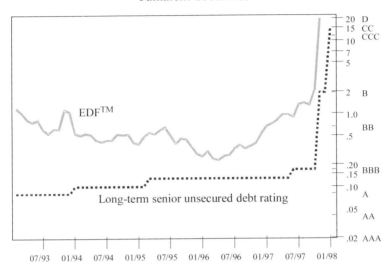

Siam City Bank

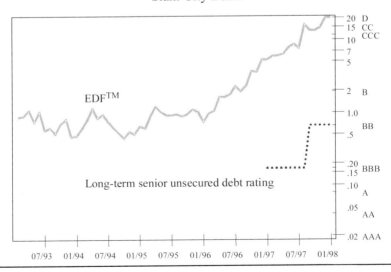

Figure 9.16

First Central Financial Corp, a US property and casualty insurance company, filed for Chapter 11 protection on March 5, 1998. First Bangkok City Bank, Thailand, was taken over in February 1998.

First Central Financial Corp

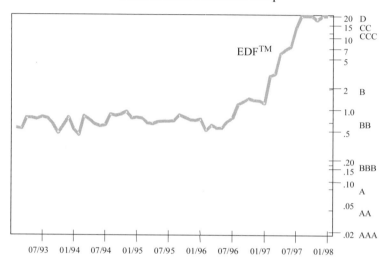

First Bangkok City Bank

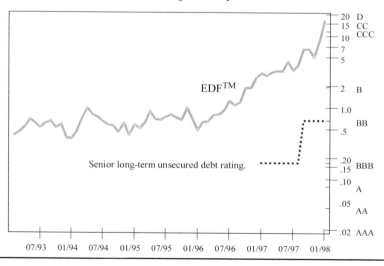

uses a broad set of comparables and essentially determines an appropriate EBIDTA[9] multiple. That is, given the set of comparables, what is a reasonable multiple to apply to the private firm's EBITDA to determine its asset value.

In spite of the obvious challenges that the absence of market data poses, overall, the PFM^{TM} does rather well. For example, in Figure 9.17 we plot the EDF^{TM} from CM^{TM} and PFM^{TM} along with senior unsecured debt rating for two public firms. Marvel Entertainment, a US publishing company that defaulted in December 1996, and Ben Franklin Retail Stores, a US retail company that defaulted in July 1997. As you would expect, at any point in time, the correspondence between the public and private EDF^{TM} is far from perfect. However, longitudinally, the correspondence can be quite remarkable, as it is in both of these cases.

PFM^{TM}'s performance on truly private companies has been tested extensively in the US and efforts are underway to extend this testing to Europe and Asia. There are some sectors in which the PFM^{TM} does not do well at all. Most notably, it cannot be used on financial institutions. The operating cash flow for these firms is a very poor indicator of asset value.

The public market comparables tie the PFM^{TM}'s EDF^{TM} into the credit cycle. That is, because the EBITDA multiples adjust to reflect the current market conditions and outlook, the EDF^{TM} from the PFM^{TM} change over time even if the financial statements of the firm remain stable. This is obviously a key property of the model and within the limitations of financial statement data keeps the EDF^{TM} as forward looking as possible.

9.7   Testing the Default Measure's Performance

Determining the performance of a default measure is both a theoretical and an empirical problem. For example, what exactly do we mean by performance or predictive power? In practice, we can only hope to estimate probabilities of default. That is, we will not be able to definitively classify firms into will default and will not default categories. As a result, in assessing the performance of a model, we face the task of assessing its ability to discriminate between different levels of default risk.

For example, consider the policy of never lending to firms below 2% EDF^{TM}, around a B rating. The benefit of this policy is that we avoid lending to firms that have a relatively high probability of default and thus avoid lending to a lot

---

[9]   We use EBITDA — earnings before interest, taxes, depreciation, and amortization — as a proxy for the firm's free cash flow

Figure 9.17

Marvel Entertainment Group

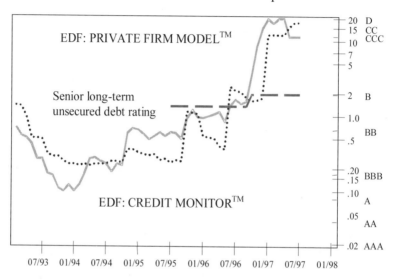

Ben Franklin Retail Stores

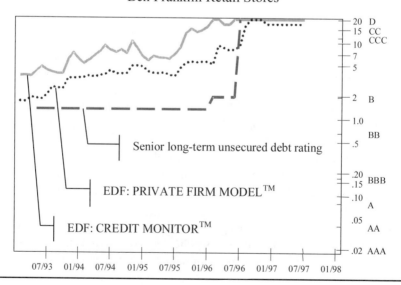

of firms that do eventually default. The cost of this policy is that we do not lend to any firms below a B rating, and many of these firms, about 98%, do not default. Thus, one measure of a model's performance is the trade-off between the defaulting firms we avoid lending to and the proportion of firms we exclude. This trade-off is commonly called the power curve of a model.

For example, in Figure 9.18 we plot the power curves for EDF^{TM} and the senior unsecured debt rating from a major bond rating agency. The cut-off points for the population are plotted along the horizontal axis and the proportion of defaults excluded at each cut-off point is plotted on the vertical axis. If we rank all firms by their EDF^{TM} and impose a cut-off at the bottom 10%, then we avoid lending to 50% of the defaulting firms. That is, by not lending to the bottom 10% as ranked by EDF^{TM}, we can avoid 50% of all defaulting firms. At a cut-off of 30%, we are able to avoid lending to 85% of defaulting firms and, of course, if we do not lend to anybody a cut-off of 100%, we avoid lending to all of the defaulting firms. Hence, for a given cut-off, the larger the proportion of defaults that are excluded, the more powerful is the model's ability to discriminate high default risk firms from low default risk firms.

Figure 9.18   Default Predictive Power EDF^{TM} and Bond Ratings Rated Universe

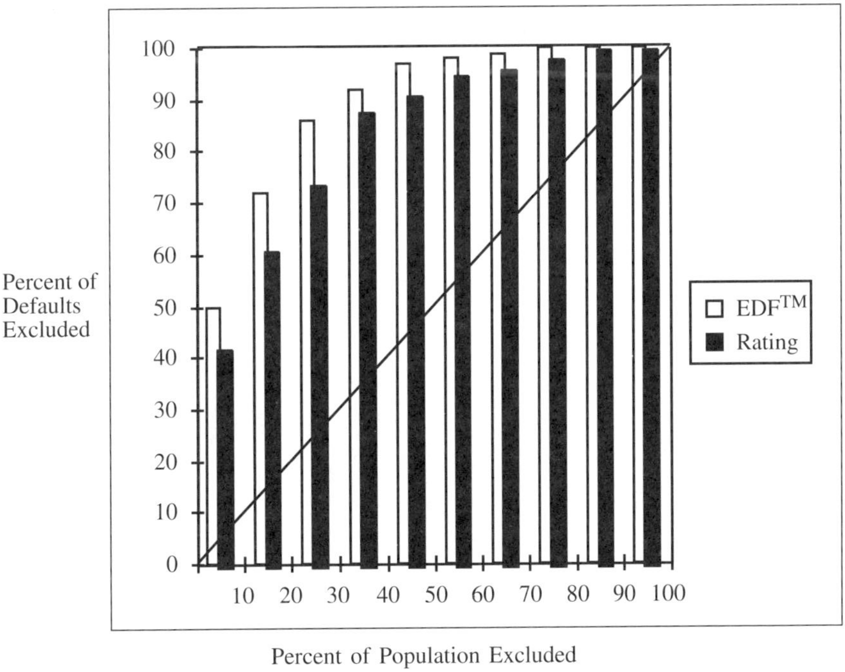

Percent of Population Excluded

The overall default rate, and thus the default probability of firms, varies considerably over time. Figure 9.19 plots the default history for the US from 1973 through 1997. The chart shows that as a general rule of thumb, we can expect the default rate to double or triple between the high and low of the credit cycle. Thus, an effective measure of default risk cannot average default rates over time; instead, it must reflect the changes in default risk over time. Because EDF^{TM} incorporates asset values based on information from the equity market, it naturally reflects the credit cycle in a forward-looking manner. For example, Figure 9.20 shows the median EDF^{TM} for US BBB rated firms from February 1993 through January 1997, and Figure 9.21 shows the EDF^{TM} quartiles for financial institutions in South Korea and Thailand over the same period.

At the individual firm level, the model's ability to reflect the current credit risk of a firm can be assessed by observing the change in the EDF^{TM} of a firm as it approaches default. Figure 9.22 plots the medians and quartiles of

Figure 9.19   US Bankruptcies and Defaults, 1973–1997

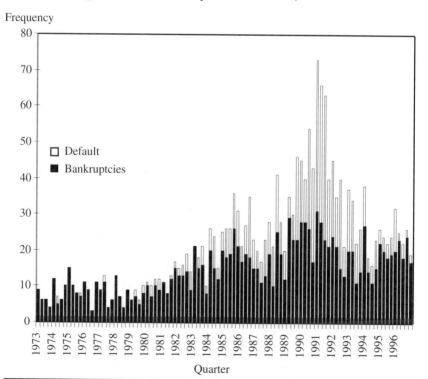

Figure 9.20 Median EDF^{TM} Rated US Corporations,
February 1993–January 1997

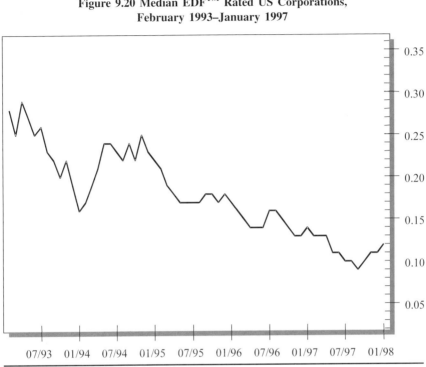

the EDF^{TM} for five years prior to the dates of default for rated companies. Default dates are aligned to the right such that the time moving to the left indicates years prior to default. EDF^{TM} is plotted along the vertical axis. The level of EDF^{TM} is sloping upward, towards increasing levels of default risk, as the date of default draws closer. Moreover, the slope increases as the date of default approaches.

Five years prior to default, the median EDF^{TM} of defaulting companies is approximately 1%, around BB. One year prior to default, the median EDF^{TM} has increased to over 6%. During the time of this sample, the median EDF^{TM} for all rated companies, both default and non-default, was around 0.16%. (The median and percentiles for the rated universe are the straight lines running parallel to the horizontal axis at the bottom of the chart.) Two years prior to default, the lower quartile of EDF^{TM} (the riskiest 25%) of the defaulting firms breaks through the upper quartile of the rated universe (the safest 25% as measured by the rating agency). Thus, two full years prior to default, 75% of the defaulting firms had EDF^{TM} in the bottom quartile of the universe.

Figure 9.21

Thai Financial Institutions

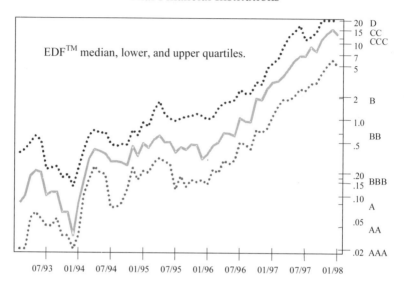

South Korean Financial Institutions

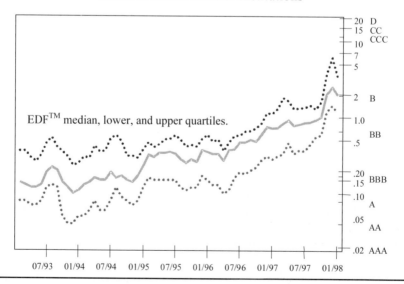

Figure 9.22   EDF™ Prior to Default Rated Companies Only

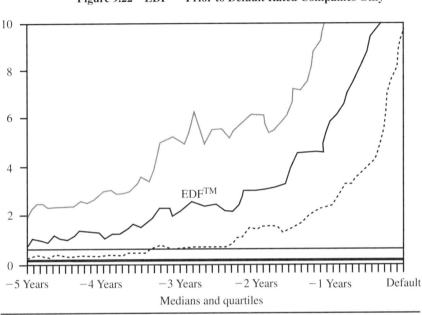

There is no single measure of performance for default measures such as an EDF™. Performance must be measured along several dimensions including discrimination power, ability to adjust to the credit cycle, and the ability to quickly reflect any deterioration in credit quality. The EDF™ generated from the equity market and financial statement information of a firm does all of these things well. The dynamics of EDF™ come mostly from the dynamics of the equity value. It is simply very hard to hold the equity price of a firm up as it heads towards default. The ability to discriminate between high and low default risks comes from the distance-to-default ratio. This key ratio compares the firm's net worth to its volatility and thus embodies all of the key elements of default risk. Moreover, because the net worth is based on values from the equity market, it is both a timely and superior estimate of the firm's value.

9.8   Summary

A three-step process is used to calculate EDF™:
1.   Estimate the market value and volatility of the firm's assets
2.   Calculate the distance-to-default, the number of standard deviations the firm is away from default

3.   Scale the distance-to-default to an EDF^{TM} using an empirical default distribution

Because EDF^{TM} are based on market prices, they are forward-looking and reflect the current position in the credit cycle. They are a timely and reliable measure of credit quality. As a final example of the forward-looking strength of EDF^{TM}, Figure 9.23 shows Venture Stores, which defaulted in January 1998. (Venture Stores was presented in our first example, Figure 9.1.) The first sign of a serious deterioration in the credit quality was in October 1994, when the EDF^{TM} jumped from 2% to 5% (B to B$-$). The EDF^{TM} climbed as high as 11% in February 1996, recovering a little as Venture Stores secured additional financing before finally reaching 20% (D) in February 1997, 11 months prior to default.

EDF^{TM} is an effective tool in any institution's credit process. Accurate and timely information from the equity market provides a continuous credit monitoring process that is difficult and expensive to duplicate using traditional credit analysis. Annual reviews and other traditional credit processes cannot maintain the same degree of vigilance that EDF^{TM} calculated on a monthly or a daily basis can provide. Continuous monitoring is the only effective early

Figure 9.23   Venture Stores Inc.

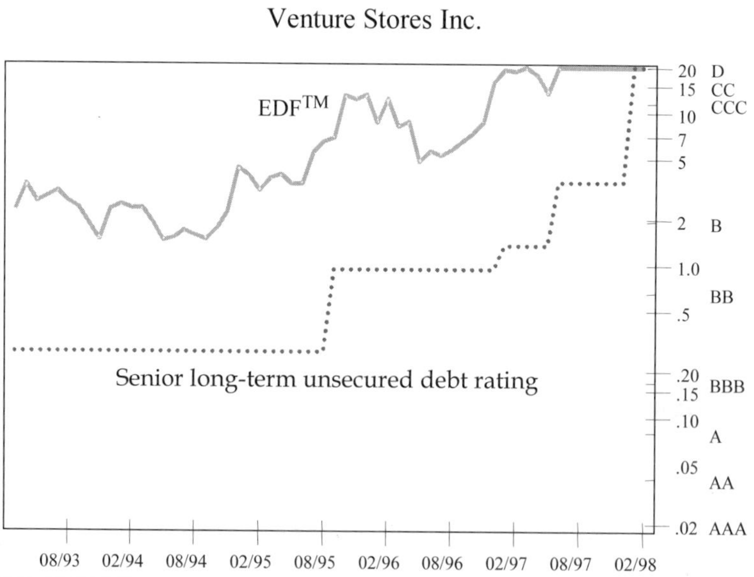

Venture Stores Inc.

warning protection against deteriorating credit quality. EDF^{TM} is also often used to help the focus of the efforts of traditional credit processes. They provide a cost-effective method to screen credits quickly and to focus credit analysis where it can add the most value. Further, because EDF^{TM} is real probabilities, it is the key data items in many institutions' provisioning, valuation, and performance measurement calculations.

10

Historical Defaults and Recoveries for Corporate Bonds

Sean C Keenan, David T Hamilton, and Lea V Carty
Moody's Risk Management Services

10.1 Introduction

Moody's corporate bond default research began in 1986 in our structured finance group as part of an effort to ensure the comparability of our long-term debt ratings across asset classes. Since then, we have continued to upgrade and expand that research to examine in greater detail the performance of our ratings as indicators of credit quality, and to provide the statistical inputs required by risk management practitioners.

This chapter encapsulates this research, and is divided into two parts. Section 10.2, "Historical Default Rates of Corporate Bond Issuers, 1920–1998," presents results from Moody's renowned annual default study for 1999. In addition to documenting defaults for 1920–1998, this section also studies patterns and correlations in the incidence of default and rating changes between industries, domiciles, and rating categories. The appendix to this chapter contains several statistical tables of default rates that serve both to document the performance of Moody's ratings and to quantify their meaning in terms of the frequency of default.

Section 10.3, "Debt Recoveries for Corporate Defaults and Bankruptcies," investigates loss in the event of default. We use two different approaches in estimating the historical recoveries investors have received. One method, which use the same data set as in Section 10.2, estimates recoveries and loss rates by using the price of defaulted bonds one month after the default date as a proxy for the bonds' recoveries. We also measure recovery values using an entirely new data set that measures actual recovery values for obligors in bankruptcy, not just for bonds, but for all debt obligations in the capital structure. This section documents the payouts, nature, timing, and relative value of these recoveries.

10.2   Historical Default Rates of Corporate Bond Issuers, 1920–1998

In the first half of this chapter we present a general overview of defaults and default rates, as well as descriptive statistics describing the industrial and geographic evolution of Moody's-rated universe. We continue to pay special attention and provide extra detail on the more recent period extending from 1970 to the present, under the rationale that more recent experience is of greater interest to investors. We first present a summary of 1998's default activity. In subsequent parts, we explore the entire period from 1920 through to 1998.

10.2.1   1998 Default and Bond Market Activity

Both the number and magnitude of bond defaults were approximately doubled in 1998, which, tempered by robust growth in issuance, produced percentage increases of 63% and 87% for the all-corporate and speculative-grade default rates, respectively. Moody's trailing 12-month default rate for all corporate issuers jumped from 0.68% at the start of 1998 to 1.27% at the start of 1999 after holding steady at around 1.0% for most of the year. Moody's speculative-grade trailing 12-month default rate ended the year at 3.31% versus 2.02% for 1997. These rates remain below the averages since January 1970 of 1.04% for all corporates and 3.37% for speculative-grade. For US-only speculative-grade issuers, the trailing 12-month default rate climbed to 3.84% as of January 1, 1999, versus 2.14% a year ago.

Globally, 128 corporate and sovereign issuers defaulted on US$29.3 billion of long-term publicly held corporate bonds in 1998. Even excluding the Russian Federation's massive US$9.7 billion default, this represents increases of 97% in issuer terms and 115% in terms of the dollar amount of defaulted debt, from 1997 when 70 issuers defaulted on US$9.3 billion. Figure 10.1 presents a breakdown of 1998's defaults by issuer domicile. While total default activity was fairly steady throughout the year, US-issuer defaults were clustered toward the end of the year with 25, or 47%, occurring in the fourth quarter.

Figure 10.1   1998 Defaulters by Domicile*

United States	53
Indonesia**	33
Thailand	7
Canada	6
Malaysia	6
Argentina	3
Korea	3
British Virgin Islands	2
Cayman Islands	2
Hong Kong	2
Russia	2
Netherlands	1
Belgium	1
China	1
Ireland	1
Japan	1
Pakistan	1
Philippines	1
United Kingdom	1
Venezuela	1

*   Includes Moody's-rated and unrated defaulters
** Includes Netherlands-based Indonesian issuers

In 1998, we saw the default of one issuer which began the year with an investment grade rating. Guangdong International Trust & Investment Corporation (GITIC), headquartered in Guangzhou, China, held a Baa2 rating as of January 1, and was downgraded to Ba1 on August 30. GITIC was established in 1980 by the government of Guangdong province to raise funds in support of the province's investment plans and economic strategy. On October 6, 1998, the People's Bank of China closed down GITIC due to its reported inability to service maturing obligations and announced that the repayment of all GITIC's debt obligations will be suspended until January 6, 1999.

An additional noteworthy default was that of CRIIMI MAE Inc., a Maryland-based real estate investment trust involved in the acquisition of subordinate commercial mortgage-backed securities and the securitization, and servicing of multifamily and commercial mortgages. Because CRIIMI MAE is a trust and not a corporate issuer, it does not fall under the scope of this report. However, its importance in the commercial mortgage-backed market—the company reported total assets of approximately US$2.8 billion and total equity of approximately US$700 million on June 30, 1998—made its October default on US$100 million of long-term debt a stark reminder that weakness in the market for a given asset class may ultimately translate into defaults on bonds backed by those assets.

Industrial Composition of Defaulters

The industrial composition of defaulters shifted again in 1998. Industrial issuers remained the primary source of defaulting issuers, contributing 38, or 30% of the total. Defaults by non-bank financial institutions rose from fourth place to second, with 20, or 16% of the total, as fallout from the Asian financial crisis continued to affect this sector. Technology and communications firms contributed 14, or 11% of the total, taking third place for the second consecutive year. Retail sector defaults were also up from last year at 10, or 8% of the total, while the remaining one-quarter of the total were dispersed across sectors, with banking, healthcare, hotels and casinos, sovereigns and transportation issuers all contributing. The recent trend in default counts by sector is presented in Figure 10.2.

In terms of the dollar amount of debt affected, sovereign issuers, led by the Russian Federation, comprised the largest component (35%) with defaults on over US$10.3 billion. Non-bank financial issuers came in second (17%) contributing over US$5.1 billion in 1998, up from US$1.4 billion last year. Following in third place were industrial issuers (12%), which contributed another US$3.6 billion, while the fourth place slot was filled by the retail sector

Figure 10.2   Number of Defaulters by Industry Group, 1994–1998*

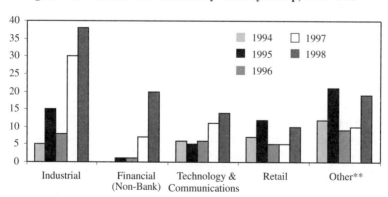

*   Includes rated and unrated defaulters.
** Includes Transportation, Banking, Media, Hotel & Gaming, and Utilities.

which defaulted on US$2.9 billion (10%). Figure 10.3 gives more detail of the composition of 1998's defaults by dollar amount.

Sovereign Defaults

The defaults by Venezuela in 1998, the Russian Federation, and Pakistan represented three of only 10 defaults by sovereign governments on long-term publicly held debt documented by Moody's since World War II (WWII). Other post-WWII sovereign defaulters include Argentina, Costa Rica, Guatemala, Panama, Poland, Rhodesia (Zimbabwe), and Uruguay.[1]

Of 1998's sovereign bond defaults, both Venezuela's US$270 million domestic currency default and Pakistan's US$300 million Euronote default involved delayed interest payments — defaults according to the operational definition of this report — which were ultimately disbursed within the specified grace period.

Of far greater magnitude in terms of the amount, severity, and effect on the debt markets was the default by the Russian Federation who announced on

Figure 10.3   1998's Defaulted Debt by Industry

($29.3 billion = 100%)*

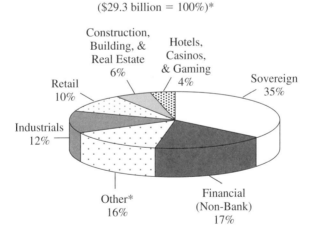

* Includes rated and unrated defaulters.
** Includes Transportation, Real Estate, Healthcare, Banking, & Miscellaneous.

---

[1]   For an overview of the long-term history of sovereign defaults on bonds and loans, see Truglia, Vincent, Levey, David, and Mahoney, Christopher, "Sovereign Risk: Bank Deposits vs. Loans," Moody's Special Comment, October 1995

August 17 a "de-facto" devaluation of the domestic currency and payment moratorium on an array of obligations. The Russian Federation, which became fully independent in December 1991 after the break-up of the Soviet Union, has been in a prolonged economic slump since its inception. While economic reform has been a top priority for policy makers, significant institutional and cultural barriers have frustrated the transition from the old centralized planning system to a free market economy. The Russian Federation's continuing problem has been the fiscal deficit, which resulted from the government's inability to collect taxes.

The August "de-facto" devaluation also carried with it a forced rescheduling of short-term treasury debt issues (GKOs) and long-term treasury debt issues (OFZs), and a 90-day moratorium on principal repayment of foreign-originated syndicated loans, settlements of foreign currency forward contracts, and margin calls on repurchase transactions. The rescheduling of rouble-denominated government debt constituted an outright default on 33 separate GKOs with face values totaling over US$33 billion, and 12 separate OFZs with face value totaling US$9.7 billion. The loan moratorium affected five multi-lateral loans originated under the London Club restructuring agreement totaling US$22 billion, as well as a US$100 million facility originated by ING Bank N.V. for the Republic of Tartarstan, a Russian Republic.

In addition to the Russian central government's default on treasury debt and post-Soviet restructured debt, 49 Russian autonomous republics and other municipalities (oblasts) defaulted on coupon and principal repayment on rouble denominated agrocultural bonds (agrobonds) totaling US$336.2 million over the period from late May through mid-Ocober. Agrobonds, issued by nearly all Russian regions in mid-1997, were created by the Russian Ministry of Finance as means of solving the severe non-payment problem on agricultural loans extended to the regions by the central government.

1998 Bond Market Activity

The bond market activity in 1998 was marked by two distinctive features. The most striking was the difference between market conditions for investment-grade versus speculative-grade issuers. Buoyed by strength in the US Treasury market where for the seven-year Treasury Note yields fell steadily from 5.48% to 4.71% over the course of the year, median yields for investment-grade bonds fell from 6.32% in January to 6.07% in December. However, the investment-grade rally did not keep pace with Treasuries and consequently spreads widened about 51 bp to 136 bp. Still, this segment's strength was evident in its ability to absorb larger and larger issues; 1998 saw over 100 separate investment-grade corporate issues with face values in excess of US$1billion.

The speculative-grade market began the year with a median yield of 8.76% for seven-year maturities. This produced a spread over Treasuries of 329 bp, which was only 17 bp higher than the average for 1996–97, and seemed to bode well for investor confidence in this segment in the face of continuing credit problems in Southeast Asia and their potential spillover effects. As shown on the cover of this report, speculative-grade spreads began to widen significantly in May and continued to widen, jumping from 349 bp to 502 bp in August alone, reaching a peak of 588 bp in October. This marked the widest spread level since December 1991, a point at which the speculative-grade default rate stood at 11.34%. As Figure 10.4 shows, default rates had already begun to creep higher, but the relationship between speculative-grade yields and default frequency experienced a fundamental shift in August as liquidity fell and investors demanded a higher credit risk premium than had been the case since 1992.

The pattern of new issuance reflected this third quarter shift in investor posture. Investment-grade issuance outpaced speculative-grade issuance for most of last year, and although slowing in August, September and October, finished the year on a high note, with over US$40 billion coming to market in November and December. Speculative-grade issuance began to weaken in May as problems with the Russian Federation began to surface, plunging to its lowest levels of the year by October, and remaining virtually flat throughout the fourth quarter.

The total US new issuance in 1998, including bonds issued under rule 144a, was US$297.3 billion, an increase of 17% over 1997's record total, comprised

Figure 10.4   Speculative-Grade Yield Spread vs. Speculative-Grade Default Rate

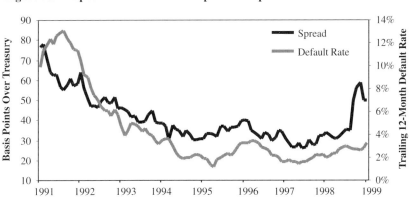

of US$176.6 billion and US$120.8 billion of investment-grade and speculative grade, respectively. Year-on-year, speculative-grade issuance growth outpaced investment-grade growth, rising by US$22.7 billion or 23% from 1997 while investment-grade issuance rose by US$21.2 billion, or 14% from the previous year. The total number of Moody's-rated corporate and sovereign issuers grew by a more modest 11% over the year.

10.2.2   Data and Methodology

Moody's bases the results of this study on a proprietary database of ratings and defaults for industrial and transportation companies, utilities, financial institutions, and sovereigns that have issued long-term debt to the public. Municipal debt issuers, structured finance transactions, private placements, and issuers with only short-term debt ratings are excluded. In total, the data cover the credit experiences of over 15,200 issuers that sold long-term debt publicly at some time between 1919 and the start of 1999. As of January 1, 1999, over 4,600 of those issuers held Moody's ratings. These issuers account for the bulk of the outstanding dollar amount of US public long-term corporate debt and a substantial part of public issuance abroad.

Figure 10.5 details the number of firms included in our ratings database as of the start of each decade since 1920. The downward trend from 1920 to 1950 reflects the public bond market's retrenchment following the Great Depression and WWII, increasing financial intermediation, and consolidation in the railroad and utilities industries. Since 1950, however, the number of rated firms has increased steadily, with sharp increases during the 1980s and 1990s due in part, to the development of the junk bond market in the US and Moody's expansion

Figure 10.5   Moody's-Rated Corporate Bond Issuers, 1920–1999

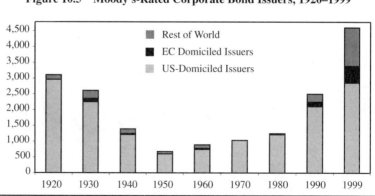

into non-US markets. It was not until 1994 that Moody's again rated as many corporate issuers as it did in 1920.

Non-US issuers comprised nearly as large a percentage of the Moody's-rated universe in January 1930 (15%) as they did in January of 1990 (18%). The portion of rated issuers domiciled outside of the US began to fall with the decline in international trade that accompanied the Great Depression and continued until it hit an all-time low in 1970. Since then, this fraction has grown significantly, rebounding to 1930 levels by 1990 and exceeding 38% as of the beginning of 1999.

Before 1980, the non-US issuers that Moody's rated were predominantly those that tapped the US bond market. In recent years, however, Moody's has extended ratings to many more issuers placing debt in non-US markets. Currently, the three non-US countries contributing the largest number of Moody's-rated issuers are the United Kingdom (5.6% of the total), Japan (5.5%), and Canada (3.8%). Two countries that specialize in providing havens for corporate residence — the Netherlands and the Cayman Islands — are the fifth and seventh largest contributors of rated bond issuers, at 3.6% and 1.7% of the total, respectively.

Historically, the industrial composition of Moody's-rated bond issuers has shifted with broad patterns in the capital formation process. In the early part of the century, railroads commanded large amounts of investment capital. As of 1920, more than half of the issuers Moody's rated were railroad companies, followed by utilities, industrials, and financial companies. Since then industrials have become the largest sector representing 39% of the total number of rated firms while non-bank financial companies risen to the number two spot comprising 17% of the Moody's rated universe, with banking institutions third at 14%, as of the start of 1999.

Geographically, two of the fastest growing components of the Moody's-rated universe are the European Community (EC) and Emerging Market (EM) countries. The growth in the number of EC-domiciled issuers has averaged just under 20% per year since 1990, while the average for all other countries combined was just under 6%. As shown in Figure 10.6, EC growth outpaced the rest of the world in every year since 1990, including a strong performance in 1998. Non-EC issuer growth was negative in 1990 and 1991 and minimal in 1992 largely as a result of the collapse of the US junk-bond market. Optimism surround the European Monetary Union helped stimulate new EC debt issuance last year and should provide even greater stimulus going forward.

While emerging market-based issuers still make up a relatively small proportion of Moody's-rated universe, this component grew by nearly 45%

Figure 10.6   Growth of Moody's-Rated, EC-Domiciled Issuers vs Rest of World

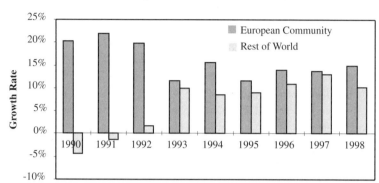

annually from 1993 through 1997. Poor borrowing conditions for speculative-grade issuers in general and investor apprehension toward EM issuers resulting from the Asian financial crisis, restrained 1998's growth in the EM issuer base to a modest 17%, with most of that growth coming from Asian countries. Since most EM issuers carry speculative-grade ratings, this growth has had a significant impact on the geographic composition of the speculative-grade universe. The proportion of speculative-grade issuers that are EM-based has risen from just 2% in 1993 to over 13% at the beginning of 1998.

Moody's Definition of Default

Moody's default database covers over 3,200 long-term bond defaults by issuers both rated and unrated by Moody's. We compiled these default histories from a variety of sources, including our own Industrial, Railroad, and Public Utilities Manuals; reports of the National Quotation Service; various issues of The Commercial and Financial Chronicle; our library of financial reports; press releases; press clippings; internal memoranda; and records of analyst contact with rated issuers. We also examined documents from the Securities and Exchange Commission, The Dun & Bradstreet Corp., the New York Stock Exchange, and the American Stock Exchange.

Moody's defines a bond default as any missed or delayed disbursement of interest and/or principal, bankruptcy, receivership, or distressed exchange where (i) the issuer offered bondholders a new security or package of securities that amount to a diminished financial obligation (such as preferred or common stock, or debt with a lower coupon or par amount), or (ii) the exchange had the apparent purpose of helping the borrower avoid default.

Moody's Default Rate Calculation Methodology

Moody's ratings incorporate assessments of both the likelihood and the severity of default. So, in order to calculate default rates, which are estimates of the default probability component of ratings, we must hold severity considerations constant. We do this by considering the rating on each company's senior unsecured debt or, if there is none, by statistically implying such a rating on the basis of rated subordinated or secured debt. In most cases, this will yield an assessment of risk that is relatively unaffected by special considerations of collateral or of position within the capital structure. We dub these ratings "implied senior unsecured ratings" or, more concisely, "implied senior ratings." It is important to note that because implied senior ratings are derived statistically and are not associated with an actual debt instrument, they do not directly benefit from the full scope of analysis that a regular Moody's bond rating would enjoy.

To calculate default rates, we use the issuer as the unit of study rather than individual debt instruments or outstanding dollar amounts of debt. Because Moody's intends its ratings to support credit decisions, which do not vary with either the size or number of bonds that a firm may have outstanding, we believe this methodology produces more meaningful estimates of the probability of default. In summary, because the likelihood of default is essentially the same for all of a firm's public debt issues, irrespective of size, weighting our statistics by the number of bond issues or their par amounts would simply bias our results towards the characteristics of large issuers.

The default rates we calculate are fractions in which the numerator represents the number of issuers that defaulted in a particular time period and the denominator represents the number of issuers that could have defaulted in that time period. In this study, the numerators are the numbers of issuers defaulting on Moody's-rated debt. The denominators are the numbers of issuers that potentially could have defaulted on Moody's-rated debt. Hence, if all of an issuer's ratings are withdrawn, it is subtracted from the denominator. Failing to correct the denominators in this way generates artificially low estimates of the risk of default. It is important to note that Moody's does not withdraw ratings because of deterioration in credit quality. In such cases, the issuer's bonds are simply downgraded.

We define default rates for any rating classification in a manner analogous to that used for calculating overall corporate default rates. For the B rating, for example, the one-year default rate is the number of Moody's-B-rated issuers that defaulted over the following one-year period divided by the number of Moody's-B-rated issuers that could have defaulted over that period. The issuer-weighted average of default rates (defined as of the start of each year) represents an estimate of the risk of default within any one-year period. (The underlying one-year default rates for each rating category from 1970 through the present are included in Figure 10.42 of the appendix.)

Moody's employs a cohort approach to calculating multi-year default rates. A cohort consists of all issuers holding a given senior implied rating at the start of a given year. These issuers are then followed through time, keeping track of when they default or leave the rated universe for non credit-related reasons (e.g., maturing of debt). Thus the cohorts are dynamic and allow the estimation of cumulative default risk over multi-year horizons. For each cumulation period, default rates based on dynamic cohorts express the ratio of issuers who did default to issuers who were in a position to default over that period. This allows for the comparison and averaging of default rates over different periods. Also, by forming and tracking cohorts of all Moody's-rated issuers with debt outstanding as of January 1 of each year, we replicate the experience of a portfolio of both seasoned and new-issue bonds purchased in a given year.

Cohort-based default rates can answer questions like "What was the probability that a Baa-rated issuer with bonds outstanding as of January 1, 1985 would default by 1998?" The answer to this question — 6.46% — is found in Figure 10.42 (appendix), in the last row and last column headed "14" of the section labeled "Cohort Formed January 1, 1985." In cases in which an investor feels that the business conditions of the current year are similar to those of some previous year, she may consult that year's cohort directly to ascertain what default patterns to expect.

To estimate the average risk of default over time horizons longer than one year, we calculate the risk of default in each year since a cohort was formed. The issuer-weighted average of each cohort's one-year default rate forms the average cumulative one-year default rate. The issuer-weighted average of the second-year default rates cumulated with that of the first year yields the two-year average cumulative default rate. In this manner, we compute average cumulative default rates for one to 20 years for each rating category. To illustrate how the weighted average smoothes out the variations and irregularities in the default experience of individual cohorts, Figure 10.7 presents cumulative default rates from one to twelve years for two Ba cohorts, 1977 and 1987, as well as for the weighted average cumulative default rate from 1970 to present.

10.2.3 Default Activity Since 1920

The incidence of default by both rated and unrated issuers is spread unevenly

Figure 10.7   Cumulative Default Rates for Ba Category

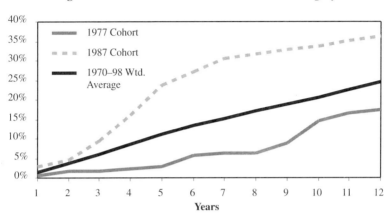

over this century, with large numbers of defaults in the 1920s, the depression of the 1930s, and again in the late 1980s and early 1990s. Figure 10.8, which portrays a monthly time-series of the 12-month trailing default rate for all Moody's-rated corporate issuers, provides an overall picture of how aggregate corporate default risk has ebbed and flowed since 1920.

January 1920 through mid-1929 was a period of cyclical and declining default risk that resembled the 1980s in terms of the average default rate. However, the next period, from mid-1929 through December 1939, produced the heaviest default activity of this century. The Great Depression generated a 79-year high, one-year corporate default rate of 9.2% in July 1932, indicating that nearly one in 10 Moody's-rated corporate issuers defaulted over the following year.

The severity of the depression and its characteristic asset depreciation ensured that such high rates of default did not quickly subside. For the eight-year period beginning in January 1930, the default rate averaged 3.7% — nearly as high as the recent 4.1% peak set in July 1991. The default rate again jumped at the beginning of WWII, reflecting the war-related defaults of Italian, German, French, Japanese, Czechoslovakian, and Austrian companies. Following the war, however, default risk subsided to very low levels. These low levels persisted until 1970, when the defaults of Penn Central Railroad and 25 of its affiliates shook fixed-income markets. After 1970, default risk again ebbed and was moderate-to-low by historical standards until 1982, when the modern period of relatively high default risk began.

Figure 10.8   Trailing 12-Month All-Corporate Issuer Default Rate, 1920–1998

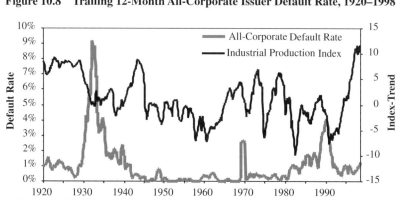

Figure 10.8 also plots the US Industrial Production Index (IP) in terms of its deviation from trend,[2] whose correlation with the all-corporate default rate is a fairly weak — 0.14. From 1920 through 1965 significant increases in the default rate were typically preceded by weakness in the overall economy as reflected in total IP. Since 1965, it has more often been the case that increases in the default rate occur in advance of a weakening in the general economy. For example, in the worst episode of the post war era, the default rate began to rise in June 1988 rising from 0.85% to its peak of 4.08% in July of 1990. IP, on the other hand, peaked in January of 1989 but did not fall below trend until July of 1989. While the default rate was back to its pre-junk bond collapse levels by July of 1991, IP remained weak through the end of 1993. More recently, robust economic growth and low default rates have gone hand in hand. Nevertheless, the shifting of this lead-lag relationship is a typical example the instability of the relationship between corporate bond default rates and macroeconomic variables generally.

Defaults by Industry

The contributions made by different industries to the total number of defaults have varied substantially through time. Figure 10.9 portrays the total number of defaults, sorted by broad industry group, in each of five decades that span the period from 1920 through the present. At 47%, industrials account for the largest percentage of the total number of defaults over the last 79 years. The remaining

---

[2]   The trend here is estimated as a smooth function of time. The correlation between the index and this trend is 0.993

Figure 10.9   Moody's Rated Default Count by Industry and Time Period

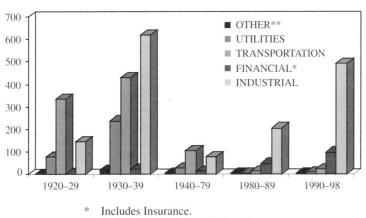

*   Includes Insurance.
**   Includes Sovereign and Miscellaneous.

defaulters are divided between transportation companies (30%), utilities (12%), financial companies (6%), and miscellaneously affiliated firms (5%). In the 1920s, transportation companies made up the majority of defaulters, with industrial firms coming in a distant second place. However, the number of industrials defaulting surged past those for other industries after the depression years of the 1930s to exceeding 600 for the period 1930–39.

Over time, changes in the raw numbers of defaulting issuers by sector have occurred simultaneously with changes in the industrial composition of Moody's rated universe. Default rates for broad industry categories, shown in Figure 10.10, capture both patterns and highlight the differences in the timing of high default activity. As the exhibit shows, high default episodes may primarily affect a few related sectors, as in 1970, or may affect many sectors but with differing timing as was the case during the 1989–91 period.

Recent Credit Quality Trends

Overall, the rating composition of speculative-grade issuance continued to deteriorate in 1998. As a result, the proportion of Moody's-rated issuers holding speculative-grade ratings climbed to 42%, a level not reached since 1953, while A- and Baa-rated issuers fell from 48% to 44% over the year, and Aaa and Aa rated issuers fell to 15%, a post-WWII low, as shown in Figure 10.11. While part of this reflects the continued outpacing of investment-grade new issuance by speculative-grade new issuance during 1998, part of it reflects negative rating drift for existing issuers.

Figure 10.10   Default Rates by Broad Industry Group, 1970–1998

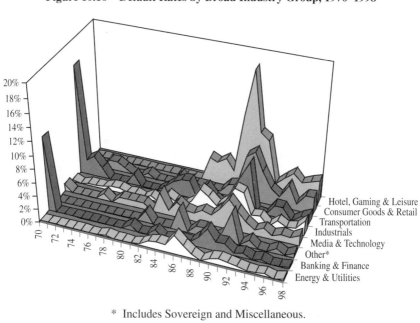

* Includes Sovereign and Miscellaneous.

Figure 10.11   Ratings Composition of Moody's Rated Bond Issuers, 1989–1998

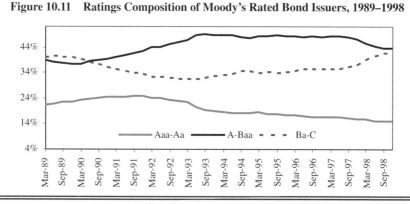

This negative drift is summarized by the overall upgrade/downgrade ratio, which was less than one for the last three quarters of 1998. This marked the first instance of three consecutive quarters with downgrades outnumbering upgrades since 1993, and the annual average of 0.90 was the worst since 1992.

One of the sectors that experienced a more severe downgrade bias was the non-US financial sector. Exposure by Japanese and European financial institutions to the devastated Southeast Asian corporate loan market contributed to the downward pressure on long-term debt ratings for this sector. Figure 10.12 compares one-year negative credit event frequency by rating category, for non-US financial issuers in 1998, with all-issuers 1998 and with the all-issuer average for 1980–1998, where negative credit events are defined as downgrades or defaults within one-year of holding a given rating.

The chart shows that credit risk is fairly evenly distributed across rating categories with the exception of the Caa-C categories where downgrades or defaults affect one out four issuers on average. The last set of bars plots the same information for non-US financial institutions. This latter group differs from the total Moody's-rated universe in that its initial credit quality is above average. None of its 722 obligors began the year with a rating lower than B, and only one defaulted during the year. Nevertheless, nearly 20% of these obligors experienced negative credit events, with most of the downgrades affecting the A, Baa, and Ba categories.

Size Distribution of Defaulting Bond Issues

The average size of defaulting corporate bonds has followed a choppy but steady upward trend since 1970, averaging about US$100 million over the past five years. Much of the volatility of the annual average default size derives from a small number of special events including the huge 1987 defaults of Texaco Capital, Inc and Texaco Capital N.V. on US$3.7 billion and US$2.7 billion, respectively, Flagstar's US$1.5 billion 1997, and Penn Traffic's US$1 billion default in 1998. One component contributing to the gradual increase in the size of defaults is the steadily increasing size of new issues, which grew from an average

Figure 10.12   Negative Credit Event Frequency by Rating

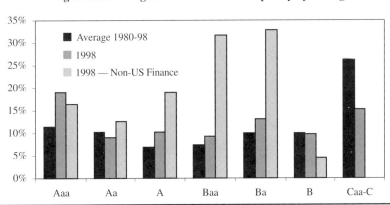

of US$144 million in 1987 to US$160 million in 1997. Increasing average issue size is not merely a reflection of overall price inflation, however. In fact, the 11% growth in average issue size, has lagged significantly behind the 41% increase in the overall price level for the same period, as measured by the CPI.

Skewness in the average distribution of default size, resulting from the small number of very large defaults and larger number of much smaller defaults, is a characteristic of the debt market as a whole. To gauge the relationship between the size distribution of bond defaults and the size distribution of bonds outstanding, we compared the size distributions for bonds issued over the past five years, with the distribution of the defaulted subset of those bonds (226 separate issues), shown in Figure 10.13. The chart shows issue size on a logarithmic scale to reduce the skewness, and shows that the distribution of defaulted issues lies slightly to the right of the overall market distribution for this period. These data suggest that for this particular sample, the smallest issues have been somewhat less likely to default than the larger issues. However, even for sub-samples in which default rates by size differ from the overall population, we find little evidence of a comparable relationship between loss rates and issue size. Over the period 1970–1998, the correlation between the face value of defaulting issues and the post-default prices of those issues is very low, just 0.02%.

10.2.4 Ratings as Indicators of Default Probability

Over 2,200 of the more than 15,200 corporate issuers that Moody's has rated since 1920 defaulted at some point in time. One year prior to default, less than

Figure 10.13 Negative Credit Event Frequency by Rating

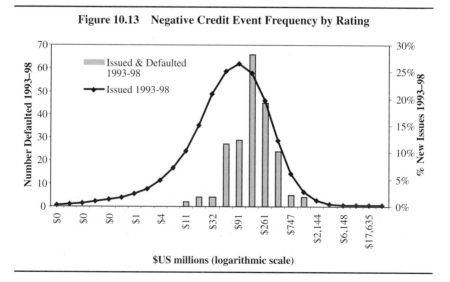

$US millions (logarithmic scale)

9% of these carried actual or implied senior unsecured ratings at the investment-grade level. However, at various lengths of time before default, more issuers carried investment-grade ratings.

To summarize the extent of rating decay in advance of default, we calculated the median and average senior or implied senior unsecured rating of issuers between zero and 60 months before default, shown in Figure 10.14. The average rating is constructed by translating Moody's rating symbols onto a scale from 1 to 21 where Aaa=1 and C=21 and simply taking the average of the numbers to produce a smooth series.[3] Thus, while the value of this "average rating" has no simple interpretation, it can be translated back onto the original symbolic scale and its changes do reflect improvement and deterioration in the underlying pool of future defaulters, capturing finer gradations than does the median rating.

Figure 10.14 shows that, five years prior to default, the median rating of defaulting companies is speculative-grade. The downward slope of the average shows that, as a group, these future defaulters are already seeing downward rating pressure five years in advance of default. At 24 months before default, the median rating has fallen to Ba2 and falls further to Ba3 12 months prior to default. The average rating falls faster and farther than the median rating, reaching Ba3 16 months prior to default. Moreover, the fact that the average lies everywhere below the median rating indicates that the rating distribution for issuers that ultimately default is skewed toward the lower end of the rating scale. The level of rating has become lower and the rate of rating decline has increased over recent years as precipitous rating drops prior to default have been rare. For

Figure 10.14   Median and Average Ratings Before Default, 1920–1998

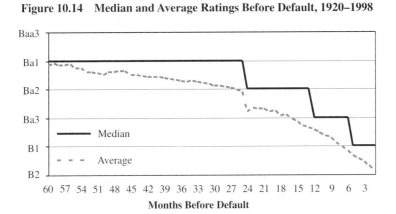

---

[3]   A linear mapping is used here for simplicity only

example, for issuers defaulting in 1998, the median rating both one and two years prior to default was B2, well below the historical average.

Outliers: Moody's Highest-Rated Defaulters

Of the more than 900 defaults on Moody's-rated debt since 1937, only three issuers have defaulted while holding investment-grade ratings. Since 1970, twenty-five issuers have defaulted within one year of holding an investment grade rating.

The highest rating ever to be held by a Moody's-rated defaulter at the time of default was A3, held in 1982 by Johns Manville, which sought protection under Chapter 11 after being found liable for massive asbestos-related damages. This marked the first ever strategic bankruptcy filing by an issuer that was solvent, thereby raising defensive Chapter 11 filings as a new category of credit risk associated with certain types of issuers. One year prior to its default (before the introduction of numerical rating-modifiers), Manville's rating was A.

The second highest rated issuer to default was Columbia Gas System, which defaulted in June 1991 while holding a Baa1 rating at the senior unsecured level.[4] The company's financial position deteriorated during the 1980's as regulatory revisions left it locked into high-priced purchase contracts with producers, while facing competitive and falling end market prices. The record warmth of the 1990 and 1991 heating seasons further depressed gas prices, and the company, unable to service its debts, filed for bankruptcy after failing to re-negotiate its bank credit facilities. Although the firm did not emerge from bankruptcy until November of 1995, secondary market pricing would have allowed investors to recover 85% of par, one month after the bankruptcy petition was filed. Ultimately, investors received principle, interest, and interest on interest generating a recovery rate of 100%. The third investment-grade rated defaulter was Green Bay & Western Railroad who defaulted in February 1938 while holding a Baa rating.

In October 1989, two New Zealand-based firms, DFC Financial Overseas and DFC Overseas Investments, defaulted while holding Ba1 ratings. These defaulters had begun the year with Aa3 ratings and so, as members of the Aa3 cohort for that year, contributed to the one-year default rates for the Aa3 category. These investment-grade ratings reflected, in part, Moody's expectation of support from the government of New Zealand. However, the Government of New Zealand's failure to support the notes resulted in their default in October

---

[4]   Technically, Columbia Gas System was downgraded to below investment grade one day prior to the bankruptcy filing

1989. This example illustrates the value of implicit, as opposed to explicit, sovereign guarantees on the credit ratings of sovereign-related issuers.

Default Rates by Rating Category

Weighted average default rates shown in Figure 10.15 clearly show an increased risk of default associated with lower rating categories. Since 1970, an average of 3.27% of speculative-grade issuers have defaulted per year, compared with just 0.17% of investment-grade issuers. For all but 28 of the past 79 years, the one-year default rate for the investment-grade sector was zero.

Figure 10.39 (in the appendix) likewise demonstrates a clear pattern of higher default risk associated with the speculative-grade rating categories. The last four rows of the exhibit give the one-year default rates for investment-grade issuers, speculative-grade issuers, US only speculative-grade issuers, and all corporate issuers since 1970. As these data indicate, the default rate for all speculative-grade issuers has averaged 3.32% higher than that for investment grade issuers since 1970, and 4.00% higher since 1980.

The results presented in Figure 10.15 suggest that the relationship between ratings and default likelihood holds for numerically modified rating categories as well as for the non-modified categories. Figure 10.39 and Figure 10.40 (in the appendix) present one-year and weighted average one-year default rates for each of these rating categories. The latter rates are drawn from the relatively high default risk period extending from 1983 through the present. Over that time period, average one-year default rates climbed from 0.0% for Aaa to 12.4% for B3. The default rate for US domiciled speculative-grade issuers has remained slightly above the total speculative-grade rate since 1992.

Figure 10.15   One-Year Default Rates by Alpha-Numeral Ratings, 1983–1998

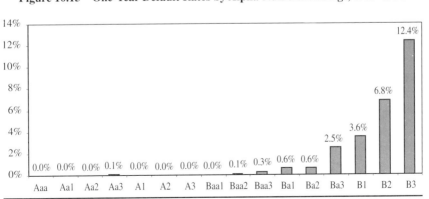

In June 1997, Moody's announced the assignment of numerical modifiers to long-term issues rated Caa. These rating categories were expanded to include three numerical modifiers each in order to provide finer gradations of credit risk evaluation. Caa-rated issues are characterized by high levels of risk with respect to principle and interest payments. Issuers include both young companies whose credit histories are sparse, as well as established players with declining fundamentals. The Caa category also encompasses defaulted obligations with high expected recoveries.

Figure 10.16 shows default rates for the numerically modified Caa ratings for 1998, the first and only cohort year for these sub categories, as well as the B3 category for the same period. The default rates increase smoothly over the entire range, from B3 through Caa3.

Multi-Year Default Rates

Although the one-year default rates presented up to this point are of greatest interest to many market participants, some find default rates for longer time horizons more relevant. A 10-year default rate, for example, estimates the share of a portfolio of bonds that can be expected to default over a 10-year period.

Figure 10.17 presents average cumulative default rates for 5-, 10-, 15-, and 20-year time horizons based on all data available since 1920. Figure 10.17 also shows that higher default risk for lower rating categories remains evident over investment periods as long as 20 years. For example, average default rates for five-year holding periods climb from 0.1% for the Aaa rating category to 27.7% for the B rating category. Figure 10.17 also shows that the pattern recurs for average default rates for 10-year and 15-year holding periods. Figure 10.40 in

Figure 10.16   1998 One-Year Default Rates for B3 and Numerically Modified Caa Ratings

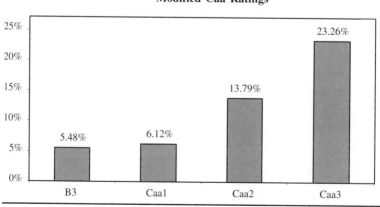

Figure 10.17   5-, 10-, 15- and 20-Year Average Cumulative Default Rates, 1970–1998

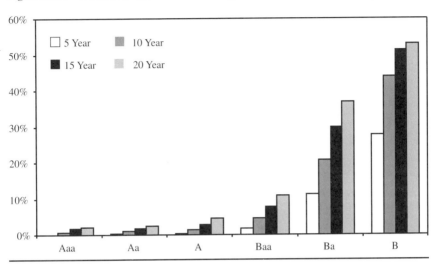

the appendix presents these data in detail for the period from 1970 to the present, and Figure 10.41 presents average cumulative default rates by numerically modified ratings for up to eight years.

Hazard Rates of Default

Defaults are complex events that involve issuers at different stages of their evolution as firms. Moody's default rates characterize the relationship between the credit rating of issuers at a point in time and the probability of default over different time horizons, with lower ratings generally linked to higher defaults rates. However, default rate statistics calculated using our cohort methodology do not identify the relationship between default frequency and the life-cycle of corporate bond issuers. More precisely, all the issuers that enter a cohort at a particular point in time belonged to the healthy population previously, but may have arrived at that point via credit histories of differing length and credit quality.

In this section we attempt to identify regularities in default dynamics by describing the time spent by an issuer in the healthy group before default occurs. Thus we are considering the hazard rate of issuer default, as opposed to default rates. The issuer-based hazard rate of default is the default frequency as a function of the length of issuer's credit rating history[5] which emphasizes the decision making

---

[5]   Carty, Lea V., 1997, "An Empirical Investigation of Default Risk Dynamics," Columbia University, doctoral thesis

characteristic of issuers, opposed to the issue-based hazard rate which is the bond-level default frequency as a function of the life of the individual bond.[6] Our approach allows us to gauge the relative risk of default for issuers with many years of credit experience versus those in the early stages of their evolution as corporations.

We consider the hazard rate of default of all Moody's-rated issuers over the period 1988–1998, comparing this to the average length of credit history over the same period. We also consider separate mortality rates for investment-grade and speculative-grade issuers. Because the credit rating of an issuer can significantly change over the years, generally deteriorating in advance of default, it is not possible to assign a single average rating to an issuer's rating history. We resolve this problem by assigning issuers into categories defined by the period of time the issuer's credit quality remains of investment or speculative grade before default, described further below.

Figure 10.18 shows the hazard rate for issuers at different stages of their credit history, plotted against the length of credit history, for the period 1988–1998. Similar results were found for other periods. The interpretation is as follows; if the curve for all- defaulters were perfectly flat, the risk of default would be constant over the issuer's life. The default rate is quite low for issuers in their first two years as rated borrowers, reflecting the fact that their initial rating is usually accompanied by a successful debt issue, bolstering their financial position in the short run. Default risk increases sharply in the third year, reaching a peak in the fourth year and tapering off thereafter. For guidance purposes, the dashed line represents the average annual number of issuers for a given length of credit history.

Figure 10.18 also breaks out the mortality rates by broad credit quality. While it is impossible to assign a single unambiguous credit quality measure to a changing rating history, we use a simple rule to group issuers' rating histories by average credit quality. The subgroups are defined as investment-grade — issuers whose credit rating remained of investment quality at least 80% of the time before default, and speculative-grade — issuers whose credit rating remained of speculative quality at least 80% of the time before default. Because these identification schemes exclude some borrowers they do not sum to the total. Nevertheless, they do show important differences in the mortality profile of issuers of varying credit quality. Specifically, the speculative-grade subset exhibits a significantly higher default risk in the 3–5 year range of its credit history and is thus a major contributor to the shape

---

[6] Altman, Edward I., February 1998, "Measuring Corporate Bond Mortality and Performance," *Journal of Finance*.

Figure 10.18   Distribution of Default Frequency by Length of Rated Credit History

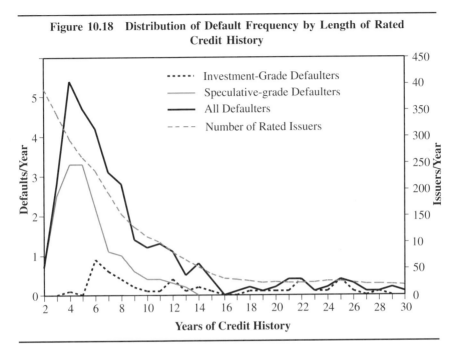

of the all-issuer mortality profile. The investment-grade profile is much flatter, indicating a more constant level of default risk over the credit history of the issuer. The modest peak that is evident is also further out and broader than that of the speculative-grade group.

Default Rate Volatility by Rating

An examination of the cohorts presented in Figure 10.42 (in the appendix) reveals the extent to which aggregate default rates vary from one year to the next for a given rating category. For the B rating category in the period from 1920 through 1998, for instance, the one-year default rate ranged from a low of zero in several years to a high of 23.4% in 1970. The sources of the year-to-year variation in aggregate default rates for a given rating category are many, but macroeconomic trends are certainly among the most influential factors. To quantify this variability, Moody's calculated the standard deviations of the one-year default rates for each letter rating category. Figure 10.18 presents these statistics defined over the periods from 1920 and from 1970 to the present.

Figure 10.19 highlights a pattern of higher default rate volatility for lower credit ratings for both time periods examined. That is, while the average risk of default is higher for lower rating categories, the chances of the default rate

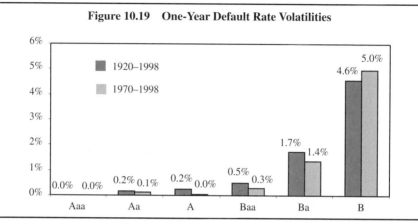

Figure 10.19   One-Year Default Rate Volatilities

differing significantly from the average in any given year is also higher. The greater investment-grade default rate volatility — except the Aaa rating — for the period including the Great Depression, reflects the uncertainty over default rates provoked by the extreme economic circumstances of that time.

The volatility of default rates has important implications for bond pricing. The returns investors earn on lower-rated debt must not only compensate them for the higher average risk of default, but also for the increased risk that the default rate could differ substantially from its historical average.

Volatility increases for cumulative default rates at horizons greater than one-year, with standard deviations for 10-year cumulative default rates being roughly three times higher than the one-year volatilities shown in Figure 10.19. However, while volatility tends to increase linearly with the default rate itself for investment-grade categories, for speculative-grade categories default rate standard deviations are significantly lower than the average cumulative default rates. Figure 10.20 plots 10-year cumulative default rates along with their standard deviations, for a representative period which covers 1920–1998 but excludes the post-WWII low default rate period where default rates near zero exert a downward bias on volatility calculations.

10.3   Debt Recoveries for Corporate Defaults and Bankruptcies

A critical aspect of a default or bankruptcy is the severity of the loss incurred. Eventually, most default resolutions provide debt holders with some amount of recovery, which may take the form of cash, other securities, or even a physical

Figure 10.20   Ten-Year Cumulative Default Rates & Volatilities, 1920–98*

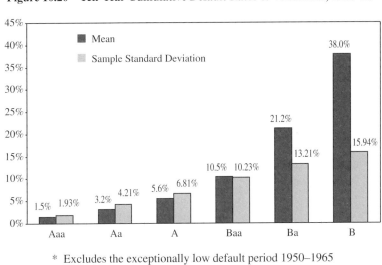

* Excludes the exceptionally low default period 1950–1965

asset. The recovery rate, defined as the percentage of par value returned to the bondholder, is a function of several variables. These variables include the seniority of the issue within the issuer's capital structure, the quality of collateral (if any), the overall state of the economy, and the market for corporate assets.

10.3.1   Default Severity and Recovery Rates

In this section, we use the trading price of the defaulted instrument as a proxy for the present value of the ultimate recovery. To do so, we collected from several sources prices for many of the bonds that defaulted between January 1, 1920, and December 31, 1998. For each defaulted issue, we considered the seniority, date of default, and the price approximately one month after default. Although this information provides only an estimate of the actual recovery, it has the advantage of being the definite measure of the recovery realized by those debtholders who liquidated a position soon after default.

We translate defaulted debt prices into recovery rate estimates by presenting them as percentages of par, not as percentages of original issue prices or accreted values. Investors are entitled to receive face value at maturity, even though they may have paid somewhat less or more for the bond either at issue or in the secondary market. Expressing recoveries as a fraction of some price other than par could improperly bias recovery rates. Because discount bonds and convertible bonds have unique pricing features, we have removed them from the sample.

The resulting data reveal correlations of recovery rates with macroeconomic variables and the risk of default. The lows in defaulted bond prices of US$21 and US$30 hit in 1932 and 1990, respectively, correspond to peaks in the corporate default rate, suggesting a negative correlation of defaulted bond prices with the incidence of default. Additionally, the low values during the late 1970s and early 1980s suggest a negative correlation with interest rates. Last year's average of US$45.02 is slightly above the long term average since 1970 of US$41.02. Defaulted bond price volatility has remained low since 1992, as shown in Figure 10.21, partly as a result of the development of deeper and more efficient markets for distressed debt instruments.

Figure 10.22 breaks out the average recovery estimates since 1970 by seniority of claim and includes Moody's estimate of the recovery investors can expect to receive on senior secured bank loans and preferred stock.[7] Recoveries, on average, decline as priority of claim declines, lending support to Moody's practise of assigning lower ratings to an issuer's subordinated debt. The average senior secured bank loan recovery estimate is US$70 per US$100 defaulted par amount. Considering prices for 118 senior secured bonds, our recovery estimate

**Figure 10.21   Yearly Average Defaulted Bond Prices, 1970–1998
(Per $100 Par Amount)**

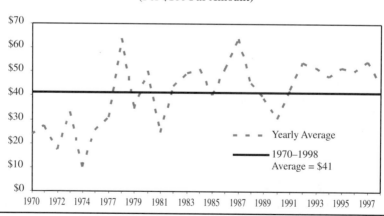

---

[7]   See Keenan, Sean C., Carty, Lea V., Shtogrin, Igor, and Fons, Jerome S., March 1998, "Moody's Preferred Stock Ratings and Credit Risk", Moody's Special Comment, and Carty, Lea V., Hamilton, David T., Keenan, Sean C., et. al., 1998, "Bankrupt Bank Loan Recoveries," Moody's Special Comment, June 1998

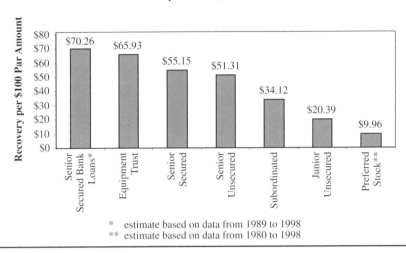

Figure 10.22   Defaulted Debt Recovery Estimates by Seniority and Security of Claim, 1997–1998

*   estimate based on data from 1989 to 1998
**   estimate based on data from 1980 to 1998

is US$55; prices for 338 senior unsecured bonds generate a recovery estimate of US$51. The 252 subordinated bonds sold for US$39 on average, while 19 junior subordinated bonds sold for US$20 on average. Preferred stock holders can only expect to retrieve about US$10 per US$100 par or liquidation value of defaulted preferred stock.

Over the past decade, about half of long-term public bond defaults resulted from bankruptcy filings, with missed payments accounting for about 43%, and distressed exchanges accounting for about 7%. However distressed exchange incidence has trended lower over recent years while missed payment incidence has trended higher, rising sharply during the past year. In 1998, payments were missed or delayed on 111 separate Moody's-rated issues or 62% of all defaulting rated issues, versus 24 for 46% in 1997. Because missed payments do not have the immediate and dramatic effect on prices that bankruptcy filings do, the sharp increase in the proportion of less severe default events in 1998 has helped to support average recovery estimates based on market prices for defaulted bonds. But, while default events that avoid immediate bankruptcy may bode well for post-default prices, ultimate recovery depends on whether or not the issuer can right his financial ship and either continue to make timely interest and principal payments on notes outstanding or re-negotiate a less burdensome debt package.

To gauge the likelihood of success for these issuers, we counted the number of missed payment and distressed exchange defaults by year, and grouped them by whether or not they filed for Chapter 11 within two years of the initial default

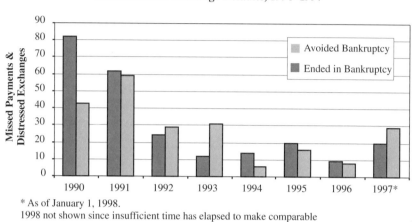

Figure 10.23   Resolution Within Two Years of Missed-Payment and Distressed Exchange Defaults, 1990–1997

* As of January 1, 1998.
1998 not shown since insufficient time has elapsed to make comparable

event. Figure 10.23 plots these resolutions and shows that, with the exceptions of 1990 where bankruptcy incidence was high and 1993 where bankruptcy incidence was low, roughly half of those issuers who miss or delay payments, or who negotiate distressed exchanges file for bankruptcy within two years of the initial default event.

Defaulted Bond Price Volatility

An additional important consideration in assessing recovery rates is the variability of defaulted bond prices. As shown in Figure 10.22, the average defaulted bond price for the 79-year period from 1920–1998 is US$41, although recovery values over various shorter time horizons vary significantly. The problem then with choosing averages as an indicator is that they approximate the most likely bond price to arise from a particular default, but they do not convey the range of possible outcomes. For example, while the estimated recovery for all subordinated bonds is US$34 per US$100 par amount, one of the underlying issues had a price of just US$1 while several had prices above par.

Equipment trust obligations have median post-default prices significantly higher than other debt classes. This reflects, in part, bankruptcy statutes that accelerate the transfer of assets pledged as security when those assets consist of transportation equipment, the main type of asset used to support equipment trust issues. Across debt types, median prices of defaulted bonds tend to fall as seniority declines, while variances first widen and then tighten. This pattern of greater variance on senior unsecured bonds reflects, in part, the greater number of defaults involving this type of bond relative to equipment trusts and junior subordinated bonds. It also suggests that although the more subordinated investor can expect to receive less in the event of default, there is less uncertainty as to how much the defaulted bond price will vary from its mean. Subordinated debt prices also exhibit a number of high value outliers, indicating that subordination by itself does not always lead to economic loss in the event of default.

Loss Rates

Moody's long-term debt ratings are statements about protections against credit loss. Conceptually, expected credit loss depends upon both the probability of a default occurring and the extent of the loss investors can expect to incur upon default. As Moody's ratings are designed to capture both default probability and severity, the credit loss one can expect to incur is higher for lower ratings.

By multiplying Moody's estimates of the risk of default by our estimate of the severity of loss for senior unsecured debt we can derive estimates of the credit losses historically associated with each rating category. Figure 10.24 presents these estimates using both the 1920–1998 and 1970–1997 average default rates and the 1989–1997 average recovery rate estimate for senior unsecured debt. (The 51% recovery rate implies a 49% loss rate.)

Figure 10.24 indicates that expected credit loss increases dramatically as Moody's credit opinion slips from investment-grade to speculative-grade. The safest speculative-grade rating category, Ba, has generated more than four times the credit loss of the riskiest investment-grade rating category, Baa.

Figure 10.24   Average One-Year Loss Rates

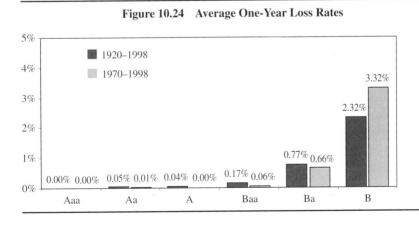

10.3.2   Measuring Realized Recoveries

In this section we analyze recoveries for financial instruments and claims on firms that have undergone formal bankruptcy proceedings. The distinction between bankruptcy and default is an important one. Bankruptcy (effectively Chapter 11s) is a subset of the broader class of corporate defaults, and is an objectively defined state in that the beginning and ending dates are clearly defined by the legal process. The time over which a financial obligation may be considered to be in default is, on the other hand, often only subjectively defined.[8]

Relying on market prices as recovery indicators (as above) does not allow us to describe the timing, value, and nature of debtholders' realized recoveries. This section concerns the recoveries actually experienced by a sample of corporate obligations. It analyzes the value (as of the date of emergence from bankruptcy) of actual payouts associated with the bankruptcy's resolution.

The difficulties associated with this approach are significant. Bankruptcy resolutions often satisfy creditor claims with a variety of debt, equity, derivative, or other claims and assets, many of which have no active secondary market in which the payments' true values can be discovered. Because the payment amount, type, and the maturity of bankruptcy claims is uncertain, accurate modeling of the instruments' values is also difficult. These difficulties do not, however, neutralize the value of the research, and the need persists for a more complete understanding of the bankruptcy resolution process and its effects on corporate obligations.

The recovery rate in this study is defined as the value of the payout to each obligation in accordance with the resolution of the firm's bankruptcy presented as a fraction of the obligation's pre-petition claim amount. The two primary components required to calculate these recovery rates are: 1) prepetition par value and accrued interest and dividends; and, 2) the value, nature and timing of any distribution returned to the creditor.

Prepetition par value, accrued interest and dividends. In researching the first component, which includes the face value of the claim plus any pre- and post-bankruptcy accrued interest and dividends, we consulted a number of sources. These include reorganization plan summaries, Moody's proprietary documents taken from our library of financial reports, press releases, press clippings,

---

[8]   Consider for example, the case of a distressed exchange default. While the date of the exchange qualifies as the end date of the default, the beginning date — the date the distress began — can only be determined subjectively

internal memoranda and our proprietary database of defaults and bankruptcies. We also examined Securities and Exchange Commission documents.

Value, nature and timing of distributions. The second component can be obtained only more subjectively because actual prices for many resolution payments are not available. Payments awarded to each creditor class varied widely across reorganizations and included such financial instruments as cash, debt, equity, derivatives, and enhancements to the terms of any surviving liability. Moody's was able to document the nature and timing of a majority of these instruments, but valuing them required additional subjective analysis.

We used a number of approaches to value these items as consistently as possible across each bankruptcy resolution in our sample. Moody's preferred approach to valuing debt instruments is to rely on market pricing after the bankruptcy's resolution. Our primary sources for obtaining equity, preferred, warrant, and debt prices were Bloomberg, IDC, Citibank, Goldman Sachs, BDS Securities, Lehman Brothers, Merrill Lynch, Loan Pricing Corporation, the borrower's financial statements, and the libraries of certain domestic stock exchanges. When possible, we took prices as of the borrower's exit date from bankruptcy. However, when a quote was not available immediately after the borrower had exited bankruptcy, we discounted the price of the new security by the total return of an applicable market benchmark.

In cases where reliable pricing was not available, we used a discounted cash flow approach to value certain distributions. Moody's recognizes the limitations of this approach and used it only to value new or amended debt instruments. To derive the discount rate, we used an historical Moody's rating or an estimated rating (based on a Moody's analyst's opinion of the reorganized borrower's credit quality) on the new or amended security. The discount rate was the median yield for similarly rated debt instruments in the market at the time.

In certain cases, Moody's valued some payments based on appraisals by Moody's analysts and independent, qualified agents. While acknowledging the subjectivity and limitations of this technique, we believe that our expertise in securities analysis and the bankruptcy process limits any distortions introduced and enables us to conduct a meaningful study of loan recoveries.

10.3.3 Data Set

This section is based on a data set of 829 financial obligations associated with the 159 bankruptcy cases of 155 borrowers.[9] All but one of the firms in our

---

[9] Four of the companies included in our sample filed for bankruptcy twice

sample are large, US-domiciled, public corporations.[10] Eighteen companies' debt financing is entirely private. Figure 10.25 summarizes the industrial cross-section of the firms in the sample. Industrials, retailers and consumer products companies accounted for 60%. No other single industry accounted for more than 9% of the sample, a pattern that is roughly consistent with Moody's database of bond defaults in the same period.

The bankruptcies we analyzed cover, for the most part, the second half of the 1980s, the recession of the early 1990s (and the coincident junk bond market crash) as well as the boom years since. Figure 10.26 shows that the majority of bankruptcies occurred in the early 1990s. Most borrowers filed for regular Chapter 11 protection, though a significant portion, 27%, filed prepackaged Chapter 11s. The earliest bankruptcy in this sample is UNR Industries' July 2, 1982 Chapter 11 filing. The most recent is Payless Cashways, Inc.'s July 21, 1997 Chapter 11.

Figure 10.26 also highlights the increased popularity of prepackaged Chapter 11s since the early 1990s. Prepackaged Chapter 11 bankruptcy filings are an expedited form of the standard Chapter 11 bankruptcy in which debtor and creditors negotiate and develop a plan before filing a bankruptcy case. The bankruptcy petition is then filed, the resolution plan proposed, and typically the plan is confirmed with less time and expense than a standard Chapter 11.

Figure 10.25   Bankruptcies by Industry

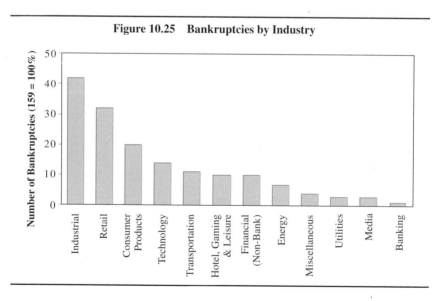

---

[10] The exception is Memorex Telex, based in the Netherlands

Figure 10.26 Bankruptcy Count by Year, 1982–1997

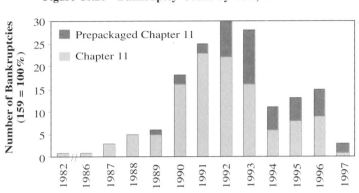

This pattern is consistent with the observations of Chatterjee, Dhillon, and Ramirez,[11] who suggest that in the early 1990s, prepackaged bankruptcies solved the problem of choosing between a formal Chapter 11 proceeding and an informal workout. Chapter 11 has the benefits of protecting debtors from creditors, but is expensive. Informal workouts, while less costly, are marred by collective action problems.[12] The 1990 Revenue Reconciliation Act made them even less attractive by making income realized from debt forgiveness taxable. Prepackaged bankruptcies take advantage of the Chapter 11 process to mitigate the holdout problem and of pre-filing negotiations to speed the process to completion, thus limiting costs.

The composition of the sample broken out by debt type is presented in Figure 10.27. Public corporate bonds comprise the majority of the sample, 46% on an issue count basis and 60% as a percentage of the total claim amount.[13] Bank loans make up 24% of the sample both as a percentage of issues and as a percentage of total claim amount. Private placements represent 19% and 9% of the sample as a percentage of the total number of issues and claim amount,

---

[11] Chatterjee, Sris, Dhillon, Upinder S., and Ramirez, Gabriel G., 1996, "Resolution of Financial Distress: Debt Restructurings via Chapter 11, Prepackaged Bankruptcies, and Workouts," *Financial Management*, Vol. 25, No. 1, Spring 1996, p. 5–18, and July 1995, "Coercive Tender and Exchange Offers in High Yield Debt Restructurings: An Empirical Analysis," *Journal of Financial Economics*.

[12] For example, in a workout involving a tender, tendering bondholders bear the cost of selling their bonds at a discount while non-tendering bondholders enjoy the benefits of the restructuring through higher prices for their bonds

[13] Claim amounts include accrued pre- and post-petition (where allowed) interest and dividends in addition to the principal due

Figure 10.27   Sample Obligation Types

Debt Type	Count	Total Claim (US$ Billions)	Percent of Total Count	Total Claim
Corporate Bonds	381	45.7	46.0	59.7
Bank Loans	195	17.9	23.5	23.4
Private Placements	153	6.9	18.5	9.0
Preferred Stock	79	5.0	9.5	6.5
Trade Claims	21	1.0	2.5	1.4
Total	829	$76.5	100.0%	100.0%

respectively. Together, the 82 preferred stock claims and 21 trade claims account for 12% of the financial obligations analyzed in this study, or about 8% of the total claim amount.

10.3.4   Characteristics of Bankruptcy Resolutions

Our analysis of bankruptcy recoveries proceeds on two levels: at the firm level and at the obligation level. Some aspects of bankruptcy occur only at the firm level; the choice of bankruptcy type and bankruptcy duration are obvious examples, which we explore in the first section. The composition of bankruptcy resolutions, which occupies our interest in the second section, is necessarily examined at the obligation level.

Bankruptcy Type and Duration

The length of time that a bankruptcy takes to resolve is a critical aspect of recovery. The workout process imposes direct and indirect costs on a bankrupt firm's claimants. Direct costs, such as legal fees, reduce creditors' payout, and these costs increase with the duration of the bankruptcy. Furthermore, the longer the workout period, the greater the cost to unsecured debtholders whose claims to interest typically do not accrue during the course of a bankruptcy. Even secured debtholders are not always paid post-petition interest, although it may accrue during the course of the bankruptcy to the extent that the underlying collateral is deemed adequate. Hence, even if the debtholders are confident that their claim will be satisfied, the uncertain timing of settlement may limit the appeal of bankrupt debt to many investors, especially those seeking current income.

Prepackaged Chapter 11 filings attempt to lower these costs in part by shortening the length of bankruptcy through a pre-negotiated plan. If prepackaged Chapter 11 cases are successful at this, then the duration of bankruptcy for "prepacks" should be less than for standard Chapter 11 cases, everything else equal, and the corresponding costs lower.

Overall, the shortest workout period for the bankruptcies in our sample is a little over one month for the prepackaged Chapter 11 of Vista Properties, Inc. The maximum is just over 7 years for UNR Industries, and the average is about one year and 8 months. The median duration of bankruptcy is a slightly lower eighteen months.[14]

Figure 10.28   Descriptive Statistics for the Length of Time Spent in Bankruptcy

Bankruptcy Type	Count	Average (yrs)	Median (yrs)	Minimum (yrs)	Maximum (yrs)	Standard Deviation (yrs)
Chapter 11	116	1.68	1.43	0.19	7.01	1.20
Prepackaged Chapter 11	43	0.29	0.18	0.09	1.76	0.29
All	159	1.30	1.15	0.09	7.01	1.20

The distribution of time to recovery varies in the expected way with the bankruptcy type. Prepackaged bankruptcies require less time on average to resolve, about 3.5 months, compared to 1.7 years on average for regular Chapter 11 filings (almost 6 times longer).

Furthermore, the distribution of resolution times varies more widely for Chapter 11 filings than for Prepackaged Chapter 11s. The longest time any of the borrowers that filed for a prepackaged Chapter 11 spent in bankruptcy is one year nine months, compared to seven years for Chapter 11 filers. Another measure of a distribution's dispersion is the standard deviation, which is much greater for Chapter 11s (1.20 years) than for prepacks (0.29 years).

The Composition of Typical Bankruptcy Resolutions

Almost by definition, bankruptcy resolution requires the relaxation of the

---

[14] The average of the resolution times may overstate the amount of time one can expect a typical filing to take to resolve. This is because the distribution of times to resolution is necessarily truncated at zero. The median is a more reliable measure of the center of similarly skewed distributions' centers. In each case shown in Figure 10.28, the median length of time to resolution is less than the average reflecting this fact

current financial commitments of the firm.[15] Financial reorganization typically requires extending debt maturity, eliminating, diminishing, deferring, or otherwise modifying interest payable (e.g., making payment-in-kind), and diminishing the principal or replacing the claim with contracts that place less strain on the firm's short-term contractual cash flow (e.g., preferred stock, equity, warrants, right, options, or other derivative instruments).

Figures 29 and 30 summarize how often the bankruptcy claims of debt of differing security and type were resolved using various types of financial instruments. Claims may be paid with a variety of new securities, cash, or "other" payments; or claims could be cancelled outright. The "other" category is composed of various types of assets, including securing collateral or claims to income generated by future legal settlements. Figure 10.29 shows how often the claim type in the left-most column was satisfied by the payment type in the top row. Figure 10.30 shows how often asset claims were satisfied as a percentage of recovery value. For example, 35.9% of the claims of secured bank loans were satisfied with new bank loans (see the upper left corner of Figure 10.29). As a percentage of the recovery value, though, senior secured bank loans were satisfied with new bank loans 42.8% of the time (see the upper left corner of Figure 10.30).

Figure 10.29   Instrument Use in Bankruptcy Resolution

(Weighted by Recovery Instrument Type)

Claim Satisfied With:

Claim Type:	Bank Loans	Public Bonds	Private Debt	Trade Claims	Preferred Stock	Equity	Options	Other	Cash	Claim Cancelled*
Secured Bank Loans	35.9%	4.5%	3.7%	0.0%	0.4%	16.3%	1.6%	4.1%	33.5%	0.0%
Secured Public Bonds	3.4%	28.6%	4.1%	0.0%	3.4%	25.9%	2.0%	1.4%	31.3%	0.0%
Secured Private Placements	1.7%	14.3%	31.1%	0.0%	0.0%	26.9%	2.5%	5.9%	17.6%	0.0%
Unsecured Bank Loans	7.9%	7.9%	2.6%	0.0%	10.5%	23.7%	0.0%	2.6%	39.5%	5.3%
Unsecured Public Bonds	0.0%	14.9%	0.2%	0.0%	7.9%	42.3%	12.8%	2.5%	18.0%	1.4%
Unsecured Private Placements	0.9%	11.2%	1.7%	0.0%	6.0%	40.5%	12.9%	0.9%	20.7%	5.2%

---

[15] Exceptions could occur in cases where firms strategically file for court protection though financially solvent (e.g. Johns Manville)

Trade Claims	0.0%	0.0%	4.2%	8.3%	0.0%	29.2%	0.0%	0.0%	58.3%	0.0%
Preferred Stock	0.0%	2.2%	1.1%	0.0%	2.2%	46.1%	20.2%	2.2%	2.2%	23.6%

* Percentage of issues cancelled

Figure 10.30 Instrument Use in Bankruptcy Resolution

(Weighted by Recovery Value)

					Claim Satisfied With:					
Claim Type:	Bank Loans	Public Bonds	Private Debt	Trade Claims	Preferred Stock	Equity	Options	Other	Cash	Claim Cancelled*
Secured Bank Loans	42.8%	11.4%	8.1%	0.0%	0.0%	15.1%	0.2%	1.9%	20.4%	0.0%
Secured Public Bonds	2.4%	55.8%	4.8%	0.0%	2.0%	13.0%	0.0%	0.4%	21.5%	0.0%
Secured Private Placements	0.1%	7.1%	24.1%	0.0%	0.0%	10.4%	0.5%	0.2%	57.6%	0.0%
Unsecured Bank Loans	7.4%	44.3%	1.1%	0.0%	6.3%	8.9%	0.0%	0.3%	31.7%	5.3%
Unsecured Public Bonds	0.0%	41.3%	0.1%	0.0%	2.8%	36.4%	1.8%	0.6%	17.1%	1.4%
Unsecured Private Placements	0.1%	16.2%	0.0%	0.0%	0.8%	56.5%	2.1%	7.5%	16.8%	5.2%
Trade Claims	0.0%	0.0%	0.3%	6.9%	0.0%	41.0%	0.0%	0.0%	51.9%	0.0%
Preferred Stock	0.0%	0.8%	0.9%	0.0%	0.4%	25.9%	3.4%	64.1%	4.6%	23.6%

* Percentage of issues cancelled

Equity and equity-like assets, such as warrants and options, were more frequently used to satisfy claims further down the capital structure. Equity was used only 25.9% of the time to satisfy the claims of secured public bonds, compared with 46.1% for preferred stock claims. The use of equity is also strongly correlated with a claim's security. 42.3% of the unsecured public bond claims were paid in new equity securities. The same pattern holds for private debt. Secured private debt was paid in new equity only 26.9% of the time; this figure rises to 40.5% for senior unsecured private debt.

Security also plays an important role in the percentage of claims cancelled outright. Preferred stocks showed the highest cancellation rate, 23.6%. Secured claims and trade claims were not cancelled in our sample. The cancellation rate for unsecured claims, on the other hand, was not trivial. 5.3% of unsecured bank loans were cancelled outright, which is very close to the 5.2% cancellation rate for unsecured private debt. Unsecured public bonds showed a cancellation rate of only 1.4%, however.

The basic patterns we saw in Figure 10.29 also show up in Figure 10.30, with a few differences, however. Figure 10.30 shows that the value of some of the new assets paid to investors was, at times, large. We saw above that secured public bonds were paid with new public bonds 28.6% of the time. The value of those bonds causes this proportion to rise to 55.8%. Secured private placements, 17.6% whose claim was paid in cash on a issue count basis, took a much larger 57.6% share as a percentage of total recovery value.

10.3.5 Recovery Rates

Several factors affect bankrupt debt recovery rates including bankruptcy timing, bankruptcy type, and obligation seniority and security. Bankruptcy duration and bankruptcy type affect overall firm-level recoveries. For instance, during an economic recession we would expect all claims in a firm's capital structure to receive lower recoveries than they might during an economic boom. In the following analyses we use the weighted-average firm-level recovery rate. The firm-level recovery is a claim value-weighted average of the recoveries of each issue belonging to the firm. For the 829 debt obligation claims in our sample, we derive 159 firm-level recovery rates.

Average firm-level recovery rates fluctuate over time, as seen in Figure 10.31, which plots the average firm-level recovery rates by the year of bankruptcy resolution. Average firm-level recovery rates have range from a low of 42.0% in 1994, to a high of 74.1% in 1989. Firm-level recovery rates for the 1995–97 period are well above the 55.9% average for the sample period. In 1998, however, firm-level recovery rates fell precipitously to 31.5% as high-yield spreads widened and investor sentiment on risky debt turned bearish in the wake of Russia's default on various domestic currency debts.

Figure 10.32 displays the distribution of our sample of firm-level recovery rates. Recovery rates range from a low of essentially 0% for Grand Union Capital Corp. to a high of 131.9% for TIE/Communications, Inc.[16] The average firm-level recovery rate is 56.7%; the median firm-level recovery rate is very close to the average rate at 56.0%. The standard deviation of the distribution is 29.3%, indicating a high dispersion of firm-level recovery rates.

---

[16] Recovery rates over 100% are possible. Consider the following example. A claim to a high coupon yield bond which is realized over a period of falling interest rates, and for which post-petition interest accrues, will be worth more than par upon the resolution of bankruptcy

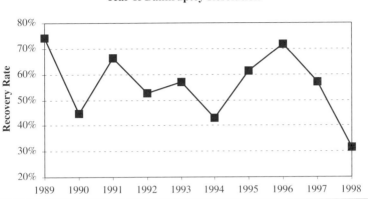

Figure 10.31   Firm-Level Recovery Rates by Year of Bankruptcy Resolution

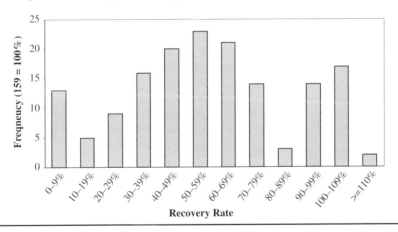

Figure 10.32   Weighted-Average Firm-Level Recovery Rate Distribution

The most notable and important feature of the distribution is the high concentration of recoveries in the lowest and the highest categories. Thirteen firms (8.2%) in our sample emerged from bankruptcy worth less than 10% of their pre-petition value, while 19 (11.9%) survived bankruptcy to emerge at 100% of its pre-petition value or higher. Moreover, these extreme values lie within the 95th percentile, and so do not represent outliers (see Figure 10.34 below for more).

The shape of the distribution implies that firm-level recovery rates can fall into one of three regimes: the extremely low (less than 10%) with low likelihood; the "normal" (between 10% and 89%) occurring most often; and, the extremely high (90% or greater), also with low likelihood.

Some of the variance of the distribution above is correlated to the capital structures of the firms. Presumably, the costs of bankruptcy are positively correlated to the complexity of a firm's capital structure. Conceptually, a large and fractious group of bond holders can be expected to incur greater costs in overcoming their conflicts than can a smaller more homogeneous group of private creditors. With this idea in mind, we form a proxy for capital structure complexity by constructing a dummy variable that signals whether a firm had any public, wholesale debt financing. If so, we consider the firm's capital structure to be complex.

We find that median firm-level recovery rates vary with our proxy for capital structure complexity in the expected manner. Figure 10.33 plots the distribution of firm-level recovery rates for firms funded purely with private debt against the distribution of recovery rates for firms that issued at least some public debt. When compared in this way, we find that the private/public nature of the firm exerts a strong influence on the distribution of firm-level recoveries, and explains much of the overall distribution of firm-level recoveries in Figure 10.32. The median firm-level recovery rate for firms with entirely private wholesale debt financing is 82.6% (78.4% average) — much higher than the public/private firms' 50.6% median recovery rate (50.4% average).

**Figure 10.33   Firm-Level Recovery Rates Distribution
(Firms with No Public Debt versus Those with Some Public Debt)**

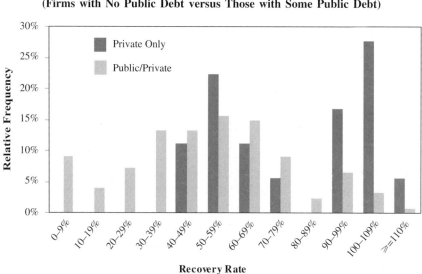

Recovery Rate

Figure 10.34   Firm-Level Recovery Rates by Bankruptcy Type

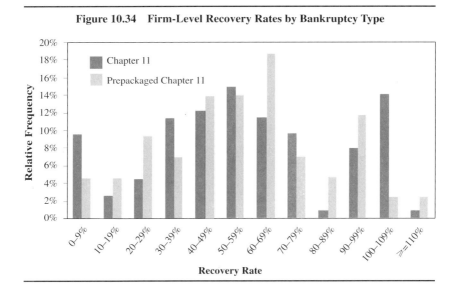

We noted above that prepackaged Chapter 11 cases are filed in an attempt to mitigate bankruptcy costs. If this strategy is successful, we should observe higher median and/or average firm-level recovery rates for firms that file prepackaged Chapter 11 cases than for Chapter 11 filers. Figure 10.34 plots these distributions. Although the distribution of firm-level recovery rates for prepackaged Chapter 11 cases appears to be slightly skewed toward higher recovery rates, closer analysis of the characteristics of the distributions reveals that there is no material difference between prepacks and standard Chapter 11s.

The median firm-level recovery rate for prepackaged Chapter 11s is 55.6%, slightly less than the 56.1% recovery rate for Chapter 11 filers. The difference in the average firm level recovery rates between prepacks and Chapter 11s is even smaller, 56.1% and 56.9% respectively. The dispersion in the distributions are also very close. The standard deviation of firm-level recovery rates for prepackaged Chapter 11 cases is 28.6%, 1.1% less than Chapter 11's 29.7% standard deviation.

The section above analyzed how firm-level factors, such as bankruptcy type and the public/private debt composition affect firm-level recoveries. We now turn our attention to the distributions of recovery rates at the obligation level. At this level, the most important factors affecting the recovery rate are the seniority and security of the claim. Figure 10.35 presents box plots for the distributions of recovery rates by seniority and security.

The patterns demonstrated in Figure 10.35 corroborate Moody's findings using recovery rates based on market prices in the previous section. As expected, an obligation's position in the capital structure of a bankrupt firm has a direct effect on its recovery rate: the more senior and secure an issue, the higher its recovery rate.

There is a smooth, monotonic relationship between median and average recovery rates and seniority/security. Senior and secured obligations' median recovery rate is 100%, or 84.3% on average. The median recovery rate falls to 85.6% (70.1% average) for senior unsecured obligations, 37% (43.1% average) for senior subordinated assets, 18.7% (25.3% average) for subordinated, and 5.8% (18% average) for junior subordinated obligations. Trade claims generated a relatively high median recovery rate of 92% (74% average), falling between the median recovery rates for senior secured and senior unsecured obligations. Preferred stock's median recovery, on the lowest rung of the capital structure ladder in our sample, was only 2.2%, or 11.6% on average.

Across seniority/security types, the dispersion of recovery rates (as measured by the inter-quartile range, and ignoring outliers) tends to first widen then contract as seniority declines. For senior secured assets, not only is the median recovery rate high, but the probability that the recovery rate of a particular obligation will differ from the median is relatively low. For preferred stocks, the distribution is also tightly centered around the median, implying that it is a

Figure 10.35   Recovery Rate Distributions by Seniority/Security

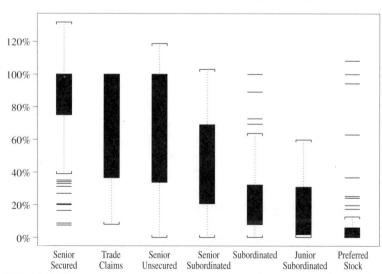

relatively reliable estimate of the recovery value for a particular asset drawn from that class at random. Senior unsecured and senior subordinated bonds exhibit much more variability in their recoveries.

The more senior and secured the claim, the more highly skewed the distribution toward high recovery rates. Similarly, the lower the priority of the claim in the capital structure, the distributions become more skewed toward lower recovery values. Senior subordinated claims, in the middle of the capital structure for the priorities we are analyzing, have a distribution of recovery rates that is most symmetric.

Recovery rates sometimes deviate substantially from their expected value. The outliers in the plot for senior secured claims shows that in rare instances (statistically speaking less than 5% of the time) senior secured claims have recovery rates as low as 7.5% (EUA Power Company). The converse is true for preferred stocks. In a few rare instances, recovery rates for preferred stock claims have been as high as 108% (Standard Brands Paint Co.).

The Relative Value of Seniority and Security in Bankruptcy

While the findings presented above are useful in confirming conventional wisdom, they only imprecisely address the value of seniority and security because the particular circumstances of individual bankruptcies were not controlled. In order to accurately quantify the value — in terms of recovery — of moving up or down a given firm's capital structure we must control for the circumstances of each bankruptcy, and compare realized recoveries for claims of differing seniorities and securities for the same bankruptcy.

Figure 10.36 summarizes the average differences between the recovery rates of debt obligations of the same bankrupt firm, but of different levels of seniority and security within the firm's capital structure. To derive this matrix, we first averaged the recovery rates of each obligation for each seniority/ security grouping and bankruptcy, producing 159 matrices — one for each case. Figure 10.36 represents the component-wise average of the differences between the most senior and secured claim class and each other for the 159 individual matrices. The cells in Figure 10.36 show the average difference in recovery between the row seniority/security type and the column seniority/security type. For example, senior unsecured claims (second row) recovered 21.3% less — in absolute recovery — than senior secured claims (first column), on average.

The table tells a compelling story about the importance seniority and security plays in the recovery debtholders can expect to receive. Average recovery rates decrease rapidly as one moves down in seniority/security. For example, senior

Figure 10.36   Average Absolute Recovery Rate Differences For Bankrupt Debt Obligations of the Same Obligor

	Sr. Secured	Sr. Unsecured	Sr. Subordinated	Subordinated	Jr. Subordinated	Preferred Stock
Senior Secured	0.0%					
Senior Unsecured	−21.3%	0.0%				
Senior Subordinated	−43.4%	−27.2%	0.0%			
Subordinated	−58.0%	−39.2%	−22.9%	0.0%		
Junior Subordinated	−67.4%	−56.3%	−21.1%	−11.6%	0.0%	
Preferred Stock	−72.9%	−52.0%	−38.5%	−17.4%	−9.5%	0.0%

unsecured claims recover 21.3% less than senior secured claims. The difference doubles one level lower: senior subordinated claims recover 43.4% less than senior secured claims. Preferred stock, at the bottom of the seniority/security hierarchy in our sample, recovered 72.9% less than senior secured claims.

In Figure 10.37, we see the effects of seniority and security on relative recovery rates. This matrix was constructed in a way similar to that of Figure 10.37, which showed absolute differences in recovery. Rather than the row recovery rate minus the column recovery rate, this table shows the row recovery rate divided by the column recovery rate.[17] Senior secured debts' (first row) average recovery relative to itself (first column) is by construction, 100%; senior unsecured debts' average recovery relative to senior secured debt is 76.3%. That is, senior unsecured debt recovered 76.3% of the value of senior secured debt on average.

Figure 10.37 shows that relative recovery rates are somewhat stable. That is, the recovery of senior subordinated debt relative to senior secured debt is comparable to the recovery of subordinated debt relative to senior unsecured debt. This, in turn, is similar to the recovery of junior subordinated debt relative to senior subordinated debt. A similar pattern holds for the recoveries of subordinated debt relative to senior secured, junior subordinated relative to senior unsecured, and preferred stock relative to senior subordinated debt.

---

[17]   Relative recovery rates where the denominator is zero were set to 100%.
Historical Default Rates 3

Figure 10.37   Average Relative Recovery Rates For Bankrupt Debt Obligations of the Same Obligor

	Sr. Secured	Sr. Unsecured	Sr. Subordinated	Subordinated	Jr. Subordinated	Preferred Stock
Senior Secured	100.0%					
Senior Unsecured	76.3%	100.0%				
Senior Subordinated	49.7%	58.2%	10.0%			
Subordinated	30.7%	45.9%	56.6%	100.0%		
Junior Subordinated	26.8%	34.7%	53.9%	63.5%	100.0%	
Preferred Stock	13.2%	10.9%	24.1%	20.2%	37.2%	100.0%

Figure 10.37 also indicates that large-sample average recovery rates may not yield accurate estimates of the relative value of seniority, particularly for more junior claims. For example, the full sample average recovery rate for preferred stock is 12%, while it is 25% and 18% for subordinated and junior subordinated claims respectively. Hence, the recovery rate of preferred stock relative to subordinated and junior subordinated bonds is 46% and 64%. However, once we control for the circumstances of each particular bankruptcy, as in Figure 10.37, we see that preferred stock's recovery relative to subordinated and junior subordinated bonds is much lower at just 20% and 37% respectively. Similarly, not considering the circumstances of each bankruptcy may lead to over estimation of the recovery rate of subordinated and junior subordinated bonds relative to senior unsecured bonds.

10.4   Summary

Our estimation of both the likelihood and the severity of default permits the estimation of the default losses that have historically been associated with each of our ratings. Over the post-1970 period, default rates and average default losses increase with lower rating categories, reaching averages of 6.47% default rate and 3.32% loss rate for the single B category. Average default rates increase smoothly even when measured over numerically modified ratings from 1983-1998. Finally, the comparability of default rates over long and short time horizons is evidence that Moody's has consistently differentiated debt on the basis of the credit risks facing investors for the better part of this century.

Default rate volatility also increases with lower rating categories, with the standard deviation of one-year default rates ranging from zero for the Aaa category to about 5% for the B category. These volatilities have been quite stable over long time horizons.

Our results on recovery rates also broadly support Moody's practise of making rating distinctions between different debt obligations of the same company based on factors such as seniority and security. Average prices for defaulted debt vary with the seniority and security of the instrument and have varied considerably over time. Since 1992, however, average defaulted bond prices have been fairly stable, hovering slightly above their post-1970 average of US$41 per US$100 par value.

Our research also sheds new light on the importance of a claim's position in the capital structure on the type and amount of payout it is likely to receive at the bankruptcy resolution date. The higher an obligation's position in the firm's capital structure, the more likely it is to receive new assets of at least the same priority as the prepetition claim or cash. Similarly, claims lowest in the capital structure were more likely to receive contingent assets, such as new equity or warrants.

Capital structure complexity (public/private debt composition of the firm) explains much of the variation in the distribution of firm-level recoveries. The median recovery rate for a firm funded entirely with private debt is significantly higher than that for a firm with both public and private debt. Bankruptcy type was not found to have a significant impact on firm-level recovery rates.

Recovery rates at the obligation level were found to increase smoothly with seniority and security. Relative recovery rates — the value of moving up or down a firm's capital structure — were also found to increase smoothly with seniority and security.

10.4.1 Footnote

The data underlying the results of this chapter and Chapter 11 are available from Moody's Investors Service. Moody's *Corporate Bond Default Database* provides you access to our ratings and default/recovery experience, the largest and most comprehensive in the world. It gives you the power to measure credit risk and credit quality correlations by their most significant determinants — rating, geography, industry and time frame. And you can use it independently or to supprot any software program you're currently using. In addition, with our

Corporate Bond Default Database, you also have access to our Credit Risk Management Services Group. In other words, you can work with the Moody's people who know and understand the database, which is a distillation of Moody's rating experience.

To learn more about Moody's *Corporate Bond Default Database* and related Default Risk Services, call Steven Liebling in New York, 212-553-4052, or Francesso Faiola in London, 44-171-772-5328.

Figure 10.38   One-Year Default Rates by Year and Letter Rating, 1970-1998 (Percent)

Rating	1970	1971	1972	1973	1974	1975	1976	1977	1978	1979	1980	1981	1982	1983	1984
Aaa	0.00	0.00	0.00	0.00	0.00	0.00	0.00	0.00	0.00	0.00	0.00	0.00	0.00	0.00	0.00
Aa	0.00	0.00	0.00	0.00	0.00	0.00	0.00	0.00	0.00	0.00	0.00	0.00	0.00	0.00	0.00
A	0.00	0.00	0.00	0.00	0.00	0.00	0.00	0.00	0.00	0.00	0.00	0.00	0.26	0.00	0.00
Baa	0.27	0.00	0.00	0.45	0.00	0.00	0.00	0.27	0.00	0.00	0.00	0.00	0.30	0.00	0.36
Ba	4.12	0.42	0.00	0.00	0.00	1.02	1.01	0.52	1.08	0.49	0.00	0.00	2.73	0.91	0.83
B	23.38	4.00	7.41	3.92	10.34	6.15	0.00	3.39	5.56	0.00	5.06	4.60	2.41	6.36	6.78
Investment-Grade	0.14	0.00	0.00	0.23	0.00	0.00	0.00	0.11	0.00	0.00	0.00	0.00	0.21	0.00	0.09
Speculative-Grade	9.12	1.11	1.88	1.24	1.31	1.74	0.88	1.35	1.79	0.42	1.61	0.70	3.54	3.82	3.32
US Only Speculative-grade	9.72	1.52	1.94	1.28	1.36	1.79	0.89	1.36	1.80	0.42	1.62	0.71	3.58	3.90	3.40
All Corporates	2.72	0.28	0.45	0.45	0.27	0.36	0.17	0.35	0.35	0.09	0.34	0.16	1.02	0.95	0.91

Rating	1985	1986	1987	1988	1989	1990	1991	1992	1993	1994	1995	1996	1997	1998
Aaa	0.00	0.00	0.00	0.00	0.00	0.00	0.00	0.00	0.00	0.00	0.00	0.00	0.00	0.00
Aa	0.00	0.00	0.00	0.00	0.61	0.00	0.00	0.00	0.00	0.00	0.00	0.00	0.00	0.00
A	0.00	0.00	0.00	0.00	0.00	0.00	0.00	0.00	0.00	0.00	0.00	0.00	0.00	0.00
Baa	0.00	1.33	0.00	0.00	0.60	0.00	0.28	0.00	0.00	0.00	0.00	0.00	0.00	0.12
Ba	1.75	2.05	2.72	1.24	2.98	3.32	5.25	0.30	0.55	0.23	0.67	0.00	0.19	0.61
B	8.28	11.80	5.86	6.02	9.17	16.11	14.66	9.00	5.76	3.81	4.84	1.45	2.10	4.08
Investment-Grade	0.00	0.32	0.00	0.00	0.28	0.00	0.07	0.00	0.00	0.00	0.00	0.00	0.00	0.04
Speculative-Grade	3.90	5.67	4.10	3.47	6.02	9.80	10.45	4.83	3.50	1.93	3.30	1.66	2.02	3.31
US Only Speculative-grade	4.24	5.82	4.04	3.77	5.75	9.85	10.53	5.13	3.84	2.07	3.65	1.92	2.14	3.84
All Corporates	1.06	1.89	1.44	1.31	2.42	3.51	3.29	1.33	0.96	0.57	1.07	0.54	0.68	1.27

Figure 10.39 One-Year Default Rates by Year and Alpha-Numeric Rating, 1983-1998 (Percent)

	1983	1984	1985	1986	1987	1988	1989	1990	1991	1992	1993	1994	1995	1996	1997	1998
Aaa	0.00	0.00	0.00	0.00	0.00	0.00	0.00	0.00	0.00	0.00	0.00	0.00	0.00	0.00	0.00	0.00
Aa1	0.00	0.00	0.00	0.00	0.00	0.00	0.00	0.00	0.00	0.00	0.00	0.00	0.00	0.00	0.00	0.00
Aa2	0.00	0.00	0.00	0.00	0.00	0.00	0.00	0.00	0.00	0.00	0.00	0.00	0.00	0.00	0.00	0.00
Aa3	0.00	0.00	0.00	0.00	0.00	0.00	1.40	0.00	0.00	0.00	0.00	0.00	0.00	0.00	0.00	0.00
A1	0.00	0.00	0.00	0.00	0.00	0.00	0.00	0.00	0.00	0.00	0.00	0.00	0.00	0.00	0.00	0.00
A2	0.00	0.00	0.00	0.00	0.00	0.00	0.00	0.00	0.00	0.00	0.00	0.00	0.00	0.00	0.00	0.00
A3	0.00	0.00	0.00	0.00	0.00	0.00	0.00	0.00	0.00	0.00	0.00	0.00	0.00	0.00	0.00	0.00
Baa1	0.00	0.00	0.00	0.00	0.00	0.00	0.00	0.00	0.76	0.00	0.00	0.00	0.00	0.00	0.00	0.00
Baa2	0.00	0.00	0.00	0.00	0.00	0.00	0.80	0.00	0.00	0.00	0.00	0.00	0.00	0.00	0.00	0.33
Baa3	0.00	1.06	0.00	4.82	0.00	0.00	1.07	0.00	0.00	0.00	0.00	0.00	0.00	0.00	0.00	0.00
Ba1	0.00	1.16	0.00	0.88	3.73	0.00	0.80	2.69	1.07	0.00	0.81	0.00	0.00	0.00	0.00	0.00
Ba2	0.00	1.61	1.63	1.21	0.96	0.00	1.82	2.74	0.00	0.00	0.00	0.59	0.00	0.00	0.00	0.58
Ba3	2.61	0.00	3.77	3.44	2.95	2.58	4.69	3.90	9.73	0.73	0.75	1.93	1.71	0.00	0.47	1.09
B1	0.00	5.84	4.38	7.61	4.93	4.34	6.24	8.59	6.04	1.03	3.32	1.93	4.43	1.19	0.00	2.09
B2	11.11	20.00	7.69	16.67	4.30	6.90	8.16	21.82	12.58	1.54	4.96	3.61	6.31	0.00	1.48	7.16
B3	17.91	2.90	13.86	16.07	8.89	9.59	19.40	28.93	28.42	24.24	11.29	7.84	4.10	3.38	7.49	5.48
Investment-Grade	0.00	0.09	0.00	0.32	0.00	0.00	0.28	0.00	0.07	0.00	0.00	0.00	0.00	0.00	0.00	0.04
Speculative-Grade	3.82	3.32	3.90	5.67	4.10	3.47	6.02	9.80	10.45	4.83	3.50	1.93	3.30	1.66	2.02	3.31
All Corporates	0.95	0.91	1.06	1.89	1.44	1.31	2.42	3.51	3.29	1.33	0.96	0.57	1.07	0.54	0.68	1.27

Figure 10.40   Average Cumulative Default Rates by Letter Rating From 1 to 20 Years (Percent) — 1970–1998

Rating	1	2	3	4	5	6	7	8	9	10	11	12	13	14	15	16	17	18	19	20
Aaa	0.00	0.00	0.00	0.04	0.14	0.24	0.35	0.47	0.61	0.77	0.94	1.13	1.35	1.47	1.59	1.73	1.88	2.05	2.05	2.05
Aa	0.03	0.04	0.09	0.23	0.36	0.50	0.64	0.80	0.91	0.99	1.08	1.18	1.30	1.56	1.63	1.72	1.92	2.04	2.17	2.32
A	0.01	0.06	0.20	0.35	0.50	0.68	0.85	1.05	1.29	1.55	1.81	2.09	2.35	2.56	2.86	3.19	3.52	3.86	4.24	4.45
Baa	0.12	0.38	0.74	1.24	1.67	2.14	2.67	3.20	3.80	4.39	5.04	5.71	6.35	7.02	7.72	8.46	9.19	9.88	10.44	10.89
Ba	1.29	3.60	6.03	8.51	11.10	13.37	15.20	17.14	18.91	20.63	22.50	24.54	26.55	28.21	29.86	31.70	33.28	34.66	35.88	36.99
B	6.47	12.77	18.54	23.32	27.74	31.59	35.04	37.97	40.70	43.91	45.98	47.25	48.53	49.69	51.07	52.20	52.90	52.90	52.90	52.90
Investment-Grade	0.05	0.15	0.33	0.58	0.81	1.06	1.34	1.63	1.94	2.27	2.62	2.99	3.35	3.72	4.10	4.52	4.95	5.36	5.73	5.99
Speculative-Grade	3.82	7.69	11.27	14.44	17.49	20.14	22.33	24.46	26.38	28.32	30.16	31.96	33.74	35.23	36.74	38.36	39.73	40.87	41.87	42.80
All Corporates	1.15	2.30	3.37	4.33	5.21	5.99	6.66	7.31	7.93	8.55	9.17	9.77	10.37	10.91	11.47	12.07	12.65	13.16	13.62	13.98

Figure 10.41 Average Cumulative Default Rates from 1 to 8 Years (Percent) — 1983–1998

	1	2	3	4	5	6	7	8
Aaa	0.00	0.00	0.00	0.07	0.22	0.30	0.40	0.53
Aa1	0.00	0.00	0.00	0.25	0.25	0.42	0.42	0.42
Aa2	0.00	0.00	0.07	0.23	0.50	0.61	0.74	0.89
Aa3	0.07	0.11	0.21	0.32	0.45	0.61	0.61	0.61
A1	0.00	0.03	0.37	0.59	0.75	0.93	1.01	1.10
A2	0.00	0.03	0.16	0.43	0.66	0.88	1.01	1.38
A3	0.00	0.15	0.28	0.38	0.45	0.60	0.88	0.99
Baa1	0.04	0.29	0.59	1.02	1.45	1.66	2.05	2.36
Baa2	0.08	0.28	0.41	0.85	1.29	1.84	2.24	2.40
Baa3	0.31	0.75	1.28	2.21	2.79	3.65	4.53	5.39
Ba1	0.64	2.14	3.77	6.11	8.45	10.93	12.63	14.30
Ba2	0.59	2.84	5.46	7.75	9.66	11.22	12.76	13.77
Ba3	2.55	6.95	11.76	16.38	20.76	24.66	28.40	32.39
B1	3.56	9.17	15.03	20.36	25.56	30.85	35.90	39.70
B2	6.85	13.83	19.85	24.78	28.52	31.34	32.93	34.34
B3	12.41	20.97	27.79	32.56	37.49	40.55	43.75	48.34
Caa1-C	18.31	25.94	31.38	35.76	38.30	42.79	42.79	47.37
Investment-Grade	0.04	0.15	0.32	0.59	0.82	1.06	1.27	1.47
Speculative-Grade	3.67	8.19	12.60	16.58	20.26	23.54	26.44	29.17
All Corporates	1.18	2.59	3.95	5.19	6.25	7.17	7.94	8.64

Figure 10.42   Cumulative Default Rates for Cohorts Formed Since 1970 (Percent)

Years:	1	2	3	4	5	6	7	8	9	10	11	12	13	14	15	16	17	18	19	20
Cohort formed January 1, 1970																				
Aaa	0.00	0.00	0.00	0.00	0.00	0.00	0.00	0.00	0.00	0.00	0.00	0.00	0.00	0.00	0.00	0.00	0.00	2.70	2.70	2.70
Aa	0.00	0.00	0.00	0.00	0.00	0.00	0.00	0.00	0.00	0.00	0.00	0.00	0.90	1.42	1.42	1.42	2.88	2.88	2.88	2.88
A	0.00	0.00	0.00	0.00	0.00	0.43	0.43	0.43	0.43	0.43	0.90	0.90	0.90	0.90	0.90	0.90	1.41	1.41	2.53	2.53
Baa	0.27	0.27	0.27	1.14	1.43	1.43	1.74	2.39	3.06	3.06	3.42	3.42	4.59	5.00	5.42	6.29	7.67	8.68	9.77	10.36
Ba	4.12	4.55	4.99	5.45	6.39	7.37	7.89	8.44	9.60	9.60	9.60	11.07	13.42	14.25	14.25	17.13	21.22	22.37	22.37	23.77
B	23.38	26.02	28.66	28.66	28.66	28.66	28.66	28.66	28.66	28.66	28.66	28.66	35.98	35.98	35.98	35.98	35.98	35.98	35.98	35.98
Investment-Grade	0.14	0.14	0.14	0.56	0.71	0.86	1.01	1.31	1.63	1.63	1.96	1.96	2.48	2.84	3.02	3.40	4.36	4.97	5.83	6.06
Speculative-Grade	9.12	10.16	11.96	12.70	13.47	14.28	14.70	15.59	16.53	16.53	16.53	17.69	20.79	21.45	21.45	23.69	26.92	27.83	27.83	28.95
All Corporates	2.72	3.02	3.52	4.03	4.35	4.67	4.89	5.35	5.81	5.81	6.07	6.33	7.41	7.83	7.97	8.71	10.09	10.74	11.43	11.80
Cohort formed January 1, 1971																				
Aaa	0.00	0.00	0.00	0.00	0.00	0.00	0.00	0.00	0.00	0.00	0.00	0.00	0.00	0.00	0.00	0.00	2.78	2.78	2.78	2.78
Aa	0.00	0.00	0.00	0.00	0.00	0.00	0.00	0.00	0.00	0.00	0.00	0.00	0.00	0.00	0.00	0.00	0.00	0.00	0.00	1.75
A	0.00	0.00	0.00	0.00	0.38	0.38	0.38	0.38	0.38	0.79	0.79	1.21	1.63	1.63	1.63	2.08	2.08	3.04	3.04	3.04
Baa	0.00	0.00	0.80	1.07	1.07	1.36	1.96	2.58	2.58	2.92	2.92	4.03	4.41	4.81	5.63	6.94	7.88	8.90	9.44	10.59
Ba	0.42	0.86	1.31	2.24	3.70	4.21	4.75	5.91	5.91	5.91	7.34	9.64	10.45	10.45	13.24	18.22	19.36	19.36	20.74	20.74
B	4.00	8.00	8.00	8.00	8.00	8.00	8.00	8.00	8.00	8.00	8.00	20.27	20.27	20.27	20.27	20.27	20.27	20.27	20.27	20.27
Investment-Grade	0.00	0.00	0.39	0.53	0.66	0.80	1.09	1.38	1.38	1.69	1.69	2.34	2.68	2.85	3.19	3.91	4.48	5.28	5.49	6.14
Speculative-Grade	1.11	3.02	3.82	4.64	5.93	6.38	7.34	8.35	8.35	8.35	9.59	12.92	13.63	13.63	16.03	20.33	21.30	21.30	22.50	22.50
All Corporates	0.28	0.77	1.26	1.56	1.98	2.19	2.63	3.08	3.08	3.32	3.58	4.75	5.16	5.29	6.01	7.33	7.96	8.63	8.98	9.53

Figure 10.42 (Cont'd)

Years:	1	2	3	4	5	6	7	8	9	10	11	12	13	14	15	16	17	18	19	20
Cohort formed January 1, 1972																				
Aaa	0.00	0.00	0.00	0.00	0.00	0.00	0.00	0.00	0.00	0.00	0.00	0.00	0.00	0.00	0.00	2.70	2.70	2.70	2.70	2.70
Aa	0.00	0.00	0.00	0.00	0.00	0.00	0.00	0.00	0.00	0.00	0.00	0.00	0.00	0.00	0.00	0.00	0.00	0.00	1.67	1.67
A	0.00	0.30	0.30	0.00	0.00	0.00	0.00	0.00	0.00	0.00	0.39	0.78	0.78	0.78	1.19	1.19	2.08	2.08	2.56	3.07
Baa	0.00	0.73	0.98	1.23	1.50	2.05	2.63	2.63	3.25	3.25	3.94	4.30	4.67	5.43	6.63	7.51	8.46	9.47	11.09	13.33
Ba	0.00	0.45	1.37	2.80	3.31	3.84	4.96	4.96	4.96	6.34	9.28	10.06	10.89	14.40	19.11	20.16	20.16	21.42	22.74	29.64
B	7.41	7.41	7.41	7.41	7.41	7.41	7.41	7.41	7.41	7.41	18.30	18.30	18.30	18.30	18.30	18.30	18.30	18.30	18.30	18.30
Investment-Grade	0.00	0.37	0.49	0.62	0.74	1.01	1.28	1.28	1.57	1.57	2.02	2.33	2.49	2.82	3.48	4.01	4.76	5.15	6.17	7.21
Speculative-Grade	1.88	2.66	3.47	4.73	5.17	6.10	7.08	7.08	7.08	8.26	12.04	12.71	13.43	16.47	20.54	21.45	21.45	22.55	23.72	29.88
All Corporates	0.45	0.92	1.20	1.59	1.79	2.20	2.62	2.62	2.85	3.09	4.19	4.57	4.82	5.62	6.86	7.45	8.07	8.56	9.60	11.37
Cohort formed January 1, 1973																				
Aaa	0.00	0.00	0.00	0.00	0.00	0.00	0.00	0.00	0.00	0.00	0.00	0.00	0.00	0.00	2.70	2.70	2.70	2.70	2.70	2.70
Aa	0.00	0.00	0.00	0.00	0.00	0.00	0.00	0.00	0.00	0.00	0.00	0.00	0.00	0.00	0.00	0.00	0.00	1.56	1.56	1.56
A	0.00	0.00	0.00	0.00	0.00	0.00	0.00	0.00	0.00	0.38	0.76	0.76	0.76	1.16	1.16	2.03	2.03	2.50	2.99	3.51
Baa	0.45	0.68	1.16	1.40	1.91	2.45	2.45	3.03	3.03	3.67	4.33	5.01	6.07	7.19	7.99	8.87	9.81	11.82	13.92	13.92
Ba	0.00	0.97	1.99	2.52	3.09	4.27	4.27	4.27	5.70	9.49	10.29	10.29	12.94	17.70	19.85	19.85	21.11	22.44	30.67	32.15
B	3.92	3.92	3.92	3.92	3.92	3.92	3.92	3.92	3.92	15.22	15.22	15.22	15.22	15.22	15.22	15.22	15.22	15.22	15.22	15.22
Investment-Grade	0.23	0.35	0.59	0.71	0.96	1.21	1.21	1.49	1.49	1.92	2.36	2.66	3.13	3.76	4.27	4.98	5.35	6.52	7.52	7.73
Speculative-Grade	1.24	2.10	3.00	3.47	4.46	5.49	5.49	5.49	6.73	11.31	12.00	12.00	14.34	18.54	20.42	20.42	21.55	22.76	30.29	31.63
All Corporates	0.45	0.73	1.10	1.30	1.70	2.11	2.11	2.33	2.56	3.74	4.23	4.47	5.25	6.45	7.15	7.76	8.23	9.40	11.28	11.65

Figure 10.42 (Cont'd)

Years:	1	2	3	4	5	6	7	8	9	10	11	12	13	14	15	16	17	18	19	20
Cohort formed January 1, 1974																				
Aaa	0.00	0.00	0.00	0.00	0.00	0.00	0.00	0.00	0.00	0.00	0.00	0.00	0.00	2.44	2.44	2.44	2.44	2.44	2.44	2.44
Aa	0.00	0.00	0.00	0.00	0.00	0.00	0.00	0.00	1.24	1.24	1.24	1.24	1.24	1.24	1.24	1.24	2.74	2.74	2.74	2.74
A	0.00	0.00	0.00	0.00	0.00	0.00	0.00	0.00	0.38	0.76	0.76	0.76	1.16	1.16	2.02	2.02	2.48	2.96	3.47	3.47
Baa	0.00	0.47	0.71	1.21	1.74	1.74	2.31	2.31	2.94	3.60	4.27	5.32	5.69	6.49	7.37	8.30	9.80	11.89	11.89	11.89
Ba	0.00	1.06	1.62	2.22	3.47	3.47	3.47	4.22	8.18	9.01	9.01	11.75	18.62	20.83	20.83	22.14	24.87	33.30	34.81	36.53
B	10.34	10.34	10.34	10.34	10.34	10.34	10.34	14.72	23.94	23.94	23.94	23.94	23.94	23.94	23.94	23.94	23.94	23.94	23.94	23.94
Investment-Grade	0.00	0.23	0.35	0.60	0.85	0.85	1.12	1.12	1.69	2.12	2.42	2.87	3.18	3.68	4.38	4.74	5.69	6.67	6.88	6.88
Speculative-Grade	1.31	2.23	2.71	3.73	4.79	4.79	4.79	6.06	10.74	11.46	11.46	13.85	19.85	21.77	21.77	22.93	25.41	33.20	34.59	36.15
All Corporates	0.27	0.65	0.84	1.23	1.64	1.64	1.86	2.09	3.37	3.86	4.10	4.86	6.05	6.75	7.35	7.82	8.96	10.82	11.18	11.37
Cohort formed January 1, 1975																				
Aaa	0.00	0.00	0.00	0.00	0.00	0.00	0.00	0.00	0.00	0.00	0.00	0.00	1.96	1.96	1.96	1.96	1.96	1.96	1.96	1.96
Aa	0.00	0.00	0.00	0.00	0.00	0.00	0.00	1.04	1.04	1.04	1.04	1.04	1.04	2.23	2.23	3.47	3.47	3.47	3.47	3.47
A	0.00	0.00	0.00	0.00	0.00	0.00	0.00	0.00	0.37	0.37	0.37	0.76	0.76	1.60	1.60	2.05	2.99	3.50	4.05	4.05
Baa	0.00	0.25	0.78	0.78	0.78	1.35	1.35	2.30	2.95	3.61	4.66	5.02	5.81	6.24	7.16	9.11	11.15	11.15	11.15	11.15
Ba	1.02	2.10	3.23	3.83	3.83	3.83	4.54	8.35	9.14	9.14	11.77	18.34	20.46	21.63	22.88	24.19	30.90	32.34	33.93	33.93
B	6.15	6.15	6.15	9.45	9.45	9.45	13.30	21.37	21.37	21.37	21.37	21.37	21.37	21.37	21.37	31.19	42.66	42.66	42.66	42.66
Investment-Grade	0.00	0.12	0.36	0.36	0.36	0.62	0.62	1.16	1.57	1.85	2.28	2.58	3.05	3.71	4.05	5.13	6.23	6.43	6.64	6.64
Speculative-Grade	1.74	2.65	4.08	5.08	5.08	5.08	6.27	10.71	11.38	11.38	13.64	19.32	21.13	22.12	23.20	25.49	32.64	33.91	35.30	35.30
All Corporates	0.36	0.54	0.92	1.31	1.31	1.52	1.73	2.96	3.41	3.65	4.37	5.50	6.16	6.86	7.31	8.53	10.43	10.77	11.14	11.14

Figure 10.42 (Cont'd)

Years:	1	2	3	4	5	6	7	8	9	10	11	12	13	14	15	16	17	18	19	20
Cohort formed January 1, 1976																				
Aaa	0.00	0.00	0.00	0.00	0.00	0.00	0.00	0.00	0.00	0.00	0.00	1.59	1.59	1.59	1.59	1.59	1.59	1.59	1.59	1.59
Aa	0.00	0.00	0.00	0.00	0.00	0.00	0.97	0.97	0.97	0.97	0.97	0.97	2.09	2.09	3.26	3.26	3.26	3.26	3.26	3.26
A	0.00	0.00	0.00	0.00	0.00	0.00	0.00	0.64	0.64	0.64	1.32	1.32	2.44	2.44	2.84	4.10	4.10	4.59	4.59	5.65
Baa	0.00	0.27	0.55	0.55	0.86	0.86	2.19	2.88	3.59	4.69	5.08	5.91	5.91	6.88	8.95	10.56	11.12	11.12	11.12	11.12
Ba	1.01	2.07	3.19	3.19	3.81	4.47	7.31	8.05	8.05	10.49	16.57	18.54	19.63	20.79	21.99	29.48	30.82	32.29	32.29	32.29
B	0.00	0.00	3.77	3.77	3.77	8.47	18.36	18.36	18.36	18.36	18.36	18.36	18.36	18.36	33.21	49.90	49.90	49.90	49.90	49.90
Investment-Grade	0.00	0.11	0.23	0.23	0.35	0.35	0.98	1.50	1.76	2.17	2.59	3.03	3.65	3.98	4.99	6.03	6.22	6.42	6.42	6.86
Speculative-Grade	0.88	2.26	2.70	3.70	4.24	5.39	9.07	9.72	9.72	11.91	17.39	19.15	20.13	21.17	23.38	31.44	32.68	34.02	34.02	34.02
All Corporates	0.17	0.53	0.90	0.90	1.10	1.30	2.45	2.99	3.21	3.90	5.09	5.72	6.38	6.80	7.97	9.92	10.24	10.59	10.59	10.97
Cohort formed January 1, 1977																				
Aaa	0.00	0.00	0.00	0.00	0.00	0.00	0.00	0.00	0.00	0.00	1.59	1.59	1.59	1.59	1.59	1.59	1.59	1.59	1.59	1.59
Aa	0.00	0.00	0.00	0.00	0.00	0.90	0.90	0.90	0.90	0.90	0.90	1.96	1.96	3.05	3.05	3.05	3.05	3.05	3.05	3.05
A	0.00	0.00	0.00	0.00	0.00	0.00	0.60	0.60	0.60	1.25	1.25	3.02	3.02	3.78	4.98	4.98	5.45	5.45	6.47	6.47
Baa	0.27	0.56	0.56	0.56	0.56	1.90	2.60	3.32	4.44	4.83	5.67	5.67	6.65	8.20	9.82	10.38	10.38	10.38	10.38	10.38
Ba	0.52	1.62	1.62	2.23	2.88	5.63	6.36	6.36	8.73	14.62	16.50	17.54	18.64	19.79	27.03	28.33	29.77	29.77	29.77	29.77
B	3.39	6.97	6.97	11.40	16.19	27.00	27.00	27.00	27.00	27.00	27.00	27.00	27.00	43.22	62.15	62.15	62.15	62.15	62.15	62.15
Investment-Grade	0.11	0.22	0.22	0.22	0.22	0.83	1.34	1.59	1.99	2.40	2.83	3.74	4.06	5.04	6.05	6.23	6.43	6.43	6.86	6.86
Speculative-Grade	1.35	2.76	2.76	3.81	4.95	8.57	9.21	9.21	11.36	16.71	18.41	19.35	20.35	22.48	30.29	31.49	32.81	32.81	32.81	32.81
All Corporates	0.35	0.71	0.71	0.90	1.10	2.22	2.74	2.96	3.63	4.79	5.40	6.31	6.71	7.84	9.74	10.05	10.39	10.39	10.76	10.76

Figure 10.42 (Cont'd)

Years:	1	2	3	4	5	6	7	8	9	10	11	12	13	14	15	16	17	18	19	20
Cohort formed January 1, 1978																				
Aaa	0.00	0.00	0.00	0.00	0.00	0.00	0.00	0.00	0.00	1.39	1.39	1.39	2.80	2.80	2.80	2.80	2.80	2.80	2.80	2.80
Aa	0.00	0.00	0.00	0.00	0.82	0.82	0.82	0.82	0.82	0.82	1.74	1.74	1.74	1.74	1.74	1.74	1.74	1.74	1.74	1.74
A	0.00	0.00	0.00	0.00	0.00	0.61	0.61	0.61	1.27	1.27	2.74	2.74	3.93	4.77	4.77	5.26	5.26	6.31	6.31	6.31
Baa	0.00	0.00	0.00	0.00	1.31	1.65	2.35	3.44	3.82	4.63	5.07	6.02	7.51	9.58	10.13	10.13	10.13	10.13	10.13	10.13
Ba	1.08	1.08	1.08	1.74	4.50	5.96	5.96	9.12	14.95	16.81	17.84	18.94	21.24	28.45	29.75	32.62	32.62	32.62	32.62	32.62
B	5.56	5.56	12.07	15.52	23.03	23.03	27.69	27.69	33.72	40.35	40.35	40.35	50.29	64.49	64.49	64.49	64.49	64.49	64.49	64.49
Investment-Grade	0.00	0.00	0.00	0.00	0.60	0.96	1.21	1.60	2.00	2.42	3.30	3.61	4.72	5.71	5.88	6.07	6.07	6.49	6.49	6.49
Speculative-Grade	1.79	1.79	2.80	3.88	7.32	8.54	9.18	11.87	18.32	20.71	21.59	22.53	25.53	32.97	34.13	36.66	36.66	36.66	36.66	36.66
All Corporates	0.35	0.35	0.53	0.73	1.81	2.32	2.64	3.39	4.74	5.45	6.32	6.72	8.08	9.92	10.22	10.71	10.71	11.07	11.07	11.07
Cohort formed January 1, 1979																				
Aaa	0.00	0.00	0.00	0.00	0.00	0.00	0.00	0.00	1.30	1.30	1.30	2.61	2.61	2.61	2.61	2.61	2.61	2.61	2.61	2.61
Aa	0.00	0.00	0.00	0.00	0.80	0.80	0.80	0.80	0.80	1.71	1.71	1.71	1.71	1.71	1.71	1.71	1.71	1.71	1.71	1.71
A	0.00	0.00	0.00	0.00	0.60	0.60	0.60	1.25	1.25	2.69	2.69	3.47	4.29	4.29	4.77	4.77	5.80	5.80	5.80	5.80
Baa	0.00	0.30	0.30	1.59	1.93	2.27	3.35	3.35	4.15	4.59	5.53	8.03	10.12	10.66	10.66	10.66	10.66	10.66	10.66	10.66
Ba	0.49	0.49	1.05	3.39	5.84	9.09	11.79	18.19	19.75	20.61	21.52	24.41	31.56	32.65	35.02	35.02	35.02	35.02	35.02	35.02
B	0.00	0.00	10.19	17.83	17.83	22.53	27.69	40.27	47.73	47.73	47.73	60.80	60.80	60.80	-	-	-	-	-	-
Investment-Grade	0.00	0.11	0.11	0.70	1.05	1.18	1.55	1.81	2.22	3.09	3.39	4.64	5.61	5.78	5.97	5.97	6.37	6.37	6.37	6.37
Speculative-Grade	0.42	1.31	2.26	5.26	7.37	10.75	13.69	21.22	23.30	24.05	24.86	28.34	34.90	35.91	38.12	38.12	38.12	38.12	38.12	38.12
All Corporates	0.09	0.35	0.54	1.58	2.26	2.96	3.79	5.30	5.98	6.82	7.20	8.78	10.56	10.85	11.33	11.33	11.67	11.67	11.67	11.67

Figure 10.42   (Cont'd)

Years:	1	2	3	4	5	6	7	8	9	10	11	12	13	14	15	16	17	18	19	20
Cohort formed January 1, 1980																				
Aaa	0.00	0.00	0.00	0.00	0.00	0.00	0.00	1.14	1.14	1.14	2.31	2.31	2.31	2.31	2.31	2.31	2.31	2.31	2.31	
Aa	0.00	0.00	0.00	0.00	0.00	0.00	0.00	0.91	1.83	1.83	1.83	1.83	1.83	1.83	1.83	1.83	1.83	1.83	1.83	
A	0.00	0.00	0.28	0.86	0.86	0.86	1.79	2.11	3.16	3.16	3.91	4.69	4.69	5.15	5.15	6.14	6.14	6.14	6.14	
Baa	0.00	0.00	0.94	1.27	1.61	3.01	3.01	3.40	4.24	5.57	7.95	9.93	10.96	10.96	10.96	10.96	10.96	10.96	10.96	
Ba	0.00	0.53	3.33	4.99	8.64	11.81	17.85	20.05	20.86	23.55	26.38	34.50	36.74	39.15	39.15	39.15	39.15	40.55	40.55	
B	5.06	7.74	16.25	22.34	28.95	32.60	45.64	50.58	50.58	50.58	62.94	71.17	71.17	71.17	71.17	71.17	71.17	71.17	71.17	
Investment-Grade	0.00	0.00	0.45	0.80	0.91	1.40	1.77	2.30	3.13	3.56	4.76	5.68	6.01	6.19	6.19	6.59	6.59	6.59	6.59	
Speculative-Grade	1.61	2.47	6.52	8.41	12.42	15.58	22.89	25.36	26.04	28.27	32.24	40.05	41.99	44.08	44.08	44.08	44.08	45.28	45.28	
All Corporates	0.34	0.51	1.68	2.33	3.19	4.17	5.81	6.67	7.47	8.19	9.82	11.76	12.32	12.77	12.77	13.10	13.10	13.27	13.27	
Cohort formed January 1, 1981																				
Aaa	0.00	0.00	0.00	0.00	0.00	0.00	1.14	1.14	1.14	2.32	2.32	2.32	2.32	2.32	2.32	2.32	2.32	2.32		
Aa	0.00	0.00	3.00	0.00	0.00	0.00	0.84	2.52	2.52	2.52	2.52	2.52	2.52	2.52	2.52	2.52	2.52	2.52		
A	0.00	0.27	0.27	0.27	0.27	1.19	1.51	2.21	2.21	2.95	3.74	3.74	4.20	4.20	5.20	5.20	5.20	5.20		
Baa	0.00	0.60	1.86	2.51	3.53	3.53	3.91	4.71	6.00	8.28	9.70	10.67	10.67	10.67	10.67	10.67	10.67	10.67		
Ba	0.00	3.59	5.00	7.98	12.14	18.81	20.66	21.35	24.36	28.38	36.44	38.47	40.67	40.67	40.67	40.67	41.98	43.32		
B	4.60	11.84	16.95	25.12	28.06	41.44	41.44	41.44	41.44	52.09	58.48	58.48	58.48	58.48	58.48	58.48	58.48	58.48		
Investment-Grade	0.00	0.32	0.77	0.99	1.35	1.71	2.22	3.03	3.45	4.62	5.37	5.69	5.86	5.86	6.24	6.24	6.24	6.24		
Speculative-Grade	0.70	4.77	6.71	10.42	14.31	22.20	24.25	24.82	27.30	32.04	39.63	41.35	43.23	43.23	43.23	43.23	44.33	45.47		
All Corporates	0.16	1.33	2.10	3.09	4.19	6.11	6.93	7.69	8.49	10.27	12.12	12.65	13.00	13.09	13.40	13.40	13.57	13.75		

Figure 10.42 (Cont'd)

Years:	1	2	3	4	5	6	7	8	9	10	11	12	13	14	15	16	17	18	19	20
Cohort formed January 1, 1982																				
Aaa	0.00	0.00	0.00	0.00	0.00	1.13	1.13	1.13	2.31	2.31	2.31	2.31	2.31	2.31	2.31	2.31	2.31			
Aa	0.00	0.00	0.00	0.00	0.00	0.75	2.28	2.28	2.28	2.28	2.28	2.28	2.28	3.37	3.37	3.37	3.37			
A	0.26	0.26	0.26	0.26	1.15	1.15	1.82	1.82	2.92	3.68	3.68	4.13	4.13	4.13	4.13	4.13	4.13			
Baa	0.30	0.30	1.30	2.34	2.70	3.48	4.30	5.62	7.95	9.39	10.39	10.39	10.39	11.00	11.00	11.00	11.00			
Ba	2.73	5.22	7.86	11.99	18.83	20.45	21.05	23.71	28.07	32.97	34.83	36.84	36.84	36.84	36.84	38.13	39.50			
B	2.41	9.92	15.14	17.92	30.31	30.31	30.31	30.31	35.67	60.18	60.18	60.18	60.18	60.18	60.18	60.18	60.18			
Investment-Grade	0.21	0.54	0.88	1.36	1.86	2.65	3.06	4.35	5.10	5.41	5.58	5.58	5.96	5.96	5.96	5.96	5.96			
Speculative-Grade	3.54	7.63	10.52	14.29	21.95	23.72	24.22	26.43	30.70	37.60	39.17	40.87	40.87	40.87	40.87	41.95	43.08			
All Corporates	1.02	2.00	2.93	4.07	6.18	6.95	7.68	8.45	10.29	12.09	12.61	13.03	13.03	13.34	13.34	13.50	13.67			
Cohort formed January 1, 1983																				
Aaa	0.00	0.00	0.00	0.00	2.06	2.06	2.06	3.20	3.20	3.20	3.20	3.20	3.20	3.20	3.20	3.20				
Aa	0.00	0.00	0.00	0.00	0.48	1.98	1.98	1.98	1.98	1.98	1.98	1.98	2.68	2.68	2.68	2.68				
A	0.00	0.00	0.00	0.26	0.26	0.83	0.83	1.76	2.74	3.42	3.79	3.79	3.79	3.79	3.79	3.79				
Baa	0.00	1.16	1.56	3.27	3.74	4.26	5.36	6.52	7.73	7.73	7.73	7.73	7.73	7.73	7.73	7.73				
Ba	0.91	2.39	5.58	13.22	13.91	17.05	20.68	25.83	31.49	31.49	32.93	32.93	34.53	34.53	36.37	38.27				
B	6.36	11.12	18.03	25.39	28.70	29.90	32.68	40.79	50.82	55.74	58.51	58.51	58.51	58.51	58.51	58.51				
Investment-Grade	0.00	0.30	0.40	0.93	1.39	2.11	2.35	3.13	3.81	4.10	4.26	4.26	4.43	4.43	4.43	4.43				
Speculative-Grade	3.82	6.97	11.32	18.64	20.68	23.00	26.21	32.33	39.31	40.92	42.73	42.73	43.73	43.73	44.92	46.18				
All Corporates	0.95	1.93	3.02	5.08	5.88	6.92	7.72	9.42	11.08	11.56	11.96	11.96	12.25	12.25	12.40	12.56				

Figure 10.42 (Cont'd)

Years:	1	2	3	4	5	6	7	8	9	10	11	12	13	14	15	16	17	18	19	20
Cohort formed January 1, 1984																				
Aaa	0.00	0.00	0.00	1.21	1.21	1.21	2.57	2.57	2.57	2.57	2.57	2.57	2.57	2.57	2.57					
Aa	0.00	0.00	0.00	0.88	1.80	1.80	1.80	1.80	1.80	1.80	1.80	2.44	2.44	2.44	2.44					
A	0.00	0.22	0.46	0.71	1.48	1.75	2.59	3.47	4.09	4.09	4.09	4.09	4.09	4.09	4.09					
Baa	0.36	0.36	0.77	1.23	1.74	2.81	3.94	5.73	5.73	6.43	6.43	6.43	6.43	6.43	6.43					
Ba	0.83	4.38	13.05	14.14	17.87	22.12	26.89	33.81	34.78	35.87	35.87	37.10	37.10	38.60	38.60					
B	6.78	12.88	20.29	24.20	27.39	32.39	42.79	50.06	52.28	57.30	57.30	57.30	57.30	57.30	61.37					
Investment-Grade	0.09	0.19	0.39	0.93	1.61	1.96	2.71	3.48	3.76	3.91	3.91	4.07	4.07	4.07	4.07					
Speculative-Grade	3.32	7.69	15.87	17.96	21.47	25.98	32.69	39.65	40.99	43.23	43.23	44.07	44.07	45.10	46.24					
All Corporates	0.91	2.07	4.20	5.10	6.42	7.63	9.50	11.37	11.82	12.31	12.31	12.59	12.59	12.74	12.89					
Cohort formed January 1, 1985																				
Aaa	0.00	0.00	0.00	0.00	0.00	1.36	1.36	1.36	1.36	1.36	1.36	1.36	1.36	1.36						
Aa	0.00	0.00	0.00	0.79	0.79	0.79	0.79	0.79	0.79	0.79	1.39	1.39	1.39	1.39						
A	0.00	0.21	1.33	2.28	2.53	3.57	4.39	4.68	4.68	4.68	4.68	4.68	4.68	4.68						
Baa	0.00	1.20	1.20	1.70	2.77	3.34	5.12	5.75	6.46	6.46	6.46	6.46	6.46	6.46						
Ba	1.75	7.05	9.64	12.62	18.72	23.71	30.55	32.06	32.90	32.90	34.84	34.84	35.98	35.98						
B	8.28	17.78	23.23	26.68	31.00	43.17	50.06	52.33	57.63	57.63	57.63	57.63	57.63	61.86						
Investment-Grade	0.00	0.36	0.85	1.58	1.92	2.61	3.33	3.59	3.74	3.74	3.90	3.90	3.90	3.90						
Speculative-Grade	3.90	10.55	14.13	17.57	23.01	30.14	36.84	38.49	40.33	40.33	42.46	42.46	43.29	44.21						
All Corporates	1.06	3.10	4.39	5.81	7.32	9.39	11.29	11.81	12.26	12.26	12.78	12.78	12.92	13.06						

Figure 10.42   (Cont'd)

Years:	1	2	3	4	5	6	7	8	9	10	11	12	13	14	15	16	17	18	19	20
Cohort formed January 1, 1986																				
Aaa	0.00	0.00	0.00	0.00	0.00	0.00	0.00	0.00	0.00	0.00	0.00	0.00	0.00							
Aa	0.00	0.00	0.79	0.79	1.24	1.24	1.24	1.24	1.24	1.84	1.84	1.84	1.84							
A	0.00	0.19	0.79	1.20	1.86	2.31	2.31	2.31	2.31	2.31	2.31	2.31	2.31							
Baa	1.33	1.33	3.00	3.87	5.25	6.70	7.75	8.34	8.34	8.34	8.34	8.34	8.34							
Ba	2.05	6.29	8.53	14.02	20.21	28.24	30.08	32.85	33.60	34.40	34.40	36.32	36.32							
B	11.80	16.60	20.62	24.69	34.60	44.29	48.80	52.33	52.33	54.78	54.78	54.78	57.90							
Investment-Grade	0.32	0.40	1.22	1.60	2.29	2.81	3.04	3.16	3.16	3.30	3.30	3.30	3.30							
Speculative-Grade	5.67	10.04	13.11	18.04	25.31	33.67	36.22	39.13	39.66	41.41	41.41	42.79	43.56							
All Corporates	1.89	3.22	4.66	6.20	8.46	10.69	11.39	12.06	12.17	12.60	12.60	12.84	12.97							
Cohort formed January 1, 1987																				
Aaa	0.00	0.00	0.00	0.00	0.00	0.00	0.00	0.00	0.00	0.00	0.00	0.00								
Aa	0.00	0.00	0.00	0.39	0.39	0.39	0.39	0.39	0.93	0.93	0.93	0.93								
A	0.00	0.00	0.40	1.25	1.68	1.68	1.68	1.68	1.68	1.68	1.68	1.68								
Baa	0.00	1.04	1.78	3.34	4.97	6.27	7.23	7.23	7.23	7.23	7.87	7.87								
Ba	2.72	4.48	9.56	15.98	23.72	27.14	30.64	31.76	32.99	33.68	35.26	36.14								
B	5.86	12.72	19.62	31.27	42.61	46.09	48.16	48.16	49.54	49.54	49.54	51.48								
Investment-Grade	0.00	0.25	0.59	1.39	1.95	2.25	2.47	2.47	2.59	2.59	2.72	2.72								
Speculative-Grade	4.10	7.86	13.52	21.67	30.49	33.87	36.83	37.58	39.24	39.70	40.75	41.94								
All Corporates	1.44	2.89	4.96	8.00	10.85	11.93	12.81	12.99	13.45	13.55	13.85	14.07								

Figure 10.42 (Cont'd)

Years:	1	2	3	4	5	6	7	8	9	10	11	12	13	14	15	16	17	18	19	20
Cohort formed January 1, 1988																				
Aaa	0.00	0.00	0.00	0.00	0.00	0.00	0.00	0.00	0.00	0.00	0.00									
Aa	0.33	0.67	0.67	0.67	0.67	0.67	0.67	1.14	1.14	1.14	1.14									
A	0.38	0.99	1.40	1.40	1.40	1.40	1.40	1.40	1.40	1.40	1.40									
Baa	0.33	1.33	2.49	3.65	4.50	4.50	4.50	4.50	4.50	5.06	5.06									
Ba	1.24	6.98	12.83	20.58	23.61	26.79	27.70	28.70	29.81	31.07	31.77									
B	6.02	13.07	25.73	37.00	41.18	46.30	47.16	50.21	50.21	51.49	57.28									
Investment-Grade	0.00	0.31	0.80	1.32	1.59	1.79	1.79	1.90	1.90	2.02	2.02									
Speculative-Grade	3.47	9.64	18.01	26.95	30.34	34.14	35.02	36.98	37.72	38.95	41.24									
All Corporates	1.31	3.75	6.96	10.17	11.36	12.55	12.78	13.35	13.52	13.88	14.36									
Cohort formed January 1, 1989																				
Aaa	0.00	0.00	0.00	0.00	0.00	0.00	0.00	0.00	0.00	0.00										
Aa	0.61	0.61	0.61	0.61	0.61	0.61	1.05	1.05	1.05	1.05										
A	0.00	0.18	0.56	0.56	0.56	0.56	0.56	0.56	0.56	0.56										
Baa	0.60	1.23	1.88	2.93	2.93	2.93	2.93	2.93	3.40	3.40										
Ba	2.98	10.00	18.13	20.82	23.99	24.40	25.31	26.84	28.58	30.54										
B	9.17	22.97	33.39	38.44	44.07	46.10	50.06	50.06	52.17	57.07										
Investment-Grade	0.28	0.51	0.82	1.06	1.06	1.06	1.17	1.17	1.28	1.28										
Speculative-Grade	6.02	15.85	24.93	28.50	32.54	33.54	35.53	36.49	38.30	41.19										
All Corporates	2.42	6.05	9.28	10.56	11.75	12.02	12.60	12.84	13.32	13.92										

Figure 10.42 (Cont'd)

Cohort formed January 1, 1990

Years:	1	2	3	4	5	6	7	8	9
Aaa	0.00	0.00	0.00	0.00	0.00	0.00	0.00	0.00	0.00
Aa	0.00	0.00	0.00	0.00	0.00	0.36	0.36	0.36	0.36
A	0.00	0.00	0.00	0.00	0.00	0.00	0.00	0.00	0.00
Baa	0.00	0.63	0.63	0.63	0.63	0.63	0.63	0.63	0.63
Ba	3.32	11.71	14.22	17.16	17.91	19.17	20.07	22.06	23.73
B	16.11	27.79	34.73	39.84	41.52	44.19	44.99	46.90	51.47
Investment-Grade	0.00	0.14	0.14	0.14	0.14	0.23	0.23	0.23	0.23
Speculative-Grade	9.80	19.57	23.86	27.61	28.71	30.71	31.55	33.43	35.93
All Corporates	3.51	6.91	8.28	9.40	9.71	10.31	10.52	10.97	11.51

Cohort formed January 1, 1991

Years:	1	2	3	4	5	6	7	8	9
Aaa	0.00	0.00	0.00	0.00	0.00	0.00	0.00	0.00	
Aa	0.00	0.00	0.00	0.00	0.31	0.31	0.31	0.31	
A	0.00	0.00	0.00	0.00	0.00	0.00	0.00	0.00	
Baa	0.28	0.28	0.28	0.28	0.28	0.28	0.28	0.28	
Ba	5.25	6.50	8.29	8.70	10.09	11.09	12.73	14.58	
B	14.66	23.84	30.75	32.96	36.23	37.00	39.74	44.05	
Investment-Grade	0.07	0.07	0.07	0.07	0.15	0.15	0.15	0.15	
Speculative-Grade	10.45	15.11	19.02	20.16	22.51	23.38	25.33	27.94	
All Corporates	3.29	4.66	5.75	6.05	6.69	6.89	7.32	7.84	

Cohort formed January 1, 1994

Years:	1	2	3	4
Aaa	0.00	0.00	0.00	0.00
Aa	0.00	0.00	0.00	0.00
A	0.00	0.00	0.00	0.00
Baa	0.00	0.21	0.21	0.43
Ba	0.23	1.76	2.04	2.95
B	3.81	9.13	12.28	14.09
Investment-Grade	0.00	0.06	0.06	0.12
Speculative-Grade	1.93	5.31	7.17	8.39
All Corporates	0.57	1.58	2.09	2.46

Cohort formed January 1, 1995

Years:	1	2	3	4
Aaa	0.00	0.00	0.00	0.00
Aa	0.00	0.00	0.00	0.00
A	0.00	0.00	0.00	0.00
Baa	0.00	0.00	0.00	0.43
Ba	0.67	0.92	1.98	3.77
B	4.84	7.37	10.24	13.50
Investment-Grade	0.00	0.00	0.00	0.11
Speculative-Grade	3.30	5.05	6.88	9.67
All Corporates	1.07	1.61	2.16	3.02

Figure 10.42 (Cont'd)

Years:	1	2	3	4	5	6	7	8	9
Cohort formed January 1, 1992									
Aaa	0.00	0.00	0.00	0.00	0.00	0.00	0.00		
Aa	0.00	0.00	0.00	0.28	0.28	0.28	0.28		
A	0.00	0.00	0.30	0.00	0.00	0.00	0.00		
Baa	0.00	0.00	0.00	0.00	0.00	0.00	0.00		
Ba	0.30	1.00	1.00	2.34	2.83	3.90	5.70		
B	9.00	17.46	20.80	24.77	27.07	29.70	33.78		
Investment-Grade	0.00	0.00	0.00	0.08	0.08	0.08	0.08		
Speculative-Grade	4.83	8.90	10.26	12.83	13.98	15.90	18.43		
All Corporates	1.33	2.39	2.72	3.37	3.62	4.01	4.50		
Cohort formed January 1, 1993									
Aaa	0.00	0.00	0.00	0.00	0.00	0.00			
Aa	0.00	0.00	0.00	0.00	0.00	0.00			
A	0.00	0.00	0.00	0.00	0.00	0.00			
Baa	0.00	0.26	0.26	0.26	0.26	0.55			
Ba	0.55	0.55	2.94	3.68	4.93	6.34			
B	5.76	9.98	14.83	16.67	19.48	22.70			
Investment-Grade	0.00	0.07	0.07	0.07	0.07	0.14			
Speculative-Grade	3.50	5.13	8.78	10.12	11.89	13.91			
All Corporates	0.96	1.38	2.33	2.65	3.05	3.52			

Years:	1	2	3	4
Cohort formed January 1, 1996				
Aaa	0.00	0.00	0.00	
Aa	0.00	0.00	0.00	
A	0.00	0.00	0.00	
Baa	0.00	0.00	0.18	
Ba	0.00	0.70	2.26	
B	1.45	4.45	8.86	
Investment-Grade	0.00	0.00	0.05	
Speculative-Grade	1.66	3.81	7.20	
All Corporates	0.54	1.21	2.24	
Cohort formed January 1, 1997				
Aaa	0.00	0.00		
Aa	0.00	0.00		
A	0.00	0.00		
Baa	0.00	0.15		
Ba	0.19	1.42		
B	2.10	7.31		
Investment-Grade	0.00	0.04		
Speculative-Grade	2.02	5.84		
All Corporates	0.68	1.93		

Figure 10.42 (Cont'd)

Years:	1	2	3	4	5	6	7	8	9	Years:	1	2	3	4
Cohort formed January 1, 1998														
Aaa	0.00													
Aa	0.00													
A	0.00													
Baa	0.12													
Ba	0.61													
B	4.08													
Investment-Grade	0.04													
Speculative-Grade	3.31													
All Corporates	1.24													

11

Credit Rating Dynamics — Moody's Watchlist, Rating Migration, and Credit Quality Correlation

Sean C Keenan, Jerome S Fons, and Lea V Carty, Moody's Investors Service

11.1 Introduction

Chapter 10 explored Moody's corporate default and recovery research in detail. The probability of default and likely recovery rates are of great interest to investors who are involved in the pricing of risky debt instruments, credit derivatives, and structured transactions.

However, default and recovery, the two fundamental components of a Moody's rating, describe only part of the broader credit rating spectrum. Moody's rating process includes both the initial assignment of ratings, and the monitoring of those ratings over the life of the security. Ratings are monitored continuously and, when circumstances warrant, are raised or lowered. Default can be considered one state in this credit rating spectrum that a debt obligation could assume. Debt instruments do not begin in default, but over time their credit quality deteriorates, and in terminal cases results in default.

This chapter examines credit rating dynamics. Like Chapter 10, it is divided into two parts. The first part, "An Historical Analysis of Moody's Watchlist," is a statistical analysis of Moody's Watchlist and the ratings of securities and issuers of those securities that have been placed on review for a rating revision. Such reviews precede formal rating changes, and are therefore the proper place to begin a discussion on credit rating dynamics.

In the second part, "Moody's Rating Migration and Credit Quality Correlation," we present an analysis of official rating actions and correlations of ratings movements. The rating transitions presented in this section describe various aspects of the probability of rating changes and default for corporate debt issuers. We also consider rating transitions in a portfolio context by describing the likelihood of joint rating changes and defaults.

11.2   An Historical Analysis of Moody's Watchlist

As part of the rating monitoring process, an issue may be placed on a formal "rating review",[1] typically for upgrade or downgrade, although the direction may also be uncertain. Moody's has been publishing a Watchlist of ratings on review since 1985. However, Watchlist assignments were not considered formal rating actions until 1991. This chapter documents the history of the Watchlist since then, and summarizes the subsequent rating changes.

The Watchlist is designed to inform investors of Moody's opinion that the credit quality of an obligation or obligor may be changing, and conveys important credit risk information. Given the significant percentage of issues that are on the Watchlist at any time — about 10% since 1995 — a detailed measurement and description of the associated rating dynamics can both serve to improve investors' understanding of Moody's ratings in general and of Watchlist assignments in particular, as well as to provide useful input to the quantification and management of credit risk for a portfolio of Moody's-rated obligations.

11.2.1   Moody's Rating Reviews

Moody's Rating Review Process

Rating reviews are formal rating actions and, like all Moody's rating actions, the decision to place an issue on the Watchlist is made by a rating committee. The rating review has a well-defined beginning and conclusion. The length of the review period will vary with the issuer and the reasons that triggered the review, but all rating reviews have a specific date of conclusion.

Moody's is cautious about putting ratings under review if the likelihood of a change is low in order to avoid unnecessarily increasing uncertainty in the

---

[1]   The terms "on the Watchlist", and "on rating review" are equivalent and are used interchangeably in this book

market place. During the course of a rating review, Moody's solicits information from the issuer in order to understand plans either for addressing the problem, or for taking advantage of the opportunities that have inspired the review. The desire to obtain information directly from the issuer occasionally delays conclusion of the review. While Moody's prefers to conclude rating reviews within 90 days, this is not always possible.

A rating may be put on review for possible upgrade, downgrade, or, more rarely, with direction uncertain in any of several possible scenarios including:

- the issuer has announced plans which Moody's believes would materially affect credit quality, but which are not certain to come to fruition. The direction (possible upgrade or downgrade) of the review indicates the effect on credit quality that we believe the plans will have, given our expectation of how likely they are to occur.
- trends in the issuer's operations or financial strength, in its industry or regulatory regime, or in the macroeconomic fundamentals of its country of domicile or region of operation may develop that could affect-positively or negatively — the issuer's willingness and ability to pay its debts on time.
- an event suddenly occurs which changes the issuer's operating environment, but the magnitude of its effect on the issuer is not clear. In this case, a review focuses on putting the dimension of the change into perspective vis-à-vis the issuer's current credit quality, and evaluating whether or not the change is likely to effect future credit quality making the existing rating inappropriate.

In some cases, Moody's changes a rating and keeps it under review. This is to signal both the irrevocable nature of the change and that the change may be more substantial in nature than we can immediately determine.

It is important to distinguish between a formal rating review and a "rating outlook" opinion. Both are designed to convey Moody's credit opinion to the investment community, but each carries different information and different rating implications. A change in rating outlook is neither a rating change nor a review for potential change. Rather, rating outlooks are designed to convey Moody's perspective on forces that might prompt a rating review over the next 6 to 18 months, and are expressed as positive, negative, or stable.

Rating outlooks are intended to keep investors abreast of analysts' perspectives on the possible direction, if any, of subtle current or anticipated changes in an issuer's creditworthiness. On the other hand, rating reviews are part of the formal committee-based process by which ratings are assigned, monitored, and changed over time. Therefore, the rating outlook may be viewed as a useful early indicator, but a weaker signal than a formal rating review.

Moody's Watchlist Activity

Since September 30, 1991, there have been 39,975 Watchlist actions affecting 38,359 ratings and representing 4,398 distinct issuers. The placement of ratings on the Watchlist affects all types of instruments rated by Moody's in roughly the proportion in which they comprise Moody's-rated universe. Oof the ratings placed on the Watchlist, 80% have been long-term debt ratings and 5% have been preferred stock ratings. The remainder is divided among shelf registrations, short-term debt, and other Moody's ratings, as shown in Figure 11.1. Moody's Watchlist also includes structured transactions although these make up only a small fraction of ratings placed on watch — just 3.5% of long-term ratings placed on watch are structured.

Typically, the reasons that trigger a security's rating review will cause all or most of the securities issued by that issuer to be placed on review. Moreover, short-term debt ratings are assigned at the issuer or program level, rather than to each obligation sold under a short-term program. For analytical purposes, such as calculating Watchlist default rates, it is often useful to consider the number of separate obligors who have any of their outstanding ratings on review, as opposed to the number of ratings on review.

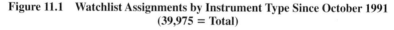

Figure 11.1   Watchlist Assignments by Instrument Type Since October 1991
(39,975 = Total)

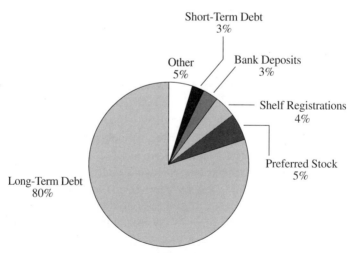

* Other includes Preferred Stock Shelf, Letters of Credit, Insurance Company, and Bank Financial Strength ratings

The number of obligors on the Watchlist at any point in time has risen since 1992, roughly in line with the growth in the number of obligors with Moody's ratings. For bond issuers (as indicated in Figure 11.1, bond ratings comprise 80% of ratings placed on review), the number of issuers on review has averaged about 11% of the total number of Moody's-rated bond issuers, with a low of 5.07% in July 1994 and a high of 11.86% in March 1998. The volatility of the number of bond issuers on the Watchlist is highlighted in Figure 11.2, which plots the number of bond issuers on watch versus the on-watch count as a percentage of all Moody's-rated bond issuers.

March 1998 was the high water mark for the number of obligors of all types on review at 680, with 501 on review for downgrade, 145 on review for upgrade, and 34 on review with direction uncertain. At 218, the US was the major contributor to the March 1998 total of obligors on review for downgrade, France was the second largest contributor at 39, and the Asian crisis was also a factor, with 127 Asian-domiciled obligors on review for downgrade.

As can be seen in Figure 11.3, the number of obligors on review for downgrade has exceeded the number on review for upgrade in all but three months since October 1991. The total number of ratings placed on review has also been skewed toward the downgrade side, with 60% of all ratings placed on review since October 1991 being placed on review for downgrade, 36% placed on review for upgrade, and 4% placed on review with the outlook uncertain.

Figure 11.2   Number and Percentage of Bond Issuers On Watch

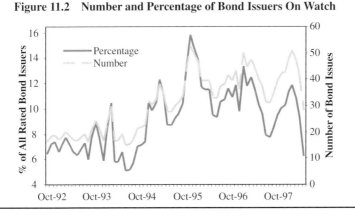

Figure 11.3   Monthly Total of Obligors on Watchlist by Direction

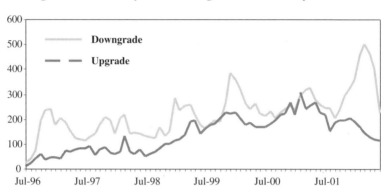

The Duration of Watchlist Status

An important component of the rating dynamics associated with the Watchlist is the length of time that ratings remain on review before the review is resolved, either with a rating change or a rating confirmation. We refer to the amount of time that any given rating remains on watch as its Watchlist duration. Since rating review status implies greater rating volatility, the distribution of Watchlist durations will be a key input for investors seeking to forecast the future distribution of ratings for a portfolio.

Although Moody's strives to resolve rating reviews within 90 days, the median duration of a rating review is 91 days, while the mean is 108 days. There is some variation in duration with respect to the initial Watchlist placement direction. Ratings placed on review for downgrade have the shortest duration with a median of 85 days and an average 103 days, followed by ratings placed on review for upgrade at 93 and 115 days, and uncertain direction issues at 92 and 133 days, for the median and average respectively. The mean, median, 10th and 90th percentiles for Watchlist durations are presented in Figure 11.4 below. In each case, and particularly for the uncertain direction category, the medians lie well below the averages, indicating that the distribution of duration times is skewed to the right. The skew is driven by the fact that the resolution times are bounded by zero on the left, but is also aggravated by the presence of a small number of rating reviews which took an abnormally long time to resolve.

The long average duration associated with reviews of uncertain direction stems from the fact that these reviews are frequently connected with the announcement by the issuer of new plans, either for mergers or acquisitions or for other changes in business strategy. Moody's extends an invitation to these issuers to provide information relevant for the reassessment of the enterprise's credit quality and the review of the issuer's debt ratings. The value of obtaining input from the issuer can often outweigh the desire for speedy resolution and so delays associated with obtaining issuer input may lead to longer resolution times. Even when Moody's can quickly assess the effect of the announced plans on the issuer's credit quality, there is frequently a long delay between the date plans are announced and the point at which it can be conclusively determined that the issuer will proceed with those plans as announced.

Figure 11.4   Watchlist Durations

	10th Percentile	Median	Mean	90th percentile
All Watchlist	22	91	108	204
Review for Upgrade	21	93	115	218
Review for Downgrade	22	85	103	95
Direction Uncertain	36	92	133	260

Watchlist Assignments by Direction

All types of Moody's ratings are placed on the Watchlist. The extent to which there is a relationship between the initial rating and the direction of the rating review, gives us insight into the credit dynamics of each rating category, for different types of securities. In the following sections, we focus on the Watchlist rating dynamics of bonds, commercial paper, and preferred stock.

While bank deposit ratings, bank financial strength ratings, insurance company financial strength ratings, and shelf registration ratings are also placed on review, bonds, commercial paper and preferred stock make up over 88% of all Watchlist assignments. Moreover, efforts to measure and manage credit risk are primarily directed toward these tradable securities. Finally, separate statistical analyses of these three instrument types establishes a complement between this chapter and Moody's bond, commercial paper and preferred stock studies.

When examining rating changes by rating initial rating category, the limits of the rating scale will impose certain regularities; e.g. Aaa-rated bonds may only be placed on review for downgrade and C-rated bonds can only be reviewed for upgrade. Other than these constraints, it is important to know if there is any systematic variation, or other unusual characteristics in the distribution of Watchlist assignments by rating. These distributions are presented in Figures 11.5–11.7. An understanding of these distributions will help us interpret the rating transition statistics in the following section.

Figure 11.5   Initial Review Direction by Rating for Long-term Debt

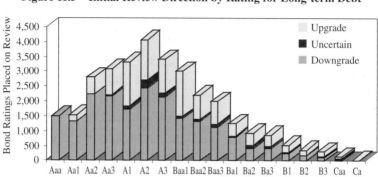

Figure 11.6   Initial Review Direction by Rating for Short-term Debt

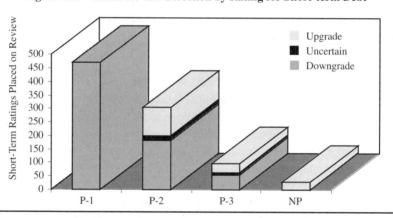

Figure 11.7   Initial Review Direction by Rating for Preferred Stock

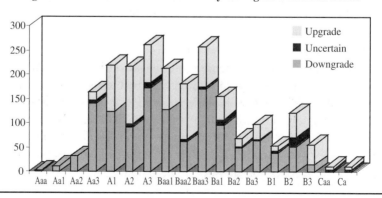

As is evident in Figure 11.5, the distribution of initial Watchlist directions does not show any untoward variation by rating for bonds. Downgrade assignments dominate overall, with only the Baa1, B3, Caa, and C categories being placed on watch for upgrade more frequently than for downgrade. For each of the Aa categories, reviews for downgrade outnumber reviews for upgrade by more than two to one.

For short-term debt, as shown in Figure 11.6, there is a clear dominance of reviews for downgrade, even at the P-3 rating. In fact, pessimistic reviews are far more common for short-term debt than for other types of debt, with over 78% of all short-term Watchlist assignments being reviews for downgrade. This reflects, in part, the important role that ratings play in the orderly exit mechanism associated with short-term debt markets described in a previous Moody's study.[2] In that report it was noted that over 88% of all Moody's-rated CP programs carry the highest possible P-1 rating, so it natural that the direction of Watchlist assignments will heavily favor downgrades.

Figure 11.7 shows the assignment distribution by rating for preferred stock. Here the relationship between Watchlist assignments and ratings is much more erratic than for bonds. In practice, most preferred stock ratings are placed on review simultaneously with ratings on that issuer's long-term debt. Thus, the choppiness of the overall distribution of ratings for preferred stocks on the Watchlist stems largely from variations in the relationship between issuers' preferred stock and long-term debt ratings.

Watchlist Resolutions

Issues that have been placed on review for rating change experience rating changes at a greater rate than the population of bonds as a whole. Given the significant percentage of issues that is on the Watchlist at any time — approximately 10% since 1995 — a detailed measurement and description of these rating dynamics is an important input to the understanding and management of credit risk for a portfolio of rated securities.

One way to gauge the rating volatility differential associated with the Watchlist is through a comparison of rating transition matrices. We compare transition matrices over a 90-day period, versus the same fraction for securities on the Watchlist. Figure 11.8 plots these historical rating transition frequencies, for bond issuers, by rating category.

---

[2] See Keenan, Sean C., Carty, Lea V., and Shtogrin, Igor, 1998 "Commercial Paper Defaults and Rating Transitions, 1972–1998," A Moody's Special Report.

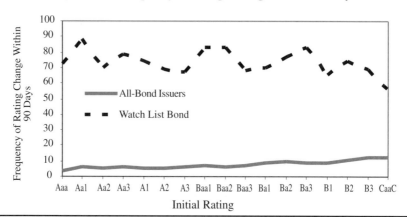

Figure 11.8   Frequency of Ratings Changed Within 90 Days

Figure 11.8 highlights several key features about Moody's ratings. First is the stability of Moody's ratings for all bonds over short time horizons. For investment-grade bonds, the average probability of a rating change over 90-days is 5.9%. Moody's ratings are intended to see through short-term fluctuations in a business' operating environment and the economy as a whole, and so the average rating variation over 90-days should be low. Bonds on the Watchlist, on the other hand, have a high probability of experiencing a rating change with investment-grade bonds on watch having a 75.6% chance of changing over the duration of the review.

We also examined general Watchlist rating dynamics based on the initial direction of the review, and the directional outcome of the review's resolution. This allows us to sum across all security types, and provides an indication of the overall strength of the credit signal provided by the placement on review for downgrade or upgrade, and of the likely outcomes associated with the placement for review with direction uncertain. A convenient representation for these rating dynamics is a rating transition matrix.

The all-issue Watchlist transition matrix presented in Figure 11.9 shows the frequency with which ratings (all types of ratings) placed on review for upgrade, downgrade, or with direction uncertain, will be resolved with a rating change, a confirmation, a rating withdrawal, or a continuation of review status. The latter are temporary confirmations of the original rating with an acknowledgment that the reasons which triggered the initial placement on watch are unresolved and that the issue remains on watch. Thus, the frequency with which ratings placed on review for downgrade are in fact downgraded is 66.77% — lower than the

				Watchlist Resolution		
		Upgrade	Downgrade	Confirm	Continue	WR
Watchlist	Upgrade	76.44%	0.13%	14.27%	2.03%	7.14%
Placement	Downgrade	0.17%	65.77%	24.37%	5.92%	3.77%
Direction	Uncertain	7.06%	27.12%	35.78%	23.45%	6.60%

Figure 11.9   All-issue Watchlist Transition Matrix

76.44% upgrade frequency for ratings placed on review for upgrade. The frequency with which ratings assigned to the Watchlist with direction uncertain remain unchanged is the sum of continue to review and confirm, or 35.78% + 23.45% = 59.23%.

Interestingly, issues placed on watch with direction uncertain have a 34.18% chance of experiencing a rating change, making a rating change of any direction a less likely outcome than a confirmation of the original rating, which happens 35.78% of the time. Issues placed on watch with direction uncertain no rating change are more than three times as likely to be downgraded than to be upgraded. Issues placed on review for upgrade or downgrade experience rating changes in the opposite direction only 0.13% and 0.17%, respectively.

Figures 11.25–11.28 in the appendix present rating transition matrices for bonds that have been placed on rating review. These are constructed with the initial rating on the left vertical axis and the final rating on the horizontal axis. Since rating resolution times are tightly clustered around 90-days, we can safely include all review episodes, interpreting the result as either the transition probability for Watchlist assignments, or as an approximate 90-day transition matrix. For example, Figure 11.25, presents the frequency with which Aa2-rated bonds placed on review for upgrade, downgrade, or with direction uncertain, end up being downgraded to A1 is 13.36%.

In general, rating volatility tends to increase as credit quality declines. For example, for all speculative-grade bonds, the average probability of a rating change is more than 10.2%, significantly higher than the 5.9% for all investment-grade bonds. This reflects the fact that lower-rated issues are more susceptible to short-term business fluctuations, and consequently are managed with respect to a shorter time horizon. For bonds on the Watchlist however, the relationship between rating stability and credit quality is fairly weak and varies from rating to rating. In fact, on average, rating stability actually increases across lower initial rating categories with speculative-grade issuers on watch exhibiting a 70.7% chance of a rating change over the review period, compared to 75.6% for investment-grade issuers.

The unconditional transition matrix shown in Figure 11.25 lumps together all bond ratings placed on review regardless of direction, and highlights the range of credit movement than can occur as a result of corporate restructuring and strategic maneuvering, mergers and acquisitions, and catastrophic events. Multi-notch rating changes within the review resolution period are not uncommon. For example, there is a 0.32% frequency associated with a B3-rated bond being upgraded all the way to Aaa as a result of a single upgrade affecting the senior subordinated notes of Outlet Broadcasting, Inc. The company's debt was put on the Watchlist in June of 1996, after it agreed to be acquired by General Electric Corp., and when GE entered into a supplemental indenture unconditionally guaranteeing the notes, the rating was raised to Aaa. There is a 0.20% frequency associated with an Aaa-rated bond falling four notches to A2 after being placed on rating review.

Figures 11.26–11.28 break these rating transitions out by the direction of the initial rating review. Figures 11.25 and 26 demonstrate that for each rating category, the direction in which the review is assigned gives a good indication that the rating will be changed in that direction. In all but one case (Aa2 bonds on review for upgrade), there has been better than 50% frequency of the rating being changed as indicated. There have been very few instances of the rating being changed in the opposite direction, although the chances of this are slightly better if the initial direction is down. As shown in Figure 11.28, bond placed on review with direction uncertain have higher probability than other Watchlist bonds of not experiencing a rating change. Where they do, bonds rated Baa2 and higher tend to have a greater likelihood of being downgraded while bonds rated Ba3 and lower are more likely to be upgrade.

Figure 11.29 in the appendix presents similar transition matrices for short-term debt, including all short-term paper on watch, as well as separate matrices broken out by the direction of the initial Watchlist assignment. Here again, multi-notch rating changes within the resolution period are not uncommon. Figure 11.10 shows the 90-day rating volatility for short-term debt on the Watchlist versus all short-term debt. Comparing Figure 11.10 with the chart on the cover shows that the difference in volatility between Watchlist ratings and all ratings is lower for short-term debt than is the case for long-term debt.

Figurs 11.25–11.29 show that rating dynamics for issuers on Moody's Watchlist are different from those not on the Watchlist. Rating dynamics have important consequences for the measurement of bond and bond portfolio credit risk. An example is afforded by JP Morgan's approach to portfolio credit risk measurement, CreditMetrics^{TM}, reliance on rating migration matrices.

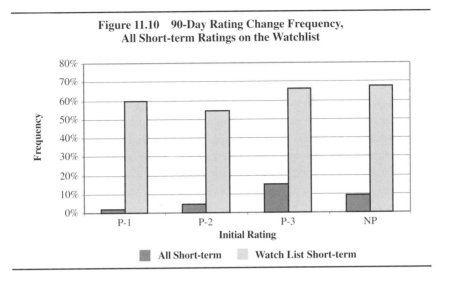

**Figure 11.10   90-Day Rating Change Frequency,
All Short-term Ratings on the Watchlist**

In order to facilitate the use of this study's results in risk management systems, and to allow comparisons between the results of this section with those of part II of this chapter, we present one-year rating transition matrices based on the ratings of long-term bond issuers, as opposed to the number of individual bond ratings. These matrices, presented in Figure 11.30 in the appendix, show the historical average rate at which issuers are upgraded or downgraded over a one-year period from the date that the issuer was placed on watch. We present one-year transition matrices by direction of initial Watchlist assignment, i.e. upgrade, downgrade or review with direction uncertain, and for comparison, we include a one-year transition matrix for all issuers calculated over the period spanned by the Watchlist.

Figure 11.30 highlights differences in the rating dynamics associated with Moody's Watchlist over a one-year time horizon. The "All-Issuers" matrix provides an estimate of how likely various rating changes are to occur over a one-year time horizon in the absence of any information beyond the rating level. However, if we knew that the issuer were on review for and upgrade, we could revise upward our outlook for the issuer's one-year forward credit quality. The second matrix, "Issuers Placed on Review For Upgrade," portrays one-year rating migration patterns for issuers on review for upgrade. As is highlighted in bold text, the greater likelihood of upgrade for these issuers results in an essentially lower-triangular transition matrix. A similar matrix shows the one-year migration patterns for issuers placed on review for downgrade. Here, the higher risk of downgrade results in an essentially upper-triangular transition matrix. Finally, the one-year migration matrix for issuers placed on review with direction uncertain displays the greater rating variability for these issuers.

Except for issuers placed on review for upgrade, the one-year default rates are also higher for Watchlist issuers than for all issuers, and are more than four times higher for issuers placed on review for downgrade. Thirty-eight issuers defaulted within one year of having been placed on the Watchlist since 1991. There was even one default by an issuer, Anchor Glass Container Corporation, in September 1996, who had been placed on review for upgrade less than a year earlier in December 1995. Another rating transition that stands out is Baby Superstore, Inc, which was raised all the way to A2 in March 1997 after having been placed on review for downgrade while at B3 in August 1996. In fact, this issuer was placed back on review, this time for upgrade in October 1996, in anticipation of its acquisition by Toys R' Us, so the eventual upgrade was not counter to the direction of the more recent Watchlist assignment, although it did occur within one-year of a review for downgrade.

That rating dynamics are substantially different for issuers placed on the Watchlist is evidenced by the essentially triangular matrices of Figure 11.30. This fact may have important implications for risk managers modeling credit risk with rating transition matrices, as issuers placed on review for upgrade (downgrade) experience much lower rates of downgrade (upgrade).

Watchlist Defaults

Since 1991, just eight obligors have defaulted while on the Watchlist. These defaulters are detailed in Figure 11.31 in the appendix. Seven defaulted on long-term debt, while one, Navistar International Corp. omitted dividends on preferred stock in December of 1992. Of the bond defaulters, all had initial Watchlist ratings in the Caa-C range except Greyhound Lines, Inc., which had an initial rating of B3. All the bond defaulters were on review for downgrade at the time of default. Navistar's preferred stock was rated "caa" when it was placed on watch, but the review direction was uncertain.

Watchlist bond default frequencies show up in the default columns of the long-term debt rating transition matrices in Figures 11.25–11.28 and Figure 11.30. Because these transition matrices are based on ratings on Watch as opposed to obligors, it is not possible to directly compare these default frequencies with historical issuer-based bond default rates presented in Chapter 10. Other differences between default rates contained in that chapter and those presented in Figures 11.25–11.28 include the short period of time spent on watch, differences in the time period, and slight differences in the population of issuers. Nevertheless, the default rate for Caa-C rated bonds the Watchlist for downgrade is higher than that for the issuer-based corporate bond default rate. The average one-year default rate for Caa-C rated bond issuers from 1983–1997 is 19.42%, which suggests a 90-day default rate of nearly 4.86%. The 90-day default rate for bonds rated Caa-C but on review for downgrade from October 1991-June 1998 is 11.94%.

For higher rating categories, the default frequencies for ratings on watch are low in absolute terms (0.0% except for the B3 category). Simply calculating the ratio of defaulted Watchlist obligors to total Watchlist obligors October 1991 yields a default rate 0.18%. The average annual all-corporate default rate over the same period is 1.12%. The low incidence of default by obligors on the Watchlist reflects, in part, the fact that placing a rating on review is a weaker signal than an outright rating change, which is an available alternative. New information about deterioration in an issuer's credit position, whose affect is clear enough and significant enough, will tend to produce an outright downgrade rather than a assignment to the Watchlist. Only for ratings in the lowest categories, where the rating itself has already expressed Moody's doubt as to the current debt servicing ability of the obligor, do Watchlist default frequencies come close to matching those for all issuers.

11.3   Rating Migration and Credit Quality Correlation

A factor critical to understanding the future distribution of the value of a credit sensitive investment is the likelihood that a change in credit quality will occur. The rating transition matrices presented in this section describe various aspects of the probability of rating changes and default for corporate debt issuers for some or all of the last 77 years. A factor critical to understanding the future distribution of the value of a portfolio of credit sensitive investments is the likelihood that changes in the credit quality of several issuers will occur jointly. We therefore present additional statistics — summarized in joint rating transition matrices — that describe the likelihood of various joint rating changes and defaults.

11.3.1   Data and Methodology

Moody's bases the results of this study on its proprietary database of ratings and defaults for industrial and transportation companies, utilities, financial institutions, and sovereigns that issued long-term debt to the public, as described in detail in Chapter 10.

As in Chapter 10, the unit of study is the long-term, public corporate debt issuer, as opposed to either the par amount of debt or the number of debt issues. The rationale for this methodology is that Moody's intends its ratings to support credit decisions. Separately tabulating multiple issues or the par amounts of a single issuer would bias the results toward the default characteristics of issuers with multiple issues or large amounts of outstanding debt and would therefore be of less utility to an investor contemplating credits without these features. We have also omitted firms whose rated debt consists solely of issues backed by entities which are not members of the issuer's corporate family, since the ratings of such debt would reflect that support and not the credit quality of the issuing firm.

In order to count each legal entity separately, we track each issuer's actual, or implied, senior unsecured long-term debt rating. If the issuer has rated senior unsecured debt, we use that rating as the measure of the issuer's credit quality for as long as such an obligations' ratings are outstanding. In cases where an issuer does not have senior unsecured debt, we estimate what this debt would most likely be rated if it did exist. We derive the estimated senior unsecured rating from actual ratings assigned to an issuer's other rated debt via a simple notching algorithm intended to reflect observed ratings relationships. While correct on average, in any particular case, the estimated senior unsecured ratings may differ from what Moody's would have actually rated a particular senior unsecured obligation. The estimated senior unsecured ratings have not been examined by Moody's analysts and benefit only indirectly from the full scope of analysis underlying Moody's bond ratings.

11.3.2 Rating Migration

Trends in Corporate Credit Quality, 1920–1996

In order to measure general trends in the credit quality of the Moody's-rated corporate universe through time, we consider annual rating drift. To calculate annual rating drift we subtract from the total number of upward rating changes (weighted by the number of ratings changed per upgrade) per year, the total number of downward rating changes (similarly weighted) per year, and divide this difference by the number of non-defaulted issuers at risk of a rating change during the course of the year.[3] Rating drift summarizes the overall increase or decrease in the credit quality of the rated universe as a percentage of one rating grade per issuer.

We measure annual rating activity in this section by computing the sum of all upward and downward letter rating changes (again, weighted by the number of ratings changed) and dividing by the number of non-defaulted issuers at risk of a rating change during the course of the year. This measurement captures both the effects of multiple rating changes for a single issuer within a given year and the relative sizes of rating changes. In effect, it shows the pace at which ratings change, based on units of ratings changed per issuer.

Figure 11.11 details annual rating drift and activity from 1920 through 1996 and is based upon letter rating changes as opposed to changes of alphanumeric ratings. Moody's altered its long-term rating scale in April 1982. The traditional nine-tiered letter rating scale (Aaa, Aa, A, Baa, Ba, B, Caa, Ca, C) was expanded by attaching three numerical modifiers (a "1," "2," or "3," in order of increasing credit risk) to each of the ratings from Aa through B. The new alphanumeric rating system is comprised of 19 grades (Aaa, Aa1, Aa2, Aa3, A1, … etc.). Because the alphanumeric ratings did not exist before April 1982, none of the statistics reported for these rating categories are based upon pre-April, 1982 ratings data. Statistics reported for the original letter rating scale are extended through the post April 1982 period by collapsing the alphanumeric ratings into the original letter rating categories. For example, the Baa1, Baa2, and Baa3 ratings all would be simply considered Baa.

Since 1920, annual rating drift has averaged a negative 6% while annual rating activity has averaged 15%. The rating drift time series illustrates prolonged deterioration (represented by negative values) in overall corporate credit quality during the depression of the 1930s and the 16-year period beginning 1980. Annual rating drift averaged -24% during the 1930s and -9% during the eighties and the first half of the nineties, versus an average of just -1% for the period from 1940 to 1979. Annual rating drift was non-negative in 1996 for the first time since 1975.

The negative average annual drift for the 1930s reflects the most severe economic contraction of this century, coupled with severe asset deflation. This combination put even highly creditworthy borrowers at considerable risk of default. The increased risk of default was reflected by an increase in the incidence and size of downgrades relative to upgrades.

---

[3] The number of issuers at risk of a rating change during the course of the year is the number of non-defaulted issuers holding ratings as of the start of the year less one half of the number of issuers whose ratings were withdrawn during the course of the year. The adjustment for the issuers whose ratings were withdrawn reflects the assumption that, on average, such issuers were at risk of a rating revision for only one half of one year

Figure 11.11   Long-Term Rating Activity and Drift, 1920–1996[4]

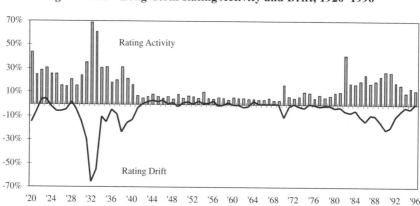

The significant credit deterioration beginning in 1980 was the result of a slew of special events and an overall trend towards increased corporate leverage. The recession of 1982 proved to be the most severe of the post-World War II era. Sharply lower oil prices in the mid-1980s prompted large numbers of industrial and financial company downgrades. Concerns about problem loans in the banking system led to numerous downgrades in 1989, just one year before the onset of another recession.

Rating Change Magnitude

We define the magnitude of a rating change as the number of rating categories that a rating change spans. For example, an upgrade from Ba to Baa covers one letter rating category while a downgrade from Ba to Caa covers 2 categories. This same concept applies analogously to our alphanumeric ratings.

---

[4] Figures for 1982 are straight-line interpolations between 1981 and 1983. We use this interpolation because our algorithm for implying senior ratings artificially inflated the numbers of upgrades and downgrades during our 1982 adoption of numerically modified ratings. For example, an issuer with subordinated debt rated Ba prior to 1982 has a senior implied rating of Baa. If, upon adoption of the modified rating system, this issue comes in at the lower end of the Ba scale, say Ba3, then its senior implied rating is now Ba1. This corresponds to the letter rating Ba. Hence our algorithm has artificially created a downgrade from Baa to Ba even though there has been no rating revision. The actual numbers occurred in nearly the same ratio as those presented here

Figures 11.12 and 11.13 display the frequency of rating revisions by the magnitude of change for the entire period spanned by our database.

Changes of smaller magnitude are relatively more frequent than are large rating revisions. Rating changes of three ratings or more have occurred historically only about 2% of the time. For the alphanumeric ratings, changes of more than four rating notches have occurred historically only about 3% of the time.

**Figure 11.12   Frquency of Letter Rating Changes of Various Magnitudes
January, 1920 – March, 1997**

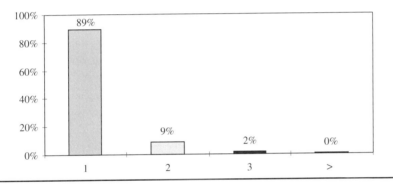

**Figure 11.13   Frequency of Alpha-Numeric Rating Changes of
Various Magnitudes
April, 1982 – March, 1997**

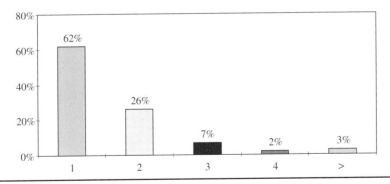

Rating Change Magnitude and Direction — Rating Transition Matrices

Unlike the charts above, an average transition matrix is a concise representation not only of the size, but also the direction of typical rating changes. Figure 11.14 below depicts an average rating transition matrix defined for a one-year time horizon. Each row indicates the rating group at the beginning of a one-year time period. Each column corresponds to a rating group, default, or withdrawn rating (WR) as of the end of the one-year period. Each cell entry, excluding the "Default" and "WR" columns, is the average fraction of issuers who held the row rating at the beginning of the time period and the column rating or status at the end of the time period.

The upper left-hand corner, for example, indicates that on average over the period from 1920 to the present, 88.32% of Aaa's have remained at that level over the course of one year. The next percentage to the right indicates that 6.15% of Aaa's have, on average, suffered a downgrade to Aa. Also, by way of example, the chart indicates that 2.30% of all A-rated companies enjoyed a net improvement of one letter rating (to Aa) by the end of any one year period.[5]

The largest values in the transition matrix are along the diagonal, indicating that the most likely rating for an issuer at the end of a one-year time horizon is the rating with which the issuer started the period. Moving off of the diagonal, the values fall off very quickly as very large changes in credit quality over a one-year period are infrequent.

The patterns in the alphanumeric rating transition matrix in Figure 11.15 are roughly similar to those of the average one-year letter rating transition matrix. However, note that the estimated likelihood that an Aaa rating is maintained over the course of one year is just 84.64% versus an estimated 88.32% in Figure 11.14. Part of the reason for this difference is that the alphanumeric transition matrices are estimated on data available since April 1982, when Moody's adopted the current alphanumeric rating scale. From 1982 until just recently, there has been an overall trend towards decreasing credit quality as documented by Moody's rating drift statistics in Figure 11.11. Hence, while the average letter rating transition matrices incorporate the entire post-WW II to

---

[5] The increase in credit quality is net since a rating transition matrix is a snapshot of the evolution of the rating profile at a specific point in time. Therefore, they do not address the dynamics of how the hypothetical A-rated issuer arrived at the Aa rating one year later. It may well have been upgraded to Aaa and then downgraded to Aa between the beginning and end of the one-year period

Figure 11.14   Average One-Year Rating Transition Matrix, 1920–1996

		Rating To: Aaa	Aa	A	Baa	Ba	B	Caa-C	Default	WR
Rating	**Aaa**	88.32%	6.15%	0.99%	0.23%	0.02%	0.00%	0.00%	0.00%	4.29%
From:	**Aa**	1.21%	86.76%	5.76%	0.66%	0.16%	0.02%	0.00%	0.06%	5.36%
	A	0.07%	2.30%	86.09%	4.67%	0.63%	0.10%	0.02%	0.12%	5.99%
	Baa	0.03%	0.24%	3.87%	82.52%	4.68%	0.61%	0.06%	0.28%	7.71%
	Ba	0.01%	0.08%	0.39%	4.61%	79.03%	4.96%	0.41%	1.11%	9.39%
	B	0.00%	0.04%	0.13%	0.60%	5.79%	76.33%	3.08%	3.49%	10.53%
	Caa-C	0.00%	0.02%	0.04%	0.34%	1.26%	5.29%	71.87%	12.41%	8.78%

1979 period of very low credit risk and volatility, the average alphanumeric rating transition matrices are estimated over a period characterized by historically high credit risk.

Additionally, the diagonal elements of Figure 11.15 are smaller than those of Figure 11.14. This is because the alphanumeric ratings represent a finer gradation of credit risk than the letter rating scale. Consequently, finer movements in credit quality that would not have been substantial enough to warrant an entire letter rating change can be registered by rating changes of one or two notches. Because finer changes in credit quality are being measured, more rating changes are registered and the average rating transition rates estimated below reflect the greater rating change volatility of the alphanumeric ratings.

Withdrawn Ratings

The withdrawn rating category (column heading WR) in the preceding (average) rating transition matrices corresponds to cases where Moody's has withdrawn all of an issuer's ratings. The likelihood of a rating withdrawal generally increases as credit quality decreases. Figure 11.14 indicates that over a one-year time period, Aaa-rated issuers have an average 4.29% risk of rating withdrawal while B-rated issuers have more than double the risk, 10.53%. At least part of the reason for this pattern is that private debt markets are relatively more attractive for many of the smaller borrowers that generally carry lower ratings. Consequently, such issuers have been more likely to replace rated public bonds with unrated private debt.

Figure 11.15 Average, One-Year Alphanumeric Rating Transition Matrix, 1983–1996

Rating From:	Rating To: Aaa	Aa1	Aa2	Aa3	A1	A2	A3	Baa1	Baa2	Baa3	Ba1	Ba2	Ba3	B1	B2	B3	Caa	Default	WR
Aaa	84.64%	5.53%	3.13%	0.67%	0.77%	0.36%	0.14%	0.00%	0.00%	0.00%	0.05%	0.00%	0.00%	0.00%	0.00%	0.00%	0.00%	0.00%	4.71%
Aa1	2.53%	74.04%	8.63%	7.87%	2.61%	0.23%	0.00%	0.24%	0.00%	0.00%	0.12%	0.00%	0.00%	0.00%	0.00%	0.00%	0.00%	0.00%	3.74%
Aa2	0.61%	2.54%	76.97%	9.15%	4.30%	1.15%	0.73%	0.21%	0.00%	0.00%	0.00%	0.00%	0.07%	0.07%	0.00%	0.00%	0.00%	0.00%	4.20%
Aa3	0.10%	0.43%	2.90%	76.85%	10.25%	3.83%	0.85%	0.10%	0.25%	0.22%	0.00%	0.05%	0.12%	0.00%	0.00%	0.00%	0.00%	0.00%	4.06%
A1	0.04%	0.10%	0.65%	4.45%	78.75%	7.25%	2.93%	0.70%	0.22%	0.18%	0.37%	0.37%	0.07%	0.17%	0.00%	0.00%	0.00%	0.00%	3.76%
A2	0.03%	0.04%	0.20%	0.63%	5.46%	77.32%	7.23%	3.04%	0.76%	0.28%	0.20%	0.13%	0.13%	0.03%	0.07%	0.00%	0.03%	0.00%	4.42%
A3	0.03%	0.11%	0.00%	0.20%	1.53%	8.56%	71.59%	6.47%	3.68%	1.43%	0.45%	0.18%	0.26%	0.41%	0.04%	0.00%	0.00%	0.00%	5.06%
Baa1	0.06%	0.00%	0.09%	0.11%	0.15%	3.11%	8.49%	69.73%	7.61%	3.03%	0.95%	0.38%	0.45%	0.62%	0.12%	0.00%	0.00%	0.06%	5.05%
Baa2	0.00%	0.12%	0.16%	0.15%	0.14%	0.93%	3.58%	7.49%	69.65%	7.41%	1.89%	0.40%	0.68%	0.40%	0.47%	0.29%	0.00%	0.06%	6.20%
Baa3	0.04%	0.00%	0.00%	0.06%	0.24%	0.57%	0.44%	4.09%	9.89%	64.87%	6.53%	2.94%	1.90%	0.89%	0.31%	0.07%	0.13%	0.52%	6.52%
Ba1	0.11%	0.00%	0.00%	0.00%	0.16%	0.10%	0.62%	0.84%	2.77%	6.12%	68.60%	4.49%	3.75%	0.76%	1.27%	0.91%	0.11%	0.81%	8.59%
Ba2	0.00%	0.00%	0.00%	0.00%	0.00%	0.17%	0.12%	0.30%	0.47%	2.22%	7.23%	66.67%	5.59%	1.25%	3.85%	1.60%	0.24%	0.68%	9.62%
Ba3	0.00%	0.03%	0.03%	0.00%	0.00%	0.21%	0.13%	0.13%	0.20%	0.77%	2.31%	4.59%	69.25%	2.45%	5.69%	2.41%	0.49%	2.69%	8.62%
B1	0.03%	0.00%	0.03%	0.00%	0.06%	0.05%	0.18%	0.08%	0.31%	0.39%	0.33%	2.42%	5.88%	70.45%	1.48%	4.88%	0.90%	4.04%	8.48%
B2	0.00%	0.00%	0.08%	0.00%	0.15%	0.00%	0.06%	0.15%	0.11%	0.00%	0.23%	1.95%	3.42%	5.35%	62.02%	7.30%	2.53%	8.67%	7.99%
B3	0.00%	0.00%	0.06%	0.00%	0.00%	0.00%	0.00%	0.10%	0.16%	0.18%	0.21%	0.29%	1.37%	4.52%	2.28%	64.57%	3.84%	13.36%	9.05%
Caa-C	0.00%	0.00%	0.00%	0.00%	0.00%	0.00%	0.00%	0.00%	0.60%	0.60%	0.79%	0.00%	2.17%	2.14%	1.34%	2.54%	51.08%	28.33%	10.41%

The rationale for the withdrawal of all of a company's debt ratings could be important in the overall understanding of the credit dynamics implied by the rating transition matrices given above. For example, Moody's might withdraw a debt rating because the underlying issue has been retired. In this case, the withdrawn ratings simply reflect the issuer's exit from the public bond market and have no negative credit implications. On the other hand, in some cases, Moody's withdraws ratings because the information necessary to accurately rate the company's debt is not available. In such cases, it is conceivable that the withdrawn rating may correlate with increased credit risk.

In order to better understand the reasons why ratings are withdrawn, we examined Moody's corporate bond ratings database. Of the over 35,000 withdrawn long-term individual debt ratings considered, 92% were withdrawn because either an issue had matured or had been called. In the remaining 8% of cases, the reason for the withdrawn rating was not specified or the rating withdrawal was associated with any of a variety of situations including conversions, mergers, defeasances, bankruptcies, or the lack of sufficient information to accurately rate the debt. Of the 8% of all rating withdrawals that were not related to debt maturities, calls, or defaults,[6] one-half were withdrawn for unspecified reasons and an additional 1% of the total number of withdrawals occurred for reasons that could be connected with negative credit developments (e.g. insufficient information to maintain the rating or an indenture amendment). In total, 95% of the rating withdrawals were not associated with any deterioration in credit quality. An additional 4% occurred for unspecified reasons and so may have been associated with a credit deterioration. However, this category also includes cases in which the par amount of the obligation outstanding has fallen to such a low level that there is little or no trading or investor interest in the maintenance of the rating. In only 1% of the cases is a deterioration in credit quality likely.

The ratings examined in this report are not Moody's published individual debt ratings, but instead senior unsecured, or estimated senior unsecured, ratings for firms. The circumstances that lead Moody's to withdraw ratings on all of a company's debts may be different from those that lead Moody's to withdraw a rating on any particular debt. To explore this possibility, we looked at each withdrawn rating in Moody's database of senior unsecured, and estimated senior

---

[6] We do not consider withdrawals associated with a default in this analysis under the rationale that a default has already occurred in such cases and the question of whether the withdrawn rating carries information about the future creditwortiness of the issuer is moot

unsecured, rating histories. In 87% of the cases in which Moody's has withdrawn all of a company's debt ratings, the withdrawal was the result of debt maturity, call, conversion or other means consistent with the debts' indentures. Therefore, in only 13% of all cases were ratings withdrawn under circumstances that could be correlated with an increase in credit risk. In 9% of the cases, the reason for the rating withdrawal was unspecified. In the remaining 4% of the cases, ratings were withdrawn because of a lack of sufficient information. The increases in the percentages of rating withdrawals associated with either unspecified, and therefore possibly risky developments, or developments likely associated with a credit deterioration indicates that the reasons that lead Moody's to withdraw a bond's rating are not necessarily the same as those that lead Moody's to withdraw all ratings on debt that a company may have outstanding.

An important use of rating transition data is in the modeling of the prices of credit sensitive securities. In many cases, an investor enters into a long-term agreement and would like to summarize the likely credit position of a counterparty at the end of the transaction. Because the withdrawn rating is most commonly associated with exit from the debt markets, such investors are interested in rating transition matrices that are estimated for rating histories that do not include rating withdrawals. Because rating withdrawals are not directly related to increased default risk, a transition matrix can be created that excludes such withdrawals without generating significant distortion. Such a matrix can be created by distributing the probability mass associated with rating withdrawal across the remaining categories on a probability weighted basis. Another approach, demonstrated in Figure 11.16, is to estimate rating transition matrices that are conditioned upon the issuer's rating remaining outstanding over the entire period spanned by the matrix. The two methodologies yield similar results.

Multi-Year, Rating Transition Matrices

We can define average rating transition matrices over a variety of time horizons. Figure 11.32 in the appendix to this chapterincludes average letter rating transition matrices similar to those previously shown, but defined over two- through 10-year, and 15-year time horizons. Figure 11.33 of the appendix presents alphanumeric average rating transition matrices for two- through 10-year time horizons. These transition matrices include rating withdrawal as a possible transition state. For those readers interested in estimating a transition matrix that does not include rating withdrawal as a state, a simple approximation

Figure 11.16   Average One-Year Rating Transition Matrix, 1920–1996 (Conditional Upon No Rating Withdrawal)

		Rating To:							
		Aa	Aa	A	Baa	Ba	B	Caa-C	Default
Rating	**Aa**	92.18%	6.51%	1.04%	0.25%	0.02%	0.00%	0.00%	0.00%
From:	**Aa**	1.29%	91.62%	6.11%	0.70%	0.18%	0.03%	0.00%	0.07%
	A	0.08%	2.50%	91.36%	5.11%	0.69%	0.11%	0.02%	0.14%
	Baa	0.04%	0.27%	4.22%	89.16%	5.25%	0.68%	0.07%	0.31%
	Ba	0.02%	0.09%	0.44%	5.11%	87.08%	5.57%	0.46%	1.25%
	B	0.00%	0.04%	0.14%	0.69%	6.52%	85.20%	3.54%	3.87%
	Caa-C	0.00%	0.02%	0.04%	0.37%	1.45%	6.00%	78.30%	13.81%

is obtained by distributing the probability associated with the rating withdrawal across the remaining ratings on a probability weighted basis. As mentioned in the previous section, because rating withdrawal is not directly related to credit deterioration, the error introduced by this technique is generally small.

Higher ratings are more likely to be maintained than are lower ratings over the two to 15 year time horizon presented in these matrices. The higher likelihood of ratings remaining unchanged for higher credit ratings indicates that not only are the higher rating categories associated with lower default risk (as indicated by the default transition rates posted in the "Default" column) but that they are also more stable.

Considering the matrices listed in Figure 11.32 of the appendix, one sees that for the Aa and A ratings, the frequency of net downgrades generally exceeds that of net upgrades. For any of the given time horizons, it is more likely for an issuer starting with one of these ratings to have a lower rating at the end of the period than a higher rating. For issuers rated Baa that have not defaulted, however, this pattern is not as pronounced. Within a one-year horizon, Baa-rated issuers are only slightly more likely to be rated below Baa as above. As the time horizon covered by the transition matrix expands, Baa-rated issuers that have not defaulted are more likely to have a higher rating than lower until, after ten years, there is nearly two times as great a chance of having a single-A rating (11.71%) as there is of having a Ba rating (6.36%). Continuing down the credit spectrum, there is a relatively greater chance of a non-defaulted B-rated issuer enjoying a net upgrade than there is for a Ba-rated issuer. Caa-and-lower rated issuers, however, tend to be too weak to make the uphill climb and tend to fall into default.

11.3.3   Rating Transition Rate Volatility and Credit Quality Correlation

Rating Transition Rate Volatility

The rating transition matrices above summarize the average risk of changes in credit quality over a specified time period. However, the risk of a change of credit quality varies from year to year as unexpected changes in macroeconomic variables and the business environment in general alter firms' credit outlooks. Consequently, there is volatility in rating transition rates from year to year. The average rating transition matrices reported above are calculated over as many as 77 years, they smooth over variations in the year-to-year rating transition rates caused by fluctuating macroeconomic and business conditions. To investigate rating transition rate volatility, we have, by way of example, expanded the average, one-year, A-to-Baa transition rate into its 77 constituent observations — one for each year since 1920 as shown in Figure 11.17. The gray bars indicate years for which the annual growth rate of real US gross domestic product was negative, hinting at downgrade risk countercyclicality — that is, economic contractions seem to be associated with greater downgrade risk.

As presented in the A-row, Baa-column of Figure 11.16, the average fraction of issuers downgraded from A to Baa over the course of one year is 5.11%. However, in three different years during the long period of very low default risk extending from WWII to the 1970s (1942, 1944, and 1956), no issuer (with an A, or estimated A, senior unsecured debt rating) experienced this downgrade. At the height of the Great Depression, 1932, 32% of A-rated issuers were downgraded to Baa.

Statistically, the median value of 3.68% is a more insightful measure of the center of the distribution of A-to-Baa transitions (shown in Figure 11.18) than is the mean. Figure 11.18 reveals that the annual risk of downgrade from A to Baa is concentrated in the 0% to 10% range, but that substantially larger fractions have not been uncommon historically. The frequency distribution of this rating transition rate is truncated on the left at zero and has a long right-hand tail. Consequently, reliance on the mean and standard deviation statistics to describe the distribution's center and dispersion is questionable.

The standard deviation of the transition rates pictured above, 5.33%, coupled with the assumption that rating transition rates are normally distributed generates negative transition rates at the 90% level of confidence. Specifically, a 90% confidence interval for the average transition rate, 5.11%, is (−1.73%, 11.94%). Considering the data directly, approximately 90% of the observations

(69 of the 77) lie between 0.56% on the low side and 16.44% on the high side. This indicates that not only are A-to-Baa transition rates below 0.56% relatively rare, but that transition rates greater than 11.94% are not rare. This highlights the limitations of the mean and standard deviation in describing the distribution of transition rates.

The asymmetry of the A-to-Baa transition rate is not unique. Figure 11.34 of the appendix provides selected summary statistics describing the distributions of all of the one-year transition rates. The medians listed in that table can be

**Figure 11.17   Yearly Fraction of Issuers Downgraded from A to Baa
(Gray bars indicate years of negative growth in real US GDP)**

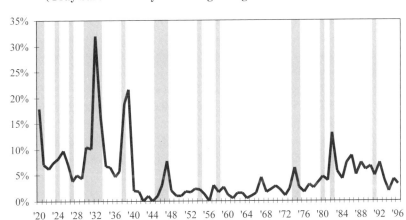

Figure 11.18   Histogram of Yearly A-to-Baa Rating Transition Rates, 1920–1996

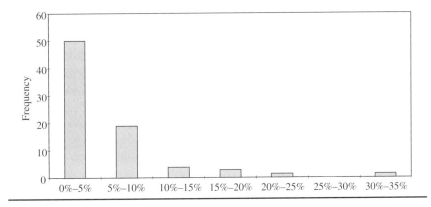

compared with the average values presented in Figure 11.16. The averages presented there may be used in conjunction with the standard deviation and the 5%- and 95%-tiles to gain a better understanding of the asymmetry of each one-year transition rate's distribution.

Credit Quality Correlation

Differences in the outlooks for firms' credit risks arise as conditions in firms' factor and output markets, and macroeconomic and regulatory environments adjust. For example, Figure 11.17 highlights the sensitivity of the risk of downgrade for A-rated issuers to economic growth. Because operating conditions adjust dynamically and movement in any one macroeconomic variable may affect several issuers, the credit ratings of different obligors are likely to be linked and therefore to move together. In this section, we examine some of the evidence ratings provide on the existence of credit quality correlation and provide some indication of their economic importance to the understanding of the portfolio characteristics of credit risk.

To examine the question of whether credit quality is correlated across firms, we first examine the patterns in the co-movements of ratings that we would expect to see if credit quality were not correlated. We then examine actual rating co-movements in our database of rating histories. Finally, we compare the two results to answer to the question of whether the credit qualities of different firms is likely to be correlated or not.

Consider, for example, two issuers with Baa-rated senior unsecured debt. Historically, over the course of one year, Baa-rated issuers have maintained the same rating, moved to another rating category, or defaulted with the probabilities reported in the Baa row of the one-year transition matrix in Figure 11.16. Because there are eight possible transitions (seven different rating groupings + default) for each of the two issuers, there are a total of 64 (8 × 8) possible credit quality combinations for the two issuers at the end of one year. If we impose the assumption that the credit qualities of these issuers are uncorrelated, the likelihood of each possible credit quality combination for the two issuers at the end of one year are easily calculated. They are simply the products of the likelihood of each issuer making the specified transition. For example, the probability of the first Baa-rated issuer moving to the A rating over a one-year time horizon is estimated to be 4.22% (the Baa-A entry of Figure 11.16). The probability of the second Baa-rated issuer moving to the Ba rating over a one-year time horizon is estimated to be 5.25% (the Baa-Ba entry of Figure 11.16). Assuming no credit quality correlation, the likelihood of the first issuer's rating changing to A and the second issuer's rating changing to Ba over the course of one year is simply the product of these two likelihood, 0.22%. If we perform this calculation for each of the 64 possible rating combinations, we obtain a matrix describing the joint probability distribution of rating migrations for the portfolio of two issuers at the end of one year. These are detailed in Figure 11.19.

Each cell entry of Figure 11.19 is an estimate of the likelihood that the first Baa-rated issuer will move to the corresponding row rating and the second issuer will move to the corresponding column rating. The first row of numbers represents the sum of each column of probabilities and identically sums to our likelihood estimate that a Baa-rated issuer will move to the corresponding column rating over the course of one year (the Baa row of the one-year rating transition matrix of Figure 11.16).[7] Similarly, the first column of numbers represents the sum of each row of probabilities and also sums to our likelihood estimate that a Baa-rated issuer will move to the corresponding row rating over the course of one year. The 64 interior cells of the joint rating transition matrix above sum to 100%. They completely describe the probabilities associated with the range of possible joint rating outcomes at the end of one year for the two Baa-rated issuers under the assumption that their credit qualities are not correlated. The most likely outcome for the two initially Baa-rated issuers at the end of one year is that they both remain at the Baa rating. The likelihood of this outcome is estimated at 79.49% (the entry in the Baa row and the Baa column

**Figure 11.19   Joint Rating Transition Matrix Assuming
No Credit Quality Correlation
(Two, initially Baa-rated, issuers. Based on data available since 1920)**

			Aaa	Aa	A	Baa	Ba	B	Caa-C	Default
			0.04%	0.27%	4.22%	89.16%	5.25%	0.68%	0.07%	0.31%
	Aaa	0.04%	0.00%	0.00%	0.00%	0.03%	0.00%	0.00%	0.00%	0.00%
First	Aa	0.27%	0.00%	0.00%	0.01%	0.24%	0.01%	0.00%	0.00%	0.00%
Issuer's	A	4.22%	0.00%	0.01%	0.18%	3.76%	0.22%	0.03%	0.00%	0.01%
End-of-	Baa	89.16%	0.03%	0.24%	3.76%	79.49%	4.68%	0.61%	0.06%	0.28%
Period	Ba	5.25%	0.00%	0.01%	0.22%	4.68%	0.28%	0.04%	0.00%	0.02%
Rating	B	0.68%	0.00%	0.00%	0.03%	0.61%	0.04%	0.00%	0.00%	0.00%
	Caa-C	0.07%	0.00%	0.00%	0.00%	0.06%	0.00%	0.00%	0.00%	0.00%
	Default	0.31%	0.00%	0.00%	0.01%	0.28%	0.02%	0.00%	0.00%	0.00%

Second Issuer's End-of-Period Rating

of Figure 11.19). The next most likely outcome is for one issuer to be downgraded to Ba while the other remains at Baa, 4.68%. This can happen in either of two ways: the first issuer could be the one downgraded, while the second maintains its Baa rating (this likelihood is given in the Ba row, Ba column cell of Figure 11.19) or vice versa (the Baa row, Ba column cell). There is an estimated 0.00% risk that both issuers default by the end of one year.

We derived Figure 11.19 under the assumption of no credit quality correlation. We obtain evidence about the true nature of credit quality correlation by comparing these results with those we obtain directly from our database of rating histories.

In Figure 11.20 we directly estimate an empirical joint rating transition matrix without imposing the assumption of no correlation. To do that, we formed a dataset of all possible pairs of Baa-rated issuers as of the start of each year since 1920 and then examined the ratings combinations of those pairs at the ends of each one-year period. The relative frequency of the actual historically observed ratings co-movements for each pair of issuers are estimates of the joint migration probabilities. These are presented in Figure 11.20.

The first row and the first column of numbers are the same as those of Figure 11.19 and give the "stand alone" likelihood of each issuer moving to each rating category. Each cell entry gives an estimate of the probability that, of a pair of Baa-rated issuers, the first will move to the row rating while the second will move to the column rating. For example, the entry in the Aa row and Baa column is 0.21%, indicating that there is an estimated 0.21% chance that the first issuer will move to Aa and that the second will remain at Baa.

A comparison of Figure 11.19 with Figure 11.20 provides evidence that the credit qualities of these two Baa-rated issuers are positively correlated. Positive credit quality correlation between the two Baa-rated issuers would imply that if one issuer improves in credit quality over the course of one year, the other issuer would be more likely also to improve in credit quality. Similarly, if one issuer deteriorates in credit quality, the other issuer would be more likely also to deteriorate in credit quality. The shaded cells in the upper left-hand quadrants of Exhibits 19 and 20 correspond to the probabilities that both issuers will experience an improvement in their credit ratings. The shaded cells in the lower right hand quadrants correspond to the probabilities that both issuers will experience a deterioration in their credit ratings. If the credit quality of Baa-rated

---

[7] The columns of this matrix, as reported here, do not all sum exactly to the corresponding entry of the first row because of the roundoff error associated with reporting only four decimal points of accuracy

**Figure 11.20   Empirical Joint Rating Transition Matrix
(Two, initially Baa-rated, issuers. Based on data available since 1920)**

			Second Issuer's End-of-Period Rating							
			Aaa	Aa	A	Baa	Ba	B	Caa-C	Default
			0.04%	0.27%	4.22%	89.16%	5.25%	0.68%	0.07%	0.31%
	Aaa	0.04%	0.00%	0.00%	0.00%	0.03%	0.00%	0.00%	0.00%	0.00%
First	Aa	0.27%	0.00%	0.00%	0.03%	0.21%	0.03%	0.00%	0.00%	0.00%
Issuer's	A	4.22%	0.00%	0.03%	0.36%	3.46%	0.31%	0.04%	0.00%	0.02%
End-of-Period	Baa	89.16%	0.03%	0.21%	3.46%	80.50%	4.14%	0.52%	0.05%	0.25%
Rating	Ba	5.25%	0.00%	0.03%	0.31%	4.14%	0.63%	0.10%	0.01%	0.04%
	B	0.68%	0.00%	0.00%	0.04%	0.52%	0.10%	0.02%	0.00%	0.00%
	Caa-C	0.07%	0.00%	0.00%	0.00%	0.05%	0.01%	0.00%	0.00%	0.00%
	Default	0.31%	0.00%	0.00%	0.02%	0.25%	0.04%	0.01%	0.00%	0.00%

obligors is positively correlated, then the total likelihood that both obligors' ratings improve (the sum of the shaded cells in the upper left-hand corner) or deteriorate (the sum of the shaded cells in the lower right-hand corner) should be larger than those calculated under the assumption of no correlation. The total likelihood of an upgrade for both issuers under the assumption of no correlation is 0.21%, versus the 0.42% actually observed. The total likelihood of downgrades or default for both issuers under the assumption of no correlation is 0.40%, versus the 0.97% actually observed

The joint rating transition matrix derived under the assumption of no credit quality correlation and the empirical joint rating transition matrix, together with the issuer counts used to generate them, can be combined in a more rigorous statistical test of the assumption of no credit quality correlation.[8] Under this test, we can reject the hypothesis of no credit quality correlation at the 1% level of confidence.

The discussion above reveals evidence of credit quality correlation for Baa-rated issuers over the better part of this century. It does not, however, address variations in this outcome across different combinations of rating categories, industries, geographies, or time periods, nor does it provide an indication of the economic impact of such correlation. In the following sections, we provide some indicative calculations that more directly quantify the effects of the credit quality correlation explored above and provide an example of how correlations may vary across rating categories, industries, geographies, and the period considered.

The Impact of Credit Quality Correlation

The correlation of credit quality movements has implications for the credit risk characteristics of portfolios of credit exposures. In general, the higher the correlation, the greater the volatility of a portfolio's value that is attributable to credit risk. Figures 11.19 and 11.20 yield evidence of positive credit quality correlation for Baa-rated obligors. It is of interest to determine how meaningful this correlation is. Towards that end, we consider one measure of the volatility of a portfolio's value — the standard deviation.[9] We also consider a hypothetical, portfolio consisting of two similar obligations: Baa-rated, 7.5% bonds with 20 years remaining to maturity.[10] We estimate the values of these securities at the end of a one-year time horizon under each possible change in credit quality.[11] Figure 11.21 presents these valuations. If a 7.5% bond were upgraded to A, for example, we estimate that the note's value would climb to $102.06 (the figure on the row corresponding to the Baa-rated note, under the A column).

A portfolio consisting of two of these bonds can then be easily valued under each possible joint credit outcome. For example, if one bond experienced an upgrade to Aa, we estimate its value would climb to $104.26. If the other bond were downgraded to Ba, we estimate its value would be $81.18. The portfolio's value would then be $185.44 ($104.26 + $81.18).

Under the assumption of no credit quality correlation, the expected value and standard deviation of the portfolio's value may be calculated using the probabilities given in the joint rating transition matrix estimated under the assumption of no credit quality correlation (Figure 11.19). However, we need not impose the assumption of no credit quality correlation between these bonds. We can re-estimate the expected value and standard deviation of the portfolio's value without imposing any assumptions about how credit quality moves by instead using the probabilities reported in the empirical joint rating transition matrix instead (Figure 11.20). Figure 11.22 below presents the results of these calculations.

---

[8] We used Pearson's Chi-square statistic to test the hypothesis of no credit quality correlation

[9] The standard deviation is only one of many possible measures of portfolio risk (volatility). We examine it here not because we feel that it is the most appropriate measure but because its wide usage promotes easy understanding

[10] We consider debt of similar characteristics here in order to focus attention on the effects of credit quality correlation

Figure 11.21   Estimated Bond Values at the End of One Year

Ratings/Status at end of year

Rating at Start of Year	Debt	Description	Aaa	Aa	A	Baa	Ba	B	Caa-C	Default
Baa	7.5%	20-year bond	$104.96	$104.26	$102.06	$100.31	$81.18	$75.47	$58.59	$44.00

Figure 11.22   Mean and Standard Deviation of Portfolio Value

	Expected	Standard
Without correlation	$198.04	$8.12
With correlation	$198.04	$8.43

The positive credit quality correlation manifests itself here as an increase in the standard deviation (risk) of the portfolio's future value from $8.12 under the assumption of no credit quality correlation to $8.43, a 3.8% increase. The greater standard deviation implies more variability, or risk, in the distribution of the portfolio's future value.

The difference between the standard deviation calculated using historical credit quality correlations and that calculated under the assumption of no credit quality correlation increases with the number of exposures. In the example above, if we were to include another similar bond, the difference between the standard deviation as calculated with correlation and without climbs to 7.5%. After adding 40 exposures, the standard deviation as calculated with correlation is double that calculated without.

Industrial and Geographic Considerations for Credit Quality Correlations

The ambient business environment, including capital market conditions, regulatory considerations, and economic growth are likely to contribute to the credit quality correlation highlighted by the empirical joint rating transition matrix above. However, prevailing business conditions vary across countries, industries, and time. For these reasons, the correlation of credit qualities can be

---

[11]   We estimate these values by discounting the bonds' remaining promised cash flows along a forward, zero coupon spot yield curve for that bond's rating. The valuation calculation is not central to this discussion and so we do not comment on it in detail here

expected to vary across industries, geographies, and time. Rather than explore the gamut of possible rating and joint rating transition matrices presented by industrial, geographic, and temporal segmentation, we present a sample calculation that suggests that these factors are, in fact, important determinants of the rating and joint rating migrations.

To explore industry- and geography-specific credit quality correlation further, we have appealed to patterns in ratings movements between debt issuers of different industries and geographies. Proceeding as in the previous sections, we estimated a joint rating transition matrix for two issuers, except this time we chose one A-rated European financial company and one A-rated US industrial company (see Figure 11.23). These results have been obtained from ratings data available since January 1990.

As in the discussion of the previous section, the first row of numbers represents the sum of each column and hence, the stand alone likelihood of a US Industrial issuer's (estimated) senior unsecured rating migrating to each other rating category or default. We estimate that an A-rated US industrial will maintain that rating over the course of one year with about 94.33% probability. The first column of numbers represents the sum of each row and so presents the stand alone likelihood of an A-rated European Financial issuer's (estimated) senior unsecured rating migrating to each other rating category or default. Note that these values differ from those of the A-rated US industrial.

At first glance, the evidence in favor of a credit quality correlation between A-rated US industrials and A-rated European financials does not appear to be as strong as the evidence considered earlier for all Baa-rated issuers. Based on the assumption that the credit qualities of these firms are uncorrelated, the total probability of joint upgrade comes to four basis points, while the total risk of joint downgrade amounts to 23 basis points. Figure 11.23 reveals that the historically observed probability of joint rating upgrade also amounts to four basis points, while that observed for joint downgrade climbs slightly to 27 basis points.

To quantify the effects of any possible correlation in these data, consider a portfolio of two A-rated bonds — one issued by a US industrial firm and one issued by a European financial firm. For the sake of simplicity, assume that the terms of these bonds are the same as those of the previous section. We can then re-construct the calculations of that section using the same bond and portfolio valuations, but replacing the Baa-Baa one-year, joint rating transition matrix with the joint rating transition matrix presented in Figure 11.23. The results are presented below in Figure 11.24.

Figure 11.23   Empirical Joint Rating Transition Matrix
(One A-rated European financial issuer and one A-rated US industrial issuer)

			A-rated US industrial issuer							
			Aaa	Aa	A	Baa	Ba	B	Caa-C	Default
			0.07%	1.46%	94.33%	3.89%	0.25%	0.00%	0.00%	0.00%
	Aaa	0.00%	0.00%	0.00%	0.00%	0.00%	0.00%	0.00%	0.00%	0.00%
A-rated	Aa	2.29%	0.00%	0.04%	2.15%	0.09%	0.01%	0.00%	0.00%	0.00%
European	A	92.13%	0.06%	1.34%	86.96%	3.54%	0.23%	0.00%	0.00%	0.00%
Financial										
Issuer	Baa	5.57%	0.00%	0.00%	5.22%	0.26%	0.01%	0.00%	0.00%	0.00%
	Ba	0.00%	0.00%	0.00%	0.00%	0.00%	0.00%	0.00%	0.00%	0.00%
	B	0.00%	0.00%	0.00%	0.00%	0.00%	0.00%	0.00%	0.00%	0.00%
	Caa-C	0.00%	0.00%	0.00%	0.00%	0.00%	0.00%	0.00%	0.00%	0.00%
	Default	0.00%	0.00%	0.00%	0.00%	0.00%	0.00%	0.00%	0.00%	0.00%

Figure 11.24   Mean and Standard Deviation of Portfolio Value
(Two, initially Baa-rated, issuers. Based on data available since 1920)

	Expected Value	Standard Deviation
Without correlation	$203.99	$1.56
With correlation	$203.99	$1.55

Using the rating and joint rating migration patterns documented in Figure 11.23, the expected value of this portfolio climbs to $203.99. This is as expected since we have effectively upgraded both bonds in the previous example from Baa to A. The standard deviation in both cases falls considerably. This is due, in part, to the increase in ratings from Baa to A. However, it is also because we have estimated these joint rating transition matrices over the period from 1990 to the present, during which there have been very few situations in which either a US industrial or a European financial with the A rating has suffered a large downgrade.

The relative difference in the portfolio's risk, as measured by the standard deviation, is very small in absolute value and suggests a slight negative correlation (thereby reducing the portfolio standard deviation in the case with correlation). This small degree of correlation between these two very different companies hints at the importance of industrial and geographic considerations when estimating the effects of credit quality correlations.

11.4 Summary

This chapter analyzed credit rating dynamics. From initial assignment, to placement on the Watchlist, to a formal rating change, the rating transitions presented in this chapter shed light on the evolution of credit ratings, and quantify credit quality dynamics by rating category. Risk practitioners requiring detailed knowledge of the statistical characteristics of credit quality will no doubt find these transitions useful.

That rating changes for issuers placed on the Watchlist are different from issuers not on the Watchlist, implies that the Watchlist is an important source of information for market participants interested in measuring credit risk. This study has shown that the Watchlist is an important leading indicator of future Moody's rating changes. As expected, the frequency and magnitude of rating transitions is markedly higher for issues on the Watchlist than for the general population of Moody's-rated debt.

Issues on review represent a significant subset of Moody's-rated debt; a subset defined by its higher than average rating volatility. This rating volatility can be measured effectively with rating transition matrices, both for all issues of an asset class placed on watch, or by subdividing the Watchlist issues by the direction of the Watchlist assignment.

The results indicate that not only are Moody's higher ratings associated with a lower incidence of default, but they are also more stable in the sense that they are generally less likely than lower rating categories to be revised over any time period from 1 to 15 years.

We also examined the variability of rating transition rates. The distribution of rating transition rates is necessarily asymmetric and there is evidence suggesting that the distribution is affected by macroeconomic factors. That macroeconomic variables may affect the credit quality of many borrowers in turn suggests that different issuers' credit qualities may be linked. A statistical test rejected the hypothesis that the credit quality of Baa-rated issuers is not correlated at the 99% level of confidence, providing additional evidence of credit quality correlation.

The results suggest that such correlation is an important feature for those wishing to understand the credit risk characteristics of credit portfolios. Finally, we performed simple indicative calculations suggesting that credit quality correlations are, in part, determined by factors specific to both the issuer's industry and geographic domain.

Figure 11.25   Unconditional* Watchlist Transition Matrix for Long-Term Debt Ratings, 10/91–6/98

	Aaa	Aa1	Aa2	Aa3	A1	A2	A3	Baa1	Baa2	Baa3	Ba1	Ba2	Ba3	B1	B2	B3	Caa	WR	Default
Aaa	27.02%	57.42%	3.44%	8.41%	0.26%	0.20%	0.00%	0.00%	0.00%	0.00%	0.00%	0.00%	0.00%	0.00%	0.00%	0.00%	0.00%	3.25%	0.00%
Aa1	14.41%	11.30%	53.17%	11.89%	4.46%	0.19%	0.19%	0.00%	0.00%	0.00%	0.00%	0.00%	0.00%	0.00%	0.00%	0.00%	0.00%	4.39%	0.00%
Aa2	1.60%	5.20%	30.11%	41.80%	13.36%	2.32%	0.50%	0.11%	0.00%	0.00%	0.00%	0.00%	0.00%	0.00%	0.00%	0.00%	0.00%	4.99%	0.00%
Aa3	0.65%	0.55%	21.68%	21.13%	38.96%	10.23%	0.78%	0.49%	0.06%	0.00%	0.00%	0.00%	0.00%	0.00%	0.00%	0.00%	0.00%	5.47%	0.00%
A1	0.12%	0.15%	0.48%	29.41%	25.39%	27.73%	10.92%	0.63%	0.24%	0.00%	0.00%	0.00%	0.00%	0.00%	0.00%	0.00%	0.00%	4.92%	0.00%
A2	0.15%	0.00%	0.20%	3.89%	23.10%	31.38%	30.74%	5.71%	0.71%	0.07%	0.00%	0.00%	0.00%	0.00%	0.00%	0.00%	0.00%	4.04%	0.00%
A3	0.06%	0.09%	0.15%	0.68%	2.88%	22.53%	32.40%	23.82%	11.90%	1.67%	0.06%	0.06%	0.12%	0.00%	0.00%	0.00%	0.00%	3.58%	0.00%
Baa1	0.13%	0.03%	0.20%	0.13%	0.13%	7.43%	38.30%	16.67%	25.40%	6.83%	1.27%	0.00%	0.13%	0.00%	0.07%	0.00%	0.00%	3.30%	0.00%
Baa2	0.00%	0.00%	0.05%	0.05%	0.50%	0.81%	7.42%	24.56%	17.14%	29.35%	12.94%	2.26%	0.41%	0.72%	0.00%	0.14%	0.09%	3.57%	0.00%
Baa3	0.15%	0.00%	0.30%	0.00%	0.25%	0.75%	1.30%	5.60%	24.55%	31.55%	21.05%	8.65%	1.65%	0.50%	0.30%	0.10%	0.65%	2.65%	0.00%
Ba1	0.00%	0.00%	0.32%	0.08%	0.55%	0.16%	0.16%	0.63%	4.11%	24.98%	30.04%	15.73%	12.41%	4.90%	0.55%	0.16%	0.24%	4.98%	0.00%
Ba2	0.00%	0.00%	0.00%	0.00%	0.21%	0.32%	0.11%	2.77%	1.60%	6.40%	22.20%	23.16%	25.29%	5.87%	3.31%	1.28%	0.00%	7.47%	0.00%
Ba3	0.23%	0.00%	0.15%	0.00%	0.11%	0.69%	0.34%	0.23%	2.64%	1.03%	5.86%	26.18%	16.88%	13.78%	18.94%	1.49%	2.18%	9.41%	0.00%
B1	0.00%	0.00%	0.00%	0.00%	0.00%	0.19%	0.19%	0.56%	2.43%	2.06%	1.31%	7.12%	15.92%	34.08%	17.79%	5.06%	2.43%	10.86%	0.00%
B2	0.00%	0.00%	0.00%	0.00%	0.00%	0.00%	0.54%	0.54%	1.63%	1.63%	3.27%	2.45%	3.81%	20.16%	25.89%	15.53%	14.71%	9.81%	0.00%
B3	0.32%	0.00%	0.00%	0.00%	0.00%	0.64%	0.32%	0.96%	0.96%	2.24%	0.64%	1.28%	2.88%	7.69%	12.50%	30.45%	21.47%	17.31%	0.32%
Caa-C	0.00%	0.00%	0.00%	0.79%	0.00%	0.00%	0.00%	0.00%	0.00%	0.00%	0.00%	0.79%	0.79%	5.56%	4.76%	7.14%	41.27%	32.54%	6.35%

*Unconditional includes ratings placed on review for upgrade, downgrade and with direction uncertain

Figure 11.26 Review for Upgrade Watchlist Transition Matrix for Long-Term Debt Ratings, 10/91–6/98

	Aaa	Aa1	Aa2	Aa3	A1	A2	A3	Baa1	Baa2	Baa3	Ba1	Ba2	Ba3	B1	B2	B3	Caa	WR	Default
Aaa	NA	NA	NA	NA	NA	NA	NA	NA	NA	NA	NA	NA	NA	NA	NA	NA	NA	NA	NA
Aa1	96.52%	0.87%	0.00%	0.00%	0.00%	0.00%	0.00%	0.00%	0.00%	0.00%	0.00%	0.00%	0.00%	0.00%	0.00%	0.00%	0.00%	2.61%	0.00%
Aa2	7.88%	25.39%	53.94%	0.00%	0.00%	0.00%	0.00%	0.00%	0.00%	0.00%	0.00%	0.00%	0.00%	0.00%	0.00%	0.00%	0.00%	12.78%	0.00%
Aa3	2.29%	1.95%	76.63%	13.06%	0.00%	0.00%	0.00%	0.00%	0.00%	0.00%	0.00%	0.00%	0.00%	0.00%	0.00%	0.00%	0.00%	6.07%	0.00%
A1	0.27%	0.34%	1.08%	65.97%	26.20%	0.00%	0.00%	0.00%	0.00%	0.00%	0.00%	0.00%	0.00%	0.00%	0.00%	0.00%	0.00%	6.14%	0.00%
A2	0.44%	0.00%	0.37%	11.58%	68.55%	14.15%	0.44%	0.00%	0.00%	0.00%	0.00%	0.00%	0.00%	0.00%	0.00%	0.00%	0.00%	4.47%	0.00%
A3	0.18%	0.26%	0.44%	2.02%	8.33%	66.78%	18.32%	0.00%	0.00%	0.00%	0.00%	0.00%	0.00%	0.00%	0.00%	0.00%	0.00%	3.68%	0.00%
Baa1	0.20%	0.07%	0.40%	0.20%	0.27%	14.39%	75.07%	6.23%	0.00%	0.00%	0.00%	0.00%	0.00%	0.00%	0.00%	0.00%	0.00%	3.18%	0.00%
Baa2	0.00%	0.00%	0.12%	0.12%	1.34%	2.19%	19.93%	65.98%	6.32%	0.00%	0.00%	0.00%	0.00%	0.00%	0.00%	0.00%	0.00%	4.01%	0.00%
Baa3	0.39%	0.00%	0.79%	0.00%	0.66%	1.97%	2.89%	14.59%	63.73%	12.35%	0.00%	0.00%	0.13%	0.00%	0.00%	0.00%	0.00%	2.50%	0.00%
Ba1	0.00%	0.00%	0.94%	0.23%	1.64%	0.47%	0.47%	1.87%	11.48%	73.77%	3.51%	0.00%	0.00%	0.23%	0.00%	0.00%	0.00%	5.39%	0.00%
Ba2	0.00%	0.00%	0.00%	0.00%	0.50%	0.75%	0.25%	6.47%	3.73%	14.93%	48.76%	13.93%	0.00%	0.00%	0.00%	0.00%	0.00%	10.70%	0.00%
Ba3	0.51%	0.00%	0.00%	0.00%	0.26%	1.53%	0.77%	0.51%	5.87%	2.30%	11.99%	52.81%	11.22%	0.00%	0.00%	0.00%	0.00%	12.24%	0.00%
B1	0.00%	0.00%	0.00%	0.00%	0.00%	0.40%	0.40%	1.21%	5.24%	4.44%	2.82%	15.32%	29.44%	26.61%	0.81%	0.00%	0.00%	13.31%	0.00%
B2	0.00%	0.00%	0.00%	0.00%	0.00%	0.00%	1.13%	1.21%	3.39%	3.39%	6.78%	5.08%	7.34%	40.68%	15.82%	0.00%	1.69%	13.56%	0.00%
B3	0.57%	0.00%	0.00%	0.00%	0.00%	1.14%	0.00%	1.71%	1.14%	4.00%	1.14%	2.29%	5.14%	13.71%	21.71%	24.57%	2.86%	20.00%	0.00%
Caa-C	0.00%	0.00%	0.00%	1.16%	0.00%	0.00%	0.00%	0.00%	0.00%	0.00%	0.00%	1.16%	1.16%	8.14%	4.65%	13.95%	31.40%	38.37%	0.00%

Figure 11.27   Review for Downgrade Watchlist Transition Matrix for Long-Term Debt Ratings, 10/91–6/98

	Aaa	Aa1	Aa2	Aa3	A1	A2	A3	Baa1	Baa2	Baa3	Ba1	Ba2	Ba3	B1	B2	B3	Caa	WR	Default
Aaa	27.02%	57.42%	3.44%	8.41%	0.26%	0.20%	0.00%	0.00%	0.00%	0.00%	0.00%	0.00%	0.00%	0.00%	0.00%	0.00%	0.00%	3.25%	0.00%
Aaa	26.96%	57.57%	3.32%	8.43%	0.27%	0.20%	0.00%	0.00%	0.00%	0.00%	0.00%	0.00%	0.00%	0.00%	0.00%	0.00%	0.00%	3.25%	0.00%
Aa1	0.08%	13.13%	62.44%	13.96%	5.24%	0.23%	0.23%	0.00%	0.00%	0.00%	0.00%	0.00%	0.00%	0.00%	0.00%	0.00%	0.00%	4.70%	0.00%
Aa2	0.00%	0.04%	23.69%	52.72%	16.85%	2.92%	0.63%	0.13%	0.00%	0.00%	0.00%	0.00%	0.00%	0.00%	0.00%	0.00%	0.00%	3.01%	0.00%
Aa3	0.00%	0.00%	0.05%	24.75%	53.52%	14.62%	1.11%	0.69%	0.09%	0.00%	0.00%	0.00%	0.00%	0.00%	0.00%	0.00%	0.00%	5.18%	0.00%
A1	0.00%	0.00%	0.00%	0.17%	24.44%	49.57%	20.15%	1.22%	0.46%	0.00%	0.00%	0.00%	0.00%	0.00%	0.00%	0.00%	0.00%	4.00%	0.00%
A2	0.00%	0.00%	0.00%	0.00%	0.04%	34.61%	50.43%	9.58%	1.20%	0.12%	0.00%	0.00%	0.00%	0.00%	0.00%	0.00%	0.00%	4.01%	0.00%
A3	0.00%	0.00%	0.00%	0.00%	0.05%	0.00%	37.90%	37.53%	18.95%	1.73%	0.09%	0.09%	0.19%	0.00%	0.00%	0.00%	0.00%	3.46%	0.00%
Baa1	0.07%	0.00%	0.00%	0.00%	0.00%	0.42%	1.20%	26.19%	53.36%	14.51%	0.71%	0.00%	0.28%	0.00%	0.14%	0.00%	0.00%	3.11%	0.00%
Baa2	0.00%	0.00%	0.00%	0.00%	0.00%	0.00%	0.00%	0.00%	23.05%	46.99%	20.82%	3.72%	0.67%	1.19%	0.00%	0.22%	0.15%	3.20%	0.00%
Baa3	0.00%	0.00%	0.00%	0.00%	0.00%	0.00%	0.00%	0.00%	0.00%	40.04%	36.70%	15.19%	2.81%	0.88%	0.35%	0.18%	1.23%	2.63%	0.00%
Ba1	0.00%	0.00%	0.00%	0.00%	0.00%	0.00%	0.00%	0.00%	0.00%	0.00%	41.21%	25.00%	19.72%	7.66%	0.88%	0.25%	0.38%	4.90%	0.00%
Ba2	0.00%	0.00%	0.00%	0.30%	0.00%	0.00%	0.00%	0.00%	0.00%	0.00%	0.48%	31.83%	40.14%	12.59%	7.36%	2.85%	0.00%	4.75%	0.00%
Ba3	0.00%	0.00%	0.00%	0.00%	0.00%	0.00%	0.00%	0.00%	0.00%	0.00%	0.74%	0.49%	20.20%	25.12%	39.66%	3.20%	4.68%	5.91%	0.00%
B1	0.00%	0.00%	0.00%	0.00%	0.00%	0.00%	0.00%	0.00%	0.00%	0.00%	0.00%	0.00%	0.00%	41.73%	35.43%	9.06%	5.12%	8.66%	0.00%
B2	0.00%	0.00%	0.00%	0.00%	0.00%	0.00%	0.00%	0.00%	0.00%	0.00%	0.00%	0.00%	0.00%	1.18%	33.14%	33.14%	29.59%	2.96%	0.00%
B3	0.00%	0.00%	0.00%	0.00%	0.00%	0.00%	0.00%	0.00%	0.00%	0.00%	0.00%	0.00%	0.00%	0.00%	0.00%	37.93%	53.45%	7.76%	0.86%
Caa-C	0.00%	0.00%	0.00%	0.00%	0.00%	0.00%	0.00%	0.00%	0.00%	0.00%	0.00%	0.00%	0.00%	0.00%	0.00%	0.00%	71.64%	16.42%	11.94%

Figure 11.28   Review with Uncertain Direction Watchlist Transition Matrix for Long-Term Debt Ratings, 10/91–6/98

	Aa2	Aa3	A1	A2	A3	Baa1	Baa2	Baa3	Ba1	Ba2	Ba3	B1	B2	B3	Caa	WR	Default
Aa2	100.00%	0.00%	0.00%	0.00%	0.00%	0.00%	0.00%	0.00%	0.00%	0.00%	0.00%	0.00%	0.00%	0.00%	0.00%	0.00%	0.00%
Aa3	0.00%	7.27%	85.45%	0.00%	0.00%	0.00%	0.00%	0.00%	0.00%	0.00%	0.00%	0.00%	0.00%	0.00%	0.00%	7.27%	0.00%
A1	0.00%	0.00%	29.03%	54.84%	12.90%	0.00%	0.00%	0.00%	0.00%	0.00%	0.00%	0.00%	0.00%	0.00%	0.00%	3.23%	0.00%
A2	1.09%	0.00%	0.73%	88.36%	7.64%	0.00%	0.00%	0.00%	0.00%	0.00%	0.00%	0.00%	0.00%	0.00%	0.00%	2.18%	0.00%
A3	0.00%	0.00%	1.59%	3.97%	66.67%	7.14%	0.00%	15.87%	0.00%	0.00%	0.00%	0.00%	0.00%	0.00%	0.00%	4.76%	0.00%
Baa1	0.00%	0.00%	0.00%	0.00%	0.00%	45.57%	10.13%	0.00%	35.44%	0.00%	0.00%	0.00%	0.00%	0.00%	0.00%	8.86%	0.00%
Baa2	0.00%	0.00%	0.00%	0.00%	0.00%	0.00%	39.53%	39.53%	13.95%	0.00%	0.00%	0.00%	0.00%	0.00%	0.00%	6.98%	0.00%
Baa3	0.00%	0.00%	0.00%	0.00%	3.96%	0.99%	5.94%	80.20%	2.97%	0.00%	0.00%	0.00%	1.98%	0.00%	0.00%	3.96%	0.00%
Ba1	0.00%	0.00%	0.00%	0.00%	0.00%	0.00%	7.14%	2.38%	88.10%	0.00%	0.00%	0.00%	0.00%	0.00%	0.00%	2.38%	0.00%
Ba2	0.00%	0.00%	0.00%	0.00%	0.00%	0.00%	0.00%	0.00%	8.77%	23.68%	59.65%	1.75%	0.00%	0.00%	0.00%	6.14%	0.00%
Ba3	0.00%	0.00%	0.00%	0.00%	0.00%	0.00%	0.00%	0.00%	1.37%	26.03%	28.77%	24.66%	5.48%	0.00%	0.00%	13.70%	0.00%
B1	0.00%	0.00%	0.00%	0.00%	0.00%	0.00%	0.00%	0.00%	0.00%	0.00%	37.50%	31.25%	9.38%	12.50%	0.00%	9.38%	0.00%
B2	0.00%	0.00%	0.00%	0.00%	0.00%	0.00%	0.00%	0.00%	0.00%	0.00%	4.76%	0.00%	52.38%	4.76%	4.76%	33.33%	0.00%
B3	0.00%	0.00%	0.00%	0.00%	3.70%	0.00%	3.70%	0.00%	0.00%	0.00%	0.00%	0.00%	3.70%	29.63%	22.22%	37.04%	0.00%
Caa-C	0.00%	0.00%	0.00%	0.00%	0.00%	0.00%	0.00%	0.00%	0.00%	0.00%	0.00%	0.00%	7.69%	0.00%	61.54%	30.77%	0.00%

Figure 11.29   Watchlist Transition Matrices for Short-Term Debt Ratings, 10/91–6/98

Unconditional

	P-1	P-2	P-3	NP	WR
P-1	40.12%	57.17%	0.21%	0.00%	2.49%
P-2	22.19%	45.36%	23.51%	0.99%	7.95%
P-3	4.26%	21.28%	34.04%	36.17%	4.26%
NP	0.00%	10.71%	39.29%	32.14%	17.86%

Review for Upgrade

	P-1	P-2	P-3	NP	WR
P-1	NA	NA	NA	NA	NA
P-2	64.42%	25.96%	0.00%	0.00%	9.62%
P-3	12.90%	64.52%	22.58%	0.00%	0.00%
NP	0.00%	12.50%	45.83%	20.83%	20.83%

Review for Downgrade

	P-1	P-2	P-3	NP	WR
P-1	39.23%	58.00%	0.21%	0.00%	2.56%
P-2	0.00%	51.40%	39.66%	1.68%	7.26%
P-3	0.00%	0.00%	35.71%	58.93%	5.36%
NP	NA	NA	NA	NA	NA

Review with Direction Uncertain

	P-1	P-2	P-3	NP	WR
P-1	75.00%	25.00%	0.00%	0.00%	0.00%
P-2	0.00%	94.74%	0.00%	0.00%	5.26%
P-3	0.00%	0.00%	71.43%	14.29%	14.29%
NP	0.00%	0.00%	0.00%	100.00%	0.00%

Figure 11.30   Issuer-Based One-Year Rating Transition Matrices, 1/1/92–12/31/97

All-issuers

	Aaa	Aa	A	Baa	Ba	B	Caa-C	Default
Aaa	92.30%	7.20%	0.50%	0.00%	0.00%	0.00%	0.00%	0.00%
Aa	0.66%	92.53%	6.50%	0.31%	0.00%	0.00%	0.00%	0.00%
A	0.07%	2.11%	93.54%	3.64%	0.62%	0.02%	0.00%	0.00%
Baa	0.04%	0.09%	6.34%	89.95%	2.96%	0.39%	0.19%	0.04%
Ba	0.00%	0.05%	0.93%	6.30%	86.05%	5.72%	0.51%	0.43%
B	0.04%	0.08%	0.24%	0.57%	7.98%	84.89%	2.81%	3.40%
Caa-C	0.00%	0.00%	0.00%	0.00%	1.94%	8.41%	78.20%	11.44%

Issuers placed on review for upgrade

	Aaa	Aa	A	Baa	Ba	B	Caa-C	Default
Aaa	NA	NA	NA	NA	NA	NA	NA	NA
Aa	17.54%	82.46%	0.00%	0.00%	0.00%	0.00%	0.00%	0.00%
A	0.78%	22.66%	75.78%	0.78%	0.00%	0.00%	0.00%	0.00%
Baa	0.46%	2.29%	48.17%	48.62%	0.46%	0.00%	0.00%	0.00%
Ba	0.00%	0.51%	9.18%	40.31%	50.00%	0.00%	0.00%	0.00%
B	0.72%	0.72%	2.88%	8.63%	41.73%	45.32%	0.00%	0.00%
Caa-C	0.00%	0.00%	0.00%	4.17%	4.17%	45.83%	41.67%	4.17%

Issuers placed on review for downgrade

	Aaa	Aa	A	Baa	Ba	B	Caa-C	Default
Aaa	27.14%	70.00%	2.86%	0.00%	0.00%	0.00%	0.00%	0.00%
Aa	0.00%	52.99%	45.38%	1.63%	0.00%	0.00%	0.00%	0.00%
A	0.00%	0.48%	67.57%	26.36%	5.27%	0.32%	0.00%	0.00%
Baa	0.00%	0.00%	2.02%	60.52%	31.12%	4.90%	0.86%	0.58%
Ba	0.00%	0.00%	0.36%	1.08%	60.65%	26.35%	8.66%	2.89%
B	0.00%	0.00%	1.48%	0.00%	2.22%	54.81%	23.70%	17.78%
Caa-C	0.00%	0.00%	0.00%	0.00%	0.00%	0.00%	42.86%	57.14%

Issuers placed on review with direction uncertain

	Aaa	Aa	A	Baa	Ba	B	Caa-C	Default
Aaa	0.00%	0.00%	0.00%	0.00%	0.00%	0.00%	0.00%	0.00%
Aa	0.00%	100.00%	0.00%	0.00%	0.00%	0.00%	0.00%	0.00%
A	0.00%	8.11%	86.49%	5.41%	0.00%	0.00%	0.00%	0.00%
Baa	0.00%	0.00%	18.75%	65.63%	12.50%	3.13%	0.00%	0.00%
Ba	0.00%	0.00%	0.00%	11.76%	67.65%	20.59%	0.00%	0.00%
B	0.00%	0.00%	6.90%	3.45%	6.90%	68.97%	6.90%	6.90%
Caa-C	0.00%	0.00%	0.00%	0.00%	0.00%	20.00%	60.00%	20.00%

Figure 11.31   Alphabetical List of Watchlist Defaulters Since 1991

Obligor	Obligation	Initial Rating	Direction	Watchlist Date	Resolution Date	Default/ Div. Omission Date
Bibb Company	Long Term	Caa	Downgrade	12-Dec-94	04-Apr-95	03-Apr-95
FPA Medical Management, Inc.	Long Term	Caa2	Downgrade	03-Jun-98	18-Jun-98	15-Jun-98
Grand Union Company	Long Term	Caa	Downgrade	29-Nov-94	26-Jan-95	15-Jan-95
Greyhound Lines, Inc.	Long Term	B3	Downgrade	27-Sep-94	04-Oct-94	30-Sep-94
Lomas Financial Corporation	Long Term	Ca	Downgrade	04-Oct-95	13-Nov-95	10-Oct-95
Navistar International Corp.	Pref. Stock	"caa"	Uncertain	04-Dec-92	15-Oct-93	18-Dec-92
Stratosphere Corporation	Long Term	Caa	Downgrade	19-Aug-96	16-Dec-96	15-Nov-96
Unison HealthCare Corporation	Long Term	Caa3	Downgrade	28-Jul-97	05-Feb-98	01-Nov-97

Figure 11.32   Average Letter Rating Transition Matrices for 2 Through 10 and 15-Year Time Horizons

Two-year average rating transition matrix, 1920 to 1995

		Rating To:								
		Aaa	Aa	A	Baa	Ba	B	Caa-C	Default	WR
Rating	**Aaa**	79.70%	9.51%	2.01%	0.45%	0.15%	0.01%	0.00%	0.00%	8.16%
From:	**Aa**	2.00%	76.26%	9.50%	1.43%	0.42%	0.03%	0.02%	0.16%	10.18%
	A	0.10%	3.77%	75.79%	7.17%	1.28%	0.22%	0.04%	0.28%	11.34%
	Baa	0.05%	0.42%	6.42%	69.73%	6.71%	1.29%	0.12%	0.73%	14.53%
	Ba	0.03%	0.14%	0.74%	7.50%	63.73%	7.06%	0.81%	2.37%	17.62%
	B	0.00%	0.05%	0.23%	1.18%	8.63%	60.42%	3.95%	6.32%	19.22%
	Caa-C	0.00%	0.02%	0.03%	0.77%	2.07%	6.97%	56.11%	18.11%	15.92%

Three-year average rating transition matrix, 1920 to 1994

		Rating To:								
		Aaa	Aa	A	Baa	Ba	B	Caa-C	Default	WR
Rating	**Aaa**	72.27%	12.33%	2.89%	0.66%	0.32%	0.02%	0.00%	0.03%	11.48%
From:	**Aa**	2.65%	6Af47%	12.47%	2.17%	0.65%	0.08%	0.02%	0.25%	14.25%
	A	0.15%	4.88%	67.66%	8.63%	1.84%	0.38%	0.06%	0.53%	15.87%
	Baa	0.06%	0.61%	8.19%	60.24%	7.63%	1.69%	0.21%	1.23%	20.14%
	Ba	0.04%	0.19%	1.22%	9.16%	52.22%	7.99%	1.09%	3.56%	24.52%
	B	0.01%	0.07%	0.32%	1.66%	10.04%	48.37%	4.11%	8.84%	26.58%
	Caa-C	0.00%	0.00%	0.02%	0.82%	3.06%	7.97%	44.74%	22.17%	21.23%

Four-year average rating transition matrix, 1920 to 1993

		Rating To:								
		Aaa	Aa	A	Baa	Ba	B	Caa-C	Default	WR
Rating	**Aaa**	66.18%	13.91%	3.68%	0.79%	0.46%	0.07%	0.00%	0.08%	14.82%
From:	**Aa**	3.07%	60.24%	14.52%	2.85%	0.94%	0.14%	0.02%	0.40%	17.81%
	A	0.18%	5.54%	61.07%	9.65%	2.28%	0.49%	0.07%	0.82%	19.91%
	Baa	0.07%	0.76%	9.30%	52.93%	7.95%	1.95%	0.28%	1.79%	24.95%
	Ba	0.04%	0.24%	1.63%	9.95%	43.41%	8.26%	1.19%	4.81%	30.47%
	B	0.01%	0.09%	0.39%	2.15%	10.45%	39.06%	3.89%	11.12%	32.84%
	Caa-C	0.00%	0.00%	0.02%	1.31%	3.40%	8.04%	36.26%	25.54%	25.44%

Figure 11.32 (cont'd)

Five-year average rating transition matrix, 1920 to 1992

		Rating To: Aaa	Aa	A	Baa	Ba	B	Caa-C	Default	WR
Rating	Aaa	60.78%	15.21%	4.33%	0.96%	0.49%	0.09%	0.03%	0.14%	17.96%
From:	Aa	3.43%	54.14%	15.93%	3.42%	1.16%	0.20%	0.02%	0.58%	21.12%
	A	0.20%	5.85%	55.74%	10.34%	2.58%	0.69%	0.08%	1.08%	23.43%
	Baa	0.09%	0.92%	10.01%	47.06%	8.03%	2.00%	0.32%	2.28%	29.28%
	Ba	0.04%	0.26%	1.92%	10.40%	36.48%	8.09%	1.29%	5.90%	35.62%
	B	0.02%	0.09%	0.48%	2.41%	10.25%	32.12%	3.53%	12.91%	38.19%
	Caa-C	0.00%	0.00%	0.02%	1.57%	4.03%	7.77%	29.60%	27.98%	29.04%

Six-year average rating transition matrix, 1920 to 1991

		Rating To: Aaa	Aa	A	Baa	Ba	B	Caa-C	Default	WR
Rating	Aaa	56.03%	16.24%	4.97%	1.12%	0.58%	0.09%	0.03%	0.21%	20.72%
From:	Aa	3.74%	48.82%	17.00%	3.93%	1.40%	0.24%	0.03%	0.78%	24.06%
	A	0.21%	6.05%	51.35%	10.67%	2.88%	0.84%	0.10%	1.31%	26.59%
	Baa	0.10%	1.04%	10.52%	42.42%	7.79%	2.09%	0.32%	2.75%	32.98%
	Ba	0.05%	0.26%	2.13%	10.64%	31.00%	7.73%	1.32%	6.89%	39.98%
	B	0.02%	0.07%	0.64%	2.42%	9.81%	26.73%	3.15%	14.43%	42.73%
	Caa-C	0.00%	0.00%	0.00%	2.01%	3.72%	7.44%	24.82%	30.17%	31.84%

Seven-year average rating transition matrix, 1920 to 1990

		Rating To: Aaa	Aa	A	Baa	Ba	B	Caa-C	Default	WR
Rating	Aaa	51.82%	17.14%	5.30%	1.44%	0.61%	0.13%	0.01%	0.27%	23.28%
From:	Aa	4.01%	44.24%	17.82%	4.28%	1.62%	0.30%	0.03%	0.97%	26.72%
	A	0.23%	6.13%	47.55%	10.77%	3.08%	0.94%	0.13%	1.54%	29.63%
	Baa	0.07%	1.14%	10.88%	38.74%	7.36%	2.12%	0.32%	3.20%	36.17%
	Ba	0.06%	0.26%	2.36%	10.55%	26.66%	7.35%	1.34%	7.69%	43.74%
	B	0.03%	0.06%	0.73%	2.34%	9.28%	22.47%	2.77%	15.81%	46.50%
	Caa-C	0.00%	0.00%	0.00%	2.50%	2.89%	7.05%	21.13%	31.97%	34.46%

Figure 11.32 (cont'd)

Eight-year average rating transition matrix, 1920 to 1989

		Rating To:								
		Aaa	Aa	A	Baa	Ba	B	Caa-C	Default	WR
Rating	Aaa	48.19%	17.90%	5.60%	1.62%	0.71%	0.14%	0.01%	0.38%	25.45%
From:	Aa	4.22%	40.36%	18.64%	4.43%	1.80%	0.40%	0.05%	1.16%	28.94%
	A	0.25%	6.28%	44.28%	10.92%	3.17%	1.00%	0.16%	1.76%	32.17%
	Baa	0.06%	1.23%	11.22%	35.58%	6.95%	2.08%	0.32%	3.64%	38.92%
	Ba	0.07%	0.25%	2.62%	10.51%	23.12%	6.98%	1.29%	8.50%	46.66%
	B	0.03%	0.07%	0.86%	2.40%	8.82%	19.03%	2.52%	16.89%	49.39%
	Caa-C	0.00%	0.02%	0.00%	2.54%	2.52%	6.53%	18.53%	33.87%	36.00%

Nine-year average rating transition matrix, 1920 to 1988

		Rating To:								
		Aaa	Aa	A	Baa	Ba	B	Caa-C	Default	WR
Rating	Aaa	44.96%	18.39%	5.95%	1.84%	0.70%	0.15%	0.01%	0.50%	27.50%
From:	Aa	4.35%	36.93%	19.27%	4.64%	1.98%	0.50%	0.08%	1.30%	30.96%
	A	0.27%	6.44%	41.43%	11.03%	3.20%	1.06%	0.18%	1.99%	34.41%
	Baa	0.07%	1.27%	11.56%	32.79%	6.62%	2.08%	0.31%	4.04%	41.26%
	Ba	0.07%	0.29%	2.81%	10.38%	20.05%	6.58%	1.28%	9.16%	49.37%
	B	0.03%	0.08%	0.85%	2.60%	8.27%	16.28%	2.36%	17.71%	51.82%
	Caa-C	0.00%	0.02%	0.00%	2.33%	2.94%	5.39%	16.10%	35.63%	37.60%

Ten-year average rating transition matrix, 1920 to 1987

		Rating To:								
		Aaa	Aa	A	Baa	Ba	B	Caa-C	Default	WR
Rating	Aaa	41.57%	19.00%	6.09%	2.11%	0.77%	0.19%	0.02%	0.64%	29.62%
From:	Aa	4.48%	33.35%	19.84%	4.88%	2.21%	0.59%	0.13%	1.45%	33.08%
	A	0.30%	6.52%	38.62%	11.07%	3.28%	1.10%	0.20%	2.24%	36.65%
	Baa	0.08%	1.33%	11.71%	30.00%	6.36%	2.05%	0.30%	4.41%	43.76%
	Ba	0.07%	0.32%	3.00%	10.13%	17.06%	6.08%	1.26%	9.91%	52.18%
	B	0.02%	0.06%	0.81%	2.74%	7.78%	13.75%	2.10%	18.62%	54.11%
	Caa-C	0.00%	0.02%	0.00%	2.12%	3.21%	5.06%	13.50%	36.92%	39.17%

Figure 11.32 (cont'd)

Fifteen-year average rating transition matrix, 1920 to 1982

		Rating To:								
		Aaa	Aa	A	Baa	Ba	B	Caa-C	Default	WR
Rating	Aaa	32.12%	20.88%	8.10%	2.70%	1.23%	0.31%	0.00%	1.11%	33.55%
From:	Aa	4.39%	24.10%	20.38%	6.18%	3.07%	0.84%	0.28%	2.13%	38.64%
	A	0.36%	6.69%	31.07%	11.15%	3.37%	1.05%	0.22%	3.23%	42.86%
	Baa	0.09%	1.34%	12.43%	22.71%	5.26%	1.79%	0.31%	5.69%	50.39%
	Ba	0.04%	0.38%	3.71%	8.97%	10.62%	4.49%	0.97%	12.27%	58.56%
	B	0.03%	0.05%	0.65%	4.00%	4.99%	7.88%	1.56%	20.98%	59.87%
	Caa-C	0.00%	0.02%	1.17%	1.02%	3.46%	4.03%	7.11%	41.11%	42.09%

Figure 11.33   Average Alphanumeric Rating Transition Matrices for 2 Through 10-Year Time Horizons

2-year average rating transition matrix, 1983–1995

Rating From: \ Rating To:	Aaa	Aa1	Aa2	Aa3	A1	A2	A3	Baa1	Baa2	Baa3	Ba1	Ba2	Ba3	B1	B2	B3	Caa-C	D	WR
Aaa	72.7%	8.1%	5.2%	2.3%	0.9%	1.0%	0.2%	0.0%	0.0%	0.0%	0.3%	0.0%	0.0%	0.0%	0.0%	0.1%	0.0%	0.0%	9.2%
Aa1	3.8%	53.7%	13.5%	11.9%	5.7%	1.7%	0.4%	0.3%	0.0%	0.3%	0.7%	0.0%	0.0%	0.0%	0.0%	0.0%	0.0%	0.0%	8.1%
Aa2	1.2%	4.6%	58.4%	13.8%	6.7%	4.0%	1.6%	0.9%	0.2%	0.0%	0.0%	0.0%	0.1%	0.1%	0.0%	0.0%	0.1%	0.0%	8.4%
Aa3	0.2%	0.9%	4.0%	58.6%	16.6%	6.7%	2.4%	0.8%	0.4%	0.4%	0.2%	0.2%	0.4%	0.1%	0.0%	0.0%	0.0%	0.0%	8.3%
A1	0.1%	0.2%	1.6%	7.6%	62.4%	11.1%	4.6%	1.7%	0.8%	0.4%	0.3%	0.4%	0.4%	0.5%	0.0%	0.0%	0.0%	0.0%	7.7%
A2	0.1%	0.1%	0.2%	1.5%	8.3%	59.9%	11.6%	4.5%	2.0%	0.8%	0.7%	0.3%	0.4%	0.3%	0.2%	0.0%	0.1%	0.0%	9.1%
A3	0.1%	0.1%	0.1%	0.5%	3.3%	13.2%	51.6%	9.7%	5.7%	2.7%	0.9%	0.3%	0.8%	0.3%	0.1%	0.1%	0.0%	0.2%	10.3%
Baa1	0.1%	0.0%	0.3%	0.3%	0.9%	6.1%	11.5%	49.0%	10.6%	4.8%	1.9%	0.7%	1.3%	0.8%	0.5%	0.1%	0.2%	0.3%	10.5%
Baa2	0.1%	0.3%	0.2%	0.3%	0.7%	2.2%	6.5%	9.9%	50.0%	9.2%	3.8%	0.9%	1.2%	0.8%	0.8%	0.6%	0.1%	0.2%	12.4%
Baa3	0.0%	0.0%	0.1%	0.1%	0.4%	0.9%	2.0%	7.4%	13.3%	44.4%	7.6%	3.7%	1.9%	2.5%	0.9%	0.3%	0.4%	1.1%	12.9%
Ba1	0.2%	0.0%	0.0%	0.0%	0.2%	0.5%	1.1%	1.3%	5.1%	8.6%	46.0%	6.3%	5.2%	1.2%	2.1%	1.5%	0.5%	2.3%	17.8%
Ba2	0.0%	0.0%	0.1%	0.0%	0.0%	0.3%	0.3%	0.9%	1.5%	3.0%	10.2%	43.7%	7.6%	2.1%	5.7%	2.5%	0.7%	3.0%	18.4%
Ba3	0.0%	0.1%	0.0%	0.1%	0.0%	0.2%	0.2%	0.5%	0.4%	1.0%	3.9%	6.0%	47.4%	3.9%	7.6%	3.9%	0.8%	6.7%	17.2%
B1	0.0%	0.0%	0.1%	0.0%	0.1%	0.2%	0.2%	0.2%	0.5%	0.8%	1.2%	3.7%	6.4%	50.1%	2.4%	6.8%	1.2%	9.7%	16.2%
B2	0.0%	0.0%	0.1%	0.0%	0.3%	0.1%	0.1%	0.2%	0.2%	0.4%	0.8%	2.3%	6.6%	6.6%	40.1%	9.5%	3.0%	15.1%	14.5%
B3	0.0%	0.0%	0.0%	0.0%	0.0%	0.0%	0.0%	0.1%	0.2%	0.2%	0.9%	0.6%	2.6%	6.8%	2.9%	41.9%	4.1%	21.5%	18.5%
Caa-C	0.0%	0.0%	0.0%	0.0%	0.0%	0.0%	0.0%	0.8%	0.0%	2.4%	0.2%	0.0%	1.9%	2.8%	2.2%	2.8%	32.0%	33.9%	21.0%

Figure 11.33 (cont'd)

3-year average rating transition matrix, 1983–1994

Rating From: \ Rating To:	Aaa	Aa1	Aa2	Aa3	A1	A2	A3	Baa1	Baa2	Baa3	Ba1	Ba2	Ba3	B1	B2	B3	Caa-C	D	WR
Aaa	62.9%	9.5%	6.8%	3.4%	0.8%	1.5%	0.4%	0.0%	0.0%	0.0%	0.6%	0.0%	0.0%	0.0%	0.0%	0.1%	0.0%	0.0%	13.8%
Aa1	4.5%	40.2%	14.8%	12.5%	9.6%	2.6%	0.8%	1.1%	0.1%	0.6%	0.7%	0.0%	0.0%	0.0%	0.0%	0.0%	0.0%	0.0%	12.5%
Aa2	1.6%	5.4%	44.8%	16.1%	9.0%	5.9%	2.6%	1.6%	0.6%	0.0%	0.0%	0.0%	0.2%	0.1%	0.0%	0.0%	0.1%	0.1%	12.0%
Aa3	0.5%	1.2%	4.5%	45.7%	18.4%	9.3%	3.6%	1.5%	0.7%	0.6%	0.4%	0.2%	0.5%	0.2%	0.0%	0.0%	0.0%	0.1%	12.6%
A1	0.3%	0.3%	2.0%	9.2%	51.0%	12.3%	5.6%	2.4%	1.7%	1.0%	0.2%	0.5%	0.4%	0.7%	0.1%	0.2%	0.2%	0.4%	11.7%
A2	0.0%	0.1%	0.2%	1.9%	10.0%	47.3%	13.9%	5.1%	3.3%	1.4%	0.9%	0.6%	0.6%	0.3%	0.2%	0.0%	0.1%	0.2%	13.9%
A3	0.1%	0.1%	0.1%	1.1%	4.1%	15.5%	39.3%	11.0%	6.2%	3.1%	1.4%	0.7%	1.3%	0.4%	0.4%	0.0%	0.0%	0.4%	14.8%
Baa1	0.1%	0.0%	0.5%	0.3%	1.5%	7.0%	14.7%	37.3%	11.0%	5.4%	2.1%	0.7%	1.6%	1.0%	0.7%	0.3%	0.3%	0.7%	15.0%
Baa2	0.1%	0.4%	0.2%	0.5%	1.3%	3.3%	6.6%	10.1%	39.3%	9.9%	3.8%	1.1%	1.8%	1.0%	1.0%	0.8%	0.3%	0.3%	18.2%
Baa3	0.1%	0.0%	0.1%	0.1%	0.5%	1.7%	2.7%	9.1%	14.8%	32.3%	7.6%	3.7%	2.7%	2.7%	0.4%	0.6%	0.5%	1.8%	18.7%
Ba1	0.2%	0.0%	0.0%	0.0%	0.2%	1.2%	1.5%	1.9%	6.8%	9.4%	31.7%	6.3%	5.8%	1.8%	2.7%	1.5%	0.6%	3.7%	24.7%
Ba2	0.0%	0.0%	0.1%	0.0%	0.1%	0.4%	0.8%	1.1%	1.6%	4.2%	10.2%	29.6%	8.6%	2.2%	5.6%	2.7%	1.2%	5.4%	26.2%
Ba3	0.0%	0.1%	0.0%	0.1%	0.0%	0.3%	0.4%	0.7%	0.9%	0.8%	4.6%	6.8%	32.5%	4.6%	7.6%	4.3%	0.8%	10.4%	25.2%
B1	0.1%	0.0%	0.2%	0.0%	0.1%	0.1%	0.2%	0.6%	0.7%	1.0%	1.8%	3.5%	6.0%	36.7%	3.4%	7.1%	0.9%	14.1%	23.6%
B2	0.0%	0.0%	0.1%	0.0%	0.1%	0.1%	0.1%	0.2%	0.2%	1.1%	1.4%	2.8%	5.4%	7.7%	26.3%	8.9%	3.1%	21.1%	21.4%
B3	0.0%	0.0%	0.0%	0.0%	0.0%	0.0%	0.3%	0.3%	0.4%	0.5%	0.5%	1.1%	2.9%	7.4%	2.4%	28.0%	3.9%	26.2%	26.2%
Caa-C	0.0%	0.0%	0.0%	0.0%	0.0%	0.0%	0.0%	0.0%	0.7%	0.9%	0.0%	0.3%	3.4%	4.2%	1.5%	2.8%	22.1%	36.3%	27.6%

Figure 11.33 (cont'd)

4-year average rating transition matrix, 1983–1993

Rating From: \ Rating To:	Aaa	Aa1	Aa2	Aa3	A1	A2	A3	Baa1	Baa2	Baa3	Ba1	Ba2	Ba3	B1	B2	B3	Caa-C	D	WR
Aaa	54.9%	10.3%	7.5%	3.8%	2.2%	1.5%	0.5%	0.0%	0.0%	0.0%	0.4%	0.0%	0.1%	0.1%	0.0%	0.1%	0.0%	0.1%	18.4%
Aa1	4.7%	32.4%	13.3%	13.1%	11.7%	3.4%	1.3%	1.5%	0.7%	0.2%	0.3%	0.0%	0.0%	0.2%	0.0%	0.0%	0.2%	0.4%	16.6%
Aa2	1.6%	5.2%	36.6%	16.3%	9.6%	7.0%	3.6%	2.5%	0.7%	0.5%	0.0%	0.1%	0.2%	0.2%	0.1%	0.0%	0.1%	0.2%	15.6%
Aa3	0.7%	1.1%	4.7%	38.9%	17.5%	10.7%	3.9%	2.4%	0.9%	0.7%	-0.4%	0.2%	0.7%	0.3%	0.0%	0.0%	0.0%	0.2%	16.7%
A1	0.3%	0.4%	2.1%	9.6%	43.5%	12.8%	6.4%	3.0%	1.6%	1.4%	0.5%	0.5%	0.5%	0.6%	0.2%	0.2%	0.2%	0.7%	15.5%
A2	0.0%	0.2%	0.1%	2.2%	10.3%	40.0%	14.6%	5.8%	3.8%	1.7%	1.1%	0.6%	0.6%	0.4%	0.2%	0.0%	0.1%	0.4%	17.9%
A3	0.1%	0.1%	0.1%	1.7%	4.1%	16.6%	32.3%	10.0%	6.7%	3.8%	1.6%	1.0%	1.5%	0.7%	0.5%	0.0%	0.0%	0.5%	18.7%
Baa1	0.0%	0.0%	0.5%	0.3%	2.5%	7.0%	14.9%	30.8%	10.5%	5.9%	2.0%	1.2%	1.4%	1.1%	0.8%	0.4%	0.3%	1.1%	19.2%
Baa2	0.1%	0.4%	0.3%	0.6%	1.4%	4.0%	6.4%	10.6%	34.2%	9.0%	3.1%	1.4%	1.8%	1.0%	1.0%	0.8%	0.4%	0.7%	22.6%
Baa3	0.2%	0.0%	0.1%	0.1%	0.5%	2.0%	4.0%	8.6%	14.6%	26.4%	6.8%	3.7%	3.2%	2.5%	0.6%	0.5%	0.7%	2.4%	23.2%
Ba1	0.2%	0.0%	0.1%	0.1%	0.2%	1.3%	1.5%	2.5%	7.4%	8.9%	24.4%	5.5%	5.6%	2.1%	3.1%	1.3%	0.4%	5.3%	30.4%
Ba2	0.0%	0.1%	0.0%	0.0%	0.2%	0.7%	0.8%	1.3%	2.2%	4.1%	9.6%	21.3%	7.8%	2.4%	5.5%	2.5%	1.1%	7.5%	33.0%
Ba3	0.0%	0.1%	0.0%	0.1%	0.1%	0.4%	0.3%	0.4%	1.0%	1.1%	4.4%	6.5%	23.9%	4.5%	6.9%	4.4%	0.6%	13.3%	32.0%
B1	0.1%	0.1%	0.2%	0.0%	0.2%	0.1%	0.4%	0.4%	1.1%	0.9%	1.7%	3.8%	5.4%	27.2%	3.4%	7.2%	0.7%	17.5%	29.7%
B2	0.0%	0.0%	0.0%	0.2%	0.1%	0.1%	0.2%	0.3%	0.2%	0.8%	1.2%	2.8%	4.7%	8.4%	19.2%	7.7%	3.9%	24.0%	26.5%
B3	0.1%	0.0%	0.0%	0.0%	0.0%	0.0%	0.5%	0.5%	0.4%	0.7%	0.3%	1.0%	3.1%	6.7%	2.0%	19.4%	3.9%	29.0%	32.3%
Caa-C	0.0%	0.0%	0.0%	0.0%	0.0%	0.0%	0.0%	1.4%	0.0%	0.2%	0.0%	0.7%	3.1%	5.4%	0.8%	3.1%	15.4%	38.2%	31.6%

Figure 11.33 (cont'd)

5-year average rating transition matrix, 1983–1992

Rating From: \ Rating To:	Aaa	Aa1	Aa2	Aa3	A1	A2	A3	Baa1	Baa2	Baa3	Ba1	Ba2	Ba3	B1	B2	B3	Caa-C	D	WR
Aaa	48.8%	9.9%	8.0%	4.0%	3.3%	1.4%	0.8%	0.3%	0.0%	0.0%	0.0%	0.1%	0.1%	0.2%	0.0%	0.1%	0.2%	0.3%	22.7%
Aa1	4.7%	28.3%	11.8%	14.1%	9.6%	3.5%	2.6%	3.0%	1.2%	0.1%	0.2%	0.5%	0.2%	0.0%	0.0%	0.0%	0.0%	0.4%	19.7%
Aa2	1.4%	4.5%	31.4%	16.7%	9.8%	7.6%	3.9%	2.7%	1.0%	0.7%	0.3%	0.3%	0.3%	0.5%	0.0%	0.0%	0.0%	0.5%	18.9%
Aa3	0.7%	1.1%	5.1%	33.6%	17.6%	11.1%	4.5%	2.8%	0.9%	0.7%	0.4%	0.3%	0.3%	0.6%	0.0%	0.0%	0.1%	0.4%	20.0%
A1	0.4%	0.3%	2.0%	9.5%	39.5%	13.7%	6.2%	3.3%	1.8%	1.4%	0.8%	0.1%	0.5%	0.6%	0.3%	0.2%	0.2%	0.9%	18.4%
A2	0.0%	0.2%	0.1%	2.1%	10.1%	35.9%	14.5%	6.3%	4.0%	1.8%	1.1%	0.7%	0.7%	0.4%	0.2%	0.0%	0.1%	0.6%	21.3%
A3	0.1%	0.1%	0.2%	1.7%	4.7%	16.2%	28.7%	9.3%	6.8%	3.6%	1.8%	1.1%	1.8%	0.8%	0.3%	0.1%	0.1%	0.5%	22.1%
Baa1	0.0%	0.0%	0.5%	0.3%	2.8%	6.9%	14.7%	27.1%	10.1%	5.7%	1.8%	1.2%	1.6%	0.9%	0.7%	0.2%	0.2%	1.4%	23.6%
Baa2	0.2%	0.4%	0.3%	0.8%	1.2%	3.9%	6.7%	10.8%	30.7%	9.0%	2.5%	1.6%	1.5%	1.0%	0.7%	0.4%	0.6%	1.1%	26.6%
Baa3	0.3%	0.0%	0.1%	0.1%	0.8%	2.2%	4.0%	8.4%	14.6%	22.7%	6.3%	3.9%	3.4%	1.9%	0.9%	0.6%	0.3%	2.9%	26.6%
Ba1	0.1%	0.0%	0.1%	0.1%	0.3%	1.2%	1.5%	3.0%	7.6%	8.1%	19.6%	4.9%	5.5%	2.2%	3.1%	1.2%	0.5%	6.3%	34.8%
Ba2	0.0%	0.1%	0.2%	0.0%	0.4%	0.7%	0.9%	1.2%	2.4%	4.0%	8.8%	16.8%	6.4%	2.7%	5.0%	2.6%	0.7%	9.0%	38.2%
Ba3	0.0%	0.1%	0.0%	0.1%	0.1%	0.3%	0.2%	0.5%	0.7%	1.2%	4.1%	5.9%	19.0%	4.7%	6.1%	4.1%	0.5%	15.4%	37.0%
B1	0.1%	0.1%	0.3%	0.0%	0.2%	0.2%	0.8%	0.1%	0.7%	0.9%	2.0%	3.6%	4.9%	20.8%	3.1%	6.2%	0.7%	20.1%	35.2%
B2	0.1%	0.0%	0.0%	0.2%	0.0%	0.2%	0.3%	0.2%	0.2%	0.6%	1.4%	2.6%	3.1%	9.0%	16.1%	6.3%	3.6%	25.6%	30.4%
B3	0.1%	0.0%	0.0%	0.0%	0.0%	0.1%	0.7%	0.7%	0.4%	0.5%	0.4%	1.0%	2.4%	6.2%	2.1%	14.7%	3.5%	31.0%	36.2%
Caa-C	0.0%	0.0%	0.3%	0.0%	0.0%	0.0%	0.0%	1.4%	0.0%	0.2%	0.0%	1.3%	2.8%	4.7%	0.5%	3.1%	12.3%	39.5%	34.3%

Figure 11.33 (cont'd)

6-year average rating transition matrix, 1983–1991

Rating From: \ Rating To:	Aaa	Aa1	Aa2	Aa3	A1	A2	A3	Baa1	Baa2	Baa3	Ba1	Ba2	Ba3	B1	B2	B3	Caa-C	D	WR
Aaa	43.9%	9.7%	8.0%	4.7%	3.8%	2.1%	1.0%	0.4%	0.1%	0.0%	0.0%	0.1%	0.1%	0.1%	0.0%	0.1%	0.1%	0.3%	25.6%
Aa1	4.6%	26.1%	11.3%	13.2%	8.6%	2.3%	3.0%	4.6%	1.6%	0.5%	0.0%	0.5%	0.4%	0.0%	0.1%	0.0%	0.0%	0.6%	22.7%
Aa2	1.3%	4.2%	28.2%	16.0%	10.2%	7.5%	4.3%	2.4%	1.5%	0.9%	0.4%	0.4%	0.2%	0.3%	0.1%	0.0%	0.0%	0.5%	21.6%
Aa3	0.7%	0.8%	5.5%	30.1%	17.1%	10.9%	5.5%	3.0%	1.1%	0.6%	0.4%	0.2%	0.1%	0.3%	0.0%	0.0%	0.1%	0.6%	23.0%
A1	0.4%	0.2%	1.8%	8.9%	36.3%	15.0%	6.5%	3.0%	1.9%	1.8%	0.6%	0.1%	0.4%	0.3%	0.4%	0.2%	0.1%	1.1%	21.1%
A2	0.0%	0.2%	0.1%	2.2%	9.6%	33.4%	14.1%	6.5%	4.0%	1.9%	1.0%	0.9%	0.8%	0.4%	0.1%	0.0%	0.1%	0.8%	23.8%
A3	0.1%	0.1%	0.2%	1.6%	5.0%	15.4%	26.9%	9.0%	6.5%	3.8%	1.5%	1.0%	2.1%	0.6%	0.4%	0.1%	0.1%	0.6%	25.1%
Baa1	0.0%	0.0%	0.3%	0.3%	3.3%	7.1%	13.8%	25.1%	9.6%	5.4%	1.5%	1.4%	1.3%	0.5%	0.8%	0.2%	0.2%	1.6%	27.4%
Baa2	0.1%	0.4%	0.3%	0.6%	1.3%	3.6%	6.4%	11.2%	28.7%	8.1%	2.7%	1.9%	1.7%	0.8%	0.6%	0.3%	0.4%	1.4%	29.3%
Baa3	0.3%	0.0%	0.2%	0.3%	0.8%	2.3%	4.3%	8.0%	14.0%	20.9%	6.1%	3.7%	3.1%	1.9%	1.1%	0.4%	0.3%	3.4%	28.9%
Ba1	0.1%	0.1%	0.1%	0.1%	0.2%	1.5%	1.5%	3.4%	7.9%	7.3%	16.2%	4.6%	5.0%	2.4%	2.9%	1.0%	0.4%	7.3%	38.0%
Ba2	0.1%	0.1%	0.3%	0.0%	0.5%	0.7%	1.0%	1.2%	2.6%	4.1%	8.0%	13.8%	5.5%	3.0%	4.6%	2.4%	0.4%	9.8%	42.0%
Ba3	0.0%	0.0%	0.1%	0.0%	0.2%	0.2%	0.3%	0.3%	0.9%	1.3%	4.2%	5.4%	15.8%	5.0%	5.3%	3.5%	0.4%	17.2%	40.0%
B1	0.1%	0.1%	0.3%	0.0%	0.2%	0.5%	0.8%	0.2%	0.5%	1.0%	1.8%	3.4%	4.6%	16.1%	2.9%	5.6%	0.6%	22.5%	39.0%
B2	0.2%	0.0%	0.0%	0.1%	0.0%	0.3%	0.2%	0.2%	0.1%	0.6%	2.3%	2.6%	2.9%	8.5%	13.1%	5.6%	3.2%	27.4%	32.8%
B3	0.1%	0.0%	0.0%	0.0%	0.0%	0.1%	0.7%	0.9%	0.2%	0.3%	0.4%	1.3%	2.5%	5.6%	1.9%	11.2%	3.5%	32.0%	39.4%
Caa-C	0.0%	0.0%	0.0%	0.0%	0.0%	0.0%	0.0%	1.4%	0.0%	0.2%	0.0%	2.0%	1.5%	4.7%	1.1%	2.8%	9.7%	40.2%	36.5%

Figure 11.33 (cont'd)

7-year average rating transition matrix, 1983–1990

Rating From:	Rating To: Aaa	Aa1	Aa2	Aa3	A1	A2	A3	Baa1	Baa2	Baa3	Ba1	Ba2	Ba3	B1	B2	B3	Caa-C	D	WR
Aaa	40.3%	9.3%	7.3%	5.9%	4.1%	2.2%	1.2%	0.3%	0.3%	0.0%	0.1%	0.1%	0.0%	0.2%	0.0%	0.0%	0.1%	0.4%	28.4%
Aa1	4.6%	24.7%	11.1%	12.6%	7.0%	2.7%	3.0%	4.9%	1.8%	1.1%	0.0%	0.6%	0.5%	0.0%	0.0%	0.1%	0.0%	0.6%	24.8%
Aa2	1.1%	3.6%	26.0%	15.7%	10.8%	7.2%	4.5%	2.7%	1.6%	0.9%	0.3%	0.4%	0.2%	0.2%	0.0%	0.0%	0.1%	0.6%	24.1%
Aa3	0.7%	0.7%	5.4%	27.5%	16.5%	10.5%	6.6%	2.9%	1.0%	0.5%	0.4%	0.1%	0.0%	0.3%	0.0%	0.0%	0.1%	0.6%	26.1%
A1	0.4%	0.1%	2.1%	8.3%	33.9%	15.7%	6.7%	3.1%	1.9%	1.2%	0.7%	0.1%	0.5%	0.2%	0.4%	0.1%	0.0%	1.1%	23.5%
A2	0.0%	0.2%	0.1%	2.2%	9.4%	31.3%	14.2%	6.5%	4.1%	2.1%	0.7%	1.1%	0.7%	0.5%	0.0%	0.1%	0.2%	0.9%	25.8%
A3	0.1%	0.1%	0.0%	1.7%	5.0%	14.9%	25.4%	8.7%	6.0%	3.4%	1.6%	0.9%	2.3%	0.8%	0.4%	0.0%	0.1%	0.8%	27.8%
Baa1	0.0%	0.0%	0.1%	0.3%	3.7%	7.3%	13.2%	23.4%	9.3%	5.4%	1.6%	1.3%	0.9%	0.2%	0.9%	0.2%	0.3%	1.9%	30.1%
Baa2	0.0%	0.4%	0.3%	0.3%	1.7%	3.2%	5.8%	11.8%	26.9%	7.6%	2.7%	2.4%	1.4%	1.0%	0.7%	0.3%	0.2%	1.6%	31.7%
Baa3	0.3%	0.0%	0.2%	0.5%	0.6%	2.5%	4.3%	8.1%	14.1%	19.5%	5.1%	3.1%	2.8%	1.7%	1.4%	0.5%	0.4%	3.9%	31.0%
Ba1	0.0%	0.1%	0.0%	0.1%	0.2%	1.4%	1.5%	3.9%	8.1%	6.7%	14.2%	4.9%	4.4%	2.7%	2.9%	0.5%	0.3%	7.9%	40.1%
Ba2	0.3%	0.1%	0.0%	0.0%	0.6%	0.7%	0.9%	1.3%	2.6%	4.5%	7.6%	12.0%	5.3%	3.2%	3.8%	1.8%	0.5%	10.6%	44.3%
Ba3	0.0%	0.0%	0.1%	0.0%	0.2%	0.2%	0.3%	0.4%	0.7%	1.4%	4.0%	5.2%	13.1%	4.8%	5.0%	3.0%	0.5%	18.7%	42.3%
B1	0.1%	0.1%	0.3%	0.0%	0.1%	0.5%	0.8%	0.3%	0.5%	0.9%	1.6%	3.2%	4.5%	12.7%	2.6%	5.2%	0.6%	24.3%	41.7%
B2	0.3%	0.0%	0.0%	0.0%	0.0%	0.4%	0.3%	0.1%	0.3%	0.9%	1.7%	2.8%	3.9%	7.5%	11.7%	5.1%	2.4%	28.3%	34.3%
B3	0.1%	0.0%	0.0%	0.0%	0.0%	0.1%	0.7%	0.7%	0.2%	0.0%	0.4%	1.0%	3.1%	5.2%	1.8%	9.4%	3.5%	32.7%	41.2%
Caa-C	0.0%	0.0%	0.3%	0.0%	0.0%	0.0%	0.0%	0.0%	1.4%	0.2%	0.0%	2.0%	0.8%	4.7%	1.7%	2.8%	6.8%	40.5%	39.1%

Figure 11.33 (cont'd)

8-year average rating transition matrix, 1983–1989

Rating From: \ Rating To:	Aaa	Aa1	Aa2	Aa3	A1	A2	A3	Baa1	Baa2	Baa3	Ba1	Ba2	Ba3	B1	B2	B3	Caa-C	D	WR
Aaa	37.1%	8.3%	7.4%	6.6%	4.3%	2.1%	1.5%	0.4%	0.3%	0.1%	0.1%	0.1%	0.0%	0.0%	0.0%	0.0%	0.0%	0.5%	31.1%
Aa1	4.0%	24.2%	11.0%	12.5%	6.8%	2.3%	3.3%	4.4%	1.9%	1.4%	0.0%	0.0%	0.6%	0.0%	0.0%	0.0%	0.0%	0.6%	26.9%
Aa2	1.1%	3.1%	24.6%	15.0%	10.9%	7.4%	4.8%	2.7%	1.6%	0.9%	0.3%	0.2%	0.2%	0.2%	0.0%	0.0%	0.2%	0.7%	26.2%
Aa3	0.7%	0.5%	5.4%	26.1%	15.9%	10.8%	6.8%	2.9%	0.9%	0.3%	0.4%	0.2%	0.0%	0.2%	0.1%	0.0%	0.1%	0.6%	28.0%
A1	0.3%	0.1%	2.2%	8.2%	31.7%	16.3%	6.6%	2.6%	2.1%	1.2%	0.6%	0.1%	0.5%	0.3%	0.2%	0.0%	0.0%	1.2%	25.7%
A2	0.0%	0.2%	0.1%	2.2%	9.3%	29.8%	14.3%	6.5%	3.9%	2.2%	0.6%	1.0%	0.6%	0.5%	0.1%	0.0%	0.2%	1.1%	27.4%
A3	0.1%	0.1%	0.0%	1.5%	5.0%	14.8%	24.3%	8.1%	6.1%	3.3%	1.7%	1.1%	1.6%	1.0%	0.3%	0.1%	0.2%	0.8%	29.9%
Baa1	0.0%	0.0%	0.1%	0.3%	3.6%	7.2%	12.7%	22.4%	8.8%	5.8%	1.7%	0.9%	0.7%	0.2%	0.7%	0.2%	0.2%	2.4%	32.0%
Baa2	0.0%	0.4%	0.2%	0.4%	1.8%	3.1%	5.5%	11.9%	25.6%	7.2%	2.8%	2.0%	1.4%	1.1%	0.9%	0.2%	0.1%	1.8%	33.7%
Baa3	0.2%	0.0%	0.1%	0.6%	0.6%	2.7%	4.3%	8.3%	13.5%	19.0%	4.6%	3.0%	2.6%	1.4%	1.4%	0.5%	0.4%	4.2%	32.7%
Ba1	0.0%	0.1%	0.0%	0.1%	0.2%	1.4%	1.4%	4.2%	8.1%	6.5%	13.0%	5.1%	4.3%	3.0%	2.3%	0.5%	0.3%	8.4%	41.2%
Ba2	0.3%	0.1%	0.0%	0.0%	0.7%	0.6%	0.6%	1.3%	2.7%	4.7%	7.1%	11.0%	5.2%	3.0%	3.5%	1.5%	0.5%	11.0%	46.1%
Ba3	0.0%	0.0%	0.1%	0.0%	0.3%	0.3%	0.3%	0.4%	0.7%	1.3%	3.9%	5.2%	11.4%	4.6%	4.9%	2.4%	0.5%	20.0%	43.8%
B1	0.1%	0.1%	0.3%	0.0%	0.1%	0.5%	0.8%	0.4%	0.5%	0.8%	1.6%	3.3%	4.1%	10.8%	2.5%	4.4%	0.7%	25.4%	43.6%
B2	0.4%	0.0%	0.0%	0.0%	0.0%	0.5%	0.3%	0.0%	0.5%	0.9%	1.6%	2.9%	3.9%	6.4%	10.3%	4.9%	2.5%	28.7%	36.2%
B3	0.1%	0.0%	0.0%	0.0%	0.0%	0.1%	0.7%	0.8%	0.2%	0.0%	0.3%	0.8%	2.6%	4.7%	1.6%	8.4%	3.3%	33.9%	42.5%
Caa-C	0.0%	0.0%	0.0%	0.0%	0.0%	0.0%	0.0%	0.0%	0.0%	1.6%	0.0%	2.0%	0.1%	4.0%	2.4%	2.8%	6.7%	40.5%	39.9%

Figure 11.33 (cont'd)

9-year average rating transition matrix, 1983–1988

Rating From: \ Rating To:	Aaa	Aa1	Aa2	Aa3	A1	A2	A3	Baa1	Baa2	Baa3	Ba1	Ba2	Ba3	B1	B2	B3	Caa-C	D	WR
Aaa	34.7%	7.5%	7.6%	6.8%	4.2%	2.1%	1.8%	0.4%	0.3%	0.1%	0.2%	0.1%	0.0%	0.0%	0.0%	0.0%	0.0%	0.5%	33.8%
Aa1	3.7%	23.8%	10.5%	12.6%	6.9%	3.2%	3.7%	3.1%	2.1%	1.3%	0.0%	0.0%	0.0%	0.0%	0.0%	0.0%	0.0%	0.6%	28.4%
Aa2	1.0%	2.9%	23.6%	14.3%	11.0%	7.7%	4.5%	3.1%	1.3%	1.1%	0.3%	0.1%	0.0%	0.1%	0.0%	0.0%	0.2%	0.7%	28.0%
Aa3	0.7%	0.5%	5.1%	24.8%	15.8%	10.8%	6.8%	3.1%	0.9%	0.4%	0.6%	0.1%	0.0%	0.1%	0.1%	0.0%	0.0%	0.6%	29.5%
A1	0.3%	0.1%	2.4%	8.0%	30.3%	15.5%	6.6%	2.6%	2.5%	1.0%	0.5%	0.2%	0.5%	0.2%	0.2%	0.0%	0.0%	1.2%	27.8%
A2	0.0%	0.3%	0.1%	1.9%	9.3%	29.2%	14.2%	6.3%	3.8%	2.1%	0.7%	1.1%	0.4%	0.4%	0.1%	0.0%	0.1%	1.2%	28.7%
A3	0.1%	0.1%	0.1%	1.3%	5.1%	14.5%	23.3%	8.0%	6.5%	3.4%	1.7%	1.0%	0.9%	1.3%	0.2%	0.2%	0.2%	0.9%	31.4%
Baa1	0.0%	0.0%	0.1%	0.4%	3.4%	7.0%	12.7%	21.2%	8.6%	5.9%	1.6%	0.9%	0.6%	0.2%	0.7%	0.2%	0.2%	2.7%	33.8%
Baa2	0.0%	0.3%	0.2%	0.3%	1.7%	3.5%	5.6%	12.0%	24.2%	6.7%	2.9%	2.1%	1.1%	1.1%	1.1%	0.2%	0.1%	1.9%	35.1%
Baa3	0.1%	0.0%	0.0%	0.7%	0.7%	2.8%	4.8%	8.0%	13.4%	18.5%	4.1%	2.6%	2.7%	1.3%	1.2%	0.5%	0.3%	4.6%	33.6%
Ba1	0.0%	0.1%	0.0%	0.1%	0.3%	1.4%	1.2%	4.7%	7.9%	6.5%	11.9%	5.5%	4.0%	2.9%	2.2%	0.6%	0.2%	8.6%	42.1%
Ba2	0.3%	0.1%	0.0%	0.0%	0.5%	0.5%	0.4%	1.5%	2.8%	4.2%	7.5%	10.3%	5.0%	2.9%	3.6%	1.3%	0.5%	11.2%	47.3%
Ba3	0.0%	0.0%	0.1%	0.0%	0.3%	0.3%	0.2%	0.5%	0.6%	1.4%	3.9%	5.0%	9.8%	4.7%	4.9%	1.8%	0.6%	21.0%	45.1%
B1	0.1%	0.1%	0.4%	0.0%	0.1%	0.5%	0.8%	0.5%	0.6%	0.7%	1.5%	3.4%	4.1%	9.8%	2.4%	3.6%	0.6%	26.1%	44.8%
B2	0.4%	0.0%	0.0%	0.0%	0.0%	0.5%	0.3%	0.0%	0.8%	1.1%	1.4%	1.8%	3.9%	5.2%	8.8%	5.1%	2.9%	29.0%	38.7%
B3	0.1%	0.0%	0.0%	0.0%	0.0%	0.1%	0.7%	0.9%	0.2%	0.0%	0.2%	1.1%	1.5%	4.6%	1.8%	8.0%	3.1%	34.8%	42.9%
Caa-C	0.0%	0.0%	0.0%	0.0%	0.0%	0.0%	0.0%	0.0%	0.0%	0.2%	0.7%	2.0%	0.8%	3.3%	2.4%	2.8%	6.7%	40.5%	40.5%

Figure 11.33 (cont'd)

10-year average rating transition matrix, 1983–1987

Rating From:	Rating To: Aaa	Aa1	Aa2	Aa3	A1	A2	A3	Baa1	Baa2	Baa3	Ba1	Ba2	Ba3	B1	B2	B3	Caa-C	D	WR
Aaa	29.2%	6.8%	7.9%	7.3%	4.6%	2.3%	1.9%	0.4%	0.0%	0.4%	0.3%	0.0%	0.0%	0.0%	0.0%	0.0%	0.0%	0.6%	38.3%
Aa1	3.4%	20.3%	10.9%	12.6%	7.0%	4.2%	4.2%	2.5%	2.2%	0.5%	0.0%	0.0%	0.0%	0.0%	0.0%	0.0%	0.0%	0.6%	31.6%
Aa2	1.1%	2.4%	19.4%	13.8%	12.0%	8.1%	4.3%	3.8%	0.9%	1.1%	0.2%	0.0%	0.0%	0.1%	0.1%	0.0%	0.1%	0.9%	31.7%
Aa3	0.6%	0.4%	5.0%	21.8%	15.0%	10.9%	7.4%	3.5%	1.0%	0.5%	0.7%	0.2%	0.1%	0.1%	0.1%	0.0%	0.0%	0.6%	32.3%
A1	0.2%	0.1%	2.7%	7.2%	27.8%	15.3%	6.5%	2.9%	2.7%	0.8%	0.5%	0.1%	0.5%	0.3%	0.2%	0.0%	0.0%	1.3%	30.8%
A2	0.0%	0.3%	0.1%	2.0%	8.9%	27.0%	13.9%	6.6%	4.0%	2.2%	0.8%	0.9%	0.4%	0.4%	0.2%	0.0%	0.1%	1.3%	31.1%
A3	0.1%	0.1%	0.1%	0.9%	4.8%	14.0%	21.5%	7.4%	6.6%	3.5%	1.8%	1.3%	0.8%	1.3%	0.0%	0.2%	0.2%	1.1%	34.4%
Baa1	0.0%	0.0%	0.1%	0.4%	3.5%	6.1%	11.7%	18.5%	9.1%	5.7%	1.7%	1.1%	0.5%	0.5%	0.6%	0.2%	0.2%	2.9%	37.3%
Baa2	0.0%	0.2%	0.2%	0.3%	1.7%	3.9%	5.6%	11.7%	20.7%	6.5%	2.9%	2.1%	0.7%	1.1%	1.2%	0.4%	0.1%	2.2%	38.6%
Baa3	0.1%	0.0%	0.0%	0.7%	0.9%	2.5%	5.4%	8.0%	13.0%	16.1%	3.1%	2.9%	2.9%	1.2%	1.1%	0.5%	0.2%	4.8%	36.6%
Ba1	0.0%	0.1%	0.0%	0.0%	0.3%	1.5%	1.2%	4.9%	7.7%	6.0%	9.5%	5.1%	3.5%	2.8%	2.3%	0.8%	0.2%	9.4%	44.8%
Ba2	0.3%	0.1%	0.0%	0.0%	0.5%	0.4%	0.3%	1.2%	2.9%	4.0%	7.0%	8.4%	4.0%	2.8%	3.5%	1.2%	0.6%	12.2%	50.8%
Ba3	0.1%	0.0%	0.1%	0.0%	0.3%	0.4%	0.2%	0.3%	0.7%	1.4%	3.7%	3.7%	7.9%	4.5%	4.4%	1.5%	0.7%	22.8%	47.5%
B1	0.0%	0.0%	0.4%	0.0%	0.1%	0.4%	0.7%	0.7%	0.5%	0.6%	1.4%	2.8%	3.6%	7.8%	2.3%	3.0%	0.5%	28.0%	47.1%
B2	0.4%	0.0%	0.0%	0.0%	0.0%	0.5%	0.4%	0.3%	0.9%	0.9%	2.8%	1.3%	2.7%	3.8%	8.5%	3.9%	3.3%	30.7%	39.6%
B3	0.1%	0.0%	0.0%	0.0%	0.0%	0.1%	0.5%	1.1%	0.1%	0.0%	0.2%	1.2%	0.9%	4.5%	1.5%	6.1%	2.5%	36.8%	44.3%
Caa-C	0.0%	0.0%	0.0%	0.0%	0.0%	0.0%	0.0%	0.0%	0.0%	0.0%	0.0%	3.0%	0.1%	3.6%	2.4%	2.6%	4.9%	42.0%	41.4%

Figure 11.34 Rating Transition Rate Distribution Summary

Each table entry is comprised of the following (5th-percentile, Median, Standard deviation, 95th-percentile). All numbers in percents

	Aaa	Aa	A	Baa	Ba	B	Caa-C	Default
Aaa	(78.2,94.1,8.3,100.0)	(0.0,5.6,6.5,18.3)	(0.0,0.0,2.7,5.8)	(0.0,0.0,0.8,1.5)	(0.0,0.0,0.1,0.0)	(0.0,0.0,0.0,0.0)	(0.0,0.0,0.0,0.0)	(0.0,0.0,0.0,0.0)
Aa	(0.0,1.2,1.2,3.4)	(81.0,92.2,7.1,98.8)	(0.0,4.8,5.7,16.6)	(0.0,0.0,1.3,3.0)	(0.0,0.0,0.5,0.8)	(0.0,0.0,0.1,0.2)	(0.0,0.0,0.0,0.0)	(0.0,0.0,0.2,0.6)
A	(0.0,0.0,0.2,0.4)	(0.0,1.9,2.6,8.3)	(72.4,94.8,8.4,98.9)	(0.6,3.7,5.3,16.7)	(0.0,0.0,1.3,2.4)	(0.0,0.0,0.3,0.7)	(0.0,0.0,0.1,0.2)	(0.0,0.0,0.4,1.0)
Baa	(0.0,0.0,0.1,0.3)	(0.0,0.0,0.5,1.5)	(0.7,2.7,4.4,12.1)	(73.0,91.2,10.2,98.5)	(0.0,3.2,6.1,18.3)	(0.0,0.2,1.2,2.7)	(0.0,0.0,0.2,0.3)	(0.0,0.0,0.5,1.5)
Ba	(0.0,0.0,0.1,0.0)	(0.0,0.0,0.2,0.6)	(0.0,0.2,0.6,1.6)	(1.5,3.9,3.9,13.7)	(70.9,90.4,9.9,96.8)	(0.0,3.4,6.4,16.9)	(0.0,0.2,0.8,1.8)	(0.0,0.6,2.0,4.8)
B	(0.0,0.0,0.0,0.0)	(0.0,0.0,0.2,0.3)	(0.0,0.0,0.3,1.0)	(0.0,0.0,1.1,3.2)	(0.0,4.7,5.6,16.2)	(65.4,86.7,10.5,98.0)	(0.0,2.3,4.7,12.1)	(0.0,2.4,4.7,15.8)
Caa-C	(0.0,0.0,0.0,0.0)	(0.0,0.0,0.2,0.0)	(0.0,0.0,0.0,2.0)	(0.0,0.0,2.1,1.3)	(0.0,0.0,3.4,7.9)	(0.0,4.5,6.0,15.6)	(46.4,82.5,20.1,100.0)	(0.0,8.3,18.1,50.0)

PART FOUR
CREDIT PORTFOLIO MANAGEMENT

12

Overview to Credit
Risk Modeling

Andrew Hickman, eRisks.com

12.1 Introduction

The purpose of this chapter is to provide the foundation for the following several chapters, each of which describes a particular credit risk portfolio model in depth. In these passages, the reader is likely to encounter quite technical algorithms and terminology specific to a particular model. In order to achieve an understanding of what these models are doing and why, and to meaningfully compare their differences and similarities, the models must be placed in the context of the modeling objectives and features common to all credit risk portfolio models.

This chapter will provide a framework for analytic comparison of the credit risk portfolio models. However, the model comparison will include neither empirical comparisons, e.g. results for sample portfolios, nor "pros and cons." Such comparisons depend more on user-specific issues than modeling theory.

12.2 Modeling Objectives — What is Credit Risk?

Credit risk can be defined broadly as the possibility of losses exceeding expectations in a portfolio of credit assets. The objective of a credit risk model is to provide estimates of the probability and magnitude of losses, graphically expressed by a chart of the probability density function (or distribution), as in Figure 12.1.

Figure 12.1   Example of Portfolio Loss Distribution

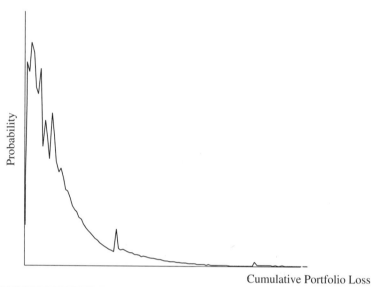

Following are several of the key sources of risk, and hence key modeling variables:

- **Default:** Defined as a situation in which the owner of credit asset receives the Exposure Amount times the Recovery Rate.
- **Credit quality:** Prior to maturity, the value of a credit asset may decline due to an increase in the likelihood of default, observed as a change in either or both of the following:
  - Rating — an ordinal categorization of default risk, either from an external agency or internal review. Ratings upgrades and downgrades are discrete by definition. The likelihood of ratings changes is often represented by a "ratings migration" table, which gives the frequency of end-of-period rating conditional on the beginning-of-period rating. Changes in rating usually reflect issues specific to the obligor rather than general market conditions; instead, the default rate for a given rating class tends to vary with market conditions.
  - Credit spread — the yield premium to a riskless security with similar cash flows. Credit spreads may widen or tighten either because of issues specific to the obligor or general market conditions. Under normal market conditions, changes in credit spread are continuous, but in extreme circumstances spreads may exhibit virtually discrete ("gap") moves.

Note, however, that accrual accounting ignores changes in value due to worsening credit quality unless the change is so severe that an asset becomes impaired.

- **Recovery rate:** In the event of a default, the actual economic loss may vary from almost zero to substantially all of the exposure amount.
- **Exposure amount:** Unfunded commitments may draw down, mark-to-market value of derivatives contracts may vary with underlying financial markets, etc.

Default is generally the primary modeling concern due to the relatively much more severe impact of default events as opposed to variation in other key credit risk variables. However, lessons of the recent past (e.g. Russia crisis in September 1998) suggest that credit spread gapping risk should not be ignored.

12.3   Empirical Observations

A useful credit risk model must be capable of reflecting whatever "stylized facts" we can observe about credit risk. In particular, we are interested in the magnitude of different forms of credit risk and the degree of correlation of that risk amongst obligors.

12.3.1   Default Rate Data

Default data presents a challenge in that the default rate of an individual obligor level is unobservable — only the state of defaulted or not defaulted can be observed. We are forced then to make inferences from data representing the default rate on some pool of obligors. A quick glance at such a time series of default rates reveals "clustering" of defaults to a greater degree than would be expected by random chance (see Figure 12.2). In an hypothetical portfolio of N obligors with no interdependence of default, the expected behavior of the portfolio default rate is a stationary distribution around the mean default rate (μ), with a standard deviation approximately given by $\sqrt{\mu / N}$. In the example data, the standard deviation is 0.92% vs. approximately 0.32% for independent with mean 1.04% and size on the order of 1000 issuers.

Further, this clustering appears to persist from period to period (e.g. high default rates from 1989 to 1991). Such effects may be even more pronounced in particular industries, geographies, etc.

While this default clustering can probably be ascribed to various background

Figure 12.2   Default Rate Time Series

Moody's One-Year Default Rates, 1970–1998
All Corporates

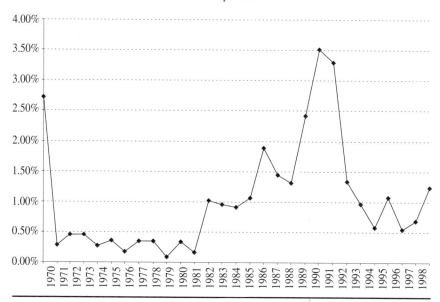

economic effects such as overall demand, input costs, etc., it is not necessary that this link be explicit. It is sufficient to say that we can infer from this data that there is a strong systematic component to default rates in a diversified portfolio, and that there may be a structure of systematic factors relevant to different segments of the portfolio. Aside from credit risk modeling, this observation has a powerful implication: some, but not all, credit risk can be diversified away by spreading exposure across more obligors.

12.3.2   Credit Spread Data

Credit spread data, where available, are much richer since they are observable at the individual obligor level, as often as market prices are observed.

Credit spread changes translate into asset price changes in a way similar to the effect of change in yield on a fixed coupon bond; the severity of change in price for a given change in spread increases with the maturity of the asset. A time series of an individual obligor's credit spread (see Figure 12.3 for example) reveals that credit spread movements can be quite large over time, and often

Figure 12.3   Example of Credit Spread Gapping

Brazil 10-1/8 11/27 vs US Treasury 6-1/2 11/26
yield spread (bp)

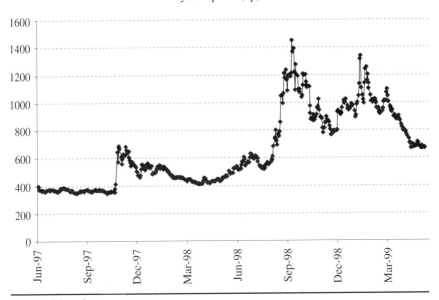

Source: Bloomberg

over a very short period of time (i.e., "gaps"). Credit spread risk is clearly material at the individual obligor level for assets with medium to long maturity.

Some changes in an individual obligor's credit spread may correspond to ratings revisions. However, significant credit spread movements can easily occur without ratings revisions, within the band of spreads corresponding to a single discrete rating category, or even off the scale beyond the spread corresponding to any defined rating. "Ratings migration" is thus able to capture credit spread risk only partially.

Credit spread data can also be pooled for a number of obligors to gauge the degree of systematic risk in credit spread changes (see Figure 12.4 for example). The data suggest that the credit spread across broad classes of obligors can move as a result of general market conditions. Interestingly, even this systematic risk factor exhibits occasional "gaps," such as in the September 1998 Russia crisis.

Note that this systematic credit spread risk is not captured by "ratings migration." Ratings class indices such as in Figure 12.4 are constructed of

Figure 12.4   Systematic Credit Spread Risk

BBB Industrial 10-yr Bond vs 10-yr US Treasury
yield spread (bp)

Source: Bloomberg

issuers with the same rating; issuers are dropped from the index if upgraded or
downgraded.

12.4   Applying Modern Portfolio Theory

At first pass, it is tempting to force credit risk into the Markowitz variance/
covariance framework, which has realized such great success in modeling
market risk (i.e. Value-at-Risk). In fact, variance/covariance is the basis for an
older generation of credit risk models which calculate loss volatility
(Unexpected Loss) at the obligor level, and then aggregate to the portfolio loss
volatility by way of default correlations. However, key features of credit risk
may not be amenable to such application:

• Default is characterized by nearly binary outcomes with relatively low
  probability, so that the distribution of losses tends not to be normal, but rather
  quite skewed. Variance-based disutility for risk may not be appropriate for
  such skewed distributions, in which case risk is often represented by
  percentiles in the "tail" of the distribution.

- The key parameters — volatility and correlation — are usually not directly observable from market data as with equities, for example.

Nonetheless, two important results of portfolio theory do pertain:
- Systematic risk (or "correlated" risk) is additive
- Non-systematic risk (or "uncorrelated" or "specific" or "idiosyncratic" risk) is [not additive — risk increases roughly proportional to square root of sum of exposure squared] [diversifiable — in percentage terms, non-systematic risk diminishes roughly proportional to square root of number of exposures]

To illustrate, consider a CAPM-style model of equity-returns where the return on any asset is decomposed into one portion perfectly correlated to the "market" return and one part with no correlation to the market return or that of any other asset:

$$R_n = \beta_n R_m + \varepsilon_n$$

A portfolio of such assets has a return equal to the weighted sum of individual asset returns:

$$R_p = \sum \omega_n R_n$$

and a volatility given by the following:

$$\sigma(R_p) = \left(\sum \omega_n \beta_n\right) \sigma(R_m) + \sqrt{\sum \omega_n^2 \sigma(\varepsilon_n)^2}$$

(ignoring non-zero means for simplicity, without loss of generality).
The proportion of systematic risk (the first term in the equation above) to non-systematic risk (the second term) rises quickly as the number of assets increases, as in Figure 12.5.

Though these results are strictly applicable only to variance, the concept that systematic risk is additive but non-systematic risk diversifies holds true approximately for other relevant distribution statistics (e.g. percentiles in the tail of the distribution). This has two significant implications for credit risk modeling:

First, though systematic risk may be a small portion of an individual obligor's

Figure 12.5   Proportion of Systematic Risk vs Number of Exposures

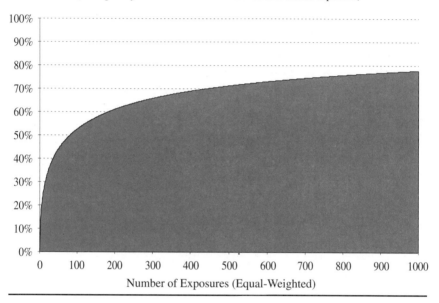

Systematic Risk % of Portfolio Risk
(example: systematic = 10% of risk for individual exposure)

Number of Exposures (Equal-Weighted)

risk, it may be the dominant portion of a portfolio's risk if the portfolio is sufficiently diversified. Systematic sources of credit risk should be a central feature of a successful credit risk model. Indeed, as diversification increases, the portfolio loss distribution tends toward the systematic risk distribution, as in Figure 12.6.

The second credit risk modeling implication is that sources of non-systematic risk are significant at the portfolio level only if extremely significant at an individual obligor level (e.g. default, credit spreads), or in a quite poorly diversified portfolio. Hence variability of recovery rates and exposure amounts are likely to be material only to the extent they have systematic components which are correlated to systematic default rate risk. In other words, to merit significant modeling attention, recovery rates would need to have the property that they not only tend to be lower or higher than expected for all obligors at the same time, but further, that they tend to be lower when the default rate is higher, and vice versa.

Figure 12.6   Portfolio Distribution vs Systematic Distribution with
Increasing Diversification

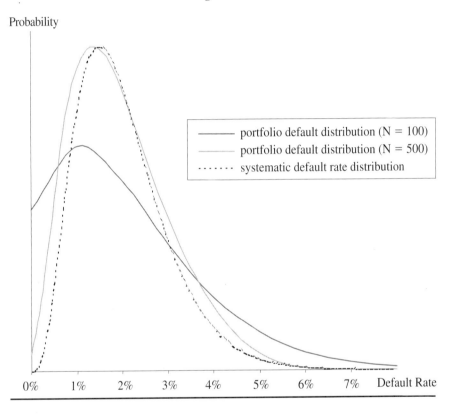

12.5   Generalized Credit Risk Portfolio Model[1]

The empirical and theoretical observations above suggest a basic two-part
framework for credit risk portfolio modeling:

1. **Systematic risk distribution:** Defines the probability associated with each
   possible "state of the world" for all relevant factors not specific to an
   individual obligor. These "states of the world" might define general economic
   variables, asset prices, etc., which are then linked to the key credit risk
   modeling variables. More practically, they define the conditional expected

---

[1]   This section draws heavily from Hickman and Koyluoglu, 1998, which is a somewhat
more technical exposition of the issues herein

values of those credit risk variables — mean default rate, ratings-class credit spread change, expected recovery rate, etc. The degree of "concentration" or "correlation" in the portfolio is reflected by the extent to which the borrowers' conditional credit risk variables vary together in different "states of the world."

2. **Conditional loss distribution:** Defines the probability associated with each possible loss outcome given conditional expectations of the key credit risk variables for a particular "state of the world" from the systematic risk distribution. Because the systematic risk distribution accounts for all common sources of risk, the outcomes from the conditional loss distribution are independent amongst obligors.

The discussion which follows will describe this framework in greater detail, focusing primarily on modeling default risk. Other significant credit risks can and should be incorporated in this framework. However, to do so herein would introduce significant complexity at the cost of explanatory value and ability to meaningfully compare models which incorporate differing aspects credit risk other than default.

12.5.1 Systematic Default Rate Distribution

The exact distribution of systematic default risk is not known, but several desirable properties can be established:

- **Bounding and shape:** Intuitively, we know that the distribution should not enable default rates to fall below 0% or above 100% (the zero bound being the more relevant since default rates are generally low). Further, as a result of the zero bound, the distribution will generally be skewed, with the skew increasing as the mean default rate decreases.

- **Economic rationale:** An underlying theory or process which generates the systematic default rate distribution provides some confidence that the distribution approximates the unknown "true" systematic default rate distribution. For example, CreditPortfolioView[TM] explicitly models default rates as a function of normally-distributed macroeconomic variables; CreditMetrics[TM] models default rates as a function of normally-distributed asset values using the Merton model.[2] This modeling approach can be

---

[2] For more details on CreditPortfolioView[TM] and CreditMetrics[TM], see Wilson (1997) and Gupton, Finger, and Bhatia (1997), respectively

represented by passing a normally-distributed systematic factor distribution through a convex transformation function, as in Figure 12.7.

- **Tractability:** The systematic default rate distribution is the centerpiece to a complex calculation, and its functional complexity will impact directly on the speed and stability of the overall calculation.

The following are several examples of generic systematic default rate distributions, which happen to correspond to those implied in some of the public domain credit risk portfolio models:

- **Gamma (CREDITRISK⁺):** A two-parameter distribution, bounded by zero with infinite positive support, given by the following probability density function:

$$f(p) = \frac{1}{\beta^{\alpha}\Gamma(\alpha)} e^{-\frac{p}{\beta}} p^{\alpha-1}$$

$$\text{where } \Gamma(\alpha) = \int_{x=0}^{\infty} e^{-x} x^{\alpha-1} dx.$$

Figure 12.7 Generating a Systematic Default Rate Distribution

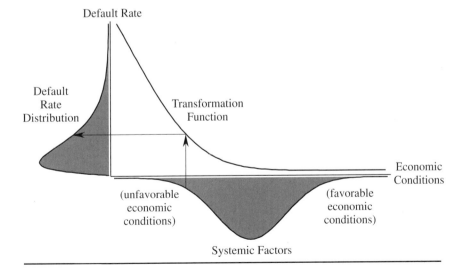

- **Probit (CreditMetrics^{TM}):** A two-parameter distribution bounded by zero and one, where the systematic default rate is a function of a standard normal variable:

$$p = \Phi[\alpha + \beta m]$$

where $\Phi[x]$ is the cumulative density function of the normal distribution and $m \sim N[0.1]$.

- **Logistic (CreditPortfolioView^{TM}):** A two-parameter distribution bounded by zero and one, where the systematic default rate is a function of a standard normal variable:

$$p = \frac{1}{1 + e^{\alpha + \beta m}}$$

where $m \sim N[0.1]$.

12.5.2 Conditional Loss Distribution

By virtue of isolating all sources of systematic risk to the systematic default rate distribution, the remaining non-systematic risks can be considered completely independent. Given the conditionally fixed value of the mean default rate from the systematic distribution, the exact conditional loss distribution for a portfolio of equal-weighted exposures[3] is known: the Binomial distribution which provides the probability that k defaults will occur in a portfolio of n borrowers given that each has probability of default p:

$$B(k; n, p) = \frac{n!}{k!(n-k)!} p^k (1-p)^{n-k}.$$

The Binomial distribution is often approximated by the more tractable Poisson distribution, which provides the probability that k defaults will occur in a portfolio of n borrowers given that each occurrence has a rate of intensity per unit time p:

$$P(k; pN) = \frac{(pn)^k}{k!} e^{-pn}.$$

---

[3] A portfolio of unequal-sized exposures can be expressed as the sum of equal-sized exposure sub-portfolios, each of which has an independent Binomial Conditional loss distribution.

The differences in approximation will generally be immaterial if default rates are reasonably low and the portfolio is reasonably well-diversified.

12.5.3   Convolution

The systematic risk distribution and the conditional loss distribution are combined by convolution, represented graphically in Figure 12.8. For each value from the systematic rate distribution, we calculate the conditional loss distribution. The unconditional portfolio loss distribution is then the average of these conditional loss distributions, weighted by the probability from the systematic risk distribution. While this sounds easy enough, in practise this step can be the most significant algorithmic challenge in designing a model. In some rare cases, the two distributions are amenable to analytic convolution, resulting

Figure 12.8   Convolution

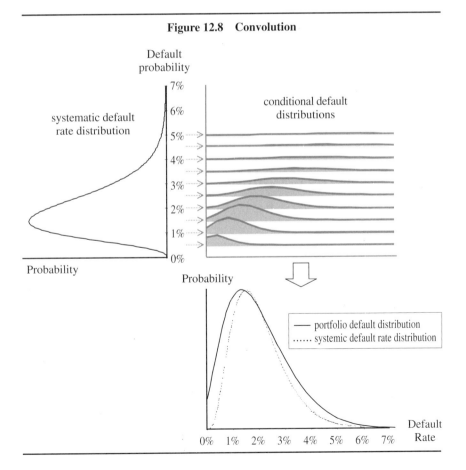

in a closed-form equation for the portfolio loss distribution. More commonly, convolution must be carried out through numerical techniques such as Monte Carlo simulation.

12.6   Model Comparison

The structure of the general modeling framework presented above allows for a straightforward analytic comparison between models. Differences in the conditional loss distribution or convolution technique are unlikely to have significant impact on the overall model result, so the key comparison point between models is the systematic default rate distribution. In order to compare the models' systematic default rate distributions, they must first be derived and then parameterized to an equivalent expression of default rate behavior. The comparison will be illustrated for a homogeneous[4] portfolio with an unconditional mean default rate $\bar{p}$ equal to 116bp and a standard deviation of default rate σ equal to 90 bp.[5] Since each model produces a two-parameter default rate distribution, the mean and standard deviation are sufficient statistics to define the parameters for any of the models.

The following sections derive the systematic default rate distributions and parameters for three credit risk portfolio models in the public domain. Note that the techniques herein are not limited to these three models, and can be applied to compare virtually any proposed credit risk portfolio models.

12.6.1   CreditMetrics[TM] Systematic Default Rate Distribution

CreditMetrics[TM],[6] using the Merton model, assumes that a borrower's default is motivated by a normally distributed change in asset value ΔA, which is correlated with the change in asset value of other borrowers in the portfolio. This change in asset value can be decomposed into a normally distributed systematic factor[7] x, and a normally distributed non-systematic component ε:

$$\Delta A = px + \sqrt{1 - p^2}\,\varepsilon,$$

---

[4]   All obligors having the same mean default rate, exposure size, correlation structure, etc

[5]   These parameters were selected to match Moody's "All Corporates" default experience for 1970–1995, as reported in Carty & Lieberman (1996)

[6]   See Gupton, Finger, and Bhatia (1997) for detail

[7]   This is presented in single-factor form for illustration, but is easily extended to multiple systemic factors (corresponding to a pairwise asset correlation matrix)

where p is the asset correlation, and x, $\varepsilon \sim N[0,1]$ and independent. Consequently, $\Delta A \sim N[0,1]$.

If the values of the systematic factors are known, then the change in asset value will be normally distributed with a mean determined by the systematic factor values, and a standard deviation given by the coefficient of the non-systemic factor.

According to the Merton model, default occurs when $\Delta A_i \leq c$, where the "critical value" c is calibrated to provide the correct unconditional default probability $\bar{p}$; that is $\Phi(c) = \bar{p}$, where $\Phi(x)$ is the cumulative density function of the normal distribution. The default rate, conditioned on the values of systematic factors, can then be expressed as[8]

$$p|m = \Phi\left[\frac{c - \sqrt{p}m}{\sqrt{1-p}}\right],$$

which may be recognized as the Probit distribution described in section 5.1.

The probability density function for the default rate can be derived explicitly as it is related to the probability density function of systematic factors by the following:

$$f(p) = \varphi(m(p))\left|\frac{dm}{dp}\right| = \frac{\varphi(m(p))}{\left|\frac{dp}{dm}\right|}.$$

Applied to the Merton model's transformation function and normally-distributed systematic factors, this yields

$$f(p) = \frac{\sqrt{1-p}\ \varphi\left(\frac{c - \sqrt{1-p}\ \Phi^{-1}(p)}{\sqrt{p}}\right)}{\sqrt{p}\ \varphi\left(\Phi^{-1}(p)\right)},$$

where $\varphi(z)$ is the standardized normal density function.

---

[8] Vasicek (1987) develops this representation of the Merton model for a single factor

As above, the critical value c is defined in terms of the unconditional default probability:

$$c = \Phi^{-1}(\bar{p})$$

In order to yield $\bar{p} = 116$bp, we set $c = -2.27$.

Calculating default rate volatility by

$$\sigma^2 = \int_{-\infty}^{\infty} (p|m - \bar{p})^2 \; \varphi(m)dm = \int_{-\infty}^{\infty} \left(\Phi\left[\frac{c - \sqrt{pm}}{\sqrt{1-p}} \right] - \bar{p} \right)^2 \varphi(m)dm,$$

we set $p = 0.073$ in order to yield $\sigma = 90$ bp.

12.6.2   CreditPortfolioView^{TM} Systematic Default Rate Distribution

CreditPortfolioView^{TM}[9] defines the borrower's default probability as a function of an index value:

$$P_{i,t} = \frac{1}{1 + e^{y_{i,t}}}.$$

This index value in turn depends on macroeconomic variables, and can be restated in terms of a constant plus a normally distributed systematic variable m, as follows:

$$y_{i,t} = U_i + V_i m_i,$$

where $m \sim N[0,1]$.

The conditional default rate function can then be expressed as

$$P|m = \frac{1}{1 + e^{U + V_m}},$$

which is the Logistic distribution described in section 5.1.

---

[9]   See Wilson (1997) for further details

Deriving the implied probability density function for the default rate proceeds just in section 6.1, yielding

$$f(p) = \frac{1}{Vp(1-p)} \varphi\left(\frac{\ln\left(\frac{1-p}{p}\right) - U}{V}\right).$$

The two parameters U and V are then set by solving the following system of equations:

$$\bar{p} = \int_{-\infty}^{\infty} \frac{1}{1 + e^{U + V_m}} \varphi(m)dm, \text{ and}$$

$$\sigma^2 = \int_{-\infty}^{\infty} \left(\frac{1}{1 + e^{U + V_m}} - \bar{p}\right)^2 \varphi(m)dm.$$

In order to yield $\bar{p} = 116$bp and $\sigma = 90$bp, $U = 4.684$ and $V = 0.699$.

12.6.3 CREDITRISK$^+$ Systematic Default Rate Distribution

CREDITRISK^{+10} explicitly assumes that the systematic default rate distribution is a Gamma distribution $\Gamma(\alpha, \beta)$ as in section 5.1. The two parameters of the Gamma distribution are related to mean and variance by:

$$\alpha = \frac{\bar{p}^2}{\sigma^2}, \text{ and } \beta = \frac{\sigma^2}{\bar{p}}.$$

In order to yield $\bar{p} = 116$bp and $\sigma = 90$bp, we set $\alpha = 1.661$ and $\beta = 0.0070$.

12.6.4 Results of Model Comparison

Calculating the systematic default rate distribution for each model as above yields distributions which are quite similar (see Figure 12.9).

---

[10] Detailed description may be found in Credit Suisse Financial Products (1997)

Figure 12.9   Comparison of Systematic Default Rate Distributions

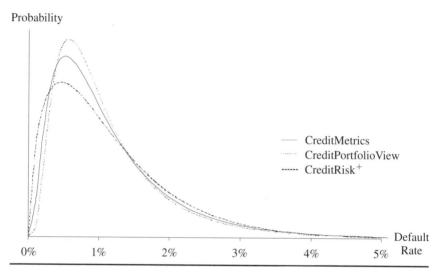

From this we may conclude that, despite the appearance of vast differences in underlying theory and algorithms, the models are not terribly different at core. An important caveat to this analysis is that the model parameters were set such that the models describe similar mean and volatility of default rates. In practise, the model's parameters are stated in quite different terms and measured from quite different types of data. Hence the models may have quite different results in empirical comparisons.

12.7   Summary

The preceding discussion has established several key non-obvious features of credit risk (systematic default risk, systematic credit spread risk and non-systematic credit spread risk. These features need not necessarily be contained within a single model so long as each is accounted for somewhere, e.g. one model for default risk model and another separate model for credit spread "Value-at-Risk," and combined prudently.

The analysis has also established that the available default risk models, once placed in a common framework and parameterized appropriately, can be shown to be quite similar. Hence, beyond the issue of model completeness, the model selection decision need not focus on the theoretical "correctness" of a model. Instead, model selection should focus on user-specific issues such as appropriateness to risks in the portfolio, availability of data for inputs, ease of use.

References

Carty, Lea and Dana Lieberman, January 1996, "Corporate Bond Defaults and Default Rates 1938–1995," Moody's Investors Service Global Credit Research.

Credit Suisse Financial Products, 1997, "CREDITRISK$^+$ — A Credit Risk Management Framework".

Gupton, Greg, Christopher Finger, and Mickey Bhatia, 1997, "CreditMetrics Technical Document," Morgan Guaranty Trust Co.

Hickman, Andrew and H. Ugur Koyluoglu, 1998, "A Generalized Framework for Credit Risk Portfolio Models" working paper; an abridged version was published in *Risk*, October 1998 as "Reconcilable Differences".

Merton, Robert, 1974, "On the Pricing of Corporate Debt: The Risk Structure of Interest Rates", *Journal of Finance*, Vol. 2.

Moody's Investors Service (Global Credit Research), January 1999, "Historical Default Rates of Corporate Bond Issuers, 1920–1998".

Vasicek, Oldrich, February 12 1987, "Probability of Loss on Loan Portfolio," KMV Corporation.

Wilson, Tom, September 1997 (part I) and October 1997 (part II), "Portfolio Credit Risk", *Risk*.

13

CreditMetrics™— Assessing the Marginal Risk Contribution of Credit

Greg M Gupton, *J.P. Morgan*

Since its launch by J.P. Morgan in April 1997, CreditMetrics™ has become the most widely applied value-at-risk (VaR) methodology for credit risk. Its details and data are fully disclosed and freely available in its continued development by The RiskMetrics™ Group, a J.P. Morgan spin-off.[1] This follows in the same open spirit that J.P. Morgan published RiskMetrics™ before to address market risks. What is extraordinary about this event is the broad and immediate endorsement that other major institutions gave to this methodology. There are currently 25 co-sponsors comprising a dozen financial institutions, six consultants, and three rating agencies, among others.[2] Why has CreditMetrics™ gained such broad industry support? What can it do for you? This chapter gives a brief overview of the methodology. It outlines how CreditMetrics™ can help guide your use of credit derivatives.

13.1 Overview

Credit risk assessment has traditionally been a matter of evaluating each individual (e.g. borrower, issuer, counterparty, or customer). We call all of these

---

[1] A downloadable data set and full documentation of the CreditMetrics™ methodology is available on the Internet at www.creditmetrics.com

[2] See www.creditmetrics.com/cm/cosponsors for this and the most recent list of the co-sponsors of CreditMetrics™

different types of creditors, obligors. How likely is the obligor to default, and in default, is there a source of recovery? The result is an estimate of the expected average (statistical mean) amount of default losses. This type of analysis has a long-standing tradition, and CreditMetrics™ does not displace it. However, banking institutions that themselves have come close to insolvency have done so, not because of the default of one of their borrowers, but because many of their borrowers were in trouble at the same time. Traditional credit risk systems do not address well these "correlated" concentrations of unexpected losses (statistical standard deviation). This is where CreditMetrics™ adds most value. Indeed, portfolio-concentration differences among market participants' drive their perceptions of credit derivative valuations. This means that a credit derivative trade can be the proverbial "win-win." Consider the transfer of risk to Corp XYZ from a portfolio with a heavy concentration on that name to a portfolio with little concentration. The party with heavy concentration on Corp XYZ will gladly sell the risk to a party with little or no concentration on Corp XYZ and both parties would stand better.

This chapter will briefly explain how CreditMetrics™ works and what it achieves, but it is worth while initially to list the scope and limits of its application. J.P. Morgan developed CreditMetrics™ to primarily cover debt outstanding directly to corporate borrowers. Therefore, it does not directly address debt to consumers and asset backed securities. The reason for this is that CreditMetrics™ uses data collected by the bond markets, rating agencies, academics, and others, which is most applicable to corporate obligors. A consumer borrower may have little data to describe credit quality (such as a credit rating). Similarly, asset backed securities depend upon more than just the credit quality of the issuers — such as prepayments.

CreditMetrics™ is not a high-level top-down index-tracking scheme. Rather, it builds a bottom-up portfolio risk estimate from the details of each specific exposure. Thus, it tailors risk management information to the specific names, industries, and sectors in the portfolio under analysis.

However, with this extra effort comes additional benefit. These are perhaps the Top 10 benefits that a credit portfolio manager gains from CreditMetrics™.

- Quantify aggregate credit risk: How much might be lost due to credit events?
- Identify risk sources: How much exposure is there to specific events?
- Set risk limits: How much risk is too much?
- Improve the risk-return trade-off: How can better returns be earned for the same risk — or lower risk for the same returns?

- Marginal what-if risk sources: How much marginal risk is contributed to the portfolio by: a small change in a position, a proposed transaction or an arbitrary group of positions?
- Quantify economic capital: How much buffer for unexpected losses is appropriate in a business sense?
- Calculate regulatory capital: How much capital is required under either the existing Basel Capital Accord or the June 1999 proposal?
- Evaluate managers' performance: Did the emerging markets desk perform well enough to compensate for the high risk?
- Understanding diversification/correlations: Am I less diversified than I think?
- Stay current, economically: How can I stay current with advances in credit risk management systems, regulations, data and methodologies?

CreditMetrics™ builds up the risk statistics that support these risk management decisions from the point of view of the portfolio as an interactive whole. This means that the correlations (or likelihood of joint defaults) are tailored to the specific names in the portfolio. Thus, the resulting portfolio will have greater (lesser) risk depending upon whether those correlations are higher (lower). In addition, marginal risk estimated for a new candidate transaction will depend upon the existing portfolio. Consider the example of a credit derivative to sell Ford risk. If this is added to a portfolio that is already concentrated in the automobile industry — not just Ford — then the realized marginal hedging benefit will be greater than if there were no existing concentration in automobiles.

Being able to quantify the marginal risk of concentrations — not just sum exposure amounts — by name, industry, geography, and sector is a powerful tool for risk managers. For instance, it is common practise to set credit limits by committee according to notional exposure amounts or credit ratings. As judicious as this may be, in the end, this type of limit-setting is arbitrary. CreditMetrics™ calculates marginal risk contributions according to the amount of diversification or concentration that each name brings to the portfolio and thus offers a rational approach to credit risk limits.

Indeed, an important use of credit derivatives is to divert risk of an over-concentrated name to alleviate the risk. After this concentration risk has been relieved, an institution can originate more primary business to the previously over-concentrated name. In this way, an organization's core business activity (e.g. lending, investing, and selling) can expand without suffering the risk (and cost) of its own naturally occurring over concentrations.

In the remainder of this chapter, we will: (1) build the case for the necessity of taking a portfolio view, (2) describe and illustrate the approach taken in CreditMetrics to construct the process of valuation changes due to credit quality changes, (3) statistically quantify this process, and (4) illustrate the real-world applications.

13.2   The Portfolio Context of Credit

Credit risk has perhaps become the essential challenge in risk management as we enter the new millennium. Globally, institutions are taking on an increasing amount of credit risk. As credit exposures have multiplied, the need for more sophisticated risk management techniques for credit risk has also increased.

Of course, credit risk can be managed — as it has been — by a more rigorous enforcement of traditional credit processes such as stringent underwriting standards, limit enforcement, and obligor monitoring. However, risk managers are increasingly seeking to quantify and integrate the overall credit risk assessment within an objective VaR statement that captures exposure to market, rating change, and default risks. For example, a risk adjusted return on capital (RAROC)[3]-type management approach would use this VaR estimate. In our view, RAROC has limited use unless the estimate of economic capital buffer is sufficiently accurate. CreditMetrics provides this better estimate of risk for credit.

In the end, a better estimate of risk across the credit portfolio will help portfolio managers identify pockets of concentration and opportunities for diversification. Over time, portfolio managers can put on positions that best use risk-carrying capacity — which is a scarce and costly resource. Managers can then make risk versus return trade-offs with the knowledge of not only the expected credit losses, but also the unexpected losses.

13.2.1   The Need for a Portfolio Approach

The primary reason for adopting a quantitative portfolio approach to credit risk management is to enable a more systematic addressing of concentration risk. Concentration risk refers to additional portfolio risk resulting from increased exposure to one obligor or groups of correlated obligors (e.g. by industry and by location).

---

[3] Throughout this chapter, we use the term risk adjusted return on capital (RAROC) in its generic sense to refer to asset management according to a risk versus return trade-off across diverse exposures. We do not mean to specify any particular implementation

Traditionally, portfolio managers have relied on a qualitative feel for the concentration risk in their credit portfolios. Intuitive — but arbitrary — exposure-based credit limits have been the principal defense against unacceptable concentrations of credit risk. However, credit limits based on exposures rather than risk do not recognize either the dynamics of portfolio correlations or the relationship between risk and return.

A quantitative approach, as in CreditMetrics™, allows a portfolio manager to state credit lines and limits in units of marginal portfolio volatility. Furthermore, such a model creates a framework within which to consider concentrations along almost any dimension (e.g. individual name, industry, sector, country, and instrument type).

Another important reason for taking a portfolio view of credit risk is to address more rationally and accountably portfolio diversification. The decision to take on ever higher exposure to an obligor will meet ever higher marginal risk — risk that grows geometrically with the concentration on that name. Conversely, similar additional exposure to an equally rated obligor who has relatively little existing exposure will entail less risk. Indeed, such names may be individually risky, but offer a relatively small marginal contribution to overall portfolio risk due to diversification benefits.

Finally, a portfolio credit risk methodology can be the foundation for a rational risk-based capital allocation process. Generically, this systematic approach takes a mark-to-market view, captures changes in value due to upgrades (downgrades) as well as defaults, and addresses portfolio effects (diversification benefits and concentration risks). In addition, there are practical considerations for a quantitative approach to credit risk:

- Financial products have become more complex. The growth of derivative activity (e.g. swaps, forwards, and options) has created uncertain and dynamic counterparty exposures that are significantly more challenging to manage than the static exposures of more traditional instruments such as bonds or loans. End users and providers of these instruments need to identify such exposures and understand their credit risks, as well as related market risks.

- The proliferation of credit enhancement mechanisms — third-party guarantees, posted collateral, margin arrangements, and netting — make it increasingly necessary to assess credit risk at the portfolio level as well as at the individual exposure level.

- Active credit risk management is becoming more practical due to improved liquidity in secondary cash markets and the rapidly growing use of credit derivatives. Each has served to increase the market efficiency of credit pricing. Proper standards of due diligence require that institutions thoroughly review existing risks before hedging or trading them.

- Innovative new credit instruments explicitly derive value from correlation estimates or credit events such as upgrades, downgrades, or default. We can best understand these in the context of a portfolio model that also explicitly accounts for credit quality migrations.

We have discussed why a portfolio approach to credit risk is necessary. In the following section, we discuss why estimating portfolio credit risk is a much harder problem than estimating portfolio market risk.

13.2.2 Challenges in Estimating Portfolio Credit Risk

Modeling concentration risk in credit portfolios is neither analytically or practically easy. It is true that modern portfolio theory has taken great strides in its application to equity price risks. Nevertheless, fundamental differences between credit risks and equity price risks make modern portfolio theory problematic when applied to credit portfolios. There are two problems: non-normality and correlation estimation.

The first problem is that credit returns are generally non-normal and specifically, they are highly skewed and fat-tailed (Figure 13.1). In contrast, equity returns are relatively symmetric and are well approximated by normal distributions (also called Gaussian distribution). Thus, the two statistical portfolio measures — mean (average) and standard deviation — are sufficient to characterize fully market risk, but these measures would not characterize the long downside "tail" of credit risk. Thus, to understand the full loss distribution of a credit portfolio, we need more than just the mean and standard deviation. Defaults and downgrades to sub-investment grade ratings cause this long downside tail of the distribution of credit returns. Credit returns typically have a large likelihood of earning a (relatively) small profit through net interest earnings (NIE), coupled with a (relatively) small chance of losing a large amount of investment. Across a large portfolio, there is likely to be a blend of these two forces creating the smooth but skewed (lopsided) distribution shape seen in Figure 13.1.

The second problem is the difficulty of estimating correlations. For equities, high-frequency, liquid market price observations allow us to estimate directly the correlations. For credit quality, the lack of data makes it difficult to estimate any type of credit correlation directly from history. Alternative approaches include:

Figure 13.1   Comparison of Distribution of Credit Returns and Market Returns

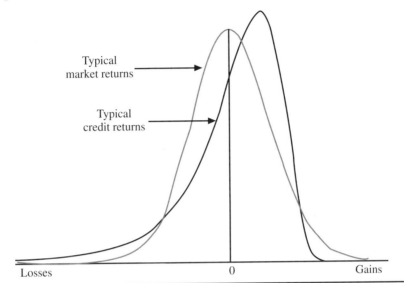

- Setting correlations at a uniform average level across the portfolio,
- Deriving a model to capture credit-quality correlations that has more readily estimated parameters, and
- Bypassing correlations entirely in favor of directly tabulating probabilities of changes in joint credit quality.

CreditMetrics™ currently offers the first two of these. The third approach offers the advantage of sidestepping the use of a correlation parameter entirely. However, it carries the disadvantage of the noise of the available data.

In summary, measuring risk across a credit portfolio is as necessary as it is difficult. With the CreditMetrics™ methodology, we address these difficulties. In the next section, we step through a detailed illustration of CreditMetrics™ risk estimation for a single standalone bond. In later sections, we will then consider the broader portfolio calculation to incorporate diversification benefits due to correlation.

13.3   Methodology

Estimating credit value volatilities is inherently challenging because credit events (rating changes and defaults) are infrequent. Thus, observing bond prices over, the previous year, for example, is unlikely to incorporate the volatility of value introduced by all possible changes in credit quality. Simply put, traditional methods may not fully capture credit risk, including default volatility, since the observed bonds have — by definition — not (yet) defaulted. To overcome this, the CreditMetrics^{TM} methodology constructs the full process of potential changes to credit quality. This complexity has led to a technical document of about 200 pages that details the methodology. To simplify, things we outline the three main components of CreditMetrics^{TM}.

- **Internal positions:** These are commonly kept in any number of systems within an institution whether they are in investment portfolios or trading books and on-or-off the balance sheet. So long as these positions are on a consistent basis, CreditMetrics^{TM} can account for credit risk differences across credit instrument types.

- **Volatilities of value due to credit quality events:** These include not only default events, but also upgrades (downgrades) in credit rating. These volatilities of value are first calculated on an individual basis before constructing the risk of the whole portfolio.

- **Correlations:** Since our goal is to calculate the risk across the entire portfolio, it is essential to estimate co-movements between different obligors (counterparties, borrowers, or issuers).

We can illustrate these three components in the road map illustrated in Figure 13.2. In truth, each step in the process is simple although there are many steps.

Figure 13.2 A Road Map of the Analytics Within CreditMetrics^{TM}

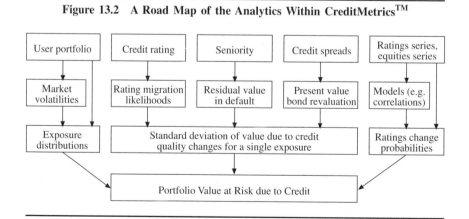

13.3.1 Exposures

Credit risk is present in a variety of instruments. CreditMetrics™ offers seven credit instrument types, which capture the substantial majority of risk found in typical portfolios. These are: loans, bonds, commitments to lend, financial (also called stand-by) letters of credit, receivables (also called trade credit), freely user defined Cash flow Streams and market-driven instruments such as swaps, forwards, and options. In addition, a Generic Exposure-type allows full user control for inputting exotic structures. For this, any proprietary credit-pricing model may be used to pre-calculate the instrument value in all possible grades of credit quality including default. CreditMetrics™ can then incorporate this position and calculate diversification effects. More importantly, CreditMetrics™ can show any of these exposure types as a short position, so the direct hedging impact of a credit derivative instrument, such as a credit swap, can be assessed.

For several of these exposure types — loans, letters of credit, and receivables — the amount of risk to changes in credit quality is simply the principal amount. The principal amount is the largest value that could be lost in default: it is known and constant over time. As an interesting contrast, this is not the case with commitments to lend or market-driven instruments.

For loan commitments, there is a distinction between the amount currently drawn versus the amount not yet drawn under the line. In general, the amount drawn is at risk and the remainder under the line may be at risk. In particular, there is a commonly observed link between the amount drawn and credit rating changes. Lower-rated credits tend to have a greater percentage draw. The most conservative assumption is that, regardless of the amount currently drawn, the full line will be drawn at the time of default. An intermediate assumption is that drawdowns increase "linearly" as credit quality decreases across rating categories through default. These two approaches, though common, are quite arbitrary. A more historically based approach can be taken by using data published in the Asarnow & Edwards [1995] study, which shows average drawdown experience for each rating and in default. CreditMetrics™ offers the user a choice among these three approaches.

For market-driven instruments, such as swaps and forwards, credit risk and market risk are intertwined. For these instruments, changes in market rates and yields can have an enormous impact on credit risk, even if all credit-related factors remain constant. The reason for this is that the amount exposed to default will change as market rates change. Moreover, it is only the degree to which an institution is "in the money" to the counterparty that there is a credit exposure. To address this, we must first calculate the profile of netted exposures across each counterparty's own "portfolio" of deals. This profile is then imported into CreditMetrics^{TM} for the consideration of credit risk. The RiskMetrics^{TM} Group offers a credit exposure calculator using the RiskMetrics^{TM} framework, which we implement in our FourFifteen software.

Finally, for a bond, CreditMetrics^{TM} allows the credit exposure to be treated in either of two ways. For simplicity, the exposure can be taken in at its estimated current market value. However, in concept, the value of a bond is volatile just like a swap. Thus, we allow bonds to be included with all other market-driven instruments to generate its credit exposure profile. Of course, the swings in value of a bond are small when compared to swaps, so this observation is merely a refinement rather than a practical concern.

For credit derivative structures, the notional "exposure amount" deserves greater consideration. Consider the case of a fixed payment upon default versus an alternative structure that pays the actual loss value of the reference bond. If the historical recovery rate were 50% of par, then a fixed payment rate in default of 50% would make the notional exposure of the credit derivative roughly comparable to the target position. However, this payoff is identical to a credit derivative of half the bond value if the payoff in default is quoted at 100%. This flexibility can be an important economic consideration for on-balance-sheet positions.

13.3.2 Volatility of Value Due to Credit Quality Changes

So far, we have established how much is at risk. Note that, unlike alternative approaches, we have not sought to estimate "risk equivalent units." Rather, we address directly: (1) the likelihood of default, (2) the chance of upgrades (downgrades), and (3) the changes in value that occur for each of these credit events. Each of these steps in the process deserves to be modeled fully as we estimate the volatility of value due to credit quality changes. Alternative methodologies that commingle these dimensions of the credit process into "equivalents" inevitably lose details that are needed to fully estimate risk. We need four types of data:

- **Transition Matrices:** For each credit rating agency (or for a bank's own internal rating system), how likely is it for obligors to "migrate" from one credit rating to another — or default? In our view, these probabilities are the only measures that give true meaning to qualitative letter categories.
- **Recovery Rates in Default:** For each seniority class and instrument type (and perhaps country and industry sectors), how much is recovered in the event of default and what is the typical range of recoveries?

- **Risk-free Yield Curve:** For each currency in the portfolio, what is the government yield curve?
- **Credit Spreads:** For each maturity and credit rating, where would the instrument typically trade over the risk-free yield curve? More generally, how would the instrument re-price upon upgrade (downgrade)?

The major credit rating agencies publish annually the first two types of data, transition matrices, and recovery rates. However, any institution may feel it is more appropriate to compile and use its own information to represent their own situation. The last two types of data can be observed in the market and can be purchased from suppliers such as Reuters, Bridge, or Bloomberg. Alternatively, these can also be supplied by each institution's understanding of its own markets. A data set of all this information is also available from The RiskMetrics™ Group's CreditMetrics™ Internet site at www.creditmetrics.com.

Before moving on to describe how this data is used, we briefly describe what this data is. First, the transition matrices are best thought of as a square table of probabilities, as illustrated in Figure 13.3. They show the likelihood of "migrating" from one credit rating today to any other credit rating (or default) in one period. So, as in the example shown here, each row of the table sums up to 100%. An example of how to read the table is that there is a 4.96% chance that a BBB-rated firm today will become a BB firm in one year. This particular table is adapted from Standard & Poor's historically tabulated annual migrations of senior unsecured long-term credit ratings.

Figure 13.3   Standard & Poor's One-Year Transition Matrix (adjusted for removal of N.R.)

Initial Rating	Rating at year-end (%)							
	AAA	AA	A	BBB	BB	B	CCC	Default
AAA	90.82	8.26	0.74	0.06	0.11	0	0	0
AA	0.65	90.88	7.69	0.58	0.05	0.13	0.02	0
A	0.08	2.42	91.30	5.23	0.68	0.23	0.01	0.05
BBB	0.03	0.31	5.87	87.46	4.96	1.08	0.12	0.17
BB	0.02	0.12	0.64	7.71	81.16	8.40	0.98	0.98
B	0	0.10	0.24	0.45	6.86	83.50	3.92	4.92
CCC	0.21	0	0.41	1.24	2.67	11.70	64.48	19.29

Source: Standard & Poor's Ratings Performance 1996 Stability & Transition

Since these probabilities are simple tabulations of historical data — in this case, 17 years' worth — there are some notable oddities. First, notice that the CCC row shows a 0.21% chance of a CCC upgrading to a AAA in one year. This represents merely one instance in the historical record that seems large only because of the relatively small number of CCC observations. Second, notice that AAA and AA show zero likelihood of default. Although this has been historically true, it is unlikely that this must remain true forever. In the CreditMetrics Technical Document,[4] we offer a technique to "smooth" a transition matrix to condition upon anticipated long-term behavior. Although this discussion is beyond the scope of this chapter, the technique is useful to avoid otherwise anomalous pricing calculations.

Second, recovery rate experience can also be historically tracked. In Figure 13.4, taken from the same 1995 Asarnow & Edwards' study, the first thing that is immediately apparent is that recovery is uncertain. It is understandable that managers throw up their hands and say: "We cannot predict recoveries so there is nothing to be done." Nevertheless, a risk management system must incorporate not only the expected average (mean), but also the historical uncertainty (standard deviation) in order to model a complete estimate of the volatility of value.[5]

Figure 13.4   Distribution of Bank Facility Recoveries

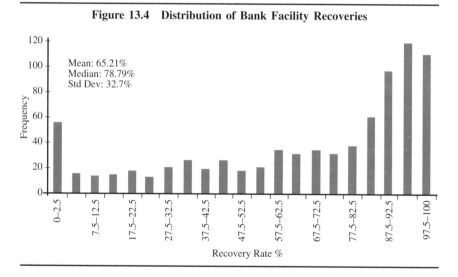

---

[4]   See pp 66–76 of the CreditMetrics[TM] Technical Document

[5]   When doing simulations, CreditMetrics[TM] models the full distribution of possible recovery rates, and not just the mean and standard deviation. The distributions of recoveries are well approximated by a Beta distribution since this addresses the 0%-to-100% bounded nature of recovery rates

There are a number of rating agencies and academic studies of historical recovery rate experience. Four of these — two for bonds and two for bank facilities — are broadly stated, and so are included in the CreditMetrics™ data set. In addition to the initial breakout between bonds versus bank facilities, these studies catalog recovery rates by seniority standing and sometimes by industry.

Third and fourth are the base yield curve and credit spreads. The base yield curves are supplied from J.P. Morgan's RiskMetrics™ government yield curve data set and are taken to be default-free. Bridge Information Systems supplies the credit spread curves. Both are listed across maturities while credit spreads are also listed across credit rating categories and industry sectors. The credit spreads at the time of this writing are compiled across non-callable US corporate bonds.

These yield and spread data are updated periodically in the CreditMetrics™ data set. Figure 13.5 illustrates an example of these data. We will use the data in Figure 13.5 as we progress through an illustration of the methodology.

**Figure 13.5   Base Yield Curve and Credit Spreads
(as downloaded from the CreditMetrics™ Internet site)**

Input Base Government Yield Curve, as of July 1997

Year	1	2	3	5	7	10	20	30
US Govt	5.95%	5.80%	5.92%	6.06%	6.12%	6.23%	6.48%	6.47%

Input Industrial US Bond Credit Spread Curves as of July 1997

Year	1	2	3	5	7	10	20	30
AAA	0.16%	0.18%	0.22%	0.25%	0.30%	0.35%	0.38%	0.40%
AA	0.20%	0.22%	0.26%	0.30%	0.37%	0.41%	0.46%	0.50%
A	0.27%	0.30%	0.32%	0.37%	0.45%	0.49%	0.55%	0.61%
BBB	0.44%	0.46%	0.50%	0.52%	0.65%	0.75%	0.83%	0.91%
BB	0.89%	1.06%	1.20%	1.41%	1.56%	1.71%	1.94%	2.16%
B	1.50%	1.63%	1.83%	2.11%	2.41%	2.63%	2.89%	3.15%
CCC	2.55%	3.00%	4.00%	5.00%	6.00%	7.00%	8.00%	9.00%

This yield and spread data are used to estimate possible changes in value of credit instruments. Estimating possible changes in value at the risk horizon is not difficult, but there are several steps. Consider, for example, a four-year bond from a BBB-rated obligor. At the risk horizon, it will then be a three-year bond and its rating may be anything from AAA to CCC, or even default. To estimate its value at the risk horizon one year from now we discount all remaining cash flows at the forward corporate yield curves — one curve for each possible rating. Figure 13.6 shows the resulting curves that were from derived the data in Figure 13.5.

**Figure 13.6   Derived Forward Yield Curves
(as calculated in the spreadsheet*)**

Derived Forward Par Coupon US Treasury Bond Curve

Year	1	2	3	5	7	10	20	29
US Govt	5.64%	5.90%	6.00%	6.12%	6.19%	6.30%	6.53%	6.51%

Derived Forward Zero Coupon US Corporate Bond Curves

Year	1	2	3	5	7	10	20	29
AAA	5.80%	6.08%	6.22%	6.37%	6.49%	6.65%	6.90%	6.91%
AA	5.84%	6.12%	6.26%	6.42%	6.56%	6.71%	6.98%	7.01%
A	5.91%	6.20%	6.32%	6.49%	6.64%	6.79%	7.08%	7.11%
BBB	6.08%	6.36%	6.50%	6.64%	6.84%	7.05%	7.36%	7.41%
BB	6.53%	6.96%	7.20%	7.53%	7.75%	8.01%	8.46%	8.65%
B	7.14%	7.53%	7.83%	8.23%	8.60%	8.93%	9.42%	9.63%
CCC	8.19%	8.90%	10.00%	11.12%	12.19%	13.30%	14.53%	15.41%

As we derive these yield curves for re-pricing one year forward, we make the following modeling choices. First, the risk-free curve is projected to follow the "expectations hypothesis." This means that forward rates are projected to be future spot rates. Second, in contrast to the risk-free curve, we project credit spreads to be "persistent." This means that the best forecast of the forward period credit spread is today's credit spread.

Thus, we start with a par coupon risk-free curve, convert it to a zero coupon curve and take the rates one year forward to be next year's spot rates. This is then restated as a par coupon curve so that today's credit spreads can be sensibly

---

*   The Excel spreadsheet is on the disk that accompanies this book

added to it. Separate credit spread curves are maintained for each credit rating category and so — for seven major rating grades — we construct seven corporate forward par coupon curves. Since these curves are to be used for re-pricing, it is convenient to restate them as zero coupon curves as shown in Figure 13.6. All of these calculations are performed in the Excel spreadsheet, which is on the disk that accompanies this book. Refer to "Calculate Yield Curves" page of this spreadsheet for the numerical example above.

With this information, we have fully specified the distribution of possible changes in value due to credit quality changes at the risk horizon. We can construct the volatility of value due to credit quality changes, as Figure 13.7 shows. An exposure is tagged with its obligor's senior unsecured long-term credit rating. Then, in the coming risk horizon — commonly set to one year — there is some likelihood of credit quality migration. For each possible migration, there is an historical estimate of its likelihood. Also, for each possible migration there is an estimate of the possible change in value. For upgrades (downgrades), this is done by rediscounting the remaining cash flows at the estimated corporate curve for that new rating. For the case of default, it is done by looking to the recovery rate distribution as seen in Figure 13.4.

Figure 13.7   Summary of Standlone Value-at-Risk (VaR) Calculation for One Exposure

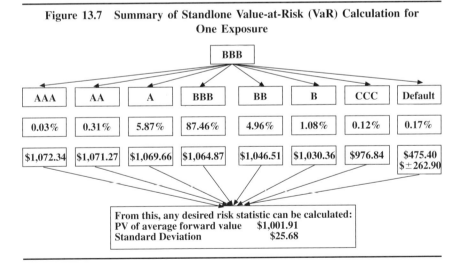

The calculation here of each exposure's possible distribution of value is a necessary step, but it is not a complete picture of the risk in this one exposure. To capture the full picture, we must know how this exposure contributes to the diversification, or perhaps over concentration, across all other names in the portfolio. Once we know this, then we can state the true marginal risk of this exposure — the amount that the risk of the portfolio would change if this exposure was added or subtracted from the portfolio.[6]

To do this, we must estimate correlations of credit quality changes between each pair of names in the portfolio. This is difficult. Its difficulty is perhaps why such a comprehensive approach to credit risk has seldom been taken before. In the next section, we give an overview of how correlations can be estimated for use in CreditMetrics[TM].

13.3.3   Correlations

Correlations are as controversial as they are necessary. Do correlations really exist in the real world? Intuitively, there is reason to argue for correlations since several firms within the same industry can be downgraded at the same time and for essentially the same reason; for example, high fuel costs hitting many airlines at once or poor real estate prices hitting many local bank lenders at once. Alternatively, one might claim that each firm is in many ways unique and its changes in credit quality are often driven by events and circumstances specific to that firm. This would argue for little correlation between different firms' rating changes and defaults. Thus, it is worthwhile to determine whether correlations in credit quality can be observed using real world data and, if so, what the likely levels of correlation are.

The historical default rate studies performed by the major rating agencies are an obvious first place to start looking for evidence of correlations. Although the agencies have not conducted correlation studies themselves, we can still infer whether there are correlations of defaults by observing the volatility of defaults over many years.

These agency studies are based on a large population of all bonds rated by that agency for as many as 26 years. Thus, if defaults were uncorrelated, then we would expect to observe aggregated default rates that are very stable from year to year. On the other hand, if defaults were correlated, then we would observe some years where default rates were much higher than average — firms defaulting together. This is what we observe; a wide fluctuation in default rates. There are some years when many firms default together and other years when far less than average are defaulting. This is good evidence of some positive correlation.

---

[6]   CreditMetrics[TM] can do three levels of marginal risk analysis: (1) a small size change to an existing position, (2) the removal of an entire existing position, or (3) a change to a user-defined number of positions simultaneously

We can make this observation more precise by examining the numbers. We use the formula here to compute average default correlations, (, from default rates taken from, in this case, a Moody's default rate study.

$$\rho = \frac{N\left(\dfrac{\sigma^2}{\mu - \mu^2}\right) - 1}{N - 1} \qquad \text{where} \begin{cases} \rho & \text{inferred default correlation within rating} \\ N & \text{number of years of observation} \\ \mu & \text{average default rate across all years} \\ \sigma & \text{standard deviation of annual default rates} \end{cases}$$

The formula itself is unimportant. What it says is that, if there is a binomial process (bonds either default or they do not) and the default rate and correlation are uniform across all bonds within a rating class, then the ratio of the observed default rate variance to the zero-correlation default rate variance is the inferred default correlation. This formula is robust in that it imposes few assumptions. It is however limited by the small amount of default rate data available.

Both Moody's and S&P publish default rate statistics, which could be used to make this type of statistical inference of average default correlations. In Figure 13.8, we use data from a Moody's default study (see Carty & Lieberman [1996a]). We can infer from Moody's default rates that the number of firm-years supporting the average default rate, μ, is in the thousands for the five credit rating categories addressed here. More importantly however, there are only 26 yearly observations supporting the calculation of σ, which itself is reported with significant rounding. Thus, the confidence levels around the resulting inferred correlation are wide.

There are at least four caveats to this approach:

- The standard deviations of default rates, μ, are calculated over a very limited number of observations which lead to wide confidence levels;
- The underlying periodic default rates for investment grade categories are not normally distributed; thus the confidence levels for the investment grades will be wider than those calculated;
- The average default rate, σ, is assumed to be constant across all firms within the credit rating category and constant across time; and
- The approach is sensitive to the proportion of recession versus growth years which — in the 26-year sample — may not be representative of the future.

Figure 13.8   Inferred Default Correlations with Confidence Levels

Credit rating category	Default Rate defaults	Standard deviation correlation	Implied default	Lower confidence	Upper confidence
	μ	σ	ρ	$\Pr\{\rho < X\} = 2.5\%$	$\Pr\{\rho > X\} = 2.5\%$
Aa	0.03%	0.1%	0.33%	0.05%	1.45%
A	0.01%	0.1%	1.00%	0.15%	4.35%
Baa	0.13%	0.3%	0.69%	0.29%	1.83%
Ba	1.42%	1.4%	1.40%	0.79%	2.91%
B	7.62%	4.8%	3.27%	1.95%	6.47%

Source: Moody's 1970–1995 1-year default rates and volatilities
(Carty & Lieberman [1996a])

The inferred default correlations shown in Figure 13.8 are all positive and — by examination of the confidence intervals — are all statistically greater than zero to the 97.5% level. This is a strong indication that default events have statistically significant correlations that a risk assessment model such as CreditMetrics cannot ignore.

Joint Likelihood of Credit Quality Moves

Proving, as we have, that credit correlations exist is not sufficiently useful. What is important is that these correlations have meaning in terms of increased chance of multiple defaults. The greatest treat to a lending institution is not when one obligor defaults, but when, many obligors default together. It is the joint likelihood of defaults that is important and it is these statistics that CreditMetrics needs. Correlations are merely a means to this end. Figure 13.9 illustrates how these historical correlations effect joint default likelihood. For the case of two Baa rated names, the joint default likelihood rises by a factor of six when historical correlations are taken into account. By themselves, these joint default probabilities may appear small, but across a portfolio, they can very materially effect the calculation of all measures of portfolio risk.

Figure 13.9   Correlation Determines Joint Credit Quality Likelihoods

	Baa					Baa		
	No Default	Default	Total			No Default	Default	Total
No Default	99.7402%	0.1298%	99.87%		No Default	99.741%	0.1289%	99.87%
Baa					Baa			
Default	0.1298%	0.0002%	0.13%		Default	0.1289%	0.0011%	0.13%
Total	99.87%	0.13%	100%		Total	99.87%	0.13%	100%

It is tables of probabilities like these — probabilities of joint credit quality changes — that CreditMetrics uses to estimate the portfolio effects of credit risk. However, since CreditMetrics addresses upgrades (downgrades) in addition to defaults, it is necessary to examine more than a 2×2 table of default versus non-default. We must estimate the joint likelihood of any possible combination of credit quality outcomes. Thus, if the credit rating system recognizes eight states (i.e., AAA, AA ... , CCC plus default), then — between two obligors — there are 8x8 or 64 possible joint states whose likelihoods must be estimated. Thus, just as the migration probabilities of credit quality can be compiled for a single name in a transition matrix (see Figure 13.3) so also can joint credit quality migration probabilities be compiled for pairwise names.

This method of "correlation" estimation has the advantage that it does not make assumptions as to the underlying process, the joint distribution shape, or rely on distilling the data down to a single parameter — the correlation. However, this technique may not be able to distinguish between any division finer than broad industry sectors. So two banks might be deemed to have the same relationship as a bank and a, say, securities firm. In the following sections, we discuss methods of estimating credit quality correlations, which are sensitive to the characteristics of individual firms.

Estimating Credit Quality Correlations through Bond Spreads

A second way to estimate credit quality correlations using historical data would be to examine price histories of corporate bonds. Because it is intuitive that some movements in bond prices reflect changes in credit quality, it is reasonable to believe that correlations of bond price moves might allow for estimations of correlations of credit quality moves. Such an approach has two requirements: adequate data on bond price histories and a model relating bond prices to credit events (i.e., upgrades, downgrades, and defaults).

Where bond price histories are available, it is possible to estimate some type of credit correlation by first extracting credit spreads from the bond prices, and then estimating the correlation in the movements of these spreads. It is important to note that such a correlation only describes how spreads tend to move together. To arrive at the parameters we require for CreditMetrics^{TM} (that is, likelihoods of joint credit quality movements), it is necessary to adopt a model which links spread movements to credit events.

Models of risky bonds typically have three state variables: the first is the risk-free interest rate, the second is the credit spread and the third indicates whether the bond has defaulted. A typical approach (see for example Duffee [1995] or Nielsen and Ronn [1994]) is to assume that the risk-free rate and credit spread evolve independently and that defaults are linked to the credit spread through some pricing model. This pricing model allows us to infer the probability of the issuer defaulting from the observed bond spread. An extension of this type of model to two or more bonds would allow for the inference of default correlations from the correlation in bond spread moves.

While an approach of this type is attractive because it is consistent with other models of risky assets, its biggest drawback is practical. Bond spread data is notoriously scarce, particularly for issues of low credit quality, thus making the estimation of bond spread correlations impossible in practise. Even within the US, prices typically reported for corporate bonds are dealers' "matrix prices" — prices that are indicative only rather than based on actual trades. These data problems would only become worse outside of the US. Thus, we abandon this approach.

Asset Value Model

Finally, we present an approach that we use in practice to model joint probabilities of upgrades, downgrades, and defaults. We are motivated to pursue such an approach by the fact that practical matters (such as the lack of data on joint defaults) make it difficult to make direct estimates. Our approach here then will be indirect. It involves two steps:

1. Propose an underlying process, which drives credit-rating changes. This will establish a connection between the events that we ultimately want to describe (rating changes), but which are not readily observable, and a process, which we understand and can observe.

2. Estimate the parameters for the process above. If we have been successful in the first part, this should be easier than estimating the joint rating change probabilities directly.

For this, we propose that a firm's underlying asset value be the process that drives its credit rating changes and defaults. This model is essentially the option theoretic model of Merton [1974], which is discussed further in Kealhofer [1995]. We then describe the model which links changes in asset values to credit rating changes and explain how we parameterize the asset value model.

It is evident that the value of a firm's assets determines its ability to pay its debt holders. We suppose then that there is a specific level such that if the firm's assets fall below this level, it will be unable to meet its debt obligations and will default. If CreditMetrics™ only addressed value changes due to default, then this would be a sufficient model. However, since CreditMetrics™ addresses portfolio value changes resulting from upgrades (downgrades) as well, we need to extend this framework.

Extending the intuition above, we say that there are a series of thresholds for underlying firm asset value corresponding to the firm's credit rating by the risk horizon of, say, one year. Figure 13.10 illustrates this for the case of a Baa-rated firm. We assume that underlying firm value is normally distributed, which is reasonable given firm valuations in our data set. Overlaid on this distribution of firm values are the thresholds for each credit rating category including default. We take the likelihoods of each possible migration in credit quality from the transition matrix, see Figure 13.10. Thus, these thresholds are different depending upon the current credit rating of the firm.

Figure 13.10   Model to Map Underlying Firm Value to Credit Rating Grades

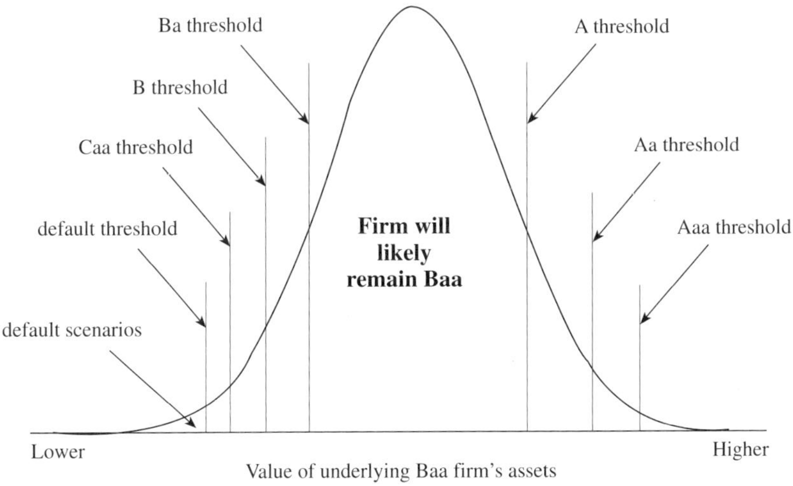

At this point, it is worth noting a methodology difference between CreditMetrics^{TM} and alternative approaches. Some approaches diligently pursue the Merton model, which values debt as a put option on the underlying value of the firm's assets. This approach would use the volatility of unlevered equity prices compared to the debt level of the firm to give an estimate of default likelihood. In contrast, CreditMetrics^{TM} takes the default likelihood as given by the credit rating for the firm (and the transition matrix from the rating agency). In our view, the default likelihood is dependent upon more than equity volatility and debt leverage. These additional determiners of credit quality are better captured in credit ratings.

Having achieved this mapping from firms' equity to credit quality states, we can now use estimates of equity correlation to imply correlations of credit quality changes. This allows a more tailored statement of correlation levels that are dependent upon each firm's own characteristics.

As a practical matter, there are choices to be made as to how best to empirically estimate equity-type correlations. We have chosen an open system that uses publicly available data that can easily be extended to firms not specifically named in our pre-compiled data set. This same openness allows non-publicly traded firms to be mapped into the correlation framework. Rather than focus on individual firm-level equity correlation, we can capture nearly all the "signal" and cancel most of the "noise" by examining higher-level equity aggregates. Thus, we look to equity aggregates compiled by industry and country.

To apply correlations, we characterize obligors by not only the industries in which they participate but also the countries in which they reside. In addition, all obligors have a unique or "firm-specific" volatility. By firm-specific, we mean the volatility of firm value that is not explained by the broad industry and country equity aggregates. We have determined that small firms have high firm-specific volatility versus large firms who are better explained by the broad equity indices. Thus, we use the obligor's total asset level to estimate the proportion of volatility that is firm specific and finally correlations for that firm.

A diagram outlining this approach to correlations is shown in Figure 13.11. CreditMetrics^{TM} addresses industry and countries/regions groups, but three of each is enough for illustration. In Figure 13.11, Philips Electronics and Sony are mapped first to their respective industries and then to their respective countries or regions. These industry and country assignments are real and are taken directly from a CreditMetrics^{TM} data set that is being offered by Bridge.

Since industry and country assignments are open to interpretation, CreditMetrics^{TM} offers two separate data sets based upon two different

Figure 13.11   Individual Firm Correlations Depend Upon Industries and Countries

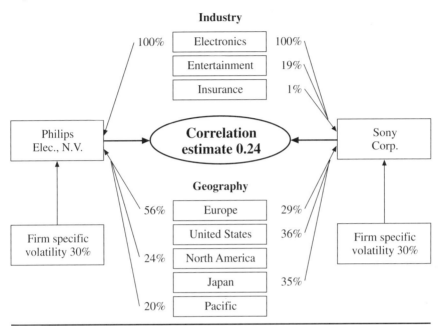

approaches. Of course, individual users are also free to make their own assignments. The first data set takes a fundamental approach of proportions of sales and assets in each industry or country. The second data set takes a purely statistical approach and, for public companies, regresses the equity series of the firm against the broad industry and country aggregates. Those indices that show the highest correlation receive the industry and country assignment(s). This approach is generated by Bridge. The two approaches are illustrated in an example list of 200 companies that have been generated by both methods. Our intent is to allow users to evaluate and chose between these alternative approaches based on which they felt is most appropriate for their own use. Assignment of further names beyond the initial list of 200 is available on an as-requested basis from Bridge. CreditMetrics offers this equity based correlation approach, the option of stating a uniform correlation across all names (useful for stress testing) and a correlation stress scenario wizard.

In summary, the methodology of CreditMetrics™ can best be summarized by its goal, approach and output. It has the goal of being an open framework that can easily allow diverse data, valuation models, periods and instrument types. It has the approach of going down to the details of both stepping through the process that leads credit value changes (hence, risk) and building up the details of each individual name and exposure. It has the output of showing both marginal risk changes to an existing portfolio viewable on several what-if levels as well as the big picture of portfolio risk at multiple levels of portfolio aggregation. This latter feature of output reports is most interesting and most important. We discuss outputs and resulting actions in the following section.

13.4 Applications

There are many ways of using the outputs of CreditMetrics^{TM} to guide the use of credit derivatives. On the strategic level, an institution can assess the aggregated amount of risk and typically set a buffer against these possible adverse outcomes. Across the industry, this buffer is becoming thought of as "economic capital" and in time, it may be regulatory capital. Importantly, an institution needs assurance that it can survive adverse credit events. This buffer carries an economic cost. This cost must be factored into any valuation of all credit exposures as well as credit derivatives used to hedge this risk.

On a finer level of detail, an institution or its departments can more rationally set credit risk limits and perform RAROC type analysis. In addition, concentration analysis can identify pockets of excess risk — risk that would be a clear candidate for hedging or diversification via credit derivatives. Finally, at the level of new exposure origination, the marginal risk of a new proposed transaction can be assessed within the context of the diversification it would provide to the portfolio. In this way, new exposures coupled with a credit derivative hedge can be accurately assessed. In this section, we will discuss further three specific applications: (i) assessing the buffer of economic capital, (ii) determining sources of over concentration, and (iii) rational credit risk limit setting.

13.4.1 Economic Capital Buffer

Financial institutions face various regulatory guidelines that specify required capital levels as a buffer against losses. For banks, the Bank for International Settlements (BIS) guidelines of 1988 are still in force although the new Amendment Proposals issued in June 1999 are receiving widespread attention.[7] This change in regulation underscores the advantage of seeking an economically

---

[7] See www.bis.org/wnew.htm, Consultative paper on a new capital adequacy framework, 3 June 1999

reasoned approach to credit risk, such as CreditMetrics™. An institution should find it in their own self-interest to be aware of the level of capital buffer that is indicated by these additional characteristics within the credit portfolio. In practise, there are two broadly used measures of risk: standard deviation and percentile level. These two measures of risk are illustrated in Figure 13.12. This institution may chose to hold buffer at the X% percentile level or a buffer of X-times the standard deviation.

CreditMetrics™ can calculate both measures. There are however computational tradeoffs between the two measures. The percentile level is intuitively appealing because it shows a precise downside limit. However, the percentile level requires a simulation, which may take a long time to estimate distant tails. On the other hand, it is computationally straightforward to calculate the standard deviation. However, the standard deviation measure does not address the irregularities in credit loss tails.

Either method can be highly valuable. By capturing portfolio effects of diversification, recognizing mark-to-market changes in value, and treating credit risk consistently across asset classes, a portfolio credit risk model can yield

Figure 13.12   Distribution of Credit Returns via CreditManager™ Simulation

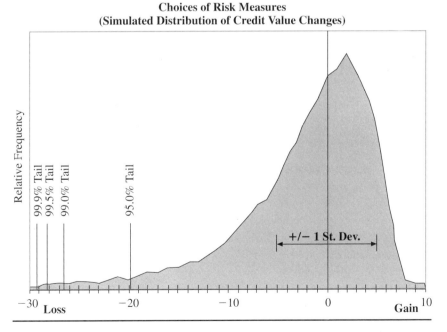

Choices of Risk Measures
(Simulated Distribution of Credit Value Changes)

rational risk-based capital allocations. CreditMetrics^{TM} can measure risk in terms of its threat to shareholder capital and the stability of an organization. A manager would likely reduce the risk of the portfolio if he found that there was, say, a ten-percent chance of a portfolio loss occurring in the next year that might cause organization-wide insolvency. Even for a portfolio with reasonable risk levels, the manager cannot add new exposures indiscriminately, since eventually the portfolio risk will surpass the "comfort level." Thus, each additional exposure uses a scarce (and costly) resource, which might be thought of as risk-taking capability, or alternatively, as economic capital.

This output from CreditMetrics^{TM} is equally appropriate for economic and regulatory capital purposes, but would differ fundamentally from the capital measures currently mandated for bank regulation by the BIS. For a portfolio of positions not considered to be trading positions, the old BIS rules require capital that is a simple summation of the capital required on each of the individual transactions of the portfolio. In turn, each transaction's capital requirement depends on a broad categorization (rather than the specific credit rating) of the obligor, on the transaction's exposure type (e.g. drawn loans versus undrawn commitments) and, for off-balance-sheet exposures, on whether the transaction's maturity is more or less than one year.

The weaknesses of this old regulatory structure — such as its one-size-fits-all risk weight for all corporate loans and its inability to distinguish between diversified and undiversified portfolios — are increasingly apparent to regulators and market participants. Particular financial industry concern as to the uneconomic incentives created by the regulatory regime and the inability of regulatory capital adequacy ratios to accurately portray actual bank risk levels. In response, the BIS's proposed framework is a nod in the direction of CreditMetrics^{TM} type models and the discipline they require.

13.4.2 Identifying Sources of Concentration

The portfolio aggregate risk is important, but for the specific management of the portfolio, it is necessary to learn more details as to where the sources of risk originate. In CreditMetrics^{TM}, and its software implementation called CreditManager^{TM}, there are over 1,000 different ways of "slicing and dicing" a credit portfolio to investigate how risk arises in different pockets of exposures. Risk concentrations can be tracked and potentially hedged, limited or sold only after they are identified. We show one example of this type of analysis in Figure 13.13.

Figure 13.13, taken from a CreditManager^{TM} report, illustrates how pockets of concentration can be identified. The cones show the marginal contribution to portfolio standard deviation across all obligors and exposure types within each country and maturity "bucket." Taller cones indicate greater contribution to portfolio risk from a given country-maturity bucket, and hence the greater the concentration risk. Thus, in this example, short-term Japanese exposures contribute the most risk as measured by marginal standard deviation.

Only when risk concentration are identified can they be acted upon. The portfolio manager can use this framework to explore concentration risks along a number of different dimensions, including for example, instrument type, rating category, maturity, industry and country. For each of these it is then possible to see any number of measures of risk, including for example, current exposure, standard deviation, mean default losses, marginal X% downside distribution tails, and regulatory capital.

Figure 13.13 Screen Shot from CreditManager™, Marginal Risk Analysis

Marginal Standard Deviation %: Country by Maturity

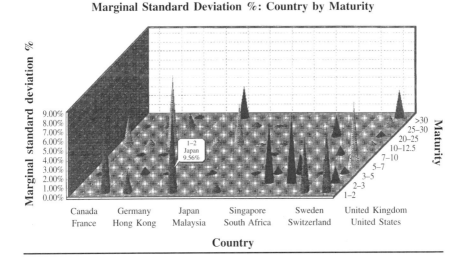

13.4.3 Credit Risk Limit Setting

The primary purpose of any risk management system is to direct and prioritize actions. Figure 13.14 illustrates marginal risk versus size of exposures within a typical credit portfolio, taken from a CreditManager™ report. This immediately allows a systematic and rational assessment of the risk contributed by exposures or obligors on a fully marginal basis. It is this information that is necessary for rational credit limit setting. Additional reporting, not illustrated here, is a comparison of marginal risk against projected returns. This is a necessary step towards maximizing the Sharpe ratio of the portfolio.

Intuitive — but arbitrary — notional limit should not therefore limit the amount of exposure taken to any obligor. Instead, looking at all other exposures and their projected returns should set limits. The risk is not the amount of a single exposure, but the volatility of all the exposures. Consequently, a portfolio model should be used to create rational risk-based credit limits that are an output from the risk management paradigm rather than an input to it.

It is within this framework of systematic quantitative analysis, that a risk manager can identify concentrations, make more accurate pricing and limit decisions and evaluate and prioritize investment decisions, credit extension and risk mitigating actions more precisely. This in turn leads to the ultimate objective of improved investment performance.

Figure 13.14   Three Alternative Credit Limit Policies

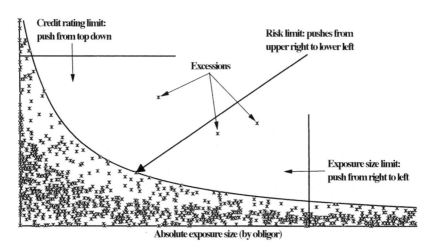

When considering risk-mitigating actions, there are various features of risk worth targeting, including perhaps obligors having the largest:
- Absolute size (lower right hand corner of Figure 13.14)
- Absolute amount of risk (upper right hand corner of Figure 13.14)
- Marginal level of risk (upper left corner of Figure 13.14)

Although each approach is valid, the last is most appealing since it sets as priority those obligors who are both relatively high percentage risk and relatively large exposure. In practise, such outliers may be the result of fallen-angels, whose now excessive exposures were appropriate when originated, or simply relationship-driven concentrations. Clearly, the CreditMetrics™ framework can readily identify such targets.

Traditionally, credit risk limits have been based on intuitive — but arbitrary — exposure amounts. This approach is unsatisfactory because resulting decisions are not risk-driven on a marginal basis. Naturally, the next step beyond using risk statistics for prioritization is to use them for limit setting. This slide illustrates how we can use marginal risk statistics to make credit limits sensitive to risk.

In Figure 13.14, we argued that it is best to first address exposures contributing marginally the highest level of risk, since these have the greatest impact on the total portfolio risk. Similarly, it is most sensible to set credit limits in terms of absolute contribution to portfolio risk. This would correspond to a limit resembling the curve defined by the boundary of non-outlying scatter points in the chart above. Such a limit would prevent the addition to the portfolio of any exposure, which increased portfolio risk by more than a given amount, rather than limiting absolute exposure size (a vertical line) or absolute riskiness (a horizontal line).

Limiting absolute risk of marginal transactions is consistent with the natural tendencies of portfolio managers; intuitively, exposures posing a greater chance of decreases in value due to credit should be smaller, while those with less chance of depreciating should be greater. Thus, setting limits based on marginal risk simply formalizes and better structures the qualitative intuition currently driving credit decisions.

It is worth mentioning that such risk limits are not meant to replace existing limits to individual names. Limits based on the notion that there is a maximum amount of desired exposure to a given counterparty, regardless of this counterparty's credit standing, are still appropriate. Such limits may be thought of as conditional, in that they reflect the amount we are willing to lose conditioned on a counterparty's defaulting, regardless of the probability that the counterparty actually defaults. The limits proposed in this section should supplement, but not replace, these conditional limits.

13.5   Software Implementation

One practical criticism of any new approach to risk management is the difficulty of actual implementation. It is all very well to read about complex mathematics, but if there is no practicable way to apply it, then it is of little use. J.P. Morgan originated CreditMetrics^{TM}, but Morgan is not a software vendor. As a response to the success of CreditMetrics^{TM} — and its predecessor, RiskMetrics — Morgan has spun both of these risk tools off as The RiskMetrics Group, see http://www.creditmetrics.com. The CreditMetrics^{TM} methodology is fully implemented in CreditManager^{TM}, which is available for sale. The author would be pleased to provide further information on CreditMetrics^{TM} and its implementation or simply give advice to those who wish to pursue their own implementations.

13.6 Summary

There is a broad industry move towards a more sophisticated — and more active — approach to credit risks and credits portfolio management. This new awareness and quantification of volatility of losses and benefits of diversification will likely lead to three major trends. First, credit portfolio management will become more active with increased liquid in the secondary markets for credit. Second, the use of liquid instruments such as credit derivatives will increase. Third, the banking regulation, as highlighted by the BIS's recent proposal will continue to evolve.

References

Asarnow, Elliot, and David Edwards, Mar-1995, "Measuring Loss on Defaulted Bank Loans: A 24-Year Study," *Journal of Commercial Lending*

Asarnow, Elliot, and James Marker, Spring 1995, "Historical Performance of the U.S. Corporate Loan Market: 1988-1993," *Journal of Commercial Lending*, Vol. 10, No. 2, pp.13–32

Carty, Lea V, and Dana Lieberman, Jan 1996, "Corporate Bond Defaults and Default Rates 1938-1995," Moody's Investors Service, Global Credit Research

Carty, Lea V, and Dana Lieberman, Nov 1996, "Defaulted Bank Loan Recoveries," Moody's Investors Service, Global Credit Research, Special Report

Duffee Gregory R, Sept 1995, "Estimating the price of default risk," Working Paper, Federal Reserve Board of Governors

Gupton, Greg M, Aug 1997, "The New Talk of the Town: CreditMetrics^{TM}, a Credit Value-at-Risk Approach," *The Journal of Lending & Credit Risk*

Management, Vol. 79, No. 12, pp. 44–54

Gupton, Greg M, Christopher Finger, and Mickey Bhatia, April 2 1997, "CreditMetrics™ — Technical Document," J.P. Morgan

Kealhofer, Stephen, 1995, "Managing Default Risk in Portfolios of Derivatives," *Derivative Credit Risk: Advances in Measurement and Management*, Renaissance Risk Publications

Merton, Robert C, 1974, "On the Pricing of Corporate Debt: The Risk Structure of Interest Rates," *Journal of Finance*, Vol. 29, No. 2, pp. 449–470

Nielsen, Soren S, and Ehud I. Ronn, Oct-1994, revised 13-Feb-96, "The Valuation of Default Risk in Corporate Bonds and Interest Rate Swaps," Working Paper, University of Texas at Austin

Standard & Poor's, 1996, *Standard & Poor's Ratings Performance 1996 Stability & Transition*

14
CREDITRISK$^+$[1]

Tom Wilde, Credit Suisse First Boston

14.1 Introduction

This chapter is about CREDITRISK$^+$, the credit portfolio modeling methodology published by Credit Suisse Financial Products in October 1997. The chapter is a technical overview of the CREDITRISK$^+$ methodology and related areas of interest. The following topics are included:
- discussion of the technical aspects of the model
- suggestions and hints for implementing the model
- statement of the main formulae in concise form
- related interesting topics

The following important topics are outside the scope of this chapter:
- relationships between credit risk modeling and economic and regulatory capital
- provisioning and accounting for credit risk
- the details of the relationship between the CREDITRISK$^+$ methodology and other models

Of these topics, the first two are beyond the scope of any purely technical exposition, while the third, the setting out of a uniform framework for understanding credit risk portfolio models, is the subject of Chapter 12.

---

[1] The CREDITRISK$^+$ document and example files illustrating the implementation of the model are available at www.csfb.com/creditrisk/

14.1.1   Credit Risk Modeling

The concepts underlying the CREDITRISK$^+$ methodology are simplifications, while data availability, quality, and interpretation are dominant aspects of the problem of practical credit risk modeling. For this reason, traditional means of credit risk measurement and management remain indispensable in the real world. The value of the portfolio modeling concepts presented below is the language they provide with which to clearly express and discuss credit risk in simple, general terms — a valuable approach in a subject where any alleged precision is doubtful. Before beginning the technical discussion, some of the most important basic concepts will be described.

14.1.2   Loss Distribution

Various meanings are attached in market risk and credit risk measurement to the terms value at risk and portfolio risk. The following meanings are all useful measures of risk:

- 99% percentile (or a higher percentile) loss due to defaults, over a one-year horizon
- 99% percentile loss due to defaults and credit rating migration, over a one-year horizon
- one of the above measures over a longer or shorter time horizon
- 99% percentile loss due to credit spread movement over a ten-day or one-year horizon
- expected excess loss, being the average loss due to defaults, given that the loss is greater than some set threshold

Each of these measures can be calculated once the loss distribution from the portfolio is known (over the specified time horizon). The loss distribution is the statistical outcome of losses (or returns given by income less losses) with the probability that each level of loss will occur. A full portfolio model is a model of credit risk that facilitates calculation of the loss distribution (as opposed to merely calculating the expected loss or some other measure that is a function of the loss distribution but contains less data). CREDITRISK$^+$ is an example of a full portfolio model for default risk, but there are many others, publicly available or privately implemented.

14.1.3   What Risks Go Into the Loss Distribution?

Loss distribution can take account of any or all of default risk, recovery rate volatility, credit spread volatility and credit rating migrations. These sources of risk can be compared (Figure 14.1).

The characteristics of different risks can be compared by organizing them according to severity and systematic behavior. The high severity, high correlation events are the most difficult to model. This is shown in Figure 14.2. Systemic event risk fits into this framework as a high severity, high correlation event. Systemic risk is briefly discussed below.

14.1.4 Credit Rating Migration and Credit Spread Risk

Credit rating migrations are low — frequency events giving rise to measured profits or losses if the portfolio is marked-to-market dependent on credit. For example, the spread on a bond may widen, and its price will then fall if the bond or its issuer is downgraded.

Because credit rating migrations are (by definition) discrete events and have

Figure 14.1   Sources of CREDITRISK$^+$

Risk	Characteristics	CREDITRISK$^+$ Treatment
Defaults	• Large loss • Low correlation	• Modeled explicitly • Often very material
Credit Spread Risk	• Small profit/loss • High correlation	• Regarded as part of market risk • Often very material
Migrations	• Small profit/loss • Low correlation	• Can be included • Normally not material
Recovery Rate Risk	• Small profit/loss • Low correlation	• Can be included • Normally not material

Figure 14.2   Classification of CREDITRISK$^+$

	Severity	
Correlation	High	Low
High	Systemic event (not captured)	Credit spread
Low	Default	Credit migration Recovery rate

low frequency, they can be regarded as being like defaults. Alternatively, because they directly impact credit spreads, they can be thought of as being like credit spread movements. Perhaps the first of these approaches is more reasonable because, like default events, credit rating migration events have low correlation. In contrast, if the value of the portfolio depends on credit spreads, then there is a more material risk due to the higher market risk levels of correlation between the spreads on all the assets. Modeling credit migration does not cover this more material risk. In fact, because credit rating migrations are events of both low value and low correlation, their impact on total portfolio risk is often immaterial.

14.1.5 Systematic Risk, Systemic Risk, and Contagion

Systematic risk is the part of total portfolio risk that is due to correlated behavior across the portfolio. The other ingredient of total risk is non-systematic risk, which should be thought of as risk due to pure randomness. Systematic risk can be measured by default correlation and is normally the critical component of total risk — this explains the emphasis on correlation that is seen in credit modeling. Non-systematic risk can be thought of as more to do with "single name concentration," i.e. having a very large single exposure to one obligor, or a very small portfolio.

Systemic risk is used interchangeably with systematic risk, but a distinction can be made between the two. "Systemic" describes risk due to the chance of a structural collapse. This may be much more severe than a mere economic downturn. For instance, some institutions (large banks and multinational companies) are extremely governmental in their importance to business that their default could reasonably only arise as a symptom of a much wider collapse.

Another phenomenon connected with systemic risk is contagion. Again, this is not well defined, but could be described loosely as the effect an economic downturn in one country has on market confidence in other countries in the same region or economic situation. Arguably, much of this correlation is found in the behavior of credit spreads and not in default rates themselves — if so, then contagion can be regarded as part of the behavior of credit spread risk.

14.1.6 Scenario Analysis

CREDITRISK$^+$ does not have the facility to deal with systemic risk in the above sense. The problem with systemic risk as described above is it deals with circumstances whose likelihood (although clearly remote) is not quantifiable. The best way to attempt to measure systemic risk is through scenario analysis, which allows a more complex description of the feared event and does not worry itself over the precise probability that the event will materialize.

14.1.7 Loss Distribution Shape and Size

It is sometimes helpful to think of a high percentile of the loss distribution as having a given value because of three factors:

- average loss level
- standard deviation = size of risk
- skewness = shape of risk

This is expressed in the following formula, which uses the 99% percentile as an example:

99% percentile loss = expected loss + multiplier × standard deviation

This formula is mere language — it does not help to calculate anything, but it is helpful as a way to discuss the shape and size of the loss distribution. For a normal distribution the multiplier to 99% is well known to be approximately 2.33. For credit loss distributions such as the ones that are calculated by CREDITRISK$^+$, the multiplier is normally greater than this; the characteristic of credit loss distributions known as "fat tails." The multiplier is theoretically only bound by Chebyshev's inequality, from which it follows that the upper bound for the multiplier to the $(1 - p)$ percentile is $1/\sqrt{p}$. In the case of the 99% percentile, this bounds the multiplier at 10, and in fact this multiplier is almost achieved in the extreme case of a single loan with default probability 1%, for which the multiplier is 9.95. For realistic portfolios, however, the multiplier is often in the range 3–4. When the multiplier is well-behaved, there is much relevant information in the standard deviation, which can be regarded as the main driver of portfolio risk. For most models, including CREDITRISK$^+$, the standard deviation is given more or less by a formula (the CREDITRISK$^+$ formula is shown in Appendix A to this chapter) while models generally have to resort to the Monte-Carlo simulation (or in the case of CREDITRISK$^+$, probability generating functions and recurrence relations) to obtain the multiplier. Another way to look at it is to say that the standard deviation encapsulates the pairwise correlation behavior in the portfolio while the multiplier looks at more subtle joint behavior of multiple obligors.

14.1.8 Pricing versus Risk Management

CREDITRISK$^+$ is a risk-management methodology, not a pricing methodology. For

| Figure 14.3   Pricing versus Risk Management ||
Pricing	Risk Management
• Transaction specific • Arbitrage free methodology • Uses current market prices • Variety of different models • Precise approach	• Portfolio based • Offsets for market risk • Diversification for credit default risk • Statistical methodology • Uses historic data • VaR model for market risk • e.g CREDITRISK$^+$ model for credit default risk • Prudent approach

credit risk, as for market risk, the objectives of pricing and risk management are different (Figure 14.3).

Pricing is connected with hedging strategies and the avoidance of risk, which gives rise to the risk neutral arguments familiar in derivatives. Portfolio credit risk models do not contain useful information about the prices of credit derivatives because they use historic rather than "risk neutral" data.

14.2   Modeling Credit Default Risk

14.2.1   Overview of CREDITRISK$^+$

CREDITRISK$^+$ is not dissimilar to other publicly available models in the way risk is modeled. The essential modeling stages for CREDITRISK$^+$ are:
• Each obligor is represented by a Poisson process, reflecting the discrete nature of the default event.
• The parameters for each obligor are the exposure, recovery rate, recovery rate volatility, and average default rate. These parameters determine entirely the behavior of the obligor considered singly.
• The realized actual default probability for each obligor has to be allowed to differ from the average to allow for systematic risk. This is modeled by having a structure of random variables on which each default probability depends. Figure 14.4 summarizes the modeling steps. The sections to follow treat each aspect of modeling in greater detail.

14.2.2   Individual Default Behavior — The Poisson Process

CREDITRISK$^+$ is an event risk model. This means that CREDITRISK$^+$ tries to capture the discrete nature of credit losses. To achieve this, mathematics that is different from the theory of diffusive processes (common in finance) is used. The Poisson process is used to describe the sudden occurrence of a gap or default event in the way that the Wiener process is used in finance to describe the volatility of markets (Figure 14.5).

The Poisson process is a mathematical model of a process in which events arrive at random and are counted. Analogously, the Wiener process or Brownian motion is the mathematical model for a process in which small movements in either direction accumulate at random over time.

Figure 14.4   Credit Risk Modeling Steps

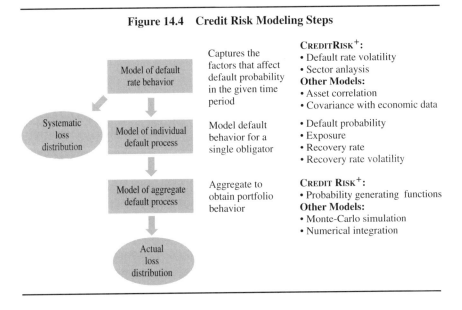

Figure 14.5   Diffusive and Event Risk

Risk Type	Diffusive	Event
Key concept	• Wiener process	• Poisson process
Applicable to	• Pricing options • Market risk measurement	• Credit risk measurement • Gap risk measurement
Related distribution	• Normal distribution	• Poisson distribution

14.2.3   Insurance Mathematics

Like much of the mathematics discussed in this chapter, the Poisson process is a key modeling technique in insurance, having been used throughout this century. An account of these techniques, including the definition and properties of the Poisson process can be found in *Panjer and Wilmot 1992* (see References at end of Chapter).

14.2.4   Probability Generating Functions

CREDITRISK^{+} uses probability generating functions to achieve an analytic solution to the full loss distribution. Suppose we have a random variable that can take only non-negative integer values. We will see later how we can ensure that the random variables we come across are like this. The probability generating function (PGF) is the formal power series defined by:

$$F(z) = \sum_{n=0}^{\infty} p(n)z^{n}$$

For sufficiently small z, the series for $F(z)$ actually converges and so defines $F(z)$ as a function of z. In CREDITRISK^{+}, the PGFs turn out to be very tractable functions.

Example: The PGF for the Poisson distribution

Let us calculate the PGF of the Poisson distribution. By definition, the probability that a Poisson variable takes the integer value n is given by:

$$p(n) = \frac{e^{-\mu}\mu^{n}}{n!}$$

We can calculate the PGF explicitly as:

$$PGF(z) = \sum_{n=0}^{\infty} \frac{e^{-\mu}\mu^{n}}{n!} z^{n} = e^{-\mu} \sum_{n=0}^{\infty} \frac{\mu^{n}z^{n}}{n!} = e^{-\mu+\mu z}$$

Note how simple the form of the PGF is. This simplicity is the key to the analytic tractability of the CREDITRISK^{+} model.

14.2.5   From Defaults to Losses

The Poisson distribution is naturally suited to modeling default events because they are counting events — you must have a whole number of them, and the Poisson distribution takes only integer values. But when we turn to losses, there is a problem that the loss amounts need not be whole numbers. We can still use the Poisson distribution, however, by the simplest possible means. We round up the exposures to nearest integer multiples of a fixed unit of loss. Why is this acceptable?

- Intuitively, the exact exposure amounts in the portfolio should not matter when determining the likelihood of large losses — knowing roughly what the exposures are should suffice.
- Imagine using a Monte-Carlo simulation to perform the same analysis as CREDITRISK$^+$. The results would be sorted into buckets, or ranges of loss amounts, for analysis, hence, rounded just as here.

These observations are borne out by showing that, in fact, when a certain unit size is chosen, the loss distribution itself is only in error by an amount comparable with the unit. See Section A4.2 in the CREDITRISK$^+$ document, Credit Suisse Financial Products October 1997 (see References at end of the chapter).

For example, suppose defaults were Poisson distributed in a portfolio, where each obligor owed an amount E, which is expressed in units. (Say, the unit is $1 million, and everyone owes between $4–5 million, which we have rounded up to $5 million. Then E would be 5.) What is the PGF of losses? It is easy to see that it is:

$$PGF(z) = \sum_{n=0}^{\infty} \frac{e^{-\mu}\mu^n}{n!} z^{nE} = e^{-\mu + \mu z^E}$$

because a loss of nE dollars in this portfolio is exactly the same as a default of n obligors. Of course, generally, each obligor does not owe the same amount, but the method still holds.

14.2.6 Incorporating Correlation in CREDITRISK$^+$

Defaults and losses in a credit risky portfolio with independent behavior can be modeled very simply by using the Poisson distribution. However, obligors are not independent and Poisson process modeling alone fails to capture systematic risk, the largest single component of risk in most cases. CREDITRISK$^+$ incorporates default correlation by stating that in the absence of an actual pairwise link between obligors (such as legal ownership or a shared business interest), the correlation between them is due to their shared dependence on the economic environment.

- If default probabilities were known, it would be appropriate to use the approach outlined in Sections 14.2.2–14.2.5 to model the portfolio using Poisson processes.
- However, default probabilities are not known because they depend on the state of the economy. Moreover, default rates across the whole portfolio depend in a similar way on the economy, giving rise to a correlation between them.

The mathematical approach is just a formulation of these steps:
- Assuming a given level of default rates, the PGF of the loss distribution is derived as in Section 14.2.5.
- This is a conditional PGF — it is a function of the default rates of each obligor, which are as yet unspecified.
- The default rates of each obligor are modeled as random variables, whose joint distribution is determined by default rate volatilities and sector analysis.
- The conditional PGF is integrated over possible levels of default rates for each obligor, weighted according to how likely they are.

The last step is encapsulated in the equation for the PGF in Appendix A to this chapter. The conditional PGF is literally integrated over possible default rates, weighted according to their joint density function:

$$G(z) = \int_{x_1 K \, x_N} G(z \,|\, X_k) f_1(x_1) \mathrm{L} \; f_N(x_N) dx_1 \, \mathrm{L} \; dx_N$$

It turns out that the unconditional PGF, though not Poisson, has a tractable mathematical form and can easily be turned back into the desired loss distribution — how this is done is described in Section 14.2.8. First, to convince the reader that default rate volatility really is intimately connected with default correlation, we derive the relation between them in a special case.

14.2.7 Correlation and the Volatility of Default Rates

The variance of the default distribution for a single obligor is $\sigma^2 = p_A(1 - p_A)$. (This follows straight from the definition of variance.) Provided the probability of default is small, $\sigma^2 = p_A$ approximately. The standard deviation of the default distribution for a portfolio is, therefore:

$$\sigma^2 = \sum_{A,B} \rho_{AB} \sigma_A \sigma_B = \sum_{A,B} \rho_{AB} (p_A p_B)^{1/2}$$

where ρ_{AB} is the default correlation between A and B.

Note that this equation contains no "modeling," — it holds true whichever model you use, and is correspondingly useless on its own as it requires all the ρ_{AB} to be known. Now, assume constant correlation $\rho_{AB} = \rho$ and constant default rate p between all obligors, and assume the total number N of obligors is large. Then the formula reduces to, very nearly:

$$\sigma^2 = N^2 p \rho \quad \text{or} \quad \rho = \frac{\sigma^2}{N^2 p}$$

Writing $\mu = Np$ for the average number of defaults and $\omega = \sigma/\mu$ for the proportional volatility of default rates (the standard deviation as a percent of the average), we get:

$$\rho = p \frac{\sigma^2}{\mu^2} = pw^2$$

The correlation formula in the CREDITRISK$^+$ methodology, ([10], equation (138)) is just a generalization of this result. Hence, default rate volatility is intimately linked to default correlation. This connection is also pointed out in the CreditMetrics^{TM} technical document [6], Appendix F.

14.2.8 Obtaining the Answer

In CREDITRISK$^+$, the integration described above is actually performed, resulting in a closed-form expression for the PGF of the loss distribution (Appendix A). However what we want is not the PGF but the distribution itself. From the definition of the PGF it is clear that:

$$p(n) = \frac{1}{n!} \frac{d^n G}{dz^n} (0)$$

But this is generally not a helpful formula, as differentiating rapidly becomes complicated and n, the loss at the percentile relative to the unit size, may be very large.

Fortunately however, for the types of PGF obtained in CREDITRISK$^+$, there is a recurrence relation between the terms of the Taylor series.[1] The simplest

---

[1] These recurrence techniques are widely used in the insurance industry. The recurrence relation in CREDITRISK$^+$ is closely related to Panjer's relation, which is well known to actuaries. Panjer's relation and many other recurrence techniques similar to the CREDITRISK$^+$ technique are discussed in *Panjer and Willmot 1992* (see References at the end of the chapter)

example is the Poisson distribution itself, for which it is easy to check directly that:

$$p(n) = \frac{e^{-\mu}\mu^n}{n!} = \frac{\mu}{n} p(n-1)$$

Combined with $p(0) = e^{-\mu}$, the relation is enough to calculate the whole distribution. Moreover, even for the Poisson distribution, it is the quickest way to calculate the distribution.

As a further example, take the loss distribution we discussed in Section 14.2.5, where each obligor has exposure E. For this loss distribution:

$$p(n) = \frac{\mu}{n} p(n-E)$$

and $p(0) = e^{-\mu}$ as before (assuming we have not included any zero exposures; no loss is the same as no default).

14.3   Systematic Risk and the Systematic Loss Distribution in CREDITRISK$^+$

14.3.1   Systematic Variance in CREDITRISK$^+$

Systematic risk was mentioned in Section 14.1.5 as the component of risk due to correlation across the portfolio. The variance of a loss distribution divides naturally into two summands, representing the systematic and non-systematic risk respectively. Thus

$$\sigma^2 = \sum_{A,B} \rho_{AB}\sigma_A\sigma_B = \sum_A \sigma_A^2 + \sum_{A \neq B} \rho_{AB}\sigma_A\sigma_B$$

This decomposition into diagonal and off-diagonal terms corresponds exactly with the split between non-systematic and systematic risk, respectively. In CREDITRISK$^+$, the formula for variance is:

$$\sigma^2 = \sum_A p_A E_A^2 + \sum_{k=1}^{N} \beta_k \left(\sum_A \theta_{Ak} p_A E_A \right)^2$$

and the systematic summand is: $\displaystyle\sum_{k=1}^{N} \beta_k \left(\sum_A \theta_{Ak} p_A E_A \right)^2$

and the non-systematic summand is: $\sum_A p_A E_A^2$ respectively.

14.3.2 The Systematic Loss Distribution in CREDITRISK$^+$

There is more to systematic risk than just a component of variance. There is a natural random variable, whose distribution we call the systematic loss distribution, whose variance is the systematic component of variance. When the systematic component of variance is a good approximation to the total variance, the systematic loss distribution is a good approximation to the actual loss distribution. This enables the systematic risk versions of all the concepts associated with the loss distribution to be defined, for example, percentiles and higher moments, which are often much simpler to deal with than the full versions to which they are good approximations.

Systematic portfolio

A systematic portfolio is one in which any individual exposure is small relative to the total exposure. The systematic equivalent of a given portfolio is obtained by replacing each obligor in the portfolio with n obligors, each having ($1/n \times$ the exposure of the original) and the same risk characteristics as the original obligor.

Systematic loss distribution

The systematic loss distribution is the distribution of losses from the systematic equivalent portfolio.

These definitions are really limits as $n \to \infty$, but to avoid abstract complication, we just think of n being large, so that put more intuitively, the systematic portfolio is one without unduly large exposures or "single name concentrations."

The systematic loss distribution is easy to determine in CREDITRISK$^+$. There is one complication: because we wish to divide the exposures indefinitely, it is inappropriate to stick to integer multiples of a given unit. Accordingly, we temporarily swap to the moment generating function (MGF) instead of the PGF. The MGF for any random variable X is given by:

$$MGF(z) = E(e^{zX}) = PGF(e^z) \text{ (here } E \text{ denotes expectation).}$$

Hence, for CREDITRISK$^+$, the MGF, conditional on the values of the default rate drivers X_k, is given by:

$$MGF(z|X_k) = G(e^z|X_k) = e^{\sum_A P_A(e^{E_A z}-1)} = e^{\sum_A \sum_{k=1}^{N} \theta_{Ak} P_A X_k (e^{E_A z}-1)}$$

(using the notation in Appendix A).

Now, suppose each exposure E_A is divided into n exposures of size E_A/n. For the new portfolio, the MGF is:

$$MGF(z|X_k) = e^{\sum_A \sum_{k=1}^{N} \theta_{Ak} P_A n X_k (e^{\frac{E_A z}{n}}-1)}$$

As $n \to \infty$,

$$n(e^{z E_A/n} - 1) \to z E_A;$$

Hence $MGF(z|X_k) \to e^{z \sum_A E_A P_A \left(\sum_{k=1}^{N} \theta_{Ak} x_k \right)}$

This MGF corresponds to a random variable that takes the value:

$$\sum_A E_A P_A \left(\sum_{k=1}^{N} \theta_{Ak} X_k \right)$$

This is nothing more than the expected loss, given the values of the driving variables X_k. We can conclude that in the limit as each exposure is subdivided into smaller exposures, the loss distribution is just the distribution of expected losses, depending on the variables driving default rates.[2]

Inspecting the derivation above, the particular dependence of the expected loss on the random variables X_k was not used neither were any properties of X_k — they could be any random variables. In Section 14.3.4, we use this to compare CREDITRISK$^+$ with a simple form of the Merton or Vasicek systematic loss distribution, and in Section 14.4.2, we once again draw on the universality of this argument to compare risk contributions with examples of these two models.

For a real portfolio without unduly large single name exposures, the convergence referred to above effectively occurs, and the loss distribution is close to the systematic loss distribution. For example, in the CREDITRISK$^+$ model

---

[2]   A rigorous version of this argument can be given

with one sector, the loss distribution for a portfolio that is not too small and does not have unduly large exposures is simply a gamma distribution. Figure 14.6 below illustrate the convergence:

- For the small portfolio (taken from the CREDITRISK$^+$ example spreadsheet with 20 exposures), the actual loss distribution is quite different from the systematic loss distribution, and has a much fatter tail.
- For the large portfolio (with about 2,000 exposures), the two distributions are nearly identical.

The systematic risk distribution will be important in a later section where we discuss risk contributions. It also provides a useful platform for comparing models.

14.3.3   The Variance of the Systematic Loss Distribution

We have already seen a natural division of the variance into systematic and non-systematic components, namely the diagonal and off-diagonal terms of the variance-covariance expression. The concepts of the systematic loss distribution and the systematic portfolio, which we have already discussed, tie in neatly with this decomposition because of the following important principle:

Variance of the systematic loss distribution = Systematic component of variance

To see this for the CREDITRISK$^+$ model, compute directly the variance of the systematic random variable:

Figure 14.6   Systematic and Full Loss Distributions

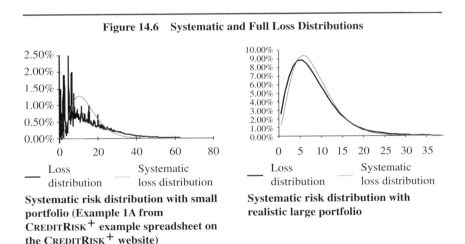

Systematic risk distribution with small portfolio (Example 1A from CREDITRISK$^+$ example spreadsheet on the CREDITRISK$^+$ website)

Systematic risk distribution with realistic large portfolio

$$\sum_A p_A E_A \left(\sum_{k=1}^{N} \theta_{Ak} X_k \right)$$

The variance is:

$$\sigma^2 = \sum_{k=1}^{N} \beta_k \left(\sum_A \theta_{Ak} p_A E_A \right)^2$$

This is just the systematic component of variance from Section 14.3.1. The result can be seen directly by considering what happens to the variance-covariance formula as exposures are subdivided to obtain the systematic portfolio. Note the importance of the fact that all of the off-diagonal risk remains in the systematic loss distribution. Only the non-systematic component of loss is not captured by this technique.

14.3.4   The Most Likely Default Rate in a
Homogeneous Portfolio

The derivation of the systematic loss distribution in Section 14.3.2 does not depend on the form of the random variables X_k. Hence, we use the same argument for other models as well as CREDITRISK$^+$. The comparison of models is not the subject of this chapter, so we shall confine ourselves to a slightly unusual comparison with the Vasicek (also known as Merton) model, with the excuse that we will thereby introduce this model, which will also be discussed in Section 14.4.2. The Vasicek or Merton systematic loss distribution is based on the Merton model of default, as follows:

• The Merton model of default relates default probabilities to asset values.
• In the single factor case we assume asset values depend on participation on a random index.
• This supplies the dependence of default rates on a random variable.
• The argument from Section 14.3.2 gives the systematic loss distribution.

The asset value of an obligor is modeled as the normally distributed random variable $X_A = (1 - \rho_A)^{1/2} Y_A + \rho_A^{1/2} Y_0$, where X_A, Y_A, and Y_0 are each normally distributed with mean 0 and variance 1. These variables describe, respectively, the asset price movement over the period for obligor A, the non-systematic component of this, and the systematic component. The obligor defaults if:

$$X_A \leqslant c_A, \text{ where } c_A = N^{-1}(p_A)$$

is chosen so that the probability of this happening is the required default probability. It is easy to see then that the default probability random variable is given by:

$$P_A = N\left(\frac{N^{-1}(p_A) - \rho_A^{1/2}Yo}{(1 - \rho_A)^{1/2}}\right)$$

Here, $N(x)$ is the cumulative normal distribution, defined in Figure 14.7 graph below.

Figure 14.7   Definition of N(x)

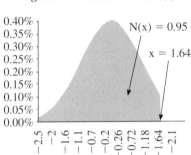

Consider a homogeneous portfolio in which each obligor has the same default rate $p = p_A$ and systematic component $\rho^{\text{asset}} = \rho_A$. There is an elegant formula for the most likely value of the systematic loss distribution under the Vasicek model:

$$P_{\text{mode}} = N\left(N^{-1}(p)\frac{(1 - \rho^{\text{asset}})^{1/2}}{1 - 2\rho^{\text{asset}}}\right)$$

In view of our discussion in Section 14.3.2, this is the most likely loss level in a large homogeneous portfolio without unduly large exposures. The equivalent formula in CREDITRISK$^+$ with one sector is:

$$P_{\text{mode}} = \max(0, p - \rho^{\text{default}})$$

where ρ^{default} is the corresponding uniform default correlation. Perhaps surprisingly, the two different models are closely aligned. The graph shows the most likely level of default in a large portfolio with uniform average default rate

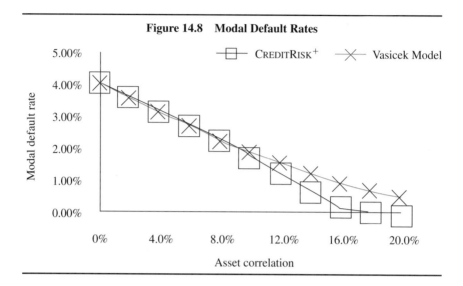

Figure 14.8   Modal Default Rates

equal to 5%, as a function of the uniform asset correlation (from which the uniform default correlation can be calculated):

The corresponding rule-of-thumb is that the most likely default rate is approximately the average default rate net of the default rate correlation in a large portfolio.

14.4   Risk Contributions

Risk contributions are the means by which portfolio level risk is allocated to individual transactions or obligors in the portfolio. The type of risk contributions used depends on the measure of risk being allocated; some measures are harder to allocate. The "natural definition" for any given measure of risk is the change in the total risk on removing that obligor or transaction. A desirable characteristic of risk contributions is that they should add up to the total portfolio risk — however, there is no reason why these definitions should be compatible. Two types of risk contribution will be discussed that can be both defined for all models and show how approximately they can be made to add up nicely.
- Contributions to the standard deviation
- Contributions to systematic risk

The additive behavior or otherwise of these contributions can be summarized as follows:
- Contributions to the standard deviation are not additive, but they can be approximated to the first order by a convenient expression that is additive.
- Contributions to systematic risk are exactly additive in a one-factor model.

14.4.1 Risk Contributions to the Standard Deviation

The definition is (minus) the change in the portfolio standard deviation when the obligor is removed. Suppose we approximate this by writing $RC_A = E_A \partial\sigma/\partial E_A$ — clearly, this is an approximation to the first order.[3] Fortunately, for most models (specifically those for which the pairwise default correlations do not depend on the exposure sizes including CREDITRISK$^+$), we have:

$$\sum_A \frac{E_A \partial\sigma}{\partial E_A} = \sigma$$

In other words, the approximated risk contributions add up to total risk. This has nothing to do with credit risk modeling, and is really due to the variance-covariance formula expressing the variance as a homogeneous quadratic form in the exposures.[4] In CREDITRISK$^+$, a simple formula exists for the variance that enables writing down these risk contributions directly. This is shown in Appendix A.

14.4.2 Systematic Risk Contributions

Suppose that X is a random variable that drives all default rates (as is the case for a one-factor model). Assume that in a portfolio of obligors, each default rate depends on X via a monotonic function, $p_A = f_A(X)$. Then, the contribution to the 99% percentile of the systematic loss distribution (defined in Section 14.3.2) can be defined. We call this the systematic risk contribution, and it is simply:

---

[3] Unfortunately, this is genuinely only an approximation to the first order. The exact contributions to the standard deviation do not add up to the standard deviation in the same nice way. This can be seen using the simplest portfolio of two independent assets.

[4] It is not hard to show more generally that the nth central moment and the nth moment about the origin of the CREDITRISK^1 distribution are homogeneous polynomials of degree n in the exposures. As a result, it is possible to define contributions adding up to the nth root of the nth central moment, where the analysis above is the special case $n = 2$.

$$RC_A = E_A f_A(X_{99\%})$$

where the term in brackets is the 99% percentile worst value of X. This follows from the fact that was demonstrated in Section 14.3.2, that the systematic loss distribution is simply the distribution of expected loss as a function of the driving variables — in this case, the single variable X. Nevertheless, it is a powerful observation for two reasons:

• The systematic risk contribution in a large portfolio without unduly large single exposures is a good approximation to the true 99% percentile contribution, as discussed in Section 14.3.2.
• The sum of the exact risk contributions is exactly the 99% percentile on the systematic loss distribution — no approximation is required.

Note that for one-factor models, the risk contributions to the standard deviation discussed in Section 14.4.1 exist as well, but as already discussed they are not exactly additive. Moreover, they can be extremely complicated.[5]

As examples of systematic risk contributions, we show how to compute these contributions for three different one-factor model:

• CREDITRISK$^+$ with one sector
• Vasicek model, which was discussed in Section 14.3.4
• CREDITRISK$^+$ with two sectors.

In each case, to avoid extra notation, assume the required confidence is 99%.

Example 1: CREDITRISK$^+$ with one sector

Here, X is gamma distributed with unit mean and standard deviation equal to the proportional volatility of default rates. Default rates are simply multiplied by this variable. Therefore:

$$RC_A = E_A p_A X_{99\%}$$

Note that in this simple case, the risk contribution for each obligor in the portfolio will be a fixed multiple of its expected loss. Assuming that a proportional volatility of default rates of approximately 100% is broadly consistent with the historical experience for speculative grade portfolios. For the

---

[5] For example, try writing down risk contributions to the standard deviation in a one-sector CREDITRISK^1 model with volatile recovery rates correlated to default rates (Section 14.5.5).

99% value of a gamma random variable with unit mean and standard deviation, $X_{99\%} = 4.6$ (approximately), so the risk contribution is about 4.6 times the expected loss in this simple model.

Example 2: Vasicek distribution

This model was introduced in Section 14.3.4. Default probability is given by:

$$P_A = N\left(\frac{N^{-1}(p_A) - \rho_A^{1/2}X}{(1-\rho_A)^{1/2}}\right)$$

Again, this is just a monotonic function of the systematic variable X. Hence:

$$RC_{A,99\%} = E_A N\left(\frac{N^{-1}(p_A) + 2.33\rho_A^{1/2}}{(1-\rho_A)^{1/2}}\right)$$

where the factor comes from $N(2.33) = 0.99$ approximately. Unlike Example 1, these risk contributions are not a constant multiple of the expected loss, but tend to be a higher multiple of expected loss for higher quality obligors (i.e. for lower default rates), provided the asset correlation is considered constant. The general consensus of evidence seems to support the idea that this is more realistic, and relates to the idea that constant asset correlation (which means higher proportional default rate volatility for more highly rated companies) is more realistic than constant proportional default rate volatility.

Example 3: CREDITRISK$^+$ with two sectors
In this version of CREDITRISK$^+$, default rates are parameterized by:

$$P_A = p_A(\theta_A + (1 - \theta_A)X)$$

where $0 \leq \theta_A \leq 1$ and X is gamma-distributed. The risk contribution of obligor A is therefore:

$$RC_A = E_A p_A(\theta_A + (1 - \theta_A)X_{99\%})$$

The parameter θ_A corresponds conceptually to the asset correlation parameter in the Vasicek model in Example 2.

14.5   Implementing CREDITRISK$^+$

This section discusses some of the issues and problems faced when implementing the CREDITRISK$^+$ methodology. These are the impact of the approximations that appear in the modeling, impact of rounding errors in the calculation and sources of data for default rates, default rate volatility, and sector analysis, and how to incorporate recovery rate volatility.

14.5.1 Approximations in CREDITRISK$^+$

Two key approximations are embedded in the CREDITRISK$^+$ methodology:
- The rounding of exposures to multiples of a unit size
- Using the Poisson approximation for individual defaults

Usually, each approximation presents no problem, but could give rise to error for "wrong" combinations of the variables. There is a way to manage the impact of these approximations, relying on the fact that although the approximations are required for the calculation of the full loss distribution, the standard deviation is given by a formula for which an exact version can be stated. Comparison of the exact and approximated standard deviations gives an estimate of how important the approximations have become for any given set of input data.

The exact standard deviation formula

The exact standard deviation in the CREDITRISK$^+$ framework but using the binomial instead of the Poisson distribution, and exact exposure figures are given by the following formula (in the notation of Appendix A):

$$\sigma^2_{\text{exact}} = \sum_A p_A E_A^2 - \sum_A (p_A^2 + \sigma_A^2) E_A^2 + \sum_{k=1}^{N} \beta_k \left(\sum_A \theta_{Ak} p_A E_A \right)^2$$

Let's compare this with the formula for the standard deviation in Appendix A:

One sees that $\sigma^2_{\text{exact}} = \sigma^2 - \sum_A (p_A^2 + \sigma_A^2) E_A^2$ where $\sigma_A = p_A \left(\sum_{k=1}^{N} \theta_{Ak}^2 \omega_k^2 \right)^{1/2}$

is the standard deviation of the default rate of obligor A as determined by the sector decomposition and the sector volatilities chosen for that obligor. For normal data, the terms p_A and σ_A are of approximately equal size for each obligor and their squares are very small (of the order of 0.1%). This explains why the methodology is accurate in this range. In general, the error term can be calculated and used to control the inaccuracy introduced.

Michael Gordy's paper (see References at the end of the chapter), in addition to discussing the quantitative relationship between CREDITRISK$^+$ and

CreditMetrics^{TM}, discusses the practical impact of these approximations. Hickman and Koyluoglu [3] also discuss these topics.

14.5.2 Computational stability using CREDITRISK$^+$

A problem that arises when using a large number of sectors and obligors in a CREDITRISK$^+$ calculation is that rounding errors in the calculation may become unstable. Most calculations on a normal personal computer use 15 significant figures of accuracy, for which, unfortunately, rounding errors can become a problem for moderately large portfolios and numbers of sectors. Surprisingly, the number of exposures does not in itself determine whether the calculation will be stable — the stability criterion presented below is more closely related to the expected loss from the portfolio.

To see how rounding errors affect the calculation, consider the equation for the logarithmic derivative from Appendix A, with N sectors, namely:

$$\frac{dG(z)/dz}{G(z)} = \sum_{k=1}^{N} \frac{\sum_A \theta_{Ak} p_A E_A z^{E_A - 1}}{\left(1 - \beta_k \sum_A \theta_{Ak} p_A (z^{E_A} - 1)\right)}$$

The performance of this summation is described in Appendix B to this chapter, but it results in a polynomial fraction whose denominator is the product:

$$\prod_{k=1}^{N} \left(1 - \beta_k \sum_A \theta_{Ak} p_A (z^{E_A} - 1)\right)$$

Clearly, when $z = 1$, the value of this polynomial is 1. But in the summation, and to perform the recurrence relation, the coefficient of each power of z in this polynomial must be known explicitly. This is where the problem arises. The coefficient of this polynomial can be very large positive and negative numbers whose net value is the relatively small number 1. If the coefficients are too large, then the restricted number of significant figures available will mean that the net result of summing them will be very inaccurate. To see why, two 17-digit numbers whose difference is, say, of the order of 100. On a personal computer with a 15-significant-figure accuracy, subtraction of one number from another would give zero because the last 2 digits of each would be ignored. In the current situation, for example, the coefficient of 1 in the polynomial is:

$$\prod_{k=1}^{N} \left(1 + \beta_k \sum_A \theta_{Ak} p_A \right)$$

This can be very large if the number N of sectors is large, the sector variances β_k are large, the default rates p_A are large or the number of obligors is large. The other coefficients in the polynomial $\displaystyle\prod_{k=1}^{N} \left(1 - \beta_k \sum_A \theta_{Ak} p_A (z^{E_A} - 1) \right)$ tend to be of similar order. From this an empirical criterion can be suggested, provided

$$\prod_{k=1}^{N} \left(1 + \beta_k \sum_A \theta_{Ak} p_A \right) < 10^8$$ holds, rounding errors do not empirically arise,

while if this condition does not hold there is a risk that the calculation will be very inaccurate. (This is not, of course, a proof, but merely an observation that seems to work in practice.)

In addition to this criterion, the presence of rounding errors can always be checked after the loss distribution has been calculated. If a rounding error due to the above effect is present, then the expected loss calculated directly from the distribution will not agree closely to the expected loss calculated directly from the input data. The standard deviation of the distribution can, of course, also be checked directly (the explicit equation is given in Appendix A), to provide an additional comfort that the portfolio distribution is accurate.

14.5.3 Sources of Data

The practical difficulty with using any credit risk portfolio model is obtaining data. In this section, we briefly suggest historical data sources. These tend to relate to US corporate data.

General remarks

The original idea of CREDITRISK$^+$ was to emphasize direct estimation of data from historical default experience. This approach has the benefit that it does not rely on translation from some other data source, and so does not require a model of default. In contrast, for example, to obtain default statistics from equity prices, one requires a model of default such as Merton's model. On the other hand, the benefit of using other data is that it allows much richer data sources to be tapped. There is not a great deal of direct default experience, and as a result, one has to be careful about how direct default data is used, and if necessary, supplement this data with inferences from other sources. As a general rule:

- For speculative grade obligors (at least in the US), there is sufficient data to obtain meaningful estimates of the parameters required for CREDITRISK$^+$ (default rate, default rate volatility, and to some extent, sector analysis).
- For investment grade obligors, there is not sufficient data, and estimates of the required parameters have to be inferred from other sources.

Rules-of-thumb

Given that other sources of data, such as equity prices, are available for many obligors, they should always be used (via an appropriate model) to compare with historical experience. In general, where both equity price data and historical default data are available, the following rules of thumb seem to apply, showing a considerable, though not perfect, agreement among the various modeling approaches:
- Asset correlation between US corporations averages 10–20%.
- Default correlation between US corporations averages 1–5%.
- Default rate volatility (as used in CREDITRISK$^+$) for speculative grade US corporations as a whole is 70–100%.

Default rate data

The US rating agencies publish annual statistics of default rate data, for example, Moody's (Carty and Lieberman February 1998) and Standard and Poor's (Brand and Bahar January 1998) (see References at the end of chapter) from which average default rates can be inferred by rating grade. Alternatively, a firm could use its own data, for example for a retail portfolio, where defaults are more common and internal data is likely to be richer.

Default rate volatility data

Default rate volatilities by rating can be inferred directly by calculating the standard deviation of the time series of historical default rates for each rating grade. Doing this for speculative grade corporations gives rise to the rule-of-thumb mentioned above, namely that default rate standard deviation for these obligors is 70–100% of the default rate. A simple but robust implementation of CREDITRISK$^+$ is to use one sector, and assume that the default rate volatility for each obligor is about 100% of the mean.

For more detailed extraction of default rate volatility, two problems arise:
- Bias — for a small sample size, the observed volatility includes the effect of both systematic and non-systematic risk, creating an overestimate.

- Estimation uncertainty — for a small sample size, there is no confidence in the estimate obtained.

For investment grade obligors, estimation uncertainty swamps the data, and it is not realistic to directly estimate default rate volatility. An alternative approach is to use asset behavior to calculate theoretical default rate volatility for higher-rated corporations. Under an assumption of constant asset correlation, theoretical proportional default rate volatility for investment grade obligors seems to be higher than default rate volatility for speculative grade obligors, although it is still not as high as directly observed default rate volatility.

14.5.4 Sector Analysis

Sector analysis is about finding independent "drivers" beneath default rate behavior, or in other words, determining appropriate values for the allocations θ_{Ak} and sector volatilities ω_k. To implement CREDITRISK$^+$ with more than one sector, it is necessary to find a way of estimating these parameters. The benefits this brings over the one-factor version of CREDITRISK$^+$ are as follows:
- More accurate reflection of a portfolio which is genuinely diversified, i.e. contains exposure to obligors in different regions whose economic fortunes are genuinely independent
- More accurate calculation of individual risk contributions

Care must be taken with sector analysis for two reasons:
- CREDITRISK$^+$ sectors have to be independent while industry sectors are certainly not independent.
- Default rate volatility estimates obtained from historical data already reflect industry diversification, which may be "double counted" by introducing sector analysis.

To examine the second point, suppose a default rate volatility is derived from Moody's time series of default rates published in *Carty and Lieberman November 1996* (see References at end of chapter). The portfolio from which this default rate data was obtained is the Moody's-rated Universe, which, of course, is already a diversified corporate portfolio. If one then introduces sectors, there is a risk of double counting. To use more than one sector, one should expect to compensate for this with higher individual sector volatilities, giving a similar overall estimate of risk.

To show the danger of using large numbers of sectors without transforming the data so that it is independent, consider dividing the portfolio for one sector into N sectors by equally dividing each obligor among sectors. The formula for correlation is the easiest way to see the impact on risk of doing this. Namely:

$$\rho_{AB} = (p_A p_B)^{1/2} \sum_{k=1}^{N} \theta_{Ak} \theta_{Bk} \omega_k^2$$

(see Appendix A). With one sector, this simplifies to

$$\rho_{AB} = (p_A p_B)^{1/2} \omega^2,$$

while with N sectors and the same default rate volatility the correlation is:

$$\rho_{AB} = (p_A p_B)^{1/2} \omega^2 \sum_{k=1}^{N} \left(\frac{1}{N}\right)^2 = \frac{(p_A p_B)^{1/2} \omega^2}{N}$$

In other words all the correlations have been reduced by a factor of N, which is equivalent to dividing the default rate volatility used by N. If the volatility estimate already reflects levels of correlation from a diversified portfolio, then this is clearly inappropriate.

To avoid this error, an approach to sector analysis has to:

• Ensure that the used data is transformed so that the sectors are independent
• Calculate default rate volatilities for the sectors that are consistent with the sectoring used

One should find that after doing this:

• There tends to be one large sector with small "residual sectors" and each industry maps largely into the large sector.
• Default rate volatilities are higher than observed ones, so that they counteract the tendency of sectors to reduce default rate volatility.
• The loss distribution looks much like the result of using one sector in total — but the risk contributions and pairwise correlations should be more accurate at the transaction level.

14.5.5 Incorporating Recovery Rate Volatility

In this section, we examine recovery rate volatility and show how to implement recovery rate volatility in CREDITRISK$^+$. We briefly consider what happens when recovery rate volatility is systematic. Throughout, recovery is defined as a proportion of notional rather than Market Value. In other words, for a marked-to-market (MTM) position such as a bond:

$$\text{Loss given default} = \text{MTM} - \text{Recovery Rate} \times \text{Notional}$$

Consistency between recovery rates and default rates

Recovery rates and default probabilities are parameters of the same event of default. Both, however, depend on how that event is defined. For example, the rating agencies publish recovery rate statistics consistent with their published default rate statistics. For example in *Gordy, A, 1998* (see References at end of chapter), a report on recovery rates by Moody's, contains a table of recovery rate data for defaulted bonds rated by Moody's, and may, therefore, be reasonably used with Moody's default rates. Standard and Poor's have published similar reports, for example *Hickman and Koyluoglu October 1999*. Another often quoted source of recovery rate data is Altman and Kishore's document *J.P. Morgan April 1997*.

Effect of recovery rate volatility on portfolio standard deviation

Consider a portfolio in which each exposure has a random recovery rate. We express this as each having exposure E_A, notional N_A, expected recovery rate R_A and suppose each recovery rate is represented by $R_A + Y_A$ where Y_A is a random variable with mean zero and standard deviation σ_{Y_A}. The loss in the event of default is then $E_A - N_A(R_A + Y_A)$, depending on Y_A.

For example, a particular exposure might have notional of 10, mark-to-market exposure of 9.195, expected recovery rate of 40%, and recovery rate standard deviation of 25%. Then $N_A = 10$, $E_A = 9.195$, $R_A = 0.4$ and $\sigma_{Y_A} = 0.25$. We make the crucial assumption that recovery rates are independently distributed or, in other words, there is no systematic component that could cause all recovery rates to be high or low. It can be shown that, under these circumstances, the variance of the loss distribution under CREDITRISK^{+} with one sector is given by:

$$\sigma^2 = \sum_A p_A (E_A - N_A R_A)^2 + \omega^2 \left(\sum_A p_A (E_A - N_A R_A) \right)^2$$
$$+ \sum_A N_A^2 \sigma_{Y_A}^2 (p_A + (\omega^2 + 1)p_A^2)$$

The CREDITRISK^{+} variance formula in this case (with fixed recovery rates) is:

$$\sigma^2 = \sum_A p_A (E_A - N_A R_A)^2 + \omega^2 \left(\sum_A p_A (E_A - N_A R_A) \right)^2 .$$

This formula is derived from the variance formula in Appendix A, by substituting in the average exposure after recovery. Comparing the formula above with volatile recovery rates, one sees that the term:

$$\sum_A N_A^2 \sigma_{Y_A}^2 (p_A + (\omega^2 + 1) p_A^2)$$

is the contribution to portfolio variance due to recovery rate volatility. This is of the same order as the non-systematic risk term, so that in a large portfolio recovery rate volatility can be expected to make only a small contribution to overall risk.

Incorporating recovery rate volatility into CREDITRISK$^+$

It was shown above that, based on variance considerations, the contribution to overall portfolio risk made by recovery rate volatility is not significant. Recovery rate volatility can nevertheless be implemented in CREDITRISK$^+$ in a simple way, if desired, by modifying the input data as follows:

The idea is to approximate the recovery rate distribution by a discrete set of alternative values, assuming that the exact shape of the distribution does not matter that much. We can assume that the random element of recovery takes two values, each with probability of 1/2, corresponding to low or high recovery. Using the above notation, let

$$E_A - N_A (R_A \pm \sigma_{Y_A})$$

be the possible losses in the event of default, each equally likely given default.[6] Hence, from each exposure in the input portfolio, two "exposures" are prepared for CREDITRISK$^+$ as follows:

- Exposure 1 = MTM Value − Notional × (Recovery Rate + Volatility)
- Exposure 2 = MTM Value − Notional × (Recovery Rate − Volatility)

---

[6] Other combinations or more states are, of course, possible, but we use two equally likely states here to keep the example simple. The exact choice of the number of possible recovery rates and the probabilities of each has very little effect on the loss distribution.

Using the exposure data above this gives:

- Exposure 1 for input to CREDITRISK$^+$ = 9.195–10 × (40% + 25%)
  $$= 2.695$$
- Exposure 2 for input to CREDITRISK$^+$ = 9.195–10 × (40% − 25%)
  $$= 7.695$$

The default probabilities corresponding to each exposure are set to half the obligor default probability, reflecting the fact that each event is half as likely as the default as a whole. The sector analysis for each of the "sub-events" should be the same as that of the original obligor. The same expected loss is obtained in both cases.[7]

Systematic recovery rate volatility

The above analyses assume that recovery rates are random but vary independently between obligors. We showed how to implement such randomness in CREDITRISK$^+$, but suggested that the effect is not likely to be material precisely because the additional risk is non-systematic.

More realistically, recovery rate volatility might have two components: non-systematic misspecification risk reflecting the fact that actual recoveries depend on the diverse terms of individual transactions, and so differ from each other, and more seriously, a systematic component connected with the health of the economy. The systematic component might also be correlated to default rates. Three broad cases can be distinguished:

- Recovery rate volatility is totally non-systematic
- Recovery rate volatility is systematic but not correlated with default rates
- Recovery rate volatility is systematic and correlated with default rates

---

[7] The standard deviation retrieved from CREDITRISK$^+$ using this method and one sector agrees to the exact formula above except for the last term. The discrepancy is due to the fact that in the standard deviation formula, the different recovery outcomes are (correctly) assumed to be mutually exclusive, while in the implementation they are not. The difference is not material

[8] The third possibility could be modeled in a one-factor context as described in Section 14.4.2 , by setting the exposure in the systematic risk contribution to the loss in the event of default with 99% worst-case recovery. This would clearly have a significant impact on risk

The method of incorporating recovery rate volatility in CREDITRISK$^+$ described above only models the first possibility. The other two give rise to a bigger impact on risk but do not seem to have been studied in a modeling context.[8]

Appendix A: CREDITRISK$^+$ Technical Summary

This appendix sets out the technical essentials of the CREDITRISK$^+$ methodology and provides an explicit example calculation.

A.1 Notation

The notation differs from the notation in the CREDITRISK$^+$ document *Credit Suisse Financial Products October 1997* (see References at the end of chapter). The notation here is more condensed and perhaps slightly simpler. The main differences between the notation here and in the CREDITRISK$^+$ document are:

- In this chapter, sector standard deviations are quoted as proportional via gamma distributions with unit mean. In the CREDITRISK$^+$ document, standard deviations were quoted as absolute numbers.
- here, equations are summed at the obligor level and it is assumed that all exposures are rounded off (expressed as multiples of the unit). In the CREDITRISK$^+$ document, equations are expressed with coefficients aggregated over common exposure levels.

Care must, therefore, be taken in comparing the equations here with those in the CREDITRISK$^+$ document.

A.2 Summary of CREDITRISK+ Formulae (N sectors)

Element of methodology	Expression
Probability generating function (PGF) for a single obligor conditional on the default rate	$G_A(z\|X_A) = e^{-P_A + P_A z^{E_A}}$
Average default rate (= mean of P_A)	P_A
Default probability P_A, as a function of the N default rate drivers.	$P_A = p_A \sum_{k=1}^{N} \theta_{Ak} X_k$
Gamma distributed default rate driver	$X_k \equiv \Gamma(\alpha_k, \beta_k)$ mean $\alpha_k \beta_k = 1$, variance $\beta_k = \varpi_k^2$
Density function of default rate driver	$f_k(x) = \dfrac{e^{-x/\beta_k} x^{\alpha_k - 1}}{\beta_k^{\alpha_k} \Gamma(\alpha_k)}$
Conditional PGF for the loss distribution	$G(z\|X_k) = \displaystyle\prod_A G_A(z\|X_k) = e^{\sum_A P_A(z^{E_A}-1)} = e^{\sum_A \sum_{k=1}^{N} \theta_{Ak} p_A X_k (z^{E_A}-1)}$
Unconditional PGF – expression as integral	$G(z) = \displaystyle\int_{x_1 \cdots x_N} G(z\|X_k) f_1(x_1) \cdots f_N(x_N) dx_1 \cdots dx_N$

Statistical information (without calculating the full loss distribution)

Element of methodology	Expression
Mean of the loss distribution	$\mu = \dfrac{dG}{dz}(1) = \displaystyle\sum_{k=1}^{N}\sum_{A}\theta_{Ak}p_A E_A = \sum_{A} p_A E_A \sum_{k=1}^{N}\theta_{Ak} = \sum_{A} p_A E_A$
Standard deviation of the loss distribution	$\sigma^2 = \dfrac{d^2G}{dz^2}(1) + \mu - \mu^2 = \dfrac{d}{dz}\left(\dfrac{dG/dz}{G}\right)(1) + \mu$ Hence: $\sigma^2 = \displaystyle\sum_{A} p_A E_A^2 + \sum_{k=1}^{N}\beta_k\left(\sum_{A}\theta_{Ak}p_A E_A\right)^2$
Risk contribution to the standard deviation	$RC_A = \dfrac{E_A\partial\sigma}{\partial E_A} = \dfrac{E_A p_A}{\sigma}\left(E_A + \displaystyle\sum_{k=1}^{N}\beta_k\theta_{Ak}\left(\sum_{B}\theta_{Bk}p_B E_B\right)\right)$
Pairwise default correlation	$\rho_{AB} = (p_A p_B)^{1/2}\displaystyle\sum_{k=1}^{N}\theta_{Ak}\theta_{Bk}\omega_k^2 = (p_A p_B)^{1/2}\sum_{k=1}^{N}\theta_{Ak}\theta_{Bk}\beta_k$

Calculation of the full loss distribution

Element of methodology	Expression
Probability of no losses	$P(\text{no losses}) = G(0) = \prod_{k=1}^{N} \left(1 + \beta_k \sum_A \theta_{Ak} p_A \right)^{-a_k}$
Recurrence relation for full distribution	$A_{n+1} = \dfrac{1}{b_0(n+1)} \left(\displaystyle\sum_{i=0}^{\min(r,\,n)} a_i A_{n-i} - \displaystyle\sum_{j=0}^{\min(s-1,\,n-1)} b_{j+1}(n-j) A_{n-j} \right)$
	where $\dfrac{\dfrac{d}{dz} G(z)}{G(z)} = \dfrac{a_0 + a_1 z + \text{L} + a_r z^r}{b_0 + b_1 z + \text{L} + b_s z^s}$

A.3 Example Calculation

This section presents a simple example calculation, illustrating the calculation of the PGF and the use of the recurrence relation to extract the loss distribution. The example portfolio consists of three obligors with two sectors. The portfolio is summarized in the table below.

			Sector 1	Sector 2
	ω_k		100%	200%
	$\beta_k = \omega_k^2$		1.00	4.00
	$\alpha_k = 1/\beta_k$		1.00	0.25
Obligor	E_A	p_A	θ_{A1}	θ_{A2}
A	5	0.4%	30%	70%
B	2	1.2%	20%	80%
C	1	2.0%	60%	40%

Assume for simplicity that the exposures are net of recovery and have already been rounded off to multiples of the unit (to be realistic, think of the unit size as, say, US$1 million).

Expected Loss

The expected loss, which will be a useful check for later, can be calculated immediately:

$$\text{Expected Loss} = 5 \times 0.4\% + 2 \times 1.2\% + 1 \times 2.0\% = 0.064$$

Using the notation of this Appendix, the PGF can be written down immediately. Hence:

$$G(z) = G_1(z) \times G_2(z)$$

where

$$G_1(z) = (1 - 1 \times (0.0012(z^5 - 1) + 0.0024(z^2 - 1) + 0.012(z - 1)))^{-1}$$

and

$$G_2(z) = (1 - 4 \times (0.028(z^5 - 1) + 0.0096(z^2 - 1) + 0.008(z - 1)))^{-0.25}$$

The logarithmic derivative is then:

$$\frac{dG/dz}{G} = \frac{0.006z^4 + 0.0048z + 0.012}{1 - 0.0012(z^5 - 1) - 0.0024(z^2 - 1) - 0.0012(z - 1)}$$

$$+ \frac{0.014z^4 + 0.0192z + 0.008}{1 - 4 \times (0.0028(z^5 - 1) + 0.0096(z^2 - 1) + 0.008(z - 1))}$$

The expected loss is a useful check:

$$\frac{dG/dz}{G}(1) = \frac{0.006 + 0.0048 + 0.012}{1} + \frac{0.014 + 0.0192 + 0.008}{1} = 0.064$$

Before the recurrence relationship can be used to generate the full loss distribution, the sum of two fractions representing the logarithmic derivative must be added up. This is the execution of equation (80), in *Credit Suisse Financial Products October 1997* (see References at the end of the chapter), namely we need to find polynomials $A(z)$ and $B(z)$ such that:

$$\frac{A(z)}{B(z)} = \frac{0.006z^4 + 0.0048z + 0.012}{1 - 0.0012(z^5 - 1) - 0.0024(z^2 - 1) - 0.0012(z - 1)}$$

$$+ \frac{0.014z^4 + 0.0192z + 0.008}{1 - 4 \times (0.0028(z^5 - 1) + 0.0096(z^2 - 1) + 0.008(z - 1))}$$

How this is in code is explained in Appendix B, but the summation can be performed manually, giving:

$$\frac{A(z)}{B(z)} = \frac{\begin{array}{c}(-0.0001z^9 - 0.0003z^6 - 0.0005z^5 - 0.0207z^4 - 0.0002z^3 \\ - 0.0009z^2 + 0.0242z + 0.0211)\end{array}}{\begin{array}{c}(0.00001z^{10} + 0.00007z^7 + 0.00017z^6 - 0.0127z^5 + 0.00009z^4 \\ + 0.0005z^3 - 0.0412z^2 - 0.0455z + 1.0985)\end{array}}$$

The coefficients of the polynomials A and B determine the recurrence relation, which in turn is used to derive the full loss distribution together with the probability of no losses. To determine the probability of no losses, we evaluate the PGF at zero:

$$P(\text{no losses}) = G(0) = (1 + 0.0012 + 0.0024 + 0.012)^{-1}$$
$$\times (1 + 4 \times (0.0028 + 0.0096 + 0.008))^{-0.25}$$

Hence:

$$P(\text{no losses}) = G(0) = 1.0156^{-1} \times 1.0816^{-0.25} = 0.965519$$

The final problem is to write out the loss distribution in full using the recurrence relation. Following the formula for the recurrence relation

$$A_{n+1} = \frac{1}{b_0(n+1)} \left(\sum_{i=0}^{\min(r,n)} a_i A_{n-i} - \sum_{j=0}^{\min(s-1,n-1)} b_{j+1}(n-j)A_{n-j} \right)$$

gives:

$$\begin{aligned}
A_{n+1} = \; & 1/(1.0985(n+1))(-0.0001A_{n-9} - 0.0003A_{n-6} - 0.0005A_{n-5} \\
& + 0.0207A_{n-4} - 0.0002A_{n-3} - 0.0009A_{n-2} + 0.0242A_{n-1} + 0.0211A_n \\
& - 0.00001(n-9)A_{n-9} - 0.00007(n-6)A_{n-6} - 0.00017(n-5)A_{n-5} \\
& + 0.0127z^5 - 0.00009(n-3)A_{n-3} - 0.0005(n-2)A_{n-2} \\
& - 0.0412(n-1)A_{n-1} + 0.0455nA_n)
\end{aligned}$$

The first few values are as follows:

Term	Recurrence relation	Value
A_0	determined above	0.965519
A_1	$1/(1.0985)(0.0211A_0)$	0.018550
A_2	$1/(1.0985 \times 2)(0.0242A_0 + 0.0211A_1 - 0.0455A_1)$	0.011203
A_3	$1/(1.0985 \times 3)(-0.0009 + 0.0242A_1 + 0.0211A_2 + 0.0412A_1 + 0.0455 \times 2A_2)$	0.000496

Appendix B — Executing Equation 80 in Code

This section is about performing practically the summation that is implied by equation (80) in the CREDITRISK$^+$ document *Credit Suisse Financial Products October 1997* (see Reference at the end of chapter). In Appendix A, this equation is rephrased in slightly simpler notation than in the original document. In the notation of this chapter, the formula for the logarithm derivative of PGF is:

$$\frac{dG(z)/dz}{G(z)} = \sum_{k=1}^{N} \frac{\sum_{A} \theta_{Ak} p_A E_A z^{E_A - 1}}{\left(1 - \beta_k \sum_{A} \theta_{Ak} p_A E_A (z^{E_A} - 1)\right)}$$

The problem is simply to sum up the N rational functions on the right hand side of this equation, where N is the number of sectors, to arrive at:

$$\frac{dG(z)/dz}{G(z)} = \sum_{k=1}^{N} \frac{P_k(z)}{Q_k(z)} = \frac{A(z)}{B(z)}$$

from which the recurrence relation can be executed. The simple approach to performing this in code as described below is recursive. The summands are added one by one, keeping a record of the partial sums as the addition proceeds.

Recursive Addition

To obtain the sum, we work with a running total. We start with $R = P_1$ and $T = Q_1$ and suppose recursively that the first $r - 1$ summands have been added together, so that now:

$$\frac{R(z)}{T(z)} = \sum_{k=1}^{r-1} \frac{P_k(z)}{Q_k(z)}$$

To add on the next summand, note that:

$$\frac{R(z)}{T(z)} + \frac{P(z)}{Q(z)} = \frac{R(z)Q(z) + P(z)T(z)}{Q(z)T(z)}$$

Therefore, we need to perform, via a subroutine, the following replacements:

$$R \rightarrow RQ_r + TP_r$$
$$T \rightarrow TQ_r$$

The order in which these replacements are performed matters — they must be performed in the given order because T, which appears in the first one, is altered by the second transformation.

Coding

There are two obvious ways to hold polynomial information in code:

- As a one-dimensional array: $R(z) = \displaystyle\sum_{n=1}^{100} R(n)z^n$

- As a two-dimensional array: $R(z) = \displaystyle\sum_{i=1}^{100} R(i, 2)z^{R(i,1)}$

The second approach is more efficient, especially for the sort of polynomials one encounters in this context, which typically have high degree (i.e. there are large powers of z with non-zero coefficient) but are "sparse" (i.e. have lots of zero terms). If the first method of storing polynomials is adopted, the code is clogged with many operations with zero coefficients.

Assuming the second method is adopted, in the earlier example expression, 100 is the maximum number of non-zero terms in the polynomial (there is no bound on the exponent of the largest term). In practise, an upper bound for the maximum number of non-zero terms in the total can be obtained, provided the maximum degree of each of the summands is known. This simply depends on the size of the exposures relative to the chosen unit size.

We show in detail how to perform the replacement $R \rightarrow RQ_r + TP_r$. The replacement $T \rightarrow TQ_r$ is then similar. To perform the replacement $R \rightarrow RQ_r + TP_r$ we have to introduce a temporary array to store the answer in the one- dimensional array format. Let this array be $X(1000)$.

There are three steps:
- Clear X to have zero entries
- Perform two operations, namely:

$$X \rightarrow X + RQ_r$$

then:

$$X \rightarrow X + TP_r$$

after which $X(\ )$ contains the polynomial in the one-dimensional format.
- Repopulate the two-dimensional array $R(\ )$ from $X(\ )$

The first addition to $X(\ )$ is performed by:

$$X(R(t, 1) + Q_r(u, 1)) \rightarrow X(R(t, 1) + Q_r(u, 1)) + R(t, 2)Q_r(u, 2) \text{ for } 1 \leq t, u \leq 100$$

and the second by the similar operation:

$$X(T(t, 1) + P_r(u, 1)) \rightarrow X(T(t, 1) + P_r(u, 1)) + T(t, 2)P_r(u, 2) \text{ for } 1 \leq t, u \leq 100$$

The array $X(\ )$ must be sufficiently large to avoid overflow — a sufficient size will be $\max_{t,u}(T(t, 1) + Q(u, 1))$, which again can be determined in terms of the base exposure data and the unit size. Above, a size of 1 000 has been chosen for example.

In the third step, the following condensation is performed. The array T is populated from X via the operation:

$$(c, 1) = i \quad \text{and} \quad (c, 2) = X(i)$$

for each i with $X(i) <> 0$. Here c is a counter which is advanced by 1 every time a non-zero $X(i)$ with $X(i) <> 0$ is found.

Once these steps have been achieved, the replacement of R has been performed. The replacement $T \rightarrow TQ_r$ is performed in the same way, except that there is only one term on the right-hand side.

References

Altman and Kishore January 1997, *Defaults and Returns on High Yield Bonds: Analysis through 1996*, Stern School of Business, New York University

Brand and Bahar January 1998, *Ratings Performance 1997 Stability and Transition*, Standard and Poor's

Brand and Bahar August 1998, *Recoveries on Defaulted Bonds Tied to Seniority Rankings*, Standard and Poor's Special Report

Carty and Lieberman November 1996, *Defaulted Bank Loan Recoveries*, Moody's Investors Service

Carty and Lieberman February 1998, *Historical Default Rates of Corporate Bond Issuers 1920–1997*, Moody's Investors Service Special Comment

Credit Suisse Financial Products October 1997, CREDITRISK^{+TM}

Gordy, A 1998, *Comparative Anatomy of Credit Risk Models*, Finance and Economics Discussion Series 1998 — 47, Federal Reserve Board, Washington

Hickman and Koyluoglu October 1998 , *Reconciliable Differences*, RISK

J.P. Morgan April 1997, CreditMetrics™

Panjer and Willmot 1992, *Insurance Risk Models*, American Society of Actuaries

PART FIVE
MARKETS

15

The Market for Credit Derivatives

Robert Reoch, Bank of America

15.1 Introduction

The credit derivative market completed its sixth year of activity in 1999. It has evolved from a product used primarily for *ad-hoc* hedging of the credit risk associated with interest rate and currency swap activity, to a range of products addressing the simple and complex credit needs of a broad universe of users. The size of the market has exceeded the best guesses of market practitioners; the extent of usage continues to surprise market commentators as a wider range of users find applications increasingly removed from the simple ones that were prevalent in 1994. The credit crisis of 1997–98 awakened and heightened people's awareness of credit risk and of the credit derivative tools available for managing it. Complex models are now being used or developed to help institutions to identify and quantify the credit risk associated with their businesses. Such analysis has rationalized the pricing of credit risk and closed the gap between the cost of hedging and the benefit of extending credit to favored clients. The investment community has embraced credit derivatives as a new and innovative asset class. Popular structures have evolved from the plain vanilla products that emulate corporate bonds and asset swaps, to complex synthetic variations of Collateralized Debt Obligations (CDO).

This chapter discusses the market for credit derivatives with particular focus on the make up of the market itself, on investor and risk management applications, and on the business issues that continue to play a major part in the market's evolution.

15.2   The Market

There now exists most of the key components that one would expect to see when describing a "market" in the financial services sector:

- The basic products and their applications are well-documented and understood
- There is a broad range of users on a global basis
- Legal documentation for usage of the main product is standardized
- There is an initiative to extend this to other products
- Key regulators have issued guidelines for credit derivative usage
- There is evidence from broker screens and user commentary that there is trading of plain vanilla structures

All of this ensures that a newcomer is presented with standardized products and usage in a market, with sufficient depth and transparency, to ensure independent verification of the structures and pricing that are being offered.

There has been much discussion about the size of the market based on a combination of official releases from the Office of the Comptroller of the Currency (OCC) annual surveys conducted by the British Bankers Association, and *ad-hoc* surveys done by financial journals and inter-dealer brokers. At the end of the second quarter of 1999, the OCC reported a contract notional of US$258 billion for credit derivative transactions declared by the banks that report to the OCC. Since many active credit derivative participants in the US do not report to the OCC and there are credit derivatives markets in Europe and Asia that, according to the surveys, could in aggregate exceed the US market, it is possible that the market has outstanding transactions with notionals exceeding US$500 billion.

The larger banks and securities houses dominate the market, and there are a number of active "end users" who, on the basis of notional of outstanding contracts, would appear to be active market participants. The former are best distinguished from the the active end users by the presence of a credit derivatives desk with professionals solely dedicated credit derivatives and its related structured credit activities. But even this distinction is becoming a bit blurred as institutions that have historically invested in credit instruments, realize how easy it is to bolt on a credit derivative capability. These institutions include smaller banks, reinsurance companies, mutual funds, and hedge funds.

The market's end-user group includes the so-called market participants or dealers who, from time to time, execute for their own balance sheet. It also includes a rapidly growing number of mutual funds and a sprinkling of corporations. The funds are active buyers of credit linked notes and some can write default swaps and total return swaps; the corporations have similar investment capabilities, but also use credit derivatives to isolate commercial risks such as the credit risk in their receivables portfolio or in emerging country projects.

Whether a transaction is initiated through the broker market or directly with a client, the process that follows is now well-established. The initial contact typically involves an exchange of basic exposure preferences and indicative pricing. Once participants have established that they are in the same ball park, more detailed negotiations begin. How quickly the transaction proceeds is very much a function of the complexity of the transaction, the sophistication of the counterparties and the extent to which they have transacted before. Complex transactions, by definition, normally require tailored structuring and documentation. Dealing with such a transaction or indeed with a plain vanilla transaction tends to proceed faster if the counterparty is a seasoned credit derivative user or, best of all, if one has had previous dealings with the counterparty . The release of standard documentation has contributed to a much faster execution process. In addition, the options contained within the legal confirmation limit and focus the universe of structuring variations, and this in turn keeps the negotiating dialogue short.

A significant proportion of transactions are initiated in the broker market, providing participants with increased confidence in the secondary market and providing the market with the beginnings of reliable pricing information. In mid-1999, the first discussions concerning the use of the Internet for initiating such transactions were conducted, and as of October 1999, one such transaction was completed. Where this new medium will lead, remains to be seen. But it does offer some distinct benefits as, among other things, more initial information can be exchanged on a website than over a broker's screen.

One characteristic that illustrates the growing maturity within the credit derivative market relates to the emergence of a secondary market for credit derivative structures. Due to the increasing number of professional participants and to the elements of standardization, it is now much easier to buy a structure from one party and sell it to another.

15.3 Credit Derivative Opportunities and Applications

The many uses of credit derivatives can best be divided by looking at the opportunities and applications for risk managers (risk reduction) and those for asset managers (investment opportunities). Clearly, for every seller of risk (risk manager or buyer of protection, i.e. buyer), there is a counterparty (risk taker or seller of protection, i.e. seller) on the other side. But often, the rationale and the structure used on either side of the transaction differ considerably, and this merits further explanation.

15.3.1   Opportunities

Risk Reduction

A buyer may be motivated by a range of benefits, some of which have little to do with mitigating credit risk. The one common feature in all so-called risk management transactions is that credit risk is synthetically transferred from one party to another. Herein lies the somewhat revolutionary benefit of credit derivatives — the ability to move credit risk without touching the underlying asset. Given the lack of liquidity in the credit markets as a whole and the close linkage between a lender and a borrower, financial institutions have historically assumed that once an asset is on the balance sheet, the credit risk is there to stay (as opposed to the currency and interest-rate risk that of course can be hedged). Risk reduction activity tends to evolve from the simple to the more complex; the following paragraphs summarize four such activities showing this evolutionary process.

- **Transaction Specific:** The use of credit derivatives for risk reduction, i.e. transaction specific, represents a broad section of product applications. The main driver behind such activity is the simplicity: a profitable trade is anticipated, one or more risk components need to be hedged, if the cost of all the hedges leaves satisfactory profitability, then the trade can proceed. Since complex transactions generally need one-off approvals, the incremental work to include a credit derivative transaction does not seem onerous. Further, since in many cases the economics of the transaction is the only obstacle that needs to be overcome, the credit derivative discussion does not get mired by topics such as regulatory capital.

- **Line Management:** A natural extension of transaction specific hedging is client specific hedging — the use of credit derivatives to reduce the overall credit line allocated to a particular client. In the early days of credit derivative marketing, this was a compelling argument for usage. But so often, it failed when the cost of such hedging was factored in — it was always cheaper to just increase the line. Since the credit crisis of 1998, this approach has changed and credit committees seem less willing to keep on increasing the line. As a result, there has been an increased use of credit derivatives for line management.

In many situations, the cost of hedging line usage is greater than the income earned from using the line. This is particularly true where the line is used for loans — default swap pricing only falls below the spread on a loan where the loan is held at a higher spread than market due to a substantial increase in the credit quality of the issuer or of the credit markets as a whole from the time when the loan was taken on the books. Other situations where credit derivative usage is compelling for line management is where the line has been exceeded and senior management are screaming for the situation to be rectified.

The most compelling use of credit derivatives for line management occurs when a client relationship is appraised not only on the basis of revenue earned, but also on the basis of the risk assumed for earning such revenues. The so-called relationship Risk Adjusted Return on Capital (RAROC) is used by a number of banks and, if tied into the compensation process, incents client managers to optimize their use of economic capital. Massive lending activity may look good from a revenue perspective, but it tends to use up much capital, resulting in a low relationship RAROC. If this lending is complemented by, for example, a mandate for cash management and maybe, results in some fee income from mergers and acquisitions activity, then the client manager will ultimately see revenue increase for no incremental use of capital. This is clearly good for the relationship RAROC. Where the client manager believes that the next loss-leading loan is going to result in additional zero-risk fee income, then he/she may be inclined to buy sufficient credit line today (using credit derivatives) to free up the line for a new facility tomorrow.

- **Balance Sheet Management:** One of the so called risk management application that has little bearing on actual risk mitigation, is the use of credit derivatives for balance sheet management. This involves the selling of balance sheet assets to a third party and the simultaneous selling of a credit derivative (normally a Total Return Swap) to retain the return of the sold assets. Since the assets are truly sold and there is no contractual obligation to repurchase them, the assets will no longer be on balance sheet, but the full economic benefits (and risks) will be retained.

This activity has had a somewhat volatile history due to the ebb and flow of banking crises in various corners of the globe. In 1997 and 1998, the entire Japanese banking sector faced significantly higher borrowing costs due to liquidity problems faced by a number of troubled banks. For the stronger banks affected by the so-called Japan premium, using credit derivatives to rent the balance sheet of non-Japanese banks was efficient from a cost perspective (the collateralized nature of the structure reduced the spread) and resulted in a contracted balance sheet and improved ratios.

Regular-flow business in this sector continues as banks seek to optimize their funding and use of balance sheet. Investors find this business attractive as they are able to take collateralized bank exposure at much better rates than they could achieve using uncollateralized bank deposits.

- **Regulatory Capital Banks:** Regulating capital banks and insurance companies are required by their respective regulators to set aside capital to support the risks associated with their businesses; this is generally referred to as regulatory capital. In addition to this regulatory requirement, many institutions choose to calculate their own capital requirements by using far more sophisticated models than those currently employed by regulators; this is generally referred to as economic capital.

Traditionally, it has been hard for financial institutions to manage their use of capital; the extension of a new loan to a corporate client will attract capital equal to 8% of the notional of the loan. Until this loan matures, it remains on balance sheet and continues to attract regulatory capital. A sale of the loan would of course release the capital, but such action would likely harm the client relationship. A number of regulators have accepted that credit derivatives can be used to effectively transfer the risk of a loan to the credit derivative counterparty and, if the counterparty is an OECD bank, have granted a reduction in capital from 8% to 1.6%, recognizing that such a counterparty would normally only attract a 20% risk weighting rather than the 100% used for corporations.

The use of credit derivatives for managing regulatory capital is divided between regular activity and one-off large transactions. Over the last two years, regulators have gotten wiser to large one-off step-up structures that secure the benefits of capital management for the key few days over quarter end, without the cost of hedging the risk to maturity. Although this activity has stopped, there has been no let up in regulatory capital management transactions. One can only speculate how busy this sector of the market will be if, and when, the regulators relax the rules relating to offsets.

Investment Opportunities

The seller in a credit derivative transaction is assuming credit risk by way of a derivative contract or a structured note. Aside from the structure itself, the seller is not faced with anything too revolutionary when investing in a credit derivative since the underlying credit risk is often identical to the risk found in corporate bonds. Contrast a risk manager who, as discussed earlier, is faced with many new concepts when first embarking on credit risk management with credit derivatives. That is not to say that credit derivatives have not changed the face of asset management, indeed the innovations are such that many fund managers see credit derivatives as an entire new assets class. But the investment community has met many new asset classes over the years, and the culture and infrastructure is well developed to deal with the inevitable obstacles. The following sections focus on the areas where credit derivatives have enhanced credit investment opportunities.

- **Access to New Assets:** For many buyers of credit derivative assets, the appeal lies merely in the underlying asset; that is to say, it is the supply of exposure to the reference credit that is the novelty brought by the credit derivative market. Not the excitement one would have hoped for in a new derivative market, but one of the fundamental changes that credit derivatives have brought to the credit markets is the ability to move assets across previously insurmountable obstacles. Many issuers conduct the bulk of their borrowing in a selected number of markets: some corporations may only borrow in the loan market and only from a few favored banks. For banks that are not in that group and for fund managers who cannot buy loans (even if they were available), access to such a corporation's debt may be limited to the occasional bond issuance. All this could change if one of the "favored banks" decided that, for whatever reasons, it wanted to reduce its corporate exposure. It may choose to target one of the other banks or indeed a mutual fund (by structuring the loan hedge as a synthetic bond) and for these institutions the attraction may be access to the asset itself.

  Freeing up loan risk for wider distribution is perhaps the most common scenario, where an investor appears to gain access to "new assets." The same occurs when credit derivatives are used to hedge the credit risk resident in a portfolio of interest rate swaps or are used to hedge corporate risk from a pool of receivables or the sovereign risk in a project finance transaction. In these and other situations, the hedging entity will chose its counterparties carefully, with due consideration for counterparty risk and correlation, structuring and legal robustness, and of course, price. The latter can vary significantly depending on the hedge counterparty's appetite for the reference credit. So, from a commercial perspective, the hedging entity is clearly going to favor the investors who have poor access to the reference credit and who would, for that reason, find it attractive.

- **Innovative Structures:** While the credit markets may present an investor with a vast array of investment opportunities, it is often the case that a particular investment does not quite meet particular investment criteria. The risk may come in the wrong form (bond vs loan), the maturity may be too long, the currency may be wrong, and so on. Some of these cash market shortcomings can be rectified using credit derivatives. Providing loan risk in bond format by embedding a default swap in a bond issuance vehicle is a common application. Embedding a currency swap provides the investor with a different currency, where perhaps an asset swap is not available or authorized. Transacting with a sophisticated credit derivative counterparty that can manage forward starting credit risk (or that wants to put on a synthetic short position) enables the first few years of a longer-dated asset to be bought in derivative format. The list of innovations is long but should be expected given the very nature of derivative instruments. One only needs to look at the interest rate swap market to gain an idea of where credit derivatives may be heading.

There is one structuring benefit that accounts for significant credit derivative activity and this is the benefit of taking credit risk through the relative simple mechanism of a swap. For many institutions, there are whole classes of cash assets that are unattractive because of the form that they come in. The best example of this would be loans — the systems required for booking loans are far more complex that those required for booking bonds. Receiving loan risk through a default swap or total return swap is no more complex than where the underlying asset is a bond. Periodic cash flows are paid and received through the same derivative back office that processes interest rate and currency swap cash flows. For some institutions, this is a major attraction of the credit derivative markets and for some it is the only mechanism available for investing in complex credit instruments.

- **Risk Profile:** The third factor that distinguishes credit derivative investment products from traditional cash market products relates to risk profile. What will ultimately be the main driver behind this sector of the market is the ability to "cut and dice" credit risk so that it meets the risk return criteria of the investor. As is discussed in more detail in the section, *Tranched Portfolio Applications*, there are some compelling benefits for a portfolio manager when a basket of risks is sold off in different risk packages, but this is only possible because of the needs of the investors. The portfolio manager is catering to sophisticated structuring requests and in doing, so is achieving overall cheaper hedging.

The use of credit derivatives to change the risk profile broadly falls into three categories: leverage, principal protection, and tranched loss. Leverage exposes the investor to more risk by way of a "first-to-default" structure but provides a return commensurate with this increased risk. Principal protection, as the name would suggest, embeds the risky part of the transaction in the coupon (which may change to zero) but provides a strong guarantor of the final par redemption. Leverage and principal protection are discussed further in the section, *Credit Linked Notes*. Tranched loss is discussed in the section *Portfolio Management Applications and Related Investor Products*. It describes an important sector of the market that produces structures and returns similar to those seen in the CDO market.

The main rationale for looking at these structures is the logical extension of a process that is fundamental to the management of risky assets — the constant balancing of risk-reward within the portfolio. In most cases, the underlying assets are well understood by the investor, the opportunity lies in structuring innovations that use the investor's capital in a more efficient way.

15.3.2 Applications

Single-Name Hedges

The use of credit derivatives for hedging the risk of single credits is well established, and for some of the more liquid credits, it is a well-developed and a relatively mature market. A combination of user sophistication, documentation

Figure 15.1 Single-Name Default Swap

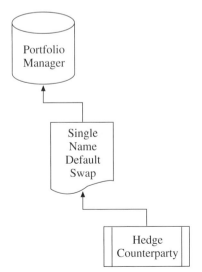

standardization, and convergence with the asset swap market has contributed to the development of this important sector of the traded credit markets.

As already discussed, there is a growing broker market which, in both London and New York, covers an increasing universe of credits and provides indicative pricing. The rationale for use is normally not a factor in this market — there is a seller and a buyer, and in most cases, the reason for trading can only be guessed. The benefit to a portfolio manager may be risk mitigation, whereas the hedge counterparty may be motivated by the financing benefits of the off-balance-sheet structure. As a result of these differing motivations, pricing may vary noticeably between different potential counterparties. Exceptions to this would include periods of market turmoil in, for example, the emerging markets, or where a particular issuer is reported to be in trouble or where the market is trying to stomach an unusually large new issue and uses credit derivatives to manage the hold levels. In these situations, user appetite tends to converge and the market sees similar pricing in all corners. Liquidity can increase noticeably and, as was observed in the South Korean credit crisis in 1997, credit derivative liquidity can even exceed cash market liquidity.

The process for executing single-name hedges is becoming increasingly standardized. Most transactions use an official ISDA standard (in the case of default swaps) or a "market standard" (in the case of Total Return Swaps) that has evolved through usage over the past five years of borrowing, where applicable, definitions from the default swap standard. The process of inquiry is faster as participants are familiar with which salient points need to be exchanged and when they need to be exchanged. As a result, "long-shot" trades tend to get dismissed earlier than they used to, and plain vanilla trades tend to proceed very quickly. For many institutions with standard documentation already agreed upon, the trade is originated and completed by telephone.

Portfolio Management Applications and Related Investor Products

The term portfolio management covers many topics, and within the credit derivatives market, it is not used consistently. At its basic level, it represents bundling together a number of single-name transactions to create one "portfolio" transaction. At a complex level, it represents the structuring of a portfolio of assets to provide investors with exposure to different tranches of loss (1st loss, 2nd loss, etc.). At most complex level, it applies to risks that are inherent in a portfolio, namely correlation and concentration risk. In all cases, portfolio management activity generates a product that, by necessity, is structured and priced to suit investor demand.

• **Bundled Transactions:** Combining a number of single-name transactions to create one larger transaction does not represent the cutting edge of the credit derivative market. But it is an important stepping stone in the path towards true portfolio management. Of the banks that developed a program of periodically using credit derivatives, many were frustrated by the time and effort needed to complete a US$25 million hedge of one exposure. Given that much of the work revolved around agreeing on the structure and the documentation, it becomes more efficient to offer the counterparty 10 or more names within the same structure. The protection bought is identical to that achieved through individual transactions, the only noticeable difference is the pricing, which is typically quoted as a basis-point charge on the total notional (rather than individual charges for each credit). This charge would ratchet down on a pro-rata basis should any of the basket of assets default or redeem early. Individually, the Buyer and Seller still build up to the price by analyzing each of the credits, but for negotiation and booking purposes, the price for the whole portfolio is used.

This is a significant development in the area of deal negotiation as it removes the somewhat tortuous process of agreeing on levels at an asset level. Institutions will have preferred and less-preferred credits according to their views on the strength of the borrower, the exposure that they currently

Figure 15.2   Multiple-Name Default Swap

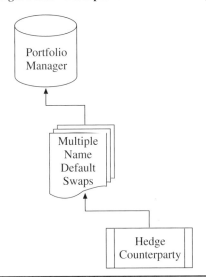

have, and the effect that the change in exposure will have on the portfolio. No two institutions will see a credit in exactly the same light, this being one of the difficulties of pricing credit. By aggregating credits in this way, many of the different views will even out, and often two institutions can agree on the price for a basket of credits, where agreeing on the component parts would be less successful.

In most cases, the Portfolio Manager achieves a price that is less than the sum of the component parts, but, since all of the risk is being hedged, the cost is still very high. Once the necessary infrastructure for basket transactions is in place, the institution can consider more sophisticated ways of selling off the risk. The following section looks at how the cost is mitigated by splitting the total risk into different components.

- **Tranched Portfolio Applications:** Where the Portfolio Manager chooses to hedge all of the risk associated with a portfolio of assets, a number of structures have emerged whereby the risk is tranched into first, second, and sometimes mezzanine pieces for distribution to investors. One of the motivations for such structures is the needs of the investor. For institutions with different or no regulatory capital guidelines, a particular tranche may look more attractive to that institution than it would to a bank. Careful choice of counterparty and careful structuring enable the Portfolio Manager to achieve a full portfolio hedge in an efficient and cost effective way.

  Changing the structure can also give the Portfolio Manager a wider universe of potential investors. By embedding the First Loss piece into a security, the security can be sold as such to fund managers who would not normally be able to assume the risk by way of a swap. Varying the currency opens up new potential investors who, for example, may be restricted when buying US dollar assets.

  In certain circumstances, Regulators have been prepared to allow some capital relief where the hedging bank retains a Second Loss position. Such relief, if any, is on a case-by-case basis and is dependent on a number of factors. First, the sophistication of the Portfolio Manager is taken into account. If it can be shown that complex models such as CreditMetrics^{TM} or KMV are being used to calculate portfolio risks, it is likely to work in the manager's favor. Second, the structure of the transaction is taken into account. The First Loss protection must be robust and sufficient to provide at least as much protection as that provided by regulatory capital.

  Whether or not there is economic-capital relief is, for the time being, an internal decision and a function of the internal models used by the Portfolio Manager and the structure of the transaction. Depending on the model and the

Figure 15.3   Tranched Portfolio Applications

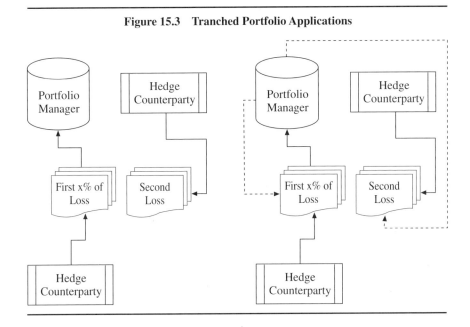

treatment of economic-capital internally, it may be beneficial, from an economic capital perspective, to retain some of the First Loss tranche.

- **Mitigation of "portfolio" risk:** A number of models are now being used to analyze the credit risk, other than direct issuer risk, that resides in a portfolio. The two risks that receive the most attention are concentration risk — the exponentially higher risk that is assumed as exposures are increased linearly and correlation risk — the risk that some industry, market, and geographic sectors are linked to each other such that a problem within one sector will increase the risk of others in that sector or related sectors.

CreditMetrics™ can be used to model the exposures in a credit portfolio and can graphically illustrate the risks arising from issuer risk as well as from concentration and correlation risks. Figure 15.4 shows the risk return output for a hypothetical portfolio before and after a credit risk management transaction using credit derivatives. As can be seen, the portfolio has excess exposure to the UK airline sector and the French pharmaceutical sector. This excess risk could be due to the riskiness of a particular borrower, to the risk associated with having a particularly large exposure to a borrower, or due to high correlation with other assets within the portfolio.

The model suggests the allocation of a certain amount of economic capital is necessary to support the risks within the portfolio. As can be seen from the

Figure 15.4   CreditMetrics™ Output Before and After Portfolio Hedging

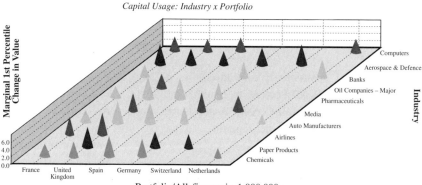

Capital (Equity) Usage = US$102.75 million on US$2.22 billion portfolio (4.63%)

Capital (Equity) Usage = US$84.15 million on US$1.96 billion portfolio (4.29%)
Reclaimed US$18.6 million by buying US$260 million on protection (7.15%)

capital numbers shown on each figure, by hedging the excess risks in the
portfolio, capital can be reclaimed in a very efficient way. The ratio of
notional reduction to capital released indicates how much capital was being
used by the peak exposures illustrated. The same would be true if some of
the "holes" in the portfolio (where there is no exposure) were filled by
appropriate lending, bond purchases, or default swap sales. The model would
indicate where additional exposure is so beneficial to overall portfolio
diversification that the incremental capital used to support the new exposure
is proportionately much less that the capital supporting the whole portfolio.

So, just as excess capital is freed up when the peaks are hedged, so minimal capital is used when the troughs are filled.

The use of a credit model in this way is very compelling, but in the absence of an environment where banks are appraised for prudent use of economic capital, such activity remains optional. As will be discussed later, once the regulatory environment changes and the risk management culture within banks evolves, it is likely that the output from models such as the example shown here, will be a major driver behind the use of credit derivatives.

Credit Linked Notes

The Credit Linked Note (CLN) is often referred to as the third main credit derivative product after Credit Default Swaps (CDS) and Total Return Swaps (TRS). From a structuring point of view, CLN should be looked at as a subset of these two products as, in most cases, it is merely a CDS or TRS embedded into a Trust structure or Medium Term Note (MTN) issuance. However, from a usage perspective, CLN does exhibit some unique characteristics which will be discussed in this chapter.

Plain Vanilla

The basic plain-vanilla version might involve a CDS indexed to one Reference Credit embedded in an MTN issued by an AA-rated bank. The spread paid on the notes would be a blended return for the risk embedded in the CDS plus, of course, the risk of the MTN issuer. It is interesting to note that even this so-called plain vanilla structure gives the investor a relatively complex credit instrument. For every $100 invested, some or all of it can be lost if either the Reference Credit or the MTN issuer defaults, but no more that the $100 can be lost. This is not the same as investing in the two credits separately as, in this case, the investment would be $200 and the maximum loss would be $200, nor is it the same as writing two CDSs, as, although no capital is invested, up to $200 could be lost if both credits were to fail.

The plain-vanilla structure does, therefore, have an element of leverage, and it can best be understood by looking at the situation where a CDS is written giving the investor exposure to the Reference Credit, and bonds issued by the MTN issuer are posted as collateral. Hence, for every $100 of CDS notional, $100 of MTN would be posted. The investor would receive the spread on the CDS, would continue to receive the MTN coupon (and hence receives the "blended return" mentioned earlier), and in the event of a default, the CDS could lose up to $100, some or all of which could be realized by selling the MTN. While this is a closer approximation to the risk profile of a CLN, it is different in the situation where both the Reference Credit and the MTN default. For the CLN holder, the maximum loss is still $100. In the example of the CDS with collateral, even if the MTN is worthless, the investor is still liable for up to $100 due under the CDS, resulting in a maximum $200 loss.

In the US market, this problem is alleviated by using a trust structure that holds US Treasuries as assets. For most investors, the MTN issuer risk described in the previous paragraphs is considered *de-minimis* as the issuer is normally rated a strong Double-'AA' or better and the Reference Credit is generally at best rated a weak A.

Leveraged and Principal Protected Credit Linked Notes

By combining multiple credits in the embedded default swap or by modifying the default swap structure itself, more complex CLNs can be created. These either provide the investor with more risk for an incrementally higher return or limit the risk and return by restricting the cash flows at risk to just the coupons. The leverage is introduced by applying the notional of the CLN against the first-to-default of a basket of two or more credits. As already discussed even the double-named risk (Issuer and Reference Credit) in a plain-vanilla CLN is non-trivial; where additional credits are added-even the conceptual risk structure is hard to understand. Modeling the risk correctly is very complex. The principal protected structure is particularly attractive where the Reference Credit is risky. Unfortunately, due to the complexity of embedding all of the risk in the coupon but none in the principal, such structures only work for a limited number of credits in maturities of greater than five years.

15.4   Business Issues

A number of obstacles still frustrate the credit derivative activities of risk managers and investors. Some relate to structural inefficiencies within the credit markets, some to the regulatory environment, and others to the slowness of financial institutions to embrace credit risk management and credit risk in a derivative format. As with other derivative products, the credit derivatives market has shown great agility during its six years of rapid growth — to the extent that obstacles have been created by the product itself, solutions have normally been found quickly and efficiently. The initiative taken to produce standard documentation is a good example of this agility — to the extent that obstacles have been created by external factors, the credit derivatives market has done its best through education, marketing, lobbying, and so on, to bring about a change. For example, the releases and revisions of regulatory guidelines around the world have normally been brought about by intense lobbying directly, via trade associations, and by the inclusion of regulatory representatives to *ad-hoc* committees set up to help market development.

The following sections discuss these and other business issues by focusing on the role of the credit culture within an institution, the systems and operation challenge, and the legal and regulatory environments.

15.4.1 Reforming the Credit Culture

For most institutions, the concept of credit portfolio manager is a new one. A few institutions can boast an active process of portfolio manager and some can boast work in progress; for the rest, such a function is not even on the drawing board. But this does not come as a huge surprise, if we consider the steps necessary.

Identification of Risks

Credit risk comes in many forms: foreign exchange settlement, lending, bond trading, interest rate swaps, etc. For most institutions, the process of pulling together these different types of credit risk is a major task in itself. Counterparty risk is clearly very different from direct issuer risk, and since counterparty risk may be contingent on conditions in the interest rate, currency, and equity and credit markets, the calculation of this risk is complex, particularly where correlation is a significant factor. Historically, financial institutions have set up risk management functions to monitor the credit risks in different business units. Because of this, the systems that track these risks are often not compatible across business units, and the risk managers tend to have skills specific to their unit. Initially, a significant systems project has to be completed merely to bring about a consolidation of the various forms of credit risk within the institution.

Quantification of Risks

The process of quantifying the credit risks within a large portfolio is not an easy task either. The methodologies are relatively new and tend to vary depending on which academic basis is preferred. The creation of models that invoke these methodologies is, for most institutions, an entirely new process, often requiring specialist quantitative skills that are hard to come by. And the linkage of these models to the portfolio information system already discussed above is also complex. As a result, a number of financial institutions have devoted one or two years to this process and have yet to produce a working system. If one considers the process that took place in the world of interest rate swaps, it is likely that there are still some years to go.

Management of Risks

Once identified and quantified, credit risk can be managed in a number of ways. Risk can be assumed by buying bonds and planning how credit will be extended through lending and so on, and risk can be laid off by selling bonds and restricting or terminating lending relationships. In practise, while the buying and selling of bonds is relatively straightforward, the planning of how exposure will be assumed through lending is notoriously unreliable. A client's request for credit is normally unpredictable, and reducing exposures where a relationship is at stake (bearing in mind that the reduction may, in the eyes of the relationship manager, be for seemingly esoteric portfolio benefits) can be hard to achieve without harming future business.

When the portfolio rationale for hedging (as opposed to issuer risk hedging) is explained to a corporate lending relationship, there tends to be a higher tolerance for the apparent selling of the borrower's risk. This acceptance, however, is generally contingent on the structure being cash settled. A corporation's biggest worry about credit derivative activity undertaken in its own name is the risk that in a work-out situation, the lending group turns out to be filled with unknown institutions that received debt by way of physically settled credit derivatives. Many of these may be less concerned with the long-time viability of the borrower and more concerned with a near-term high payout on their recently acquired debt.

The use of credit derivatives, for the purpose of not alerting the issuer that the risk is being hedged, is a much needed and welcome addition to the rather empty credit risk management tool box. However, while for the concept of using credit derivatives in this way may be compelling, in practise, the actual usage has been held up by institutional skepticism. In a nutshell, a dated or traditional credit-culture has been slow to embrace a form of risk reduction that includes the word "derivative." Issues such as documentation, counterparty credit, and booking have further stalled the process.

A more genuine concern relates to basis-risk: where positions are hedged with cash-settled structures or the deliverable asset differs from the hedged asset, then the hedging entity is open to the risk that the underlying loss exceeds the payout on the hedge. While this risk is generally small (a function of both the default probability and the difference in recovery rates), there is a need to book and report it and this represents a challenge for most institutions.

Another issue relates to the availability and pricing of a credit derivative hedge. In many situations, there just isn't a hedge available (there are lots of credits out there out only a few institutions may be familiar with the credits that need to be hedged) or the price being quoted is uneconomic (often reflecting the lack of enthusiasm by the hedging entity or complete lack of liquidity in the underlying issuer). Given the substantial amount of work before a trade is even contemplated, it can come as a big disappointment to find that the market still only caters to relatively well-known and preferably rated names. This is changing, but not as fast as the increasing desire for hedges.

Reporting of Risks and Recognizing the Benefit

Despite the sometimes tortuous route from concept to execution, many financial institutions have successfully navigated this course and have an ongoing credit risk management program. There is, however, a final obstacle that, more often than not, appears after the completion of a few transactions. This obstacle relates to recognizing the benefit of any risk reduction. It stems from the regulatory blockage that was already discussed, where regulatory capital can only be reduced in a limited number of situations. It further extends to sovereign transactions such that few regulators will permit banks to report their sovereign exposure net of any credit derivative benefits. For senior management, this has been very frustrating as the rationale for reducing emerging market sovereign exposure is often split between a desire to actually reduce the risk and a desire to report such reductions. If the latter cannot be done, then the benefits of the transaction are reduced significantly.

While an inability to report externally that the hedging benefit is an obstacle to growth, a bigger obstacle often comes in the form of senior management's reluctance to recognize risk reduction internally. Traditionally, management has monitored direct issuer risk by seeing periodic exposure reports generated from, for example, the loan booking system. As will be discussed in the next section, it has proved a challenge to modify these systems to report offsets due to credit derivative hedges. It has also been a management challenge, as there is still some lingering doubts as to whether the risk has actually been transferred. Many institutions have preferred to leave the exposure reports as they are, and to add in footnotes to highlight where protection has been bought.

Alternatives to these include reporting the net exposure and including footnotes on the gross exposure or reporting the net exposure and picking up the contingent exposure (potentially resulting from the hedger's inability to provide the promised cover) in the system that reports counterparty exposure due to interest rate swaps and so forth. These alternatives represent the correct way forward, but often senior management prefers to see the gross positions due to a reluctance to fully commit to the benefits brought by credit derivatives.

Reluctance on the part of senior management is also responsible for limited hedging at a portfolio and relationship level. Until the portfolio manager and the relationship manager believe that their risk reduction efforts — which result in the improved use of capital (see earlier discussion on relationship RAROC in the section *Line Management*) — will actually be reported somewhere, there will always be lingering doubts as to whether such activities will ever be rewarded. At the end of the day, revenue is still king, and mild increases in return on equity, often resulting in lower revenue, are considered of secondary importance in a tight year. This can only be resolved by a significant cultural change that results in a review process which rewards less tangible benefits than revenue.

15.4.2   Systems and Operations

There is little discussion in the public domain about systems and operations for credit derivatives, suggesting that it either is not a problem, that nobody has thought about it yet, or that nobody wants to talk about it. Depending on the institution, it is likely that all three are true. Where very few trades have been done, typically all bookings were done manually, and the resulting exposures combined with manual scrutiny are unlikely to present a booking or reporting problem. For most institutions, this is how the early trades were dealt with, and in the absence of a dramatic increase in business, there was no impetus to change this. Hence, as more and more "occasional" trades were completed, the same manual process was used. For some institutions, the fact that a fair number of trades are still being monitored manually has escaped the notice or concern of senior management. Those that have figured out that there might be a problem have naturally refrained from broadcasting it to the world at large.

The nature of the potential problem is easy to understand. Credit derivatives involve the synthetic transfer of credit risk emanating from a broad range of cash instruments and resulting in a change to reported credit risk and capital numbers. Creating a system that captures or replicates cash flows from the bond and loan systems and that feeds portfolio information and capital systems is, for most financial institutions, a completely new systems initiative. Consider a TRS referencing a loan: loan cash flows can be very complex, especially where a

Revolver is concerned. Rather than manually mirror the various resets, etc. in the derivatives systems, it makes better sense to take a direct feed from the loan system and leverage off the infrastructure in the loan department that has resources specially dedicated to managing Revolvers, etc. There are few reasons why such a feed should already exist. Having used the derivative system to process the payments to and from the counterparty (standard matter), the next step is to ensure that the exposure and capital reductions resulting from the trade are captured by the relevant systems. Links to these systems are unlikely to exist for this particular purpose. As more and more departments seek out and use credit derivatives, the need increases for a centralized credit derivative system with multiple links to most other systems.

15.4.3   Legal and Documentation

In contrast to systems and operation, legal and documentation have probably been the most discussed aspects of the credit derivative market. Some would argue that it runs neck-and-neck with regulatory discussions — often vaunted as the Gordian knot of the credit derivatives market. In practise, regulatory issues do not obstruct many trades, whereas legal certainty is key for every trade. Institutions have lost significant payouts from valuable credit protection due to incomplete documentation, losses due to unfavorable regulatory treatment pale in comparison.

Market practitioners have worked closely with the ISDA and legal counsel to produce standard documentation. Since the process started in 1995, there have been two releases of standard documentation by ISDA. Both of these covered non-sovereign default swaps. Following the release of the first ISDA standard documents and the realization that, given the change in market conditions, this standard was not sufficient, market practitioners worked fast and hard to assist the ISDA in producing the new booklet on confirmations and definitions. This has been in use since the second half of 1999.

The main beneficiaries of standard confirmations are new market entrants and participants in traded default swaps. It goes without saying that, given some of the obstacles that newcomers face when embarking on their first credit derivative transaction, having a painstakingly produced and widely used document as a basis for a draft confirmation represents a great bonus. It also represents a valuable tool to be taken to a doubting senior management that needs convincing that there is consistency within the credit derivatives market.

At the other end of the user spectrum, traders that are enjoying the convergence between cash instruments and credit derivatives, increasingly can trade credit spreads will little concern for the form that it comes in (cash or derivative). It is interesting to note that the first Internet site to be used for a "brokered" credit derivative has a mechanism to enable its users to compare ISDA confirmations (the document has a number of optional terms that may or may not be included) in an efficient graphical way. At a glance, the trader can check whether a potential counterparty uses the same optional terms. With time, maybe the choice of options will become a standard to further optimize the process.

For many transactions, however, the standard confirmation is at best a starting point, and at the end of the process, the confirmation is often hardly recognizable from the original. The whole of the TRS market uses documentation that differs substantially from the default swap confirmation (due primarily to the mechanism within a TRS that allows for changes in underlying price to be paid or received — a mechanism that does not exist in a default swap). Furthermore, most complex structures (such as some of the portfolio applications already discussed) require tailored confirmations. This is not as bad as it may sound when one considers what makes up a credit derivative confirmation. The key sections relate firstly to *when* there should be a payout and, secondly, to *how much* the payout should be. Generally speaking, there are two types of payout: those that are expected and wanted — default swap fees, total return payments, funding payments — and those that are unexpected and only wanted by the party buying protection — default payments. The crucial "when" clauses are those relating to the Credit Event and these, where possible, are taken from the ISDA standard. The crucial "how much" clauses are those relating to Cash and Physical Settlement, and here again, these are taken from the ISDA standard.

If these crucial legal building blocks survive within complex transactions, then it is likely that the structure will be as robust as the plain-vanilla structures. Most credit derivative disputes have centered on misunderstandings about the Credit Event and Settlement terms. These were brought to light by the numerous defaults during 1998 that triggered many credit derivative payouts, and for the first time in the market's history, seriously tested the robustness of the documentation. Most of the changes in the second ISDA version related to the holes that were brought to light by these disputes.

15.4.4   The Regulatory Environment for Credit Derivatives

The credit derivative market has met and overcome many obstacles in its six years of development. Its most significant obstacle that has yet to be overcome is the 1988 Basel Accord. Due to the accord's increasingly dated capital guidelines, there is a limit to which a national regulator can interpret the provisions to provide users of credit derivatives with capital offsets. Within this narrow band of interpretations, there are a number of interesting variations, particularly with regard to maturity mismatches and asset mismatches.

The conservative treatment of maturity mismatches (normally where the derivative protection is for a shorter maturity than the asset being hedged) allows for capital offsets (reduction of risk weighting from 100% to 20%) during the life of the hedge but requires additional capital to be held for the future exposure that will revert when the derivative matures. Such forward exposure is 50% risk weighted and when added to the standard offset gives a somewhat disappointing restated risk weighing of 70%. The more progressive treatment looks at the ratio of the maturity of the hedge to the maturity of the stub exposure and reduces the capital allocation by the same fraction. Hence a 10-year asset hedged with a 9-year default swap gets a far greater offset than the same asset hedged with a 5-year default swap.

The issue of asset mismatches applies to those situations where the Reference Credit isn't quite the same as the asset being hedged. The more conservative treatment is to provide no offsets unless the two are the same. The more liberal approach allows offsets so long as the two assets are of similar seniority, maturity, currency etc. and from the same issuer.

Changes to the Accord, currently under discussion following the release of a new framework by the Basel Committee, may or may not improve the situation. Certainly any change that introduces a relationship between capital allocated and underlying risk is going to encourage far more hedging and hence fuel the frustration faced by banks in the current environment. But since any change is unlikely to happen within two years, the market will have to tolerate the current capital rules and continue to lobby regulators to lean towards the more liberal interpretations.

15.5 Summary and Future Developments

There is little doubt that the credit derivative market will continue to grow and develop. Questions remain as to how quickly this will happen and how profound the changes could be. For all the nimbleness of the derivatives market the underlying credit markets represent a super-tanker that will be slow to turn. A major influence on the direction of this market continues to be the regulatory environment. The credit derivative market is mobilizing credit risk and the investing community will continue to consume many of the structures that come its way. The blockage, if any, will be at the bank level where there is, understandably, reluctance to voluntarily shed credit risk. The day that banks are required to allocate capital in support of risk rather than notional, will mark the beginning of active "risk management" by all banks rather than by the dozen or so that currently manage economic capital. The first changes to the regulatory capital environment are unlikely to bring about an environment of economic capital — there will likely be a compromise with current regulations. However the changes ahead are bound to form part of a general convergence towards true economic capital and close on its heals will be the constantly evolving credit derivative market.

PART SIX
RATINGS, DOCUMENTATION ACCOUNTING, & TAXATION ISSUES

16

Rating Implications of Credit Derivatives

Nels Anderson, Moody's Investors Service

16.1   Introduction

Credit derivatives fundamentally alter the role of credit risk in the financial markets by transforming credit from a strictly negative element — the possibility that a promise to pay will not be kept — into a market variable in its own right. This transformation challenges rating agencies to determine how existing rating scales and analytical approaches should be adapted to credit derivatives, especially to credit derivative-based synthetic securitizations, which now constitute a significant portion of the market for securitized corporate debt.

16.2   A Quantitative Approach to Rating Structured Securities

To develop an approach for assigning credit ratings to credit derivatives, we begin with the rating scale that has been applied to plain vanilla corporate debt since the beginning of this century. The familiar triple-A–to–single-C rating scale used by Moody's for rating long-term debt is shown in Figure 16.1. This system is essentially qualitative and relative, rather than absolute. For example, bonds rated Aaa are of the best quality and feature large or exceptionally stable margins of protection, while Aa-rated bonds are of high quality, but there may be elements which make the long-term risk appear somewhat larger.

The value of this system to the market is demonstrated by its longevity. It is not immediately clear, however, how it should be applied to credit derivatives and other structured notes developed since the 1980s. Consider, for example, a

Figure 16.1   Moody's Long-Term Rating Scale

	Rating	Description
Investment Grade	**Aaa**	Of the best quality; large or exceptionally stable margins of protection
	Aa1 **Aa2** **Aa3**	Of high quality by all standards; may be elements present which make the long-term risk appear somewhat larger than the Aaa securities
	A1 **A2** **A3**	Possess many favorable investment attributes; elements may be present which suggest a susceptibility to impairment some time in the future
	Baa1 **Baa2** **Baa3**	Interest payments and principal security appear adequate; certain protective elements may be lacking
Speculative Grade	**Ba1** **Ba2** **Ba3**	Have speculative elements; future cannot be considered as well-assured
	B1 **B2** **B3**	Lack characteristics of the desirable investment; assurance of interest and principal payments over any long period may be small
	Caa1 **Caa2** **Caa3**	Of poor standing; may be in default
	Ca	Speculative in a high degree
	C	Poor prospects of ever attaining any real standing

simple asset swap in which an A1-rated asset produces dollar LIBOR cash flows which are swapped into yen LIBOR by a Aa3-rated swap counterparty. Appealing to the traditional definitions, we see that the underlying asset, by virtue of its single-A rating, "possesses many favorable investment characteristics," while the swap counterparty is of "high quality." All very well, but how can we sensibly combine these qualitative definitions into one overall assessment of credit risk?

Several different approaches are used by various players in the credit-analysis business. Simplest is the weak-link approach, in which the credit rating of the structure is determined by its weakest element. In the case of the asset swap package, the weakest link is the A1 asset, so the package would be rated A1. While this approach does have the advantage of simplicity and may be meaningful for basic structures, it fails badly in complex cases. Consider, for example, another asset swap package consisting of not just one A1 asset, but of several, and suppose that investors will suffer losses if any one of the assets defaults. In the weak-link view, this more complex package has the same credit risk as the simpler single-asset version. This is clearly inaccurate; the multi-asset package represents a greater credit risk by any sensible definition.

More sophisticated than the weak-link approach is the probability-of-loss approach, in which a structure is evaluated according to the likelihood that it will inflict losses on investors. In the case of the simple asset swap example above, we see that the investor may suffer a loss as a result either of default of the underlying asset or of the swap counterparty. The probability of loss to the investor is greater than the probability of default of either component. The multi-asset package considered in the previous paragraph has a still higher default probability. Thus, the probability-of-loss approach is more powerful for analyzing complex structures than the weak-link approach.

A third approach is based on the concept of expected loss, which is, loosely speaking, the probability of loss multiplied by the severity of loss. More precisely, it is the probability-weighted average credit loss. The expected-loss approach offers the same analytical advantages over the weak-link approach that the probability-of-loss approach does. It also succeeds in circumstances where probability-of-loss fails. For example, consider two securities each having a default probability of 1%. Suppose that detailed analysis shows that default of the first security is likely to be catastrophic, with investors losing nearly 100% of their investment. In the case of the second security, however, default is likely to be relatively mild, perhaps because of a partial guarantee from a highly rated entity. Other things being equal, a rational investor would choose the second security. Credit ratings of the two based solely on the probability of loss, however, would be identical.

This example illustrates the greater power of the expected-loss approach over the weak-link and probability-of-loss approaches. Expected-loss is also the only one of the three that is consistent with the common practise of rating subordinated corporate debt lower than senior debt. Expected-loss, unlike weak-link or probability-of-loss, is also consistent with arbitrage-free pricing of credit risk in multi-tranche structures. For all of these reasons, Moody's has adopted the expected-loss approach for rating structured products.

16.3   Assigning a Rating to a Structured Security

Having selected a quantitative criterion, the expected loss, for comparing securities, we must calibrate the criterion to the traditional bond rating scale. To this end, Moody's conducts a study of corporate bond defaults on an on-going basis. Discussed in detail elsewhere in this volume, the study provides two important inputs for the present discussion. The first is an estimate of the default probabilities over various time horizons of issuers of various senior unsecured credit ratings. The second is an estimate of typical default severities, in particular the observation that senior unsecured debt on average suffers a loss of 55% upon default (i.e., a recovery rate of 45% for debt with a pre-default price near par). Multiplying this 55% severity by the default probability associated with issuers of a particular rating, we obtain a quantitative expected-loss benchmark for each rating category as a function of time horizon.

Not all factors in a complex credit structure can be quantified. Sometimes ratings are adjusted qualitatively to account for withholding tax risks, legal risks or other elements which cannot be included in the numerical analysis.

Although the rating of a structured security is tied to an expected-loss benchmark, the rating of a structured security should be thought of as relative indication of credit risk rather than as an absolute measure of expected loss. This is so because, while the benchmark is based on a historical average over many variables — economic cycles, industries, geographical areas — the performance of an individual security is likely to be sensitive to a narrower set of influences.

16.4   Adaptations of the Approach for Credit Derivatives

Before this approach may be applied to credit derivatives, one additional issue must be settled: how are credit risks arising from explicit credit indexation to be treated? Should the rating of a credit linked note indicate only the ability of the issuer of the note to pay as promised, regardless of amount that may be due under the terms of the credit linkage? Or should the rating reflect risks inherent in the credit linkage itself?

Although reasonable arguments can be made in favor of either position, Moody's has chosen to consider credit indexation in assigning ratings. The simple example of the "wolf in sheep's clothing" repackaged bond illustrates the most important reason for taking this tack. Suppose a Aaa-rated entity issues a note under which the holder of the note is entitled to receive whatever cash flows are produced by a B1-rated reference bond, including any recoveries that may be made following the default of the reference. If the credit rating assigned to the new note is based solely on the issuer's ability to pay, the note must be rated Aaa. Yet, if an investor were to purchase the reference bond itself, he would be buying a B1 risk. A Aaa rating might allow an asset manager who is normally forbidden to purchase speculative grade assets to obtain exposure to such assets anyway. By considering both embedded credit risks and issuer performance, one prevents this abuse of ratings.

A second reason for considering both issuer performance and embedded credit in assigning ratings to credit derivatives is consistency with older instruments. Consider, for example, a collateralized bond obligation, or CBO. In the simplest example of such a structure, a bankruptcy-remote special-purpose vehicle is created for the sole purpose of purchasing a pool of bonds and passing the cash flows produced by the bonds on to one or more classes of investors. Once the bankruptcy remoteness of the issuer has been established, verifying the issuer's ability to perform is relatively simple. If CBOs were rated solely on the basis of the issuer's performance, most, if not all, would be rated Aaa, and credit ratings of CBOs would be of little value. Investors therefore demand that CBO ratings address not only the issuer's ability to perform as promised, but also the risk that the investor may suffer losses because of credit risks in the pool of bonds. Thus, with CBOs as well as credit derivatives, ratings are much more useful if they address embedded credit risk as well as issuer performance.

Although Moody's ratings of credit derivatives do address credit risks arising from indexation to reference credits, they do not address risks arising from indexation to market variables. Thus, an obligation of a Aaa issuer with coupons linked to the dollar-yen exchange rate would be rated Aaa. Aside from foreign exchange rates, other market variables that do not by themselves constitute credit risks include interest rates, commodity prices, common equity prices or indices based on any of these. Variables that do constitute credit risks include prices or yields of debt instruments, events of default on individual debt instruments, and events of default by issuers of debt. For these purposes, debt includes both bonds and preferred stock.

It may at first seem surprising that while debt is regarded as a credit risk, common equity is not. Although equity might conceivably be thought of as a highly subordinated form of debt, it involves no particular credit promise. Therefore, linkage to equity prices is not regarded as a credit issue.

Although indexation to market variables, as defined above, does not by itself constitute a credit risk, interplay between market variables and credit variables may alter credit risk, as will be illustrated in the next section.

16.5   Example Structures

To put theory into practice, we now consider a few concrete examples, which represent the sorts of credit derivatives that Moody's is most often asked to rate. In assigning a rating, Moody's frequently performs detailed cash flow modeling under a variety of default scenarios in order to determine the expected credit loss inherent in a particular structure. We forgo such detailed analysis here in order to concentrate on the major ideas.

16.5.1   The Wolf in Sheep's Clothing

Already mentioned above, this simple yet deceptive structure requires careful treatment. Suppose that a Aaa-rated issuer promises to pay to investors all principal and interest paid by the on a particular B1-rated corporate bond. Except in the very unlikely event that the Aaa issuer defaults, the investor will receive cash flows identical to what he would receive if he purchased the corporate debt directly. Because Moody's considers embedded credit risks as well as issuer credit risks, this structure will be rated B1. If the issuer were rated well below Aaa, it is possible that, after considering the risks arising from the issuer and from the embedded credit, the rating for the credit derivative would be lower than B1. In particular, if the issuer were rated below B1, the rating of the note would be at best that of the issuer.

16.5.2   Note with Embedded Credit Call

Consider again a Aaa issuer promising to pay a coupon of US$ LIBOR plus a spread for five years followed by par at maturity, unless a particular B1-rated reference credit defaults during the five-year lifetime of the note. If the reference credit defaults, the note matures early at 80% of par. Although detailed cash flow modeling may be required in some situations, in the first approximation what we have is a note with a loss probability equal to that of the B1 reference credit, and a loss severity of 20%. Given that a standard loss severity is about 60%, this note has approximately one-third the expected loss of a standard B1 obligation of five years' maturity. This would be sufficient to push the rating up to the Ba range.

Note that we have implicitly assumed here that the B1 reference credit has a "normal" default probability. This would need to be verified by consultation with the analyst who assigned the B1 rating.

The credit risk introduced by the Aaa issuer is negligible and may be ignored for purposes of assigning the rating. If the issuer's rating is comparable or lower than that of the reference credit, scenarios including default of the issuer would need to be analyzed in assigning the rating.

Now suppose the terms of the note are altered, so that the redemption value of the note following default of the reference credit is not 80% of par, but rather the lesser of 80% and the 80% plus the percentage change in the dollar-mark exchange rate since the date of issuance of the note. Thus, if the exchange rate had dropped by 5% between issuance and early redemption, the early redemption value would be 75% of par rather than 80%. In this case, estimation of the expected loss requires consideration of the volatility of the exchange rate. A high volatility would lead to a larger loss severity, and consequently a lower rating for the note. This is an example of a market variable affecting a credit rating, even though market risks themselves are not addressed by the rating.

16.5.3   Note with Embedded Total Return Swap

This is the credit derivative that Moody's is most often asked to rate. In the absence of default of a specified reference security, the issuer pays a coupon and par at maturity. If, however, the reference security defaults, the note matures early at the post-default price of the obligation. If the coupons and maturities of the note and the reference obligation are comparable, the default risk faced by the investor is similar to that confronting an investor who simply buys the reference credit itself (again assuming that the issuer's credit rating is substantially higher than that of the reference). In this case, the note will likely receive the same rating as the reference credit. It may be, however, that the characteristics of the reference credit are very different from those of the credit linked note being rated. For example, if the reference credit is a zero-coupon obligation with a term much longer than that of the note, it is likely to have a low market price even before default. Following default, its value could well be effectively zero. This increase in severity of loss would likely lower the rating of the note by a notch or so.

16.5.4   Principal Guaranteed Emerging Market Note

Another frequently proposed structure consists of a principal payment provided by a highly rated institution and a coupon supplied by an emerging-market sovereign. Typically, the present values of the principal and interest components are roughly equal. To assign a rating, Moody's would likely need to perform detailed cash flow modeling, including all possible default scenarios. As a quick estimate, however, we can simply add the expected losses arising from the principal and interest components. Suppose, for example, that the principal provider has a rating of Aa2, while the emerging-market interest source is B2. Many people would expect the resulting rating to fall halfway between Aa2 and B2, i.e., at about Baa2. In fact, the rating is likely to be lower, because expected loss increases quite rapidly as one goes down the rating scale. As a rough guide, we note that the historical default rate of Aa2 credits over 5 years is about 0.6%, while for B2 credits it is about 31%. If principal and interest are each about half the value of the note, the expected loss is about 11%, assuming a 70% default severity. This is far higher than the losses historically associated with Baa credits, where typical default rates over five years are in the neighborhood of a couple of percent. A five-year expected loss of 11% is a consistent with a rating in the Ba range. Thus, the fact that default rates increase rapidly as one goes down the rating scale means that when two ratings are blended together, the rating of the resulting product is likely to be nearer that of the lower of the two.

16.5.5 Basket Linked Notes

Some notes are linked not just to one reference credit, but to several. For example, a note linked to five credits may lose one-fifth of its value each time a reference defaults. In another case, it may be that investors suffer no losses until two of five credits default but lose their entire investment if more than two default. In analyzing these and other basket structures, Moody's applies the same expected-loss approach that it applies in the case of notes linked to a single credit. Two additional factors often arise, however. First of all, it can be difficult to define the "promise" that is being made to investors; careful consideration is needed to define the "zero-loss" scenario against which default scenarios are compared. An additional factor is that of correlation. In many cases it is not sufficient merely to specify the default probabilities of all reference credits; one must also know their joint probabilities of default. For example, the probability that two credits in different industries and widely separated parts of the globe will both default is likely to be simply the product of their individual default probabilities. If the credits are in the same industry in the same country, however, a bad year in that industry may cause them to default together. Therefore, the probability of them both defaulting will be higher than simply the product of their individual default probabilities. Default correlation can be difficult to estimate, especially for highly rated credits where single defaults are rare enough, let alone multiple defaults. Moody's has developed an approach to default correlation for CBO analysis. This approach has a successful 20-year track record to its credit, enabling Moody's to rate credit derivatives involving multiple reference credits with confidence. Nonetheless, this is an area in which further research is worthwhile.

16.6   Credit linked MTN Issues

Moody's focus on embedded credit risks in credit derivatives has required an important change in its approach to medium-term note (MTN) programs. Previously, all drawdowns under a rated MTN program carried the credit rating of the program. In order to properly assess MTN issues containing embedded credit derivatives, however, Moody's now rates each MTN drawdown of at least a year's maturity individually. Desks have been established in New York and London to examine drawdowns and assign the program rating if there is no credit linkage. Where credit linkages do exist, the desks forward issues to analysts for rating.

16.7   Synthetic Securitization

Synthetic securitizations now dominate the rated portion of the credit derivatives market. As a basis for understanding the application of credit derivatives in securitization, we first briefly review securitization itself. The focus will be on the securitization of corporate debt, since this is at present the dominant type of transaction in which credit derivative technology has appears.

16.7.1   Collateralized Loan Obligations (CLOs)

In a typical corporate loan securitization—known as a collateralized loan obligation (CLO)—a bank sells the credit risk on a portfolio of loans to a bankruptcy-remote special-purpose vehicle (SPV) or trust created solely for the purpose of undertaking the securitization. The SPV funds its purchase of the loan exposures through the issuance of bonds which are secured by the loan exposures. Payments of interest and principal from the loans are applied to pay interest and principal due on the SPV's bonds. The bonds are typically issued in several classes of differing seniority, the more senior bonds having first claim on the SPV's assets in the event of shortfalls. Often, though not always, the bank itself purchases the most subordinated of the bonds.

By selling the loan exposures to the SPV, the bank may realize a number of benefits. It may free itself of some of the economic risk in the portfolio, though the amount if risk actually transferred is likely to be limited if the bank itself purchases the most subordinated bonds. It may achieve a reduction in regulatory capital. Finally, the securitization provides funding for the loan portfolio.

The most problematic aspect of loan securitization is the transfer of the loan exposures from the bank to the SPV. While in many other types of securitization assets may be transferred by outright sale, this is often infeasible for corporate loans. Often the bank may fear that sales of loans would damage its relationships with its borrowers, who are frequently important customers for many banking services besides lending. In addition, loan agreements often prohibit sale.

A number of solutions to the transfer problem have traditionally been used, including subparticipation, contingent perfection, and declaration of trust. Each approach, the feasibility of which depends on the relevant legal jurisdictions, has its own advantages and disadvantages. Subparticipation, for example, introduces a large element of the risk of the default of the bank into the transaction. Other approaches may reduce the element of bank risk but are usually more complex and expensive to implement from the legal point of view. This is particularly important in the European context, where loans in many jurisdictions may be involved.

16.7.2   Synthetic CLOs

Synthetic CLOs, in which credit derivative contracts serve to transfer loan risk, have recently become a popular solution to the transfer problem. In the prototypical synthetic transaction, all loans remain fully on the balance sheet of the originating bank. The bank enters a credit default swap with the SPV under which the bank pays a periodic premium to the SPV and in turn receives payments from the SPV whenever losses occur on the loan portfolio associated with the transaction. The SPV issues bonds as in the traditional structure, but it uses the proceeds of the bond issuance to buy not loan exposures but Aaa-rated bonds. If no losses occur in the reference loan pool, the interest received by the SPV on the Aaa bonds together with the swap payments from the bank are sufficient to pay the interest due on the notes issued by the SPV. Furthermore, at maturity the principal payments on the Aaa bonds will suffice to repay all outstanding principal on the SPV's notes. If loan losses do occur, however, the SPV will either liquidate or deliver collateral to the bank to cover the losses, and the SPV's outstanding notes will be written down.

From the bank's point of view, the economic effect of the synthetic CLO just described is similar to that of the traditional funded CLO: credit risk on the loan portfolio is transferred to buyers of the SPV's notes. Thus, the synthetic structure allows the bank to offload economic risk and, depending on the disposition of the relevant regulators toward credit derivatives, may reduce the bank's regulatory capital requirements as well. Unlike the traditional CLO, however, the synthetic structure does not provide funding; the significance of this fact will depend on the needs of the bank.

From the point of view of the investor, both the traditional and synthetic structures create exposure to the underlying loan pool. The two alternatives may differ, however, in the degree to which the investor is exposed directly to the credit of the bank. Some of the traditional loan transfer mechanisms mitigate this risk and some do not. Synthetic structures easily allow for mitigation. For example, if the bank is required to make its swap payments in advance and the swap terminates following a failure by the bank to make such payments, then the transaction may simply be unwound in the event of a bank default. Provided that the collateral is puttable, investors need suffer no loss as a result of such an early unwind (except for possible reinvestment risk).[1]

This ease of limiting the investor's exposure to the bank's credit is not the only advantage of the synthetic CLO over the traditional type. The maturity profile of the synthetic structure need not match that of the underlying loan pool, allowing tailoring of the transaction to the needs of investors and the bank. In addition, the fact that the SPV's income does not derive from the loans simplifies the analysis and may allow greater flexibility in selecting loans for inclusion in the pool.

The popularity of synthetic CLOs demonstrates the importance of these advantages. It should be remembered, however, that there are some potential drawbacks to the synthetic approach. As noted previously, synthetic structures do not provide funding. The other major disadvantage is the difficulty in defining and analyzing credit events. Narrowly defined credit events, such as bankruptcy and failure to pay on particular reference obligations, are closely linked to the fundamental credit quality of the reference credits. With such narrowly defined credit events, it is often possible to infer the probability of a credit event occurring with respect to any given reference credit in much the same way that one would infer the probability of the same asset defaulting in the context of a traditional CLO. On the other hand, if the definition of credit event includes failure to pay on obligations of any sort or includes a restructuring of the borrower, the probability of a credit event occurring may be significantly higher.

The significance of the definition of a credit event also depends on the structure of the synthetic CLO. Following a credit event, the loss arising from

---

[1] From the point of view of the bank, all that is needed to affect risk transfer is a credit-worthy counterparty for the default swap; whether that counterparty in turn issues credit-linked notes or not is not of importance. Indeed, in most synthetic CLOs, the most senior portion of the credit risk is placed directly with a highly rated financial institution or insurer in the form of a default swap, and only the more subordinated exposure is converted into credit linked notes

the event must be determined. If the loss is fixed at, for example, 50% of the notional value of the asset triggering the credit event, then "spurious" credit events, i.e., those triggered by causes that are not truly related to credit, are serious. In contrast, if the consequence of a credit event is that loss is determined by pricing the relevant asset in the market, then the significance a spurious credit event may be reduced by the fact that it may not hurt the price of the asset much.

Once the nature of the credit event and the loss-determination mechanism are understood, the analysis of a synthetic CLO may proceed much as in the case of a traditional CLO. In either case, Moody's employs the same expected-loss approach that it applies to other credit derivatives securities and structured notes.

References

A number of publications available from Moody's may be of interest. Regarding credit derivatives themselves and Moody's approach, please refer to:
* *A Review of the Credit Linked EMTN Market* (April 1998)
* *Moody's Extends New Medium-term Note Rating Process to the Euro MTN Markets* (Feb. 1997)
* *Moody's Announces New Medium-term Note Rating Process* (Jan. 1996)
* *Weighing the Added Credit Risks of Credit linked Securities: Update on Moody's Rating Approach* (Jan. 1996)

Several additional publications contain fundamental statistical information on defaults and recoveries that is useful in evaluating credit derivatives:
* *Historical Default Rates of Corporate Bond Issuers 1920–1998* (Feb. 1999)
* *Bankrupt Loan Recoveries* (June 1998)
* *Commercial Paper Defaults and Rating Transitions, 1972–1998* (June 1998)
* *Moody's Preferred Stock Dividend and Credit Risk* (March 1998)
* *Moody's Rating Migration and Credit Quality Correlation, 1920–1996* (Nov. 1997)

Finally, several articles discuss the analysis of collateralized debt obligations, including synthetic CLOs:
* *Subordination, Diversification, and the Expected-Loss Approach to Credit Risk* (Feb. 1997)
* *The Binomial Expansion Method Applied to CBO/CLO Analysis* (Dec. 1996)
* *Emerging Market Collateralized Bond Obligations: An Overview* (Oct. 1996)
* *Rating Cash-Flow Transactions Backed by Corporate Debt* (April 1995)

17

Credit Derivatives — Documentation and Legal Issues

Christopher Whiteley, Allen & Overy[1]

17.1 Introduction

Credit derivatives have pushed the boundaries of the law as much as they have forced a new perspective on financial analysis. However, the legal world is not necessarily as fast on its feet as the financiers. This can partly mean that inappropriate regulations or laws are applied to credit derivatives: for example, in the field of capital adequacy. It can also partly mean that the commercial world overlooks valid legal concerns in the hurry to get things done. Finally, it can mean much head scratching and industry on the part of lawyers without any tangible result other than an all-clear signal. Of these three possibilities, the latter is clearly the most valuable result (for all concerned).

In this chapter, I am going to discuss some of the common legal issues affecting derivatives generally and credit derivatives in particular. Although my background is that of common law (anglophone) jurisdictions, I try to avoid focusing too much on any one jurisdiction. Necessarily, however, many of the references are to English law. The discussion is not technical, in the sense that my main aim is to raise issues that may be relevant, rather than to give a detailed

---

[1] The views expressed by the author are his own and do not necessarily reflect the views of Allen & Overy or any of its partners. I am grateful to Edward Murray for having reviewed and commented on the chapter in draft form, but I remain solely responsible for the views expressed. Nothing written in this chapter constitutes definitive advice and should not be relied on as definitive advice. The law is stated as of October 1, 1999

analysis of applicable laws or exemptions. Many readers of this book will not be lawyers and so may not find a detailed analysis interesting. I do not discuss purely regulatory issues such as the characterization of credit derivatives in the US or the rights of "passporting" credit institutions to enter into cross-border transactions in the European Union (EU). Although interesting, these issues are sufficiently complex to require their own separate review.

Secondly, I will discuss the documentation of credit derivatives, particularly in the privately-negotiated (OTC) markets, and I include sample documentation. I do, therefore, review common contractual terms in detail. Since a derivative transaction is no more than a set of promises, it is important to understand what these promises are from a legal perspective. I focus on the OTC markets because, in terms of legal technology, this is an area of both great innovation and significant standardization of terms. In addition, it is a market where the negotiating positions of the two parties, if not equal, are balanced, and where each counterparty may regularly take different sides of a similar deal.

I also include sample terms and conditions for a credit linked note. This will enable readers to compare differences in documentation and will show the similarities. Structured notes and OTC products are often viewed as economic equivalents. Credit derivatives in particular are often issued in structured note form. However, from a lawyer's point of view, they involve quite different requirements, and, in terms of the way a law firm runs its business, are often dealt with by different teams.

Credit derivatives such as credit default products, differ from other forms of derivatives in that the trigger for payments is usually defined as a legal event rather than a price-related event. The protection seller will make a payment if a "credit event" occurs: that is, for example, if the reference entity goes bankrupt, defaults on its obligations, or repudiates or is subject to a moratorium on its obligations — it is not a question of comparing one set of prices and/or index levels with another and calculating the difference. This means that the drafting of credit events is an intrinsic part of the financial deal. It has also meant, on occasion, that market participants have needed to instruct (internal or external) lawyers to determine whether a payment is due.

17.2 General Legal Issues

17.2.1 Characterization

Although credit derivatives are relatively new, credit risk and techniques for mitigating or transferring credit risk have been around for much longer.

Therefore, laws or principles of case law have developed that address issues raised by credit risk and the mitigation of credit risk. Sometimes, this can be a problem.

Credit risk mitigation products involving third parties include: guarantees (where a third party agrees to pay the creditor on a default, usually as a result of some connection with the debtor); letters of credit (where a financial institution agrees to pay the creditor on a default in return for payment of a fee, usually by the debtor); credit insurance (where an insurance company agrees to pay the creditor on a default in return for payment of a fee, usually by the debtor); participation agreements (where a financial institution buys a debt owed under a loan at a discount of its face value); and the factoring of receivables (where a finance house buys a trade debt owed to a company at a discount to its face value). In certain circumstances jurisdictions have promoted such techniques or required such techniques to be used: for example, by the creation of export credit guarantee schemes and deposit guarantee schemes.

Quite often, the challenges to the credit derivatives industry posed by these laws are the result of old words or concepts not fitting the new business environment. A clear example of this is the debate over whether credit derivatives are caught by regulations concerning insurance contracts (discussed below). However, sometimes credit derivatives are used as a form of regulatory arbitrage. Like other derivatives, credit derivatives create a synthetic exposure to an underlying risk. If regulations exist that control economic activity with respect to that risk, then it is important that any credit derivative transaction does not infringe those requirements or does not fall within their scope.

For example, there are restrictions on banks in the People's Republic of China (PRC) regulating both borrowing from and lending money to overseas investors (and indeed only banks are able to enter into any derivative transaction with an overseas entity and then only for hedging purposes). These restrictions may apply to a PRC bank agreeing to a credit derivative transaction that exposes the PRC bank to the risk of an overseas credit, or agreeing to a credit derivative transaction which is itself devised as a synthetic loan (as may be the case with a self-referenced transaction, that is one where the counterparty is also the reference entity). In these circumstances, it is necessary to look not only at regulations affecting the derivative markets (such as the PRC requirement that transactions are hedged), but also at regulations that might apply if the transaction were agreed as a cash market transaction.

In each case, the issue is partly characterization. Can the credit derivative transaction be recharacterized (by a court, regulator, or tax inspector) as something different from what it purports to be, and as a result will this affect the enforceability of the obligations and enable one party to escape from its obligations? Other consequences may also follow from recharacterization, such as criminal liability. This may be more than a purely commercial risk since it clearly carries risk to an institution's overall reputation. On a personal note, it might even extend to potential imprisonment of the board of directors of a financial institution. Understanding the legal risks involved is not just a question of their financial implications.

Derivative transactions are usually contracts governed by English or New York law, and the starting point for any analysis will be their characterization under the governing law. Common law jurisdictions tend to look at the intention of the parties. This can be a double-edged sword. It generally allows the parties to organize their affairs in a way that avoids the application of inconvenient regulations. It does not allow arrangements that amount to a sham or a fraud. To determine whether arrangements are in fact sham, the court may seek to look through statements by the parties at the time they are entering into the transaction, and apply objective criteria to establish whether those statements are true or not.

In the Singapore case *Thai Chee Ken & Others (Liquidators of Pan-Electric Industries Ltd) v Banque Paribas*,[2] which considered whether an equity repurchase transaction (repo) should really be characterized as a secured loan, the court held that different legal forms can be used to achieve the same economic result, and that some legal forms may legitimately fall outside statutory provisions. The court said that the object of a transaction is distinct from its nature in law and that the courts must take notice of developments in financing arrangements. In this case, although there were some inconsistencies in the documentation and records, beneficial ownership of the shares concerned was transferred to the counterparty, subject to an obligation to redeliver equivalent securities at maturity.

On the other hand, in the English case *Re Curtain Dream plc*[3] where a financing company purported to enter into a buy/sell-back arrangement in relation to fabric stored in a back room by a curtain shop and used to make curtains for customers, the court held that the failure of the financing company to take possession or otherwise use the curtain material for its own benefit meant that really there was never any intention to sell the material to the financing company. Instead the transaction should really be characterized as a secured loan and had been expressed to be a buy/sell-back arrangement only to avoid

---

[2]   [1993] 2 SLR 609
[3]   [1990] BCLC 925

breaking certain restrictive covenants. In this case, the security interest was unenforceable due to a failure to comply with required formalities.

It should also be noted that when it comes to the interpretation of legislation, a court may be able to review contemporaneous debates or statements by the legislature when the relevant legislation was enacted, particularly if this is necessary to interpret any ambiguities (as with the rule in *Pepper v Hart*[4] in English law). This may be helpful if the issue is a technical one as to whether a credit derivative transaction falls within the letter of legislation, which was clearly not designed to deal with credit derivatives. It may be less helpful if the credit derivative is designed purely to avoid breaking some rule or regulation that would otherwise be applicable to a similar transaction using a different structure.

17.2.2 Insurance Contracts

As mentioned in the first edition of this book, much has been written about whether credit derivatives may be insurance contracts.[5] The issue is sufficiently important that the International Swaps and Derivatives Association, Inc. (ISDA) commissioned and made available an opinion from Robin Potts QC[6] as to whether credit derivatives were insurance contracts under English law (and also whether they might be characterized as gaming contracts). In May 1997, the Financial Law Panel (an English body whose remit is to identify and research areas of uncertainty in the law affecting financial markets) also published a paper on the topic.

Insurance is a legal issue for all derivative transactions. It was an issue that was discussed in the first major swaps litigation in England, *Hazell v Hammersmith and Fulham*.[7] It is also an element in the development of the derivative markets themselves. Insurance or re-insurance companies have made significant investments in creating or being a partner in derivatives firms so as

---

[4] [1993] 1 All ER 42

[5] Benton D. et al., November 1997, "Credit Derivatives are not insurance products," *International Financial Law Review;* Firth S., September 1997, "Recent developments in credit derivatives," *Compliance Monitor;* Lawless J., September 1998, "Irish-legal issues affect credit derivatives," *International Financial Law Review;* E. Twomey, June 1998, "Legal and Regulatory Aspects of Credit Derivatives," *Presentation at the Irish Centre for Commercial Law Studies;* Henderson S., May 1999, "Credit Derivatives Part 3: Selected Legal Issues," *Butterworth's Journal of International Banking and Financial Law*

[6] Opinion of May 19, 1997 available from ISDA to its members

to benefit from the risk management expertise of the two different disciplines. In legal terms in the UK, the consequences of a derivative transaction being an insurance rather than a financial contract are that the protection seller may commit a crime (the carrying on of an unauthorized insurance business), the contract may be unenforceable (except for the benefit of the protection buyer), and the seller would be prohibited from both carrying on an insurance business without a license and from carrying on any other sort of business. All these consequences flow from the UK Insurance Companies Act 1982. In addition, in many jurisdictions, contracts of insurance are subject to a separate tax regime.

These adverse consequences are the result of the carrying on of insurance business rather than resulting from the status of individual contracts. The problem is that there is no definition in the Insurance Companies Act of what amounts to carrying on a business (including an insurance business). The Insurance Companies Act does specify different types of insurance contract, which presumably should be used to determine whether the provisions of the Insurance Companies Act apply. So far as credit derivatives are concerned, a particular issue is raised by the inclusion of credit insurance and suretyship in Classes 14 and 15 of the classes of insurance contract set out in Part 1 of Schedule 2 of the Act. In a non-UK context, the regulatory structure adopted by the Insurance Companies Act is significant both because it derives from the EU Non-life Insurance Directive[8] and has served as the model for legislation in other common law jurisdictions. Credit insurance and suretyship are specified as Classes 14 and 15 of the classes of insurance contract contained in Part 3 of the First Schedule to the Insurance Companies Ordinance[9] in Hong Kong,[10] which also prohibits the carrying on of insurance business without a licence but does not define what this is.

The response of the Financial Law Panel is to adopt a purposive analysis to the question of whether entering into credit derivative transactions might require a financial institution to be authorized. Essentially their argument is that whether or not a credit derivative transaction is an insurance contract is a red herring. The Financial Law Panel points out that a number of financial products could also be a form of insurance in its broadest sense since they involve transfers of risk. This does not mean that a business that involves entering into such contracts amounts to insurance business under the Insurance Companies Act.

---

[7]   [1991] 1 All ER 545

[8]   73/239/EEC

[9]   Cap. 41

[10] the Hong Kong Special Administrative Region of the PRC

The Financial Law Panel points to the fact that financial institutions are regulated by (what was then) the UK Securities and Futures Authority,[11] as being sufficient legal reason for their (regulated) business not to fall also within the ambit of the Insurance Companies Act. However, as discussed below in relation to gaming, not all credit derivatives may fall within an institution's regulated business under the UK Financial Services Act 1986.

The other approach taken by commentators has been to focus on the commercial differences between the two types of contract. In particular, this was the reasoning behind the opinion of Potts QC.[12] It was also the approach suggested in a Bank of England discussion paper "Developing a Supervisory Approach to Credit Derivatives"[13] (although this was mainly concerned with capital adequacy issues). There are several ways in which a credit derivative is legally distinct from a contract of insurance. Whereas a party buying protection under a credit derivative transaction is not required to hedge its position, or to do so by holding the underlying reference obligation, the party buying protection under a contract of insurance must have an insurable interest in the underlying risk. No payment will become due from the insurer to the insured if this is not the case. As a result, the amount of the payment under an insurance contract is linked to the specific loss suffered. Although it is possible for the insurer to cap any payment at a particular amount, it cannot easily set a floor to payments: if the loss suffered is less than the nominal amount insured, then any payment will be reduced accordingly. Unlike other forms of contract, the English common law imposes a duty on the buyer of protection under an insurance contract to act with the utmost good faith (*uberrimae fides*). The buyer of protection must, therefore, report if it has been able to mitigate its loss in any way.

By contrast, none of these characteristics apply to a credit derivative whether as a matter of contract or as a matter of the parties' commercial understanding. In the English case *Deutsche Bank AG v ANZ Banking Group Ltd*[14] the court considered the terms of two credit derivative transactions where the underlying obligation was a loan by Daiwa Europe (Daiwa) to the City of Moscow. The City of Moscow repaid 75% of the loan on August 17, 1998 but did not repay the remaining balance until the next day. Although, the court did not discuss whether the contracts were insurance contracts,[15] the case is interesting both for its facts and because the court held that there was no triable issue in ANZ

---

[11] now, the Financial Services Authority
[12] Ibid.
[13] November 1996
[14] Judgment of Langley J, QBD May 28, 1999

Banking Group's (ANZ's) defense. Daiwa used late payment as the basis for a claim against Deutsche Bank under the credit default swap between them, even though ultimately it suffered no loss. Deutsche Bank claimed a similar payment under a back-to-back transaction with ANZ. The court granted Deutsche Bank summary judgement for its claim, enforcing the contract strictly in accordance with its express terms.[16]

The absence of a need for the protection buyer to suffer any loss under a credit derivative also applies as an argument in other jurisdictions. In France,[17] there is no definition of insurance contracts or insurance business under the Code Civil[18] or under legislation specifically relating to the regulation of insurance.[19] However, French law does require that there be an underlying risk — whether this is categorized as a chance event; uncertainty as to the timing of a known event (such as death); or the risk of unpredictable consequences following on from an event. French law also expressly requires that any compensation paid by an insurer is calculated on an indemnity basis.[20] In other words, the amount paid cannot be greater than the actual loss of the insured. In addition, French law treats insurance business as equivalent to a form of mutualization. An insurer is seen as a facilitator who enables several people to pool a portion of their resources in order to protect themselves against risk. As conceived, this assumes there can be a mathematically pure premium (the Platonic ideal) based on factors such as statistical probabilities, the amount of insured, the term of the insurance, and interest rates. To this is added other factors such as the level of profits or the cost of the overheads of the insurance company, which explain the differences between competing insurers. This approach is true to the commercial reality in that changes in the levels of premiums and the insurance company's return on investments are the traditional

---

[15] Indeed, quite apart from the market impact, there would be little point in a protection seller arguing this

[16] The court decided that a payment obligation was triggered by a technical as well as a more substantive default by the Reference Entity; that a Protection Buyer is entitled to rely on a self-serving publication of information unless this was expressly excluded by the terms of the transaction; and that Publicly Available Information did not need to set out all the required facts to evidence the Credit Event

[17] See, in relation to French law, Gauvin A, February 2000, "La nouvelle geotian du risque finanaier," *LADY*

[18] Which refers to insurance contracts in Article 1964

[19] the Law of July 13, 1930, as amended and consolidated under L.111-1 of the Insurance Code

[20] L.113-5 of the Insurance Code

ways in which risk is managed by the insurance industry. Payments by a protection buyer under a credit derivative transaction are calculated differently. Of course there is some cross-over of risk-management techniques between insurers and other financial institutions. However, in my view, this distinction remains as important as any.

In Irish law, the Irish High Court considered the nature of insurance in *International Commercial Bank plc v Insurance Corporation of Ireland plc.*[21] In that case, the issue was whether a "credit guarantee insurance agreement" was an insurance contract under applicable Irish legislation. The court held that it was not. The decision focused on the need for an insurable loss, the duty of utmost good faith in an insurance contract, and also the commercial nature of the parties involved.

In those jurisdictions where there is a statutory definition of what is meant by the term "insurance," the definition is also likely to focus on insurable interest and loss. In Belgium, legislation first set out the definition of an insurance contract in 1874. This stated that:

> An insurance contract is one under which the insurer is obliged in return for payment of a premium to indemnify the insured against any loss or damages suffered by the insured [*qu'éprouverait celui-ci*] as a result of agreed fortuitous events [*évènements fortuits*] or force majeure.[22]

Although a more modern definition was recently enacted (in 1992) the legislation is still framed in terms of the interest of the insured. The legislation now reads that an insurance contract is:

> ... a contract as a result of which one party (the insurer) in return for payment of a fixed or variable premium promises another party (the purchaser of the insurance) to pay an agreed amount if a chance event [*un évènment incertain*] occurs and which the insured or the beneficiary of the policy, as appropriate, has an interest in its not occurring [*a intérêt à ne pas voir se réaliser*].[23]

The legal analysis in the US is complicated by the fact the insurance industry is generally regulated by state legislation.[24] Although certain provisions of federal law (for example tax laws) will override state insurance legislation,

---

[21] [1991] ILRM 726
[22] Article 1 of the Law of June 11, 1874

provisions relating to the regulation of the insurance business are essentially matters of state law. Only where there is no state legislation will federal legislation apply. Moreover, if one is trying to adapt the approach advocated by the Financial Law Panel to the US, the potential for the competencies of different regulators to overlap makes this analysis even more complex.

In relation to New York, the carrying on of an insurance business gives rise to a licensing requirement.[25] As with Belgium and unlike the position under English law, there are definitions of insurance business and insurance contract. The legislation defines insurance business generally and also both by reference to a definition of an insurance contract[26] and by listing different "kinds of insurance."[27] As is to be expected, the different categories of insurance listed include some that could overlap with credit derivatives. On the other hand, the definition of an insurance contract is defined in terms of protection against the risk of a "fortuitous event" beyond the control of the parties. This definition also emphasizes the requirement for the insured to have a material interest in the underlying risk and that the insured is expected to be adversely affected by the happening or event that triggers a payment. The concept of insurance imposes the need for there to be an insurable interest. Again, this is a fundamental distinction from credit derivatives.

To my mind, even if not expressly defined, the concept of mutualization is also part of the legal analysis in these jurisdictions. The definition of an insurance contract under the Belgian and New York legislation refers to an uncertain or fortuitous event. This, like French law, presupposes that the relevant event cannot be controlled and is unpredictable on an individual level. Control is exercised, and the risk mitigated, by calculating the statistical probability across a wider spectrum. An insurer usually protects itself against underwriting such risks by adjusting the levels of premiums. A bank, however, will actively manage the risk under a derivative transaction by its trading activities. When deciding how to characterize a contract, it is important to keep the commercial context in mind. There is a qualitative difference between a derivatives trading floor and an insurance company (or a bookie). A similar difference is recognized

---

[23] The Law of June 25, 1992

[24] As a result of the McCarran-Ferguson Act Recognizing State Regulation of Insurance (15 USCS Chapter 20)

[25] Section 1102(a) of the Insurance Law (Chapter 28 of the New York State Consolidated Laws)

[26] Section 1101(a)(1) of the Insurance Law

[27] Section 1113 of the Insurance Law

in the way that regulators distinguish between parts of a bank's business. This means that a derivatives lawyer must understand not just the terms of a contract, but the way in which a client intends to manage or is able to absorb any financial risks that result.

17.2.3 Gaming

As well as insurance, Potts QC was also asked to consider whether a credit derivative transaction might be unenforceable as a gaming contract under English law. He gave several reasons why not. As with insurance, gaming is an issue that haunts derivative transactions generally, and not just credit derivatives. There is legislation in many countries that makes gaming contracts unenforceable in order to protect public morality. The technical arguments, at least in common-law countries, are mainly derived from Victorian case law[28] and particularly concern cash-settled transactions (since these involve a payment of differences between different prices or levels of an index). Often this has led to legislative amendment exempting derivative transactions. In the UK, there is statutory protection[29] for transactions that fall within the scope of the term "investment business" (as defined in the UK Financial Services Act).

A significant concern in relation to gaming legislation is its effect in emerging-market jurisdictions. These jurisdictions may not have been so prompt to provide a safe harbor for financial contracts. Gaming legislation may also be left unamended as a convenient way to prevent derivative transactions from being enforceable, when an outright prohibition would provoke too strong a political debate. One notable feature of the credit derivatives market (partly as a result of capital adequacy risk weightings that favored dealing with banks over corporations) has been the importance of emerging-market reference entities and counterparties in transactions, often in the same jurisdiction.

There is also an additional concern in all jurisdictions in relation to credit derivatives, which is whether credit derivatives fall within safe harbor provisions drafted without them in mind. For example, Section 63 of the UK Financial Services Act only applies to investments listed in Schedule 1. These may include many types of credit derivative (Schedule 1 clearly includes total

---

[28] See Gower, 1984, "Review of Investor Protection," *Her Majesty's Stationery Office*, Cmnd. 9125

[29] Section 63 of the Financial Services Act

return swaps),[30] but possibly exclude some types of transactions.[31] This can also be seen in France, where there have been several successive pieces of legislation[32] passed to ensure (*inter alia*) that different types of financial (including derivative) transactions do not fall within the prohibition on enforcement of gambling contracts in Article 1965 of the Civil Code.

Theoretical concerns about legislation or safe harbor provisions are often allayed by court decisions. Since courts in common-law jurisdictions may find persuasive decisions or commentary from other common-law jurisdictions, decisions of the English courts are helpful in this regard. Apart from one remark from Lord Hailsham[33] in *Hazell v Hammersmith and Fulham*, there have now been a number of English decisions[34] that derivative transactions are not gaming contracts. These cases support the view that for a contract to be a gaming contract both parties must have an intention to wager.[35] Where one of the parties to a derivative transaction is a financial institution, and as a result actively manages any market exposure resulting from the transaction, this is clearly not the case.

There have also been positive decisions for the financial markets in other jurisdictions, for example Hong Kong.[36] In France, there was a decision as early as 1881 in which a division of the Cour de Cassation recognized that financial contracts "even though they were concluded with a view to profiting from changes in prices ... may be serious and legitimate."[37] However, this is not

---

[30] Which would be contracts for differences under Schedule 1, Part I, paragraph 9

[31] To be an option within Schedule 1, Part I, paragraph 7 of the Financial Services Act a contract must relate to an underlying risk, price, or index which is itself an investment; although bonds, loan stock, CDs, debentures and similar instruments are specified as investments in paragraph 2, credit is not listed as a separate item and loans themselves are not; also a transaction may not be a future under Schedule 1, Part I, paragraph 8 of the Financial Services Act if it is physically settled (q.v. Note 4(b))

[32] Acts of July 11, 1986, 91-716 of July 26, 1991, 93-1444 of December 31, 1993, and the Financial Activity Modernisation Act no. 96-597 of July 2, 1996

[33] Lord Hailsham said that interest rate swaps were "more akin to gambling than insurance," which was perhaps appropriate in the context of the trading strategies of the local authorities concerned

[34] *City Index v Leslie* 1992 QB 98 and *Morgan Grenfell v Welwyn Hatfield District Council* 1995 1 All ER 1; it is also noticeable that the court in *Hazell v Hammersmith and Fulham* refrained from holding that derivative transactions are gaming contracts

[35] Potts QC cites *Carlill v Carbolic Smoke Ball Company* (1892) 2 QB 489 as holding that a gaming contract is one where both parties intend to wager and agree what one party will "win" from the other depending on the outcome of a future uncertain event

[36] *Richardson Greenshields of Canada (Pacific) Ltd v Keung Chak-Kui and Hong Kong Futures Exchange Ltd* [1989] 1 HKLR 476

[37] Cass Req December 19 1881, 1882, I. page 262

always the case. Notoriously, courts in Russia have recently held non-deliverable forward contracts to be void gaming contracts. Similarly, in the Philippines,[38] it was held (in 1993) that a forward transaction was void under Article 2018 of the Civil Code.[39] It appears that this was because neither party had an economic interest in the underlying risk.

Derivatives, even if speculative, are different from pure gaming contracts, as with insurance, because of the ways in which the parties lay off their risks. Derivatives allow the parties to transfer selected risks between themselves. End users profit because this allows them to invest more efficiently. The profit for dealers lies in the fact that they have the skills and technological resources (and economies of scale) to manage these risks more efficiently.

17.2.4 Guarantees

Whether a credit derivative transaction might be a guarantee has been less debated. For certain regulatory purposes it is argued that credit default products should be treated like guarantees. This is particularly true in relation to capital adequacy requirements. There have also been arguments that derivatives should be treated like guarantees where a country[40] has foreign-exchange controls that do not directly address new types of transaction such as credit derivatives, but do, for example, have regulations dealing with guarantees as a more traditional technique for transferring credit risk. However, just as it would be a problem for the market if insurance terms (such as a duty of utmost good faith and an inability to go short credit risk by buying protection without holding the underlying asset) were implied into the contract for a credit derivative transaction, so likewise, issues would arise if a credit derivative transaction were deemed to be a contract of guarantee.

A guarantor is usually connected in some way to the underlying obligor. The guarantee is given in order to enhance the credit of the obligor and so induce the guaranteed party to deal with the obligor on more favorable terms. Often this in itself is the quid pro quo: the guarantor receives no other payment than this.

---

[38] *Onapal Philippine Commodities Inc. v Court of Appeals* 218 SCRA

[39] Article 2018 of the Philippines Civil Code provides that if a contract which purports to be for the delivery of goods, securities, or shares of stock is entered into with the intention that the difference between the price stipulated and the exchange or market price at the time of the pretended delivery shall be paid by the loser to the winner, the transaction is null and void, and the loser may recover any payments paid to the winner

[40] As the Republic of Korea (South Korea) formerly did.

From the point of view of the guaranteed party, this results in a high degree of correlation of risk with respect to the guarantor and the obligor. If a parent company goes bust, it is quite likely that the subsidiary will also become credit-impaired and vice versa. The advantage of the guarantee is that it may allow the guaranteed party to treat its exposure as exposure to the group as a whole rather than individual companies (by allowing access to operating revenues), and it may give enhanced rights of set-off on insolvency.

Notwithstanding any connection between the guarantor and the obligor, English law favors the guarantor and not the guaranteed party. This is because of the (quasi) gratuitous nature of many guarantees and the doctrine of separate corporate personality. The precise terms of a guarantee will therefore be construed strictly in favor of the guarantor. The guaranteed party may have duties of disclosure to the guarantor, and, unless the guarantee is expressed to be a continuing guarantee, any change in the legal obligations of the obligor (including a waiver or reduction of its obligations) will result in the discharge of the guarantor. As with an insurance contract, the guaranteed party must show the extent of its loss. If these requirements are not satisfied, no payment will become due. One further point to note is that an English law guarantee can only be agreed in writing.[41]

Under English law, a guarantor will also usually have a right of indemnity against the obligor with respect to any amounts paid by the guarantor to the guaranteed party (this will arise as a matter of law). If the obligor discharges the guaranteed obligation in order to avoid the guarantor having to pay when the obligor is insolvent or may subsequently become insolvent, payment of the guaranteed obligation may itself be set aside as a preference. That is, there would be an intention to prefer the guarantor (with its claim under the indemnity) which taints the guaranteed party. Although such circumstances would be rare, this creates a considerable theoretical risk for the guaranteed party. Given the connection between the guarantor and the obligor, the suspect period for such a preference may be much longer than normal.[42] Under a credit derivative there is no indemnity and so the same risk does not arise.

Regulators sometimes wish to treat credit derivatives as banking book instruments like guarantees. This is to prevent reporting institutions arbitraging the differences in capital requirements between banking and trading book (usually trading book instruments require less capital because of the short-term nature of the exposures). However, in relation to off-sets (the ability to reduce

---

[41]   Section 4 of the Statute of Frauds 1877

[42]   Two years rather than six months under Section 239 of the UK Insolvency Act 1986

capital charges relating to the underlying exposure) regulators resist guarantee treatment for credit derivatives because they are suspicious that a credit derivative transaction does not afford the same protections as a guarantee. In particular, they focus on the close-out netting provisions of the ISDA Master Agreement[43] as provisions which may terminate the protection afforded by a credit derivative transaction and require it to be valued as of a particular date. The netting of credit derivatives is discussed below. In other contexts, close-out netting is seen as a protection for the creditor that enhances that creditor's overall rate of return and enables the creditor to manage better other risks (such as market risk) resulting from the default. It is accepted as necessary to guard against systemic risk, including in jurisdictions where the overall insolvency environment is hostile to set-off. In the context of credit derivatives, regulators are concerned about a potential mismatch between the valuation of the transaction on close-out and the value of the unsecured claim against the protection seller, which would otherwise result if the underlying reference entity eventually were to default.[44]

In fact the risks associated with each are different, but neither a credit derivative nor a guarantee gives a risk-free right of full recovery. Although capital adequacy requirements do not necessarily distinguish in this way, the treatment of a guarantee on insolvency will depend on the jurisdiction of the insolvency proceedings. Since guarantee treatment relates to banking book exposures under the Basle Capital Accord,[45] the only relevant underlying transactions are those of a type held in the banking book: guarantees in relation to trading book exposures such as derivative transactions may fall within the express terms of close-out netting legislation (for example, see the Irish legislation discussed later). Some jurisdictions may only allow a claim under the guarantee in any insolvency proceedings if the contingency specified in the guarantee (default by the underlying obligor) has actually occurred. The nominal value of the claim may be for the full amount at the outset of the proceedings, but nothing will be received unless an obligation would have been triggered under the terms of the guarantee by the time the proceedings are complete. I

---

[43] 1992 ISDA Master Agreement (Multicurrency — Cross Border) or (Local Currency — Single Jurisdiction)

[44] See the notice of June 17, 1998 of the French Commission Bancaire on the Interim Capital Treatment of Credit Derivatives, paragraph II.2

[45] Committee on Banking Regulations and Supervisory Practices (1988) International Convergence of Capital Measurement and Capital Standards, implemented in the EU by the Solvency Ratio Directive 89/647/EEC and the Own Funds Directive 89/299/EEC

understand this is the position in France.[46] The alternative approach is to allow a creditor to claim for contingent obligations such as a guarantee by giving an estimate of the value. English law adopts a mixture of the two. Of course, notwithstanding any valuation, payment under the guarantee will be made at the same rate as payments of claims by the other creditors of the insolvent (the insolvency dividend rate) as is also the case with the net amount owed under the ISDA Master Agreement.

Under English law,[47] insolvency set-off is mandatory[48] and is deemed self-executing without any further action by creditor or debtor, taking effect automatically on the date the court makes a winding-up order.[49] The effect is that all outstanding obligations between the parties are set off and converted into a net claim, the proof in insolvency, which is treated as a new legal right separate from the original obligations. This set-off will include any contingent obligations of the insolvent under a guarantee.[50] To this extent, a guarantee will be no different to exposures under an ISDA Master Agreement with the insolvent. The difference between a guarantee and close-out netting under English law comes in the timing of valuations. Whereas the ISDA Master Agreement gives an immediate value to any claim, claims under a guarantee may be subject to later adjustment. It is this lack of flexibility under the ISDA Master Agreement that causes some regulators a concern.

In principle, valuations of terminated transactions under an ISDA Master Agreement are made on or as soon as reasonably practical after the relevant early termination date. The valuation will be equal to the market valuation or loss/gain of the non-defaulting party. Where a contingent obligation such as a guarantee needs to be valued for the purposes of proving in English insolvency proceedings, the value must be estimated based on all factors, including the likelihood of the contingency occurring. Usually, this will be calculated as at the date of winding up. However, if the contingency occurs before a final dividend is declared by the liquidators, or if the obligation is limited in time and that time elapses without the contingency occurring, then an English court will look to the facts as they have occurred to calculate the value of the claim and not rely on

---

[46] Under Article 58 of the first law of January 25, 1985
[47] English insolvency proceedings will be likely to apply if the guarantor is incorporated in England or acts through a branch in England for the purposes of the guarantee and has assets in England
[48] Rule 4.90 of the 1986 Insolvency Rules (SI 1986 No. 1925)
[49] Per Lord Hoffmann in *Stein v Blake* [1995] 2 All ER 961
[50] *MS Fashions v BCCI* [1993] Chapter 425

earlier estimations. As a result, valuation of a guarantee is flexible and not necessarily fixed as at the date of the winding-up order.

Whether credit derivatives are eligible for guarantee treatment in the banking book, as with other questions about the capital adequacy treatment of credit derivatives, is likely to continue to be an area of debate between the derivatives industry and regulators for some time. Although the debate may be obviated by credit risk models, until these are fully recognized, the derivatives industry needs to convince regulators that credit derivatives offer similar standards of credit protection, both legally and commercially, as guarantees. Valuation of claims under an ISDA Master Agreement may not be as flexible as that of claims under a guarantee; but equally, the ISDA Master Agreement does at least give some value to the expectation if a contingency has not occurred: and this is tested against the market so that the value should be as objective as possible. Of course, even if they offer similar levels of protection credit derivatives should not be considered the same as guarantees — at least in relation to their legal terms. Otherwise the parties would risk importing into the contract, terms which are incompatible with their commercial objectives.

17.2.5   Netting and Counterparty Insolvency

Netting (and set-off) is "the discharge of reciprocal obligations to the extent of the smaller obligation."[51] The effect is that a creditor may be able to recover amounts owed to it in full or to a greater extent than perhaps other creditors. To this extent, it is functionally like taking security. However, unlike taking security, there are none of the legal formalities, registration requirements, or transfer of assets associated with execution of a netting agreement. As a result, some jurisdictions treat netting agreements as an interference with the *pari passu* (equal) treatment of creditors and make such agreements unenforceable on insolvency. Equally, to the extent that enforcement of security interests may be subject to stays during corporate rescue/rehabilitation proceedings (such as proceedings under Chapter 11 of the US Federal Bankruptcy Code)[52] some jurisdictions also apply stays to set-off and netting rights. Of course, it is precisely in circumstances of bankruptcy of a counterparty (when by definition there is not enough money to pay all creditors in full) that netting is needed to work.

For a lawyer, OTC derivatives and netting are closely connected. One of the first concerns of the derivatives industry was to reduce credit risk with

---

[51]   Wood Philip, 1989, *English and International Set-off*, Sweet & Maxwell
[52]   Bankruptcy Code 1978

counterparties by netting exposures under outstanding transactions: allowing the credit risk to be managed on a portfolio basis. This became both possible and necessary because of the development of mark-to-market pricing for derivative transactions, which allowed trading technology to be applied to these instruments despite their long-term nature. Although derivative transactions themselves are typically non-transferable, dealers are ready to quote prices for terminating a transaction before its scheduled termination date. This price can be compared to those of other dealers by seeking quotes for an equal and opposite transaction, which would have the effect of reversing out the market risk on the existing transaction.

Initially, efforts to promote netting focused on the development of standardized agreements, most notably the ISDA Master Agreement and its precursor the 1987 Interest Rate and Currency Exchange Agreement (also published by ISDA). Other standard agreements have been published, most notably in the international arena by the British Bankers Association (BBA),[53] but also for local markets where participants wish to deal under documentation in their own language and subject to local law.[54] Secondly, sponsors of such agreements (ISDA in particular) have commissioned legal opinions from law firms in jurisdictions all around the globe to confirm that these master agreements are enforceable. These opinions have subsequently been used as the basis for satisfying regulators that netting should be allowed to calculate capital adequacy requirements.[55] Thirdly, where these opinions indicated doubt about the enforceability of netting in a particular jurisdiction, ISDA and others have lobbied for legislative reform and ISDA has published a form of Model Netting Act[56] to promote this.

Insolvency, because it involves choices between who gets paid and who does not, is an area of law where there are fundamental differences in philosophy. Jurisdictions tend to be either pro-creditor or pro-debtor. It is also an area where national laws tend to prevail over principles of international comity. However, ISDA has often been successful in persuading authorities in jurisdictions that are traditionally hostile to set-off to initiate reforms giving express rights of set-off/

---

[53] For example, the International Currency Options Markets Master Agreements (ICOM) and the International Foreign Exchange Markets Master Agreements (IFEMA)

[54] For example, the 1994 Master Agreement for forward market transactions published by the Association Française des Banques in France, the Rahmenvertrag published by the Zentraler Kreditausssschuss in Germany, and the Korean Master Agreement in South Korea

netting to participants in the derivative markets. This has been because of the huge volumes of transactions in the financial markets and the perceived threat of systemic risk to the financial sector as a whole if a liquidator were able to cherry-pick between transactions: that is able to choose to perform transactions profitable to the insolvent (requiring the creditor to pay any amounts due from it in full) and disclaim onerous contracts (requiring the creditor to claim damages at the insolvency dividend rate). Netting has, therefore, been encouraged not just by netting legislation being enacted in these jurisdictions, but also by allowing financial institutions to calculate capital adequacy requirements based on the net exposure under, for example, an ISDA Master Agreement, rather than the gross amount. However, credit derivatives is an area where a similar consensus has not yet been reached.

The ISDA Model Netting Act gives a laundry list of common types of derivative transaction that are defined to be "qualified financial contracts" that should benefit from the legislation. The list given reflects the list of possible privately-negotiated derivative transactions that are known in the marketplace today. However, the problem with this approach is that a list may become out of date. This can be seen, with hindsight, with the definition of Specified Transaction in the ISDA Master Agreement itself (which is discussed below).

The structures used for transactions in the derivative markets are relatively unchanging. Most transactions can be broken down into options, forwards, or a combination of these (and to the extent it is a funding transaction may also include a spot sale of an asset). A swap is the same as a series of cash-settled forwards; a barrier option is the same as one party writing a put option and the other writing a call option with different strike prices. It is the types of underlying risk which are always expanding. Given the relative novelty of credit derivatives, the problem is that they are often not specifically enumerated in netting legislation as eligible transactions. It, therefore, becomes necessary to rely on any catch-all wording in the legislation. This creates legal uncertainty. In addition, because the approach taken is often to focus on a list of all possible products, rather than to distinguish between types of structure and types of underlying, it involves asking the question: "Is a credit derivative really similar to an interest rate swap?"

By way of example, rights of set-off and netting are stayed in Ireland in the event of examination proceedings (the Irish equivalent of corporate rescue

---

[55] See the 1994 amendment to the Basle Capital Accord
[56] Which can be accessed on the Internet at www.isda.org

proceedings). This is disapplied in relation to derivatives by the Netting of Financial Contracts Act 1995. It is drafted widely not only to include specified financial contracts, but also any guarantees and any collateral (such as cash collateral or collateral transferred under the 1995 ISDA Credit Support Annex).[57] However, it does not expressly include credit derivatives in the definition of financial contracts. That definition does include bonds, and so credit derivatives, where the reference obligation is a bond, are likely to be included within the scope of netting.[58] On the other hand, credit derivatives where the reference obligation is some other obligation (such as a loan) or where there is only a reference entity (and no reference obligation) may not be included. The Act also requires that only exposures arising from financial contracts that are part of a netting agreement between the parties can be netted on insolvency. Transactions governed by and forming part of an ISDA Master Agreement would satisfy this requirement. However, ISDA's Irish counsel believe that there is a significant risk that if an ISDA Master Agreement incorporates transactions that are not "financial contracts" (for example, the wrong sort of credit derivative) this will taint the whole agreement and mean that it will not be a netting agreement within the terms of the Act.[59] Therefore, none of the transactions will be able to be netted.

Similar problems exist in New York although with different results. New York netting legislation is perhaps the most complex netting legislation in the world. Different provisions apply depending on whether the relevant entity is incorporated in the US or overseas, and whether it is a regulated financial institution or not, including whether it is regulated at federal level or state level. Under the US Bankruptcy Code it is possible to net swap agreements, forward contracts or securities contracts where the insolvent counterparty is a financial institution but this will create three separate pools of exposure.[60] It should then be possible to set off these three remaining amounts against each other, although this may not be possible immediately. In addition, rights exist under other legislation to net "qualified financial contracts" with financial institutions. This legislation includes the Federal Deposit Insurance Act (FDIA), the Federal Deposit Insurance Corporation Improvement Act of 1991 and the New York

---

[57] (Bilateral Form — Transfer) (ISDA Agreements Subject to English law)

[58] See the opinion of McCann FitzGerald given to ISDA on October 9, 1996 and updated on December 8, 1997 and January 20, 1999

[59] Opinion of McCann FitzGerald of January 20, 1999 ibid

[60] See the opinion of Cravath Swaine & Moore given to ISDA on March 12, 1998 and updated on February 22, 1999

Banking Act. The term "qualified financial contracts" includes securities contracts, forward contracts, and swap agreements (and certain other agreements). Although the definitions contained in each Act are not exactly the same, swap agreement under the Bankruptcy Code is defined to include:

> ...a rate swap agreement, basis swap, forward rate agreement, commodity swap, interest rate option, forward foreign exchange agreement, spot foreign exchange agreement, rate cap agreement, rate floor agreement, rate collar agreement, currency swap agreement, cross-currency rate swap agreement, currency option, any other similar agreement (including any option to enter into any of the foregoing.[61]

Credit derivatives are not specifically enumerated, but ISDA's New York counsel believe that they should be included in this definition as they are similar agreements. Alternatively, to the extent that the underlying reference obligation is a bond or similar instrument, credit derivatives should fall within the definition of a securities contract. It is likely that a credit derivative linked to a loan would not be a securities contract; it might be a forward contract, but there is no precedent to support (or undermine) this.

Legislation was proposed in 1998 to confirm that credit derivatives are swap agreements for these purposes but failed to be passed in the Senate.[62] However, even if credit derivatives are not included the opinion does not take the same approach as the Irish opinion in relation to the question of a non-nettable transaction tainting the whole agreement. Instead, the other transactions can still be netted. Although the basic cause of the problems are similar for each, the solutions to the problem, and therefore the extent to which one exists, in Ireland and the US are quite different.

By contrast, in France, the approach has focused on practise in the financial markets and the type of structure, rather than the type of underlying risk.[63] Generally, under French law[64] the acceleration of outstanding contracts purely as a result of insolvency is prohibited and rights of set-off are likely to be unenforceable except to the extent they relate to obligations under the same

---

[61] 11 USC section 101 (53B)

[62] The draft Financial Contract Netting Improvement Act of 1998 (HR 4393)

[63] See Chapter 6 "Les aspects juridiques des dérivés de crédit," P. Gissinger in — "Les Dérivés de Crédit," P. Mathieu, P. d'Herouville, *Eds. Economica*, 1998

[64] The Business Reorganisation and Bankruptcy Act no. 85–98 of January 25, 1985

transaction. This was amended in so far as it applies to transactions in the financial markets by the Financial Activity Modernization Act,[65] which provides that netting agreements shall be enforceable if one of the counterparties is a financial institution (or exempt institution) in relation to any financial instruments.[66] The definition of "financial instruments" includes:[67]

1. forward contracts involving any bills, securities, indices, or currencies, including equivalent cash-settled instruments,
2. forward interest-rate agreements
3. swaps
4. forward commodities and goods agreements
5. options to acquire or dispose of financial instruments, and all other futures and forward market instruments

The Act provides that a netting agreement must be "a market master agreement in keeping with the general principles of a national or international master agreement".[68] The Governor of the Bank of France has confirmed that this would include the ISDA Master Agreement.[69]

Equally, the position in England is very simple: netting is mandatory in respect of all mutual dealings whether or not these relate to derivative transactions (Rule 4.90 of the 1986 Insolvency Rules).[70] Therefore, the netting of credit derivatives is also enforceable, and indeed required.

The legal enforceability of netting in relation to credit derivatives obviously has a direct impact on the credit risk being run by a financial institution entering into such transactions. This should in any case have a financial implication when pricing the transaction. However, the general uncertainty outlined above means that, even where netting is legally enforceable, regulators may refuse to recognize this in terms of the capital adequacy treatment of the transaction. The Guide to Banking Supervisory Policy published by the UK Financial Services Authority states that exposures arising from "total return swaps and other credit derivatives" are not eligible for net treatment in relation to capital adequacy requirements.[71] This is despite the very clear application of insolvency set-off

---

[65] Ibid.

[66] Article 52

[67] Article 3

[68] Article 52

[69] Letters to the President of the French Association of Credit Institutions (AFEC) dated August 7, 1995 and March 23, 1998

[70] Ibid.

[71] Volume 2, Chapter NE, paragraph 5(a) of Section 5.1

in England. Given the interests of the financial community and the momentum that has already built up from earlier lobbying, this is an area where there is likely to be further reform. However, the real need is to move away from lists of transactions which need constant updating to the establishment of basic principles that can apply to all transactions whatever the underlying risk.

17.3 ISDA Documentation

One of the purposes behind the creation of ISDA was to produce standard documentation for the derivatives industry, the most famous example of which is the ISDA Master Agreement. The ISDA Master Agreement is a credit agreement. It creates a general set of terms and conditions which are incorporated in all Transactions,[72] unless specifically altered. These terms regulate the exposure that each counterparty has to the other in terms of credit risk (chiefly by netting) and deal with the consequences of Transactions being agreed on a cross-border basis. It, therefore, specifies the governing law of the agreement, the venue for any litigation, a covenant that payments can be made free of taxes, and a requirement to gross up any payments in respect of tax that must be withheld.

However, it is more than just a simple set of general terms and conditions. The ISDA Master Agreement deems that it, and each Confirmation[73] evidencing a Transaction, are part of a single agreement. This means that, if an Event of Default[74] occurs, all the outstanding Transactions are terminated (or if the event is a Termination Event,[75] the Affected Transactions[76] are terminated), valued, and a single amount becomes payable by one party to the other that is equal to the net value of the Terminated Transactions.[77] This is close-out netting. The obligation to pay this net amount following termination is a new obligation that arises by virtue of Section 6(d) and is completely distinct from the obligation to make the payments agreed under any Transaction (which is specified in Section 2(a)(i)) and the settlement netting that applies to such payments (under Section 2(c)).

---

[72] As defined in the preamble to the ISDA Master Agreement
[73] As defined in the preamble to the ISDA Master Agreement
[74] As defined in Section 5(a) of the ISDA Master Agreement
[75] As defined in Section 5(b) of the ISDA Master Agreement
[76] As defined in Section 14 of the ISDA Master Agreement
[77] As defined in Section 14 of the ISDA Master Agreement

There is no limit to the types of transactions that may be agreed under the ISDA Master Agreement. It is as suitable for a credit derivative transaction as an interest rate swap. This is the unique advantage of the ISDA Master Agreement. There is a misconception that the definition of Specified Transaction[78] in the ISDA Master Agreement means this is not the case. A Specified Transaction is any transaction that is:

> a rate swap transaction, basis swap, forward rate transaction, commodity swap, commodity option, equity or equity index swap, equity or equity index option, bond option, interest rate option, foreign exchange transaction, cap transaction, floor transaction, currency swap transaction, cross-currency rate swap transaction, currency option, or any other similar transaction

or any combination of these, or any option to enter into such transactions. Again this is a list that rehearses those transactions that were common at the time it was written (1992) and does not expressly include credit derivatives.

On first reading, it is assumed that this is meant to define the types of transaction that will form part of the agreement. In fact, Specified Transaction is included in Section 5(a)(v) of the ISDA Master Agreement as triggering an Event of Default if the counterparty defaults under any Specified Transaction between the parties (or certain related entities). Section 5(a)(v) is, therefore, intended to allow a cross-default where a counterparty has defaulted on other derivative transactions not part of the ISDA Master Agreement. However, in so far as any cross-default is concerned, whether or not credit derivatives fall within the Specified Transaction definition may still be an issue, particularly if, for example, credit derivatives are documented separately to avoid tainting the ISDA Master Agreement under any netting legislation.

It has been argued that Section 5(a)(v) will extend to Transactions under the ISDA Master Agreement as well transactions outside it. Unlike the other Events of Default, Section 5(a)(v) includes any repudiation, rejection, disclaimer or disaffirmation of the relevant transaction. There is no other event of default in the ISDA Master Agreement that would easily apply if a party were simply to repudiate the legality of its obligations under a Transaction that forms part of the agreement. If this argument is used in relation to a credit derivative transaction, the fact that credit derivatives are not expressly included in the relevant list might be a problem.

---

[78] As defined in Section 14 of the ISDA Master Agreement

The ISDA Master Agreement envisages that the parties will enter into Transactions orally and will subsequently evidence the Transaction by means of a Confirmation.[79] A Confirmation may be any "document or other confirming evidence... exchanged between the parties,"[80] and it is expressly contemplated that Confirmations may be in electronic form. Because the ISDA Master Agreement is a single agreement, each Confirmation is treated as binding supplement to that agreement.

ISDA has published figures that show that the total nominal amount of outstanding interest rate swaps, currency swaps, and interest rate options as at the end of 1998 was US$50.997 trillion. This was a 76% increase on the amount outstanding as at the end of 1997. In relation to credit derivative transactions, the BBA estimates the nominal value of outstanding transactions to be US$350 billion as at the end of 1998 and that this will grow to US$740 billion by 2000.[81] In order to document such a huge volume of transactions, banks need to be able to produce confirmations quickly. Only the terms of the more complex, structured transactions can be negotiated between the parties. Therefore, ISDA has published sample confirmations to enable parties to document those products on standard terms.

In general, ISDA's practise has been to wait for a market to establish itself, and for the major participants to standardize their own documentation before setting up an ISDA working-group to produce standard confirmations for the industry as a whole. These confirmations are usually long-form confirmations that set out the terms of each transaction in full. The long-form confirmations are road-tested before being used to produce a set of Definitions that are published by ISDA and allow any confirmation to focus on the key commercial terms, incorporating general provisions by reference to the relevant set of Definitions. This was the case with equity derivatives,[82] bond options,[83] and credit derivatives, where the 1998 Confirmation of OTC Credit Swap

---

[79] Section 9(c)(ii) of the ISDA Master Agreement
[80] Page 1 of the ISDA Master Agreement
[81] Merchant, Khozem, August 17, 1999, "Watershed rules offer greater liquidity," *Financial Times*
[82] The 1992 Confirmation of OTC Equity Index Option Transaction and the 1994 Confirmation of OTC Single Share Option Transaction — Physical Settlement being used as the basis for the 1994 ISDA Equity Option Definitions, which were in turn superseded by the 1996 ISDA Equity Derivatives Definitions
[83] The 1997 ISDA Government Bond Option Definition. The 1993 Confirmation of OTC Bond Option Transaction being used as the basis for

Transaction (Single Reference Entity) (Non-Sovereign) (the long-form Credit Swap Confirmation) was used as the basis for the 1999 ISDA Credit Derivatives Definitions (the Credit Definitions).

In each case, new working groups are assembled to prepare the Definitions, and often the scope is expanded to include new products. These short-form confirmations are meant to be easier for traders and end users to read and effectively hide away much of the legal provisions in the Definitions. They do not mean that legal provisions are irrelevant or that the parties do not have to make choices about how they apply. In the next part of this chapter is a discussion of the Credit Definitions and in particular, how different elections and variables are made when drafting a confirmation. Also included is a sample short-form confirmation as Appendix I. ISDA intends to publish a user's guide for the Credit Definitions, which will go through these points in greater detail.

17.4   1999 ISDA Credit Derivatives Definitions

17.4.1   Reference Entity and Obligations

The Credit Definitions are principally aimed at "default" transactions, where the underlying Obligation[84] of the Reference Entity[85] is a bond or a loan. A default transaction is a transaction where the trigger to payment by the protection Seller[86] is the occurrence of a specified Credit Event.[87] Although the Credit Definitions do not exclude other types of credit derivative transactions, for example, a transaction where the underlying Obligation is a swap, they may not contain all the provisions necessary for such transactions. They also assume a single Reference Entity, whether the original obligor with respect to a specified Obligation or an entity acting as guarantor. They do not make provision for transactions that refer to a basket of Reference Entities, although they could be amended to do this. They do, however, expand on the long-form Credit Swap Confirmation in that they cover both Sovereign[88] and non-sovereign Reference Entities. They also permit the parties to refer to more than one Obligation of the same Reference Entity.

Like the long-form Credit Swap Confirmation, the Credit Definitions require the parties to specify a Reference Entity whose credit is the subject of the

---

[84] As defined in Section 2.14 of the Credit Definitions
[85] As defined in Section 2.1 of the Credit Definitions
[86] As defined in Section 1.19 of the Credit Definitions
[87] As defined in Article IV of the Credit Definitions
[88] As defined in Section 2.23 of the Credit Definitions

derivative transaction, and distinguish between the concepts of that entity's general Obligations, any Excluded Obligations,[89] one or more Reference Obligations,[90] and Deliverable Obligations.[91] Where the underlying risk is sovereign credit risk, the parties should consider carefully which entity to use as the Reference Entity. Emanations of the state can take different forms in different jurisdictions, and more than one entity or agency may be used for fund-raising. This may particularly be the case in countries with, or with the legacy of, a centrally planned economy.

In terms of the Obligations, the key definition is the definition of Reference Obligation: a Reference Obligation must be specified by the parties in the confirmation if the transaction is to be cash-settled. Both the definitions of Obligation and Deliverable Obligation take the fall-back position that these will be only the Reference Obligation unless otherwise specified. Deliverable Obligations are those Obligations that the protection Buyer[92] can deliver to the protection Seller where the transaction is to be settled by physical delivery. Excluded Obligations are Obligations that the parties agree are not to be included in the definition of Reference Obligations or Deliverable Obligations (or both). The Credit Events (as a result of which payments are made by the protection Seller) are triggered, except in the case of Bankruptcy,[93] by the specified events occurring with respect to any Obligation. In the case of Bankruptcy, the Credit Event is defined by any events happening to the Reference Entity itself.

The Credit Definitions also provide that the transaction may be terminated (as if an Additional Termination Event[94] had occurred under the ISDA Master Agreement) if the Reference Entity and the protection Seller merge or become part of the same group of companies.[95] This provision will need to be amended if the transaction is self-referenced, that is, at the outset of the transaction, the Reference Entity is also a party (for example, the protection Seller in relation to a synthetic refinancing). Other definitions (such as Section 3.5 relating to the definition of "Publicly Available Information") provide for the Reference Entity perhaps being a party to the transaction. However, the definition of Calculation

---

[89] As defined in Section 2.16 and 2.17 of the Credit Definitions
[90] As defined in Section 2.3 of the Credit Definitions
[91] As defined in Section 2.15 of the Credit Definitions
[92] As defined in Section 1.18 of the Credit Definitions
[93] As defined in Section 4.2 of the Credit Definitions
[94] As defined in Section 5(b)(v) of the ISDA Master Agreement
[95] Section 2.28 of the Credit Definitions

Agent[96] assumes that, unless otherwise specified, the protection Seller will be the Calculation Agent. The parties may consider this inappropriate if the Reference Entity is the protection Seller. The parties may also wish to amend the fall-back provisions[97] relating to Quotations[98] (discussed later). Apart from this, if the Reference Entity is also a party, then there are complex legal issues that will result. It is important that any such structure is subject to a detailed legal review.

The Credit Definitions allow the definitions of Obligation and Deliverable Obligation to be expanded beyond the Reference Obligations by a menu of categories and characteristics[99] set out in tabular form. Each category is mutually exclusive, being different degrees of generality, and so only one category should ever be specified. However, the characteristics allow the parties to define in detail different elements which should apply, from the ranking of the Obligation in the insolvency of the Reference Entity to the currency or market of issuance (onshore/offshore). The Credit Definitions also provide for Deliverable Obligations to be in different currencies from the base currency of the transaction. This is a change from the long-form Credit Swap Confirmation, where there was no set of choices to define Obligations or Deliverable Obligations, and so each transaction required detailed drafting. The long-form Credit Swap Confirmation did provide sample wording for different categories of obligation, but this was not done in the methodical way as set out in the Credit Definitions.

The categories of Obligation included in the Credit Definitions[100] are any payment obligation (Payment); any borrowed money—which is defined to include deposits and drawings under a letter of credit (Borrowed Money); only those obligations specified to be reference obligations (Reference Obligation); any amounts issued under a certificated debt security (Bond); any loan—whether a term loan or revolving (Loan); and a combination of the last two terms (Bond or Loan). Only one of these categories should be used. The different types of characteristics[101] that can apply are: *Pari Passu* Ranking; Specified Currency; Not Sovereign Lender; Not Domestic Currency; Not Domestic Law; Listed; Not Contingent; and Not Domestic Issuance. This allows

---

[96] Section 1.13 of the Credit Definitions
[97] See Section 7.8 of the Credit Definitions
[98] As defined in Section 7.8 of the Credit Definitions
[99] See Section 2.19 of the Credit Definitions
[100] As defined in Section 2.18(a) of the Credit Definitions
[101] As defined in Section 2.18(b) of the Credit Definitions

the parties to choose, for example, whether Obligations must rank (*pari passu*) with the most senior Reference Obligation or (if none is specified) other unsecured debt of the Reference Entity; or the currency of denomination of any Obligation. If Specified Currency applies and no further details are given, the Credit Definitions state that the Standard Specified Currencies[102] shall be those of Canada, Japan, the UK, the US, and the Euro: and an Obligation may be denominated in any of these. Equally, the parties may require that any Obligation is not owed to a Sovereign or Supranational Organization[103] (the Credit Definitions give the example of Paris Club debt),[104] or that Obligations are listed on an exchange (whatever category of obligation is chosen, this characteristic will apply only to Bonds). If Not Contingent applies, this means only Obligations where payment is not structured by reference to a formula or index, or which is not subject to a contingency are eligible. The Not Domestic Currency and Not Domestic Law characteristics each refer to the Reference Entity's own jurisdiction (if it is a Sovereign) or jurisdiction of organization (if it is not). However, the definition of Domestic Currency[105] carves out the currencies of Canada, Japan, the UK, the US, as well as the Euro (which are the Standard Specified Currencies listed earlier) if one of these is subsequently adapted in a jurisdiction. Therefore domestic currency restrictions cannot apply to Obligations in one of these currencies unless the currency was the domestic currency at the time the transaction was agreed. On the other hand, Not Domestic Issuance refers not to the Reference Entity's jurisdiction of incorporation, but to its domestic market.

In addition, in relation to Deliverable Obligations (that is where the transaction is to be settled by physical delivery), the Credit Definitions permit further characteristics to be stated. These are:[106] Assignable Loan; Consent Required Loan, Direct Loan Participation; Indirect Loan Participation; Transferable; Maximum Maturity; Accelerated or Matured; and Not Bearer. The Assignable Loan and Consent Required Loan definitions are used to distinguish between those Loans that are freely transferable and those that require the consent of the Reference Entity or borrower (if different) or a third party before any assignment can take place. Where a Loan cannot be assigned, the economic

---

[102] See Section 2.18(b)(ii) of the Credit Definitions
[103] As defined in Section 2.25 of the Credit Definitions
[104] See Section 2.18(b)(iii) of the Credit Definitions
[105] See Section 2.26 of the Credit Definitions
[106] As defined in Section 2.19 of the Credit Definitions

interest in the Loan can be transferred through a participation: that is a back-to-back arrangement, where receipts under the Loan are paid over by the original lender. Since this involves credit risk not only on the borrower but also on the original lender, the Credit Definitions distinguish between Direct Loan Participation (where payments are received from a person with a direct relationship with the borrower) and an Indirect Loan Participation (where payments are received down a chain of persons involving credit risk on each one). The parties may also agree a maximum maturity for any Deliverable Obligations or may agree that delivered Obligations must be due and payable (whether or not as a result of the relevant Credit Event). The Credit Definitions also permit the parties to agree that Deliverable Obligations may not be in bearer form (that is payable to bearer and so, transferable by a mere transfer of physical possession of the Obligation) or may be transferable in any way. In relation to the requirement that Obligations be Transferable, the test is only whether they can be transferred to institutional investors, and expressly ignores whether there are selling restrictions or other restrictions, which mean that the relevant Obligations cannot be transferred to the protection Seller. If this is the case, the illegality provisions in Section 9.4 may apply (resulting in cash settlement).

Although it is possible for more than one characteristic to be applied to a given category of Obligations or Portfolio[107] of Deliverable Obligations, certain characteristics are only suitable for certain categories. Under the Credit Definitions, Not Bearer and Listed can only apply to Bonds; Assignable Loan and Consent Required Loan can only apply to Loans. Equally, the parties should consider whether categories are suitable, given the nature of the Reference Entity. It may not be appropriate to specify Not Contingent where the Reference Entity is (acting) as guarantor. Similarly, it may not be possible to apply requirements that Obligations not be domestic to a Supranational Organization as Reference Entity without further defining this. The parties may also wish to define more narrowly or broadly the concept of a Reference Entity's domestic market, perhaps if the domestic jurisdiction is part of a federal structure or, for example, in relation to capital markets, by reference to a single currency or other criteria.

17.4.2   Credit Events

The Credit Events included as triggers for payment in the Credit Definitions are:[108] bankruptcy of the Reference Entity (Bankruptcy); a failure by a Reference

---

[107] As defined in Section 8.6 of the Credit Definitions
[108] As defined in Article IV of the Credit Definitions

Entity to make payments due under any Obligation (Failure to Pay); any Obligation becoming capable of being declared due and payable as a result of an event of default under the terms of such Obligation (Obligation Default); any Obligation being declared due and payable as a result of an event of default under the terms of such Obligation (Obligation Acceleration); a Reference Entity or Governmental Authority[109] repudiating any Obligations or imposing a moratorium or similar (whether *de facto* or *de jure*) on payments under any Obligation (Repudiation/Moratorium); and a Restructuring, being a restructuring of the payment terms of any Obligations, or any Obligations being subject to a mandatory exchange for other obligations, securities, or assets with different terms (Obligation Exchange). In each case, the Credit Event only applies to the Obligations agreed by the parties, and also only to the extent that the Obligations affected are in excess of the specified threshold amount. The Credit Definitions do not include as Credit Events two that were included as potential choices in the long-form Credit Swap Confirmation. These are Downgrade and Credit Event Upon Merger.[110] Both were left out as they were not popular enough. The Credit Definitions also use amended definitions of Failure to Pay, Restructuring and Repudiation compared to those used in the long-form Credit Swap Confirmation.

The Bankruptcy language is modeled on the language used in Section 5(a)(vii) of the ISDA Master Agreement. This wording is comprehensive and tries to cover the various types of insolvency proceedings in any jurisdiction. It is important to note, however, that the precise application of this clause will depend on the jurisdiction of incorporation of the Reference Entity. Problems may arise when a jurisdiction has not developed comprehensive bankruptcy laws, and in particular, has not developed forms of corporate rescue proceedings. This is most likely to be the case in jurisdictions that have enjoyed periods of sustained growth, since the legal infrastructure relating to business failures will not have kept up to date with the more developed economic environment. This may require spontaneous action by the state to protect creditors. In fact, there have been examples of government authorities seeking outside legal advice to determine in advance what the effect of their actions will be in relation to standard documentation such as the ISDA Master Agreement. The result is that certain actions may fall within the definition of a Repudiation/Moratorium and it is important, therefore, to review the two Credit Events together. Of course these are not the only provisions applicable to the

---

[109] As defined in Section 4.8(b) of the Credit Definitions
[110] In each case, as defined in the long-form Credit Swap Confirmation

Bankruptcy of the Reference Entity, since the terms and conditions of most Obligations will contain (whether express or implied) events of default in relation to bankruptcy.

To take an example, on October 6, 1998, the People's Bank of China (PBOC) gave notice that Guangdong International Trust and Investment Corp (GITIC) was unable to pay its debts and that PBOC had decided to require GITIC to cease business in order to protect creditors. PBOC, therefore, revoked various regulatory licenses and appointed the Bank of China and Guangfa Securities Co Ltd as custodians of the assets of the banking and securities businesses of GITIC, respectively. Non-financial parts of GITIC's business (which were being run profitably) would continue with the same management. PBOC also set up a liquidation committee to wind up GITIC under PRC law. There was no precedent for this action under PRC law.

In terms of the Bankruptcy Credit Event, these events probably fell within a number of different headings. Firstly, PBOC had stated (fortunately) that GITIC was unable to pay its debts (such a statement being itself a Credit Event under Section 4.2(b)), and second, arguably, winding-up proceedings had been instituted (Section 4.2(c)) (although this requires certain additional events such as the making of a court order or 30 days to pass without any petition being dismissed). However, PBOC acted independently of any judicial authorities. Potentially also, an event had occurred under Section 4.2(f) (or to the extent analogous thereto under PRC law Section 4.2 (h)). Section 4.2(f) refers to the appointment of an administrator, provisional liquidator, conservator receiver, trustee, custodian, or a similar official over all (or substantially all of) the assets of the Reference Entity. There is difficulty in interpreting these words since they have different meanings under English or New York law (one of which will be the governing law of the ISDA Master Agreement and/or Confirmation). So far as English law is concerned, these appointees are usually appointees of the court, whereas the custodians appointed by PBOC, were appointed in PBOC's capacity as regulatory authority. Moreover Section 4.2(h) requires the appointment of only one official over all the assets of the Reference Entity, whereas PBOC separately appointed two officials over different parts of GITIC's business, and these two did not control all of the assets, some of which were left in the hands of GITIC's incumbent management. It is not clear how significant these distinctions are. It is important to stress that a Credit Event would have occurred as a result of one of these events under a transaction using the Credit Definitions with GITIC as Reference Entity. The point is merely that the analysis as to why, or as to which precise facts should be cited in any Credit Event Notice,[111] may be complex.

Bankruptcy is the only Credit Event that does not refer to the Reference Entity's Obligations. The others refer to an event that involves defined Obligations (as agreed between the parties) of the Reference Entity subject to a threshold amount (the Default Requirement,[112] which is deemed to be US$10 million unless otherwise specified). The events relating to Obligation Acceleration and Obligation Default are the same as a cross-acceleration or cross-default clause. In the case of Obligation Acceleration, it is that creditors have taken action to require immediate payment of amounts owed under the relevant Obligation. In the case of Obligation Default, it is that creditors have the right to do this, but may or may not have done so. Obviously the first is primarily a factual question and reasonably easy to determine; the second is more of a legal question, but there should usually be a consensus about what the position is. Where Reference Obligations are individually specified, it is important to note how these rights might be exercised. In some instances, an event of default (giving rights of acceleration) only occurs after a breach of the terms of the agreement has been notified to the debtor[113] (and therefore, the Obligation Default will not occur until this point).

The Credit Definitions also separately specify a failure by the Reference Entity to make payments when due under an Obligation. This clearly is sufficiently important that it should be specified as a Credit Event whatever the underlying terms of the Obligation. However the Credit Event only occurs when the Reference Entity fails to pay. If the Reference Entity is acting as guarantor of the Obligation, this may have an impact on the timing of the Credit Event since amounts may not again be payable by the guarantor until certain steps have been taken to notify it or enforce any claims. The Credit Definitions also deem (in most circumstances) that at least a minimum three-day Grace Period[114] is included in the terms of any Reference Obligation. Even if the Reference Obligation does not contain a Grace Period for non-payment, a Credit Event still will not occur until at least three days after the payment was due. This avoids a Credit Event being triggered by a Failure to Pay arising from some technical or administrative error, when the money was available anyway. Any Grace Period presents a problem where the Potential Failure to Pay[115] occurs close to

---

[111] As defined in Section 3.3 of the Credit Definitions

[112] As defined in Section 4.8 of the Credit Definitions

[113] This is the position under Paragraph 10 of the 1995 PSA/ISMA Global Master Repurchase Agreement

[114] As defined in Section 1.11 of the Credit Definitions

[115] As defined in Section 1.12 of the Credit Definitions

the maturity of the transaction. Therefore, the Credit Definitions contain complex provisions relating both to the deemed Grace Period and to any express Grace Period under the terms of an Obligation where this would run over the Scheduled Termination Date.[116] Like the other Credit Events, the Failure to Pay Credit Event is also subject to a threshold amount (the minimum Payment Requirement),[117] which may be agreed by the parties, but in this case, the Credit Definitions contain a fall-back provision that if none is specified, then the parties are deemed to have agreed on US$1 million or its equivalent in any currency.

The Credit Definitions move the provisions in the long-form Credit Swap Confirmation relating to a moratorium from the definition of Restructuring to be included as part of the wording regarding a repudiation. It should be noted that the wording of the relevant Credit Event (Repudiation/Moratorium) includes any repudiation or challenge to the legal validity of Obligations. The definition of Credit Event itself in Section 4.1 also states that the occurrence or otherwise of a Credit Event is not affected by any challenge to the enforceability of an Obligation by the Reference Entity including any alleged lack of capacity or due authority and is also not affected by an intervening illegality (that is any change in applicable law). As a result, the Credit Definitions transfer not just credit risk to the protection Seller but also certain legal risks. Under Repudiation/Moratorium, a Credit Event will also occur following any declaration or imposition of a moratorium on payments on Obligations whether *de facto* or *de jure*. If the Reference Entity seeks to negotiate with creditors in anticipation of a potential breach but before Obligations become due, this Credit Event may still be triggered (depending on what is said and how strongly by the Reference Entity). This may be early in any restructuring process. The parties should therefore consider at which point they want the obligations of the protection Seller to be triggered. As will be discussed later, these events may result from the absence of any proscribed insolvency procedures in the jurisdiction of the Reference Entity. In this case, authorities or the Reference Entity itself will need to take spontaneous actions outside the field of any existing law to protect creditors generally. Depending on the jurisdiction of incorporation of the Reference Entity, it may therefore be sensible also to apply Repudiation/Moratorium to the extent the parties wish Bankruptcy to apply.

A significant amount of time was spent agreeing on a revised definition of Restructuring for the Credit Definitions. The Restructuring Credit Event set out

---

[116] As defined in Section 1.6 of the Credit Definitions
[117] As defined in Section 4.8 of the Credit Definitions

in the long-form Credit Swap Confirmation was dependent on whether: (a) there had been any restructuring of the payment obligations under the Reference Obligation (or a forced substitution of new obligations as will be discussed later) and (b) this was material. The question of whether this type of event was material in a given situation proved difficult to work in practise and gave rise to disputes. Whether the parties agree to include Restructuring as a Credit Event may depend on how the protection Seller is to settle its obligations under the transaction. As will be discussed later, if the protection Seller simply pays a cash amount without acquiring underlying Obligations from the protection Buyer, it will not benefit from any potential upside to the restructuring and also may not be represented in negotiations with the Reference Entity. On the other hand, if the protection Buyer delivers Obligations to the protection Seller, the protection Seller will acquire with those Obligations all the rights of the Buyer (direct or indirect) against the Reference Entity but may be exposed to the downside if the restructuring is unsuccessful.

The Credit Definitions expand the definition of a Restructuring. They still include materiality as a concept and require that the Restructuring results from a deterioration in creditworthiness, but they also specify: (a) changes in the terms of the Reference Obligation that are considered important (including the ranking of the debt, a change in the currency of payment, or a change in the date of payment or amount of any interest or principal) and (b) changes that are not material (such as conversion of a payment obligation to payments in Euro when the Obligation was originally denominated in a legacy currency).

Restructuring also includes any Obligation Exchange, which is separately defined to be the mandatory transfer of new assets, securities, or obligations in exchange for existing Obligations (other than in accordance with the terms of the existing Obligations). Since any transfer must be mandatory, this may not include an arrangement to defer or restructure debt agreed to by holders of the relevant Obligation (but such an arrangement may fall within the definition of the Bankruptcy Credit Event). This will also be the case in relation to Obligation Acceleration or Obligation Default or any Failure to Pay, if, before the relevant Credit Event has occurred, the holders of the relevant Obligation agree with the Reference Entity to renegotiate the terms of the Obligation.

Two credit events included in the long-form Credit Swap Confirmation are left out of the Credit Definitions. The downgrade Credit Event enabled the parties to agree a minimum rating with a payment potentially being triggered if a Reference Obligation fell below that rating or if the public debt of the Reference Entity ceased to be rated by any specified rating agency. Transactions based on this type of provision had proved difficult to price — particularly in the light of perceived inconsistencies in the ratings of emerging markets issuers. Credit Event Upon Merger reflected the similar provision, which is a Termination Event under the ISDA Master Agreement.[118] A Credit Event would occur if the Reference Entity were to merge with or transfer its assets to another entity and the resulting entity were materially weaker. The problem with this is that the test is too subjective. It is difficult to say with any precision what is meant by "materially weaker."

17.4.3   Cash and Physical Settlement

Although the occurrence of a Credit Event is the trigger for payments by the protection Seller, the Credit Event itself does not crystallize that payment as being due (that is, there is no immediate binding obligation on the protection Seller). Instead, an obligation to pay only becomes binding on the protection Seller once the conditions specified in Article III[119] of the Credit Definitions have been satisfied, and in the case of Cash Settlement,[120] once the Reference Obligations are valued, or in the case of Physical Settlement,[121] when the protection Seller receives any Deliverable Obligations (on a delivery versus payment basis).

The requirements in Article III are notice requirements. The terms of the transaction will specify whether the Buyer or both the Buyer and Seller of credit protection should deliver notice of any credit event which occurs. To the extent also required, the same party or parties must also give notice of any Publicly Available Information[122] confirming that a Credit Event exists. The date notice of a Credit Event is effective (or if both notices are required on which both notices are effective) is the Event Determination Date[123] under the Credit Definitions. If Cash Settlement applies the Calculation Agent is then required to value any payment to be made by the protection Seller. If Physical Settlement applies, the protection Buyer must then deliver a further notice[124] detailing the obligations it intends to deliver (described as the Portfolio) within 30 days. The Credit Definitions do not contain any requirements in relation to the timing of

---

[118] See Section 5(b)(iv) of the ISDA Master Agreement

[119] Tthe Conditions to Payment

[120] As defined in Section 7.1 of the Credit Definitions

[121] As defined in Section 8.1 of the Credit Definitions

[122] As defined in Section 3.5 of the Credit Definitions

[123] As defined in Section 1.8 of the Credit Definitions

[124] The Notice of Intended Physical Settlement as defined in Section 3.4 of the Credit Definitions

notices following a Credit Event, and there is no requirement that the Credit Event has both occurred and is continuing. In theory, therefore, a notice is possible at any time during the remainder of the transaction.

In relation to Cash Settlement, the Calculation Agent is required to value each Reference Obligation. The provisions relating to valuation allow the parties to choose either that a single Valuation Date[125] should apply or that multiple Valuation Dates be used. They also contemplate that there may be more than one Reference Obligation. A valuation is calculated by seeking Quotations[126] from reference Dealers[127] for a specified amount[128] of the relevant Reference Obligation. The parties may agree whether Quotations used should be the Highest[129] given or a Market[130] value based on the average of Quotations from several Dealers. In addition, the parties may agree whether Quotations should be based on a Dealer's Bid or Offer prices or that Dealer's Mid-market" price.[131] The Calculation Agent may equally be required to calculate an average value over several Valuation Dates if multiple Valuation Dates apply. The amount payable by the protection Seller (the Cash Settlement Amount[132]) will equal the product of the notional amount[133] of the transaction multiplied by the difference between the Reference Price agreed at the outset of the transaction and the Final Price[134] resulting from the Calculation Agent's valuations.

Quotations are to be given by Dealers for a transaction in the Reference Obligation with a face (due and payable) value equal to or greater than the Quotation Amount agreed by the parties. If no amount is otherwise specified the Credit Definitions, assume this will be the same as the nominal amount of the credit swap itself. If it is impossible to get such Quotations, then the Calculation Agent can calculate a value based on Weighted Average Quotations[135] for a sale or purchase of a lesser amount of the Reference Obligation. Again, the parties

---

[125] As defined in Section 7.5 of the Credit Definitions
[126] As defined in Section 7.8 of the Credit Definitions
[127] As defined in Section 7.15 of the Credit Definitions
[128] The Quotation Amount as defined in Section 7.12 of the Credit Definitions
[129] As defined in Section 7.11(a)(ii) of the Credit Definitions
[130] As defined in Section 7.11(a)(i) of the Credit Definitions
[131] Each as defined in Section 7.6 of the Credit Definitions
[132] As defined in Section 7.3 of the Credit Definitions
[133] The Floating Rate Payer Calculation Amount as defined in Section 2.13 of the Credit Definitions
[134] As defined in Section 7.4 of the Credit Definitions
[135] As defined in Section 7.10 of the Credit Definitions

can specify a minimum amount[136] for any such Quotations. Unless otherwise stated, this minimum amount is deemed to be the lower of the nominal amount of the transaction and US$1 million. The level of the minimum amount for Weighted Average Quotations is important because if no such Quotation is available, then the value of the relevant Reference Obligation is deemed to be zero.

If there are more than one Reference Obligations specified, the parties will need to agree on a Minimum Quotation Amount for Quotations (and Weighted Average Quotations) for each Reference Obligation. The Calculation Agent will seek Quotations for a transaction for each relevant Reference Obligation based on these amounts. Again, the same possibilities apply as to whether the Highest or a Market value be calculated. Where there are multiple Reference Obligations and Quotations are not available for a particular Reference Obligation, this Reference Obligation will be deemed to have a value of zero even if Quotations are available for the other Reference Obligations. The Credit Definitions require that the eventual valuation be a blended[137] Final Price based on the unweighted arithmetic mean of the different values. This is because the Credit Definitions require there to be a single Final Price to calculate the Cash Settlement Amount (and in this sense, the definition of Final Price assumes a single Reference Obligation). When the parties agree on a single Reference Price at the outset of the transaction, it will, therefore, also apply as a blended price to all Reference Obligations.

The Reference Price agreed at the outset may sometimes require other terms to be modified. The Cash Settlement Amount is defined by reference to the "difference" between the Reference Price and the Final Price. Since the difference is always positive, if the Reference Price is below the Final Price a positive number will still result. In practice, this should not usually happen because the Credit Events require the Reference Entity to be Bankrupt or Obligations to be in default, or not be being repaid. Where the Credit Event is a Restructuring of the Reference Obligation, then a materiality requirement is imposed before the Credit Event is triggered. These events should lead to a drop in the value of the Reference Obligation. However, if at the outset of the transaction the underlying Reference Obligation is already trading as distressed credit-impaired debt, so that the Reference Price is only a fraction of the face

---

[136] The Minimum Quotation Amount, as defined in Section 7.13 of the Credit Definitions
[137] Blended Market, Blended Highest, Average Blended Market, or Average Blended Highest, each as defined in Section 7.11 of the Credit Definitions

value, then the Final Price may end up higher than the Reference Price. If this is a possibility, the definition of Cash Settlement Amount should be amended to refer to the excess (if any) of the Reference Price over the Final Price.

Cash Settlement may raise particular issues for the protection Seller if the relevant Credit Event is a Restructuring. So far as its rights under the Credit Definitions are concerned, the protection Seller does not have any representation in negotiations with the Reference Entity or an ability to influence the outcome of negotiations (for example, by a right to vote on any proposal). This follows from the fact that there is no requirement for the protection Buyer to have an interest in any Obligations, or indeed to suffer any loss as a result of the Credit Event. The protection Seller (or Buyer if it does hold any Obligations) may therefore be exposed in the sense that the negotiations surrounding a Restructuring may eventually improve the position of the Reference Entity, or at least put a floor under the potential downside (or vice versa). Of course the protection Seller, or one of its affiliates, may have other relationships with the Reference Entity and may take a leading role in dealings between creditors and the Reference Entity (for example, if the protection Seller is the administrative agent under a Loan, or trustee of a Bond). However, any such rights would be completely distinct from rights under the Credit Definitions.

If the protection Seller wishes to avoid being left out of negotiations and acquire rights against the Reference Entity, directly or indirectly, the easiest solution is for the parties to agree that Physical Settlement should apply. To the extent that the protection Seller is required to make any payment, it will then acquire Obligations of the Reference Entity, and so will be able to exercise all the rights attached to them. Alternatively, if Cash Settlement applies, the parties may agree that the protection Buyer will exercise any rights attaching to (a specified amount of) Obligations it holds as directed by the protection Seller. This may be the preferred approach from a commercial point of view: particularly if the transaction is, say, a total return swap (discussed below). The problem is that the protection Buyer should not be required to hold any Obligations implicitly or expressly under the terms of the transaction. If such a requirement does exist then it is arguable that there is a requirement that the protection Buyer suffers a loss before any payment is due from the protection Seller. If this is required, the contract comes closer to resembling an insurance contract. Recharacterization in this way would cause far more significant damage to the interests of the protection Seller than not being represented in negotiations. To the extent that the terms of the transaction clearly state that the protection Buyer is not required to hold Obligations, the covenant is of course significantly weaker, although this may avoid the transaction being treated as something other than a credit derivative transaction.[138]

On the other hand, the protection Seller or protection Buyer's concern may only be that a single valuation of the Reference Obligations may not accurately reflect the change in creditworthiness of the Reference Entity. If this is the case, then a possible solution is to provide that multiple Valuation Dates be used and that the Cash Settlement Amount be calculated based on an average of the different Quotations (or as otherwise agreed between the parties). However, the benefits of this will be limited if the restructuring is a drawn-out affair.

If it applies, Physical Settlement must take place within the usual time-frame based on market practice for the Obligations being delivered unless the number of days is specified. Since the protection Buyer has control of the make-up of the Portfolio, it can decide whether to exercise its rights in relation to the full nominal amount of the transaction, or only in part. If the protection Buyer chooses to deliver Obligations denominated in currencies other than the agreed base currency,[139] the value of the Obligations will be converted into the base currency at spot exchange rates.[140]

On delivery, the protection Buyer makes representations that it can deliver full title to the relevant Obligations and that they are generally free of any set-off, counterclaim, or defense that the Reference Entity might have against the protection Buyer (except to the extent that such a counterclaim or defense relates to the legality or validity of the Obligation itself).[141] Problems may arise where delivery turns out to be difficult to effect, but only after the protection Buyer has given notice. This is particularly an issue in relation to Loans that may not be easily transferable. The Credit Definitions provide that any failure to deliver by the protection Buyer does not create an Event of Default under the ISDA Master Agreement (which would otherwise be the case under Section 5(a)(i)).[142] Instead, the transaction will terminate with no further obligation on either party, except that there is a fall-back to Cash Settlement in certain circumstances. Where the fall-back applies, the parties will settle by physical

---

[138] This is the approach taken in relation to voting rights on shares to avoid the risk of recharacterization as a secured loan under the 1997 Equity Annex to the 1995 PSA/ISMA Global Master Repurchase Agreement

[139] The Settlement Currency as defined in Section 6.3 of the Credit Definitions which provides a fall-back of the currency of the Floating Rate Payer Calculation Amount

[140] The Currency Rate as defined in Section 8.9 of the Credit Definitions

[141] See Section 9.3 of the Credit Definitions

[142] See Section 9.3(c)(ii) of the Credit Definitions

delivery to the extent possible and will settle the remaining part by payment of a proportionate Cash Settlement Amount.

Cash Settlement will apply if the protection Buyer is unable to deliver any or all of the Obligations specified in the Portfolio as a result of some supervening illegality or impossibility.[143] An illegality or impossibility is defined as any event occurring that affects the obligations of either the protection Seller or the protection Buyer and that is beyond their control. Unlike the ISDA Master Agreement,[144] the Credit Definitions do not expressly require the illegality or impossibility to arise as a result of any changes in law. Impossibility expressly includes clearance system failure and illegality expressly includes the effect of any law, regulation, or court order. The wording expressly excludes market conditions or a failure to obtain consent to assignment in relation to a Loan. Of course there may be borderline situations. In these situations, the parties may choose instead to effect or receive delivery through an Affiliate[145] in accordance with Section 9.3 (for example, where the problem is selling restrictions in the terms of an Obligation).

The Credit Definitions also permit the parties to elect that Cash Settlement will apply as a fall-back where it proves impossible to assign any Loans or to transfer Loans via participations. The parties may distinguish between those Loans that are expressed to be assignable only by consent and those that do not require assent, and between Direct Loan Participations and Indirect Loan Participations, where the economic interest in a loan is transferred by a participation agreement involving credit risk on the other person (direct) or persons (indirect) in the chain.

Physical Settlement may be a particular problem if the Credit Event that occurs is Bankruptcy of the Reference Entity. In terms of the legal landscape, bankruptcy involves a sea change. A bankruptcy requires the rights of all creditors against the insolvent to be accelerated and valued as of the same date. As a result, although their economic terms do not change, the obligations of the Reference Entity metamorphosize. Whereas before bankruptcy, claims against the Reference Entity may take different legal forms (whether a loan, a negotiable security, or a claim for damages), after bankruptcy each creditor has the same right to prove in the liquidation proceedings for payment at the insolvency dividend rate. The value of the proof is defined by reference to whatever

---

[143] See Section 9.4 of the Credit Definitions

[144] Section 5(b)(i) of the ISDA Master Agreement

[145] As defined in Section 14 of the ISDA Master Agreement (see Section 1.17 of the Credit Definitions)

previously existed, but the legal nature of the proof is a totally new claim with different rights.

The question in each jurisdiction will be the date as of which this legal fiction takes place. For example, in England or Hong Kong, it is the date that a final winding-up order is made. The petition to wind up Peregrine Fixed Income Ltd (PFIL) was filed with the Hong Kong courts on January 15, 1998 and the next day the court gave an order appointing provisional liquidators. Then on March 18, 1998 there was a further hearing at which the winding-up order was made. From March 18, 1998, in theory, each claim against PFIL became a proof in the liquidation.

This may mean that the protection Buyer cannot deliver the Reference Obligation any more and the proof itself may also not be assignable. In practise, liquidators should not be too concerned about the identity of a claimant, and so should accept any assignment, except in two circumstances. First, liquidators may not wish to waste valuable resources where proofs are already submitted (and perhaps accepted) and would need to be resubmitted in the name of a different party. Second, the liquidators will be concerned if the transfer potentially changes rights of set-off. Under English law, a proof in liquidation is calculated on a net basis, that is for the net amount of all mutual obligations between the parties. Liquidators will not wish a transfer to proceed if a right of set-off exists between the insolvent and the transferor. Any set-off would in any case make it impossible for the protection Buyer to make representations that the delivered Obligations are free of any set-off by the Reference Entity. It is possible this will amount to an illegality or impossibility so that the Cash Settlement fall-back applies. However, problems regarding transferability of an Obligation may also affect Cash Settlement. Although some form of gray market in the Reference Obligations may exist, and liquidators may even announce an anticipated insolvency dividend rate, it may still prove difficult to get Quotations. It is quite likely, therefore, that the deemed valuation of the Reference Obligations will be zero.

The parties should also note that liquidators will not allow the protection Seller acquiring delivered Obligations to use this to create rights of set-off in its favor. Rules against any such build-up of set-off exist in probably all jurisdictions, and will have retroactive effect which may even predate the insolvency proceedings. As a result, a protection Seller should not consider that it is hedged merely by the fact that it owes any amounts to the Reference Entity. Such a hedge might be effective if Physical Settlement can take place before bankruptcy proceedings (including any retroactive provisions) take effect. However, this is not within the control of the protection Seller.

17.4.4   Confidentiality and Publicly Available Information

The Credit Definitions[146] and the long-form Credit Swap Confirmation both contain representations regarding the relationship between the parties and the Reference Entity. These make clear that, notwithstanding the existence of the transaction, the parties remain free to enter into any private arrangements with the Reference Entity, including contingent liability transactions such as derivative transactions, or to extend credit to the Reference Entity or take any steps to enforce rights against the Reference Entity, including steps that might trigger a Credit Event.

This reflects concerns that the contract should not be recharacterized as one that requires disclosure by the protection Buyer to the protection Seller, or that any duty of disclosure should not be implied as a term of the transaction. It also reflects concerns that a bank may owe a duty of confidentiality to the underlying Reference Entity if it has had any dealings with the Reference Entity. Whether or not this is the case will depend on the local jurisdiction. This would be a serious problem if a counterparty were required to breach confidentiality as a result of the credit derivative transaction and particularly if this would give rise to any criminal liability. However, it is difficult to see what problems can arise if any duty of disclosure is properly excluded, as is the case under the Credit Definitions.

Confidentiality does raise issues in terms of the contractual requirements to determine whether a Credit Event has occurred. A Buyer of protection, by virtue of its dealings with the Reference Entity, may have knowledge that a Credit Event has occurred but be unable to use this because it cannot give the relevant information to the protection Seller. Section 3.3 of the Credit Definitions states that any notice of a Credit Event to the other party must contain a description in reasonable detail of the relevant facts. If the parties desire, the Credit Definitions allow the terms of the transaction to exclude the use of such information altogether. The parties may elect that notice of a Credit Event may only be given when information about the relevant event is publicly available. If this is the case then, as well as notice of the Credit Event, the relevant party must also give notice confirming that the information is publicly available as one of the conditions before any payment becomes due from the protection Seller.

The Credit Definitions define Publicly Available Information to include the contents of any official court papers where proceedings are begun to wind up the

---

[146] See Article IX of the Credit Definitions

Reference Entity, or the contents of any judicial order, or decree of any regulatory authority. Publicly Available Information also includes information that is made available by a trustee or administrative agent for the relevant Obligation(s) (in which case this is likely to be a Bond or a Loan) or that is published by any news service. The Credit Definitions contain a list of standard news services.[147] However, a party cannot rely on any information where it, or any associated company, is cited as the sole source of the information by the news service unless the information is corroborated, or unless it was provided while acting in a fiduciary capacity, for example, as trustee of a Bond. Although information about the event must be publicly available, the information does not itself need to detail whether all relevant criteria have been satisfied: such as Grace Periods, threshold amounts, or any subjective criteria about materiality. These issues must be resolved by the Calculation Agent.

Publicly Available Information is sometimes referred to as a "bright line" evidencing whether payment is due. This reflects concerns of the regulators in the early days of the market that it would be impossible to tell when the obligations of the protection Seller were triggered and the resulting concern that credit derivatives would not be effective hedging instruments. Of course Publicly Available Information does serve an evidential purpose. However, this argument does have disadvantages. At the fringes, there have been instances where one party argued that a payment was due based on press rumors where subsequently no Credit Event was found to have occurred. More importantly, this approach may lead to an assumption that Publicly Available Information should set out all the required facts (such as the expiration of Grace Periods or the amount of a default) before the occurrence of a Credit Event is established.

In fact, the effect of the Publicly Available Information requirement is as much to delay payments that would otherwise be due as to confirm the obligation to pay. This protects the protection Seller so that it is able to use information about the Credit Event under any hedging transaction by which it has sought to lay off its risk. Otherwise, the protection Seller may be prevented from using such information, for example, by confidentiality requirements. In *Deutsche Bank AG v ANZ Banking Group Ltd*,[148] the information about a default by the City of Moscow was placed with a news service at the instigation of Daiwa Europe (a protection Buyer) to trigger a claim against Deutsche Bank AG. Deutsche Bank then (successfully) sought to use this information in making

---

[147] See the definition of Public Source in Section 3.7 of the Credit Definitions
[148] Ibid

a claim under a back-to-back transaction with ANZ. In this sense, it does not matter how the information got into the public domain (apart from, of course, from the point of view of the Reference Entity and any person releasing the information in breach of its obligations) or whether it clearly evidences every detail. The defenses raised by ANZ on these points were roundly dismissed. On the other hand, it still matters that the information is true.

17.4.5   Dispute Resolution

Both the long-form Credit Swap Confirmation and the Credit Definitions contain separate dispute resolution language.[149] The Credit Definitions also state that ISDA intends to publish the ISDA Dispute Resolution Guidelines[150] and the Credit Definitions allow the parties to incorporate these by reference if they are published as at the Trade Date[151] of the transaction: draft guidelines are not yet available. Credit derivatives were caught up in the crisis surrounding the Russian moratorium in August 1998 before standardized documentation was widely used. Such stress-testing of the economic terms of transactions early on in the life of a new derivative product has not been experienced before. Currently, it is, therefore, intended that the ISDA Dispute Resolution Guidelines will be directed specifically at credit derivatives, and once published will supersede the language currently in Section 10.2 of the Credit Definitions, which will no longer be applicable.

In fact, the Russian crisis provoked disputes across a broad range of transactions. For example, in relation to currency transactions, price sources disappeared when the Russian central bank suspended trading in the rouble at the Moscow Interbank Currency Exchange. However, credit derivatives are unusual in that the trigger for payment (usually) depends on a legal analysis rather than movements in prices or an index. This makes the role of Calculation Agent more difficult, because it may be required to make subjective decisions on these points. Section 1.13 of the Credit Definitions sets out a list of the different areas in which the Calculation Agent is required to act.

The dispute resolution language in Section 10.2 (and which was previously in the long-form Credit Swap Confirmation) is relatively narrow in scope. It applies in the event that one party disputes any determination (or failure to make a determination) by the Calculation Agent; the effect is that a disinterested third-

---

[149] See Section 10.2 of the Credit Definitions
[150] As defined in Section 10.1 of the Credit Definitions
[151] As defined in Section 1.5 of the Credit Definitions

party financial institution be appointed Calculation Agent instead and should then review any decision retroactively exercising its discretion.

However, the Credit Definitions significantly expand the role played by each of the parties in the Calculation Agent's deliberations. Under the 1991 ISDA Definitions[152] (as amended by the 1998 Supplement),[153] the Calculation Agent is required to act in good faith and "after consultation with ... the parties"[154] when seeking quotations.[155] By contrast, the Credit Definitions provide that if the Calculation Agent cannot obtain Quotations to establish a value for any Obligations, then either or both parties can seek Quotations. The Calculation Agent will then use any Quotations the parties obtain in making its determinations. The Credit Definitions specify a fall-back if Quotations are still unobtainable, that the value will be deemed to be zero.

Valuation is only one issue that may give rise to a dispute. The ISDA Dispute Resolution Guidelines are likely to be more wide-ranging and cover issues such as whether a Credit Event has been triggered. Although ISDA's current project relates only to credit derivatives, there is no reason why future guidelines should not be more generic. As a genre, dispute resolution guidelines are aimed primarily at disputes between financial institutions. Where the problem is a dispute between a financial institution and an end user, it is more likely that the appropriate forum should be a court. Such disputes are less likely to focus on the express terms of the trade and more on the relationship between the parties and their respective states of knowledge. However, when disputes occur regarding the terms of a transaction, the same issues will usually affect a large number of transactions with similar characteristics. Ultimately, the market needs these issues to be resolved with speed and consistency, whatever the type of underlying risk. A counterparty that has hedged its exposure with another transaction will wish to ensure that the same decisions are reached on the interpretation of the terms of each transaction. To allow this, counterparties will also need to make sure that the transactions are drafted in the same way and so avoid "legal basis risk" that is, a mis-match. The Credit Definitions should help in this respect.

---

[152] Which are primarily designed for interest rate and currency transactions but which may be incorporated in the long-form Credit Swap Confirmation by reference

[153] The 1998 Supplement to the 1991 ISDA Definitions

[154] See Section 4.14 of the 1991 ISDA Definitions

[155] For example, to determine a Floating Rate under Article 7 of the 1991 ISDA Definitions

17.5   Other Documentation

17.5.1   Price and Spread Materiality

As well as the Credit Definitions, ISDA is working on a Materiality Annex. A final draft of this was not available at the time of writing. However, Materiality language was included in the long-form Credit Swap Confirmation and the first drafts of the Materiality Annex use the same approach. ISDA's Materiality wording allows the parties to build into the terms of the transaction a price or spread related element. The ISDA documentation conceives this as supplemental to any specified Credit Event: once the Credit Event has happened, the Calculation Agent will determine whether or not it is material by reference to changes in the price or spread of the Reference Obligation compared to a benchmark. However, Materiality has proved difficult to apply in practice. Generally, the market still prefers to use defined Credit Events, rather than a price or spread-related event.

Price Materiality[156] is kept relatively simple in relation to a floating rate Reference Obligation by the long-form Credit Swap Confirmation. It requires the Calculation Agent to compare the spot price[157] to a reference price[158] and determine whether the difference between the two exceeds the specified Price Decline Requirement.[159] In relation to a fixed rate Reference Obligation, the long-form Credit Swap Confirmation requires the price to be adjusted first to take into account changes in floating rates of interest,[160] before a comparison of the change in price of the Reference Obligation and the Price Decline Requirement can be effected. To do this, changes in the floating rate of interest are backed-out by valuing a hypothetical fixed/floating rate swap where the fixed leg is equal to the fixed return on the Reference Obligation. However, although the procedure is complex, the result is still not precise. It assumes that swap prices are not affected by anything other than anticipated interest rate movements. Of course this is not true. It also assumes that the price of a floating rate instrument does not adjust to reflect other concerns apart from credit risk on the issuer. Again, this is not quite true.

---

[156] As defined in the long-form Credit Swap Confirmation
[157] The Market Price as defined in the long-form Credit Swap Confirmation
[158] The Initial Price as defined in the long-form Credit Swap Confirmation
[159] As defined in the long-form Credit Swap Confirmation
[160] By the Interest Rate Adjustment Amount as defined in the long-form Credit Swap Confirmation

Spread Materiality[161] relates not to the price of the Reference Obligation, but the yield. The formula used requires the Calculation Agent to calculate a yield for the Reference Obligation expressed as a percentage and based on the Reference Obligation's maturity. This may not work if the Reference Obligation has already matured (and the issuer has defaulted on payments of principal) or has been accelerated. Spread Materiality should, therefore, only be used following certain Credit Events. For example, for a transaction documented using the Credit Definitions, it should not apply if the Credit Event that has occurred is Bankruptcy (which, depending on the relevant insolvency law, may result in the automatic acceleration of Obligations) or Obligation Acceleration. In these circumstances, the parties will probably accept that the Credit Event is material or will need to establish some other way of determining its materiality. There are provisions built into the definition of Bankruptcy in the Credit Definitions that guard against any Credit Event occurring merely as a result of a technical breach. For example, in relation to the presentation of a petition to wind up the Reference Entity, there is a requirement that the petition results in a court order in favor of the petitioner or is not dismissed within 30 days. As far as Obligation Acceleration is concerned, there is a threshold amount that applies, so that the Credit Event only triggers if the affected Obligations are of sufficient value.

Whether a Spread Materiality exists is determined by comparing this yield[162] to a benchmark yield and noting the difference. If the difference is greater than that at the outset of the transaction by the agreed Spread Widening Requirement[163] then a payment will become due. The benchmark yield used in the ISDA documentation is an Interpolated Swap Rate.[164] This represents the rate usually used to determine funding costs in the derivatives business and is commonly determined as a spread over US Treasury securities. The language in the long-form Credit Swap Confirmation assumes a US dollar calculation, although this is likely to be changed in the draft Materiality Annex. As with Price Materiality, there will also be an element of basis risk (or mis-match) in comparing different spreads. Swap spreads may vary depending not only on the credit quality of the potential counterparty, but also market factors such as the strength of corporate bond issuance and the availability and cost of hedging instruments.

---

[161] As defined in the long-form Credit Swap Confirmation
[162] The Reference Obligation Yield as defined in the long-form Credit Swap Confirmation
[163] As defined in the long-form Credit Swap Confirmation
[164] As defined in the long-form Credit Swap Confirmation

17.5.2   Credit Spread Transactions

A credit spread transaction refers to a transaction where payments are calculated based on the difference in yield between a reference obligation and a benchmark obligation. These are not covered by the Credit Definitions. However, the Spread Materiality concept discussed earlier is based on the same principles, even though it is used only to calculate whether a payment is due and not the amount of a payment. In fact, a credit spread transaction is used to refer only to the way in which the amount of any payment is calculated, and such transactions may be structured in a number of different ways. In each case, this will require separate drafting of a confirmation not using the Credit Definitions, but (in theory at least) this should be relatively straightforward. Although there is no generally accepted language addressing the relevant points, the legal technology often exists in relation to other types of derivative transaction. It is just a question of transferring it.

Payment obligations under a credit spread transaction may be asymmetric, with a payment only becoming due from one party if a "strike yield" is breached. In this case, the structure will be similar to ISDA's Spread Materiality language, although without reference to any Credit Event. Comparison of the current yield with a strike yield is effectively the same as the calculation of the Spread Widening Requirement. However, the Materiality provisions drafted by ISDA are not intended to be used to calculate payments, but only to validate or invalidate a Credit Event. They, therefore, allow the Calculation Agent a high degree of discretion in fixing a price or yield. Where the calculation is used to quantify payments, this may not work. The Calculation Agent is allowed to use its own judgement in most instances in converting screen rates to a market rate and is not required to seek quotations from dealers. It is also required to exercise its judgement on how rates should be interpolated without any detailed provisions determining how this is done. Therefore, although ISDA's language is a useful precedent, the parties will probably require these procedures to be set out in more detail. On a commercial level, the parties will also need to consider which benchmark yield and which other parameters (such as the timing of valuations of both legs and the applicable day count fraction) are appropriate. Alternatively, a credit spread transaction may be structured as a forward or as a swap with a series of payments due from each party. In that case, one party will pay amounts based on the yield of the reference obligation and the other party will pay amounts based on a benchmark. The benchmark will usually be a risk-free rate (for example, the yield on US government securities). It could, however, be another more liquid obligation of the reference entity (or a correlating risk), if the transaction is an arbitrage on the way these are priced. The same considerations will apply to calculating the yield for payments by each party as are discussed in relation to a strike yield above. In other respects, the structure will be similar to a standard swap with Floating Amounts payable by one or both of the parties.

Since the trigger for payments under a credit spread transaction is based on price rather than a legal event, the parties will also need to consider what adjustments or extraordinary events may need to apply. The Credit Events listed in the Credit Definitions are events that may affect the transaction in this sense. If an obligation is accelerated, it will not have a yield. The terms of an obligation may also be relevant. The obligation may contain an express right for the issuer to redeem or convert the securities in certain circumstances. The parties should decide what will happen in these circumstances. Will the transaction continue by reference to some other obligation or underlying Reference Entity? Or will it terminate, and if so, on what terms? Given the ongoing nature of the calculations, the parties may also prefer to use price sources other than reference banks, for (parts of) the Calculation Agent's determinations for such transactions. In that case, it will be necessary to specify what will happen in the event of any price source disruption. Equally, language to deal with price source disruption has been standardized for transactions with many other types of underlying risk.

17.5.3 Total Return Transactions

The Credit Definitions also do not contain provisions relating to total return transactions. There is, therefore, no standard market language for credit derivative transactions that are total return transactions. However, a total return transaction is very similar to an unfunded subparticipation agreement. These have traditionally been used between banks to transfer loan risk on an indemnity basis. In fact, a participation is one way in which the parties may arrange for Physical Settlement of a credit default swap with a Loan as the underlying risk under the Credit Definitions. The protection Seller receives manufactured payments equal to interest on the loan adjusted to reflect funding costs and in return for giving an indemnity if the borrower defaults. If the participation is funded, then the protection Seller stumps up a cash amount equal to the interest in the loan being acquired; the protection Seller then receives amounts equal to all payments of interest in full and repayment of the cash at maturity to the extent the borrower repays. The difference between a credit derivative and a participation agreement mainly comes in the way the two agreements are documented and the underlying risks managed. A participation agreement has always been treated as a banking book product for capital adequacy purposes, whereas a credit derivative may be treated as a trading book product.

Total return language is included in the 1996 ISDA Equity Derivatives Definitions (the Equity Definitions). The Equity Definitions define Total Return[165] to be a combination of income received and the change in price of the reference securities. It is equally possible to apply this formula to credit derivatives. The change in price is measured as the product of the number of reference securities multiplied by their Initial Price (their price as at the date this was previously calculated) multiplied by a Rate of Return. The Rate of Return is a fraction where the numerator is the spot price[166] minus the Initial Price and the denominator is the Initial Price calculated ((Spot Price − Initial Price) ÷ Initial Price). The reason for using this particular formula (rather than a more simple version) is that it works well with all types of transaction, including baskets and transactions where income is reinvested (to increase the nominal amount).

In fact, credit derivatives are easier than equity derivatives in the sense that concerns about changes to the capital structure or ownership of the issuer are not as prevalent. To the extent that there may be adjustments to the terms and conditions of a debt obligation these are defined in the Credit Events included in the Credit Definitions. As with credit spread products, it is still important for the parties to decide in advance the outcome for the transaction if, for example, there is a restructuring, mandatory exchange of assets, securities or obligations, or repudiation of the underlying obligation. Given the parallels with participation agreements, it is tempting for the protection Seller to want issues to be resolved in the same way. In terms of adjustments, a protection Seller which is a bank may also wish to reserve the right to adjust pricing if the capital adequacy treatment of the transaction changes, in the same way that an "increased costs" clause under an underlying loan may allow the lender of record to pass on capital adequacy costs to the borrower. This might make sense if the protection buyer would otherwise benefit from a windfall profit: that is, if the terms of an underlying loan could be adjusted without any corresponding adjustment to a total return transaction hedging the exposure. However, the capital adequacy treatment of the two transactions may be quite different. The biggest factor affecting the capital adequacy cost for a credit derivative transaction is whether it is treated as a banking book or trading book exposure.

---

[165] See Section 7.1 of the Equity Definitions
[166] The Final Price as defined in Section 7.10 of the Equity Definitions

Another example, the protection Seller may seek to impose covenants that votes relating to the underlying reference obligation will only be exercised in accordance with its instructions in a creditors' meeting. The temptation to do this may be stronger the less liquid the underlying Reference Obligation. On the other hand, in order to benefit from the regulatory, tax, and accounting regimes that apply to derivative transactions, the parties will want to make the terms of the transaction as synthetic (and therefore, as standard as possible). As discussed above in relation to Cash Settlement under the Credit Definitions, it is difficult to put the protection Seller in the shoes of a holder of the underlying reference obligation (for example, by imposing covenants on the protection Buyer regarding exercise of rights against the reference entity) without disturbing the legal analysis of the transaction. At its worst, this can make it much more likely that the transaction will be recharacterized as something else (such as an insurance contract) with unacceptable consequences.

17.5.4   Credit Linked Notes

Attached as Appendix II to this Chapter is a form of credit linked note. A credit derivative transaction may take the form of a credit linked note for a number of reasons: often these will be connected with the investor (the purchaser of a note is usually the protection Seller). Compared with an OTC transaction, the issue of a structured note involves greater expense and effort. Documentation will usually involve external lawyers, and fees will need to be paid to a paying agent and registrar and, if applicable, for listing of the note on an exchange. However, notes differ from OTC derivatives in the way that they are regulated. While the OTC market is essentially a wholesale market for professionals, notes can be sold to many different types of investor.

A credit linked note may, therefore, be used if the investor has the capacity and authority to purchase notes (including structured notes) but not to enter into OTC transactions. This is often the case with trustees or managers of a collective investment scheme whose powers of investment are limited. Often, investment managers operate under powers that have been granted under outdated documentation or are prescribed by legislation. However, these restrictions may be justified for other reasons. Unlike an OTC transaction, the holder of a note can (in theory) realize his investment by selling it and so can control the risk. A credit linked note is also likely to appear on the purchaser's balance-sheet (although the contingent nature of the return may not) whereas an OTC transaction will probably be treated as off-balance sheet.

From the point of view of the issuer, a credit linked note has the same economic effect as taking collateral for an OTC transaction. The issuer can use the subscription moneys for the note to discharge any contingent liability of the investor (as protection Seller) under the credit derivative transaction embedded in the terms of the note. The proceeds of redemption that are returned to the investor at maturity are reduced accordingly. The issuer, therefore, takes no credit risk on the investor. However, unlike an OTC transaction where the obligations of each party are personally enforceable by the other party, no further obligation beyond the initial payment of the subscription moneys can be imposed on the holder of a note. This is because a note is by definition transferable, and could simply be abandoned if its terms were onerous. As a result, there is always a cap on the liability of the holder.

Calculations required under a credit linked note will be the responsibility of the issuer. Moreover, since the issuer is responsible for drafting the documentation, it can make exercise of its discretion subject to such contractual duties of good faith and fair dealing as it thinks appropriate. Although the purchaser may be keen to check that the commercial terms match those set out in any indicative terms sheet, there is unlikely to be much negotiation of the legal terms. This favors the issuer, allowing documentation to be more one-sided (by, for example, not including any events of default).

17.6 Summary

The law relating to credit derivatives is a sizable and complex topic. In this chapter, I have tried to do two quite different things. The first is a discussion of general legal issues. In this, much of the ground I have covered has already been substantially debated before, and on a number of points, a consensus is beginning to emerge about how credit derivatives should be treated. No doubt there are other points that have not yet been raised or discussed in detail and that are also relevant. (These can be saved for the next edition.) Usually, the issues are not big issues in so far as they do not affect whether credit derivatives are legal or illegal. They involve placing credit derivatives in context and in particular how existing regulations should apply or not apply to them as a result.

In the second part of the chapter, I have discussed the documentation of credit derivatives, both in terms of publications that are intended to help with or standardize this, and in terms of the requirements of different types of transaction. This does more than simply illustrate the points made earlier in the chapter and so there is often no link between the two parts. However credit derivatives are still very new and so the relevant documentation is not yet well-known. This newness is the overriding theme of this chapter.

Appendix I — Annotated Form of Credit Swap Confirmation

[LETTERHEAD OF PARTY A]

[Party B]
[Address of Party B]

February 16, 2000

Dear Sirs,

Transaction Ref: XJS

The purpose of this letter (this "Confirmation") is to confirm the terms and conditions of the Credit Derivative Transaction entered into between us on the Trade Date specified below (the "Transaction"). This Confirmation constitutes a "Confirmation" as referred to in the ISDA Master Agreement specified below.

The definitions and provisions contained in the 1999 ISDA Credit Derivatives Definitions (the "Credit Derivatives Definitions") as published by the International Swaps and Derivatives Association, Inc., are incorporated into this Confirmation. In the event of any inconsistency between the Credit Derivatives Definitions and this Confirmation, this Confirmation will govern.

This Confirmation evidences a complete and binding agreement between you and us as to the terms of the Transaction to which this Confirmation relates. In addition, you and we agree to use all reasonable efforts promptly to negotiate, execute and deliver an agreement in the form of the ISDA Master Agreement (Multicurrency-Cross Border) (the "ISDA Form"), with such modifications as you and we will in good faith agree.[167] Upon the execution by you and us of such an agreement, this Confirmation will supplement, form part of, and be subject to that agreement. All provisions contained in or incorporated by reference in that agreement upon its execution will govern this Confirmation except as expressly modified below. Until we execute and deliver that

---

[167] This language is recommended where the parties have not yet agreed to an ISDA Master Agreement. It seeks to benefit as much as possible from the standard provisions of the ISDA Master Agreement (including close-out netting) by deeming that this Transaction and all other outstanding Transactions are part of the same hypothetical agreement

agreement, this Confirmation, together with all other documents referring to the ISDA Form (each a "Confirmation") confirming transactions (each a "Transaction") entered into between us (notwithstanding anything to the contrary in a Confirmation), shall supplement, form a part of, and be subject to, an agreement in the form of the ISDA Form as if we had executed an agreement in such form (but without any Schedule except for the election of English Law[168] as the governing law and the Euro as the Termination Currency)[169] on the Trade Date of the first such Transaction between us. In the event of any inconsistency between the provisions of that agreement and this Confirmation, this Confirmation will prevail for the purpose of this Transaction.

The terms of the Transaction to which this Confirmation relates are as follows:

1. General Terms

Trade Date:	February 14, 2000
Effective Date:	February 16, 2000
Scheduled Termination Date:[170]	February 17, 2001
Floating Rate Payer:	Party A (the "Seller")[171]
Fixed Rate Payer:	Party B (the "Buyer")[172]
Calculation Agent:	Seller[173]
Calculation Agent City:[174]	London[175]

---

[168] There is no fall-back for governing law

[169] The fall-back is US$ dollars

[170] The Termination Date may be extended to allow for settlement of the Transaction if a Credit Event occurs prior to the Scheduled Termination Date or to provide for a Grace Period if a Potential Failure to Pay occurs prior to the Scheduled Termination Date

[171] The protection Seller

[172] The protection Buyer

[173] The fall-back is that the Seller will be the Calculation Agent

[174] The Calculation Agent City is used to determine the timing of valuations and the effectiveness of any notices following a Credit Event

[175] The fall-back is the city in which the relevant branch of the Calculation Agent is situated

Business Day:[176]	A day on which the Trans-European Automated Real-Time Gross Settlement Express Transfer (TARGET) System is open[177]
Business Day Convention:	Modified Following[178] (which shall apply to any date referred to in this Confirmation that falls on a day that is not a Business Day[179] unless otherwise specified)
Reference Entity:	Uh-Oh PLC
Reference Obligation:[180]	The obligations identified as follows:

Primary Obligor:	Uh-Oh Finance NV
Guarantor:	Reference Entity
Maturity:	2004
Coupon:	9%
CUSIP/ISIN:	●
Original Issue Amount:	€100 million

Reference Price:[181]	100%[182]

---

[176] The Credit Definitions require valuations and payments to be made on a Business Day

[177] Additional language is necessary for Euro-zone Business Days to apply. The fall-back is the principal financial center for the currency of the Floating Rate Payer Calculation Amount

[178] The fall-back is the Modified Following Business Day Convention (that is the following Business Day unless the new date will be in the next calendar month in which case it is the preceding Business Day). The alternatives are the Following or Preceding Business Day Conventions

[179] The Credit Definitions suggest applying a Business Day Convention to all dates specified in the Confirmation in this way

[180] A Reference Obligation must be specified for Cash Settlement to apply

[181] The Cash Settlement Amount will be the difference between the Reference Price and the Final Price of the Reference Obligation

[182] The fall-back is 100%

2. Fixed Payments[183]

Fixed Rate Payer Calculation Amount:	Floating Rate Payer Calculation Amount[184]
Fixed Rate Payer Period End Dates:[185]	February 17, August 17. Not subject to adjustment[186]
Fixed Rate Payer Payment Dates:	February 17, August 17
Fixed Rate:	3% pa
Fixed Rate Day Count Fraction:[187]	Actual/360[188]

3. Floating Payment

Floating Rate Payer Calculation Amount:	€ 100,000
Conditions to Payment:[189]	Credit Event Notice
	Notifying Party: Buyer[190]
	Notice of Intended Settlement if Physical Settlement applies[191]
	Notice of Publicly Available Information: Applicable

---

[183] The Buyer makes one or more payments of a Fixed Amount during the life of the Transaction. If one payment is made, this is similar to a premium. If regular payments are made, these payments are often based on the yield on the Reference Obligation on the Trade Date. In the latter case, the Buyer may wish to match the calculation of any Fixed Amounts (such as the dates) to the terms of the Reference Obligation

[184] The fall-back is the Floating Rate Payer Calculation Amount

[185] Period End Dates are used to determine the Calculation Period for which a Fixed Amount is payable

[186] The fall-back is Fixed Rate Payer Payment Dates. The difference between the two in this Confirmation is the lack of adjustment for days which are not Business Days

[187] The Day Count Fraction is used to determine the number of days in the Calculation Period for which a Fixed Amount is payable

[188] The fall-back is Actual/360. The alternatives are Actual/Actual; Actual/365 (fixed); 30/360 (Bond Basis); and 30E/360 (Eurobond Basis)

[189] These requirements must be met before any payment is due from the Seller following a Credit Event

[190] The fall-back is Buyer. The alternative is Buyer or Seller

[191] If Physical Settlement applies the Buyer must give notice of the Portfolio it intends to deliver

Public Source(s): Standard Public Sources[192]

Specified Number: 2^{193}

Credit Events: The following Credit Events shall apply to this Transaction:[194]

Bankruptcy[195]
Failure to Pay[196]

Grace Period Extension:[197]   Applicable[198]

Grace Period: 30 calendar days[199]

Payment Requirement:[200]   € 1 million[201] or its equivalent in the relevant Obligation Currency as of the occurrence of the relevant Failure to Pay

---

[192] The fall-back is Standard Public Sources: these are Bloomberg Services, Dow Jones Telerate Service (now Bridge Telerate Service), Reuter Monitor Money Rules Services, Dow Jones News Wires, *Wall Street Journal*, *New York Times*, *Nikon Keizai Shimbun*, and *Financial Times*

[193] The fall-back is two

[194] The parties must elect which Credit Events apply. Possible Credit Events are Bankruptcy, Failure to Pay, Obligation Default, Obligation Acceleration, Repudiation/Moratorium, Restructuring

[195] Bankruptcy means bankruptcy of the Reference Entity

[196] Failure to Pay means a failure to make payments in excess of the Payment Requirement when due under any Obligations

[197] If Grace Period Extension applies and a Potential Failure to Pay occurs before the Scheduled Termination Date, the party responsible may deliver a Credit Event Notice with respect to a Failure to Pay occurring within the Grace Period even if this is after the Scheduled Termination Date

[198] The fall-back is that Grace Period Extension doesn't apply

[199] If Grace Period Extension applies, the fall-back is that the Grace Period will be no more than 30 calendar days

[200] Payment Requirement is a threshold amount that applies to the Failure to Pay Credit Event

[201] The fall-back is US$1 million

Obligation Default[202]
Obligation Acceleration[203]
Repudiation/Moratorium[204]
Restructuring[205]

Default Requirement:[206] €10 million[207] or its equivalent in the relevant Obligation Currency as of the occurrence of the relevant Credit Event

Obligations:[208]

Obligation Category:[209]	*Obligation Characteristics:*[210]
Bond or Loan	*Pari Passu* Ranking Not Contingent[211] Listed

---

[202] Obligation Default means Obligations in excess of the Default Requirement become capable of being declared due and payable as a result of an event of default or similar event

[203] Obligation Acceleration means Obligations in excess of the Default Requirement are declared due and payable as a result of an event of default or similar event

[204] Repudiation/moratorium means any repudiation of Obligations in excess of the Default Requirement by the Reference Entity or any government or self-imposed moratorium on payments under Obligations in excess of the Default Requirement

[205] Restructuring means any unilateral change to material terms of any Obligation or the mandatory exchange of Obligations for new Obligations with different terms

[206] Default Requirement is a threshold amount that applies to all Credit Events apart from Failure to Pay

[207] The fall-back is US$10 million

[208] Whether or not a Credit Event has occurred (other than Bankruptcy) will be determined by reference to any Obligations in the category and with the characteristics specified

[209] The parties should select only one category from Payment, Borrowed Money, Reference Obligations Only, Bond, Loan, or Bond or Loan

[210] The parties should select any characteristics from *Pari Passu* Ranking, Specified Currency, Not Sovereign Lender, Not Domestic Currency, Not Domestic Law, Listed, Not Contingent, Not Domestic Issuance

[211] Not Contingent excludes Obligations where payments are subject to a contingency or determined by reference to a formula or index

Excluded Obligations: None[212]

4. Settlement Terms
Settlement Method: Cash Settlement unless on or before the third Business Day following the Event Determination Date; Seller (by notice given in accordance with Section 3.9) requires Buyer to deliver a Notice of Intended Settlement[213]

Terms Relating to
  Cash Settlement:
Valuation Dates:[214]   Multiple Valuation Dates: Five Business Days[215] and each five Business Days thereafter
Number of Valuation Dates: Three[216]
Valuation Time: 11.00am, London time[217]
Quotation Method:[218]   Bid[219]
Quotation Amount:[220]   Floating Rate Payer Calculation Amount[221]
Minimum Quotation   Floating Rate Payer Calculation Amount[223]
  Amount:[222]

---

[212] The fall-back is none

[213] I have provided for cash or physical settlement to apply for purposes of illustration only. This would not normally be the case

[214] Valuation Dates are used to determine the Cash Settlement Amount by calculating a Final Price for Reference Obligation(s). The parties may choose the number of Valuation Dates. The valuation will be based on Quotations from Dealers

[215] The fall-back is five

[216] The fall-back is five

[217] The fall-back is 11:00AM in the Calculation Agent City

[218] The parties must choose between Bid, Offer, and Mid-market

[219] The fall-back is Bid

[220] Dealers will be asked to give Full Quotations for the Quotation Amount of the Reference Obligation

[221] The fall-back is the Floating Rate Payer Calculation Amount

[222] If Full Quotations are not available, dealers will be asked to give quotations for at least the Minimum Quotation Amount of the Reference Obligations. A Market Value calculated using such quotations will be the Weighted Average Quotation. If no Weighted Average Quotation is available, the Market Value will be deemed to be zero

Dealers:	Megabank, NA; Farmers Bank[224]
Settlement Currency:[225]	Euro[226]
Cash Settlement Date:	Three Business Days[227]
Cash Settlement Amount:[228]	The greater of: (a) Floating Rate Payer Calculation Amount multiplied by the excess of the Reference Price over the Final Price (if a positive amount) and (b) zero[229]
Market Value:	Exclude Accrued Interest[230]
Valuation Method:	Average Highest[231]

Terms Relating to
  Physical Settlement:

Physical Settlement Period:	Five Business Days[232]
Portfolio:[233]	Exclude Accrued Interest[234]

---

[223] The fall-back is the lesser of the Quotation Amount and US$1 million

[224] If no Dealers are specified they will be selected by the Calculation Agent in consultation with the parties

[225] The Cash Settlement Amount will be payable in the Settlement Currency

[226] The fall-back is the currency of the Floating Rate Payer Calculation Amount

[227] The fall-back is three Business Days following calculation of the Final Price

[228] If the parties agree at the outset to fix any payments by Seller following a Credit Event, this should be specified here, and the Cash Settlement Date will be three Business Days following satisfaction of all applicable Conditions to Payment

[229] The Credit Definitions refer to the difference between the Reference Price and the Final Price

[230] If not specified, the Calculation Agents will determine whether Quotations should include or exclude accrued interest

[231] Depending on the number of Reference Obligations and Valuation Dates, the parties must choose from among Market, Highest Average Market, Average Highest, Blended Market, Blended Highest, and Average Blended Market

[232] The fall-back is whatever is usual market practise for the Obligations concerned

[233] Following a Credit Event Notice, Buyer must give Seller notice of the Portfolio and amount of Deliverable Obligations it intends to deliver

[234] The fall-back is to exclude accrued interest

Deliverable Obligations:[235]

Deliverable Obligation Category:[236]	*Deliverable Obligation Characteristics:*[237]

Bond or Loan	*Pari Passu* Ranking
	Specified Currency:
	  US dollars or
	  the Euro
	Assignable Loan
	Direct Loan
	  Participation[238]
	Qualifying
	  Participation
	  Seller: any bank
	    rated at least
	    AA or
	    higher[239]
	Maximum Maturity:
	  10 years[240]
	  Not Contingent[241]

---

[235] Buyer may include in the Portfolio delivered to Seller any Obligations in the category and with the characteristics specified

[236] The parties should select only one category from Payment, Borrowed Money, Reference Obligations Only, Bond, Loan, or Bond or Loan

[237] The parties should select any characteristics from *Pari Passu* Ranking, Specified Currency, Not Sovereign Lender, Not Domestic Currency, Not Domestic Law, Listed, Not Contingent, Not Domestic Issuance, Assignable Loan, Consent Required Loan, Direct Loan Participation, Indirect Loan Participation, Transferable, Maximum Maturity, Accelerated or Matured, and Not Bearer

[238] A loan participation is a back-to-back arrangement where the lender of record manufactures payments to the participating party equal to receipts on the loan in return for funding or an indemnity

[239] The Seller will take counterparty credit risk on any Participation Seller

[240] The maximum period to maturity for any delivered Obligation is calculated from the Physical Settlement Date

[241] See above

Excluded Deliverable Obligations:	None[242]
Partial Cash Settlement of Loans:[243]	Applicable[244]
Partial Cash Settlement of Participations:[245]	Applicable[246]
Escrow:[247]	Not Applicable[248]

5. **Dispute Resolution:**[249]   Applicable[250]

6. **Notice and Account Details:**

Telephone, Telex and/or Facsimile Numbers and Contact Details for Notices:	●
Account Details	
Account Details of Buyer:	For account of Party B
Account Details of Seller:	For account of Party A

---

[242] The fall-back is none

[243] Partial Cash Settlement will apply if Physical Settlement is illegal or impossible, but the parties must elect if they also wish Partial Cash Settlement to apply where a Loan cannot be assigned due to lack of any requisite consents

[244] The fall-back is not applicable

[245] Partial Cash Settlement will apply if Physical Settlement is illegal or impossible, but the parties must elect if they also wish Partial Cash Settlement to apply where a Participation cannot be effected for any Loan

[246] The fall-back is not applicable

[247] Physical Settlement is on a delivery versus payment basis, but either party may require that Physical Settlement takes place using an escrow agent. The Schedule to an ISDA Master Agreement may contain additional provisions relating to the appointment of an escrow agent, but unless otherwise stated these provisions will over-ride in the event of any inconsistency (Section 1(b) of the ISDA Master Agreement)

[248] The fall-back is not applicable

[249] ISDA intends to publish Dispute Resolution Guidelines for Credit Derivatives.-If these are published as at the Trade Date, they may be incorporated into the terms of the Transaction. Section 10.2 of the Credit Definitions contains limited provisions relating to resolution of any disputes

[250] The fall-back is not applicable

Please confirm your agreement to be bound by the terms of the foregoing by executing a copy of this Confirmation and returning it to us by facsimile.

Yours sincerely,

PARTY A

By: _____

    Name:

    Title:

Confirmed as of the date
first above written:

PARTY B

By: _____

    Name:

    Title:

Appendix II — Form of Credit Linked Note

Reference No.: ●

THIS NOTE HAS NOT BEEN AND WILL NOT BE REGISTERED UNDER THE SECURITIES ACT OF 1933, AS AMENDED, (THE "SECURITIES ACT"), AND THIS NOTE MAY NOT BE OFFERED SOLD, PLEDGED OR OTHERWISE TRANSFERRED EXCEPT IN A TRANSACTION EXEMPT FROM, OR NOT SUBJECT TO, THE REGISTRATION REQUIREMENTS OF THE SECURITIES ACT AND ONLY WITH THE PRIOR CONSENT OF THE ISSUER.

POTENTIAL PURCHASERS OF THIS NOTE SHOULD BE AWARE THAT THE RETURN OF PRINCIPAL ON THIS NOTE IS LINKED TO THE VALUE OF SECURITIES. MOVEMENTS IN THE VALUE OF THOSE SECURITIES MAY ADVERSELY AFFECT THE VALUE OF THIS NOTE AND COULD RESULT IN PURCHASERS RECEIVING SECURITIES THE VALUE OF WHICH IS LESS THAN THE PRINCIPAL AMOUNT OF THIS NOTE.

THIS NOTE CONTAINS REPRESENTATIONS AND ACKNOWLEDGEMENTS TO BE MADE TO THE ISSUER BY ANY PURCHASER OF THIS NOTE — SEE CONDITION 7.

— NOTE —

SOUTH BANK LIMITED

£10,000,000
28 per cent. IGD Linked Notes due 2000

This Note forms one of a Series of Notes issued as registered Notes in the denomination of £100,000 each or an integral multiple thereof, in an aggregate principal amount of £10,000,000.

This is to certify that Orsino Nominees Limited is the registered holder of this Note (the "holder") in the principal amount of £100,000 (One Hundred Thousand Illyrian Pounds).

The Issuer for value received promises:

(i) if the Notes become due and redeemable in accordance with Condition 3(a)(i)(1), to redeem each Note at its principal amount on August 8, 2000; and

(ii) if the Notes become due and redeemable in accordance with Condition 3(a)(i)(2), the Issuer shall have no obligation to make any payment of principal to the holder and in such event the Issuer shall procure the delivery of the IGD Amount, to be made in accordance with and subject to the Conditions, together with any other amounts as may be patable, all subject to and under the Conditions.

THIS NOTE DOES NOT REPRESENT A BANK DEPOSIT OR SAVINGS ACCOUNT. IT IS AN UNSECURED OBLIGATION OF THE ISSUER AND IS NOT INSURED BY THE DEPOSIT INSURANCE FUND OR ANY OTHER GOVERNMENTAL AGENCY OR INSTRUMENTALITY.

This Note is issued subject to and with the benefit of the Conditions endorsed hereon.

This Note shall not be valid for any purpose unless and until it has been authenticated by or on behalf of The Trustee Company Limited, Verona branch as Registrar.

IN WITNESS WHEREOF this Note has been executed on behalf of the Issuer.

Dated August 2, 1999

SOUTH BANK LIMITED
By:

CERTIFICATE OF AUTHENTICATION
This is one of the Notes described
in the Agency Agreement

By or on behalf of
The Trustee Company Limited,
Verona branch as Registrar
(without recourse, warranty
or liability)

CONDITIONS OF THE NOTES

The issue of £10,000,000 28 per cent. IGD Linked Notes due 2000 (the "Notes") was authorized by a resolution of the board of directors of Issuer (the "Issuer") on January 15, 1998. Payments in respect of the Notes will be made pursuant to the terms of an Agency Agreement (the "Agency Agreement") dated August 2, 1999 made between the Issuer and The Trustee Company Limited, Verona branch as registrar (the "Registrar") and paying agent (the "Agent", which expression shall include any of its successors as such agent).

1. FORM, TITLE AND TRANSFERS

(a) **Form and Denomination**

The Note is in registered form in the denomination of £100,000 each or an integral multiple thereof.

(b) **Title**

Title to the Notes passes only by registration in the register of Noteholders. The holder of a Note will (except as otherwise required by law) be treated as its absolute owner for all purposes (whether or not it is overdue and regardless of any notice of ownership, trust or any interest in it, any writing on it, or its theft or loss) and no person will be liable for so treating the holder. In these Conditions "Noteholder" and (in relation to a Note) "holder" each means the person in whose name the Note is registered in the register of Noteholders.

(c) **Transfers**

Transfers of the Notes in whole or in part (in the denomination of £100,000) may be made in accordance with the regulations for transfer of the Notes from time to time in force maintained by the Agent.

2. **STATUS OF THE NOTES**

The Notes are direct, unconditional, and unsecured obligations of the Issuer and will rank *pari passu* with all other outstanding unsecured and unsubordinated obligations of the Issuer, present and future, but, in the event of insolvency, only to the extent permitted by applicable laws relating to creditors' rights.

3. **REDEMPTION AND PURCHASE**

(a) **Final redemption**

(i)   Unless previously purchased and cancelled as provided below, the Issuer may, in its sole and absolute discretion, determine on the Determination Date either to:

(1) redeem each Note at its principal amount, being £100,000, on August 8, 2000 (the "Maturity Date"); or

(2) procure in respect of each £100,000 principal amount of the Notes, the delivery of the IGD Amount on or after the Maturity Date, subject to and in accordance with these Conditions. Upon such delivery, the Issuer shall have no further obligations in respect of the redemption of this Note.

(ii)   If Condition 3(a)(i)(2) applies, the holder of the Notes will be required to pay an amount in Illyrian Pounds equal to all the expenses payable by the Issuer, including but not limited to any stamp duty, agent's expenses, scrip fees, levies, registration charges and other expenses payable on or in respect of or in connection with the purchase or agreement to purchase an amount of IGD to which such Notes relate (together, the "Transfer Expenses"). An amount equivalent to the Transfer Expenses must be paid by the Noteholder in accordance with Condition 3(a)(iii).

(iii)   If Condition 3(a)(i)(2) applies, in order to obtain delivery of the IGD Amount in respect of the Notes, the Noteholders must deliver to the specified office of the Agent on a Bank Business Day in Verona on or after the Determination Date such Notes and a duly completed Assets Transfer Notice (an "Assets Transfer Notice") which is obtainable from the specified office of the Agent. If Condition 3(a)(i)(2) applies, the Issuer will pay any trade taxes imposed in Illyria in respect of the transfer of the IGD Amount in respect of such Notes.

Each Assets Transfer Notice shall:

(a) specify the name(s) of the Noteholder(s) and the principal amount of the Notes to which such notice relates;

(b) specify the name and address of the person or persons to be shown on the instrument of transfer for the IGD Amount to be delivered and the name and address of the bank or broker or other person in Illyria to whom the relevant documents of title relating to the IGD Amount are to be delivered;

(c) be accompanied by payment in Illyrian Pounds by way of banker's draft or other payment, in each case in immediately available funds, in favor of the Issuer, for such of the Transfer Expenses as may be determined by the Calculation Agent at that time or, if later, as soon as the same shall have been determined by the Calculation Agent; and

(d) contain a certification as to non-U.S. beneficial ownership with respect to the person or persons to be shown on the instrument of transfer for the IGD Amount to be delivered.

Delivery of an Assets Transfer Notice in accordance with this Condition 3(a)(iii) shall constitute an irrevocable authority to the Issuer to execute all relevant contract notes and IGD transfer form(s) on the Noteholder's behalf in relation to the IGD Amount.

Failure properly and completely to deliver an Assets Transfer Notice may result in such Notice being treated as null and void. Any determination as to whether an Assets Transfer Notice has been properly and completely delivered as provided above shall be made by the Issuer and shall be conclusive and binding on the holder of the Note.

Subject as provided in this Condition, document(s) of title relating to the IGD Amount will be delivered at the risk and expense of the Noteholder to such bank or broker or such other person in Illyria as each Noteholder has specified in the Assets Transfer Notice as soon as practicable and no later than fifteen Illyria Business Days following the Illyria Business Day on which the Assets Transfer Notice was delivered (the "Notice Date"). Notwithstanding the foregoing, such delivery shall not take place until the Noteholder shall have accounted to the Issuer for the amounts payable in accordance with Condition 3(a)(iii) to the extent that they were not or could not be paid prior to the Notice Date.

If on the Notice Date or on any date thereafter prior to the delivery in accordance with this Condition of the IGD Amount to which such Assets Transfer Notice relates (i) there is a suspension of trading in the IGD or a general suspension of trading on the Stock Exchange as a result of which the Calculation Agent determines (in its absolute discretion) that it is unable to deliver the IGD Amount pursuant to Condition 3(a)(i)(2), or (ii) if otherwise a transfer of IGD cannot be effected, delivery of the relevant IGD Amount shall be postponed until the date on which such register of members is open or such delivery may be effected or transfer can be recorded and notice thereof shall be given to the Noteholders in accordance with Condition 11.

(iv)   The Issuer shall not be obliged to account to any Noteholder for any entitlement received or that is receivable in respect of the IGD comprising the IGD Amount if the date on which the IGD are first traded on the Stock Exchange ex such entitlement is on or prior to the Maturity Date. The Calculation Agent shall determine the date on which the IGD are so first traded on the Stock Exchange ex any such entitlement.

(v)   Where the provisions of Condition 3(a)(i)(2) apply and the IGD Amount would otherwise consist of a fraction of an IGD, the Issuer shall not be obliged to deliver such fraction provided that any fraction shall, subject to Condition 4, be rounded to the nearest IGD.

(vi)   If the IGD Amount comprises a number of IGD which does not correspond with the board lot for such IGD at such time or an integral multiple thereof, then (a) the Issuer shall not deliver and the holder shall cease to be entitled to receive in respect of the Note, that number of IGD (the "Excess IGD") which exceeds the amount of such board lot or the relevant integral multiple thereof, and (b) the relevant holder shall be entitled to receive a cash amount from the Issuer (to be paid at the same time as the IGD certificates relating to IGD to which that holder has become entitled are, in accordance with these Conditions, to be delivered) equal to the fair market value of the Excess IGD on the Determination Date, as determined by the Calculation Agent in its sole and absolute discretion.

(vii) For the purposes of these Conditions:
       "Bank Business Day" means a day (excluding Saturday) on which commercial banks are open for business in the relevant location;

"IGD Amount" means £100,000 principal amount of the IGD subject to adjustment in accordance with Condition 4, the IGD Amount to be represented by the documents of title relating thereto;

"Calculation Agent" means South Bank Limited;

"Determination Date" means 2nd August, 2000 or if such day is not an Illyria Business Day the immediately preceding Illyria Business Day;

"IGD" means 28 per cent. Illyrian Government Debt due 2000, which are registered with the Bank of Illyria pursuant to the Law concerning Government Debt;

"Stock Exchange" means the Illyria Stock Exchange; and

"Illyria Business Day" means a day (excluding Saturday) on which the Stock Exchange is open for dealing and which is also a Bank Business Day in Illyria.

(b) **Purchase**

The Issuer may at any time purchase Notes in the open market or otherwise at any price. Any Note so purchased may, at the option of the purchaser, be held, resold or surrendered for cancellation.

(c) **Cancellation**

A Note so redeemed or purchased and surrendered for cancellation will be cancelled and may not be reissued or resold.

4. ADJUSTMENTS

(a) **Adjustments**

Following each Potential Adjustment Event (as defined below), the Calculation Agent shall, in its sole discretion, determine the appropriate adjustment, if any, to be made to any of the terms of the Notes necessary to preserve the economic equivalent of the rights of the Noteholder under the Notes immediately prior to that Potential Adjustment Event, such adjustment to be effective as of the date determined by the Calculation Agent.

For the purposes of these Conditions, "Potential Adjustment Event" means the declaration by the Illyrian Ministry of Finance or other relevant authority, of the terms of any of the following:-

(i)   a subdivision, consolidation or reclassification of IGD; or

(ii) any change to the terms and conditions relation to payment of interest or principal under the IGD or the mandatory transfer of any other securities, obligations or assets to holders of the IGD in exchange for such IGD.

In determining whether an adjustment should be made as a result of the occurrence of a Potential Adjustment Event, if options contracts or futures contracts on the IGD are traded on the Stock Exchange or any other exchange, the Calculation Agent may have regard to, but shall not be bound by, any adjustment to the terms of the relevant options contract or futures contract made and announced by the Stock Exchange or any other exchange.

(b) **Notification of Adjustments and Determinations**

The Issuer shall as soon as practicable notify Noteholders of any determinations and/or adjustments, as the case may be, made pursuant to Condition 4(a) in accordance with Condition 11.

5. INTEREST

(a) The Note bears interest from and including 2nd August, 1999 at the rate of 28 per cent. per annum payable in arrears on the Maturity Date.

The Note will cease to bear interest from and including its due date for redemption unless, upon due presentation, payment of the principal in respect of the Note is improperly withheld or refused or unless default is otherwise made in respect of payment.

(b) When interest is required to be calculated in respect of a period of less than a full year, it shall be calculated on the basis of a 360 day year consisting of 12 months of 30 days each.

6. PAYMENTS

(a) **Method of Payment**

Payments of principal and interest will be made upon presentation of certificates as to non-U.S. beneficial ownership by transfer to the registered account (in the case of payment to a non-resident of Illyria, a non-resident account) of each Noteholder or by Illyrian Pounds cheque drawn on a bank in Illyria mailed to the registered address of each Noteholder if it does not have a registered account. Payments will only be made against surrender of the Notes to the specified office of the Agent and upon presentation of certificates as to non-U.S. beneficial ownership in the relevant form(s) scheduled to the Agency Agreement.

Interest (if any) on the Notes due on the Maturity Date will be paid to the holder shown on the register of Noteholders at the close of business on the date being the seventh day before the due date for payment of interest.

(b) **Payments subject to fiscal laws**

All payments are subject in all cases to any applicable fiscal or other laws and regulations. In the event of withholding tax being imposed, the Issuer is under no obligation to gross up any amounts payable under these Conditions and the Noteholders will only be entitled to the net amount after deduction of any such withholding. In such circumstances, the Agent shall only be obliged to pay such net amount to the Noteholders upon receipt of such amount from the Issuer.

(c) **Payments on Bank Business Days**

The Note may only be presented for payment on a day which is a Bank Business Day in London, Verona and Illyria. If any date on which a payment is due is not a Bank Business Day in London, Verona and Illyria, then payment shall be made on the immediately succeeding Bank Business Day in London, Verona and Illyria. No additional interest or other payment will be made as a consequence of the Note being presented for payment under this paragraph after the due date.

7. REPRESENTATIONS AND ACKNOWLEDGEMENTS

THE PURCHASER (BEING, IN THE CASE OF A NOTE HELD BY A NOMINEE OR HELD IN A CLEARANCE SYSTEM, THE BENEFICIAL OWNER OF THE NOTE) BY PURCHASING THE NOTES OR AN INTEREST IN THE NOTES, CONFIRMS THAT ALL OF THE FOLLOWING STATEMENTS WITH RESPECT TO IT ARE TRUE AND CORRECT ON THE DATE OF ISSUE OF THE NOTES AND THE PURCHASER ACKNOWLEDGES THAT THE ISSUER HAS RELIED ON SUCH CONFIRMATION AND UNDERSTANDING IN ISSUING THE NOTES.

(a) It has itself been, and will at all times continue to be, solely responsible for making its own independent appraisal of and investigation into the business, financial condition, prospects, creditworthiness, status and affairs of the Issuer and the Government of Illyria.

(b) It has not relied and will not at any time rely, on the Issuer or any other member of the Issuer's group of companies (the "Group") to provide it with any information relating to, or to keep under review on its behalf, the business, financial conditions, prospects, creditworthiness, status of affairs of the Government of Illyria or conducting any investigation or due diligence into the Government of Illyria.

(c)   In issuing the Notes, the Issuer is not making, and has not made, any representations whatsoever as to the Government of Illyria or any information contained in any document filed by the Government of Illyria with any exchange or with any governmental entity regulating the purchase and sale of securities.

(d)   It acknowledges that the Notes are not and do not represent or convey any interest in, a direct or indirect obligation of the Government of Illyria and that the Issuer is not an agent of the holder for any purpose.

(e)   The Issuer and each Group company may accept deposits from, make loans or otherwise extend credit to, and generally engage in any kind of commercial or investment banking business with the Government of Illyria or any other person or entity connected with or having obligations relating to the Government of Illyria and may act with respect to such business without accountability to the holder in the same manner as if the Notes did not exist, regardless of whether any such action might have an adverse effect on the holder.

(f)   The Issuer and each Group company may, whether by virtue of the types of relationships described above or otherwise, at the date hereof or at any time hereafter be in possession of information in relation to the Government of Illyria which is or may be material in the context of the Notes and which is or may not be known to the general public or the purchaser. The Notes do not create any obligation on the part of the Issuer or any Group company to disclose to the purchaser any such relationship or information (whether or not confidential) and neither the Issuer nor any other Group company shall be liable to the holder by reason of such non-disclosure.

(g)   It is purchasing the Notes as principal for its own account for investment purposes and not with a view to, or for resale in connection with, any distribution or any disposition thereof, and no other person has or will have a direct or indirect beneficial interest in the Notes (other than by virtue of such person's direct or indirect beneficial interest in the purchaser).

8.   NOTE REGISTER

The Registrar will keep a register in which the Registrar will provide for the registration of the Notes and the registration of transfers thereof. The Issuer and the Registrar may treat the person in whose name the Notes are registered on such register as the owner thereof for all purposes.

9. REPLACEMENT OF THE NOTES

Should any Note be lost, stolen, mutilated, defaced or destroyed, it may be replaced at the specified office of the Agent upon payment by the claimant of the expenses incurred in connection therewith and on such terms as to evidence and indemnity as the Issuer may reasonably require. A mutilated or defaced Note must be surrendered before replacements will be issued.

10. PRESCRIPTION

Claims in respect of principal, interest and the IGD Amount will become void unless presented for payment or delivery within a period of ten years (in the case of principal and the IGD Amount) and five years (in the case of interest) after the date upon which payment or delivery becomes due.

11. NOTICES

All notices regarding the Notes shall be sent by mail to the holder of each Note at its address appearing in the register.

12. ASSIGNMENT

Notwithstanding any other provision of the Notes, the Issuer may, without the consent of the holders, designate any company affiliated with the Issuer to assume or undertake in lieu of the Issuer any right or obligation which the Issuer may have under the Notes, to purchase, sell, receive or deliver securities, provided that such designation shall not relieve the Issuer of any liability for failure of performance by such designee. The Issuer shall be discharged of its obligations to the holder to the extent of the performance by such designee.

13. GOVERNING LAW AND SUBMISSION

The Notes are governed by, and shall be construed in accordance with, English law.

The Issuer irrevocably agrees for the benefit of the holders that the courts of England are to have jurisdiction to settle any disputes which may arise out of or in connection with the Notes and that accordingly any suit, action or proceedings arising out of or in connection therewith (together referred to as "Proceedings") may be brought in the courts of England.

The Issuer irrevocably and unconditionally waives and agrees not to raise any objection which it may have now or subsequently to the laying of the venue of any Proceedings in the courts of England and any claim that any Proceedings have been brought in an inconvenient forum and further irrevocably and unconditionally agrees that a judgement in any Proceedings brought in the courts of England shall be conclusive and binding upon the Issuer and may be enforced in the courts of any other jurisdiction. Nothing in this Condition shall limit any right to take Proceedings against the Issuer in any other court of competent jurisdiction, nor shall the taking of Proceedings in one or more jurisdictions preclude the taking of Proceedings in any other jurisdiction, whether concurrently or not.

The Issuer irrevocably and unconditionally appoints South Bank (England) Limited at its registered office for the time being as its agent for service of process in England in respect of any Proceedings and undertakes that in the event of it ceasing so to act it will appoint another person in England as its agent for that purpose.

Specified Office of the Agent and the Registrar

The Trustee Company Limited
Verona

FORM OF TRANSFER

FOR VALUE RECEIVED the undersigned sell(s), assign(s) and transfer(s) to:

....

....

....

(Please print or type name and address (including postal code) of transferee)

£............................. amount of this Note and all rights under this Note, irrevocably constituting and appointing .... as attorney to transfer the principal amount of this Note in the register maintained by ● with full power of substitution.

Signature(s) ....

....

18
Accounting for Credit Derivatives

PricewaterhouseCoopers

18.1   Accounting for Credit Derivatives — Australia
by Ian Hammond and Regina Fikkers

18.1.1   Introduction

There is currently no Australian accounting standard dealing comprehensively with accounting for derivatives.

Standards dealing with accounting for derivatives have been issued in the United States and by the International Accounting Standards Committee (IASC). Additionally a joint working group (the JWG) of national standard setters are working together to develop a longer term standard on financial instruments. The JWG includes representatives from the IASC, Australia, Canada, France, Germany , Japan, New Zealand, Nordic Countries, the United Kingdom and the United States.

The Australian Accounting Standards Board (AASB) have begun a project to develop an accounting standard for the measurement and recognition of financial instruments including derivatives. The AASB project will be based on the recommendations of March 1997 IASC Discussion Paper "Accounting for Financial Assets and Financial Liabilities" and the tentative views of the JWG. The AASB has a policy of harmonizing Australian standards with IAS. However the Board has not announced an intention to adopt IAS 39 "Financial Instruments: Recognition and Measurement" or an interim measure, preferring to await the outcome of the JWG.

Australia has already adopted a disclosure standard developed by the IASC. The disclosure requirements of this standard cover credit derivatives including credit default swaps and total rate of return swaps.

Until a standard is developed, there are two relevant methods of accounting for credit derivatives in Australia, market value accounting and hedge accounting (or accrual accounting).

18.1.2   Market Value Accounting vs Hedge Accounting

Under the Australian GAAP reference must first be made to the accounting standards dealing with particular industries. Market value accounting is prescribed by specific accounting standards, regulatory rules and/or industry practise on a broad base for the life insurance industry, general insurance industry, investment trust industry and superannuation funds. This means that any counterparty to a credit derivative from these industries would use market value accounting.

For all other industries existing Australian practise would require the question of intent to be considered. Where a counterparty uses credit derivatives as a trading position including where they are used as a mechanism to increase risk, market value accounting is appropriate.

Where a financial institution uses credit derivatives to reduce or modify exposures on an underlying position such as a loan or security, hedge accounting is used on the basis that the underlying position is similarly accounted for on an accrual basis. Particularly for financial institutions, the onus is to prove that the criteria for hedge accounting has been met otherwise, if there is any doubt, market value accounting should be adopted. To qualify for hedge accounting there must be designation and a high correlation of risk between the underlying position and the credit derivative.

18.1.3   Credit Default Swaps

A protection buyer would be eligible for hedge accounting for a credit default swap (CDS) where they hold loans or securities whose change in value is highly correlated to changes in value of the reference asset and management intent has been documented. Under hedge accounting payments made or received would generally be accrued over the period of protection. Payments received on the occurrence of the credit event on the reference asset would be recognized in the same period that a provision for loan loss on the underlying loan is also recognized.

Under market value accounting periodic assessment of the market value of the CDS is required and changes in that value along with the current periods cash flows are recognized in the profit and loss statement. Where the protection buyer is market valuing both the underlying loan or security and the CDS, the expectation would be that any credit loss would be matched by a gain on the CDS in that same period.

18.1.4 Total Return Swaps

Hedge accounting for total rate of return swaps (TRR) requires periodic interest exchanges to be accrued on a regular basis in line with the accrual of interest revenue on the underlying loan or security.

Under Australian GAAP, the accruals under the TRR are not netted against interest revenue from a designated loan or security but are simply recognized on a consistent basis in the profit and loss statement. Any payments received from actual or expected changes in value are recognized consistently with changes in value of the designated loan or security as with CDSs.

Market value accounting requires access to periodic market values or fair values with changes in the values recognized in the profit and loss statement as they occur.

18.1.5 Disclosure

Australian Accounting Standards AASB 1033 "Presentation and Disclosure of financial instruments" was issued in December 1996 and initially applied for years ending on or after 31 December 1997. Compliance with AASB 1033 also ensures conformity with International Accounting Standard IAS 32 "Financial Instruments; Disclosure and Presentation".

For credit derivatives along with similar disclosures for loans or securities, the following information would need to be summarized in the notes to the financial statements:

- Accounting policies and methods adopted including the basis for recognition whether market value accounting or hedge accounting had been applied.
- Significant terms and conditions that may effect the amount, timing and certainty of future cash flows. This would include disclosure of notional amounts under credit derivatives, stated interest terms, maturity dates and any related security.
- The objectives for holding or issuing the credit derivative financial instruments including the context needed to understand those objectives and strategies.
- Information about exposure to interest rate risk including effective interest rates and contractual re-pricing dates.
- The amount that best represents the maximum credit risk exposure at the reporting date on the basis that the counterparty fails to perform their

obligations under the credit derivatives. Any concentrations of credit risk that arise from a single counterparty or group of counterparties must also be disclosed.

- Net fair values i.e. market values must be disclosed at balance date. Separate disclosure is also made of the aggregate of fair values for those financial assets or financial liabilities which are not readily tradable on organized markets in standardized form.
- The methods adopted in determining market values and any significant assumptions made.
- Where a financial asset has been recognized at an amount in excess of market value, details of this need to be disclosed and the reasons why management expects the carrying amounts to be recovered.

18.1.6   Proposed Guidance

The AASB accounting standard project will be based on the recommendations of March 1997 IASC Discussion Paper "Accounting for Financial Assets and Financial Liabilities" and the tentative views of the JWG. The discussion paper explores the issues of a wider use of market value accounting for all financial instruments.

The measurement proposals included in this discussion paper would require all financial assets and liabilities including derivative contracts such as the credit derivatives, to be accounted for on a market value basis with gains and losses included in the profit and loss statement. There are some proposed exceptions for gains and losses arising on market valuing of hedges of anticipated transactions, however these exceptions are not likely to be relevant to credit default swaps nor total return swaps.

The significant increase in use of market values or fair values obviously assumes that these values can be either obtained directly from liquid and organized markets or estimated on a reasonable basis.

18.1.7   Summary

While Australian Accounting Standards clearly deal with the disclosure requirements arising from the use of credit derivatives there is only limited guidance available on accounting for credit derivatives. The whole area of market value versus hedge accounting is determined by reference to current market practise adopted for accounting for all derivatives. The ability of counterparties to credit derivatives to observe market values or estimate using appropriate indices and observable interest rates will be a critical factor in the acceptance of an increased use of market value accounting.

18.2 Taxation Considerations in Australia
by Bill Testa

18.2.1 Introduction

Current Australian income tax law contains no systematic way of dealing with derivatives and other financial transactions. A potpourri of general and specific legislative provisions, Court decisions and Australian Taxation Office rulings need to be considered for even the most basic transactions and considerable uncertainty exists in many instances.

18.2.2 Status of the Taxpayer

To a large degree, the tax treatment of a derivative transaction depends on the status of the taxpayer – namely the nature of the taxpayer's business activities, the part played by the transaction in those business activities, and the purpose for which the taxpayer enters into the transaction. This will determine whether the transaction and/or its component cash flows is to be characterized as being of a "revenue" or "capital" nature.

Where a transaction has a "revenue" character, gains and losses will be recognized as ordinary income and expense under the general assessing provisions.

Where a transaction has a "capital" character, the tax issues are more complex. Generally speaking, the capital gains tax (CGT) provisions will apply to tax a gain where a relevant "CGT event" can be identified. However, the practical application of the CGT provisions to derivatives is not clear in all cases. Losses under the CGT provisions are quarantined and may only be offset against capital gains.

Certain specific provisions may tax gains and losses on derivatives as if they were ordinary income or deductions, even if on capital account – for example, the foreign exchange gain or loss provisions.

Generally speaking, where a taxpayer trades, deals or otherwise enters into derivatives as part of its day-to-day business activities (e.g. financial institutions, arbitragers or derivatives traders), then the resulting gains or losses will be of a revenue nature.

However, for a taxpayer not carrying on such activities but using a derivative for hedging purposes, the character of the gain and loss on the derivative will generally follow the character of the underlying transaction or cash flow being hedged. For example, a derivative entered into by such a taxpayer to hedge interest rate risk would typically be on revenue account whereas a hedge of the underlying value of a capital asset (e.g. a long term investment portfolio) would typically be on capital account. For a taxpayer in the business of moneylending who enters into a derivative to hedge the principal value of loans, the derivative will ordinarily be on revenue account on the basis that the underlying loans being hedged are essentially revenue assets for a moneylender. However, these comments do over-generalize the position. It may be possible for a hedge which is prima facie on capital account to be treated as on revenue account on the grounds of being speculative. For example, in Income Tax Ruling IT 2228 on futures, the ATO states that it may not accept excess hedging as a genuine hedge.

It is possible for a capital/revenue mismatch to arise as between a hedge and an underlying transaction. For example, a gain on a bond held by a taxpayer on capital account (e.g. where the taxpayer is not a financial institution and is not in the business of trading in securities) could be taxed as ordinary income under the "traditional securities" provisions notwithstanding it is inherently of a capital nature. However, the corresponding loss on the hedge would be on capital account and could be either non-deductible or (at best) quarantined under the CGT provisions, unless the "traditional securities" provisions also apply to the hedge.

Given the complexities and uncertainties applying to derivatives on capital account, and the fact that principal demand for credit derivative products is generally from banks, financial institutions and moneylenders, **the following discussion will limit itself to the tax treatment of credit derivatives entered into by a taxpayer on "revenue" account.**

18.2.3   Taxation of Receipts and Deductibility of Payments on Credit Derivatives

General

The existing Australian tax regime is generally based upon the "form" rather than the "substance" of a transaction. Consequently, the tax treatment of a derivative can be quite different from the applicable financial accounting rules or economics of the transaction.

However, there are instances where the Australian Taxation Office (ATO) attempts to apply a substance over form approach in respect of financial transactions. For example, if the cash flows of a derivative instrument suggest that it is really an "in substance loan" or an "in substance investment", the ATO may seek to challenge the purported tax treatment of the arrangement (for example, by recharacterizing the cash flows as being principal and interest).

The timing of recognition of income and expense for tax purposes does not generally follow financial accounting principles. Rather, the usual approach is to recognize either gross receipts and outgoing, or a net profit or loss on a "realization" basis, (e.g. on completion of the transaction) depending on the nature of the transaction.

It is necessary to break down the transaction into its individual components and apply the timing rules applicable to each individual element. In particular, where a derivative is used for hedging purposes or is otherwise used in conjunction with an underlying asset or liability, there may be a lack of symmetry in the timing of recognition of income or deductions on the derivative and the recognition of income or deductions on the underlying transaction. This can result in significant and often unacceptable timing mismatches and distortions.

The tax legislation does contain some specific provisions dealing with timing of recognition of income or expense, however, in practise they have limited relevance for derivatives.

Total Return Swaps

Under a total return swap, one party agrees to pay the other the return on a loan asset (comprising interest, fees and any capital appreciation or depreciation) in return for a regular floating rate payment of say LIBOR plus a spread based on the underlying loan balance. Such a product is essentially a variation on the traditional interest rate swap transaction.

The ATO has set out its views on the tax treatment of interest rate swap transactions in Taxation Rulings IT 2050, IT 2682 and Draft Taxation Ruling TR 1999/D13. The ATO concludes that payments and receipts under "bona fide" interest rate swaps are inherently of a revenue nature and hence assessable or deductible under the general assessing provisions. As to timing, it is generally accepted that for swaps transacted under the standard ISDA agreement:

- swap payments and receipts in arrears which are set at the beginning of a calculation period are assessable/deductible on a straight line daily accruals basis;
- swap payments and receipts in arrears but which are not set (i.e. able to be calculated) at the beginning of calculation period are typically only assessable or deductible when they are due and payable or due and receivable, although a case for an accruals basis could be made in certain circumstances;
- swap payments and receipts received in advance (i.e. at the beginning of the calculation period) are considered wholly assessable at that point;

- Swap payments made in advance are generally considered deductible over the period to which the payment relates (or ten years if less); however, various special rules may apply to accelerate the deductions for payments covering a period of up to thirteen months.

It is important to note that the above rules are only applied to what the ATO terms as "bona fide" interest rate swaps. Swaps which are "in substance" loans or investments would not be treated as "bona fide" and the ATO would seek to characterize some portion of the swap cash flows as loan or investment principal and only the "interest" return component would be on revenue account.

The ATO has not issued any public guidance on its views as to the tax rules for other kinds of swaps. Further, following the decision in Bellinz Pty Ltd v FCT (98 ATC 4634), ATO rulings in respect of a particular arrangement cannot be relied on in relation to other (albeit similar) arrangements. Nevertheless, it is likely that the principles discussed above would equally apply to total return swaps entered into under the standard ISDA Agreement format, at least in so far as the swap cash flows reflect interest flows. However, the position in relation to swap payments which reflect fees, principal repayments and capital appreciation/depreciation is less than clear. Difficult and uncertain issues of characterization and timing arise, with results possibly varying depending on the taxpayer's specific circumstances.

For example:

- It is not clear whether swap payments relating to fee revenue on the underlying loan asset are to be assessable or deductible on a daily accruals basis, given that the fee income itself would not ordinarily be assessable until due and receivable. The ATO's comments on "swap fees" at paragraph 5 of IT 2682 (i.e. that such fees are assessable/deductible only when due and payable) may be relevant. However, it is not clear whether these payments would constitute swap fees of the type envisaged in the ruling.
- It is not clear whether swap payments relating to principal repayments are to be treated as items of capital and therefore not to be recognized as income or deductions per se. For the counterparty using the credit derivative in relation to an actual loan or loan portfolio, this might be an arguable position. For other counterparties (e.g. a swap trader), the position may be different. If not assessable or deductible per se, then presumably they are to be taken into account in calculating any assessable net profit or loss on the principal cash flows but then there is the further difficulty of determining *when* that net profit or loss is to be recognized for tax purposes.
- It is also not clear whether any payments between the parties relating to

capital appreciation/depreciation of the underlying loan asset are assessable/deductible as and when received/paid. If these payments reflect the fact that principal repayments have occurred on the loan, similar issues arise as for principal repayment swap cash flows discussed above. If unrelated to principal repayments (e.g. if related purely to market value movements), then it may be possible that these are ordinarily assessable or deductible. This could create timing mismatch problems for, say, a bank which receives such a payment under the swap, but where its offsetting loss on the loan asset is not yet deductible (e.g. because the loan is not yet capable of being written off as bad or has not yet been disposed of). Questions also arise as to the ability to apportion between principal repayment and market valuation components, if a different treatment is to be afforded to each component.

Credit Spread Products

Credit spread products are typically structured as forward rate agreements or options, which involve a net cash settlement based on the difference between an agreed spread and the actual spread between two securities.

A gain or loss on credit spread products would typically be on revenue account and taxed under the ordinary assessing provisions, regardless of the type of taxpayer. This is because the products relate to interest yields, which are inherently of a revenue nature.

If structured as a forward rate agreement, the gain or loss will generally be wholly recognized for tax purposes upon maturity or any earlier termination or close out of the transaction (i.e. at the time the cash settlement between the parties is due). Unlike financial accounting, it is not possible for tax purposes to amortize the payment or receipt over the period of any underlying or related asset.

If structured as an option, then any option premium received or paid would normally be assessable or deductible in its own right at the time the premium is due, with any cash settlement on exercise or close out (apart from the premium) being recognized as a separate profit or loss at the time settlement is due.

Credit Default Products

Credit default products generally involve one party making regular payments based on a notional principal amount, in return for the other party making an agreed default payment if a defined "credit event" occurs. The wide range of credit default products makes it difficult to comment specifically on their tax treatment. However, some general comments may be made for taxpayers on revenue account.

The periodic payments or fees would be assessable or deductible under the ordinary assessing provisions. The timing of recognition would depend on the terms of each contract. However, payments in arrears would usually be assessable or deductible on a straight line daily accruals basis in appropriate cases (as with interest rate swap payments under IT 2682). Payments received in advance would typically be assessable when received. Depending on the terms, payments made in advance would typically be deductible over the relevant period (or 10 years, if less), subject to certain special rules affecting pre-payments for periods of up to 13 months.

The agreed default payment would generally be assessable or deductible at the time it is due and payable. This could raise an unfavorable timing mismatch for the counterparty which is using the product to obtain default protection, as any loss on the underlying credit asset may not yet be available until a later time (e.g. when the credit asset is written off as bad or is otherwise disposed of). That counterparty could seek to argue that the default payment received is on account of principal (i.e. not separately assessable or deductible but merely taken into account in calculating the eventual loss on the underlying credit asset). However, the reluctance of the courts and the ATO to adopt an "integrated" approach in relation to linked transactions could create difficulties for this argument. Ultimately, however, the desired result might be achieved by careful structuring or wording of the credit default product agreement.

18.2.4 Withholding Tax Issues

Payments made under credit derivatives would not normally be "interest" or "amounts in the nature of interest" for interest withholding tax purposes, as they are independent of the interest on any underlying loan obligations. This is consistent with the ATO's view on interest rate swap payments as expressed in Tax Ruling IT 2050. However, the ATO might seek to take a different approach if the credit derivative was in essence a form of financial accommodation (i.e. a "disguised" lending transaction between the swap counterparties).

Technically, there is a question as to whether the non-resident insurer "withholding" tax provisions may apply to some credit default products if they are seen to be "insurance contracts" having a specified nexus with Australia. However, at the practical level, these provisions are unlikely to be applied by the ATO to most credit derivatives documented under the standard ISDA Agreement format. It is understood that the ATO's policy on these provisions is that they are anti-avoidance provisions that should be confined to contracts of insurance at common law (i.e. contracts involving indemnity).

18.2.5   Government's Proposals for Reform

The Australian Government has announced proposals for a complete overhaul of the tax treatment of financial arrangements including derivatives.

It is expected that an optional mark-to-market approach may be allowed in certain circumstances, or an accrual approach where relevant. However, given the complexity of the issues and the fact that further public consultation is envisaged, a start date and final content of the proposals are difficult to predict as at the time of writing (March 31, 2000).

18.3   Accounting for Credit Derivatives — Germany
by Manfred Kühule

18.3.1   Introduction

In Germany, the credit derivatives market is of small, but growing importance. The contracts are traded OTC, not standardized and sometimes very complex. A secondary market for credit derivatives is currently non-existing. Trading almost exclusively takes place between international banks and their foreign subsidiaries.

In respect to the accounting principles so far neither a legal basis nor specific directive have been developed in Germany. Two of the most important standard setting bodies (German Accounting Standards Committee (GASC)) and The Institute of Certified Accountants (Institut der Wirtschaftsprüfer IdW) have not yet published statements concerning the accounting treatment of credit derivatives. The Banking Technical Committee of the IdW (Bankenfachausschuß — BFA) has issued a pronouncement (#2/95) entitled "Accounting Treatment of Options" (original title "Bilanzierung von Optionsgeschäften") which provides guidance and background information for the accounting treatment and valuation of options in general. The Federal Banking Supervisory Office (Bundesaufsichtsamt für das Kreditwesen – BAK) has recently issued a circular of supervisory regulations concerning credit derivatives (Circular 10/99).

Therefore the accounting treatment of credit derivatives is based on the general regulations of the German Commercial Code (HGB) as well as the generally accepted accounting principles (Grundsätze ordnungsmäßiger Buchführung — GoB).

In the following we will give an overview of the general accounting, valuation and regulatory rules and of the existing types of credit derivatives. Finally we will describe the treatment of credit derivatives in detail, depending on their assignment to the banking or trading book.

18.3.2   General Accounting and Valuation Basis

The accounting treatment of credit derivatives generally corresponds to that of classical market-risk derivatives such as swaps and options as well as credit-risk related products such as guarantees etc. The correct treatment must be determined case by case, depending for instance on the assignment to the banking or trading book.

Commercial law basis

The regulations of the German Commercial Code (HGB) are applicable for all industry sectors and contain special regulations for credit institutions and insurance companies. The accounting rules for both bookkeeping purposes and the annual financial statements are based on the principle that the books have to reflect a true and fair view of the economic situation of the company. This common principle is specified by the principles explained below:

No set-offs and valuation on an item-by-item basis – a netting of neither assets and liabilities nor income and expenses in the financial statements is permitted. In general assets and liabilities must be valued at the balance sheet date on an item-by-item basis. The creation of valuation units is permissible, if it serves the principle of a true and fair view e.g. for hedged positions. Because of the lack of special rules the creation of valuation units has to be examined case by case. In such cases the unrealized gains may be netted against unrealized losses (only to the extent of these losses). Any amount of unrealized losses remaining must be reported in the financial statements; any remaining unrealized gains exceeding losses may not be included in the financial statements of the reporting period.

Principle of realization — according to this principle gains and losses must not be reported until they are realized. Upon realization, they are recorded in the profit and loss account. The realization takes place generally upon the creation of a legal claim. This means that neither the signing of a contract nor the payment of a debt can be considered as realization event. If no payments are made until the due date or the closing of a position (e.g. for an option), the maturity date or the date of exercise, respectively, is considered to be the realization event.

Principle of imparity — the principle of imparity prevents unrealized gains from being taken into account, but requires unrealized losses to be shown in the profit and loss account by the creation of provisions for risks and threatening losses.

Principle of historical cost — the principle of historical cost provides that an asset must be valued at the lower of the market value on balance sheet date or its historical cost.

Principle of periodicity — income and expenses of the financial year must be recorded in the financial statements regardless of the point in time of the related payments. The principle of periodicity is in partial contradiction to the principle of realization.

Supervisory law basis for financial institutions

The German Banking Act (KWG) contains several regulations for financial institutions which are supplemented and concretized by principles and guidelines of the Federal Banking Supervisory Office.

Capital adequacy — the Federal Banking Supervisory Office has issued principles regulating adequate liable capital and liquidity of banks. Credit institutions have to cover the credit risk arising from the banking and the trading book with liable capital/own funds. If a banks trading book volume exceeds a certain level, the market risks arising from the trading book have to be covered with liable capital/own funds as well. The protection seller has to cover credit risks arising from credit derivatives like a position in the underlying asset. The protection seller may consider the risk mitigating effects of credit derivatives, if certain conditions for their acknowledgement are fulfilled (effective transfer of risk, ...).

Large exposure (Article 13 of the KWG) — all exposures to one counterparty exceeding 10% of the liable capital/own funds have to be reported to the Central Bank upon granting of the credit and once every following year. A further report is necessary should the credit be increased by more than 20%. Large credits may only be granted on an unanimous decision of all managers. Credit derivatives are included in the definition of large credits as provided for by Article 13 of the KWG. Depending on the type of contract credit derivatives have to be treated either as guarantees, financial swaps or options.

Exposures exceeding DM 3 million (Article 14 of the KWG) — the banks have to report all debtors owing DM 3 million or more to the Central Bank every 3 months. Credit derivatives are included in the definition of credits provided for by Article 14 of the KWG. Depending on the type of contract, credit derivatives are to be treated either as guarantees, financial swaps or options.

18.3.3   Basic Structures of Credit Derivatives

Credit Default Option

A credit default option gives the protection buyer the right to receive a predefined payment in case of a credit event. Usually credit event is defined as bankruptcy or default of a reference asset. The credit event payment is either cash settlement of the credit loss or sale of the reference asset at its nominal value. The option premium is paid as an upfront or annual fee. The credit default option is also known as the credit default swap.

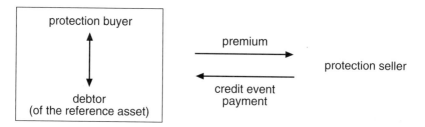

Credit Spread Option

A credit spread option is similar to a credit default option as described above. The credit event is defined as an increase of the spread of the reference asset, caused by a deterioration of the original debtors credit quality.

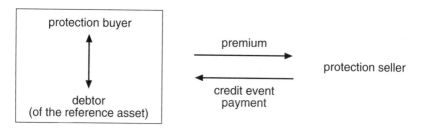

Total Return Swap

A total return swap is a financial instrument, with which credit risk and market risk of an underlying asset is transferred to the protection seller. The protection buyer pays interest and (unrealized) market value gains of the underlying asset and receives a variable rate plus (unrealized) market value losses. It is not relevant whether a market value change results from a change of the bond issuer's credit rating or from a change of the average market conditions.

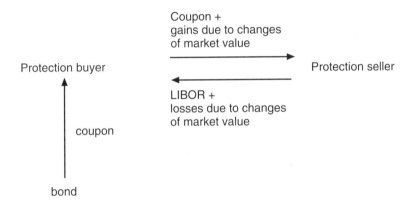

Credit Linked Note

A credit linked note is a debt security issued by the protection buyer, which is to be repaid at the nominal amount less the credit loss of a reference asset. Unlike all other types of credit derivatives the protection buyer not only hedges his original credit risk, but also refinances his lending. Thus the credit linked note can be considered as a combination of a long position in a floating rate note issued by the protection seller and a short position in a credit default option on the reference asset.

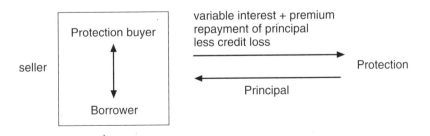

18.3.4 Accounting and Valuation of Banking Book Items

Protection Buyer

If the credit derivative hedges an original credit risk (proven by intention, qualification and documentation), the formation of a valuation unit is allowed. A credit loss of the underlying asset is covered by the credit derivative, thus no provision has to be established. If the credit quality of the protection seller deteriorates, a provision must be established.

If **credit default options** or **credit spread options** are assigned to the banking book, they are treated like classical guaranties. The premium has to be amortized over the time to maturity and is recorded as fee expense. A credit event payment compensates the depreciation of the underlying asset and should be recorded as negative loan loss expenses.

In the case of a **total return swap** market value losses are covered as well and do not result in provisions for the underlying asset. An increase of the underlying assets value results in a provision for the increased liability against the protection seller, whereas the valuation of the asset is restricted to the lower of purchase cost or market value. The swap itself is a pending transaction and must not be initially recognized in the balance sheet. The interest received or paid is to be recorded as interest expense or income. The payments resulting from market value changes are recorded corresponding to the underlying asset.

A **credit linked note** is treated like a combination of a short position in a floating rate note and a long position in a credit default option. The FRN is to be recorded as issued debt security. The coupon interest has to be recorded as interest expense and the risk premium as fee expense. In case of a credit event, no provision for credit losses of the underlying asset is required.

Protection Seller

The option premium for **credit default options** or **credit spread options** is recorded as fee income and has to be amortized over the time to maturity. The credit risk has to be recorded as contingent liability off-balance sheet. If a credit event is likely to occur, a provision for anticipated losses related to incomplete contracts has to be established.

A **total return swap** as an off-balance sheet transaction is not recorded in the balance sheet. A decrease of the underlying assets value results in a provision for the increased liability against the protection buyer. The current payments are recorded corresponding to those of the protection buyer.

The **credit linked note** is treated like a combination of a floating rate note and a credit default option. The protection seller records the note as a long-term investment. The valuation follows the general accounting rules applicable for investments held as fixed assets. If the original borrower defaults, the protection seller has to write down the note. The amount has to be recorded as write-down on investments.

18.3.5 Accounting and Valuation of Trading Book Items

Protection Buyer

If **credit default options** or **credit spread options** are assigned to the trading book, they are treated like market-risk related options. They have to be recorded as other assets and are valued at the lower of cost or market value on an item-by-item basis. The option premium and credit event payments are recorded as net revenue of trading activities at maturity or exercise date.

A **total return swap** as an off-balance sheet transaction is not recorded in the balance sheet. An increase of the underlying assets value results in a provision for the increased liability against the protection seller. The current payments are recorded as net revenue of trading activities. The interest payments may also be recorded as interest income or expense.

A **credit linked note** is treated like a combination of a short position of a floating rate note and a long position of a credit default option. The FRN is recorded as issued debt security. The interest payment has to be recorded as interest expense. The option premium is first recorded as other asset and booked as net revenue of trading activities at maturity or exercise date.

Protection Seller

The option premium for **credit default options** or **credit spread options** has to be recorded as other liability. If a credit event is likely to occur, a provision has to be established. The option premium and credit event payments are booked as net revenue of trading activities at maturity or exercise date.

A **total return swap** as a market-risk related transaction is not recorded in the balance sheet. A decrease of the underlying assets value results in a provision for the increased liability against the protection buyer. The current payments are recorded as net revenue of trading activities. The interest payments may also be recorded as interest income or expense.

A **credit linked note** is treated like a combination of a long position of a floating rate note and a short position of a credit default option. The FRN is recorded as security held for trading. The option premiums are first recorded as other liability and booked as net revenue of trading activities at maturity or exercise date. The interest payment has to be recorded as interest income. If the credit quality of the underlying asset deteriorates, a provision should be made.

18.4   Tax Considerations in Germany
by Georg Klusak and Steffen Gnutzmann

18.4.1   Taxation of Receipts and Deductibility of Payments on Credit Derivatives

There are no statutory provisions dealing with the taxation of derivatives in Germany. The taxation principles are basically developed on the basis of isolated tax letter rulings or court decisions. Otherwise the taxation of corporate investors with respect to derivative instruments will follow the treatment in the financial accounts. On the level of German financial accounting rules there is also a complete absence of specific legislation on derivatives so that ultimately German GAAP will determine both the taxation and the accounting of derivatives. Even though there are isolated statements of the revenue or court decisions on certain derivative instruments no such guidance exists with respect to credit derivatives of the type described above. The taxation of credit derivatives would therefore have to be determined on the basis of an analogy to existing instruments such as options (on other underlyings), swaps or plain vanilla guarantees.

It is likely that the (premium) income received by the protection seller has to be taxed by analogy to the tax treatment of option premiums received and/or income received for providing a guarantee. In both cases the income would have to be recognized as taxable when payable, i.e. on a current basis. The analogy to the treatment of option premiums where the revenue requires income recognition upon inception of the contract, would be stringent where a protection *seller* enters into the contingent obligation to acquire an underlying asset at an agreed upon amount in case of a credit event.

In the case of qualification as a guarantee the income recognition of the consideration received by the guarantor would be on a pro-rata basis depending on the life of the contract.

If the credit derivative was treated as the sale of an option any unrealized loss reflecting the contingent liability under the derivative would not be tax deductible prior to the actually default event, i.e. when the loss is actually realized.

If the credit derivative is incorporated in a credit linked note or other debt instrument the income recognition would follow the recognition of the interest received, i.e. be taxed on an accruals basis. Any unrealized loss resulting from a write-down of the credit linked note or other is deductible to the extent that it is permanent. There should be no other limitations as to the deductibility of payments made by the protection *buyer*. In any case deductions should only be available on a pro-rata basis depending on the life of the protection agreement.

18.4.2 Withholding Tax Issues

Where structured or simple *loans* are used in credit derivative structures (credit linked notes, credit linked Schuldscheine, credit linked loans) any interest paid by a German bank will be subject to a 30% withholding tax if the recipient of the payment is also a German resident.

There are, however, various exemptions which may apply, the most relevant of which are

• the interest is paid to another German bank
• the interest is below 1%
• the interest is paid to insurance companies having a specific exemption certificate

Where the credit derivative element is incorporated in a credit linked *bond* or other securities the German interest withholding tax of 30% applies where such a security is deposited in a securities account with a German bank which pays out or credits the interest to the German holder of the bond. Again there are exemptions for banks and certain insurance companies holding the bonds.

Payments made by a German protection buyer would not be subject to a German withholding tax if they will qualify or treated like option premiums received. The same will apply if the credit derivative was treated as a guarantee or a comparable instrument.

18.4.3 Potential Distribution Treatment

Although a number of credit derivative structures involve the use of loans into which the credit derivative is embedded there would normally be no danger that the interest paid on the loan would be reclassified into dividends or profit participating loans for German tax purposes.

Thus, all payments made on such loans should be tax deductible (with a limitation for interest payments on long-term debt for trade tax purposes, see above).

18.4.4 VAT and Transfer Taxes

VAT

Payments under credit derivatives are exempt for the purposes of German VAT law. This will apply irrespective of the qualification as interest, as option premium or as the consideration for a guaranty. All types of payments would be tax-exempt under German VAT law.

Transfer Taxes

There are no applicable transfer taxes in Germany.

18.5   Tax Consideration in Switzerland

by *Dr Urs Landolf, Dr Andreas Risi, and Marc Bertschy*

18.5.1   Introduction

A derivative transaction is a contractual agreement determined by the underlying asset. Derivatives facilitate the separate trading of individual components of the asset in isolation from the asset itself. Possible underlying 'assets' are shares, bonds, precious metals, interest rates, exchange rates, etc. In principle any good or right may serve as the underlying asset. However, these instruments do not allow the separate trading of changes in the risk margin and the risk of default.

One of the main advantages of credit derivatives is the 'isolation of credit view': By focusing on the spread between a credit-risk-sensitive instrument and a non-credit-risk-sensitive instrument (for example a treasury bond) a credit derivative can isolate credit risks from market risks.

The scope for standardised credit derivatives is limited: a contract designed to separate credit from an underlying asset is a special arrangement between two contract parties and therefore very individual, private, complex and heavily negotiated. It is difficult to group the different products traded today but the principal products encompass the following instruments:
• Total return swap or loan swap;
• Credit default products (credit default swaps and credit options);
• Credit spread products (credit spread forward and credit spread option).

This report is concerned with the basic taxation and accounting rules of credit derivatives in Switzerland.

Legal basis for the taxation of credit derivatives

- **Commercial law basis:** The commercial law valuation provisions of the Swiss Code of Obligation ("CO') are applicable for all sectors of business. In addition, banks must comply with the provisions of the Federal Banking Law Statute, the ordinance of the Federal Council and the circular letters of the Federal Banking Commission (the banking control authority) based thereon, as well as the guidelines of the association of bankers. Additionally, the legal requirements of the Federal Law on Stock Exchanges (BEHG) have to be considered. These contain both commercial and supervisory regulations.

- **Supervisory law basis:** There is in principle free access to the capital markets. A special permit is, however, necessary to obtain bank status, to participate regularly in securities trading activities, to be a stock broker or to be an insurer. Additionally, all securities traders require a stock exchange license according to the BEHG.

In connection with derivative financial instruments, pension funds must fulfil the investment provisions of the Occupational Pension Plan Statute and the ordinances belonging thereto. Investment funds are limited with respect to their investments by the restrictions of the Investment Fund Statute.

In Switzerland, there exists no capital movement limitation which would hinder the outflow of capital in connection with credit derivatives. The requirement of obtaining a banking law permit as well as a stock exchange license is, as a rule, not a problem. In addition, there are no regulations which would, in principle, forbid parties from entering into contracts on derivatives.

Tax law basis

The Swiss tax system consists of many types of taxes. Their impact on the taxation of credit derivatives is described below:

- **Direct taxes**
    - income tax and net wealth tax (individuals)
      progressive tax rates dependent on total income and net wealth respectively;
    - income tax and capital tax (corporate entities)
      The Federal government, cantons and municipalities collect direct taxes. Capital tax is levied on the cantonal and communal level but not on the federal level. The tax statutes of the cantons are autonomously passed. They are in many respects often very different from another. The cantons have until 2001 to adjust their tax statutes in order to fulfil the

requirements of the Federal Tax Harmonisation Statute.

- **Special taxes on income and net assets**
  - withholding tax (mainly on income from securities);
  - no capital gains tax (the increase in value on moveable private property is on the federal level and all cantons tax-free).
- **Stamp taxes on certain legal transactions**
  - issuance tax (Emissionsabgabe) on certain issuances of securities;
  - transfer tax (Umsatzabgabe) on certain transfers of securities.
  - stamp tax on insurance premiums
- **Other business transaction taxes**
  - value added tax (VAT).

Many legal sources address in a broader sense the issue of the taxation of credit derivatives. Specific legislation on the tax treatment of credit derivatives does not, however, exist.

The legislature has neither addressed directly in its tax statutes the issue of the taxation of credit derivatives nor derivative financial instruments (DFI) in general. This philosophy is based on the tendency to keep the tax statute simple as opposed to problem specific. Furthermore, the legislature wants to give more discretion to the tax authorities given the fact that they have more detailed knowledge regarding singular tax issues. The goal is thus that the tax authorities can better address specific tax problems, and as a result, quicker react to new circumstances. Therefore, the taxpayer is more dependant on the administration, especially since the courts differ from the opinion of the tax authorities rarely.

18.5.2   *Taxation of Credit Derivatives Under Swiss Tax Law*

Taxation of Private Assets of Individuals

Basic principles
Individuals are taxed on their total net income. Investment income is in principle considered taxable with an allowance being made for tax permissible deductions.

In Swiss tax law, there is a fundamental difference between business assets and private assets. While companies have only business assets according to tax law classifications, individuals can have both private assets as well as business assets (e.g. a sole proprietorship, a participation in a partnership).

With respect to business assets, capital gains (losses) are like all other types of income taxable. One refers to the so-called *book value principle* because the income tax value (which as a rule conforms to the book value) serves as a basis for the determination of capital gains. When speaking about business assets, there is no relevant difference between investment income and capital gains.

Investment income from private assets are taxable. In contrast, capital gains on movable private assets (except for real estate) are tax-free. Liquidation payments which are higher than the nominal value of the security are also considered investment income. The investor may under certain circumstances be subject to tax with respect to fictitious profit, if he bought the securities above the nominal value.

The delineation between what constitutes investment income and capital gains has been developed in the tax practise over a long period of time and refined as specific problems have arisen.

The distinction between private and professional asset management
The increased potential for the production of tax-free capital gains as opposed to taxable investment income has created great concern among the tax authorities that the tax base will be reduced to an unacceptable level. The attempt to consider capital gains on options as taxable income from a game or a bet has found no acceptance by the tax courts. The newest trend is to characterise private asset transactions as a gainful activity with the result that the assets no longer belong to one's private assets, but rather one's business assets. This has the effect that capital gains are then taxable while capital losses can be deductible.

According to decisions of the Swiss Federal Supreme Court, the distinction between gainful activities and private asset management can not conclusively be determined on the basis of a single factor rather the entire picture is decisive. The Swiss Federal Supreme Court has adopted the following essential criteria when distinguishing between private and gainful real estate and securities trade:
- systematic planning;
- frequency of securities/real estate transactions;
- relationship to a primary profession;
- usage of third party funds;
- usage of sale proceeds;
- a commercial course of action;
- a short ownership period.

Not decisive is the appearance of the activity towards third parties, e.g., active participation in the course of business, the making of public offers.

Taking all factors into account, the tax subject is lacking legal certainty due to the scope of discretion that the tax authorities have. The consequences are grave since it is an all or nothing issue, e.g. the full taxation of capital gains or the non-taxation thereof.

The canton of Zurich has distanced itself for cantonal tax purposes from the decision of the Swiss Federal Supreme Court. The canton instead relies *on the appearance of the activity in normal business transactions towards third parties* as the only capable criteria for differentiation between an independent business activity and private asset management. The appearance of the activity shall be considered a business activity when the taxpayer is entered in the commerce register or a trade register, conducts a business, or advertises for the activity of his business.

In our opinion, the management of one's own assets is in principle a private matter. Otherwise the freedom from tax on capital gains and the goals of the legislature would be undermined. In attempting to find clear differentiating criteria, the Federal Supreme Court has succeed in applying unsuitable criteria, e.g., amount of assets, number of transactions, use of borrowed funds etc. The fear of a loss of the tax base is in our opinion not justified because capital losses are also tax neutral in the case of private asset management.

Individuals enter the market for DFI predominantly as investors managing their own private assets. Thus they do not as a rule have the function of market-makers. Instead they purchase DFI which are supplied by banks and other financial intermediaries. Because most of the credit derivatives traded today are custom made and because we expect companies enter the credit derivatives market mainly we renounce to describe tax implications in relation to individuals more detailed.

However, the question of the individual's taxation would become relevant if e.g. banks would securitize the credit derivatives, i.e. if the credit derivatives would be converted into tradable securities. The tax authorities have increased their focus on income derived from DFI and, in this regard, especially on the distinction between investment income and capital gains. The federal tax authorites have recently issued the circular letter of April 1999 which regulates the taxation of income derived from DFL. If investment income and capital gains can be separated clearly the taxation follows the general rules as described above. In case the income derived from DFI consists of both, investment income and capital gains and a clear separation of these "income" components can not be done, than the whole income is considered taxable.

Taxation of Business Assets

Introduction

In Swiss tax law, capital gains on business assets are subject to income tax. The main question for business assets is the time of the taxation and the qualification as ordinary or extraordinary income.

The difference between ordinary and extraordinary income is primarily of importance at the beginning and at the end of the tax liability period as well as upon a tax statute revision. The differentiation must take into consideration all circumstances in each case. In particular, the type of transaction and its relationship to the goals of the company are of critical importance.

The *adherence to accounting rules principle* is applicable for income and capital tax purposes. This principle stands for the proposition that the accounting balance sheet is decisive for tax purposes unless the tax law provides otherwise.

Thus we will examine in a first step the accounting rules, and subsequently, the specific tax rules.

Swiss accounting principles

The accounting rules for both bookkeeping purposes and the annual financial statements are based on the principle that the books *shall accurately reflect the economic situation of the company* (Art. 959 CO). This principle is realised by other principles which are derived from the CO.

Principle of conservatism

The principle of conservatism requires that risks are to be weighed heavily and opportunities lightly in order to protect the creditors.

Principle of realization

The principle of realization provides that gains and losses may not be reported until they are realised. Upon realization, they are included in the income statement. The realization event occurs generally upon the creation of a legal claim. This means that neither the signing of a contract nor the payment of a debt can be considered the realization event.

If no payments are made until the due date or the closing of a position (e.g., for options, forwards etc.) other than down payments like commissions, the maturity date or the date of exercise, respectively, is considered to be the realization event.

Additional mid-term net compensation payments in connection with swap contracts are considered to be partial realizations of a contract. On the other side, pure collateral payments are to be booked as debits or credits and have no influence on the timing of realization.

The principle of realization is overruled by the principle of imparity and the possibility to value securities at market value pursuant to Art. 667 CO.

Principle of imparity/lower of cost or market value rule
The principle of imparity forbids unrealised gains from being taken into account, but requires unrealised losses to be shown in the balance sheet by the creation of reserves and provisions for risks and threatening losses.

The lower of cost or market value rule provides that an asset may generally not be valued higher than its purchase price *or* the lower market value on the date of the balance sheet.

The principle of imparity is overruled by Art. 667 CO which permits quoted securities to be valued at market value.

Exceptions to the principles of realization and imparity: quoted securities
Quoted securities must not be valued at a price higher than their average stock exchange price during the month prior to the date of the balance sheet (Art. 667 CO). Thus, it is permissible to show unrealised book gains for certain assets.

Two conditions must be met to show market value:
• securities must be current asset rather than long-term assets (the latter thus being forbidden to use the mark-to-market approach);
• securities must have a quoted price.

In recent years, the importance of physical existence of securities according to the wording of article 667 CO has rapidly decreased so that today the fact that *a right is no longer embodied in a security's instrument* has no influence on its market valuation. Mark-to-market valuation is certainly admissible for non-physically existing options and futures traded on EUREX.

Furthermore, the interpretation of a quoted price is more liberal today. The decisive factor is whether a liquid market exists, and thus, the securities can be traded on a regular basis and sold easily.

The decisive issue with respect to DFI is not so much the liquidity of DFI, but rather the liquidity of the risk attached. If the liquidity of an attached risk exists (e.g., an option on a listed stock), the requirement of the quoted price is met.

The market value can easily be determined, if the DFI are traded regularly on a stock exchange.

The contract volume of a future contract is not shown in the balance sheet.

Instead the balance of the margin account is to be shown in the balance sheet. The margin account consists of the initial margin plus the unrealised gain/loss.

A theoretical value must be determined for complex OTC products, in particular, for options. The value can be determined with the help of arbitrage prices and mathematical formulas.

Banks and securities dealers subject to stock exchange law are required to apply the mark-to-market approach with regard to trading securities.

The principle of periodicity
Gains and losses have to be booked in the year of occurrence according to the principle of periodicity.

The principle of periodicity is in partial contradiction to the principle of realization and the principle of conservatism. The law requires that the principle of conservatism is superior.

No set-offs
It is not permissible to balance assets and liabilities or income and expenses in the financial statements. It is permissible, however, to value fungible goods of similar assets as a whole.

The safeguarding is complete pursuant to hedge accounting if the correlation between the transaction to be hedged and the hedging transaction is -1. In other words, the increase in value of the former transaction is compensated by a corresponding loss in the latter transaction.

The creation of valuation units is permissible, if it helps to show the economic reality correctly. This is the case of complete or almost complete safeguarding of a position. Neither the law nor the practise provides a fixed solution to the admissibility of valuation units. Thus, the admissibility of valuation units has to be examined on a case-by-case basis. According to general practise and in compliance with international accounting principles the following conditions have to be fulfilled for the use of hedge accounting:
- The hedging transaction must be clearly marked as such at the signing.
- The hedged position poses a clear and identifiable risk for the company.
- The hedging transaction must effectively reduce the risk position. A negative correlation close to 21 between base and hedging position is necessary.

The creation of valuation units must be disclosed in the annex to the annual financial statements.

Tax treatment of credit derivatives

Credit default swap

Credit default swaps are designed to isolate the risk of default on credit obligations. In a typical credit swap, the protection seller receives a periodic fee, normally expressed in basis points on the notional. If there is a credit event by the reference credit, then the protection seller would pay to the counterparty the agreed default payment. A clear and uniform definition of default does not exist, but dealers usually interpret it as a bankruptcy, insolvency, failure to meet a payment obligation when due or even ratings downgrade below agreed threshold. In the case of basket linked credit default derivatives, the credit event is linked to the first default within the basket.

The notional amount of swap contracts is not to be shown in the balance sheet, but for negative replacement values a provision has to be made. However, the payment flow during the term of the swap contract has to be considered, i.e. the periodic fee received by the protection seller has to be recorded as income for the protection seller and as expense for the counterparty.

Swap contracts are neither subject to issuance stamp tax nor subject to withholding tax. It has to be considered, however, whether a certain contract may be subject to stamp tax on insurance premiums. In general the stamp tax law does not apply; nevertheless we recommend to check a credit default swap contract with the federal tax authorities to receive their approval.

Provisions commercially required due to a feasible default payment are accepted for tax purposes.

Total return swap/loan swap

The central concept of this credit derivative structure is the replication of the total performance of a loan asset. One counterparty pays out the total return of an asset by passing through all payments of the underlying asset including any interest payments, capital appreciation, loan repayments and any loan fees to the other counterparty. In return the first counterparty receives a regular floating-rate payment such as LIBOR plus or minus an agreed margin. Total return or loan swaps are typically for terms of 1 to 3 years. The terms need not to coincide with the maturity of the underlying credit asset.

Total return or loan swaps are treated like credit default swaps. They are neither subject to issuance stamp tax nor subject to withholding tax.

Regular payments and all payments in connection with the underlying asset have to be recorded as income or expense.

Provisions commercially required due to the development of the swap spread have to be accepted for tax purposes.

Credit option

A credit option is much the same as a credit default swap. The protection buyer pays an option price in return for receiving an agreed payment in the event that a third-party reference credit defaults. The option is only exercised if the credit defaults. Neither of the counterparties has to maintain a credit agreement with a third party; the credit option can be related to a loan of a company to which neither of the counterparties has business relations.

The buyer pays at the beginning of the term an option premium which can be entered in the balance sheet. Incurred costs can be immediately deducted or depreciated over the term. The valuation of these options requires the use of complicated math formulas. Thus the valuation based on quoted prices pursuant to Art. 667 CO is only possible for such companies which are capable of performing such a valuation or which can rely on information by third parties or the writer.

In applying the principle of the lower of purchase price or market value, the market value has to be determined. If the valuation based on quoted prices is not possible, the market value has to be estimated since it cannot be required from everybody, not even the tax authorities, to develop complicated math formulas. If the counterparty, generally a bank, cannot provide a current market value, the value of the option has to be determined by the method of approximation. Assuming that no provision for bad debts needs to be taken into account, the so-called inner-value (e.g., the difference between current spot price for the good underlying the option and the exercise price) can be used as the lower limit. If the valuation is commercially sound, it will be accepted by the tax authorities. A global valuation method for all cases does not exist.

The **option seller** has to record the option price as income. A provision for the agreed payment in the event that a third-party reference credit defaults is to be accepted at least at the amount of the tax allowed valuation allowance on the underlying credit.

Regarding issuance stamp tax, withholding tax and stamp tax on insurance premiums credit option contracts are much the same as credit default swaps: they are neither subject to issuance stamp tax nor subject to withholding tax but it has to be considered whether a certain contract may be subject to stamp tax on insurance premiums. In general the stamp tax law does not apply; nevertheless we recommend to check a credit default swap contract with the federal tax authorities to receive their approval.

Credit spread forward and credit spread option
The central concept of credit spread products is to use credit spread derivatives to trade, hedge or monetise expectations on future credit spreads. With a credit

spread product the change of the difference between the yield of a security or loan and the yield of a corresponding asset has been isolated to make it tradable. The corresponding asset itself can be either a risk free security or loan (e.g. a risk free benchmark or a treasury) or another credit sensitive asset.

The result of a credit spread forward transaction is that the investor receives a fixed percentage of the notional amount for every basis point that the spread on a bond (difference between a bond yield and a reference security yield) decreases relative to the strike spread (strike spread is pre-agreed in the credit spread forward contract). If the spread increases, the investor pays a fixed percentage of the notional amount.

Credit spread options allow the creation of non-linear payoffs on the underlying credit spread change, where the buyer has the right to buy the spread and benefits from a decreasing spread (call option) or where the buyer has the right to sell the spread and benefits from an increase in the spread (put option).

The contract volumes of futures contracts are not shown in the balance sheet. It is not disputed that margins (reflecting payments made or received as collateral) have to be included in the balance sheet. When entered as either debits or credits, they do not influence income. Transactional costs are tax deductible.

Gains on such contracts are considered capital gains. Thus, no withholding tax applies.

Provisions commercially required due to the development of the bond spread have to be accepted for tax purposes. The tax authorities do not have to approve a change in the valuation method. The tax authorities will accept in practise a one time change, if this does not result in tax avoidance. Global provisions for futures contracts are generally not accepted for tax purposes with the exception of the rules enumerated for specific trades.

Tax Structuring Possibilities

Waiver of market valuation

The trend of modern accounting is towards market valuation (compulsory mark to market valuation for securities in the trading books of banks and registered brokers). Nevertheless it must be pointed out that the taxpayer (except banks and brokers) is permitted to record quoted securities as part of current assets in the balance sheet at either purchase price or their lower value without concern of any revaluation by the tax authorities.

Besides having a tax postponement effect, waiving market valuation has other advantages as well. In particular, it minimises capital tax liability. In addition, unrealised gains must not be taxed. Likewise in view of a possible change to the market valuation principle, the potential is created for tax purposes to absorb any losses. Depending on the particular tax circumstances, the progressive cantonal tax rates may be lowered.

The prerequisite for taking advantage of these tax opportunities is that the purchase price or current lower market value of securities has to be recorded in the commercial balance sheet.

Set-up of provisions
The set-up of provisions required by the business is generally permitted for tax purposes. Except for bad debt provisions and sector specific provisions, global corrections in value or provisions in connection with DFI are added for income tax purposes.

The planning of the annual financial statements requires, therefore, to analyse carefully business needs when making provisions in connection with DFI and record them accordingly. Discretion may be used in view of the principle of conservatism.

18.5.3 International Aspects of Credit Derivatives Taxation in Switzerland

Switzerland as the Source Country

In general
The withholding tax (Federal Tax Statute concerning withholding tax dated October 13, 1965) is a source based tax on income from Swiss sources which secures the tax payment by domestic recipients and taxes foreign recipients. Foreign recipients have the right to claim the return of taxes paid, or a portion thereof, based only upon an applicable double tax treaty.

Considered the applicability of Art. 4, para 1 of the Withholding Tax Statute, any interest income and profit share are considered income from movable assets. Corresponding to the function of the withholding tax as a security tax, the meaning of income from capital is in principle to be considered the same as by the income tax.

Withholding tax on gains in connection with DFI
No withholding tax is due on income from pure derivative financial instruments (futures contracts, swaps and options, credit derivatives). For example swap payments in connection with interest rate swaps are not considered interest in connection with the Withholding Tax Statute.

In the case of mixed derivative financial instruments the delineation between capital gains and investment income is in the practise today not very precise. Payments subject to withholding tax are considered interest, and therefore, taxable investment income. Payments not covered by the withholding tax are considered capital gains.

Application of certain provisions of double tax treaties
Switzerland has entered into double taxation treaties with a multitude of countries. These treaties largely follow the OECD Model Tax Agreement.

In cases where Switzerland levies withholding tax, any recipient who is a resident of a country with which Switzerland has a double tax treaty, can claim a partial or complete refund of the withholding tax.

Payments based on credit derivatives can be qualified as follows:

- **interest income** (subject to withholding tax), Art. 11 OECD Model Tax Agreement;
- **capital gains income** (withholding tax-free), Art. 13 OECD Model Tax Agreement;
- **all other income** (withholding tax-free), Art. 21 OECD Model Tax Agreement.

Switzerland as the Recipient Country

In general
For Swiss income tax purposes, domestic and foreign source income are in principle treated equally. The character of income is determined according to internal Swiss law. In so far as Switzerland unilaterally or in its tax treaties seeks the avoidance of double taxation, Switzerland shall follow the principle of exemption from tax with inclusion for rate determination. The factors generally used world-wide are authoritative for the determination of the actual tax rate. Switzerland, however, only taxes income based on internal Swiss law or allocated by the double tax treaties to Swiss tax jurisdiction. In particular, profits from foreign permanent establishments are allocated to the country of the permanent establishment.

Unilateral taxation in Switzerland
Since the domestic characterisation of a payment is generally authoritative for income tax purposes, income from pure derivative financial instruments is generally characterised as capital gains. In the case of mixed financial instruments, the respective income statute is authoritative for the differentiation between investment income and capital gains income.

Based on internal regulations only, foreign withholding tax can not be credited against Swiss income. In contrast, foreign withholding tax which may neither be reclaimed nor credited may be deducted as business expenses from taxes independently of whether the asset is allocated to private or business assets.

Application of certain provisions of tax treaties
According to the provisions of the applicable double tax treaty, the foreign withholding tax can be reduced (relieved) at source or later reclaimed.

In principle, the characterisation of the payment is determined (with respect to the recipient) based on the law of the recipient country while the reduction of withholding tax is determined according to the law of the source country. Double taxation resulting from characterisation problems shall be solved by the mutual agreement procedures in the respective double tax treaty.

According to the provisions of most double tax treaties non-reclaimable foreign withholding tax is creditable against Swiss taxes (lump sum tax credit). The maximum credit for withholding tax is limited to the amount which would be due on the same income if Swiss direct taxes were to be paid. In the case of a lump sum tax credit, a different legal classification of income in Switzerland and the country of source does not result in double taxation, given that:

- both investment income and capital gains are taxed in Switzerland at the same rates in the case of business assets;
- the global tax credit for assets belonging to private assets does not apply in the case of different classifications (i.e. either there is no withholding tax or no income tax in Switzerland, so that the maximum tax credit amount is always zero).

18.5.4   Summary

A contract designed to separate credit from an underlying asset is a special arrangement between two contract parties and therefore very individual, private, complex and heavily negotiated. It is difficult to group the different products traded today but the principal products encompass total return swap, credit default products (credit default swaps and credit options) and credit spread products (credit spread forward and credit spread option).

There are no particular supervisory regulations other than the capital requirements for banks, the license requirement for securities dealers and the investment regulations for pension funds and life insurance companies.

The Swiss commercial law permits (except for banks and brokers) for accounting purposes, valuation based on purchase price or market value (for quoted securities which form part of the current assets).

Income from derivative financial instruments is generally considered a capital gain.

Capital gains on business assets are taxable as company profits. The tax treatment of derivative financial instruments follows general accounting rules. Commercially unjustified value adjustments and global provision are not accepted for tax purposes.

The Swiss Double Tax Treaty is modelled after the OECD Model Tax Agreement. Income from DFI is not subject to any withholding tax so long as the income stream is not qualified as dividends or interest payments. According to the provisions of most double tax treaties, Switzerland allows a global credit for non-refundable foreign withholding tax. All remaining double taxation due to differing characterisations of the income in the source and receiving countries should seldom occur and are to be solved through mutual agreement proceedings.

18.6 Accounting for Credit Derivatives — United Kingdom
by Jonathan Davies

18.6.1 Introduction

There are no specific reporting standards currently issued in the UK that cover the measurement of credit derivatives. Accordingly, when considering the accounting issues impacting these products, we seek to draw analogies between credit derivatives and other established products that encompass similar economic risks. In addition, the underlying business intent of the transaction has to be considered. An accounting treatment that is consistent with generally accepted market practice can then be developed. This process should be supported by referring to guidance, that although not specific, may be relevant for determining an acceptable accounting approach. This guidance is detailed below:

British Bankers Association (BBA) Statement of Recommended Practise (SORP) on Derivatives

For banks, the first recommendation to consider is the British Bankers Association Statement of Recommended Practise on Derivatives which was published in February 1997. SORPs are recommended practise for banks only and, while not mandatory, do reflect best practice and would be considered by the Financial Reporting Review Panel as such. However if a bank includes a statement in its annual accounts that it has complied with the SORPs then it is not acceptable for that bank to depart from recommended practice. Although not mandatory, the SORP is good guidance for non-banks to follow.

The SORP defines "derivative" as a generic term that covers a wide range of financial instruments that derive their value from an underlying rate or price (such as interest or exchange rates, equity or commodity prices). There are three basic structures - futures and forwards, swaps and options. The SORP encompasses all exchange rate derivatives including forwards, futures and other financial instruments with similar characteristics, such as interest rate caps and floors. The SORP does not extend to on balance sheet receivables and payables or to derivatives embedded within them. The SORP pre-dates the emergence of credit derivatives and therefore does not address them specifically.

The SORP gives guidance on how profits/losses are recognized by differentiating between transactions which are used for hedging purposes and transactions used for trading activities.

Hedging transactions are defined in the SORP as "transactions entered into with the purpose of matching or eliminating the risk of loss or reduction in profit as a result of movements in interest rates, exchange rates, equity prices or commodity prices. These transactions should be clearly identified and their purpose properly documented at the outset and an ongoing assessment should be undertaken to confirm that such transactions do in fact manage risk to the degree sought". If a derivative is used to hedge a transaction the accounting treatment for the derivative should be consistent with that of the underlying. Hence if a loan which is accrual accounted is hedged using a default swap and this swap is deemed to be an effective hedge, then the credit derivative should be accrual accounted. This means that the premium would be amortized over the life of the credit derivative.

However if the transaction does not meet the hedging criteria, then the derivative instrument should be carried at fair value. In addition any bank which is trading these instruments will carry them at fair value. Fair value is defined as the amount at which the instrument could be exchanged in an arms length transaction between informed and willing parties. The fair value should be determined by reference to the quoted market price, if available, for an instrument, and should take account of future costs including the cost of credit and other risks, close-out costs and administrative costs. The daily price fluctuations of credit derivatives that are traded will be included in the profit and loss account.

BBA SORP on Contingent Liabilities and Commitments

This SORP defines contingent liabilities and commitments and also covers guarantees, which are contracts written by a bank in support of the performance of a customer. In the event that the customer defaults on payments due to a third party, the bank, which is guaranteeing the transaction will have to make good any loss incurred by the bank with the underlying exposure. Sale and option to resell transactions such as repos and reverse repos are considered commitments. The SORP does not cover credit derivatives specifically.

The SORP requires that certain principles of SSAP 2, namely accruals and prudence, be followed. Fees which represent remuneration for credit risk borne should be credited to the profit and loss account on a time-apportioned basis over the period of the risks.

Any position that is similar to a guarantee, such as writing default protection under a credit default swap, should be treated in a manner consistent with a guarantee for accounting purposes. Hence an institution which writes default protection could accrual account for the premium and the position should be off balance sheet. However the protection seller's intention of holding the instrument for the longer term is critical to such an analysis. A long-term holding is normally defined as an instrument where the intention is to hold the instrument to maturity. A short-term position or a position purchased to resell should be carried at fair value.

Financial Reporting Standard (FRS) 5 "Reporting the Substance of Transactions"

FRS 5 specifically excludes derivatives from its scope, unless they form part of a larger transaction that is within the standard's scope. The underlying principles however are generally regarded as best practise for complex transactions and structures and, as such, the principles should be considered for transactions involving credit derivatives.

The basic concept of this standard is "substance over legal form." In other words the intent of the transaction or, a series of transactions if deemed linked, and its exact purpose should be the basis for determining the accounting treatment, rather than specific legal form. A transaction is considered linked with others if the commercial effect can be understood only by considering the series of transaction as a whole.

FRS 5 is an extremely complex and detailed financial reporting standard but will be relevant when institutions use total return swaps or quasi securitization structures.

FRS 13 "Derivatives and Other Financial Instruments – Disclosure"

This standard discusses specifically the disclosure requirements for derivatives and accordingly must be considered when credit derivative positions exist. There is a requirement for both qualitative and quantitative disclosure together with comparatives. Qualitative disclosures include the purpose for which financial instruments are used, a description of the major financial risks which the institution is subject and the approach to managing those risks and the main types of instruments used to do so. Quantitative disclosures include details of notional and fair value of all financial instruments and the value of instruments held for trading and any net gains or losses. The reader will need to review the FRS directly for the full disclosure requirements, which are very detailed.

In this chapter two of the most common credit derivative transactions are discussed, namely credit default swaps (CDS) and total rate of return swaps (TRORS).

18.6.2   Key Considerations — Type of Instrument and Intent

Although credit derivatives represent a new category of derivative transactions, from an accounting perspective the current accounting treatment is a function of two criteria: type of instrument and intent. At present, where an institution uses credit derivatives as an end-user to hedge an existing loan portfolio, provided certain criteria are met, accrual accounting is typically followed. For credit derivative transactions where the institution acts solely as a market maker or a credit exposure is taken with trading intent, fair value accounting is followed.

It can be argued that the cash-flow characteristics of a CDS are similar to other derivative contracts such as options. Thus, one approach is to determine its accounting treatment by analogy to the treatment of such derivatives. Alternatively, where CDSs are economically similar to guarantee contracts, the accounting treatment could be determined by reference to the reporting of such contracts. However, the similarity is not perfect. For instance, unlike guarantees, the pay-out under the CDS is determined by reference to the change in value of a reference asset or an agreed percentage of the notional amount rather than the actual loss incurred by the buyer.

On the other hand, TROR's have a different economic profile to the CDS. They are similar to equity swaps because, in terms of cash flows, market appreciation/depreciation is added to the periodic exchange of coupon and funding payment or receipt. Accordingly they have characteristics similar to these derivative contracts and their accounting treatment could be determined by analogy to the treatment of derivatives.

The principal reporting issue for these types of instruments is whether the instruments should be carried at fair value with changes in fair value reflected in current income or whether, and in what circumstances, accrual or hedge accounting would be appropriate.

18.6.3 UK GAAP — Suggested Application

General guidance is that trading derivative contracts should be marked to market and fair value calculated from this figure. Due regard should be made to the size of the position, liquidity and other factors which may affect the price that could be achieved to close out the position. Relevant provisions should be made in this regard. Changes in the fair value should be recognized in income as they occur. However, when the derivative is considered to be a hedge for reporting purposes (having satisfied both management intentions and risk reduction criteria) hedge accounting may be considered appropriate. Under this alternative, the gain, loss or cash flow from the derivative is recorded in income in the same period as flows arising from the underlying instrument being hedged.

Credit Default Swap (CDS)

If a CDS is viewed as a trading asset, fair value accounting is generally applied for accounting purposes. However, if the protection buyer has purchased the CDS to hedge another asset it may be eligible for hedge accounting. This treatment would be appropriate for example when the protection buyer holds loans or securities whose change in value is expected to be negatively correlated to changes in the value of the CDS and where management has documented their intent to reduce the risks of such loans or securities. Note that if the credit default swap has a shorter duration than the underlying asset, no account of the hedge should be taken until there is protection to maturity in place. This is because even though there may be a fall in value of the underlying asset, a credit event may not necessarily trigger during the covered period and thus further protection would be required.

If viewed as a guarantee, the fee received/paid for providing/receiving protection would be recorded as income/expense over the life of the contract. Any payments that are made by the protection seller are recorded as a loss at the time that is probable that such a payment will be required and the amount payable can be reasonably estimated. Amounts to be received are considered contingent gains which are recorded as income only on crystallization. This income would coincide with the related write-down or provision against the item being hedged.

Total Rate of Return Swap (TRORS)

When considering TRORs, we refer to the accounting treatment adopted for accounting for swaps. Again, fair value accounting would generally be applied and a position in the TRORS would be recorded at its fair value with changes in fair value recorded in income as they occur. However, hedge accounting may be applied if, for example, the total return payer holds a loan or security whose change in value is negatively correlated to the TRORS and the intent is to hedge the underlying risk of such a loan or security. Payments or receipts attributed to any actual cash flows or change in value of the designated loan or security will offset the opposite movements under the TRORS. In this way the profit and loss effect is mitigated representing a hedged position.

There are specific rules on netting for accounting purposes that would make it difficult for a protection buyer to net down a hedged position on its balance sheet. One such requirement is the ability to have legal right of offset. This is unlikely as the protection seller is not expected to be the same as the issuer of the security or the borrowing entity.

18.6.4 ASB's Discussion Paper — Derivatives and Financial Instruments

Additional thinking on the accounting for derivatives is likely to develop from the ASB discussion paper on derivatives and financial instruments which was published in July 1996. This paper addresses three main issues — measurement, hedge accounting and disclosure. The disclosure proposals have been discussed above.

The proposals in the discussion paper relating to the measurement of financial instruments and hedge accounting are summarized below.

18.6.5 Measurement

The ASB proposes that all financial instruments should be measured at current value and all gains and losses recognized in the financial statements as they occur. It is accepted, however, that it is inappropriate to recognize all of these gains and losses in the P&L itself, as they often do not result from the ongoing operations of the enterprise. As a result, the ASB propose that both realized and unrealized gains and losses associated with the following instruments should be reported in the statement of gains and losses (STRGL), i.e. fixed rate borrowings, interest-rate derivatives used to manage the interest basis of borrowings, currency borrowings and derivatives used to manage the currency translation risk of investments in overseas operations.

18.6.6 Hedge Accounting

The discussion paper also considered whether hedge accounting should be permitted. It was noted that some board members believe that no hedge accounting treatment should be used, as allowing an exception to normal accounting rules is not justified. This approach would therefore disallow the use of accrual accounting for credit derivative instruments which are considered hedges. However, although there are opponents to hedge accounting other members of the ASB would permit some hedge accounting.

The ASB has proposed two solutions in relation to hedge accounting and envisage that either one or a combination of the two will be incorporated into a standard in the future. The proposed accounting treatments are as follows:

(a)   The hedge should be measured at its current value in the balance sheet and the resulting gain or loss should be recorded in the balance sheet within liabilities or assets respectively. The effect of this is that a loss will be recorded as an asset whereas a gain will appear as a liability.

(b)   The hedge should be measured at is current value in the balance sheet, and any resulting gain or loss should be recorded in the STRGL to the P&L account in a later period when the hedged transaction occurs.

18.6.7   Summary

It should be noted that under UK GAAP, the recommended accounting treatment for accounting for financial instruments is still under review and minimum authoritative guidance is currently available, although this is likely to change in the future. The accounting treatment discovered above is based on the current market practise adopted for accounting derivatives.

18.7   Tax Considerations in the United Kingdom
by Emma Lubbock and Matthew Davidson

18.7.1   Introduction

This section is intended to outline the key taxation issues from a United Kingdom (UK) perspective. In recent years there has been considerable changes made to the UK tax system due to the ever increasing complexity and diversity of financial instruments. The intention of these changes is to bring the taxation of financial instruments within a statutory code, rather than a combination of statute law, case law principles and Inland Revenue practise.

Specifically, legislation in relation to financial instruments, foreign exchange and loan relationships has been enacted. Essentially this legislation seeks to remove the income/capital distinction and tax payments and receipts falling within the new legislation on revenue account, as opposed to capital account. The majority of this legislation is contained in the Finance Act 1993 (FA93), the

Finance Act 1994 (FA94) and the Finance Act 1996 (FA96) and is discussed below. Transactions which do not meet the requirements of FA93, FA94 and FA96 will continue to be subject to the traditional rules which are also discussed below.

This section addresses the taxation of credit derivatives based on the law as it applies from 1 April 1996 and concentrates on the position of typical companies resident in the UK for tax purposes. The taxation implications of taxpayers such as individuals, pension funds, investment trusts, insurance companies and the like is not addressed.

It is not intended that this section provide a definitive treatment of the taxation of credit derivatives, but rather it is intended to identify key taxation issues to be considered. Notably, where a credit derivative transaction is taxable under the "new" provisions the taxation treatment is relatively straightforward. Where the transaction is taxable under the "old" provisions, the taxation treatment can be complex and uncertain. As such, where taxpayers are seeking certainty and simplicity of taxation treatment it may be preferable to ensure transactions are taxable under the new provisions.

18.7.2 General Taxation Aspects of Credit Derivatives

When considering the taxation implications of credit derivatives, as with any financial instrument, it is important to consider the legal rights and obligations of the parties, and not simply the label applied to the transaction or the economic result achieved. As there is no legislation dealing specifically with the general category of credit derivatives, it is only once these rights and obligations have been determined that appropriate tax legislation can be applied to the transaction.

As credit derivatives seek to mimic the economic risks and rewards of credit assets without transferring or creating a credit asset, correctly understanding the legal rights and obligations arising from the transaction is essential. These rights will depend on the type of credit derivative, being total return, credit spread and credit default products. The general taxation aspects associated with these products are discussed below.

Total Return Products

Total return products seek to replicate the total performance of a loan asset. These products are often variations of traditional swap transactions. Under a total return swap the investor will assume all risk and cash flow associated with the credit asset. Typically the investor and the counter party enter into an agreement such that price changes and cash flows under the contract will be borne by the investor, whilst the investor pays the counter party (for example, a bank) some other rate of return such as LIBOR.

The taxation treatment of total return products will depend on whether the investor obtains (or may obtain) rights and liabilities corresponding with those that would exist if the investor were party to a "loan relationship". Legislation addressing the taxation of loan relationships was introduced as part of FA96. Essentially, a loan relationship will exist where a company stands in the same position as a creditor or debtor in relation to a money debt which has arisen from the actual or deemed lending of money. A money debt is essentially a debt which falls to be settled by payment of money, or by transfer of a right to settlement under a money debt. The taxation of loan relationships is not discussed in this book.

Where the investor has obtained rights and liabilities corresponding with a loan relationship, it is necessary to consider whether the investor has entered into a debt contract (possibly combined with a qualifying interest rate contract) and is now subject to the provisions of FA94. Where the investor has not obtained rights and liabilities corresponding with a loan relationship, or the transaction does not satisfy the definition of either a debt contract or an interest rate contract, the traditional provisions that applied prior to the introduction of FA94 will apply.

It is important to note that total return products do not generally disturb the underlying credit asset, and therefore, the taxation treatment of the lender and borrower will continue unaltered.

Credit Spread Products

Credit spread products seek to isolate and capture value from expectations on future credit spreads. These transactions may be structured in a number of ways, however typically involve a net cash settlement based on the difference between an agreed spread and the actual spread between two securities.

The taxation treatment of credit spread products will depend on whether the investor has become party to an interest rate contract under FA94. Where the investor is not party to an interest rate contract the provisions that applied prior to the introduction of FA94 will apply.

Credit Default Products

Credit default products seek to isolate and capture value from expectations on the risk of default on credit obligations. These transactions may be structured as default swaps or options, or as indemnity agreements. In the absence of careful structuring these transactions are unlikely to be classified as debt contracts or interest rate contracts, and thus will be subject to the traditional taxation provisions which operated prior to the introduction of FA94.

18.7.3 Taxation Treatment of Credit Derivatives – Taxation Treatment under FA94

As noted above, the purpose of the new legislation is to remove the traditional income/capital distinction, and tax all qualifying transactions on revenue account. Transactions specifically captured by FA94 are interest rate contracts, currency contracts and debt contracts. The calculation and treatment of profits and losses arising on these contracts is similar, and is summarized below. FA94 applies to accounting periods ending on or after 1 April 1996.

What is a Debt Contract?

A debt contract will exist, firstly, where a company enters into a contract such that the company has any entitlement, or is subject to any duty, to become a party to a "loan relationship" (s. 150A(1) FA94). Secondly, a debt contract will exist where a company enters into a contract such that the company becomes entitled to rights and liabilities corresponding to those of a party to a "loan relationship" (s. 150A(2) FA94).

It is not necessary for a credit asset (i.e. loan relationship) to physically exist for there to be a debt contract. Rather, as noted above, a company must simply obtain rights and liabilities which correspond with those that would exist if it were party to a loan relationship. As such, where an investor is party to a total return product which is structured such that the credit risk (i.e. price movements) associated with the credit asset will be borne by the investor, it is likely the debt contract legislation will apply to the transaction.

A final requirement for the debt contract legislation to apply is that the only payments made under the contract are "qualifying payments". The term "qualifying payment" is defined in s. 153 FA94. In relation to debt contracts this term includes the following types of payments:

(i)   Payments to become a party to an actual loan relationship;
(ii) Payments by reference to the value at any time of the underlying money debt related to an actual loan relationship; and
(iii) Settlement payments calculated by reference to the value of the underlying credit asset at the beginning and end of the debt contract period (whether

or not the underlying is an actual loan relationship or only equivalent to a loan relationship).

In addition the payment of reasonable fees and costs associated with arranging, altering and terminating the debt contract will also be regarded as qualifying payments under FA94.

Where an agreement to acquire an actual loan relationship exists, the legislation will deem there to be a separate debt contract with all the cash flows constituting qualifying payments.

What is a Qualifying Interest Rate Contract?

An interest rate contract will exist where a company enters into a contract such that the company becomes entitled to a right to receive, or become subject to a duty to pay, an amount established by applying a variable rate of interest to a notional principal sum. The contract may also allow for other qualifying payments such as fixed rate payments, lump sum payments and payment of fees. Whilst the point has not been tested, it might be possible to structure periodic payments which depend on the credit standing of a borrower as a variable rate of interest.

Calculation of Profits and Losses

Where a transaction is taxed under FA94 profits and losses arising must be calculated using either a mark to market basis or an accruals basis in accordance with normal accountancy practise. Where a company has prepared its accounts using either method, this method must also be used for tax purposes. However, where a company has not used one of these methods in preparing its accounts, the company must prepare its tax computations using either a mark to market or accruals methods as agreed with, or alternatively notified to, the Inland Revenue.

In practise the effect of these calculations will be to bring the net of the following amounts to account on an accruals basis in respect of each asset:

(i)   Price movements;
(ii)   Interest receipts;
(iii)   Fees and costs; and
(iv)   Exchange gains losses

Treatment of Profits and Losses

Where a transaction is entered into in the course of a company's trade, any income or expense arising under the transaction will be assessed/relieved as either a trading expense or trading income under Schedule D Case I. Where a transaction is entered into other than in the course of a trade, income from the contract will be assessed as a "non-trading credit", whilst expenses will be relieved as a "non-trading debit" under comprehensive loss relief rules.

18.7.4 Taxation Treatment Under Traditional Provisions

As it is anticipated that many of the above transactions will now be dealt with under FA94, the provisions which apply to transactions conducted in financial years ending before April 1, 1996, and for transactions not covered by FA94, have not been discussed in detail as this is a relatively complex area.

However, where a transaction is not subject to the provisions of FA94, or was entered into in an accounting period ending before April 1, 1996, it is necessary to determine whether or not the transaction is entered into in the course of a trade. Where a company enters into a credit derivative transaction as part of its trade, the taxation treatment will generally be in line with the accounting treatment. This will not be the case however if the transaction is for a non-trade purpose or the instrument is on capital account.

Where a company enters into a credit derivative transaction that is non-trading, it will normally be treated as a capital transaction and taxed under the capital gains provisions. As such, net capital gains, after allowing for inflation, will be brought to account in the company's tax computation, whilst capital losses may only be offset against capital gains of the same or later years making effective relief difficult to obtain. Furthermore the capital gains regime only applies to assets and if loss making contracts are regarded as liabilities they will fall outside the scope of the UK tax regime.

In addition contracts which have a capital nature may generate cash flows with a revenue characteristic. In the absence of trading treatment there is no clear basis for securing relief for such payments. Finally the cost of credit derivatives may be treated as wasting away over their lives without giving rise to a tax deduction. Although these rules are disapplied for financed futures and options, credit derivatives may not be within the definitions particularly in the case of option contracts.

Where a company enters into a transaction that is non-trading, and not capital in nature, it is possible that any gain or loss would be accounted for under Case VI of Schedule D. This is historically an unattractive taxation treatment as Case VI losses cannot be offset against trading or capital gains, and may only be offset against future Case VI income. Changes in the Finance Act 1997 may have alleviated this difficulty since it should not be relatively straight forward to generate Case VI income and thus gain relief. In practise Case VI will only rarely apply to unconditional contracts if they are "futures" for UK tax purposes. (The term future is not defined). This is because futures entered into with regulated entities will be treated as capital if not a trading item. There is an equivalent rule for options but the relevant definition is unhelpful and careful consideration would need to be given to the structure of the credit derivative if the rule is to be applied.

18.7.5 Anti-avoidance Provisions

Where a qualifying contract results in the transfer of value between associated companies, or is conducted other than on an arm's length basis, specific provisions within FA94 act to adjust the respective contract values to ensure all parties to the contract are taxed as if the contract had been entered into on an arm's length basis. The traditional capital gains rules also incorporate adjustments to arm's length values although the rules are less detailed than the FA 94 regime.

18.7.5 Value Added Tax (VAT)

A typical credit derivative will, in principal, be an exempt financial product for VAT purposes so no VAT is chargeable on payments passing under the contract. Difficulties arise, however, in determining whether supplies are being made by either party to the contract for a consideration. Customs tend to view contracts of this nature as not giving rise to consideration for VAT purposes unless a premium or fee is charged for the derivative contract. The payments made by either party under the contract itself are, generally, not viewed as consideration (unlike interest rate or currency swaps).

This may impact on the VAT recovery position of the parties to the contract as VAT incurred on expenditure that relates directly or indirectly to these non-taxable contracts will be irrecoverable. This treatment can be contrasted with that of a contract that does give rise to consideration for VAT purposes where the payer of the consideration is outside the EU. In this case any VAT on attributable costs, both direct and indirect, would be recoverable.

18.8   Accounting for Credit Derivatives — United States
by John T. Lawton and Nabi Niang

18.8.1   The New Accounting Framework

Accounting standards worldwide continue to evolve in an effort to address the most recent capital markets products. Given their relative newness in relation to many other types of derivatives, credit derivatives in particular have had little authoritative accounting guidance devoted to them. As a result, a variety of paradigms have been used to develop accounting guidance for the variety of transactions that developed in the market place. Soon, however, there will be a uniform model for addressing derivative transactions, including most credit derivatives. With the issuance by the Financial Accounting Standards Board in June 1998 of Statement of Financial Accounting Standards No. 133, "Accounting for Derivative Instruments and Hedging Activities," (FAS 133) comprehensive, definitive guidance has been provided on accounting for derivatives in the US. That statement becomes effective for most entities at the beginning of 2001. Other standard setters have proposals in various stages of development, and it is virtually certain that a steady flow of additional accounting guidance will be issued in the foreseeable future with implications for the accounting for credit derivative transactions. Consultation with a locally qualified accountant is recommended when considering how to account for a specific transaction. This chapter focuses on this new accounting standard, which will become applicable in the US.

Prior to the release of FAS 133, specific US GAAP guidance for credit derivatives had been virtually nonexistent. General guidance was clear that non-hedging derivative contracts should be marked to market and that changes in fair value should generally be recognized in the profit and loss account as they occur. Questions arose, however, as to whether certain credit derivatives should be considered as "derivatives" for accounting purposes. Other accounting models, such as the accounting for guarantees, were applied by analogy in some circumstances. In addition, where a credit derivative might be considered to be part of a hedge transaction or a synthetic instrument, it was unclear what criteria should be applied to qualify for specialized accounting treatment.

FAS 133 gives greater definition to the accounting for most credit derivative transactions. It establishes criteria for determining which products should be considered derivatives for accounting purposes and which products should be afforded treatment under other accounting models. It also provides for consistency between the treatment for embedded credit derivatives and those that are free standing. FAS 133 prohibits synthetic instrument accounting and requires embedded derivatives that are not clearly and closely related to the host contract in which they are embedded to be bifurcated from that host and treated as if the embedded instrument was a stand-alone instrument. FAS 133 also establishes rules for credit derivatives used in hedging transactions, allowing special accounting only when a series of criteria for both the hedging instrument and the item being hedged are met.

Under the new accounting guidance, credit derivative instruments generally will be marked-to-market and the corresponding change in fair value for each period will be reported in earnings. Special accounting treatment is possible if the credit derivative instrument is part of a qualifying accounting hedge transaction. When the credit derivative is part of an effective cash flow hedge, the portion of the change in value that is effective as an offset to the change in cash flows being hedged may be reported in other comprehensive income. Later, when the hedged cash flows affect reported earnings, other comprehensive income will be released into reported earnings as well. If the credit derivative product is part of an effective fair value hedge, the basis of the hedged item may be adjusted for changes in fair value attributable to the risk being hedged. The change in earnings from the basis adjustment thus offsets, to the extent effective, the earnings effect of the change in the fair value of the credit derivative product.

Figure 18.1 demonstrates how the range of credit derivative transactions can be categorized for accounting purposes and describes the respective accounting treatments. While each of the decision points in the diamonds seems straightforward, there are in fact detailed criteria for making each of the determinations. The criteria do not always render the intuitive result. In addition, there are many ambiguities that have not been resolved in interpreting the new guidance. So, despite the improved clarity of the accounting model, it is not always clear what the appropriate accounting treatment for a transaction should be. Rather than attempt to decipher all the intricacies of whether an instrument should be bifurcated from its host or what contracts qualify as a derivative, the remainder of this chapter will attempt to demonstrate how the basic accounting model is applied to two of the most commonly traded credit derivatives: total return swaps and credit default swaps.

Total Return Swaps

In general, a total return swap buyer exchanges the economic performance (i.e., all due contractual amounts and observed price appreciation) of a reference asset, or index, for a return that typically — but not necessarily always - approximates the protection seller's short-term borrowing costs, plus any observed price depreciation of the reference asset. The observed price differential component may be determined periodically or at contract maturity. Total return swaps can be structured for a notional amount different to that of the reference security, with the exchange of payments adjusted proportionally. During the life of a total return swap, the protection buyer can effectively exchange its credit risk on the reference asset obligor for the credit risk of the protection seller on the contract's notional amount.

Figure 18.1   Basis of Recognition of Credit Derivative Contracts

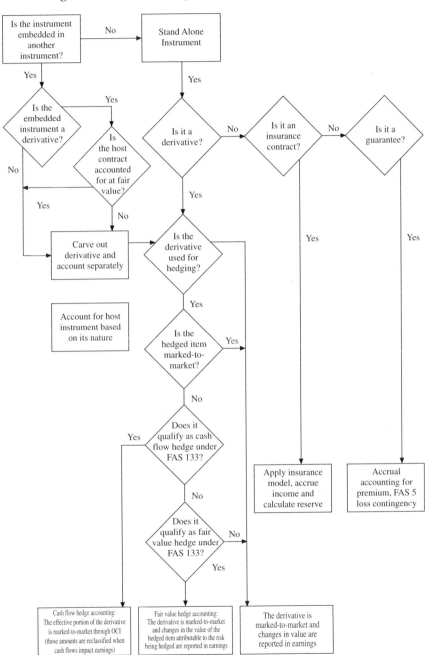

The economic characteristics of total return swaps are significantly different from those of credit default products. Total return swaps can be compared to equity swaps, because in terms of cash flows, market appreciation or depreciation is added to the periodic exchange of coupon payments. Total return swaps will most likely meet the definition of a derivative under FAS 133, and will therefore be covered by the new Standard.

Let us consider the following example in Figure 18.2:

Figure 18.2

Total return swap between Bank A and Bank B with the loan between Bank A and Company C as the "reference asset." At each payment date or at the date of default on the loan, any depreciation or appreciation in the value of the reference asset is calculated as the difference between the notional principal balance of the reference asset and the dealer price determined by reference to the average of quotes by a group of specified dealers. The dealer price will reflect changes in the credit profile of the reference obligor and the reference asset.

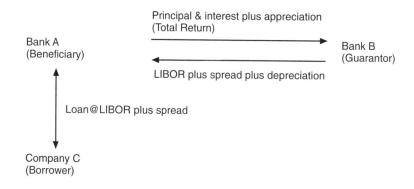

Contractual Cash Flows on Loan (Assuming no Default)	Bank A $'m	Company C $'m
Let us assume that the loan by Bank A to Company C has a principal balance of $100 million, carries a rate of interest of 7%, and matures with a bullet payment at the end of 5 years. As such the expected cash flows would be as follows:		
Year 0	(100)	100
Year 1	7	(7)

Year 2		7	(7)
Year 3		7	(7)
Year 4		7	(7)
Year 5		107	(107)

Let us assume that the terms of the Total Return Swap between Bank A and Bank B are such that Bank A makes a single annual payment to Bank B of all receipts (i.e., principal and interest payments) from Company C, as well as any increases in the value of the loan (based on dealer quotes). In exchange, Bank B pays annually to Bank A, LIBOR plus 1.25% on $100 million. In addition, Bank B makes a payment to Bank A for any diminution in the secondary market value of the loan.

In addition, let us assume that Company C's debt value on the secondary market decreases in price by 10% from year 1 to year 3, and by 5% in year 4 and 5, and that the company defaults on termination and that the final repayment in Year 5 is only $60 million.

Company A decides to hedge its exposure to changes in the fair value of the loan. At the inception of the hedge, there is formal documentation of the hedging relationship and the entity's risk-management objective and strategy for undertaking the hedge. Both at the inception of the hedge and on an ongoing basis (at a minimum every three months), the hedging relationship is expected to be highly effective in achieving offsetting changes in fair value during the 5 years. The company measures the degree of ongoing effectiveness by comparing the change in the fair value of total return swap to the change in the fair value of the loan. The hedging relationship is deemed to be effective since the changes in the fair value of the total return swap are between 80 percent and 125 percent of the inverse changes in the fair value of the loan.

Year	Transaction	LIBOR + 1.25%	Bank A Carrying Value of Loan at End of Year***	Movement in Bank A's Profit & Loss	Movement in Bank B's Profit & Loss
0	Loan Disbursement		100		
1		6.90%	90		
	Loan:				
	Interest received			7	
	Basis adjustment**			(10)	
	Total Return Swap:				

Payment to Bank B			(7)	7
Receipts from Bank B:				
• Interest			6.90	(6.90)
• Loan depreciation			10	(10)
TRS mark-to-market change*			0.2	(0.2)
2	6.95%	80		
Loan:				
Interest received			7	
Basis adjustment**			(10)	
Total Return Swap:				
Payment to Bank B			(7)	7
Receipts from Bank B:				
• Interest			6.95	(6.95)
• Loan depreciation			10	(10)
TRS mark-to-market change*			0.2	(0.2)
3	6.80%	70		
Loan:				
Interest received			7	
Basis adjustment**			(10)	
Total Return Swap:				
Payment to Bank B			(7)	7
Receipts from Bank B:				
• Interest			6.80	(6.80)
• Loan depreciation			10	(10)
TRS mark-to-market change*			0.25	(0.25)
4	6.85%	65		
Loan:				
Interest received			7	
Basis adjustment**			(5)	
Total Return Swap:				
Payment to Bank B			(7)	7
Receipts from Bank B:				
• Interest			6.85	(6.85)
• Loan depreciation			5	(5)
TRS mark-to-market change*			0.30	(0.30)

5		6.95%	60		
Loan:					
Interest received				7	
Basis adjustment**				(5)	
Total Return Swap:					
Payment to Bank B				(7)	7
Receipts from Bank B:					
• Interest				6.95	(6.95)
• Loan depreciation				5	(5)
TRS mark-to-market change*				0.95	(0.95)

*   Period change in the swap mark-to-market adjusted for settlements (mostly reflects change in spread on the total return swap).

** The basis adjustments are passed to adjust the loan's carrying value for changes in its market value during each reporting period.

*** Carrying values are presented net of the basis adjustment recorded at the end of the period.

Under FAS 133, the entire gain or loss on the total return swap is recognized into earnings. The change in the fair value of the loan, based on market price, is recorded as a basis adjustment and is also recognized in earnings. As such, any ineffectiveness in the hedging relationship is necessarily reflected currently in earnings.

An asset that has been designated as being hedged and accounted for in accordance with FAS 133 remains subject to the applicable requirements in generally accepted accounting principles for assessing impairment for that type of asset. The impairment requirements of FAS 114, "Accounting by Creditors for Impairment of a Loan," will be applied by Company A after hedge accounting has been applied for the period and the carrying amount of the loan has been adjusted.

As illustrated in example I, Bank A earns a stable income through its hedging strategy, although there is some earnings volatility to the extent that the changes in the swap mark-to-market and the adjustments of the basis of the loan do not offset each other perfectly. Overall Bank A achieves its goal of hedging the risks related to changes in market value of the underlying loan. However, it is important to note that if the total return swap does not continue to be effective as a hedge of the loan, subsequent derivative gains or losses would be directly recognized into income and changes in value of the hedged item would no longer be recorded in income. This situation could potentially result in volatile earnings.

If company A decided not to apply hedge accounting, mark-to-market accounting would be applied and a position in the total return swap would be recorded at its fair value with changes in fair value recorded in income as they occur. An allowance for loan losses would be set aside on the loan if there were a significant likelihood of Company A not recovering the full value of the loan, in accordance with US GAAP (i.e., FAS 114).

Credit Default Swaps

A credit default product is intended to provide some protection against credit losses associated with a default event on a specific reference asset. The product buyer pays a premium to the seller for a future event, such as a rating downgrade or non-performance of the reference asset, which is typically an asset held by the protection buyer. The conditional payment may be an amount fixed at contract inception or an amount determined at the time of a credit event, usually based on observed depreciation in the market price of the reference asset or of a similar debt of the obligor.

The cash flow characteristics of a credit default swaps are similar to derivative contracts with optionality. Alternatively, where credit default swaps are economically similar to financial guarantee contracts, the accounting treatment could be determined by reference to the reporting of such contracts.

FAS 133 establishes guidance for determining which contracts should be considered derivatives and which should be analogized to other types of products such as financial guarantees. A contract may be considered a financial guarantee only if one party to the contract will receive payment as a reimbursement for actual losses incurred because the underlying debtor fails to make payment when due.

This guidance will cause many contracts that have previously been treated by analogy to standby letters of credit and other credit products to be considered derivatives from the date of adoption of FAS 133. That means that contracts which were accounted for by amortizing premiums through date of maturity on a systematic basis and reporting loss accruals when losses become probable will suddenly be accounted for at market value.

Credit default swaps that are within the scope of FAS 133 will be accounted for just the same as other options. Consequently, they will be marked-to-market each period and reported on the balance sheet at fair value. If the entity opts to designate the credit default swap as a hedge, the effectiveness of the hedging relationship for option products can be determined by comparing the change in value of the hedged item to:

- the change in the total fair value of the credit default swap
- the change in the intrinsic value of the option
- the change in the minimum value, that is intrinsic value plus the effect of discounting

In each circumstance above, changes in the fair value of the excluded component would be included currently in earnings, together with any ineffectiveness that results under the entity's defined method of assessing ineffectiveness.

To the extent that the option will have no intrinsic value unless there is a default event (i.e., when the credit default swap is exercised), entities will most likely choose to measure effectiveness based on changes in the full fair value of the option, consisting only of time value. Due to the volatility of the time value component of the credit default swap, the effectiveness test requirements of FAS133 will be hard to meet.

Let us consider the scenario set out in **Figure 18.3**:

Figure 18.3

Credit Default Swap between Bank A and Bank B with the loan between Bank A and Company C as the "reference asset." At each payment date, Bank A pays to Bank B a fee of a number of basis points on the par value of the reference asset. In return Bank B agrees to pay Bank A an agreed upon, market-based, post-default amount or a predetermined fixed percentage of the value of the reference asset if there is a default. Bank B makes no payment until there is a default as defined in the legal agreement, and involves the absorption of a specified level of loss by Bank A before any payment is made by Bank B.

As in Example 1, let us assume that the loan by Bank A to Company C has a principal balance of $100 million, carries a rate of interest of 7%, and matures with a bullet payment at the end of 5 years.

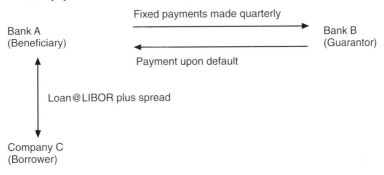

Let us assume that the terms of the Credit Default Swap between Bank A and Bank B are such that Bank A makes a single annual payment to Bank B of 0.7% of the principal of the loan. These payments are made for the duration of the swap, or until default occurs if that is earlier. In exchange, Bank B agrees to reimburse Bank A, in the amount of the difference between the principal outstanding and the market value of the loan, at the date of default by Company C.

In addition, let us assume that Company C defaults on the loan from Bank A midway through Year 3, and that Bank A sells the loan in Year 4 for $75 million.

The contract does not require, as a precondition for payment of a claim, that Bank A be exposed to a loss on the referenced asset due to the debtor's failure to pay when payment is due. Consequently, the credit default swap cannot be considered a financial guarantee, and must be accounted for in accordance with the requirements of FAS 133. Company A decides not to opt for hedge accounting. The mark to market of the credit default swap is thus recorded into income and the loan is accounted for in accordance with US GAAP.

Year	Transaction	Market Value of the Loan	Bank A Carrying Value of Loan	Movement in Bank A's Profit & Loss	Movement in Bank B's Profit & Loss
0	Loan Disbursement	100	100		
1		100	100		
	Loan:				
	Loan interest received			7	
	Credit Default Swap:				
	Payment to Bank B			(0.7)	0.7
	Receipt from Bank B:			0	0
	Change in mark-to-market			0.5	(0.5)
2		98	100*		
	Loan:				
	Loan interest received			7	
	Credit Default Swap:				
	Payment to Bank B			(0.7)	0.7
	Receipt from Bank B:			0	0
	Change in mark-to-market			2.2	(2.2)

3		70	70		
	Loan:				
	Loan interest received				
	Loan Loss Reserve**			(30)	
	Credit Default Swap:				
	Payment to Bank B			(0.7)	0.7
	Receipt from Bank B:			30	(30)
	(default payment)				
	Change in mark-to-market			(2.7)	2.7
4		75	70		
	Loan:				
	Loan interest received				
	Recovery on loan sale			5	
	Credit Default Swap:				
	Payment to Bank B				
	Receipt from Bank B:			0	
	Change in mark-to-market			0	
				N/A	N/A
5		N/A	N/A	N/A	N/A
	Loan:				
	Loan interest received				
	Loan Principal received				
	Credit Default Swap:				
	Payment to Bank B				
	Receipts from Bank B:				

*   Reduction in market value believed to be temporary
** At the end of the reporting period, Bank A does not anticipate any improvement on the loan credit risk and thus records a charge – off of $30 million

If a credit default product is viewed as a guarantee rather than an option contract, the fee for providing protection is recorded as income by Bank B and as expense by Bank A. Any payment made by the protection seller (i.e. Bank B) is recorded as a loss at the time that it is probable that such a payment will be required and can be reasonably estimated. Amounts to be received by Bank A from Bank B are considered contingent gains and are recorded as income only on realization. This treatment is consistent with the reporting treatment of letters of credit and guarantees under FAS 5 "Accounting for Contingencies."

Disclosure

For credit derivatives that are considered to be derivatives and subject to the requirements of FAS 133, an entity is required to disclose its objectives for holding or issuing such instruments, the context needed to understand those objectives, and its strategies for achieving those objectives. The disclosure should distinguish between instruments designated as fair value hedges, cash flow hedges and all other types of credit derivatives. It should also include a summary of the risk management policy for each type of hedge, including a description of the transactions or items for which risks are hedged.

For those instruments not designated as hedging instruments, the purpose of the credit derivative activity should be described. Additional quantitative disclosure is required for credit derivatives that have been designated as fair value or cash flow hedge instruments.

The disclosure requirements of FAS 5 "Accounting of Loss Contingencies" will have to be considered for credit derivatives accounted for as financial guarantees. This standard establishes disclosure requirements for both gain and loss contingencies.

In addition, pursuant to FAS 107 "Disclosures about Fair Value of Financial Instruments" (as amended by FAS 133), an entity has to disclose:

- the fair value of the financial instruments, both assets and liabilities recognized and not recognized in the statement of financial position, for which it is practicable to estimate fair value. If estimating fair value is not practicable, the Statement requires disclosure of descriptive information pertinent to estimating the value of a financial instrument.
- all significant concentrations of credit risk arising from all financial instruments, whether from an individual counterparty or a group of counterparties.

18.9 Taxation Considerations in the United States
by Viva Hammer

In the past five years, the US has developed a fairly comprehensive regime for the taxation of derivative products. The key questions of timing and source of income or loss can be answered with some degree of certainty for most derivative products, although the issue of the character of income remains controversial because of the lack of statutory or regulatory guidance. The US federal tax system generally taxes a transaction according to its classification as debt or equity, an option, forward/future or a swap. For transactions that have the characteristics of more than one of these financial building blocks, it becomes more difficult to conduct tax analysis, since neither bifurcation nor integration of instruments is generally acceptable to characterize the transaction (except when specifically permitted by the Internal Revenue Code or Regulations thereunder).

The three kinds of products that are collectively called "credit derivatives" will be analyzed below more or less comfortably using existing US federal taxation models, and we will discuss each separately below.

18.9.1   Timing

Total return products

Under these products, one party agrees to pay to the other the return on a public or private loan/bond, or a basket of loans/bonds, in exchange for a Libor-based return on the outstanding loan balance or face value on the bond. The most pertinent guidance in regard to this product is the regulation governing "notional principal contracts."

A notional principal contract is a financial instrument that provides for payment of amounts by one party to another at specified intervals calculated by reference to a specified index upon a notional principal amount in exchange for specified consideration or a promise to pay similar amounts.[1] Several elements of this definition deserve further discussion:

1. A notional principal contract only requires one party to make regular payments. As long as the other party makes some promise, or transfers other good consideration, there is no need for both parties to make regular payments.

2. A specified index can be a rate, price, or amount that is constant throughout the life of the contract, or changes from period to period. It can also be an index that is based on current, objectively determinable financial information that is not within the control of any of the parties to the contract and is not unique to one of the party's circumstances (e.g., one of the party's dividends, profits or the value of its stock)[2].

3. A notional principal amount is any specified amount of money or property that, when multiplied by a specified index, measures a party's rights and obligations under the contract, but is not borrowed or loaned between the parties as part of the contract. The notional amount can vary over the term

---

[1]   Reg. §1.446-3(c)(1)(i)
[2]   Reg. §1.446-3(c)(2) and Reg. §1.446-3(c)(4)(ii)

of the contract, provided that it is set in advance or varies based on objective financial information.[3]

Many total return swaps will fall under this definition. However, if the agreement provides for bullet payments by both parties at the maturity of the contract (analagous to a zero coupon bond on both sides) there is no "payment of amounts by one party to another at specified intervals," and the contract will not be a notional principal contract.

Payments under notional principal contracts are taken into income under three different regimes, depending on whether they are "periodic" payments, "nonperiodic" payments or "termination" payments.

Periodic payments are payable at intervals of one year or less during the entire term of the contract, are based on a specified index and on a single notional principal amount or a notional principal amount that varies over the term of the contract in the same proportion as the notional amount that measures the other party's payments.[4] Taxpayers are required to recognize the daily portion of a periodic payment for the taxable year to which that portion relates.[5] This means that the total periodic payment due by each party is netted, then divided by the number of days in the payment period, and then multiplied by the number of days of that payment period that fall within the taxpayer's tax year.

A termination payment is one made or received to extinguish or assign all or a proportionate part of the remaining rights and obligations of any party to a notional principal contract. It includes a payment made between the original parties to the contract (an extinguishment), a payment made between one party to the contract and a third party (an assignment), and any gain or loss realized on the exchange of one notional principal contract for another. A nonassigning counterparty under a notional principal contract will have a taxable event if the assignment results in a deemed exchange of contracts and a realization event under the general sale or exchange principles of the tax law.[6] A party to a

---

[3] Reg. §1.446-3(c)(3)

[4] Reg. §1.446-3(e)(1)

[5] Reg. §1.446-3(e)(2)(i)

[6] Reg. Sss1.446-3(h). The general sale or exchange rules are found in Sss1001 Regulations promulgated under that code section provide that substitution of a new party under a notional principal contract is not treated as a deemed exchange by the nonassigning party if the party assigning its rights and obligations and the party to whom the rights and obligations are assigned are both swap dealers, and the terms of the contract permit the substitution. Reg. Sss1.1001-4(a)

notional principal contract recognizes a termination payment in the year the contract is extinguished, assigned, or exchanged.[7]

The third type of payment under a notional principal contract is a nonperiodic payment, which is defined as a payment that is neither a periodic nor a termination payment.[8] The regulations require taxpayers to recognize the ratable daily portion of a nonperiodic payment for the taxable year to which the payment relates, in a manner that reflects the economic substance of the transaction. The general rule is that a nonperiodic payment must be recognized over the term of the contract by allocating it in accordance with the forward rates of a series of cash-settled forward contracts that reflect the specified index and the notional principal amount.[9]

Credit Default Products

Credit default products generally provide for one party to make regular interest payments based on a notional principal amount and the other party to make a payment if a defined "credit event" occurs. As explained above, this kind of contract will fit within the definition of a notional principal contract as long as at least one party makes regular payments. If both parties agree to make payments only on the occurrence of the credit event, the contract will not be a notional principal contract.

Although accounting for the periodic payments under the credit default contracts is fairly clear, particular problems arise when trying to account for the contingent (nonperiodic) payment which may or may not be made at termination. For example, one party agrees to pay a fixed percentage of the notional principal amount throughout the life of the contract, and the other party agrees to pay the notional principal amount if country X defaults on its public obligations. Since there is a possibility that country X will never default, the final payment is considered contingent. The preamble to the notional principal contract regulations explicitly excludes contingent nonperiodic payments from the notional principal contract rules. This may indicate that the IRS will not require taxpayers to amortize contingent nonperiodic payments into income throughout the life of contingent payment swaps, as is required for all other nonperiodic payments. However, in Notice 89-21, 1989-1 C.B. 651, the Service required amortization of lump-sum payments made under a swap, and did not make any exception for contingent payments. Basing their analysis on clear

---

[7] Reg. §1.446-3(h)(2)
[8] Reg. §1.446-3(f)(1)
[9] Reg. §1.446-3(f)(2)(ii)

reflection of income principles, Notice 89-21 states that recognizing a lump-sum payment in the year of receipt is not appropriate, and that some kind of amortization over the life of the swap will be required. Since Notice 89-21 is the only real guidance in this area, a conservative position would be to amortize the nonperiodic payment using, for example, one of the following methods:

1. Treat the swap on day one as if it provided for a single up-front payment equal to the present value of the anticipated nonperiodic payment, and a loan of that amount between the parties. The deemed up-front payment is amortized by assuming it equals the present value of a series of identical payments made throughout the term of the swap contract. When the contract expires, any unamortized amounts of the deemed up-front payment would be taken into account, together with amounts due or from the counterparty as a result of the final determination of the nonperiodic payment (if any).
2. Compute an annual mark-to-market adjustment of the final swap payment, with any difference between the mark-to-market value and the original value of the deemed up-front payment amortized over the remaining life of the contract. Any unamortized amount would be taken into account upon expiration or termination of the contract.
3. Mark the swap to market annually, recognizing the mark-to-market adjustment each year. This method may not be viewed favorably by the IRS as it could result in front-loading, which is inconsistent with clear reflection principles.

However, because of the contingent nature of the nonperiodic payment, some taxpayers have taken the "wait and see" approach and take the nonperiodic payment into income when and if it is paid.

Alternatively, credit default products can be structured such that one party makes only a single payment to the other in exchange for a promised payment in the event of default. Such a product would not classify as a notional principal contract. It may, however, be classified as an option for federal income tax purposes. Under general principles, the grantor (recipient of credit default income) under the credit default contract does not include the payment in income at the time it is made.[10] If the option expires unexercised, the premium income, less fees and commissions,[11] becomes income to the grantor on the date of expiration, and is included in income in the year of the expiration.[12] The

---

[10] Rev. Rul. 78-182, 1978-1 CB 265, Rev. Rul. 58-234, 1958-1 CB 279, Rev. Rul. 71-521, 1971-2 CB 313
[11] Rev. Rul. 58-234, 1958-1 CB 279, Rev. Rul., 68-151, 1968-1 CB 363
[12] Rev. Rul. 78-182, 1978-1 CB 265

amount of income realized by the option grantor upon the exercise of an option is the amount of the premium less commissions and fees.

The treatment of option purchasers mirrors that of option grantors. The mere payment of a premium plus commissions and fees for an option does not trigger any tax consequences. If the option expires unexercised, the taxpayer is treated as if it disposed of the option on the expiration date.[13] Purchasers will therefore have a loss for the amount of the option premium plus commissions and fees in the year the option expired.

Derivatives That Are Part of a Tax Straddle

The US tax law provides for special treatment of "offsetting positions in personal property."[14] Most particularly, a taxpayer may not take a loss on one of the positions in a straddle to the extent of unrealized gains in any other offsetting positions;[15] it must capitalize all expenses associated with carrying positions that are part of a straddle;[16] and its holding period on any position that is part of a straddle does not begin to run until the position ceases to be part of the straddle.[17]

For these purposes, a taxpayer will be considered to hold "offsetting positions with respect to personal property" if holding one of the positions substantially diminishes the taxpayer's risk of loss from holding any other position.[18] "Personal property" is any property of a kind that is actively traded.[19] Actively traded personal property includes any personal property for which there is an established financial market. A notional principal contract constitutes personal property of a type that is actively traded if contracts based on the same or substantially similar specified indices are purchased, sold, or entered into on an established financial market.[20] An established financial market includes:

- A national securities exchange
- An interdealer quotation system
- A domestic board of trade

---

[13] §1234(a)(2)
[14] §1092
[15] §1092(a)(1)(A)
[16] §263(g)
[17] Reg. §1.1092(b)-2T(a)(1)
[18] §1092(c)(2)
[19] §1092(d)(1)
[20] Reg. §1.1092(d)-1(a)

- A foreign securities exchange or board of trade that satisfies analogous regulatory requirements to their US counterparts (such as the LIFFE, Frankfurt Stock Exchange, Tokyo Stock Exchange).
- An Interbank Market
- An Interdealer Market.[21]

Within the past year, the level of trading of credit derivatives may have risen to the level of being actively traded by institutions and brokers. Therefore, they could be caught by the straddle rules. Some practitioners have argued that a swap can be disaggregated into its component parts, and if one of the legs of the swap payments is based on an actively traded index (e.g., Libor leg), this is sufficient to bring the instrument within the ambit of the straddle rules. This, however, may be an unnecessarily broad interpretation of the straddle rules, and would seem to go beyond the purpose of the rules, which was to curb tax abuses accomplished with transactions involving liquid instruments.

Even if the broad interpretation under the straddle rules prevailed, the taxpayer[22] would also have to hold offsetting property that also constitutes an "interest in personal property". In this context, that would be either another credit derivative, or a debt instrument. A debt instrument will be considered actively traded if price quotations for the instrument are readily available from brokers, dealers or traders, with a number of exceptions.[23]

---

[21] Reg. §1.1092(d)-1(b)

[22] or the taxpayer's spouse, or entity with which the taxpayer files a consolidated return, or held by certain flowthrough entities. §1092(d)(4)

[23] Reg. §1.1092(d)-1(b)(2)(ii). A debt market does not exist with respect to a debt instrument if —

(A) No other outstanding debt instrument of the issuer (or of any person who guarantees the debt instrument) is traded on an established financial market described in paragraph, or

(B) The original stated principal amount of the issue that includes the debt instrument does not exceed $25 million;

(C) The conditions and covenants relating to the issuer's performance with respect to the debt instrument are materially less restrictive than the conditions and covenants included in all of the issuer's other traded debt (e.g., the debt instrument is subject to an economically significant subordination provision whereas the issuer's other traded debt is senior); or

(D) The maturity date of the debt instrument is more than 3 years after the latest maturity date of the issuer's other traded debt.

The straddle rules do not apply in many cases, for example, where a tax hedging election is made, an identified straddle election is made, a mixed straddle account is established, and in a number of other circumstances.

The straddle rules may be avoided most particularly in the credit derivative context through the operation of the integration provisions of Reg. § 1.1275-6. A credit derivative may be integrated with an underlying debt if:

> the combined cash flows of the financial instrument and the qualifying debt instrument permit the calculation of a yield to maturity ... or the right to the combined cash flows would qualify under §1.1275-5 as a variable rate debt instrument that pays interest at a qualified floating rate or rates ... A financial instrument is not a §1.1275-6 hedge, however, if the resulting synthetic debt instrument does not have the same term as the remaining term of the qualifying debt instrument.[24]

Both notional principal contracts and options are qualifying "financial instruments" for this purpose. The taxpayer's biggest hurdle will be to ensure that a "yield to maturity" can be calculated on the integrated instrument. In the case of total return swaps, if one side's payments are based on a floating or fixed interest rate, and the credit derivative is coterminous with the underlying debt, integration should be possible, and the straddle rules can be avoided. However, if one party's payments are based on market value changes in the underlying debt, it will not be possible to calculate a yield to maturity (since it is not possible to draw up a schedule in advance stating what the payments will be).

Dealers in Securities

Taxpayers which are considered "dealers in securities" are subject to mark-to-market treatment on their securities portfolio. A "dealer" is very broadly defined as a taxpayer who regularly purchases securities from or sells securities to customers in the ordinary course of a trade or business, or regularly offers to enter into, assume, offset, assign or otherwise terminate positions in securities with customers in the ordinary course of a trade or business.[25] A security includes stock, evidence of indebtedness, swap, or other derivative instrument

---

[24] Reg. §1.1275-6(b)(2)(i)
[25] §475(c)(1)

on stock or debt.[26] A credit derivative could be part of a dealer's portfolio, and unless the derivative is held by the taxpayer as an investment,[27] or is a hedge of an security held for investment,[28] the taxpayer treats the derivative as if sold for its fair market value on the last business day of the taxable year, and takes the resulting gain or loss into account for that year.[29]

18.9.2   Character

Notional Principal Contracts

In General

There has been controversy over the character of swap payments ever since they became a popular financing tool. The general principle is that in order to obtain capital gain or loss, there must be a sale or exchange of a capital asset. Alternatively, under §1234A of the Internal Revenue Code, gain or loss attributable to the cancellation, lapse, expiration or other termination of a derivative will be treated as a capital gain or loss if the derivative is a right or obligation with respect to property.

Periodic Payments

There is no direct guidance on the character of periodic payments under NPCs. It is generlaly believed that they should be treated as ordinary.

It has been argued that with respect to resetting swaps, i.e., those whose market value resets to zero every time a periodic payment is made, the periodic payments should generate capital gain. This is because, economically, all rights and obligations under the swap are terminated each time the swap is reset.[30]

This argument was recently the subject of a technical advice memorandum (TAM) released by the IRS in July 1997. The taxpayer which was the subject of the TAM had entered into a nonresetting commoditiy swap and treated all the periodic payments as capital. The taxpayer put forward the argument outlined above, that the swap is a series of cash-settled forward contracts, and since the underlying property is a capital asset, the termination of each forward results in capital gain or loss treatment.

---

[26]   §475(c)(2)

[27]   §475(b)(1)(A)

[28]   §475(b)(1)(C)

[29]   §475(a)(2)

[30]   Klienbard E.D., 1991 "Equity Derivative Products: Financial Innovation's Newest Challenge to the Tax System," 69 *Tex. Law Rev.* 1319

The IRS disagreed with this conclusion for a number of reasons. It said that although a swap is economically equivalent to a series of forward contracts, it is considered a single, indivisible contract for tax and other legal purposes. The IRS states that a periodic payment under a swap does not constitute a sale or exchange of an asset. Whether or not the swap itself is a capital asset to the taxpayer, the payments under the swap do not meet the requirements for capital treatment.

The IRS does not explain its conclusion. The TAM does not address the possibility that because a swap is constituted entirely by the payments provided for under its terms, at least a right or obligation is terminated when a payment is made. Taxpayers will probably keep taking positions that certain swap payments are capital, based on the wording of §1234A (discussed above) and without a clear basis for the IRS' conclusion.

Nonperiodic Payments

The character of the appreciation/depreciation payment is uncertain. As discussed earlier, if the payment is made according to the terms of the contract, there is no "sale or exchange" as required by Section 1221. The question is whether the appreciation/depreciation payment would fall under one of the terms of Section 1234A, i.e., "cancellation, lapse, expiration, or other termination." It appears that the Internal Revenue Service does not support this position, stating in the preamble to the NPC regulations, "Nothing in the regulations supports characterizing either periodic or nonperiodic payments as attributable to the settlement, exercise, cancellation, lapse, expiration, or other termination of forward or option contracts."[31] Practitioners take both views on this matter, and the IRS and Treasury Department are examining the issue carefully. We expect rules out in this area sometime in the new decade!

Termination Payments

Termination payments, i.e., those made to extinguish all or a part of the rights under the contract appear to fit more easily within the Section 1234A rubric, and therefore would most likely receive capital treatment if the contract itself is a capital contract.

---

[31] TD 8491, November 8, 1993

Options

Gain and loss associated with the sale, disposition, lapse, exercise, etc., of an option takes on the character of the property which is the subject of the option.[32] Therefore, if the debt to which the option relates is a capital asset in the taxpayer's hands, the gain or loss from the option will also be capital. This is true whether the option is cash or physically settled.

Therefore, the purchaser of the option will have a capital loss in the amount of the premium for the credit default option if it expires due to nondefault in the reference obligation. If the option purchaser also receives payments from the counterparty, those payments may also be capital in character under the newly expanded §1234A.[33]

If the credit default option is a "security" in the hands of a dealer (as defined in the tax law), or a hedge of ordinary property held by the dealer, gain and loss with respect to the option will be ordinary.[34]

Withholding

There are specific rules governing the source of income from notional principal contracts. Although as originally proposed, these rules only covered contracts with payments tied to an interest rate index, the final regulations expanded the ambit of the rules.[35] The regulations on source of income are now expressed to cover contracts that fit under the same definition as contracts governed by the timing regulations of Reg. §1.446-3, discussed above.

The general rule is that income from a notional principal contract is sourced according to the residence of the recipient of the income. Therefore, if a US person makes a net payment to a foreign person under the swap, the payment will be sourced outside the US and will attract no withholding tax. However, if the income from the notional principal contract is effectively connected with a US trade or business, the income will be US source.[36] If a foreign person makes a net payment to US counterparty under a national principle payment, the payment will generally be US source.

---

[32] §1234(a)(1)

[33] §1234A no longer requires an interest in actively traded property for capital treatment to apply, merely an interest in property

[34] §§1221, Reg. §1.1221-2.

[35] See the proposed rules T.D. 8258, 54 Fed. Reg. 31672 (1989), and the final regulations Reg. Sss. 1.863-7

[36] Reg. Sec. 1.864-4(c)

There is no authority as to whether income received by a foreign person upon sale, or cash settlement of an option constitutes FDAP and is therefore subject to withholding tax. Moreover, there are no specific rules relating to the sourcing of income realized with respect to an option. The US Treasury has authority to issue sourcing rules for option, forward and futures contracts, but this authority has not been exercised. Therefore, income realized under option, forward and futures contracts is sourced under the general sourcing provisions of the Internal Revenue Code.

For many taxpayers, the question of withholding is resolved by Treaty rather than domestic law. Under the 1996 US Model Treaty,[37] income from financial instruments not specifically covered by another Treaty article will be covered by "Other Income" Article 21 and will be subject to income tax only in the country of residence of the recipient. For taxpayers whose option gains or losses are generated by a business in dealing in such instruments the income or loss may be covered by the "Business Profits" articles of the Model or other relevant treaty.[38]

---

[37] The U.S. Model Income Tax Convention of September 20, 1996
[38] Article 7 of the 1996 Model Treaty

19

Credit Derivatives and Credit Linked Notes — Regulatory Treatment

Satyajit Das

19.1 Overview[1]

The central focus of credit derivatives and credit linked notes is the transfer of credit risk. This transfer of risk can be considered at two separate levels:

- **Economic capital relief:** That is, the reduction in economic capital required to be held against a position where entry into a credit derivative transaction provides an effective hedge against the risk of loss as a result of credit events (spread changes and default).
- **Regulatory capital relief:** That is, the entry into a credit derivatives transaction which provides economic relief results in a corresponding reduction in regulatory capital required to be held against the credit risk incurred.

The relief from regulatory capital is pivotal to the operation of the market for credit derivatives and credit linked notes. This reflects the use of these instruments to manage both economic and regulatory capital arising from credit risk.

---

[1] The views expressed in this chapter are merely indications of possible methods of treatment and are not intended to be definitive. It is recommended that institutions seeking to enter into credit derivatives obtain appropriate professional advice from their own advisers regarding the required treatment of these transactions for regulatory purposes in the relevant jurisdictions

There are currently limited definitive guidelines to the treatment of credit derivatives for regulatory purposes. This reflects the recent emergence of the market. Users of credit derivatives must consequently evaluate appropriate regulatory capital treatment independently. This is done primarily on the basis of reliance on the various discussion papers issued by individual regulatory authorities.

This chapter deals with the regulatory issues arising from credit derivative transactions. The primary focus is the impact on regulatory capital required to be held against credit risk. The structure of the chapter is as follows: the overall position of regulators to date is examined; the existing credit risk capital framework is considered; the regulatory issues are isolated; the suggested regulatory position (as evinced in the various discussion papers) is analyzed; and, the longer terms implications for the credit capital framework arising from the growth in credit derivatives is finally outlined.

19.2   Credit Derivatives — Regulatory Approach

The emergence of a market in credit derivatives has been greeted with cautious support by regulators. This support is predicated on recognition of the significant potential benefits that these instruments offer to financial institutions in the management of credit risk. To date, there has been a number official pronouncements on the regulation of credit derivatives (see Figure 19.1 for a listing of some of the publications).[2]

---

[2]   For an overview of the regulatory announcement, see Brown, Claude "Developments In The Legal Documentation and Regulatory Issues for Credit Derivatives" in Storrow, Jamie, 1999, *Credit Derivatives: Key Issues (2nd Edition)*, British Bankers Association, London

Figure 19.1   Credit Derivatives — Regulatory Announcements

Regulator	Pronouncement
Federal Reserve Board (FRB)	Supervisory Letter SR 96-17 (August 1996); "Application of Market Risk Capital Requirements" (SR 97-16 (GEN)) (July 1997)
Office of the Comptroller of the Currency (OCC)	OCC Bulletin OCC 96-43 (August 1996)
Federal Deposit Insurance Corporation (FDIC)	Supervisory Guidance Letter FIL-62-96 (August 1996)
Bank of England (BOE)	Discussion paper "Developing A Supervisory Approach to Credit Derivatives" (November 1996)
Financial Services Authority (FSA) [Previously Securities and Futures Authority (SFA)][3]	Board Notice 414 Guidance on Credit Derivatives (April 1997); Board Notice 482 — Guidance on Credit Derivatives (July 1998); Chapter CD of Banking Supervisory Policy; Consultation Report on Appropriate Supervisory Treatment of Credit Derivatives
Commission Bancaire — France	Credit Derivatives: Issues for Interim Treatment (June 1997); Traitment Prudentiel Des Instruments Derives De Credit (April 1998)
Office of the Superintendent of Financial Institutions — Canada	Policy for Credit Derivatives Statement # 1997-04 (October 1997)
Bundesaufsichsamt fur das Kreditwesen (BAKred) — Germany	Rundschreiben/98 — Behandling von Kreditderivaten" Draft under Principal 1 of Sections 10 and 10a of the Banking Act

The basic approach taken by the regulators is to draw analogies with more conventional instruments for which a well developed regulatory framework already exists.

---

[3]   In the UK, the FSA has been established as a single financial regulator subsuming the responsibilities of the Bank of England and the SFA

In reviewing the regulatory framework, it is important to note that regulators of other active participants in capital markets, primarily, insurance company regulators, have also begun to review the treatment of credit derivatives. The attitude of the National Association of Insurance Commissioners (NAIC) has not been to discourage the use of credit derivatives either to hedge credit exposure within investment portfolios or as a form of investments (for example, in the form of credit derivatives). The NAIC investment committee in 1996 released a document discussing the use of derivatives (including credit derivatives).

19.3   BIS Capital Adequacy Guidelines

In understanding the regulatory approach to credit derivatives, it is essential to review the existing framework under which capital is held against credit risk. As discussed below, this framework itself is under review.

Credit capital requirements are determined under the BIS Capital Adequacy Accord released in 1988.[4] The guidelines are predicated on regulated banks holding a minimum level of capital (8%) against credit risk. Credit risk is determined in accordance with the conversion of all transactions into risk asset equivalents (based on a system of risk weighting determined by type of transaction and maturity) and the quality (based on broad guidelines) of the counterparty/obligor. Specifically, the guidelines do not specifically recognize credit derivatives.

The basic regulatory capital position in respect of credit risk in terms of the BIS credit capital accord as expressed in the risk weighting calculations is as follows:

- Term loans and the funded component of revolving credit facilities to a corporate counterparty are 100% risk weighted.
- Unfunded commitments have risk weighting of 50%.

For off-balance-sheet/derivative transactions, the calculation is:

- The mark-to-market on the transactions (if positive) plus an add-on factor calculated as a percentage of notional principal of the transaction for future exposure (based on volatility of rates/prices).

---

[4] Bank of International Settlements (1988) *Proposals for International Convergence of Capital Measurement and Capital Standards*

- The prescribed add-on factors are:

Residual Maturity	Rates	Forex	Equity	Precious Metals	Commodities
Under 1 Year	0.0%	1.0%	6.0%	7.0%	10.0%
1–5 Years	0.5%	5.0%	8.0%	7.0%	12.0%
Over 5 Years	1.5%	7.5%	10.0%	8.0%	15.0%

The methodology outlined is used to derive risk asset equivalent that is then weighted within a general framework according to the risk of the counterparty. The counterparty risk weights are as follows:[5]

Risk Weighting	Types of Obligation
0%	Central governments of OECD countries
10%	Public-sector entities (other than the central government) located in the same country as the regulated bank
20%	OECD Banks Non-OECD for obligations less than one year Public-sector entities within OECD outside the bank's home country Multilateral development agencies
50%	Housing finance Foreign exchange and interest rate transaction
100%	All other counterparties and assets.

The counterparty risk weighting system limits the maximum risk weighting for a counterparty to a derivative transaction to 50%. This represents a specific exception to the 100% weight applicable to non-bank counterparties.

The basic position under this regime is that banks have to hold the following capital against the following credit risk:

---

[5] Care is needed when interpreting this matrix, as individual regulators have discretion regarding treatment of certain types of obligations

Type of Transaction	20% Risk-Weighted Counterparty (e.g. OECD Bank)	100% Risk-Weighted Counterparty (e.g. Corporation)
Fully drawn Loan (> 1 year in maturity)	Face value × 100% × 20%	Face value × 100% × 100%
Unfunded Loan (> 1 year in maturity)	Face value × 50% × 20%	Face value × 50% × 100%
Derivative transaction	[Mark-to-market + (Notional Face value × Variable Add-On Factor)] × 50%	[Mark-to-market + (Notional Face value × Variable Add-On Factor)] × 20%

The regime described has significant weaknesses that are considered below.

Parallel to the credit capital regime is the market risk capital guidelines that require the banks to hold 8% capital against the risk of loss from movements in market rates and prices. The market risk is required to be calculated using either standard models prescribed by the BIS or internal models (in effect, VaR models). Banks are required to hold capital against market risk (in their trading books) from January 1, 1998.[6]

19.4   Credit Derivatives and Regulatory Capital — Overview

19.4.1   Key Issues

In reviewing the issues in incorporating credit derivatives within a regulatory capital framework, a fundamental distinction is necessary. This relates to the difference between:

- **The issuer/counterparty credit:** This refers to the credit risk on a loan/bond obligation or the credit exposure on a derivative transaction. This exposure is the traditional credit risk that is inherent in all financial transactions arising from the risk of non performance of the counterparty.
- **The reference asset or underlying reference entity:** This refers, in the context of credit derivatives, to the reference asset or entity the change in value of which manifests itself in the payoffs of the credit derivative transaction.

---

[6]   Basel Committee on Banking Supervision (January 1996) *Amendment to the Capital Accord To Incorporate Market Risks*

In the context of credit derivatives, both levels of credit exposure have to be dealt with. This contrasts with traditional financial instruments where only issuer or counterparty credit risk is relevant.

The issues in relation to the regulatory requirements of credit derivatives revolve around the treatment of these instruments for regulatory capital. There are several distinct issues:

- Whether credit derivatives should be included in either the banking or the trading books of financial institutions?
- The treatment of the underlying reference asset or entity in the books of the entity seeking protection or transferring the economic risk of the credit assets.
- The treatment of the underlying reference asset or entity in the books of the entity providing protection or acquiring the economic risk of the credit assets.
- The treatment of the counterparty risk on the credit derivative itself.
- The degree to which the underlying reference asset in the credit derivative transaction matches any asset held by an institution (which the credit derivative seeks to hedge) — the basis risk on the transaction.

19.4.2   Regulatory Approach

The regulatory treatment problems are different as between the credit spread products, total return loan swaps, and credit default swaps.

Total return loan swaps and credit default swaps transfer the credit risk of the underlying credit assets. This necessarily means that these transactions impact more directly on the credit risk and therefor on the regulatory credit capital position. Treatment approaches are considered in the next Section.

Credit spread products are analogous to positions in the underlying assets (a long or short securities position in a risky asset and an offsetting position in a risk free security). This decomposition should logically allow the market risk of the position to be determined and the regulatory market risk capital requirement to be calculated. The counterparty credit risk should be derived by analogy with interest rate products. This would dictate that the counterparty risk be treated as the mark-to-market of the position plus the usual add-on factor for interest rate products.

In examining the potential regulatory treatment of credit derivatives (primarily, total return swaps and credit default swaps), there are two important preliminary issues:

- The difference in the risk transfer characteristics of total return swaps as against credit default swaps.
- The issue of basis risk.

The difference in risk transfer characteristics revolves around the fact that a total return swap necessarily transfers both the price risk and the risk of loss upon default. The first is important insofar as there is a change in credit risk which manifests itself as a change in credit spread which, in turns, results in a changes in the market value of the security. In the case of a total return swap, the price change is transferred through the final settlement. In contrast, where the change in credit risk is short of default (or specified credit event under the credit default swap), there is no corresponding settlement in the case of a credit default swap.

In relation to total return swaps and credit default swaps, a further issue relates to the treatment of security based credit derivatives and loan based credit derivatives. Most regulators do not differentiate between the two classes of instruments. For example, the FSA specifically permits the introduction of loan based credit derivatives in the trading book in its most recent policy stance. Earlier proposals did not allow such inclusion on the basis that it would create an anomaly in respect of credit derivatives that were a synthetic version of the loans themselves. However, the German regulators have not recognized this treatment explicitly.

The issue of basis risk relates to the degree of correspondence between the asset being hedged and the reference asset underlying the credit derivative transaction itself.

This asymmetry will typically arise from one of a number of the following sources:

- **Size mismatch:** This relates to any mismatch between the face value of the underlying transaction and the notional principal of the credit derivative. The central issue is whether partial protection should be regarded as a hedge at least up to the face value of the credit derivative transaction.
- **Maturity mismatch:** This relates to the mismatch between the final maturity of the underlying transaction and that of the credit derivative. The problem situation arises where the maturity of the credit derivative is shorter than that of the underlying transaction. This prompts the issue whether the hedge is treated as effective given that the risk on the underlying transaction reverts to the original holder at the maturity of the credit derivative.
- **Reference asset mismatch:** This relates to where the credit derivative transaction is referenced to a reference asset that is different to the underlying transaction being hedged. This creates complexity in determining the extent of the mismatch and the degree to which risk transfer should be recognized.
- **Currency Mismatch:** This relates to where the credit derivative is denominated in a different currency to that of the underlying obligation being hedged.

- **Default payment amount and timing mismatch:** This relates to the calculation of the default payment under the credit derivative and the timing of the payment of any amounts due and payable. Other than where a fixed payment amount (the binary payout structure) is utilized, there is some level of uncertainty as to both amount and payment. Similarly, the specification of default may in fact create timing uncertainties — for example, where a materiality test is specified. This creates issues of the degree to which the risk transfer should be recognized.

Importantly, the identified issues are relevant to both issues of regulatory and economic capital. Economic capital in this context refers to the extent of "true" risk transfer and therefor the level of risk carried by an institution and therefor the amount of capital required to be held to manage that risk (separate to any issue regarding the amount of capital to held against that position under regulations).

In practise, the most important issues relate to maturity and default payment mismatches. The size mismatch can be dealt with by allowing recognition of the risk transfer only for an amount equal to the notional principal of the credit derivatives. The reference asset mismatch can be dealt with by specifying rules that are designed to determine the extent to which an asset can act as a proxy for the transaction or asset sought to be hedged. Key factors would logically include:

- Correspondence in obligor or effective guarantor as between the reference asset and the underlying transaction.
- Equivalent seniority in bankruptcy as between the reference asset and the underlying transaction.
- Similar terms and conditions (including default conditions) and mutual cross default provisions as between the reference asset and the underlying transaction.

The currency issue in practise is dealt with by according recognition to protection and therefore capital to held against the underlying asset only to the extent of the daily revaluation of the credit derivative at current market rates.

The maturity mismatch issue is more problematic. In effect, upon maturity of the credit derivatives, the party which has used the transaction to hedge its credit exposure effectively re-acquires the credit exposure to the underlying asset (in essence a "rollover" risk). The problem is somewhat different as between total return swaps and credit default swaps. In the case of a total return swap, the exposure is re-acquired at the market price at the time the total return swap matures (this is because the final settlement is based on marking the underlying asset to market even where there has been no default). In contrast, in the case of a credit default swap, the exposure is re-acquired without any price adjustment unless there has been a credit event. This means that where there has been deterioration in the credit of the obligor short of default the party using the swap to hedge re-acquires the exposure at original price levels.

The issue regarding the default payment relates to both certainties of amount and timing and also the relationship between the loss suffered on the underlying transaction and the payout on the credit derivative.

In practice, regulators have dealt with these issues by reference to the concept of virtually complete credit protection; that is, the protection afforded by a credit derivative will only be recognized where it provides an effective guarantee of the risk of loss on the underlying transaction. Risk transfer short of this level of protection and certainty is disregarded for the purpose of regulatory capital. The specific approach adopted in respect of these mismatches varies significantly as between regulators.[7]

19.5   Regulatory Framework — Total Return Loan Swaps

19.5.1   Overview

Figure 19.2 sets out an example of a total return swap.

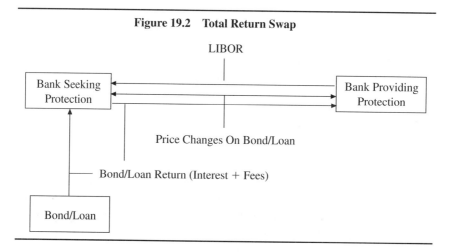

Figure 19.2   Total Return Swap

LIBOR

Bank Seeking Protection

Bank Providing Protection

Price Changes On Bond/Loan

Bond/Loan Return (Interest + Fees)

Bond/Loan

---

[7]   For an innovative approach to dealing with the maturity offset problem, see Hattori, Paul and Varotsis, Paul, April 1999, "The Maturity Offset Problem," *Risk,* pp 60–61

In the case of the total return swap, the bank providing protection incurs two separate credit exposures against which capital must be held:
- Exposure to the underlying asset.
- Exposure to the total return swap counterparty.

The exposure to the underlying is analogous to that under guarantees or standby letters of credit. The exposure on the swap itself is analogous to the credit risk on a swap.

The credit capital requirement for the bank seeking protection against the credit exposure through the swap has the exposure on the counterparty in relation to the swap plus the issue of the exposure on the underlying credit asset which continues to be held on the balance sheet of the bank. There are two possible approaches:
- A conservative approach whereby the bank seeking protection must continue to hold existing capital against that asset.
- A more reasonable approach whereby the bank seeking protection is allowed to substitute the risk of the bank providing protection for the risk of the obligor of the underlying loan.

In practise, as a general approach, the regulators have adopted the second view where the degree of protection is deemed to be sufficient to effect the transfer of credit risk.

19.5.2   Banking vs Trading Book Treatment

Total return swaps are to be treated in the bank's trading books. The treatment is conditional on the liquidity of the underlying asset rather than the issue of the isolation of the credit risk. In order to qualify for trading book treatment, the dealer institution must be able to mark to market the underlying reference asset. Where the liquidity of the underlying asset is not demonstrable, the swap will be included in the banking book. Inclusion in the trading book is conditional upon establishment of a trading intent and compliance with the regulated entity's general trading book policy statement agreed with the relevant regulator.

The ability to include the transactions in the trading book has significant capital benefits as traded instruments are risk capital weighted at between 0.25% and 1.6% of the notional value of the transaction compared to 8% if included in the banking book (see discussion below).

19.5.3   Trading Book Treatment

Where the transaction qualifies for inclusion in the trading book, the total return swap is decomposed into synthetic long or short positions in the underlying asset and an offsetting position in a FRN for the interest payments. There is an additional charge for counterparty credit risk on the swap.

The essential issue under this approach is whether the specific risk charge on the synthetic position in the swap is able to be offset against a position in the asset (that is, the holding being hedged). The offset is allowed where the reference asset is identical as between the physical holding and the swap. This would be the case only where the issuer, seniority in bankruptcy, currency of the issues, coupon, and maturity are identical as between the underlying asset and the reference asset.

Where the reference asset is of the same asset class but not identical to the asset being hedged, the position is as follows:

- The general risk charges on the two positions are offsetting within the general risk calculations (leaving either zero or a small general market risk charge).
- There is no reduction in the specific risk charge. In fact there could be two full specific risk charges plus the additional counterparty risk charge to be set against the benefit of the reduced general market risk charge. A variety of regulatory approaches have developed for offsetting positions:
  1. Standard specific risk charges should only apply to the largest leg of the offsetting credit derivative and underlying asset position (that is, standard specific risk charges are not to be applied to each leg separately).[8]
  2. An alternative approach that has been suggested is the allowing of an initial offset between the hedged positions plus a residual unhedged forward credit exposure after netting as a forward commitment to purchase the reference asset. This approach results in a single specific risk charge remaining (that is no benefit is recognized in terms of the specific risk charge for a maturity mismatched hedge), but no additional specific risk charge is applied for the hedge.[9]

---

[8]   See Federal Reserve Board (13 June 1997) SR 97-18 (Gen) Application of Market Risk Capital Requirements to Credit Derivatives, pp 4

[9]   See FSA Board Notice 482 — Guidance on Credit Derivatives (July 1998), paragraphs 34–37

The specific risk charge would be calculated as follows:
- Internal model based determination of specific risk.[10]
- Using the BIS standardized measurement method[11] (see Figure 19.3).

Figure 19.3   BIS Specific Risk Capital Charges

Under the BIS approach there is a specific risk capital charge to protect against an adverse movement in the price of an individual security deriving from factors related to an individual obligor (as distinguished from market events — general market risk). The specific risk charge is set as follows:

Government	0.00%
Qualifying	0.25% (residual maturity six months or less)
	1.00% (residual maturity between six and 24 months)
	1.60% (residual maturity exceeding 24 months)
Other	8.00%

The category "government" would include all forms of government paper (including, at national discretion, local and regional governments subject to a zero credit risk weight in the Basel Accord) including bonds, treasury bills and other short-term instruments. National authorities reserve the right to apply a specific risk weight to securities issued by certain foreign governments, especially to securities denominated in a currency other than that of the issuing government.

The category "qualifying" would apply to securities issued by public sector entities and multilateral development banks, plus other securities that are:
- Rated investment grade (rates Baa or higher by Moody's and BBB or higher by Standard & Poor's) by at least two credit agencies specified by the relevant supervisor;
- Rated investment grade by one rating agency and not less than investment grade by any other rating agency specified by the supervisor (subject to supervisory oversight);

---

[10] For example see Goldman Sachs/SBC Warburg Dillion Read, 1998, *The Practice of Risk Management: Implementing Processes For Managing Firmwide Market Risk*, Euromoney Books, London, pp 101–107

[11] See Basel Committee on Banking Supervision (January 1996) Amendment to the Capital Accord To Incorporate Market Risks, pp 9–10

- Unrated, but deemed to be of comparable investment quality by the bank or securities firm, and the issuer has securities listed on a recognized stock exchange (subject to supervisory approval).

The supervisors would be responsible for monitoring the application of these qualifying criteria, particularly in relation to the last criterion where the initial classification is essentially left to The reporting institutions.

Maturity mismatches may be allowed with shorter dated swaps being able to be utilized to hedge a longer dated position in the physical asset. The regulators are divided on the later issue. Some regulators (the FSA and the Federal Reserve) accept maturity mismatches on a qualified basis. However, the process is far from clear. The contrasting approaches include partial recognition of protection where the maturity of the credit derivative is less than that of the underlying obligation or no recognition of protection. In the case of partial recognition, there would be expected to be some reduction in the specific risk charge (for example, the higher of the two specific charges may be applied). In the case of no recognition, two specific risk charges would be incurred (one on the position in the asset and an additional charge on the offsetting position in the credit derivative).

19.5.4   Banking Book Treatment

Where the total return swap is included in the banking book, the treatment is as follows:
- If the swap exactly offsets another position in the same asset, the issuer risk on both positions exactly offset leaving only counterparty risk on the swap.
- If the swap does not exactly match the underlying asset, then whether or not it is recognized as reducing exposure will depend on how closely it matches the underlying asset. There is uncertainty about the treatment under this scenario with the suggested treatment being that of a guarantee or letter of credit with the risk weight being reduced to that of the counterparty. The matching process requires satisfaction of the following criteria:
  1. **Reference asset:** The correlation as between the asset being hedged and the reference asset underlying the swap (involving consideration of the factors identified above).
  2. **Maturity match:** The correspondence between maturities of the positions.
- If the swap is not hedging an underlying position, then:

1. If the swap entails a short position — it is ignored.
2. If the swap entails a long position — it is treated as a direct credit substitute and the risk weight is that of the reference asset.

The position on maturity mismatches is interesting. There is a wide diversity of approaches:
- No recognition of any reduction in risk.
- One option (adopted by the FSA) allows a maturity mismatch subject to the following conditions:
  1. The residual maturity of the credit derivative is at least one year.
  2. An additional charge is made for the unhedged forward exposure at maturity of the credit derivative. This is treated as a 50% credit conversion factor against the risk weight of the underlying asset.
- Another option (adopted by the Commission Bancaire) is to recognize protection subject to a 10% deduction of the amount of protection recognized unless these is a currency mismatch in which case the deduction is 20%.

However, the current consensus seems to favor recognition of protection subject to some additional capital requirement for the forward exposure.

19.5.5 Treatment of Counterparty Risk

There is also the issue of the counterparty credit risk against which capital must also be held. The credit capital required is calculated as follows:

Current exposure plus add-on for future exposure.

The replacement cost of the contract is self evident although absence of liquidity may make it difficult to establish the true market values of the contract. There is uncertainty about the add-on factor for potential future exposure.

The regulators appear to favor the a variety of approaches:
- **BOE/FSA Approach:** Interest rate add-ons for qualifying (for specific risk purposes) reference assets and equity products add-ons for non qualifying reference assets.[12]
- **Fed/OCC Approach:** Equity add-ons for investment grade assets and commodity add-ons for non-investment grade assets.

---

[12] See FSA Board Notice 482 — Guidance on Credit Derivatives (July 1998), paragraph 71

- **Germany:** Equity add-ons irrespective of asset status.
- **France:** An asymmetric approach is proposed. The seller of protection uses interest rate add-ons for qualifying (for specific risk purposes) reference assets and equity product add-ons for non qualifying reference assets. The purchaser of protection uses equity rate add-ons for qualifying reference assets and commodity products add-ons for non qualifying reference assets

No clear consensus has emerged regarding the add-on factors for potential future exposure.

19.6   Regulatory Framework — Credit Default Products

19.6.1   Overview

Figure 19.4   sets out an example of a default swap.

The issues in relation to the default swap are similar to those encountered in relation to total return swaps. From the perspective of the bank selling protection, capital is required to be held against the underlying credit asset (as described above). There should logically be no exposure on the counterparty (the bank-seeking protection) as there is no performance obligation on this party under the terms of the transaction. This assumes that the fee for the default swap is payable in full at the commencement of the transaction. If the fee is payable over the term of the transaction, the bank selling protection has an exposure to the other party equivalent to the receivable of the fee.

Figure 19.4   Credit Default Swap

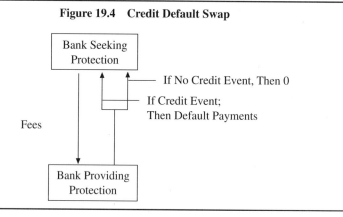

The major issue therefore relates to the capacity of the bank seeking protection to reduce the risk weighting of the credit asset being hedged to that of the counterparty where the counterparty providing protection has a lower risk weighting. This will be the case in most cases for corporate credit risk as the protection where it is provided by a bank will result in the substitution of a 20% risk weighting versus the 100% risk weighting for the underlying corporate obligation.

The consensus that is emerging seems to favor the capacity to substitute the counterparty credit risk for the underlying credit risk only where the credit derivative transaction provides "virtually complete credit protection." This should be contrasted with transaction that provide "severely limited or uncertain" protection".[13] Factors that may result in the credit protection being regarded as less than complete would include:

- The term of the hedge being shorter in maturity than the asset or obligation being hedged.
- The reference asset underlying the credit derivative is not identical to the hedged asset.
- The payout under the credit derivative may not accurately reflect the actual loss under the asset being hedged as a result of the mechanism for determining payout under the credit derivative being an average of dealer prices or a fixed amount agreed in advance.
- Uncertainty about the timing of the recovery under the credit derivatives because of the terms of the agreement dictate payment after the pre-determined event or after the occurrence of the event plus satisfaction of additional conditions.

The issue of maturity mismatch is more difficult in the case of a credit default swap as identified above. In regard to the maturity mismatch, a logical form of treatment would allow the risk weighting to be reduced allowing capital relief for the period of the hedging credit derivative transaction. The capital requirement and exposure would revert upon the credit derivative expiring. The bank seeking protection would also be required to hold some additional capital against the implied commitment to repurchase the credit asset after the credit hedge expires.

---

[13] See Office of the Comptroller of the Currency , Administrator of National Banks "Guidance for Credit Derivatives" OCC Bulletin 96–43, August 12, 1996

19.6.2   Banking vs Trading Book Treatment

For credit default products, the initial regulatory position required inclusion in the banking book. Subsequently, regulators appear to have amended the treatment of default products to allow a trading book treatment of credit default swaps.[14] The reason for the change was comments by regulated banks that challenged the regulator's suggestions that credit default products lacked clarity in valuation methodology and liquidity/tradability. They were able to persuade the central bank that default products should be eligible for inclusion in the trading book. It should be noted that default products whereby the underlying asset is a loan may still be excluded in certain jurisdictions.

19.6.3   Trading Book Treatment

The treatment of a credit default swap where it is eligible for inclusion in the trading book follows the logic applicable to other credit derivatives, such as total return swaps. Using this framework, where a credit default swap is referenced to a traded security issued by the relevant issuer, it is treated in the trading book as equivalent to the specific risk of a long or short position in the bond with the maturity of the credit default swap. Where the swap offsets an existing position in the security (that is, the issuer, seniority, and terms are identical) and where the maturities of the security and the swap is the same, the specific risk charges of the two positions will offset. Where the credit default swap has a shorter maturity, no specific risk offset is allowed and a specific risk charge is applied to either both positions or to the larger of the positions as specified above. No general interest rate charge is applied to credit default swaps in the trading book.

19.6.4   Banking Book Treatment

Where the credit default swap is included in the banking book, the required treatment is:
- If protection is sold, the exposure is treated as a direct credit substitute and the risk weight is that of the reference asset.
- If protection is purchased, then the protection conferred will be incorporated in any capital calculation only where certain conditions are met.

---

[14] See FSA Board Notice 482 — Guidance on Credit Derivatives (July 1998), paragraph 20, 71

The criteria that must be met include:
- The asset match must demonstrate high correlations.
- The protection must cover the full life of the underlying asset.
- The payment structure must have minimal uncertainties. Fixed payment and physical delivery options are regarded as certain payment structures. Par less recovery rate structures are regarded as uncertain structures.

Where all three criteria are met, the capital charge will be recognized and based on a full or partial guarantee or letter of credit (depending on the extent of protection conferred) with the risk weight being reduced to that of the counterparty. Where there is a maturity mismatch exists the approach adopted is identical to that applicable to total return swaps. Where an uncertain payment structure is utilized or where a mark to market regime is difficult to implement, an additional charge may be levied to cover the payment uncertainty.[15]

19.7 Regulatory Framework — Credit Linked Notes

The regulatory position in respect of credit linked notes recognizes that the issuer of the credit linked notes effectively purchases protection against loss through default or specified credit event that is fully cash collateralized. The treatment of credit linked transactions is similar to that of a credit default swap. The important difference is that the presence of cash as collateral removes the capital requirement in respect of the credit exposure on the asset sought to be hedged without adding a capital requirement in respect of the counterparty risk of the seller of default protection. The problems in relation to mismatch of reference asset, maturity and/or default payment mechanism identified above are still present.

For the seller of protection, the credit linked note creates exposure to both the issuer and the underlying reference credit. The seller of protection is required to hold capital against the higher of the reference obligation and the issuer. The rationale is that the recovery of the principal of the note is most affected by the riskier of these two parties.[16]

---

[15] For example, the FSA appear to take a position that all credit derivatives referenced to illiquid underlying assets including loans will be subject to an appropriate reserve against valuation uncertainties

[16] A credit derivative that was fully cash collateralized would presumably be accorded similar treatment

19.8   Regulatory Framework — Other Issues

The other major issues include:
- **Credit or default baskets:** In the original formulation of the guidelines, regulators took a worst case approach with the seller of protection being required to hold capital against an exposure to the highest possible payout amount under the contract, that is, to the issuer in the basket with the highest risk weighting. The buyer of protection would be regarded as having purchased protection against only one issuer (one in the basket with the lowest risk weighting) for an amount equal to the lowest possible payout amount under the contract. More recent proposals allow protection against one asset but with allowance for the bank/firm with a short position in a multiple — name credit default product to choose the single asset recognized as a short position for calculating regulatory capital. For the seller of protection, regulatory capital may have to be held against all the names in the basket.[17] However, the position in respect of these structures is far from clear in a number of jurisdictions.
- **Large exposures:** Protection sold and received is recognized for the purpose of calculating large exposures. For example, under the BOE guidelines, the banks continue to report both the gross and the guaranteed exposures with the bank being able to choose to count towards its large exposure limits either the exposure to the protected asset or the exposure to the guarantor.

19.9   Regulatory Position — Implications

The regulatory approach to credit derivatives transactions recognizes that these transactions, at least when held in the trading book, create or reduce exposure to counterparty credit risk and general market risk and specific risk (depending on structure).

The exposure created or transferred depends on the nature and purpose for which the transaction is entered into. Where the transaction is not matched or offsetting (an open transaction), it creates exposure to the relevant risks, functioning as a means to create synthetic credit exposure. Where the transactions are entered into for the purpose of transferring or hedging, the treatment is conditional upon the level of correspondence between the asset being hedged and the credit derivative. The degree of protection conferred depends on whether the transactions are matched (that is, long and short position

---

[17] See FSA Board Notice 482 — Guidance on Credit Derivatives (July 1998), paragraphs 26–32, 71

in identical assets with the maturity of the underlying transaction and the credit derivatives being exactly the same) or offsetting (where there are mismatches in reference asset or maturity). Figure 19.5 sets out the risk elements for each type of situation.

Within the regulatory framework, individual regulators have sought innovative mechanisms for dealing with the issue of basis risk, particularly, reference asset and maturity mismatches. For example, the French authorities have sought to deal with this problem through the imposition of an extra charge (50% of the underlying) where the protection is for a period shorter than the maturity of the transaction sought to be hedged. For example, if a bank holding a US$100 million position in a corporate loan (100% risk weighted) bought protection from an OECD bank, in the normal case, the bank would have achieved a reduction in capital required to be held to 20% (that is, US$20 million risk weighted asset). In the event, that the protection is purchased for a period shorter than the term of the loan, the risk on the loan is offset but a 50% additional charge would be introduced. This would mean that the credit exposure would be recorded as US$70 million (the US$20 million plus the additional charge of US$50 million). Similarly, where the reference assets are similar but not identical an offset is allowed but with an adjustment of either 10% (in the same currency) or 20% (in a different currency). This methodology provides some degree of recognition (however approximate) of the effect of the hedge.

Figure 19.5   Credit Derivatives — Market Risk Capital Framework

Type of Position	General Market Risk		Specific Risk		Counterparty Credit Risk	
	Buyer	**Seller**	**Buyer**	**Seller**	**Buyer**	**Seller**
Open	Yes	Yes	Yes	Yes	Yes	No
Matched	Yes	No	Yes	No	Yes	No
Offsetting	Yes	Partial	Yes	Partial	Yes	No

Notes:
1. Yes refers to presence of risk.
2. No refers to absence of risk
3. Partial refers to the fact that there is some offset of risk depending on the extent of offset (basis risk)
4. The above assumes that the Seller has a position in the underlying asset and enters into the credit derivatives.

The regulatory position in respect of credit derivative though far from definitive already points to significant anomalies. These exist at two levels:

- The fact that credit derivatives which can be used to replicate traditional loan or bond credit exposures are capable of being treated in the trading books as distinct from the banking book.[18]
- The fact that the capital treatment in some jurisdictions in some circumstances creates a disincentive to hedge.
- Differences between the treatment of *different types of credit derivatives* and different types of instruments that achieve economically similar outcomes.

The problems identified can be illustrated easily. For example, a traditional bank loan to a corporation would traditionally have been booked in the institution's banking book and attract a capital charge of 8%. However, if the transaction is restructured as a total return swap or credit default swap with the same loan (assuming it is traded), then it could be booked in the bank's trading book and would attract a lower capital charge (1.6%). The advantage of a lower capital charge would be partially offset by the following:

- The position would have to be marked to market (resulting in greater volatility in earnings).
- There would be a counterparty risk charge (in the case where the trade was structured as a total return swap).

It is important to note that this precise same treatment (except for the counterparty risk charge) could be engineered by re-structuring the transaction as a tradable security (a bond).

The distortion may impact upon banking practise in determining *how* specific transactions are structured as distinct from the fundamental economics of the transactions.

Where a transaction does not qualify for a risk offset, the proposed treatment may actually increase capital requirements. For example, where there is reference asset or maturity mismatch the hedge even if it provides an economic reduction in risk will generally result in *higher capital charges*. This is because the entity will be required to hold capital potentially against *both* the transaction being hedged and the credit derivative. This clearly creates an incentive *not to hedge*.

---

[18] The French authorities have clarified the basis of classification as between the banking and the trading book. In order to include a transaction in the trading book, the instrument must be subject of an intention to trade and it must be tradable (that is it is must be quoted daily in a liquid market or otherwise freely tradable)

The differences between the treatment of the types of credit derivatives is more subtle but affect such issues as maturity mismatches and default payment mismatches. This may distort the trading in total return swaps as against credit default swaps. The differences as between different types of instruments that are used to achieve economically similar results can be illustrated with the example of securitization. Structures such as Collateralized Loan Obligation (CLO) transactions can be used in a manner analogous to credit default swaps to hedge the economic credit exposures within portfolios. However, the regulatory capital treatment of the two structures is not consistent.

These anomalies are not derived from the regulatory treatment of credit derivatives but from weaknesses in the treatment of credit risk generally within the regulatory capital framework.

19.10 Credit Capital Framework

19.10.1 Current Regulatory Framework — Weaknesses

The currently used credit capital regime is relatively dated. Developed in the early 1980s, it was a landmark step at the time enabling the establishment of an international supervisory standard. While the framework has evolved over time, market developments have exposed its weaknesses increasingly. In particular, the introduction of the market risk capital guidelines, including the innovation of allowing internal models as an alternative to the use of standardized rules, has created a discontinuity between the treatment of credit risk and market risk. This is particularly noticeable in an era when market risk and credit risk has increasingly begun to overlap as credit risk has become tradable firstly through securitization and subsequently through the advent of credit derivatives.

The weaknesses of the current credit capital guidelines include:

- **Simplified measure of credit exposure:** The credit exposure on instruments is measured within a simplified static framework based on fixed percentages applied to the face value of the transaction. For example, for an undrawn commitment the exposure is measured as 50% and for a derivatives the transaction mark-to-market plus a pre-determined factor for future exposure.
- **Limited Differentiation:** Counterparty risk is differentiated only into broad categories with significant anomalies. For example, the treatment of OECD versus non OECD banks irrespective of credit quality.
- **Lack of term structure of credit risk:** The existing guidelines are relatively independent of the maturity structure of obligations and in addition do not differentiate between current and forward exposures.

- **Static capital charge:** The existing guidelines are predicated on a fixed static capital charge of 8%.
- **Limited recognition of credit enhancement:** Only limited recognition of credit enhancement is accorded. The only form of collateral that is recognized as providing full protection is OECD central government securities and cash which allows the risk weighting to be reduced to O%.
- **Limited recognition of offsets:** The existing rules give only limited recognition to offsetting long and short risk positions.
- **Absence of recognition of portfolio and diversification effects:** The existing system is predicated on the concept of credit exposure to individual counterparties/obligors with no overriding adjustment for the portfolio which may provide diversification benefits.
- **Lack of integrated view of risk:** Credit risk is calculated with reference to specific arbitrary categories — banking book risk, trading book risk (in effect, general market risk and specific risk), and counterparty risk. These risk classes are not fully integrated in determining the overall risk of an entity.

The impact of these weakness on banking practise include:
- **Macro effects:** Such as mispricing of credit and creation of disincentives for credit risk management.
- **Micro effects:** Such as the incorrect or anomalous treatment of specific instruments and transactions and the creation of opportunities for significant regulatory arbitrage.

19.10.2 *Amending The Credit Regulatory Framework — ISDA Proposals Overview*

It is inevitable that the existing regulatory capital framework for credit risk will need to be revised. The weaknesses identified, improvements in the modeling technology for credit risk and the continued development of the market for credit derivatives make it likely that the existing framework will need to be amended radically. ISDA has proposed a possible methodology for such a change.[19]

The basic proposal is for an evolutionary models-based approach. The essential element of the proposed structure includes:

---

[19] See (March 1998) *Credit Risk And Regulatory Capital*, International Swaps and Derivatives Association

- The existing structure is to be maintained but supplemented by certain measures that would facilitate a gradual evolution of capital calculation methods consistent with internal risk management practise.
- The structure would have three essential tiers designed to allow this migration to increasingly more sophisticated methodologies for measuring credit risk:
  1. Tier 1 (Standardized Rules) would be the existing Basel credit capital rules supplemented by a modification that allows increased risk offsets.
  2. Tier 2 (Simplified Modeling) would be based on simplified credit risk modeling (not dissimilar to the Standard Models Approach of the Market Risk Capital Guidelines) which would incorporate greater differentiation of credit risk (by credit rating), term structure, and recognition of offsets.
  3. Tier 3 (Full Portfolio Modeling) would be based on more sophisticated credit risk modeling (analogous to the Internal Models Approach to market risk — in effect a credit value at risk) which would incorporate all the elements of the Tier-2 approach as well as portfolio correlation effects.

The ISDA approach is depicted in Figure 19.6.

Figure 19.6   An Evolutionary Model-based Approach to Credit Risk Capital

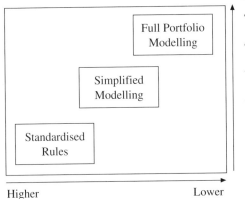

Risk Management Accuracy

- Correlation recognised, diversification rewarded
- Consistent integrated risk measure

- Differentiation of risk weighting by rating
- Term structure
- Offsets

- Existing Basel rules
- Modification for offsets

Higher   Lower
Overall Capital Charges

Note: The intended overall calibration of capital changes is shown here; for particular low credit quality portfolios, model approaches could lead to higher changes.

Source: (March 1998) *Credit Risk And Regulatory Capital,* International Swaps and Derivatives Association, 12

The ISDA approach is predicated on a gradual development of credit modeling by financial institutions allowing incremental improvements in modeling technology and sophistication. In particular, it is designed to allow individual institutions to adopt an approach consistent with its business focus and level of sophistication. The approach avoids the imposition of sophisticated credit modeling, favored by larger more sophisticated banks (many of which already have in place or are in the process of putting in place such systems), on smaller entities. However, the objective remains to increasingly achieve a better alignment of economic and regulatory capital required to be held against credit risk.

Standardized Rules

As noted above, the standardized rules would continue to be utilized supplemented by an expanded set of guidelines in respect of offsets. This is designed to overcome the deficiencies within the existing guidelines that do not recognize the impact of economic hedging. The proposed guidelines are as follows:

- **Maturity mismatches:** A straight line method is proposed whereby the position is reduced by an appropriate percentage under a sliding scale and subject to standardized specific risk charges at the residual maturity of the unhedged term of the instrument. For examples, a 10-year bond hedged by a 9-year credit derivative would be accorded a 90% offset (9/10 years) with the full risk reverting after year 9. This approach is applied irrespective of whether the residual risk is back end (an instrument being hedged by a shorter maturity instrument) or front end (an instrument hedged by a forward commencing transaction).
- **Instrument mismatches:** These are handled in a number of ways depending upon the nature of the mismatch:
  1. Different seniority (where the two instruments have different seniority) — offset would only be allowed where the seniority of the instrument being used to hedge is above that of the instrument being hedged.
  2. Different instruments (for example, a loan being offset by a bond) — offset would be permitted subject to the seniority rule set out above.
  3. Counterparty risk on a transaction — offset permitted subject to seniority rule set out above.
  4. Banking versus trading book transactions — offset permitted subject to inclusion of a counterparty risk charge (if appropriate, such as with a credit derivative).

The approach adopted relies, primarily, on payout levels and the transaction structure which allows a default on the underlying to trigger a credit event payment on the offsetting transaction to determine offsets.

Simplified Modeling

The simplified modeling approach is predicated on a two step approach:
- A more differentiated assessment of credit risk to determine risk weights based on either credit ratings or internal credit rankings being mapped to external credit rating.
- A term structure of credit risk involving specified time/term buckets to differentiate different types of credit risks.
  The basic model steps are set out in Figure 19.7.

The more differentiated credit system is based on three rating classes: AAA/AA; A/BBB; and, less than BBB. The rating would be applicable where the obligor is publicly rated. Where the obligor is not publicly rated, banks would utilize internal ratings that are then mapped into one of the specified categories. The simplified model parameters are set out in Figure 19.8.

Figure 19.7   An Evolutionary Models — Based Approach to Credit Risk Capital

Step 1
Assign positions for each name to buckets depending on maturity and rating

⇓

Step 2
Apply offset rules (see Figure 19.9)

⇓

Step 3
Apply Capital Charges (see Figure 19.8)
• Default risk charges for long positions
• Spread risk charges for long and short positions

⇓

Step 4
Sum capital charges
• For default and spread risk for each name, then
• Of all individual names

Source: (March 1998) *Credit Risk And Regulatory Capital*; International Swaps and Derivatives Association at 47

Figure 19.8   Simplified Model Parameters

Default risk charge per period for long positions with an exposure within 1 year

Class	AAA/AA	A/BBB	< BBB
Spot	0.00%	0.33%	4.00%
1 day–1 month	0.00%	0.27%	3.20%
1 month –3 months	0.00%	0.20%	2.40%
3 months – 6 months	0.00%	0.13%	1.60%
6 months – 1 year	0.00%	0.07%	0.80%
Sum of charges for one year position		1.00%	12.00%

Spread charges *per annum* for long positions

Class	AAA/AA	A/BBB	< BBB
0–5 years	0.15%	0.30%	0.75%
5 years –10 years	0.10%	0.20%	0.50%
10 years –15 years	0.05%	0.10%	0.25%
15 years +	0.00%	0.00%	0.00%

Spread charge *per annum* for short positions

Class	AAA/AA	A/BBB	< BBB
>=spot	0.05%	0.15%	0.15%

Max (calculated charge, present value of credit spread) to be applied for short positions

Source: (March 1998) *Credit Risk And Regulatory Capital*, International Swaps and Derivatives Association, 49

Within this framework, default and spread charges are applied as follows:
- Default risk charges are made against long positions and applies to any position which falls within the first year.
- Spread risk charges are made on both long and short position based on the risk of changes in both the market price of credit risk as well as the risk of changes in the individual entities credit spread. Spread charges are based on maturity and all relevant spread charges are summed. The system specifically caters for forward credit exposures.

The offset of positions is based on firstly permitting full offsetting between long and short positions within the same time band and secondly partial offsetting where the position are mismatched in accordance with the offset rules specified in Figure 19.9.

Figure 19.9   Simplified Model Offset Rules

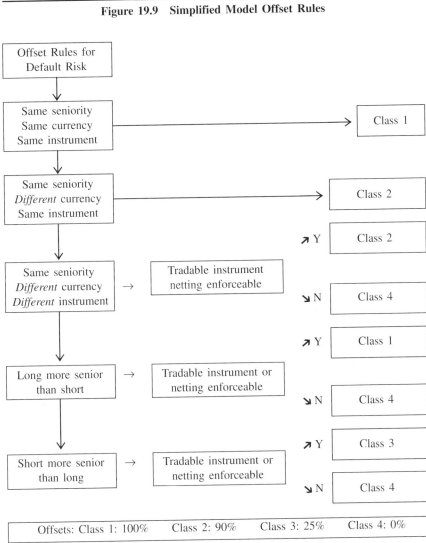

Offsets: Class 1: 100%   Class 2: 90%   Class 3: 25%   Class 4: 0%

Source: (March 1998) *Credit Risk And Regulatory Capital,* International Swaps and Derivatives Association, pp 50

Full Portfolio Modeling

Full portfolio modeling is based on a credit value at risk approach which is designed to generate the expected loss for the credit portfolio as well as assigning economic capital against the unexpected loss through the application of a confidence interval related to tolerance for risk. The basic model steps would include:

- Determining the actual credit exposure on individual transactions and the portfolio.
- Establishing the risk of default and recovery rates for obligors within the portfolio as well as the risk of migration in default probabilities over a prescribed holding period. This can be done using credit transition models or default/credit spread volatility.
- Deriving the expected loss and distribution of portfolio losses allowing the derivation of the level of unexpected loss due to credit risk based on a prescribed confidence level.

The process would be reinforced by stress testing techniques, to cover for tail events.

ISDA proposes the following minimum parameters for the full portfolio modeling approach:

- one year holding period.
- An observation period of 5–10 years.
- 99% confidence interval.[20]

Significantly, ISDA have resisted the three times multiple factor applied by the BIS in determining capital to be held against market risk as calculated by internal (VaR) models.

The use of internal models for credit risk are subject to similar controls as applicable to market risk capital calculations utilizing internal models including:

- Qualitative assessment and pre qualification of the internal model by the relevant regulator including consideration of high level qualitative controls.
- Backtesting and validation of the credit risk model.
- Regular stress testing.

---

[20] Note that because of the non-log normal distribution of credit losses, a percentage confidence level rather than number of standard deviations would be utilized

Quantitative Analysis of Credit Modeling

As part of its proposal, ISDA conducted a quantitative analysis of the proposed approach with three model portfolios. The portfolios utilized were as follows:
- Each portfolio was US$66.3 billion
- Portfolio A was a high credit quality diversified (500 name) portfolio
- Portfolio B was a low credit quality diversified (500 name) portfolio
- Portfolio C was a high credit quality concentrated (100 name) portfolio
- The portfolios consisted of 1 year drawn term loans to 100% risk weighted corporation with all exposures being of equal size
- Different recovery rate and recovery rate uncertainties were utilized. Modeled correlation as well as a zero correlation case was utilized

The regulatory capital requirement was assessed using a number of models:
- The current standardized rules
- The Simplified Model
- CreditMetrics^{TM} (J.P. Morgan) and CREDITRISK$^+$ (CSFP) (both were used at 99% confidence levels for a one year holding period)
- Two proprietary models of ISDA members

The results are summarized in Figure 19.10.

The results that are consistent with expectations show:
- The impact of portfolio diversification that is not revealed under the current rules
- The impact of difference in credit quality that is not sufficiently differentiated under existing models

The results highlight the important benefits of portfolio credit risk modeling as well as the weaknesses of the existing simple capital regime.

Figure 19.10   Comparison of Capital Calculation Methodologies

Correlation assessed, zero recovery (US$m)

| | Capital Charge | | |
	Portfolio A	Portfolio B	Portfolio C
Current standardized rules*	5,304	5,304	5,304
Simplified Model	1,407	5,351	1,407
CreditMetrics^{TM}	2,264	11,436	2,941
CREDITRISK$^+$	1,638	10,000	2,574
SBC ACRA	1,373	9,654	2,366

Correlation assessed, 50% recovery rate, zero recovery uncertainty (US$m)

| | Capital Charge | | |
	Portfolio A	Portfolio B	Portfolio C
Current standardized rules*	5,304	5,304	5,304
Simplified Model	1,407	5,351	1,407
CreditMetrics^{TM}	1,132	5,718	1,471
CREDITRISK$^+$	819	5,000	1,287
SBC ACRA	686	4,827	1,183

Zero correlation, zero recovery (US$m)

| | Capital Charge | | |
	Portfolio A	Portfolio B	Portfolio C
Current standardized rules*	5,304	5,304	5,304
Simplified Model	1,407	5,351	1,407
CreditMetrics^{TM}	777	1,989	2,093
CREDITRISK$^+$	789	2,074	2,020
SBC ACRA	767	1,907	1,967
Internal Model A	724	1,756	1,906

* Same charges would arise if modified to recognize offsets, as no short positions are included.

Source: (March 1998) *Credit Risk And Regulatory Capital*; International Swaps and Derivatives Association, pp 29

19.10.3   Proposals For Reform — Issues

The ISDA proposals are to be welcomed as a far-reaching and thoughtful attempt to reform the existing credit capital framework. While the proposal addresses some of the weaknesses of the existing system, the proposal does not address certain structural issues. These include:

- **The banking and trading book distinction:** The distinction between the banking and trading book is somewhat artificial. It is in practise difficult to define and monitor. This difficulty is compounded by the fact that the trading book is both much more generous and flexible in its treatment of credit risk. This creates an incentive for regulated institutions to seek to migrate assets into the trading book for the purpose of claiming favorable capital treatment. The migration creates, if this is in practise what occurs, increased pressure on regulators to re-examine the issue of the banking book and apply the same mark to market discipline on both the banking book and the deposit liabilities funding it.
- **The problem of data sources:** The ISDA approach and in fact any credit modeling approach is reliant on the availability of data which allows the credit risk to be accurately measured. The ISDA proposal is predicated on the ability of banks to fair value all positions to which credit risk models are to be applied. ISDA analyzed the data sources in its proposal[21] and specified a number of asset classes for credit risk modeling as set out in Figure 19.11. ISDA concluded that the data available provided the capacity to model credit risk in a number of markets and industries although further improvements were necessary. The views expressed may well be overly optimistic about the availability of data and also it quality. The key problems with data available include: problems of sample size (in the case of default events in certain rating classes; the non normal distribution of recovery rates and credit losses; and the lack of data outside markets such as the United States.

---

[21] See (March 1998) *Credit Risk And Regulatory Capital*, International Swaps and Derivatives Association at Annex III

Figure 19.11   Possible Asset Classes For Credit Risk Modeling

Asset Class	Comments
Traded debt and equity	• Good public data • Credit risk already covered under specific risk modeling rules
Traded loans	• Good public data
Large corporate loans	• Good to patchy public data • Good internal data
Mid-market loans	• Patchy to no public data • Variable internal data
Homogenous retail (mortgages, car loans, credit cards etc)	• Good aggregate data • Top-down (behavioral/actuarial) modeling
Counterparty risk	• Good data • More complex modeling

Source: (March 1998) Credit Risk And Regulatory Capital; International Swaps and Derivatives Association at 16

- **Other risks:** An aspect of the existing credit capital regime which is often highlighted by regulators is that the existing 8% capital charge is simple and moreover designed to cover other risk which cannot be separately measured or identified. These would include various operational risks encountered by banks in their operations. This means that any move to a more sophisticated credit-modeling framework would necessitate a separate capital charge to cover these risks.[22]

There are other specific problems in any reformation of the credit capital guidelines including the structure of the European Union (EU) Capital Adequacy Directive (CAD). The problem of the CAD stems from the fact that it is an EU directive and must be first approved by the European parliament and then by

---

[22] See D. Jones and J. Mingo (26–27 February 1998) "Industry Practices in Credit Risk Modelling and Internal Capital Allocations: Implications For A Models-Based Regulatory Capital Standard;" a paper presented at the Federal Reserve Bank of New York

national parliaments before it can take effect. This makes for a particularly cumbersome process of change in regulations which further complicates the process of amending the credit capital framework.[23]

19.11 BIS Review of Credit Capital Requirements

In September 1998, the Basel Committee on Banking Supervision (chaired by William McDonough, vice chairman of the US Federal Reserve Bank) announced a review of the BIS Capital Adequacy Accord with a focus on the treatment of credit risk.[24] This much-awaited review is expected to clarify the regulatory capital treatment of credit derivatives in the context of the treatment of credit risk and credit capital generally.

The review process was expected to publish a consultative paper in April 1999. The paper was not intended as a new accord but as a discussion paper designed to provide the framework for a consultative process which involved the markets.[25] However, release of the paper was delayed. The delay was rumored to be the result of disagreements among the central banks. One difficulty related to the special position of German mortgage banks. These banks enjoy a number of capital advantages including 50% risk weighting for commercial property lending, 10% risk weighting for Pfandbriefe issues, and 20% risk weighting for bank senior debt which is subordinated to the claims of Pfandbriefe holders. It was rumored that reluctance to remove these advantages were among the causes of the delay in release of the document.[26] The Consultative Paper was released in June 1999. The proposed reforms are discussed in the next section.

In April 1999, the Basel Committee released a separate paper on internal credit models and modeling processes.[27] The paper prepared by the Models Task Force presented the results of the review conducted on credit risk modeling and the potential to use internal credit risk models in supervisory oversight of banking organizations. The report was based on an extensive survey conducted by the task force of credit modeling practises in 20 large international based in 10 countries.

---

[23] See Brian Scott-Quinn and Julian K. Walmsley, 1998, *The Impact of Credit derivatives On Securities Markets*, ISMA, Zurich, Switzerland

[24] See Rhode, William, August 1998, "Basel Credit Review," *Risk*, 7

[25] See Dunbar, Nicholas, March 1999, "Basel Ready With Consultative Paper," *Risk*, 7; Crabbe, Matthew, June 1999, "Basel: Reform Or Reinvention," *Risk*, pp 29–31

[26] See Walker, Marcus, May 1999, "Punch Up In Basel," *Risk*, 7

[27] See (April 1999) *Credit Risk Modelling: Current Practices And Applications*, Basel Committee on Banking Supervision, Basel

The task force took the view that regulators would have to be confident that credit models were conceptually sound, empirically valid and produce capital requirements that are comparable across institutions prior to allowing such models to be used in the formal process of setting regulatory capital requirements for credit risk. The report's conclusion was that credit risk modeling was not a simple extension of the internal model approach enshrined in the market risk capital regulations. The report expressed significant concerns regarding data limitations and difficulties with validation of credit risk models. Figure 19.12 summarizes some of the issues identified by the task force.

The report is useful in providing descriptions of current practises and issues in credit risk modeling. However, it is inconclusive as to whether the doubts expressed by The task force will act as a barrier to adoption of internal credit models as the one of the basis for determining credit capital requirements for financial institutions.[28]

19.12 BIS Proposal for Reform of the Capital Adequacy Accord

19.12.1 Overview

As noted above, the Basel Committee on Banking Supervision issued its paper on reformation of the existing Capital Adequacy Accord in June 1999.[29] The paper proposes significant reform of the original 1988 Capital Accord (originally published in July 1988).

The central premise of the consultative paper is the acceptance that the original accord needs to be updated if it is to remain an efficient and economically relevant basis for global bank prudential regulation. The committee acknowledges that the accord is outdated in a number of key respects. The committee also acknowledges that the accord has been superseded by the development of the credit risk management and mitigation techniques being used by international financial institutions. The committee recognizes that these factors have led to an increasing divergence between market practise and actual regulatory requirements. This has resulted in regulatory arbitrage exploiting divergences between true economic risk/capital and regulatory risk/capital. The consultative paper is viewed by The committee as a first step in this process of the credit capital requirements to overcome these deficiencies.

---

[28] See Rhode, William, December 1998, "Regulators Cool On Credit Models," *Risk,* 6
[29] See (June 1999) A New Capital Adequacy Framework; Consultative Paper issued by Committee on Banking Supervision, Basel

Figure 19.12 Issues In Credit Risk Modeling

Conceptual Issues

Item	Description	Range of Practice	Issues/Concerns
Credit Loss Definition	How is loss defined?	• Both mark-to-market (MTM) and default mode (DF) processes are used/promoted. • Some banks include workout expenses and carrying costs while others do not.	• Materiality of loss definition (i.e. to use MTM or DM) not clear.
Time Horizon	Over what time period should losses be measured?	• Most use one-year horizon.	• Very little sensitivity analysis done to date. • What horizon should be used for capital (e.g. one-year, life of loan, etc)?
Credit Risk Aggregation	The distinction between entering individual loan attributes versus attributes of pool.	• Most banks enter individual characteristics of commercial credits and pool real portfolios.	• Reliability of pooled data. • Pooled data hide "credit specific" risks.
Probability Density Function (PDF)	The method used to generate and the use of PDF.	• Models do not specify the specific distribution.	• No agreement on the "family" of distributions to use.

Figure 19.12 (cont'd)

Item	Description	Range of Practice	Issues/Concerns
Credit Quality Correlations	How co-movement among credit ratings and defaults is considered.	• Implicit versus explicit • Explicit (ratings versus sector)	• Is one method better than the other? • Is there significant difference in reported results?
Conditional vs Unconditional	Are the results of the model dependent on the current state of the economy?	• Currently most models are unconditional and a few are conditional.	• Depending on the method chosen, risk can be overstated or understated depending on the location within the business cycle.
Internal Applications	Does the process provide companywide application/ use of the model, or is it only applied to exposures within certain businesses? How are banks using their credit models internally?	• Very few (if any) banks have developed a fully integrated company-wide model to measure credit risk. • Usage varies significantly. Some of uses noted include: credit concentration limits, ALL guideline and RAROC input.	• If banks do not use these systems for internal allocations of credit, how much confidence can be placed in these processes?
Loss Given Default Rates (LGDs)	Determination of how much loss will occur once a credit has defaulted?	• Most banks use a combination of historical data and intuition to determine LGD rates. • LGD modeling methodology varies; however, most models use beta distribution.	• Lack of sensitivity. • Lack of historical information.

Figure 19.12 (cont'd)

Item	Description	Range of Practice	Issues/Concerns
Risk Ratings and Expected Default Frequency	Determination of what the expected default risk is within individual credits and/ or pools of assets.	• Internal risk and public debt ratings are used in most cases for individual credits. • For pools of credits, the bank's internal historical charge-off rates are typically used.	• Public debt rating transition matrices may not be appropriate for bank credits. • Internal systems may not be accurate or have enough history.
Risk Rating Transitions	Projection of future movements in risk ratings and to default.	• A number of banks rely on public debt rating information (i.e. Historical information). • Other banks have produced transition matrices based on internal historical information.	• Questionable accuracy of internal systems being able to determine EDF. Most systems combine EDF and LGD.
Credit Correlations	Determine the co-movement between assets. For MTM process need to measure correlation between risk rating movements as well as default.	• Most models use correlation data generated from equity price movements. • Other banks rely on their judgement to establish correlations.	• Is it reasonable to use equity information to estimate correlations for bank credits? • Lack of historical data is a very significant problem for this parameter. • Outside the United States, there is even less information.
Credit Spreads	Determine the appropriate credit spreads to use to discount future cash flows for MTM purposes.	• Banks tend to use credit spreads commonly quoted in the market for loans that fall into public debt rating buckets.	• How is "liquidity" element of credit spreads taken into consideration?

Figure 19.12 (cont'd)

Item	Description	Range of Practice	Issues/Concerns
Exposure Levels (e.g.. amount drawn at default)	Determine the appropriate exposure amount to use within the model.	• Banks attempt to determine a credit equivalency when the exposure is not known with certainty (e.g. Undrawn commitments). • Banks attempt to determine future and average exposure amounts or estimate a credit equivalent amount on market driven instruments.	• Accuracy of estimates.
Characterization of Credit	Determine the appropriate industry and country in which to slot the data.	• Banks use a combination of judgement and financial statement information based on sales and assets.	• Accuracy of judgement based characterizations. • Lack of information to fully support industry/ country assignments.
System Capacity	Are bank systems able to capture needed data and can data from multiple systems be combined?	• Significant differences in how information is collected and what is collected.	• Insufficient information being collected. • Significant system upgrades/ changes needed if information is to be collected.
Management Information Systems	Is accurate, timely and understandable information being prepared for management?	• Reporting processes tend to be in very early stages of development.	• Some applications take a great length of time to run analysis.

Figure 19.12 (cont'd)

Item	Description	Range of Practice	Issues/Concerns
Management Oversight	What is the current state of bank management's ability to provide reasonable oversight to this area?	• Most knowledge/expertise of modeling process currently lies in backroom analytics.	• Line management and senior management need to gain understanding of strengths and weaknesses.
Backtesting	Verification that actual losses correspond to projected losses.	• No banks have completed any significant backtesting. • Limited availability of historical data is a big hurdle.	• To date there is no way to verify accuracy. • Questions remain as to how to adequately backtest.
Stress testing	Determine the model results to changes in the inputs (parameters)	• Some institutions are doing work in this area; however, to date, we have not seen comprehensive work.	• Few institutions are doing stress testing.
Sensitivity Analysis	Assess the sensitivity of results to changes in the inputs (parameters)	• Very limited work completed in this area to date.	• Sensitivity information is very limited. Significant enhancements needed to understand effects of parameter changes.
Internal Review And Audit Of Models	Does bank have an independent review process to determine the reasonableness of the models?	• Most banks do not have an internal review process in place.	• Lack of independence in reviewing these processes.

Source: (April 1999) *Credit Risk Modeling: Current Practices And Applications*; Basel Committee on Banking Supervision, Basel, Appendix

The objectives of the proposed framework (which are similar to those underlying the original accord) include:
- Promotion of safety and soundness in the financial system
- Enhancement of competitive equality
- Comprehensive approach to addressing risks
- The universal applicability of the existing Accord equally to smaller banks and highly sophisticated financial institutions

In addition, the committee identified two important collateral objectives:
- Maintain the overall level of capital currently in the banking system and possibly increase it
- Improve the correlation between supervisory risk and economic risk

In order to achieve these objectives, the new framework will be based on three pillars
- Minimum capital requirements
- Supervisory review of capital adequacy
- Market discipline

The consultative paper has been circulated inviting comment from market participants. The paper does not set out detailed proposals on all the areas that need to be amended. Instead, the paper sets out a number of areas in which The committee will be consulting with the banking industry. The deadline for responses to the paper is March 31, 2000. Responses may be made either to national bank regulators or direct to the Basel Committee. Thereafter, definitive proposals are to be produced later in the year. The probable target date for an agreed revised accord is unlikely to be before 2001.

In this section, the proposals for amendment are identified and examined. The impact on credit derivatives is then considered.

19.12.2   Minimum Capital Requirements

Approach

The key element of the proposed amendments is the alteration in the credit risk weighting in banking book assets. Under the proposed systems, the approach taken is:
- A more carefully differentiated set of risk weighting for sovereigns, banks, corporations and securitization vehicles is proposed
- The system relies on external credit ratings and potentially internal credit scoring techniques

The proposed risk weighting system is summarized in Figure 19.13.

Sovereigns

Under the current accord, all claims on sovereigns, central banks, and supranational organizations are 0% risk-weighted. This risk weighting is applicable where the sovereign country concerned is a member of the OECD, has concluded special lending arrangements with the International Monetary Fund associated with the fund's General Arrangements to Borrow and has not rescheduled its external sovereign debt within the past five years. The new proposals involve a five-level risk weighting categorization as set out in Figure 19.13.

Figure 19.13   BIS Risk Weightings — Proposed

Credit Rating	AA− or above	A+ to A−	BBB+ to BBB−	BB+ to B−	B− and below	Unrated
Sovereign	0%	20%	50%	100%	150%	100%
Bank (Option 1)	20%	50%	100%	100%	150%	100%
Bank (Option 2)	20%	50%	50%	100%	150%	50%
Corporate	20%	100%	100%	100%	150%	100%
Securitization SPV	20%	50%	100%	150%	Full deduction	Full deduction

The proposed risk weighting's will only automatically apply to foreign currency borrowing. Banks' exposures to their own sovereign (or central bank) denominated in the domestic currency of that sovereign and funded in that currency may, at the national supervisor's discretion, be zero weighted.

Claims on non-central government public-sector entities (PSEs) may be treated as a claim on a bank incorporated in the country of the government concerned. By concession, national supervisory authorities may treat claims on their own PSEs in the same way as claims against their sovereign.

Banks

The current accord provides that all claims on banks incorporated in OECD countries may be 20% risk weighted. Claims of less than one year maturity on banks incorporated in non-OECD countries are also 20% risk weighted. All other claims on banks are 100% risk weighted. The new proposals involve a five-level risk weighting categorization as set out in Figure 19.13.

The revised accord suggests two possible alternative mechanisms:

- **Option 1:** This option gives claims on banks a weighting that is one category less favorable than that applied to its country of incorporation, subject to a cap of 100%. The exception is for claims on banks of the lowest-rated countries, where the risk weight would be capped at 150%. The country risk weighting would be the foreign currency risk weighting. It would not be the concessionary zero weighting available for domestic own currency borrowing by sovereigns.

- **Option 2:** The second option is to use a base 50% risk weighting for all bank exposures, modified by reference to credit ratings assigned by an external credit assessment institution. Claims of a short original maturity (6 months or less) would receive a risk weighting which is one category more favorable than the ordinary risk weighting. The minimum risk weighting for all claims would be 20%. No claim could receive a risk weighed less than that applied to claims on its sovereign.

The potential application of these two options is illustrated in Figure 19.14.

Figure 19.14   BIS Bank Risk Weighting's — Proposed

Credit Rating	AA− or above	A+ to A−	BBB+ to BBB−	BB+ to B−	B− and below	Unrated
Option 1 (sovereign plus)	20%	50%	100%	100% (or 150% if incorporated in a B− country)	100% (or 150% if incorporated in a B− country)	100%
Option 2 (own rating) The higher of the weighting of the relevant sovereign or	20%	50% (20% if less than 6m original maturity)	50% (20% if less than 6m original maturity)	100% (50% if less than original maturity)	150% (100% if less than original maturity)	50%

Claims of multilateral development banks would continue to be weighted at 20%

The committee proposes that claims on securities firms should generally be risk weighted the same as claims on banks.[30]

Corporations

Under the existing terms of the accord, all claims on corporations are 100% risk weighted. The committee's proposals are that the standard weighting on claims on corporations should remain at 100%. However, two changes are proposed:

- Concessional risk weighting of 20% is given to claims on corporations of a very high quality (i.e.. those with a rating of AA−).
- Higher risk weighting of 150% is given to claims on corporations of a rating of below B−.

The new proposals involve a five-level risk weighting categorization as set out in Figure 19.13.

Securitization Vehicles

The proposals are predicated on the principle that securitization can serve as an efficient way to redistribute credit risk. The committee regards securitization as a potential arbitrage technique that is employed to avoid maintaining capital commensurate with the risk exposure of a given financial entity.

The primary proposal is that securitization tranches should be weighted in accordance with the risk weighting categorization set out in Figure 19.13. The most important change is that holdings of securitization tranches rated B+ or below and all unrated tranches will be deducted in full from capital.

Treatment of Derivatives Transactions

Under the existing accord, exposures in respect of OTC derivative transactions are calculated by marking the transaction itself to market and applying an "add-on" to reflect the potential future credit exposure (PFCE). The PFCE is based on the outstanding duration of the derivative and the underlying asset. The risk weighting of the counterparty is calculated as the lower of the risk weighting (determined normally) or 50%. The original justification for the 50% reduction was that the OTC derivative business is usually conducted between highly creditworthy entities. The revised accord proposes to remove this 50%

---

[30] In the European Union, the bank capital adequacy regime is applied in full to investment firms. This should ensure that claims on all European-incorporated securities firms will be treated worldwide as equivalent to claims on banks

risk weighting. This is based on the fact that higher rated institutions will benefit from the lower risk weighting provided for in the revised Accord.[31]

Undrawn Commitments

Under the current accord, commitments with an original maturity of up to one year or commitments that can be unconditionally cancelled at any time are 0% risk weighted. Commitments with a maturity of over one year are recognized in full subject to the application of a 50% credit conversion factor. The committee expressed concern with the explosive growth in the market for 365-day commitments that this substantial distinction has produced.

The committee, therefore, proposes that a credit conversion factor of 20% be applied to all commitments. The sole exception being commitments that are unconditionally cancelable which effectively provide for automatic cancellation on a deterioration of the borrower's creditworthiness without prior notice.

Loans Secured by Real Property

The proposal preserves the existing position that residential property lending should be risk weighted at 50%. However, commercial property lending should be 100% risk weighted.

Higher Risk Assets

The committee proposes that a higher risk category than 150% may be introduced for even riskier assets. No indication is given as to what categories of assets would be contained in such a class with submissions being invited on the point.

Credit Risk Mitigation

The committee takes the view that the existing rules are highly restrictive in terms of allowing the use of collateral, security, hedging, or other techniques reduce the amount of credit risk on the banking book. The committee accepts that the existing system may provide a regulatory disincentive to hedge risk . The proposals in respect of credit risk mitigation cover a number of separate

---

[31] This proposal is consistent with the recommendation made in the BIS paper published in the wake of the LTCM crisis, see (January 1999) "Bank's Interactions with Highly Leveraged Institutions," Consultative Paper issued by Committee on Banking Supervision, Basel

areas including imperfect hedges, guarantees, and treatment of collateral.

• *Imperfect Hedge*

  In an important concession, the committee accepts that imperfect hedges are accepted. This is predicated on the basis that any reduction of credit risk in the banking book is. The committee segregates imperfect hedge risk into three categories:

  • **Maturity mismatch:** A maturity mismatch arises where a hedging instrument does not match the maturity of the underlying assets. Such imperfect hedges are to be recognized subject to an additional capital requirement in the form of an add-on to deal with the unhedged risk involved in the position (effectively the forward risk). The committee takes the view that hedging is only valuable if it covers a substantial proportion of the risk. Accordingly, it is considering specifying a minimum remaining maturity for the hedge (one year is the suggested period). Below this minimum period the hedge would not be recognized. The add-on would be waived if the remaining maturity of the hedge were to be longer than two or three years.

  • **Basis risk:** Basis risk is taken to arise where the exposure on the hedging instrument is subject to potential changes in market price that could create a shortfall in the value of the hedge. In practise, this is sought to be dealt with by over-collateralization and frequent marking to market. However, The committee accepts that the collateral that the regulated person has at any given time is the collateral that is relevant. The committee suggests two potential methods of addressing basis risk:

    1. An add-on approach (as for derivative contracts).
    2. A haircut approach.

    Both of these methods have potential deficiencies. The committee invites comments on both approaches.

  • **Asset mismatch:** Where the reference asset and the underlying asset of a credit derivative are not identical then there is the potential for asset mismatch risk. The credit derivative will function as a hedge only if the hedger is satisfied that there is perfect (or near perfect) correlation between the two instruments. This would be supported by the existence of cross default clauses between them. The committee does not accept that this technique will be sufficient. It proposes to disallow credit protection based on distinct and separate assets.

• *Guarantees*

  Under the current approach, where an obligation is collateralized by another asset with a lower risk weighting the regulatory treatment involves a simple substitution of the higher risk weighted asset by the lower risk weighted asset. This assumes that there is a perfect correlation between the two liabilities (that is, either both will not default or both will default at the same time). The potential credit portfolio diversification benefit (that is, some credit should be given for the fact that the availability of two claims is more valuable than either single claim) is accepted by The committee. The committee identifies very substantial technical concerns with giving credit for this sort of approach. The committee does not permit a reduced credit risk weighting in these circumstances.

Treatment of Collateral

The existing accord adopts a highly restrictive approach to collateral. Cash and government securities are treated as the only acceptable types of collateral for risk reduction purposes. The committee notes that over the last few years there has been an increase in the use of collateral by banks to reduce counterparty credit risk. The committee identifies the need for recognition of the use of this credit exposure reduction technique.

The reforms proposed that eligible collateral might be extended to all financial assets. This would cover all assets that attract a lower risk weighting than the underlying exposure. Recognition is condition upon the collateral being supported by appropriate legal opinion and having a readily determinable. This would include all trading book securities, but might also include amounts receivable from derivative contracts.

The committee states that the effect of such an expansion in types of eligible collateral could be "significant". It seeks comment on the point. It also indicated that, subject to certain conditions, the scope of on balance sheet netting should be expanded to all assets and liabilities in the banking book.

Other Issues

There are a number of other issues in relation addressed in the proposal including:
- **Interest rate risk in the banking book:** The committee noted that several entities have significantly higher exposure to interest rate risk in their banking books than the industry norm. The committee intends to impose a higher weight of capital charge for such banks.[32] One approach might be to

---

[32] The mechanisms for identifying such banks were set out in the BIS paper, see (April 1999) "Measurement of Banks Exposure to Interest Rate Risks;" Consultative Paper issued by Committee on Banking Supervision, Basel

extend either of the two approaches contained in the market risk amendment of the current Accord or apply a model based approach.

- **Trading book:** The proposed changes do not specifically indicate changes to the trading book rules. The committee states its intent to update and modify the rules relating to the trading book in order to bring them into line with rules relating to the banking book where necessary. The committee states that the regulatory treatment of reverse repo transactions in the trading book has now become an area of special concern. It intends to specify adequate capital requirements to reflect price volatility of the underlying security in the frequency with which positions are marked for market.[33]

- **Operational risk:** The committee accepts the difficulty in the quantification of such risks. The committee accepts that in the absence of industry standard practise it would be difficult to incorporate operational risk into the existing capital framework. It solicits submissions on this point. The primary approach suggested is a straightforward percentage of growth revenue/ operating costs/managed assets. This would be qualified by an anchoring reference to the balance sheet. The proposal is clearly targeted at custodians, fund managers, securitization advisory firms and other entities who conduct operations which affect a large nominal value of securities who do not carry those securities directly on their balance sheet. Other suggested mechanisms for assessing operational risk include earnings at risk models, cost volatility models, brand values, non-quantitative self assessment, or loss events dependent on business volumes. A combination of these cross-referenced to loss benchmarks is also mooted. A model based approach may well also be considered based on The committee being satisfied as to the validity of the models themselves.

- **Bank regulatory capital instruments:** The committee does not propose any amendments to the definition of capital.

19.12.3   Supervisory Review of Capital Adequacy

There is marked shift in the actual supervisory approach to capital adequacy. The committee recognizes that minimum capital requirements play a central role in bank regulation. However, these minimum capital requirements are required to operate within an internal control framework appropriate to the regulated institution. This would include the markets in which banks operate, size,

---

[33] This is another consequence of the work done by the committee on relations with hedge funds in the aftermath of the LTCM collapse

sophistication and other factors. The committee identifies four principles on which supervisory review of capital adequacy should be based:

- Supervisors should expect banks to operate above the minimum capital ratios and should have the power to require banks to hold capital in excess of the minimum
- Banks should have a process for assessing overall capital adequacy in relation to risk profile as well as a strategy for maintaining capital levels
- Supervisors should review and evaluate a bank's internal capital adequacy assessment and strategy as well as compliance with capital ratios
- Supervisors should seek to intervene as early as possible to prevent capital falling below prudent levels

These proposals are potentially very significant. The ability for the supervisor to prescribe a capital requirement above the regulatory minimum is a radical innovations. Bank supervisors traditionally conduct formal prudential regulation by requiring compliance with only the minimum ratio (currently 8% of risk assets). The emphasis on supervisory monitoring of a bank's internal capital control systems as much as the regulatory minimum is a very significant change in supervisory approach. In some jurisdictions, discrimination between banks by the regulator based on the regulator's subjective perception may amount to illegal discrimination against individual institutions.

The committee's objective in the consultative paper has been to enunciate principles for the review process. It is in essence giving national regulators a range of approaches in order to cover the variety of banks and take their individual business focus into account in arriving at a required capital position.

19.12.4 Market Discipline

The third pillar of the supervisory approach is based on an initiative on transparency carried out by the bank in 1998.[34] The committee takes the view that it is in the interests of all banks to be perceived as safe and well-managed. The committee takes the view that regular public disclosure will assist in this process. This disclosure should cover key features of capital held against losses and the risk exposures. It should include all relevant details on the bank's financial condition and performance, business activities, risk profile and risk management activities. It should provide information on a bank's loss-absorbing

---

[34] See (September 1998) "Enhancing Bank Transparency;" Consultative Paper issued by Committee on Banking Supervision, Basel

capacity, details of capital maturity, level of seniority, step-up provisions, interest or dividend deferrals, use of Special Purpose Vehicles and terms of derivatives embedded in hybrid capital instruments. The committee states that such information should at a minimum be provided in annual financial reports.

The consultative paper acknowledges that regulators have differing legal powers to set such disclosure standards.

19.12.5   Application of Capital Adequacy Regime

The original accord was intended to apply on a consolidated basis to banks only. The revised accord proposes two amendments to expand its scope to address solo and holding company supervision issues:

- It is proposed that the accord be extended to include holding companies that are parents of banking groups
- The accord is applied to international active banks at every tier within the banking group, also on a fully consolidated basis

The committee proposes that this consolidation should include group members that conduct financial activities. This is intended to cover all non-bank financial subsidiaries. However, as an alternative. The committee proposes a system whereby each individual component of the group can be considered on a stand-alone basis. Under this approach, the assets and liabilities of any consolidated subsidiaries should be de-consolidated and the amount of the investment in the subsidiary should be deducted from capital. Insurance subsidiaries would be excluded from the scope of this consolidated supervision through deduction. Significant minority and equity investments in regulated financial entities should be consolidated on a pro-rata basis in accordance with local accounting and/or regulatory practises.

The revised accord proposes a three-year transitional period for applying full sub-consolidation for those countries where there is not currently a requirement.

19.12.6   Assessment

Specific Comments

The proposals for reform are interesting. The proposals seek to address some significant weaknesses in the existing capital adequacy framework. This aspect of the proposals is welcome. As noted below, the proposals are not as far reaching and comprehensive as the banking industry, at least the larger multi-national banks, were seeking. In assessing the proposal, it is useful to assess individual aspects of the proposals as well the approach taken by the committee. There are several individual aspects of the proposal that merit comment:

- **Sovereign risk weighting:** The capacity for national regulators to specify zero risk weighting for claims on the sovereign in its domestic currency has the potential to create considerable difficulties. If this discretion is exercised to any degree, then there is a chance that there will be a flow on effect. For example, if a particular country with a middle-rank external debt credit rating permits the banks of that country to treat claims on that sovereign at a zero weighting, then the local banks would enjoy a substantial competitive advantage in transaction with that sovereign. The accord states that where this discretion is exercised in a particular jurisdiction other supervisory authorities may allow their banks to apply similar risk weighting in respect of claims on the sovereign concerned in the currency concerned. Thus, transaction with the particular sovereign in its own currency would become cheaper than transactions with other sovereigns with similar credit ratings.[35] The supervisory authorities in those other sovereign countries would face pressure to adopt a similar treatment. The result may be adoption of this policy by all supervisors located in countries with credit ratings of less than AA−. There is a second anomaly in the treatment of sovereign entities. If the grant of discretion is based on the fact that the sovereign can never become insolvent in its own currency,[36] then the discretion should not be available to regulators in countries which are participant in the European Monetary Union and the Euro. This reflects the fact that these governments no longer have money-creating. It is not clear that regulators in these countries take this view. This is because the basis for the grant of the discretion is not spelt out in the proposed changes to the Accord.

- **Bank risk weighting:** The most important issue raised by these proposal is in relation to European banks. Article 6 of the Treaty of Rome prohibits discrimination by any government body (including a bank regulator) of a European Member State government against a bank incorporated in any other Member State by virtue only of its state of incorporation. This would prevent one regulator imposing a higher capital weighting on banks based in a

---

[35] National regulators could, therefore, find themselves in the position that exposures to two different sovereign borrowers with identical credit ratings could be carried at substantially different capital charges depending on the discretion of the regulator in those jurisdictions to claims in domestic currency on sovereign entities

[36] An assumption which was mercilessly exposed in the case of the default by Russia on its rouble denominated debt instruments (GKOs)

different country purely on the basis of relative credit ratings.[37] Discrimination is inherent in Option 1. However, it is incidentally present in Option 2. This may favor the adoption of Option 2 in respect of bank risk weightings.

- **Corporation risk weighting's:** The committee's proposals will result in the majority of claims on corporations remaining in the 100% risk weighting category. However, there is one anomaly. A corporation that has a credit rating below B− can reduce the risk weighting on its transactions by becoming unrated.

- **Derivative transactions:** The proposals correct an anomaly that was embedded in the original accord. The effect of the changes will be interesting. The effect of the removal of the 50% cap will increase the amount of capital required to be held in respect of each OTC derivative transaction. For high-quality bank counterparties the underlying exposure will continue to be rated at 20%. Where the exposure is to a highly rated bank that is incorporated in a lower rated country, the total amount of capital required to be held in respect of certain derivative transactions and counterparties may increase very significantly.

- **Rating basis:** The system proposed uses external credit ratings in the assessment of bank capital. The committee does not intend to produce a global list of acceptable agencies. The committee intends to allow national supervisors to determine the agencies that will be permitted to be used by their regulated. The committee provides general guidelines as to how individual supervisors should go about this assessment of individual rating agencies. The committee does not at this stage accept that internal rating techniques are sufficiently validated to be eligible for use as part of the supervisory process. However, it proposes the use of a mapping process whereby the relevant bank's internal ratings may be allocated to external rating categories. The committee is concerned also about the capacity of external rating agencies to rate sovereigns. The issue is that the credit analysis of a sovereign borrower is different to the analysis of a corporate or private sector entity. The committee suggests that this problem may be addressed in part by utilizing ratings given by entities other than the established bond market rating agencies. The real issue with the use of rating is the low number of firms that have external credit rating assessments outside of the US. This problem is made more difficult by the fact that two

---

[37] The accord concedes in a footnote that neither of these options can be adopted within the European Union without modification

potential approaches to default risk modeling (credit modeling and internal credit scoring) are both considered as being insufficiently developed for implementation at this stage. The committee has requested views on methods by which differentiation amongst corporations in particular may be achieved in practice.

General Comments

In assessing the overall approach of the proposals, it is useful to use the weaknesses in the existing capital accord identified above as a benchmark. The proposals address the following existing weaknesses:
• Simplified measure of credit exposure but only in respect of undrawn commitments and derivatives
• Limited differentiation of credit risk
• Recognition of credit enhancement of credit enhancement and offsets.
  The proposals do not address:
• Lack of term structure of credit risk
• Static capital structure
• Absence of recognition of portfolio and diversification effects
• Lack of an integrated view of risk

The major criticism of the proposals is that as a result of The committee concern about internal credit models (see discussion above) it appears unlikely that a model based approach to credit risk capital is unlikely to be an option for larger banks in the near term.

As a transitional matter, the proposals create significant short term uncertainty in markets. This uncertainty derives primarily from the potential increase in capital requirements on a large range of transactions. This affects existing transactions with long maturities and also proposed transactions.

19.12.7   Impact On Credit Derivatives

The proposals do clarify the position in respect of credit derivative transactions to any significant degree. The major proposals of relevance are the proposals in respect of "Imperfect Hedges."

The proposals seem to pave the way for accepting maturity mismatches in credit risk mitigation transactions. This is subject to holding additional capital against any residual forward risk. The amount of the capital required to be held has not been specified. For transactions where the hedge has a long remain maturity (two to three years), this add-on may not be applicable.

The issue of basis risk and asset mismatches. The proposals appear to recognize basis risk on the hedge and will accord (some) capital relief based on the amount of basis risk. The proposals appear to specifically disallow credit protection based on distinct and separate assets. The recognition of protection will require the same obligor, the reference asset must rank pari passu or more junior than the underlying asset and cross default clauses must apply.

The major impact on credit derivative markets derives from the proposed changes to the credit risk weighting framework. Under the existing Accord framework, the capital requirements have limited the purchase of credit protection from OECD banks or through cash collateralized structures (credit linked notes). This is the case where regulatory capital considerations are relevant to the design and execution of the transaction. The proposals open up the market significantly. Any counterparty with a credit rating higher than the obligation being hedged is theoretically available to provide the hedge against credit risk. This means that large insurers (either directly or through their financial products operations) and well-rated corporation emerge as potential participants in credit derivative markets as sellers of credit protection. Highly rated banks continue to have a competitive advantage in credit derivative transactions.

In summary, the BIS proposals for the reformation of credit capital have little direct impact on the treatment of such transactions. The major impact is indirect through introduction of a new group of potential participants who may add significantly to the liquidity of the market and the portfolio diversification opportunities available in the management of credit risk.

19.13   Summary

In summary, the regulatory position remains unsettled. Early resolution of the regulatory uncertainty is an important element in allowing expansion of the applications of credit derivatives. Current practice favors the calculation of regulatory capital based on analogy with more conventional derivatives.

The evolution of regulatory frameworks, as evident with the adoption of the internal models approach to determination of market risk capital requirements, favors, at least in the longer term, a revision of the credit capital requirements, set out under the BIS Capital Adequacy Accord. The process has already commenced. However, the outcomes remain uncertain. Credit derivatives, it is hoped, will be accorded fuller recognition for regulatory purposes under this framework. However, the complexity of issues dictates that the process of change is likely to be measured.

PART SEVEN
CONCLUSIONS

20

Credit Derivatives and Credit Risk Management — Evolution and Prospects

Satyajit Das

20.1 Overview

The credit derivatives market is of relatively recent origin. Since inception, the credit derivatives market has grown at a rapid rate over the year. This growth is predicated on the fundamental value of credit derivatives in creating a new mechanism for transferring and hedging credit risk (both spread and default risk) and also for assuming credit risk.

This chapter examines the evolution and future prospects for the market for credit derivative products. The origin and key phases of market development are first considered. The estimated size of the market is then examined. The structure of the market, in particular the nature of the participants, is analyzed. Two special sub-sectors of the market — the role of credit derivatives in the US leveraged loan market and credit derivatives in emerging markets is described. Some key developmental problems, including the organization of the credit derivative function within an organization, are set out. Potential areas of development in the market are considered.

20.2 Origins and Key Factors in Development

20.2.1 Market Origins

The origins of the market for credit derivatives are not clear. The market appears to have evolved out of the market for secondary loan trading which has developed since the early 1990s. The earliest transactions appear to have been completed around 1991/92.[1] The early transactions entailed total return loan swap transactions with credit spread and default products. The basic motivation driving the market was the desire to reduce credit risk to a specific counterparty to free up credit lines. This spawned the use of first-to-default baskets as a mechanism for transferring the risk on a basket of obligors to investors. It also spawned the concept of total return swaps as a mechanism for shifting the economic risk of the asset without the necessity for trading in the asset itself.

20.2.2   Key Factors in Development

The key factors underlying the development of the market include:
- Concern about concentration of credit risk in bank asset portfolios
- Developments in the management of credit risk
- Focus on overcoming the inefficiency and illiquidity of available structures for transferring and trading credit risk
- Incompleteness of the credit risk spectrum
- Recognition of the need to develop structures which would facilitate attracting new investment risk capital into assumption of credit risk

The deterioration of credit quality in the asset portfolios in the early 1990s served to emphasis both the importance of credit risk and the often poorly diversified structure of these portfolios. These concentration problems initially became evident not only in loan portfolios but also in portfolios of derivatives.

The concentration in real estate or related borrowers and also in certain cyclical industries who were adversely affected by the global macro-economic recession were prominent examples of this problem of concentration within credit portfolios. However, the problem in relation to credit concentration was not confined to problem credits at the lower levels of credit ratings. There was increased scrutiny of credit concentration *to higher quality counterparties.*

For example, this period of scrutiny of credit exposures served to highlight very quickly the large concentrations of exposures to a number of prominent sovereigns and multi-national entities. These exposures derived not only from traditional transactions but also from term derivatives transactions (interest rate and currency swaps) completed in connection with capital market issues. The exposures to individual counterparties were in many cases extremely large and caused significant scrutiny amongst the financial institutions regarding

---

[1]   For an interesting view of the development of the credit derivatives market, see Falloon, William, December 1997, "Freundian Analysis". *Risk*, pp 60–62

mechanisms for managing this exposure. A prime concern in this regard was the ability to continue to deal with these counterparties but *without significantly increasing the exposure to these parties*.

The problems of concentration of credit exposure relating to derivatives and other market risk sensitive instruments became evident around 1992/93 peaking in 1994/95. A combination of market factors (the appreciation of the yen and falling yen interest rates) and credit factors (the decline in the credit quality of a number of Japanese banks evidenced by credit rating downgrades) resulted in a sharp increase in credit risks on these portfolios. In certain cases, internal credit limits and absolute prudential limits on exposures to individual counterparties were reached and, in some cases, exceeded.

The problems of concentration were reinforced in the 1997–1999 period with the rapid deterioration in the credit quality of emerging market obligors. A combination of weaker local currency values, high interest rates, asset quality problems in local bank portfolios and the flight of foreign capital from emerging markets caused severe solvency problem for emerging markets obligors. The high level of exposure to these emerging countries and sovereign and corporate obligors in these emerging countries became evident in the portfolios of major financial institutions in the world. The problem of rapid changes in the level of exposure in certain derivatives contract also emerged as a serious problem. For example, the mark-to-market credit exposure on currency swaps undertaken with Thai, Korean and Indonesian counterparties where the local entity was paying US$ and receiving the local currency (baht, won or rupiah) increased dramatically. As the local currency devalued (often by 100% or more), the currency swap counterparty's credit risk to the local obligor increased rapidly to levels often *in excess of the notional principal value of the swap*.[2]

The increasing concern about the level of credit risk and concentration risk in credit portfolios was paralleled by increasing focus on improving systems for risk adjusted performance measurement in banks and financial institutions. Implementation of these approaches rapidly highlighted the risk and relative returns on these credit portfolios. The result of these processes served to highlight the dynamic nature of credit risk and the need to manage it actively. The inefficiency and illiquidity of the traditional mechanisms for credit trading prompted focus on credit derivatives as a mechanism for active management of these types of risks.

As these products started to become available, two factors added to the impetus for growth. Firstly, the capacity of developing products that extended

---

[2]   These swaps have come to be known as "wrong way" swaps

the range of credit risks available created new applications. The second factor related to the flexibility of these structures and the ability to allow participation by non bank investors. This reflected the fact that the synthetic nature of the instruments allowed institutions with little or none of the traditional infrastructure of banks to assume credit risks.

The participation of non bank investors coincided with a period of low nominal interest rates and low credit spreads which encouraged investors to identify new sources of return and yield enhancement. The new markets that developed in response to investor demand were the emerging market segment and the bank loan market (in particular, the leveraged loan market).[3] Credit derivatives rapidly developed as a flexible mechanism for packaging and distributing the credit risk of both these market segments to investors.

The early stages of the market emphasized the following types of transactions:

- The ability to isolate and transfer credit risk on specific assets allowing banks to hedge their credit risks
- The opportunity to access new classes of credit assets (such as bank loans and emerging market assets) which had traditionally not been directly available to non bank investors
- Interest in investors generating yield enhancement through investment in credit risks through loans and derivatives exposures

As the market has evolved, other types of transactions that extend the range and focus of applications have emerged including:

- Opportunities to increase the spectrum of credit risks, including the term of such risks, types of credit risk assumed and recovery rates, and assume specific combinations of risks considered acceptable
- Use of credit derivatives to manage credit risk within portfolios in order to reduce risk concentrations, improve management of credit capital to optimize returns on available credit lines, and generally seek to enhance risk adjusted returns on credit assets on a portfolio basis

---

[3]   As at mid-1997, in the US domestic market, institutional investor participation totaled 40–50% of the bank loan market, particularly focused on the lower credit-rated and leveraged loan markets. This included prime rate mutual funds, crossover investors from the high-yield market and special purpose asset repackaging vehicles (such as CBOs). See Lee, Peter, September 1997, "Hybrids Take Root", *Euromoney*, 12

20.2.3   Key Phases in Market Development[4]

The development of the market was to a large degree spasmodic. At each phase, particular factors and a type of transaction appear to have dominated the evolution of the market.[5] These can be loosely divided into the following phases:

- **To 1992:** A period dominated by banks primarily seeking to reduce exposures to particular counterparties developing credit derivatives as a mechanism for transferring credit risk.
- **1993 to 1994:** A period dominated by a funding arbitrage exploited by total rate of return investors (such as hedge funds) to take highly leveraged views on certain credits and markets (particularly, emerging markets) and specific transactions, such as the Italian tax arbitrage transactions.
- **1995 to 1996:** A period dominated by:
  - Low interest rates and low and falling credit spreads forcing investors to leverage their positions to earn satisfactory returns.

---

[4]   I am indebted to Paul Hattori for drawing to my attention aspects of market evolution and some of the ideas discussed here are drawn from Hattori, Paul "Credit Derivatives — A View Of The Market" a speech given to a Seminar on Credit Derivatives (Lanesborough Hotel, London, March 1997)

[5]   For a discussion on the evolution of the market, see Smith, Terry, March 1993, "The New Credit Derivatives", *Global Finance*, pp 109–110; Falloon, William, March 1994, "Credit Where Credit's Due", *Risk*, Vol 7, No 3, pp 9–11; July 1993, "A Wealth of Stealth," *Risk*, Vol 6, No 7, pp 29–33; van Duyn, Aline, April 1995, "Credit Risk For Sale. Any Buyers?" *Euromoney*, pp 41–43; 17 August 1995, "Taking Credit," *IFR Swaps* Issue 82 1, 10; 6 September 1995, "Credit Without Charity," *IFR Financial Products Issue* 25, pp 14–16; Parsley, Mark, March 1996, "Credit Derivatives Get Cracking", *Euromoney*, pp 28–34; 3 April 1996, "Regulating Credit Derivatives," *IFR Financial Products*, Issue 39, pp 16–17; Irving, Richard, July 1996, "Credit Derivatives Come Good", *Risk*, Vol 9, No 7, pp 22–26; Banks, Jim, July 1996, "Comfy With Credit?", *Futures & Options World*, pp 30–33; 4 September 1996, "Credit Where It's Due," *IFR Financial Products*, Issue 49, pp 1–3; Murphy, David, September 1996, "Keeping Credit Under Control", *Risk*, Vol 9, No 9, pp 123–126; McDermott, Robert, December/January 1997, "The Long Waited Arrival of Credit Derivatives", *Derivatives Strategy*, pp 19–26; Ghose, Ronit (Editor), 1997, *Credit Derivatives: Key Issues*, British Bankers Association, London; Lee, Peter, July 1997, "Masters of Credit or Hype", *Euromoney*, pp 44–49; Beder, Tanyo Styblo, and Iacono, Frank, July 1997, "The Good, The Bad — And The Ugly", *Risk, Credit Risk Supplement*, pp 30–33; July–August 1997, "Credit Derivatives — Five Years Out," *Derivatives Strategy*, pp 48–55; Covill, Laura, February 1999, "Getting Hooked On Credit Derivatives", *Euromoney*, pp 31–32; Storrow, Jamie, 1999, *Credit Derivatives: Key Issues* (2nd Edition), British Bankers Association, London

- Increased investment interest in emerging markets using credit derivative formats.
- Increased interest in leveraged loan markets using credit derivatives.
- **1997 to 1998:** The collapse of asset values in emerging markets, the Long Term Capital Management crisis and the liquidity crisis in capital markets generally.
- **Post 1998:** The expansion of use of credit derivatives and credit linked notes to manage bank credit portfolios and the incorporation of credit derivatives into the main stream of capital markets.

There is a lack of delineation as between the phases and there is substantial overlap between the market phases. However, the division into the identified phases does serve to highlight the nature of the development of the market for credit derivatives.

In Phase 1 (to 1992), the driving factor was the *internal* requirement for certain leading banks to reduce their credit exposure to certain counterparties. These counterparties included a number of Scandinavian and European sovereign entities that had been active borrowers in international markets. Another prominent group was the Japanese banks as the "bubble economy" of the late 1980s came to an end heralding a period of concern about the credit quality of the banking system.

The transactions were structured in a number of ways. These included: total return swaps, credit default swaps as well as credit linked structured notes. The structured notes included first-to-default basket structures with a fixed payout in case of default where the investor was rewarded by an enhanced return over LIBOR. The value dynamics were dictated by the cost of reduction in the credit exposures to the banks and the enhanced returns to investors seeking higher return in a period of low rates and very low credit spreads.

Phase 2 (1993 to 1994) was driven by two groups of investors. The first — total return investors — were seeking exposure to certain credit risks. These were to the domestic US high yield market and also to emerging markets. The investments were driven by the objective of both positive carry on the investment and the prospect of capital appreciation (usually from spread tightening resulting from economic recovery for the domestic high yield market or the re-rating of emerging markets sovereigns. Credit derivatives, in the form of total return swaps, offered these investors the capacity to both fund the assets at a competitive cost and leverage their positions significantly. In this regard, credit derivatives were competing with the repo market in providing funding for these investors. These total return swaps (usually collateralized by around

5–10% and providing funding at around 80 bp over LIBOR) became a prominent part of the market.

The second group of investors was driven by a tax anomaly in the Italian tax system (involving withholding tax). This combined with anomalies in the bond and swap market allowed investors to purchase Italian domestic bonds that were then swapped to an attractive margin over LIBOR.[6] These transactions were undertaken in significant size totaling US$billions.[7]

The problem with this form of arbitrage was the increasing concentration of credit risk and the lack of availability of credit limits to keep exploiting this anomaly. This prompted the use of credit default swaps to shield the purchaser of the assets from the underlying Italian credit risk. The typical structure that evolved entailed a credit default swap on one designated Italian BTP to maturity in return for the payment of a fee (usually around 20/25 bp pa). Even after incorporating the credit default swap (usually to generate a AAA rated asset), investors were able to generate earning of around US$LIBOR plus 25–30 bp.[8]

Phase 3 (1995 to 1996) was fuelled by the sharp decline in credit spreads that took place in 1995/96. This spread contraction was evident in both developed and emerging markets. This lead to traders wanting to continue to be exposed to spreads but wanting to fund these position off balance sheet. This was due to the fact that at low spreads it was more and more difficult to fund the positions profitably and to also limit their exposure to a widening of spreads. At the same time investors were unable to achieve target return levels at current spread levels and were willing to take some additional risk in order to increase returns to closer to acceptable levels. Investors increasingly sought higher returns from either sale of hidden optionality on credit risk (credit spreads) or taking default risk in formats which allowed them to incorporate leverage to enhance returns. Investors also increased their credit risk by investing in emerging market and/ or leveraged loan markets.

In this environment, a number of products evolved. The first group entailed selling the investor assets (either securities or asset swaps) at a higher than market spread in return for the investor having an option to repurchase the asset

---

[6] For a discussion on the Italian bond arbitrage, see Das, Satyajit, 1994, *Swaps And Financial Derivatives*, LBC Information Services, Sydney, McGraw-Hill, Chicago, pp 591, 592, 844–846

[7] For an insight into activity in this type of trade by certain hedge funds, see Muehring, Kevin, November 1996, "John Meriwether By The Numbers", *Institutional Investor*, pp 50–63

[8] See Irving, Richard, July 1996, "Credit Derivatives Come Good", *Risk*, Vol 9, No 7, pp 22–26

at par within 12 months (callable asset swaps). If spreads continued to decrease the dealer exercised the call option to repurchase the asset which could be sold at a tighter spread. Investors were able through the sale of optionality enhance returns. The second group essentially was structured as protection against increasing spreads. They took the form of asset swaptions, synthetic lending facilities or volume/size options. The essential feature of all of these trades was the ability to place asset swaps with the seller of the option at a pre-agreed spread in the event of rises in credit spreads. The dealers obtained protection on their positions and the investors received a yield which when the option premium was incorporated was acceptable.

Investors also began to aggressively trade credit default correlations with first-to-default baskets and utilize total return swaps to leverage their credit views.

The entry into emerging and leveraged bank loan markets was driven as noted above by an altered risk return profile. However, the *format* of the investment was driven by the increasing availability of credit derivative structures.[9] This reflected a variety of structural considerations. In emerging markets, these considerations included:

- **Maturity:** The emerging market assets were generally of long duration while investor demand was for shorter term risk. Total return swaps and credit default swaps were used to synthesize these types of shorter tenor assets for investors.

- **Regulatory factors:** The complex regulatory factors and investment mechanics discouraged foreign direct investment in many emerging markets. These included regulations preventing foreign ownership, withholding taxes, high transactions costs (stamp taxes, custody costs, high foreign exchange transaction margins), lack of liquidity of the asset market and currency convertibility risk. Total return swaps and to a lesser extent credit default swap structures were used to overcome these issues.

- **Trading factors:** Trading strategies such as the desire to merely trade the credit spread of emerging market paper or short emerging market issues were practically difficult to implement. This reflected the absence of well developed markets to finance assets or borrow securities (the repo market). In addition, the requirement for leveraged transaction structures to further enhance returns also became a major driving factor. Total return swaps, credit

---

[9] See "Credit Derivatives Come Alive In Asia" (22 January 1997) *IFR Financial Products*, Issue 58, pp 10–12; Crossman, Alex, 15 November 1997, "Credit Notes Harvest Asian Interest", *International Financial Review*, Issue 1209, pp 40

default products and credit spreads forwards and options rapidly emerged to act as the vehicle instruments for emerging market issuers.

Credit derivatives use among financial institutions and emerging market traders also was important. The major driver was the need to manage credit exposures, both at a sovereign and individual counterparty level. As activity in emerging markets developed, banks and traders active in these market segments rapidly increased their exposure to individual countries and counterparties. This increase was to a point when the need to hedge some of the economic credit risk become a major factor in allowing these institutions to continue to transact business with counterparties in the relevant jurisdiction. Total return swaps and credit default swaps rapidly emerged as a mechanism for this hedging.

In leveraged loan markets, the factors driving the use of the credit derivative format included all of the above factors as well as the following additional factors:

- **Structural flexibility:** The investor often sought to assume one or other part of often complex packages of loans. The actual loan participation were sometimes structured as strips — that is, lenders had to participate in more than one tranche.[10] In addition, these investors may have been interested in a specific component of the overall risk of the transaction only. In addition, initial participation amounts may have been well above the optimal investment amount for individual investors in the context of an overall diversified portfolio. In some cases, restrictions on assignments or loan sales may also have limited the scope for risk transfer. The use of total return swaps and credit default swaps was adaptable to the identified investor objectives and overcame some of the barriers to risk transfer.
- **Administrative flexibility:** Institutional investors typically did not possess the loan administration infrastructure to participate directly in loans. The total return swaps, credit default swaps and synthetic lending facility/asset swaption structures were ideally suited to transferring the risk while allowing the originating or participation bank to remain the lender of record for the transaction.

The use of credit derivatives in both emerging market and leveraged loan markets is specifically considered below.

---

[10] For example, a lender might have to take a participation in the senior secured, unsecured, and mezzanine (subordinated) debt facilities. This structure is designed to align lender and equity investor interests and lower the agency costs of the transaction

Phase 4 (1997 to 1998) was dominated by the crisis in emerging markets and the flow on into capital markets generally.[11] The crisis had its origins in Asia. In July 1997, the Thai Baht was uncoupled from the US\$ to which had been pegged and promptly plunged in value. The situation was repeated in quick succession in a series of other Asian economies such as Korea, Indonesia, and Malaysia. The situation also affected to a varying degree other regional economies such as Philippines, Taiwan, India, Hong Kong and Singapore. The rapid depreciation in the value of the local currency was accompanied by a series of events:

- Unhedged foreign currency borrowings (in US\$, DEM and yen) showed significant foreign exchange losses. Both sovereign and corporate borrowers in Asia had large amounts of unhedged foreign currency debt which had been undertaken to capitalize on large favorable interest rate differentials in the belief that the local currency was effectively linked to the US\$ and unlikely to depreciate significantly.
- There was a sharp decline in local currency stock markets and in asset prices generally.
- Local currency interest rates increased to very high levels.
- There was a flight of capital from these markets. This reflected withdrawal of short term financing lines by foreign lenders as well as liquidation of portfolio investments.

The combination of these events triggered a massive collapse in economic activity and a recession in these countries. The solvency of many borrowers was completed undermined by these events with the default risk rising sharply. The crisis triggered massive intervention by the International Monetary Fund.

The crisis rapidly affected other markets. The immediate effect was in other emerging markets. Russia and Eastern Europe was first affected. Russia defaulted on it rouble obligations in the second half of 1998.[12] Latin America

---

[11] For a discussion on the impact of the emerging market crisis, see Clow, Robert, December 1997, "Past Due", *Institutional Investor*, pp 159–163; Wilson, Neil, January 1998, "Credit Derivatives," *Futures & Options World*, pp 51; Paul-Choudury, Sumit, March 1998, "Strength Through Adversity", *Risk — Credit Risk Supplement*, pp 6–9; Elliot, Margaret, April 1998, "Waking Up To Credit Risk", *Derivatives S   t   r   a   t   e   g   y* pp 32–38; Louis, Jack, February 1999, "Tonic For The Troops", *Risk*, pp 18–23

[12] For an analysis of the Russian default, see Stoakes, Christopher, November 1998, "Ways Out Of Russia's Big Freeze", *Euromoney*, pp 20; Dyson, Jack, March 1999, "Every Man For Himself" *Euromoney*, pp 25–28

was also affected with Brazil being forced to float the Real that promptly fell sharply in value.[13]

The crisis in emerging markets rapidly affected capital markets more generally. The key transmission mechanism was a general reduction in liquidity, a contraction in available capital particularly in other than the highest credit quality categories and a sharp increase in credit spreads. These factors triggered major problems for banks and investors. The most serious victim of the spreading crisis was Long Term Capital Management (LTCM) (a very large and well known hedge fund) which had to seek an infusion of new capital to survive a serious erosion in the net asset value of the fund.

The impact on the banking system was immediate and massive. Bank credit losses rose sharply as provisions were made against exposures to emerging market and hedge fund counterparties. In addition, banks active in emerging market trading sustained serious trading losses as emerging market financial assets well sharply in value.

This period with its unprecedented volatility had a negative impact on the development of credit derivatives markets. The major problems arose because the credit derivative format had begun to become established as a favored method for taking on emerging market exposure (as noted above). For example, investment in the Russian GKO market was substantially structured in the form of credit linked notes.

As the crisis developed, credit default swaps were triggered and total returns swaps were terminated and a cash or physical settlement effected. Initially there was considerable confusion about the actual mechanics of these actions. There was also acrimony about the economic effect. This ranged from counterparties seeking to disown transactions on the basis that they had not understood the transaction and its risks to concern about the mismatch between the actual loss suffered and the payout under the default hedge. The problems encountered created significant negative publicity and also concern about the actual efficacy of credit derivatives.

---

[13] For an interesting analysis of the behavior of the market for emerging debt, see Kulesz, Javier, November 19, 1998, "Contagion: Did The Market Discriminate?" *Financial Products*, Issue 102, pp 14–15; Currie, Anthony, November 1998, "Back To The Age Of Defaults", *Euromoney*, pp 60–63

However, as the initial problems with existing transactions were resolved, the credit derivatives market received considerable impetus from the effects of the crisis.[14] This impetus came from a number of sources:

- **Necessity for credit risk management:** The crisis served to highlight the need for active management of credit risks. At a macro level, this reinforced interest in using credit derivatives to hedge and manage credit risk, particularly concentration risk within portfolios. At a micro level, as limits to emerging countries and individual obligors were reduce, there was an immediate need to seek mechanisms for hedging existing positions to ensure compliance with limits. Credit derivatives markets (total return swaps and credit default swaps) rapidly became a means for achieving these objectives.
- **Emerging market debt portfolio management:** In the aftermath of the crisis, traders in emerging market debt were faced with large inventory positions that were both illiquid and also showing large mark to market losses. Traders seeking to liquidate position found it necessary to develop new and innovative mechanisms for selling down this risk. Structures such as total return swaps and credit linked notes (CBOs and basket structures) were utilized to seek to repackage and liquidate these positions. The motivation was both to increase the value achieved and also to access liquidity.
- **Access to liquidity:** For borrowers in emerging markets, financing and access to cash was an urgent issue. The prospect of selling prime marketable assets (such as equities and bonds) at distress prices was unattractive. Total return swaps emerged as a means for accessing cash while maintaining the desired price exposure to the underlying assets. These structures often allowed access to funding at more economic costs than direct funding (if available).
- **Repatriation of investment to home markets:** As investors disinvested from emerging markets, the liquidity was directed into other assets. After an initial period of concern, markets such as the leveraged loan market and even the domestic US high yield market attracted investment. The increase in spreads, the robust state of the US economy and the perception that investment returns were in excess of the expected default risk drove this investment. Credit derivative formats were again extensively utilized to

---

[14] See Quist, Robert, February 1998, "Credit Derivatives Ease Asia's Debt Crisis" , *Risk*, pp 4–5; Horsewood, Rachel, Gailey, Colin, and Yu, Daniel, March 1998, "Back To Basics", *AsiaMoney*, pp 20–24; Rhode, William, August 1998, "Brave New World", *Asia Risk*, pp 10–13; Abed, Kamal, November 1998, "It Ain't What You Do...", *Futures & OTC World*, pp 55

access these markets. In addition, some more aggressive investment began to seek re-investment opportunities in emerging markets on a selected basis. This included purchase of financial assets as well as distressed bonds. Credit derivative structures were often used to create the appropriate format for these investments that primarily focused on recovery rates and credit spread movements.

- **Portfolio liquidation:** The capital losses suffered by banks forced some banks to seek to adjust their balance sheets. For example, Japanese banks already weakened by credit losses in Japan suffered large credit losses on their significant loan portfolios to Korean, Thai and Indonesian obligors. These banks used credit derivatives in a number of ways. Japanese banks used credit derivatives to shed risk over key balance dates to "window dress" balance sheet and risk profiles. More fundamentally, Japanese banks undertook the securitization of loans assets through either credit linked notes (CLOs) or sought economic hedges through credit default swaps or synthetic securitization transactions.
- **Concern about currency transferability risk:** The imposition of currency controls by Malaysia served to reinforce already evident concerns about currency convertibility risk in emerging markets. Interest in currency conversion protection increased during this period from both investors (both portfolio and direct) as well as emerging market traders.[15]

In essence, the crisis was important to the evolution of the credit derivatives market in a number of ways:
- It served to highlight that these hedges actually functioned as intended, albeit with some problems. The triggering of defaults and the need to settle default payments served to highlight key issues in the operation of these structures. This lead to significant enhancements and improvements in documentation, structuring and design of transactions.
- It highlighted the necessity of active credit management in a dramatic manner.
- It illustrated that credit derivatives could provide some assistance in the management of credit risks. In reality, they could be part of the way in which the crisis needed to be dealt with rather than as a causal factor in the crisis.

It is arguable that this phase of activity in credit derivatives was pivotal in establishing these instruments as a significant factor in capital markets.

---

[15] See Kirby, James, October 1998, "Capital Controls Raise Risk", *Asia Risk* 9

Phase 5 (1999 to the present) is characterized by increasing maturity at both a product level and in the application of these products to credit risk management. Following the emerging market crisis, credit derivatives have become accepted at two levels within capital markets:

- For banks and financial institutions, the various structures have become a more accepted means of managing tactical credit risk to individual counterparties as well as a strategic portfolio management tool (primarily, in the form of credit linked notes and portfolio securitization structures).
- For non financial institutions and investors, the instruments have come to be seen as a way of selectively managing credit risk or as an alternative means for synthesizing assets and establishing relative value positions in sovereign and other credit risks.

Key drivers have included the increased standardization of structures, terminology and documentation. Increased pricing transparency and the availability of information on pricing techniques has also assisted this process. Increased liquidity and the rise in volumes of transactions outstanding have all contributed to the acceptance of these products. An additional driver for banks has been their increased focus on regulatory and economic capital management. The presence of significant regulatory capital arbitrage opportunities has also been a factor.

The discussion of the points of focus in the evolution of the market in credit derivatives highlights the eclectic pattern of the market's development. It also highlights the intricate manner in which specific imperatives that have prevailed in different guises at different times have gradually allowed the development of the products and elicited the participation of different banks and investor groups.

20.3   Market and Activity Levels

The size of the market and activity levels is difficult to gauge. The difficulties are the result of a number of factors including:

- The absence of any specific survey data on these types of transactions, until recently.
- The wide variety of transaction structures utilized, including structured notes, off balance sheet derivative transactions, and other forms (indemnities). This has prompted significant debates as to the types of transactions that should be treated as credit derivatives.
- The lack of standardization of credit derivative structures which creates inherent difficulties of characterization and collation of data.

- The generally secretive nature of this market and its lack of transparency which impedes assessment of the markets size.

In 1996, one commentator estimated the size of the market as at 1996 at around US$40 billion.[16] Other estimates range from around US$30–100 billion in annual volume.

In late 1996, the British Bankers' Association (BBA) published the results of a survey of 15 London based financial institutions.[17] The average estimate of market outstanding was around US$20 billion. This, it is assumed, is the outstanding among London-based institutions. The survey also revealed that the surveyed institutions believed that the market was based in London and the New York credit derivatives market was somewhat smaller than that in London. Growth rates were also high reflecting the low current volume base but also reflecting the strong underlying demand and interest in the product and potential applications. The BBA survey identified significant interest in using credit derivatives projecting a market size by 2000 of US$100 billion. At the end of 1997, the BBA published the results of a follow up survey of 44 institutions. Based on this survey, the market size was estimated at around US$180 billion as at end 1997 of which London was estimated at US$70 billion.[18] In a further survey as at the end of 1998. the BBA estimated at US$350 billion (this was the average size with an estimated range of US$100 to 750 billion.[19]

The current market size as at end-1999 is estimated at in excess of US$750 billion. Growth in the market very rapid with the market having effectively doubled in size in each of the last few years. Major trading centers continue to be New York (focused on the large domestic US market) and London (focused on European and international transactions). Activity is distributed fairly evenly between these two centers. A smaller but significant center of activity is Hong Kong that has emerged as an important hub for Asian, including Japanese, credit derivatives activity.

---

[16] See Smithson, Charles with Holappa, Hal and Rai, Shaun, June 1996, "Credit Derivatives (2)", *Risk*, Vol 9, No 6, pp 47–48

[17] See 1996, BBA Credit Derivatives Report 1996, British Bankers Association

[18] See 8 October 1998, "BBA Counts Up Credit Trades", *Financial Products*, Issue 99, pp 7

[19] See Storrow, Jamie, 1999, *Credit Derivatives: Key Issues (2nd Ed)*, British Bankers Association, London, pp 127

20.4   Market Sectors

20.4.1   Overview

The market for credit derivatives is capable of dissection in a number of ways including the type of underlying assets, the liquidity of underlying assets, specific types of credit risk (investment grade, non investment grade, distressed credits and emerging market credits) as well as geographically.

20.4.2   Liquidity of Underlying Assets

It is important in dissecting the market for credit derivatives to separate the universe of underlying reference credit obligations into liquid and illiquid assets.

Liquid assets refers to securities (such as bonds) as well as tradable loans (sometimes in the form of Transferable Loan Certificates (TLCs) or in more traditional formats such as assignments, novation and risk and sub participations).[20] Illiquid assets encompass all other credit obligations such as non traded loans as well as non static exposures, arising typically from derivatives and other market risk related instruments. The illiquidity may be a function of the form of the obligations (such as the exposure on a derivative, for example, a swap), particular conditions impacting upon the issuer or obligor (such as distressed credits) or the lack of trading interest in the type of obligations (due to size or the limited range of investors in emerging markets). Estimates typically classify approximately 5% of outstanding credit risk as liquid. The remaining 95% is treated as substantially illiquid.

Originally, the credit derivative markets were focused on liquid credit assets. This reflected the ease of obtaining prices, marking positions to market, the need to establish payouts on the transactions in case of a credit event and the ease in dealer hedging of positions. However, as the market has evolved there is much greater interest in the larger and more interesting illiquid market segments. The fact that it is in relation to the illiquid credit markets that the advantages of credit derivatives are greater has come to be appreciated. These advantages include creation of liquidity by allowing trading in these assets, reduction in transaction costs and market frictions, and enhancing efficiency in the management of portfolios containing these types of assets.

---

[20] There is an increasingly liquid secondary loan market in the US, particularly in leveraged loans. In 1997, one estimate put the volume traded at around US$40 billion, with dealers making prices in US$5 million lots and active participation from loan investors; see Lee, Peter, September 1997, "Hybrids Take Root", *Euromoney*, 12

The distinction is also reflected in both the nature of the participation and the types of products favored. The liquid market sector has attracted investment banks and securities dealers. This reflects the fact that the credit derivatives business is a natural extension of their underlying securities and trading business. It is also most relevant to their traditional client bases, particularly fixed income investors. The illiquid asset sectors have attracted great interest from commercial banks. This reflects the fact that their own balance sheets contain significant levels of these illiquid assets. Credit derivatives are a natural extension of traditional methods of managing these risks within their portfolios.

20.4.3   Types of Exposure — Static vs Non Static

The early phases of the market emphasized traditional static credit exposures such as those generated by loans and other credit extension transactions. These obligations were fully funded and had no market price sensitivity.

However, as the market has developed, credit derivatives, particularly default swaps, linked to non static exposures such as those generated by derivatives has emerged. The differentiating factors of these types of exposures include:

- Non funded exposures.
- Market price sensitivity of the credit exposure.
- The *actual* credit exposure is not capable of exact estimation at the commencement of the transaction.

These factors create major problems for the management of credit exposures in financial institutions. The problems arise from the fact that while the expected credit exposure is estimated prior to entry into the transaction and appropriate limits are established changes in market rates could result in the exposure being significantly different from that forecast. The changes in the level of credit exposure have a number of implications:

- Causing a breach of internal credit limits.
- Creating undesired concentration of credit risk within the entity's credit portfolios.
- Reducing trading liquidity through increased utilization of counterparty credit limits thereby potentially increasing the market risk of the entity.

The fact that this is more than a theoretical possibility was graphically illustrated during 1994/95. The appreciation of the yen and the drop in Japanese interest rates lead to a dramatic change in the mark-to-market values of currency swap and long dated forward foreign exchange positions increasing the counterparty credit risk dramatically. The fact that this market rate change coincided with a decline in the credit rating of several prominent Japanese financial institutions served to highlight the dynamic nature of credit exposure in these types of transactions. The experience was repeated in 1997/98 when the sharp depreciation in the value of some Asian currencies had a similar impact on existing derivative positions.

The issues identified above combined with the dramatic growth in the volume of derivatives and other off balance sheet transactions sensitive to market risk has created increased interest in credit derivatives to manage the exposure of these types of transactions.

20.4.4   Market Sectors

The credit derivatives market can also be sub-divided into sectors based on the credit quality of the underlying reference assets or obligations. The usual categories are as follows:

- **Investment grade credit:** This category covers higher quality credits. Lower grade investments credits (BBB/Baa) while technically investment grade are generally closer to the non investment credits in terms of credit derivatives activity. The risk of default is relatively low in this market segment prompting focus on other aspects of risk, such as credit spreads. The primary motivations for transactions in this segment include:
  - Reducing the impact of market friction, such as withholding taxes and regulatory factors.
  - Creating customized forms of exposure.
  - Completing the available credit spectrum.

  The type of products most frequently encountered include:
  - Credit spread transactions.
  - Credit default derivatives, particularly, focusing on first to default structures and other structures for yield enhancement or diversification of credit.
- **Non-investment grade credit:** The dynamics of lower rated investment grade credits and non investment grade credits is significantly different to that of investment grade credits. The higher default risk and the higher level of barriers to participation in this investment sector are significant factors in this market segment. The primary motivations in this sector include:
  - Facilitating access to credit assets where direct exposure is otherwise difficult.
  - Reduction in transaction costs.

- Yield enhancement applications including assumption of credit exposures.
- Facilitating funding to overcome market imperfections such as the absence of a liquid repo market in these securities.

The products most frequently used include

- Total return loan swaps, including structures indexed to individual loans/bonds or high yield index products.
- Credit spread products.
- Default products, including capital structure arbitrage (as between secured, senior and subordinated tranches of transactions) and recovery rates plays.
- **Distressed credits:** This market sector focuses on obligations where the issuer has defaulted or is anticipated to be in financial distress and where the underlying credit obligations are being rescheduled or restructured. The primary motivation for transactions in this sector include:
- Opportunistic loan trading.
- High risk return trading transactions, such as leveraged distressed loan plays.
- Industry, sector or geographic plays based on anticipated macro-economic cycle transactions.
- Recovery rate expectations driven transactions.
- The capacity to finance positions off balance sheet.

The activity in this sector is an extension of loan/asset trading where credit derivatives provides amore efficient *mechanism* for creating or reducing exposure to the underlying credit. The full range of products are likely to be encountered in this sector.

- **Emerging markets:**[21] This market sector focuses on obligations where the issuer is domiciled in emerging markets (primarily, Latin America, Eastern Europe and Asia). The dynamics of this market segment are dictated by the predominant role of sovereign credit risk in these sectors and the difficulties of or inefficiencies in obtaining direct exposures to the underlying credit assets. The nature of investment risk (higher political risk and regulatory risks, e.g. currency inconvertibility) in these markets is also different. The primary motivation for transactions in this sector include:

---

[21] For a discussion on credit derivatives in an emerging-market context, see Watzinger, Hermann "Credit Derivatives In Emerging Markets" in Ghose, Ronit (Ed), 1997, *Credit Derivatives: Key Issues*, British Bankers Association, London; van der Maas, Paul and Naqui, Nabeel "Credit Derivatives Structures Within An Emerging Markets Framework" in Storrow, Jamie, 1999, *Credit Derivatives: Key Issues (2nd Ed)*, British Bankers Association, London

- Attempts to isolate and capture returns from instruments without direct exposure to the underlying credit risk of the exposure (e.g. through an emerging market index or securities etc where the return is indexed to the price performance of a reference underlying bond).
- Lowering transaction costs, particularly those arising from taxation and other regulations (for example, using total return swaps to synthesize direct investments to avoid withholding taxes).
- Capturing value from spread movements that can often be very dramatic (through credit spread products).
- Relative value performance strategies.
- Creating customized risk reward profiles (e.g. through targeted put selling and covered call writing).
- Managing aspects of the political and regulatory risk of these operating environments.

The full range of products are likely to be encountered in this sector.

20.4.5   Geographic Structure

An interesting aspect of the market is its geographic structure. The key market sectors are the US/North American market, the European market, the Japanese market and the emerging markets (notable, Latin America, Eastern Europe and Asia).

The most noteworthy aspect of the geographical structure is the surprising proliferation of credit derivative products across *all* the market segments. Credit derivatives, involving emerging market issuers, is a significant component of the market. This continues to be the case albeit at more subdued levels even after the 1997/98 crisis. However, the bulk of this activity is non indigenous in nature being undertaken between investor, corporations and banks based outside the emerging markets themselves.

There are a number of significant differences in the pattern of development of each of these market segments. The US market is dominated by commercial and investment banks and institutional investors. The banks are primarily involved in managing their asset portfolios or selling down loan positions acquired in the primary markets. Institutional investors are involved in order to acquire indirect exposure to certain sectors, such as the non investment grade loan markets, or to manage their portfolio risks. Other participants like hedge funds have emerged as significant contributors of capital to credit risk based on specific credit views, either on an individual issuer or sector, or based on economy wide views. The US market contains several unique sectors. One such sector where credit derivatives have emerged as a significant factor is the leveraged loan market (see discussion below).

The European market[22] is focused on banks, particularly, those outside the major banking institutions. These banks are concerned with the management of portfolio concentration (arising from their strong market positions in their home markets) and either funding cost advantages or disadvantages. The opportunities to acquire credit exposure synthetically to diversify their credit risks while maximizing their returns relative to their funding cost positions has provided a strong impetus to growth. Investor participation in Europe has also been a factor. The capacity to trade credit spreads and to take default risk or to hedge default risk has been increasingly a center of focus, although the level of participation has not been comparable to that in the US. The ability to optimize bank capital management has also emerged as a significant factors, albeit at a slower pace than in corresponding organization in the US. Factors that have impeded the rate of adoption of credit derivatives include:

- The higher degree of bank intermediation in most European markets that has the effect of reduced available traded reference assets which underlie much of credit derivative structures. This is compounded by a higher proportion of small to middle market loans in many European countries.
- The absence of meaningful historical data on European loan portfolios and a lower portion of rated obligors reduced the ability to price and trade credit risk generally.

Increasingly, European market development has come to focused on the impact of the introduction of the Euro.[23] Initially, the surge of trading on the convergence of interest rates between the countries destined to become part of Euroland created credit derivatives opportunities. This reflected the often very large positions assumed by investors in government and sovereign securities of particular countries in anticipation of convergence in interest rates. The resulting concentration in credit exposure forced some investors to use synthetic structures (credit spread transactions) or use credit default swaps to manage credit concentration risk and credit limit utilization.

---

[22] See Theodore, Samuel S. and Madelain, Michel, March 1997, *Modern Credit Risk Management And The Use Of Credit Derivatives: European Banks' Brave New World (And Its Limits)*, Moody's Investors Service

[23] See Paul-Choudhury, Sumit, November 1998, "New Tricks For The Old World", *Risk, — Credit Risk Special Report*, pp 8–9

In the longer term, the advent of the euro is likely to have significant implications for the development of the credit derivatives. The elimination of currency risk between 11 European nations has the inadvertent effect of creating not only a large single and unified market but one where credit differentiation as expressed by spread to the strongest credit quality issuer is the dominant market variable. In effect, the euro creates a highly structured and large bond or securities market. The use of credit spread derivative structures to trade and monetize credit expectations (effectively the spread to the German euro securities yield) between Euroland countries are logically set to grow.[24] In addition, the creation of a unified single bond market has the potential to create a market comparable to the US domestic market. The emergence of an embryonic high yield and leveraged loan market in Europe is the initial tentative steps in that direction.[25] This promise to allow the development of credit derivatives products in Europe similar to those actively traded in the parallel US markets.

The credit derivatives market in Japan is less developed than in either Europe or the US. That is not say that Japanese banks are not active. However, the nature of the activity is narrowly focused in two specific areas: non Japanese credits and Japanese banks. Japanese banks have been active in using credit derivative structures (total return swaps, credit default swaps and credit linked notes) to manage the risk on their foreign loan portfolios. This is particularly in relation to exposures in Asia and other emerging market. The activity in relation to Japanese banks is more complex. This consists of both use of credit derivatives (such as credit default swaps and credit linked notes, for example, step up callable credit linked structure) to manage credit risk. This type of activity has both been of a genuine economic risk transfer nature and balance date "cosmetic" risk profile management nature. The second type of activity has been in the credit risk of the Japanese banks themselves. A large part of that activity has focused on non Japanese counterparties seeking to shed credit risk to Japanese banks as default risk levels have risen. This has taken traditional forms including credit default swaps and credit linked notes. A component of that activity has been the activity of non bank Japanese counterparties (highly

---

[24] See Nicholls, Mark, November 1997, "Credit Plays In Vogue As Europe Mulls EMU", *Risk*, pp 8

[25] See Adams, Jeremy and Ball, Matthew, August 1997, "The Banks Behind The High Yield Hype", *Corporate Finance*, pp 33–38; Paul-Choudhury, Sumit, April 1998, "Jewels In The Junk", *Risk*, pp 32–34; Brewis, Janine, May 1998, "Growing Gains And Pains Of The High Yield Market", *Corporate Finance* pp 38–42

rated corporations and insurance companies, particularly, fire and marine insurance companies) selling default protection on Japanese banks. One element of this activity is the arbitrage of information or knowledge gaps between these Japanese entities and non Japanese banks.[26]

The development in emerging markets has been linked primarily to the difficulties faced by banks, dealers and investors and to a lesser extent non financial corporations in relation to their growing sovereign risk exposures. For banks, dealers and investors, the use of default swaps to cap exposures to individual credits has provided a significant impetus to the market. For investors, the opportunity to capture value from the change in emerging market credit spreads has also been a factor in their participation. Some special factors in relation to the role of credit derivatives in emerging markets is considering in the next section.

20.4.6   Emerging Markets — The Role of Credit Derivatives[27]

As already set out above, credit derivatives play an important role in emerging markets. The primary motivation for transactions in this sector include the ability to create *indirect* exposure to the underlying credit risk, lowering transaction costs, tax and regulatory efficiency and managing aspects of the political and regulatory risk of these operating environments.

Investment in or trading with emerging market counterparties entails assuming both traditional risks and certain risk which are unique to this market sector. The risks of emerging markets can be classified as set out in Figure 20.1.

---

[26] See Reed, Nick, December 1995, "Credit Products Come To The Fore In Japan", *Risk*, pp 15–17

[27] For a perspective on the use of credit derivatives in emerging markets, see Gheerbant, Mark "Managing Country Risk Using Credit Derivatives" in 1998, *Credit Derivatives: Applications for Risk Management, Investment and Portfolio Optimisation*, Risk Books, London, Chapter 3; Van Der Maas, Paul and Naqui, Nabeel "Credit Derivatives Within An Emerging Market Framework" in Storrow, Jamie, 1999, *Credit Derivatives: Key Issues (2nd Ed)*, British Bankers Association, London, Chapter 6

Figure 20.1 Emerging Market Risk Hierarchy	
Type of risk	**Definition**
Asset price risk (interest rate; currency; equity)	Exposure to changes in the value of the underlying variable.
Credit risk	Exposure to risk of counterparty default
Regulatory risk	Exposure to changes in the regulations applicable to the transaction (securities legislation, tax regulations etc)
Sovereign risk	Exposure to political risk, including risk of currency inconvertibility or non transferability, expropriation/ confiscation etc

Transactions involving emerging market counterparties tend, in general, to be characterized by higher degrees of credit (often reflecting the lower credit rating of the country and its impact on the rating of individual counterparties), regulatory and sovereign risk. Credit derivative applications have increasingly been used to manage these risks.

Typical applications have included:

- Use of credit default swaps and total return swaps to hedge counterparty risk reflecting the lower credit capacity available to be deployed in these markets as well as the volatile outlook of these markets.
- Use total return swaps to replicate emerging market investments.
- Use of currency inconvertibility protection structures to manage this aspect of sovereign risk.

Some special types of applications warrant mention:

- **Incorporation of credit derivatives in repackaging emerging market securities (in particular, Brady bonds):** The basis of these transactions has entailed Brady bonds (with their high yield and irregular cash flows) being placed in an asset repackaging vehicle. The cash flows of the Brady bond are then swapped into European currencies, say deutschemark. The objective is to create a higher yielding emerging market security for European investors, arbitraging against the pricing of emerging market debt issued directly in the Eurobond market. These structures create a contingent exposure in relation to default on the Brady Bonds for the swap counterparty as the residual value of the Brady bonds may not be sufficient to cover any loss resulting from the termination of the cross currency swap used to re-profile the cash flows. In several cases, a credit default where the default payment is linked to the current mark-to-market value of the swap has been used to reduce this risk. Counterparties capable of evaluating the joint probability of market and default risk and then assuming this risk for a fee which still allows the arbitrage to be executed are not numerous dictating that these applications are opportunistically executed.

- **Incorporating default protection in financing transactions:** Figure 20.2 sets out an example of a typical emerging market structured transaction. The transaction highlights the factors identified prompting the use of credit derivatives in repackaging credit risk to facilitate access to certain types of investments.

- **Funding transactions:** Emerging market companies often use the sale of assets combined with a total return swap (where the borrower receives the return on the asset and pays an interest rate amount) to raise funds at a cost which is lower than that available in other markets. Similar transactions entailing the use of equity swaps are also common.[28] The structure enables the borrower to continue to maintain exposure to the underlying asset (including any potential price application) while generating lower cost funding. The lower borrowing cost derives from the fact that the lender effectively extends credit secured by the assets and the reduction in counterparty risk to the exposure on the swap (which is a fraction of the face value of the transaction). The lender also benefits from the lower joint default probability of the counterparty and the underlying asset. This allows the spread charged to be often significantly lower than the normal credit spread charged to the borrower.

---

[28] See Das, Satyajit, 1994, *Swaps And Financial Derivatives*, LBC Information Services, Sydney, McGraw-Hill, Chicago, Chapter 17

Figure 20.2   Emerging Market Financing Structure Incorporating Credit Derivatives

In the period 1997–98, a number of financing structures evolved which embedded credit default swaps. The transaction set out below involving Korean won denominated bonds was typical of these structures.[29]

The diagram set out below sets out the basic structure:

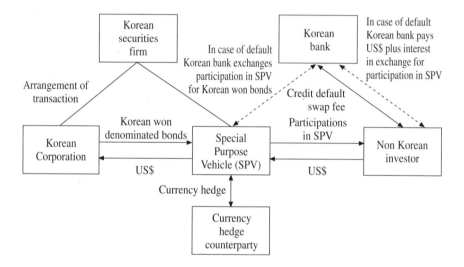

The transaction structure operates as follows:
- The transaction was typically arranged by a Korean securities firm.
- Korean Corporations issued won denominated bonds in the domestic market.
- The bonds were transferred via the arranger to a special purpose vehicle ("SPV"). The SPV utilized was a unit trust based in Dublin, Ireland. The use of Dublin was predicated on the double taxation treaty between Korea and Ireland.
- The SPV issued participations collateralized by the assets of the SPV. The trust issued units in the trust collateralized by the won denominated bonds. The units were issued in US$ and were structured to be serviced and redeemed in US$.
- The structure exposed the investor in the SPV to two levels of risk: credit risk to the Korean Corporation and the won/US$ currency risk. Each of these was hedged in separate transactions.
- In order to manage the credit risk, the investor in the SPV entered into a credit default swap with a banks (typically, a Korean bank). The credit default swap operated in the following manner. The investor in the SPV pays a fee to the bank selling default protection. In the case of default, the bank providing default protection makes a

---

[29] See Rhode, William, February 1998, "Banks Face Losses On Esoteric Korean Notes", *Asia Risk*, 8–9

payment equal to the face value of investment and interest. In return, the investor transfers the participations in the SPV to the bank. In effect, it is a physical settlement of the credit default swap. The bank providing credit default protection can then exchange the participations in the SPV for the underlying won denominated bonds (which are presumably in default).

- The currency risk was managed by a currency hedge entered into by the SPV with a bank. The hedge was structured as a cross currency swap where the SPV pays won denominated cash flows in return receiving US$ cash flows.

The basic rationale of this structure was facilitating fund raising by Korean corporations and allowing foreign investors to access investment opportunities in the Korean domestic bond market. Factors favoring this structure included:

- The then applicable regulations preventing foreign investor access to the domestic won bond market.[30]
- The structure avoided the 27.5 % withholding tax on bond interest because of the Ireland-Korea double taxation treaty.

Some risk aspects of the structure merit comment:

The use of Korean banks to provide protection ultimately created problems. Given the high risk of default by the underlying won bond issuer, the investor in reality was heavily reliant on the default swap. However, as proved to be the case, the risk of a Korean bank defaulting in that situation was high. This reflected both broad macro-economic inter-relationships and the often complex ownership and business relationships between Korean companies (within the *chaebol* groupings). In effect, the default correlation were higher than desirable which increased the risk of credit risk loss to the investor.

The credit risk on the currency hedge is interesting. The bank providing the hedge is paying US$ and receiving won. This means that in a domestic crisis the swap may not expose the bank to credit risk. This is because the payments to be received are of lower value (reflecting the decline in the value of the local currency) relative to payments to be made (the US$ payments).

---

[30] The structure was based on similar equity financing transactions that had been previously completed. Subsequently, under the IMF-imposed reform scheme access to the domestic won bond market for foreign investors was allowed

20.4.7   Leveraged Loan Market — The Role of Credit Derivatives[31]

The role of credit derivatives in relation to the high yield or non investment grade credit market in the US has already been noted. In a parallel development, a market in leveraged loans has emerged. This market overlaps significantly with and complements the high yield *bond* market.[32] The role of credit derivatives in the leveraged loan market warrants analysis.

The leveraged loan market is generally defined as loan priced at LIBOR plus 150 bp or more. This market has developed as a non investment grade bank loan market providing funding for lower credit rated organizations. The market has existed since the late 1980s but has in recent years begun to assume increased importance. The key factor of interest in the leveraged loan market is its evolution as a *public capital market* exhibiting the characteristics of *bond markets* rather than the *traditional bank loan market*. Importantly, the leveraged loan market has attracted greater investment from institutional investors than traditional loan market and also features greater levels of secondary market trading, independent credit ratings and credit research than conventional loan markets. It also has attracted greater credit derivatives activity.

The driving force in this market has been institutional investor participation. This has been driven by a number of factors:

* **Attractive returns relative to risk:** Compared to the investment grade loan market where surplus liquidity saw a progressive fall in credit spreads until the sharp reversal in 1997, the leveraged loan market provided high returns. The returns were attractive on a risk adjusted basis in view of the covenant protection incorporated in these loans. This protection include seniority in capital structure, collateral and mandatory repayments from excess cash flows and assets sales. The fact that such loans are often pre-paid prior to maturity also serves to lower the risk profile.

---

[31] See Asarnow, Elliot "Credit Derivatives: Linking Loan Portfolio Management and Bank Loan Investment Programs" in (1998) *Credit Derivatives: Applications for Risk Management, Investment and Portfolio Optimisation*, Risk Books, London, Chapter 6

[32] See Barnish, Keith, Miller, Steve, and Rushmore, Michael, Spring 1997, "The New Leveraged Loan Syndication Market", *Journal of Applied Corporate Finance*, Vol 10, No 1, pp 79–88; Culp, Christopher, and Neves, Andrea M.P. "Financial Innovations In Leveraged Commercial Loan Markets," *Journal of Applied Corporate Finance*, Vol 11, No 2, pp 79–94

- **Loans as a separate asset class:** Participation has been based, at least in part, on the emergence of loan assets as a specific and distinct asset class. The performance of various bank loan indexes highlights the higher returns available and the modest risk of bank loans as a fixed interest asset class (see Figure 20.3). In particular, the higher recovery rates in case of default and low volatility (in part because of the floating rate structure of loans that minimizes interest rate risk) means that such assets are attractive. The fact that investment in bank loans effectively, in a portfolio context, can enhance return on a risk adjusted basis on fixed income portfolios has attracted institutional investor interest.[33]

- **Rating of loan:** The large credit rating agencies now provide credit ratings for *loans*. Importantly, the credit rating process for loans is different for loans and reflects risk analysis of the loan's structural characteristics (security, covenants etc) and differential recovery rates.[34] Significant differences (up to 2 to 3 rating levels) may exist between loans and bonds issued by the same obligor. The ratings have developed in response to investor demand as both participation and trading has increased.

- **Alternative to high yield market:** The leveraged loan market has emerged as an alternative to the high yield market and provided investment assets even when the high yield market has been less active.[35]

- **Liquidity:** Secondary market liquidity has also grown rapidly. One research documents records the secondary market trading volume at US$60 billion in 1997.[36]

---

[33] See Asarnow, Elliot, Summer 1996, "Corporate Loans As An Asset Class", *Journal of Portfolio Management*, Marker, Jim and Rapoport, Michael R. (1996) Historical Performance of Corporate Loans: An Update" Citibank's Corporate Loan Market Review And Outlook — 1st Quarter 1996

[34] Carty, Lea V., Hamilton, David T., Keenan, Sean C., Moss, Adam, Mulvaney, Michael, Marshela, Tom and Subhas, M.G., June 1998, *Bankrupt Loan Recoveries*, Moody's Investors Service Globala Credit Research

[35] Leveraged loan volume has on occasion outstripped high-yield bond issuance. For example, in 1996, leveraged loans totaled US$135 billion against US$60 billion in high-yield issuance. See Barnish, Keith, Miller, Steve, and Rushmore, Michael, Spring 1997, "The New Leveraged Loan Syndication Market", *Journal of Applied Corporate Finance* Vol 10 No 1 pp 79–88

[36] See Garman, M. Christopher, and Fridson, Martin S., 13 April 1998, "Highlights of Loan Trading: 1997 Review" Merrill Lynch Global Securities Research & Economics Group

Figure 20.3   Comparative Performance of Leveraged Loans as an Asset Class

Monthly returns June 1992 to 1997

Asset class	Average monthly return (%)	Standard deviation	Sharpe ratio
3 month Treasury Bills	0.38	0.09	Not Applicable
Leveraged Loans	0.73	0.51	0.68
Mortgage Backed Securities	0.61	0.95	0.24
10 Year Treasury Notes	0.62	1.94	0.14
High Grade Corporate Bonds	0.74	1.40	0.25
High Yield Bonds	0.95	1.08	0.52
Small Stocks	1.34	3.65	0.26
Big Stocks	1.53	3.00	0.38

Correlation of monthly returns June 1992 to 1997

	Leveraged loans	High yield bonds	Mortgage backed	10 year T-bonds	3 Month T bills	Big stocks	Small stocks	High grade corporations
Leveraged Loans	1.000							
High Yield Bonds	0.148	1.000						
Mortgage Backed	0.040	0.805	1.000					
10 year Treasuries	0.054	0.751	0.887	1.000				
3 month Treasuries	0.145	0.276	0.357	0.294	1.000			
Large Stocks	0.077	0.598	0.527	0.511	0.289	1.000		
Small Stock	0.052	0.387	0.156	0.147	0.108	0.652	1.000	
High Grade corporate	0.087	0.764	0.900	0.985	0.276	0.537	0.151	1.000

Notes: Leverage Loans are calculated as the LPC Leveraged Loan Index. Mortgage Backed securities is calculated as the Merrill Lynch Mortgage Backed Master Index. High grade corporate bonds are calculated as the Merrill Lynch High Grade Corporate Master Index. High yield bonds are calculated as the Merrill Lynch High Yield Master Index. Small stock and big stock are calculated as the Russell 2,000 index and the Standard & Poor's Index of 500 common stock.

Source: Garman, M. Christopher, and Fridson, Martin S., 13 April 1998, "Highlights of Loan Trading: 1997 Review" Merrill Lynch Global Securities Research & Economic Group at 4, 5.

A further factor influencing US institutional participation in loan asset markets is in part the result of the increasing involvement of investment banks in the origination, syndication and distribution of loan assets. This development has a number of factor driving it. In the early 1990s, the market for leveraged finance (for LBO/MBOs and other corporate restructuring) came to be dominated by the high yield bond market. Banks in an effort to compete expanded their loan activities to gradually encompass these types of leveraged financing (by increasing their risk appetite and becoming involved in leveraged loans). This development resulted in bank loans and high yield bonds essentially becoming close substitutes for each other in these types of transactions blurring the previous distinction between bank and bond markets.

The investment banks reacted to this development by both increasingly committing their own capital to financing leveraged transactions but in also setting up loan origination and distribution activities. However, the investment banks remain reluctant to commit long term funding to such transactions. To economize on using their own capital, the investment banks set up a number of funds, usually combining their capital with that of institutional investors, to provide this term loan capital. The development of these vehicles allowing investors to indirectly participate in the bank loan market has attracted increased institutional interest. For the investment banks, it has provided a large and efficient funding source for loan capital.[37]

This institutional investment has, in the main, been synthetic, entailing the use of credit derivatives due to barriers to direct participation. In particular, total returns swaps, credit default swaps and credit linked note structures have been important in allowing this investment to be channeled into this sector.[38] The use of credit derivatives has been driven by the ability to introduce leverage to enhance returns and reduced administration burdens (processing loan repayment, prepayments etc). some credit linked note structures have been driven by the necessity to create baskets of loans which can carry an investment grade rating which is crucial for insurance companies (to avoid higher capital requirements under insurance guidelines) and mutual funds (which have minimum credit quality requirements). For the investors, the credit derivative format provides an attractive and liquid manner to obtain exposure to this type of asset.

---

[37] For a discussion on these developments, see Atlas, Riva, February 1997, "You Gotta Have Leverage", *Institutional Investor*, pp 134–142

[38] See Mahtani, Arun, 28 November 1998, "Synthetic Structure Facilitate Leveraged Loan Boom", *International Financing Review*, Issue 1261, pp 85

20.5   Market Participants

20.5.1   Overview

The range of participants in the credit derivatives market is large. It would cover: commercial banks; investment banks; fixed interest investors; and non financial corporations. Each group is motivated to participate for quite different reasons and the range of transactions for each group, both current and potential, is very different.

However, underlying the different types of applications are: the isolation of the underlying credit risk; the attempts (somewhat tentative) at increasing the liquidity and therefor the tradability of credit risk; and, to a lesser extent the transformation of credit into a more generic asset class. The ability to utilize the standard ISDA agreement and the resultant standardization of documentation is also an important factor in the participation of individual types of organizations.

20.5.2   Commercial Banks

Commercial bank activity is predicated on the fact that these organizations are holders of substantial credit risk through their normal operations. In this regard, the emerging market for credit derivatives is best regarded as an adjunct to both traditional methods of management of credit exposures and loan asset trading and distribution activities. Figure 20.4 sets out a comparison of credit derivatives (primarily, total return swaps and credit default products) to more traditional methods of transferring credit risk.

The major focus of applications will typically emphasize:
- **Transferring credit risk** — as an alternative to traditional forms of selling down credit risk.
- **Hedging credit risk** — in effect, purchasing default protection sometimes financing the cost of protection by the assumption of credit risk on a different counterparty.
- **Credit portfolio management** — in particular, reducing portfolio credit concentration and improving the utilization of credit capital.

Figure 20.4   Credit Derivatives vs Conventional Credit Risk Sale Transactions[39]

Instrument Impact	Credit derivatives	Loan sale	Participation	Guarantee/ Letter of credit
Type of risk	Market traded securities and loans preferred	Loans	Loans	Varied
Financing	No financing (as off balance sheet)	Funding achieved	Funding achieved in case of funded sub-participations	No financing
Pricing	Market driven (based on securities/loan traded prices)	Private without transparency	Private without transparency	Private without transparency
Counterparty credit risk	On credit derivative	No	Yes	Yes
Default costs	Low	Loan recovery costs	Loan recovery costs	Loan recovery costs
Accounting	No impact	Realization of gain or loss	Realization of gain or loss	No impact
Ongoing costs	Minimal	Present	Present	Minimal
Documentation	Standard (ISDA)	Customized	Customized	Customized
Confidentiality	Confidential	Requires involvement of borrower	Requires involvement of borrower	Confidential

20.5.3   Investment Banks/Dealers

Investment bank/dealer participation in the market for credit derivatives is motivated by a broader range of factors. Investment banks, at least traditionally, have not been long term holders of credit risk. The bulk of the risk assumed has been market risk from inventory holdings of securities and trading in financial institutions. In more recent times, investment banks have assumed higher level of credit exposures from two primary sources:

- Entry into term derivatives transactions as an adjunct to new issues of securities.
- The entry into loan/credit syndications and increased emphasis on loan trading (reflecting in some part the increased liquidity of these markets).

---

[39] This table draws on but is not identical to Hattori, Paul "Credit Derivatives — A View Of The Market," a speech given to a Seminar on Credit Derivatives, Lanesborough Hotel, London, March 1997

The credit risk arising from traditional sources has also undergone a metamorphosis as a result of the increased importance of trading and distribution of non investment grade securities and emerging market paper. The fact that both these types of securities have higher levels of credit risk than more traditional government and corporate securities has served to increase the level of credit risk in inventories.

Against this background, investment bank applications of credit derivatives have evolved into two distinct areas of activity:
- Hedging credit exposures in their own portfolios or arising from its activities.
- Trading in credit derivatives as a new activity, complementing trading activities in other assets.

The hedging activity has focused on hedging both default risk and credit spread risk. Default risk hedging by investment banks can be illustrated by the following examples:
- Assume an investment bank has a large counterparty credit exposure to a sovereign issuer (AA/Aa rated). The exposure arises under term (final maturity 10 years; average maturity 5 years) swap contracts associated with securities issues underwritten by the bank. The current exposure is at the limit that the bank can prudently assume. The inability to either increase the credit exposure limits or free up the existing credit lines will clearly constrain further new issue business with this issuer. Under these circumstances, the investment bank can purchase default protection through a default swap to reduce its credit exposure to the issuer. The protection would typically be bought for short terms and rolled as required with the level of protection being adjusted to the run off of existing positions.
- Assume an investment bank has a large holding of the debt securities of an emerging market sovereign issuer (BBB/Baa rated) in connection with an underwriting. The position is difficult to liquidate quickly without creating significant losses. The holding has the effect of increasing the credit exposure to this issuer and to the country beyond prudential limits. The credit exposure can be hedged using a default swap to allow the credit risk to be reduced to acceptable levels until the securities are distributed.

The other source of risk is the significant credit spread risk incurred by investment banks in its securities inventories and underwriting activities. Credit spread products can be utilized to hedge these risks.

The trading focus is more straightforward in objective. As credit has emerged as a more liquid commodity, investment banks have perceived opportunities to trade in and distribute credit risk in a manner analogous to trading in other assets classes such as debt, equities, foreign exchange and commodities. A significant factor in this focus has been the demand for credit linked products from fixed income investors who constitute a significant client base for these banks.

20.5.4   Fixed Income Investors

Fixed income investors have traditionally assumed credit risk in a variety of forms. The largest component of credit risk assumed has been in the form of issuer default risk in debt and equity securities and counterparty default in off balance sheet/derivative transactions. Credit derivatives provide investors with the capacity to isolate and purify credit risk (both default and spread risk) and to either hedge this risk away or assume specific risk as desired.

The participation of institutions has been motivated by a variety of factors that varies as between types of institutions. Traditional investors, such as insurance companies, pension funds and investment managers, have viewed credit derivatives as a mechanism for more completely and efficiently disaggregating credit risk and allowing trading in this risk attribute. Other investors, such as special purpose funds (e.g. prime rate funds) and hedge funds, have seen credit derivatives as providing the capacity to participate in certain market segments which traditionally would have excluded their participation. The inherent leverage potential in the derivative format has been particularly attractive for hedge funds enabling them to create leveraged credit views.

All parties have been attracted by the inefficiencies in credit pricing both as between credits of similar default characteristics and between market segments for the same issuer (bank loan market, securities/bond markets and the equity markets). The fact that credit derivatives allow effective arbitrage between these markets has motivated participation.

The primary applications to emerge for fixed income investors includes:

- **Replication applications:** Focused on creating synthetic exposure to the high yield/non investment grade and emerging markets to overcome barriers to or the high costs of direct access.
- **Yield enhancement:** Primarily generated by assuming spread risk or the risk of credit default in return for higher income.
- **Trading:** Emphasizing targeted buying or selling of securities at defined spread levels to capture premium income from sale of options, trading spread expectations and assuming specific types of default exposures on a risk return basis.

The nature of participation of fixed income investors is different as between jurisdictions. Most investor participation has been opportunistic predicated on the above factors. However, there are significant differences as between market segments.

20.5.5 Non-Financial Corporations

The participation of non financial corporation to date has been limited. This reflects the poorly developed framework for credit risk management within corporations. The major applications currently include:

- **Managing funding costs:** Particularly, the risk from potential movements in credit spreads.
- **Credit risk management:** Primarily, in the context of international projects (located in emerging markets) and reduction of counterparty risk in derivative transactions, sometimes with the objective of broadening the range of counterparties with which an institution with credit constraints can enter into transactions.

20.5.6 Trading in Credit Derivatives

The market for credit derivatives is still some way from existing as a highly liquid and fully tradable market in credit risk. The level of trading in the secondary market is still low. Corresponding to this structure of the market, most business is conducted on matched basis with limited warehousing of positions. The warehousing of positions, to the extent that this is done, is integrated with the institution's overall credit risk management and/or credit spread trading. The limits on warehousing and market making in credit is driven by the lack of available instruments to hedge the and the uncertain liquidity of the market itself.

However, the market is likely to become more liquid as time elapses. This increase will reflect a variety of factors including:

- The entry of new dealers expanding the range of traders and participants. In recent years, a number of major banks made significant commitments to the credit derivatives business with the making of key hires to establish and operate substantial credit trading operations. These new entrants included a number of major European (Deutsche Bank, Dresdner Bank) and Japanese houses (Nomura Securities, Daiwa Securities). These entrants compete with the major US commercial and investment banks (JP Morgan, BT, Chase, Citibank, Morgan Stanley, Merrill Lynch, Lehman Brothers, Bear Stearns) and Credit Suisse Financial Products, who had been the major players in the early phase of the market. While the market difficulties experienced in 1997 and 1998 has affected some of these dealers resulting in some retrenchment of trading capacity, the activity levels have continued to increase steadily.

- The gradual acceptance of credit derivatives and their movement into core credit risk management has meant that most major banks have begun to use these instruments to manage their credit risk to individual counterparties as well as the portfolio overall. This has meant increase in trading volumes and overall enhancement of market liquidity and trading volumes.
- The entrance of a number of interbank brokers seeking to facilitate trading in these products. Prebon Yamane and Tullet & Tokyo as well as others have begun broking credit derivatives products interbank. This will undoubtedly assist in increasing liquidity by providing greater price discovery and transparency. At least two electronic exchanges focused on credit derivatives have emerged – Creditrade and Creditex.[40] These are relatively new and are evolving rapidly to combine a mix of voice and electronic broking services.
- The continued standardization of documentation and product structures will facilitate trading by increasing the homogeneity of the underlying that is being traded.

A central issue to trading is the need for most dealers to optimize the location of the credit trading function and its relationship to the credit function more generally. To date, the credit derivatives function has been either located with the derivatives trading or in the securities trading/capital markets areas, including asset swaps or structured products (essentially less liquid or non standard products). In some houses, it is located within the bank's loan syndication/loan or asset sales area.

The lack of familiarity with credit risk and the lack of availability of natural hedges in a lot of cases makes the use of the derivatives desks to trade credit derivatives problematic. Similarly, the use of securities trading as the focus of credit trading activity is also not ideal as its tends to bias activity to traded securities. In reality, as discussed in greater detail below, the credit trading function has a more central role in financial institutions. However, until the location issue is resolved the integration of credit trading to the credit risk

---

[40] Abed, Kamal, October 19–25, 1999, "Credit Brokers Plan To Counter Threat Of Online Intermediation", *Financial Products 1*, 10; Abed, Kamal, November 1999, "Battle For e-Credit Begins", Futures & OTC World 14; Faloon, William, November 1999, "Creditex And The Internet Revolution", *Risk*, pp 33–35

management of the entity is not likely to be complete. This will manifest itself in lower liquidity and secondary market trading in these products.

20.6   Developmental Issues

The current strong growth in the market reflects increased comfort with several aspects of these products:

- **Documentation:** The publication of the ISDA default confirmation has assisted in standardizing the documentation of these types of transactions. However, there remain some significant differences in opinion as to key documentary terms (such as the inclusion of materiality and the sampling process for determining the default payment).
- **Regulatory treatment:** While falling short of an unified framework for treating credit derivatives, the positive attitude of regulatory authorities to the market developments and the fact that a reduction in capital held against exposures is achievable in most circumstances has helped the market develop.
- **Default experience:** This has been at both a theoretical and practical level. The interest in credit risk has prompted modeling efforts that have greatly increased the understanding of credit risk generally. At a practical level, the experience of default or financial distress (particularly as a result of the emerging market and Japanese monetary crises) has served to enhance participants understanding of the instruments and their practical application (including the determination of default and the default settlement of these types of transaction).

However, a number of issues remain unresolved:

- **Pricing:** The lack of an accepted pricing model (such as Black-Scholes for options) creates an inherent lack of transparency that discourages participation and trading. In addition, the difficulties in modeling parameters like default risk, recovery rates and default correlations (for portfolios) remains significant.
- **Systems issues:** The availability of appropriate technology and systems to deal with credit risk also impedes development.
- **Organization:** The fact that credit occupies a central role in most organizations and also transcends product or geographic boundaries create significant difficulties in developing an organization of the credit derivatives trading function within the institutions. This prevents the maximization of the capability to manage credit risk within the firm. It may also generate

inefficiency in interaction between units, which further reduces the utility of these products.

- **Operations:** The nature of these products (the primacy of credit issues) means that traditional derivative operations areas are not always well equipped to manage the settlement and payment determination aspects of these products. This creates impediments to growth.

The issues of organization and operations are particularly important for banks and financial institutions. These are considered below.

20.7   Organisation of the Credit Derivatives Function

20.7.1   Current Organization

As noted above, a significant problem in the growth and development of credit derivatives trading within a bank/financial institution is the proper location of this function within the organization.[41]

Most organizations have a number of areas that have a legitimate claim to and do in reality trade credit derivative instruments. These may include:

- Fixed income desks
- High-yield/non-investment grade desks
- Emerging market desks
- Repo or finance desks
- Asset swaps desks
- Syndication/asset sales desks
- Distressed debt trading
- Securitization desks
- Equity desks (particularly convertible trading)
- Individual credit officers/account managers
- Credit portfolio management.

As is evident, the potential users of the products cross product and functional boundaries. The purpose and products traded are summarized in Figure 20.5.

---

[41] For examples, see Drzik, John P. and Kuritzkes, Andrew, July 1997, "Credit Derivatives: The Tip Of The Iceberg", *Risk Credit Risk Supplement Sponsor's Statement*; Nason, Rick, Cromarty, Christine, and Maglic, Stevan, March 1998, "Credit Derivatives: An Organisational Dilemma", *Risk Credit Risk Supplement Sponsor's Statement*; Varotsis, Paul, 1999, "Where Do Credit Derivatives Fit In" in Storrow, Jamie, *Credit Derivatives: Key Issues (2nd Ed)*, British Bankers Association, London, Chapter 8

Figure 20.5   Potential Users of Credit Derivatives within a Financial Institution.

Desk	Purpose	Products			
		Total return swaps	Credit default swap	Credit spread products	Other
Fixed Income	• Trading • Risk Management • Client driven products (including those not available directly)	• To finance positions for clients	• Trade/manage credit risk assumed • Synthesize fixed income product for clients	• Trade/manage spread risk • Synthesize credit spread product for clients	
High Yield	• Trading • Risk Management • Client driven products (including those not available directly)	• To finance positions for clients	• Trade/manage credit risk assumed • Synthesize fixed income product for clients	• Trade/manage spread risk • Synthesize credit spread product for clients	
Emerging Markets	• Trading • Risk Management • Client driven products (including those not available directly)	• To finance positions for clients	• Trade/manage credit risk assumed • Synthesize fixed income product for clients	• Trade/manage spread risk • Synthesize credit spread product for clients	• Trade currency inconvertibility protection for clients/ own account
Repo/Finance	• Finance inventory • Assist clients fund assets	• To finance position synthetically (non government obligations) • Arbitrage against repo rates			

Figure 20.5 (cont'd)

Desk	Purpose	Products			
		Total return swaps	Credit default swap	Credit spread products	Other
Asset Swaps	• Trading • Risk management of asset swap inventory • Client drive products (including those not available directly) • Use as hedge against credit derivatives products	• Leveraged/unfunded asset swap product for clients	• Manage credit risk of inventory • Synthesize from asset swaps • Arbitrage against asset swap pricing	• Manage spread risk of inventory • Synthesize from asset swaps • Arbitrage against asset swap pricing	• Embed credit spread optionality in asset swaps
Syndications/Loan Sales	• Selling down/acquiring loan risk	• Utilize as defacto unfunded risk participations	• Utilize as defacto unfunded risk participations	• Manage syndication spread risks	• Use synthetic lending facilities/assets swaptions to synthesize revolving credit facilities for investors
Distressed Debt	• Trading distressed debt • Funding distressed debt position	• To finance position synthetically	• Assume risks (identical to selling puts on the distressed debts) • Assume recovery rate positions		

Figure 20.5 (cont'd)

Desk	Purpose	Products			
		Total return swaps	Credit default swap	Credit spread products	Other
Securitization	• Securitizing credit portfolios • Enhancing the credit of securitized assets		• Alternative to monoline insurers as a form of credit enhancement		• Credit linked notes as alternatives to CB/CLO structures
Equity (Convertible) Trading	• Funding convertible positions • Repackaging the credit risk of convertible	• To finance position synthetically	• Hedging/managing the risk of convertible portfolios • Synthesize fixed income product for clients		
Individual Account Managers	• Manage exposure to individual credits	• Sell down/acquire exposure to clients as part of maximizing client revenues	• Sell down/acquire exposure to clients as part of maximizing client revenues		
Credit Portfolio Management	• Manage aggregate portfolio risk characteristics • Manage concentration risk • Manage return on economic credit capital • Manage regulatory credit capital	• Sell down/acquire exposure to clients as part of maximizing client revenues	• Sell down/acquire exposure to clients as part of maximizing client revenues		• Use of credit linked notes to manage total portfolio in terms of economic returns and regulatory capital • Trade credit risk

The complexity of these relationships is evident from the diversity and similarity of the motivations of individual desks in their use of credit derivative structures. This makes it difficult to optimally structure the credit derivatives unit from an operational perspective. This structural dilemma derives in part from the actual evolution of the product itself.

20.7.2   Organizational Options[42]

The required organization of the credit derivative function within an entity requires consideration of a banking process model in the future. This is best understood by following the transaction flow in such a banking model.

Assume a bank wishes to enter into any transaction — a loan, purchase a security, or enter into a derivative transaction. In the present model, credit approval is sought from the credit function. Under current practise, this approval is binary (yes or no) and may have pricing guidelines for the transaction. The transaction is then booked against credit risk limits allocated either for the transaction or to the entity.

Under the future banking process model, the steps are somewhat different:

1.   The originator would seek approval from the credit function.

2.   The credit function would base its approval not on the traditional binary approval process but would indicate to the originator the price it would charge the originator as a credit capital charge for allocating lines to do the transaction. This explicit charge would be attributed against the profit and loss account of the originator of the transaction (whether it is a relationship manager, trader or capital markets desk).

3.   The credit function would price the credit charge from the lower of two sources:

   — Internal — this would be based on the marginal contribution to portfolio risk of the proposed transaction. The return would equate to that required to cover the incremental expected and unexpected losses of the portfolio resulting from the transaction.

   — External — this would be based on the market price for purchasing default protection (through a credit default swap) from an acceptable financial counterparty.

---

[42]   For a detailed discussion of this issue, see Das, Satyajit, September 1999, "The Credit Revolution", *Futures & OTC World*, 52–61

4. If the transaction were undertaken, then the credit risk would be treated internally as a credit default risk swap written between the credit function (the seller of protection) and the transaction originator (the buyer of protection).

5. The credit function then would have the responsibility for managing the credit risk assumed. This may take the following forms:

    — Creating provisions and holding capital against the risk.
    — Purchasing protection against the risk through a credit derivative transaction.
    — Packaging up selected credit risks and selling them down through securitization structures (CBO/CLOs) or by issuing credit linked notes.

In essence, the approach requires the creation of a centralized "credit warehouse" to both centralize and manage the credit risk incurred by the institution.

Several aspects of this process dynamic require comment:

• The structure separates the transaction from the credit risk inherent in the transaction. Both are then managed separately.

• The essential element of this process is there is a price at which any transaction can be done, at least in terms of credit risk. This price is never higher than the market price for the credit risk adjusted for counterparty risks on the credit derivative transactions. This means that in effect no organization is ever full on counterparty. It can continue to do business with a particular entity but lay off its credit risk where it is no longer (because of concentration risk) able to assume additional exposure economically.

• The process of managing the credit risk of the institution becomes more rigorous. This covers provisioning policy and managing returns on risk capital. It also covers management of regulatory capital.

• The credit function becomes essentially a credit trading desk with its own profit and loss. It manages its risk dynamically based on its portfolio and its evolving expectations on default risk, default correlations and recovery rates. For example, it may short credit risk in anticipation of a change in the credit cycle by buying protection. It may seek to originate exposures to particular entities, industries or geographic sectors either through the origination teams (primary credit market) or through the credit derivative markets (secondary credit market).

• The specific risk charge to the origination desk allows the relationship dividend to be measured. For example, an originator willing to do the transaction at an economic loss (in terms of compensation for credit risk) would immediately see the negative impact on his or her profit and loss account. The extent to which other transactions compensate for this loss leading transaction could now be explicitly measured.

The most significant impact of this change is the migration of the credit derivative function from the derivative to the credit desk within the institution. It also requires a shift in the philosophy of credit risk management. A number of organizations have made this transition, at least in part.

It will also require a significant degree of integration of credit and market risk. For example, when a currency swap or any market sensitive instrument is traded, the credit exposure is dynamic. The exposure is modeled and limits established. However, changes in market rates beyond those forecast can rapidly lead to the actual exposure exceeding the forecast exposure. This risk is inherent in all credit risk management of market value instruments but is not explicitly and systematically managed. In the new process model, the exposure could be managed by the credit risk function estimating worst case and average exposures and then purchasing protection against movements in rates beyond the forecast levels. This protection would be in the form of out-of-the-money options purchased from the relevant market risk desk. It would allow the accurate quantification of these risks and the capital costs of assuming these risks. This would in turn allow more accurate pricing of these risks.

The process described above relates to the overall re-structure of the capture and management of credit risk within the institution. At a different level, credit derivative instruments will become fairly generic building block tools for financial engineering across the entire business unit. This may include the following applications:

- **Total return loan swaps:** The non funded nature of these structure will make them generic devices to finance assets and arbitrage markets across various desks.
- **Credit default products:** The non funded nature of the structure and the ability to shift the exposure to default risk will make them useful a ways of repackaging assets or customizing risk attribute bundles for investors.
- **Credit spread products:** The ability to trade and monetize expectations of spread movement independent of absolute interest rate movements will make these useful across various desks as a mechanism for managing or acquiring exposure to spread risk.

In effect, credit derivatives will be embedded in the organization structure at two distinct levels:

- A centralized credit trading and management function that manages the total credit risk of the institution's portfolio in an integrated fashion.
- The instruments will increasingly be homogenous and absorbed into the trading or financial engineering disciplines across all business activities.

In essence this process is not radically different from that which has and continues to take place currently whereby derivatives trading is gradually being merged with the cash markets for the underlying.

20.8   Operational Issues

The shift to the new paradigm requires a major re-engineering of financial institutions and their credit functions. The major operational issues include:

- **Investment in credit portfolio management models:** The release of CreditMetrics^{TM} and CreditRisk^{+TM} as well as increased interest in products like KMV's EDF default prediction models has advanced the debate about credit portfolio models. However, considerable work still remains to be done in this area.
- **Systems:** The availability of credit risk management systems currently lags market risk management systems. The availability of software to price and trade credit risks and credit derivatives as well as manage credit portfolios remains an important factor in enabling the market to develop further.
- **Middle office and operational structures:** The ability of traditional middle offices or operations areas to settle and monitor credit derivative transactions is questionable. The complexity of default language, the options for calculating the default payments and the very different demand on counterparties in such transactions as compared to traditional market risk derivatives means that traditional middle offices or operations are not equipped to deal with these trades. The lack of transparency and difficulty in marking to market individual transaction also creates problems. Approaches currently being used include establishment of a separate middle office function for credit derivatives, merging credit derivatives operations with loan administration, or re-engineering the credit monitoring function to encompass these products.

20.9   Potential Areas of Development

20.9.1   Overview

The market for credit derivatives to date has evolved in response to the requirements of two primary groups of participants: the banks/financial institutions and the fixed income investors.

The primary objective of the banks/financial institutions to date has been to reduce the concentration of credit risk in the portfolio and increase liquidity of credit risk. This has been driven by the desire to improve the management of credit risk, the management of credit capital (both economic and regulatory) and allow access to credit risk to other institutions and investors where the bank holds the asset. The investors have primarily sought synthetic access to markets (loan markets, high yield and emerging markets) and capacity to trade pure credit risk attributes. The pricing inefficiencies of credit risk have created an environment where attractive transaction possibilities consistent with the above objectives have been feasible.

As the market continues to develop, the growth is increasingly likely to be derived from additional sources and the credit derivative market will evolve in a number of directions.

20.9.2   Financial Institutions

Further impetus to the development of this part of the market is likely to come from several sources. The most important areas are:

- Changes in the way credit risk is managed within financial institutions — increasingly, financial institutions are focusing on managing credit exposures incurred more actively, This ranges from concentration risks to a specific counterparty, industry or geographic area to sophisticated analysis of a *portfolio*. The later approach seeks to identify the risk characteristics of the *aggregate* exposures and relating the return earned *to the credit risk capital required to be dedicated to the specific risks taken.*
- Changes in regulatory capital required to be held against credit risk — it now appears inevitable that the BIS Capital Accord of July 1988 which governs the capital required to be held against credit risk will be altered.[43] The flat 8% (1.6%) required to be held against corporate credit exposures (OECD Bank exposures) *irrespective of* individual credit quality or type/tenor of the obligation which currently applicable is clearly illogical. Moreover, the introduction of the market risk capital guidelines means that sophisticated credit models can be used in the Trading Book to model specific risk (primarily, default risk as manifested in credit spread behavior). This inconsistency will, it seems, be addressed in the near future. The most logical

---

[43] See discussion in Chapter 19

solution is to *"harness for supervisory purposes the market oriented tolls already in use by banks for management purposes"*.[44] This will create a more favorable environment for credit portfolio management and, indirectly, activity in credit derivatives.

The current focus of applications of credit derivatives is the transfer and hedging of credit risk and credit portfolio management. These applications are capable of extensions in a number of areas:

- Utilizing credit derivatives for the purpose of credit risk enhancement in structured finance projects (e.g. securitization, project finances etc). This would be as a substitute to other form of credit enhancement.
- Allow assumption of credit risks outside normal risk criteria.

However, there is significant potential for application of credit derivatives beyond these types of applications.

The shift in structure and processing model for credit risk will dictate that the growth in credit derivatives will increasingly be derived from additional sources (particularly for commercial banks):

- A more unified and consistent methodology for pricing credit risk uniformly across markets allowing increasing efficiency of credit pricing. Credit derivatives may emerge as a synthetic measurement tool.
- The management of credit risk within banks/financial institutions and investors and, to a lesser degree, non-financial institutions on a portfolio basis with institutions separating out the process of credit origination from the assumption and management of credit risk. Banks may shift focus from the assumption of credit risk to the origination and distribution of credit risk.
- The emergence of credit risk as a separate asset class for investors that is traded in a manner similar to trading in other assets.
- Systematic arbitrage across capital markets to assume credit risk in the most efficient form — either direct or indirect — based on optimization of transaction costs, market friction, and regulatory factors.

The use of credit derivatives as a synthetic measurement tool focuses on a number of separate elements. The use of credit derivatives to value credit risk within financial institutions allows increased accuracy of and consistency in default risk pricing. Combined with portfolio management concepts it allows measurement and management of credit concentration issues within loan portfolios.

---

[44] The words in italics are those of Alan Greenspan, Chairman of the US Federal Reserve

The development of more accurate measures of credit risk within financial institution portfolios allows improved credit risk management in the following respects:

- Credit loss performance can be benchmarked against the cost of obtaining default protection through a default swap.
- Improve capital management allowing credit capital allocation on a more accurate risk-reward basis.
- Improved performance measurement and management as return on capital committed against default risk becomes transparent.

A major impetus to these potential applications is the implementation of Risk Adjusted Performance Measurement ("RAPM") systems within banks, such as RAROC. The implementation of these systems requires accurate estimates of credit capital and the risk of credit losses to be effective. The use of credit derivatives as a synthetic measure of credit risk assists in overcoming some of these problems.

There is increasing interest in using credit derivatives to actively *trade* credit risk. This entails taking views on and positions in credit spreads or default risk of issuers. This entails taking positions on the risk of default, the recovery rate and the correlation between default risk in portfolios and comparing it to the return for that risk. The net result is that credits where the return provides excess compensation for the estimated credit risk are assumed and credits where the return is lower than the risk is sold. In essence, it is designed to convert credit from a *necessary consequence* of financial transactions to a specific market parameter that can be traded.

The objective of trading can be either for profit from correctly predicting market movements or for broader competitive positioning. The latter could take the form of, for example, selling forward low spreads against future underwriting and hedging default risk at attractive costs levels to enable aggressive market expansion at a future date without exposure to the credit risk.

The ultimate potential application entails a shift in emphasis for financial institutions from *holders* of credit risk to *originators* and *distributors* of credit risk. The primary analogy here is to the impact of securitization on asset portfolios of banks and other financial institutions. The advent of securitization has enabled the conversion of assets traditionally considered illiquid, such as mortgages and credit card receivables, into tradable securities. This change has altered the role of financial institutions into one of asset originators and asset distributors rather than classical take-and-hold investors in these loans. Figure 20.6 sets out a number of possible models of banking practise.

Credit derivatives has the potential to convert the role of financial institutions to that of *originators of credit risk*. Under this altered paradigm, banks/financial institutions would originate the credit risk asset, either in on balance sheet form or in off balance sheet form. The credit risk then would be distributed to other parties. The distinction between this process and that of classical securitization is the unbundling of credit and liquidity risk and the separation of the decision to sell down these individual elements.

The process could entail two separate types of activity:

- The transfer of credit risk to *other financial institutions*. This would overcome the credit paradox allowing bank's to diversify their credit portfolios beyond their own credit origination capabilities to reduce concentration risks as well as improve their risk return characteristics.
- The transfer of credit risk to *non-bank investors*. This would be similar to the securitization of loans through capital market instruments for distribution to direct investors. This would enable new capital to be attracted to support credit risk as well facilitating arbitrage between credit pricing in different market sectors.

Figure 20.6   Models of Banking Practice

Model 1 — Classical Banking Model

Bank originates, funds, administers and retains credit risk of borrower

Model 2 — Investment Banking/Securities Model

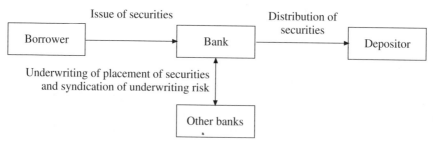

Bank originates transaction and may administer it as payment agent.
Funding and credit risk of borrower is transferred to investor.
Primary risk is underwriting which is syndicated to reduce risk level.

Model 3 — Securization Model

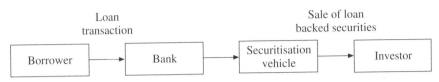

Sale of loan to securitisation vehicle

Bank originates and administers the loan. Bank sells loan to securisation vehicle which issues loan asset backed securities. Funding and credit risk of borrower is borne by investor. Bank risk is confined to credit risk pre-sale to securisation vehicle and any underwriting risk on the placement of the loan asset backed securities.

Model 4 — Economic Risk Transfer Model

Bank originates, funds and administers the loan. Credit risk of borrower is transferred to investors or other banks. Bank credit risk is pre economic hedge only.
Where a credit linked note is issued the investor/other bank also provides funding.

The major advantages of this change in credit emphasis includes:

- The capacity for banks to leverage their existing credit infrastructure more effectively.
- Allowing liquefaction of bank balance sheets.
- Improve the efficiency of credit risk pricing.

20.9.3 Institutional Investors

Institutional investor applications have focused primarily on using credit derivatives for the purpose of yield enhancement or credit diversification. The investor groups, in the main, have been fixed income portfolio managers although there has been some limited participation from equity investors. The latter have viewed credit derivatives as an alternative mechanism for assuming default risk and have focused on volatility level disparities as between equity markets and default risk markets.

The potential extension of applications for investors focuses on the evolution of credit and default risk as a separate asset class. While definitive research evidence is not available, separate investment in credit or default risk may add return to portfolio in excess of that required to compensate for the additional risk based on the low correlation of default risk to other market risk factors.

The addition of credit risk as a separate asset class would encourage investors to deploy capital to take on credit risk, increase trading in credit risk and allow the development of both new generations of credit derivative products and applications.

In an interesting development in March 2000, J.P. Morgan introduced the European Credit Swap Index (ECSI).[45] The index will track the performance of credit swaps on 100 large corporations in Europe. The ECSI is designed as an index of the market's valuation of pure credit risk (stripped of interest rate risk and swap spread movements). J.P. Morgan hopes that the index will become a vehicle for investment, active management and benchmarking of corporate credit exposure. An attraction of the ECSI is that it offers investors access to a more diversified, liquid and better balanced (less skewed to high grade credit) portfolio of credit risk relative to corporate cash bond indices. The index is based on the prices of credit default swaps and investors could use credit default swaps and/or credit linked notes to replicate exposure to the index or components thereof. Exchanges traded futures and options as well OTC derivative structures on the ECSI are also feasible. The development of the ECSI will be closely followed as a precursor to similar innovation in investing in credit risk in other markets.

20.9.4   Non Financial Corporations

Existing applications of credit derivatives amongst non financial corporations is narrowly focused on the management of financing risk (particularly, issuance spread risk) and the management of credit risk associated with investments or projects (particularly, sovereign risk in emerging countries). The potential for further applications for non financial corporation focus on the operational integration of credit risk within the overall financial and strategic/economic risk framework of these organizations.

To understand the potential for these additional applications, it is necessary to categorize the credit risks inherent in the normal operations of any non financial corporation:

---

[45] See 11 February 2000, *Introducing The J.P. Morgan European Credit Swap Index*, J.P. Morgan, London and New York

- **Financing risk:** This relates to primarily the cost of new funding for the issuer.
- **Default risk on financial counterparties:** This covers both financial transactions (counterparty exposures on derivative etc transactions) as well as extensions of credit either directly (receivables, vendor finance) or indirectly (pre-payments).
- **Default risk of major business relationships:** This covers the business and strategic impact of the financial distress of a major supplier of inputs, purchaser of products, or distributor on the organization.

The first two types of exposure are relatively ease to quantify. They are similar to the types of credit risk already discussed and are similar to the types of exposures encountered by banks/financial institutions or investors. The last is more difficult to measure but is likely, in reality, to be the most important of the credit exposures encountered by corporations.

A review of most corporations tends to reveal a high degree of concentration of credit risk. As in the case of financial institutions, business or strategic considerations drive this concentration risk. However, this concentration has the potential to create problems for the entity by either limiting the potential for expansion of these business relationships (because they represent unacceptable increases in credit exposure) or expansion of the trading relationship which exposes the entity to higher overall risk levels. The latter may ultimately impact upon the rating of the company itself.

Against this background, an understanding of the potential of credit derivatives where there is an operational integration of credit risk allows the development of the following range of applications:

- Increasing the range of clients with whom the organization can trade (as the default risk can be hedged at a known cost) allowing reduction of concentration as well as allowing expansion of business relationships.
- Hedging against the potential losses to the company resulting from the default of a major supplier, client or distributor.
- Use credit derivatives to disaggregate the profitability/earnings of commercial transaction and attribute sources of earnings allowing improved analysis of risk reward attributes of transactions. For example, a sale of capital equipment on deferred payment terms to a lower credit quality entity may seem superficially profitable but part of the earnings is directly attributable to the credit risk assumed in the vendor financing provided. Disaggregation of each element of profitability is very important in allowing appropriate pricing decisions to be made.

The concentrated nature of credit risk in corporate portfolios dictates that these entities will generally benefit from both purchasing and selling protection against default risk. In addition, for large well capitalized entities, entry into credit swaps whereby they sell protection against default may emerge as an attractive investment for surplus liquidity of these organizations.

20.10   Summary

The market for credit derivatives is still relatively new and immature. However, this immaturity does not detract from either the rapid development of the products and applications or it current significant volumes. Given the central role played by credit risk in financial markets the potential for this market is undoubted and it would be surprising if the market did not ultimately rival derivative markets in other assets.

However, it is clear that there are significant issues in the development of the market currently including:

- Lack of standardization of products and documentation.
- The limited range of credits available, in particular, the concentration on traded bonds and loans.
- The (perceived) expensive pricing of these products.
- The lack of underlying price discovery, reflecting a lack of liquidity in these instruments.
- The absence of standardized default risk models.
- The regulatory uncertainty as well as ambiguities in accounting and taxation of these structures.

It is clear that many of these issues reflect the emergent nature of the products. Many of the issues identified are also being dealt with and, as the market develops, these barriers to participation will become increasingly less significant.

The development of the market to date has already exceeded expectations and there are considerable expectations as to both growth in volumes and the impact that credit derivatives will ultimately have on the nature of credit risk in financial markets. Central elements underlying these developments are the capacity to isolate and separate credit risk and trade these attributes allowing a marked increase in the liquidity of credit risk and the ability to access new sources of risk capital to support credit risk.

The emergence of credit derivatives has the potential to change banking and credit risk management in a profound manner. The obvious parallel in this regard is the way in which the emergence of derivatives generally has altered the markets for debt, foreign exchange, equity and commodities. The ultimate structure and size of the market for credit derivatives is, to an extent, less consequential than probably imagined. The process of development and analysis prompted by the emergence of credit derivatives, in the areas of credit risk pricing, portfolio concentration and management of credit risk, will in itself profoundly affect capital markets.

Index

For information about the CD-ROM, refer to Chapter 13.